PAGE 50

ON THE ROAD

N GUIDE

ings

S MAP NEXT PAGE

PAGE 837

SURVIVAL GUIDE

YOUR AT-A-GLANCE REFERENCE
How to get around, get a room, stay safe, say hello

Public Holidays
In England and Wales, most businesses and banks close on these official public holidays (hence the term 'bank holiday').
New Year's Day 1 January
Easter March/April (Goo
iday to Easter Monda
ive)

THIS EDITION WRITTEN AND RESEARCHED BY

David Else,

Oliver Berry, Joe Bindloss, Fionn Davenport, Marc Di Duca, Belinda Dixon, Peter Dragicevich, Etain O'Carroll, Neil Wilson

England

Top Experiences

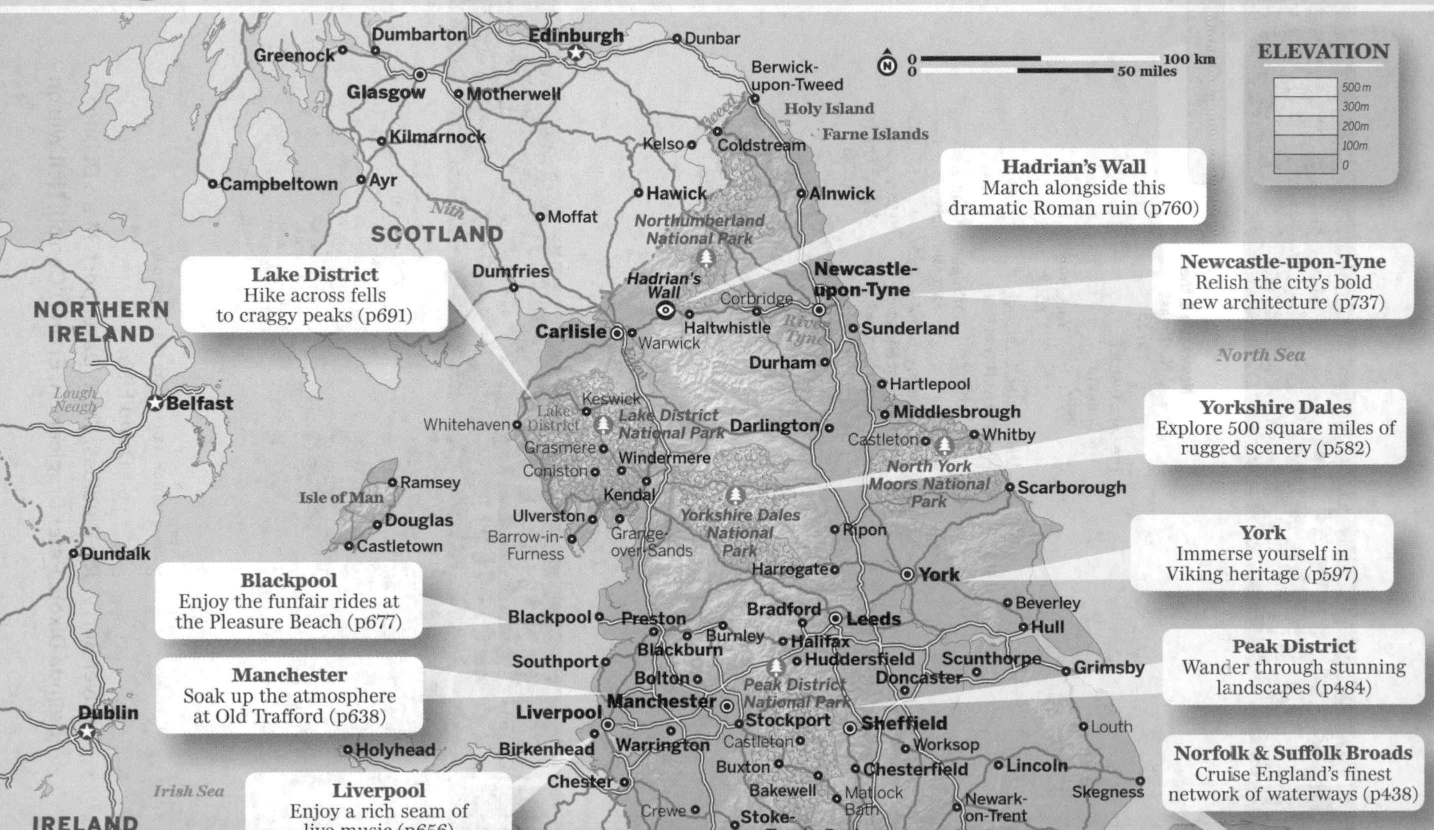

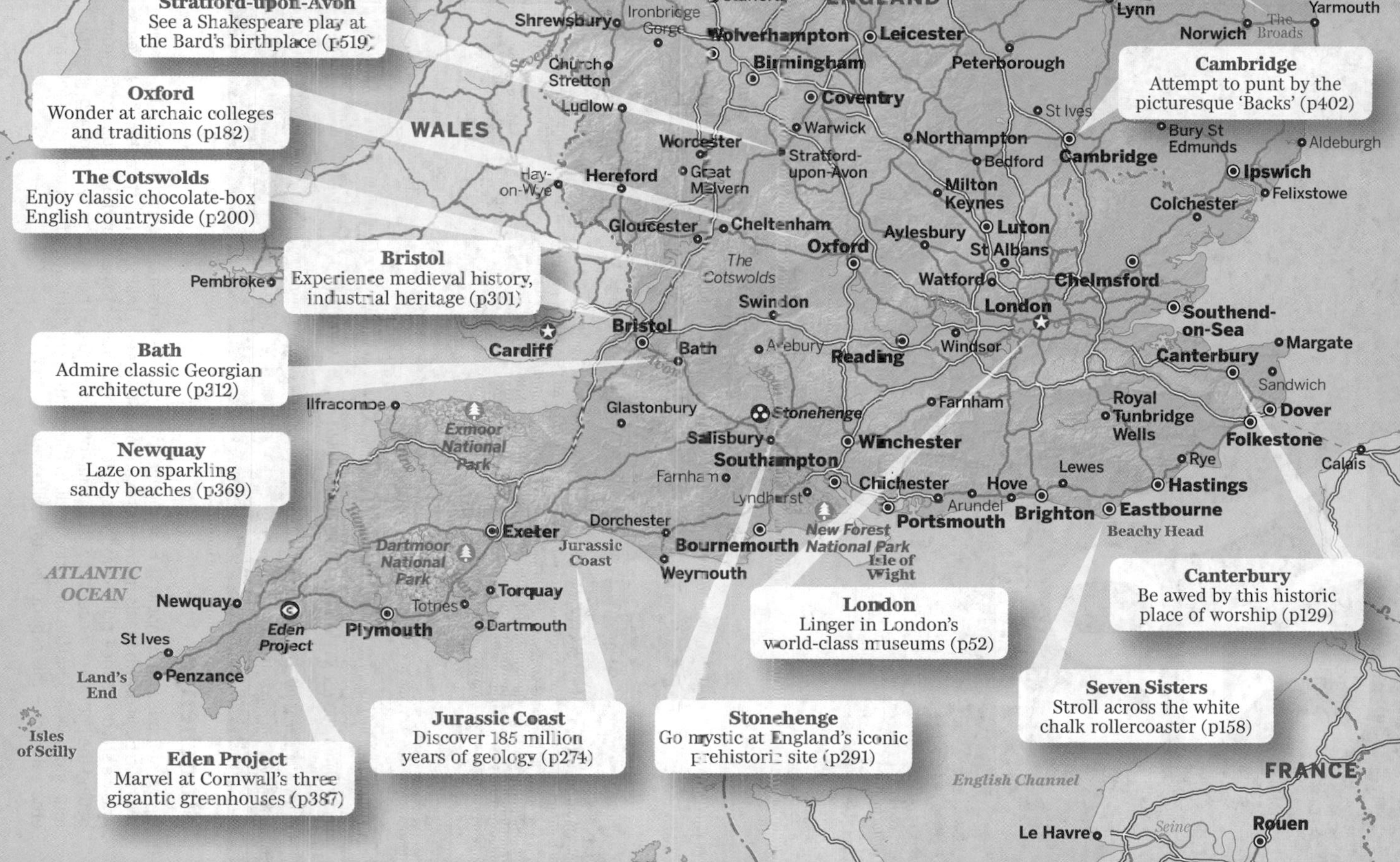

Stratford-upon-Avon
See a Shakespeare play at the Bard's birthplace (p519)
Oxford
Wonder at archaic colleges and traditions (p182)
The Cotswolds
Enjoy classic chocolate-box English countryside (p200)
Bristol
Experience medieval history, industrial heritage (p301)
Bath
Admire classic Georgian architecture (p312)
Newquay
Laze on sparkling sandy beaches (p369)
Eden Project
Marvel at Cornwall's three gigantic greenhouses (p387)
Jurassic Coast
Discover 185 million years of geology (p274)
Stonehenge
Go mystic at England's iconic prehistoric site (p291)
London
Linger in London's world-class museums (p52)
Seven Sisters
Stroll across the white chalk rollercoaster (p158)
Canterbury
Be awed by this historic place of worship (p129)
Cambridge
Attempt to punt by the picturesque 'Backs' (p402)
ENGLAND
WALES
FRANCE
ATLANTIC OCEAN
English Channel
Shrewsbury
Ironbridge Gorge
Wolverhampton
Leicester
Lynn
Norwich
The Broads
Yarmouth
Church Stretton
Birmingham
Peterborough
Ludlow
Coventry
St Ives
Warwick
Northampton
Cambridge
Bury St Edmunds
Aldeburgh
Worcester
Stratford-upon-Avon
Bedford
Ipswich
Felixstowe
Hay-on-Wye
Hereford
Great Malvern
Milton Keynes
Colchester
Gloucester
Cheltenham
Luton
Aylesbury
St Albans
Oxford
The Cotswolds
Pembroke
Watford
Chelmsford
Swindon
London
Southend-on-Sea
Cardiff
Bristol
Bath
Avebury
Reading
Windsor
Margate
Canterbury
Sandwich
Ilfracombe
Glastonbury
Stonehenge
Farnham
Royal Tunbridge Wells
Dover
Exmoor National Park
Salisbury
Winchester
Folkestone
Southampton
Rye
Calais
Farnham
Lewes
Chichester
Hove
Hastings
Lyndhurst
Arundel
Brighton
Eastbourne
Portsmouth
Dorchester
Exeter
New Forest National Park
Beachy Head
Bournemouth
Jurassic Coast
Dartmoor National Park
Isle of Wight
Weymouth
Torquay
Newquay
Totnes
Eden Project
Plymouth
Dartmouth
St Ives
Land's End
Penzance
Isles of Scilly
Le Havre
Seine
Rouen

27 TOP EXPERIENCES

Stonehenge

1 Mysterious and compelling, Stonehenge (p291) is England's most iconic ancient site. People have been drawn to this myth-rich ring of bluestones and trilithons for more than 5000 years. And we still don't know quite why it was built. Most visitors get to gaze at the 50-ton stones from behind the perimeter fence, but with enough planning you can book an early morning or evening tour and walk around the inner ring itself. In the slanting sunlight, away from the crowds, it's an ethereal place – this experience stays with you.

ANDREW MARSHALL & LEANNE WALKER

Hadrian's Wall

2 Hadrian's 2nd-century wall (p760) is one of England's most revealing and dramatic Roman ruins, its procession of abandoned forts, garrisons, towers and milecastles marching across a wild and lonely landscape. But walls are always about much more than the stones from which they are built – this edge-of-empire barrier symbolised the boundary of civilised order. To the south was the bridled Roman world of underfloor heating, bath-houses and orderly taxpaying, to the north the unruly land of the marauding Celts.

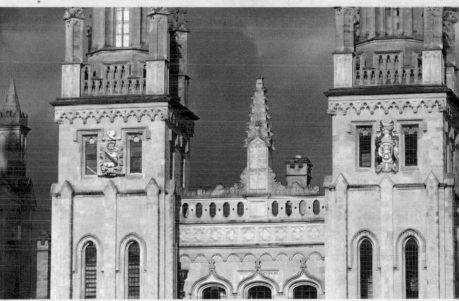

Oxford's Glorious Architecture

3 For most of us a visit to Oxford (p184) is as close as we're going to get to the brilliant minds and august institutions that have made this city famous across the globe. But you'll get a glimpse of this other world in the hushed quads and cobbled lanes where student cyclists and dusty academics roam. The beautiful college buildings, archaic traditions and stunning architecture have changed little over the centuries leaving the city centre much as Einstein or Tolkien would have found it.

DAVID TOMLINSON

The Lake District

4 William Wordsworth and his Romantic chums were the first to champion the charms of the Lake District (p691) and it's not hard to see what stirred them. Pocked by whale-backed fells, razor-edge valleys and misty mountain tarns (as well as the nation's highest peak), this craggy corner of northwest England is still considered by many to be the spiritual home of British hiking. Strap on the boots, stock up on mintcake and drink in the views: inspiration is sure to follow.

Historic York

5 With its Roman and Viking heritage, ancient city walls, spectacular Gothic cathedral and maze of medieval streets, York (p597) is a living showcase for the highlights of English history. Join one of the city's many walking tours and plunge into the network of snickelways (narrow alleys), each one the focus of a ghost story or historical character, then explore the intricacies of York Minster, the biggest medieval cathedral in all of Northern Europe. And don't miss the Flying Scotsman at the National Railway Museum, the world's largest collection of historic locomotives.

CHRIS MELLOR

London's live entertainment scene

6 Can you hear that, music lovers? That's London calling – from the numerous theatres, concert halls, nightclubs, pubs and even tube stations, where on any given night, hundreds if not thousands of performers are taking to the stage (p115). Search out your own iconic London experience, whether it's a big-name West End musical or a low-key East End pub sing-along, the Proms at the Royal Albert Hall, a superstar DJ set at Fabric or a floppy-fringed guitar band at a Hoxton boozer.

RCCCO FASA-IC

London's museums

7 Institutions bright and beautiful, great and small, wise and wonderful – London (p56) has them all. The range of museums is vast: from generalist collections (British Museum, V&A) to specific themes (Imperial War Museum, London Transport Museum, Natural History Museum); from intriguing private collections (Sir John Soane's Museum, Wallace Collection) to those celebrating people associated with the city (Handel, Dickens, Freud). Seriously, you could spend weeks without even scratching the surface. And most of it is free!

Bristol

8 It might not have London's loot or Bath's beauty, but make no mistake: Bristol (p301) is one of Britain's most innovative cities. The southwest's major metropolis has a history stretching back to medieval times, but it was the pioneering engineer Isambard Kingdom Brunel who really put the place on the map, and built two of the city's most celebrated landmarks, the Clifton Suspension Bridge and the transatlantic steamship SS *Great Britain*. These days Bristol is known for its creativity and culture: keep your eyes peeled for the work of the guerrilla graffitist Banksy as you wander the city's streets.

NEIL SETCHFIELD

DAVID TOMLINSON

Jurassic Coast

9 Some shorelines offer so much more than just a spot to soak up the sun. Devon's and Dorset's Jurassic Coast (p274) traces 185 million years of geological time in just 95 miles. Here russet-red and creamy-white cliffs have been carved by the sea into a string of bewitching bays, stacks and rock arches. Whether you're swimming or kayaking through the immense Durdle Door (p275) or fossil hunting in Lyme Regis (p282), the dinosaur era has never been so much fun. And the memories linger longer than any tan.

Bath

10 In a nation awash with pretty cities, Bath (p312) still stands out as the belle of the ball. Founded by the Romans, who established the spa resort of Aquae Sulis to take advantage of the area's hot springs, Bath hit its stride in the 18th century when the rich industrialist Ralph Allen and two architects, John Wood Elder and Younger, oversaw the city's reinvention as a model of Georgian architecture. Awash with amber townhouses, sweeping crescents and Palladian mansions (not to mention a cutting-edge 21st-century spa), Bath demands your undivided attention.

GLENN BEANLAND

The Eden Project

11 Looking like a cross between a lunar landing station and a James Bond villain's lair, the three gigantic greenhouses of the Eden Project (p387) have become a symbol of Cornwall's renaissance. Dreamt up by ex-record producer Tim Smit, and built in an abandoned clay pit near St Austell, Eden's three biomes recreate the world's habitats in microcosm, from the lush jungles of the Amazon rainforest to the temperate plains of the African savannah.

HOLGER LEUE

Newquay & Cornwall's North Coast

12 Cornwall (p364) boasts more miles of unbroken coastline than anywhere else in Britain, but if it's rugged cliffs and sparkling bays you're looking for, there's only one place that fits the bill: Newquay. The cluster of white sandy beaches around Newquay (p369) are some of the loveliest in England, favoured by everyone from bucket-and-spaders to beach-bronzed surfers. Visit in early spring or late autumn and you might even have the sands to yourself.

The Cotswolds

13 The most wonderful thing about the Cotswolds (p200) is that no matter where you go or how lost you get, you'll still end up in an impossibly quaint village of rose-clad cottages and honey-coloured stone. And when you do, there'll be a charming village green, a pub with sloping floors and fine ales, and a view of the lush green hills. It's easy to leave the crowds behind and find your very own slice of medieval England – and some of the best boutique hotels in the country.

BARBARA VAN ZANTEN

Punting the Cambridge 'Backs'

14 No trip to Cambridge (p402) would be complete without an attempt to punt by the picturesque 'Backs', the leafy, green lawns behind the city's finest colleges. Hop off to marvel at the intricate vaulting of King's College Chapel, a show-stopping Gothic concoction, glide under the curious-looking Mathematical Bridge, or down a pint in one of the city's many historic pubs. You'll soon wonder how you could have studied anywhere else.

CHRIS MELLOR

Blackpool Pleasure Beach

15 The queen bee of the bucket-and-spade holiday, Blackpool (p677) has forgone the genteel pleasures of the Victorian holiday for the kind of no-holds barred adrenaline kick that comes from going on one of the Pleasure Beach's fairground rides. The Big One is just as its name describes – the tallest, fastest roller coaster in Europe, but the real stomach churn comes on the 75m vertical descent aboard the Ice Blast... at 85mph. And then there are the 'woodies,' as nostalgic and unthreatening as the others are hair-and-lunch-raising.

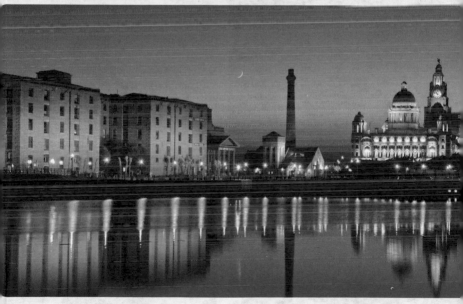

Albert Dock Museums, Liverpool

16 After a decade of development the reborn waterfront is once again the heart of Liverpool. Head for Albert Dock (p660), a World Heritage Site of iconic and protected buildings, including a batch of top museums: the Merseyside Maritime Museum and International Slavery Museum ensure the good and bad sides of Liverpool's history are not forgotten, while the Tate Liverpool and the Beatles Story museum celebrate popular culture and the city's (still) most famous musical sons.

Shakespeare at Stratford-upon-Avon

17 What could be more English than taking in a Shakespeare play in the birthplace of the Bard? The pretty town of Stratford-upon-Avon (p519) is also where the world's most famous playwright shuffled off this mortal coil, and its tight knot of Tudor streets form a living street-map of Shakespeare's life and times. Huge crowds of theatre-lovers and would-be thespians congregate here to visit the five historic houses owned by Shakespeare and his relatives, with a respectful detour to the old stone church where the Bard was laid to rest.

The Yorkshire Dales

18 From well-known names such as Wensleydale and Swaledale, to obscure and evocative Langstrothdale and Arkengarthdale, these glacial valleys (p582) are characterised by a distinctive landscape: high heather moorland and stepped skylines, and flat-topped hills rising above green valley floors patchworked with dykes and dotted with barns, where sheep and cattle still graze on village greens. Pull on your hiking boots or hire a mountain bike and explore the 500 miles of footpaths, bridleways and green lanes, many of them following ancient routes – even Roman roads – between remote villages.

DENNIS JOHNSON

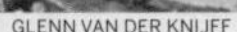

GLENN VAN DER KNIJFF

Eating in England

19 England is packed with high quality eateries – from Michelin-starred restaurants and welcoming gastropubs, to classic city cafes and quaint country teashops – with a choice of food to match. Tuck into national favourites such as fish and chips or toad-in-the-hole, followed of course by rhubarb and custard, or spotted dick. Then move onto regional specialities such as Cumberland sausage, Stilton cheese or the quintessential multicultural dish of northern England: a big fresh Yorkshire pudding filled with curry.

Peak District Playground

20 Curiously, you won't find many peaks in the Peak District (p484), just pocket-sized stone villages and blissful miles of tumbling moorland, plunging valleys and eroded gritstone crags. This stunning landscape is an adventure playground for cyclists, hikers, cavers and rock climbers, attracting a veritable army of outdoor enthusiasts on summer weekends. Set amongst all this natural wonder are some charming towns, including the genteel spa of Buxton with its Regency pump rooms and Victorian pavilions.

EIL SETCHFIELD

DAVID ELSE

Canterbury Cathedral

21 Few other English cathedrals come close to Canterbury's (p132), top temple of the Anglican Church and a place of worship for over 15 centuries. Its intricate tower dominates the Canterbury skyline. At its heart lies a 12th-century crime scene, the very spot where Archbishop Thomas Becket was put to the sword – an epoch-making event that launched a million pilgrimages and still pulls in the crowds today. A lone candle mourns the gruesome deed, the pink sandstone before it smoothed by 800 years' worth of devout kneeling.

ORIEN HARVEY

NEIL SETCHFIELD

Newcastle-upon-Tyne

22 Nowhere else in the northeast is the renaissance of this once proud industrial region more obvious than in rejuvenated Newcastle (p737). Revamped, rebranded and regenerated, Newcastle's (and Gateshead's) bold new architecture peers across the old river, scantily attired pleasure seekers knock back Technicolor cocktails in retro-styled bars, and high-brow culture pulls in a sophisticated crowd. But amid the excitement, clear-headed reminders of the past remain, from the honey-hued stone of the Georgian city streets to the symbol of all things Geordie, the magnificent Tyne Bridge.

Seven Sisters Chalk Cliffs

23 Dover's iconic white cliffs grab most attention, but Sussex' Seven Sisters (p158) are a much more spectacular affair. This four-mile roller-coaster ride in flint-flecked chalk undulates from Cuckmere Haven to Beachy Head, a chalk colossus rising 162m above the Channel. The rolling cliffs are best photographed from Cuckmere Haven, but a clifftop hike also provides wide sea views, breathtaking in every sense. The area is also home to rare flower and butterfly species, as well as thousands of gulls that swoop down to pilfer hikers' lunches.

DAVID TOMLINSON

Football

24 The rest of the world may call it 'soccer' but to the English the name of the national sport is definitely 'football'. And despite what the fans may say in Italy or Brazil, the English Premier League has some of the finest football teams in the world, with many of the world's best – and richest – players. Big names include the globally renowned Arsenal, Liverpool and Chelsea – plus of course THE most famous club on the planet: Manchester United. Tickets are like gold dust – but most stadiums are open to visitors outside match-days.

ORIEN HARVEY

A Pint down the Pub

25 The pub is still the centre of social life in England, and the best traditional drink has to be beer. Not your fizzy lager, but honest to goodness English ale. To outsiders it may be 'warm and flat', but give it a chance and you'll soon learn to savour the complex flavours before setting off to explore the country's many regional varieties, from Wiltshire's 6X to Cumbria's Sneck-lifter. And these days you can usually get good pub grub to wash down with your pint as well.

RICHARD I'ANSON

Historic Buildings

26 England's history is rich and turbulent, and nowhere is this more apparent than in the mighty castles and stately homes that dot the landscape. From romantic clifftop ruins like Corfe (p274) and Dunstanburgh (p771), surrounded by fields or overlooking the sea, to the sturdy fortresses still at the heart of towns like Skipton (p582) and Richmond (p588). And when the English aristocracy no longer needed castles, they built 'stately homes' at the heart of for their country estates. Classics of the genre include Blenheim Palace, Castle Howard and Chatsworth House.

Slow Boat England

27 If you want to slow down and see the best of England from a new angle, you can't beat hiring a boat and cruising down the country's network of rivers and canals. Day-trips are possible in many areas, but for the real deal you can hire a gaily painted narrow boat, complete with cabins, galley and saloon, and ply the English waterways for a week or more. Favourite destinations include the River Thames, the canals of Shropshire and Cheshire, and the Norfolk and Suffolk Broads – an enchanting network of rivers, water-meadows, freshwater lakes and saltwater marshes.

CHRIS MELLOR

welcome to England

Tower Bridge, Buckingham Palace, Manchester United, The Beatles. England does icons like no other place on earth, and travel here is a fascinating mix of famous names and hidden gems.

Variety Packed

From the Roman remains of Hadrian's Wall to the stunning architecture of Canterbury Cathedral, England's astounding variety is a major reason to travel here. City streets buzz day and night, with tempting shops and restaurants, and some of the finest museums in the world. After dark, cutting-edge clubs, top-class theatre and formidable live music provide a string of nights to remember. Next day, you're deep in the English countryside or enjoying a classic seaside resort. In England, there really is something for everyone, whether you're eight or 80, going solo or travelling with your friends, your kids or your grandma.

Time Travel

Along with variety, a journey through England is a journey through history. But not the history that's dull and dusty. History you can feel and re-live. You can lay your hands on the ancient megaliths of a 5000-year-old stone circle, or walk the battlements of a medieval fortress – just as they were patrolled by knights in armour many centuries ago. Then fast forward to the future and you're admiring 21st-century architecture in Manchester, or exploring the space-age domes of Cornwall's Eden Project.

English Spoken Here

And while England boasts a culture and tradition that may appear complex, on the surface at least it's familiar to many visitors thanks to a vast catalogue of British film and TV exports. The same applies when it comes to communication; this is home turf for the English language. For many visitors this means no need to carry a phrasebook – although you might get a little confused by local accents in places such as Devon or Liverpool.

Easy Does It

A final thing to remember while you're planning a trip to England: travel here is a breeze. Granted, it may not be totally effortless, but it's easy compared with many parts of the world. And although the locals may grumble (in fact, it's a national pastime) public transport is pretty good, and a train ride through the English landscape can be a highlight in itself. But whichever way you get around, in this compact country you're never far from the next town, the next pub, the next restaurant, the next national park or the next impressive castle on your hit-list of highlights. The choice is endless, and we've hand-picked the best places to create this book. Use it as a guide – to steer you from place to place – and mix it with making your own discoveries. You won't be disappointed.

need to know

Currency

» Pound – also called 'pound sterling' (£)

Language

» English

When to Go

Carlisle
GO May-Sep

York
GO May-Sep

Liverpool
GO May-Sep

Norwich
GO May-Sep

Warm to hot summers, mild winters

London
GO Any time
many attractions indoors

Exeter
GO Apr-Sep

High Season (Jun–Aug)

» Weather at its best. Accommodation rates at their highest (especially for August school holidays).

» Roads busy, especially in seaside areas, national parks and popular cities such as Oxford, Bath and York.

Shoulder (Easter to end May, mid-Sep to end Oct)

» Crowds reduce. Prices drop.

» Weather often good; sun mixes with sudden rain March to May, while balmy 'Indian summers' can feature September to October.

Low Season (Dec–Feb)

» Wet and cold is the norm. Snow falls in mountain areas, especially up north.

» Opening hours reduced October to Easter; some places shut for the winter. Big-city sights (especially London's) operate all year.

Your Daily Budget

Budget less than

£50

» Dorm beds from £10–25

» Cheap meals in cafes and pubs £5–9

» Long-distance coach £10–30 for 200-mile journey

Midrange

£50–100

» Midrange hotel or B&B £50–130 (London £80–180) per double room

» Main course in midrange restaurant £9–18

» Long-distance train £15–50 for 200-mile journey

» Car rental from £30 per day for a small car

Top end over

£100

» Accommodation in a 4-star hotel room from £200

» A 3-course meal in a good restaurant around £40 per person

Money

» Change bureaus and ATMs widely available, especially in cities and major towns.

Visas

» Not required by most citizens of Europe, Australia, NZ, USA and Canada.

Mobile Phones

» Phones from most other countries operate in England, but attract roaming charges. Local SIM cards cost from £10; SIM and basic handset around £30.

Driving

» Traffic drives on the left. Steering wheels on the right. Most hire (rental) cars have manual gears (stick-shift).

Websites

» **BBC** (www.bbc.co.uk) News and entertainment from the national broadcaster.

» **Enjoy England** (www.enjoyengland.com) Official tourism website.

» **Lonely Planet** (lonelyplanet.com) Destination information, hotel bookings, traveller forums and more.

» **Seize the Days** (lonelyplanet.com/132days) Weekly updates on UK activities and events.

» **National Traveline** (www.traveline.org.uk) Great portal site for all public transport around England.

Exchange Rates

Australia	A$1	£0.60
Canada	C$1	£0.62
Eurozone	€1	£0.83
Japan	Y100	£0.75
New Zealand	NZ$1	£0.47
USA	US$1	£0.64

For current exchange rates see www.xe.com.

Important Numbers

Omit the code if you're inside that area. Drop the initial 0 if you're calling from abroad.

Country code	☎+44
International access code	☎00
Emergency (police, fire, ambulance, mountain rescue or coastguard)	☎999

Arriving in England

» **Heathrow airport**
Train to Paddington station every 15 minutes (from £16) p124

» **Gatwick airport**
Train to Victoria station every 15 minutes (from £15) p124

» **Eurostar trains from Paris or Brussels**
Arrive at St Pancras International station in central London p846

» **Buses from Europe**
Arrive at London Victoria Coach Station p846

» **Taxis from airports**
Trips to central London run from £40 (Heathrow) to £90 (Luton); more at peak hours. p124 or p127

England on a Shoestring

If you're a shoestring traveller, there's no getting around it – England isn't cheap. Public transport, admission fees, restaurants and hotel rooms all tend to be expensive compared to many other European countries. But with some careful planning, that doesn't mean an English trip has to break the bank. You can save money by staying in B&Bs instead of hotels, or hostels instead of B&Bs. Another option is the chain of motels along motorways and outside large towns. You can also save considerably, by prebooking long-distance travel by coach or train – and by avoiding the times when everyone else is on the move (such as Friday afternoon). Many attractions are free (or offer discounts on quiet days (eg Mondays). And don't forget that you won't have to stump up a penny to enjoy England's best asset: the wonderful countryside and coastline.

what's new

For this new edition of England, our authors have hunted down the fresh, the transformed, the hot and the happening. Here are a few of our favourites. For up-to-the-minute recommendations, see lonelyplanet.com/england

Darwin Centre, Natural History Museum, London

1 One of the world's finest museums, the Natural History Museum has been attracting visitors for 100 years. Inside the museum's striking new Darwin Centre (a seven-storey, egg-shaped structure inside a glass pavilion), biologists study the 20 million animal and plant specimens stored here. Visitors can snoop through windows at the boffins hard at work and interact with displays explaining the science (p78).

Ashmolean Museum, Oxford

2 Britain's oldest public museum re-opened in late 2009 after a massive £61 million redevelopment (p188).

Galleries of Modern London, Museum of London

3 Covering London's more recent history – from the Great Fire to the present day – the Galleries of Modern London have recently reopened after a £20-million overhaul (p68).

Agatha Christie's Greenway, Devon

4 The famous crime writer's riverside holiday home opened to visitors in 2009. Rooms still looking much as she left them (p349).

Fallen Angel Hotel, Durham

5 Bed-down in a sleeper train compartment or in your own personal cinema at the one of the northeast's newest (and most bizarre) hotels (p752).

Nottingham Contemporary

6 A David Hockney retrospective was the opening event at the Midlands' newest art centre in November 2009. Edgy architecture pays tribute to Nottingham's vanished lace markets (p451).

Gray's Court, York

7 One of York's oldest medieval buildings is now open to the public as an atmospheric cafe, where you can enjoy lunch in an oak-panelled Jacobean gallery (p605).

English Whisky Company, Norfolk

8 The first new whisky distillery in England in 120 years started bottling spirits in November 2009. Take a tour and sample the dram (p438).

Turner Contemporary

9 Launching in 2011, Margate's brand new state-of-the-art gallery stands right on the seafront, bathed in the sea-refracted light that the artist JMW Turner loved so much. The first exhibition, naturally, focuses on Turner himself (p141).

if you like...

Castles

England's turbulent history bequeaths a landscape dotted with defensive masterpieces of the medieval era, complete with moats, keeps, battlements, dungeons and all the classic features we know from history books or legends of knights in armour.

Tower of London Built as a castle, used as a palace, perhaps most famous as a prison – 1000 years of history in one iconic building (p67)

Windsor Castle The largest and oldest occupied fortress in the world, a majestic vision of battlements and towers used for state occasions and as the Queen's weekend retreat (p237)

Richmond Castle Among England's oldest castles, with fantastic views from the top of the medieval keep (p588)

Warwick Castle One of the finest castles in England; preserved enough to be impressive, ruined enough to be romantic (p515)

Tintagel Castle The atmospheric ruins of King Arthur's legendary birthplace (p367)

Skipton Castle Little known, but probably the best-preserved medieval castle in the country (p582)

Cathedrals

Along with castles, the cathedrals of England are the country's most impressive and inspiring historic structures. Many were works in progress for centuries, so display an eclectic mix of styles, with solid Norman naves later enjoying the addition of graceful Gothic arches or soaring spires, and – most beautiful of all – epic extents of stained-glass windows.

St Paul's Cathedral A symbol of the city for centuries, and still an essential part of the London skyline (p67)

York Minster One of the largest medieval cathedrals in all of Europe, especially renowned for its windows (p597)

Canterbury Cathedral The mothership of the Anglican Church, still attracting pilgrims and visitors in their thousands (p132)

Salisbury Cathedral A truly majestic cathedral, and English icon, topped by the tallest spire in England (p286)

Ely Cathedral Visible for miles across the flatlands of eastern England, and locally dubbed the 'Ship of the Fens' (p414)

Ruined Abbeys

Thanks to the hard work of industrious monks in the 12th to 14th centuries, great abbeys are a feature of the English landscape. Thanks to Henry VIII's spat with the Catholic Church around 1540, many are now in ruins – but no less impressive for today's visitor.

Fountains Abbey Extensive ruins set in more recently landscaped water-gardens make this one of the most beautiful sites in England (p610)

Rievaulx Abbey Tranquil remains hidden away in a secluded valley (p620)

Whitby Abbey A stunning clifftop ruin with an eerie atmosphere that inspired the author of *Dracula* (p623)

Glastonbury Abbey The legendary burial place of King Arthur and Queen Guinevere (p325)

>> Known as the 'Palace of the Peak', Chatsworth House (p497) has been occupied by the earls and dukes of Devonshire for centuries

GLENN BEANLAND

Stately Homes

Where France has endless chateaux, and Germany a schloss on every corner, England boasts a raft of stately homes – vast mansions where the landed gentry have lived for generations, recently opening their doors so the rest of us can admire the fabulous interiors.

Blenheim Palace A monumental baroque fantasy and one of England's greatest stately homes (p196)

Castle Howard Another impressive baroque edifice, best-known as the setting for *Brideshead Revisited* (p608)

Harewood House A vast mansion with superb grounds by Capability Brown (p577)

Leeds Castle One of the world's most romantic stately homes, just a short hop from London (p151)

Chatsworth House The quintessential stately home; a treasure trove of heirlooms and works of art (p497)

Kingston Lacy Smothered with gold and graced by an overwhelming fresco, this is Dorset's must-see stately home (p272)

Village Idylls

If you want to see the England of your imagination (or of period costume dramas), you'll love England's villages. Though different in character from region to region, all are a reminder of a simpler, more bucolic age.

Castle Combe Overlooked for centuries, this place won the 'Prettiest Village in England' award and starred in the original *Dr Dolittle* movie in the 1960s. It remains unchanged today, and film crews still stop by (p296)

Lavenham One of England's most beautiful spots: a collection of exquisitely preserved medieval buildings virtually untouched since the 15th century (p423)

Painswick The Cotswold Hills has many pretty villages, with hilltop Painswick an absolute gem, unassuming and gloriously uncommercial (p214)

Hutton-le-Hole One of Yorkshire's loveliest villages, with sheep grazing on a wide green amid a scattering of cottages (p621)

Hawkshead Surrounded by dramatic natural scenery, this is the Lake District's most handsome village – a maze of cobbled lanes and whitewashed cottages, with connections to William Wordsworth and Beatrix Potter (p706)

Moors & Mountains

For a crowded country, England has a surprising proportion of countryside, some of it even more surprisingly high and wild – a playground for hikers, bikers, birdwatchers and other lovers of the great outdoors.

North York Moors National Park Wild and windswept, with whaleback hills stretching all the way to the sea, topped by England's largest expanse of heather (p618)

The Lake District A feast of mountains, valleys, views and – of course – lakes; the place to hike the hilltops that inspired William Wordsworth (p691)

Yorkshire Dales National Park With scenic valleys, high hills and deep caves, the Dales are designed for hiking, biking and caving (p582)

Peak District OK, so it's the most visited national park in Europe, but all these outdoor enthusiasts can't be wrong (p484)

Dartmoor Exhilarating wilderness, hidden valleys and southern England's highest hills (p356)

If you like... weird stuff
Forbidden Corner is a bizarre labyrinth of miniature castles, caves, temples and gardens (p613)

Industrial Heritage

England's history is not all about big castles or twee cottages; this nation also drove the world's industrialisation in the 18th and 19th centuries. This golden (though rather grimy) era is sometimes forgotten, but it's celebrated at several sites – an excellent opportunity to get beneath the skin of the destination.

Ironbridge The place where it all started, the crucible of the Industrial Revolution; today, 10 museums for the price of one give fascinating insights (p549)

National Railway Museum A cathedral to the great days of steam, plus trains of a later vintage; for railway fans of all ages it's the perfect place to go loco (p599)

SS Great Britain The pride of Bristol, this iconic transatlantic steamer is now lavishly restored (p301)

Derwent Valley Mills The River Derwent powered the first factories, and the valley is now a World Heritage Site (p483)

Roman Remains

For 400 years England was part of the Roman Empire, a legacy still visible at various sites around the country – from sturdy defences for soldiers to fancy houses for wealthy citizens.

The Roman Baths at Bath Perhaps the most famous Roman remains in England – a complex of bathhouses around the natural thermal waters – plus additions from the 17th century when restorative waters again became fashionable (p312)

Hadrian's Wall Snaking coast-to-coast across the lonely hills of northern England, this 2000-year-old fortified line once marked the northern limit of Imperial Roman jurisdiction (p760)

Chedworth Roman Villa One of the largest Roman villas in England, built as a stately home around AD 120, with exquisite mosaics (p209)

Hardknott Fort High on the Cumbrian fells sits one of Roman Britain's most remote outposts, still an evocative site today (p711)

Outdoor Art

Many of the great stone sculptures by well-known English artists are from, and of, the earth so it's fitting that we can now admire many of them in a natural setting. Works in steel and other materials complete the picture.

Yorkshire Sculpture Park England's biggest outdoor sculpture collection, dominated by the works of Henry Moore and Barbara Hepworth (p578)

Barbara Hepworth Museum The studio of St Ives' most celebrated sculptress is now a museum, and the attached garden contains many examples of her work (p373)

Tout Quarry An unsung artistic gem: 50 rock-carved sculptures still in situ, including works by Antony Gormley and Dhruva Mistry (p279)

Angel of the North England's best-known public work of art spreads its rusty wings and stands sentinel near Newcastle (p747)

If you like... clifftop drama
The Minack is a unique theatre, carved into the sheer rocks overlooking the sea in wild west Cornwall. With the Atlantic as a backdrop it's dramatic in every sense. The classic play to catch – and the theatre's signature piece – is *The Tempest*. (p379)

Shopping

For every identikit megastore in England, there's an independent shop with soul and character – whether you're in the market for books, clothes, jewellery, arts and crafts, retro handbags or 1960s vinyl.

Hay-on-Wye The self-proclaimed secondhand book capital of the world boasts over 30 bookshops and millions of volumes, attracting browsers, collectors and academics from around the world (p539)

Victoria Quarter, Leeds These lovely arcades of wrought ironwork and stained glass are home to several top fashion boutiques (p576)

Brighton's North Laine The perfect place to pick up essential items such as vegetarian shoes, Elvis outfits and circus monocycles (p170)

Tetbury An upper-class shopping experience, with stylish crafts and antique shops, and even an outlet for goodies from the Prince of Wales' estate at nearby Highgrove (p212)

Ludlow Epicurean delights await in this foodie heaven, where almost everything is organic, artisan, sustainable or locally sourced (p557)

Galleries

Fans of the visual arts are spoilt for choice in England. Galleries abound, from long-standing classics in London and the larger cities exhibiting some of the most famous paintings in the world, to quirky and off-beat locations featuring experimental and up-and-coming artists. Some of the galleries are works of art in themselves.

Tate Britain The best-known gallery in London, full to the brim with the finest works (p77)

Tate Modern London's other Tate focuses on modern art in all its wonderful permutations (p73)

Baltic Gateshead The 'Tate of the North' features work by some of contemporary art's biggest show-stoppers (p741)

Barber Institute of Fine Arts, Birmingham With works by Rubens, Turner and Picasso this provincial gallery is no lightweight (p505)

Towner Gallery The south coast's newest art space occupies a purpose-built structure next to the sea. Look out too for the Turner Contemporary in nearby Margate, due to open in 2011 (p141)

Arts & Music Festivals

Whatever your taste in music or the arts, there's a festival for you somewhere in England.

Notting Hill Carnival London's Caribbean community shows the city how to party (p94)

Glastonbury Thirty years on and still going strong, Britain's biggest and best-loved music festival (p325)

Brighton Festival You know a festival's matured when it grows a fringe, and this gathering of all things arts is now firmly placed on the calendar (p163)

Latitude An eclectic mix of music, literature, dance, drama and comedy, with stunning location and manageable size (p429)

Birmingham Artsfest A cultural extravaganza, featuring ballet and bhangra to rhythm and blues (p506)

Reading Festival Venerable rock gathering that traces its roots back to the 1960s (p237)

Leeds Festival Northern companion to the long-established Reading Festival (p571)

>> The Tate Britain (p77) is crammed with the art of British heavyweights, such as Blake, Hogarth, Gainsborough, Whistler and Turner

NEIL SETCHFIELD

Coastal Beauty

It won't have escaped your notice that England is part of the island of Britain. Surrounded by the sea, the country boasts a nautical heritage and a long coastline with many beautiful spots.

Holkham Bay This pristine 3-mile beach is one of England's best; the vast expanse of sand gives a real sense of isolation with giant skies stretching overhead (p443)

The Jurassic Coast An exhilarating 3-D geology lesson, with towering rock stacks, sea-carved arches and fossils a-plenty (p268)

Beachy Head & Seven Sisters Where the South Downs plunge into the sea, these mammoth chalk cliffs provide a dramatic finale (p158)

Spurn Head National nature reserve amid a string of sand dunes, and a paradise for birdwatchers (p594)

Beach Action

Maybe you want to do more than just look at England's wonderful coastal scenery. Down on the beach, or out in the swell, you can be a bit more active.

Newquay Beautifully positioned above a cluster of golden beaches, this is the undisputed capital of UK surfing, and Cornwall's premier party town (p369)

Burnham Deepdale Eastern England's unexpected centre for wind-powered beach activities, thanks to strong breezes and big stretches of flat sand (p443)

Perranporth Over a mile of golden beach, and endless opportunities for surfing, kite-buggying and bodyboarding (p372)

Longsands, Tynemouth This once-overlooked seaside resort enjoys great breaks and new status as the venue for the National Surfing Championships (p747)

Classic Seaside Resorts

Quiet coves or surfy beaches are one thing, but for a different view of England's coast you have to sample a traditional seaside resort. This is the place for Victorian piers, buckets and spades, candy floss and a stroll along the prom-prom-prom...

Scarborough The original British seaside resort, where it all began back in the 17th century (p614)

Southwold A genteel seaside resort with lovely sandy beach, charming pier and rows of colourful beach huts (p429)

Bournemouth Seven miles of sandy beach, 3000 deckchairs, 1800 beach huts and a pair of Edwardian cliff lifts (p268)

Brighton Away from the ubercool scene there are still plenty of naughty postcards and kiss-me-quick hats in 'London-by-the-Sea' (p162)

Eastbourne A south coast favourite, once known as the nation's retirement home, where new attractions and lively ambience now attract a considerably younger crowd (p157)

month by month

Top Events

1 **Brighton Festival,** May

2 **Glastonbury Festival,** Late June

3 **Glyndebourne,** Late May–August

4 **Notting Hill Carnival,** Late August

5 **Trooping the Colour,** Mid-June

January

After the festivities of Christmas and New Year's Eve, the first few weeks of the year can feel a bit of an anticlimax – never helped by the often bad weather.

The London Parade

A ray of light in the gloom, the New Year's Day Parade in London (to use its official title) is one of the biggest events of its kind in the world, featuring marching bands, street performers, classic cars, floats and displays winding their way through the streets, watched by over half a million people. See www.londonparade.co.uk.

February

February is mid-winter in England. The country may be scenic under snow and sunshine, but more likely grey and gloomy. Festivals and events to brighten the mood are still thin on the ground.

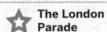

Jorvik Viking Festival

In chilly mid-February, the ancient Viking capital of York becomes home once again to invaders and horned helmets galore, with the intriguing addition of longship races (p603).

March

Spring starts to show itself, with daffodil blooms brightening up the month. Some people cling to the winter mood, but hotels and inns offer special weekend rates to tempt them out from under their duvets.

Crufts Dog Show

Coiffured canines strut their stuff in early March, locked in a struggle to be awarded 'Best in Show' at Birmingham's historic doggy gathering (p506).

University Boat Race

Annual race down the River Thames in London between the rowing teams from Cambridge and Oxford Universities – an institution (since 1856) that still captures the imagination of the country. Late March (p92).

April

The weather is looking up, warmer and drier days bringing out the spring blossoms. Sights and attractions that closed for the low season open up around the middle of the month or at Easter.

Grand National

Half the country has a flutter on the highlight of the three-day horse race meeting at Aintree, a steeplechase with a testing course and high jumps. First Saturday in April (p662).

London Marathon

In early April, super-fit athletes cover 26 miles, 385 yards in just over two hours. Others dress up in daft costumes and take considerably longer (p92).

Camden Crawl

This is your chance to spot the next big thing in the music scene or witness a secret gig by an established act, with 40 of Camden's venues given over to live music for two full days in late April/early May (p92).

May

With sunny spring days, the calendar fills with more events. There are two May public holidays (the first and last Mondays) so road traffic is very busy over the corresponding long weekends.

FA Cup Final

The highlight of the football season for over a century. All winter, teams from all of England's foot ball divisions have been battling it out in a knock-out tournament, culminating in this heady spectacle at Wembley Stadium – the home of English footy. Held in early May (p835).

Brighton Festival

The lively three-week arts fest takes over the streets of buzzy south-coast resort Brighton during May. Alongside the mainstream performances there's a festival fringe as well (p163).

Chelsea Flower Show

The Royal Horticultural Society flower show at Chelsea in late May is the highlight of the gardener's year. Top garden designers take gold, silver and bronze medals (and TV accolades), while the punters take the plants in the last-day give-away (p92).

Glyndebourne

From late May til the end of August, this open-air festival of world-class opera enlivens the pastoral surroundings of Glyndebourne House in East Sussex (p162).

June

Now it's almost summer. You can tell because June sees the music festival season kick off properly, while sporting events – from rowing to racing – fill the calendar.

Derby Week

Horse racing, people-watching and clothes-spotting are on the agenda at this week-long race meeting in Epsom, Surrey, in early June. See www.epsomderby.co.uk.

Download Festival

Expect ear-splitting feedback and fists thrust aloft at this heavy-metal fest in Donington Park, Derbyshire, in early June. Online, see www.downloadfestival.co.uk

The Cotswolds Olimpicks

Welly-wanging, pole-climbing and shin-kicking are the key disciplines at this traditional Gloucestershire sports day in early June, held every year since 1612 (p205).

Isle of Wight Festival

Originally held at the height of the Summer of Love in 1968, this musical extravaganza was resurrected in 2002. Today it attracts top bands, especially from the indie and rock fraternities. Held in mid-June (p263).

Trooping the Colour

Military bands and bear-skinned grenadiers march down London's Whitehall in this mid-June martial pageant to mark the monarch's birthday (p92).

Royal Ascot

It's hard to tell which matters more – the fashion or the fillies – at this highlight of the horse-racing year, held in mid-June at Berkshire's Royal Ascot racetrack. Expect top hats, designer frocks and plenty of frantic betting (p241).

Wimbledon Lawn Tennis Championships

Correctly titled the All England Club Championship, and the best-known grass-court tennis tournament in the world, Wimbledon attracts all the big names. The crowds cheer on the stars and eat tons of strawberries-and-cream. No sign of a British winner coming through any time soon, though... Held in late June (p92).

Glastonbury Festival

England's favourite pop and rock fest held (nearly) every year on a dairy farm in Somerset in late June. Invariably muddy and still a rite of passage for every self-respecting British teenager (p328).

Meltdown Festival

In late June, London's Southbank Centre hands

over the curatorial reigns to a legend of contemporary music (David Bowie, Morrissey, Patti Smith) to pull together a full program of concerts, talks and films. See www.southbankcentre.co.uk.

Royal Regatta

In late June or early July, boats of every description take to the water for Henley's upper-crust river regatta (p198).

Pride

The big event on the gay-and-lesbian calendar happens in late June or early July: a technicolour street parade heading through London's West End, culminating in a concert in Trafalgar Sq (p92).

July

This is it: summer, with weekly festivals and country shows. Schools break up at the end of the month, so there's a holiday tingle in the air, dulled only by ridiculously busy Friday-evening roads.

Great Yorkshire Show

In July, the charming town of Harrogate plays host to one of England's largest county shows. Expect Yorkshire grit, Yorkshire tykes, Yorkshire puddings, Yorkshire beef... See www.greatyorkshireshow.co.uk.

International Birdman Competition

In the first weekend in July, competitors dressed as batmen, fairies and flying machines compete in an outlandish celebration of self-powered flight at West Sussex' Bognor Regis. The furthest flight takes home a £30,000 prize. So far noone's got near the hallowed 100m goal. See www.birdman.org.uk.

Latitude Festival

A small but fast-growing art gathering in the lovely Suffolk seaside town of Southwold. There's theatre, cabaret, art, literature and poetry readings, plus top names from the alternative music scene. Held in mid-July (p429).

World Snail Racing Championships

Three hundred of the nation's sportiest snails gather in the town of Congham for this annual speedfest, held in mid-July. The prize? A tankard of lettuce leaves, of course (p418).

Cowes Week

The country's biggest yachting spectacular hits the choppy seas around the Isle of Wight in late July (p265).

Womad

In late July, roots and world music take centre stage at this former Reading-based festival, now in a country park near Melmesbury in the south Cotswolds. See www.womad.org.

Truck

Held in late July, this indie music festival in Steventon, Oxfordshire, has a loyal following and is known for its eclectic acts. See www.thisistruck.com.

August

Schools and colleges are closed, parliament is in recess, the sun is shining (hopefully), most people go on holiday for a week or two (some of them abroad), and England is in a holiday mood.

Notting Hill Carnival

A multicultural, Caribbean-style street carnival in late August in the London district of Notting Hill. Steel drums, dancers, outrageous costumes, rastas and police officers having a laugh together (p92).

Reading Festival

England's second-oldest music festival. Originally a rock fest, it veers a bit more towards pop these days, but it's still a good bet for big-name bands. Happens in late August (p237).

Leeds Festival

Leeds' major music festival, and Reading's northern sister. The festivals are the same late-August weekend, with the same line-up. If they play Reading on the Friday they'll play Leeds on Saturday, and vice versa (p571).

Manchester Pride

One of England's biggest celebrations of gay, bisexual and transgender life. Happens in late August; see www.manchesterpride.com.

Mathew Street Festival

In last week of August, the world's biggest tribute to The Beatles features six days of music, a convention and a memorabilia auction. Online see www.mathewstreetfestival.org.

September

The first week of September feels more like August, but then the schools open up again, motorway traffic returns to normal and the summer party's over for another year. Good weather is still a chance.

Bestival

Quirky music festival in early September, with a different fancy-dress theme every year. Held at Robin Hill Country Park on the Isle of Wight (p263).

World Gurning Championships

Gurning is face-pulling, and this has to be one of the weirdest events of the year. Elastic-faced contestants come to Egremont in Cumbria in mid-September every year, contorting their features in a bid to pull the most grotesque expressions.

Great North Run

Britain's biggest marathon is in London, but the Great North Run in Tyneside in September is the biggest half-marathon in the world, with the greatest number of runners of any race over this distance (p746).

October

October means autumn. Leaves turn golden-brown and, unless there's an 'Indian Summer', the weather starts to get cold. Sights and attractions start to shut down for the low season, and accommodation rates drop.

Horse of the Year Show

The country's major indoor horse show, with dressage, show-jumping and other equine activities. Held in early October at the NEC arena near Birmingham (p506).

November

Winter's here, and November is dull. The weather's often cold and damp, summer is a distant memory and Christmas seems far away: suitably sombre for Remembrance Day, while Guy Fawkes Night sparks up some fun.

Guy Fawkes Night

Also called Bonfire Night and Fireworks Night, 5 November sees fireworks filling the country's skies in commemoration of a failed attempt to blow up parliament in 1605. Effigies of Guy Fawkes, the leader of the Gunpowder Plot, often burn on bonfires. See www.bonfirenight.net.

Remembrance Day

On 11 November, red poppies are worn and wreaths are laid in towns and cities around the country. The day commemorates military personal killed and injured in the line of duty, from the World Wars to modern conflicts. See www.poppy.org.uk.

World's Biggest Liar Contest

Another whacky event, and it's Cumbria again. Fibbers from all walks of life go head-to-head in a battle of mid-November mendacity at the Bridge Inn in Wasdale (p711).

December

Schools break up around mid-December, but most shops and businesses keep going until Christmas Eve. Holidaymakers hit the roads on the weekend before Christmas Day, driving to see family or heading for the airports.

New Year Celebrations

On 31 December, fireworks and street parties happen in town squares across the country, lighting up the nation to welcome in the New Year.

itineraries

Whether you've got six days or 60, these itineraries provide a starting point for the trip of a lifetime. Want more inspiration? Head online to lonelyplanet.com/thorntree to chat with other travellers.

Two Weeks
England Highlights

If you've got just two weeks to see the best of England, this tour hits most major highlights, with the occasional hidden gem as well. Start with a full day in the nation's capital, **London**, simply walking the streets to admire the world-famous sights: Buckingham Palace, Tower Bridge, Trafalgar Square and more. Then head southwest to the grand cathedral cities of **Winchester** and **Salisbury**. Next stop: ancient history – the iconic menhirs of **Stonehenge**, and their less-well-known counterpart **Avebury Stone Circle**.

A short hop west is the beautiful historic city of **Bath,** and if time allows you can branch out to neighbouring **Bristol** – the southwest's big little city. Then cruise across the classic English countryside of the **Cotswolds** to reach the ancient seat of learning, **Oxford**. Not far away is **Stratford-upon-Avon**, for everything Shakespeare.

Next, strike out north to **York** for Viking remains and the stunning Minster, before swinging south to England's other great university city, **Cambridge**. Enjoy the last few days of your tour back in **London**, immersed in galleries, museums, luxury shops, street markets, West End shows or East End cafes – or whatever takes your fancy.

One Month

The Full Monty

With a month to spare you can enjoy a trip taking in all the very best that England offers. Kick off in **London,** and spend a couple of days seeing the big-name attractions. Make the time for no fixed-program saunters as well – along the south bank of the River Thames, or through the markets of the East End. Next, go down to the sea, and the buzzy coast-resort **Brighton**; then west, via **Portsmouth** for the historic harbour, to reach the picturesque **New Forest**. From the coast head inland to the grand cathedral cities of **Winchester** and **Salisbury**, and on to England's best-known ancient site, **Stonehenge**, and nearby **Avebury Stone Circle** – bigger than Stonehenge and a more intimate experience. Onwards into deepest Wessex, via Thomas Hardy's hometown, **Dorchester**, to reach the neat little city of **Exeter** and the wide and wild expanse of **Dartmoor National Park**. Then it's time for yet another historic city, **Wells**, with its beautiful cathedral, en route to the Georgian masterpiece of **Bath** and the southwest's big little city, **Bristol**. Next comes the classic English countryside of the **Cotswolds**, with a stop at delightful **Stow-on-the-Wold**, and maybe **Broadway** or **Chipping Campden** before reaching **Oxford**, England's original seat of learning. Not far away is Shakespeare Central at **Stratford-upon-Avon** – tie in your visit here with seeing a play by the Bard himself. Continue journeying north via the heather-clad moors and tranquil limestone dales of the **Peak District** to reach England's second city **Manchester** and neighbouring cultural crossroads **Liverpool**. Then it's back to the wilds again with a short hop to the scenic wonders of the **Lake District**. From the sturdy border-town of **Carlisle**, follow the ancient Roman landmark of **Hadrian's Wall** all the way to revitalised city **Newcastle-upon-Tyne**, for a taste of England's far north. Then it's into the home stretch, south via **Durham** and its world-class cathedral, and then **York** for its Viking remains and stunning Minster, to reach **Cambridge**, England's other great university city. From here it's a hop back to **London**, to use up the last few days of your grand tour, taking in highlights such as the Trafalgar Square, the National Gallery, Tate Modern, the Tower of London, all polished off with a stroll across Westminster Bridge as Big Ben chimes the hour.

One Month

The Wild Side

Some itineraries focus on the cities, but this is a tour through the best of England's natural landscape, the inspiration for generations of poets, writers and composers. So put on your hiking boots, or have a camera at the ready, as we take a northeast–southwest meander through some of the country's finest national parks and stretches of open countryside.

Start on the achingly wild and beautiful **Northumberland coast**; the elements are unpredictable, but that's the attraction. Just a short distance inland is **Northumberland National Park**, England's final frontier, dotted with sturdy castles and wind-lashed hilltops. Then it's west via the spectacular Roman remains of **Hadrian's Wall** to the high peaks of the **Lake District**, once the spiritual home for Wordsworth and the Romantic poets, now a mecca for outdoor fans, with dramatic hikes, cosy inns and the country's highest summit **Scafell Pike**.

Travelling east from the Lakes carries you across the **Pennines** – the chain of hills known as 'England's backbone'. To the south lie the green hills and valleys of the **Yorkshire Dales**, and the moors around Haworth – inspiration for Emily Brontë's *Wuthering Heights*. Further east sit the heather-clad **North York Moors**, where humpbacked hills roll all the way to the coast to drop as sheer cliffs into the choppy waters of the North Sea.

Travel south through the moors and dales of the **Peak District** to reach the bucolic **Cotswolds** and Elgar's beloved **Malvern Hills** and then the epic dimensions of **Salisbury Plain**, home to **Stonehenge** and other archaeological intrigues. A few miles more and you're back at the sea again on Dorset's spectacular and fossil-ridden **Jurassic Coast**.

Then head west into England's toe, the counties of Devon and Cornwall, jutting deep into the Atlantic. First stop here is the lush fields and sandy coves of **Exmoor**, then it's on to the eerie granite tors of **Dartmoor** offering some of England's most bleakly beautiful views, rivalled only by the gorse-clad clifftops and sparkling bays of Cornwall's **North Coast**. Last port of call on this scenic excursion is **Land's End**, where the English mainland finally runs out of steam and plunges headlong into the restless ocean. Toodle-pip, England – next stop, America…

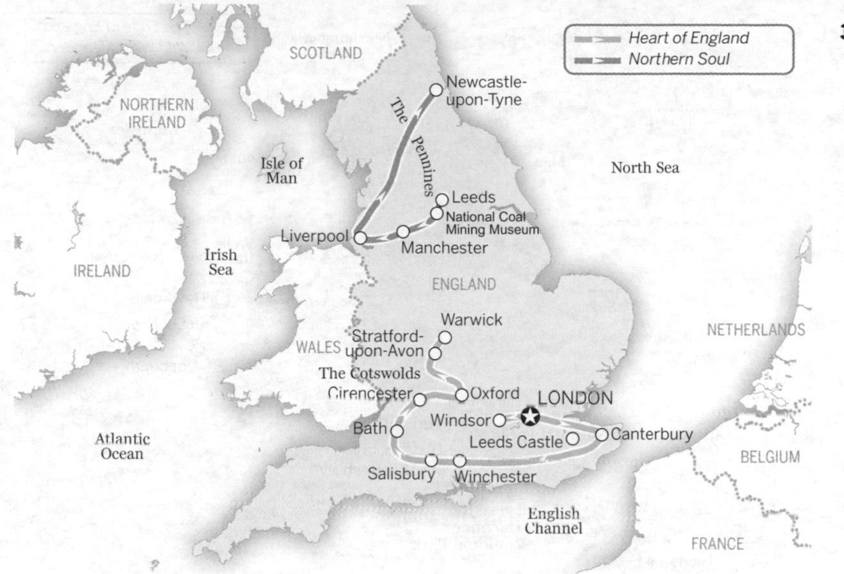

Two to Three Weeks

Heart of England

This journey through England's central regions starts in **London**, with its biggest landmarks: Trafalgar Square, Westminster Abbey, the Tower of London, St Paul's Cathedral and Buckingham Palace. Out of the centre, the gorgeous gardens at **Kew**, historic **Eton College** and regal **Windsor Castle** are also must-see sights.

Beyond the capital is old England proper, especially around the market towns of Kent, where **Canterbury Cathedral** and **Leeds Castle** are top architectural spots.

Then loop through Sussex and into Hampshire, where **Winchester**, the ancient capital, boasts another fine cathedral. Jostling for prominence is nearby **Salisbury**, whose cathedral's famous spire dominates the landscape for miles around.

Out to the west, **Bath** is crammed with landmark English architecture, while the picture-perfect **Cotswolds** conceal a host of pretty villages. On to **Oxford**, one of the country's great centres of learning, and **Stratford-upon-Avon**, home of Shakespeare. There's just time to top up on traditional English towns such as **Northleach**, **Cirencester** and **Wantage**, as well as the grand stately home of **Blenheim Palace** and historic **Warwick Castle**.

Two to Three Weeks

Northern Soul

It's grim up north (an old saying), and if England's former industrial heartland once was, this itinerary shows how things have changed. Start in **Leeds**, where run down factories and abandoned warehouses have been turned into loft apartments and ritzy boutiques. But don't forget the past completely: go deep underground at the **National Coal Mining Museum**.

Just a few miles east is 'England's second city', **Manchester**, famous for its music and a certain football team, where architectural highlights include the stunning **Imperial War Museum North**.

Nearby **Liverpool** is reinventing itself as a cultural capital, with the rebuilding and rebranding most apparent at the historic waterfront, **Albert Dock**.

Back across the Pennines, one-time king of coal and steel **Newcastle-upon-Tyne** has traded heavy industries for art and architecture. Cross the **Millennium Bridge** to Gateshead and the **BALTIC Centre for Contemporary Art**, a former grain mill turned art gallery, before catching a show at the fabulous **Sage** concert hall.

Conclude your tour with a visit to England's best-known piece of public art, the iconic (and gigantic) **Angel of the North**.

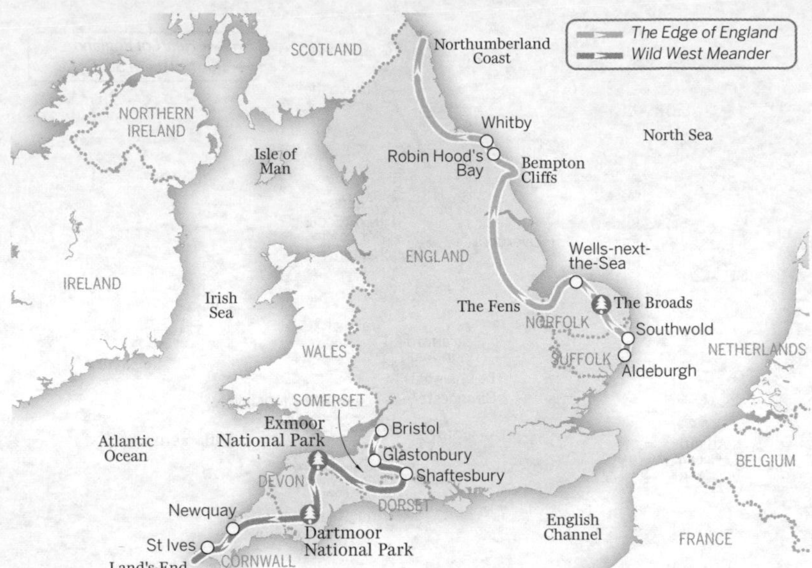

Two Weeks

The Edge of England

England's national parks are beautiful: hardly a well-kept secret. If you like your landscapes a little less hectic, try this backwater route along England's eastern fringe.

Start in sleepy **Suffolk**, a favourite spot for boaters, bikers and birdwatchers. Quaint villages and market towns such as **Sudbury** and **Lavenham** dot the landscape; along the coast are wildlife reserves, shingly beaches, fishing ports such as **Aldeburgh** and the delightfully retro seaside resort of **Southwold**.

Things get even quieter in **Norfolk**, especially around the misty lakes and windmill-lined rivers of **The Broads**. For big-sky strolls or historic country pubs head for the coastal villages near **Wells-next-the-Sea**.

Across the border in Lincolnshire lies the eerie, pan-flat landscape of **The Fens**, now a haven for otters and birdlife. Then it's north again into Yorkshire, where the massive breeding seabird colonies at **Bempton Cliffs** are one of England's finest wildlife spectacles.

Enjoy quirky **Robin Hood's Bay** and bustling **Whitby,** then round things off with a blustery stroll between the landmark castles of **Bamburgh** and **Dunstanburgh** on the wild **Northumberland Coast**.

Two Weeks

Wild West Meander

The southwest of England takes a bit of effort to reach, but repays in full with a rich green landscape surrounded by glistening seas.

Start in **Bristol**, the capital of the West-country, then saunter down through Somerset to **Glastonbury** – famous for its music festival and the best place to stock up on candles or crystals at any time of year. West leads to heathery **Exmoor**. South leads into Dorset, where highlights include picturesque **Shaftsbury**.

Onwards into Devon, there's a choice of coasts, as well as **Dartmoor**, the highest and wildest hills in southern England.

Cross into Cornwall to browse the galleries at **St Ives**, explore **Tintagel Castle**, the legendary birthplace of King Arthur, or wax your board in **Newquay**, epicentre of England's surf scene. Just inland is the **Eden Project**, where giant space-age greenhouse domes are home to a range of habitats from jungle to desert.

The natural finish to this wild west meander is **Land's End**, where the English mainland comes to a final full stop. Sink a drink in the First & Last pub, and promise yourself a return trip some day...

Outdoor England

Best Long-Distance Routes

Coast to Coast, Hadrian's Wall, Cotswold Way, South West Coast Path

Best for Short Walks

Lake District, Yorkshire Dales, The Cotswolds, Dartmoor

Best for Coast Walks

Northumberland, Devon and Cornwall, Norfolk and Suffolk, Dorset

Best for Leisurely Cycling

Norfolk and Suffolk, Wessex, The Cotswolds

Best Mountain Biking

Yorkshire, Peak District, Wessex

Best Time to Go

Summer (June to August) The best time for walking, cycling and surfing, when the weather is usually warm and dry and the water isn't too cold.

Late spring (May) and early autumn (September) The seasons either side of summer can also be good – fewer crowds and days are often sunny.

What's the best way to slow down, meet the locals and get off the beaten track as you travel around England? Simple: go for a walk, get on a bike or enjoy any other kind of outdoor activity. Becoming *actively* involved in the country's way of life is much more rewarding than staring at it through a camera lens or car window.

Walking and cycling are the most popular outdoor activities here – for locals and visitors alike – because they open up some beautiful corners of the country and can be done virtually on a whim. For walkers, there's no need to apply for trekking permits, arrange Sherpas or carry tents. If you prefer to go cycling (on- or off-road) bikes can be easily hired.

In England, these activities are not for sporty types only. How much you do is your choice. On foot or bike you can amble across plains, conquer lofty mountains, enjoy relaxed saunters or work up a sweat on long tours. There are activities suited for young and old – and often perfect for families, too.

But if waking or cycling is too gentle for your tastes, England supplies the goods for thrill-seekers too. The coastline offers up excellent spots for surfing and sailing, while rock-climbers can test their skills on sheer sea-cliffs or inland crags – and that's before we get onto cutting-edge activities like mountain-boarding and kitesurfing.

So pack your bags and your sense of adventure. Whatever your budget, a walk or ride through the English countryside – and possibly something involving more adrenaline – could be a highlight of your trip.

THREE STEPS TO HEAVEN

So you've arrived in a new area, and want to know more about local options for walking or other outdoor activities. Here's what to do:

» Step 1: Flip to the relevant regional chapter in this book for an overview of the best outdoor activities in that area.

» Step 2: Find the local tourist office, where you can pick up leaflets, maps and guidebooks, and find out about bike-hire and guided walks. Tourist offices can also supply information on other local activities, such as surf schools and riding stables.

» Step 3: Head out, and enjoy!

Walking

England can seem a crowded place, so open areas are highly valued by the English, and every weekend millions of them go walking in the countryside. It might be a short riverside stroll or a major hike over mountain ranges - or anything in between. You could do a lot worse than join them.

Every village and town in England is surrounded by a web of footpaths, while most open country is crossed by paths and tracks. You can walk from place to place, maybe following a long-distance national trial. Or you can base yourself in one spot for a week or so, and go out on walks each day to explore the surrounding countryside. The options really are limitless.

Where to Walk

Although you can walk pretty much anywhere in England, some areas are better than others. Here's a rundown of our favourites:

Lake District

» This wonderful area of soaring peaks, endless views, deep valleys and, of course, beautiful lakes is protected by the Lake District National Park (often abbreviated to simply 'The Lakes', but never the 'Lakes District') and loved by walkers, partly because of the landscape, and partly because of the history; thanks to the poet Wordsworth and his Romantic chums, this is where walking for enjoyment really began (p691).

Peak District

» Despite the name, this area has very few soaring summits. But there plenty of hills, valleys and moors, making the Peak District National Park one of the most popular walking areas in northern England. And deservedly so: access is easy, facilities are good, and there's a huge choice of routes of all lengths and standards through a variety of landscapes (p484).

Yorkshire Dales

» The green valleys and rolling hills of the Yorkshire Dales National Park make this another of the most popular walking areas in England. Paths are a little gentler and conditions a little less serious than the Lakes, with the happy addition of some delightful villages and hamlets nestling in the dales – many with pubs and tearooms that are used to providing refreshments for weary walkers (p582).

Northumberland

» On northern England's frontier lands (any further north and you're in Scotland), keen walkers love the starkly beautiful moors of Northumberland National Park (p765). For a change of scene, the high cliffs and vast empty beaches on the nearby coast are less daunting but just as dramatic – perfect for wild seaside strolls (p737).

The Cotswolds

» The favoured spot for walkers in central-southern England is the Cotswold Hills. This

FRESH-AIR FREEDOM

The absolute pleasure of walking in England is due to the 'right of way' network. In England nearly all land (including in national parks) is privately owned, but if there's a right of way, you can follow it through fields, pastures, woods, even farmhouse yards, as long as you keep to the route and do no damage. In some mountain and moorland areas, it gets even better: walkers can move freely beyond the rights of way. Known as 'freedom to roam', where permitted it's clearly advertised with markers on gates and signposts.

is classic English countryside, where lovely paths meander through neat fields and mature woodland, past pretty villages with farms and cottages of honey-coloured stone. Walks on the eastern side of the Cotswolds tend to be gentler; on the western side, especially along the Cotswold Escarpment, the paths go up and down a bit more (p200).

Dartmoor

» In the southwest, Dartmoor National Park boasts the highest hills in southern England. Much of the landscape is devoid of trees and surprisingly wild, but for walkers that's its very attraction. Other features of the high ground are the spiky granite outcrops called tors, and the remains of numerous Bronze-Age sites. Lower down, delightful valleys cut into the edge of the moor, perfect for riverside strolls in summer (p356).

Exmoor

» Just to the north of Dartmoor, the southwest's other national park is Exmoor, with heather-covered hills cut by deep valleys, edged with the added bonuses of spectacular cliffs and great beaches (p331).

North Downs & South Downs

» South of London, between the capital and the lively resorts on the coast (and within easy reach of both), the North and South Downs are two ranges of broad chalky hills, running roughly parallel, with the tranquil farmland of the Weald in between. On the map, the North Downs (p129) appear hemmed-in by motorways and conurbations, and while this area can never be described as wilderness, the walking here is often unexpectedly tranquil. The South Downs are higher, and not so cramped by urban expansion, with more options for walks. It's also one of England's newest national parks (p129).

New Forest

» In England's deep south lies the New Forest. Visitors love this name, as the area is more than 1000 years old and there aren't *that* many trees – but the beautiful open areas of gorse and grassland are ideal for easy strolls (p258).

Isle of Wight

» Off the south coast of England sits the Isle of Wight. This is a great spot if you're new to walking, or simply not looking for high peaks and wilderness. Many routes are signposted, and there's a range of short and long options. You can also choose from circular loops or linear walks, and you can always get back to your starting point using the island's excellent bus service (p263).

SAMPLING THE LONG ROUTES

Although England's long-distance trails have official start- and finish-points, you don't have to do the whole thing end-to-end in one go. Many people walk just a section for a day or two, or use the main route as a basis for loops exploring the surrounding area.

Long-Distance Walks

Many walkers savour the chance of completing one of England's famous long-distance routes, and there are so many to choose from you'd easily wear out your boots trying to do them all. Most take between one and two weeks to complete, although some are longer. As with the short walks, there are many options, and it's easy to pick a route that suits your experience and the time you have available.

Because England just doesn't have the endless tracts of wilderness found in some other countries, you're never more than a few miles from a village. This means overnight stops can be at inns or B&Bs – you don't have to camp. And you don't even have to carry your pack if you don't want to. Baggage services operate on most of the main routes, carrying your kit between each night's accommodation. It may be the soft option, but it certainly makes the walking far more enjoyable.

Some long distance walking routes are obscure and exist only in dedicated guidebooks, while others are high-profile with signposts and route-markers as well as being highlighted on Ordnance Survey maps. The most high-profile routes are the national trails, clearly marked on the ground and on the map. These are ideal for beginners or visitors from overseas (although they're not all easy; some are long and pass over tough terrain).

Coast to Coast Walk

» 190 miles – England's number-one favourite – a top-quality trial across northern England, through three national parks and a spectacular mix of valleys, plains, mountains, dales and moors.

ROUTE OF ALL KNOWLEDGE

For comprehensive coverage of a selection of long and short walking routes, we (naturally) recommend Lonely Planet's very own *Walking in Britain*, which also covers places to stay and eat along the way. If you're on two wheels, Lonely Planet also publishes *Cycling Britain*, a selection of touring routes around the country. For more ideas, *Cycling in the UK* is an excellent handbook published by the bike campaign group Sustrans, covering over 40 day-rides and a range of longer 'holiday routes'. For off-road rides, the best book is *Where to Mountain Bike in Britain*, or see www.wheretomtb.com.

Cotswold Way

» 102 miles – A delightful walk through classic picture-postcard countryside with fascinating smatterings of English history along the way.

Cumbria Way

» 68 miles – A wonderful hike through the Lake District, keeping mainly to the valleys, with breathtaking views of the mountains on either side.

Hadrian's Wall

» 84 miles – A new national trial following the famous Roman structure all the way across northern England, and giving the Coast-to-Coast a run for its money in the popularity stakes.

Pennine Way

» 256 miles – The granddaddy of them all, an epic hike along the mountainous spine of northern England.

South West Coast Path

» 610 miles – A roller-coaster romp round England's southwest peninsula, past beaches, bays, shipwrecks, seaside resorts, fishing villages and clifftop castles.

Thames Path

» 173 miles – A journey of contrasts beside England's best-known river, from rural Gloucestershire to the heart of London.

Cycling

A bike is the perfect mode of transport for exploring back-road England. Once you escape the busy main highways, a vast network of quiet country lanes winds through fields and peaceful villages, ideal for cycle-touring.

Mountain-bikers can go further into the wilds on the tracks and bridleways that cross England's hills and high moors, or head for the dedicated mountain-bike centres where specially built single-track trails wind through the forests. Options at these centres vary from delightful dirt roads ideal for families to precipitous drops for hardcore riders, all classified from green to black in ski-resort style.

Whether on-road or off-road is your thing, the options in England are truly enticing. You can cruise through gently rolling landscapes, taking it easy and stopping for cream teas, or you can thrash all day through hilly areas, revelling in steep ascents and swooping downhill sections.

You can cycle from place to place, camping or staying in B&Bs (many of which are cyclist-friendly), or you can base yourself in one area for a few days and go out on rides in different directions. All you need is a map and a sense of adventure, and the

WEATHER WATCH

While enjoying your walking in England, it's always worth remembering the fickle nature of English weather. The countryside can appear gentle and welcoming (and often is), but sometimes conditions can turn nasty – especially on the higher ground. At any time of year, if you're walking on the hills or open moors:

» carry warm and waterproof clothing (even in summer)

» take a map and compass (that you know how to use)

» bring some drink, food and high-energy stuff such as chocolate

» leave details of your route with someone responsible if you're really going off the beaten track

BOOTS & BIKES – HANDY WEBSITES

Before you set off, the website of the **Ramblers' Association** (www.ramblers.org.uk), the country's leading organisation for walkers, is a mine of background information. The annually updated *Walk Britain* handbook listing walker-friendly accommodation is also invaluable. Also great for specifics on some longer routes is www.nationaltrail.co.uk.

For two-wheeled travel, the website of the **Cyclists' Touring Club** (www.ctc.org.uk), the UK's recreational cycling and campaigning body, includes a cycle-hire directory and mail-order service for maps and books.

highways and byways of England are yours for the taking.

Where to Cycle

Here's an overview of some or our favourite English cycling areas:

Norfolk & Suffolk

» If you're not a regular cyclist, the hills in some parts of England can be daunting, so the counties of Norfolk (p431) and Suffolk (p421) are a great place to start. The landscape is generally flat, with quiet lanes winding through farmland and picturesque villages, past rivers, lakes and welcoming country pubs.

Wessex

» The counties of Somerset, Dorset and Wiltshire are good spots if you're looking for gentle cycling. There are no mountains, and most hills are fairly gentle – although there are a few steep valleys to keep you on your toes. But the main attraction here is the beautiful network of quiet lanes, making the area perfect for leisurely cycle-touring. In the same area, off-road fans can head for the tracks on the Quantock or Mendip Hills, or for the chalky byways of the Wiltshire Downs. Next door in Hampshire, the New Forest is another good spot for on- and off-road rides.

The Cotswolds

» The Cotswolds is a mostly rural area with good cycling options. From the western side of the hills you get fantastic views over the Severn Valley, but you wouldn't want to go up and down the escarpment too often. The landscape is gentler on the eastern side. There's also a difference between the north and south Cotswolds; most of the well-know scenic towns and villages are in the northern Cotswolds, so they can be crowded in summer (as can the surrounding roads). In contrast, the southern Cotswolds area sees less visitors, though still has its fair share of pretty villages and a fantastic network of country lanes, making it one of the best cycling areas in England (p200).

Cornwall & Devon

» Westcountry gems Cornwall and Devon enjoy the best of the English climate and some of the finest scenery in the country, but the rugged landscape means tough days in the saddle. Even the coast-roads go up and down all day, thanks to those beautiful rivers flowing down steep valleys to the sea. If you like a challenge on two wheels, this is the place.

Peak District

» Wedged between the industrial cities of northern England (but standing firm), the Peak District National Park is very popular for mountain-biking and road cycling, although (or perhaps, because) the hills are quite steep in places. The park falls into two distinct zones: in the south are limestone valleys, lanes and villages that are good for cycle touring or easier off-road outings; in the north are high peaty moors, generally more favoured by the mountain-bikers. If it all sounds too strenuous, take the time to explore cycle routes cutting through the landscape along disused railways – dramatic and effortless at the same time (p484).

The Marches

» To the west of the Midlands, on the borderlands where England meets Wales, the Marches is another pastoral delight, with good minor roads relatively free of cars and some off-road options in the hills.

Yorkshire

» The North York Moors and Yorkshire Dales also offer exhilarating options for cycle touring and mountain-biking – but conditions can be tough. It's no accident that many of England's top racing cyclists come from this area – the mountain roads make an excellent training ground. Mountain-bikers love hills, of course, and many

THE NATIONAL CYCLE NETWORK

Anyone riding a bike through England will almost certainly come across the National Cycle Network (NCN), a UK-wide 10,000-mile web of roads and traffic-free tracks. Strands of the network in busy cities are aimed at commuters and school kids (where the network follows city streets, cyclists normally have their own lane, separate from motor traffic); while other sections follow the most remote roads in the country and are perfect for touring.

The whole scheme is the brainchild of **Sustrans** (www.sustrans.org.uk), a name derived from 'sustainable transport'. This campaign group was barely taken seriously way back in 1978 when the network idea was first announced. But the growth of cycling, coupled with near-terminal car congestion, has earned the scheme lots of attention – not to mention serious millions from government, regional authorities and (in early 2008) the national lottery.

Several long-distance touring routes use the most scenic sections of the NCN (plus, it has to be said, a few less-than-scenic urban sections). Other features include a great selection of artworks to admire along the way. In fact, the network is billed as the country's largest outdoor sculpture gallery. The whole scheme is a resounding success and a credit to the visionaries who persevered against inertia all those years ago.

head for the dedicated trails in Dalby Forest. But on- or off-road, if you like your days out to be a tad strenuous, the superb scenery of 'God's Own Country' make it well worth the effort.

Other Outdoor Activities

While walking and cycling can be done at the drop of a hat, many other outdoor activities need a bit more organisation and often specialised equipment, guides or instructors. Coasteering, for example, is not something you can just go off and do on your own. Below are a few ideas to inform and inspire. If you need more details while you're travelling in England, tourist offices can advise about specialist local operators and adventure centres.

Coasteering

If sometimes a simple clifftop walk doesn't cut the mustard, then coasteering might appeal. It's like mountaineering, but instead of going up a mountain, you go sideways along a coast – a steep and rocky coast – with waves breaking around your feet. And if the rock gets too steep, no problem – you jump in and start swimming. The mix of sheer cliffs, sandy beaches and warm water make Cornwall and Devon prime coasteering spots. Outdoor centres provide wetsuits, helmets and buoyancy aids; you provide an old pair of training shoes and a sense of adventure. For more information see www.coasteering.org.

Kitebuggying

Bring together a wing-shaped parachute, three wheels, a good breeze, and – *whoosh!* – you're picking up serious speed across the beach. Welcome to the world of kitebuggying. Often available wherever you find big stretches of flat sand, good places to start include the beaches of Cornwall, Devon and Norfolk.

Horse Riding & Pony Trekking

If you want to explore the hills and moors but walking or cycling is too much of a sweat, seeing the wilder parts of England from horseback is highly recommended. In rural areas and national parks like Dartmoor and Northumberland, riding centres cater to all levels of proficiency, with ponies for kids and beginners and horses for the more experienced. The **British Horse Society** (www.bhs.org.uk) lists approved riding centres offering day rides or longer holidays on horseback.

Mountain-boarding & Kiteboarding

Imagine hurtling down a grassy hillside on a gigantic skateboard with four oversized wheels, and you've pretty much got mountain-boarding. If that's not enough, add a wing-shaped parachute, and it's a kite-board – so you can get the wind to pull you around whenever gravity gives up. There are mountain- and kiteboarding centres in Yorkshire, Derbyshire, Shropshire and Cornwall, among other places.

Rock Climbing & Mountaineering

England's main centre for long multipitch routes (as well as some fine short routes) is the Lake District. Other popular climbing areas are the Peak District and Yorkshire Dales – mainly single-pitch and a lot of extreme bouldering. England also offers the exhilaration of sea-cliff climbing, most notably in Cornwall (nothing makes you concentrate more on finding the next hold than waves crashing 30m below!). For more info, see website of the **British Mountaineering Council** (www.thebmc.co.uk).

Sailing & Windsurfing

England's nautical heritage means sailing is a very popular pastime, in everything from tiny dinghies to ocean-going yachts. In recent years there's been a massive surge in windsurfing too. Favourite spots include the coasts of Norfolk and Suffolk, southeast England, Devon, Cornwall and the Isle of Wight. There are also many inland lakes and reservoirs, ideal for training, racing or just pottering. The **Royal Yachting Association** (www.rya.org.uk) can provide details on training centres where you can improve your skills or simply charter a boat for pleasure.

Surfing

England may not seem an obvious place for surfing, but conditions are surprisingly good, and the huge tidal range means often a completely different set of breaks at low and high tides. If you've come from the other side of the world, you'll be delighted to learn that summer water temperatures in England are roughly equivalent to winter temperatures in southern Australia. Wetsuit-protected, you'll find many excellent surf opportunities here. Top of the list is the Atlantic-facing west coast of Cornwall and Devon (Newquay is surf-central, with all the trappings from Kombi vans to bleached hair) and there are smaller surf scenes on the west coast, notably Norfolk and Yorkshire. At the main spots, it's easy enough to hire boards and wetsuits. The **British Surfing Association** (www.britsurf.co.uk) can provide details on instruction centres, courses, competitions and so on.

BEST MAPS

Ordnance Survey (www.ordnancesurvey.co.uk), the UK's national mapping agency, produces some of the finest mapping in the world. Use the 1:50,000 *Landranger* series for cycling, and 1:25,000 scale *Explorer* maps for walking. In the mountains, **Harvey Maps** (www.harveymaps.co.uk) are excellent.

Kitesurfing

If regular surfing doesn't offer enough airtime, strap on a wing-shaped parachute and let the wind do the work. Brisk breezes, decent waves and great beaches make Cornwall a favourite spot for kitesurfing, but it's possible all round the English coastline, and there are several training centres to show you the ropes. The **British Kitesurfing Association** (www.kitesurfing.org) has more information.

RULES OF THE ROAD

Bikes aren't allowed on motorways, but you can cycle on all other public roads, although main roads (A-roads) tend to be busy with cars and trucks so should be avoided. Many B-roads suffer heavy motor traffic too. The best places for cycling are the small C-roads and unclassified roads (lanes) that cover rural England, especially in lowland areas, meandering through quiet countryside and linking small, picturesque villages.

For off-roaders, cycling is *not* allowed on footpaths in England, but it is allowed on unmade roads or bridleways (originally for horses but now for bikes too) that are public rights-of-way. For the best mountain-biking it's often worth seeking out forestry areas: among these vast plantations, signposted routes of varying difficulty have been opened up for single-track fans.

Travel With Children

Best Regions for Kids

London

Children's attractions galore; some put a strain on parental purse strings, but many others are free.

Devon, Cornwall & Wessex

Some of the best beaches in England, and fairly reliable holiday weather – though crowded in summer.

East Midlands

Former railways now traffic-free cycle routes make the Peak District perfect for family outings; Sherwood Forest is the obvious spot for Robin Hood games.

Oxford & the Cotswolds

Oxford has kid-friendly museums plus Harry Potter connections; Cotswold countryside is ideal for little-leg strolls.

West Midlands & the Marches

Historic England–Wales borderland has castles to explore, as well as excellent museums for inquisitive minds.

Lake District & Cumbria

Activity Central: longer walks, zip-wires and mountain bikes for teenagers, boat rides and Beatrix Potter for the youngsters.

England is great for travel with children because it's compact, with a lot of attractions packed into a small area. So when the kids in the back of the car say 'Are we there yet?', your answer can often be 'Yes!'. Throughout this book, we've highlighted many kid-friendly attractions. With a bit of planning ahead, and some online research to get the best bargains, having the kids on board can make a trip round England even more enjoyable.

England for Kids

Many places of interest in England cater for kids as much as adults. At the country's historic castles, for example, mum and dad can admire the medieval architecture, while the kids will have great fun striding around the battlements. In the same way, many national parks and holiday resorts organise specific activities for children. It goes without saying that everything ramps up in the school holidays (see Planning box, p43).

Bargain Hunting

Most visitor attractions offer family tickets – usually two adults plus two children– for less than the sum of the individual entrance charges. Most offer cheaper rates for solo parents and kids too. Be sure to ask, as these are not always clearly displayed.

PLANNING

When to Go

The best time for families to visit England is pretty much the best time for everyone else – anytime from April/May till the end of September. It's worth avoiding August – the heart of school summer holidays – when prices go up and the roads are busy, especially near the coast.

Places to Stay

Some hotels welcome kids (with their parents) and provide cots, toys and babysitting services, while others maintain an adult atmosphere. Many B&Bs offer 'family suites' – two adjoining bedrooms with one bathroom – and an increasing number of hostels (YHA and independent) have family rooms with four or six beds, some even with private bathroom attached. If you want to stay in one place for a while, renting a holiday cottage is ideal (see p840). Camping is very popular with English families, and there are lots of fantastic campsites, but you'll usually need all your own equipment.

On the Road

If you're going by public transport, trains are great for families: intercity services have plenty of room for luggage and extra stuff like buggies (prams), and the kids can move about a bit if they get bored. In contrast, they need to stay in their seats on long-distance coaches.

If you're hiring a car, most (but not all) rental firms can provide child seats – you'll need to check this in advance. Most will not actually fit the child seats; you need to do that yourself, for insurance reasons.

Dining, not Whining

When it comes to refuelling, most cafes and teashops are child-friendly. Restaurants are mixed: some offer highchairs and kiddy portions; others firmly say 'No children after 6pm'.

Children under 18 are not allowed in some pubs, but most serve food, making them 'family-friendly'. If in doubt, simply ask the bar-staff.

And finally, a word on another kind of feeding: England is still slightly buttoned-up about breastfeeding; older folks may tut-tut a bit if you give junior a top-up in public, but if done modestly it's usually considered OK.

Children's Highlights

Best Hands-on Action

'Please Do Not Touch'? No chance! Here are some places where grubby fingers and enquiring minds are positively welcomed:

» **Science Museum, London** Seven floors of educational exhibits at the mother of all science museums.

» **Discovery Museum, Newcastle** Tyneside's rich history on display; highlights include a buzzers-and-bells science maze.

» **Magna, Yorkshire** Formerly one of the world's largest steel works, and now a science adventure centre.

» **Action Stations, Portsmouth** Toys for the boys (and girls) with a military spin; your chance to fly a helicopter, control an aircraft carrier, or up-periscope in a submarine.

» **Enginuity, Ironbridge** Endless interactive displays at the birthplace of the Industrial Revolution.

» **Roald Dahl Museum, Great Missenden** Try on costumes, make up stories and explore the writing hut of the much-loved children's author.

HANDY WEBSITES

» **Baby Goes 2** (www.babygoes2.com) Advice, tips and encouragement (and a stack of adverts) for families on holiday.

» **Enjoy England** (www.enjoyengland.co.uk) Official tourism website for England, with lots of useful info for families.

» **Mums Net** (www.mumsnet.com) No-nonsense advice on travel and more from a gang of UK mothers.

ALL CHANGE

On the sticky topic of dealing with nappies (diapers), most museums and other attractions in England usually have good baby-changing facilities (cue old joke: I swapped mine for a nice souvenir!). Elsewhere, some city-centre public toilets have baby-changing areas, although these can be a bit grimy; your best bet for clean facilities is an upmarket department store. On the road, baby-changing facilities are usually OK at motorway service stations or out-of-town supermarkets.

Best Fresh-Air Fun

If the kids tire of England's castles and museums, you're never far from a place for outdoor activities to blow away the cobwebs:

» **Conkers, Leicestershire** Play indoors, outdoors or among the trees in the heart of the National Forest.

» **Puzzle Wood, Forest of Dean** A wonderful woodland playground with maze-like paths, weird rock formations and eerie passageways to offer a real sense of discovery.

» **Whinlatter Forest, Cumbria** Highlights include a 'Go Ape' adventure park, excellent mountain-bike trails, plus live video feeds from squirrel-cams.

» **Bewilderwood, Norfolk** Zip wires, jungle bridges, tree houses, marsh walks, boat trips, mazes and all sorts of old-fashioned outdoor adventure.

» **Lyme Regis & the Jurassic Coast, Dorset** Guided tours show you how to find your very own prehistoric fossil.

» **Tissington Trail, Derbyshire** Cycling this former railway is fun and almost effortless. You can hire kids' bikes, tandems and trailers. Don't forget to hoot in the tunnels!

Best Rainy-Day Distractions

On those inevitable gloomy days, head for the indoor attractions, including the nation's great collection of museums. Alternatively, try outdoor stuff like coasteering in Cornwall or canyoning in the Lake District – always fun, wet or dry.

» **Cadbury World, Birmingham** Your dentist may cry, but kids love the story of chocolate. And yes, there are free samples.

» **Eden Project, Cornwall** It may be raining outside, but inside these gigantic semi-spherical greenhouses it's forever tropical forest or Mediterranean climate.

» **Cheddar Gorge Caves, Wessex** Finally nail the difference between stalactites and stalagmites in the Westcountry's deep caverns.

» **Underground Passages, Exeter** Explore medieval catacombs – the only system of its kind open to the public in England.

Best Stealth Learning

Secretly exercise their minds while the little darlings think they are 'just' having fun.

» **At-Bristol** One of the best interactive science museums in England, covering space, technology and the human brain.

» **Jorvik Centre, York** An excellent smells-and-all Viking settlement reconstruction.

» **Natural History Museum, London** Animals everywhere! Highlights include the life-size blue whale and the animatronics dinosaurs.

» **ThinkTank, Birmingham** Every display comes with a button or a lever at this edu-taining science museum.

» **National Space Centre, Leicester** Spacesuits, zero-gravity toilets and mini-astronaut training – all guaranteed to fire-up little minds.

regions at a glance

London

Historic Streets ✓✓✓
Entertainment ✓✓✓
Museums ✓✓✓

Historic Streets

London's ancient streets contain many of the nation's most famous and history-steeped landmarks. The echoes of the footfalls of monarchs, poets, whores and saints can still be detected in places like the Tower of London, Westminster Abbey, St Paul's Cathedral, the Houses of Parliament and the capital's many palaces. And away from the grand buildings, pubs and coaching inns that once served the likes of Dickens, Shelley, Keats and Byron are still pouring pints today.

Entertainment

From West End theatres to East End clubs, from Camden's rock venues to Covent Garden's opera house, from tennis at Wimbledon, cricket at Lords, or football at Stamford Bridge, Highbury or any of the home grounds of the city's beloved clubs, London's world-famous venues and arenas offer a perpetual clamour of entertainment. You can rest assured that you'll never be bored.

Museums & Galleries

While the British Museum is the big crowd-puller, the capital has museums and galleries of every shape and size – and many of the very best are free. Even with London's famously wet weather it's unlikely that your supply of rainy days will ever exhaust the great many collections on offer. Many are geared equally towards children and adults, and some you'll need to dip into again and again just to scratch the surface.

p52

Canterbury & the Southeast

Cathedrals ✓✓✓
Invasion Heritage ✓✓
Food & Drink ✓✓

Cathedrals

A major reason to visit southeast England, Canterbury Cathedral is one of the finest in Europe, and one of the most holy places in Christendom. Write your own Canterbury tale as you explore its atmospheric chapels, cloisters and crypts.

Invasion Heritage

The southeast has always been a gateway for arrivals from the Continent, some more welcome than others. Castles and fortresses, the 1066 battlefield and Dover's secret wartime tunnels all tell the region's story of invasion and defence.

Food & Drink

Kent is deservedly known as the Garden of England, long celebrated for its hops, fruit, oysters, fish, lamb and vineyards – yes, vineyards! Sussex isn't far behind, with England's finest sparkling wine giving the French stuff a run for its euro.

p128

Oxford, Cotswolds & Around

Stately Homes ✓✓✓
Villages ✓✓
Cream Teas ✓

Stately Homes

Favoured by the rich and powerful for centuries, thanks to its proximity to London and the lush undulating landscape, this region is scattered with some of the finest stately homes and country houses in all of England.

Villages

Littered with implausibly picturesque 'chocolate box' scenes of honey-coloured stone cottages, thatched roofs, neat greens and cobbled lanes, the villages of the Cotswolds provide a charming snapshot of rural England, little changed since medieval times.

Cream Teas

If you're craving a proper cream tea with all the trimmings in historic surroundings, nearly every scenic village in this region has at least one tearoom – and you couldn't find a better place to indulge.

p178

Wessex

Coastline ✓✓✓
Stone Circles ✓✓✓
Architecture ✓✓

Coastline

The coasts of the rural counties of Hampshire and Dorset together boast beautiful beaches, jolly seaside resorts and wave-sculpted cliffs. Take a dip at Lulworth Cove, search for fossils at Lyme Regis, or go sailing round the Isle of Wight.

Stone Circles

Wessex is an ancient landscape, nowhere more epitomised than the mysterious stone circle of Stonehenge – older than Egypt's Pyramids of Giza and an iconic symbol of England's prehistoric period. Nearby is Avebury Stone Circle, even bigger than Stonehenge.

Architecture

Besides stone circles, Wessex delights with later constructions too: photogenic ruined castles, impossibly ornate stately homes, quaint villages and handsome country houses. All topped by the grand Georgian crescents of Bath – one of England's most beautiful cities.

p243

Devon & Cornwall

Beaches ✓✓✓
Outdoor Activities ✓✓✓
Food ✓✓✓

Beaches

England's far southwest peninsula juts determinedly into the Atlantic, with a spectacular coast on each side, and an almost endless chain of sandy beaches – some big, some small, some brash, some tranquil.

Outdoor Activities

If you like to take it nice and easy, come here to hike on the wilderness moors or tootle along cycle trails. If you prefer life fast and furious, with adrenaline on the side, come here to surf the best waves in England, or learn to sail, dive or kitesurf.

Food

Lush fields means fine farm produce and rich waters mean plenty of seafood, making this region one of the best foodie hot spots in the country. Tuck into local steak pies in stylish gastropubs, sample cones with Devon cream in friendly teashops or buy super-fresh crab direct from the fishermen.

p338

Cambridge & East Anglia

Cathedrals ✓✓✓
Coastline ✓✓
The Broads ✓✓

Cathedrals
The magnificent cathedrals of East Anglia soar above the flat landscape, a testimony to the region's past wealth and prosperity. Top highlights are Ely and Norwich (with a spire second only to Salisbury's in height) while less well-known architectural gems include the cathedrals of Peterborough and St Albans.

Coastline
With historic villages still proud of their nautical heritage, classic seaside resorts like Southwold or Great Yarmouth, wide sandy beaches, delightful old pubs and globally important bird reserves, the coastline of East Anglia is rich and varied.

The Broads
The Norfolk and Suffolk Broads are a tranquil haven of lakes and meandering waterways, a national park, and an ideal spot for boating, birding, canoeing, cycling or walking – perfect for getting back to nature at a leisurely pace.

p398

Nottingham & the East Midlands

Outdoor Activities ✓✓✓
History ✓✓✓
Stately Homes ✓✓✓

Outdoor Activities
Gem of the region is the Peak District National Park: with its high moors and deep valleys, it's a giant adventure playground full of walking trails, cycle routes, cliffs to climb and potholes to explore.

History
You can explore a wide range of historic sites, from the seminal War of the Roses battlefield at Bosworth to the pioneering factories at the Unesco World Heritage Derwent Valley Mills. And if you want to mix in a little myth, head for Nottingham and its Robin Hood connections.

Stately Homes
Stately homes like Haddon Hall, Burghley House and Chatsworth promise walls dripping with oil paintings, sprawling deer-filled grounds and more priceless heirlooms than you can shake a Chippendale at.

p447

Birmingham, the West Midlands & the Marches

Outdoor Activities ✓✓✓
History ✓✓✓
Food & Drink ✓✓✓

Outdoor Activities
Away from the conurbations, the natural landscape calls fans of the great outdoors, from the long-distance trek along Offa's Dyke National Trail to high-level rambles on the Shropshire and Malvern Hills, via mountain-biking at Cannock Chase or kayaking on the River Wye.

History
Centuries ago, the powerful Lords Marcher sealed their grip on the England–Wales borderlands, leaving us with a legacy of great castles and giving their name to the region. At the other end of the timeline, England's rich industrial heritage can be savoured at places like Birmingham and Ironbridge.

Food & Drink
Foodies take note - Birmingham is the curry capital of the country (and increasingly, a magnet for Michelin-starred chefs) and the country town of Ludlow is an epicentre of a gastronomic exploration.

p498

Yorkshire

Outdoor Activities ✓✓✓
Food ✓✓✓
History ✓✓✓

Outdoor Activities
With rolling hills, scenic valleys and high moors and a long, cliff-lined coast, all protected by two national parks, Yorkshire is a natural adventure playground. Come here for some of England's finest hiking, biking, surfing and rock-climbing.

Food & Drink
Lush pastures and a rich farming heritage means Yorkshire beef and lamb are among the most sought after in the country, while the famous twin breweries of Masham turn out some of England's most popular real ales. Where better to enjoy them than one of Yorkshire's many excellent traditional pubs?

History
From York's Viking heritage and the ancient abbeys of Rievaulx, Fountains and Whitby to the industrial archaeology of Leeds, Bradford and Sheffield, Yorkshire is steeped in the essence of England's historical narrative.

p562

Manchester, Liverpool & the Northwest

Museums ✓✓✓
Football ✓✓✓
Blackpool ✓✓

Museums
The northwest's collection of heritage sites – from the wonderful People's History Museum in Manchester to the International Slavery Museum in Liverpool's Albert Dock – is testament to the region's rich history and its ability to keep it alive.

Football
Two cities – Liverpool and Manchester – give the world four famous clubs, including the two most successful in English history. The new National Football Museum in Manchester is just another reason for football fans to visit this region.

Blackpool
The queen of England's classic seaside resorts, keeps going on the back of the rides of Pleasure Beach, England's best amusement park where adrenaline junkies can always find a fix.

p628

The Lake District & Cumbria

Mountains ✓✓✓
Lakes ✓✓✓
Walking ✓✓✓

Mountains
Cumbria is the most mountainous part of England, a stunningly beautiful region that moved Romantic poet William Wordsworth to write his ode to 'a host of golden daffodils'. Two centuries on, this landscape still inspires and delights.

Lakes
Dotted between the mountains sit numerous lakes. Some are big and famous, such as Windermere, Coniston and Ullswater, while others are small, hidden and little known. Together they give their name to the Lake District National Park that protects this striking and valuable landscape.

Walking
If anywhere is the heart and soul of walking in England, it's the Lake District. Casual strollers find gentle routes through foothills and valleys, while serious hikers hit the high fells and mountains – many heading to the top of Scafell Pike, England's highest point.

p687

Newcastle & the Northeast

Hadrian's Wall ✓✓✓
Big Landscapes ✓✓✓
Castles ✓✓✓

Hadrian's Wall

One of the world's premier Roman Empire sites, this potent symbol of power and defence strides its way for over 70 miles across the neck of England, from Tyneside to the Solway Firth. You can travel its length – by foot, bike, car, bus or train – stopping off at fascinating museums and forts along the way.

Big Landscapes

If it's widescreen vistas you're after, the northeast never fails to please, with great views from the golden windswept beaches of Northumberland to the high moors and russet dales of the Pennine uplands.

Castles

Vast Northumberland has some of England's finest castles. Some, like Bamburgh and Dunstanburgh stare reflectively out to sea, others stand isolated on the high moors, all reminders of the centuries-long scrap with the Scots over these remote borderlands.

p733

Look out for these icons:

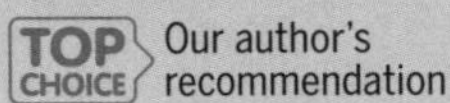

Our author's recommendation

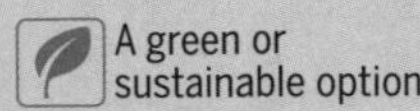

A green or sustainable option

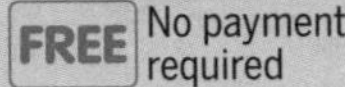

No payment required

See the Index for a full list of destinations covered in this book.

On the Road

London

TELEPHONE CODE: 020 / POP: 7.51 MILLION / AREA: 609 SQ MILES

Includes »

Best Places to Eat

» Bistrot Bruno Loubet (p109)
» Ottolenghi (p108)
» Tamarind (p102)
» Hakkasan (p107)
» St John (p109)

Best Places to Stay

» Haymarket Hotel (p94)
» Hazlitt's (p94)
» Hoxton (p101)
» Zetter Hotel (p100)
» Palmers Lodge (p101)

Why Go?

Everyone comes to London with a preconception shaped by a multitude of books, movies, TV shows and songs. Whatever yours is, prepare to have it shattered by this endlessly fascinating, amorphous city. You could spend a lifetime exploring it and find that the slippery thing's gone and changed on you. One thing is constant: that great serpent of a river enfolding the city in its sinuous loops, linking London both to the green heart of England and the world. From Roman times the world has come to London, put down roots and whinged about the weather. There is no place on earth that is more multicultural; any given street yields a rich harvest of languages. Those narrow streets are steeped in history, art, architecture and popular culture. With endless reserves of cool, London is one of the world's great cities, if not the greatest.

When to Go

April in the city sees daffodils in bloom, costumed marathon runners and London's edgiest music event, the Camden Crawl. In June you'll find the parks filled with people, Trooping the Colour, summer arts festivals, gay pride and Wimbledon. London in December is all about Christmas lights on Oxford and Regent Sts, and perhaps a whisper of snow.

History

London first came into being as a Celtic village near a ford across the River Thames, but it wasn't until after the Roman invasion, in the year 43, that the city really began to take off. The Romans enclosed their Londinium in walls that are still echoed in the shape of the City of London (the big 'C' City) today.

By the end of the 3rd century AD, Londinium was almost as multicultural as it is now, with 30,000 people of various ethnic groups and temples dedicated to a variety of cults. Internal strife and relentless barbarian attacks took their toll on the Romans, who abandoned Britain in the 5th century, reducing the conurbation to a sparsely populated backwater.

The Saxons then moved in to the area, establishing farmsteads and villages. Their 'Lundenwic' prospered, becoming a large, well-organised town divided into 20 different wards. As the city grew in importance, it caught the eye of Danish Vikings, who launched many invasions and razed the city in the 9th century. The Saxons held on until, finally beaten down in 1016, they were forced to accept the Danish leader Knut (Canute) as King of England, after which London replaced Winchester as its capital. In 1042 the throne reverted to the Saxon Edward the Confessor, whose main contribution to the city was the building of Westminster Abbey.

The Norman Conquest saw William the Conqueror marching into London, where he was crowned king. He built the White Tower (the core of the Tower of London), negotiated taxes with the merchants, and affirmed the city's independence and right to self-government. From then until the late 15th century, London politics were largely taken up by a three-way power struggle between the monarchy, the church and city guilds.

The greatest threat to the burgeoning city was that of disease caused by unsanitary living conditions and impure drinking water. In 1348 rats on ships from Europe brought the bubonic plague, which wiped out a third of London's population of 100,000 over the following year.

London was consolidated as the seat of law and government in the kingdom during the 14th century. An uneasy political compromise was reached between the factions, and the city expanded rapidly in the 16th century under the House of Tudor.

The Great Plague struck in 1665 and by the time the winter cold arrested the epidemic, 100,000 Londoners had perished. Just as the population considered a sigh of relief, another disaster struck. The mother of all blazes, the Great Fire of 1666, virtually razed the place. One consequence was that it created a blank canvas upon which master architect Sir Christopher Wren could build his magnificent churches.

London's growth continued unabated, and by 1700 it was Europe's largest city, with 600,000 people. An influx of foreign workers brought expansion to the east and south, while those who could afford it headed to the more salubrious environs of the north and west, divisions that still largely shape London today.

Georgian London saw a surge in artistic creativity, with the likes of Dr Johnson, Handel, Gainsborough and Reynolds enriching the city's culture while its architects fashioned an elegant new metropolis. At the same time the gap between rich and poor grew ever wider, and lawlessness was rife.

In 1837, 18-year-old Victoria ascended the throne. During her long reign (1837–1901), London became the fulcrum of the expanding British Empire, which covered a quarter of the earth's surface. The Industrial Revolution saw the building of new docks and railways (including the first underground line in 1863), while the Great Exhibition of 1851 showcased London to the world. The city's population mushroomed from just over two million to 6.6 million during Victoria's reign.

Although London suffered relatively minor damage during WWI, it was devastated by the Luftwaffe in WWII, when huge

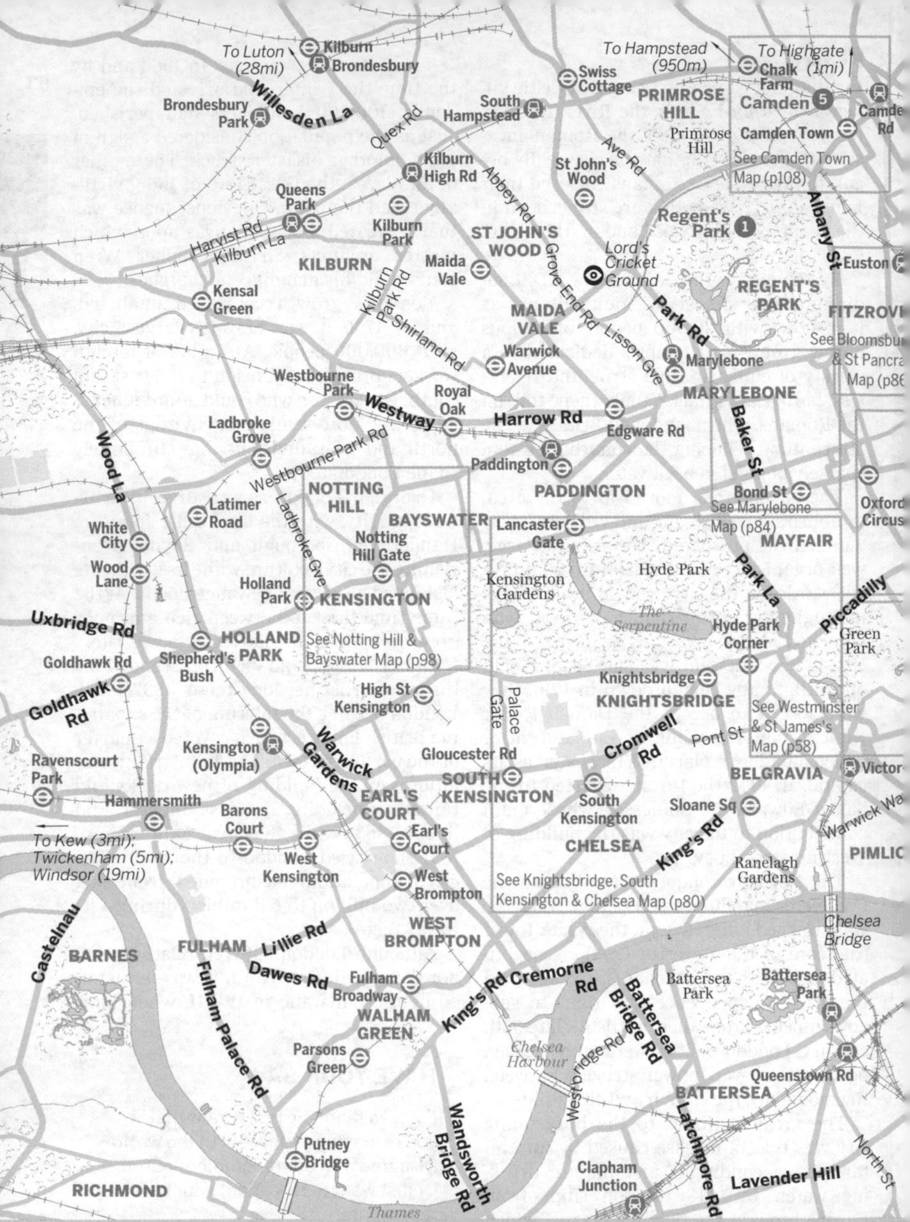

London Highlights

1. Watching the world pass by on a sunny day in **Regent's Park** (p82) or any of London's other green oases
2. Admiring the booty of an empire at the **British Museum** (p83)
3. Losing your head in history at the **Tower of London** (p67)
4. Meeting the dead famous in **Westminster Abbey** (p57)
5. Discovering the next cool thing in skinny jeans in one of Camden's **live music venues** (p117)

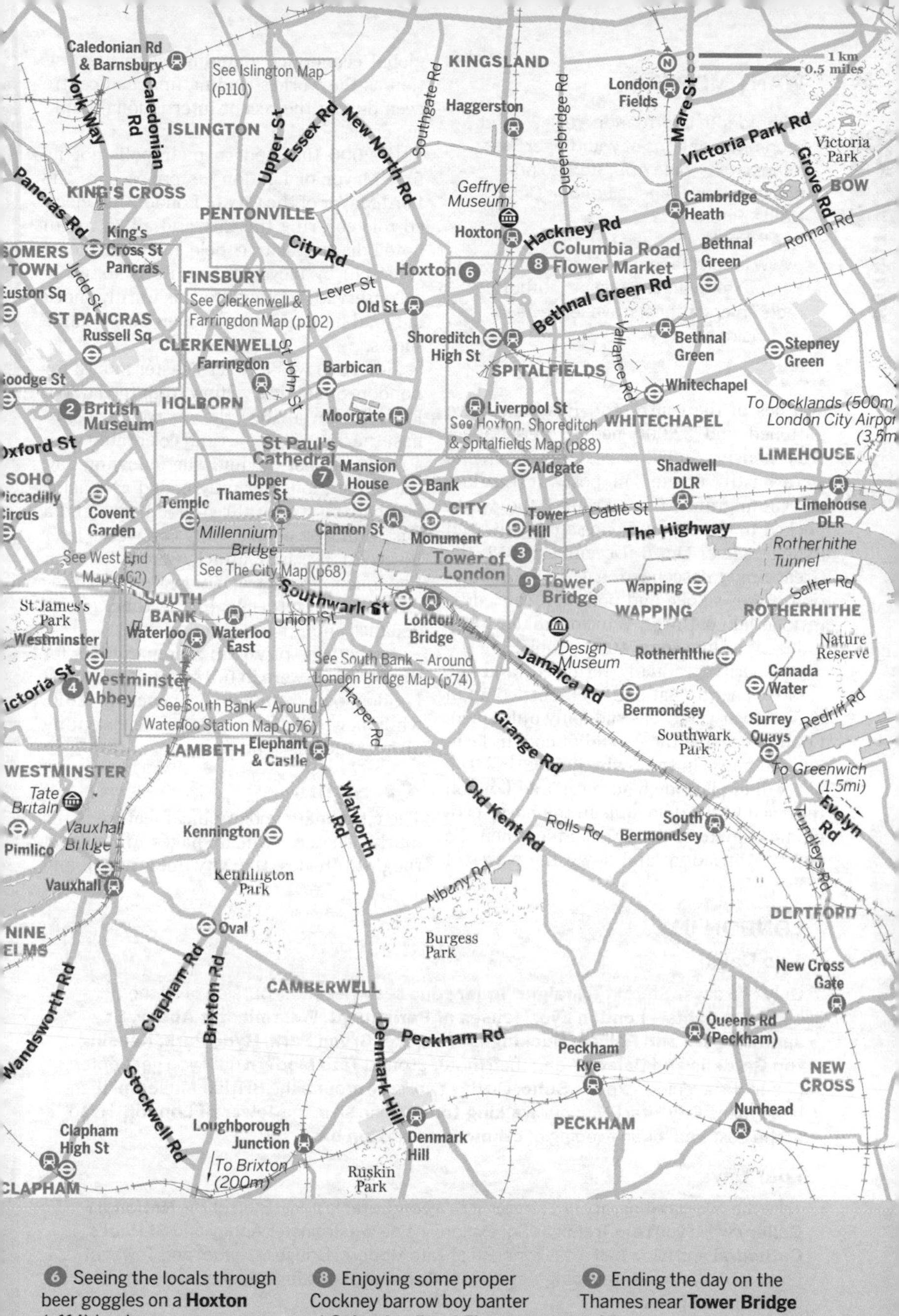

6 Seeing the locals through beer goggles on a **Hoxton** (p114) bar hop

7 Getting closer to God at the top of the dome of **St Paul's Cathedral** (p67)

8 Enjoying some proper Cockney barrow boy banter at **Columbia Road Flower Market** (p123)

9 Ending the day on the Thames near **Tower Bridge** (p67) – a Waterloo sunset's fine but one by the bridge is even better

WANT MORE?

For in-depth information, reviews and recommendations at your fingertips, head to the Apple App Store to purchase Lonely Planet's London City Guide iPhone app.

Alternatively, head to Lonely Planet (www.lonelyplanet.com/england/london) for planning advice, author recommendations, traveller reviews and insider tips.

swathes of the centre and East End were flattened and 32,000 people were killed. Ugly housing and low-cost developments were hastily erected in postwar London, and immigrants from around the world flocked to the city and once again changed its character. On 6 December 1952 the Great Smog descended, a lethal combination of fog, smoke and pollution caused by residential coal fires, vehicle exhausts and industry, killing some 4000 people.

Prosperity gradually returned, and the creative energy that had been bottled up in the postwar years was suddenly unleashed. London became the capital of cool in fashion and music in the 'Swinging Sixties'. The party didn't last long, however, and London returned to the doldrums in the harsh economic climate of the 1970s. Since then the city has surfed up and down the waves of global economics, hanging on to its position as the world's leading financial centre even during the recent international banking crisis.

In 2000 the modern metropolis got its first Mayor of London (as opposed to the Lord Mayor of the City of London), an elected role covering the City and all 32 urban boroughs, a position held (at the time of research) by bicycle-riding Boris Johnson, a Conservative known for his unruly shock of blond hair and appearances on TV game shows.

July 2005 was a roller-coaster month for London. Snatching victory from the jaws of Paris (the favourites), the city won its bid to host the 2012 Olympics and celebrated with a frenzy of flag waving. The following day, the celebrations abruptly ended as suicide bombers struck on three tube trains and a bus, killing 52 people. Only two weeks later a second terrorist attack was foiled. But Londoners are not easily beaten and they immediately returned to the tube, out of defiance and pragmatism.

At the time of writing, preparations for the Olympics were in full swing. A new East London overground line opened in 2010, while new sporting venues were sprouting all over the East End.

Sights

The city's main geographical feature is the murky Thames, which snakes around but roughly divides the city into north and

LONDON IN...

Two Days

Only two days? Start in **Trafalgar Square** and see at least the outside of all the big-ticket sights – **London Eye, Houses of Parliament, Westminster Abbey, St James's Park and Palace, Buckingham Palace, Green Park, Hyde Park, Kensington Gardens and Palace** – and then motor around **Tate Modern** until you get booted out. In the evening, explore **Soho**. On day two, race around the **British Museum**, then head to the City. Start with our **walking tour** and finish in the **Tower of London**. Head to the East End for an evening of **ethnic food** and **hip bars**.

Four Days

Take the two-day itinerary but stretch it to a comfortable pace. Stop at the **National Gallery** while you're in Trafalgar Sq, explore inside Westminster Abbey and **St Paul's Cathedral** and allow half a day for each of Tate Modern, British Museum and Tower of London. On your extra evenings, check out **Camden** and **Islington** or splurge on a slap-up dinner in **Chelsea**.

One Week

As above, but add in a day each for **Greenwich**, **Kew Gardens** and **Hampton Court Palace**.

south. The old City of London (note the big 'C') is the capital's financial district, covering roughly a square mile bordered by the river and the many gates of the ancient (long-gone) city walls: Newgate, Moorgate etc. The areas to the east of the City are collectively known as the East End. The West End, on the City's other flank, is effectively the centre of London nowadays. It actually falls within the City of Westminster, which is one of London's 32 boroughs and has long been the centre of government and royalty.

Surrounding these central areas are dozens of former villages (Camden Town, Islington, Clapham etc), each with their own High Street, which were long ago swallowed by London's sprawl.

With so much to see and do, it can be hard to know where to start. Weather will be a determining factor: the museums and galleries are great for a rainy day, but when the sun shines make like a Londoner and head to the parks – you never know whether this fine day will be your last. Otherwise, attack the sights by area using the ordering of this section as your guide.

WESTMINSTER & ST JAMES'S

Purposefully positioned outside the old City (London's fiercely independent burghers preferred to keep the monarch and parliament at arm's length), Westminster has been the centre of the nation's political power for nearly a millennium. The area's many landmarks combine to form an awesome display of authority and gravitas.

Put on your best rah-rah voice to wander around St James's, an aristocratic enclave of palaces, famous hotels, historic shops and elegant buildings. There are some 150 historically noteworthy buildings within its 36 hectares.

Westminster Abbey CHURCH

(Map p58; ☎020-7654 4834; www.westminster-abbey.org; 20 Dean's Yard SW1; adult/child £15/6, tours £3; ⏱9.30am-4.30pm Mon, Tue, Thu & Fri, to 7pm Wed, to 2.30pm Sat; ⊖Westminster) If you're one of those boring sods who boast about spending months in Europe without ever setting foot in a church, get over yourself and make this the exception. Not merely a beautiful place of worship, Westminster Abbey serves up the country's history cold on slabs of stone. For centuries the country's greatest have been interred here, including most of the monarchs from Henry III (died 1272) to George II (1760).

Westminster Abbey has never been a cathedral (the seat of a bishop). It's what is called a 'royal peculiar' and is administered directly by the Crown. Every monarch since William the Conqueror has been crowned here, with the exception of a couple of unlucky Eds who were murdered (Edward V) or abdicated (Edward VIII) before the magic moment. Look out for the strangely ordinary-looking **Coronation Chair**.

The building itself is an arresting sight. Though a mixture of architectural styles, it is considered the finest example of Early English Gothic in existence. The original church was built in the 11th century by King (later Saint) Edward the Confessor, who is buried in the chapel behind the main altar. Henry III began work on the new building in 1245 but didn't complete it; the French Gothic nave was finished in 1388. Henry VII's magnificent Late Perpendicular–style **Lady Chapel** was consecrated in 1519 after 16 years of construction.

Apart from the royal graves, keep an eye out for the many famous commoners interred here, especially in **Poets' Corner**, where you'll find the resting places of Chaucer, Dickens, Hardy, Tennyson, Dr Johnson and Kipling as well as memorials to the other greats (Shakespeare, Austen, Brontë etc). Elsewhere you'll find the graves of Handel and Sir Isaac Newton.

The octagonal **Chapter House** (⏱10.30am-4pm) dates from the 1250s and was where the monks would meet for daily prayer before Henry VIII's suppression of the monasteries. Used as a treasury and 'Royal Wardrobe', the cryptlike **Pyx Chamber** (⏱10.30am-3.30pm) dates from about 1070. The neighbouring **Abbey Museum** (⏱10.30am-4pm) has as its centrepiece the death masks of generations of royalty.

Parts of the Abbey complex are free to visitors. This includes the **Cloister** (⏱8am-6pm) and the 900-year-old **College Garden** (⏱10am-6pm Tue-Thu Apr-Sep, to 4pm Oct-Mar). Free concerts are held here from 12.30pm to 2pm on Wednesdays from mid-July to mid-August. Adjacent to the abbey is **St Margaret's Church** (⏱9.30am-3.30pm Mon-Sat, 2-4.45pm Sun), the House of Commons' place of worship since 1614. There are windows commemorating churchgoers Caxton and Milton, and Sir Walter Raleigh is buried by the altar.

Verger-led tours are held several times a day (except Sundays) and are limited to 25

Westminster & St James's

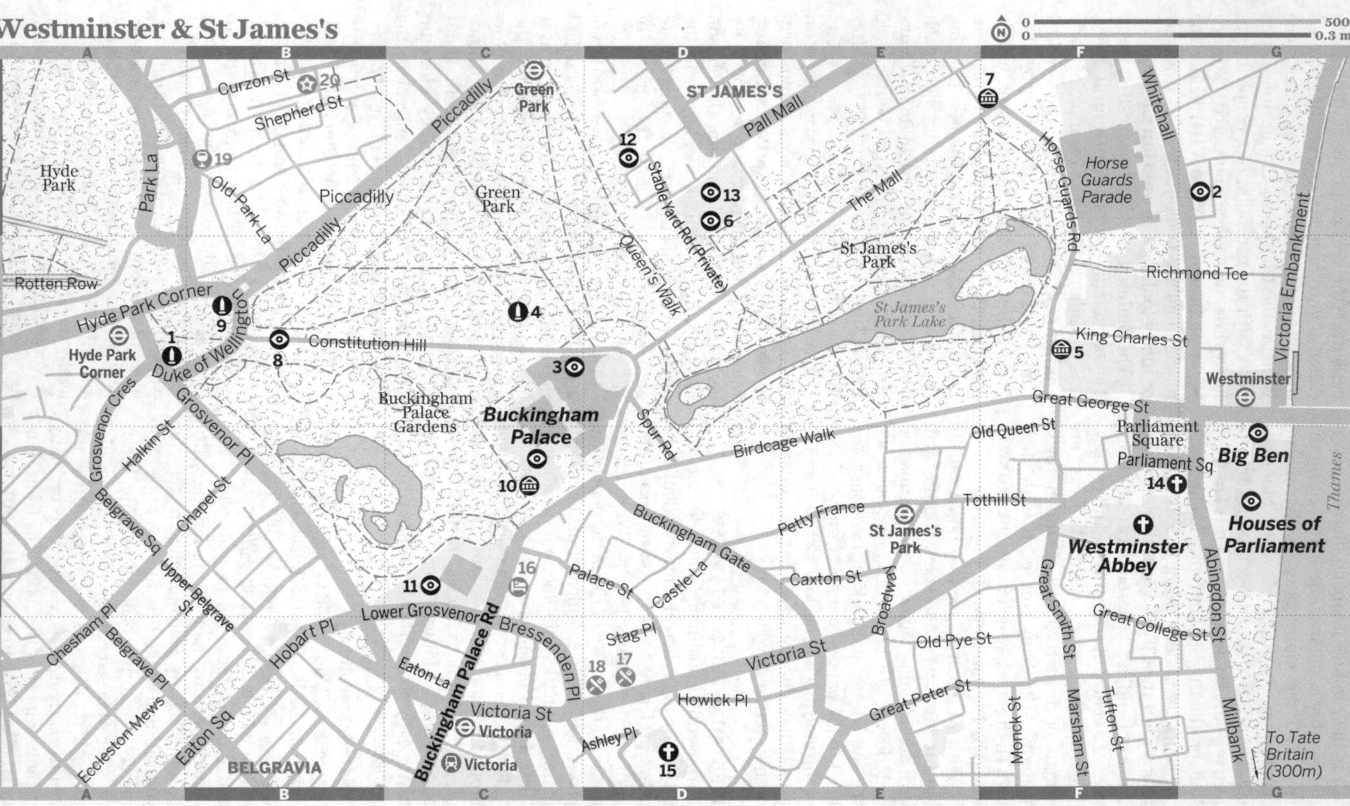

Westminster & St James's

Top Sights

Big Ben....G3
Buckingham Palace....C3
Houses of Parliament....G3
Westminster Abbey....F3

Sights

1 Australian War Memorial....A2
2 Banqueting House....G1
3 Canada Gate....C2
4 Canada Memorial....C2
5 Churchill Museum & Cabinet War Rooms....F2
6 Clarence House....D1
7 Institute of Contemporary Arts....F1
8 Memorial Gates....B2
9 New Zealand War Memorial....B2
10 Queen's Gallery....C3
11 Royal Mews....C3
12 Spencer House....D1
13 St James's Palace....D1
14 St Margaret's Church....F3
15 Westminster Cathedral....D4

Sleeping

16 Rubens at the Palace....C3

Eating

17 Wagamama....D4
18 Zizzi....D4

Drinking

19 Galvin at Windows....B1

Entertainment

20 Curzon Mayfair....B1

people per tour; call ahead to secure your place. Of course, admission to the Abbey is free if you wish to attend a service. On weekdays, Matins is at 7.30am, Holy Communion at 8am and 12.30pm, and Choral Evensong at 5pm. There are services throughout the day on Sundays. You can sit and soak in the atmosphere, even if you're not religious.

Houses of Parliament HISTORIC BUILDING
(Map p58; www.parliament.uk; Parliament Sq SW1; ⊖Westminster) Coming face to face with one of the world's most recognisable landmarks is always a surreal moment, but in the case of the Houses of Parliament it's a revelation. The BBC's standard title shot just doesn't do justice to the ornate stonework and golden filigree of Charles Barry and Augustus Pugin's neo-Gothic masterpiece (1840).

Officially called the **Palace of Westminster**, the oldest part is **Westminster Hall** (1097), which is one of only a few sections that survived a catastrophic fire in 1834. Its roof, added between 1394 and 1401, is the earliest known example of a hammerbeam roof and has been described as the greatest surviving achievement of medieval English carpentry.

The palace's most famous feature is its clock tower, aka **Big Ben** (Map p58). Ben is actually the 13-ton bell, named after Benjamin Hall, who was commissioner of works when the tower was completed in 1858.

At the business end, parliament is split into two houses. The green-hued **House of Commons** is the lower house, where the 650 elected Members of Parliament sit. Traditionally the home of hereditary bluebloods, the scarlet-decorated **House of Lords** now has peers appointed through various means. Both houses debate and vote on legislation, which is then presented to the Queen for her Royal Assent (in practice, this is a formality; the last time Royal Assent was denied was 1708). At the annual State Opening of Parliament (usually in November), the Queen takes her throne in the House of Lords, having processed in the gold-trimmed Irish State Coach from Buckingham Palace. It's well worth lining the route for a gawk at the crown jewels sparkling in the sun.

When parliament is in session, visitors are admitted to the **House of Commons Visitors' Gallery** (admission free; ⌚2.30-10.30pm Mon & Tue, 11.30am-7.30pm Wed, 10.30am-6.30pm Thu, 9.30am-3pm some Fridays). Expect to queue for at least an hour and possibly longer during Question Time (at the beginning of each day). The **House of Lords Visitors' Gallery** (admission free; ⌚2.30-10pm Mon & Tue, 3-10pm Wed, 11am-7.30pm Thu, from 10am some Fridays) can also be visited.

Parliamentary recesses (ie holidays) last for three months over summer and a couple of weeks over Easter and Christmas. When parliament is in recess there are guided **tours** (☎0844 847 1672; www.ticketmaster.co.uk/housesofparliament; 75-min tours adult/child £14/6) of both chambers and other historic areas. UK residents can approach their MPs to arrange a free tour and to climb the clock tower.

Buckingham Palace PALACE
(Map p58; ☎020-7766 7300; www.royalcollection.org.uk; Buckingham Palace Rd SW1; tours

adult/child £17/9.75; ⌚late Jul-Sep; ⊖Victoria) With so many imposing buildings in the capital, the Queen's well-proportioned but relatively plain city pad is an anticlimax for some. Built in 1803 for the Duke of Buckingham, Buckingham Palace replaced St James's Palace as the monarch's London home in 1837. When she's not off giving her one-handed wave in far-flung parts of the Commonwealth, Queen Elizabeth II divides her time between here, Windsor and Balmoral. If you've got the urge to drop in for a cup of tea, a handy way of telling whether she's home is to check whether the yellow, red and blue royal standard is flying.

Nineteen lavishly furnished State Rooms – hung with artworks by the likes of Rembrandt, van Dyck, Canaletto, Poussin and Vermeer – are open to visitors when HRH (Her Royal Highness) takes her holidays. The two-hour tour includes the **Throne Room**, with his-and-hers pink chairs initialled 'ER' and 'P'.

A Royal Day Out is a combined ticket including the State Rooms, Queen's Gallery and Royal Mews (adult/child £31/18).

Changing of the Guard

If you're a fan of bright uniforms, bearskin hats, straight lines, marching and shouting, join the throngs outside the palace at 11.30am (daily from May to July and on alternate days for the rest of the year, weather permitting), when the regiment of guards outside the palace changes over in one of the world's most famous displays of pageantry. It does have a certain freak show value but gets dull very quickly. If you're here in November, the procession leaving the palace for the State Opening of Parliament is much more impressive.

Queen's Gallery

(Map p58; adult/child £8.75/4.50; ⌚10am-5.30pm) Originally designed by John Nash as a conservatory, it was smashed up by the Luftwaffe in 1940 before being converted to a gallery in 1962, housing works from the extensive Royal Collection.

Royal Mews

(Map p58; adult/child £7.50/4.80; ⌚11am-4pm) Indulge your Cinderella fantasies while inspecting the exquisite state coaches and immaculately groomed royal horses housed in the Royal Mews. Highlights include the 1910 royal wedding's Glass Coach and the 1762 Gold Coach, which has been used for every coronation since that of George IV. We're pretty sure that these aren't about to change back into pumpkins any time soon.

St James's Park & Palace PARK

(Map p58; ⊖St James's Park) With its manicured flower beds and ornamental lake, St James's Park is a wonderful place to stroll and take in the surrounding palaces. The striking Tudor gatehouse of **St James's Palace** (Map p58; Cleveland Row SW1; ⊖Green Park), initiated by the palace-mad Henry VIII in 1530, is best approached from St James's St, to the north of the park. This was the residence of Prince Charles and his sons before they shifted next door to **Clarence House** (1828), following the death of its previous occupant, the Queen Mother, in 2002. It's a great place to pose for a photograph beside one of the resolutely unsmiling royal guards.

Green Park PARK

(Map p58; ⊖Green Park) Green Park's 47-acre expanse of meadows and mature trees links St James's Park to Hyde Park and Kensington Gardens, creating a green corridor from Westminster all the way to Kensington. It was once a duelling ground and served as a vegetable garden during WWII. Although it doesn't have lakes, fountains or formal gardens, it's blanketed with daffodils in spring and seminaked bodies whenever the sun shines. The only concessions to formality are the war memorials of various Commonwealth countries: the **Canada Memorial** near **Canada Gate**, which links the park to Buckingham Palace; the **Memorial Gates** at its western end, which recognise the contribution of various African, Caribbean and Indian subcontinent countries; and the nearby **Australian** and **New Zealand War Memorials** in Hyde Park Corner.

Westminster Cathedral CATHEDRAL

(Map p58; www.westminstercathedral.org.uk; Victoria St SW1; ⌚7am-7pm; ⊖Victoria) Begun in 1895, this neo-Byzantine cathedral is the headquarters of Britain's once suppressed Roman Catholic Church. It's still a work in progress, the vast interior part dazzling marble and mosaic and part bare brick; new sections are completed as funds allow. Look out for Eric Gill's highly regarded stone **Stations of the Cross** (1918). The **Chapel of St George and the English Martyrs** displays the body of St John Southwark, a priest who was hanged, drawn and quartered in 1654 for refusing to reject the supremacy of the Pope. The distinctive 83m red-brick and white-stone **tower** (adult/child £5/2.50) offers splendid views of London and, unlike St Paul's dome, you can take the lift.

Banqueting House PALACE

(Map p58; www.hrp.org.uk/BanquetingHouse; Whitehall SW1; adult/child £4.80/free; ⏲10am-5pm Mon-Sat; ⊖Westminster) The beautiful, classical design of the Banqueting House was conceived by Inigo Jones for James I in 1622. It's the only surviving part of Whitehall Palace after the Tudor bit burnt down in 1698. The key attraction is the ceiling, painted by Rubens in 1635 at the behest of Charles I. The king didn't get to enjoy it for long, as in 1649 he was frogmarched out of the 1st-floor balcony to lose his head for treason. A bust outside commemorates him. An audioguide is included in the price.

Churchill Museum & Cabinet War Rooms MUSEUM

(Map p58; www.iwm.org.uk/cabinet; Clive Steps, King Charles St SW1; adult/child £15/free; ⏲9.30am-6pm; ⊖Westminster) The Cabinet War Rooms were Prime Minister Winston Churchill's underground military HQ during WWII. The preserved rooms (including Churchill's bedroom) of this museum capture the drama of the time. The interactive displays offer an intriguing exposé of the public and private faces of the man.

FREE **Institute Of Contemporary Arts** GALLERY

(Map p58; www.ica.org.uk; The Mall SW1; ⏲noon 7pm Wed & Fri-Sun, to 9pm Thu; ⊖Charing Cross) A one-stop contemporary-art bonanza, the exciting program at the ICA includes film, photography, theatre, installations, talks, performance art, DJs, digital art and book readings. Stroll around the galleries, watch a film, browse the bookshop, then head to the bar for a beer.

Spencer House HISTORIC HOME

(Map p58; ☎020-7499 8620; www.spencerhouse.co.uk; 27 St James's Pl SW1; adult/child £9/7; ⏲10.30am-5.45pm Sun Feb-Jul & Sep-Dec; ⊖Green Park) The ancestral home of Princess Diana's family, Spencer House was built in the Palladian style between 1756 and 1766. It was converted into offices after the Spencers moved out in 1927, but 60 years later an £18 million restoration returned it to its former glory. Visits are by guided tour.

WEST END

Synonymous with big-budget musicals and frenzied flocks of shoppers, the West End is a strident mix of culture and consumerism.

> **ESCALATOR ETIQUETTE**
>
> The fastest way to get abused in London (apart from jumping a queue – you'd need to have a death wish to attempt that) is to block an escalator, especially at a busy tube station. Always stand in single file to the right. And make sure you have your ticket/Oyster card ready when you get to the tube exit. Fumbling in your wallet or purse is guaranteed to elicit a sharply passive-aggressive 'Excuse me!' from the person behind you.

More a concept than a fixed geographical area, it nonetheless takes in Piccadilly Circus and Trafalgar Sq to the south, Regent St to the west, Oxford St to the north and Covent Garden and the Strand to the east.

Named after the elaborate collars (picadils) that were the sartorial staple of a 17th-century tailor who lived nearby, **Piccadilly** became the fashionable haunt of the well-heeled (and collared), and still boasts establishment icons such as the Ritz hotel and Fortnum & Mason department store. It meets Regent St, Shaftesbury Ave and Haymarket at neon-lit, turbo-charged **Piccadilly Circus**, home to the popular but unremarkable Eros statue.

Mayfair hogs all of the most expensive streets on the Monopoly board, including Park Lane and Bond St, which should give you an idea of what to expect: lots of pricey shops, Michelin-starred restaurants, society hotels and gentlemen's clubs. Elegant **Regent St** and frantic **Oxford St** are the city's main shopping strips. At the heart of the West End lies **Soho**, a grid of narrow streets and squares hiding gay bars, strip clubs, cafes and advertising agencies. **Carnaby St** was the epicentre of the swinging London of the 1960s but is now largely given over to chain fashion stores. Lisle and Gerrard Sts form the heart of **Chinatown**, which is full of reasonably priced Asian restaurants and unfairly hip youngsters. Its neighbour, pedestrianised **Leicester Sq** (*les*-ter), heaves with tourists. Dominated by large cinemas, it sometimes hosts star-studded premieres. Described by Benjamin Disraeli in the 19th century as Europe's finest street, **the Strand** still boasts a few classy hotels but has lost much of its lustre. Look

West End

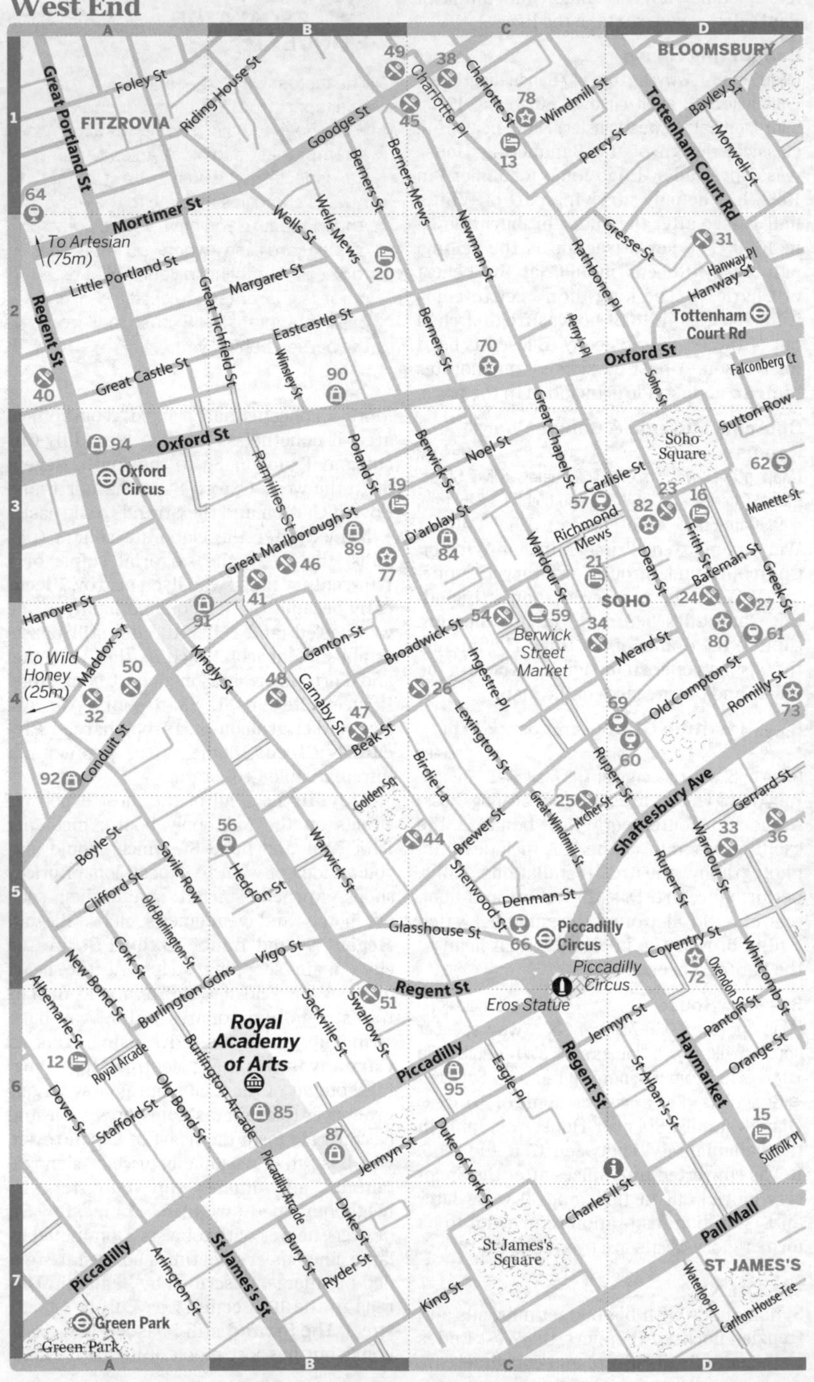

BLOOMSBURY
FITZROVIA
SOHO
ST JAMES'S
Great Portland St
Foley St
Riding House St
Goodge St
Charlotte Pl
Charlotte St
Windmill St
Tottenham Court Rd
Bayley St
Morwell St
Percy St
Berners St
Berners Mews
Wells St
Wells Mews
Newman St
Rathbone Pl
Gresse St
Hanway Pl
Hanway St
Tottenham Court Rd
Mortimer St
To Artesian (75m)
Little Portland St
Margaret St
Great Titchfield St
Eastcastle St
Winsley St
Perry's Pl
Regent St
Great Castle St
Oxford St
Falconberg Ct
Soho St
Sutton Row
Soho Square
Oxford Circus
Ramillies St
Poland St
Berwick St
Noel St
Great Chapel St
Carlisle St
Manette St
D'arblay St
Great Marlborough St
Richmond Mews
Wardour St
Dean St
Frith St
Bateman St
Greek St
Hanover St
Ganton St
Broadwick St
Berwick Street Market
Meard St
Old Compton St
Romilly St
Maddox St
To Wild Honey (25m)
Kingly St
Carnaby St
Beak St
Ingestre Pl
Lexington St
Rupert St
Conduit St
Golden Sq
Birdie La
Archer St
Great Windmill St
Shaftesbury Ave
Gerrard St
Boyle St
Savile Row
Heddon St
Warwick St
Brewer St
Sherwood St
Clifford St
Old Burlington St
Denman St
Glasshouse St
Piccadilly Circus
Coventry St
Whitcomb St
Cork St
Vigo St
New Bond St
Burlington Gdns
Albemarle St
Sackville St
Swallow St
Regent St
Eros Statue
Oxendon St
Panton St
Jermyn St
Royal Academy of Arts
Royal Arcade
Burlington Arcade
Piccadilly
Eagle Pl
St Alban's St
Haymarket
Orange St
Dover St
Stafford St
Old Bond St
Duke of York St
Suffolk Pl
Piccadilly Arcade
Charles II St
Duke St
Pall Mall
St James's Square
Arlington St
St James's St
Bury St
Ryder St
King St
Waterloo Pl
Carlton House Tce
Green Park

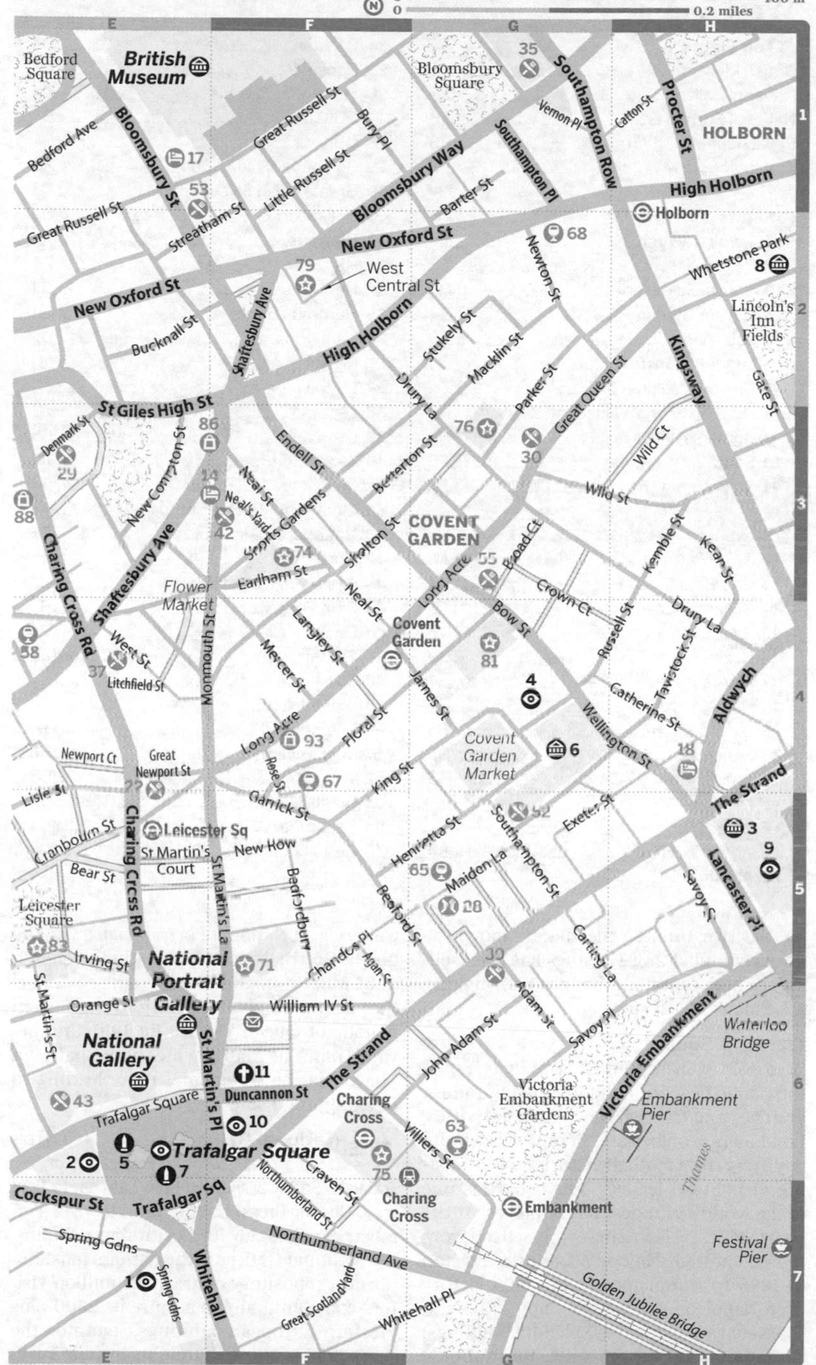
0 400 m
0 0.2 miles
E
F
G
H
Bedford Square
British Museum
Bloomsbury Square
35
Southampton Row
Procter St
HOLBORN
Vernon Pl
Catton St
Bedford Ave
Bloomsbury St
Great Russell St
Bury Pl
17
53
Little Russell St
Bloomsbury Way
Southampton Pl
Great Russell St
Streatham St
Barter St
High Holborn
Holborn
New Oxford St
68
Newton St
Whetstone Park
8
79
West Central St
New Oxford St
Lincoln's Inn Fields
Bucknall St
Shaftesbury Ave
High Holborn
Stukely St
Macklin St
Kingsway
Gate St
St Giles High St
Drury La
Parker St
Great Queen St
Denmark St
86
76
29
New Compton St
Endell St
30
Betterton St
Wild Ct
14
Neal St
Neal's Yard
Wild St
88
42
Sports Gardens
Shelton St
COVENT GARDEN
Kemble St
Kean St
Charing Cross Rd
Shaftesbury Ave
74
Long Acre
55
Broad Ct
Flower Market
Earlham St
Crown Ct
Neal St
Langley St
Bow St
Drury La
Russell St
Covent Garden
Tavistock St
West St
58
Mercer St
81
37
Litchfield St
Monmouth St
James St
4
Aldwych
Catherine St
Long Acre
Floral St
Wellington St
Covent Garden Market
6
18
Newport Ct
Great Newport St
93
Rose St
67
King St
Lisle St
22
Garrick St
The Strand
52
Exeter St
Southampton St
Cranbourn St
Leicester Sq
Charing Cross Rd
3
St Martin's Court
New Row
Henrietta St
Bear St
9
Bedfordbury
65
Maiden La
Savoy St
Lancaster Pl
Leicester Square
St Martin's La
28
Bedford St
83
Irving St
National Portrait Gallery
71
Chandos Pl
Agar St
Carting La
10
Adam St
Orange St
William IV St
Waterloo Bridge
St Martin's St
National Gallery
St Martin's Pl
The Strand
John Adam St
Savoy Pl
Victoria Embankment
11
43
Duncannon St
Charing Cross
Victoria Embankment Gardens
Embankment Pier
Trafalgar Square
10
63
Villiers St
Trafalgar Square
2
5
7
Northumberland St
Craven St
75
Thames
Cockspur St
Trafalgar Sq
Charing Cross
Embankment
Spring Gdns
Northumberland Ave
Festival Pier
1
Spring Gdns
Whitehall
Great Scotland Yard
Whitehall Pl
Golden Jubilee Bridge
1
2
3
4
5
6
7

West End

for the two Chinese merchants above the door at number 216; Twinings has been selling tea here continuously since 1787, making it London's oldest store.

Trafalgar Square SQUARE

(Map p62; ⊖Charing Cross) Trafalgar Sq is the public heart of London, hosting rallies, marches and feverish New Year's festivities. Londoners congregate here to celebrate anything from football victories to the ousting of political leaders. The square is one of the world's grandest public places. At the heart of it, Nelson surveys his fleet from the 43.5m-high **Nelson's Column**, erected in 1843 to commemorate his 1805 victory over Napoleon off Spain's Cape Trafalgar. The square is flanked by splendid buildings: **Canada House** to the west, the National Gallery and National Portrait Gallery to the north, **South Africa House** and the church of **St Martin-in-the-Fields** to the east. Further south stands **Admiralty Arch**, built in honour of Queen Victoria in 1910, and beyond that, The Mall (rhymes with 'shall', not 'shawl') is the ceremonial route leading to Buckingham Palace.

FREE **National Gallery** GALLERY

(Map p62; www.nationalgallery.org.uk; Trafalgar Sq WC2; ⏲10am-6pm Sat-Thu, to 9pm Fri; ⊖Charing Cross) Gazing grandly over Trafalgar Sq through its Corinthian columns, the National Gallery is the nation's most important repository of art. Four million visitors come annually to admire its 2300-plus Western European paintings, spanning the years 1250 to 1900. Highlights include Turn-

Drinking

56	Absolut Ice Bar	B5
57	Candy Bar	C3
58	Coach & Horses	E4
59	Flat White	C4
60	Friendly Society	D4
61	G-A-Y Bar	D4
62	G-A-Y Late	D3
63	Gordon's Wine Bar	G6
64	Heights	A1
65	Jewel Covent Garden	G5
66	Jewel Piccadilly Circus	C5
67	Lamb & Flag	F4
68	Princess Louise	G2
69	Village	D4

Entertainment

70	100 Club	C2
71	Coliseum	F5
72	Comedy Store	D5
73	Curzon Soho	D4
74	Donmar Warehouse	F3
75	G-A-Y Club @ Heaven	F6
76	Guanabara	G3
77	Lucky Voice	B3
78	Pear Shaped	C1
79	Popstarz	F2
80	Ronnie Scott's	D4
81	Royal Opera House	G4
82	Soho Theatre	D3
83	tkts	E5

Shopping

84	BM Soho	C3
85	Burlington Arcade	B6
86	Forbidden Planet	E3
87	Fortnum & Mason	B6
88	Foyle's	E3
89	Grant & Cutler	B3
90	HMV	B2
91	Liberty	A4
	Ray's Jazz	(see 88)
92	Rigby & Peller	A4
93	Stanford's	F4
94	Topshop Oxford Circus	A3
95	Waterstone's	C6

er's *The Fighting Temeraire* (voted Britain's greatest painting), Botticelli's *Venus and Mars* and van Gogh's *Sunflowers*. The medieval religious paintings in the Sainsbury Wing are fascinating, but for a short, sharp blast of brilliance, you can't beat the truckloads of Monets, Cézannes and Renoirs.

FREE **National Portrait Gallery** GALLERY
(Map p62; www.npg.org.uk; St Martin's Pl WC2; ⏲10am-6pm Sat-Wed, to 9pm Thu & Fri; ⊖Charing Cross) The fascinating National Portrait Gallery is like stepping into a picture book of English history. Founded in 1856, the permanent collection (around 11,000 works) starts with the Tudors on the 2nd floor and descends to contemporary figures (from pop stars to scientists). An audiovisual guide (£3) will lead you through the gallery's most famous pictures.

Royal Academy of Arts GALLERY
(Map p62; ☎020-7300 8000; www.royalacademy.org.uk; Burlington House, Piccadilly W1; admission depending on exhibition £6-20; ⏲10am-6pm Sat-Thu, to 10pm Fri; ⊖Green Park) Set back from Piccadilly, it hosts high-profile exhibitions and a small display from its permanent collection. The crafty academy has made it a condition of joining its exclusive club of 80 artists that new members donate one of their artworks. Past luminaries have included Constable, Gainsborough and Turner, while Sir Norman Foster, David Hockney and Tracey Emin are among the current crop.

Covent Garden SQUARE
(Map p62; ⊖Covent Garden) A hallowed name for opera fans due to the presence of the esteemed Royal Opera House (p118), Covent Garden is one of London's biggest tourist traps. Better, marginally less frenetic, shopping can be had in the atmospheric narrow streets surrounding it (eg Floral St and Neal St). In the 7th century the Saxons built Lundenwic here, a satellite town to the City of London. It reverted back to fields until the 1630s, when the Duke of Bedford commissioned Inigo Jones to build London's first planned square. Covent Garden's famous fruit, vegetable and flower market, immortalised in the film *My Fair Lady*, eventually took over the whole piazza, before being shifted to Nine Elms in South London in 1974.

TOP CHOICE **Sir John Soane's Museum** MUSEUM
(Map p62; www.soane.org; 13 Lincoln's Inn Fields WC2; ⏲10am-5pm Tue-Sat, 6-9pm 1st Tue of month, ⊖Holborn) Not all of this area's inhabitants were poor, as is aptly demonstrated by the remarkable home of celebrated architect and collector extraordinaire Sir John Soane (1753–1837). Now a fascinating

MAPS

No Londoner would be without a pocket-size *London Mini A-Z,* which lists nearly 30,000 streets. Worth getting if you're in London for more than a few weeks.

museum, the house has been left largely as it was when Sir John was taken out in a box. Among his eclectic acquisitions are an Egyptian sarcophagus, dozens of Greek and Roman antiquities and the original *Rake's Progress,* William Hogarth's set of caricatures telling the story of a late 18th-century London cad. Soane was clearly a very clever chap – check out the ingenious folding walls in the picture gallery. Tours (£5) are given at 11am on Saturdays.

London Transport Museum MUSEUM
(Map p62; www.ltmuseum.co.uk; Covent Garden Piazza WC2; adult/child £10/free; ⌚10am-6pm; ⊖Covent Garden) Newly refurbished, this museum houses vintage vehicles, ranging from sedan chairs to train carriages, along with fascinating posters, videos and photos. You can buy your tube-map boxer shorts at the museum shop.

Somerset House GALLERIES
(Map p62; www.somersethouse.org.uk; Strand WC2; ⌚7.30am-11pm; ⊖Temple) The first Somerset House was built for the Duke of Somerset, brother of Jane Seymour, in 1551. For two centuries it played host to royals (Elizabeth I once lived here), foreign diplomats, wild masked balls, peace treaties, the Parliamentary army (during the Civil War) and Oliver Cromwell's wake. Having fallen into disrepair, it was pulled down in 1775 and rebuilt in 1801 to designs by William Chambers. Among other weighty organisations, it went on to house the Royal Academy of the Arts, the Society of Antiquaries, the Navy Board and, that most popular of institutions, the Inland Revenue.

The tax collectors are still here, but that doesn't dissuade Londoners from attending open-air events in the grand central courtyard, such as live performances in summer and ice skating in winter. The riverside terrace is a popular spot to get caffeinated with views of the Thames.

Near the Strand entrance, the **Courtauld Gallery** (Map p62; www.courtauld.ac.uk; adult/child £5/free, admission free 10am-2pm Mon; ⌚10am-6pm) displays a wealth of 14th- to 20th-century art, including a room of Rubens and works by van Gogh, Renoir and Cézanne. Downstairs, the **Embankment Galleries** are devoted to temporary exhibitions; prices and hours vary.

Handel House Museum MUSEUM
(Map p84; www.handelhouse.org; 25 Brook St W1; adult/child £5/2; ⌚10am-6pm Tue, Wed, Fri & Sat, 10am-8pm Thu, noon-6pm Sun; ⊖Bond St) George Frideric Handel's pad from 1723 until his death in 1759 is now a moderately interesting museum dedicated to his life. He wrote some of his greatest works here, including the *Messiah,* and music still fills the house during live recitals (see the website for details).

From songs of praise to *Purple Haze,* Jimi Hendrix lived next door at number 23 many years (and genres) later.

Burlington Arcade SHOPPING ARCADE
(Map p62; 51 Piccadilly W1; ⊖Green Park) The well-to-do Burlington Arcade, built in 1819, is most famous for the Burlington Berties, uniformed guards who patrol the area keeping an eye out for offences such as running, chewing gum or whatever else might lower the arcade's rarefied tone.

THE CITY

For most of its history, the City of London *was* London. Its boundaries have changed little since the Romans first founded their gated community here two millennia ago. You can always tell when you're within it as the Corporation of London's coat of arms appears on the street signs.

It's only in the last 250 years that the City has gone from being the very essence of London and it's main population centre to just its central business district. But what a business district it is – despite the hammering its bankers have taken in recent years, the 'square mile' remains at the very heart of world capitalism.

Currently fewer than 10,000 people actually live here, although some 300,000 descend on it each weekday, when they generate almost three-quarters of Britain's entire GDP before squeezing back onto the tube. On Sundays it becomes a virtual ghost town; it's a good time to poke around but come with a full stomach – most shops and eateries are closed.

Apart from the big-ticket sights, visitors tend to avoid the City, which is a shame as it's got enough interesting churches, intriguing architecture, hidden gardens and atmospheric lanes to spend weeks exploring.

Tower of London CASTLE

(Map p68; ☎0844-482 7777; www.hrp.org.uk; Tower Hill EC3; adult/child £17/9.50, audioguides £4/3; ⏲9am-5.30pm Tue-Sat, from 10am Sun & Mon Mar-Oct, until 4.30pm Nov-Feb; ⊖Tower Hill). If you pay only one admission fee while you're in London, make it the Tower. One of the city's three World Heritage Sites (joining Westminster Abbey and Maritime Greenwich), it offers a window on to a gruesome and fascinating history.

In the 1070s, William the Conqueror started work on the White Tower to replace the castle he'd previously had built here. By 1285, two walls with towers and a moat were built around it and the defences have barely been altered since. A former royal residence, treasury, mint and arsenal, it became most famous as a prison when Henry VIII moved to Whitehall Palace in 1529 and started dishing out his preferred brand of punishment.

The most striking building is the central **White Tower**, with its solid Romanesque architecture and four turrets. Today it houses a collection from the Royal Armouries. On the 2nd floor is **St John's Chapel**, dating from 1080 and therefore the oldest church in London. To the north is **Waterloo Barracks**, which now contains the spectacular **Crown Jewels**. On the far side of the White Tower is the **Bloody Tower**, where the 12-year-old Edward V and his little brother were held 'for their own safety' and later murdered, probably by their uncle, the future Richard III. Sir Walter Raleigh did a 13-year stretch here, when he wrote his *History of the World*.

On the small green in front of the **Chapel Royal of St Peter ad Vincula** stood Henry VIII's **scaffold**, where seven people, including Anne Boleyn and her cousin Catherine Howard (Henry's second and fifth wives) were beheaded.

Look out for the latest in the Tower's long line of famous ravens, which legend says could cause the White Tower to collapse should they leave. Their wings are clipped in case they get any ideas.

To get your bearings, take the hugely entertaining free guided tour with any of the Tudor-garbed Beefeaters. Hour-long tours leave every 30 minutes from the bridge near the main entrance; the last tour's an hour before closing.

St Paul's Cathedral CATHEDRAL

(Map p68; www.stpauls.co.uk; adult/child £12.50/4.50; ⏲8.30am-4pm Mon-Sat; ⊖St Paul's) Dominating the City with a dome second in size only to St Peter's in Rome, St Paul's Cathedral was designed by Wren after the Great Fire and built between 1675 and 1710. Four other cathedrals preceded it on this site, the first dating from 604.

The dome is renowned for somehow dodging the bombs during the Blitz and became an icon of the resilience shown in the capital during WWII. Outside the cathedral, to the north, is a **monument to the people of London**, a simple and elegant memorial to the 32,000 Londoners who weren't so lucky.

Inside, some 30m above the main paved area, is the first of three domes (actually a dome inside a cone inside a dome) supported by eight huge columns. The walkway round its base is called the **Whispering Gallery**, because if you talk close to the wall, your words will carry to the opposite side 32m away. It can be reached by a staircase on the western side of the southern transept (9.30am to 3.30pm only). There are 528 lung-busting steps to the **Golden Gallery** at the very top, and an unforgettable view of London.

The **Crypt** has memorials to up to 300 military demigods, including Wellington, Kitchener and Nelson, whose body lies below the dome. But the most poignant memorial is to Wren himself. On a simple slab bearing his name, a Latin inscription translates as: 'If you seek his memorial, look about you'.

Audio tours lasting 45 minutes are available for £4. Guided tours (adult/child £3/1) leave the tour desk at 10.45am, 11.15am, 1.30pm and 2pm (90 minutes). Evensong takes place at 5pm (3.15pm on Sunday).

Tower Bridge LANDMARK

London was still a thriving port in 1894 when elegant Tower Bridge was built. Designed to be raised to allow ships to pass, electricity has now taken over from the original steam engines. A lift leads up from the northern tower to the overpriced **Tower Bridge Exhibition** (Map p68; www.towerbridge.org.uk; adult/child £7/3; ⏲10am-5.30pm Apr-Sep, 9.30am-5pm Oct-Mar; ⊖Tower Hill), where the story of its building is recounted within the upper walkway. The same ticket gets you into the engine rooms below the southern tower. Below the bridge on the

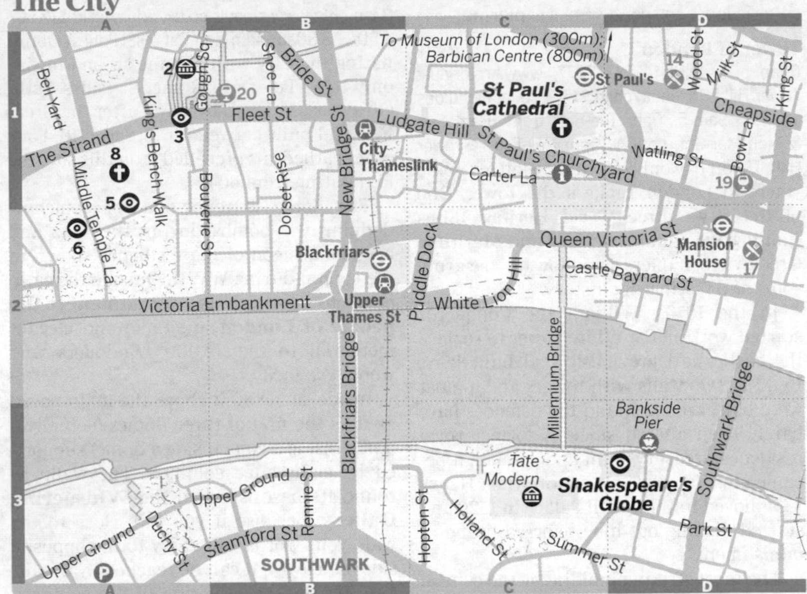

The City

Top Sights

- Shakespeare's Globe ... D3
- St Paul's Cathedral ... C1
- Tower Bridge ... H3
- Tower of London ... G3

Sights

1. Bank of England Museum ... E1
2. Dr Johnson's House ... A1
3. Fleet St ... A1
4. Guildhall ... E1
5. Inner Temple ... A1
6. Middle Temple ... A2
7. Monument ... F2
8. Temple Church ... A1
9. Tower Bridge Exhibition ... H3

Sleeping

10. Apex City of London ... G2
11. Threadneedles ... F1

Eating

12. 1 Lombard Street ... E1
13. GBK ... G3
14. Hummus Brothers ... D1
15. Konditor & Cook ... G1
16. Leon ... E2
17. Wagamama ... D2
- Wagamama ... (see 13)

Drinking

18. Vertigo 42 ... F1
19. Ye Old Watling ... D1
20. Ye Olde Cheshire Cheese ... B1

City side is Dead Man's Hole, where corpses that had made their way into the Thames (through suicide, murder or accident) were regularly retrieved.

FREE **Museum of London** MUSEUM
(www.museumoflondon.org.uk; 150 London Wall EC2; ⊙10am-6pm; ⊖Barbican) Visiting the fascinating Museum of London early in your stay helps to make sense of the layers of history that make up this place. The Roman section, in particular, illustrates how the modern is grafted onto the ancient; several of the city's main thoroughfares were once Roman roads, for instance.

The museum's £20 million Galleries of Modern London opened in 2010, encompassing everything from 1666 (the Great Fire) to the present day. While the Lord Mayor's ceremonial coach is the cen-

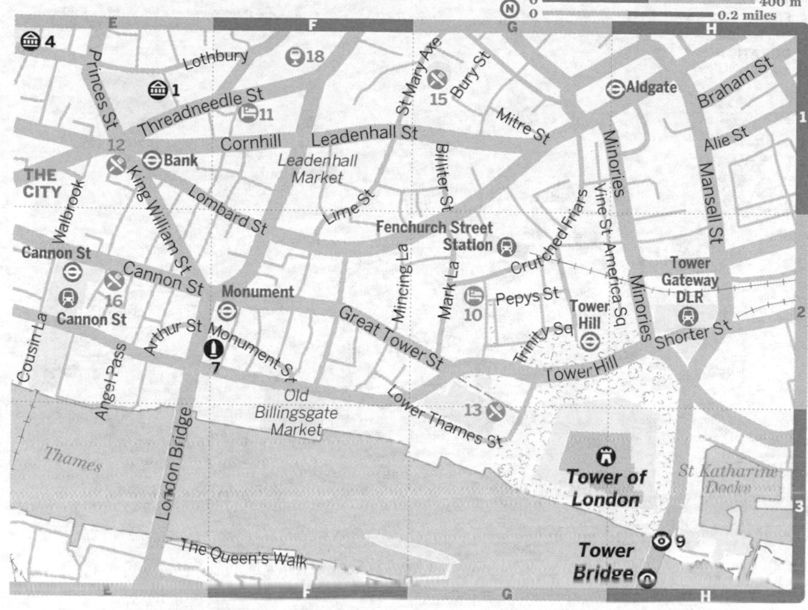

trepiece, an effort has been made to create an immersive experience: you can enter reconstructions of an 18th-century debtors' prison, a Georgian pleasure garden and a Victorian street.

FREE **Guildhall** HISTORIC BUILDING
(Map p68; ☎020-7606 3030; www.guildhall.cityoflondon.gov.uk; Gresham St EC2; ⏲10am-4pm unless in use; ⊖Bank) Plum in the middle of the 'square mile', the Guildhall has been the seat of the City's local government for eight centuries. The present building dates from the early 15th century.

Visitors can see the **Great Hall**, where the city's mayor is sworn in and where important fellows like the Tsar of Russia and the Prince Regent celebrated beating Napoleon. It's an impressive space decorated with the shields and banners of London's 12 principal livery companies, carved galleries (the west of which is protected by disturbing statues of giants Gog and Magog) and a beautiful oak-panelled roof. There's also a lovely bronze statue of Churchill sitting in a comfy chair. Beneath it is London's largest **medieval crypt** (visit by free guided tour only, bookings essential), with 19 stained-glass windows showing the livery companies' coats of arms.

The **Clockmakers' Museum** (admission free; ⏲9.30am-4.45pm Mon-Sat) charts 500 years of timekeeping with more than 600 ticking exhibits, and the **Guildhall Art Gallery** (adult/child £2.50/1; ⏲10am-5pm Mon-Sat, noon-4pm Sun) displays around 250 artworks. Included in the art gallery admission is entry to the remains of an ancient **Roman amphitheatre**, which lay forgotten beneath this site until 1988.

FREE **Bank of England Museum** MUSEUM
(Map p68; www.bankofengland.co.uk/museum; Bartholomew Lane EC2; ⏲10am-5pm Mon-Fri; ⊖Bank) Guardian of the country's financial system, the Bank of England was established in 1694 when the government needed to raise cash to support a war with France. It was moved here in 1734 and largely renovated by Sir John Soane. The surprisingly interesting museum traces the history of the bank and banking system. Audioguides are free and you even get to pick up a £230,000 gold bar.

Monument MEMORIAL
(Map p68; www.themonument.info; Monument St; adult/child £3/1; ⏲9.30am-5.30pm; ⊖Monument) Designed by Wren to commemorate the Great Fire, the Monument is 60.6m high, the exact distance from its base to the

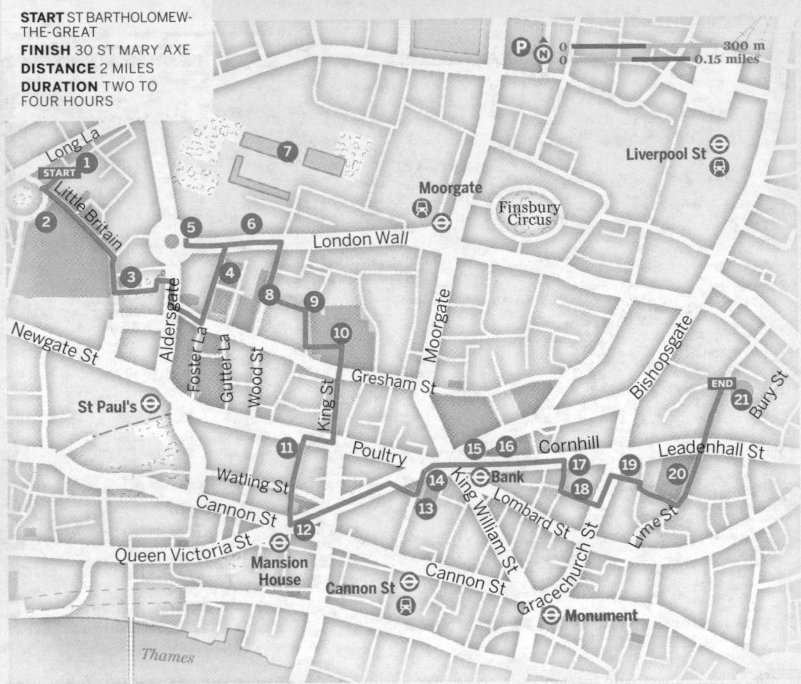

Walking Tour

City of London

The City of London has as much history and interesting architecture in its square mile as the rest of London put together. This tour focuses on the City's hidden delights (secluded parks, charming churches) in a journey from the ancient to the ultramodern.

It's fitting to start at **1 St Bartholomew-the-Great**, as this fascinating 12th-century church was once a pilgrimage stop for travellers to London. In more recent times, it's been used for scenes in *Four Weddings & A Funeral*, *Shakespeare In Love* and *Sherlock Holmes*.

Head out through the Tudor gatehouse. In the distance you'll see the Victorian arches of Smithfield's meat market, which has occupied this site just north of the old city walls for 800 years. Executions were held here, most famously the burning of Protestants under Mary I and the grisly killing of Scottish hero William Wallace (Braveheart) in 1305; a plaque on the front of **2 St Bartholomew's Hospital** commemorates him. Also note the shrapnel damage to the wall – the legacy of an attack in 1916 by a German Zeppelin.

Head back towards the gate and turn right into Little Britain. Follow it as it curves to the right and look out for the large oak marking the entrance to **3 Postman's Park**. This lovely space includes a touching legacy of Victorian socialism: a tiled wall celebrating everyday heroes.

Turn right at the end of the park, then left and left again into Noble St. You're now inside what was once the old City's **4 walls**, remnants of which you'll pass on your left. Commenced in Roman times, the fortifications were demolished in the 18th and 19th centuries, but the shape of them can be traced in street names such as Newgate, Moorgate, Bishopsgate and Aldgate. This section was only uncovered after WWII bombs destroyed the buildings covering it. Take the stairs up to the footbridge crossing the street called London Wall towards the **5 Museum of London** (p68). The museum's Roman section will give you a feel for the layout of the City.

Turn left when leaving the museum and follow the Highwalk. On your left you'll see 6 **ruins** of the barbicans (defensive towers) that once guarded the northwestern corner of the walls, with the 7 **Barbican Centre** behind them. Like Marmite, you either love or hate the concrete Barbican. Parts of it are extraordinarily ugly, particularly the forbidding high-rise tower blocks (romantically named Shakespeare, Cromwell and Lauderdale). However, in 2001 the complex became heritage-listed and more people are admitting to finding beauty in its curved roofs, brightly planted window boxes and large central 'lake'. At the time of its construction, this vast complex of offices and residences was revolutionary. At its heart is an arts centre consisting of concert halls, cinemas, galleries, eateries, a library and a school. It was designed by Chamberlain, Powell and Bon, disciples of Le Corbusier, to fill a WWII bomb–pummelled space with democratic modern housing. Sadly this dream never really materialised, and today around 80% of the flats are privately owned.

Follow the painted lines on the Highwalk for a closer look, or turn right at Pizza Express, take the escalator down to Wood St and head towards the remaining tower of 8 **St Alban's**, a Wren designed church destroyed in WWII. Turn left and you'll find a sweet garden on the site of 9 **St Mary Aldermansbury**, capped by a bust of Shakespeare. The 12th-century church was ruined in the war then shipped to Missouri where it was re-erected.

Turn right on to Aldermansbury and head to the 10 **Guildhall** (p69). Take King St down to Cheapside, cross the road and head right to elegant 11 **St Mary-le-Bow**. The church was rebuilt by Wren after the Great Fire, and then rebuilt again after WWII. The term 'Cockney' traditionally refers to someone born within the sound of this church's bell.

Backtrack to Bow Lane and follow this narrow path to beautiful 12 **St Mary Aldermary**, rebuilt in the Perpendicular Gothic style in 1682 following the fire. Turn left on to Queen Victoria St and then right into Bucklersbury, where you'll see 13 **St Stephen's Walbrook** directly in front of you. In the 3rd century, a Roman temple stood here, and in the 7th century a Saxon church. Rebuilt after the Great Fire, the current St Stephen's is one of Wren's greatest masterpieces, with elegant Corinthian columns supporting a beautifully proportioned dome. Henry Moore sculpted the round central altar from travertine marble in 1972.

Leaving the church, you'll pass 14 **Mansion House**, built in 1752 as the official residence of the Lord Mayor. As you approach the busy Bank intersection, lined with neoclassical temples to commerce, you might think you've stumbled into the ancient Roman forum (the actual forum was a couple of blocks east). Head for the 15 **equestrian statue of the Iron Duke**, behind which a metal pyramid details the many significant buildings here. Directly behind you is the 16 **Royal Exchange**, walk through it and exit through the door on the right, then turn left onto Cornhill.

If you're not churched out, cross the road to 17 **St Michael's**, a 1672 Wren design which still has its box pews. Hidden in the warren of tiny passages behind the church is its 18 **churchyard**. Head through to Gracechurch St, turn left and cross the road to wonderful 19 **Leadenhall Market**. This is roughly where the ancient forum once stood. As you wander out the far end, the famous 20 **Lloyd's building** displays its innards for all to see.

Once you turn left onto Lime St, you'll see ahead of you Norman Foster's 180m 21 **30 St Mary Axe building**. Its dramatic curved shape has given birth to many nick names (the Crystal Phallus, the Towering Innuendo), but it's the Gherkin by which it's fondly referred. Built nearly 900 years after St Bartholomew-the-Great, it's testimony to the City's ability to constantly reinvent itself for the times.

POUND SAVERS

As many of London's very best sights are free, you can easily spend a busy week without paying much on admission charges. However, if you're hanging around for longer and have particular attractions that you're keen to see, there are options for saving a few pounds.

The **London Pass** (www.londonpass.com; per 1/2/3/6 days £40/55/68/90) is a smart card that gains you fast-track entry to 55 different attractions, including pricier ones such as the Tower of London and St Paul's Cathedral. You'd have to be racing around frantically to get real value from a one-day pass, but you could conceivably save quite a bit with the two- or three-day version. You'll have to weigh up whether the money saved justifies the cramming of so much into each day. Passes can be booked online and collected from the Britain & London Visitor Centre. It also sells a version with a preloaded Transport For London (TFL) travel pass, but it's cheaper to buy this separately.

If you're a royalty buff, taking out an annual membership to the **Historic Royal Palaces** (www.hrp.org.uk; individual/joint membership £41/63) allows you to jump the queues and visit the Tower of London, Kensington Palace, Banqueting House, Kew Palace and Hampton Court Palace as often as you like. If you were intending to visit all five anyway, membership will save you £12 (£43 for a couple). There can be a lengthy wait for membership cards, but temporary cards are issued immediately.

bakery on Pudding Lane where the blaze began. Climb the 311 tight spiral steps (not advised for claustrophobes) for an eye-watering view from beneath the symbolic vase of gold-leaf flames.

Dr Johnson's House MUSEUM

(Map p68; www.drjohnsonshouse.org; 17 Gough Sq EC4; adult/child £4.50/1.50; 11am-5pm Mon-Sat; Chancery Lane) The Georgian house where Samuel Johnson and his assistants compiled the first English dictionary (between 1748 and 1759) is full of prints and portraits of friends and intimates, including the good doctor's Jamaican servant to whom he bequeathed this grand residence.

Inns of Court HISTORIC BUILDINGS

All London barristers work from within one of the four atmospheric Inns of Court, positioned between the walls of the old City and Westminster. It would take a lifetime working here to grasp all the intricacies of their arcane protocols, originating in the 13th-century. It's best just to soak up the dreamy ambience of the alleys and open spaces and thank your lucky stars you're not one of the bewigged barristers scurrying about. A roll call of former members would include the likes of Oliver Cromwell, Charles Dickens, Mahatma Gandhi and Margaret Thatcher.

Lincoln's Inn (Map p102; www.lincolnsinn.org.uk; Lincoln's Inn Fields WC2; grounds 9am-6pm Mon-Fri, chapel & gardens noon-2.30pm Mon-Fri; Holborn) still has some original 15th-century buildings. It's the oldest and most attractive of the bunch, with a 17th-century chapel and pretty landscaped gardens.

Gray's Inn (Map p102; www.graysinn.org.uk; Gray's Inn Rd WC1; grounds 10am-4pm Mon-Fri; Chancery Lane) was largely rebuilt after the Luftwaffe levelled it.

Middle Temple (Map p68; www.middletemple.org.uk; Middle Temple Lane EC4; 10-11.30am & 3-4pm Mon-Fri; Temple) and **Inner Temple** (Map p68; www.innertemple.org.uk; King's Bench Walk EC4; 10am-4pm Mon-Fri; Temple) both sit between Fleet St and Victoria Embankment. The former is the best preserved, while the latter is home to the intriguing 12th-century **Temple Church** (Map p68; 020-7353 8559; www.templechurch.com; hours vary), built by the Knights Templar and featuring nine stone effigies of knights in its round chapel. Check the church's website or call ahead for opening hours.

Fleet St FAMOUS THOROUGHFARE

(Map p68; Temple) As 20th-century London's 'Street of Shame', Fleet St was synonymous with the UK's scurrilous tabloids until the mid-1980s, when the press barons embraced computer technology, ditched a load of staff and largely relocated to the Docklands. It's named after the River Fleet, which it once crossed. This substantial river was a major feature of the London landscape until the 18th century, when it was relegated to the sewers. It now flows subterraneously from Hampstead Heath and joins the Thames near Blackfriars Bridge.

St Katharine Docks HARBOUR

(Map p68; ⊖Tower Hill) A centre of trade and commerce for 1000 years, St Katharine Docks is now a buzzing waterside area of pleasure boats, shops and eateries. It was badly damaged during the war, but survivors include the popular **Dickens Inn**, with its original 18th-century timber framework, and **Ivory House** (built 1854) which used to store ivory, perfume and other precious goods.

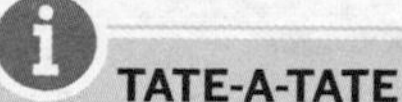

TATE-A-TATE

To get between London's Tate galleries in style, the **Tate Boat** (www.thamesclippers.com) will whisk you from one to the other, stopping en route at the London Eye. Services run from 10.10am to 5.28pm daily at 40-minute intervals. A River Roamer hop-on/hop-off ticket (purchased on board) costs £12; single tickets are £5.

SOUTH BANK

Londoners once crossed the river to the area controlled by the licentious Bishops of Southwark for all kinds of raunchy diversions frowned upon in the City. It's a much more seemly area now, but the theatre and entertainment tradition remains. While South Bank only technically refers to the area of river bank between Westminster and Blackfriars Bridges (parts of which are actually on the east bank due to the way the river bends), we've used it as a convenient catch-all for those parts of Southwark and Lambeth that sit closest to the river. In reality you'll find that many Londoners refer to sections of this largish stretch by the nearest tube station, especially Waterloo, Borough and London Bridge.

FREE **Tate Modern** GALLERY

(Map p74; www.tate.org.uk; Queen's Walk SE1; ⌚10am-6pm Sun-Thu, to 10pm Fri & Sat; ⊖Southwark) It's hard to miss this surprisingly elegant former power station on the side of the river, which is fortunate as the tremendous Tate Modern really shouldn't be missed. Focussing on modern art in all its wacky and wonderful permutations, it's been extraordinarily successful in bringing challenging work to the masses, becoming one of London's most popular attractions.

Outstanding temporary exhibitions (on the 4th floor; prices vary) continue to spark excitement, as does the periodically changing large-scale installation in the vast Turbine Hall. The permanent collection is organised into four themed sections, which change periodically but include works by the likes of Mark Rothko, Pablo Picasso, Francis Bacon, Roy Lichtenstein, Andy Warhol and Tracey Emin.

The multimedia guides (£3.50) are worthwhile for their descriptions of selected works, and there are free guided tours of the collection's highlights (Level 3 at 11am and midday; Level 5 at 2pm and 3pm). Make sure you cop the view from the top floor's restaurant and bar.

Shakespeare's Globe HISTORIC THEATRE

(Map p74; ☎020-7401 9919; www.shakespeares-globe.org; 21 New Globe Walk SE1; adult/child £11/7; ⌚10am-5pm; ⊖London Bridge) Today's Londoners might grab a budget flight to Amsterdam to behave badly. Back in Shakespeare's time they'd cross London Bridge to Southwark. Free from the city's constraints, they could hook up with a prostitute, watch a bear being tortured for their amusement and then head to a theatre. The most famous of them was the Globe, where a clever fellow was producing box-office smashes like *Macbeth* and *Hamlet*.

Originally built in 1599, the Globe burnt down in 1613 and was immediately rebuilt. The Puritans, who regarded theatres as dreadful dens of iniquity, eventually closed it in 1642. Its present incarnation was the vision of American actor and director Sam Wanamaker, who sadly died before the opening night in 1997.

Admission includes a guided tour of the open-roofed theatre, faithfully reconstructed from oak beams, handmade bricks, lime plaster and thatch. There's also an extensive exhibition about Shakespeare and his times.

From April to October plays are performed, and while Shakespeare and his contemporaries dominate, modern plays are also staged (see the website for upcoming performances). As in Elizabethan times, 'groundlings' can watch proceedings for a modest price (£5; seats are £15 to £35). There's no protection from the elements and you'll have to stand, but it's a memorable experience.

South Bank – Around London Bridge

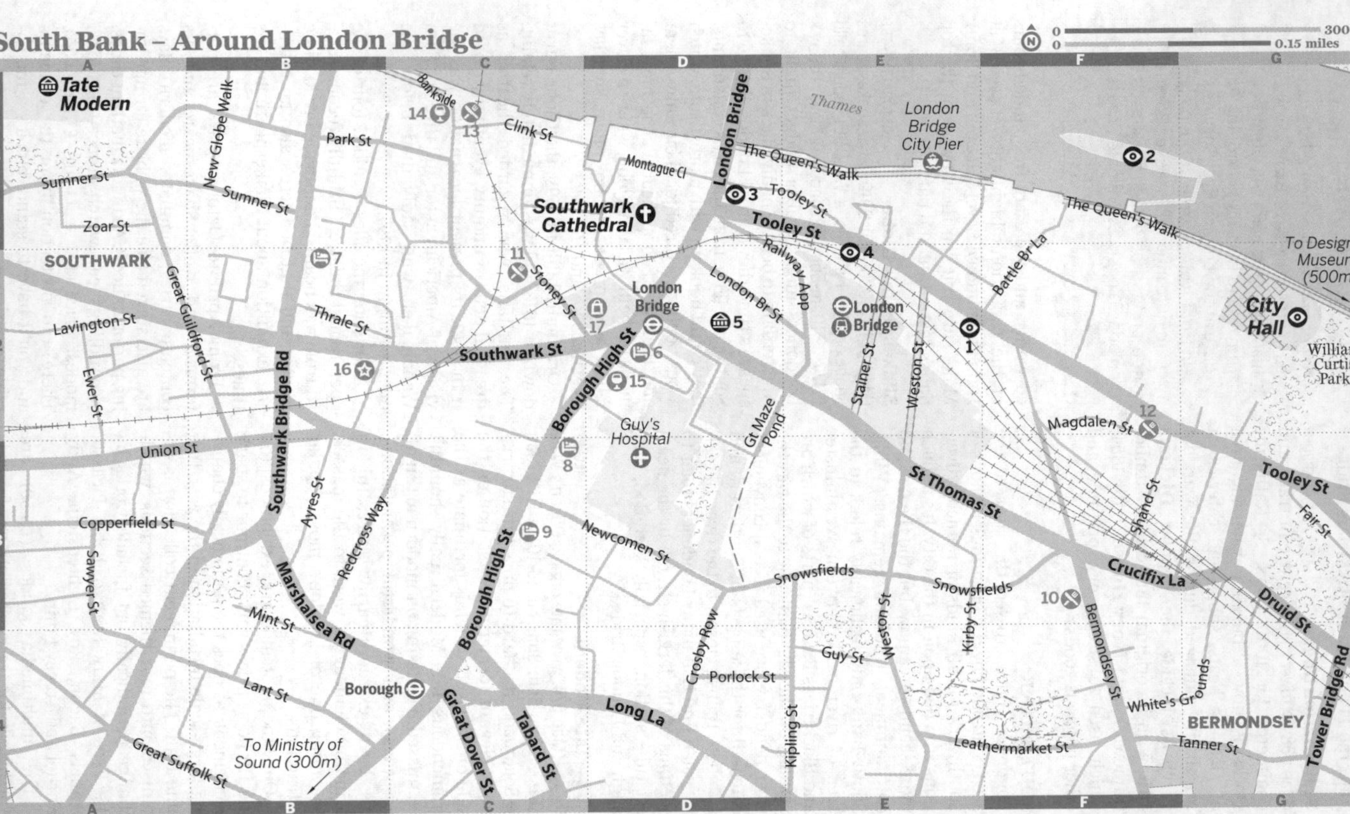

South Bank – Around London Bridge

Top Sights
City Hall G2
Southwark Cathedral D1
Tate Modern A1

Sights
1 Britain at War Experience E2
2 HMS Belfast F1
3 London Bridge Experience & London Tombs D1
4 London Dungeon E2
5 Old Operating Theatre Museum & Herb Garret D2

Sleeping
6 Orient Express D2
7 Southwark Rose Hotel B2
8 St Christopher's Inn C3
9 St Christopher's Village C3

Eating
10 Delfina F3
GBK .... (see 13)
11 Konditor & Cook C2
12 Magdalen F2
13 Wagamama C1

Drinking
14 Anchor C1
15 George Inn D2
Monmouth Coffee Company .... (see 11)

Entertainment
16 Menier Chocolate Factory B2

Shopping
17 Borough Market D2

London Eye RIDE, VIEWPOINT
(Map p76; ☎0871 781 3000; www.londoneye.com; adult/child £18/9.50; ⏲10am-8pm; ⊖Waterloo) It may seem a bit Mordor-ish to have a giant eye overlooking the city, but the London Eye doesn't actually resemble an eye at all, and, in a city where there's a CCTV camera on every other corner, it's probably only fitting. Originally designed as a temporary structure to celebrate the millennium, the Eye is now a permanent addition to the cityscape, joining Big Ben as one of London's most distinctive landmarks.

This 135m-tall, slow-moving Ferris-wheel-like attraction is the largest of its kind in the world. Passengers ride in an enclosed egg-shaped pod; the wheel takes 30 minutes to rotate completely and offers 25-mile views on a clear day. Visits are preceded by a short '4D' film offering a seagull's view of London, enhanced with bubbles, rain and snow.

Book your ticket online to speed up your wait (you also get a 20% discount), or you can pay an additional £10 to jump the queue. Joint tickets for the London Eye and Madame Tussauds (adult/child £43/31) are available, as is a 40-minute, sightseeing **River Cruise** (adult/child £12/6) with a multilingual commentary.

FREE **Imperial War Museum** MUSEUM
(Map p76; www.iwm.org.uk; Lambeth Rd SE1; ⏲10am-6pm; ⊖Lambeth North) You don't have to be a lad to appreciate the Imperial War Museum and its spectacular atrium with Spitfires hanging from the ceiling, rockets (including the massive German V2), field guns, missiles, submarines, tanks, torpedoes and other military hardware. Providing a telling lesson in modern history, highlights include a recreated WWI trench and WWII bomb shelter as well as a Holocaust exhibition.

Old Operating Theatre Museum & Herb Garret MUSEUM
(Map p74; www.thegarret.org.uk; 9A St Thomas St SE1; adult/child £5.80/3.25; ⏲10.30am-4.45pm; ⊖London Bridge) One of London's most genuinely gruesome attractions, the Old Operating Theatre Museum is Britain's only surviving 19th-century operating theatre, rediscovered in 1956 within the garret of a church. The display of primitive surgical tools is suitably terrifying, while the pickled bits of humans are just unpleasant.

It's a hands-on kind of place, with signs saying 'please touch', although obviously the pointy things are locked away. For a more intense experience, check the website for the regular 20-minute 'special events'.

Southwark Cathedral CATHEDRAL
(Map p74; www.southwark.anglican.org/cathedral; Montague Close SE1; suggested donation £4-6.50; ⏲8am-6pm; ⊖London Bridge) Although the central tower dates from 1520 and the choir from the 13th century, Southwark Cathedral is largely Victorian. Inside are monuments galore, including a Shakespeare

Memorial. Catch evensong at 5.30pm on Tuesdays, Thursdays and Fridays, 4pm on Saturdays and 3pm on Sundays.

City Hall LANDMARK

(Map p74; www.london.gov.uk; Queen's Walk SE1; ⌚8.30am-6pm Mon-Fri; ⊖London Bridge) The Norman Foster–designed, wonky-egg-shaped City Hall is an architectural feast and home to the mayor's office, the London Assembly and the Greater London Assembly (GLA). Visitors can see the mayor's meeting chamber and attend debates.

Design Museum MUSEUM

(www.designmuseum.org; 28 Shad Thames SE1; adult/child £8.50/5; ⌚10am-5.45pm; ⊖Tower Hill) The whiter-than-white Design Museum is a must for anyone interested in beautiful, practical things. The permanent collection has displays of modern British design and there are also regular temporary exhibitions including the annual *Designs of the Year* competition. To get here from Tower Bridge, head east along Shad Thames, an evocative lane between old warehouses.

HMS Belfast SHIP

(Map p74; http://hmsbelfast.iwm.org.uk; Queen's Walk SE1; adult/child £13/free; ⌚10am-5pm; ⊖London Bridge) Launched in 1938, HMS *Belfast* took part in the D-Day landings and saw action in Korea. Explore the nine decks and see the engine room, gun decks, galley, chapel, punishment cells, canteen and dental surgery.

Britain at War Experience MUSEUM

(Map p74; www.britainatwar.co.uk; 64-66 Tooley St SE1; adult/child £13/5.50; ⌚10am-5pm Apr-Oct, to 4.30pm Nov-Mar) You can pop down to the London Underground air-raid shelter, look at gas masks and ration books, stroll around Southwark during the Blitz and learn about the battle on the home front. It's crammed with fascinating WWII memorabilia.

South Bank – Around Waterloo Station

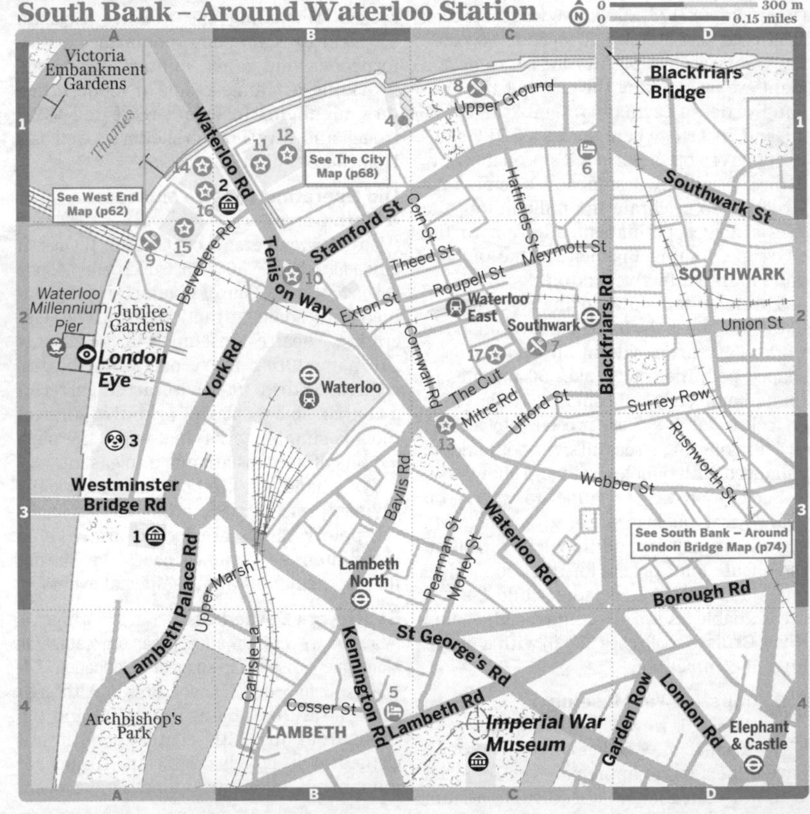

London Dungeon FRIGHT EXPERIENCE
(Map p74; ☎020-7403 7221; www.thedungeons.com; 28-34 Tooley St SE1; adult/child £20/15; ⏲10.30am-5pm, extended during holidays; ⊖London Bridge) Older kids tend to love the London Dungeon, as the terrifying queues during school holidays and weekends testify. It's all spooky music, ghostly boat rides, macabre hangman's drop-rides, fake blood and actors dressed up as torturers and gory criminals (including Jack the Ripper and Sweeney Todd). Beware the interactive bits.

London Bridge Experience & London Tombs FRIGHT EXPERIENCE
(Map p74; www.thelondonbridgeexperience.com; 2-4 Tooley St SE1; adult/child £22/17; ⏲10am-5pm; ⊖London Bridge) Another coronary-inducing attraction, similar to but not related to nearby London Dungeon. This one starts with the relatively tame London Bridge Experience, where actors bring to life the bridge's history with the assistance of plenty of severed heads. Once the entertaining educational bit is out the way, the London Tombs turns up the terror. Adding to the general creepiness is the knowledge that these were once plague pits and therefore actual tombs. The experience takes about 45 minutes, with the tombs an optional additional 25 minutes. Tickets are much cheaper if bought in advance online.

Florence Nightingale Museum MUSEUM
(Map p76; www.florence-nightingale.co.uk; 2 Lambeth Palace Rd SE1; adult/child £5.80/4.80; ⏲10am-5pm; ⊖Waterloo) The thought-provoking Florence Nightingale Museum recounts the story of 'the lady with the lamp' who led a team of nurses during the Crimean War. She established a training school for nurses here at St Thomas' Hospital in 1859.

Sea Life AQUARIUM
(Map p76; ☎0871 663 1678; www.sealife.co.uk/london; County Hall SE1; adult/child £18/13; ⏲10am-6pm; ⊖Waterloo) One of the largest aquariums in Europe, Sea Life has all sorts of aquatic creatures organised into different zones (coral cave, rainforest, River Thames), culminating with the shark walkway. Check the website for shark-feeding times and book online for a 10% discount.

Hayward Gallery GALLERY
(Map p76; www.southbankcentre.co.uk; Belvedere Rd SE1; admission prices vary; ⏲10am-6pm Sat-Thu, to 10pm Fri; ⊖Waterloo) Part of the Southbank Centre, the Hayward hosts a changing roster of contemporary art (video, installations, photography, collage, painting etc) in a 1960s Brutalist building.

PIMLICO

Handy to the big sights but lacking a strong sense of neighbourhood, the streets get prettier the further you stray from Victoria station.

FREE **Tate Britain** GALLERY
(www.tate.org.uk; Millbank SW1; ⏲10am-5.40pm; ⊖Pimlico) Unlike the National Gallery, Britannia rules the walls of Tate Britain. Reaching from 1500 to the present, it's crammed with local heavyweights like Blake, Hogarth, Gainsborough, Whistler,

South Bank Around Waterloo Station

Top Sights
Imperial War Museum C4
London Eye A2

Sights
1 Florence Nightingale Museum A3
2 Hayward Gallery B1
3 Sea Life A3

Activities, Courses & Tours
4 London Bicycle Tour Company B1
London Duck Tours Departure Point .... (see 3)

Sleeping
5 Captain Bligh House B4
6 Mad Hatter Hotel C1

Eating
7 Anchor & Hope C2
8 Oxo Tower Brasserie C1
Ping Pong .... (see 15)
9 Wagamama A2

Entertainment
10 BFI IMAX B2
11 BFI Southbank B1
12 National Theatre B1
13 Old Vic C3
Purcell Room .... (see 14)
14 Queen Elizabeth Hall A1
15 Royal Festival Hall A2
16 Southbank Centre A1
17 Young Vic C2

Spencer and, especially, Turner, whose work dominates the **Clore Gallery**. His 'interrupted visions' – unfinished canvasses of moody skies – wouldn't look out of place in the contemporary section, alongside the work of David Hockney, Francis Bacon, Tracey Emin, Angela Bulloch and Damien Hirst. The always-controversial annual Turner Prize is exhibited in the gallery from October to January.

There are free hour-long guided tours, taking in different sections of the gallery, held daily at midday and 3pm (as well as 11am and 2pm on weekdays). The popular **Rex Whistler Restaurant** (020-7887 8825; mains £14 to £21), featuring an impressive mural from the artist, is open for breakfast, lunch and snacks.

CHELSEA & KENSINGTON

Known as the royal borough, residents of Chelsea and Kensington are certainly paid royally, earning the highest incomes in the UK (shops and restaurants will presume you do too). Kensington High St has a lively mix of chains and boutiques. Thanks to the surplus generated by the 1851 Great Exhibition, which allowed the purchase of a great chunk of land, South Kensington boasts some of London's most beautiful and interesting museums all on one road.

FREE **Victoria & Albert Museum** MUSEUM

(V&A; Map p80; www.vam.ac.uk; Cromwell Rd SW7; 10am-5.45pm Sat-Thu, to 10pm Fri; South Kensington) A vast, rambling and wonderful museum of decorative art and design, the V&A is part of Prince Albert's legacy to Londoners in the wake of the Great Exhibition. It's a bit like the nation's attic, comprising four million objects collected from Britain and around the globe. Spread over nearly 150 galleries, it houses the world's greatest collection of decorative arts, including ancient Chinese ceramics, modernist architectural drawings, Korean bronzes, Japanese swords, cartoons by Raphael, spellbinding Asian statues and Islamic carpets, Rodin sculptures, actual-size reproductions of famous European architecture and sculpture (including Michelangelo's *David*), Elizabethan gowns, ancient jewellery, an all-wooden Frank Lloyd Wright study and a pair of Doc Martens. Yes, you'll need to plan. To top it all off, it's a fabulous building, with an attractive garden cafe as well as the original, lavishly decorated V&A cafe.

Natural History Museum MUSEUM

(Map p80; www.nhm.ac.uk; Cromwell Rd SW7; 10am-5.50pm; South Kensington) Let's start with the building itself: stripes of pale blue and honey-coloured stone are broken by Venetian arches decorated with all manner of carved critters. Quite simply, it's one of London's finest.

A sure-fire hit with kids of all ages, the Natural History Museum is crammed full of interesting stuff, starting with the giant dinosaur skeleton that greets you in the main hall. In the dinosaur section, the fleshless fossils are brought to robotic life with a very realistic 4m-high animatronic Tyrannosaurus Rex and his smaller, but no less sinister-looking, cousins.

The other galleries are equally impressive. An escalator slithers up and into a hollowed-out globe where two exhibits – The Power Within and Restless Surface – explain how wind, water, ice, gravity and life itself impact on the earth. For parents unsure of how to broach the facts of life, a quick whiz around the Human Biology section should do the trick.

The **Darwin Centre** houses a team of biologists and a staggering 20-million-plus species of animal and plant specimens. Take a lift to the top of the Cocoon, a seven-storey egg-shaped structure encased within a glass pavilion, and make your way down through the floors of interactive displays. Glass windows allow you to watch the scientists at work.

FREE **Science Museum** MUSEUM

(Map p80; www.sciencemuseum.org.uk; Exhibition Rd SW7; 10am-6pm; South Kensington) With seven floors of interactive and educational exhibits, the Science Museum covers everything from the Industrial Revolution to the exploration of space. There is something for all ages, from vintage cars, trains and aeroplanes to labour-saving devices for the home, a wind tunnel and flight simulator. Kids love the interactive sections. There's also a 450-seat **Imax cinema**.

Kensington Palace PALACE

(Map p98; www.hrp.org.uk/Kensingtonpalace; Kensington Gardens W8; adult/child £13/6.25; 10am-6pm; High St Kensington) Kensington Palace (1605) became the favourite royal residence under the joint reign of William and Mary and remained so until George III became king and moved across the park to Buckingham Palace. It still has private apartments where various members of the royal extended family live. In popular imagination it's most associated with three intriguing princesses: Victoria (who was born here in 1819 and lived here with her domineering mother until her accession to the throne), Margaret (sister of the current queen, who lived here until her 2002 death) and, of course, Diana. More than a million bouquets were left outside the gates following her death in 1997.

The building is undergoing major restoration work until January 2012. Rather than closing completely, sections of the palace have been transformed into a giant art installation. Leading artists and fashion designers have been given free rein to create their own enchanted spaces within the ornately painted and gilded rooms, which are changed every six months. All museum-like elements have been removed – there are no information panels, display cases, audioguides or tours. If you're hungry for historical information, ask the warders, who have been rebranded 'explainers' for this very purpose.

Kensington Gardens PARK

(Map p98; ⏲dawn-dusk; ⊖Queensway) Blending in with Hyde Park, these royal gardens are part of Kensington Palace and hence popularly associated with Princess Diana. Diana devotees can visit the **Diana, Princess of Wales Memorial Playground** in its northwest corner, a much more restrained royal remembrance than the over-the-top **Albert Memorial** (Map p80). The latter is a lavish marble, mosaic and gold affair opposite the Royal Albert Hall, built to honour Queen Victoria's husband, Albert (1819–61).

The gardens also house the **Serpentine Gallery** (Map p80; www.serpentinegallery.org; admission free; ⏲10am-6pm), one of London's edgiest contemporary art spaces. The **Sunken Garden** (Map p98), near the palace, is at its prettiest in summer, while tea in the **Orangery** (Map p98) is a treat any time of the year.

Hyde Park PARK

(Map p80; ⏲5.30am- midnight; ⊖Marble Arch, Hyde Park Corner or Queensway) At 145 hectares, Hyde Park is central London's largest open space. Henry VIII expropriated it from the Church in 1536, when it became a hunting ground and later a venue for duels, executions and horse racing. The 1851 Great Exhibition was held here, and during WWII the park became an enormous potato field. These days, it serves as an occasional concert venue and a full-time green space for fun and frolics. There's boating on the **Serpentine** for the energetic, while **Speaker's Corner** is for oratorical acrobats. These days, it's largely nutters and religious fanatics who address the bemused stragglers at Speaker's Corner, maintaining the tradition begun in 1872 as a response to rioting. Nearby **Marble Arch** was designed by John Nash in 1828 as the entrance to Buckingham Palace. It was moved here in 1851. The infamous Tyburn Tree, a three-legged gallows, once stood nearby. It is estimated that up to 50,000 people were executed here between 1196 and 1783.

A soothing structure, the **Diana, Princess of Wales Memorial Fountain** is a circular stream that cascades gently and reassembles in a pool at the bottom; paddling is encouraged. It was unveiled in mid-2004, instigating an inevitable debate over matters of taste and gravitas.

FREE **Royal Hospital Chelsea** HISTORIC BUILDING

(Map p80; www.chelsea-pensioners.co.uk; Royal Hospital Rd SW3; ⏲10am-noon Mon-Sat & 2-4pm daily; ⊖Sloane Sq) Designed by Wren, the Royal Hospital Chelsea was built in 1692 to provide shelter for ex-servicemen. Today it houses hundreds of war veterans known as Chelsea Pensioners, charming old chaps who are generally regarded as national treasures. As you wander around the grounds or inspect the elegant chapel and interesting museum, you'll see them pottering about in their winter blue coats or summer reds. The Chelsea Flower Show takes place in the hospital grounds in May.

Chelsea Physic Garden GARDEN

(Map p80; www.chelseaphysicgarden.co.uk; 66 Royal Hospital Rd SW3; adult/child £8/5; ⏲noon-5pm Wed-Fri, noon-6pm Sun; ⊖Sloane Sq) One for the garden obsessives (the less hardcore should head to the many free parks or Kew), this historic botanical garden is one of the oldest in Europe, established in 1673 for apprentice apothecaries to study medicinal plants. An audioguide is included in the price, and tours commence at 3pm on Sundays.

MARYLEBONE

Hip Marylebone isn't as exclusive as Mayfair, its southern neighbour, but it does have one of London's nicest high streets and the very famous, if somewhat disappointing, Baker St. Apart from being immortalised

Knightsbridge, South Kensington & Chelsea

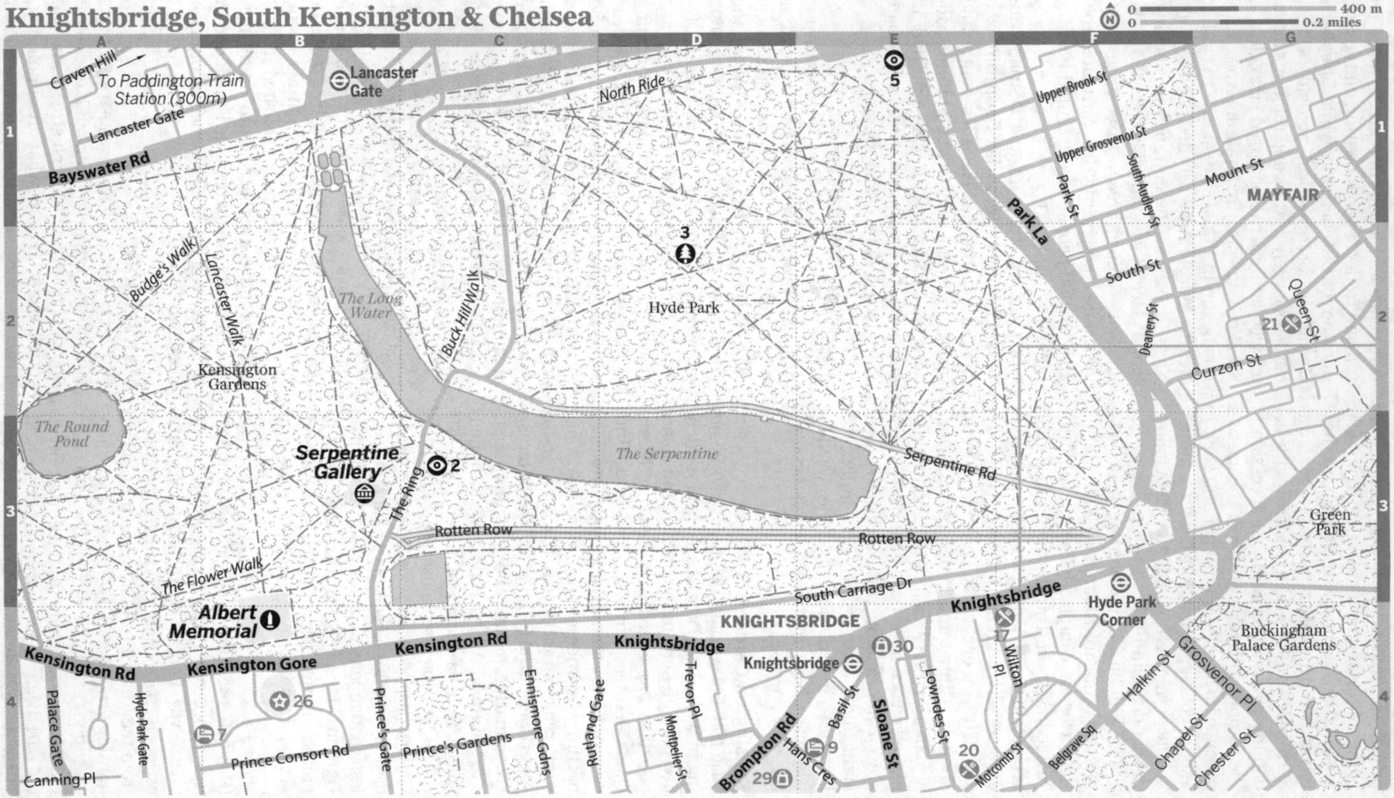

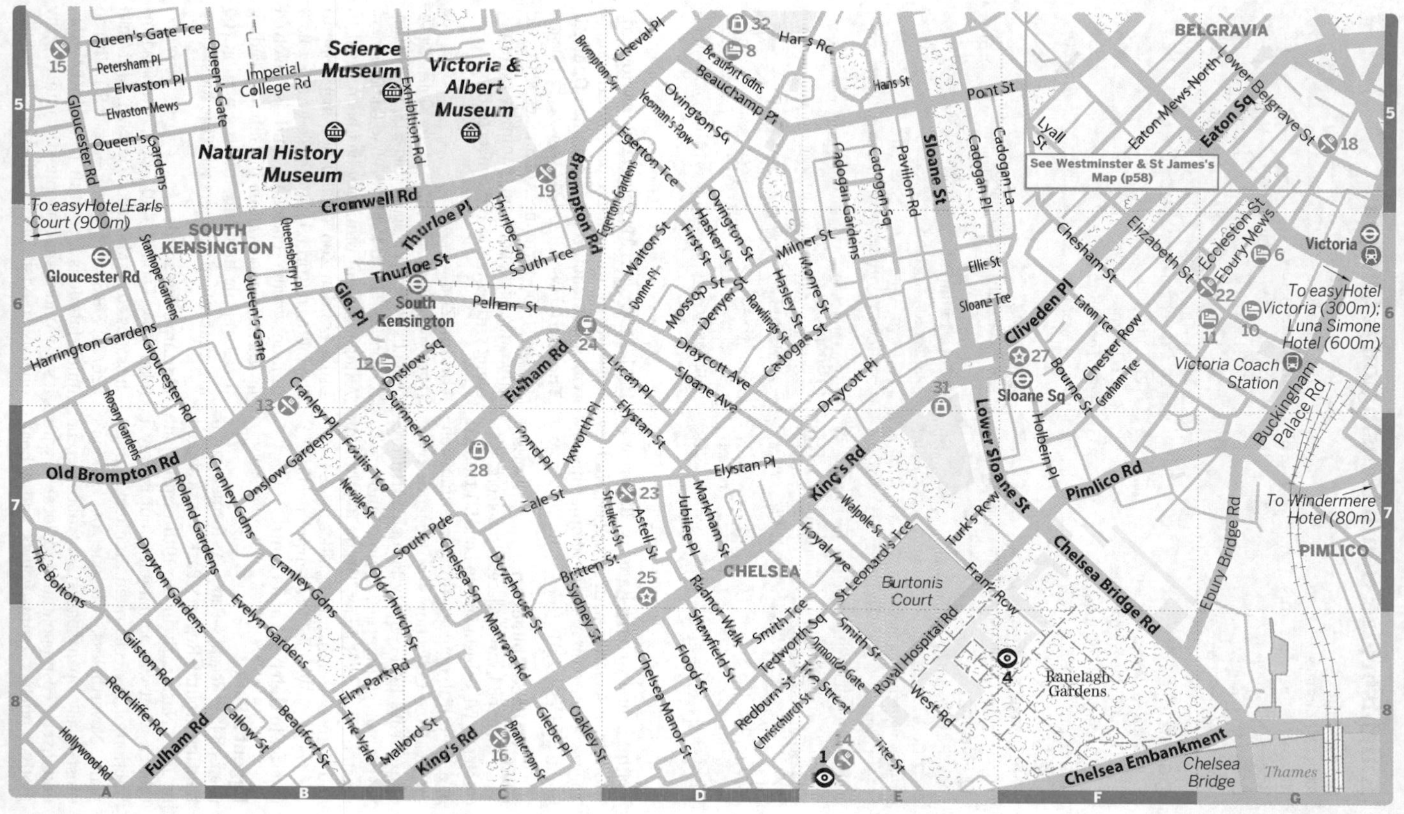
BELGRAVIA
Eaton Sq
Lower Belgrave St
Eaton Mews North
18
Lyall St
See Westminster & St James's Map (p58)
Victoria
6
Eccleston St
Ebury Mews
22
11
10
To easyHotel Victoria (300m); Luna Simone Hotel (600m)
Victoria Coach Station
Buckingham Palace Rd
To Windermere Hotel (80m)
PIMLICO
Ebury Bridge Rd
Thames
Chelsea Bridge
Chelsea Embankment
Ranelagh Gardens
4
Chelsea Bridge Rd
Pimlico Rd
Elizabeth St
Chesham St
Cliveden Pl
Eaton Tce
Chester Row
Graham Tce
Bourne St
27
Sloane Sq
Holbein Pl
Lower Sloane St
Turk's Row
Franklin Row
Burtonis Court
Royal Hospital Rd
West Rd
Tite St
14
1
Pont St
Cadogan La
Cadogan Pl
Ellis St
Sloane Tce
31
Sloane St
Pavilion Rd
Cadogan Sq
Cadogan Gardens
Hans St
Hans Rd
32
8
Beaufort Gdns
Beauchamp Pl
Ovington Sq
Yeoman's Row
Cheval Pl
Brompton Sq
Egerton Tce
Egerton Gardens
Ovington St
Hasker St
First St
Walton St
Donne Pl
Mossop St
Denyer St
Rawlings St
Hasley St
Moore St
Milner St
Cadogan St
Draycott Ave
Sloane Ave
Draycott Pl
King's Rd
Walpole St
Royal Ave
St Leonard's Tce
Smith St
Ormonde Gate
Tite Street
Smith Tce
Tedworth Sq
Redburn St
Christchurch St
Elystan Pl
Markham St
Jubilee Pl
Radnor Walk
Shawfield St
Flood St
CHELSEA
Chelsea Manor St
Astell St
St Luke's St
23
25
Britten St
Sydney St
Oakley St
Glebe Pl
Bramerton St
16
Brompton Rd
19
24
Lucan Pl
Elystan St
Ixworth Pl
Pond Pl
Cale St
Dovehouse St
Manresa Rd
Chelsea Sq
South Pde
Old Church St
Elm Park Rd
The Vale
Mallord St
King's Rd
Science Museum
Victoria & Albert Museum
Natural History Museum
Exhibition Rd
Imperial College Rd
Queen's Gate Tce
Petersham Pl
Elvaston Pl
Elvaston Mews
Queen's Gate
Queen's Gardens
15
Gloucester Rd
To easyHotel Earls Court (900m)
SOUTH KENSINGTON
Cromwell Rd
Thurloe Pl
Thurloe Sq
South Tce
Thurloe St
Glo. Pl
South Kensington
Pelham St
Fulham Rd
Onslow Sq
12
Sumner Pl
Foulis Tce
Neville St
28
Queensberry Pl
Stanhope Gardens
Harrington Gardens
Gloucester Rd
Rosary Gardens
13
Cranley Pl
Onslow Gardens
Cranley Gdns
Old Brompton Rd
Roland Gardens
Drayton Gardens
Evelyn Gardens
The Boltons
Gilston Rd
Redcliffe Rd
Hollywood Rd
Fulham Rd
Callow St
Beaufort St
A
B
C
D
E
F
G
5
6
7
8

Knightsbridge, South Kensington & Chelsea

Top Sights

Albert Memorial B4
Natural History Museum B5
Science Museum B5
Serpentine Gallery B3
Victoria & Albert Museum C5

Sights

1 Chelsea Physic Garden E8
2 Diana, Princess of Wales Memorial Fountain C3
3 Hyde Park D2
4 Royal Hospital Chelsea F8
5 Speaker's Corner E1

Sleeping

6 B&B Belgravia G6
7 Gore B4
8 Knightsbridge Hotel D5
9 Levin E4
10 Lime Tree Hotel G6
11 Morgan House G6
12 Number Sixteen B6

Eating

Boxwood Cafe .... (see 17)
13 GBK B6
14 Gordon Ramsay E8
15 L'Etranger A5
16 Made in Italy C8
17 Marcus Wareing at the Berkeley F4
18 Olivomare G5
19 Orsini C5
20 Ottolenghi Belgravia E4
21 Tamarind G2
22 Thomas Cubitt G6
23 Tom's Kitchen D7
Wagamama .... (see 30)

Drinking

24 Bibendum Oyster Bar C6

Entertainment

25 Curzon Chelsea D7
26 Royal Albert Hall B4
27 Royal Court Theatre F6

Shopping

28 Butler & Wilson C7
29 Harrods D4
30 Harvey Nichols E4
31 Rigby & Peller E6
32 Rigby & Peller D5

in a hit song by Gerry Rafferty, Baker St is strongly associated with Sherlock Holmes (there's a museum and gift shop at his fictional address, 221B).

FREE **Wallace Collection** MUSEUM
(Map p84; www.wallacecollection.org; Manchester Sq W1; ⌚10am-5pm; ⊖Bond St) Housed in a beautiful, opulent, Italianate mansion, the Wallace Collection is a treasure trove of exquisite 18th-century French furniture, Sèvres porcelain, arms, armour and art by masters such as Rubens, Titian, Rembrandt and Gainsborough. Audioguides are £4. Oliver Peyton's Wallace Restaurant occupies a glassed-in courtyard at its centre.

Regent's Park PARK
(Map p84; ⊖Regent's Park) A former royal hunting ground, Regent's Park was designed by John Nash early in the 19th century, although what was actually laid out is only a fraction of the celebrated architect's grand plan. Nevertheless, it's one of London's most lovely open spaces – at once serene and lively, cosmopolitan and local – with football pitches, tennis courts and a boating lake. **Queen Mary's Gardens**, towards the south of the park, are particularly pretty, with spectacular roses in summer. **Open Air Theatre** (☎0844 826 4242; www.openairtheatre.org) hosts performances of Shakespeare and other classics here on summer evenings, along with comedy and concerts.

London Zoo ZOO
(Map p108; www.londonzoo.co.uk; Outer Circle, Regent's Park NW1; adult/child £18/14; ⌚10am-5.30pm Mar-Oct, to 4pm Nov-Feb; ⊖Camden Town) A huge amount of money has been spent to bring London Zoo, established in 1828, into the modern world. It now has a swanky £5.3 million gorilla enclosure and is involved in gorilla conservation in Gabon. Feeding times, reptile handling and the petting zoo are guaranteed winners with the kids.

Madame Tussauds WAXWORKS
(Map p84; ☎0870 400 3000; www.madame-tussauds.co.uk; Marylebone Rd NW1; adult/child £26/22; ⌚9.30am-5.30pm; ⊖Baker St) With so much fabulous free stuff to do in London, it's a wonder that people still join lengthy queues to visit pricey Madame Tussauds,

but in a celebrity-obsessed, camera-happy world, the opportunity to pose beside Posh and Becks is not short on appeal. The life-size wax figures are remarkably lifelike and are as close to the real thing as most of us will get. It's interesting to see which are the most popular; nobody wants to be photographed with Richard Branson, but Prince Charles and Camilla do a brisk trade.

Honing her craft making effigies of victims of the French revolution, Tussaud brought her wares to England in 1802. Her Chamber of Horrors still survives (complete with the actual blade that took Marie Antoinette's head), but it's now joined by Chamber Live, where actors lunge at terrified visitors in the dark. The Spirit of London ride is wonderfully cheesy.

Tickets are cheaper when ordered online; combined tickets with London Eye and London Dungeon are also available (adult/child £65/48).

BLOOMSBURY & ST PANCRAS

With the University of London and British Museum within its genteel environs, it's little wonder that Bloomsbury has attracted a lot of very clever, bookish people over the years. Between the world wars, these pleasant streets were colonised by a group of artists and intellectuals known collectively as the Bloomsbury Group, which included novelists Virginia Woolf and EM Forster and the economist John Maynard Keynes. Russell Square, its very heart, was laid out in 1800 and is one of London's largest and loveliest.

Most people are content to experience Kings Cross St Pancras subterraneously, as it's a major interchange on the tube network, but the conversion of spectacular St Pancras station into the new Eurostar terminal and a ritzy apartment complex seems to be reviving the area's fortunes. The streets are still grey and car-choked, but some decent accommodation options and interesting bars have sprung up.

FREE **British Museum** MUSEUM
(Map p62; 020-7323 8000; www.britishmuseum.org; Great Russell St WC1; 10am-5.30pm Sat-Wed, to 8.30pm Thu & Fri; Russell Sq) The country's largest museum and one of the oldest and finest in the world, this famous museum boasts vast Egyptian, Etruscan, Greek, Roman, European and Middle Eastern galleries, among many others.

Begun in 1753 with a 'cabinet of curiosities' bequeathed by Sir Hans Sloane to the nation on his death, the collection mushroomed over the ensuing years partly through the plundering of the empire. The grand **Enlightenment Gallery** was the first section of the redesigned museum to be built (in 1823).

Among the must-sees are the **Rosetta Stone**, the key to deciphering Egyptian hieroglyphics, discovered in 1799; the controversial **Parthenon Sculptures**, stripped from the walls of the Parthenon in Athens by Lord Elgin (the British ambassador to the Ottoman Empire), and which Greece wants returned; the stunning **Oxus Treasure** of 7th- to 4th-century-BC Persian gold; and the Anglo-Saxon **Sutton Hoo** burial relics.

The **Great Court** was restored and augmented by Norman Foster in 2000 and now has a spectacular glass-and-steel roof, making it one of the most impressive architectural spaces in the capital. In the centre is the **Reading Room**, with its stunning blue-and-gold domed ceiling, where Karl Marx wrote the *Manifesto of the Communist Party*.

You'll need multiple visits to savour even the highlights here; happily there are 15 half-hour free 'eye opener' tours between 11am and 3.45pm daily, focussing on different parts of the collection. Other tours include the 90-minute highlights tour at 10.30am, 1pm and 3pm daily (adult/child £8/5), and audioguides are available (£4.50).

FREE **British Library** LIBRARY
(Map p86; www.bl.uk; 96 Euston Rd NW1; 9.30am-6pm Mon & Wed-Fri, 9.30am-8pm Tue, 9.30am-5pm Sat, 11am-5pm Sun; King's Cross St Pancras) You need to be a 'reader' (ie member) to use the vast collection of the library, but the Treasures gallery is open to everyone. Here you'll find Shakespeare's first folio, Leonardo da Vinci's notebooks, the lyrics to 'A Hard Day's Night' scribbled on the back of Julian Lennon's birthday card, Oscar Wilde's handwritten 'Ballad Of Reading Gaol', religious texts from around the world and, most importantly, the 4th-century *Codex Sinaiticus* (one of the earliest Bibles) and 1215 *Magna Carta*.

FREE **Wellcome Collection** MUSEUM
(Map p86; www.wellcomecollection.org; 183 Euston Rd NW1; 10am-6pm Tue, Wed, Fri & Sat, 10am-10pm Thu, 11am-6pm Sun; Euston Sq) Focussing on the interface of art, science and medicine, this clever museum is surprisingly fascinating. There are interactive displays

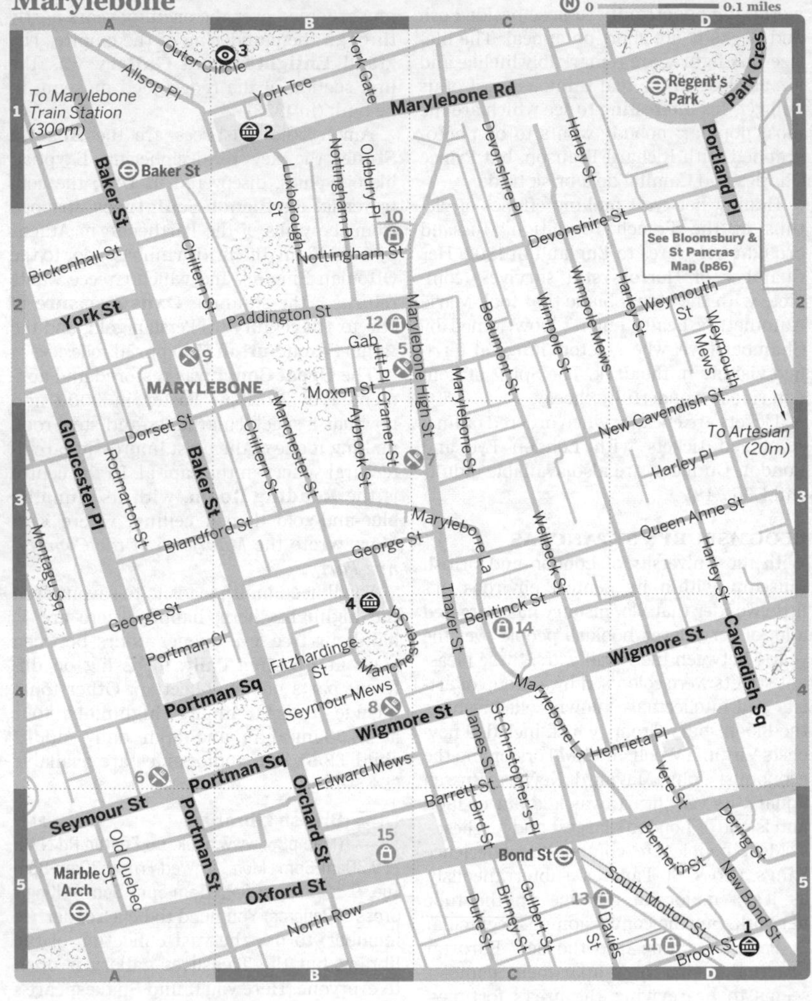

where you can scan your face and watch it stretched into the statistical average; wacky modern sculptures inspired by various medical conditions; and downright creepy things, like an actual cross-section of a body and enlargements of parasites (fleas, body lice, scabies) at terrifying proportions.

Foundling Museum MUSEUM

(Map p86; www.foundlingmuseum.org.uk; 40 Brunswick Sq WC1; adult/child £7.50/free; ⏲10am-5pm Tue-Sat, 11am-5pm Sun; ⊖Russell Sq), The Foundling Hospital opened in 1741 at a time of such extreme poverty that a thousand babies were abandoned annually. Hogarth was a founding governor, and in order to raise funds he hung his own artwork in the hospital's picture gallery and encouraged other artists to do the same – creating the first permanent exhibition space in Britain. The hospital closed and was demolished in 1928, but this neighbouring building recalls its social and artistic legacy.

Leading-edge artists still exhibit their work here, along with art from throughout the hospital's history. Most affecting is the display of the trinkets and tokens that mothers left as a parting gift to their children; they were never passed on.

Marylebone

Sights

1 Handel House Museum....D5
2 Madame Tussauds....B1
3 Regent's Park....B1
4 Wallace Collection....B4

Eating

5 La Fromagerie....B2
6 Locanda Locatelli....A4
7 Providores & Tapa Room....C3
8 Zizzi....B4
9 Zizzi....A2

Shopping

10 Apartment C....B2
11 Butler & Wilson....D5
12 Daunt Books....B2
13 Grays....C5
14 KJ's Laundry....C4
15 Selfridges....B5

The top floor is devoted to a collection of Handel memorabilia – including concert programs, tickets and the composer's handwritten will. Handel staged an annual performance of his greatest work, *Messiah,* as a fundraiser for the hospital.

Charles Dickens Museum MUSEUM
(Map p86; www.dickensmuseum.com; 48 Doughty St WC1; adult/child £6/3; ⊙10am-5pm Mon-Sat, 11am-5pm Sun; ⊖Russell Sq) Dickens' sole surviving London residence is where his work really flourished – *The Pickwick Papers, Nicholas Nickleby* and *Oliver Twist* were all written here. The handsome four-storey house opened as a museum in 1925, and visitors can stroll through rooms choc-a-bloc with fascinating memorabilia.

CAMDEN TOWN

Once well outside the city limits, the former hamlets of North London have long since been gobbled up by the metropolis, and yet they still maintain a semblance of a village atmosphere and distinct local identity. Not as resolutely wealthy as the west or as gritty as the east, the 'Norf' is a strange mix of genteel terrace houses and council estates, and contains some of London's hippest neighbourhoods.

Technicolor hairstyles, facial furniture, intricate tattoos and ambitious platform shoes are the look of bohemian Camden Town, a lively neighbourhood of pubs, live-music venues, interesting boutiques and, most famously, Camden Market. There are often some cartoon punks hanging around earning a few bucks for being photographed by tourists, as well as none-too-discreet dope dealers.

HOXTON, SHOREDITCH & SPITALFIELDS

Fans of the long-running TV soap *Eastenders* may find it hard to recognise its setting in traditionally working-class but increasingly trendy enclaves like these. The fact is you're more likely to hear a proper Cockney accent in Essex these days than you are in much of the East End. Over the centuries waves of immigrants have left their mark here, and it's a great place to come for diverse ethnic cuisine and vibrant nightlife.

TOP CHOICE **Dennis Severs' House** MUSEUM
(Map p88; ☎020-7247 4013; www.dennissevershouse.co.uk; 18 Folgate St E1; ⊖Liverpool St) This extraordinary Georgian House is set up as if its occupants had just walked out the door. There are half-drunk cups of tea, lit candles and, in a perhaps unnecessary attention to detail, a full chamber pot by the bed. More than a museum, it's an opportunity to meditate on the minutiae of everyday Georgian life through silent exploration.

Bookings are required for the Monday evening candlelit sessions (£12, 6pm to 9pm), but you can just show up on the first and third Sundays of the month (£8; noon to 4pm) or the following Mondays (£5; noon to 2pm).

FREE **Geffrye Museum** MUSEUM
(www.geffrye-museum.org.uk; 136 Kingsland Rd E2; ⊙10am-5pm Tue-Sat, noon-5pm

WORTH A TRIP

ABBEY ROAD

Beatles aficionados can't possibly visit London without making a pilgrimage to **Abbey Road Studios** (3 Abbey Rd) in posh St John's Wood. The fence outside is covered with decades of fans' graffiti. Local traffic is by now accustomed to groups of tourists lining up on the zebra crossing to recreate the cover of the fab four's 1969 album *Abbey Road*. To get here, take the tube to St John's Wood, cross the road, follow Grove End Rd to its end and turn right.

Bloomsbury & St Pancras

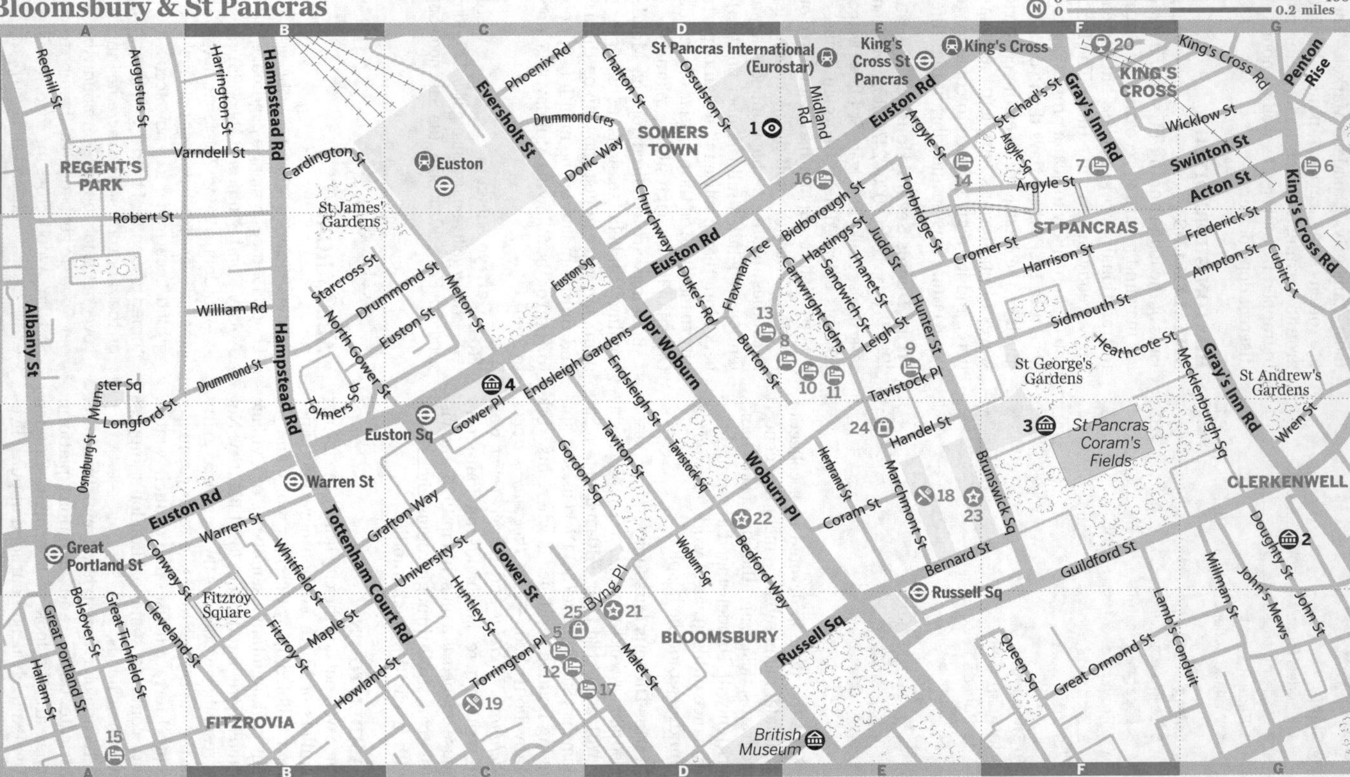

Bloomsbury & St Pancras

Sights
1 British Library D1
2 Charles Dickens Museum G3
3 Foundling Museum F3
4 Wellcome Collection C2

Sleeping
5 Arosfa Hotel C4
Arran House Hotel .... (see 5)
6 Clink78 .... G1
7 Clink261 .... F1
8 Crescent Hotel E2
9 Generator E2
10 George E2
11 Harlingford Hotel E2
12 Hotel Cavendish C4
13 Jenkins Hotel D2
14 Jesmond Dene Hotel E1
15 London Central YHA A4
16 London St Pancras YHA E1
17 Ridgemount Hotel D4

Eating
18 GBK E3
19 Planet Organic C4

Drinking
20 Big Chill House F1

Entertainment
21 Barfly D4
22 Bloomsbury Bowling Lanes D3
23 Curzon Renoir E3

Shopping
24 Gay's the Word E3
25 Waterstone's C4

Sun; Old St) If you like nosing around other people's homes, the Geffrye Museum will be a positively orgasmic experience. Devoted to middle-class domestic interiors, these former almshouses (1714) have been converted into a series of living rooms dating from 1630 to the current Ikea generation. On top of the interiors porn, the back garden has been transformed into period garden 'rooms' and a lovely walled herb garden (April to October only).

The museum is three blocks along Kingsland Rd, the continuation of Shoreditch High St.

FREE **White Cube** GALLERY
(Map p88; www.whitecube.com; 48 Hoxton Sq N1; 10am-6pm Tue-Sat; Old St) Set in an industrial building with an impressive glazed-roof extension, White Cube has an interesting program of contemporary-art exhibitions, from sculptures to video, installations and painting.

DOCKLANDS

Dockland's Canary Wharf and Isle of Dogs, to the east of the City, are now an island of tower blocks, rivalling those of the City itself. London's port was once the world's greatest, the hub of the enormous global trade of the British Empire. Since being pummelled by the Luftwaffe in WWII, its fortunes have been topsy-turvy, but the massive development of Canary Wharf has replaced its crusty seadogs with battalions of dark suited office workers. It's an interesting if slightly sterile environment, best viewed while hurtling around on the DLR (Docklands Light Railway).

FREE **Museum of London Docklands** MUSEUM
(www.museumoflondon.org.uk/docklands; Hertsmere Rd, West India Quay E17; 10am-6pm; DLR West India Quay) Housed in a heritage-listed warehouse, this outpost of the Museum of London uses a combination of artefacts and multimedia to chart the history of the city through its river and docks. There's a lot to see here, including an affecting section on the slave trade. The museum faces West India Quay; head west (towards the city) from the DLR station.

GREENWICH

Simultaneously the first and last place on earth, Greenwich (*gren*-itch) straddles the hemispheres as well as the ages. More than any of the villages swamped by London, Greenwich has retained its own sense of identity based on splendid architecture and strong connections with the sea and science. All the great architects of the Enlightenment made their mark here, leaving an extraordinary cluster of buildings that have earned 'Maritime Greenwich' its place on Unesco's World Heritage list.

Greenwich is easily reached on the DLR or via train from London Bridge. **Thames River Services** (020-7930 4097; www.thamesriver

Hoxton, Shoreditch & Spitalfields

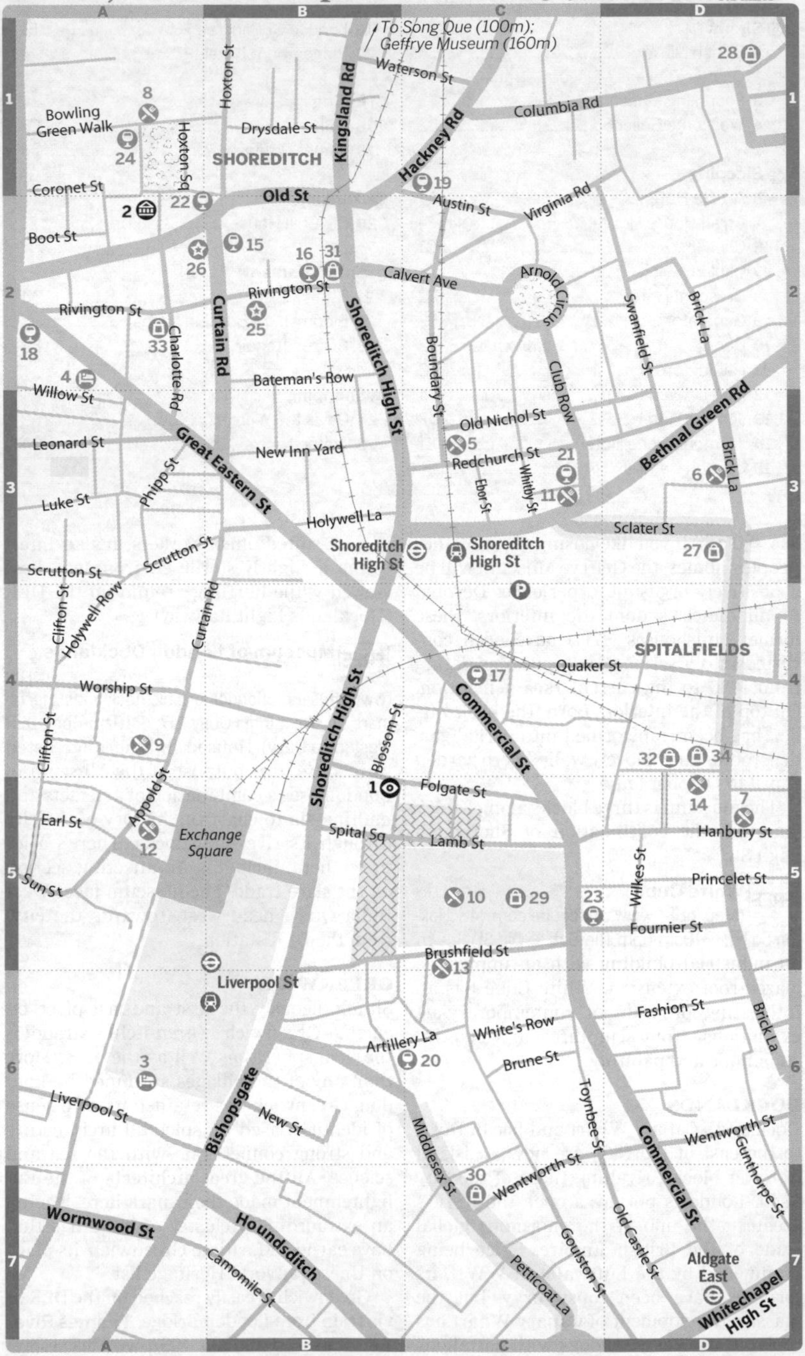

0 — 200 m
0 — 0.1 miles

A B C D

To Song Que (100m); Geffrye Museum (160m)

Waterson St
28
Bowling Green Walk
8
24
Hoxton Sq
Hoxton St
Drysdale St
Kingsland Rd
Hackney Rd
Columbia Rd
SHOREDITCH
Coronet St
2
22
Old St
19
Austin St
Virginia Rd
Boot St
15
26
16
31
Calvert Ave
Arnold Circus
Rivington St
Rivington St
25
18
33
Charlotte Rd
Curtain Rd
Shoreditch High St
Boundary St
Swanfield St
Brick La
Club Row
4
Willow St
Bateman's Row
Bethnal Green Rd
Leonard St
Great Eastern St
New Inn Yard
Old Nichol St
5
Redchurch St
21
Whitby St
Ebor St
11
6
Brick La
Phipp St
Luke St
Holywell La
Sclater St
Scrutton St
Shoreditch High St
Shoreditch High St
27
Scrutton St
Holywell Row
Curtain Rd
Clifton St
SPITALFIELDS
Quaker St
17
Worship St
Commercial St
Blossom St
Shoreditch High St
9
Clifton St
32
34
Appold St
1
Folgate St
14
7
Earl St
Exchange Square
Spital Sq
Lamb St
Hanbury St
12
Sun St
Wilkes St
Princelet St
10
29
23
Fournier St
Brushfield St
13
Liverpool St
Fashion St
Brick La
White's Row
Artillery La
20
Brune St
3
Liverpool St
New St
Bishopsgate
Toynbee St
Commercial St
Wentworth St
Middlesex St
Gunthorpe St
30
Wentworth St
Wormwood St
Houndsditch
Old Castle St
Goulston St
Camomile St
Petticoat La
Aldgate East
Whitechapel High St

services.co.uk) has boats departing from Westminster Pier (single/return £9.50/12.50, one hour, every 40 minutes), or alternatively take the cheaper Thames Clippers ferry. The *Cutty Sark,* a famous Greenwich landmark, remains closed while repairs continue on the boat, which was damaged by fire in 2007.

FREE Old Royal Naval College HISTORIC BUILDINGS

(www.oldroyalnavalcollege.org; 2 Cutty Sark Gardens SE10; ⏲10am-5pm; DLR Cutty Sark) Designed by Wren, the Old Royal Naval College is a magnificent example of monumental classical architecture. Parts are now used by the University of Greenwich and Trinity College of Music, but you can visit the **chapel** and the extraordinary **Painted Hall**, which took artist Sir James Thornhill 19 years of hard graft to complete.

The complex was built on the site of the 15th-century Palace of Placentia, the birthplace of Henry VIII and Elizabeth I. This Tudor connection, along with Greenwich's industrial and maritime history, is explored in the **Discover Greenwich** centre. The tourist office is based here, along with a cafe and microbrewery. Tours of the complex leave at 2pm daily, taking in areas not otherwise open to the public (£5, 90 minutes). You can also buy 'walkcards' (50p) for themed self-guided tours of Greenwich: *Highlights* (40 minutes), *Royal* (80 minutes), *Viewpoints*, and *Architecture* (both 90 minutes).

Greenwich Guided Walks (☎0757-577 2298; www.greenwichtours.co.uk; adult/child £6/5; ⏲12.15pm & 2.15pm) leave from the tourist office.

FREE National Maritime Museum MUSEUM

(☎020-8858 4422; www.nmm.ac.uk; Romney Rd SE10; ⏲10am-5pm; DLR Cutty Sark) Directly behind the old college, the National Maritime Museum completes Greenwich's trump hand of historic buildings. The museum itself houses a large collection of paraphernalia recounting Britain's seafaring history. Exhibits range from interactive displays to humdingers like Cook's journals and Nelson's uniform, complete with a hole from the bullet that killed him. The mood changes abruptly between galleries (one is devoted to toy ships while another examines the slave trade).

At the centre of the site, the elegant Palladian **Queen's House** has been restored to something like Inigo Jones' intention when he designed it in 1616 for the wife of Charles I. It's a refined setting for a gallery focusing on illustrious seafarers and historic Greenwich.

Hoxton, Shoreditch & Spitalfields

Sights

1 Dennis Severs' House ... B5
2 White Cube ... A2

Sleeping

3 Andaz ... A6
4 Hoxton ... A2

Eating

5 Albion ... C3
6 Brick Lane Beigel Bake ... D3
7 Cafe Bangla ... D5
GBK ... (see 10)
8 Hoxton Apprentice ... A1
9 L'Anima ... A4
10 Leon ... C5
11 Les Trois Garçons ... C3
12 Ping Pong ... A5
13 S&M Cafe ... C5
14 Story Deli ... D5
Wagamama ... (see 10)

Drinking

15 Bar Music Hall ... B2
16 Cargo ... B2
17 Commercial Tavern ... C4
18 Favela Chic ... A2
19 George & Dragon ... C1
20 Grapeshots ... C6
21 Loungelover ... C3
22 Mother ... A2
23 Ten Bells ... C5
24 Zigfrid Von Underbelly ... A1

Entertainment

25 Comedy Cafe ... B2
26 Plastic People ... A2

Shopping

27 Brick Lane Market ... D3
28 Columbia Road Flower Market ... D1
29 Old Spitalfields Market ... C5
30 Petticoat Lane Market ... C7
31 Present ... B2
32 Rough Trade ... D4
33 Start ... A2
34 Sunday (Up)Market ... D4

Behind Queen's House, idyllic **Greenwich Park** climbs up the hill, affording great views of London. It's capped by the **Royal Observatory** (same hours as rest of museum, until 7pm May-Aug), which Charles II had built in 1675 to help solve the riddle of longitude. Success was confirmed in 1884 when Greenwich was designated as the prime meridian of the world, and Greenwich Mean Time (GMT) became the universal measurement of standard time. Here you can stand with your feet straddling the western and eastern hemispheres.

If you arrive just before lunchtime, you will see a bright-red ball climb the observatory's northeast turret at 12.58pm and drop at 1pm – as it has every day since 1833 when it was introduced for ships on the Thames to set their clocks by.

The observatory's galleries are split into those devoted to astronomy and those devoted to time. There's also a 120-seat **planetarium** (adult/child £6.50/4.50) screening a roster of digital presentations; the website is updated daily with details.

O2 PERFORMANCE VENUE

(www.theo2.co.uk; Peninsula Sq SE10; North Greenwich) The world's largest dome (365m in diameter) opened on 1 January 2000, at a cost of £789 million, as the Millennium Dome, but closed on 31 December, only hours before the third millennium began. Renamed the O2, it's now a 20,000-seat sports and entertainment arena surrounded by shops and restaurants. It has hosted some massive concerts, including the one-off Led Zeppelin reunion and a 21-night purple reign by Prince; but alas not Michael Jackson's sold-out 50-show run that was imminent at the time of his death. There are ferry services from central London on concert nights.

HAMPSTEAD & HIGHGATE

These quaint and well-heeled villages, perched on hills north of London, are home to an inordinate number of celebrities.

Hampstead Heath PARK

(Gospel Oak or Hampstead Heath) With its 320 hectares of rolling meadows and wild woodlands, Hampstead Heath is a million miles away – well, approximately four – from central London. A walk up **Parliament Hill** affords one of the most spectacular views of the city, and on summer days it's popular with picnickers. Also bewilderingly popular are the murky brown waters of the single-sex and mixed bathing ponds (basically duck ponds with people splashing about in them), although most folk are content just to sun themselves around London's 'beach'.

Kenwood House (www.english-heritage.org.uk; Hampstead Lane NW3; admission free; 11.30am-4pm) is a magnificent neoclassical mansion (1764) on the northern side of the heath that houses a collection of paintings by English and European masters including Rembrandt, Vermeer, Turner and Gainsborough.

Highgate Cemetery CEMETERY

(020-8340 1834; www.highgate-cemetery.org; Swain's Lane N6; Archway) The cemetery weaves a creepy kind of magic, with its Victorian symbols – shrouded urns, obelisks, upturned torches (life extinguished) and broken columns (life cut short) – eerily overgrown graves and the twisting paths of the **West Cemetery** (adult/child £7/3; tours 2pm Mon-Fri Mar-Nov, hourly 11am-3pm Sat & Sun year-long), where admission is by tour only; bookings are essential for weekday tours. In the less atmospheric **East Cemetery** (adult/child £3/2; 10am-5pm Mon-Fri, 11am-5pm Sat & Sun Mar-Oct, to 4pm Nov-Feb), you can pay your respects to Karl Marx and George Eliot.

From Archway station, walk up Highgate Hill until you reach Waterlow Park on the left. Go through the park; the cemetery gates are opposite the exit.

Freud Museum MUSEUM

(www.freud.org.uk; 20 Maresfield Gardens NW3; adult/child £6/3; noon-5pm Wed-Sun) After fleeing Nazi-occupied Vienna in 1938, Sigmund Freud lived the last year of his life here. The fascinating Freud Museum maintains his study and library much as he left it, with his couch, books and collection of small Egyptian figures and other antiquities. Excerpts of dream analyses are scattered around the house, and there's a video presentation upstairs.

OUTSIDE CENTRAL LONDON

Kew Gardens PARK

(020-8332 5655; www.kew.org.uk; Kew Rd; adult/child £14/free; 9.30am-6.30pm, earlier closing in winter; Kew Gardens) In 1759 botanists began rummaging around the world for specimens they could plant in the 3-hectare plot known as the Royal Botanic Gardens. They never stopped collecting, and the gardens, which have bloomed to 120 hectares, provide the most comprehensive botanical collection on earth (including the world's largest collection of orchids). It's now recognised as a Unesco World Heritage Site.

You can easily spend a whole day wandering around, but if you're pressed for time, the **Kew Explorer** (adult/child £4/1) is a hop-on/hop-off road train that leaves from Victoria Gate and takes in the gardens' main sights.

Highlights include the enormous **Palm House**, a hothouse of metal and curved sheets of glass; the impressive **Princess of Wales Conservatory**; the red-brick, 1631 **Kew Palace** (www.hrp.org.uk/kewpalace; adult/child £5/free; ⏲10am-5pm Easter-Sep), formerly King George III's country retreat; the celebrated **Great Pagoda** designed by William Chambers in 1762; and the **Temperate House**, which is the world's largest ornamental glasshouse and home to its biggest indoor plant, the 18m Chilean Wine Palmand.

The gardens are easily reached by tube, but you might prefer to take a cruise on a riverboat from the **Westminster Passenger Services Association** (☎020-7930 2062; www.wpsa.co.uk), which runs several daily boats from April to October, departing from Westminster Pier (return adult/child £18/9, 90 minutes).

Hampton Court Palace PALACE

(www.hrp.org.uk/HamptonCourtPalace; adult/child £14/7; ⏲10am-6pm Apr-Oct, to 4.30pm Nov-Mar; 🚉Hampton Court) Built by Cardinal Thomas Wolsey in 1514 but coaxed out of him by Henry VIII just before the chancellor fell from favour, Hampton Court Palace is England's largest and grandest Tudor structure. It was already one of the most sophisticated palaces in Europe when, in the 17th century, Wren was commissioned to build an extension. The result is a beautiful blend of Tudor and 'restrained baroque' architecture.

Take a themed tour led by costumed historians or, if you're in a rush, visit the highlights: **Henry VIII's State Apartments**, including the Great Hall with its spectacular hammer-beamed roof; the **Tudor Kitchens**, staffed by 'servants'; and the **Wolsey Rooms**. You could easily spend a day exploring the palace and its 60 acres of riverside gardens, especially if you get lost in the 300-year-old **maze**.

Hampton Court is 13 miles southwest of central London and is easily reached by train from Waterloo. Alternatively, the riverboats that head from Westminster to Kew continue here (return adult/child £23/12, three hours).

Richmond Park PARK

(⊖Richmond) London's wildest park spans more than 1000 hectares and is home to all sorts of wildlife, most notably herds of red and fallow deer. It's a terrific place for birdwatching, rambling and cycling.

To get there from Richmond tube station, turn left along George St then left at the fork that leads up Richmond Hill.

Tours

One of the best ways to orientate yourself when you first arrive in London is with a 24-hour hop-on/hop-off pass for the double-decker bus tours. The buses loop around interconnecting routes throughout the day, providing a commentary as they go, and the price includes a river cruise and three walking tours. You'll save a couple of pounds by booking online.

Original London Sightseeing Tour BUS TOURS

(☎020-8877 1722; www.theoriginaltour.com; adult/child £25/12)

Big Bus Company BUS TOURS

(☎020-7233 9533; www.bigbustours.com; adult/child £26/10)

LONDON FOR CHILDREN

London has plenty of sights that parents and kids can enjoy together, and many of them are free, including the Natural History Museum, Science Museum and all of the city's parks, many of which have excellent playgrounds. Pricier but popular attractions include London Dungeon (for older children), London Zoo, Madame Tussauds, Tower of London, Sea Life and the London Eye. On top of that, there are city farms (see www.london-footprints.co.uk/visitfarms.htm) and the big galleries have activities for children. However, don't expect a warm welcome in swanky restaurants or pubs.

All top-range hotels offer in-house babysitting services. Prices vary enormously from hotel to hotel, so ask the concierge about hourly rates. Alternatively try www.sitters.co.uk: membership costs £12.75 for three months, then sitters cost around £8 per hour plus a £4 booking fee.

Citisights WALKING TOURS
(☎020-8806 3742; www.chr.org.uk/cswalks.htm) Focuses on the academic and the literary.

London Beatles Walks WALKING TOURS
(☎07958 706329; www.beatlesinlondon.com) Following the footsteps of the Fab Four.

London Walks WALKING TOURS
(☎020-7624 3978; www.walks.com) Harry Potter tours, ghost walks and the ever popular Jack the Ripper tours.

London Mystery Walks WALKING TOURS
(☎07957 388280; www.tourguides.org.uk)

City Cruises FERRY TOURS
(☎020-7740 0400; www.citycruises.com; single/return trips from £8/11, day pass £13) Ferry service between Westminster, Waterloo, Tower and Greenwich piers.

Black Taxi Tours of London TAXI TOURS
(☎020-7935 9363; www.blacktaxitours.co.uk; 8am-6pm £100, 6pm-midnight £110, plus £5 on weekends) Takes up to five people on a two-hour spin past the major sights with a chatty cabbie as your guide.

London Bicycle Tour Company CYCLING TOURS
(Map p76; ☎020-7928 6838; www.londonbicycle.com; 1A Gabriel's Wharf, 56 Upper Ground SE1; tour incl bike £16-19; ⊖Waterloo) Themed 2½- to 3½-hour tours of the 'East', 'Central' or 'Royal West'.

City Jogging Tours JOGGING TOURS
(☎0845 544 0433; www.cityjoggingstories.co.uk; tours £26) Combine sightseeing with keeping fit on a 6km route, graded for 'gentle joggers' or 'recreational runners'.

London Duck Tours AMPHIBIOUS-VEHICLE TOURS
(Map p76; ☎020-7928 3132; www.londonducktours.co.uk; County Hall SE1; adult/child from £20/16; ⊖Waterloo) Cruise the streets in the same sort of amphibious landing craft used on D-Day before making a dramatic plunge into the Thames.

Festivals & Events

Chinese New Year ETHNIC CELEBRATION
Late January or early February sees Chinatown snap, crackle and pop with fireworks, a colourful street parade and eating aplenty.

University Boat Race BOAT RACE
(www.theboatrace.org) A posh-boy grudge match held annually since 1829 between the rowing crews of Oxford and Cambridge Universities (late March).

London Marathon MARATHON
(www.london-marathon.co.uk) Up to half a million spectators watch the whippet-thin champions and bizarrely clad amateurs take to the streets in late April.

Camden Crawl MUSIC FESTIVAL
(www.thecamdencrawl.com; 1-/2-day pass £39/62) Your chance to spot the next big thing on the music scene or witness a secret gig by an established act, with 40 of Camden's venues given over to live music for two full days (late April/early May).

Chelsea Flower Show HORTICULTURAL SHOW
(www.rhs.org.uk/chelsea; Royal Hospital Chelsea; admission £19-42) Held in May, arguably the world's most renowned horticultural show attracts green fingers from near and far.

Trooping the Colour ROYAL PAGEANT
Celebrating the Queen's official birthday (in June), this ceremonial procession of troops, marching along the Mall for their monarch's inspection, is a pageantry overload.

Royal Academy Summer Exhibition ART EXHIBITION
(www.royalacademy.org.uk; adult/child £9.50/5) Running from mid-June to mid-August, this is an annual showcase of works submitted by artists from all over Britain, mercifully distilled to 1200 or so pieces.

Meltdown Festival MUSIC FESTIVAL
(www.southbankcentre.co.uk) The Southbank Centre hands over the curatorial reigns to a legend of contemporary music (such as David Bowie, Morrissey or Patti Smith) to pull together a full program of concerts, talks and films in late June.

Wimbledon Lawn Tennis Championships TENNIS TOURNAMENT
(www.wimbledon.org) Held at the end of June, the world's most prestigious tennis event is as much about strawberries, cream and tradition as smashing balls.

Pride GAY & LESBIAN PARADE
(www.pridelondon.org) The big event on the gay and lesbian calendar, a Technicolor street parade heads through the West End in late June or early July, culminating in a concert in Trafalgar Sq.

GAY & LESBIAN LONDON

London's had a thriving scene since at least the 18th century, when the West End's 'Mollie houses' were the forerunners of today's gay bars. The West End, particularly Soho, remains the visible centre of gay and lesbian London, with numerous venues clustered around Old Compton St and its surrounds. However, Soho doesn't hold a monopoly on gay life. One of the nice things about the city is that there are local gay bars in many neighbourhoods.

Despite, or perhaps because of, its grimness and griminess, Vauxhall's taken off as a hub for the hirsute, hefty and generally harder-edged sections of the community. The railway arches are now filled with dance clubs, leather bars and a sauna. Clapham (South London), Earl's Court (West London), Islington (North London) and Limehouse (East End) have their own miniscenes.

Generally, London's a safe place for lesbians and gays. It's rare to encounter any problem with sharing rooms or holding hands in the inner city, although it would pay to keep your wits about you at night and be conscious of your surroundings.

The easiest way to find out what's going on is to pick up the free press from a venue *(Pink Paper, Boyz, QX)*. The gay section of *Time Out* is useful, as are www.gaydarnation.com (for men) and www.gingerbeer.co.uk (for women). The hardcore circuit club nights run on a semiregular basis at a variety of venues: check out **DTPM**, **Fiction** (both at www.dtpmevents.co.uk), **Matinee**, **SuperMartXé** (both at www.loganpresents.com) and **Megawoof!** (www.megawoof.com).

Some venues to get you started:

Candy Bar (Map p62; www.candybarsoho.co.uk; 4 Carlisle St W1; ⊖Tottenham Court Rd) Long running lesbian hang-out.

Friendly Society (Map p62; 79 Wardour St W1; ⊖Piccadilly Circus) Soho's quirkiest gay bar, this Bohemian basement is bedecked in kid's-room wallpaper and Barbie dolls.

G-A-Y (Map p62; www.g-a-y.co.uk) Bar (30 Old Compton St W1; ⊖Leicester Sq); Late (5 Goslett Yard WC2; ⌚11pm-3am; ⊖Tottenham Court Rd); Club @ Heaven (The Arches, Villiers St WC2; ⌚11pm-4am Thu-Sat; ⊖Charing Cross) Too camp to be restricted to one venue, G-A-Y now operates a pink-lit bar on the strip, a late-night bar a few streets away and club nights at one of gaydom's most internationally famous venues, Heaven. Cover charges vary; entry is usually cheaper with a flyer from G-A-Y Bar.

Gay's the Word (Map p86; 66 Marchmont St WC1; ⊖Russell Sq) Books and mags of all descriptions.

George & Dragon (Map p88; 2 Hackney Rd E2; ⊖Old St) Appealing corner pub where the crowd is often as eclectically furnished as the venue.

Popstarz (Map p62; www.popstarz.org; The Den, 18 West Central St WC1; ⌚10pm-4am Fri; ⊖Tottenham Court Rd) London's legendary indie pop club night. The online flyer gets you in free.

Royal Vauxhall Tavern (RVT; www.rvt.org.uk; 372 Kennington Lane SE11; admission free-£9; ⊖Vauxhall) Much-loved pub with crazy cabaret and drag acts. Head under the arches from Vauxhall tube station onto Kennington Lane, where you'll see the tavern immediately to your left.

Two Brewers (www.thetwobrewers.com; 114 Clapham High St SW4; admission free-£5; ⊖Clapham Common) Popular bar with regular acts and a nightclub out the back. From the tube station, head north along Clapham High St (away from the common).

Village (Map p62; www.village-soho.co.uk; 81 Wardour St W1; ⊖Piccadilly Circus) Glitzy gay bar with excellent, lengthy happy hours.

Lovebox MUSIC FESTIVAL
(www.lovebox.net) London's contribution to the summer music festival circuit, held in Victoria Park in mid-July.

Notting Hill Carnival ETHNIC CARNIVAL
(www.nottinghillcarnival.biz) Held over two days in August, this is Europe's largest and London's most vibrant outdoor carnival, where London's Caribbean community shows the city how to party. Unmissable and truly crazy.

Sleeping

Take a deep breath and sit down before reading this section because no matter what your budget, London is a horribly pricey city to sleep in – one of the most expensive in the world, in fact. Anything below £80 per night for a double is pretty much 'budget', and at the top end, how does a £3500 penthouse sound? For this book we've defined the price categories for London differently than for the other chapters. Double rooms ranging between £80 and £180 per night are considered midrange; cheaper or more expensive options fall into the budget or the top-end categories, respectively.

Ignoring the scary money stuff for a minute, London has a wonderful selection of interesting hotels, whether brimming with history or zany modern decor. Most of the ritzier places offer substantial discounts on the weekends, for advance bookings and at quiet times (if there is such a thing in London).

Public transport is good, so you don't need to be sleeping at Buckingham Palace to be at the heart of things. However, if you're planning some late nights and don't fancy enduring the night buses (a consummate London experience, but one you'll want only once) it'll make sense not to wander too far from the action.

London's a noisy city, so expect a bit of the din to seep into your room. If you're a light sleeper, earplugs are a sensible precaution, as is requesting a room back from the street and higher up.

It's now becoming the norm for budget and midrange places to offer free wireless internet. The expensive places will offer it, too, but often charge. Hostels tend to serve free breakfast (of the toast-and-cereal variety). If your hotel charges for breakfast, check the prices; anything over £8 just isn't worth it when there are so many eateries to explore.

Budget accommodation is scattered about, with some good options in Southwark and St Pancras. For something a little nicer, check out Bloomsbury, Fitzrovia, Bayswater and Earl's Court. If you've the cash to splash, consider the West End, Clerkenwell and Kensington.

WESTMINSTER & ST JAMES'S

A bed in the Queen's own hood can be as ritzy as the Ritz, but there are some surprisingly affordable options.

Rubens at the Palace HOTEL ££
(Map p58; ☎020-7834 6600; www.rubenshotel.com; 39 Buckingham Palace Rd SW1; r from £149; @; ⊖Victoria) Opposite Buckingham Palace, it's perhaps not surprising to find that Rubens is a firm favourite with Americans looking for that quintessential British experience. The rooms are monarchist chic: heavy patterned fabrics, dark wood, thick drapes and crowns above the beds.

WEST END

Like on the Monopoly board, if you land on a Mayfair hotel you may have to sell a house, or at least remortgage. This is the heart of the action, so naturally accommodation comes at a price, and a hefty one at that. A couple of hostels cater for would-be Soho hipsters of more modest means.

TOP CHOICE **Haymarket Hotel** HOTEL £££
(Map p62; ☎020-7470 4000; www.haymarkethotel.com; 1 Suffolk Pl SW1; r/ste from £250/1750; @; ⊖Piccadilly Circus) The building was designed by John Nash (Buckingham Palace's main man) but the rest is Kit Kemp all the way. We love the gold loungers around the sunset-lit indoor swimming pool.

Hazlitt's HOTEL £££
(Map p62; ☎020-7434 1771; www.hazlittshotel.com; 6 Frith St W1; s £206, d/ste from £259/646; @; ⊖Tottenham Court Rd) Staying in this charming Georgian house (1718) is a trip back into a time when four-poster beds and claw-foot baths were the norm for gentlefolk. Each of the individually decorated 30 rooms is packed with antiques and named after a personage connected with the house.

One Aldwych HOTEL £££
(Map p62; ☎020-7300 1000; www.onealdwych.com; 1 Aldwych WC2; d/ste from £195/440; @; ⊖Covent Garden) Granite bathrooms, long swimming pool with underwater music, majestic bar and restaurant, modern

art, and a lift that changes colour to literally lift your mood.

Brown's Hotel HOTEL £££
(Map p62; ☎020-7493 6020; www.brownshotel.com; 30 Albemarle St W1; d £340-645, ste £885-3200; @📶; ⊖Green Park) Rudyard Kipling penned many of his works here, Kate Moss has frequented the spa and both Queen Victoria and Winston Churchill dropped in for tea. There's a lovely old-world feel to Browns, but without the snootiness of other Mayfair hotels. The rooms have every modern comfort.

Soho Hotel HOTEL £££
(Map p62; ☎020-7559 3000; www.sohohotel.com; 4 Richmond Mews W1; d £290-360, ste £400-2750; @📶; ⊖Oxford Circus) Hello Kitty! This Kit Kemp–designed hotel has a giant cat sculpture in a reception that looks like a psychedelic candy store; try to refrain from licking the walls.

Covent Garden Hotel HOTEL £££
(☎020-7806 1000; www.coventgardenhotel.co.uk; 10 Monmouth St WC2; d/ste from £240/395; @📶; ⊖Covent Garden) Well-positioned Firmdale hotel (see p95) with gym and private cinema.

Oxford St YHA HOSTEL £
(☎0845 371 9133; www.yha.org.uk; 14 Noel St W1; dm/tw from £18/44; @📶; ⊖Oxford Circus) In most respects, this is a bog-standard YHA hostel, with tidy rooms and all the usual facilities (kitchen, TV room, laundry). What it's got going for it are a terrific (albeit noisy) location and decent views over London's rooftops from some of the rooms.

THE CITY

Bristling with bankers during the week, you can often pick up a considerable bargain in the City on weekends.

Threadneedles HOTEL ££
(Map p68; ☎020-7657 8080; www.theetoncollection.com; 5 Threadneedle St EC2; r weekend/weekday from £175/345; @📶; ⊖Bank) The incredible stained-glass dome in the lobby points to Threedneedles' former status as a bank HQ. Today it's still popular with suits, but the atmosphere is chic rather than stuffy. Request one of the two deluxe rooms with balconies.

Apex City of London HOTEL ££
(Map p68; ☎020-7702 2020; www.apexhotels.co.uk; 1 Seething Lane EC3; r from £100; 📶; ⊖Tower Hill) Business-focussed but close enough to the Tower to hear the heads roll, the Apex offers particularly enticing weekend rates, a gym, huge TVs, free wi-fi and a rubber ducky in every room.

> **THE KIT KEMP CLUB**
>
> Kit Kemp's interiors purr loudly rather than whisper. She's waved her magically deranged wand over all the hotels of London's boutique **Firmdale chain** (www.firmdalehotels.com), creating bold, playful spaces full of zany fabrics, crazy sculpture and sheer luxury. Yet somehow she manages to create an old-fashioned feel from a thoroughly modern sensibility. While nonconformity is the norm, key values are shared throughout the chain: welcoming staff, inviting guest lounges with honesty bars, a dressmaker's dummy in each bedroom (some in miniature) and beautiful grey-flecked granite bathrooms.

SOUTH BANK

Immediately south of the river is a good spot if you want to immerse yourself in workaday London and still be central.

Captain Bligh House B&B ££
(Map p76; ☎020-7928 2735; www.captainblighhouse.co.uk; 100 Lambeth Rd SE1; s/d £58/80; 📶; ⊖Lambeth North) The blue disk by the door confirms that this 1780 house, opposite the Imperial War Museum, belonged to the unfortunate Bligh, of Mutiny on the Bounty and Rum Rebellion infamy. No such bad luck awaits guests who manage to snag one of the two comfortable, reasonably priced rooms nowadays.

Mad Hatter Hotel HOTEL ££
(Map p76; ☎020-7401 9222; www.fullershotels.com; 3-7 Stamford St SE1; r £155; ⊖Southwark) There's nothing particularly mad (or even unusual) about it, but this is a good hotel with decent-sized rooms and unassuming decor hiding behind a lovely Victorian frontage. Prices fall considerably on weekends.

Southwark Rose Hotel HOTEL ££
(Map p74; ☎020-7015 1480; www.southwarkrosehotel.co.uk; 47 Southwark Bridge Rd SE1; r/ste from £85/115; @📶; ⊖Borough) Though it's somewhat pricey during the week, this

BOOKING SERVICES

At Home in London (020-8748 1943; www.athomeinlondon.co.uk) B&Bs.

GKLets (020-7613 2805; www.gklets.co.uk) Apartments.

British Hotel Reservation Centre (020-7592 3055; www.bhrconline.com)

London Homestead Services (020-7286 5115; www.lhslondon.com) B&Bs.

LondonTown (020-7437 4370; www.londontown.com) Hotel and B&Bs.

Uptown Reservations (020-7937 2001; www.uptownres.co.uk) Upmarket B&Bs.

Visit London (0871 222 3118, per min 10p; www.visitlondonoffers.com) Hotels.

generic but comfortable business hotel drops its rates considerably to attract the weekender visitors.

St Christopher's Village HOSTEL £
(Map p74; 020-7939 9710; www.st-christophers.co.uk; 163 Borough High St SE1; dm/r from £14/62; @; London Bridge) The Village – a huge, up-for-it party hostel, with a club that opens until 4am on the weekends and a roof terrace bar – is the main hub of three locations on the same street. It's either heaven or hell, depending on what side of 30 you're on. The others are much smaller, quieter and, frankly, more pleasant. **St Christopher's Inn** (121 Borough High St) is above a very nice pub, while **Orient Express** (59 Borough High St) is a dude-free zone.

PIMLICO

Luna Simone Hotel B&B ££
(020-7834 5897; www.lunasimonehotel.com; 47-49 Belgrave Rd SW1; s £70-75, d £95-120; @; Pimlico) The blue-and-yellow rooms aren't huge, but they're clean and calming; the ones at the back are quieter. Belgrave Rd follows on from Eccleston Bridge, directly behind Victoria Station.

Windermere Hotel B&B ££
(Map p80; 020-7834 5163; www.windermere-hotel.co.uk; 142-144 Warwick Way SW1; s £105-155, d £129-165; @; Victoria) Chintzy but comfortable early-Victorian town house. The cheapest rooms share bathrooms.

BELGRAVIA

Lime Tree Hotel B&B ££
(Map p80; 020-7730 8191; www.limetreehotel.co.uk; 135-137 Ebury St SW1; s £95, d £135-160; @; Victoria) A smartly renovated Georgian town house hotel with a beautiful back garden to catch the late afternoon rays. Contemporary renovations have left it the best of the Belgravia crop.

Also recommended:

B&B Belgravia B&B ££
(Map p80; 020-7259 8570; www.bb-belgravia.com; 64-66 Ebury St SW1; s/d £99/120; @; Victoria) This small hotel's unassuming facade belies a contemporary interior, although a new coat of paint wouldn't go astray.

Morgan House B&B £
(Map p80; 020-7730 2384; www.morganhouse.co.uk; 120 Ebury St SW1; s £58, d £78-98; ; Victoria) Pleasant Georgian town house with homely rooms, some en suite.

KNIGHTSBRIDGE

Knightsbridge is where you'll find some of London's best-known department stores, including Harrods and Harvey Nicks.

Levin HOTEL £££
(Map p80; 020-7589 6286; www.thelevinhotel.co.uk; 28 Basil St SW3; r £285-485; Knightsbridge) As close as you can get to sleeping in Harrods, the Levin knows its market. Despite the baby-blue colour scheme, there's a subtle femininity to the decor, although it's far too elegant to be flouncy.

Knightsbridge Hotel HOTEL £££
(Map p80; 020-7584 6300; www.knightsbridgehotel.com; 10 Beaufort Gardens SW3; s/d from £170/220; @Knightsbridge) Another Firmdale property (see p95), the Knightsbridge is on a quiet, tree-lined cul-de-sac very close to Harrods.

CHELSEA & KENSINGTON

Classy Chelsea and Kensington offer easy access to the museums and fashion retailers. It's all a bit sweetie-darling, along with the prices.

Number Sixteen HOTEL £££
(Map p80; 020-7589 5232; www.numbersixteenhotel.co.uk; 16 Sumner Pl SW7; s/d from £120/205; @; South Kensington) The least

pricey of the Firmdale hotels (see p95), with a lovely garden tucked away.

Gore HOTEL ££
(Map p80; ☎020-7584 6601; www.gorehotel.com; 190 Queen's Gate SW7; r from £135; @📶; ⊖Gloucester Rd) A short stroll from the Royal Albert Hall, the Gore serves up British grandiosity (antiques, carved four-posters, a secret bathroom in the Tudor room) with a large slice of camp. How else could you describe the Judy Garland, Dame Nellie and Miss Fanny rooms, named after famous former occupants?

Vicarage Private Hotel B&B ££
(Map p98; ☎020-7229 4030; www.londonvicaragehotel.com; 10 Vicarage Gate W8; s/d £95/125, without bathroom £56/95; @📶; ⊖High St Kensington) You can see Kensington Palace from the doorstep of this grand Victorian town house, which opens on to a cul-de-sac. The cheaper rooms (without bathrooms) are on floors three and four, so you may get a view as well as a workout.

EARL'S COURT & FULHAM

West London's Earl's Court is lively, cosmopolitan and so popular with travelling Antipodeans it's been nicknamed Kangaroo Valley. There are no real sights, but it does have inexpensive digs and an infectious holiday atmosphere.

Barclay House B&B ££
(☎020-7384 3390; www.barclayhouselondon.com; 21 Barclay Rd SW6; s/d £69/89, @📶; ⊖Fulham Broadway) A proper homestay B&B, the two comfy bedrooms in this charming Victorian town house share a bathroom and an exceptionally welcoming hostess. You'll be well set up to conquer London with helpful tips, maps, umbrellas and a full stomach. From the tube station head west on Fulham Broadway and then look out for Barclay Rd on your left.

Twenty Nevern Square HOTEL ££
(☎020-7565 9555; www.20nevernsquare.com; 20 Nevern Sq SW5; r from £95; @📶; ⊖Earl's Court) An Ottoman theme runs through this Victorian town-house hotel, where a mix of wooden furniture, luxurious fabrics and natural light helps maximise space – even in the cheaper bedrooms, which are not particularly large. Exit the tube station from the rear and turn right into Warwick St and then take the second right.

Base APARTMENT HOTEL ££
(☎020-7244 2255; www.base2stay.com; 25 Courtfield Gardens SW5; s/d from £93/99; @📶; ⊖Earl's Court) With smart decor, power showers, flatscreen TVs with internet access and artfully concealed kitchenettes, this boutique establishment feels like a four-star hotel without the hefty price tag. Enter the tube station from the front entrance, cross Earl's Court Rd and take Earl's Court Gardens, turning right at the end.

easyHotel CAPSULE HOTEL £
(www.easyhotel.com; r from £25; @📶); Earls Court (44 West Cromwell Rd SW5; ⊖Earl's Court); Paddington (10 Norfolk Pl W2; ⊖Paddington); South Kensington (14 Lexham Gardens W8; ⊖Gloucester Rd); Victoria (36 Belgrave Rd SW1; ⊖Victoria) Run along the same principles as its sibling business easyJet, this no-frills chain has tiny rooms with even tinier bathrooms, all bedecked in their trademark garish orange.

NOTTING HILL, BAYSWATER & PADDINGTON

Don't be fooled by Julia Roberts and Hugh Grant's shenanigans, Notting Hill and the areas immediately north of Hyde Park are as shabby as they are chic. There are some nice gated squares surrounded by Georgian town houses, but the area is better exemplified by the Notting Hill Carnival, where the West Indian community who made the area their home from the 1950s party up big time.

Scruffy Paddington has lots of cheap hotels, with a major strip of unremarkable ones along Sussex Gardens, worth checking if you're short on options.

Vancouver Studios APARTMENT HOTEL ££
(Map p98; ☎020-7243 1270; www.vancouverstudios.co.uk; 30 Prince's Sq W2; apt £89-170; @📶; ⊖Bayswater) It's the addition of kitchenettes and a self-service laundry that differentiate these smart, reasonably priced studios (sleeping from one to three people) from a regular Victorian town-house hotel. In spring, the garden is filled with colour and fragrance.

New Linden Hotel HOTEL ££
(Map p98; ☎020-7221 4321; www.newlinden.co.uk; 58-60 Leinster Sq W2; s/d from £79/105; @📶; ⊖Bayswater) Cramming in a fair amount of style for the price, this terrace house hotel has interesting modern art in the rooms and carved wooden fixtures in the guest lounge. The quiet location, helpful staff and monsoon shower heads in

the deluxe rooms make this an excellent proposition.

FITZROVIA

Sanderson HOTEL £££

(Map p62; ☎020-7300 1400; www.sandersonlondon.com; 50 Berners St W1; r from £253; @; Goodge St) Liberace meets Philippe Starck in an 18th-century French bordello – and that's just the reception. A 3-D space scene in the lift shuttles you into darkened corridors leading to blindingly white rooms complete with sleigh beds, oil paintings hung on the ceiling, en suites behind glass walls and pink silk curtains.

Charlotte Street Hotel HOTEL £££

(Map p62; ☎020-7806 2000; www.charlottestreethotel.com; 15 Charlotte St W1; d/tw/ste from 270/340/447; @; Goodge St) Another of the Firmdale clan (see p95), this one's a favourite with media types, with a small gym and a screening room.

London Central YHA HOSTEL £

(Map p86; ☎0845 371 9154; www.yha.org.uk; 104-108 Bolsover St W1; dm £21-32, q from £70; @; Great Portland St) One of London's new breed of YHA hostels, most of the four- to six-bed rooms have en suites. There's a flash cafe-bar attached to recep-

Notting Hill & Bayswater

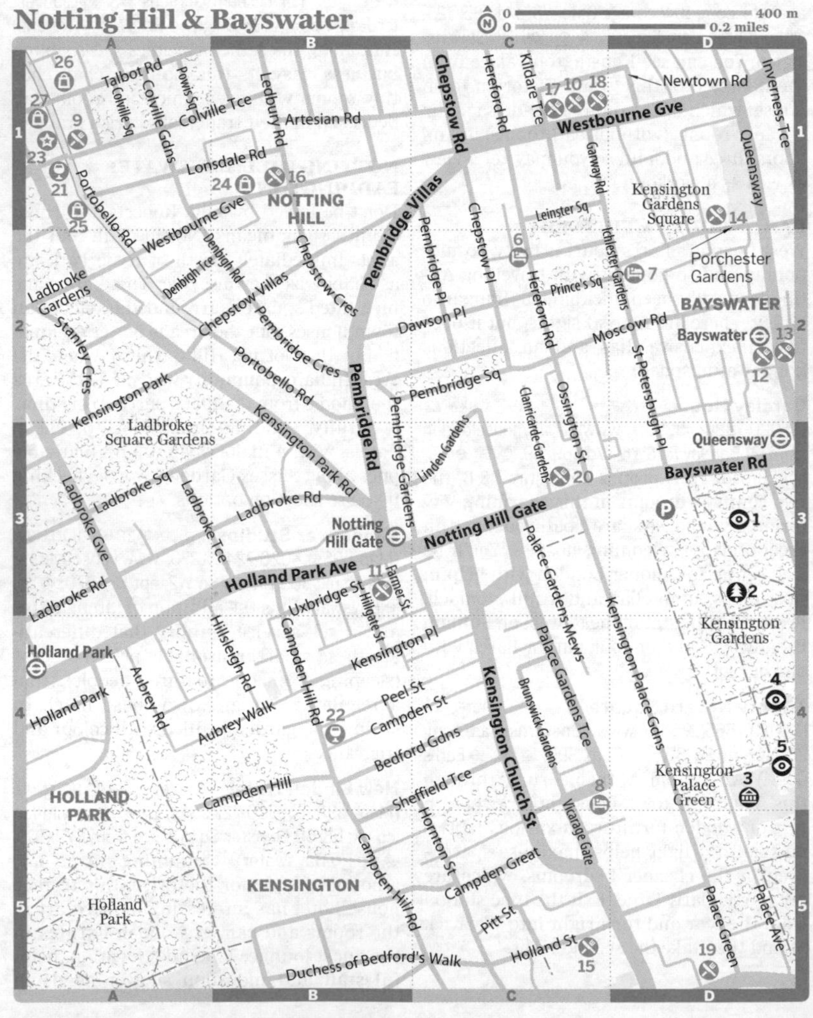

tion and a wheelchair-accessible kitchen downstairs.

BLOOMSBURY & ST PANCRAS

Only one step removed from the West End and crammed with Georgian town-house conversions, these neighbourhoods are much more affordable. You'll find a stretch of lower-priced hotels along Gower St and on the pretty Cartwright Gardens crescent. While hardly a salubrious location, St Pancras is handy to absolutely everything and has some excellent budget options.

Arran House Hotel B&B ££

(Map p86; ☎020-7636 2186; www.arranhotel-london.com; 77-79 Gower St WC1; s/d/tr/q £70/110/128/132, without bathroom £60/80/105/111; @📶; ⊖Goodge St) Period features such as cornicing and fireplaces, a pretty pergola-decked back garden and a comfy lounge with PCs and TV lift this hotel from the average to the attractive. Squashed en suites or shared bathrooms are the trade-off for these reasonable rates.

Arosfa Hotel B&B ££

(Map p86; ☎020-7636 2115; www.arosfalondon.com; 83 Gower St WC1; s £60-65, d/tr/q £90/102/110; @📶; ⊖Goodge St) While the decor of the immaculately presented rooms is unremarkable, Arosfa's guest lounge has been blinged up with chandeliers, clear plastic chairs and a free-internet terminal. Recent refurbishments have added en suites to all 15 bedrooms, but they're tiny (putting the 'closet' back into water closet).

Jesmond Dene B&B £

(Map p86; ☎020-7837 4654; www.jesmonddenehotel.co.uk; 27 Argyle St; s/d incl breakfast from £60/65; P@📶; ⊖Kings Cross) A surprisingly pleasant option for a place so close to busy Kings Cross station, this modest hotel has clean but small rooms, some of which share bathrooms.

London St Pancras YHA HOSTEL £

(Map p86; ☎020-7388 9998; www.yha.org.uk; 79 Euston Rd NW1; dm/r from £20/61; @📶; ⊖Kings Cross) A renovation in 2009 has made this 185-bed hostel one of the best in central London – even if it is on a busy road. Rooms range from private doubles to six-bed dorms; most have bathrooms. There's a good bar and cafe but no kitchen.

Ridgemount Hotel B&B £

(Map p86; ☎020-7636 1141; www.ridgemounthotel.co.uk; 65-67 Gower St WC1; s/d/tr/q £55/78/96/108, without bathroom £43/60/81/96; @📶; ⊖Goodge St) There's a comfortable, welcoming feel at this old-fashioned, slightly chintzy place that's been in the same family for 40 years.

Harlingford Hotel B&B ££

(Map p86; ☎020-7387 1551; www.harlingfordhotel.com; 61-63 Cartwright Gardens WC1; s/d £86/112; @📶; ⊖Russel Sq) This family-run

Notting Hill & Bayswater

Sights

1	Diana, Princess of Wales Memorial Playground	D3
2	Kensington Gardens	D3
3	Kensington Palace	D4
4	Orangery	D4
5	Sunken Garden	D4

Sleeping

6	New Linden Hotel	C2
7	Vancouver Studios	D2
8	Vicarage Private Hotel	C4

Eating

	Electric Brasserie	(see 23)
9	GBK	A1
10	GBK	C1
11	Geales	B3
12	Kam Tong	D2
13	Kiasu	D2
14	Le Café Anglais	D1
15	Ottolenghi	C5
16	Ottolenghi	B1
17	Ping Pong	C1
18	Planet Organic	C1
19	Wagamama	D5
20	Zizzi	C3

Drinking

21	Trailer Happiness	A1
22	Windsor Castle	B4

Entertainment

23	Electric	A1

Shopping

24	EC One	B1
25	Portobello Road Market	A1
26	Rough Trade	A1
27	Travel Bookshop	A1

hotel sports refreshing, upbeat decor: bright-green mosaic-tiled bathrooms (with trendy sinks), fuchsia bedspreads and colourful paintings. There's lots of stairs and no lift; request a 1st-floor room.

Jenkins Hotel B&B ££

(Map p86; ☎020-7387 2067; www.jenkinshotel.demon.co.uk; 45 Cartwright Gardens WC1; s/d from £52/95; ⊖Russell Sq) This modest hotel has featured in the TV series of Agatha Christie's *Poirot*. Rooms are small but the hotel has charm.

Morgan Hotel B&B ££

(Map p62; ☎020-7636 3735; www.morganhotel.co.uk; 24 Bloomsbury St WC1; s/d £95/115; ⊖Tottenham Court Rd) In a row of Georgian town houses alongside the British Museum, the Morgan has 20 guestrooms at its disposal. Don't fret about the busy location, though – the windows are double-glazed. The warmth and hospitality more than make up for the slightly cramped quarters.

Crescent Hotel B&B ££

(Map p86; ☎020-7387 1515; www.crescenthoteloflondon.com; 49-50 Cartwright Gardens WC1; s/d from £52/105; @; ⊖Russell Sq) There's a homely feel to this humble hotel, despite the odd saggy bed. It's one of the cheaper options on the crescent overlooking Cartwright Gardens.

Clink78 HOSTEL £

(Map p86; ☎020-7183 9400; www.clinkhostel.com; 78 Kings Cross Rd WC1; dm/r from £12/60; @; ⊖Kings Cross) If anyone can think of a more right-on London place to stay than the courthouse where The Clash went on trial, please let us know. You can watch TV from the witness box or sleep in the cells, but the majority of the rooms are custom-built and quite comfortable.

Clink261 HOSTEL £

(Map p86; ☎020-7833 9400; www.ashleehouse.co.uk; 261 Grays Inn Rd WC1; dm/r £12/50; @; ⊖Kings Cross) This hostel is a cheery surprise in a gritty but central location. It's not as massive as its sister, the 740-bed Clink around the corner, but neither does it have its historic import.

Generator HOSTEL £

(Map p86; ☎020-7388 7666; www.generatorhostels.com/london; 37 Tavistock Pl WC1; dm/r from £18/55; @; ⊖Russell Sq) Lashings of primary colours and shiny metal are the hallmarks of this futuristic hostel. This former police barracks has 820 beds; a bar that stays open until 2am and hosts quizzes, pool competitions, karaoke and DJs; safe-deposit boxes; and a large eating area (but no kitchen). Come to party.

George B&B £

(Map p86; ☎020-7387 8777; www.georgehotel.com; 58-60 Cartwright Gardens WC1; s/d from £55/69; @; ⊖Russell Sq) A friendly chap, this George, if a little old-fashioned. Cheaper rooms share bathrooms.

Hotel Cavendish B&B ££

(Map p86; ☎020-7636 9079; www.hotelcavendish.com; 75 Gower St WC1; s/d/tr/q £75/90/120/140; @; ⊖Goodge St) Bedrooms have flatscreen TVs and compact en suite shower rooms (some have pretty tiles and bumper mirrors). The two gardens at the back are a good place to catch some rays.

CLERKENWELL & FARRINGDON

In these now fashionable streets, it's hard to find an echo of the notorious 'rookeries' of the 19th century, where families were squeezed into damp, fetid basements, living in possibly the worst conditions in the city's history. This is the London documented so vividly by Dickens. It was also the traditional place for a last drink on the way to the gallows at Tyburn Hill – fitting, as many of the condemned hailed from here, as did many of those who were transported to Australia.

The availability of accommodation hasn't kept pace with Clerkenwell's revival, but it's still a great area to stay in. The best pickings aren't exactly cheap.

TOP CHOICE **Zetter Hotel** HOTEL £££

(Map p102; ☎020-7324 4444; www.thezetter.com; 86-88 Clerkenwell Rd EC1; d £180-423; @; ⊖Farringdon) A slick 21st-century conversion of a Victorian warehouse. The furnishings and facilities are cutting edge. You can even choose the colour of your room's lighting.

Rookery HOTEL £££

(Map p102; ☎020-7336 0931; www.rookeryhotel.com; Peter's Lane, Cowcross St EC1; s £205, d £258-582; @; ⊖Farringdon) Taking its name from London's notorious slums (Fagin's house in *Oliver Twist* was nearby), this antique-strewn luxury hotel recreates an 18th-century ambience with none of the attendant grime or crime. For a bird's-eye view of St Paul's, book the Rook's Nest, but be warned: Fagin never had a lift.

HOXTON, SHOREDITCH & SPITALFIELDS

It's always had a rough-edged reputation, but London's East End is being gentrified faster than you can say 'awrigh' guv'. Staying here, you'll be handy to some of London's best bars.

TOP CHOICE Hoxton HOTEL £
(Map p88; ☎020-7550 1000; www.hoxtonhotels.com; 81 Great Eastern St; d & tw £59-199; @ 📶; ⊖Old St) A novel approach to pricing means that while all the rooms are identical, the first ones on any given day are offered at £59: an absolute steal for a hotel of this calibre. The reasonably sized rooms all have comfy beds, quality linen and TVs that double as computers.

Andaz HOTEL ££
(Map p88; ☎020-7961 1234; www.london.liverpoolstreet.andaz.com; 40 Liverpool St EC2; r from £145; @ 📶; ⊖Liverpool St) The former Great Eastern Hotel is now the London flagship for Hyatt's youth-focussed Andaz chain. There's no reception here, just black-clad staff who check you in on laptops. Rooms are a little generic but have free juice, snacks and wi-fi.

GREENWICH

If you'd rather keep the bustle of central London at arm's length and nightclubbing is your idea of hell, Greenwich offers a villagey ambience and some great old pubs to explore.

Number 16 B&B ££
(☎020-8853 4337; www.st-alfeges.co.uk; 16 St Alfege Passage SE10; s/d £75/90; @ 📶; DLR Cutty Sark) Both the house and the host have personality plus, so much so that they were featured on TV's *Hotel Inspector* series. The two double rooms are elegant and comfortable, but the single would only suit the vertically challenged and going to the toilet in the wardrobe might take some getting used to. From the DLR station head up Greenwich High St and look for St Alfege Passage on your left – it's the lane that skirts the church.

HAMPSTEAD & HIGHGATE

A little further out but still in transport Zone 2, the following are excellent options within walking distance of Hampstead Heath.

Palmers Lodge HOSTEL £
(☎020-7483 8470; www.palmerslodge.co.uk; 40 College Cres NW3; dm £18-38; P @ 📶; ⊖Swiss Cottage) Reminiscent of a period murder mystery (in a good way), this former children's hospital has bags of character. Listed by English Heritage, it's stuffed with cornicing, moulded ceilings, original fireplaces and imposing wooden panelling. Ceilings are high, rooms are spacious, there's a chapel bar with pews, a grand stairway and a roomy lounge. Privacy curtains make the 28-bed men's dorm bearable (imagine you're in the hold of a pirate ship), but they don't shut out the amorous noises in the couples dorm. From Swiss Cottage tube station, cross Finchley Rd, turn left and take College Crescent which heads straight up the hill.

Hampstead Village Guesthouse B&B ££
(☎020 7435 8679; www.hampsteadguesthouse.com; 2 Kemplay Rd NW3; s £55-75, d £80-95, apt £100-175; @ 📶; ⊖Hampstead) Eclectic and thoroughly charming, this grand Victorian house has an easygoing hostess, comfy beds and a delightful back garden. There's also a studio flat, which can accommodate up to five people. From the tube station, turn left down Hampstead High St. After a few streets and lanes turn left into Willoughby Rd and then first right into Kemplay Rd.

AIRPORTS

Yotel CAPSULE HOTEL ££
(☎020-7100 1100; www.yotel.com; s/d £69/85, or per 4hr £29/45 then per additional hr £8; @ 📶) Gatwick (South Terminal); Heathrow (Terminal 4) The best news for early-morning flyers since coffee-vending machines, Yotel's smart 'cabins' offer pint-sized luxury: comfy beds, soft lights, internet-connected TVs, monsoon showers and fluffy towels. Swinging cats isn't recommended, but when is it ever?

Eating

Dining out in London has become so fashionable that you can hardly open a menu without banging into some celebrity chef or other: at the time of writing, London's eateries had 59 Michelin stars between them. The range and quality of eating options has increased exponentially over the last few decades, with waves of immigrants bringing with them the flavours of their respective homelands. You'll still find relics of the London food scene's stodgy, surly past, but these days Londoners expect better.

In this section, we steer you towards restaurants and cafes distinguished by their location, value for money, unique features, original settings and, of course, good food. Vegetarians needn't worry; London has a host of dedicated meat-free joints, while most others offer at least a token dish.

There are supermarkets absolutely everywhere in central London. Look out for the big names: Waitrose, Tesco, Sainsbury's, Marks & Spencer, Morrisons and Asda.

WEST END

Mayfair, Soho and Covent Garden are the gastronomic heart of London, with stacks of restaurants and cuisines to choose from at budgets to suit both booze hounds and theatre-goers. If you're craving a decent coffee, this is the place to come.

TOP CHOICE **Hibiscus** FRENCH, BRITISH £££

(Map p62; ☎020-7629 2999; www.hibiscusrestaurant.co.uk; 29 Maddox St W1; 3-course lunch/dinner £30/70; ⊖Oxford Circus) Claude and Claire Bosi have generated an avalanche of praise and two Michelin stars since moving their restaurant from Shropshire to Mayfair. Expect adventurous, intricate dishes and perfect service.

Tamarind INDIAN ££

(Map p80; ☎020-7629 3561; www.tamarindrestaurant.com; 20 Queen St W1; mains £14-26; ⊖Green Park) A mix of spicy Moghul classics and new creations have earned this northwest Indian

Clerkenwell & Farringdon

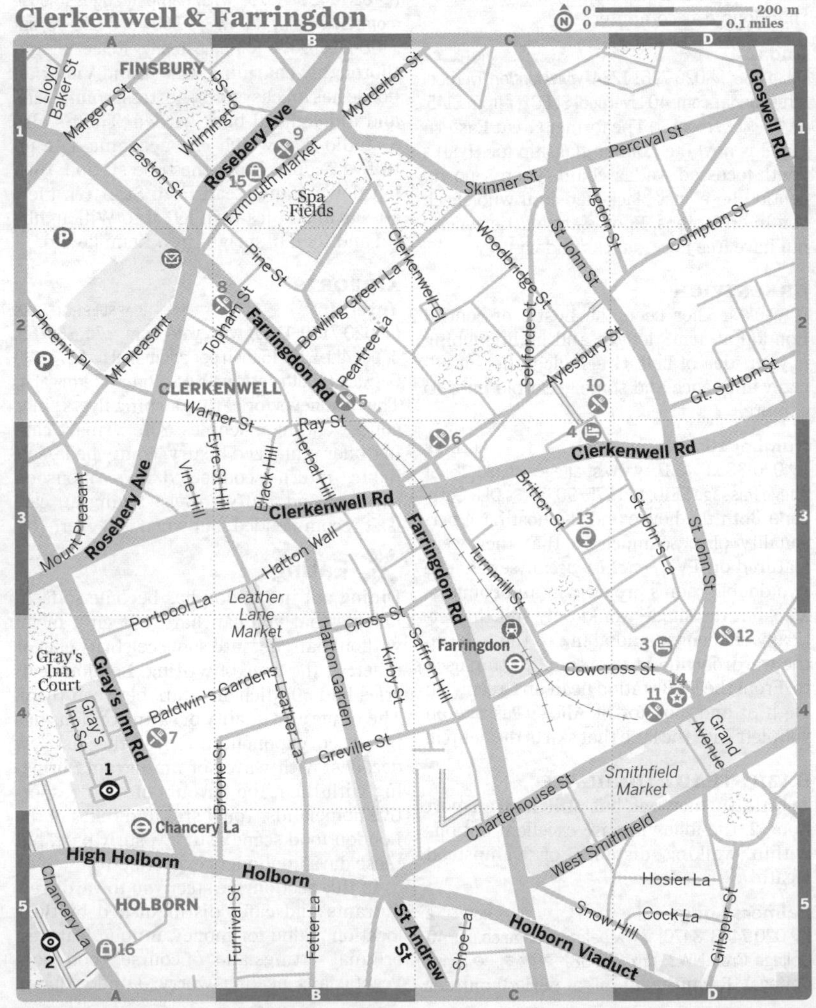

restaurant a Michelin star. The set lunches are a good deal (two-/three-courses £17/19).

Polpo ITALIAN ££

(Map p62; www.polpo.co.uk; 41 Beak St W1; dishes £1-7; closed dinner Sun; Piccadilly Circus) Come early or late, or expect to queue: this hip Venetian place doesn't take bookings and it's often as packed as a rush-hour tube. The friendly young staff maintain the waiting list efficiently and help you negotiate the delicious tapas-style menu. Serendipitously, Venetian painter Canaletto once resided here.

Great Queen Street BRITISH ££

(Map p62; 020-7242 0622; 32 Great Queen St WC2; mains £9-19; lunch daily, dinner Mon-Sat; Holborn) There's no tiara on this Great Queen, her claret-coloured walls and mismatched wooden chairs suggesting cosiness and informality. But the food's still the best of British, including lamb that melts in the mouth and Arbroath smokie (a whole smoked fish with creamy sauce).

Veeraswamy INDIAN ££

(Map p62; 020-7734 1401; www.veeraswamy.com; 99 Regent St W1; mains £15-30, pre- & post-theatre 2-/3-course £18/21; Piccadilly Circus) Since 1926 Veeraswamy has occupied this prime 1st-floor location, with windows looking over Regent St – making it Britain's longest-running Indian restaurant. The excellent food, engaging service and exotic, elegant decor make for a memorable eating experience. The entrance is on Swallow St.

Wild Honey MODERN EUROPEAN ££

(020-7758 9160; www.wildhoneyrestaurant.co.uk; 12 St George St W1; mains £15-24; Oxford Circus) If you fancy a relatively affordable meal within the oak-panelled ambience of a top Mayfair restaurant, Wild Honey offers excellent lunch and pre-theatre set menus (respectively, £19 and £22 for three courses).

Sketch FRENCH £££

(Map p62; 020-7659 4500; www.sketch.uk.com; 9 Conduit St W1; Parlour mains £5-16, Gallery mains £11-32, Lecture Room 2-course lunch/8-course dinner £30/95; Oxford Circus) A design enthusiast's dream, with shimmering white rooms, video projections, designer Louis XIV chairs and toilet cubicles shaped like eggs. And that's just the Gallery, which becomes a buzzy restaurant and bar at night. The ground-floor Parlour has decadent cakes and decor, but is surprisingly affordable: perfect for breakfast, or afternoon tea served on fine bone china. The swanky Lecture Room upstairs is the realm of Pierre Gagnaire, whose book *Reinventing French Cuisine* gives a hint of what to expect.

Giaconda Dining Room MODERN EUROPEAN ££

(Map p62; 020-7240 3334; www.giacondadining.com; 9 Denmark St WC2; mains £12-15; Mon-Fri; Tottenham Court Rd) Blink and you'll miss this 10-table restaurant (we did at first). It's well worth hunting down for quality British, French and Italian dishes and attentive service. Pig trotters are a specialty but for those less au fait with offal, there's always a choice of fish dishes.

Abeno Too JAPANESE £

(Map p62; www.abeno.co.uk; 17-18 Great Newport St WC2; mains £8-13; Leicester Sq) This restaurant specialises in soba (noodles) and *okonomi-yaki* (Japanese-style pancakes), which are cooked in front of you on a hotplate. Sit at the bar or by the window and feast.

Yauatcha CHINESE ££

(Map p62; 020-7494 8888; www.yauatcha.com; 15 Broadwick St W1; dishes £3-17; Piccadilly

Clerkenwell & Farringdon

Sights

1	Gray's Inn	A4
2	Lincoln's Inn	A5

Sleeping

3	Rookery	D4
4	Zetter Hotel	C3

Eating

5	5ifty 4our	B2
	Bistrot Bruno Loubet	(see 4)
6	Dans le Noir	C3
7	Konditor & Cook	A4
8	Little Bay	B2
9	Medcalf	B1
10	Modern Pantry	C2
11	Smiths of Smithfield	D4
12	St John	D4

Drinking

13	Jerusalem Tavern	C3

Entertainment

14	Fabric	D4

Shopping

15	EC One	B1
16	London Silver Vaults	A5

Circus) Dim sum restaurants don't come much cooler than this, and the menu is fantastic and Michelin-starred. It's housed in an architecturally interesting building, with a choice of light-filled ground floor tables or a hip basement area.

Arbutus MODERN EUROPEAN ££
(Map p62; ☎020-7734 4545; www.arbutusrestaurant.co.uk; 63-64 Frith St W1; mains £14-20; ⊖Tottenham Court Rd) Focussing on seasonal produce, inventive dishes and value for money, Anthony Demetre's Michelin-starred restaurant just keeps getting better.

L'Atelier de Joël Robuchon FRENCH ££
(Map p62; ☎020-7010 8600; www.joel-robuchon.com; 13 West St WC2; mains £16-34; ⊖Leicester Sq) Superchef Robuchon has 25 Michelin stars to his name – and two of them are derived from this, his London flagship. A wall of living foliage adds lushness to the dimly lit dining room, with a sparkling open kitchen as its showcase. Degustation (£125) and set lunch and pre-theatre menus (two-/three-courses £22/27) are available.

Sacred CAFE £
(Map p62; www.sacredcafe.co.uk; mains £4-6); Ganton St (13 Ganton St W1; ⊙7.30am-8pm Mon-Fri, 10am-7pm Sat & Sun; ⊖Oxford Circus); Covent Garden (Stanfords, 12-14 Long Acre; ⊙9am-7.30pm Mon-Fri, 10am-8pm Sat, noon-6pm Sun) The spiritual paraphernalia and blatant Kiwiana don't seem to deter the smart Carnaby St set from lounging around this eclectic cafe. That's down to the excellent coffee and appealing counter food.

National Dining Rooms BRITISH £££
(Map p62; ☎020-7747 2525; www.thenationaldiningrooms.co.uk; Sainsbury Wing, National Gallery WC2; 2-/3-course meals £23/26; ⊙10am-5pm Sat-Thu, 10am-8.30pm Fri; ⊖Charing Cross) It's fitting that this acclaimed restaurant should celebrate British food, being in the National Gallery and overlooking Trafalgar Sq. For a much cheaper option with the same views, ambience, quality produce and excellent service, try a salad, pie or tart at the adjoining bakery.

Fernandez & Wells DELICATESSEN CAFE £
(Map p62; www.fernandezandwells.com; 73 Beak St W1; mains £4-5; ⊖Piccadilly Circus) With its sister deli around the corner, there's no shortage of delicious charcuterie and cheese to fill the fresh baguettes on the counter of this teensy cafe. The coffee's superb.

HK Diner CHINESE £
(Map p62; 22 Wardour St W1; mains £6-13; ⊙11am-4am; ⊖Piccadilly Circus) If you've a hankering for soft-shell crab or barbecue pork in the wee hours of the morning, this Hong Kong–style cafe (delicious food, no-nonsense decor) is the place to come.

Nordic Bakery SCANDINAVIAN £
(Map p62; www.nordicbakery.com; 14a Golden Sq W1; snacks £3-5; ⊙8am-8pm Mon-Fri, 9am-7pm Sat, 11am-6pm Sun; ⊖Piccadilly Circus) As simple and stylish as you'd expect from the Scandinavians, this small cafe has bare wooden walls and uncomplicated Danish snacks, such as sticky cinnamon buns and salmon served on dark rye bread.

Bocca di Lupo ITALIAN ££
(Map p62; ☎020-7734 2223; www.boccadilupo.com; 12 Archer St W1; mains £11-25; ⊖Piccadilly Circus) A new Italian restaurant that has sent ecstatic tremors down Londoners' taste buds, Bocca di Lupo hides down a dark Soho backstreet and radiates elegant sophistication.

Barrafina SPANISH ££
(Map p62; ☎020-7813 8016; www.barrafina.co.uk; 54 Frith St W1; tapas £4-13; ⊖Tottenham Court Rd) They may not be as reasonably priced as you'd get in Spain, but the quality of the tapas served here is excellent.

Hummus Bros BUDGET £
(Map p62; www.hbros.co.uk; mains £4-8; 📶); Soho (88 Wardour St W1; ⊖Piccadilly Circus); Holborn (Map p62; 37-63 Southampton Row W1; ⊖Holborn); Cheapside (Map p68; 128 Cheapside EC2; ⊖St Pauls) Don't come here if you're chickpea-challenged, because this informal place is hummus heaven. It comes in small or regular bowls with a choice of meat or veggie toppings and a side of pita bread.

THE CITY

You'll be sorely dismayed if you've got an empty belly on a Sunday morning in the City. Even during the busy weekdays, the chain eateries are often your best option.

1 Lombard St FRENCH ££
(☎020-7929 6611; www.1lombardstreet.com; 1 Lombard St EC3; mains £15-30; ⊖Bank) Cassoulet goes head-to-head with bangers-and-mash in the brasserie, under the domes of a heritage-listed bank building, and both the French and the Brits come out winners.

CHAIN-CHAIN-CHAIN, CHAIN OF FOODS

It's an unnerving, but not uncommon, experience to discover the idiosyncratic cafe or pub you were so proud of finding on your first day in London popping up on every other high street. But among the endless Caffe Neros, Pizza Expresses and All-Bar-Ones are some gems, or, at least, great fallback options. The following are some of the best:

GBK GOURMET BURGERS

(Map p98, p86, p80, p68, p88, p74, p62; www.gbk.co.uk) Gourmet Burger Kitchens dishing up creative burger constructions, including lots of vegetarian options.

Konditor & Cook BAKERY

(Map p102, p68, p74, p62; www.konditorandcook.com) London's best bakery chain, serving excellent cakes, pastries, bread and coffee.

Leon BISTRO

(p68, p88, p62; www.leonrestaurants.co.uk) Focussing on fresh, seasonal food (salads, wraps and the like).

Ping Pong CHINESE

(Map p98, Map p76, p88, p62; www.pingpongdimsum.com) Stylish Chinese dumpling joints.

S&M Cafe BRITISH

(Map p110, Map p88; www.sandmcafe.co.uk) The sausages and mash served in these retro diners won't give your wallet a spanking.

Wagamama JAPANESE

(Map p110, p68, p58, p98, p108, p88, p80, p62,p76, p74; www.wagamama.com) Japanese noodles taking over the world from their London base.

Zizzi ITALIAN

(Map p98, p58, p62,p84; www.zizzi.co.uk) Wood-fired pizza.

SOUTH BANK

You'll find plenty of touristy eateries on the riverside, making the most of the constant foot traffic and iconic London views. For a feed with a local feel, head to Borough Market or Bermondsey St.

Oxo Tower Brasserie FUSION £££

(Map p76; ☎020-7803 3888; www.harveynichols.com; Barge House St SE1; mains £18-26; ⊖Waterloo) The spectacular views are the big drawcard, so skip the restaurant and head for the slightly less extravagantly priced brasserie, or if you're not hungry, the bar. The food is excellent, combining European and East Asian flavours. Set-price menus (two-/three-courses £23/27) are offered at lunchtime, before 6.15pm and after 10pm.

Magdalen BRITISH ££

(Map p74; ☎020-7403 1342; www.magdalenrestaurant.co.uk; 152 Tooley St SE1; mains £14-18, lunch 2-/3-course £16/19; ⊙lunch Mon-Fri, dinner Mon-Sat; ⊖London Bridge) Roasting up the best of the critters that walk, hop, flap and splash around these fair isles, Magdalen isn't the place to bring a vegetarian or a weight-conscious waif on a date. Carnivorous couplings, however, will appreciate the elegant room and traditional treats presented in interesting ways.

Delfina MODERN EUROPEAN ££

(Map p74; ☎020-7357 0244; www.thedelfina.co.uk; 50 Bermondsey St SE1; mains £10-15; ⊙lunch Sun-Fri, dinner Fri; ⊖London Bridge) This white-walled restaurant in a converted Victorian chocolate factory serves delicious modern cuisine to a backdrop of contemporary canvases. Sunday roasts are popular.

Anchor & Hope GASTROPUB ££

(Map p76; 36 The Cut SE1; mains £12-17; ⊙lunch Tue-Sun, dinner Mon-Sat; ⊖Southwark) The hope is that you'll get a table without waiting hours because you can't book at this quintessential gastropub. The Anchor serves gutsy, unashamedly meaty British food.

BELGRAVIA

Olivomare ITALIAN ££

(Map p80; ☎020-7730 9022; www.olivorestaurants.com; 10 Lower Belgrave St SW1; mains £14-21; ⊖Victoria) The Sardinian seaside comes to Belgravia in a dazzling white dining room with flavoursome seafood dishes, regional wines and impeccable service.

Thomas Cubitt BRITISH ££

(Map p80; ☎020-7730 6060; www.thethomascubitt.co.uk; 44 Elizabeth St SW1; mains £17-23; ⊖Victoria) The bar below gets rammed to the impressively high rafters with the swanky Belgravia set, but don't let that put you off this excellent, elegant dining room. The culinary focus is thoroughly British and deftly executed. The downstairs menu is cheaper (£10 to £17).

KNIGHTSBRIDGE

Marcus Wareing at the Berkeley FRENCH £££

(Map p80; ☎020-7235 1200; www.marcus-wareing.com; Berkeley Hotel, Wilton Pl SW1; 3-course lunch/dinner £38/75; ⊖Knightsbridge) A very public spat between Marcus Wareing and his former boss Gordon Ramsay has added an entertaining frisson of drama to the London scene. Wareing now runs this one-time Ramsay restaurant under his own name, and its reputation for exquisite food and exemplary service has only been enhanced.

Boxwood Cafe BRITISH, FRENCH £££

(Map p80; ☎020-7235 1010; www.gordonramsay.com/boxwoodcafe; Berkeley Hotel, Wilton Pl SW1; mains £18-25; ⊖Knightsbridge) An accessible entry point into Gordon Ramsay's eating empire, Boxwood offers set-price lunch and pre-7pm menus (two/three courses £21/25). It's intended as an informal option – although you wouldn't guess it from the attentive staff, faultless food and staid decor.

CHELSEA & KENSINGTON

These highbrow neighbourhoods harbour some of London's very best (and priciest) restaurants. Perhaps the Chelsea toffs are secretly titillated by the foul-mouthed telechefs in their midst.

Tom's Kitchen FRENCH ££

(Map p80; ☎020-7349 0202; www.tomskitchen.co.uk; 27 Cale St SW3; breakfast £4-15, mains £15-30; ⏲breakfast Mon-Fri, lunch & dinner daily; ⊖South Kensington) A much more informal and considerably cheaper option than Tom Aikens' eponymous restaurant, just around the corner, the firebrand chef's kitchen maintains the magic throughout the day. The breakfasts are excellent.

L'Etranger FRENCH, JAPANESE ££

(Map p80; ☎020-7584 1118; www.etranger.co.uk; 36 Gloucester Rd SW7; mains £15-29; ⊖Gloucester Rd) A refined grey and burgundy interior (echoed in waitress uniforms that are part kimono, part Parisian runway) sets the tone for a romantic formal dining experience. While most of the menu is mainly French, it's also possible to blow the budget on sashimi and five types of caviar. The two-/three-course set weekday lunch and pre-6.45pm dinner are £17/20.

Made in Italy ITALIAN £

(Map p80; ☎020-7352 1880; www.madeinitalygroup.co.uk; 249 King's Rd SW3; pizzas £5-11, mains £8-17; ⏲lunch Sat & Sun, dinner daily; ⊖Sloane Sq) Pizza is served by the tasty quarter-metre at this traditional trattoria. Sit on the Chelsea roof terrace and dream of Napoli.

Orsini ITALIAN ££

(Map p80; www.orsiniristorante.com; 8a Thurloe Pl SW3; snacks £2-6, mains £9-16; ⏲8am-10pm; ⊖South Kensington) Marinated in authentic Italian charm, this tiny family-run eatery serves excellent espresso and deliciously fresh baguettes stuffed with Parma ham and mozzarella. More substantial fare is offered in the evenings.

Gordon Ramsay FRENCH £££

(Map p80; ☎020-7352 4441; www.gordonramsay.com; 68 Royal Hospital Rd SW3; 3-course lunch/dinner £45/90; ⊖Sloane Sq) Like or loathe the ubiquitous Scot, his eponymous restaurant is one of Britain's finest – one of only four in the country with three Michelin stars. Book ahead and dress up: jeans and T-shirts are forbidden – if you've seen the chef on the telly, you know not to argue.

NOTTING HILL, BAYSWATER & PADDINGTON

Notting Hill teems with good places to eat, from cheap takeaways to atmospheric pubs and restaurants worthy of the fine-dining tag. Queensway has the best strip of Asian restaurants this side of Soho.

Kiasu SOUTHEAST ASIAN £

(Map p98; www.kiasu.co.uk; 48 Queensway W2; mains £6-9; ⊖Bayswater) Local Malaysians and Singaporeans rate this place highly, as do those who know a tasty cheap thing when they see it. Kiasu serves 'Food from the Straits of Malacca'. You'll also find Thai and Vietnamese food on the menu, but it's hard to go past the delicious and filling laksa.

Geales SEAFOOD ££

(Map p98; ☎020-7727 7528; www.geales.com; 2 Farmer St W8; 2-course lunch £10, mains £10-18;

closed lunch Mon; Notting Hill Gate) It may have opened in 1939 as a humble chippy, but now it's so much more. Fresh fish stars in a variety of guises – either battered and British or with an Italian sensibility. Tables spill out onto the pleasant side street.

Electric Brasserie FRENCH ££
(Map p98; 020-7908 9696; www.electricbrasserie.com; 191 Portobello Rd W11; breakfasts £5-13, mains £11-20; Ladbroke Grove) The leather-and-cream look is suitably cool for the brasserie that's attached to the Electric Cinema. And the food's very good, too; head to the back area for a darker, more moody dinner. The two-/three-course pre-7pm dinner (£14/17) is served Monday to Friday.

Kam Tong CHINESE £
(www.kam-tong.co.uk; mains £8-17) Bayswater (Map p98; 59-63 Queensway W2; Bayswater) Chinatown (Map p62; 14 Lisle St WC2; Leicester Sq) When most of the clientele are actually Chinese, you know you're on to a good thing. Kam Tong serves genuine Cantonese and Szechuan dishes and wonderful yum cha (£3 to £4).

Satay House MALAYSIAN £
(020-7723 6763; www.satay-house.co.uk; 13 Sale Pl W2; mains £5-19; Edgware Rd) Authentic Malaysian cuisine, including some dishes that will blow your head off, have been served here for nearly 40 years. Book ahead for an upstairs table, although the communal tables in the basement can be fun. Sale Pl is one block along Sussex Gardens from Edgware Rd.

Le Café Anglais MODERN EUROPEAN ££
(Map p98; 020-7221 1415; www.lecafeanglais.co.uk; 8 Porchester Gardens W2; mains £13-25, 3-course menu £30; Bayswater) This bustling restaurant has a very eclectic menu (from gigantic roasts to Thai curries) that means to please everybody and usually does.

MARYLEBONE

You won't go too far wrong planting yourself on a table anywhere along Marylebone's charming High Street.

Providores & Tapa Room FUSION £££
(Map p84; 020-7935 6175; www.theprovidores.co.uk; 109 Marylebone High St W1; 2-/3-/4-/5-course meals £30/43/53/60; Baker St) New Zealand's greatest culinary export since kiwi fruit, chef Peter Gordon works his fusion magic here, matching his creations with NZ wines. Downstairs, in a cute play on words, the Tapa Room (as in the Polynesian bark-cloth) serves sophisticated tapas, along with excellent breakfasts.

La Fromagerie CAFE, DELI £
(Map p84; www.lafromagerie.co.uk; 2-6 Moxon St W1; mains £6-13; Baker St) This deli-cafe has bowls of delectable salads, antipasto, peppers and beans scattered about the long communal table. Huge slabs of bread invite you to tuck in, and all the while the heavenly waft from the cheese room beckons.

Locanda Locatelli ITALIAN ££
(Map p84; 020-7935 9088; www.locandalocatelli.com; 8 Seymour St W1; mains £11-30; Marble Arch) Known for its sublime pasta dishes, this dark but quietly glamorous restaurant in an otherwise unremarkable hotel is one of London's hottest tables.

FITZROVIA

Tucked away behind busy Tottenham Court Rd, Fitzrovia's Charlotte and Goodge Sts form one of central London's most vibrant eating precincts.

Hakkasan CHINESE ££
(Map p62; 020 7927 7000; www.hakkasan.com; 8 Hanway Pl W1; mains £11-58; Tottenham Court Rd) Hidden down a lane like all fashionable haunts need to be, the first Chinese restaurant to get a Michelin star combines celebrity status, a dimly lit basement dining room, persuasive cocktails and sophisticated food.

Salt Yard SPANISH, ITALIAN ££
(Map p62; 020-7637 0657; www.saltyard.co.uk; 54 Goodge St W1; tapas £4-8; Goodge St) Named after the place where cold meats are cured, this softly lit joint serves delicious Spanish and Italian tapas. Try the roasted chicken leg with gnocchi, wild garlic and sorrel, or flex your palate with courgette flowers stuffed with cheese and drizzled with honey.

Lantana CAFE £
(Map p62; www.lantanacafe.co.uk; 13 Charlotte Pl W1; mains £4-10; breakfast & lunch Mon-Sat; Goodge St) Excellent coffee and substantial, inventive brunches induce queues on Saturday mornings outside this Australian-style cafe.

CAMDEN TOWN

Camden's great for cheap eats, while neighbouring Chalk Farm and Primrose Hill

Camden Town

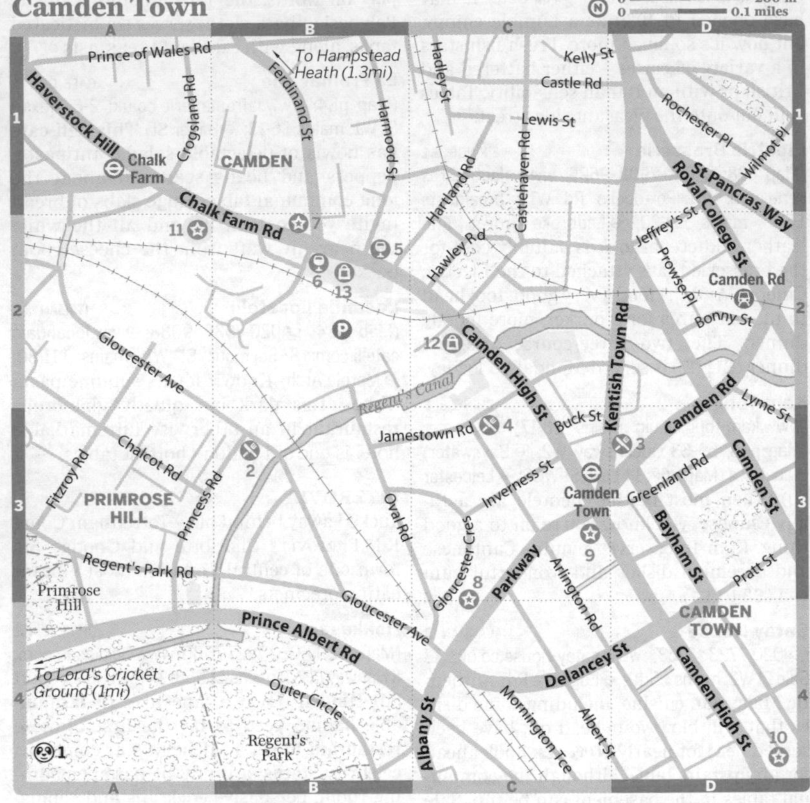

are salted with gastropubs and upmarket restaurants.

Engineer GASTROPUB ££

(Map p108; ☎020-7722 0950; 65 Gloucester Ave NW1; mains £13-21; ⊖Chalk Farm) One of London's original gastropubs, the Engineer has been serving up consistently good international cuisine to hip north Londoners for a fair while now. The courtyard garden is a real treat on balmy summer nights.

Mango Room CARIBBEAN ££

(Map p108; ☎020-7482 5065; www.mangoroom.co.uk; 10-12 Kentish Town Rd NW1; mains £11-14; ⊖Camden Town) With exposed-brick walls hung with bright cartoonish paintings, Mango Room is an upmarket Caribbean experience serving a mix of modern and traditional dishes: Creole fish, goat curry, jerk chicken etc. The rum-based happy hour cocktails (£4, 6pm to 8pm) will get you in the tropical mood.

ISLINGTON

Allow at least an evening to explore Islington's Upper St, along with the lanes leading off it.

TOP CHOICE **Le Mercury** FRENCH £

(Map p110; ☎020-7354 4088; www.lemercury.co.uk; 140A Upper St N1; mains £7-10; ⊖Highbury & Islington) A cosy Gallic haunt ideal for cash-strapped Casanovas, given that it appears much more expensive than it is. Sunday lunch by the open fire upstairs is a treat, although you'll have to book.

Ottolenghi BAKERY, MEDITERRANEAN ££

(www.ottolenghi.co.uk; mains £10-15; ⌚8am-8pm Mon-Sat, 9am-6pm Sat); Islington (Map p110; ☎020-7288 1454; 287 Upper St N1; ⌚8am-11pm Mon-Sat, 9am-7pm Sun; ⊖Angel); Belgravia (Map p80; 13 Motcomb St SW1); ⊖Knightsbridge); Kensington (Map p98; 1 Holland St W8; ⊖High St Kensington) Notting Hill (Map p98; 63 Ledbury Rd W11; ⊖Notting Hill Gate) Mountains of mer-

Camden Town

Sights

1 London Zoo A4

Eating

2 Engineer B3
3 Mango Room D3
4 Wagamama C3

Drinking

5 Lock Tavern B2
6 Proud B2

Entertainment

7 Barfly B2
8 Dublin Castle C3
9 Jazz Cafe C3
10 Koko D4
11 Roundhouse A2

Shopping

12 Camden Lock Market C2
13 Camden Stables Market D2

ingues tempt you through the door, where a sumptuous array of bakery treats and salads greet you. Meals are as light and tasty as the oh-so-white interior design. Vegetarians are well catered for. The Islington branch is open till later – until 11pm, and 7pm on Sundays.

Regent PIZZA £
(Map p110; 201 Liverpool Rd N1; mains £7-11; ⊖Angel) Delicious crispy-based pizza with deli toppings is what the regular crowd of youngish Islingtonians come here for. The ambience is more pub than gastropub, and the jukebox is loaded with indie pop gems.

Duke of Cambridge GASTROPUB ££
(Map p110; ☎020-7359 3066; www.dukeorganic.co.uk; 30 St Peter's St N1; mains £14-18; ⊖Angel) Pioneers in bringing sustainability to the table, this tucked-away gastropub serves only organic food, wine and beer, fish from sustainable sources and locally sourced fruit, vegetables and meat.

Planet Organic GROCERIES
(www.planetorganic.co.uk); Islington (Map p110; 64 Essex Rd, N1; ⊖Angel); Bayswater (Map p98; 42 Westbourne Grove W2; ⊖Bayswater); Fitzrovia (Map p86; 22 Torrington Pl WC1; ⊖Goodge St) As the name suggests, everything in this cafe/supermarket is organic. Fresh veggies are sourced (where possible) directly from British farms.

CLERKENWELL & FARRINGDON

Clerkenwell's hidden gems are well worth digging for. Pedestrianised Exmouth Market is a good place to start.

TOP CHOICE **Bistrot Bruno Loubet** FRENCH ££
(Map p102; ☎020-7324 4455; www.bistrotbrunoloubet.com; 86-88 Clerkenwell Rd EC1; mains £12-17; ⊙breakfast, lunch & dinner; ⊖Farringdon) There are London restaurants that charge double as much for food half as good as what's on offer at this informal but stylish bistro below the Zetter Hotel. Top quality ingredients, surprising taste combinations and unfaultable execution all come together – in the food, the cocktails and the home-infused aperitifs.

St John BRITISH ££
(Map p102; ☎020-7251 0848; www.stjohnrestaurant.com; 26 St John St EC1; mains £14-22; ⊖Farringdon) Bright whitewashed brick walls, high ceilings and simple wooden furniture keep diners free to concentrate on the world-famous nose-to-tail offerings. Expect offal, ox tongue and bone marrow.

5ifty 4our MALAYSIAN ££
(Map p102; ☎020-7336 0603; www.54farringdon.com; 54 Farringdon Rd; mains £11-16; ⊖Farringdon) Britain and Malaysia go back a long way and this smart-looking restaurant celebrates that fact with tasty fusion dishes such as lamb shanks with a spicy *redang* sauce.

Smiths of Smithfield BRITISH ££
(Map p102; ☎020 7251 7950; www.smithsofsmithfield.co.uk; 67-77 Charterhouse St EC1; mains 1st floor £13-15, top floor £19-30; ⊖Farringdon) This converted meat-packing warehouse endeavours to be all things to all people and succeeds. Hit the ground-floor bar for a beer, follow the silver-clad ducts and wooden beams upstairs to a relaxed dining space, or continue up for two more floors of feasting, each slightly smarter and pricier than the last.

Little Bay EUROPEAN £
(Map p102; ☎020-7278 1234; www.little-bay.co.uk; 171 Farringdon Rd EC1; mains before/after 7pm £6.45/8.45; ⊖Farringdon) The crushed-velvet ceiling, handmade twisted lamps that improve around the room (as the artist got better) and elaborately painted bar and tables showing nymphs frolicking are bonkers but fun. The hearty food is very good value.

Modern Pantry FUSION ££
(Map p102; ☎020-7553 9210; www.themodernpantry.co.uk; 47-48 St John's Sq EC1; mains £15-22; ⊙breakfast, lunch & dinner; ⊖Farringdon)

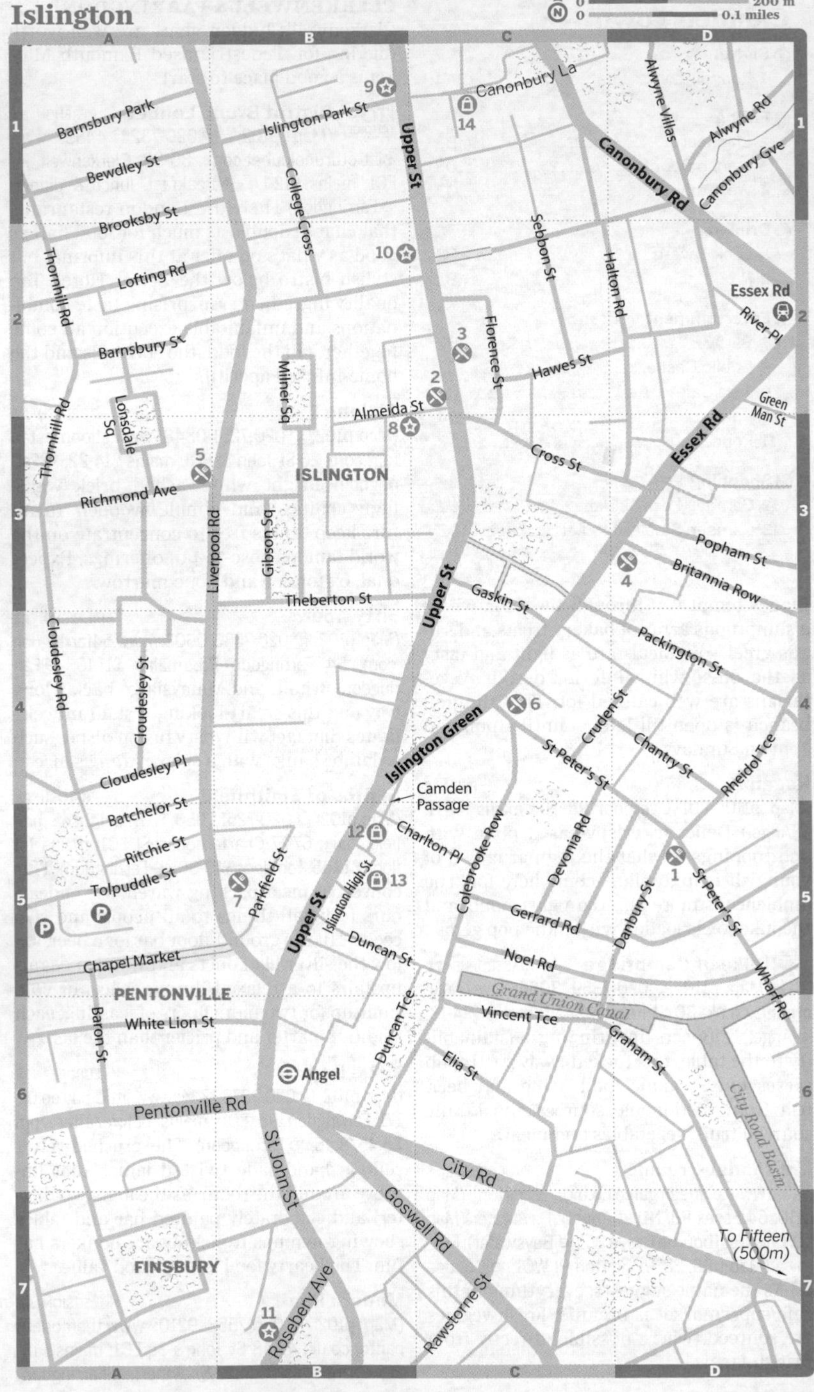

0 200 m
0 0.1 miles
Barnsbury Park
Islington Park St
Canonbury La
Upper St
Alwyne Villas
Alwyne Rd
Canonbury Rd
Canonbury Gve
Bewdley St
College Cross
Brooksby St
Sebbon St
Halton Rd
Thornhill Rd
Lofting Rd
Essex Rd
River Pl
Barnsbury St
Florence St
Milner Sq
Hawes St
Almeida St
Green Man St
Lonsdale Sq
Cross St
ISLINGTON
Richmond Ave
Liverpool Rd
Gibson Sq
Popham St
Britannia Row
Theberton St
Gaskin St
Cloudesley Rd
Cloudesley St
Packington St
Islington Green
Cruden St
Chantry St
Rheidol Tce
St Peter's St
Cloudesley Pl
Camden Passage
Batchelor St
Charlton Pl
Devonia Rd
Ritchie St
Islington High St
Colebrooke Row
Tolpuddle St
Parkfield St
Danbury St
Gerrard Rd
Duncan St
Noel Rd
Chapel Market
Wharf Rd
PENTONVILLE
Grand Union Canal
Vincent Tce
White Lion St
Baron St
Duncan Tce
Graham St
Elia St
Angel
City Road Basin
Pentonville Rd
St John St
City Rd
Goswell Rd
To Fifteen (500m)
FINSBURY
Rawstorne St
Rosebery Ave

Islington

Eating

1	Duke of Cambridge	D5
2	Le Mercury	C2
3	Ottolenghi	C2
4	Planet Organic	D3
5	Regent	A3
6	S&M Cafe	C4
7	Wagamama	B5

Entertainment

8	Almeida	B3
9	Hope & Anchor	B1
10	Lucky Voice	B2
11	Sadler's Wells	B7

Shopping

12	Camden Passage Market	B5
13	Laura J London	B5
14	Palette London	C1

Currently one of London's most talked-about eateries, this three-floor Georgian town house in the heart of Clerkenwell has a cracking innovative, all-day menu.

Medcalf BRITISH ££
(Map p102; ☎020-7833 3533; www.medcalfbar.co.uk; 40 Exmouth Market EC1; mains £10-16; closed dinner Sun; Angel) Medcalf is one of the best value hang outs on Exmouth Market. Housed in a beautifully converted 1912 butcher's shop, it serves up interesting and well-realised British fare.

Dans le Noir THEME RESTAURANT £££
(Map p102; ☎020-7253 1100; 30-31 Clerkenwell Green EC1; 2-/3-course meals £39/44; dinner Mon-Sat; Farringdon) If you've ever felt in the dark about food, eating in the pitch black might suit you. A visually impaired waiter guides you to your table, plate and cutlery. Then it's up to you to guess what you're eating and enjoy the anonymous conviviality of the dark.

HOXTON, SHOREDITCH & SPITALFIELDS

From the hit-and-miss Bangladeshi restaurants of Brick Lane to the Vietnamese strip on Kingsland Rd, and the Jewish, Spanish, French, Italian and Greek eateries in between, the East End's cuisine is as multicultural as its residents.

Fifteen ITALIAN ££
(☎0871-330 1515; www.fifteen.net; 15 Westland Pl N1; breakfast £2-8.50, trattoria mains £6-11, restaurant mains £11-25; breakfast, lunch & dinner; Old St) Jamie Oliver's culinary philanthropy started at Fifteen, set up to give unemployed young people a shot at a career. The Italian food is beyond excellent, and, surprisingly, even those on limited budgets can afford a visit. In the trattoria, a croissant and coffee will only set you back £3.50, while a £10 pasta makes for a delicious lunch. From Old St tube station, take City Rd and after 300m turn right into Westland Place.

Song Que VIETNAMESE £
(134 Kingsland Rd E2; mains £5-8; Old St) If you arrive after 7.30pm, expect to queue: this humble eatery has already had its cover blown as one of the best Vietnamese restaurants in London. There's never much time to admire the institutional-green walls, fake lobsters and bizarre horse portrait, as you'll be shunted out shortly after your last bite. Song Que is 300m along Kingsland Rd, the continuation of Shoreditch High St.

L'Anima ITALIAN ££
(Map p88; ☎020-7422 7000; www.lanima.co.uk; 1 Snowden St EC2; mains £11-32; lunch Mon-Fri, dinner Mon-Sat; Liverpool St) Sleek design meets accomplished cooking – what could be more Italian? The capacious space is divided into a formal dining room and a bar/lounge where you can drop in for a quick pasta fix.

Story Deli PIZZA ££
(Map p88; www.storydeli.com; 3 Dray Walk; pizzas £13; Liverpool St) This organic cafe, with mismatched cutlery poking out of jam jars, vintage mirrors leaning haphazardly against walls, high ceilings and solid wooden furniture (mismatched of course) is justifiably popular. The pizzas are thin and crispy, and you can rest assured that anything fishy has been sustainably caught.

Albion BRITISH ££
(Map p88; www.albioncaff.co.uk; 2-4 Boundary St E2; mains £9-13; Old St) For those wanting to be taken back to Dear Old Blighty's cuisine but with rather less grease and stodge, this self-consciously retro 'caff' serves up top-quality bangers and mash, steak-and-kidney pies, devilled kidneys and, of course, fish and chips.

Les Trois Garçons FRENCH £££
(Map p88; ☎020-7613 1924; www.lestroisgarcons.com; 1 Club Row E1; Mon-Thu 2-/3-courses £27/31, Fri & Sat £40/46, closed Sun; Liverpool St) The name may prepare you for the

French menu, but nothing on earth could prepare you for the camp decor. A virtual menagerie of stuffed or bronze animals fills every surface, while chandeliers dangle between a set of suspended handbags. The food is great, if overpriced, and the small army of bow-tie-wearing waiters unobtrusively deliver complementary bread and tasty gifts from the kitchen.

Hoxton Apprentice EUROPEAN ££
(Map p88; ☎020-7749 2828; www.hoxtonapprentice.com; 16 Hoxton Sq N1; mains £11-15; 🕑11am-11pm Tue-Sat, to 6pm Sun; ⊖Old St) Both professionals and apprentices work the kitchen in this restaurant, under the auspices of the Training For Life charity. Appropriately enough, it's housed in a Victorian school building.

Cafe Bangla BANGLADESHI £
(Map p88; 128 Brick Lane E1; mains £5-15; ⊖Liverpool St) Dining in the famous curry houses of Brick Lane is inevitably more about the experience than the food. Amongst the hordes of practically interchangeable restaurants, this one stands out for its murals of scantily clad women riding dragons, alongside a tribute to Princess Di.

Brick Lane Beigel Bake BAGELS £
(Map p88; 159 Brick Lane E2; most bagels less than £2; 🕑24hr; ⊖Liverpool St) A relic of London's Jewish East End, it's more a takeaway than a cafe and sells dirt-cheap bagels. They're a top snack on a bellyful of booze.

Drinking

As long as there's been a city, Londoners have loved to drink – and, as history shows, often immoderately. The pub is the focus of social life and there's always one near at hand. When the sun shines, drinkers spill out into the streets, parks and squares as well. It was only in 2008 that drinking was banned on the tube!

Soho is undoubtedly the heart of bar culture, with enough variety to cater to all tastes. Camden's great for grungy boozers and rock kids, although it has lost ground on the bohemian-cool front to the venues around Hoxton and Shoreditch.

Now that Princes William and Harry have hit their stride, the Sloane Ranger (cashed-up young aristocrat in the heady pre-crash 1980s) scene has been reborn in exclusive venues in South Ken(sington), although the 'Turbo Sloanes' now count megarich commoners among their numbers.

Us mere mortals will find plenty of pub-crawl potential in places like Clerkenwell, Islington, Southwark, Notting Hill, Earl's Court…hell, it's just not that difficult. The reviews below are simply to make sure you don't miss out on some of the most historic, unusual, best-positioned or excellent examples of the genre.

WEST END

Flat White CAFE
(Map p62; www.flat-white.co.uk 17 Berwick St W1; 🕑8am-7pm Mon-Fri, 9am-6pm Sat & Sun; ⊖Piccadilly Circus) Trailblazers of the unexpected but thoroughly welcome Kiwi invasion of Soho cafes, Flat White is both named after and delivers the holy grail of antipodean coffee. The beach scenes on the walls are a comfort on a cold day.

Gordon's Wine Bar BAR
(Map p62; www.gordonswinebar.com; 47 Villiers St WC2; ⊖Embankment) What's not to love about this cavernous wine cellar that's lit by candles and practically unchanged over the last 120 years? In summer, the crowd spills out into Embankment Gardens.

Princess Louise PUB
(Map p62; 208 High Holborn WC1; ⊖Holborn) This late 19th-century Victorian boozer is arguably London's most beautiful pub. Spectacularly decorated with fine tiles, etched mirrors, plasterwork and a gorgeous central horseshoe bar, it gets packed with the after-work crowd.

Coach & Horses PUB
(Map p62; www.coachandhorsessoho.co.uk; 29 Greek St W1; ⊖Leicester Sq) Regulars at this no-nonsense Soho institution have included Francis Bacon, Peter O'Toole and Lucien Freud. The Wednesday and Saturday night singalongs are tops.

Lamb & Flag PUB
(Map p62; 33 Rose St WC2; ⊖Covent Garden) Everyone's Covent Garden 'find', this historic pub is often jammed. Built in 1623, it was formerly called the 'Bucket of Blood'.

Galvin at Windows HOTEL BAR
(Map p58; www.galvinatwindows.com; The Hilton, 22 Park Lane W1; ⊖Hyde Park Corner) Drinks are pricey, but the view's magnificent from this 28th-floor eyrie.

Jewel COCKTAIL BAR
(Map p62; www.jewelbar.com); Piccadilly Circus (4-6 Glasshouse Street W1; ⊖Piccadilly Circus); Covent Garden (29-30 Maiden Lane WC2; ⊖Cov-

LOCAL KNOWLEDGE

SUE OSTLER: FLIRT DIVA

JOB Running practical 'flirtshops' in London's bars, helping women hone their man-meeting skills.

Where's the best place in London to get your flirt on?

Piccadilly Circus, because it's the gateway to London and you get all kinds of people there. If the girls say 'Hey Sue, we want a fun night out', I take them to Jewel bar (p112). It's a meat market without the trash – a m-e-e-t market, if you like.

And once you m-e-e-t, any ideas for a first date that doesn't waste any valuable sightseeing time?

Meet at the Wallace (p82) for afternoon tea among the art, then grab a bottle of bubbly at Tesco and find an enchanted corner of Regent's Park (p82) to quaff it in.

And for a meal to impress?

You'd have to be seriously loaded, but I can guarantee that if you took a date to Marcus Wareing's restaurant at The Berkeley (p106) it would certainly make an impression

ent Garden) Chandeliers, banquettes, cocktails and, in Piccadilly, sunset views.

Monmouth Coffee Company CAFE
(Mon-Sat) Covent Garden (Map p62; 27 Monmouth St WC2; Covent Garden), Borough (Map p74; 2 Park St SE1; London Bridge) While the array of treats displayed on the counter is alluring, it's the coffee that's the star, nay god, here. Chat to a caffeinated stranger on one of the tight tables at the back, or grab a takeaway and slink off to a nearby lane for your fix.

Absolut Ice Bar NOVELTY BAR
(Map p62; 020-7478 8910; www.belowzerolondon.com; 31-33 Heddon St W1; admission Thu-Sat £16, Sun-Wed £13; Piccadilly Circus) At -6°C, this bar made entirely of ice is literally the coolest in London. Entry is limited to 40 minutes, and your ticket includes a vodka cocktail served in an ice glass. It's a gimmick, sure, but a good one, and there are plenty of places nearby that charge the same for a cocktail alone. Book ahead.

THE CITY

Ye Olde Watling PUB
(Map p68; 29 Watling St; Mansion House) Atmospheric 1668 pub with a good selection of wine and tap beer.

Ye Olde Cheshire Cheese PUB
(Map p68; Wine Office Ct, 145 Fleet St EC4; Holborn) Rebuilt six years after the Great Fire, it was popular with Dr Johnson, Thackeray, Dickens and the visiting Mark Twain. Touristy but always atmospheric and enjoyable for a pub meal.

Vertigo 42 CHAMPAGNE BAR
(Map p68; 020-7877 7842; www.vertigo42.co.uk; Tower 42, Old Broad St, EC2; Liverpool St) Book a two-hour slot in this 42nd-floor bar with vertiginous views across London.

SOUTH BANK

George Inn PUB
(Map p74; www.nationaltrust.org.uk/main/w-georgeinn; 77 Borough High St SE1; London Bridge) Tucked away in a cobbled courtyard is London's last surviving galleried coaching inn, dating in its current form from 1677 and now belonging to the National Trust. Dickens and Shakespeare used to prop up the bar here (not together, obviously). There are outdoor tables for sunny days.

Anchor PUB
(Map p74; 34 Park St SE1; London Bridge) An 18th-century boozer replacing the 1615 one where Samuel Pepys witnessed the Great Fire, it has a terrace offering superb views over the Thames. Dr Johnson was once a regular.

CHELSEA & KENSINGTON

Bibendum Oyster Bar CHAMPAGNE BAR
(Map p80; www.bibendum.co.uk; 81 Fulham Rd SW3; South Kensington) If rubber-clad men happen to be your thing, slurp up a bivalve and knock back a champers in the foyer of the wonderful art nouveau Michelin House (1911). The Michelin Man is everywhere: in mosaics, stained glass, crockery and echoed in the architecture itself.

NOTTING HILL, BAYSWATER & PADDINGTON

Trailer Happiness COCKTAIL BAR

(Map p98; www.trailerhappiness.com; 177 Portobello Rd W11; ⊖Ladbroke Grove) Think shag carpets, 1960s California kitsch and trashy trailer-park glamour. Try the Tiki cocktails and share a flaming volcano bowl of Zombie with a friend to ensure your evening goes off with a bang.

Windsor Castle PUB

(Map p98; www.thewindsorcastlekensington.co.uk; 114 Campden Hill Rd W11; ⊖Notting Hill Gate) A memorable pub with oak partitions separating the original bars. The panels have tiny doors so big drinkers will have trouble getting past the front bar. It also has one of the loveliest walled gardens of any pub in London. Thomas Paine (*Rights of Man* writer) is rumoured to be buried in the cellar.

MARYLEBONE

Artesian HOTEL BAR

(www.artesian-bar.co.uk; Langham Hotel, 1C Portland Pl W1; ⊖Oxford Circus) For a dose of colonial glamour with a touch of the Orient, the sumptuous bar at the Langham hits the mark. Rum is the speciality here – award-winning cocktails (£15) are concocted from the 60 varieties on offer.

Heights HOTEL BAR

(Map p62; St George's Hotel, 14 Langham Pl W1; ⊖Oxford Circus) Take the lift up to this understated bar with huge windows showcasing the panorama. It's an unusual view, managing to miss most of the big sights, but impressive nonetheless.

KING'S CROSS

Big Chill House BAR, DJS

(Map p86; www.bigchill.net; 257-259 Pentonville Rd N1; entry £5 after 10pm Fri & Sat; ⊖King's Cross) Come the weekend, the only remotely chilled-out space in this busy bar, split over two levels, is its first-rate and generously proportioned rooftop terrace.

CAMDEN TOWN

Lock Tavern PUB, BANDS

(Map p108; www.lock-tavern.co.uk; 35 Chalk Farm Rd NW1; ⊖Camden Town) The archetypal Camden pub, the Lock has both a rooftop terrace and a beer garden and attracts an interesting crowd with its mix of ready conviviality and regular live music.

Proud BAR, BANDS

(Map p108; www.proudcamden.com; Stables Market NW1; admission free-£10; ⊖Camden Town) No, despite the name it's not a gay bar. Proud occupies a former horse hospital within Stables Market, with booths in the stalls, ice-cool rock photography on the walls and deck chairs printed with images of Pete Doherty and Blondie. Spin around the gallery during the day or enjoy bands at night.

CLERKENWELL & FARRINGDON

Jerusalem Tavern PUB

(Map p102; www.stpetersbrewery.co.uk; 55 Britton St; ⊖Farringdon) Pick a wood-panelled cubbyhole to park yourself in at this 1720 coffee shop-turned-inn, and choose from a selection of St Peter's beers and ales, brewed in Suffolk.

HOXTON, SHOREDITCH & SPITALFIELDS

TOP CHOICE **Commercial Tavern** PUB

(Map p88; 142 Commercial St E1; ⊖Liverpool St) The zany decor's a thing of wonder in this reformed East End boozer. Check out the walls coated in buttons and jigsaw puzzle pieces. The little boy's room has been wallpapered like, well, a little boy's room: Popeye, astronauts and cyclists all make an appearance.

TOP CHOICE **Loungelover** COCKTAIL BAR

(Map p88; ☎020-7012 1234; www.lestriosgarcons.com; 1 Whitby St E1; ⏲6pm-midnight Sun-Thu, 6pm-1am Fri & Sat; ⊖Liverpool St) Book a table, sip a cocktail and admire the Louis XIV chairs, the huge hippo head, the cage turned living room, the jewel-encrusted stag's head and the loopy chandeliers. Utterly fabulous.

Bar Music Hall BAR, BANDS

(Map p88; www.barmusichall.com; 134 Curtain Rd EC2; ⊖Old St) Keeping the East End music-hall tradition alive but with a modern twist, this roomy space with a central bar hosts DJs and live bands. Music runs the gamut from punk to jazz to rock and disco.

Grapeshots WINE BAR

(Map p88; www.davywine.co.uk/grapeshots; 2/3 Artillery Passage E1; ⊖Liverpool St) Half the fun of this place is walking down the Dickensian passage, complete with old street lamps, that leads to it. The old-world ambience continues inside.

Ten Bells PUB

(Map p88; cnr Commercial & Fournier Sts E1; ⊖Liverpool St) The most famous Jack the

Ripper pub, Ten Bells was patronised by his last victim before her grisly end, and possibly by the slayer himself. Admire the wonderful 18th-century tiles and ponder the past over a pint.

Other good stops on a Hoxton hop:

Favela Chic BAR, DJS
(Map p88; www.favelachic.com; 91-93 Great Eastern St EC2; entry £5-10 after 8pm; ⊖Old St) Ticks the following boxes: hip young things; crazy theme nights; lumberyard meets jungle decor; fun and funky music.

Mother BAR, NIGHTCLUB
(Map p88; www.333mother.com; 333 Old St EC1; entry free-£5; ⊖Old St) Red-and-gold flocked wallpaper, chequerboard floors and live alternative music and DJs on weekends. Downstairs, 333 is part nightclub, part live venue.

Zigfrid Von Underbelly BAR, DJS
(Map p88; www.zigfrid.com; 11 Hoxton Sq N1; ⊖Old St) Furnished like an oversize lounge room (check out the disturbing family portrait over the fireplace), it's the kookiest of the Hoxton Sq venues.

HAMPSTEAD & HIGHGATE

Spaniard's Inn PUB
(www.thespaniardshampstead.co.uk; Spaniard's Rd NW3; ⊖Hampstead, then bus 21) An enigmatic tavern that dates from 1585, complete with dubious claims that Dick Turpin, the dandy highwayman, was born here and used it as a hideout. More savoury sorts like Dickens, Shelley, Keats and Byron certainly availed themselves of its charms. There's a big, blissful garden and good food. From the tube station take Heath St and then veer left onto Spaniard's Rd.

Flask PUB
(77 Highgate West Hill N6; ⊖Highgate) Charming nooks and crannies, an old circular bar and an enticing beer garden make this 1663 pub the perfect place for a pint en route between Hampstead Heath and Highgate Cemetery. It's like a village pub in the city. From Highgate tube station, cross Archway, turn right and then left onto Southwood Lane. At the lane's end, the Flask is a block to the right.

Holly Bush PUB
(22 Holly Mount NW3; ⊖Hampstead) Dating from the early 19th century, this beautiful pub has a secluded hilltop location, open fires in winter and a knack for making you stay a bit longer than you had intended. It's above Heath St, reached via the Holly Bush Steps, which you'll find across the road and slightly up the hill from the tube station.

☆ Entertainment

From West End luvvies to End End geezers, Londoners have always loved a spectacle. With bear-baiting and public executions no longer an option, they've learnt to make do with having the one of the world's best theatre, nightclub and live-music scenes to divert them. Yet the gladiatorial contests that the Romans brought to these shores still survive on the football fields, especially when Chelsea goes head-to-head with Arsenal.

For a comprehensive list of what to do on any given night, check out *Time Out*. The listings in the free tube papers are also handy.

Theatre

London is a world capital for theatre and there's a lot more than mammoth musicals to tempt you into the West End. As far as the blockbuster musicals go, you can be fairly confident that *Les Miserables* and *Phantom of the Opera* will still be chugging along, as well as Phantom's sequel *Love Never Dies*, *Legally Blonde*, *Sister Act* and *The Wizard of Oz*.

On performance days, you can buy half-price tickets for West End productions (cash only) from the official agency **tkts** (Map p62; www.tkts.co.uk; ⊙10am-7pm Mon-Sat, noon-4pm Sun; ⊖Leicester Sq), on the south side of Leicester Sq. The booth is the one with the clock tower; beware of touts selling dodgy tickets. For a comprehensive look at what's being staged and where, visit www.officiallondontheatre.co.uk, www.theatremonkey.com or http://london.broadway.com.

The term 'West End' – as with Broadway – generally refers to the big-money productions like musicals, but also includes other heavyweights. Some recommended options:

Royal Court Theatre THEATRE
(Map p80; ☎020-7565 5000; www.royalcourttheatre.com; Sloane Sq SW1; ⊖Sloane Sq) The patron of new British writing.

National Theatre THEATRE
(Map p76; ☎020-7452 3000; www.nationaltheatre.org.uk; South Bank SE1; ⊖Waterloo) Cheaper tickets for both classics and new plays from some of the world's best companies.

Royal Shakespeare Company THEATRE COMPANY
(RSC; ☎0844 800 1110; www.rsc.org.uk) Productions of the bard's classics and other quality stuff.

NOVEL NIGHTS OUT

It seems that the cool kids are bored with simply going clubbing, listening to a band or propping up a bar with a pint. To plant your finger on the party pulse, check out some of these activity-based haunts.

Bloomsbury Bowling Lanes TENPIN BOWLING
(Map p86; ☎020-7183 1979; www.bloomsburybowling.com; Bedford Way WC1; ⏲1pm-late; ⊖Russell Sq) With eight 10-pin bowling lanes, a diner and authentic 1950s decor shipped in from America (even the carpet), this place is the real deal. And the fun doesn't stop with dubious footwear and a burger; there are also private karaoke rooms, a cinema screening independent movies, DJs and up-and-coming live bands.

Lucky Voice KARAOKE
(www.luckyvoice.com; 4-person booth per 2hr £20-50) Soho (Map p62; ☎020-7439 3660; 52 Poland St W1; ⏲5.30pm-1am Mon-Thu, 3pm-1am Fri & Sat, 3-10.30pm Sun; ⊖Oxford Circus); Islington (Map p110; ☎020-7354 6280; 173-174 Upper St N1; ⏲5pm-midnight Mon-Thu, 3pm-2am Fri & Sat, 3pm-midnight Sun; ⊖Highbury & Islington) Moulded on the private karaoke bars of Tokyo, Lucky Voice is a low-lit maze of dark walls with hidden doors revealing snug leather-clad soundproofed booths for your secret singalong. Select one of 50,000 songs from a touch screen, pick up a microphone and you're away. In the Super Lucky rooms there are wigs and blow-up guitars to enhance your performance. Drinks and bento boxes are ordered by the touch of a button; expect to spend a fortune in Dutch courage.

SRO Audiences LIVE TV
(www.sroaudiences.com) British telly is saturated with chat shows and quiz shows hosted by famous comedians with even more famous guests. It's surprisingly easy to be part of a **live TV studio audience** – for free; follow the instructions on the website and be prepared to queue, whoop and cheer on demand.

Old Vic THEATRE
(Map p76; ☎0844 871 7628; www.oldvictheatre.com; The Cut SE1; ⊖Waterloo) Kevin Spacey continues his run as artistic director (and occasional performer).

Donmar Warehouse THEATRE
(Map p62; ☎0844 871 7624; www.donmarwarehouse.com; 41 Earlham St WC2; ⊖Covent Garden) A not-for-profit company that has forged itself a West End reputation.

Off West End is where you'll generally find the most original works. Some venues to check out:

Almeida THEATRE
(Map p110; ☎020-7359 4404; www.almeida.co.uk; Almeida St N1; ⊖Highbury & Islington)

Young Vic THEATRE
(Map p76; ☎020-7922 2922; www.youngvic.org; 66 The Cut SE1; ⊖Waterloo)

Menier Chocolate Factory THEATRE
(Map p74; ☎020-7907 7060; www.menierchocolatefactory.com; 55 Southwark St SE1; ⊖London Bridge)

Nightclubs

London's had a lot of practice perfecting the art of clubbing – Samuel Pepys used the term in 1660! – and the volume and variety of venues in today's city is staggering. Clubland's no longer confined to the West End, with megaclubs scattered throughout the city wherever there's a venue big enough, cheap enough or quirky enough to hold them. Some run their own regular weekly schedule, while others host promoters on an ad hoc basis. The big nights are Friday and Saturday, although you'll find some of the most cutting-edge sessions midweek. Admission prices vary widely; it's often cheaper to arrive early or prebook tickets.

Fabric SUPERCLUB
(Map p102; www.fabriclondon.com; 77A Charterhouse St EC1; admission £8-18; ⏲10pm-6am Fri, 11pm-8am Sat; 11pm-6am Sun; ⊖Farringdon) Consistently rated by DJs as one of the world's greatest, Fabric's three dance floors occupy a converted meat cold-store opposite the Smithfield meat market. Friday's FabricLive offers drum and bass, breakbeat and hip hop, Saturdays see house, techno and electronica, while hedonistic Sundays are delivered by the Wetyourself crew.

Plastic People NIGHTCLUB
(Map p88; www.plasticpeople.co.uk; 147-149 Curtain Rd EC2; admission £5-10; ⏲10pm-3.30am Fri & Sat, 10pm-2am Sun; ⊖Old St) Taking the directive 'underground club' literally, Plastic People provides a low-ceilinged subterranean den of dubsteppy, wonky, funky, no-frills fun times.

Guanabara BRAZILIAN
(Map p62; www.guanabara.co.uk; cnr Parker St & Drury Lane WC2; admission free-£10; ⏲5pm-2.30am Mon-Sat, 5pm-midnight Sun; ⊖Covent Garden) Brazil comes to London with live music and DJs nightly.

Ministry of Sound SUPERCLUB
(www.ministryofsound.com; 103 Gaunt St SE1; admission £13-22; ⏲11pm-6.30am Fri & Sat; ⊖Elephant & Castle) Where the global brand started, it's London's most famous club and still packs in a diverse crew with big local and international names.

Cargo NIGHTCLUB
(Map p88; www.cargo-london.com; 83 Rivington St EC2; admission free-£10; ⊖Old St) A popular club with a courtyard where you can simultaneously enjoy big sounds and the great outdoors. Hosts live bands and gay bingo too.

Mass NIGHTCLUB
(www.mass-club.com; St Matthew's Church, Brixton Hill SW2; cover charges vary; ⊖Brixton) The congregation's swollen at this Brixton church under its new high priests, with regular services of live music and club nights. Turn left when leaving Brixton tube station and you'll see the church on your left, immediately after the first major intersection.

Matter SUPERCLUB
(www.matterlondon.com; The O2 Arena SE10; admission £10-20; ⊖North Greenwich) London's newest superclub, courtesy of the Fabric crew, Matter is the latest word in high-tech club design. No regular nights, just a busy roster of visiting promoters.

Rock, Pop & Jazz

While London may have stopped swinging in the 1960s, every subsequent generation has given birth to a new set of bands in the city's thriving live venues: punk in the 1970s, New Romantics in the 1980s, Brit Pop in the 1990s and the current crop of skinny-jeaned rockers and electro acts thrilling the scenesters today. You'll find interesting young bands gigging around venues all over the city. Big-name gigs sell out quickly, so check www.seetickets.com before you travel. See also the Drinking reviews, especially Bar Music Hall and Mother in Hoxton, and Proud and the Lock Tavern in Camden.

Koko CLUB
(Map p108; www.koko.uk.com; 1A Camden High St NW1; ⊖Mornington Cres) Occupying the grand Camden Palace theatre, Koko hosts live bands most nights and the regular Club NME (£5) on Friday.

O2 Academy Brixton CONCERT HALL
(☎08444772000;www.o2academybrixton.co.uk; 211 Stockwell Rd SW9; ⊖Brixton) This Grade II–listed art deco venue is always winning awards for 'best live venue' (something to do with the artfully sloped floor, perhaps) and hosts big-name acts in a relatively intimate setting (5000 capacity).

Dublin Castle PUB
(Map p108; ☎020-7485 1773; www.thedublincastle.com; 94 Parkway NW1; ⊖Camden Town) There's live punk or alternative music most nights in this pub's back room (cover usually £6).

Jazz Cafe CLUB
(Map p108; www.jazzcafe.co.uk; 5 Parkway NW1; ⊖Camden Town) Jazz is just one part of the picture at this intimate club that stages a full roster of rock, pop, hip hop and dance, including famous names.

Barfly PUB
(www.barflyclub.com; ☎0844 847 2424) Camden (Map p108; 49 Chalk Farm Rd NW1; ⊖Chalk Farm); ULU (Map p86; Byng Pl NW1; ⊖Goodge St) Pleasantly grungy, and a good place to see the best new bands. The same crew run a couple of other joints around town.

Ronnie Scott's CLUB
(Map p62; ☎020-7439 0747; www.ronniescotts.co.uk; 47 Frith St W1; ⊖Leicester Sq) London's legendary jazz club has been pulling in the hep cats since 1959.

100 Club CLUB
(Map p62; ☎020-7636 0933; www.the100club.co.uk; 100 Oxford St W1; ⊖Oxford Circus) This legendary London venue once showcased the Stones and was at the centre of the punk revolution. It now divides its time between jazz, rock and even a little swing.

Hope & Anchor PUB
(Map p110; ☎020-7700 0550; 207 Upper St; admission free-£6; ⊖Angel) Live music's still the focus of the pub that hosted the first

London gigs of Joy Division and U2 (only nine people showed up).

Roundhouse CONCERT HALL
(Map p108; ☎0844 482 8008; www.roundhouse.org.uk; Chalk Farm Rd NW1; ⊖Chalk Farm) Built in 1847 as a railway shed, Camden's Roundhouse has been an iconic concert venue since the 1960s (capacity 3300), hosting the likes of the Rolling Stones, Led Zeppelin and The Clash. It's also used for theatre and comedy.

Classical Music

With four world-class symphony orchestras, two opera companies, various smaller ensembles, brilliant venues, reasonable prices and high standards of performance, London is a classical capital. Keep an eye out for the free (or nearly so) lunchtime concerts held in many of the city's churches.

Royal Albert Hall CONCERT HALL
(Map p80; ☎020-7589 8212; www.royalalberthall.com; Kensington Gore SW7; ⊖South Kensington) A beautiful circular Victorian arena that hosts classical concerts and contemporary artists, but is best known as the venue for the annual classical music festival, the Proms.

Barbican Centre ARTS CENTRE
(☎0845 121 6823; www.barbican.org.uk; Silk St EC2; ⊖Barbican) This hulking complex has a full program of film, music, theatre, art and dance including loads of concerts from the **London Symphony Orchestra** (www.lso.co.uk), which is based here. The centre is in the City and is well signposted from both the Barbican and Moorgate tube stations.

Southbank Centre CONCERT HALLS
(Map p76; ☎0844 875 0073; www.southbankcentre.co.uk; Belvedere Rd; ⊖Waterloo) Home to the London Philharmonic Orchestra (www.lpo.co.uk), Sinfonietta (www.londonsinfonietta.org.uk) and the Philharmonia Orchestra (www.philharmonia.co.uk), among others, this centre hosts classical, opera, jazz and choral music in three premier venues: the **Royal Festival Hall**, the smaller **Queen Elizabeth Hall** and the **Purcell Room**. The precinct is a riverside people-watching mecca of shops and restaurants. Look out for free recitals in the foyer.

Opera & Dance

Royal Opera House OPERA, BALLET
(Map p62; ☎020-7304 4000; www.roh.org.uk; Bow St WC2; tickets £5-195; ⊖Covent Garden) Covent Garden is synonymous with opera thanks to this world-famous venue, which is also the home of the Royal Ballet, Britain's premier classical ballet company. Backstage tours take place on weekdays (£10, book ahead).

Sadler's Wells DANCE
(Map p110; ☎0844 412 4300; www.sadlers-wells.com; Rosebery Ave EC1; tickets £10-49; ⊖Angel) A glittering modern venue that was, in fact, first established in the 17th century, Sadler's Wells has been given much credit for bringing modern dance to the mainstream.

Coliseum OPERA
(Map p62; ☎0871 911 0200; www.eno.org; St Martin's Lane WC2; tickets £10-87; ⊖Leicester Sq) Home of the progressive English National Opera; all performances are in English.

Comedy

When London's comics aren't being terribly clever on TV, you might find them doing stand-up somewhere in your neighbourhood. There are numerous venues to choose from, and many pubs getting in on the act.

Comedy Store CLUB
(Map p62; ☎0844 847 1728; www.thecomedystore.co.uk; 1A Oxendon St SW1; admission £14-20; ⊖Piccadilly Circus) One of London's first comedy clubs, featuring the capital's most famous improvisers, the Comedy Store Players, on Wednesdays and Sundays.

Comedy Cafe CLUB
(Map p88; ☎020-7739 5706; www.comedycafe.co.uk; 68 Rivington St EC2; admission free-£15; ⊙Wed-Sat; ⊖Old St) Have dinner and watch comedy; Wednesday is free New Act Night.

99 Club MULTIVENUE CLUB
(☎0776 048 8119; www.the99club.co.uk; admission £10-30) Not quite the famous 100 Club, this virtual venue takes over various bars around town nightly, with three rival clones on Saturdays.

Soho Theatre THEATRE
(Map p62; ☎020-7478 0100; www.sohotheatre.com; 21 Dean St W1; ⊖Tottenham Court Rd) Where grown-up comedians graduate to once they start pulling the crowds.

Pear Shaped COMEDY NIGHT
(Map p62; www.pearshapedcomedy.com; Fitzroy Tavern, 16a Charlotte Street W1; admission £5; ⊙8.30pm Wed; ⊖Goodge St) Advertising themselves as 'London's second-worst

LONDON CALLING

Download these to your MP3 player before tackling the tube.

» **London in general:** Blur – 'London Loves'; Chemical Brothers – 'Hold Tight London'; The Clash – 'London Calling'; The Jam – 'Down In The Tube Station At Midnight'; Pet Shop Boys – 'London'

» **West End:** David Bowie – 'London Boys'; The Kinks – 'Lola'; Pet Shop Boys – 'West End Girls'; Roll Deep – 'Good Times'; The Who – 'Who Are You'

» **The City:** The Beatles – 'Being for the Benefit of Mr Kite'; Roxy Music – 'Do The Strand'; T-Rex – 'London Boys'

» **South London:** The Clash – 'Guns of Brixton'; Dire Straits – 'Sultans of Swing'; Eddie Grant – 'Electric Avenue'; The Kinks – 'Waterloo Sunset'; Morrissey – 'You're the One for Me, Fatty'

» **West London:** Blur – 'Fool's Day'; The Clash – 'London's Burning'; Elvis Costello – 'Chelsea'; Hard-Fi – 'Tied Up Too Tight'; Rolling Stones – 'You Can't Always Get What You Want'

» **North London:** Dizzee Rascal – 'Dream'; Morrissey – 'Come Back to Camden'; Pet Shop Boys – 'Kings Cross'; The Pogues – 'London Girl'; The Smiths – 'London'

» **East End:** Billy Bragg – 'Dreadbelly'; Morrissey – 'Dagenham Dave'; Pulp – 'Mile End'; Rolling Stones – 'Play With Fire'

comedy club', Pear Shaped is the place to destroy the hopes of enthusiastic amateurs.

Cinemas

Glitzy premieres usually take place in one of the mega multiplexes in Leicester Sq.

Electric CINEMA
(Map p98; ☎020 7908 9696; www.electriccinema.co.uk; 191 Portobello Rd W11; tickets £8-15; ⊖Ladbroke Grove) Grab a glass of wine from the bar, head to your leather sofa (£30) and snuggle down to watch a flick. All cinemas should be like this. Tickets are cheapest on Mondays.

BFI Southbank CINEMA, MEDIATHEQUE
(Map p76; ☎020-7928 3232; www.bfi.org.uk; Belvedere Rd SE1; tickets £9; ⏲11am-11pm; ⊖Waterloo) A film-lover's fantasy, it screens some 2000 flicks a year, ranging from classics to foreign art house. There's also the Mediatheque viewing stations, where you can explore the British Film Institute's extensive archive of movies and watch whatever you like for free.

BFI IMAX IMAX CINEMA
(Map p76; ☎020-7199 6000; www.bfi.org.uk/imax; Waterloo Rd SE1; tickets £9-16; ⊖Waterloo) Watch 3-D movies and cinema releases on the UK's biggest screen: 20m high (nearly five double-decker buses) and 26m wide.

Curzon Cinemas CINEMA
(www.curzoncinemas.com; tickets £8-12) Chelsea (Map p80; 206 Kings Rd SW3; ⊖Sloane Sq); Mayfair (Map p58; 38 Curzon St W1; ⊖Green Park); Renoir (Map p86; Brunswick Sq WC1; ⊖Russell Sq); Soho (Map p62; 99 Shaftesbury Ave W1; ⊖Leicester Sq) Part of a clutch of independent cinemas spread throughout the capital showing less-mainstream fare.

Sport

As the capital of a football-mad nation, you can expect London to be brimming over with sporting spectacles during the cooler months. The Wimbledon Lawn Tennis Championships (p92) is one of the biggest events on the city's summer calendar.

FOOTBALL

Tickets for Premier League football matches are ridiculously hard to come by for casual fans these days, but you could try your luck. Contacts for London's Premier League clubs:

Arsenal (www.arsenal.com)

Chelsea (www.chelseafc.com)

Fulham (www.fulhamfc.com)

Tottenham Hotspur (www.tottenhamhotspur.com)

West Ham United (www.whufc.com)

RUGBY

Twickenham (www.rfu.com; Rugby Rd, Twickenham; 🚆Twickenham) is the home of English rugby union, but as with football, tickets for tests are difficult to get unless you have contacts. The ground also has the **World Rugby Museum** (☎020-8892 8877; adult/child £6/4; ⏲10am-5pm Tue-Sat, 11am-5pm Sun), which can be combined with a tour of the stadium (adult/child £14/8, bookings recommended).

CRICKET

Cricket is as popular as ever in the land of its origin. Test matches take place at two venerable grounds: Lord's Cricket Ground (which also hosts tours) and the **Brit Oval** (☎0871 246 1100; www.britoval.com; Kennington SE11; ⊖Oval). Tickets cost from £20 to £80, but if you're a fan it's worth it. If not, it's an expensive and protracted form of torture.

Lord's Cricket Ground CRICKET GROUND
(☎020-7616 8595; www.lords.org; St John's Wood Rd NW8; tours adult/child £14/8; ⏲tours 10am, noon & 2pm; ⊖St John's Wood) The next best thing to watching a test at Lord's is the absorbingly anecdotal 100-minute tour of the ground and facilities, held when there's no play. It takes in the famous (members only) Long Room and the **MCC Museum**, featuring evocative memorabilia, including the tiny Ashes trophy.

Shopping

Napoleon famously described Britain as a nation of shopkeepers, which doesn't sound at all bad to us! From world-famous department stores to quirky backstreet retail revelations, London is a mecca for shoppers with an eye for style and a card to exercise. If you're looking for something distinctly British, eschew the Union Jack–emblazoned kitsch of the tourist thoroughfares and fill your bags with London fashion, music, books and antiques.

London's famous department stores are a tourist attraction in themselves, even if you don't intend to make a personal contribution to the orgy of consumption. If there's a label worth having, you'll find it in central London. The capital's most famous designers (Paul Smith, Vivienne Westwood, Stella McCartney, the late Alexander McQueen) have their own stores scattered about and are stocked in major department stores. Look out for dress agencies that sell second-hand designer clothes, bags and shoes – there are particularly rich pickings in the wealthier parts of town.

Nick Hornby's book *High Fidelity* may have done for London music-store workers what *Sweeney Todd* did for barbers, but those obsessive types still lurk in wonderful independent stores all over the city.

WEST END

Oxford St is the place for High St fashion, while Regent St cranks it up a notch. Carnaby St is no longer the hip hub that it was in the 1960s, but the lanes around it still have some interesting boutiques. Bond St has designers galore, Savile Row is famous for bespoke tailoring and Jermyn St is the place for Sir to buy his smart clobber (particularly shirts). For musical instruments, visit Denmark St (off Charing Cross Rd).

Selfridges DEPARTMENT STORE
(Map p84; www.selfridges.com; 400 Oxford St W1; ⊖Bond St) The funkiest and most vital of London's one-stop shops, where fashion runs the gamut from street to formal. The food hall is unparalleled, and the cosmetics hall the largest in Europe.

Fortnum & Mason DEPARTMENT STORE
(Map p62; www.fortnumandmason.com; 181 Piccadilly W1; ⊖Piccadilly Circus) The byword for quality and service from a bygone era, steeped in 300 years of tradition. It is particularly noted for its old-world basement food hall, where Britain's elite come for their marmite and bananas.

Liberty DEPARTMENT STORE
(Map p62; www.liberty.co.uk; Great Marlborough St W1; ⊖Oxford Circus) An irresistible blend of contemporary styles and indulgent pampering in a mock-Tudor fantasyland of carved dark wood.

Topshop Oxford Circus CLOTHES
(Map p62; www.topshop.com; 216 Oxford St W1; ⊖Oxford Circus) Billed as the 'world's largest fashion store', the Topshop branch on Oxford Circus is a constant frenzy of shoppers searching for the latest look at reasonable prices. It's been given a shot of cool by being home to a range by London's favourite local supermodel rock chick, Kate Moss. Topman is upstairs.

Grays ANTIQUES
(Map p84; www.graysantiques.com; 58 Davies St W1; ⊖Bond St) Top-hatted doormen welcome you to this wonderful building full of specialist stallholders. Make sure you head to the basement where the Tyburn River still runs through a channel in the floor.

Also check out:

HMV MUSIC
(Map p62; www.hmv.com; 150 Oxford St W1; ⊖Oxford Circus) Giant store selling music, DVDs and magazines.

Foyle's BOOKS
(Map p62; www.foyles.co.uk; 113-119 Charing Cross Rd WC2; ⊖Tottenham Court Rd) Venerable independent store with an excellent collection of poetry and women's literature.

Ray's Jazz JAZZ
(Map p62; www.foyles.co.uk; Foyles, 113-119 Charing Cross Rd WC2; ⊖Tottenham Court Rd) Where aficionados find those elusive back catalogues from their favourite jazz and blues artists.

Stanfords TRAVEL BOOKS
(Map p62; www.stanfords.co.uk; 12-14 Long Acre WC2; ⊖Covent Garden) The granddaddy of travel bookstores.

Waterstone's BOOKS
(www.waterstones.com) Piccadilly (Map p62; 203-206 Piccadilly W1; ⊖Piccadilly Circus); Bloomsbury (Map p80, 82 Gower St WC1; ⊖Goodge St) Beautiful branches of the chain. Check out the 5th View bar in the Piccadilly store.

Rigby & Peller LINGERIE
(www.rigbyandpeller.com) Mayfair (Map p62; 22A Conduit St W1; ⊖Oxford Circus); Knightsbridge (Map p80; 2 Hans Rd SW3; ⊖Knightsbridge); Chelsea (Map p80; 13 Kings Rd SW3; ⊖Sloane Sq); Westfield mall (see p123) Get into some right royal knickers with a trip to the Queen's corsetière.

Butler & Wilson JEWELLERY
(www.butlerandwilson.co.uk) Mayfair (Map p84; 20 South Moulton St W1; ⊖Bond St); Chelsea (Map p80; 189 Fulham Rd SW3; ⊖South Kensington) Camp jewellery, antique baubles and vintage clothing.

BM Soho DANCE MUSIC
(Map p62; www.bm-soho.com; 25 D'Arblay St W1; ⊖Oxford Circus) Your best bet for dance – if they haven't got what you're after, they'll know who has.

Forbidden Planet COMICS
(Map p62; 179 Shaftesbury Ave WC2; ⊖Tottenham Court Rd) On a different planet to our lonely one, populated by comic-book heroes, sci-fi figurines, horror and fantasy literature.

Grant & Cutler BOOKS
(Map p62; www.grantandcutler.com; 55-57 Great Marlborough St W1; ⊖Oxford Circus) Specialises in foreign languages.

KNIGHTSBRIDGE

Knightsbridge draws the hordes with quintessentially English department stores.

Harrods DEPARTMENT STORE
(Map p80; www.harrods.com; 87 Brompton Rd SW1; ⊖Knightsbridge) A pricy but fascinating theme park for fans of Britannia, Harrods is always crowded with slow tourists.

Harvey Nichols DEPARTMENT STORE
(Map p80; www.harveynichols.com; 109-125 Knightsbridge SW1; ⊖Knightsbridge) London's temple of high fashion, jewellery and perfume.

NOTTING HILL, BAYSWATER & PADDINGTON

Portobello Rd and the lanes surrounding it are the main focus, both for the famous market and the quirky boutiques and gift stores.

Travel Bookshop TRAVEL BOOKS
(Map p98; www.thetravelbookshop.com 13 Blenheim Cres W11; ⊖Ladbroke Grove) Hugh Grant's haunt in *Notting Hill* is a wealth of guidebooks and travel literature.

MARYLEBONE

Daunt Books TRAVEL BOOKS
(Map p84; 83 Marylebone High St W1, ⊖Baker St) An exquisitely beautiful store, with guidebooks, travel literature, fiction and reference books, all sorted by country.

KJ's Laundry WOMEN'S CLOTHES
(Map p84; www.kjslaundry.com; 74 Marylebone Lane W1; ⊖Bond St) Break out of the High St uniform in this women's boutique, which sources collections from up-and-coming designers.

Apartment C LINGERIE
(Map p84; www.apartment-c.com; 70 Marylebone High St W1; ⊖Baker St) 'Apartment C is about hanging out in your knickers, drinking gin out of a teacup, and reading *Last Tango in Paris* out loud.' Quite.

ISLINGTON

Curios, baubles and period pieces abound along Camden Passage. Upper and Cross Sts have an interesting mix of stores.

Palette London WOMEN'S CLOTHES
(Map p110; www.palette-london.com; 21 Canonbury Lane N1; ⊖Highbury & Islington) Fancy an original 1970s Halston dress or 1980s Chanel? Vintage meets modern and fashion meets collectables in this interesting store.

ROLL OUT THE BARROW

London has more than 350 markets selling everything from antiques and curios to flowers and fish. Some, such as Camden and Portobello Rd, are full of tourists, while others exist just for the locals.

Columbia Road Flower Market FLOWERS

(Map p88; Columbia Rd; 8am-2pm Sun; Old St) The best place for East End barrow boy banter ('We got flowers cheap enough for ya muvver-in-law's grave'). Unmissable.

Borough Market FOOD

(Map p74; www.boroughmarket.org.uk; 8 Southwark St SE1; 11am-5pm Thu, noon-6pm Fri, 8am-5pm Sat; London Bridge) A farmers' market sometimes called London's Larder, it has been here in some form since the 13th century. It's wonderfully atmospheric; you'll find everything from organic falafel to boars' heads.

Camden Market ALTERNATIVE

(Map p108; 10am-5.30pm; www.camdenmarkets.org; Camden Town) London's most famous market is actually a series of markets spread along Camden High St and Chalk Farm Rd. Despite a major fire in 2008, the **Camden Lock Market** and **Camden Stables Market** are still the places for punk fashion, cheap food, hippy chic and a whole lotta craziness.

Portobello Road Market CLOTHES, ANTIQUES

(Map p98; www.portobellomarket.org; Portobello Rd W10; 8am-6.30pm Mon-Sat, closes 1pm Thu; Ladbroke Grove) One of London's most famous (and crowded) street markets. New and vintage clothes are its main attraction, with antiques at its south end and food at the north.

Old Spitalfields Market ASSORTED

(Map p88; www.oldspitalfieldsmarket.com; 105a Commercial St E1; 10am-4pm Mon-Fri, 9am-5pm Sun; Liverpool St) It's housed in a Victorian warehouse, but the market's been here since 1638. Thursdays are devoted to antiques and vintage clothes, Fridays to fashion and art, but Sunday's the big day, with a bit of everything.

Laura J London WOMEN'S SHOES

(Map p110; www.laurajlondon.com; 114 Islington High St N1; Angel) A girlie boutique stocking shoes and accessories from a local designer.

CLERKENWELL & FARRINGDON

London Silver Vaults SILVER

(Map p102; www.thesilvervaults.com; 53-63 Chancery Lane WC2; Chancery Lane) Thirty subterranean shops forming the world's largest retail collection of silver under one roof.

EC One JEWELLERY

(www.econe.co.uk) Clerkenwell (Map p102; 41 Exmouth Market EC1; Farringdon); Notting Hill (Map p98; 56 Ledbury St W11; Notting Hill Gate) Husband-and-wife team Jos and Alison Skeates sell contemporary collections by British and international jewellery designers.

HOXTON, SHOREDITCH & SPITALFIELDS

Rough Trade ALTERNATIVE MUSIC

(www.roughtrade.com) East (Map p88; Dray Walk, 91 Brick Lane E1; Liverpool St); West (Map p98; 130 Talbot Rd W11; Ladbroke Grove) At the forefront of the punk explosion of the 1970s, it's the best place to come for anything of an indie or alternative bent.

Present MEN'S CLOTHES

(Map p88; www.present-london.com; 140 Shoreditch High St E1; Old St) Hip men's designer duds.

Start CLOTHES

(Map p88; www.start-london.com; 42-44 Rivington St EC2; Old St) Spilling over three stores on the same lane (womenswear, menswear and men's formal), your quest for designer jeans starts here.

Broadway Market FOOD
(www.broadwaymarket.co.uk; Broadway Mkt E8; 9am-5pm Sat; Bethnall Green) Graze from the organic food stalls, choose a cooked meal and then sample one of the 200 beers on offer at the neighbouring Dove Freehouse. It's a bit of a schlep from the tube. Head up Cambridge Heath Rd until you cross the canal. Turn left, following the canal and you'll see the market to the right after a few short blocks.

Brixton Market ASSORTED
(www.brixtonmarket.net; Electric Ave & Granville Arcade; 8am-6pm Mon-Sat, to 3pm Wed; Brixton) Immortalised in the Eddie Grant song, Electric Ave is a cosmopolitan treat that mixes everything from reggae music to exotic foods and spices.

Sunday (Up)market CLOTHES
(Map p88; www.sundayupmarket.co.uk; The Old Truman Brewery, Brick Lane E1; 10am-5pm Sun; Liverpool St) Handmade handbags, jewellery, new and vintage clothes and shoes, plus food if you need refuelling.

Brick Lane Market ASSORTED
(Map p88; www.visitbricklane.org; Brick Lane E1; 8am-2pm Sun; Liverpool St) An East End pearler, a sprawling bazaar featuring everything from fruit and veggies to paintings and bric-a-brac.

Camden Passage Market ANTIQUES
(Map p110; www.camdenpassageislington.co.uk; Camden Passage N1; 10am-2pm Wed, to 5pm Sat; Angel) Get your fill of antiques and trinkets galore. Not in Camden (despite the name).

Greenwich Market ASSORTED
(www.greenwichmarket.net; College Approach SE10; 10am-5.30pm Wed-Sun; DLR Cutty Sark) Rummage through antiques, vintage clothing and collectibles (Thursday and Friday), arts and crafts (Wednesday and weekends), or just chow down in the food section.

Petticoat Lane Market ASSORTED
(Map p88; Wentworth St & Middlesex St E1; 9am-2pm Sun-Fri; Aldgate) A cherished East End institution overflowing with cheap consumer durables and jumble-sale ware.

SHEPHERD'S BUSH

Westfield MALL
(http://uk.westfield.com/london; Ariel Way W12; Wood Lane) A new concept for London, this giant mall has 265 stores, restaurants and cinemas.

Information

Dangers & Annoyances

Considering its size and disparities in wealth, London is generally safe. That said, keep your wits about you and don't flash your cash unnecessarily. A contagion of youth-on-youth knife crime is cause for concern, so walk away if you sense trouble brewing and take care at night. When travelling by tube, choose a carriage with other people in it and avoid deserted suburban stations. Following reports of robberies and sexual attacks, shun unlicensed or unbooked minicabs.

Nearly every Londoner has a story about a wallet/phone/bag being nicked from under their noses – or arses, in the case of bags on floors in bars. Watch out for pickpockets on crowded tubes, night buses and streets. That friendly drunk who bumped into you may now be wandering off with your wallet.

When using ATMs, guard your PIN details carefully. Don't use one that looks like it's been tampered with as there have been incidents of card cloning.

Emergency

Police/fire/ambulance (999)

Rape & Sexual Abuse Support Centre (0808 802 9999)

Samaritans (08457 90 90 90)

Internet Access

You'll find free wireless access at many bars, cafes and hotels. Large tracts of London, notably Canary Wharf and the City, are covered by pay-as-you-go wireless services that you can sign up to in situ – and London's mayor is promising blanket wireless coverage of this sort for all of London by 2012. You'll usually pay less at the numerous internet cafes (about £2 per hour).

Internet Resources

BBC London (www.bbc.co.uk/london)

Evening Standard (www.thisislondon.co.uk)

Londonist (www.londonist.com)

Time Out (www.timeout.com/london)

Urban Path (www.urbanpath.com)

View London (www.viewlondon.co.uk)

Walk It (www.walkit.com) Enter your destination and get a walking map, time estimate and information on calories burnt and carbon dioxide saved.

Media

Two free newspapers bookend the working day – *Metro* in the morning and the *Evening Standard* in the evening – both available from tube stations. All of the national dailies have plenty of London coverage. Published every Wednesday, *Time Out* (£2.99) is the local listing guide par excellence.

Medical Services

To find a local doctor, pharmacy or hospital, consult the local telephone directory or call 0845 46 47.

Hospitals with 24-hour accident and emergency units include:

St Thomas' Hospital (Map p76; 020-7188 7188; Lambeth Palace Rd SE1; Waterloo)

University College Hospital (Map p86; 0845 155 5000; 235 Euston Rd WC1; Euston Sq)

Toilets

If you're caught short around London, public toilets can be hard to find. Only a handful of tube stations have them, but the bigger National Rail stations usually do (although they're often coin operated). If you can face five floors on an escalator, department stores are a good bet. In a busy pub, no one's going to notice you sneaking in to use the loo, but if you're spotted it would be polite to order a drink afterwards.

Tourist Information

For a list of all tourist offices in London and around Britain, see www.visitmap.info/tic.

Britain & London Visitor Centre (Map p62; www.visitbritain.com; 1 Regent St SW1; 9am-6.30pm Mon-Fri, 10am-4pm Sat & Sun; Piccadilly Circus) Books accommodation, theatre and transport tickets; *bureau de change;* international telephones; and internet terminals. Longer hours in summer.

City of London Information Centre (Map p68; 020-7332 1456; www.visitthecity.co.uk; 9.30am-5.30pm Mon-Sat, 10am-4pm Sun; St Paul's Churchyard EC4; St Paul's) Tourist information, fast-track tickets to City attractions and guided walks (adult/child £6/4).

Greenwich tourist office (0870 608 2000; www.visitgreenwich.org.uk; Discover Greenwich, 2 Cutty Sark Gardens SE10; 10am-5pm) Information plus guided tours.

Getting There & Away

London is the major gateway to England, so further transport information can be found in the main Transport chapter.

AIR For a list of London's airports see p846.

BUS Most long-distance coaches leave London from **Victoria Coach Station** (Map p80; 020-7824 0000; 164 Buckingham Palace Rd SW1; Victoria).

CAR See p848 for reservation numbers of the main car-hire firms, all of which have airport and various city locations.

TRAIN London's main-line terminals are all linked by the tube and each serve different destinations. Most stations have left-luggage facilities (around £4) and lockers, toilets (a 20p coin) with showers (around £3), newsstands and bookshops, and a range of eating and drinking outlets. St Pancras, Victoria and Liverpool St stations have shopping centres attached.

If you can't find your destination below, see the journey planner at www.nationalrail.co.uk.

Charing Cross (Map p62) Canterbury.

Euston (Map p86) Manchester, Liverpool, Carlisle, Glasgow.

King's Cross (Map p86) Cambridge, Hull, York, Newcastle, Scotland.

Liverpool St (Map p88) Stansted airport, Cambridge.

London Bridge (Map p74) Gatwick airport, Brighton.

Marylebone (Map p54) Birmingham.

Paddington (Map p54) Heathrow airport, Oxford, Bath, Bristol, Exeter, Plymouth, Cardiff.

St Pancras (Map p86) Gatwick and Luton airports, Brighton, Nottingham, Sheffield, Leicester, Leeds, Paris.

Victoria (Map p80) Gatwick airport, Brighton, Canterbury.

Waterloo (Map p76) Windsor, Winchester, Exeter, Plymouth.

Getting Around

To/From the Airports

GATWICK There are **National Rail** (www.nationalrail.co.uk) services from Gatwick's South Terminal to Victoria (from £12, 37 minutes), running every 15 minutes during the day and hourly through the night. Other trains head to St Pancras (from £12, 66 minutes), stopping at London Bridge, City Thameslink, Blackfriars and Farringdon. Fares are cheaper the earlier you book. If you're racing to make a flight, the **Gatwick Express** (☎0845 850 1530; www.gatwickexpress.com) departs Victoria every 15 minutes from 5am to 11.45pm (one way/return £16/26, 30 minutes, first/last train 3.30am/12.32am).

Prices start from £2, depending on when you book, for the **EasyBus** (www.easybus.co.uk) minibus service between Gatwick and Earls Court (£10, allow 1¼ hours, every 30 minutes from 4.25am to 1am). You'll be charged extra if you have more than one carry-on and one check-in bag.

Gatwick's taxi partner, **Checker Cars** (www.checkercars.com), has a counter in each terminal. Fares are quoted in advance (about £95 for the 65-minute ride to Central London).

HEATHROW The transport connections to Heathrow are excellent, and the journey to and from the city is painless. The cheapest option is the Underground. The Piccadilly line is accessible from every terminal (£4.50, one hour to central London, departing from Heathrow every five minutes from around 5am to 11.30pm). If it's your first time in London, it's a good chance to practice using the tube as it's at the beginning of the line and therefore not too crowded when you get on. If there are vast queues at the ticket office, use the automatic machines instead; some accept credit cards as well as cash. Keep your bags near you and expect a scramble to get off if you're hitting the city at rush hour (7am to 9am and 5pm to 7pm weekdays).

You might save some time on the considerably more expensive **Heathrow Express** (☎0845 600 1515; www.heathrowexpress.co.uk), an ultramodern train to Paddington station (one way/return £16.50/32, 15 minutes, every 15 minutes 5.12am to 11.42pm). You can purchase tickets on board (£5 extra), from self-service machines (cash and credit cards accepted) at both stations, or online.

There are taxi ranks for black cabs outside every terminal; a fare to the centre of London will cost between £50 and £70.

LONDON CITY The Docklands Light Railway connects London City Airport to the tube network, taking 22 minutes to reach Bank station (£4). A black taxi costs around £25 to/from central London.

LUTON There are regular **National Rail** (www.nationalrail.co.uk) services from St Pancras (£9.50, 29 to 39 minutes) to Luton Airport Parkway station, where a shuttle bus (£1) will get you to the airport within 10 minutes. EasyBus minibuses head from Victoria and Baker St to Luton (from £2, walk-on £10, allow 1½ hours, every 30 minutes). A taxi costs around £65.

STANSTED The **Stansted Express** (☎0845 850 0150; www.stanstedexpress.com) connects with Liverpool St station (one way/return £18/27, 46 minutes, every 15 minutes 6am to 12.30am).

EasyBus also has services between Stansted and Baker St (from £2, £10 walk-on, 1¼ hours, every 20 minutes). The **Airbus A6** (☎0870 580 8080; www.nationalexpress.com) links with Victoria Coach Station (£11, allow 1¾ hours, at least every 30 minutes).

A black cab to/from central London costs about £100.

Bike

The central city is flat and relatively compact and the traffic moves slowly – all of which make it surprisingly good for cyclists. It can get terribly congested though, so you'll need to keep your wits about you – and lock your bike (including both wheels) securely. At the time of writing, **TFL** (www.tfl.gov.uk) was about to launch a Cycle Hire Scheme, with 6000 cycles available to hire from self-service docking stations within Zone 1 (£1/6/15/35/50 for up to one/two/three/six/24hrs).

Car

The M25 ring road encompasses the 609 sq miles that is broadly regarded as Greater London. For motorists it's the first circle of hell; London was recently rated western Europe's second-most congested city (congratulations Brussels). Don't even think about driving within it: traffic is heavy, roadwork continuous, parking is either impossible or expensive, and wheel-clampers keep busy. If you drive into central London from 7am to 6pm on a weekday, you'll need to pay an £8 per day congestion charge (visit www.tfl.gov.uk for payment options) or face a hefty fine. If you're hiring a car to continue your trip, take the tube to Heathrow and pick it up from there.

Public Transport

Although locals love to complain about it, London's public transport is excellent, with tubes, trains, buses and boats conspiring to get you anywhere you need to go. **TFL** (www.tfl.gov.uk) is the glue that binds the network together. Its website has a handy journey planner and information on all services, including cabs. As a creature of leisure, you'll be able to avoid those bits that Londoners hate (especially the sardine squash of rush-hour tubes), so get yourself an Oyster card and make the most of it.

LONDON UNDERGROUND, DLR & OVERGROUND 'The tube', as it's universally known, extends its subterranean tentacles throughout London and into the surrounding counties, with services running every few minutes from roughly 5.30am to 12.30am (from 7am to 11.30pm Sunday).

LONDON'S OYSTER DIET

To get the most out of London, you need to be able to jump on and off public transport like a local, not scramble to buy a ticket at hefty rates each time. The best and cheapest way to do this is with an Oyster card, a reusable smartcard on which you can load either a season ticket (weekly/monthly £26/100) or prepaid credit. The card itself is £3, which is fully refundable when you leave.

London is divided into concentric transport zones, although almost all of the places covered in this book are in Zones 1 and 2. The season tickets quoted above will give you unlimited transport on tubes, buses and rail services within these zones. All you need to do is touch your card to the yellow sensors on the station turnstiles or at the front of the bus.

If you opt for pay as you go, the fare will be deducted from the credit on your card at a much lower rate than if you were buying a one-off paper ticket. An oyster bus trip costs £1.20 as opposed to £2, while a Zone 1 tube journey is £1.80 as opposed to £4. Even better, in any single day your fares will be capped at the equivalent of the Oyster day-pass rate for the zones you've travelled in (Zones 1-2 peak/off-peak £7.20/5.60).

Assuming you avoid peak hours (6.30am to 9.30am and 4pm to 7pm), this ready reckoner gives the cheapest options for your length of stay:

» 1-4 days: prepay
» 5-24 days: weeklies topped up with prepay for any remaining days
» 25-31 days: monthly

It's easy to use. Tickets (or Oyster card top-ups) can be purchased from counters or machines at the entrance to each station using either cash or credit card. They're then inserted into the slot on the turnstiles (or you touch your Oyster card on the yellow reader), and the barrier opens. Once you're through you can jump on and off different lines as often as you need to get to your destination.

Also included within the network are the driverless Docklands Light Railway (DLR), and the train lines shown on tube maps as 'Overground'. The DLR links the City to Docklands, Greenwich and London City Airport. It's very Jetsons-like, especially when it hurtles between the skyscrapers of Canary Wharf; try to get the front row seat.

The tube map itself is an acclaimed graphic design work, using coloured lines to show how the 14 different routes intersect. However, it's not remotely to scale. The distances between stations become greater the further from central London you travel, while Leicester Sq and Covent Garden stations are only 250m apart.

BUS Travelling round London by double-decker bus is an enjoyable way to get a feel for the city, but it's usually slower than the tube. Heritage 'Routemaster' buses with conductors operate on route 9 (from Aldwych to Royal Albert Hall) and 15 (between Trafalgar Sq and Tower Hill); these are the only buses without wheelchair access.

Buses run regularly during the day, while less frequent night buses (prefixed with the letter 'N') wheel into action when the tube stops. Single-journey bus tickets (valid for two hours) cost £2 (£1.20 on Oyster, capped at £3.90 per day); a weekly pass is £17. Children ride for free. At stops with yellow signs, you have to buy your ticket from the automatic machine (or use an Oyster) *before* boarding. Buses stop on request, so clearly signal the driver with an outstretched arm.

TRAIN Particularly south of the river, where tube lines are in short supply, the various rail companies are an important part of the public transport picture. Most stations are now fitted with Oyster readers and accept TFL travelcards. If you travel outside your zone you'll need to have enough prepay credit on your Oyster card to cover the additional charge. As not all stations have turnstiles, it's important to remember to tap-in and tap-out at the Oyster reader at the station or your card will register an unfinished journey and you're likely to be charged extra. You can still buy a paper ticket from machines or counters at train stations.

BOAT The myriad boats that ply the Thames are a great way to travel, avoiding traffic jams while affording great views. Passengers with daily, weekly or monthly travelcards (including on Oyster) get a third off all fares.

Thames Clippers (www.thamesclippers.com) runs regular commuter services between Embankment, Waterloo, Blackfriars, Bankside, London Bridge, Tower, Canary Wharf, Greenwich, North Greenwich and Woolwich piers (adult/child £5.30/2.65) from 7am to midnight (from 9.30am weekends).

Leisure services include the Tate-to-Tate boat (see p73) and Westminster–Greenwich services (p87). For boats to Kew Gardens and Hampton Court Palace, see p91.

London Waterbus Company (020-7482 2660; www.londonwaterbus.com, single/return £6.70/9.70) and **Jason's Trip** (www.jasons.co.uk; opposite 42 Blomfield Rd W9; single/return £7.50/8.50) both run canal boat journeys between Camden Lock and Little Venice; see websites for times. London has some 40 miles of inner-city canals, mostly built in the 19th century.

Taxi

London's famous black cabs are available for hire when the yellow light above the windscreen is lit. To get an all-London licence, cabbies must do 'The Knowledge', which tests them on up to 25,000 streets within a 6-mile radius of Charing Cross and all points of interest from hotels to churches. Fares are metered, with flag fall of £2.20 and the additional rate dependent on time of day, distance travelled and taxi speed. A one-mile trip will cost between £4.60 and £8.60. To order a black cab by phone, try **Dial-a-Cab** (020-7253 5000; www.dialacab.co.uk); you must pay by credit card and will be charged a premium.

Licensed minicabs operate via agencies (most busy areas have a walk-in office with drivers waiting). They're a cheaper alternative to black cabs and quote trip fares in advance. The cars are recognisable by the symbol displayed in the window. To find a local minicab firm, visit www.tfl.gov.uk.

There have been many reports of sexual assault and theft by unlicensed minicab drivers. Only use drivers from proper agencies; licensed minicabs aren't allowed to tout for business or pick you up off the street without a booking, so avoid the shady characters who hang around outside nightclubs or bars.

Canterbury & the Southeast

Includes »

Best Places to Eat

- » Deeson's (p136)
- » Allotment (p148)
- » Eddie Gilbert's (p143)
- » Terre à Terre (p167)
- » Town House (p172)

Best Places to Stay

- » Abode Canterbury (p135)
- » Jeake's House (p152)
- » Wallett's Court (p148)
- » Neo Hotel (p165)
- » Bell Hotel (p145)

Why Go?

Rolling chalk downs, venerable Victorian resorts, fields of hops and grapes sweetening in the sun – welcome to England's affluent southeast, four soothing counties' worth of country houses, fairytale castles and Cinque Ports, and with the country's finest food and drink to boot.

That fruit-ripening sun shines brightest and longest on the southeast, gently warming a string of seaside towns wedged between formidable chalk cliffs. There's something for everyone here, from the understated charm of Whitstable, to the bohemian spirit of hedonistic Brighton, to more genteel Eastbourne.

But the southeast is also pockmarked with less idyllic reminders of darker days. From the 1066 battlefield to Dover Castle's secret war tunnels to the scattered Roman ruins, the region's position as the front line against Continental invaders has left a wealth of turbulent history.

England's spiritual heart is Canterbury. Its cathedral and ancient Unesco-listed attractions are essential viewing for any camera-toting, 21st-century pilgrim.

When to Go

May is a good time to get creative at Great Britain's second-largest arts festival, held in Brighton. During June don your top hat and britches to revel in frilly Victoriana at Dickens festivals in Broadstairs and Rochester. Any time between May and October is ideal for a hike along the South Downs Way, running the length of England's newest national park. And in November head for Lewes for one of the most spectacular Guy Fawkes Night celebrations in all of England.

Activities

The southeast of England may be Britain's most densely populated corner, but there are still plenty of off-the-beaten-track walking and cycling routes to enjoy. Below are some of the highlights, but you'll find more information throughout the chapter.

CYCLING

Finding quiet roads for cycle touring takes a little extra perseverance in England's southeast, but efforts are richly rewarded. Long-distance routes on the **National Cycle Network** (NCN; www.sustrans.org.uk):

Downs & Weald Cycle Route (110 miles; NCN Routes 2, 20 & 21) London to Brighton and on to Hastings.

Garden of England Cycle Route (165 miles; NCN Routes 1, 2) London to Dover and then Hastings.

You'll also find less-demanding routes on the NCN website. Meanwhile there are plenty of uppers and downers to challenge mountain bikers on walking trails, such as the South Downs Way National Trail (100 miles), which takes hard nuts two days but mere mortals around four.

WALKING

Two long-distance trails meander steadily westward through the region, but there are plenty of shorter ambles to fit your schedule, stamina and scenery wish list.

South Downs Way National Trail (100 miles) This trail through England's newest national park is a beautiful rollercoaster walk along prehistoric drove ways between the ancient capital, Winchester, and the seaside resort of Eastbourne.

North Downs Way (153 miles) This popular walk begins near Farnham in Surrey but one of its most beautiful sections runs from near Ashford to Dover in Kent; there's also a loop that takes in Canterbury near its end.

Both long-distance routes have sections ideal for shorter walks. History buffs will revel in the 1066 Country Walk which connects with the South Downs Way. The Devil's Punchbowl (p177) offers breathtaking views, sloping grasslands and romantic wooded areas.

Information

Kent Attractions (www.kentattractions.co.uk)

Tourism South East (www.visitsoutheastengland.com) The official website for south and southeast England.

Visit Kent (www.visitkent.co.uk)

Visit Surrey (www.visitsurrey.com)

Visit Sussex (www.visitsussex.org)

Getting There & Around

The southeast is easily explored by train or bus and many attractions can be visited in a day-trip from London. Contact the **National Traveline** (☎0871 200 2233; www.travelinesoutheast.org.uk) for comprehensive information on public transport in the region.

Bus

Explorer tickets (adult/child £6.50/4.50) provide day-long unlimited travel on most buses throughout the region; you can buy them at bus stations or on your first bus.

Train

You can secure 33% discounts on most rail fares in the southeast by purchasing a **Network Railcard** (www.railcard.co.uk/network; per yr £25). Children under 15 can save 60%, but a minimum fare of £1 applies.

KENT

Kent isn't described as the garden of England for nothing. Inside its sea-lined borders you'll find a clipped landscape of gentle hills, fertile farmland, cultivated country estates and fruitful orchards. It also serves as the booze garden of England, producing the world-renowned Kent hops, some of the country's finest ales and award-winning wines from its numerous vineyards. At its heart is spellbinding Canterbury crowned by its enthralling cathedral.

Here, too, are beautiful coastal stretches dotted with beach towns and villages, from old-fashioned Broadstairs to gentrified Whitstable, to the aesthetically challenged port town of Dover, close enough to France to smell the garlic or go on a day-trip to taste it.

Canterbury

POP 43,432

Canterbury tops the charts when it comes to English cathedral cities and is one of southern England's top attractions. The World Heritage–listed cathedral that dominates its centre is considered by many to be one of Europe's finest, and the town's narrow medieval alleyways, riverside gardens and ancient city walls are a joy to explore. But Canterbury isn't just a showpiece to times past; it's a spirited place with an

Canterbury & the Southeast Highlights

1. Shopping, tanning and partying in **Brighton & Hove** (p162), bustling hedonist capital of the southeast
2. Making a pilgrimage to **Canterbury Cathedral** (p132), one of England's most important religious sites
3. Wandering the cobbled lanes of **Rye** (p152), one of England's prettiest towns

4 Being transported back to the age of chivalry at the moated marvel that is **Leeds Castle** (p151)

5 Scrambling up **Beachy Head** (p158), a spectacular headland in snow-white chalk

6 Exploring the atmospheric WWII tunnels beneath sprawling **Dover Castle** (p146)

7 Packing your thirst for a **vineyard or brewery tour** (p149)

8 Shaking out your beach towel for some seaside fun on the **Isle of Thanet** (p142)

energetic student population and a wide choice of contemporary bars, restaurants and arts. But book ahead for the best hotels and eateries: pilgrims may no longer flock here in their thousands but tourists certainly do.

The old city centre is enclosed by a bulky medieval city wall that makes a wonderful walk. The Unesco World Heritage Site encompasses the cathedral, St Augustine's Abbey and St Martin's Church. Much of the centre is pedestrianised, but there is parking inside the wall.

History

Canterbury's past is as rich as it comes. From AD 200 there was a Roman town here, which later became the capital of the Saxon kingdom of Kent. When St Augustine arrived in England in 597 to carry the Christian message to the pagan hordes, he chose Canterbury as his *cathedra* (primary seat) and set about building an abbey on the outskirts of town. Following the martyrdom of Thomas Becket, Canterbury became northern Europe's most important centre of pilgrimage, which in turn led to Geoffrey Chaucer's *The Canterbury Tales,* one of the most outstanding poetic works in English literature.

Blasphemous murders and rampant tourism thrown aside, the city of Canterbury still remains the primary seat for the Church of England.

Sights

Canterbury Cathedral CATHEDRAL

(www.canterbury-cathedral.org; adult/concession £8/7; 9am-5pm Mon-Sat, 12.30pm-2.30pm Sun) The Church of England could not have a more imposing mother church than this extraordinary early Gothic cathedral, the centrepiece of the city's World Heritage Site and repository of more than 1400 years of Christian history.

Canterbury

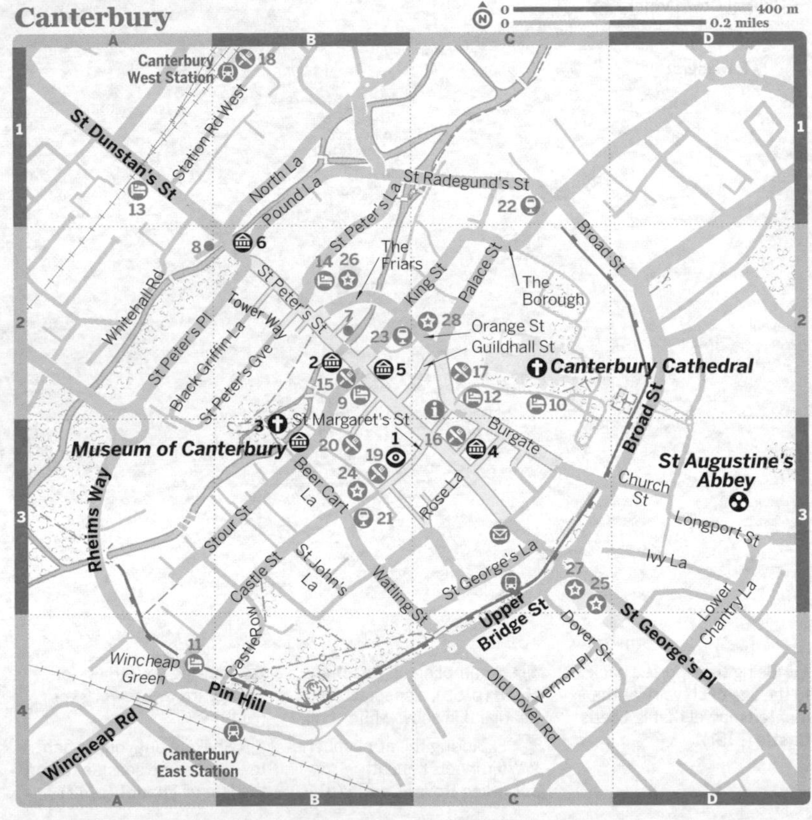

It's an overwhelming edifice filled with enthralling stories, striking architecture and a very real and enduring sense of spirituality, although visitors can't help but pick up on the ominous undertones of violence and bloodshed that whisper from its walls.

This ancient structure is packed with monuments commemorating the nation's battles. Also here is the grave and heraldic tunic of one of the nation's most famous warmongers, Edward the Black Prince (1330–76). The spot in the northwest transept where Archbishop Thomas Becket met his grisly end has been drawing pilgrims for more than 800 years and is marked by a flickering candle and striking modern altar.

The doorway to the crypt is beside the altar. This cavernous space is the cathedral's highlight, an entrancing 11th-century survivor from the cathedral's last devastating fire in 1174, which destroyed the rest of the building. Look for original carvings among the forest of pillars.

The wealth of detail in the cathedral is immense and unrelenting, so it's well worth joining a one-hour **tour** (adult/child £5/3; ⏲10.30am, noon & 2.30pm Mon-Fri, 10.30am, noon & 1.30pm Sat Easter-Oct), or you can take a 40-minute self-guided **audiotour** (adult/concessions £3.50/2.50).

Museum of Canterbury MUSEUM

(www.canterbury-museums.co.uk; Stour St; adult/child £3.60/2.30; ⏲11am-4pm Mon-Sat year-round, also 1.30-4pm Sun Jun-Sep). A fine 14th-century building, once the Poor Priests' Hospital, now houses the city's absorbing museum, which has a jumble of exhibits from pre-Roman times to the assassination of Becket, Joseph Conrad to locally born celebs. The kids' room is excellent, with a memorable glimpse of real medieval poo among other fun activities. There's also a fun **Rupert Bear Museum** (Rupert's creator, Mary Tourtel, was born in Canterbury) and a gallery celebrating that other children's favourite of old, Bagpuss. The museum will also house the Royal Museum & Art Gallery's collections until restoration work is completed there.

St Augustine's Abbey ABBEY RUINS

(EH; adult/child £4.50/2.30; ⏲10am-6pm Jul & Aug, to 5pm Apr-Jun) An integral but often overlooked part of the Canterbury World Heritage Site, St Augustine's Abbey was founded in AD 597, marking the rebirth of Christianity in southern England. Later requisitioned as a royal palace, it was to fall into disrepair and now only stumpy foundations remain. A small museum and a worthwhile audiotour (free) do their best

Canterbury

Top Sights

Canterbury Cathedral C2
Museum of Canterbury B3
St Augustine's Abbey D3

Sights

1 Canterbury Tales B3
2 Eastbridge Hospital B2
3 Greyfriars Chapel B3
Main Library .... (see 5)
4 Roman Museum C3
5 Royal Museum & Art Gallery B2
6 West Gate Towers B2

Activities, Courses & Tours

7 Canterbury Historic River Tours B2
8 Canterbury River Navigation Company A2
Ghost Tours .... (see 24)

Sleeping

9 Abode Canterbury B2
10 Canterbury Cathedral Lodge C2
11 Castle House A4
12 Cathedral Gate Hotel C2
13 House of Agnes A1
14 White House B2

Eating

15 Boho B2
16 Café Mauresque C3
17 Deeson's C2
18 Goods Shed B1
19 Tiny Tim's Tearoom B3
20 Veg Box Cafe B3

Drinking

21 Loft B3
22 Parrot C1
23 Thomas Beckett B2

Entertainment

24 Alberry's Wine Bar B3
25 Chill Nightclub C3
26 New Marlowe Theatre B2
27 Odeon Cinema C3
28 Orange St Music Club C2

CANTERBURY ATTRACTIONS PASSPORT

The **Canterbury Attractions Passport** (adult/child £19/15.25) gives entry to the cathedral, St Augustine's Abbey, the Canterbury Tales and any one of the city's museums. It's available from the tourist office.

to underline the site's importance and put flesh back on its now humble bones.

FREE **St Martin's Church** CHURCH
(North Holmes Rd; admission free; 11am-4pm Tue, Thu & Sat Apr-Sep) This stumpy little building is thought to be England's oldest parish church in continuous use, and where Queen Bertha (the wife of the Saxon King Ethelbert) welcomed Augustine upon his arrival in the 6th century. The original Saxon church has been swallowed by a medieval refurbishment, but it's still worth the 900m walk east of the abbey.

Eastbridge Hospital HISTORICAL ALMSHOUSE
(www.eastbridgehospital.org.uk; 25 High St; adult/child £1/50p; 10am-5pm Mon-Sat) A 'place of hospitality' for pilgrims, soldiers and the elderly since 1180, the Hospital of St Thomas the Martyr, **Eastbridge** is worth a visit for the Romanesque undercroft and historic chapel. The 16th-century almshouses, still in use today, sit astride Britain's oldest road bridge dating back over 800 years.

Roman Museum MUSEUM
(Butchery Lane; adult/child £3.10/2.10; 10am-4pm Mon-Sat year-round, also 1.30-4pm Sun Jun-Sep) A fascinating subterranean archaeological site forms the basis of this museum where you can walk around reconstructed rooms, including a kitchen and a market place, and view Roman mosaic floors. At the time of writing there were plans afoot to close this piece of the city's heritage for good in 2011.

West Gate Towers MUSEUM
(St Peter's St; adult/concession £1.30/80p; 11am-12.30pm & 1.30-3.30pm Sat) The city's only remaining medieval gateway – a brawny 14th-century bulk through which traffic still passes – is home to a small museum with superb rooftop views. As with the Roman Museum, this too was to become a victim of cuts in 2011.

FREE **Greyfriars Chapel** CHAPEL
(2-4pm Mon-Sat Easter-Sep) In serene riverside gardens behind the Eastbridge Hospital you'll find Greyfriars Chapel, the first English monastery built by Franciscan monks in 1267. The grounds are a tranquil spot to shake out the picnic blanket.

Canterbury Tales CHAUCER ATTRACTION
(www.canterburytales.org.uk; St Margaret's St; adult/child £7.75/5.75; 10am-5pm Mar-Oct) A three-dimensional interpretation of Chaucer's classic tales through jerky animatronics and audioguides, the ambitious Canterbury Tales is certainly entertaining but could never do full justice to Chaucer's tales. It's a lively and fun introduction for the young or uninitiated, however.

FREE **Royal Museum & Art Gallery** MUSEUM
(High St; 10am-5pm Mon-Sat) The building's mock-Tudor facade is a splendid display of Victorian foppery, with intricate carving and big wooden gables. The interior houses mostly ho-hum art and military memorabilia as well as the city's **main library**, but the whole caboodle was closed for lengthy renovation at the time of publication.

Tours

Canterbury Historic River Tours RIVER TOURS
(07790-534744; www.canterburyrivertours.co.uk; adult/child £7.50/5; 10am-5pm Mar-Oct) Knowledgeable guides double as energetic oarsmen on these fascinating minicruises that leave from behind the Old Weaver's House on St Peter's St.

Canterbury River Navigation Company RIVER TOURS
(07816-760869; www.crnc.co.uk; Westgate Gardens; adult/child £8/4; Apr-Oct) Relaxing punt trips on the River Stour.

Canterbury Walks WALKING TOURS
(01227-459779; www.canterbury-walks.co.uk; adult/under 12yr/senior & student £6/5.50/4.25; 11am daily Feb-Oct, also 2pm Jul-Sep) Chaperoned walking tours leave from the tourist office.

Ghost Tours WALKING TOURS
(0845-5190267; www.canterburyghosttour.com; adult/child £8/6; 8pm Fri & Sat) Award-winning ghost hunts departing from outside Alberry's Wine Bar (p137) on St Margaret's St. Only groups need book.

KEEP YOUR ENEMIES CLOSE...

Not one to shy away from nepotism, in 1162 King Henry II appointed his good mate Thomas Becket to the highest clerical office in the land, figuring it would be easier to force the increasingly vocal religious lobby to toe the line if he was pally with the archbishop. Unfortunately for Henry, he had underestimated how seriously Thomas would take the job, and the archbishop soon began disagreeing with almost everything the king said or did. By 1170 Henry had become exasperated with his former favourite and, after a few months of sulking, 'suggested' to four of his knights that Thomas was too much to bear. The dirty deed was done on 29 December. Becket's martyrdom – and canonisation in double-quick time (1173) – catapulted Canterbury Cathedral to the top of the premier league of northern European pilgrimage sites. Mindful of the growing criticism at his role in Becket's murder, Henry arrived here in 1174 for a dramatic *mea culpa*, and after allowing himself to be whipped and scolded was granted absolution.

Festivals & Events

Myriad musicians, comedians, theatre groups and other artists from around the world come to the party for two weeks in mid-October, during the **Canterbury Festival** (01227 787787; www.canterburyfestival.co.uk).

Sleeping

TOP CHOICE **Abode Canterbury** HOTEL ££
(01227-766266; www.abodehotels.co.uk; 30-33 High St; s/d from £89/109;) The only boutique hotel in town, the 72 rooms here are graded from 'comfortable' to 'fabulous' and for the most part they live up to their names. They come with little features such as handmade beds, cashmere throws, velour bathrobes, beautiful modern bathrooms and little tuck boxes of locally produced snacks. There's a splendid champagne bar, restaurant and tavern here, too.

House of Agnes HOTEL ££
(01227-472185; www.houseofagnes.co.uk; 71 St Dunstan's St; r from £83; @) Situated near the West Gate, this 13th-century beamed inn, mentioned in Dickens' *David Copperfield*, has eight themed rooms bearing such names as 'Marrakesh' (Moorish), 'Venice' (inevitable carnival masks), 'Boston' (light and airy) and 'Canterbury', the last in the list arguably the pick of the bunch, packed with antiques and heavy fabrics.

Cathedral Gate Hotel HOTEL ££
(01227-464381; www.cathgate.co.uk; 36 Burgate; s/d £70/105, without bathroom £44/75) This often-photographed 15th-century hotel adjoins the spectacular cathedral gate, which it predates – a fact that becomes evident upon exploring its labyrinthine passageways, where few rooms lack an angled floor, low door or wonky wall. Rooms are simple but worth it for the fantastic position.

White House B&B ££
(01227-761836; www.whitehousecanterbury.co.uk; 6 St Peter's Lane; s/d from £60/80;) This elegant white Regency town house, supposedly once home to Queen Victoria's head coachman, has a friendly welcome, seven period rooms with modern touches and a grand guest lounge. Some of the rooms would have cathedral views were it not for the New Marlowe Theatre under construction in between.

Castle House B&B ££
(01227 761897; www.castlehousehotel.co.uk; 28 Castle St; s/d from £70/95; P@) This historic guesthouse sits opposite the ruins of Canterbury's Norman castle, and incorporates part of the old city walls. The tasteful, high-ceilinged rooms have great views and bags of space and there's a secluded garden out back.

Magnolia House B&B ££
(01227-765121; www.magnoliahousecanterbury.co.uk; 36 St Dunstan's Tce; s/d from £55/95; P@) A gorgeous Georgian guesthouse, complete with smart if slightly cramped rooms, lovely gardens and big breakfasts. Head up St Dunstan's St from the West Gate for around 400m until you reach a roundabout. Turn left and St Dunstan's Terrace is the second turn on the left.

Kipp's Independent Hostel HOSTEL £
(01227-786121; www.kipps-hostel.com; 40 Nunnery Fields; dm/s/d £16/22/36; @) This red-brick town house is popular for its laid-back, homely atmosphere with friendly hosts and long-term residents, lots of communal areas, clean though cramped dorms, bike hire and garden. It's just south of the centre.

THE CANTERBURY TALES

If English literature has a father figure, then it must be Geoffrey Chaucer (1342/3–1400). Chaucer was the first English writer to introduce characters – rather than 'types' – into fiction, and he did so to greatest effect in his most popular work, *The Canterbury Tales*.

Written in the now hard-to-decipher Middle English of the day between 1387 and his death, Chaucer's *Tales* is an unfinished series of 24 vivid stories as told by a party of pilgrims on their journey from London to Canterbury and back. Chaucer successfully created the illusion that the pilgrims, not Chaucer (though he appears in the tales as himself), are telling the stories, which allowed him unprecedented freedom as an author. *The Canterbury Tales* remains one of the pillars of the literary canon, but more than that it's a collection of rollicking good yarns of adultery, debauchery, crime and edgy romance, and filled with Chaucer's witty observations of human nature.

Canterbury Cathedral Lodge HOTEL ££
(☎01227-865350; www.canterburycathedrallodge.org; Canterbury Cathedral precincts; r from £65; @📶) Located opposite the cathedral within the precinct itself, the position of this modern, circular lodge is pretty special. Modern, recently refurbished rooms – done out in white and blond wood – have excellent facilities but what really makes this place are the views and the unlimited access to the cathedral for guests. Often full, so book ahead.

Yew Tree Park CAMPSITE £
(☎01227-700306; www.yewtreepark.com; Stone St, Petham; tent & 2 adults £12.20-17.20; ⏰Mar-Sep; P@📶🏊) Set in gentle rolling countryside 5 miles southeast of the city, this lovely family-run campsite has plenty of soft grass to pitch a tent on and a heated swimming pool. Call for directions and transport information.

Canterbury YHA HOSTEL £
(☎0845 371 9010; www.yha.org.uk; 54 New Dover Rd; dm from £15.95; P@) This grand Victorian Gothic-style villa is a little way out of town, but it's spacious and organised, with a garden and cheaper, prepared-tent accommodation. It's 1¼ miles southeast of the centre, and open year-round by advanced booking. Wheelchair access available.

Eating

TOP CHOICE Deeson's BRITISH ££
(☎01227-767854; 25-27 Sun St; mains £4.50-16; ⏰lunch & dinner) Put the words 'local', 'seasonal' and 'tasty' into a make-believe restaurant search engine and this superb new British eatery would magically pop up first under Canterbury. Kentish fruit and veg, local award-winning wines, beers and ciders, fish from Kent's coastal waters and the odd ingredient from the proprietor's very own allotment, all served in a straightforward, contemporary setting a Kentish apple's throw from the Cathedral gates. What more do you want? Bookings recommended.

Boho INTERNATIONAL £
(43 St Peter's St; snacks £3-7; ⏰9am-6pm Mon-Sat) In a prime spot on the main drag, next to the Eastbridge Hospital, this hip eatery is extraordinarily popular and you'd be lucky to get a table on busy shopping days. The coolest sounds on CD lilt through the chic retro dining space as chilled diners chow down on humungous burgers, full-Monte breakfasts and imaginative, owner-cooked international mains. Boho doesn't do bookings so be prepared to queue.

Veg Box Cafe VEGETARIAN CAFE £
(1 Jewry Lane; soups £4.95, specials £6.95; ⏰9am-5pm Mon-Sat) Perched above Canterbury's top veggie food store, this welcoming, laid-back spot uses only the freshest, locally sourced organic ingredients in its dishes; served at stocky timber tables under red paper lanterns.

Tiny Tim's Tearoom TEAROOM ££
(☎01227-450793; 34 St Margaret's St; mains £7-15; ⏰9.30am-5pm Tue-Sat, 10.30am-4pm Sun) Hungry shoppers queue up outside to bag a table at this swish 1930s English tearoom. Once inside they feast on big breakfasts full of Kentish ingredients or tiers of cakes, crumpets, cucumber sandwiches and scones with clotted cream, all washed down with Canterbury's widest selection of teas. There's a sunny courtyard garden outside and chutneys, breads and local Kentish wines for sale.

Goods Shed MARKET RESTAURANT ££
(☎01227-459153; Station Rd West; mains £11-19; ⏰market 9am-7pm Tue-Sat, to 4pm Sun, restaurant breakfast, lunch & dinner Tue-Sat, lunch Sun)

Farmers market, food hall and fabulous restaurant all rolled into one, this converted station warehouse by the railway is a hit with everyone from self-caterers to sit-down gourmets. The chunky wooden tables sit slightly above the market hubbub but in full view of its appetite-whetting stalls, and country-style daily specials exploit the freshest farm goodies the Garden of England has to offer.

Cafe Mauresque NORTH AFRICAN ££
(☎01227-464300; www.cafemauresque.com; 8 Butchery Lane; mains £13-18; ⊙lunch & dinner) Fun little North African and Spanish spot with a plain cafe upstairs as well as a noisy basement swathed in exotic fabric, serving up rich tagines, couscous, paella and tapas. There are hubbly bubbly hookah pipes to finish off your meal.

Drinking

Parrot PUB
(1-9 Church Lane) Built in 1370 on Roman foundations, Canterbury's oldest boozer has a snug, beam-rich pub downstairs and a much-lauded dining room upstairs under yet more aging oak. Needless to say many a local microbrewed ale is pulled in both.

Thomas Beckett PUB
(21 Best Lane) A classic English pub with a garden's worth of hops hanging from its timber frame, several quality ales to sample and a traditional decor of copper pots, comfy seating and a fireplace to cosy up to on winter nights. It also serves decent pub grub.

Loft BAR
(516 St Margaret's St) Miles away from Canterbury's quaint alehouses, this slick bar plays chilled electronic beats in a retro-edged setting with one extremely long couch, a black granite bar and DJs spinning house at the weekend. It draws a youthful crowd and serves a medley of multicoloured cocktails.

☆ Entertainment

Alberry's Wine Bar NIGHTCLUB
(St Margaret's St) Every night is different at this after-hours music bar, which puts on everything from smooth live jazz to DJ-led drum and bass to commercial pop. It's a two-level place where you can relax over a French Kiss (cocktail or otherwise) above, before partying in the basement bar below.

Chill Nightclub NIGHTCLUB
(www.chill-nightclub.com; St George's Pl, New Dover Rd) Canterbury's most visible nightclub is a large, fun, cheesy place with a popular student night on Mondays and house anthems and old skool at the weekends.

Orange St Music Club MUSIC VENUE
(www.orangestreetmusic.com; 15 Orange St) This bohemian music and cultural venue in a 19th-century hall puts on a medley of jazz, salsa, folk, DJ competitions, comedy and even poetry and film screenings.

Odeon Cinema CINEMA
(☎0871-224 4007; cnr Upper Bridge St & St George's Pl) Canterbury's principal picture house shows mostly mainstream movies. There are two screens and things get busy here on weekend evenings.

Cinema 3 CINEMA
(☎01227-769075; University of Kent) Part of the Gulbenkian Theatre complex, this cinema shows a mix of mainstream film, arty flics and old classics. There's a pretty good cafe here too.

New Marlowe Theatre THEATRE
(☎01227-787787; www.newmarlowetheatre.org.uk; The Friars) The old Marlowe Theatre was bulldozed in 2009 and a spanking new, state-of-the-art building was being bolted together at the time of writing. When it reopens in 2011, the New Marlowe is set to become the southeast's premier venue for performing arts, attracting top companies and productions.

Gulbenkian Theatre THEATRE
(☎01227-769075; www.kent.ac.uk/gulbenkian; University of Kent) Out on the university campus, this large long-time venue puts on plenty of contemporary plays, modern dance and great live music.

Information

Canterbury Health Centre (☎01227-597000; 26 Old Dover Rd) For general medical consultations.

Dotcafe (19-21 St Dunstan's St; per hr £3; ⊙9am-9pm Mon-Sat, 10am-6pm Sun) Large cyber cafe near the Canterbury West train station.

Kent & Canterbury Hospital (☎01227-766877; Etherbert Rd) Has a minor injuries emergency unit and is a mile from the centre.

Post office (19 St George's St, 1st fl, WH Smiths; ⊙9am-5.30pm Mon-Sat)

Tourist office (01227-378100; www.canterbury.co.uk; 12 Sun St; 9.30am-5pm Mon-Sat, 9.30am-4.30pm Sun) Situated opposite the Cathedral gate; staff can help book accommodation, excursions and theatre tickets.

 Getting There & Away

The city's bus station is just within the city walls on St George's Lane. There are two train stations: Canterbury East for London Victoria; and Canterbury West for London's Charing Cross and St Pancras stations.

Bus

Canterbury connections:

London Victoria National Express, £13.40, two hours, hourly

Dover National Express, 40 minutes, hourly

Margate 48 minutes, three per hour

Ramsgate 46 minutes, twice hourly

Sandwich 37 minutes, three hourly

Whitstable 35 minutes, every 15 minutes)

Train

Canterbury connections:

London St Pancras High-speed service; £27.80, one hour, hourly

London Victoria/Charing Cross £23.40, one hour 40 minutes, two to three hourly

Dover Priory £6.50, 25 minutes, every 30 minutes

 Getting Around

Canterbury's centre is mostly pedestrianised. Car parks are dotted along and just within the walls, but due to Canterbury's traffic issues day-trippers may prefer to use one of the three Park & Ride sites, which cost £2.50 per day and are connected to the centre by bus every eight minutes (7am to 7.30pm Monday to Saturday, 10am to 6pm Sunday). Further sites are planned. **Downland Cycles** (01227-479643; www.downlandcycles.co.uk) rents bikes from the Malthouse on St Stephen's Rd. Bikes cost £15 per day with helmet.

Taxi companies:

Cabwise (01227-712929).

Canterbury Cars (01227-453333)

Around Canterbury

HOWLETT'S WILD ANIMAL PARK

This 28-hectare **wildlife park** (www.totallywild.net; Bekesbourne; adult/child £16.95/12.95; 10am-6pm Apr-Oct) is one England's best and a superb day out with tots in tow. The animals here live in an environment as close to their natural habitat as possible but are still easily spotted amid the greenery. Tigers, lemurs, African elephants, monkeys, giant anteaters and a very rare snow leopard called Marta are the highlights of the pleasant stroll around the enclosures, and when boredom strikes, there's a rope centre and face painting. The rather hefty admission goes towards funding projects to reintroduce rare and endangered animals to their natural habitat.

The park is 4 miles east of Canterbury. By car, take the A257 and turn right at the sign for Bekesbourne, then follow the signs. Several regular buses run from Canterbury bus station to Littlebourne, from where it's about a mile's walk.

CHILHAM

Five miles southwest of Canterbury on the A252, compact little Chilham is one of the best examples of a medieval village you'll see anywhere in England. Built in typical feudal fashion around a square beside the 12th-century castle, the village consists of a 13th-century church and a cluster of Tudor and Jacobean timber-framed houses.

The town makes a great destination for a lovely day's walk from Canterbury via the North Downs Way (see p129). Alternatively, hourly trains run from Canterbury (nine minutes). The centre is a half-mile walk from the station.

Rochester

POP 27,000

Romans, Saxons and Normans have all occupied this historic riverside town and their architectural remains can be seen to this day, most vividly in a grand cathedral and a ruined Norman castle that loom over the town's medieval walls, cobbled streets and half-timbered buildings. Charles Dickens spent a large chunk of his childhood and the last few years of his life here, and many of the town's streets and buildings feature (albeit disguised) in his books.

Sights

Rochester Castle CASTLE

(EH; adult/child £5/4; 10am-6pm Apr-Sep) Rising high above the River Medway, Rochester's sturdy castle is one of the finest examples of Norman architecture in England and has lived through three sieges and partial demolition. The flooring of the 12th-century, 35m-tall Norman keep is long gone, allowing awesome views of its structure and open roof from the ground. You can also climb to the top of the battlements for widescreen views across the town.

FREE **Rochester Cathedral** CATHEDRAL
(Guided tours £4; ⏲7.30am-6pm; to 5pm Sat) Founded in AD 604, this is the second-oldest cathedral in England. Although construction on the present building started in 1080 and remodelling has left a mixture of styles, much of the Norman building remains, including the high-vaulted nave. Sunday afternoons when white-robed choristers flood the building with acoustic magic are the best time to visit.

FREE **Guildhall Museum** MUSEUM
(High St; ⏲10am-4.30pm Tue-Sun) Housed in a splendid 17th-century building, this fascinating little museum contains a range of exhibitions including a Dickens room, where a short film explores the writer's links with Rochester, and a dramatic exhibition of life on hulks – prison ships used to contain convicts in the 18th century.

Swiss Chalet DICKENS' CHALET
(Eastgate House grounds, Eastgate) Rochester has many Dickens associations, but none so striking as the writer's very own Swiss chalet, brought here from Gads Hill just outside the town where Dickens' spent his final years. It's thought he penned his last in its upper room. Sadly the interior is only accessible on special occasions.

Festivals & Events

For three days in early June, the streets of Rochester take on an air of Victorian England during the town's annual **Dickens Festival** (www.rochesterdickensfestival.org.uk), when parades, music and costumed characters make his best-loved novels come to life.

Eating

Precinct Pantry CAFE £
(3 College Yard; snacks £3-6⏲10am-5pm Mon-Sat; from 11am Sun) This miniature wood-panelled cafe has a prime location next to the cathedral and opposite the castle. There's a snug dining room inside and in summer you can enjoy the great sandwiches, homemade cakes and tea on the pavement tables outside.

Topes INTERNATIONAL ££
(60 High St; mains £10-15.50; ⏲lunch Wed-Sun; dinner Wed-Sat) Deservedly popular, modern-European food served in a cosy restaurant with low-beamed slanted ceilings, wood panelling and a large, inviting fireplace. Some windows look out onto the castle.

Shopping

Baggins Book Bazaar SECONDHAND BOOKSHOP
(www.bagginsbooks.co.uk; 19 High St) If Rochester's illustrious literary connections have put you in bookish mood, this fabulous bookshop claims to stock over half a million secondhand titles, making it one of the largest in the land.

Information

Tourist office (☎01634-843666; 95 High St; ⏲9am-5pm Mon-Fri, 10am-5pm Sat, 10.30am-5pm Sun) Has details of local accommodation, a cafe and a small Dickens exhibition. Free town tours leave here at 2.15pm from Easter to September at weekends, bank holidays and Wednesdays.

Getting There & Away

Rochester train connections:

Canterbury £10.70; 50 minutes twice hourly

London St Pancras High-speed service; £16.90; 39 minutes, twice hourly

London Victoria £10.90; 45 minutes, hourly

Whitstable

POP 30,195

Best known for its succulent oysters, which have been harvested here since Roman times, charming Whitstable has morphed into a popular destination for weekending metropolitans, attracted by the weatherboard houses, shingle beach and candy-coloured beach huts. The town has nevertheless managed to retain the character of a working fishing town, its thriving harbour and fish market coexisting with boutiques, organic delis and swanky restaurants. In recent years assorted campaigns by steadfast locals have kept some of the biggest names of the retail world out of the town, thus preserving its eccentric, artisanal air.

Sights

FREE **Whitstable Museum & Gallery** MUSEUM
(www.whitstable-museum.co.uk; 8 Oxford St; ⏲10am-4pm Mon-Sat year-round, 1-4pm Sun Jul & Aug) This modest museum has glass cases examining Whitstable's oyster industry, the Crab & Winkle Railway, which once ran

WHITE HORSE OF KENT

Forget the *Angel of the North* and soon-to-be Northumberlandia (p748), the southeast is set to trump them both with the ambitious *White Horse of Kent*. Designed by Turner Prize–winner Mark Wallinger, the gargantuan life-like stallion will stand more than twice as tall (50m) as Gateshead's angel, and towering above both the Eurostar railway line and the A2 motorway near Ebbsfleet, it will eventually overtake it as the country's most viewed work of public art. This proud symbol of Kent, costing £2 million, will hopefully be finished in time to welcome spectators arriving for the 2012 Olympics.

from Canterbury, and the local fishing fleet, as well as a corner dedicated to the actor Peter Cushing, star of several Hammer Horror films and the town's most famous resident, who died in 1994.

Festivals & Events

For a week in late July, the town hosts a seafood, arts and music extravaganza, the **Whitstable Oyster Festival** (www.whitstableoysterfestival.co.uk), offering a packed schedule of events, from history walks, crab-catching and oyster-eating competitions to a beer festival and traditional 'blessing of the waters'.

Sleeping

Pearl Fisher B&B ££

(☎01227-771000; www.thepearlfisher.com; 103 Cromwell Rd; s/d £60/90; P) A few minutes' walk from the high street in a residential area, this B&B has comfortable, themed rooms and plenty of thoughtful touches, such as night caps and bedtime pillow chocolates. There's a warm welcome and filling, top-quality breakfasts.

Hotel Continental HOTEL ££

(☎01227-280280; www.hotelcontinental.co.uk; Beach Walk; s/d/huts from £62.50/85/130; P) The rooms in this elegant seaside art-deco building are nothing special – come for the quirky converted fishermen's huts right on the beach. These should be booked well in advance.

Eating & Drinking

The town's famous oysters are harvested between September and April. EU Protected Geographical Indication status means a Whitstable oyster is just that, and not an import.

Wheeler's Oyster Bar OYSTER BAR £££

(☎01227-273311; 8 High St; mains £17-22; ⊙lunch & dinner Thu-Tue) Squeeze onto a stool by the bar or into the Victorian four-table dining room of this baby-blue and pink restaurant, choose from a seasonal menu and enjoy the best seafood in Whitstable. They know their stuff – they've been serving oysters since 1856. Bookings highly recommended unless you're travelling solo.

Crab & Winkle SEAFOOD ££

(South Quay, the Harbour; mains £9.50-22.95; ⊙lunch & dinner Mon-Sat, lunch Sun) Sitting above the Whitstable Fish Market in a black clapboard house, this bright restaurant has large windows overlooking the harbour, a buzzing vibe and excellent seafood with a few options for meat lovers thrown in.

Old Neptune PUB

(www.neppy.co.uk; Marine Tce) About as far onto the beach as it's possible to be (the building has been washed away several times by high tides), Whitstable's most famous and ramshackle pub has plenty of strategically placed outdoor tables, wonky wooden floorboards, window seats and even a honkytonk piano in the corner. There's regular live music and a friendly vibe, although it can get massively crowded in summer.

Information

Whitstable has no tourist office, but you can pick up maps and other information at the **library** (31-33 Oxford St; ⊙9am-6pm Mon-Fri, to 5pm Sat, 10am to 4pm Sun), which also lays on free internet access (bring ID).

Getting There & Away

Buses 4, 5 and 6 go to Canterbury (35 minutes) several times an hour.

Margate

POP 57,000

A popular seaside resort for more than 250 years thanks to its fine-sand beaches,

Margate's tatty seafront and amusement arcades seem somewhat removed from the candy-striped beach huts and crowd-pleasing Punch and Judy puppet shows of its Victorian heyday. Major cultural regeneration projects – including the spectacular new Turner Contemporary art gallery – are slowly reversing the town's fortunes.

Sights

Shell Grotto GROTTO

(www.shellgrotto.co.uk; Grotto Hill; adult/child £3/1.50; ⏲10am-5pm Apr-Oct). Margate's unique attraction is this mysterious, subterranean grotto discovered in 1835. It's a claustrophobic collection of rooms and passageways embedded with millions of shells arranged in symbol-rich mosaics. It has inspired feverish speculation over the years but presents few answers; some think it a 2000-year-old pagan temple, others an elaborate 19th-century hoax. Either way, it's an exquisite place worth seeing.

Turner Contemporary ART GALLERY

(www.turnercontemporary.org) Due to open in spring of 2011, this long-awaited and much-delayed gallery will highlight the town's links with the artist JMW Turner. At the time of writing the state-of-the-art building was under construction on the site of the seafront guesthouse where Turner used to stay. The gallery is set to become East Kent's top attraction and the first exhibition is expected to focus on Turner and his relationship with Margate.

Tom Thumb Theatre THEATRE

(☎01843-221791; www.tomthumbtheatre.co.uk; Eastern Esplanade) Just over a mile along the seafront heading east into Cliftonville, this recently reopened theatre with its titchy stage and just 58 seats is thought to be the world's smallest working theatre.

Sleeping & Eating

Walpole Bay Hotel HOTEL ££

(☎01843-221703; www.walpolebayhotel.co.uk; 5th Ave, Cliftonville; s/d from £60/80) For Margate's most eccentric night's sleep, look no further than this peculiar part-hotel, part-shrine to interwar trinkets. The pink, flouncy rooms are furnished with antiques, while public spaces are lined with glass-cased displays of memorabilia from the early 20th century. The hotel is a mile from central Margate, in Cliftonville.

Margate YHA HOSTEL £

(☎0870 371 9130; www.yha.org.uk; 3-4 Royal Esplanade; dm from £15; P ⓦ ⓚ) Clean and family-friendly hostel in what used to be a hotel, a gentle stroll from a sandy bay and about half a mile west of the tourist office. Book a couple of days in advance.

Mad Hatter CAFE £

(9 Lombard St, mains £4-8; ⏲lunch & dinner) Insanely unmissable, this completely cuckoo eatery run by a top-hatted proprietor packs two rooms of a 1690s house with bonkers regalia and miscellaneous knick-knackery from down the ages. Christmas decorations stay up all year and the toilets are original Victorian porcelain. The yummy cakes and snacks are all homemade.

Information

Tourist office (☎01843-577577; www.visitthanet.co.uk; 12-13 The Parade; ⏲10am-5pm Apr-Sep) Following the closure of Broadstairs and Ramsgate tourist offices, the Margate office now serves all of Thanet. Surf the net for £1.50 per 30 minutes and pick up a copy of *The Isle* (£1.50), a glossy magazine crammed with listings and Thanet essentials.

Getting There & Away

Margate has good connections with London and East Kent.

Bus

Canterbury Bus 8, 48 minutes, three hourly

London Victoria National Express, £12, 2½ hours, four daily

Train

London St Pancras High-speed service; £31.40, 1½ hours, hourly

London Victoria £27, one hour 50 minutes, twice hourly

Broadstairs

POP 24,370

Unlike its bigger, brasher neighbours, the charming resort village of Broadstairs revels in its quaintness, plays the Victorian nostalgia card at every opportunity, and names every second business after the works of its most famous holidaymaker, Charles Dickens. The town's elegant clifftop buildings, neatly manicured gardens, scythe of saffron sand and colourful beach huts hide a far grittier history of smuggling and shipbuilding.

ISLE OF THANET

Margate, Ramsgate and Broadstairs are all towns on the Isle of Thanet, but you won't need a wetsuit or a ferry to reach them – the 2-mile-wide Wantsum Channel, which divided the island from the mainland, silted up in the 16th century, transforming the East Kent landscape forever. In its island days Thanet was the springboard of several epoch-making episodes in English history. It was here that the Romans kicked off their invasion in the first century AD and where Augustine landed in AD 597 to launch his conversion of the pagans.

Sights

Dickens House Museum MUSEUM
(2 Victoria Pde; adult/child £3.25/1.80; 10am-5pm Jun-Sep) Broadstairs' top attraction is this quaint museum, which was actually the home of Mary Pearson Strong, inspiration for the character of Betsey Trotwood in *David Copperfield*. Diverse Dickensiana on display includes letters from the author.

Dickens wrote parts of *Bleak House* and *David Copperfield* in the handsome, if slightly worse for wear, **clifftop house** above the harbour wall between 1837 and 1859. It's now a private property.

Festivals & Events

Broadstairs' biggest bash is the annual, nine-day-long **Dickens Festival** (www.broadstairsdickensfestival.co.uk) held in late June and culminating in a banquet and ball in Victorian fancy dress.

Sleeping & Eating

East Horndon Guesthouse B&B ££
(01843-868306; www.easthorndonhotel.com; 4 Eastern Esplanade; s £44, £80-90;) This elegant guesthouse sits on manicured lawns a few yards from the cliff edge. The eight comfortable rooms are decorated in warm colours, the front four enjoying views of the sea and the world's largest offshore wind farm.

Copperfields Guest House B&B ££
(01843-601247; www.copperfieldsbb.co.uk; 11 Queen's Rd; d & tw from £65;) This vegetarian B&B has three homely, recently refreshed rooms and a warm welcome from the owners and pet Yorkie. It also caters for vegans and all products in the bathrooms are cruelty free. It's a short hop away from the seafront and there's space to store muddy bikes.

Tartar Frigate PUB ££
(42 Harbour St; mains £14-16.50) Dating back to the 18th century, this seafront pub is a great place to be in summer when tourists and locals alike spill out onto the beach. The seafood restaurant upstairs serves excellent fare and there are great views of the bay. The pub also puts on regular live folk music.

Getting There & Away

The handy Thanet Loop bus runs every 10 minutes through the day to Ramsgate (20 minutes) and Margate (20 minutes).

Bus

Canterbury Bus 8/9, 1½ hours

London Victoria National Express, £12, three hours, four daily

Train

London St Pancras High-speed service; £31.40, 1 hour 20 minutes, hourly

London Victoria £27, two hours, twice hourly

Ramsgate

POP 39,639

The most diverse of Kent's coastal towns, Ramsgate has a friendlier feel than rival Margate and is more vibrant than quaint little neighbour Broadstairs. A forest of sails whistle serenely in the breeze below the town's handsome curved harbour walls, surrounded by seafront bars and cosmopolitan street cafes that give things a laid-back feel. One celebrity chef away from being described as 'up-and-coming', Ramsgate retains a shabbily undiscovered charm, with its superb Blue Flag beaches, some spectacular Victorian architecture and a few welcoming places to stay and eat making it worth the trip.

Sights & Activities

When the sun's out, inline skaters, surfers and sunbathers all head to the east of the main harbour where Ramsgate's reddish-sand-and-shingle beach and elegant promenade sit under an imposing cliff.

Ramsgate Maritime Museum MUSEUM
(www.ekmt.fogonline.co.uk; The Clock House, Royal Harbour; adult/child £1.50/75p; ⊙10am-5pm Tue-Sun Easter-Sep) More than 600 ships have been wrecked on the notorious Goodwin Sands off this stretch of coast, and an intriguing assortment of loot from their barnacled carcasses fills the town's 19th-century clock tower near the harbour. Here, too, is a line marking Ramsgate's meridian (the town once had its own Ramsgate Mean Time almost 6 minutes ahead of GMT).

Sleeping

Glendevon Guesthouse B&B ££
(☎01843-570909; www.glendevonguesthouse.co.uk; 8 Truro Rd; s/d from £45/65; P ☎) Run by energetic and outgoing young hosts, this comfy guesthouse takes the whole eco-friendly thing very seriously, with guest recycling facilities, ecoshowers and even energy-saving hairdryers. The hallways of this grand Victorian house, a block back from the seafront road, are decorated with watercolours by local artists, and there are bookshelves full of games, books and DVDs to borrow. All the rooms have kitchenettes and breakfast is a convivial affair taken around a communal table.

Royal Harbour Hotel HOTEL ££
(☎01843-591514; www.royalharbourhotel.co.uk; 10/11 Nelson Crescent; s/d from £78/98; ☎) Occupying two regency town houses on a glorious seafront crescent, this boutique hotel feels enveloped in warmth and quirkiness. An eclectic collection of books, magazines, games and artwork line the hotel walls, and there's a gramophone with old records and an honesty bar in the lounge. There are complimentary cheese and biscuits in the evening and hot-water bottles for when it gets chilly. Rooms range from tiny nauticalesque 'cabins' to country-house style, four-poster doubles, and most of them have postcard views over the forest of masts below.

Eating

Eddie Gilbert's SEAFOOD ££
(32 King St; mains £6-17; ⊙lunch & dinner Mon-Sat, extended lunch Sun) Indulge in England's favourite aroma (battered fish and chips) at Thanet's best seafood and gourmet fish and chips restaurant above a traditional fishmonger's. The beamed dining space decorated with lobster cages, fish nets and sea charts is the ideal setting for platters of locally caught fish prepared in some very inventive ways by a Michelin-trained chef. There's plenty to choose from even if fish is not your dish.

Bon Appetit BRITISH ££
(4 Westcliff Arcade; mains £6-19; ⊙lunch & dinner) Arguably Thanet's top nosh is plated up by head chef Mark May in the simple dining room or out on the pavement. Ingredients on the menu of Bon Appetit are of the seasonal and local-sourced ilk, with finely crafted dishes, such as pan-fried Kentish pheasant, line-caught sea bass and lamb rump with rosemary and redcurrant preserve, which attracts national attention.

Surin Restaurant ASIAN ££
(www.surinrestaurant.co.uk; 30 Harbour St; mains £4-13; ⊙lunch & dinner Mon-Sat) Ramsgate is an unlikely spot to eat some of the best Thai, Cambodian and Laotian food this side of the Hindu Kush, but sure enough, the tasty menu in this restaurant delivers. The restaurant is a dumpling's throw from the seafront and even serves its own label of microbrewed beers.

Getting There & Away

Ramsgate is linked to Margate, Broadstairs and Sandwich by frequent local bus services.

Air

The only scheduled service out of nearby **Kent International Airport** (☎08707 605 755; www.kia-m.com) is the daily flight to Edinburgh operated by **Flybe** (www.flybe.com). More may be added in coming years.

Bus

London Victoria National Express, £12, three hours, four daily

Boat

Euroferries (☎0844-4145355; www.euroferries.co.uk) Runs high-speed ferries to Boulogne (1¼ hours, from £49 per car, four daily).

Transeuropa Ferries (☎01843-595522; www.transeuropaferries.com) Operates ferries from Ramsgate New Port to Ostend in Belgium (five hours, from £49 per car, four daily).

Train

London Charing Cross £27.30, two hours, hourly

London St Pancras High-speed service; £31.40, one hour 20 minutes, hourly

Sandwich

POP 4398

With a top slice of ancient churches, Dutch gables and peg-tiled roofs, a juicy filling of medieval lanes and timber-framed houses, and a wholesome base slice of riverside strolls and great pubs, Sandwich makes a very tasty morsel for passing travellers. Today it's a sleepy little inland settlement, but the town retains a certain salty tang from its days as one of the original Cinque Ports when it ran a close second to the Port of London. Decline set in when the entrance to the harbour silted up in the 16th century, leaving this once vital gateway to and from the Continent to spend the last 400 years retreating into very quaint rural obscurity.

Of course, though the town makes precious little of it, Sandwich indirectly gave the world its favourite snack when the 4th Earl of Sandwich called for his meat to be served between two slices of bread, thus freeing him to gamble all night long without leaving the table or smudging his cards. It hence became de rigueur to ask for meat 'like Sandwich' and the rest is fast-food history.

Ageing earls might be interested in another innovation associated with the town – Viagra – developed and produced at the mammoth Pfizer pharmaceutical plant on the town's outskirts. However, true-blue conservative Sandwich is understandably a tad shy of its little-blue-pill heritage.

Sights & Activities

Sandwich's spider web of medieval and Elizabethan streets is perfect for ambling and getting pleasantly lost. **Strand Street** in particular has one of the highest concentrations of half-timbered buildings in the country. Stepped gables betray the strong influence of 350 Protestant Flemish refugees (the 'Strangers') who settled in the town in the 16th century on the invitation of Elizabeth I.

Guildhall Museum MUSEUM

(adult/child £1/50p; 10.30am-12.30pm & 2-4pm Tue, Wed, Fri & Sat, 2-4pm Thu & Sun Apr-Nov) A good place to start is the small but thorough guildhall with its exhibitions on Sandwich's rich past as a Cinque Port, the town at war and gruesome punishments meted out to felons, fornicators and phoney fishermen.

Sandwich Quay QUAY

Several attractions line the River Stour; first up is a cute little flint-chequered **Barbican** tollgate, built by Henry VIII, which controls traffic flow over the only road bridge across the river. Nearby rises the **Fishergate**, built in 1384 and once the main entrance to the town through which goods from the Continent and beyond, unloaded on the quay, once passed. On fair-weather days, hop aboard the **Sandwich River Bus** (07958-376183; www.sandwichriverbus.co.uk; adult/child 30min trip £6/4, 1hr £10/7; every 30-60min 11am-6pm Thu-Sun Apr-Sep) beside the toll bridge for seal-spotting trips along

CINQUE PORTS

Due to their proximity to Europe, southeast England's coastal towns were the front line against raids and invasion during Anglo-Saxon times. In the absence of a professional army and navy, these ports were frequently called upon to defend themselves, and the kingdom, on land and at sea.

In 1278, King Edward I formalised this already ancient arrangement by legally defining the Confederation of Cinque Ports. The five original ports – Sandwich, Dover, Hythe, Romney and Hastings – were granted numerous perks and privileges in exchange for providing the king with ships and men. At their peak, the ports were deemed England's most powerful institution after Crown and Church.

Even after shifting coastlines silted up several Cinque Port harbours, a professional navy was based at Portsmouth and the ports' real importance evaporated, the pomp and ceremony remains. The Lord Warden of the Cinque Ports is a prestigious post now given to faithful servants of the Crown. The Queen Mother was warden until she passed away, succeeded by Admiral Lord Boyce. Previous incumbents include the Duke of Wellington and Sir Winston Churchill.

'Who names us sank and not sink is a foreigner and foe' once went the saying on the south coast, describing a faux pas committed today by just about every unknowing tourist, both foreign and British (cinque, as in Cinque Port, is pronounced 'sink' and not 'sank' as the French would say).

LOCAL KNOWLEDGE

COLIN CARR: SANDWICH HARBOURMASTER & BOATMAN

You could say I've had the sea and the southeast in my blood since birth, having arrived in Sandwich via the net shops of Hastings and my own boatyard on the Medway. For the last decade I've been continuing ancient boating traditions as harbourmaster of this Cinque Port, but when I'm not overseeing the navigation way on the River Stour, you'll find me restoring my 1903 barge, which I hope to use for river tours from 2011. You can't live in Sandwich without developing a passion for local history and wildlife, so here are my tips.

Hidden gems

Sandwich is one big hidden gem! Wander aimlessly through its medieval web of streets to unearth a wealth of history and architecture or take a tour. Most atmospheric is around 8pm when the 'curfew bell' is still rung from the tower of St Peter's, as it has been for 800 years.

Must-sees

The exquisite Salutation Gardens, Sandwich's redundant Norman churches and Richborough Roman Fort, where the Romans gained their first foothold in Britain in AD 43, should be on every visitor's checklist.

Top tip

Head down the meandering River Stour towards Pegwell Bay and the Channel at low tide for the best bird- and wildlife-spotting; high tide is more picturesque.

the River Stour and in Pegwell Bay or an interesting way to reach Richborough (p146).

Salutation Gardens GARDENS
(www.the-secretgardens.co.uk; adult/child £6/3; ⏲10am-5pm) Just along from Fishergate is Sandwich's top attraction, a set of exquisite gardens laid out by leading early 20th-century garden designers Jekyll and Lutyens behind a 1912 mansion. There's a superb new tea room in the grounds.

Churches CHURCHES
Architecture buffs should head for **St Clement's Church** (Church St St Clement's), topped with a handsome Norman tower. The oldest church in Sandwich is **St Peter's** (King St), now no longer used for worship. It's a real mixture of styles and years: its tower collapsed in dramatic fashion in 1661 and it was rebuilt with a bulbous cupola by the Strangers. It houses the town's old horse-drawn fire engine and sparse displays on the often scandalous earls of Sandwich. **St Mary's** (Cnr Church St St Mary's and Strand St), the town's third church, is now a multipurpose venue, but open during the day for perusal.

Royal St George's GOLF COURSE
(www.royalstgeorges.com) Sandwich is also home to one of the most challenging golf links in England and occasional host to the Open Golf Championships. Ian Fleming of *James Bond* fame was elected captain of St George's in 1964 after setting the famous game of golf between Goldfinger and Bond on the course.

Sleeping & Eating

Sandwich once boasted a brewery and 50 pubs! That number has dropped significantly, but the town is still known for its atmospheric old taverns.

TOP CHOICE **Bell Hotel** HOTEL ££
(☎01304 613388; www.bellhotelsandwich.co.uk; the Quay; s/d from £95/110; P 📶) Today the haunt of celebrity golfers, the Bell Hotel has been sitting on the town's quay since Tudor times, though much of the remaining building is from the 19th century. A splendid, sweeping staircase leads up to luxurious rooms, some with great quay views. The service here could not be better.

King's Arms INN ££
(☎01304-617330; cnr Church St St Mary's & Strand St; light meals £3-8, mains £10.50-18; ⏲lunch & dinner) This 15th-century inn opposite St Mary's church serving quality English food and very popular Sunday lunches has a beamed dining room heated by large fireplaces. For sunny days there's a walled,

vine-covered beer garden. There are six B&B rooms upstairs.

No Name Shop DELI-CAFE £

(No Name St; snacks £2.60-4) For coffee, flavoured breads, cheeses, cakes or a quick sandwich in Sandwich, this far from anonymous deli-cafe near the bus stop is very popular among locals, some of whom seem to regularly prefer it over their own kitchens.

George & Dragon PUB

(Fisher St; mains £7-16) Another great 15th-century inn a short stroll from the quay, with a cosy beamed front bar area and a rear dining room.

Information

Tourist office (☎01304-613565; www.open-sandwich.co.uk; New St; ⏲10am-4pm Mon-Sat Apr-Oct plus noon-3pm Sun Jun-Aug) Hands out maps and audioguides (£2). In the entrance take a peek into the impressive wood-panelled Elizabethan courtroom, in use until 1951.

Getting There & Away

Trains run from Dover Priory train station (21 minutes, hourly), Ramsgate (12 minutes, hourly) and London Charing Cross (£26.90, two hours 18 minutes, hourly).

Buses also go to Ramsgate (22 minutes, hourly), Dover (47 minutes, hourly) and Canterbury (40 minutes, three hourly).

Around Sandwich

RICHBOROUGH

Roman Britain began here amid the windswept ruins of **Richborough Roman Fort** (EH; adult/child £4.50/2.30; ⏲10am-6pm Mar-Sep), just 2 miles north of Sandwich. This is the spot from which the successful AD 43 invasion of Britain was launched. To celebrate their victory, a colossal triumphal arch was planted here, the base of which remains. The fort's clearest features today – high walls and scores of deep defensive ditches that give it the appearance of a vast jelly mould – came later as the Romans were forced to stave off increasingly vicious seaborne attacks.

There's a small onsite museum and an audiotour to steer you through the rise and fall of Roman Richborough. To arrive as the Romans did – by boat – take the Sandwich River Bus from Sandwich quay.

DEAL

Julius Caesar and his armies set foot on Deal's peaceful shingle beach in 55 BC for their first exploratory dip into Britain. Today there's a gorgeous little 16th-century **castle** (EH; Victoria Rd; adult/child £4.50/2.30; ⏲10am-6pm Apr-Sep) with curvaceous bastions that form petals in a Tudor rose shape. Far from delicate, however, it is the largest and most complete of Henry VIII's defence chain along the south coast.

And hardly a mile south is another link in the 16th-century coastal defences, **Walmer Castle** (EH; Kingsdown Rd; adult/child £7/3.50; ⏲10am-6pm Apr-Sep, to 4pm Wed-Sun Mar & Oct), the much-altered and really rather lavish official residence of the warden of the Cinque Ports. Military hero the Duke of Wellington died here.

Dover

POP 39,078

Down-in-the-dumps Dover has certainly seen better days and its derelict, postwar architecture and shabby town centre of vacant shops is a sad introduction to Blighty for travellers arriving from the Continent, most of whom pass through quickly. Lucky, then, that the town has a couple of stellar attractions to redeem it. The port's vital strategic position so close to mainland Europe gave rise to a sprawling hilltop castle, with some 2000 years of history to its credit. The spectacular white cliffs, as much a symbol of English wartime resilience as Winston Churchill or the Battle of Britain, rise in chalky magnificence to the east and west.

Sights & Activities

Dover Castle CASTLE

(EH; adult/child £13.90/7; ⏲10am-6pm Apr-Sep; P) The almost impenetrable Dover Castle, one of the most impressive in England, was built to bolster the country's weakest point at this, the shortest sea-crossing to mainland Europe. It sprawls across the city's hilltop, commanding a tremendous view of the English Channel as far as the French coastline.

The site has been in use for as many as 2000 years. On the vast grounds are the remains of a **Roman lighthouse**, which date from AD 50 and may be the oldest standing building in Britain. Beside it lies a restored **Saxon church**.

The robust 12th-century **Great Tower**, with walls up to 7m thick, is filled with interactive exhibits and light-and-sound shows

Dover

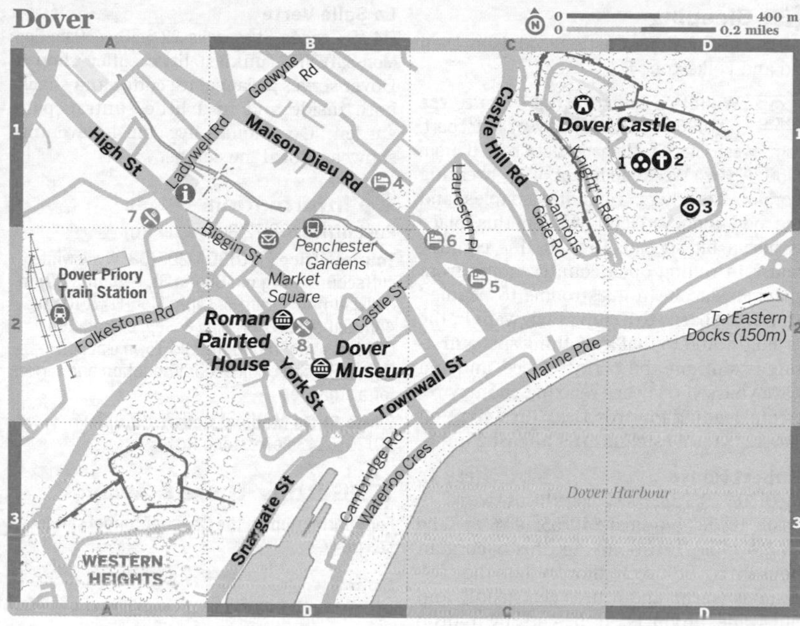

that take visitors back to the times of Henry II. But it's the warren of claustrophobic **secret wartime tunnels** under the castle that are the biggest draw. Excellent 50-minute tours delve into the hillside passageways, which were first excavated during the Napoleonic Wars and then expanded to house a command post and hospital in WWII. They now house reconstructed scenes of their wartime use, complete with sounds, smells and erratic lighting. One of Britain's most famous wartime operations, code-named Dynamo, was directed from here in 1940. It saw the evacuation of hundreds of thousands of troops from the French beaches of Dunkirk.

Dover Museum MUSEUM

(www.dovermuseum.co.uk; Market Sq; adult/child £3/2; ⏲10am-5.30pm Mon-Sat year-round, noon-5pm Sun Apr-Aug) By far the most enthralling exhibit in the town's three-storey museum is an astonishing 3600-year-old Bronze Age boat, discovered here in 1992. Vaunted as the world's oldest-known seagoing vessel, it measures a thumping great 9.5m by 2.4m and is kept in a huge, low-lit, climate-controlled glass box.

Roman Painted House ROMAN ART

(New St; adult/child £3/2; ⏲10am-5pm Tue-Sun Apr-Sep) A crumbling 1960s bunker is the unlikely setting for some of the most extensive, if stunted, Roman wall paintings north of the Alps. Several scenes depict Bacchus (the god of wine and revelry), which makes perfect sense as this large villa was built around AD 200 as a *mansio* (hotel) for travellers in need of a little lubrication to unwind.

Dover

Top Sights

Dover Castle	C1
Dover Museum	B2
Roman Painted House	B2

Sights

1 Roman Lighthouse	D1
2 Saxon Church	D1

Activities, Courses & Tours

3 Secret Wartime Tunnels	D1

Sleeping

4 East Lee Guest House	B1
5 Hubert House	C2
6 Number One Guest House	C2

Eating

7 Allotment	A1
8 La Salle Verte	B2

Sleeping

B&Bs cluster along Castle St, Maison Dieu Rd and Folkestone Rd.

TOP CHOICE **Wallett's Court** HOTEL £££
(01304-852424; www.wallettscourt.com; Westcliffe, St Margaret's-at-Cliffe; d from £150; P) Weekend haunt of de-stressing London highfliers, romantic couples and the odd moneyed cliff walker, this place is just a bit special. Digs at this country house in rolling open country range from spacious Jacobean guestrooms to beamed converted barns to a canvas wigwam in the grounds. Add to that a soothing spa, a first-rate restaurant and perky service, and you have yourself one very relaxing country retreat. Heading towards Deal, turn right off the A258 for Westcliffe after almost 2 miles.

Hubert House B&B ££
(01304-202253; www.huberthouse.co.uk; 9 Castle Hill Rd; s/d from £40/55; P@) The comfortable bedrooms in this Georgian house may be overly flowery but the welcome is warm, and it uses ecofriendly and fair-trade products. It has its own little bistro downstairs, which opens out onto a front terrace.

Number One Guest House B&B ££
(01304-202007; www.number1guesthouse.co.uk; 1 Castle Street; d from £50; P) Set in a grand Georgian town house at the foot of Dover Castle, with rooms decorated in traditional Victorian style. There's also a quaint walled garden with lovely views and breakfast is served in bed.

East Lee Guest House B&B ££
(01304-210176; www.eastlee.co.uk; 108 Maison Dieu Rd; d £60; P) This lovely terracotta-shingled town house impresses with its grand, elegantly decorated communal areas, energetic hosts, recently renovated rooms and excellent, varied breakfasts.

Eating

TOP CHOICE **Allotment** BRITISH ££
(9 High St; www.theallotmentdover.com; mains £7.50-16; 8.30am-11pm Tue-Sat) Dover's best dining spot plates up local fish and meat from around Canterbury, seasoned with herbs from the tranquil garden out back, in a relaxed, understated setting. Swab the decks with a Kentish wine as you admire the view of the Maison Dieu directly opposite through the exquisite stained glass frontage.

La Salle Verte CAFE £
(14-15 Cannon St; snacks £2-5.50; 9am-5pm Mon-Sat) The funkiest little coffee shop in Dover serves great cakes, coffee and snacks both inside and in a little suntrap patio garden. Occasional live music evenings showcase local musicians.

Information

Post office (68-72 Pencester Rd)

Tourist office (01304-205108; www.whitecliffscountry.org.uk; Biggin St; 9am-5.30pm daily Jun-Aug, 9am-5.30pm Mon-Fri & 10am-4pm Sat & Sun Apr, May & Sep, closed Sun Oct-Mar) Located in the Old Town Gaol on Biggin St; can book accommodation and ferries for a small fee.

White Cliffs Medical Centre (01304-201705; 143 Folkestone Rd)

Getting There & Away

For information on the Channel Tunnel services, see p847.

Boat

Ferries depart for France from the Eastern Docks below the castle. Fares vary according to season and advance purchase. See the websites for specials.

LD Lines (0800 917 1201; www.ldlines.co.uk) Services to Boulogne (50 minutes, up to seven daily).

Norfolk Line (0844 847 5042; www.norfolkline.com) Services to Dunkirk (two hours, every two hours).

P&O Ferries (08716 642020; www.poferries.com) Runs to Calais (1½ hours, every 40 minutes to an hour).

Seafrance (0871 423 7119; www.seafrance.com) Ferries to Calais roughly every 90 minutes.

Bus

Dover connections:

Canterbury Bus 15, 45 minutes, twice hourly

Deal Bus 15, 40 minutes, twice hourly

London Victoria Coach 007, £13.50, 2¾ hours, 19 daily

Sandwich Bus 87, 45 minutes, hourly

Train

Dover connections:

London Charing Cross £18.50, two hours, twice hourly

London St Pancras High-speed service; £31.70, one hour, hourly

Ramsgate £7.50, 35 minutes, hourly, via Sandwich

Getting Around

The ferry companies run regular shuttle buses between the docks and the train station (five minutes) as they're a long walk apart.

Heritage (☎01304-204420) Provides a 24-hour service.

Star Taxis (☎01304-228822) Also has a 24-hour service.

Around Dover

THE WHITE CLIFFS

Immortalised in song, film and literature, these iconic cliffs are embedded in the national consciousness, acting as a big, white 'Welcome Home' sign to generations of travellers and soldiers.

The cliffs rise 100m high and extend for 10 miles on either side of Dover, but it is the 6-mile stretch east of town – properly known as the Langdon Cliffs – that particularly captivates visitors' imaginations. The chalk here is about 250m deep, and the cliffs themselves are about half a million years old, formed when the melting icecaps of northern Europe were gouging a channel between France and England.

The Langdon Cliffs are managed by the National Trust, which has a **tourist office** (☎01304-202756; ⊙10am-5pm Mar-Oct, 11am-4pm Nov-Feb) and **car park** (£3 for nonmembers) 2 miles east of Dover along Castle Hill Rd and the A258 road to Deal or off the A2 past the Eastern Docks.

From the tourist office, follow the stony path east along the clifftops for a bracing 2-mile walk to the stout Victorian **South Foreland Lighthouse** (NT; adult/child £4/2; ⊙guided tours 11am-5.30pm Fri-Mon mid-Mar-Oct). This was the first lighthouse to be powered by electricity, and is the site of the first international radio transmissions in 1898.

A mile further on the same trail brings you to delightful **St Margaret's Bay**, a gap in the chalk with a sun-trapping shingle beach and the welcoming **Coastguard Pub** (www.thecoastguard.co.uk; mains £10-15; ⊙lunch & dinner). As this is the closest point to France many a cross-Channel swimmer has stepped into the briny here. From the top of the hill the hourly bus 15 shuttles back to Dover or onwards to Deal.

To see the cliffs in all their full-frontal glory, **Dover White Cliffs Tours** (☎01303-271388; www.doverwhitecliffstours.com; adult/child £8/4; ⊙daily Jul & Aug, Sat & Sun Apr-Jun & Sep-Oct) runs 40-minute sightseeing trips at least three times a day from the Western Docks.

ROMNEY MARSH

This eerie landscape of flat reed beds, sparsely populated and echoing with the whistling wind and lonely squawks of sea birds, was once a favourite haunt of smugglers and wreckers. It's now home to an incredibly cramped tourist attraction: the world's smallest-gauge public railway. Opened in 1927, the pocket-sized

A SWIG OF KENT & SUSSEX

With booze cruises over to Calais now almost a thing of the past, many Kent and Sussex drinkers are rediscovering their counties' superb home-grown beverages. Both counties produce some of the most delicious ales in the country and the south-east's wines are even outgunning some traditional Continental vintners.

Kent's **Shepherd Neame Brewery** (☎01795-532206; www.shepherd-neame.co.uk; 10 Court St, Faversham; admission £10; ⊙on request) is Britain's oldest and cooks up aromatic ales brewed from Kent-grown premium hops. Sussex's reply is **Harveys Brewery** (☎01273-480209; www.harveys.org.uk; Bridge Wharf, Lewes; ⊙tours evenings only), which perfumes Lewes town centre with a hop-laden scent. Book in advance for tours of either brewery.

Mention 'English wine' not too long ago and you'd likely hear a snort of derision. Not any more. Thanks to warmer temperatures and determined winemakers, English wine, particularly of the sparkling variety, is developing a fan base of its own.

Award-winning vineyards can be found in both Sussex and Kent, whose chalky soils are likened to France's Champagne region. Many vineyards now offer tours and wine tastings. Some of the most popular are **Biddenden Vineyards** (☎01580-291726; biddendenvineyards.co.uk; 1.2 miles from Wealden; admission free; ⊙tours 10am daily) and **Chapel Down Vinery** (☎01580-766111; www.englishwinesgroup.com; Tenterden; admission £9; ⊙tours Jun-Sep).

trains belonging to the **Romney, Hythe & Dymchurch Railway** (www.rhdr.org.uk; adult/child £14/7; ⏲daily Apr-Sep, Sat & Sun Nov-Mar) trundle and toot their way 13.5 miles from Hythe to Dungeness lighthouse and back (roughly an hour each way). Cute, undoubtedly. But prone to cramped leg space and sore heads? You better believe it.

DUNGENESS

Sticking out from the western edge of Romney Marsh is a low shingle spit dominated by a brooding nuclear power station. In spite of the apocalyptic desolation, this spot is home to the largest sea-bird colony in the southeast at the **Royal Society for the Protection of Birds (RSPB) Nature Reserve** (www.rspb.org.uk; Dungeness Rd; adult/child £3/1; ⏲9am-9pm or sunset, tourist office 10am-5pm Mar-Oct), which has displays, binocular hire, explorer backpacks for kids, and information on birdwatching hides.

Sevenoaks & Around

POP 26,699

A bland commuter town off the M25, Sevenoaks is home to one of England's most celebrated country estates. The gates to **Knole House** (NT; adult/child £9.50/4.75; ⏲10.30am-5pm Tue-Sun Apr-Oct) sit on the southern High St, and from there it's a beautiful winding walk or drive through a rolling medieval park dotted with bold deer. The estate was built in the 12th century, but in 1456 the Archbishop of Canterbury, Thomas Bouchier, snapped the property up and set about building a vast and lavish house 'fit for the Princes of the Church'. Its curious calendar design encompasses 365 rooms, 52 staircases and seven courtyards. The house was the childhood home of Vita Sackville-West, whose love affair with Virginia Woolf spawned the novel *Orlando,* set at Knole.

The house is 1.5 miles southeast of Sevenoaks train station on London Rd. Trains leave from London Charing Cross (£9.40, 35 minutes, every 15 minutes) and continue to Tunbridge Wells (£5.40, 20 minutes, two per hour) and Hastings (£16.20, one hour).

The home of Sir Winston Churchill from 1924 until his death in 1965, **Chartwell** (NT; Westerham; adult/child £10.60/5.30; ⏲10.45am-5pm Wed-Sun Mar-Oct, plus Tue Jul & Aug), 6 miles east of Sevenoaks, offers a breathtakingly intimate insight into the life of England's famous cigar-chomping bombast.

This 19th-century house and its rambling grounds have been preserved much as Winnie left them, full of books, pictures, maps and personal mementos. Churchill was also a prolific painter and his now extremely valuable daubs are scattered throughout the house and fill the garden studio.

Transport options are limited without a car. Kent Passenger Services bus 238 runs from Sevenoaks train station (30 minutes, every two hours) on Wednesdays from May to mid-September. Arriva bus 401 runs on Sundays and Bank Holiday Mondays only.

Hever Castle

The idyllic little **Hever Castle** (www.hevercastle.co.uk; adult/child £13/7.50, gardens only £10.50/6.50; ⏲noon-6pm Apr-Oct) seems to have leapt right out of a film set. It's encircled by a narrow moat and surrounded by family-friendly gardens, complete with cute topiary of woodland creatures and wandering ducks and swans.

The castle is famous for being the childhood home of Anne Boleyn, mistress to Henry VIII and then his doomed queen. It dates from 1270, with a Tudor house added in 1505 by the Bullen (Boleyn) family. The castle later fell into disrepair until 1903, when American multimillionaire William Waldorf Astor bought it, pouring obscene amounts of money into a massive refurbishment. The exterior is unchanged from Tudor times, but the interior is thick with Edwardian panelling.

WORTH A TRIP

SISSINGHURST CASTLE GARDEN

One of England's most famous and romantic gardens is at **Sissinghurst** (NT; Sissinghurst; adult/child £9.50/4.70; ⏲10.30am-5.30pm Fri-Tue Mar-Oct). Though the castle dates to the 12th century, writer Vita Sackville-West crafted the delightful gardens after she bought the estate in 1930. Highlights include the exuberant rose garden and the virginal snowy-bloomed White Garden. Sissinghurst is 2 miles northeast of Cranbrook and 1 mile east of Sissinghurst village off the A262.

WORTH A TRIP

DOWN HOUSE

Charles Darwin's home from 1842 until his death in 1882, **Down House** (EH; Luxted Rd, Downe; adult/child £9.30/4.70; ⏲11am-5pm Jul & Aug, Wed-Sun Mar, Jun, Sep & Oct) witnessed the development of Darwin's theory of evolution by natural selection. The house and gardens have been restored to look much as they would have in Darwin's time, including Darwin's study, where he undertook much of his reading and writing; the drawing room, where he tried out some of his indoor experiments; and the gardens and greenhouse, where some of his outdoor experiments are re-created. There are three self-guided trails in the area, where you can follow in the great man's footsteps.

The house, Downe village and the surrounding area has been on Unesco's tentative list for World Heritage Site status for over a decade.

Down House is in Downe, off the A21. Take bus 146 from Bromley North or Bromley South railway station, or service R8 from Orpington.

From London Bridge trains go direct to Hever (£9.40, 40 minutes, hourly), a poorly signposted 1-mile walk from the castle; and to Edenbridge (£9.10, 50 minutes, hourly), from where it's a 4-mile taxi or bike ride. If you're driving, Hever Castle is 3 miles off the B2026 near Edenbridge.

Penshurst

The pretty village of Penshurst, on the B2176, just off the A21, is lined with timber-framed Tudor houses and features a fanciful four-spired church, but most people come for grandiose medieval manor house **Penshurst Place** (www.penshurstplace.com; adult/child £9.50/6; ⏲noon-4pm Apr-Oct). Its pride and joy is the splendid **Baron's Hall**, built in 1341, where a number of royal visitors, including Queen Elizabeth I, were entertained beneath its stunning 18m-high chestnut roof. Just outside the main house is a vintage-toy museum, whose empty eyed dolls, classic rocking horses and mechanical red-eyed bear are enough to give even adults nightmares.

Outside, Penshurst's famous **walled gardens** (⏲10.30am-6pm Apr-Oct) were designed in 1346 and remain virtually unchanged since Elizabethan times. There are also lovely riverside walks in the grounds.

From Edenbridge, buses 231 and 233 leave for Tunbridge Wells via Penshurst every hour (27 minutes).

Leeds Castle

This immense moated pile is for many the world's most romantic **castle** (www.leeds castle.com; adult/child £17.50/10; ⏲10am-6pm Apr-Sep), and it's certainly one of the most visited in Britain. While it looks formidable enough from the outside – a hefty structure balancing on two islands amid a large lake and sprawling estate – it's actually known as something of a 'ladies castle'. This stems from the fact that in its more than 1000 years of history, it has been home to a who's who of medieval queens, most famously Henry VIII's first wife, Catherine of Aragon.

The castle was transformed from fortress to lavish palace over the centuries, and its last owner, the high-society hostess Lady Baillie, used it as a princely family home and party pad to entertain the likes of Errol Flynn, Douglas Fairbanks and JFK.

The castle's vast estate offers enough attractions of its own to justify a day-trip: peaceful walks, a duckery, aviary and falconry demonstrations. You'll also find possibly the world's sole **dog collar museum**, plenty of kids' attractions and a **hedge maze**, overseen by a grassy bank where fellow travellers can shout encouragement or misdirections.

Since Lady Baillie's death in 1974, a private trust has managed the property. This means that some parts of the castle are periodically closed for private events.

Leeds Castle is just east of Maidstone. Trains run from London Victoria to Bearsted (£17.10, one hour) where you catch a special shuttle coach to the castle (£5 return).

EAST SUSSEX

Home to rolling countryside, medieval villages and gorgeous coastline, this inspiring corner of England is besieged by weekending Londoners whenever the sun pops out. And it's not hard to see why as you explore the cobbled medieval streets of Rye, wander historic Battle, where William the Conqueror first engaged the Saxons in 1066, and peer over the edge of the breathtaking Seven Sisters chalk cliffs and Beachy Head near the gentile seaside town of Eastbourne. Brighton, a highlight of any visit, offers some kicking nightlife, offbeat shopping and British seaside fun. But you needn't follow the crowds to enjoy East Sussex. It's just as rewarding to get off the beaten track, linger along its winding country lanes and stretch your legs on the South Downs Way, which traverses England's newest national park, the South Downs National Park.

Rye

POP 4195

If you're searching for a perfect example of a medieval settlement, look no further than Rye, described by many as the most attractive little town in England. Once a Cinque Port, this exquisite place looks as if it's been pickled, put on a shelf and promptly forgotten about by Father Time. Even the most hardened cynic can't fail to be bewitched by Rye's cobbled lanes, mysterious passageways and crooked half-timbered Tudor buildings. Romantics can lap up the townsfolk's tales of resident smugglers, ghosts, writers and artists, and hole up in one of a slew of gorgeous accommodation in its heart.

Once an island, the town now sits high and dry atop a rocky outcrop, sheep grazing where the briny once lapped. If you do visit – and you absolutely should – try to avoid summer weekends when hoards of day-trippers dilute the town's time-warp effect.

Sights

A short walk from the Rye Heritage Centre, most start their exploration of Rye in the famous **Mermaid Street**, bristling with 15th-century timber-framed houses with quirky house names such as 'The House with Two Front Doors' and 'The House Opposite'.

Ypres Tower MUSEUM

(Tower & museum adult/child £3/free; ⌚10.30am-5pm Apr-Oct) Just off Church Sq stands the sandcastle-esque Ypres Tower (pronounced 'wipers'). This 13th-century building looks out over Romney Marsh and Rye Bay, and houses one part of Rye Museum. It's overseen by a friendly warden, who's full of colourful tales from the tower's long history as fort, prison, mortuary and museum (the last two at overlapping times). New exhibitions dedicated to women and children in Rye and a medieval garden are planned. The other branch of the **museum** (www.ryemuseum.co.uk; 3 East St; adult/child £2.50/free; ⌚2-5pm Thu, Fri & Mon, 10.30am-1pm & 2-5pm Sat & Sun Apr-Oct), a short stroll away on East St, is home to an 18th-century leather fire engine and other intriguing loot.

Lamb House HOUSE MUSEUM

(NT; West St; adult/child £4/2.10; ⌚2-6pm Thu & Sat late Mar-Oct) This Georgian town house is a favourite stomping ground for local apparitions, but not that of its most famous resident, American writer Henry James, who lived here from 1898 to 1916, during which time he wrote *The Wings of the Dove*.

Church of St Mary the Virgin CHURCH

(Church Sq; ⌚9.15am-5.30pm Apr-Sep) Rye's church is a hotchpotch of medieval and later styles and its turret clock is the oldest in England (1561) still working with its original pendulum, which swings above your head as you enter. Climb the **tower** (adult/child £2.50/1) for panoramic views of the town and surroundings.

Landgate TOWN GATE

At the northeastern edge of the village, this thickset pale-stone gate dating from 1329 is the only remaining gate out of four and is still in use. The name comes from the fact that when first built, it was the only gate linking the town to the mainland at high tide.

Activities

To combine history and a hearty hike, the well-signposted **1066 Country Walk** meanders 31 miles from Rye to Battle and Pevensey where it connects with the South Downs Way.

Sleeping

Rye boasts an exceptional choice of unique period accommodation.

TOP CHOICE **Jeake's House** HOTEL ££

(☎01797-222828; www.jeakeshouse.com; Mermaid St; s/d from £70/114; P 📶) Superbly situated on cobbled Mermaid St, this labyrinthine 17th-century town house once belonged to US poet Conrad Aitken. The '11 Rooms' are named after writers who actually stayed here, though the decor was probably slightly less bold back then, minus the bees-waxed antiques and lavish drapery. You can literally take a pew in the snug book-lined bar and, continuing the theme, breakfast is served in an 18th-century former chapel.

Mermaid Inn HOTEL £££

(☎01797-223065; www.mermaidinn.com; Mermaid St; d £160-250; P) Few inns can claim to be as atmospheric as this ancient hostelry, dating from 1420. Every room is different – but each is thick with dark beams and lit by leaded windows, and some are graced by secret passageways that now act as fire escapes. Small wonder it's such a popular spot – these days you're as likely to spot a celeb or a royal as the resident ghost.

George in Rye HOTEL £££

(☎01797-222114; www.thegeorgeinrye.com; 98 High St; d from £135; @) This old coaching inn has managed to reinvent itself as a contemporary boutique hotel while staying true to its roots. Downstairs, an old-fashioned wood-panelled lounge is warmed by roaring log fires, while the 24 guestrooms, created by the set designer from the film *Pride & Prejudice*, are chic and understated. The George's contemporary restaurant can contend with Rye's best and if you stay here, ask to see the incredible, and unexpectedly large, 18th-century ballroom.

Windmill Guesthouse B&B ££

(☎01797-224027; www.ryewindmill.co.uk; Mill La; d from £65; P) Visible from the main road, this white windmill, sails still intact, houses perhaps Rye's oddest digs. Due to the shape of the building, room sizes vary, as do standards with the two-storey 'Windmill Suite', located almost at the top of the mill and enjoying 360-degree views, one of the town's most sought-after rooms. Breakfast is served in the former granary and the octagonal guest lounge occupies the mill's base. Book well ahead.

Apothecary B&B ££

(☎01797-229157; www.bedandbreakfastrye.com; 1 East St; d from £65) Originally home to Rye's apothecary, this characterful B&B has three rooms and its own coffee shop where breakfast is taken.

Eating

Simon the Pieman TEAROOM £

(3 Lion St; snacks £1.50-5; ⏲9.30am-5pm Mon-Sat, 1.30-5.30pm Sun) Many local cream-tea cognoscenti assert that this traditional tearoom, Rye's oldest, does the best scone-cream-jam combo this side of Romney Marsh. Further foes of tooth and waistline tempt from the shop's window.

Flushing Inn RESTAURANT ££

(☎01797-223292; www.theflushinginn.com; 4 Market St; mains £9.50-20; ⏲lunch & dinner Wed-Sun) Push open the heavy oak door of this 15th-century inn for a homely experience provided by the same family for the past 50 years! A variety of menus and mains, including heaps of veggie options, is cooked and served in person by the friendly owners, who do their utmost to make sure you leave satisfied. A precious 16th-century fresco, only rediscovered in 1901, adds extra flavour to the dining room. Bookings advisable.

Haydens CAFE £

(108 High St; snacks/meals from £3/9; ⏲10am-5pm daily, dinner Fri & Sat) Staunch believers in organic and fair-trade produce, these guys dish up delicious omelettes, ploughman's lunches, salads and pancakes in their light, breezy cafe. There's a wonderful elevated terrace at the back with great views over the town and surrounding countryside.

Ypres Castle Inn PUB ££

(Gun Gardens; meals £5.50-17; ⏲lunch & dinner) You can have a match on a boules pitch, enjoy some live bands or chow down on scrumptious seasonal food like Rye bay scallops at this warm, country-style pub. The beer's not bad either.

Information

Post office (Unit 2, Station Approach)

Rye Heritage Centre (☎01797-226696; www.ryeheritage.co.uk; Strand Quay; ⏲10am-5pm Apr-Oct) Runs a town-model audiovisual history for £3.50 and upstairs is a freaky collection of penny-in-the-slot novelty machines. It also sells a *Rye Town Walk* map (£1) and rents out multilingual audiotours (adult/child £4/2).

Rye Internet Cafe (46 Ferry Rd; per hr £2; ⏲10am-9pm Tue-Thu, 10am-7pm Fri, 11am-6pm Sat & Sun)

Tourist office (☎01797-229049; www.visit1066country.com; 4/5 Lion St; ⏲10am-5pm Apr-Sep) New but rather spartan office. Can help with accommodation bookings.

Getting There & Away

Bus

Dover Bus 100, two hours, hourly

Hastings Bus 344 or 100, 40 minutes, two per hour

Train

London Charing Cross £25.80, two hours, hourly; change either in Hastings or Ashford

Getting Around

Rye Hire (01797-223033; 1 Cyprus Pl; 8am-5pm Mon-Fri, to noon Sat) You can rent all-terrain bikes for £14/10 per day/four hours. Call ahead for Sunday hire.

Battle

POP 5190

This unassuming village grew up around the spot where invading French duke William of Normandy, aka William the Conqueror, scored a decisive victory over local King Harold in 1066, so beginning Norman rule and changing the face of the country forever. If there'd been no battle, there'd be no Battle, as locals sometimes say.

Sights

Battle Abbey BATTLEFIELD

(EH; adult/child £7/3.50; 10am-6pm Apr-Sep) Another day, another photogenic ruin? Hardly. On this spot raged *the* pivotal battle in the last successful invasion of England in 1066: an event with unparalleled impact on the country's subsequent social structure, architecture and well…pretty much everything. Four years after, the conquering Normans began constructing an abbey in the middle of the battlefield, a penance ordered by the Pope for the loss of life incurred here.

Only the foundations of the original church remain, the altar's position marked by a **plaque** – also supposedly the spot England's King Harold famously took an arrow in his eye. Other impressive monastic buildings survive and make for atmospheric explorations.

The battlefield's innocently rolling lush hillsides do little to evoke the ferocity of the event, but high-tech interactive presentations and a film at the new visitors centre, as well as blow-by-blow audiotours, do their utmost to bring the battle to life.

Yesterday's World MUSEUM

(www.yesterdaysworld.co.uk; 89-90 High St; adult/child £7/5; 10am-6pm Apr-Sep) Overshadowed literally and figuratively by the abbey, this growing museum is an incredible repository of England's retail past. The first building houses entire streets of quaint old shops where costumed dummies proffer long-discontinued brands, every space in between stuffed with yester-year products, enamel advertising signs, battered toys, wartime memorabilia and general nostalgia-inducing knick-knackery. The second building is much the same except for the Royalty Room where a cardboard cut-out illustrates just how tiny Queen Victoria was (1.40m).

Sleeping & Eating

Powdermills HOTEL £££

(01424-775511; www.powdermillshotel.com; Powdermill Lane; s/d £125/140; P) Rebuilt in the late 18th century after a gunpowder works saw off the previous manor with a bang, this graceful, ivy-covered country-house hotel has rooms with classic four-poster beds, a wonderful orangery restaurant, a swimming pool and 200-acre grounds of tranquil lakes and woodland adjoining Battle Abbey's grounds.

Tollgate Farmhouse B&B ££

(01424-777436; www.tollgatefarmhouse.co.uk; 59 North Trade Rd; s/d from £40/65; P) A homely atmosphere can be found 10 minutes' walk from the centre of Battle at this large domestic residence, with a handful of florid en suite rooms adorned with embroidery and cut flowers. This must be one of only a handful of B&Bs in the country to have its own outdoor pool. Bookings are essential in summer.

Pilgrim's Restaurant BRITISH £

(1 High St; mains £6-8.50; lunch & dinner Mon-Sat, lunch Sun) Misshapen beams, rough-plastered walls and a vaulted ceiling make this 15th-century pilgrims' lodging the most spectacular place to eat in Battle. The tasty food is prepared as much as possible using Sussex produce and plated up with panache. Staff can be flustered when things are busy.

Information

The **tourist office** (01424-776789; Gatehouse; 10am-6pm Apr-Sep, to 4pm Oct-Mar) is in the entrance to Battle Abbey. The post office, banks and ATMs are also on High St.

Getting There & Away

Bus

London Victoria National Express bus 023, £13.40, 2¼ hours, daily

Hastings Bus 304/305, 26 minutes, hourly

Train

London Charing Cross £18.30, one hour 20 minutes, hourly, twice hourly

THE LAST INVASION OF ENGLAND

The most famous battle in the history of England took place in 1066: a date seared into every English schoolchild's brain. The Battle of Hastings began when Harold's army arrived on the scene on 14 October and created a three-ring defence consisting of archers, then cavalry, with massed infantry at the rear. William marched north from Hastings and took up a position about 400m south of Harold and his troops. He tried repeatedly to break the English cordon, but Harold's men held fast. William's knights then feigned retreat, drawing some of Harold's troops after them. It was a fatal mistake. Seeing the gap in the English wall, William ordered his remaining troops to charge through, and the battle was as good as won. Among the English casualties was King Harold who, as tradition has it, was hit in the eye by an arrow, and struck down by Norman knights as he tried to pull it out. At news of his death the last English resistance collapsed.

In their wonderfully irreverent *1066 and All That* (1930), WC Sellar and RJ Yeatman suggest that 'the Norman conquest was a Good Thing, as from this time onward England stopped being conquered and thus was able to become top nation...' When you consider that England hasn't been successfully invaded since, it's hard to disagree.

Around Battle

BODIAM CASTLE

Surrounded by a square moat teeming with oversized goldfish, four-towered archetypal **Bodiam Castle** (NT; adult/child £6.40/3.20; ⏲10am-6pm mid-Feb–Oct) makes you half expect to see a fire-breathing dragon appear or a golden-haired princess lean over its walls. It is the legacy of 14th-century soldier of fortune (the polite term for knights who slaughtered and pillaged their way around France) Sir Edward Dalyngrigge, who married the local heiress and set about building a castle to make sure everybody knew who was boss.

Parliamentarian forces left the castle in ruins during the English Civil War, but in 1917 Lord Curzon, former viceroy of India, bought it and restored the exterior. Much of the interior remains unrestored, but it's possible to climb to the battlements for some sweeping views.

While here you'll most likely hear the tooting of the nearby **Kent & East Sussex steam railway** (www.kesr.org.uk; day ticket adult/child £12.80/7.80), which runs from Tenterden in Kent through 11 miles of gentle hills and woods to Bodiam village, from where a bus takes you to the castle. It operates three to five services on most days from May to September and at the weekend and school holidays in October, December and February.

The castle is 9 miles northeast of Battle off the B2244. Stagecoach bus 349 stops at Bodiam from Hastings (40 minutes) once every two hours during the day Monday to Saturday.

BATEMAN'S

It was love at first sight when Mr Rudyard Kipling, author of *The Jungle Book*, set eyes on **Bateman's** (NT; adult/child £8.20/4.10; ⏲11am-5pm Sat-Wed mid-Mar–Oct), the glorious little 1634 Jacobean mansion he would call home for the last 34 years of his life, and where he would draw inspiration for *The Just So Stories* and other vivid tales.

Even today, the house is pervaded by a sense of Kipling's cosy contentment here. Everything is pretty much just as the writer left it after his death in 1936, down to the blotting paper on his study desk. Furnishings often reflect his fascination with the East, with many oriental rugs and Indian artefacts adding colour.

The house is surrounded by lovely gardens and a small path leads down to a water mill that grinds corn on Wednesdays and Saturdays at 2pm.

Bateman's is about half a mile south of the town of Burwash along the A259. The nearest railway station is three miles away at Etchingham on the Hastings to London Charing Cross line.

Hastings

POP 85,000

Forever associated with the Norman invasion of 1066 even though the crucial events took place 6 miles away, Hastings thrived as a Cinque Port, and in its Victorian heyday was one of the country's most fashionable seaside resorts. After a period of steady decline, the town is enjoying a mini renaissance, and these days it's an intriguing mix of tacky resort, fishing port and arty New Age hang-out.

Hastings last hit the news in October 2010 when its Victorian pier burnt down following an alleged arson attack. The ballroom at the end of the pier, where groups like the Clash, the Sex Pistols and the Rolling Stones once performed, was completely destroyed. It's very unlikely the money will be found to rebuild this reminder of the town's seaside holiday heyday.

Sights

The best place for aimless wandering is the **Old Town**, a hotchpotch of narrow streets and half-timbered buildings filled with junk shops, quirky boutiques, street cafes, quaint local pubs and galleries.

Down by the seafront, the **Stade** – the stretch of shingle in front of Rock-a-Nore Rd – is home to distinctive, tall black clapboard huts known as **Net Shops**, built as storage for fishing gear back in the 17th century. Some now house fishmongers where the catch brought home by Europe's largest beach-launched fishing fleet is sold.

Three nautical attractions line up one after the other on Rock-a-Nore Rd itself: the **Fishermen's Museum** (www.hastingsfish.co.uk; Rock-a-Nore Rd; admission free; ⏲10am-5pm Apr-Oct), the **Shipwreck and Coastal Heritage Centre** (www.shipwreck-heritage.org.uk; Rock-a-Nore Rd; admission free; ⏲10am-5pm) and the **Blue Reef Aquarium** (www.bluereefaquarium.co.uk/hastings; Rock-a-Nore Rd; adult/child £7.95/5.95; ⏲10am-5pm).

Two Victorian funicular railways scale the high cliffs that shelter the town, the most useful of which is the **West Hill Cliff Railway** (George St; adult/child £2.20/1.30; ⏲10am-5.30pm Apr-Sep), which takes visitors up to West Hill and the ruins of a Norman fortress built by William the Conqueror in 1069, now known as **Hastings Castle** (www.discoverhastings.co.uk; Castle Hill Rd; adult/child £4.25/3.50; ⏲10am-5pm Easter-Sep). The **Smugglers Adventure** (www.smugglersadventure.co.uk; St Clement Caves; adult/child £7.20/5.20; ⏲10am-5pm Easter-Sep) is also on West Hill. Meander through underground caverns to hear yarns of smuggling along the Sussex coast, told through interactive exhibits and a ghostly narrator. The **East Hill Cliff Railway** (Rock-a-Nore Rd; adult/child £2.20/1.30; ⏲10am-5.30pm Apr-Sep) reopened in March 2010, and once again elevates walkers and nature-lovers to the 267-hectare **Hastings Country Park**.

Sleeping & Eating

The Laindons B&B ££
(☎01424-437710; www.thelaindons.com; 23 High St; s/d from £80/110; 📶) This newcomer occupying a Georgian Grade II–listed former coaching inn is five minutes' amble from the seafront at the quieter end of High St. The three beautifully appointed rooms are flooded with sea-refracted light from the huge Georgian windows, illuminating the blend of breezy contemporary design and antique furnishings. Owner-cooked breakfasts are taken around a communal table.

Swan House B&B ££
(☎01424-430014; www.swanhousehastings.co.uk; 1 Hill St; s/d from £70/115; @📶) Inside its ancient, timbered 15th-century shell this place blends contemporary and vintage chic to perfection. Rooms feature organic toiletries, fresh flowers, hand-painted walls and huge beds. The guest lounge, where pale sofas, painted floorboards and striking modern sculpture sit alongside beams and a huge stone fireplace, is a stunner.

Dragon Bar BAR/RESTAURANT ££
(71 George St; mains £10-16; ⏲lunch & dinner Mon-Sat, lunch Sun) Atmospheric, laid-back bar full of dark walls, mismatched furniture and beaten leather sofas, attracting the younger end of the alternative old-town crowds. The eclectic menu features everything from Thai curry to Winchelsea lamb to pizzas.

Information

Tourist office (☎01424-451111; Queen's Sq; ⏲8.30am-6.15pm Mon-Fri, 9am-5pm Sat, 10.30am-4pm Sun) This large office sells all kinds of bus, ferry and train tickets as well as locally themed publications.

Getting There & Away

Bus

Eastbourne Bus 99, one hour 20 minutes, three per hour

London Victoria National Express, £13.40, 2½ to four hours, twice daily

Rye Buses 100 & 344, 40 minutes, twice hourly

Train

Brighton £11.20, one hour to 1 hour 20 minutes, three per hour, via Eastbourne

London Charing Cross £25.90, 1½ hours, twice hourly

London Victoria £25.90, two hours, hourly

Eastbourne

POP 89,667

This classic, old-fashioned seaside resort has long brought to mind images of octogenarians dozing in deck chairs. While many of Eastbourne's seafront hotels still have that retirement-home feel, in recent years an influx of students and one of the largest new Polish communities in the southeast have given the town a sprightlier feel. The creation of the new South Downs National Park to the west also means Eastbourne's pebbly beaches, scrupulously snipped seaside gardens and picturesque arcade-free promenade are likely to see increasing numbers of walkers and cyclists, finishing or embarking on a trip along the South Downs Way.

Sights & Activities

FREE **Towner Art Gallery** ART GALLERY
(☎01323-434670; www.townereastbourne.org.uk; Devonshire Park, College Rd; ⊙10am-6pm Tue-Sun, bldg tours 11.30am) Until Turner Margate is up and running, Eastbourne's Towner Gallery will be far and away the most exciting new exhibition space on the south coast. The purpose-built, state-of-the-art gallery building has temporary shows of contemporary work on the ground and second floors, while the first floor is given over to rotating themed shows created from the 4000-piece-strong Towner collection. Building tours include a peek inside the climate-controlled art store.

Pier PIER
(seafront) Eastbourne's striking filigree-trimmed pier is a lovely place to watch the sunset, and also has a curious Victorian **Camera Obscura** that projects images of the outside world into a dish within a darkened room (when it's working).

Museum of Shops MUSEUM
(20 Cornfield Tce; adult/child £4.50/3.50; ⊙10am-5pm) This small museum is swamped by an obsessive collection of how-we-used-to-live memorabilia.

Eastbourne Heritage Centre MUSEUM
(www.eastbournesociety.co.uk; 2 Carlisle Rd; adult/child £2.50/1; ⊙2-5pm Apr-Oct) Livens up exhibits on the town's history with eccentric asides, such as on Donald McGill, the pioneer of the 'naughty postcard'.

Redoubt Fortress FORTRESS
(www.eastbournemuseums.co.uk; Royal Pde; adult/child £4/2; ⊙10am-5pm Tue-Sun Apr-Nov) One in a chain of 77 strongholds built in the early 19th century to defend the south coast from Napoleon's planned invasion. It now houses a small military museum.

Tours

City Sightseeing BUS TOURS
(☎0170-886 6000; www.city sightseeing.co.uk; adult/child £5/3; ⊙tours every 30min 10am-4.30pm) Open-top bus tours around local sights and up to Beachy Head.

Allchorn Pleasure Boats BOAT TRIPS
(☎01323-410606, www.allchornpleasureboats.co.uk; adult/child £9/5.50; ⊙hourly 10.30am-3.30pm Jun-Oct) The dramatic white cliffs to the west are best viewed from the sea; tours leave from just west of the pier, weather permitting.

Sleeping

The Big Sleep DESIGN HOTEL ££
(☎01323-722676; www.thebigsleephotel.com; King Edward's Pde; s/d from £45/59; 🅦) Hip, fresh and friendly, this seafront design hotel has 50 gobsmacking rooms with big-print wallpaper, retro furnishings and curtains that look as though they might have been grazing on Beachy Head just a few hours prior. Home to Eastbourne's trendiest bar, a big basement games room and Channel views make this BN21's coolest kip.

Albert & Victoria B&B ££
(☎01323-730948; www.albertandvictoria.com; 19 St Aubyns Rd; s/d £45/70) Book ahead to stay at this delightful Victorian terraced house with opulent rooms, canopied beds, crystal chandeliers and wall frescoes in the breakfast room, mere paces from the seafront promenade.

Eastbourne YHA EASTBOURNE YHA HOSTEL £
(☎0845-371 9316; www.yha.org.uk; East Dean Rd; dm from £14) A brand new, purpose-built and ecofriendly hostel on the road into the South Downs National Park. Take bus 12 from the pier.

Eating & Drinking

Eastbourne's restaurants gather around the seafront end of Terminus Rd and along Seaside Rd.

Lamb Inn PUB ££

(36 High St; mains £9.50-12; ⌚lunch & dinner) This Eastbourne institution located less than a mile northwest of the train station in the undervisited Old Town has been plonking Sussex wet ones on the bar for eight centuries. A holidaying Dickens also left a few beer rings and smudged napkins here (he stayed across the road). Take bus 1, 1A or 10.

Dal Maestro ITALIAN ££

(☎01323-417733; www.dalmaestro.co.uk; 17 Carlisle Rd; mains £4-18; ⌚10am-5pm Mon-Sat) This chic new Italian job near the Towner Gallery has old curved-glass vitrines, an elegantly contemporary dining room and perfectly crafted meat dishes, pastas, salads and desserts.

Oastler's Pie & Mash DINER £

(22 Seaside Rd; meals from £3.80; ⌚lunch Tue-Sat) What could be more 'south coast' than good ole pie, mash, stewed oysters and liquor (parsley sauce) for the London day-tripper crowd. Austere 1950s setting and simple but delicious grub.

Shopping

Camilla's Bookshop SECONDHAND BOOKSHOP

(www.camillasbookshop.com; 57 Grove Rd) Literally packed to the rafters with musty volumes, this incredible book repository, a short amble from the train station, fills three floors of a crumbling Victorian town house. The owner claims to have over a million books for sale, making it the best stocked, if not the biggest, secondhand bookstore in England.

Information

Tourist office (☎0871-663 0031; www.visiteastbourne.com; Cornfield Rd; ⌚9.15am-5.30pm Mon-Fri, to 4pm Sat Apr-Oct) Can book accommodation for a £3 fee.

Getting There & Away

Bus

Brighton Bus 12, one hour 15 minutes, three per hour

Hastings Bus 99, one hour 20 minutes, three per hour

Train

Brighton £8.50, 30 to 40 minutes, twice hourly

London Victoria £23.90, 1½ hours, twice hourly

Around Eastbourne

After decades of campaigning, planning and deliberation, the South Downs National Park, stretching west from Eastbourne for around 100 miles, finally came into being in March 2010. Most of the sights below fall within the park's boundaries.

BEACHY HEAD

The famous cliffs of Beachy Head are the highest point in a string of chalky rock faces that slice across this rugged stretch of coast at the southern end of the South Downs. It's a spot of thrilling beauty, at least until you remember that this is also officially one of the top suicide spots in the world!

From Beachy Head, the stunning **Seven Sisters Cliffs** undulate their way west, a clifftop path (a branch of the South Downs Way) riding the waves of chalk as far as the picturesque Cuckmere Haven. Along the way, you'll stumble upon the tiny seaside hamlet of **Birling Gap**, where you can stop for a drink, snack or ice cream at the **Birling Gap Hotel** (Seven Sisters Cliffs, Birling Gap, East Dene). The secluded sun-trap beach here is popular with locals and walkers taking a breather.

Beachy Head is off the B2103, from the A259 between Eastbourne and Newhaven. Eastbourne's City Sightseeing tour bus stops at the clifftop.

THE LONG MAN

If you're travelling along the A27 between Eastbourne and Lewes, be sure to look southwards, just east of the village of Wilmington, to see the spindly **Long Man of Wilmington**. No one really knows how this leggy 70m-high geoglyph – now marked out with white concrete – arrived here or what he represents, though many assume he's a Victorian hoax.

There is a turn-off for the Long Man at Wilmington, 7 miles west of Eastbourne, from where you can get a close-up view. If you're walking this section of the South Downs Way, the path passes right over the figure's head and it's easy to miss.

PEVENSEY CASTLE

The ruins of William the Conqueror's first stronghold, **Pevensey Castle** (EH; adult/child £4.50/2.30; ⌚10am-6pm Apr-Sep), sit 5 miles east of Eastbourne, off the A259. Pictur-

THE BLOOMSBURY GROUP

The Bloomsbury Group was Britain's most influential artistic and intellectual circle to arise from the first half of the 20th century, a set of Cambridge graduates, artists and scholars who all gravitated to London's Bloomsbury area pre-WWI. Its most famous members included Virginia Woolf, Maynard Keynes, Vanessa Bell, Duncan Grant, Lytton Strachey, TS Elliot and EM Forster.

The outspokenly pacifist group gained notoriety for stunts that embarrassed the military forces during WWI, and scandalised London society with their intergroup relationships and, in several cases, bisexuality. Their tastes in post-Impressionist art and avant-garde literature were ahead of their time, and were often savaged by critics only to be later hailed as masterpieces. Woolf of course was winning herself acclaim as a novelist, and with her husband Leonard founded the Hogarth Press. Her artist sister Vanessa and Vanessa's lover Duncan Grant were two of several group members to make a name through the modernist design firm Omega Workshops. Keynes, meanwhile, became one of the foremost economic theorists of the day, and Strachey had several uncompromising biographies under his belt.

Though the group gradually drifted apart after the war and Woolf committed suicide in 1941, their once-controversial views were steadily accepted into the mainstream and their work has continued to influence generations of new writers, poets, artists and musicians.

esquely dissolving into its own moat, the castle marks the point where William the Conqueror landed in 1066, just two weeks before the Battle of Hastings. And shortly afterwards, Old Bill wasted no time in building upon sturdy Roman walls to create a castle, which was used time and again through the centuries, right up to WWII. You can roam about its decaying husk with an enlightening audioguide, free with entry.

The 14th-century **Mint House** (High St; admission £1), just across the road from the castle, is worth visiting for its nutty collection of antiques and curios.

Regular train services between London Victoria and Hastings via Eastbourne (10 minutes) stop at Westham, half a mile from Pevensey.

CHARLESTON FARMHOUSE

Five miles west of Eastbourne, **Charleston Farmhouse** (www.charleston.org.uk; Firle, off A27; adult/child £9/5; ⌚1-6pm Wed-Sat, to 5.30pm Sun Apr-Oct) was the bohemian country getaway of the influencial Bloomsbury Group. Even now that the joyous frescoes and vivid furniture have begun to fade, and the last of its pioneering occupants and visitors have long since passed away, it's still a tangible example of the rich intellectual and aesthetic life that they came to represent.

In 1916, Virginia Woolf's sister, painter Vanessa Bell, moved here with her lover Duncan Grant, and they set about redecorating with abandon in a style that owed much to the influence of the post-Impressionists. Hardly a wall, door or piece of furniture was left untouched, and the walls featured paintings by Picasso, Derain, Delacroix and others. There's also a striking garden, interesting outbuildings and medieval dovecote.

Visits are by guided tour only, except on Sunday and bank holiday Mondays. The nearest train station is at Berwick, on the Brighton to Eastbourne line, a 2-mile walk from the farmhouse.

ALFRISTON

Eight miles west of Eastbourne lies the excruciatingly quaint village of Alfriston, an essential stop for South Downs Way hikers and south coast explorers.

Most action takes place on boutique- and tavern-lined **High Street**, a crooked hodgepodge of medieval half-timbered houses, some (such as the Star Inn) still supporting their original flagstone roofs. Just off High St, in a bend in the River Cuckmere, stands musty **St Andrew's Church**, a 14th-century creation in flint known as the 'Cathedral of the Downs' due to its size. Notice the rare bell ropes that descend into the chancel crossing (where the nave meets the transepts). The **Clergy House** (NT; adult/child £4.05/2.05; ⌚10.30am-5pm Wed, Thu, Sat-Mon) is the church's old vicarage and the first property to be acquired by the National Trust in 1896.

Just across the bridge from the church is the point where the South Downs Way divides, one route heading south to the sea and the Seven Sisters, the other inland to the Long Man.

Guided tours (3pm Sat Jul & Aug) leave from the Market Cross.

Where the A27 meets the access road to the village is **Drusillas** (www.drusillas.co.uk; admission £14.30; 10am-5pm), probably the best small zoo in the country. There's heaps of turtle-stroking, cow-milking, dino-hunting fun to be had and the playgrounds and rides are superb.

Lewes

POP 15,988

Strung out along an undulating High St flanked by elegant Georgian buildings, a part-ruined castle and a traditional brewery perfuming the air with a hoppy aroma, Lewes (pronounced 'Lewis') is a charmingly affluent hillside town with a turbulent past and fiery traditions. Off the main drag, however, there's a more intimate atmosphere as you descend into twisting narrow streets called twittens – the remainder of the town's original medieval street plan.

The town made headlines in late 2008 when it introduced its own currency to encourage more money to be spent in the local economy. The Lewes Pound has the same value as sterling and is accepted by over 130 businesses.

Lewes' other claim to fame is that it straddles the 0 degrees line of longitude. An inconspicuous **plaque** in Western Rd marks the meridian, though modern measuring methods have actually placed the line around 100m to the east, running right through the Black Horse Inn.

Sights

Lewes Castle & Barbican House Museum CASTLE/MUSEUM

(www.sussexpast.co.uk; 169 High St; adult/child £6/3, with Anne of Cleves House £8.80/4.40; 10am-5.30pm Tue-Sat, 11am-5.30pm Sun-Mon) Now little more than a set of ruins, this castle was built shortly after the 1066 Norman invasion. It never saw warfare, not counting the riotous celebrations following the navy's victory over the Spanish Armada in 1588, when happy citizens blew great chunks out of the castle's walls! They left enough standing for it to remain an impressive sight, however, and its windy keep, visible for miles around, affords widescreen views across the town and beyond. The castle grounds also host summertime plays and concerts.

The attached **Barbican House Museum** has a good collection of prehistoric flint axeheads, Anglo-Saxon jewellery and medieval long swords, but the star attraction is the recently reinstated town model, glued together by an army of volunteers in the mid-1980s and showing how the town looked a century earlier.

Anne of Cleves House Museum MUSEUM

(52 Southover High St; adult/child £4.20/2.10; 10am-5pm Tue-Thu, from 11am Sun & Mon Mar-Oct) When Henry VIII divorced Anne of Cleves in 1541, he gave her this timber-framed house as part of her divorce settlement, although she never moved in. The creak-and-groan floors and spider's web wooden roof today sandwich an idiosyncratic folk museum, with everything from a witch's effigy complete with pins to a rack of Tudor costumes to try on.

Activities

Paragliders can get one step closer to heaven in the South Downs near Lewes, an excellent spot for the sport. A half-hour tandem flight costs about £100 to £120.

Companies include the following:

Airworks PARAGLIDING

(01273-858108; www.airworks.co.uk; Glynde)

Flybubble PARAGLIDING

(01273-812442; www.flybubble.co.uk; Ringmer)

Sussex Hang Gliding & Paragliding PARAGLIDING

(01273-858170; www.flysussex.co.uk; Tollgate)

Sleeping

TOP CHOICE **Langtons House** B&B ££

(01273-476644; www.langtonshouse.com; 143b High St; s £65, d £80-110) This three-room boutique newcomer opposite the Fifteenth Century Bookshop is Lewes' most luxurious B&B. The high-ceilinged rooms all have little opulent touches and the owners pull out all the stops to make guests feel welcome.

Castle Banks Cottage B&B ££

(01273-476291; www.castlebankscottage.co.uk; 4 Castle Banks; s/d £37.50/75) Tucked away in a quiet lane near the castle, this tiny, pretty guesthouse has only two rooms. The easy-

LEWES GOES FIRECRACKERS

The English enjoy an evening of frenzied pyromania nationwide on Guy Fawkes Night (5 November) in memory of a 1605 plot to blow up the Houses of Parliament. But Lewes has double the reason to host one of the craziest fireworks celebrations you're ever likely to see.

In 1555, at the height of Mary Tudor's Catholic revival, 17 Protestant martyrs were burned at the stake in the town's High St. Lewes has not forgotten, and every 5 November tens of thousands gather for the famous fireworks display, in which effigies of the pope (plus modern-day figures such as prime ministers, presidents and England football managers) are burnt in memory of the martyrs. Locals parade the streets in outlandish medieval garb and send barrels packed with bangers to crack and fizzle their way down to the river, chased by local youth.

going proprietor is a mine of information about the area's local history. Breakfast is served in the secluded garden in summer.

Berkeley House Hotel B&B ££
(☎01273-476057; www.berkeleyhouselewes.co.uk; 2 Albion St; s from £55, d £75-120;) Unexpected extras such as a roof terrace looking over the South Downs and iPod docks make this Georgian town house worth a go, as do the tastefully decorated rooms and courteous service.

Shelleys HOTEL £££
(☎01273-472361; www.the-shelleys.co.uk; High St; s/d from £135/190;) Full of old-fashioned charm, this 16th-century manor house was once home to the earl of Dorset and was owned by the Shelley family (of Percy Bysshe fame). It has cosy, country rooms and a good restaurant overlooking a lovely walled garden.

Eating & Drinking

TOP CHOICE Bill's CAFE £
(56 Cliffe High St; meals £2.50-9; lunch) Part grocers, part delicatessen, part rustic-styled cafe, this insanely popular place envelopes customers in its colours and smells then dishes up melt-in-the-mouth tartlets, gourmet pizzas, salads, desserts and other artisanal snacks. Get here early for Sunday dinner as it's normally chock-a-block.

Real Eating Company BRITISH ££
(18 Cliffe High St; mains £6-16; 11.30am-4pm Mon, to 11pm Tue-Fri, 9am-11pm Sat, 9.30am-4pm Sun) This large, airy cafe-brasserie stretches back to a lovely outside terrace and serves delicious cheese and charcuterie plates, breakfast, omelettes and substantial British meat-and-two-veg combos – such as roast pork belly with mash and Cumberland sausage with onion gravy.

John Harvey Tavern PUB
(Bear Yard) Warm and friendly place just off the high street serving a great selection of ales from the local Harveys brewery, a hop's throw away. There's decent food on offer and regular live music nights.

Shopping

Fifteenth Century Bookshop SECONDHAND BOOKSHOP
(99 High St) Rummage through antiquarian treasures and new editions at the fabulous, half-timbered bookshop housed in a former candle factory.

Old Needlemakers SECONDHAND BAZAAR
(West St) A complex of quaint craft and secondhand shops with a decent cafe.

Information

Post office (High St)

Tourist office (☎01273-483448; www.enjoysussex.info; 187 High St; 9am-5pm Mon-Fri, 9.30am-5.30pm Sat & 10am-2pm Sun Apr-Oct) Helps with accommodation bookings.

Getting There & Away

Lewes is 9 miles northeast of Brighton and 16 miles northwest of Eastbourne, just off the A27.

Bus

Brighton Bus 28/29, 34 minutes, every 15 minutes

Tunbridge Wells Bus 29, one hour 10 minutes, every 30 minutes

Train

Brighton 13 minutes, four times hourly

Eastbourne 20 minutes, four times hourly

London Victoria £21.40, 1¼ hours, twice hourly

Around Lewes

In 1934 science teacher John Christie and his opera-singer wife decided to build a 1200-seat opera house in the middle of nowhere. It seemed a magnificent folly at the time. But now **Glyndebourne** (☎01273-812321; www.glyndebourne.com) is one of England's best places to enjoy the lyric arts, with a season that runs from late May to the end of August. Tickets can be like gold dust so book well ahead. And bring your glad rags: dress code is strictly black tie and evening dress. Glyndebourne is 4 miles east of Lewes off the B2192.

Brighton & Hove

POP 247, 817

Raves on the beach, Graham Greene novels, Mods and Rockers in bank holiday fisticuffs, hens and stags on naughty weekends, classic car runs from London, the UK's biggest gay scene and the Channel's best clubbing – this city by the sea evokes many images among the British, but one thing is for certain: with its bohemian, cosmopolitan, hedonistic vibe, Brighton is where England's seaside experience goes from cold to cool.

Brighton rocks all year round, but really comes to life during the summer months, when tourists, language students and revellers from London, keen to explore the city's legendary nightlife, summer festivals and multitude of trendy restaurants, slick boutique hotels and shops, pour into the city. The city has embraced the outlandish ever since the Prince Regent built his party palace here in the 19th century. Celebrities rub shoulders with dreadlocked hippies, drag queens party next to designer-clad urbanites, and kids toddle around the tables of mocha-quaffing media types.

The town's increase in popularity over the past decade isn't all good, however. Chain bars are slowly sneaking into once staunchly alternative areas, and some long-term residents grumble that the city's trendy status and the influx of moneyed outsiders are prompting a sharp rise in prices and pretension, detracting from the very alternative spirit that makes the city unique in the first place and creating a kind of London-on-Sea in the process.

Brighton last hit the news in 2010 in the wake of the British General Election when the city centre constituency found itself with the UK's very first Green Party MP, Caroline Lucas. Perhaps more surprising to many in this supposed hip nest of alternativism is that the city's other two constituencies (Kemptown and Hove) plumped for the Tories.

Sights

Royal Pavilion ROYAL RESIDENCE

(www.brighton-hove-rpml.org.uk/royalpavilion; adult/child £9.50/5.40; 9.30am-5.45pm Apr-Sep, 10am-5.15pm Oct-Mar) The city's must-see attraction is the Royal Pavilion, the glittering party-pad and palace of Prince George, later Prince Regent then King George IV. It's one of the most decadent buildings in England and an apt symbol of Brighton's reputation for hedonism. The Indian-style domes and Moorish minarets outside are only a prelude to the palace's lavish oriental-themed interior, where no colour is deemed too strong, dragons swoop and snarl from gilt-smothered ceilings, gem-encrusted snakes slither down pillars, and crystal chandeliers seem ordered by the tonne. While gawping is the main activity, you can pick up an audiotour (included in the admission price) to learn more about the palace.

FREE **Brighton Museum & Art Gallery** MUSEUM/GALLERY

(Royal Pavilion Gardens; 10am-7pm Tue, to 5pm Wed-Sat, 2-5pm Sun) Set in the Royal Pavilion's renovated stable block, this museum and art gallery has a glittering collection of 20th-century art and design, including a crimson Salvador Dalí sofa modelled on Mae West's lips. There's also an enthralling gallery of world art, an impressive collection of Egyptian artefacts and an 'images of Brighton' multimedia exhibit containing a series of oral histories and a model of the now defunct West Pier.

Brighton Pier PIER

(www.brightonpier.co.uk) This grand old centenarian pier, full of glorious gaudiness, is the place to experience the tackier side of Brighton. There are plenty of stomach-churning fairground rides and dingy amusement arcades to keep you amused, and candy floss and Brighton rock to chomp on while you're doing so.

Look west and you'll see the sad remains of the **West Pier** (www.westpier.co.uk), a skeletal iron hulk that attracts flocks of birds at sunset. It's a sad end for a Victorian marvel upon which the likes of Charlie Chaplin and Stan Laurel once performed.

WANT MORE?

Head to **Lonely Planet** (http://www.lonelyplanet.com/england/southeast-england/brighton-and-hove) for planning advice, author recommendations, traveller reviews and insider tips.

So far there's no sign of the i360 observation tower ('Hurray!' some may cry), a spectacularly space-age piece of architecture from the creators of the London Eye that may one day loom 150m above the seafront. This would include a West Pier Heritage Centre – a pavilion where AV exhibits will relate the pier's history.

FREE **Booth Museum of Natural History** MUSEUM
(194 Dyke Rd; ⏲10am-5pm Mon-Wed, Fri, Sat, 2-5pm Sun) This odd Victorian taxidermy museum has several creepy sights such as walls full of mammoth butterflies and cabinets of birds poised to tear apart small mammals – particularly disturbing if you've seen the Hitchcock movie. The museum is about half a mile north of the train station. Buses 27 and 27A stop nearby on Dyke Rd.

FREE **Hove Museum & Art Gallery** MUSEUM/GALLERY
(19 New Church Rd; ⏲10am-5pm Mon, Tue, Thu-Sat, 2-5pm Sun) It may surprise you that Hove can justifiably claim to be the birthplace of British cinema, with the first short-film shot here in 1898. You can see it alongside other fascinating films at this attractive Victorian villa. Another highlight is the kids' room, full of fairy lights and reverberating to the snores of a wizard and the whirr of an underfloor train. Exhibits include old zoetropes, a magic lantern and a small cupboard with a periscope inside. From central Brighton take bus 1, 1A, 6 or 6A from Churchill Sq.

Brighton Sea Life Centre AQUARIUM
(www.sealifeeurope.com; Marine Pde; adult/child £15.50/10.50; ⏲10am-5.30pm) This grand old Victorian aquarium is the world's oldest operational sea-life centre, and makes for a fun hour or two pressing your nose up against glass and making fishy faces at sea horses, rays, sea turtles and other inhabitants.

Brighton Marina MARINA
(www.brightonmarina.co.uk; Marina Way) Brighton's wave-shaped marina, the largest in the UK, washes ashore 1.5 miles east of the pier. In addition to brand-name shopping and numerous chain eateries, you'll also find Brighton's Hollywood-style **Walk of Fame**, which dedicates a pavement-embedded plaque to anyone rich, famous and with a link to the city, though some associations are tenuous. Big-hitting names honoured include Graham Greene, Winston Churchill and Lewis Carroll.

Reaching the marina is half the fun when you hop aboard the **Volks Electric Railway** (www.volkselectricrailway.co.uk; single/return £1.80/2.80; ⏲10.15am-5pm). The world's oldest electric railway, opened in 1883, trundles along the seafront from just short of the pier. Otherwise take bus 7.

Activities

There is a huge range of activities on offer in Brighton, from rollerblading to beach volleyball to skateboarding to paragliding, and of course myriad water sports: ask the tourist office for details.

Tours

City Sightseeing BUS TOURS
(www.city-sightseeing.co.uk; adult/child £8/3; ⏲tours every 30min May-late Sep) Open-top hop-on/hop-off bus tours leaving from Grand Junction Rd near Brighton Pier.

Tourist Tracks MP3 TOURS
(www.tourist-tracks.com) MP3 audioguides downloadable from the website (£5) or available on a preloaded MP3 player at the tourist office (£6 per half-day).

Festivals & Events

There's always something fun going on in Brighton, from **Gay Pride** (www.brightonpride.org; ⏲early Aug;) to food and drink festivals, but the showpiece is May's three-week-long **Brighton Festival** (☎01273-709 709; www.brightonfestival.org), the biggest arts festival in Britain after Edinburgh, drawing theatre, dance, music and comedy performers from around the globe.

Sleeping

Despite a glut of hotels in Brighton, prices are relatively high and you'd be wise to book well ahead for summer weekends and for the Brighton Festival in May. Expect to pay up to a third more at weekends across the board.

Brighton's hostels are a varied bunch. Several cater to raucous stag and hen nights; others are more traditional and homely.

Brighton & Hove

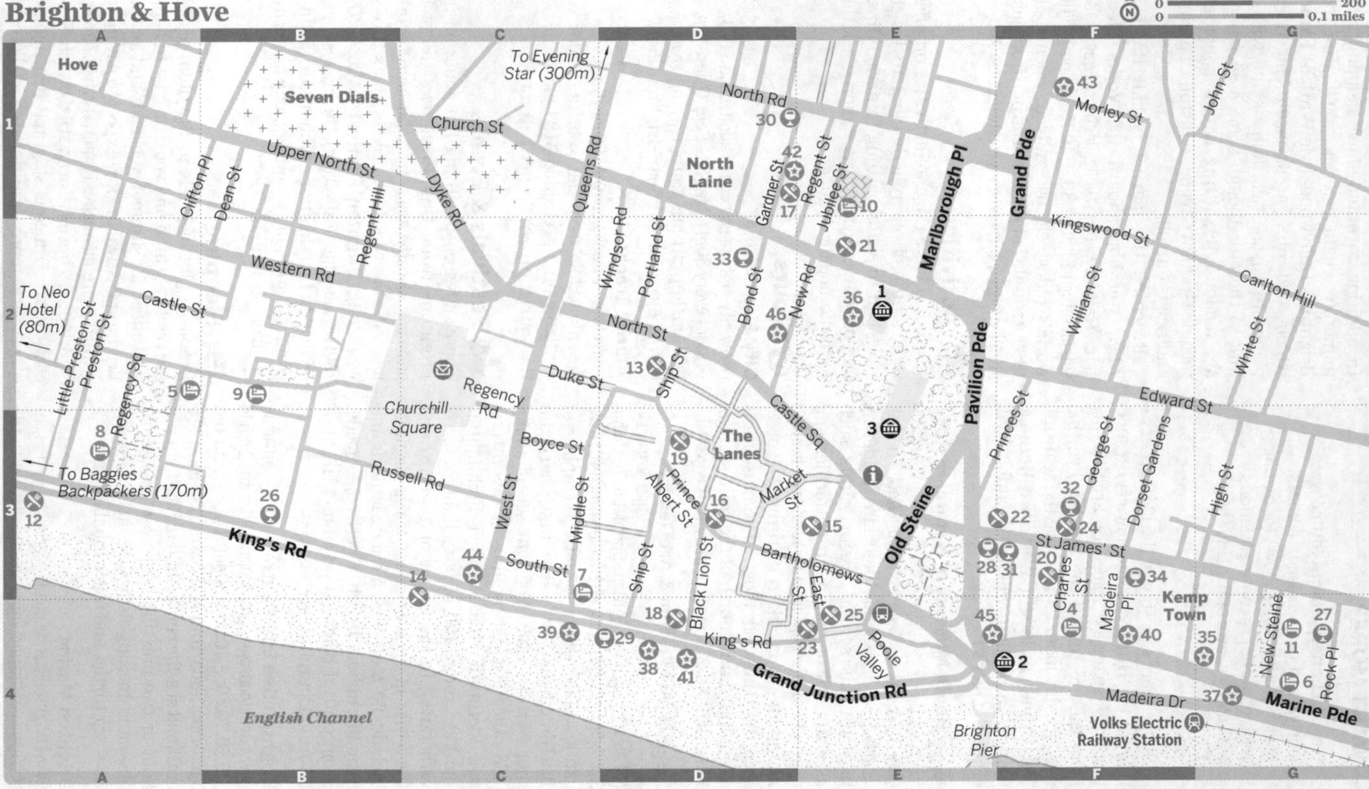

Choose wisely! Brighton is blessed with a wide selection of midrange accommodation.

TOP CHOICE **Neo Hotel** BOUTIQUE HOTEL ££
(☎01273-711104; www.neohotel.com; 19 Oriental Pl; d from £100; 📶) You won't be surprised to learn that the owner of this gorgeous hotel is an interior stylist. The nine rooms could have dropped straight out of the pages of a design magazine, each finished in rich colours and tactile fabrics, with bold floral and Asian motifs and black-tiled bathrooms. Kick back in satin kimono robes and watch a DVD on your wafer-thin-screen TV, or indulge in massage and beauty treatments. Wonderful breakfasts include homemade smoothies and fruit pancakes.

Baggies Backpackers HOSTEL £
(☎01273-733740; www.baggiesbackpackers.com; 33 Oriental Pl; dm/d £13/35; 📶) A warm familial atmosphere, worn-in charm, motherly onsite owners and clean, snug dorms have made this long-established hostel an institution. It's also blessed with a homely kitchen, an inexpensive laundry, a cosy basement music and chill-out room and a TV lounge piled high with video cassettes. The hostel only takes phone bookings and is a stag- and hen-free zone.

Snooze HOTEL ££
(☎01273-605797; www.snoozebrighton.com; 25 St George's Tce; s/d from £60/85; @📶) This eccentric Kemptown pad is very fond of retro styling. Rooms feature vintage posters, bright '60s and '70s patterned wallpaper, flying wooden ducks, floral sinks and mad clashes of colour. It's more than just a gimmick though – rooms are comfortable and spotless, and there are great veggie breakfasts. You'll find it just off St James' St about 500m east of New Steine.

Hotel Pelirocco THEME HOTEL ££
(☎01273-327055; www.hotelpelirocco.co.uk; 10 Regency Sq; s £50-65, d £95-130, ste from £230; @📶) One of Brighton's first theme hotels, this is the sexiest and nuttiest place to stay in town and the ultimate venue for a flirty weekend in style. There's a range of flamboyantly designed rooms, some by artists,

Brighton & Hove

Sights
1 Brighton Museum & Art Gallery E2
2 Brighton Sea Life Centre F4
3 Royal Pavilion E3

Sleeping
4 Amsterdam F4
5 Brighton House Hotel A2
6 Drakes G4
7 Grapevine C3
8 Hotel Pelirocco A3
9 Motel Schmotel B2
10 myhotel E1
11 Seaspray G4

Eating
12 Al Fresco A3
13 Bombay Aloo D2
14 Due South C3
15 English's Oyster Bar E3
16 Food for Friends D3
17 Infinity Foods Cafe D1
18 JB's American Diner D4
19 Piccolo's D3
20 Pomegranate F3
21 Pompoko E2
22 Red Roaster F3
23 Scoop & Crumb E4
24 Tea Cosy F3
25 Terre à Terre E4

Drinking
26 106 Bar & Brasserie D3
Amsterdam .... (see 4)
27 Brighton Rocks G4
28 Candy Bar E3
29 Coalition D4
30 Dorset D1
31 Hub F3
32 Queen's Arms F3
33 Riki Tik D2
34 St James F3

Entertainment
Audio .... (see 4)
35 Basement Club G4
36 Brighton Dome E2
37 Concorde 2 .... G4
38 Digital D4
39 Funky Buddha C4
40 Funky Fish Club F4
41 Honey Club D4
42 Komedia Theatre D1
43 Ocean Rooms F1
44 Odeon Cinema C3
45 Revenge E4
46 Theatre Royal D2

THE PRINCE, THE PALACE & THE PARTYING

It's widely known that England's George III was, to be polite, a little nuts. But you'd be forgiven for thinking that 'Mad King George's' eldest son Prince George (1762–1830) was the eccentric in the family upon visiting his princely pavilion at Brighton. The young prince began drinking with abandon and enjoying the pleasures of women while still a teenager. And to daddy's displeasure, he soon started hanging out with his dissolute uncle the Duke of Cumberland, who was enjoying himself royally by the sea in Brighton.

In 1787 George commissioned Henry Holland to design a neoclassical villa as his personal pleasure palace. While he waited to accede to the throne (when his father was declared officially insane in 1810 he was sworn in as Prince Regent), George whiled away the years with debauched parties for himself, his mistresses and his aristocratic mates.

Ever conscious of what was trendy, George decided in 1815 to convert the Marine Pavilion to reflect the current fascination with all things Eastern. He engaged the services of John Nash, who laboured for eight years to create a Mogul Indian-style palace, complete with the most lavish Chinese interior imaginable. George finally had a palace suited to his outlandish tastes and, to boot, he was now the king.

His brother and successor, William IV (1765–1837), also used the pavilion as a royal residence, as did William's niece Victoria (1819–1901). But the conservative queen never really took to the place and in 1850 sold it to the town, but not before stripping it of every piece of furniture – 143 wagons were needed to transport the contents. Thankfully, many original items were later returned and the palace is now restored to its former glory.

some by big-name sponsors, from a basic single done up like a boxing ring, to Betty's Boudoir with leopard skin throws and a big-enough-for-two bath, to the Play Room suite with a 3m circular bed, mirrored ceiling and pole-dancing area.

myhotel DESIGN HOTEL ££
(☎01273-9003000; www.myhotels.com; 17 Jubilee St; r from £94; P @) With trend-setting rooms looking like space-age pods, full of curved white walls, floor-to-ceiling observation windows and suspended flatscreen TVs, with the odd splash of neon orange or pink, there's nothing square about this place, daddio. You can even hook up your iPod and play music through speakers in the ceiling. There's a cocoon-like cocktail bar downstairs, and if you've money to burn, a suite with a steam room and harpooned vintage carousel horse.

Motel Schmotel B&B ££
(☎01273-326129; www.motelschmotel.co.uk; 37 Russell Sq; s/d from £50/60;) If you can overlook the petite rooms and minuscule bathrooms, this 11-room B&B in a Regency town house, a short stroll from virtually anywhere, is a sound and very central place to hit the sack. Rooms are accented with colourful oversize prints and an uncluttered design, and guests heap praise on the breakfast cooked by the always-around-to-help couple who run the place.

Paskins Town House B&B ££
(☎01273-601203; www.paskins.co.uk; 18/19 Charlotte St; d from £60; @) An environmentally friendly B&B spread between two elegant town houses. It prides itself on using ecofriendly products such as recycled toilet paper, low-energy bulbs and biodegradable cleaning materials. The individually designed rooms are beautifully maintained, and excellent organic and vegetarian breakfasts are served in the art deco–inspired breakfast room.

Drakes BOUTIQUE HOTEL £££
(☎01273-696934; www.drakesofbrighton.com; 43-44 Marine Pde; r £105-275; P @) Drakes oozes understated class: a stylish, minimalist boutique hotel that eschews the need to shout its existence from the rooftops (you could easily miss it). Feature rooms have giant free-standing tubs set in front of full-length bay windows with stunning views out to sea.

Blanch House BOUTIQUE HOTEL £££
(☎01273-603504; www.blanchhouse.co.uk; 17 Atlingworth St; r £100-230; @) Themed rooms are the name of the game in this boutique hotel, but there's nothing tacky about them – plush fabrics and a Victorian roll-top bath rule in the 'Decadence' suite and the 'Snowstorm' room is a frosty vision in white and tinkling ice. There's a magnificently stylish fine dining restaurant here –

all white leather banquettes and space-age swivel chairs – and a fine cocktail bar. No wonder it's the hotel of choice for celebs in transit. To reach it from New Steine, walk for 150m east along St James' St then turn right into Atlingworth St.

Seadragon Backpackers HOSTEL £
(☎01273-711854; www.seadragonbackpackers.co.uk; 36 Waterloo St; dm/tw incl breakfast £20/50; 📶) Perched on the edge of Hove, but just a short bus ride from Churchill Sq, this simple, uncluttered and well-equipped hostel lacks vibe but is ideal for budget nomads, who like to snooze in peace and party outside the hostel. The 20 beds are divided into four-bed dorms and twins with one set of facilities per six beds. The best hostel kitchen you're likely to see, memory foam mattresses and a free breakfast make these very respectable no-frills lodgings.

St Christopher's HOSTEL £
(☎01273-202035; www.st-christophers.co.uk; Palace Hotel, 10/12 Grand Junction Rd; dm £18, s/d £25/50; @) If you've come to Brighton to make merry, this is the place to stash your stuff while you do it – sleep-lovers should go elsewhere. While quiet is a rare luxury here, it does boast sea views, a spot near Brighton Pier and a pub downstairs for cheap belly filling.

Also recommended:

Seaspray BOUTIQUE HOTEL ££
(☎01273-680332; www.seaspraybrighton.co.uk; 25 New Steine; s/d/ste from £64/64/160; 📶) A light-hearted theme hotel with boutique touches and attentive owners. We dare you to come down to breakfast in the suit, wig and sunglasses provided in the Elvis room.

Amsterdam HOTEL ££
(☎01273-688825; www.amsterdam.uk.com; 11-12 Marine Pde; d £65-140) Popular gay run hotel that also welcomes tolerant straights, with tastefully decorated, spacious, bright rooms and wonderful Channel views. Request a room on higher floors if you're a light sleeper.

Brighton House Hotel B&B ££
(☎01273-323282; www.brighton-house.co.uk; 52 Regency Sq; s/d from £45/70; @📶) Honest value is the speciality at this welcoming Regency town-house B&B with immaculate and traditionally styled rooms.

Grapevine BUDGET HOTEL £
(☎01273-777717; www.grapevinewebsite.co.uk; 75-76 Middle St; per person from £15; @📶) The spartan rooms in this budget hotel have the air of an Eastern European hospital ward, but are generally clean and well kept. Popular with hen and stag nights, so it can get noisy.

Eating

Brighton easily has the best choice of eateries on the south coast, with cafes, diners and restaurants to fulfil every whim. It's also one of the UK's best destinations for vegetarians, and its innovative meat-free menus are also terrific value for anyone on a tight budget.

TOP CHOICE **Terre à Terre** VEGETARIAN ££
(71 East St; mains £10-15; ⏲noon-10.30pm Tue-Fri, to 11pm Sat, to 10pm Sun) Even staunch meat eaters will come out raving about this legendary vegetarian restaurant. Terre à Terre offers a sublime dining experience, from the vibrant, modern space, to the entertaining menus, to the delicious, inventive dishes full of rich robust flavours.

Infinity Foods Cafe VEGETARIAN £
(50 Gardner St; mains £3-7; ⏲10.30am-5pm Mon-Sat, noon-4pm Sun) The sister establishment of Infinity Foods wholefoods shop, a health-food cooperative and Brighton institution, serves a wide variety of vegetarian and organic food, with many vegan and wheat- or gluten-free options including tofu burgers, mezze plates and falafel.

JB's American Diner AMERICAN DINER £
(31 King's Rd; burgers £7, other mains £6.50-12; ⏲lunch & dinner) The waft of hotdog aroma as you push open the door, the shiny red-leather booths, the stars and stripes draped across the wall, the '50s soundtrack twanging in the background and the colossal portions of burgers, fries and milkshakes – in short, a hefty slab of authentic Americana teleported to Brighton seafront.

Food for Friends RESTAURANT ££
(www.foodforfriends.com; 17-18 Prince Albert St; mains £9-13; ⏲lunch & dinner) This airy, glass-sided restaurant attracts the attention of passers-by as much as it does the loyalty of its customers with an ever-inventive choice of vegetarian and vegan food. Children are also catered to.

Al Fresco ITALIAN ££
(Milkmaid Pavilion, Kings Rd Arches; mains £10-25; ⏲noon-midnight) Housed in a curved-glass structure with a huge, staggered outdoor terrace, the show-stopping feature

here is the wide-screen vistas out across the Channel and along the seafront. The pizzas, pastas and Italian meat dishes make a tasty accompaniment to the views.

English's Oyster Bar SEAFOOD ££
(www.englishs.co.uk; 29-31 East St; mains £11-25; ⏲lunch & dinner) A 60-year institution, this Brightonian seafood paradise dishes up everything from oysters to lobster to Dover sole. It's converted from fishermen's cottages, with echoes of the elegant Edwardian era inside and buzzing alfresco dining on the pedestrian square outside.

Pomegranate KURDISH ££
(www.eatpomegranates.com; 10 Manchester St; mains £11-15; ⏲lunch & dinner) Take your taste buds on a trip to the Middle East at this fascinating Kemptown nosh spot where mains such as Kurdish-style roast lamb, stuffed aubergine and baked swordfish are dished up in a cosy setting. There are plenty of veggie choices as well as such lip-smacking desserts as revani (semolina cake) and stuffed figs with pomegranate paste.

Due South LOCAL CUISINE ££
(www.duesouth.co.uk; 139 Kings Rd Arches; mains £12-18; ⏲lunch & dinner Mon-Sat, lunch Sun) Sheltered under a cavernous Victorian arch on the seafront, with a curvaceous front window and small bamboo-screened terrace on the promenade, this refined yet relaxed and convivial restaurant specialises in dishes cooked with the best environmentally sustainable and seasonal Sussex produce.

Pompoko JAPANESE £
(110 Church St; mains £4-5; ⏲lunch & dinner) Simple Japanese food in a small but perfectly formed little cafe. It's quick, cheap and delicious, with an emphasis on home-style curries, soups and noodle dishes.

Also try:

Bombay Aloo INDIAN BUFFET £
(39 Ship St; buffet £4.95; ⏲noon-midnight) Cheap and cheerful all-you-can-eat Indian buffet with big pots of vegetarian curry, acres of salad and mountains of rice.

Scoop & Crumb ICE-CREAM PARLOUR £
(5-6 East St; snacks £3-5, sundaes £2.50-6; ⏲10am-6pm Sun-Fri, to 7pm Sat) The sundaes (over 50 types) stacked at this ice-cream parlour, belonging to the city's artisan ice-cream producer, are second to none. Freshly cut sandwiches and monster toasties also available.

Piccolo's ITALIAN £
(56 Ship St; mains £4-8.50; ⏲lunch & dinner) Cheap, tasty pizza and pasta served in a frantic, friendly restaurant – just what everyone expects from an Italian eatery.

Red Roaster COFFEE HOUSE £
(1d St James' St; meals £3.50-5; ⏲7am-7pm Mon-Fri, 8am-7pm Sat, 9am-6.30pm Sun) You can smell the aroma of roasting coffee from across the street at this fine independent coffee house, which also serves sandwiches and salads.

Tea Cosy TEAROOM £
(3 George St; teas £3.50-12; ⏲noon-5pm Wed-Fri, 11am-6pm Sat & Sun) Barmy tearoom full of strict etiquette rules and royal family memorabilia.

Drinking

Outside London, Brighton's nightlife is the best in the south, with its unique mix of seafront clubs and bars. Drunken stag and hen parties and charmless, tacky nightclubs rule on West St, which is best avoided. For more ideas, visit www.drinkinbrighton.co.uk.

Evening Star PUB
(www.eveningstarbrighton.co.uk; 55/56 Surrey St) This cosy, unpretentious pub is a beer-drinker's nirvana, with a wonderful selection of award-winning real ales, Belgian beers, organic lagers and real ciders. It's a short stagger away from the station.

Coalition BAR/CLUB
(171-181 Kings Rd Arches) On a summer's day, there's nowhere better to sit and watch the world go by than at this popular beach bar, diner and club. It's a cavernous place with a funky brick-vaulted interior and a wide terrace spilling onto the promenade. All sorts happen here, from comedy, to live music, to club nights.

106 Bar & Brasserie BAR
(www.106brasseries.com; Kings Rd; ⏲3pm-11pm Fri, noon-11pm Sat, 11am-5pm Sun) Huge sea-view windows deluge this weekend venue in light as you sip a pre-club 'pretty Pink' or 'Flirtini' champagne cocktail and watch the sun go down. There's a limited choice of light meals available between noon and 5pm.

Dorset GASTRO PUB
(www.thedorset.co.uk; 28 North Rd; 📶) This laid-back Brighton institution throws open its doors and windows in fine weather and spills tables onto the pavement. You'll be just as welcome for a morning coffee as for

an evening pint here, and if you decide not to leave between the two, there's always the decent gastropub menu.

Riki Tik BAR

(18a Bond St; ⏲10am-late) Coffee bar by day, popular preclub venue by night, this place has been pumping out cool cocktails and funky breaks for years. It's stylish, dark and sexy and much bigger than it looks from the outside. DJs play here most nights.

Brighton Rocks BAR

(6 Rock Pl) Incongruously located in an alley of garages and used car lots, this cocktail bar is firmly on the Kemptown gay scene, but welcomes all-comers. The cocktails are tasty, there's a damn fine 'grazing' menu and the bar plays regular host to theme parties and art launches.

St James PUB

(cnr James' St & Madeira Pl) A blend of traditional Victorian boozer and hip watering hole, this popular Kemptown pub has lots of sanded wood, elaborate tiling and an ornate glass-backed bar; perfect for a peaceful pint.

☆ Entertainment

Brighton offers the best entertainment lineup on the south coast, with clubs to rival London and Manchester for cool. Keep tabs on what's hot and what's not by searching out publications such as the *List*, the *Source* and *What's On*.

Nightclubs

When Britain's top DJs aren't plying their trade in London, Ibiza or Aya Napia, chances are you'll spy them here. All Brighton's clubs open until 2am, and many as late as 5am.

Funky Buddha NIGHTCLUB

(Kings Rd Arches) Twin giant, brick, subterranean tunnels, with bars at the front and back, playing funky house, '70s, R&B and disco to a stylish and attitude-free crowd.

Audio NIGHTCLUB

(www.audiobrighton.com; 10 Marine Pde) Some of the city's top club nights can be found at this ear-numbing venue, where the music's top priority, attracting a young, up-for-it crowd. Every night is different, with music ranging from breakbeat to electro to indie. Next to the Amsterdam Hotel.

Ocean Rooms NIGHTCLUB

(www.oceanrooms.co.uk; 1 Morley St) This enduring favourite crams in three floors of dance variety, from an all-white bar to a dance floor where you can lap up the efforts of top DJs, from hip-hop to drum and bass, to breakbeat.

Funky Fish Club NIGHTCLUB

(www.funkyfishclub.co.uk; 19-23 Marine Pde) Fun, friendly and unpretentious little club playing soul, funk, jazz, Motown and old-skool breaks. No big-name DJs or stringent door policies, just cheap drinks and a rocking party atmosphere.

Digital NIGHTCLUB

(www.yourfutureisdigital.com/brighton; 187-193 Kings Rd Arches) This inconspicuous place on the Brighton seafront hosts indie, house and cheesy student nights.

Honey Club NIGHTCLUB

(www.thehoneyclub.co.uk; 214 Kings Rd Arches) A cavernous seafront club that jumps from strength to strength, almost as popular with DJs as it is with the weekly queues of clubbers who pile into its glittering depths. Dress up, party hard, then cool off on the balcony chill-out area or dip your aching feet in the sea.

Concorde 2 NIGHTCLUB

(www.concorde2.co.uk; Madeira Dr, Kemptown) Brighton's best-known and best-loved club is a disarmingly unpretentious den, where DJ Fatboy Slim pioneered the Big Beat Boutique and still occasionally graces the decks. There's a huge variety of club nights and live bands each month, from world music to rock.

Cinemas

Odeon Cinema CINEMA

(☎0871-224 4007; cnr King's Rd & West St) Check out this seafront cinema for mainstream movies.

Duke of York CINEMA

(☎0871-704 2056; Preston Circus) About a mile north of North Rd, showing art-house films, mainstream flicks and classics.

Theatre

Brighton Dome THEATRE

(☎01273-709709; www.brightondome.org; 29 New Rd) Once the stables and exercise yard of King George IV, this art-deco complex houses three theatre venues within the Royal Pavilion estate. ABBA famously won the 1974 Eurovision Song Contest here.

Theatre Royal THEATRE

(☎01273-328488; New Rd) Built by decree of the Prince of Wales in 1806, this grand venue hosts plays, musicals and operas.

GAY & LESBIAN BRIGHTON

Perhaps it's Brighton's long-time association with the theatre, but for more than 100 years the city has been a gay haven. With more than 25,000 gay men and around 15,000 lesbians living here, it is the most vibrant queer community in the country outside London.

Kemptown (aka Camptown), on and off St James' St, is where it's all at. In recent years the old Brunswick Town area of Hove has emerged as a quieter alternative to the traditionally cruisy (and sometimes seedy) scene here.

For up-to-date information on gay Brighton, check out www.gay.brighton.co.uk and www.realbrighton.com, or pick up the free monthly magazine **Gscene** (www.gscene.com) from various venues or the tourist office.

For drinking...

Hub CAFE
(129 St James' St; 8am-6pm Mon-Fri, 10am-6pm Sat & Sun) This cool coffeeshop hang-out and internet cafe is *the* place to get word on everything going on in town.

Amsterdam RESTAURANT/BAR
(www.amsterdam.uk.com; 11-12 Marine Pde; noon-2am) Hotel, sauna, restaurant and extremely hip bar above the pier; its sun terrace is a particular hit.

Candy Bar CAFE
(www.thecandybar.co.uk; 129 St James' St; 9pm-2am) Slick cafe-bar-club for the girls, with pink-lit arches, curvaceous bar, pool table and dance floor.

Queen's Arms PUB
(www.queensarmsbrighton.com; 7 George St; 3pm-late) And they don't mean Victoria or Elizabeth! Plenty of camp cabaret and karaoke at this pub.

For dancing...

Bars and pubs may be fun, but the real action takes place on and off the dance floor.

Revenge NIGHTCLUB
(www.revenge.co.uk; 32-34 Old Steine; 10.30pm-3am) Nightly disco with occasional cabaret.

Basement Club NIGHTCLUB
(31-34 Marine Pde; 9am-2am) Located beneath the Legends Hotel, arguably the best gay hotel in town and winner of the Golden Handbag award 2009.

Komedia Theatre COMEDY
(0845 293 8480; www.komedia.co.uk; 44-47 Gardner St) This former billiards hall and supermarket is now a stylish comedy, theatre and cabaret venue attracting some of the brightest stars on the stand-up circuit.

Shopping

A busy maze of narrow lanes and tiny alleyways that was once a fishing village, the **Lanes** is Brighton's most popular shopping district. Its every twist and turn is jam-packed with jewellers and gift shops, coffee shops and boutiques selling everything from antique firearms to hard-to-find vinyls. There's another, less-claustrophobic shopping district in **North Laine**, a series of streets north of the Lanes, including Bond, Gardner, Kensington and Sydney Sts, that are full of retro-cool boutiques and bohemian cafes. Head west from the Lanes and you'll hit Churchill Square Shopping Centre and Western Rd, where all the mainstream high street stores gather.

Information

Brighton City Guide (www.brighton.co.uk)

Brighton Internet Centre (109 Western Rd; per hr £1)

City Council (www.brighton-hove.gov.uk) A mine of information on every aspect of the city.

Jubilee Library (Jubilee St; 10am-7pm Mon & Tue, to 5pm Wed, Fri & Sat, to 8pm Thu, 11am-4pm Sun) Bring ID and sign up to use machines for free.

Post office (2-3 Churchill Square Shopping Centre)

Royal Sussex County Hospital (01273-696955; Eastern Rd) Has an accident and emergency department 2 miles east of the centre.

Tourist office (☎0300-300 0088; www.visitbrighton.com; Royal Pavilion Shop, Royal Pavilion; ⊙10am-5.30pm) The guys to turn to for anything Brighton-related, from tide times to train times.

visitbrighton.com (www.visitbrighton.com)

Wistons Clinic (☎01273-506263; 138 Dyke Rd) For general medical consultations, under a mile from the centre.

Getting There & Away

Brighton is 53 miles from London and transport is fast and frequent. If arriving by car, parking is plentiful but pricey, city-centre traffic bus-clogged and road layouts confusing.

Bus

Standard connections:

Arundel Bus 700, two hours, hourly

Chichester Bus 700, 2¾ hours, twice hourly

Eastbourne Bus 12, one hour 10 minutes, up to every 10 minutes

Lewes Bus 28/29, 34 minutes, every 15 minutes

London Victoria National Express, £11.80, two hours, hourly

Train

All London-bound services pass through Gatwick Airport.

Chichester £11.40, 50 minutes, half hourly

Eastbourne £8.50, 30 to 40 minutes, half hourly

Hastings £11.80, one hour, half hourly

London St Pancras £16.90, 1¼ hours, half hourly

London Victoria £13.90, 50-70 minutes, half hourly

Portsmouth £13.90, 1½ hours, hourly

Getting Around

Most of Brighton can be covered on foot. Alternatively, buy a day ticket (£3.60) from the driver to scoot back and forth on Brighton & Hove buses, or for £2 on top of the rail fare, you can get a PlusBus ticket that gives unlimited bus travel for the day.

Parking can be expensive. The city operates a pay-and-display parking scheme. In the town centre, it's usually £1.50 per half hour with a maximum stay of two hours. Alternatively, there's a Park & Ride 2.5 miles northwest of the centre at Withdean, from where bus 27 zips into town.

Cab companies include **Brighton Streamline Taxis** (☎01273-747474) and **City Cabs** (☎01273-205205), and there's a taxi rank on the junction of East St with Market St. All Brighton taxis have a distinctive white and turquoise livery.

Planet Cycle Hire (West Pier Promenade; bikes per half day/day £8/12; ⊙10am-6pm Thu-Tue), next to West Pier, rents bikes. Deposit and ID required.

WEST SUSSEX

After the fast-paced adventures of Brighton and East Sussex, West Sussex is welcome respite. The serene hills and valleys of the South Downs ripple across the county, fringed by sheltered coastline. Beautiful Arundel and cultured Chichester make good bases from which to explore the county's winding country lanes and remarkable Roman ruins.

Arundel

POP 3408

Arguably West Sussex's prettiest town, Arundel is clustered around a vast fairytale castle and its hillside streets overflow with antique emporiums, teashops, a host of eateries and the odd boutique hotel. While much of the town appears medieval – the whimsical castle has been home to the dukes of Norfolk for centuries – most of it dates back to Victorian times.

Sights & Activities

Arundel Castle CASTLE

(www.arundelcastle.org; adult/child £16/7.50; ⊙10am-5pm Tue-Sun Apr-Oct) Originally built in the 11th century, all that's left of the first structure are the modest remains of the keep at its core. Thoroughly ruined during the English Civil War, most of what you see today is the result of passionate reconstruction by the eighth, 11th and 15th dukes of Norfolk between 1718 and 1900. The current duke still lives in part of the castle. Highlights include the atmospheric keep, the massive Great Hall and the library, which has paintings by Gainsborough and Holbein. The castle does a good impression of Windsor Castle and St James' Palace in the popular 2009 film *The Young Victoria*.

Cathedral CATHEDRAL

(www.arundelcathedral.org; ⊙9am-6pm Apr-Oct) Arundel's ostentatious 19th-century Catholic cathedral is the other dominating feature of the town's impressive skyline. Commissioned by the 15th duke in 1868, this impressive structure was designed by Joseph Aloysius Hansom (inventor of the Hansom cab) in the French Gothic style, but marked with much Victorian economy and restraint. Although small for a cathedral – it only holds

500 worshippers – Hansom's clever layout makes the building seem a lot bigger.

A 1970s shrine in the north transept holds the remains of St Philip Howard, a canonised Catholic martyr who was banged up in the Tower of London by Elizabeth I until his death in 1595 for reverting to Catholicism.

Other attractions:

Arundel Ghost Experience GHOST EXPERIENCE
(www.arundeljailhouse.co.uk; High St; adult/child £5/3; ⊙noon-6pm) Hear hair-raising ghost stories and explore supposedly haunted prison cells by candlelight at this kids' attraction.

Wildfowl & Wetlands Centre WILDLIFE RESERVE
(www.wwt.org.uk; Mill Rd; adult/child £9.70/4.85; ⊙9.30am-5.30pm Easter-Oct) Bird fanciers will be rewarded by an electric boat safari through this 26-hectare reserve, a mile east of the centre as the duck flies.

FREE **Arundel Museum** MUSEUM
(www.arundelmuseum.org.uk; ⊙11am-3pm) Temporarily located in a small metal container at the Mill Rd car park, poor old Arundel Museum has been waiting for a new home to be erected on an adjacent plot for years. The modern, Lottery-funded structure should appear by 2013.

Sleeping

Arundel House HOTEL ££
(☎01903-882136; www.arundelhouseonline.com; 11 High St; d from £80;) The modern rooms in this lovely 'restaurant with rooms' may be slightly low-ceilinged but they're clean-cut and very comfortable, with showers big enough for two. The restaurant downstairs serves some of the best food in Arundel (three-course dinner £28), which happily extends to breakfast.

Norfolk Arms HOTEL ££
(☎0808-144 9494; www.norfolkarmshotel.com; High St; s/d from £60/70; P) You'll be warmly welcomed at this rambling old Georgian coaching inn built by the 10th duke. Although the rooms are spacious, they are looking dated and a little scruffy.

Arundel YHA HOSTEL £
(☎0845 371 9002; www.yha.org.uk; Warningcamp; dm £15.95; P @) Catering to South Downs Way walkers and families, this large Georgian hostel has excellent facilities and is set in sprawling grassy grounds on a charming country lane, 20 to 30 minutes' walk from town off the A27 (call for directions).

Eating

TOP CHOICE **Town House** BRITISH £££
(☎01903-883847; 65 High St; set lunch £14-18, set dinner £22-27.50; ⊙Tue-Sat) The only thing that rivals the stunning 16th-century Florentine gilded-walnut ceiling at this compact and very elegant eatery is the acclaimed British cuisine with a European twist and sparkling atmosphere. Book ahead.

Bay Tree INTERNATIONAL ££
(☎01903-883679; www.thebaytreearundel.com; 21 Tarrant St; mains lunch £7-13, dinner £12-17; ⊙lunch & dinner Tue-Sat, lunch Sun) Frequented by famished antique hunters, this uncluttered eatery keeps things surprisingly free of yesteryear knickknacks. Everything from basic panini to sophisticated dishes blending local produce with Mediterranean flavours populates the menu.

Pallant of Arundel ENGLISH DELI £
(www.pallantofarundel.co.uk; 17 High St; ⊙9am-6pm Mon-Sat, 10am-5pm Sun) Set yourself up for an English picnic by the river at this irresistible delicatessen selling crusty loaves, Sussex cheeses and bottles of ale from the Arundel Brewery.

Tudor Rose BRITISH £
(49 High St; mains £4-11; ⊙9am-6pm) This bustling, kitschy family-run tearoom is cluttered with everything from faux armour to wooden tennis rackets, to ships' wheels, to a portrait of the Queen. As well as tea and cakes, breakfasts, burgers, Sunday roasts and other substantial meals are served here.

Shopping

Arundel is antiques central as far as West Sussex is concerned and if you've come to splurge on old stuff, **Tarrant Street** must have the highest concentration of antique shops anywhere in the southeast.

Information

Tourist office (☎01903-882268; www.sussexbythesea.com; 1-3 Crown Yard Mews; ⊙10am-5pm Mon-Sat, 10am-4pm Sun Apr-Oct) Supplies maps and provides an accommodation-booking service but may close in 2011.

Getting There & Away

Trains run to London Victoria (£22.80, 1½ hours, twice hourly) and to Chichester (20 minutes, twice hourly); change at Barnham. There are also links to Brighton (£8.40, one hour 20 minutes, twice hourly); again change at Barnham. Bus 700 (two hours, twice hourly) is a slower option to Brighton.

Around Arundel

BIGNOR ROMAN VILLA

Bignor Roman Villa (www.bignorromanvilla.co.uk; adult/child £5.50/2.50; ⌚10am-5pm Mar-Oct, to 6pm Jun-Aug) is home to an astonishingly fine collection of mosaics preserved within an atmospheric thatched complex that's historic in its own right. Discovered in 1811 by a farmer ploughing his fields, the villa was built around AD 190. The wonderful mosaic floors include vivid scenes of chunky-thighed gladiators, a beautiful Venus whose eyes seem to follow you around the room and an impressive 24m-long gallery design.

While Bignor is well worth the trip, it's a devil of a place to reach without your own wheels. It's located 6 miles north of Arundel off the A29.

Chichester

POP 27,477

A lively Georgian market town still almost encircled by its medieval town walls, the administrative capital of West Sussex keeps watch over the plains between the South Downs and the sea. Visitors flock to its splendid cathedral, streets of handsome 18th century town houses, famous theatre and an annual arts festival, as well as a superb modern art gallery, and nearby Petworth House, a must-visit for culture vultures. A Roman port garrison in its early days, the town is also a launch pad to other fascinating Roman remains as well as Arundel and the coast.

Sights

Chichester Cathedral CATHEDRAL
(www.chichestercathedral.org.uk; West St; donation requested; ⌚7.15am-6pm) This understated cathedral was begun in 1075 and largely rebuilt in the 13th century. The freestanding church tower, now in fairly bad shape, was built in the 15th century and the spire dates from the 19th century when its predecessor famously toppled over. Inside, three storeys of beautiful arches sweep upwards, and Romanesque carvings are dotted around. Interesting features to track down include a smudgy stained-glass window added by Marc Chagall in 1978 and a glassed-over section of Roman mosaic flooring about a metre below ground level.

Guided tours operate at 11.15am and 2.30pm Monday to Saturday, Easter to October, and the excellent cathedral choir is guaranteed to give you goosebumps during the daily **Evensong** (⌚5.30pm Mon-Sat, 3.30pm Sun).

Pallant House Gallery ART GALLERY
(www.pallant.org.uk; 9 North Pallant; adult/child £8.25/2.30; ⌚10am-5pm Tue-Sat, 12.30-5pm Sun) A Queen Anne mansion built by a local wine merchant, handsome Pallant House, along with a recently opened modern wing, hosts this superb gallery that focuses on 20th-century, mostly British, art. Showstoppers such as Caulfield, Freud, Sutherland, Auerbach and Moore are interspersed with international names such as Filla, Le Corbusier and Kitaj. Most of these older works are in the mansion while the new wing is packed with pop art and temporary shows of modern and contemporary work.

FREE **Guildhall** CHURCH BUILDING
(Priory Park; ⌚noon-4pm Sat Jun-Sep) This church building is all that remains of a Franciscan monastery, which didn't survive Henry VIII's 1536 Dissolution. The church later served as a court of law, where William Blake was tried for sedition in 1804, and Chichester's first museum.

FREE **District Museum** MUSEUM
(29 Little London; ⌚10am-5.30pm Wed-Sat) The eclectic collections once housed at the Guildhall can now be viewed at this somewhat ramshackle museum where the ground-floor Roman finds and mosaic fragments are the clear-cut winners.

Market Cross COVERED MARKET
(crossroads of North, South, East & West Sts) Chichester's epicentre is marked by a dinky market building constructed in 1501 by the bishop of the time to enable impoverished locals to sell their wares without paying hefty market fees.

Festivals & Events

For three weeks in June and July, the annual **Chichester Festivities** (☎01243-528356; www.chifest.org.uk) puts on an abundance of terrific theatre, art, guest lectures, fireworks and performances of every musical genre.

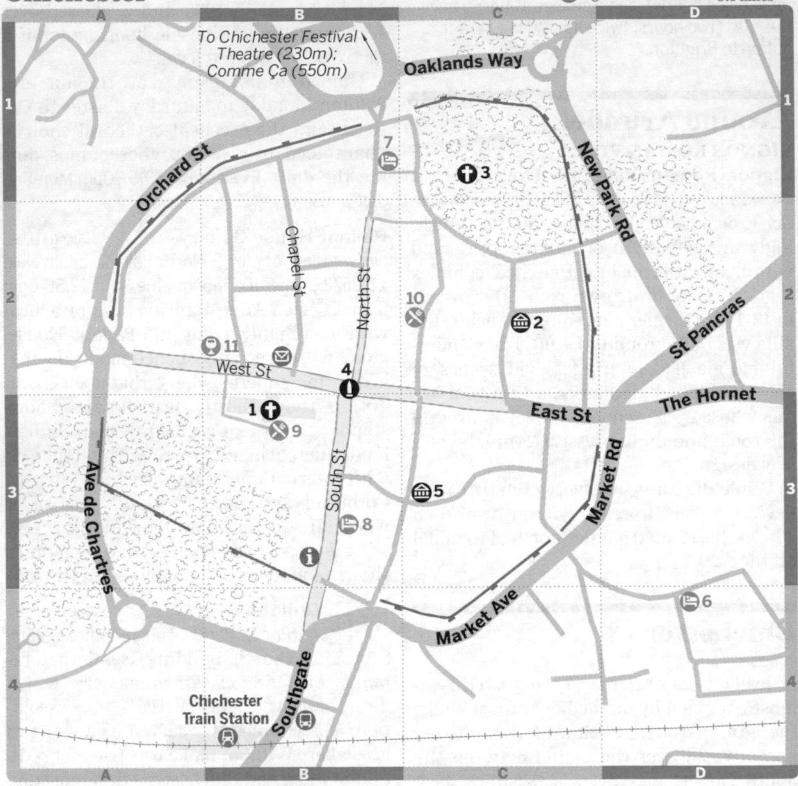

Chichester

Sights

1 Chichester Cathedral B3
2 District Museum C2
3 Guildhall C1
4 Market Cross B2

Activities, Courses & Tours

5 Pallant House Gallery C3

Sleeping

6 Old Orchard Guest House D4
7 Ship Hotel B1
8 Trents B3

Eating

9 Cloisters Cafe B3
Field & Fork .... (see 5)
10 St Martin's Tea Rooms C2

Drinking

11 Wests Bar B2

Sleeping

Chichester is about to get a spanking new Travelodge! 'So what?' you may say, but this one will be located right opposite the cathedral, meaning the views out may be worth bearing the blandness within.

Ship Hotel HOTEL ££
(01243-778000; www.theshiphotel.net; North St; s/d £75/99;) The grand central staircase in this former Georgian town house climbs to 36 fairly spacious rooms of commandingly clean-cut period chic. It's the most enticing option in the city centre and also boasts an excellent all-day brasserie.

Old Orchard Guest House B&B ££
(01243-536547;www.oldorchardguesthouse.co.uk; 8 Lyndhurst Rd; s/d from £50/70) Though not much to look at from the outside, this residential area B&B, an easy amble from the city centre, gets better on the inside

with three light and spacious, old-style rooms and a scrumptious breakfast.

Trents B&B ££
(☎01243-773714; www.trentschichester.co.uk; 50 South St; s/d from £65/85;) Right in the thick of the city centre, the five snazzy rooms above this trendy bar-restaurant are understandably popular.

Eating

St Martin's Tea Rooms TEAROOMS £
(www.organictearooms.co.uk; 3 St Martins St; mains £4-10; ⊙10am-6pm Mon-Sat) A little cocoon of nooks and crannies tucked away in a part-18th-century, part-medieval town house, this passionately organic cafe serves freshly ground coffee, wholesome, mostly vegetarian, food and a sinful selection of desserts. There's also a guest piano with which to shatter the tranquil scene if you so wish.

Field & Fork RESTAURANT ££
(9 North Pallant; snacks & meals £4-10; ⊙10am-5pm Mon-Sat, also 6-10pm Wed-Sat, 11.30am-5pm Sun) In the new wing of the Pallant House Gallery, this sophisticated eatery has paintings and display cases, and a sunny courtyard that's a good spot for sandwiches, cakes and heartier main meals.

Comme Ça FRENCH ££
(☎01243-788724; 67 Broyle Rd; mains £8-14; ⊙lunch Wed-Sun, dinner Tue-Sat) Run by a Franco-English couple, this friendly French place does traditional Normandy cuisine in a converted Georgian inn, with a lovely vine-covered alfresco area. It's a short walk north of the centre.

Cloisters Cafe CAFE £
(Cathedral Cloisters; snacks £2.50-7; ⊙9am-5pm Mon-Sat, 10am-4pm Sun) Sparkling marble-floored cafe in the cathedral grounds with sunny walled garden and airy atmosphere. It's a good spot for simple sandwiches, cakes and fair-trade drinks.

Drinking

Wests Bar BAR/RESTAURANT
(14 West St; mains £4.50-8) Occupying every nook and chapel of a large church opposite the cathedral entrance, this daytime temple to tummy-packing and evening ale sanctuary allows you to refuel and kick back in an incongruously ecclesiastical setting. The sinful menu of British pub favourites, pseudo-Italian concoctions and spicy fare is sure to bust your bible belt and invoke a holy thirst.

Entertainment

Chichester Festival Theatre THEATRE
(☎01243-781312; www.cft.org.uk; Oakland's Park) This somewhat Soviet-looking playhouse was built in 1962 and has a long and distinguished history. Sir Laurence Olivier was the theatre's first director and Ingrid Bergman, Sir John Gielgud and Sir Anthony Hopkins are a few of the other famous names to have played here.

Information

Click Computers (2 Southdown Bldg, Southgate; per hr £1; ⊙9am-7pm Mon-Fri, 11am-7pm Sat, 11am-5pm Sun) Mega-fast net access opposite the train station.

Post office (10 West St)

Tourist office (☎01243-775888; www.visitchichester.org; 29a South St; ⊙10.15am-5.15pm Mon, 9.15am-5.15pm Tue-Sat year-round, also 10.30am-3pm Sun Apr-Sep) Organises guided walks (£4) on Tuesdays at 11am and Saturdays at 2.30pm.

Getting There & Around

Bus

Brighton Bus 700, 2¾ hours, twice hourly

London Victoria National Express, £13.30, four hours, daily

Portsmouth Bus 700, one hour, twice hourly

Train

Chichester has connections to:

Arundel £4, 20 to 30 minutes, twice hourly, change at Barnham

Brighton £10.10, 50 minutes, twice hourly

London Victoria £22.80, 1½ hours, half hourly

Portsmouth £6.70, 30 to 40 minutes, twice hourly

Around Chichester

Spreading its watery tentacles to the south of town, **Chichester Harbour** is designated an Area of Outstanding Natural Beauty (AONB) and has a lovely, sandy beach west of the harbour, ideal for a spot of sea air and strolling.

At West Itchenor, 1½-hour harbour cruises are run by **Chichester Harbour Water Tours** (☎01243- 670504; www.chichesterharbourwatertours.co.uk; adult/child £7.50/3.50).

FISHBOURNE ROMAN PALACE & MUSEUM

Mad about mosaics? Then head for **Fishbourne Palace** (www.sussexpast.co.uk; Salthill Rd; adult/child £7.60/4; ⊙10am-4pm Feb-Nov, to 5pm Mar-Oct), the largest known Roman residence in Britain. Happened upon by labourers in the 1960s, it's thought that this once-luxurious mansion was built around AD 75 for a romanised local king. Housed in a modern pavilion are its foundations, hypocaust and painstakingly relaid mosaics. The centrepiece is a spectacular floor depicting cupid riding a dolphin flanked by sea horses and panthers. There's also a fascinating little museum and replanted Roman gardens.

Fishbourne Palace is 1½ miles west of Chichester, just off the A259. Bus 700 leaves from outside Chichester Cathedral and stops at the bottom of Salthill Rd (five minutes' walk away; four hourly). The museum is a 10-minute amble from Fishbourne train station.

PETWORTH

On the outskirts of its namesake village, the imposing 17th-century stately home, **Petworth House** (NT; adult/child £9.90/5; ⏰11am-5pm Sat-Wed Mar-Nov), has an extraordinary art collection, the National Trust's finest. JMW Turner was a regular visitor and the house is still home to the largest collection of his paintings outside London's Tate Gallery. There are also many paintings by Van Dyck, Reynolds, Gainsborough, Titian, Bosch and William Blake. Other highlights are the fabulously theatrical grand staircase and the exquisite Carved Room, which ripples with wooden reliefs by master chiseller Grinling Gibbons.

The surrounding **Petworth Park** (⏰11am-6pm Wed-Sun Mar-Nov) is the highlight – the fulfilment of Lancelot 'Capability' Brown's romantic natural landscape theory. It's home to herds of deer and becomes an open-air concert venue in summer.

Petworth is 5 miles from the train station at Pulborough, from where bus 1 runs to Petworth Sq (15 minutes, hourly Monday to Saturday). If driving, it's 12 miles northeast of Chichester off the A285.

SURREY

Surrey is the heart of commuterville, chosen by well-off Londoners when they spawn, move out of the city and buy a country pad. For the most part, though, it's made up of uninspiring towns and dull, sprawling suburbs. Further away from the roaring motorways and packed rush-hour trains, the county reveals some inspiring landscapes made famous by authors Sir Arthur Conan Doyle, Sir Walter Scott and Jane Austen.

Farnham

POP 37,055

Nudging the border with Hampshire and joined at the hip with the garrison settlement of Aldershot, affluent Farnham is Surrey's prettiest town and its most worthwhile destination. Blessed with lively shopping streets of Georgian symmetry, a 12th-century castle and some soothing river walks, this easy-going market town makes for an undemanding day-trip from the capital just an hour away.

Farnham has no tourist office but maps and leaflets are available from the library (28 West St), the museum (38 West St) and the town hall (South St).

Sights

Farnham Castle CASTLE

(EH; adult/child £3.20/1.60 ⏰noon-5pm Fri-Sun Mar-Sep) Constructed in 1138 by Henry de Blois, the grandson of William the Conqueror, there's not much left of the castle keep today except the beautiful old ramparts. Even if the keep is closed, it's worth walking around the outside for the picturesque views.

A residential palace house, Farnham Castle was built in the 13th century for the bishops of Winchester as a stopover on London journeys. From 1926 to the 1950s, it was taken over by the bishops of Guildford. It's now owned by the Farnham Castle International Briefing & Conference Centre, but you can visit it on a **guided tour** (☎01252-721194; adult/child £2.50/1.50; ⏰2-4pm Wed & 2.30pm Fri Apr-Aug).

Farnham Castle is located up the old steps at the top of Castle St.

FREE **Museum of Farnham** MUSEUM

(38 West St; ⏰10am-5pm Tue-Sat) This engaging little museum is located in the splendid Willmer House, a Georgian mansion built for wealthy hop merchant and maltster John Thorne in 1718.

Themed rooms trace Farnham's history from flint tool days to Bakelite nostalgia, with a corner dedicated to William Cobbett, the town's most famous son and 19th-century reformer, radical MP, writer and journalist who established *Hansard* (the official record of what is said in Parliament). Cobbett's bust takes pride of place in the peaceful garden out back where you'll also find a spanking new timber gallery housing temporary exhibitions by local artists.

Sleeping

Bush Hotel HOTEL £££

(☎01252-715237; www.mercure-uk.com; The Borough; r from £140; P ❄ 📶) This 17th-century inn is right in the heart of the action and benefits from recently renovated rooms, a cosy beamed bar and a superb restaurant that spills out into the pretty courtyard.

Bishop's Table HOTEL ££

(☎01252-710222; www.bishopstable.com; 27 West St; s/d from £60/100) Despite the trendy 'designer' feel of the lobby, clean-cut restaurant and leathery bar, rooms retain as much character as the 17th-century building in which they're housed, and range from scuffed but acceptable to antique-filled and almost luxurious. Take a peek before committing. Rates plummet at weekends.

Eating & Entertainment

Mulberry GOURMET BURGERS ££

(Station Hill; burgers £7-11; ⏰lunch & dinner) Right by the station, all this bar-restaurant does is humungous gourmet burgers, and boy does it do 'em well. There are snazzy rooms upstairs where you can sleep off any excesses and a bi-monthly local DJ open-deck night (Sundays) you may wish to avoid.

Nelson Arms PUB ££

(50 Castle St; mains £7-13) A cosily rustic, low-ceilinged bar with a few modern touches, a small terrace at the back and good-value, locally sourced food.

Farnham Maltings ARTS VENUE

(☎01252-745444; www.farnhammaltings.com; Bridge Sq) Creative, multipurpose spot with a riverside bar, live music, amateur theatre, exhibitions, workshops and comedy.

Getting There & Away

Bus

London Victoria National Express, £9.30, one hour 40 minutes, daily

Train

London Waterloo £19.30, one hour, twice hourly, change at Woking

Winchester £16.10, one hour, twice hourly, change at Woking

Around Farnham

WAVERLEY ABBEY

Said to be the inspiration for Sir Walter Scott's eponymous novel, Waverley Abbey sits ruined and forlorn on the banks of the River Wey about 2 miles southeast of Farnham. This was the first Cistercian abbey built in England (construction began in 1128) and was based on a parent abbey at Cîteaux in France.

Across the Wey is the impressive **Waverley Abbey House** (closed to the public), built in 1783 using bricks from the demolished abbey. In the 19th century it was owned by Florence Nightingale's brother-in-law, and the famous nurse was a regular visitor. Fittingly, the house was used as a hospital in WWI. Since 1973 it has been the headquarters of the Crusade for World Revival, a Christian charity.

The abbey and house are off the B3001.

HINDHEAD

The tiny hamlet of Hindhead, 8 miles south of Farnham off the A287, lies in the middle of the largest area of open heath in Surrey. During the 19th century, a number of prominent Victorians bought up property in the area, including Sir Arthur Conan Doyle (1859–1930). One of the three founders of the National Trust, Sir Robert Hunter, lived in nearby Haslemere, and today much of the area is administered by the foundation.

The most beautiful part of the area is to the northeast, where you'll find a natural depression known as the **Devil's Punchbowl**. There are a number of excellent trails and bridleways here. To get the best view, head for **Gibbet Hill** (280m), which was once an execution ground.

The **Hindhead YHA Hostel** (☎0845 371 9022; www.yha.org.uk; Punchbowl La, Thursley; dm £15.95) is a completely secluded cottage run by the National Trust on the northern edge of the Punchbowl – perfect digs for walkers.

Bus 19 runs hourly to Hindhead from Farnham.

Oxford, Cotswolds & Around

Includes »

Best Places to Eat

» Le Champignon Sauvage (p218)

» Daffodil (p218)

» Chef's Table (p212)

» Trout (p192)

» 5 North St (p207)

Best Places to Stay

» St Briavels Castle YHA (p224)

» Malmaison (p191)

» Dial House (p209)

» Old Parsonage Hotel (p191)

» Lamb Inn (p202)

Why Go?

Dripping with charm and riddled with implausibly pretty villages, this part of the country is as close to the old-world English idyll as you'll get. It's a haven of lush rolling hills, rose-clad cottages, graceful stone churches, thatched roofs, cream teas and antique shops. Add to the mix the legendary city of Oxford, and it's easy to see why the region is a magnet for tourists.

Although the roads and the most popular villages are busy in summer, it's easy to get off the tourist trail. The Cotswolds are at their best when you find your own romantic refuge and discover the fire-lit inns and grandiose manors that persuade A-list celebrities and the merely moneyed to buy property here.

Most of the area is an easy day-trip from London, but Oxford and the Cotswolds deserve at least an overnight stay.

When to Go

On 1 May you can welcome the dawn with Oxford's Magdalen College Choir, which sings hymns from the college tower. In July you can swill champagne and watch the rowing at Henley's Royal Regatta and Festival. September is the best time to sample England's finest ales at the four-day St Alban's Beer Festival.

Oxford, Cotswolds & Around Highlights

1. Following in the footsteps of Lyra, Tolkien, CS Lewis and Inspector Morse as you tour the **Oxford colleges** (p182)
2. Meandering around **Painswick** (p214), one of the most beautiful and unspoilt towns in the Cotswolds
3. Getting a glimpse of the high life at the Queen's very own hideaway, **Windsor Castle** (p237)
4. Touring the elegant cloisters at the magnificent **Gloucester Cathedral** (p221)
5. Stepping back in time as you down a pint by the fire in the **Falkland Arms** (p203)
6. Strolling the streets, soaking up the architecture and browsing the chichi shops of Regency **Cheltenham** (p215)
7. Touring the monumental **Blenheim Palace** (p196), one of the country's greatest stately homes
8. Exploring the vast collection and swanky new makeover at the **Ashmolean Museum** in Oxford (p188)

History

The Bronze Age chalk horse at Uffington and the Iron Age hill fort close by are some of the earliest evidence of settlement in this part of England. In Roman times, the region was traversed by a network of roads, some of which still exist today, and as word of the good hunting and fertile valleys spread, the area became heavily populated.

By the 11th century, the wool and grain trade had made the locals rich, William the Conqueror had built his first motte and bailey in Windsor, and the Augustinian abbey in Oxford had begun training clerics. In the 12th century, Henry II fortified the royal residence at Windsor by adding a stone tower and protective walls, and in the 13th century, Oxford's first colleges were established, along with its reputation as England's foremost centre of learning.

Meanwhile, local farmers continued to supply London with corn, wool and clothing. The Cotswolds in particular flourished and amassed great wealth. By the 14th century, the wool merchants were rolling in money and happy to show off their good fortune by building the beautiful villages and graceful wool churches that still litter the area today.

The region's proximity to London also meant that it became a popular retreat for wealthy city dwellers. The nobility and aristocracy flocked to Hertfordshire and Buckinghamshire, building country piles as retreats from the city. Today, the area remains affluent and is home to busy commuters and is a popular choice for wealthy Londoners looking for second homes.

Activities

Walking or cycling through the Cotswolds is an ideal way to get away from the crowds and discover some of the lesser-known vistas and villages of the region. You'll also find great walking and cycling opportunities in Buckinghamshire's leafy Chiltern Hills and along the meandering River Thames. There are specific suggestions for walks and rides throughout this chapter.

CYCLING

Gentle gradients and scenic vistas make the Cotswolds ideal for cycling, with only the steep western escarpment offering a challenge to the legs. Plenty of quiet country lanes and gated roads criss-cross the region, or you can follow the signposted **Thames Valley Cycle Way** (NCN Routes 4, 5).

> **WANT MORE?**
>
> Head to **Lonely Planet** (www.lonelyplanet.com/england/oxfordshire/oxford) for planning advice, author recommendations, traveller reviews and insider tips.

Mountain bikers can use a variety of bridleways in the **Cotswolds** and **Chilterns**, and in the west of the region the **Forest of Dean** has many dirt-track options and some dedicated mountain-bike trails.

WALKING

The **Cotswold Hills** offer endless opportunities for day hikes, but if you're looking for something more ambitious, the **Cotswold Way** (www.national trail.co.uk/Cotswold) is an absolute classic. The route covers 102 miles from Bath to Chipping Campden and takes about a week to walk.

Alternatively, the **Thames Path** (www.nationaltrail.co.uk/thamespath) follows the river downstream from its source near Cirencester to London. It takes about two weeks to complete the 184-mile route, but there's a very enjoyable five-day section from near Cirencester to Oxford.

Finally, the 87-mile **Ridgeway National Trail** (www.nationaltrail.co.uk/ridgeway) meanders along the chalky grassland of the Wiltshire downs near Avebury, down into the Thames Valley and then along the spine of the Chilterns to Ivinghoe Beacon near Aylesbury in Buckinghamshire, offering wonderful views of the surrounding area.

Getting There & Around

Thanks to its proximity to London and the rash of commuters who live in the area, there are frequent trains and buses here from the capital. Getting across the region by public transport can be frustrating and time-consuming, though. Renting a car gives you the most freedom, but be prepared for busy roads in the Cotswolds during the summer months and daily rush-hour traffic closer to London.

Traveline (☎0871-200 22 33; www.travelineeastanglia.org.uk) provides timetables for all public transport across the country. For specific information on travelling across the Cotswolds, try www.cotswoldsaonb.org.uk, which has downloadable guides on all bus and rail options in the region.

BUS Major bus routes are run by **Stagecoach** (www.stagecoachbus.com) and **Arriva** (www.arrivabus.co.uk), with a host of smaller companies offering services to local towns and villages. Pick up a copy of Oxfordshire County Council's *Public Transport Map & Guide*, or the *Explore the Cotswolds by Public Transport* brochures in any tourist office.

TRAIN Services in the region are limited, with the exception of the area immediately outside London. For general rail information, call **National Rail** (☎08457-48 49 50; www.nationalrail.co.uk).

OXFORDSHIRE

The whiff of old money, academic achievement and genteel living wafts from Oxfordshire's well-bred, well-preened pores. Rustic charm, good manners and grand attractions are in abundant supply here, with a host of charming villages surrounding the world-renowned university town.

Oxford is a highlight on any itinerary, with over 1500 listed buildings, a choice of excellent museums and an air of refined sophistication. Between the gorgeous colleges and hushed quads students in full academic dress cycle along cobbled lanes little changed by time.

Yet there is a lot more to the county. Just to the north is Blenheim Palace, an extravagant baroque pile that's the birthplace of Sir Winston Churchill, while to the south is the elegant riverside town of Henley, famous for its ever-so-posh Royal Regatta.

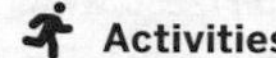

Activities

As well as the long-distance national trails, walkers may be interested in the **Oxfordshire Way**, a scenic, 65-mile signposted trail running from Bourton-on-the-Water to Henley-on-Thames, and the **Wychwood Way**, a historic, 37-mile route from Woodstock, which runs through an ancient royal forest. The routes are divided into manageable sections, described in leaflets available at most local tourist offices and libraries.

The quiet roads and gentle gradients also make Oxfordshire good cycling territory. The main signposted route through the county is the **Oxfordshire Cycleway**, which takes in Woodstock, Burford and Henley. If you don't have your own wheels, you can hire bikes in Oxford.

You'll find more information at www.oxfordshire.gov.uk/countryside.

ℹ Getting Around

You can pick up bus and train timetables for most routes at local tourist offices. The main train stations are in Oxford and Banbury and have frequent connections to London Paddington and Euston, Hereford, Birmingham, Bristol and Scotland.

ST SCHOLASTICA'S DAY MASSACRE

The first real wave of students arrived in Oxford in the 12th century, and right from the start an uneasy relationship grew between the townspeople and the bookish blow-ins. Name calling and drunken brawls escalated into full-scale riots in 1209 and 1330, when browbeaten scholars abandoned Oxford to establish new universities in Cambridge and Stamford, respectively. The riots of 10 and 11 February 1355 changed everything, however, and left a bitter scar on relations for hundreds of years.

It all began when celebrations for St Scholastica's Day grew out of hand and a drunken scuffle spilled into the street. Years of simmering discontent and frustrations were let loose, and soon students and townspeople took to one another's throats. The chancellor ordered the pealing of the university bells, and every student who heard it rushed to join the brawl. By the end of the day, the students had claimed victory and an uneasy truce was called.

The next morning, however, the furious townspeople returned with the help of local villagers armed with pickaxes, shovels and pikes. By sundown, 63 students and 30 townspeople were dead. King Edward III sent troops in to quell the rioting and eventually decided to bring the town under the control of the university.

To prove its authority, the university ordered the mayor and burgesses (citizens) to attend a service and pay a penny for every student killed on the anniversary of the riot each year. For 470 years, the vengeful practice continued, until one mayor flatly refused to pay the fine. His successors all followed suit, but it took another 130 years for the university to extend the olive branch and award a Doctorate of Civil Law to Mayor William Richard Gowers, MA, Oriel in 1955.

The main bus operators are the **Oxford Bus Company** (☎01865-785400; www.oxfordbus.co.uk) and **Stagecoach** (☎01865-772250; www.stagecoachbus.com/oxfordshire).

Oxford

POP 134,248

The genteel city of Oxford is a privileged place, one of the world's most famous university towns – it's soaked in history, dripping with august buildings and yet incredibly insular. The 39 colleges that make up the university jealously guard their elegant honey-coloured buildings, and inside their grounds, a reverent hush and studious calm descends.

Oxford is highly aware of its international standing and yet is remarkably restrained for a city driven by its student population. It's a conservative, bookish kind of place where academic achievement and intellectual ideals are the common currency. The university buildings wrap around narrow cobbled lanes, cyclists in academic gowns blaze along the streets and the vast library collections run along shelves deep below the city streets.

Oxford is a wonderful place to ramble: the oldest colleges date back almost 750 years, and little has changed inside the hallowed walls since then. But along with the rich history and tradition, there is a whole other world beyond the college walls. Oxford has a long industrial past and was the birthplace of the Morris motor car as well as of Mensa. Today, the new Mini runs off the production lines, and the real-world majority still outnumber the academic elite. Along with all the fine architecture, world-class museums and historic pubs is a working city that's home to disadvantaged council estates, the usual glut of high-street chain shops and plenty of chichi restaurants, trendy bars and expensive boutiques.

The university buildings are scattered throughout the city, with the most important and architecturally significant in the centre. Jericho, in the northwest, is the trendy, artsy end of town, with slick bars and restaurants and an art-house cinema, while Cowley Rd, southeast of Carfax, is the gritty student and immigrant area packed with cheap places to eat and drink. Further out, in the salubrious northern suburb of Summertown, you'll find more upmarket restaurants and bars.

History

Strategically placed at the confluence of the Rivers Cherwell and Thames (called the Isis here, from the Latin *Tamesis*), Oxford was a key Saxon town heavily fortified by Alfred the Great during the war against the Danes.

By the 11th century, the Augustinian abbey in Oxford had begun training clerics, and when Henry II banned Anglo-Norman students from attending the Sorbonne in 1167, the abbey began to attract students in droves. Whether bored by the lack of distractions or revolted by the ignorance of the country folk we'll never know, but the new students managed to create a lasting enmity with the local townspeople, culminating in the St Scholastica's Day Massacre in 1355. Thereafter, the king ordered that the university be broken up into colleges, each of which then developed its own traditions.

The first colleges, Balliol, Merton and University, were built in the 13th century, with at least three more being added in each of the following three centuries. Newer colleges, such as Keble, were added in the 19th and 20th centuries to cater for an ever-expanding student population. However, old habits die hard at Oxford, and it was 1877 before lecturers were allowed to marry, and another year before female students were admitted. Even then, it still took another 42 years before women would be granted a degree for their four years of hard work. Today, there are 39 colleges that cater for about 20,000 students, and in 2008 the last all-female college, St Hilda's, eventually opened its door to male students.

Meanwhile, the arrival of the canal system in 1790 had a profound effect on the rest of Oxford. By creating a link with the Midlands' industrial centres, work and trade suddenly expanded beyond the academic core. However, the city's real industrial boom came when William Morris began producing cars here in 1913. With the success of his Bullnose Morris and Morris Minor, his Cowley factory went on to become one of the largest motor plants in the world. Although the works have been scaled down since their heyday, new Minis still run off BMW's Cowley production line today.

Sights

University Buildings & Colleges

Much of the centre of Oxford is taken up by graceful university buildings and elegant colleges, each one individual in its appearance and academic specialities. However, not all are open to the public. For those that are, visiting hours change with the term and exam schedule. Check www.ox.ac.uk/colleges for full details of visiting hours and admission.

Christ Church College COLLEGE

(www.chch.ox.ac.uk; St Aldate's; adult/child £6/4.50; ⌚9am-5pm Mon-Sat, 2-5pm Sun) The largest and grandest of all of Oxford's colleges, Christ Church is also its most popular. The magnificent buildings, illustrious history and latter-day fame as a location for the Harry Potter films have tourists coming in droves.

The college was founded in 1525 by Cardinal Thomas Wolsey, who suppressed 22 monasteries to acquire the funds for his lavish building project. Over the years numerous luminaries have been educated here, including Albert Einstein, philosopher John Locke, poet WH Auden, Charles Dodgson (Lewis Carroll) and 13 British prime ministers.

The main entrance is below the imposing **Tom Tower**, the upper part of which was designed by former student Sir Christopher Wren. Great Tom, the 7-ton tower bell, still chimes 101 times each evening at 9.05pm (Oxford is five minutes west of Greenwich) to sound the curfew imposed on the original 101 students.

Mere visitors, however, are not allowed to enter the college this way and must go further down St Aldate's to the side entrance. Immediately on entering is the 15th-century cloister, a relic of the ancient Priory of St Frideswide, whose shrine was once a focus of pilgrimage. From here, you go up to the **Great Hall**, the college's magnificent dining room, with its hammerbeam roof and imposing portraits of past scholars.

Coming down the grand staircase, you'll enter **Tom Quad**, Oxford's largest quadrangle, and from here, **Christ Church Cathedral**, the smallest cathedral in the country. Inside, brawny Norman columns are topped by elegant vaulting, and beautiful stained-glass windows illuminate the walls. Look out for the rare depiction of the murder of Thomas Becket dating from 1320.

You can also explore another two quads and the **Picture Gallery**, with its modest collection of Renaissance art. To the south of the college is **Christ Church Meadow**, a leafy expanse bordered by the Cherwell and Isis rivers and ideal for leisurely walking.

Christ Church is a working college, and the hall often closes between noon and 2pm and the cathedral in late afternoon.

Magdalen College COLLEGE

(www.magd.ox.ac.uk; High St; adult/child £4.50/3.50; ⌚1-6pm) Set amid 40 hectares of lawns, woodlands, river walks and deer park, Magdalen (*mawd*-len) is one of the wealthiest and most beautiful of Oxford's colleges.

An elegant Victorian gateway leads into a medieval chapel, with its glorious 15th-century tower, and on to the remarkable cloisters, some of the finest in Oxford. The strange gargoyles and carved figures here are said to have inspired CS Lewis' stone statues in *The Chronicles of Narnia*. Behind the cloisters, the lovely **Addison's Walk** leads through the grounds and along the banks of the River Cherwell for just under a mile.

Magdalen has a reputation as an artistic college, and some of its most famous students and fellows have included Oscar Wilde, Poet Laureate Sir John Betjeman and Nobel Laureate Seamus Heaney.

The college also has a fine choir that sings *Hymnus Eucharisticus* at 6am on May Day (1 May) from the top of the 42m bell tower. The event now marks the culmination of a solid night of drinking for most students as they gather in their glad rags on Magdalen Bridge to listen to the dawn chorus.

Opposite the college and sweeping along the banks of the River Cherwell is the beautiful **Botanic Garden** (www.botanic-garden.ox.ac.uk; adult/child £3.50/free; ⌚9am-5pm). The gardens are the oldest in Britain and were founded in 1621 for the study of medicinal plants.

Sheldonian Theatre CEREMONIAL HALL

(www.sheldon.ox.ac.uk; Broad St; adult/child £2.50/1.50; ⌚10am-12.30pm & 2-4.30pm Mon-Sat) The monumental Sheldonian Theatre was the first major work of Christopher Wren, at that time a university professor of astronomy. Inspired by the classical Theatre of Marcellus in Rome, it has a rectangular front end and a semicircular back, while inside the ceiling of the main hall is blanketed by a fine 17th-century painting of the triumph of truth over ignorance. The Sheldonian is now used for college ceremonies and public concerts, but you can climb to the cupola for good views of the surrounding buildings.

Bodleian Library LIBRARY

(www.bodley.ox.ac.uk; Broad St; ⌚9am-5pm Mon-Fri, 9am-4.30pm Sat, 11am-5pm Sun) Oxford's Bodleian Library is one of the oldest public libraries in the world, and one of England's three copyright libraries. It holds more than 7 million items on 118 miles of

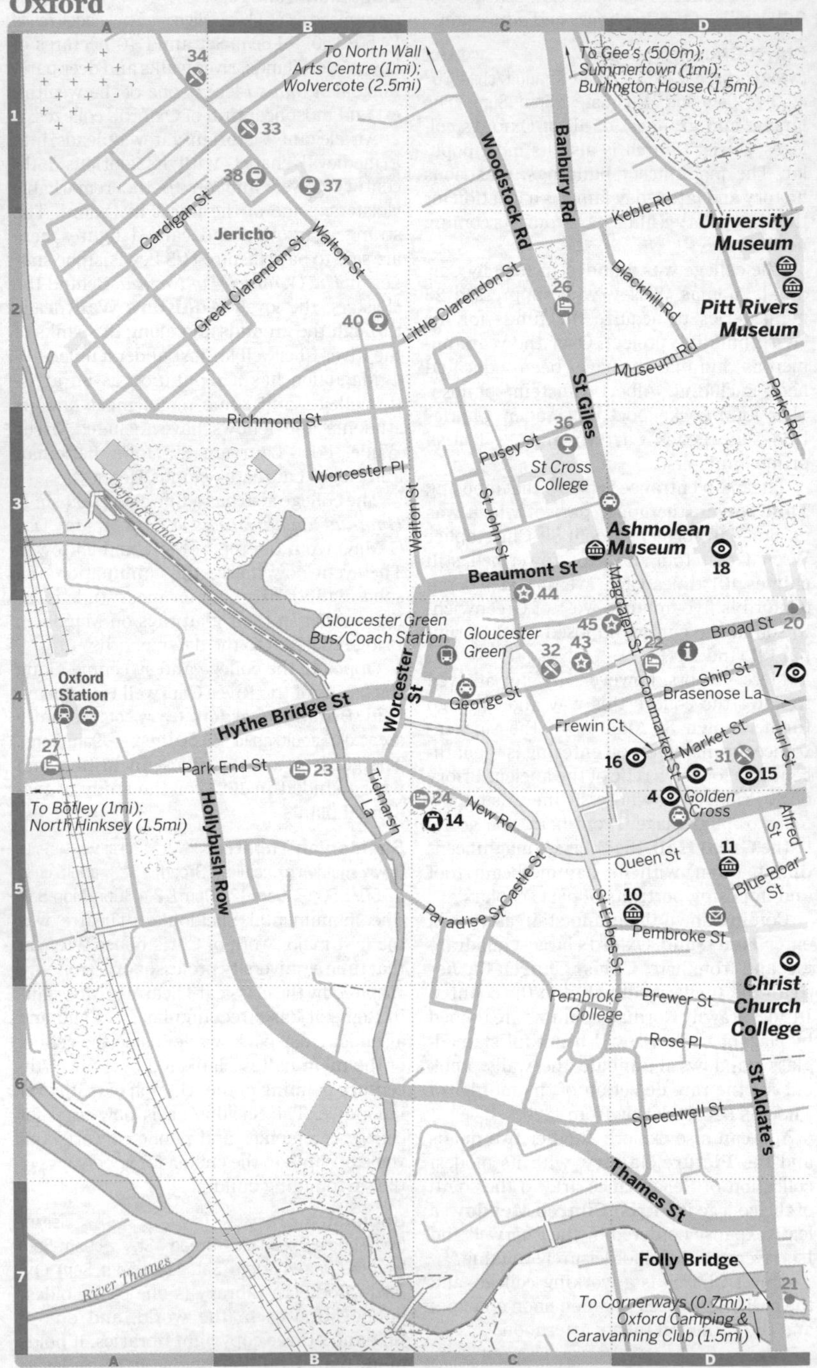
To North Wall Arts Centre (1mi); Wolvercote (2.5mi)
To Gee's (500m); Summertown (1mi); Burlington House (1.5mi)
Jericho
Cardigan St
Great Clarendon St
Walton St
Little Clarendon St
Woodstock Rd
Banbury Rd
Keble Rd
Blackhall Rd
University Museum
Pitt Rivers Museum
Museum Rd
Parks Rd
St Giles
Richmond St
Worcester Pl
Pusey St
St Cross College
St John St
Oxford Canal
Ashmolean Museum
Beaumont St
Magdalen St
Gloucester Green Bus/Coach Station
Gloucester Green
Broad St
Ship St
Brasenose La
Oxford Station
Hythe Bridge St
Worcester St
George St
Frewin Ct
Cornmarket St
Market St
Turl St
Park End St
Golden Cross
To Botley (1mi); North Hinksey (1.5mi)
Hollybush Row
Tidmarsh La
New Rd
Alfred St
Queen St
Castle St
Blue Boar St
Paradise St
St Ebbes St
Pembroke St
Pembroke College
Brewer St
Christ Church College
Rose Pl
St Aldate's
Speedwell St
Thames St
River Thames
Folly Bridge
To Cornerways (0.7mi); Oxford Camping & Caravanning Club (1.5mi)

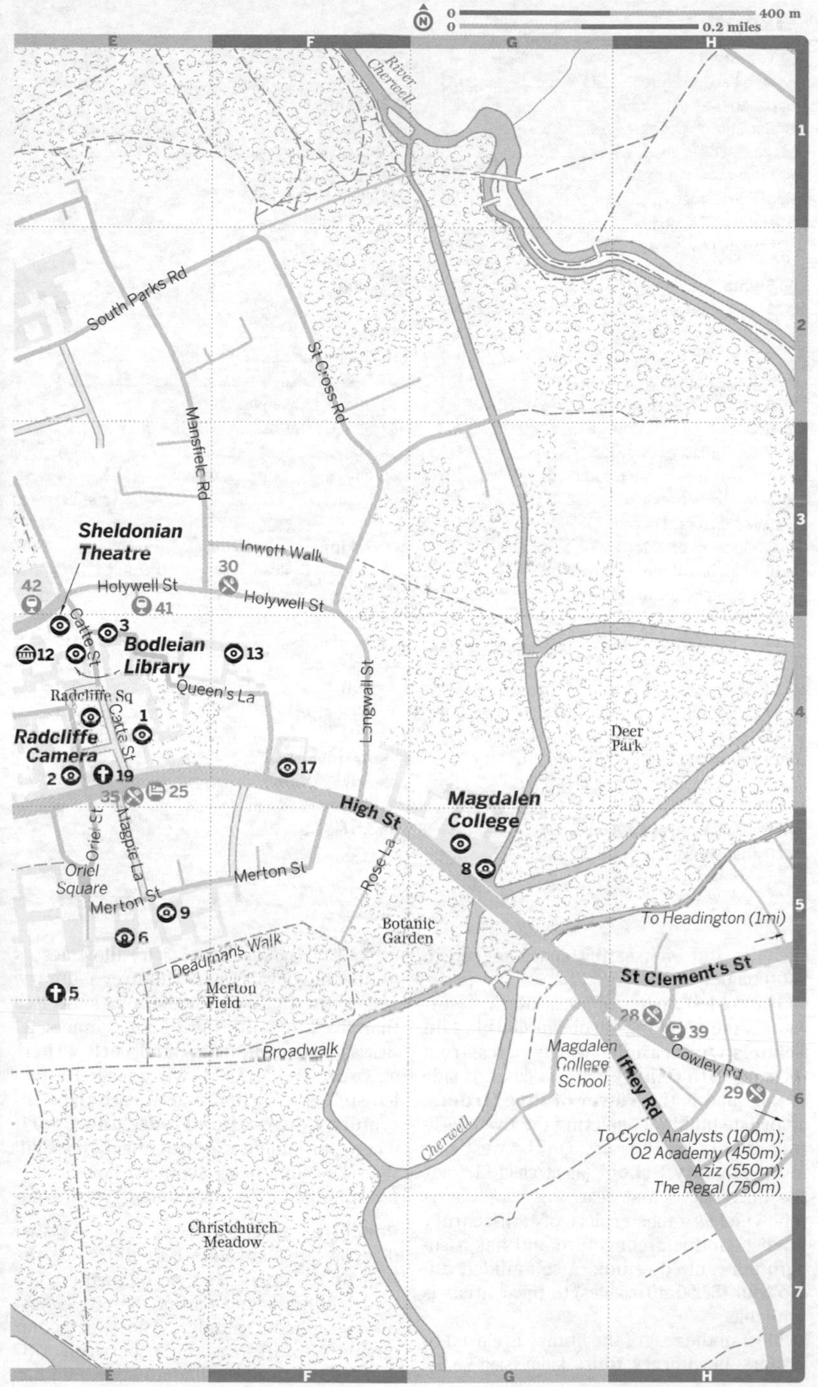

0 400 m
0 0.2 miles
River Cherwell
South Parks Rd
Mansfield Rd
St Cross Rd
Sheldonian Theatre
Jowett Walk
30
42
Holywell St
41
Holywell St
3
Catte St
12
Bodleian Library
13
Radcliffe Sq
Queen's La
Longwall St
1
Radcliffe Camera
Catte St
17
2
19
35
25
High St
Magdalen College
8
Deer Park
Oriel St
Magpie La
Merton St
Rose La
Oriel Square
Merton St
9
6
Botanic Garden
To Headington (1mi)
Deadmans Walk
St Clement's St
5
Merton Field
28
39
Broadwalk
Magdalen College School
Iffley Rd
Cowley Rd
29
Cherwell
To Cyclo Analysts (100m); O2 Academy (450m); Aziz (550m); The Regal (750m)
Christchurch Meadow

Oxford

Top Sights

Ashmolean Museum C3
Bodleian Library E4
Christ Church College D5
Magdalen College G5
Pitt Rivers Museum D2
Radcliffe Camera E4
Sheldonian Theatre E4
University Museum D2

Sights

1 All Souls College E4
2 Brasenose College E4
3 Bridge of Sighs E4
4 Carfax Tower D5
5 Christ Church Cathedral E5
6 Corpus Christi College E5
7 Exeter College D4
8 Magdalen Bridge Boathouse G5
9 Merton College E5
10 Modern Art Oxford D5
11 Museum of Oxford D5
12 Museum of the History of Science E4
13 New College F4
14 Oxford Castle C5
15 Oxford Covered Market D4
16 Oxford Union D4
17 St Edmund Hall F4
18 Trinity College D3
19 University Church of St Mary the Virgin E4

Activities, Courses & Tours

20 Blackwell D4
21 Salter Bros D7

Sleeping

22 Buttery Hotel D4
23 Central Backpackers B4
24 Malmaison C5
25 Old Bank Hotel E4
26 Old Parsonage Hotel C2
27 YHA Oxford A4

Eating

28 Café Coco H6
29 Door 74 .... H6
30 Edamame F3
31 Georgina's D4
32 Jamie's Italian C4
33 Jericho Café B1
34 Manos A1
35 Quod E4
Vaults .... (see 19)

Drinking

36 Eagle & Child C3
37 Frevd B1
38 Jericho Tavern B1
39 Kazbar H6
40 Raoul's B2
41 Turf Tavern E3
42 White Horse E3

Entertainment

43 New Theatre C4
44 Oxford Playhouse C3
45 Po Na Na D4

shelving and has seating space for up to 2500 readers.

The oldest part of the library surrounds the stunning Jacobean-Gothic **Old Schools Quadrangle**, which dates from the early 17th century. On the eastern side of the quad is the **Tower of Five Orders**, an ornate building depicting the five classical orders of architecture. On the west side is the **Divinity School** (adult/child £1/free), the university's first teaching room. It is renowned as a masterpiece of 15th-century English Gothic architecture and has a superb fan-vaulted ceiling. A self-guided **audio tour** (£2.50, 40 minutes) to these areas is available.

Most of the rest of the library is closed to visitors, but **library tours** (admission £6.50; ⌚10.30am, 11.30am, 2pm & 3pm) allow access to the medieval Duke Humfrey's library, where, the library proudly boasts, no less than five kings, 40 Nobel Prize winners, 25 British prime ministers and such writers as Oscar Wilde, CS Lewis and JRR Tolkien studied. You'll also get to see the 17th-century **Convocation House and Court**, where parliament was held during the Civil War. The tour takes about an hour and is not suitable for children under 11 years old.

Radcliffe Camera LIBRARY

(Radcliffe Sq) Just south of the library is the Radcliffe Camera, the quintessential Oxford landmark and one of the city's most photographed buildings. The spectacular circular library was built between 1737 and 1749 in grand Palladian style, and has

Britain's third-largest dome. The only way to see the library is to join an **extended tour** (£13), which also explores the warren of underground tunnels and passages leading to the library's vast book stacks. Tours take place on some Saturdays at 10am and most Sundays at 11.15am and last about an hour and a half. Check the website for up-to-date details.

For excellent views of the Radcliffe Camera and surrounding buildings, climb the 14th-century tower in the beautiful **University Church of Saint Mary the Virgin** (www.university-church.ox.ac.uk; High St; tower admission adult/child £3/2.50). On Sunday the tower does not open until about noon, after the morning service.

New College COLLEGE

(www.new.ox.ac.uk; Holywell St; admission £2; ⌚11am-5pm) From the Bodleian, stroll under the **Bridge of Sighs**, a 1914 copy of the famous bridge in Venice, to New College. This 14th-century college was the first in Oxford for undergraduates and is a fine example of the glorious Perpendicular style. The chapel here is full of treasures, including superb stained glass, much of it original, and Sir Jacob Epstein's disturbing statue of Lazarus.

During term time, visitors may attend the beautiful **Evensong**, a choral church service held nightly at 6pm. Access for visitors is through the New College Lane gate from Easter to early October, and through the Holywell St entrance the rest of the year.

William Spooner was once a college warden here, and his habit of transposing the first consonants of words gave rise to the term 'spoonerism'. Local lore suggests that he once reprimanded a student by saying, 'You have deliberately tasted two worms and can leave Oxford by the town drain.'

Merton College COLLEGE

(www.merton.ox.ac.uk; Merton St; admission £2; ⌚2-5pm Mon-Fri, 10am-5pm Sat & Sun) From the High St, follow the wonderfully named Logic Lane to Merton College, one of Oxford's original three colleges. Founded in 1264, Merton was the first to adopt collegiate planning, bringing scholars and tutors together into a formal community and providing a planned residence for them. The charming 14th-century **Mob Quad** was the first of the college quads.

Just off the quad is a 13th-century **chapel** and the **Old Library** (admission on guided tour only), the oldest medieval library in use. It is said that Tolkien spent many hours here writing *The Lord of the Rings*. Other literary giants associated with the college include TS Eliot and Louis MacNeice.

During the summer months it may be possible to join a **guided tour** (£2, 45 minutes) of the college grounds. These usually take place in the afternoon, but are dependent on the availability of the graduate students who run them. If you're visiting in summer, look out for posters advertising candlelit concerts in the chapel.

FREE **All Souls College** COLLEGE

(www.all-souls.ox.ac.uk; High St; ⌚2-4pm Mon-Fri) One of the wealthiest of Oxford's colleges and unique in not accepting undergraduate students, All Souls is primarily an academic research institution. It was founded in 1438 as a centre of prayer and learning, and today fellowship of the college is one of the highest academic honours in the country. Each year, the university's top finalists are invited to sit a fellowship exam, with an average of only two making the grade annually.

Much of the college facade dates from the 1440s and, unlike other older colleges, the front quad is largely unchanged in five centuries. It also contains a beautiful 17th-century sundial designed by Christopher Wren. Most obvious, though, are the twin mock-Gothic towers on the north quad. Designed by Nicholas Hawksmoor in 1710, they were lambasted for ruining the Oxford skyline when first erected.

Oxford Union LIBRARY

(www.oxford-union.org; Frewin Court; admission £1.50; ⌚9.30am-5pm Mon-Fri) Oxford's legendary members' society is famous for its feisty debates, heavyweight international speakers and Pre-Raphaelite murals. Although most of the building is off limits to nonmembers, you can visit the library to see the murals which were painted between 1857 and 1859 by Dante Gabriel Rossetti, William Morris and Edward Burne-Jones. The murals depict scenes from the Arthurian legends but are very difficult to see on bright days as they surround the windows. Go after dark if possible.

Brasenose College COLLEGE

(www.bnc.ox.ac.uk; Radcliffe Sq; admission £1; ⌚noon-4pm) Small and select, this elegant 16th-century place is truly charming. Look out for the door-knocker above the high table in the dining hall – and ask about its fascinating history.

FREE **Exeter College** COLLEGE
(www.exeter.ox.ac.uk; Turl St; ⏲2-5pm) Exeter is known for its elaborate 17th-century dining hall and ornate Victorian Gothic chapel housing *The Adoration of the Magi,* a William Morris tapestry.

Trinity College COLLEGE
(www.trinity.ox.ac.uk; Broad St; adult/child £1.50/75p; ⏲10am-noon & 2-4pm Sun-Fri, 2-4pm Sat) This small 16th-century college is worth a visit to see its exquisitely carved chapel, one of the most beautiful in the city, and the lovely garden quad designed by Sir Christopher Wren.

FREE **St Edmund Hall** COLLEGE
(www.seh.ox.ac.uk; Queen's Lane; ⏲noon-4pm Mon-Fri term time only) St Edmund Hall is the sole survivor of the original medieval halls, the teaching institutions that preceded colleges in Oxford. The Mohawk chief Oronhyatekha studied here in 1862 (and eloped with the principal's daughter) but it is best known for its small chapel decorated by William Morris and Edward Burne-Jones.

FREE **Corpus Christi College** COLLEGE
(www.ccc.ox.ac.uk; Merton St; ⏲1.30-4.30pm) Reputedly the friendliest and most liberal of Oxford's colleges, Corpus Christi is small but strikingly beautiful. The pelican sundial in the front quad calculates the time by the sun and the moon, although it is always five minutes fast.

Other Sights

FREE **Ashmolean Museum** MUSEUM
(www.ashmolean.org; Beaumont St; ⏲10am-6pm Tue-Sun) Britain's oldest public museum, the Ashmolean reopened in 2009 after a massive £61 million redevelopment and is now being lauded as the finest university museum in the world. The makeover has made the once intimidating building and stuffy collection a real joy to browse, with a giant atrium, glass walls revealing galleries on different levels, and a beautiful rooftop restaurant.

The museum was established in 1683 when Elias Ashmole presented the university with the collection of artefacts amassed by John Tradescant, gardener to Charles I. It contains everything from Egyptian, Islamic and Chinese art to rare porcelain, tapestries and silverware, priceless musical instruments and extensive displays of European art (including works by Raphael and Michelangelo). Set in one of Britain's best examples of neo-Grecian architecture, it is one of the region's top attractions.

FREE **University & Pitt Rivers Museums** MUSEUM
Housed in a glorious Victorian Gothic building with slender, cast-iron columns, ornate capitals and a soaring glass roof, the **University Museum** (www.oum.ox.ac.uk; Parks Rd; ⏲10am-5pm; 👪) is worth a visit for its architecture alone. However, the real draw is the mammoth natural-history collection of more than 5 million exhibits, ranging from exotic insects and fossils to a towering *T. rex* skeleton.

Hidden away through a door at the back of the main exhibition hall, the **Pitt Rivers Museum** (www.prm.ox.ac.uk; ⏲10am-4.30pm Tue-Sun, noon-4.30pm Mon; 👪) is a treasure trove of weird and wonderful displays to satisfy every armchair adventurer's wildest dreams. In the half light inside are glass cases and mysterious drawers stuffed with Victorian explorers' prized booty. Feathered cloaks, necklaces of teeth, blowpipes, magic charms, Noh masks, totem poles, fur parkas, musical instruments and shrunken heads lurk here, making it a fascinating place for adults and children.

Both museums run workshops for children almost every weekend and are known for their child-friendly attitude.

Oxford Castle Unlocked PRISON
(www.oxfordcastleunlocked.co.uk; 44-46 Oxford Castle; adult/child £7.75/5.50; ⏲10am-4.20pm) Oxford Castle Unlocked explores the 1000-year history of Oxford's castle and prison. Tours begin in the 11th-century Crypt of St George's Chapel, possibly the first formal teaching venue in Oxford, and continue into the Victorian prison cells and the 18th-century Debtors' Tower, where you can learn about the inmates' grisly lives, daring escapes and cruel punishments. You can also climb the Saxon St George's Tower, which has excellent views of the city, and clamber up the original medieval motte.

FREE **Modern Art Oxford** ART GALLERY
(www.modernartoxford.org.uk; 30 Pembroke St; ⏲10am-5pm Tue-Sat, noon-5pm Sun; 👪) Far removed from Oxford's musty hallways of history, this is one of the best contemporary-art museums outside London, with heavyweight exhibitions, a wonderful gallery space and plenty of activities for children.

LOCAL KNOWLEDGE

PETER BERRY, BLACKWELL TOUR GUIDE

Although it's a small city, Oxford is such a big world, with a wealth of famous people who have studied here. There's no shortage of material for a tour guide.

Must see:

» **Christ Church Cathedral** (p183)

» **Bridge of Sighs** (p187)

» **Radcliffe Camera** (p186)

» **Turf Tavern** (p194)

Must do:

» Climb the tower of **University Church** (p187) – it's the highest point in the city and offers great views of the dreaming spires.

Favourite chapel:

» **Exeter College** (p188) Don't miss it.

Oxford inspires:

» CS Lewis' office at **Magdalen** (p183) looked out over the deer park, and this was probably the inspiration for the fawn in the *Narnia* series.

» Tolkien lived at 99 Holywell St and neighbours can recall him coming out to the street to test his stories on the local children.

» The *Jabberwocky* tree still stands at the back of **Christ Church Cathedral** (p183); you can see it through a gate in the high wall. It's almost 400 years old.

» *Hidden gem:*

The Elizabethan murals in the **Golden Cross Inn** (now Pizza Express). The Prince's Chamber was Shakespeare's overnight Oxford stop between London and Stratford.

Things the university would rather you didn't know:

Percy Bysshe Shelley was infamous for playing schoolboy pranks, in particular, swapping babies left in prams outside the shops on the High St.

FREE **Museum of the History of Science** MUSEUM

(www.mhs.ox.ac.uk; Broad St; ⏲noon-5pm Tue-Fri, 10am-5pm Sat, 2-5pm Sun) Science, art, celebrity and nostalgia come together at this fascinating museum where the exhibits include everything from a blackboard used by Einstein to the world's finest collection of historic scientific instruments, all housed in a beautiful 17th-century building.

Oxford Covered Market INDOOR MARKET

(www.oxford-covered-market.co.uk; ⏲9am-5.30pm) A haven of traditional butchers, fishmongers, cobblers and barbers, this is the place to go for Sicilian sausage, handmade chocolates, traditional pies, funky T-shirts and expensive brogues. It's a fascinating place to explore and, if you're in Oxford at Christmas, a must for its traditional displays of freshly hung deer, wild boar, ostrich and turkey.

FREE **Museum of Oxford** MUSEUM

(www.museumofoxford.org.uk; St Aldate's; ⏲10am-5pm Tue-Sat) A bit dated but still interesting, this is the place to brush up on the history of the city and university, from Oxford's prehistoric mammoths to its history of car manufacturing.

Carfax Tower MEDIEVAL TOWER

(adult/child £2.20/1.10; ⏲10am-5.30pm) Oxford's central landmark is the sole reminder of medieval St Martin's Church and offers good views over the city centre.

THE BRAINS BEHIND THE OED

In 1879, Oxford University Press began an ambitious project: a complete re-examination of the English language. The four-volume work was expected to take 10 years to complete. Recognising the mammoth task ahead, editor James Murray issued a circular appealing for volunteers to pore over their books and make precise notes on word usage. Their contributions were invaluable, but after five years, Murray and his team had still only reached the word 'ant'.

Of the thousands of volunteers who helped out, the most prolific of all was Dr WC Minor, a US Civil War surgeon. Over the next 20 years, he became Murray's most valued contributor, providing tens of thousands of illustrative quotations and notes on word origins and usage. Murray received all of the doctor's contributions by post from Broadmoor, a hospital for the criminally insane. When he decided to visit the doctor in 1891, however, he discovered that Minor was not an employee but the asylum's longest-serving inmate, a schizophrenic committed in 1872 for a motiveless murder. Despite this, Murray was deeply taken by Minor's devotion to his project and continued to work with him, a story told in full in Simon Winchester's book *The Surgeon of Crowthorne*.

Neither Murray nor Minor lived to see the eventual publication of *A New English Dictionary on Historical Principles* in 1928. Almost 40 years behind schedule and 10 volumes long, it was the most comprehensive lexicographical project ever undertaken, and a full second edition did not appear until 1989.

Today, the updating of such a major work is no easier, and the public were again asked for help in 2006. This time, the BBC ran a TV program, *Balderdash and Piffle*, encouraging viewers to contact the Press with early printed evidence of word use, new definitions and brand-new entries for the dictionary. A second edition of the program was broadcast a year later.

For a full history of the famous dictionary and the development of printing, pay a visit to the **Oxford University Press Museum** (☎01865-267527; Great Clarendon St; ⌚by appointment only).

Activities

A quintessential Oxford experience, **punting** is all about sitting back and quaffing Pimms (the quintessential English summer drink) as you watch the city's glorious architecture float by. Which, of course, requires someone else to do the hard work – punting is far more difficult than it appears. Be prepared to spend much of your time struggling to get out of a tangle of low branches or avoiding the path of an oncoming rowing team. For tips on how to punt, see the boxed text, p409.

Punts are available from mid-March to mid-October, 10am to dusk, and hold five people including the punter (£13/15 per hour weekdays/weekends, £65 deposit).

The most central location to rent punts is **Magdalen Bridge Boathouse** (www.oxfordpunting.co.uk; High St). From here, you can punt downstream around the Botanic Garden and Christ Church Meadow or upstream around Magdalen Deer Park. Alternatively, head for the **Cherwell Boat House** (www.cherwellboathouse.co.uk; Bardwell Rd) for a countryside amble, where the destination of choice is the busy boozer, the **Victoria Arms** (Mill Lane). To get to the boathouse, take bus 2 or 7 from Magdalen St to Bardwell Rd and follow the signposts.

Salter Bros (www.salterssteamers.co.uk; Folly Bridge; boat trips adult/child £10.50/5.60; ⌚9.15am & 2.30pm Jun–mid-Sep) offer a range of trips along the Isis from Oxford. The most popular is the scenic journey to the historic market town of Abingdon. The trip takes 1¾ hours and passes the college boathouses and several popular riverside pubs en route.

Tours

The tourist office can also advise on a number of self-guided (brochure or audio) tours of the city.

Tourist Office WALKING TOURS
(☎01865-252200; www.visitoxford.org; 15-16 Broad St; ⌚9.30am-5pm Mon-Sat, 10am-4pm Sun) Runs two-hour tours of Oxford city and colleges (adult/child £7/3.75) at 10.45am and 2pm year-round, and at 11am and 1pm in July and August, Inspector Morse tours (adult/child £7.50/4) at 1.30pm on Saturdays, family walking tours (adult/child £5.75/3.50) at

1.30pm on school holidays, and a bewildering array of themed tours (adult/child £7.50/4) – including an Alice [in Wonderland] tour, a Literary Tour, and a Harry Potter tour – that run on various dates throughout the year.

Blackwell WALKING TOURS
(☎01865-333606; oxford@blackwell.co.uk; 48-51 Broad St; adult/child £7/6.50; ⊙mid-Apr–Oct) Oxford's most famous bookshop runs 1½-hour guided walking tours, including a literary tour at 2pm Tuesday and 11am Thursday, a tour devoted to 'Inklings' – an informal literary group whose membership included CS Lewis and JRR Tolkien – at 11.45am on Wednesday, and a Chapels, Churches and Cathedral tour (adult/child £9/8) at 2pm on Friday. Book ahead.

Bill Spectre's Ghost Trail WALKING TOURS
(☎07941 041811; www.ghosttrail.org; adult/child £6/3; ⊙6.30pm Fri & Sat) For a highly entertaining and informative look at Oxford's dark underbelly, join Victorian undertaker Bill Spectre on a tour of Oxford's most haunted sites. The tour lasts one hour 45 minutes and departs from Oxford Castle Unlocked.

City Sightseeing BUS TOURS
(www.citysightseeingoxford.com; adult/child £12.50/6; ⊙9.30am-6pm Apr-Oct) Hop-on/hop-off bus tours depart every 10 to 15 minutes from the bus and train stations or any of the 20 dedicated stops around town.

Oxon Carts PEDICAB TOURS
(☎07747-024600; www.oxoncarts.com; tour £20) Oxon Carts runs a fleet of pedicabs around Oxford's narrow lanes. Passengers receive a copy of a 1904 map of the city and a personal guide to its buildings and history. The 45-minute tours are fully flexible so you can follow the standard itinerary or your own suggestions.

Sleeping

Oxford accommodation is generally overpriced and underwhelming, with suffocating floral patterns as the B&B norm. The following places stand out for their value for money and good taste. Book ahead between May and September. If you're stuck, you'll find a string of B&Bs along Iffley, Abingdon, Banbury and Headington Roads.

Oxford Rooms STUDENT ROOMS ££
(www.oxfordrooms.co.uk; r from £40) Didn't quite make the cut for a place at Oxford? Well, at least you can experience life inside the hallowed college grounds and breakfast in a grand college hall by staying overnight in one of their student rooms. Most rooms are singles and pretty functional, with basic furnishings, shared bathrooms and internet access, though there are some en suite, twin and family rooms available. Some rooms have old-world character and views over the college quad, while others are more modern but in a nearby annexe.

There's limited availability during term time, but a good choice of rooms during university holidays.

TOP CHOICE **Malmaison** HOTEL £££
(☎01865-268400; www.malmaison-oxford.com; Oxford Castle; d/ste from £160/245; P@🔊) Lock yourself up for the night in one of Oxford's most spectacular settings. This former Victorian prison has been converted into a sleek and slinky hotel, with plush interiors, sultry lighting, dark woods and giant beds. If you're planning a real treat, go for the Governor's Suite, complete with four-poster bed and mini-cinema. Look out for online promotions: you might bag a room for as little as £115.

Old Parsonage Hotel HOTEL £££
(☎01865-310210; www.oldparsonage-hotel.co.uk; 1 Banbury Rd; r from £138; P@) Wonderfully quirky and instantly memorable, the Old Parsonage is a small boutique hotel with just the right blend of old-world character, period charm and modern luxury. The 17th-century building oozes style, with a contemporary-art collection, artfully mismatched furniture and chic bedrooms with handmade beds and marble bathrooms. Oscar Wilde once made it his home. Ask for a room in the old building to see just how he might have lived.

Ethos Hotel HOTEL ££
(☎01865-245800; www.ethoshotels.co.uk; 59 Western Rd; d from £80; @🔊) Hidden away off Abingdon Rd, this funky new hotel has bright, spacious rooms with bold, patterned wallpaper, enormous beds and marble bathrooms. You'll also get a minikitchen with a microwave, a breakfast basket and free wi-fi – all just 10 minutes' walk from the city centre. Some rooms open directly to the street, but with online deals for as little as £68, it's incredible value. To get here, cross Folly Bridge to Abingdon Rd and take the first right onto Western Rd.

Buttery Hotel HOTEL ££
(☎01865-811950; www.thebutteryhotel.co.uk; 11-12 Broad St; s/d from £55/95; @) Right in the heart of the city with views over the college

grounds, the Buttery is Oxford's most central hotel. It's a modest enough place, but considering its location, it's a great deal, with spacious if innocuous modern rooms, decent bathrooms and the pick of the city's attractions on your doorstep.

Oxford YHA HOSTEL £
(☎01865-727275; www.yha.org.uk; 2a Botley Rd; dm/d from £18/46; @) Bright, well kept, clean and tidy, this is Oxford's best budget option, with simple but comfortable dorm accommodation, private rooms and loads of facilities, including a restaurant, library, garden, laundry and a choice of lounges. All rooms are en suite and are bright and cheery, a far better option than some of the city's cheapest B&Bs.

Old Bank Hotel HOTEL £££
(☎01865-799599; www.oldbank-hotel.co.uk; 92 High St; r from £150; P @) Slap bang in the centre of Oxford, rooms here look over the college walls and spires into the very heart of the university. The rooms are sleek and spacious, all neutral colours and silky throws, but they lack a little soul. Downstairs there's a buzzing restaurant with brash modern art and a tumult of eager diners.

Burlington House B&B ££
(☎01865-513513; www.burlington-house.co.uk; 374 Banbury Rd, Summertown; s/d from £65/85; P @ wifi) Simple, elegant rooms decked out in restrained, classical style are available at this Victorian merchant house. The rooms are big, bright and uncluttered, with plenty of period character and immaculately kept bathrooms. The Burlington isn't central, but it has good public transport to town and is well worth the trip.

Remont Guesthouse B&B ££
(☎01865-311020; www.remont-oxford.co.uk; 367 Banbury Rd, Summertown; s/d from £70/88; P @ wifi) All modern style, subtle lighting and plush furnishings, this 25-room guesthouse has rooms decked out in cool neutrals with silky bedspreads and abstract art. There's free wi-fi and a sunny garden, making it a good bet despite the hike from the city centre.

Cornerways B&B ££
(☎01865-240135; www.oxfordcity.co.uk/accom/cornerways; 282 Abingdon Rd; s/d from £55/80; P wifi) Bright, modern rooms with simple but attractive decor make this a good bet within walking distance of town. The genial hosts can help with planning your stay, and breakfast is served in a lovely conservatory overlooking the small patio garden.

Central Backpackers HOSTEL £
(☎01865-242288; www.centralbackpackers.co.uk; 13 Park End St; dm £17-20; @) A good budget option right in the centre of town, this small hostel has basic, bright and simple rooms that sleep four to 12 people. There's a small but decent lounge with satellite TV, a rooftop terrace and free internet and luggage storage.

Oxford Camping & Caravanning Club CAMPING £
(☎01865-244088; www.campingandcaravanningclub.co.uk; 426 Abingdon Rd; sites per adult/child £8.90/2.80) This well-run campsite is conveniently close to the city centre but consequently lacks character and can be noisy. It's a popular spot, however, especially at weekends, so book well in advance. Nonmembers must pay an additional £7 per pitch.

Eating

Oxford has plenty of choice when it comes to eating out, but unfortunately the ubiquitous chain restaurants dominate the scene, especially along George St and around the pedestrianised square at the castle. Head to Walton St in Jericho, to Summertown, St Clements or up Cowley Rd for a quirkier selection of restaurants. Look out for local chain G&D's for excellent ice cream and cakes.

TOP CHOICE **Edamame** JAPANESE £
(www.edamame.co.uk; 15 Holywell St; mains £6-8; ⏲lunch Wed-Sun, dinner Thu-Sat) It may not be the place for a leisurely dinner thanks to its cramped quarters, but the queue out the door speaks volumes about the quality of the food here. This tiny Japanese joint is the best place in town for rice and noodle dishes, and the sushi (Thursday night only, £2.50 to £4) is divine. Arrive early and be prepared to wait – it's well worth it. Last orders at 8.30pm.

Trout MODERN BRITISH ££
(☎01865-510930; www.thetroutoxford.co.uk; 195 Godstow Rd, Wolvercote; mains £8-16) Possibly the prettiest location in Oxford, 2½ miles north of the city centre, this charming old-world pub has been a favourite haunt of town and gown for many years. Immortalised by Inspector Morse, it's generally crammed with happy diners enjoying the riverside garden and the extensive menu, though you can also just come for a quiet pint outside meal times. Book ahead.

Vaults CAFE £
(www.vaultsandgarden.com; Church of St Mary the Virgin; mains £3.50-5; ⏲10am-5pm) Set in a vaulted 14th-century Congregation House, this place serves a wholesome line of soups, salads, pastas and paellas with plenty of choice for vegetarians. It's one of the most beautiful lunch venues in Oxford, with a lovely garden overlooking Radcliffe Sq. Come early for lunch as it's a local favourite.

Manos GREEK £
(www.manosfoodbar.com; 105 Walton St; mains £6-8) For delicious home-cooked tastes of the Med, head for this Greek deli and restaurant where you'll find a great selection of dishes bursting with flavour. The ground floor has a cafe and deli, while downstairs has more style and comfort, with giant cushions surrounding low tables.

Door 74 MODERN BRITISH ££
(☎01865-203374; www.door74.co.uk; 74 Cowley Rd; mains £8-13; ⏲closed Mon & Sun dinner) This cosy little place woos its fans with a rich mix of British and Mediterranean flavours and friendly service. The menu is limited and the tables tightly packed, but the food is consistently good and combines classic ingredients with a modern twist. Book ahead as seating is limited.

Café Coco MEDITERRANEAN £
(www.cafe-coco.co.uk; 23 Cowley Rd; mains £6-10.50) Chilled out but always buzzing, this Cowley Rd institution is a sort of hip hangout, with classic posters on the walls and a bald plaster-cast clown in an ice bath. The food is vaguely Mediterranean and can be a bit hit-and-miss, but most people come for the atmosphere.

Jericho Café MEDITERRANEAN ££
(www.thejerichocafe.co.uk; 112 Walton St; mains £7-12) Chill out and relax with the paper over a coffee and a slab of cake, or go for some of the wholesome lunch and dinner specials, which encompass everything from sausages and mash to Lebanese lamb *kibbeh*. There are plenty of hearty salads and lots of options for vegetarians.

Quod MODERN BRITISH ££
(www.quod.co.uk; 92 High St; mains £12-15) Bright, buzzing and decked out with modern art and beautiful people, this joint dishes up modern brasserie-style food to the masses. It's always bustling and, at worst, will tempt you to chill by the bar with a cocktail while you wait. The two-course set lunch (£9.95) is great value.

Fishes MODERN BRITISH ££
(☎01865-249796; www.thefishesoxford.co.uk; North Hinksey; mains £10-17; 👪) Old and quaint on the outside but sleek and modern inside, this popular summer haunt, a couple of miles west of the city centre, is a Victorian pub with a large garden complete with playground. It's set in a quiet village enclave and makes a great destination for a quiet pint or an enjoyable meal.

Jamie's Italian ITALIAN ££
(www.jamiesitalian.com; 24-26 George St; mains £8-18) Celebrity chef Jamie Oliver's restaurant serves up some excellent rustic Italian dishes at affordable prices. The food is great and the service efficient, but you'll have to put up with the rather confused decor and a very odd choice of music.

Georgina's CAFE £
(Ave 3, Oxford Covered Market; mains £3-6; ⏲8.30am-5pm Mon-Sat, 10am-4pm Sun) Hidden up a scruffy staircase in the covered market and plastered with old cinema posters, this is a funky little cafe serving a bumper crop of bulging salads, hearty soups and such goodies as goat-cheese quesadillas and scrumptious cakes.

Gee's MODERN BRITISH £££
(☎01865-553540; www.gees-restaurant.co.uk; 61 Banbury Rd; mains £15-23.50) Set in a Victorian conservatory, this top-notch restaurant is a sibling of Quod's but much more conservative. Popular with the visiting parents of university students, the food is modern British and European and the setting stunning, but it's all a little stiff. Book ahead.

Aziz INDIAN £
(www.aziz.uk.com; 228 Cowley Rd; mains £6-9; ⏲closed Fri lunch) Thought by many to be Oxford's best curry house, this award-winning restaurant attracts vegans, vegetarians and curry-lovers in hoards. There's an extensive menu, chilled-out surroundings and portions generous enough to ensure you'll be rolling out the door.

Drinking

Oxford is blessed with some wonderful traditional pubs as well as a good selection of funky bars. Stroll along the towpaths to find a few riverside gems, or check out Cowley Rd for student haunts or George St for rowdy weekend revellers.

Isis Tavern PUB
(Iffley Lock; ⌚6-10pm Mon-Wed, 4-10pm Thu, noon-11pm Fri, 10.30am-11pm Sat, 10.30am-9pm Sun; 👪) The destination of choice on a sunny weekend, the Isis is a down-to-earth boozer serving real ales in simple surroundings. It's slowly being spruced up, but somehow its stripped walls, sticky carpet and unassuming looks neatly convey its honest character. The large garden is a great place for children, dogs and lazy afternoons. To get here walk downstream along the towpath from Folly Bridge for about a mile. If you have the time, continue to Iffley Lock and cross the river to see the pretty village of stone cottages, thatched village hall and stunning 12th-century church.

Turf Tavern TRADITIONAL PUB
(4 Bath Pl) Hidden away down a narrow alleyway, this tiny medieval pub is one of the town's best-loved and bills itself as 'an education in intoxication'. Home to real ales and student antics, it's always packed with a mix of students, professionals and the lucky tourists who manage to find it. It's one of the few pubs in town with plenty of outdoor seating.

Eagle & Child TRADITIONAL PUB
(49 St Giles) Affectionately known as the 'Bird & Baby', this atmospheric place dates from 1650 and is a hotchpotch of nooks and crannies. It was once the favourite haunt of Tolkien, CS Lewis and their literary friends and still attracts a mellow crowd.

Raoul's COCKTAIL BAR
(www.raoulsbar.co.uk; 32 Walton St; ⌚4pm-midnight) This trendy retro-look bar is one of Jericho's finest and is always busy. Famous for its perfectly mixed cocktails and funky music, it's populated by effortlessly cool customers trying hard not to spill their drinks as people squeeze by.

Kazbar BAR
(www.kazbar.co.uk; 25-27 Cowley Rd; ⌚4pm-midnight) This funky Moroccan-themed bar has giant windows, low lighting, warm colours and a cool vibe. It's buzzing most nights with hip young things sipping cocktails and filling up on the Spanish and North African tapas (£3 to £5).

White Horse TRADITIONAL PUB
(52 Broad St) This tiny old-world place was a favourite retreat for TV detective Inspector Morse, and it can get pretty crowded in the evening. It's got buckets of character and makes a great place for a quiet afternoon pint and intellectual conversation.

Jericho Tavern PUB
(www.thejericho.co.uk; 56 Walton St) Chilled out, with big leather sofas, tasselled lamps and boldly patterned wallpaper, this hip bar also has a live-music venue upstairs. Adorned with giant portraits of John Peel, Supergrass and Radiohead, it's supposedly where the latter played their first gig.

Frevd PUB
(119 Walton St) Once a neoclassical church, now a happening bar, Frevd is a cavernous place with soaring ceilings, distressed walls, quirky art and a mixed bag of barflies. It's popular with a young style-conscious crowd and cocktail-sipping luvvies by night.

☆ Entertainment

Despite its large student population, Oxford's club scene is fairly limited, with several cattle-mart clubs in the centre of town and a lot of crowd-pleasing music. If you're a fan of classical music, however, you'll be spoilt for choice, with a host of excellent venues and regular concerts throughout the year. See www.dailyinfo.co.uk or www.musicatoxford.com for listings.

Creation Theatre THEATRE COMPANY
(www.creationtheatre.co.uk) Performing in a variety of nontraditional venues including city parks, the BMW plant and Oxford Castle, this theatre company produces highly original, mostly Shakespearean shows featuring plenty of magic and special effects. If you're in town when a performance is running, don't miss it.

O2 Academy LIVE VENUE
(www.o2academy.co.uk; 190 Cowley Rd) Oxford's best club and live-music venue had a recent makeover and now hosts everything from big-name DJs and international touring artists to indie bands, hard rock and funk nights across three performance spaces. Expect a mixed crowd of students, professionals and dusty academics.

Po Na Na NIGHTCLUB
(www.oxfordponana.com; 13-15 Magdalen St; ⌚Thu-Sat) Looking a little rough around the edges now, this small cavelike place is hung with Moroccan lanterns and drapes and, in between the regular club nights, attracts some famous DJs and live events. Expect funk, soul, electro, drum and bass, house and indie rock.

Oxford Playhouse THEATRE
(www.oxfordplayhouse.com; Beaumont St) The city's main stage for quality drama also hosts an impressive selection of touring music, dance and theatre performances, and the Burton Taylor Studio has quirky student productions.

Regal PERFORMANCE SPACE
(www.the-regal.com; 300 Cowley Rd; ⏲Thu-Sat) Set in a restored art deco building, the regal hosts an eclectic mix of dance classes, live music, headline DJs, club nights and theatre performances.

Pegasus Theatre THEATRE
(www.pegasustheatre.org.uk; Magdalen Rd) Set in a sparkly new building off Iffley Rd, just five minutes' walk from the Plain, this is the place for alternative independent productions.

New Theatre THEATRE
(www.newtheatreoxford.org.uk; George St) For West End shows, ageing pop stars, comedians and plenty of fanfare.

North Wall Arts Centre ARTS CENTRE
(www.thenorthwall.com; South Parade, Summertown) For drama, dance, live music and art.

Information

Emergency

Police (☎0845 8 505 505; St Aldate's)

Internet Access

C-Works (1st fl, New Bailey House, New Inn Hall St; per 50min £1; ⏲9am-9pm Mon-Sat, to 7pm Sun)

Central Library (Westgate; ⏲9am-7pm Mon-Thu, to 5.30pm Fri & Sat) Free internet access.

Links (33 High St; per 45min £1; ⏲10am-7pm Mon-Sat, 11am-6pm Sun)

Internet Resources

Daily Info (www.dailyinfo.co.uk) Daily listings for events, gigs, performances, accommodation and jobs.

Oxford City (www.oxfordcity.co.uk) Accommodation and restaurant listings as well as entertainment, activities and shopping.

Oxford Online (www.visitoxford.org) Oxford's official tourism website.

Medical Services

John Radcliffe Hospital (☎01865-741166; Headley Way, Headington) Three miles east of the city centre in Headington.

Money

You'll find that every major bank and ATM is handily represented on or close to Cornmarket St.

Post

Post office (102 St Aldate's; ⏲9am-5.30pm Mon-Sat)

Tourist Information

Tourist office (☎01865-252200; www.visitoxford.org; 15-16 Broad St; ⏲9.30am-5pm Mon-Sat, 10am-4pm Sun)

Getting There & Away

Bus

Oxford's main bus/coach station is at **Gloucester Green**. Services to **London** (£16 return) run up to every 15 minutes, day and night, and take about 90 minutes.

Airline (www.oxfordbus.co.uk) Runs to **Heathrow** (£20, 90 minutes) half-hourly from 4am to 10pm and at midnight and 2am, and **Gatwick** (£26, two hours) hourly 5.15am to 8.15pm and every two hours from 10pm to 4am.

National Express (www.nationalexpress.com) Runs buses to Birmingham, Bath and Bristol, but all are easier to reach by train.

Stagecoach (www.stagecoachbus.com) Serves most of the small towns in Oxfordshire and runs the X5 service to **Cambridge** (£10.90, 3½ hours) roughly every half-hour.

Car

Driving and parking in Oxford is a nightmare. Use the five Park & Ride car parks on major routes leading into town. Parking is free and buses (10 to 15 minutes, every 10 minutes) cost £2.50.

Train

Oxford's train station is conveniently placed at the western end of Park End St. There are half-hourly services to **London Paddington** (£19.90, one hour) and roughly hourly trains to **Birmingham** (£27, 1¼ hours). Hourly services also run to **Bath** (£22.50, 1¼ hours) and **Bristol** (£24.50, 1½ hours), but require a change at Didcot Parkway.

Getting Around

Bicycle

Cyclo Analysts (☎01865-424444; 150 Cowley Rd; per day/week £17/54) Rents hybrid bikes.

Bus

Buses 1 and 5 go to Cowley Rd from St Aldate's, 2 and 7 go along Banbury Rd from Magdalen St, and 16 and 35 run along Abingdon Rd from St Aldate's.

A multi-operator Plus Pass (per day/week £6/19) allows unlimited travel on Oxford's bus system.

Taxi

There are taxi ranks at the train station and bus station, as well as on St Giles and at Carfax. Be prepared to join a long queue after closing time. For a green alternative, call **Oxon Carts** (☎07747 024600; info@oxoncarts.com), a pedicab service.

Woodstock

POP 2924

The charming village of Woodstock is full of picturesque creeper-clad cottages, elegant town houses, buckled roofs, art galleries and antique shops. It's an understandably popular spot, conveniently close to Oxford, yet a quintessential rural retreat. The big draw here is Blenheim Palace, the opulent country pile of the Churchill family, but the village itself is a gracious and tranquil spot even on busy summer days.

Sights

The hub of the village is the imposing **town hall**, built at the Duke of Marlborough's expense in 1766. Nearby, the **Church of St Mary Magdalene** had a 19th-century makeover but retains its Norman doorway, early English windows and a musical clock.

Opposite the church, the **Oxfordshire Museum** (www.tomocc.org.uk; admission free; Park St; ⏲10am-5pm Tue-Sat, 2-5pm Sun) has displays on local history, art, archaeology and wildlife. It also houses the **tourist office** (☎01993-813276).

Blenheim Palace PALACE

(www.blenheimpalace.com; adult/child £18/10, park & garden only £10.30/5; ⏲10.30am-5.30pm daily mid-Feb–Oct, Wed-Sun Nov–mid-Dec) One of the country's greatest stately homes, Blenheim Palace is a monumental baroque fantasy designed by Sir John Vanbrugh and Nicholas Hawksmoor between 1705 and 1722. The land and funds to build the house were granted to John Churchill, Duke of Marlborough, by a grateful Queen Anne after his decisive victory at the 1704 Battle of Blenheim. Now a Unesco World Heritage Site, Blenheim (pronounced *blen*-num) is home to the 11th duke and duchess.

Inside, the house is stuffed with statues, tapestries, ostentatious furniture and giant oil paintings in elaborate gilt frames. Highlights include the **Great Hall**, a vast space topped by 20m-high ceilings adorned with images of the first duke in battle; the opulent **Saloon**, the grandest and most important public room; the three **state rooms**, with their plush decor and priceless china cabinets; and the magnificent **Long Library**, which is 55m in length.

From the library, you can access the **Churchill Exhibition**, which is dedicated to the life, work and writings of Sir Winston, who was born at Blenheim in 1874. For an insight into life below stairs, the **Untold Story** exhibition explores the family's history through the eyes of the household staff.

If the crowds in the house become too oppressive, retire to the lavish gardens and vast parklands, parts of which were landscaped by Lancelot 'Capability' Brown. To the front, an artificial lake sports a beautiful bridge by Vanbrugh, and a minitrain is needed to take visitors to a maze, adventure playground and butterfly house. For a quieter and longer stroll, glorious walks lead to an arboretum, cascade and temple.

Sleeping & Eating

Woodstock has a good choice of accommodation, but it's not cheap. Luxurious, old-world hotels are the thing here, so plan a day-trip from Oxford if you're travelling on a budget.

Hope House BOUTIQUE HOTEL £££

(☎01993-815990; www.hopehousewoodstock.co.uk; Oxford St; d from £295; P@) Wallow in pure indulgence at Woodstock's newest accommodation option, a sumptuous place set in a stunning 18th-century town house. The whole building has been meticulously restored and furnished with effortless style. Original features blend seamlessly with high-tech gadgetry; cool neutral colour schemes abound; and service is attentive but discreet. There are three enormous suites, two of which have two bedrooms.

Kings Arms Hotel HOTEL £££

(☎01993-813636; www.kings-hotel-woodstock.co.uk; 19 Market St; s/d from £75/140; @) Set in a lovely Georgian town house, the rooms here are sleek and stylish, with warm woods, soft, neutral tones and black-and-white images on the walls. Downstairs, there's a bright bistro serving modern British fare (mains £11 to £15) and a good bar with leather sofas and cheaper snacks.

Woodstock's Own B&B ££
(☎01993-810040; www.woodstocksown.co.uk; 59 Oxford St; s/d from £45/75) The modern rooms here offer a break from the usual Cotswold chintz, and although small, they're bright and comfortable. You'll get a hearty breakfast and a very warm welcome from the amiable owners.

Hampers DELI & CAFE £
(31-33 Oxford St; snacks £1.50-5; ⏲lunch) On a fine day you couldn't do better than a picnic in the grounds of the palace, and this deli provides all the essential ingredients: fine cheeses, olives, cold meats, Cotswold smoked salmon and delicious cakes. If it's raining, pop in to the cafe and feast on the delicious soups, sandwiches and cakes instead.

La Galleria ITALIAN ££
(☎01993-813381; www.lagalleriawoodstock.com; 2 Market Pl; mains £16-22.50; ⏲closed Mon) Big windows bathe the simple interior of this much-loved restaurant in light. It's a classic kind of place, with white swag curtains, pink tablecloths and flowers on every table, but the food is divine. Primarily Sardinian, the menu ranges from silky pastas to perfectly cooked veal and fish and is well worth the price. Book ahead.

Getting There & Around

Stagecoach bus S3 runs every half-hour (hourly on Sunday) from George St in Oxford. **Cotswold Roaming** (☎01865-308300; www.cotswoldroaming.co.uk) offers a Cotswolds–Blenheim combination tour (adult £47.50), with a morning at Blenheim and a half-day Cotswolds tour in the afternoon. The price includes admission to the palace.

Dorchester-on-Thames & the Wittenhams

A winding street flanked on either side by old coaching inns, quaint cottages and timber-framed buildings flows through sleepy **Dorchester-on-Thames**. Known locally as Dorchester, this town, about 8 miles south of Oxford, is best known for its magnificent medieval church. **SS Peter & Paul** (www.dorchester-abbey.org.uk; ⏲8am-6pm), or Dorchester Abbey, as it is more commonly known, is a beautiful space, built on the site of a Saxon cathedral and home to a wonderful Jesse window, a rare Norman font and, in the Cloister Gallery, a collection of medieval decorated stones. There's also a small FREE **museum** (⏲2-5pm Apr-Sep) in the Old School Room in the grounds.

From the village you can take a pleasant 3-mile walk to **Wittenham Clumps**, two ancient tree-topped hills offering wonderful views of the surrounding area. At the bottom of the hills lies the village of Little Wittenham, a rustic idyll. Known for its beautiful cottages and the imposing **St Peter's Church**, it has made its mark on the international sporting calendar by hosting the **Pooh Sticks World Championships** in March each year. Teams from all over the world compete by dropping sticks into the river and watching them 'race' to the finish line.

Dorchester-on-Thames is on the A4074, 7 miles south of Oxford. Buses 105 and 114a connect Dorchester with Oxford (45 minutes, hourly Monday to Saturday).

Henley-on-Thames

POP 10,646

A conservative but well-heeled kind of place, Henley is an attractive town set on the banks of the river, studded with elegant stone houses, a few Tudor relics and a host of chichi shops. The town bursts into action in July when it becomes the location for the Henley Royal Regatta, a world-famous boat race and weeklong posh picnic.

The **tourist office** (☎01491-578034; www.visithenley-on-thames.com; ⏲10am-5pm Mon-Sat) is in the town hall.

Sights

Walking around Henley, you'll come across a wealth of historic buildings, with many Georgian gems lining Hart St, the main drag. You'll also find the imposing **town hall** here, and the 13th-century **St Mary's Church**, with its 16th-century tower topped by four octagonal turrets.

River & Rowing Museum MUSEUM
(www.rrm.co.uk; Mill Meadows; adult/child £7.50/5.50; ⏲10am-5.30pm; 👪) Life in Henley has always focused on the river, and this impressive museum takes a look at the town's relationship with the Thames, the history of rowing, and the wildlife and commerce supported by the river. Hands-on activities and interactive displays make it a good spot for children, and the *Wind in the Willows* exhibition brings Kenneth Grahame's stories of Ratty, Mole, Badger and Toad to life.

Festivals & Events

Henley Royal Regatta ROWING FESTIVAL
(www.hrr.co.uk) The first ever Oxford and Cambridge boat race was held in Henley in 1839, and ever since the cream of English society has descended on this small town each year for a celebration of boating, back-slapping and the beau monde.

The five-day Henley Royal Regatta has grown into a major fixture in the social calendar of the upwardly mobile and is a massive corporate entertainment opportunity. These days, hanging out on the lawn swilling champagne and looking rich and beautiful is the main event, and although rowers of the highest calibre compete, most spectators appear to take little interest in what's happening on the water.

The regatta is held in the first week of July, but you'll need contacts in the rowing or corporate worlds to get tickets in the stewards' enclosure. Mere mortals should head for the public enclosure (tickets £12 to £15), where you can lay out your gourmet picnic and hobnob with the best of them.

Henley Festival ARTS FESTIVAL
(www.henley-festival.co.uk) In the week following the regatta, the town continues its celebrations with the Henley Festival, a vibrant black-tie affair that features everything from big-name international stars to quirky, alternative acts – anything from opera to rock, jazz, comedy and swing. The main events take place on a floating stage on the Thames, and tickets vary in price from £80 for a seat in the grandstand to £35 for a space in the enclosure.

Sleeping & Eating

Henley has a good choice of accommodation, especially at the top end, but if you're planning to visit during either festival, book well in advance.

TOP CHOICE **Hotel du Vin** HOTEL £££
(01491-848400; www.hotelduvin.com; New St; d from £145; P @ wi-fi) Set in the former Brakspears Brewery, this upmarket hotel chain scores high for its blend of industrial chic and top-of-the-line designer sophistication. The spacious rooms and opulent suites are slick and stylish and are matched by a walk-in humidor, incredible billiards rooms, huge wine cellar and a popular bistro (mains £13 to £21).

Old School House B&B ££
(01491-573929; www.oldschoolhousehenley.co.uk; 42 Hart St; d £85; P) This small, quiet guesthouse in the town centre is a 19th-century schoolhouse in a walled garden, with a choice of two pretty guest rooms decked out in simple but comfortable style. Exposed timber beams and rustic furniture give it plenty of character, and the central location can't be beat at this price.

Apple Ash B&B ££
(01491-574198; www.appleash.com; Woodlands Rd, Harpsden Woods; s/d £50/70; P) Lovingly maintained and beautifully decorated, it's well worth the 2-mile trip from town to stay at this charming Edwardian country house. The rooms are spacious and dripping in period character, but the styling is modern and comfortable, with pale fabrics and plenty of scatter cushions.

Milsoms HOTEL ££
(01491-845789; www.milsomshotel.co.uk; 20 Market Pl; r £95; wi-fi) Set in an 18th-century former bakery, Milsoms offers sleek and stylish rooms, with bespoke artwork, subtle lighting and a muted colour scheme. They can be pretty compact, though, so ask for light and airy room 1 for more space. Downstairs, **Loch Fyne** (01491-845780; mains £9 to £16) serves its impeccably prepared fish dishes in bright surroundings.

Black Boys Inn FRENCH ££
(01628 824212; www.blackboysinn.co.uk; Henley Rd, Hurley; mains £14.50-19.50) A little bit of France in the English countryside, this 16th-century coaching inn is in the nearby village of Hurley, and the fantastic food is worth the trip. Simple dishes cooked with passion are the speciality here, and the owners make weekly trips to France to collect ingredients from the markets. It's a local favourite and regular award-winner. The pub is about 4 miles east of Henley just off the A4130. It's on the left just before you come into the village of Hurley.

Green Olive GREEK £
(www.green-olive.co.uk; 28 Market Pl; mezedhes £4-10) A popular Henley haunt, Green Olive dishes up piled plates of traditional mezedhes (appetisers) in a bright and airy building with a lovely garden to the rear. Choose from over 50 dishes, including *spanakopita* (spinach pie), souvlaki, mussels with feta, *stifadho* (meat cooked with onions in a tomato puree) and *mousaka* (baked layers of

eggplant or zucchini, minced meat and potatoes topped with cheese sauce).

Chez Gerard Brasserie FRENCH ££
(www.brasseriegerard.co.uk; 40 Hart St; mains £11-17) This stalwart chain of French brasseries has a chilled atmosphere, wooden floors, modern art on the walls and a selection of mismatched furniture. The menu features French classics as well as Moroccan *tagine*, fish and grills.

Getting There & Around

There are no direct train or bus services between Henley and Oxford. Trains to **London Paddington** take about one hour (£12.80, hourly).

If you fancy seeing the local area from the river, **Hobbs & Son** (01491-572035; www.hobbs-of-henley.com) runs hour-long afternoon river trips from April to September (adult/child £7.75/5) and hires five-seater rowing boats (£20 per hour) and four-seater motorboats (£25 per hour).

Wantage

POP 9767

Sleepy but handsome Wantage is a medieval market town of sturdy timber-framed buildings, old coaching inns and crooked cottages. The market square is dominated by a statue of Alfred the Great, who was born here in AD 849, and traders still peddle their wares beneath his feet every Wednesday and Saturday. To the west of the square is the beautiful 13th-century **Church of St Peter & St Paul**, with its hammer-beam roof and beautiful corbels. Wantage also provides easy access to the ancient Ridgeway trail, less than 3 miles to the south.

There's a **visitor information point** (www.visitvale.com; 10am-4pm Mon-Sat) in the **Vale & Downland Museum** (www.wantage.com/museum; Church St; adult/student under 25yr £2.50/1; 10am-4pm Mon-Sat). Set in a converted 16th-century cloth merchant's house, the museum covers local geology and archaeology, as well as everything from King Alfred and Victorian kitchens to the local Williams Formula 1 team.

Close to the church you'll find the **Betjeman Millennium Park**, which commemorates the work of the much-loved former Poet Laureate, who lived in the town for some time. It's also worth taking a trip to the picturesque Victorian estate villages of **Ardington** and **Lockinge**, which are nearby.

WORTH A TRIP

OLDE BELL

With country pubs all getting a makeover and everyone jumping on the gastropub bandwagon, it can sometimes be hard to choose where to go. Just outside Henley, however, is a gastropub extraordinaire complete with designer interior and perfectly mismatched furniture, sheepskin throws and open fires. **Olde Bell** (01628-825881; www.theoldebell.co.uk; Hurley) is within easy striking distance of London and popular with well-heeled patrons keen to dine on the superb modern British food (mains £12 to £18) dished up in chic surroundings. It's not all new-world sophistication here, though: you'll still get the exposed beams, tasteful knick-knacks and even tea cosies knitted by the local WI (Women's Institute). You can also put your head down for the night in one of the artfully uncluttered rooms (from £129) with claw-foot baths, sheepskin rugs and Ercol rocking chairs.

Hurley is on the A4130, 4½ miles east of Henley.

Sleeping & Eating

Manor Farm B&B ££
(01235-763188; www.manorfarm-wantage.co.uk; Silver Lane, West Challow; s/d £35/70; P) By far the most atmospheric place to stay in the area, this early 15th-century Queen Anne manor house makes a wonderful base and is incredible value for money. The charming rooms have high ceilings, cast-iron fireplaces, antique furniture and buckets of period style. West Challow is about 3 miles west of Wantage on the B4507.

Courthill Centre HOSTEL £
(01235-760253; www.courthill.org.uk; Court Hill; dm per adult/child £17/13) Set in a series of converted barns just 500m from the Ridgeway, this hostel is an ideal base for walkers. It has basic but spacious dorms, an oak-beamed dining room and excellent views over the Vale. There's also a choice of family rooms and camping space (£8.50). The hostel is about 2 miles south of Wantage off the A338.

Boar's Head VILLAGE PUB ££
(01235-833254; www.boarsheadardington.co.uk; Church St, Ardington; mains £15-17; P)

Tucked behind a 13th-century church in a charming village, this place is well worth the trip for its stunning location and excellent food. Choose from simple dishes in the pub or the more ambitious modern European fare in the restaurant. There's a definite emphasis on fish but plenty of choice for meat-lovers too. If you'd like to stay, there are three simple, modern rooms (s/d from £80/95). Ardington is 3 miles east of Wantage on the A417.

King Alfred's Head PUB ££
(☎01235-765531; www.kingalfredshead.com; 31 Market Pl; mains £9-12; 📶) The best bet in town for food, this rustic pub serves a decent menu of upmarket pub grub. The interior is full of old church pews and scrubbed tables, while the courtyard garden is a good bet on sunny days.

Getting There & Away

Bus X30 runs between Oxford and Wantage from Monday to Saturday (35 minutes, hourly).

Around Wantage

One of England's oldest chalk carvings, the **Uffington White Horse** is a stylised image cut into a hillside almost 3000 years ago. No-one is sure why the people of the time went to so much trouble to create the image or what exactly it is supposed to represent, but the mystery only adds to the sense of awe. This huge figure measures 114m long and 49m wide but is best seen from a distance – or, if you're lucky enough, from the air – because of the stylised lines of perspective.

Just below the figure is **Dragon Hill** – so called because it is believed that St George slew the dragon at this location – and above it the grass-covered earthworks of **Uffington Castle**. From the Courthill Centre, near Wantage, a wonderful 5-mile walk leads along the Ridgeway to the White Horse.

In the nearby village of Uffington, you can visit the lovely 13th-century **St Mary's Church**, known locally as the 'Cathedral of the Vale', and the FREE **Uffington Museum** (www.museum.uffington.net; Broad St; ⌚2-5pm Sat & Sun Easter-Oct). The museum is set in the old schoolroom featured in Thomas Hughes' *Tom Brown's Schooldays* and has displays on the author, local history and archaeology.

THE COTSWOLDS

Glorious honey-coloured villages riddled with beautiful, old mansions, thatched cottages, atmospheric churches and rickety almshouses draw crowds of tourists to the Cotswolds. The booming medieval wool trade brought the area its wealth and left it with such a glut of beautiful buildings that its place in history is secured for evermore. If you've ever craved exposed beams, dreamed of falling asleep under English-rose wallpaper or lusted after a cream tea in mid-afternoon, there's no finer place to fulfil your fantasies.

This is prime tourist territory, however, and the most popular villages can be besieged by tourists and traffic in summer. Plan to visit the main centres early in the morning or late in the evening, focus your attention on the south or take to the hills on foot or by bike to avoid the worst of the crowds. Better still, just leave the crowds behind and meander down deserted country lanes and bridleways until you discover your very own bucolic village seemingly undisturbed since medieval times.

Activities

The gentle hills of the Cotswolds are perfect for walking, cycling and riding. The 102-mile **Cotswold Way** (www.nationaltrail.co.uk/cotswold) gives walkers a wonderful overview of the area. The route meanders from Chipping Campden to Bath, with no major climbs or difficult stretches, and is easily accessible from many points en route if you fancy tackling a shorter section. Ask at local tourist offices for details of day hikes, or pick up a copy of one of the many walking guides to the region.

Away from the main roads, the winding lanes of the Cotswolds make fantastic cycling territory, with little traffic, glorious views and gentle gradients. Again, the local tourist offices are invaluable in helping to plot a route.

For more information on companies operating self-guided and guided tours of the region, see the boxed text, p207.

Information

For information on attractions, accommodation and events:

Cotswolds (www.the-cotswolds.org)

Cotswolds Tourism (www.cotswolds.com)

Oxfordshire Cotswolds (www.oxfordshirecotswolds.org)

The Cotswolds

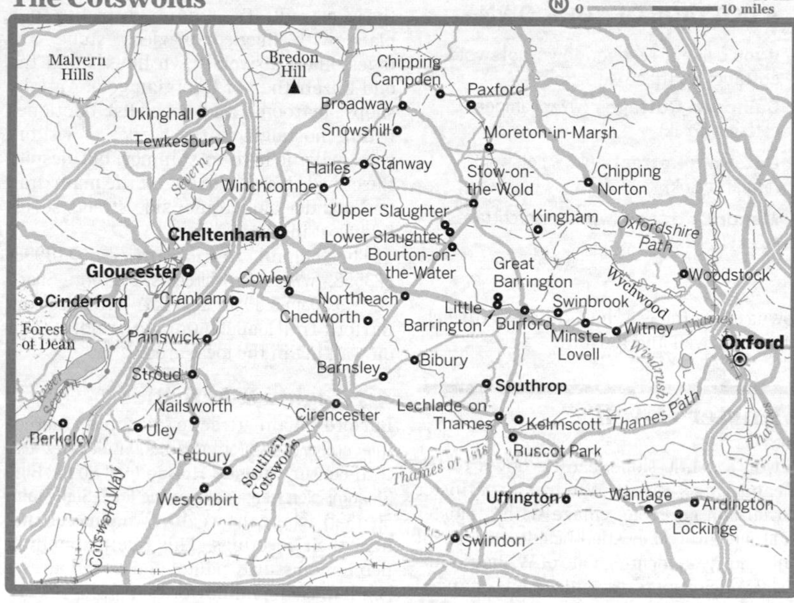

Getting Around

Public transport through the Cotswolds is fairly limited, with bus services running to and from major hubs only, and train services just skimming the northern and southern borders. However, with a little careful planning and patience, you can see all the highlights. Tourist offices stock useful *Explore the Cotswolds* brochures with bus and rail summaries.

For the most flexibility, and the option of getting off the beaten track, your own car is unbeatable; car hire can be arranged in most major centres.

Alternatively, **Cotswold Roaming** ((☎01865-308300; www.cotswold-roaming.co.uk) runs guided bus tours from Oxford between April and October. Half-day tours of the Cotswolds (£25) include Minster Lovell, Burford and Bibury, while full-day tours of the North Cotswolds (£40) feature Bourton-on-the-Water, Lower Slaughter, Chipping Campden and Stow-on-the-Wold.

Witney

POP 22,765

The sleepy town of Witney is firmly on Oxford's commuter belt, but make your way through the traffic and new housing developments to the centre of town and you'll find a charming village green flanked by pretty stone houses. At one end is a glorious wool church and 18th-century almshouses, at the other a 17th-century covered market. Witney built its wealth through blanket production, and the mills, wealthy merchants' homes and blanket factories can still be seen today. The baroque, 18th-century Blanket Hall dominates genteel High St, while at Wood Green you'll find a second village green and a cluster of stunning old stone cottages.

Pick up a copy of the *Witney Wool & Blanket Trail* from the **tourist office** (☎01993-775802; www.oxfordshirecotswolds.org; 3 Welch Way; ⊙9am-5pm Mon-Fri, 9.30am-5pm Sat) to guide you around the town.

Your best bet for a meal and a bed is the **Fleece** (☎01993-892270; www.fleecewitney.co.uk; 11 Church Green; s/d £80/90; P), a contemporary pub, restaurant and B&B on the main village green. The rooms are sleek and stylish, while the spacious brasserie (mains £9 to £17) has an ambitious modern menu.

Stagecoach bus S1 runs from Oxford to Witney roughly every 20 minutes Monday to Saturday, hourly on Sunday (30 minutes). **Swanbrook** (www.swanbrook.co.uk) runs three buses Monday to Saturday (one on Sunday) between Cheltenham (£7.50, one hour) and Oxford (30 minutes) via Witney. This service also goes to Gloucester (£7.50, 1½ hours) and serves a number of Cotswold

A COTTAGE OF YOUR OWN

If you'd like to rent your own Cotswold cottage, try these websites:

Campden Cottages (www.campdencottages.co.uk)

Cotswold Retreats (www.cotswoldretreats.co.uk)

Manor Cottages (www.manorcottages.co.uk)

towns along the way, including Northleach, Minster Lovell and Burford.

Minster Lovell

POP 1348

Set on a gentle slope leading down to the meandering River Windrush, Minster Lovell is a gorgeous village with a cluster of stone cottages nestled beside an ancient pub and riverside mill. One of William Morris' favourite spots, the village has changed little since medieval times and is a glorious place for an afternoon pit stop, quiet overnight retreat or start to a valley walk.

The main sight here is the ruins of **Minster Lovell Hall**, the 15th-century manor-house that was home to Viscount Francis Lovell. Lovell fought with Richard III at the Battle of Bosworth in 1485 and joined Lambert Simnel's failed rebellion after the king's defeat and death. Lovell's mysterious disappearance was never explained, and when a skeleton was discovered inside a secret vault in the house in 1708, it was assumed he had died while in hiding.

The **Mill & Old Swan** (☎0844-980 2313; www.deverevenues.co.uk; d from £69-170; P @) has charming period-style rooms in the 17th-century Old Swan or sleek, contemporary design in the 19th-century converted mill. The Old Swan serves decent pub food (£9 to £14).

Swanbrook coaches stop here on the Oxford to Cheltenham run. Stagecoach bus 233 between Witney and Burford stops here Monday to Saturday (10 minutes each way, 10 daily).

Burford

POP 1340

Slithering down a steep hill to a medieval crossing point on the River Windrush, the remarkable village of Burford is little changed since its glory days at the height of the wool trade. It's a stunningly picturesque place with higgledy-piggledy stone cottages, fine Cotswold town houses and the odd Elizabethan or Georgian gem. Antique shops, tearooms and specialist boutiques peddle nostalgia to the hordes of visitors who make it here in summer, but despite the crowds it's easy to get off the main drag and wander along quiet side streets seemingly lost in time.

The helpful **tourist office** (☎01993-823558; www.oxfordshirecotswolds.org; Sheep St; ⏲9.30am-5.30pm Mon-Sat) provides the Burford Trail leaflet (50p), with information on walking in the local area.

Sights & Activities

Burford's main attraction lies in its incredible collection of buildings, including the 16th-century **Tolsey House** (Toll House; High St; admission free; ⏲2-5pm Tue-Fri & Sun, 11am-5pm Sat), where the wealthy wool merchants held their meetings. This quaint building perches on sturdy pillars and now houses a small museum on Burford's history.

Just off the High St, you'll find the town's 14th-century **almshouses** and the gorgeous **Church of St John the Baptist**. The Norman tower here is topped by a 15th-century steeple, and inside you'll find a fine fan-vaulted ceiling and medieval screens dividing the chapels.

Younger visitors will enjoy a visit to the excellent **Cotswold Wildlife Park** (☎01993-823006; www.cotswoldwildlifepark.co.uk; adult/child £11.50/8; ⏲10am-4.30pm), set around a Victorian manor house. The park is home to everything from penguins to white rhinos and giant cats.

If you fancy getting away from the crowds, it's worth the effort to walk east along the picturesque river path to the untouched and rarely visited village of **Swinbrook** (3 miles), where the beautiful church has some remarkable tombs.

Sleeping & Eating

Burford has a wonderful choice of atmospheric, upmarket hotels but far fewer options at more affordable prices.

Lamb Inn HOTEL **£££**
(☎01993-823155; www.cotswold-inns-hotels.co.uk/lamb; Sheep St; r from £150; P @ 🛜) Step back in time with a stay at the Lamb, a 15th-century inn just dripping with character. Expect flagstone floors, beamed

DON'T MISS

A STEP BACK IN TIME

Squirreled away in the gorgeous village of Great Tew is a real gem of a 16th-century pub. Original flagstone floors, open fireplaces and low beams give the **Falkland Arms** (☎01608-683653; www.falklandarms.org.uk; Great Tew; r £85-115) oodles of medieval charm. The pub sits on the village green and serves a fine collection of real ales from ancient hand pumps, as well as ciders, perries and malt whiskies. There are boxes of snuff and clay pipes behind the bar, beams hung with a dusty collection of beer mugs and jugs, benches out front and a small garden at the rear. It's the kind of place where you feel instantly at home and immediately at ease, the kind of place you pray will stay the same – though regulars lament the fact that you no longer need to walk outside to get to the loo. You can also grab a decent meal (mains £9 to £17) or stay in one of the five guest rooms that come complete with four-poster or cast-iron beds and period style. On Sunday nights the pub is packed for its regular folk music sessions.

If you get the chance take a walk around the village, the stone cottages, thatched roofs and winding lanes remain virtually untouched and rival anything the rest of the Cotswolds has to offer. It simply doesn't get much more authentic than this.

Great Tew is about 4 miles east of Chipping Norton.

ceilings, creaking stairs and a charming, laid back atmosphere downstairs, and luxurious period-style rooms with antique furniture and cosy comfort upstairs. You'll get top-notch modern British food in the restaurant (three-course dinner, £35) or less formal dining (mains £9 to £16) in the bar.

Westview House B&B ££
(☎01993-824723; www.westview-house.co.uk; 151 The Hill; s/d from £60/80) This lovely old stone cottage has two bright and spacious guest rooms with plenty of period character. The Heritage Room has exposed beams, stone walls and a cast-iron bed, while the Windrush Room has its own private balcony overlooking the garden.

Cotland House B&B ££
(☎01993-822382; www.cotlandhouse.com; Fulbrook Hill; s/d from £50/80) About half a mile from town along the A361, this delightful B&B effortlessly mixes contemporary style with period charm. Although the rooms aren't spacious, they are gloriously comfortable, with cast-iron beds, crinkly white linen and soft throws.

Angel MODERN BRITISH ££
(☎01993-822714; www.theangelatburford.co.uk; 14 Witney St; mains £14.50-18) Set in a lovely 16th-century coaching inn, this atmospheric brasserie serves up an innovative menu of modern British and European food. Dine in by roaring fires in winter, or eat alfresco in the lovely walled garden in warmer weather.

ℹ Getting There & Away

From Oxford, Swanbrook runs three buses a day (one on Sunday) to Burford (45 minutes) and on to Cheltenham. Stagecoach bus 233 runs between Witney and Burford 10 times a day, Monday to Saturday (20 minutes).

Chipping Norton

POP 5972

The sleepy but attractive town of Chipping Norton – or 'Chippy' as it is locally known – is somewhat spoiled by the traffic running along the main street, but it has plenty of quiet side streets to wander and none of the Cotswold crowds. Handsome Georgian buildings, stone cottages and old coaching inns cluster around the market square, and on Church St you'll find a row of beautiful honey-coloured **almshouses** built in the 17th century. Further on is the secluded **Church of St Mary**, a classic example of the Cotswold wool churches, with a magnificent 15th-century Perpendicular nave and clerestory.

Chippy's most enduring landmark, however, is the arresting **Bliss Mill** (now converted to apartments) on the outskirts of town. This monument to the industrial architecture of the 19th century is more like a stately home than a factory, topped by a domed tower and chimney stack of the Tuscan order.

For lunch or dinner your best bet is **Wild Thyme** (☎01608-645060; www.wildthymerestaurant.co.uk; 10 New St; mains £9-19, s/d from £40/60; ⊙Tue-Sat), a simple but stylish restaurant with rooms. The menu is modern British

TOP FIVE PUBS FOR SUNDAY LUNCH

Trout (p192, Oxford) Top-notch food, old-world charm and a lovely riverside setting.

Falkland Arms (p203, Great Tew) Real ales, clay pipes and snuff behind the bar: it doesn't get more authentic than this.

Plough (Kingham) Quaint village pub with sublime food and chilled-out atmosphere.

Swan (p211, Southrop) Ambitious fare from ex-London foodies at a traditional village inn.

Olde Bell (p199, Hurley) Sophisticated country pub with designer interior and excellent nosh.

and the food is top-notch, and the three upstairs rooms are pretty and excellent value.

Alternatively, make your way 4 miles southwest of town to the pretty village of Kingham, where two fine gastropubs offer stylish rooms and sublime food. Set on the village green, **Plough** (☎01608-658327; www.thekinghamplough.co.uk; The Green, Kingham; mains £12-17, s/d from £70/85; ⊙closed Sun dinner) is a deceptively simple place serving some of the best pub food in the country. It has three stylish, clutter-free rooms.

Just around the corner is **Tollgate Inn** (☎01608-658389; www.thetollgate.com; Church St, Kingham; mains £14-16, s/d £65/95; ⊙closed Sun & Mon dinner), with contemporary but rustic rooms and sophisticated modern British fare.

Stagecoach bus S3 runs between Chippy and Oxford (55 minutes) roughly every half-hour.

Moreton-in-Marsh

POP 3198

Home to some beautiful buildings but utterly ruined by through traffic, Moreton-in-Marsh is a major road hub and useful for its transport links. On Tuesday, the town bursts into life for its weekly market.

Just east of Moreton, **Chastleton House** (NT; www.nationaltrust.org.uk; adult/child £7.85/3.65; ⊙1-5pm Wed-Sat) is one of England's finest and most complete Jacobean houses, full of rare tapestries, family portraits and antique furniture. Outside, there's a classic Elizabethan topiary garden and a lovely 12th-century church nearby.

Pulham's Coaches (www.pulhamscoaches.com) runs seven services between Moreton and Cheltenham (one hour, Monday to Saturday) via Stow-on-the-Wold (15 minutes) and Bourton-on-the-Water (20 minutes). Two Sunday services run from May to September only.

There are **trains** roughly every two hours to Moreton from London Paddington (£26.90, one hour 40 minutes) via Oxford (£7.90, 40 minutes) and on to Worcester (£9.90, one hour) and Hereford (£15.20, one hour 45 minutes).

Chipping Campden

POP 2206

An unspoiled gem in an area full of achingly pretty villages, Chipping Campden is a glorious reminder of life in the Cotswolds in medieval times. The graceful curving main street is flanked by a wonderful array of wayward stone cottages, fine terraced houses, ancient inns and historic homes, liberally sprinkled with chichi boutiques and upmarket shops. Despite its obvious allure, the town remains relatively unspoiled by tourist crowds and is a wonderful place to visit.

Pop into the helpful **tourist office** (☎01386-841206; www.chippingcampdenonline.org; High St; ⊙9.30am-5pm) to pick up a town trail guide (£1) for information on the most historic buildings and to get you off the main drag and down some of the gorgeous back streets. If you're visiting on a Tuesday between July and September, it's well worth joining a **guided tour** at 2.30pm (suggested donation £3) run by the Cotswold Wardens.

Sights & Activities

The most obvious sight is the wonderful 17th-century **Market Hall**, with multiple gables and an elaborate timber roof. Further on, at the western end of the High St, is the 15th-century **St James'**, one of the Cotswolds' great wool churches. Built in the Perpendicular style, it has a magnificent tower and some graceful 17th-century monuments. Nearby on Church St is a remarkable row of **almshouses** dating from the 17th century, and the Jacobean lodges and gateways of the now-ruined Campden House.

The surviving **Court Barn** (☎01386-841951; www.courtbarn.org.uk; Church St; adult/child £3.75/free; ⏰10.30am-5.30pm Tue-Sat, 11.30am-5.30pm Sun) is now a craft and design museum featuring work from the Arts and Crafts Movement. CR Ashbee and the Guild of Handicrafts moved to Chipping Campden in 1902, and a collection of their work is showcased here.

About 4 miles northeast of Chipping Campden, **Hidcote Manor Garden** (NT; www.nationaltrust.org.uk; Hidcote Bartrim; adult/child £8.60/4.30; ⏰10am-6pm) is one of the finest examples of Arts and Crafts landscaping in Britain.

Sleeping & Eating

Cotswold House Hotel HOTEL £££
(☎01386-840330; www.cotswoldhouse.com; The Square; r £140-650; P @) If you're after a spot of luxury, look no further than this chic Regency town house turned boutique hotel. Bespoke furniture, massive beds, Frette linens, cashmere throws, private gardens and hot tubs are the norm here. You can indulge in some treatments at the hotel spa, dine in luxuriant style at Juliana's (three-course set dinner, £49.50) or take a more informal approach at Hick's Brasserie (mains £10 to £19), a slick operation with an ambitious menu.

Chance B&B ££
(☎01386-849079; www.the-chance.co.uk; 1 Aston Rd; d £75; P) Two pretty rooms with floral bedspreads, fresh flowers and a cast-iron fireplace make this B&B a good choice. The owners are particularly helpful, and little extras such as bathrobes and hot-water bottles are waiting in the rooms.

Eight Bells PUB ££
(☎01386-840371;www.eightbellsinn.co.uk;Church St; mains £13-17) Dripping with old-world character and charm, but also decidedly modern, this 14th-century inn serves real ales and a fine selection of modern British and Continental dishes in rustic settings.

If you're willing to stray a little out of town, there are plenty of fine options well worth going the extra mile for:

Churchill Arms COUNTRY PUB ££
(☎01386-594000; Paxford; s/d £65/85) Set in a pretty village, this popular gastropub has cosy rooms and a decent menu (mains £9 to £18).

Ebrington Arms COUNTRY PUB ££
(☎01386-593223; www.theebringtonarms.co.uk; Ebrington; mains £9-14) A local favourite, this 17th-century inn is all log fires and exposed beams and has three modern guest rooms (doubles from £90).

Getting There & Around

Between them, buses 21 and 22 run almost hourly to Stratford-upon-Avon or Moreton-in-Marsh. Bus 21 also stops in Broadway. There are no Sunday services.

To catch a real glimpse of the countryside, try hiring a bike from **Cotswold Country Cycles** (☎01386-438706; www.cotswoldcountrycycles.com; Longlands Farm Cottage; per day £15) and discover the quiet lanes and gorgeous villages around town.

Broadway

POP 2496

This absurdly pretty village has inspired writers, artists and composers in times past with its graceful, golden-hued cottages set at the foot of a steep escarpment. It's a quintessentially English place pitted with antique shops, tearooms and art galleries and is justifiably popular in the summer months. But take the time to wander away from the main street and you'll be rewarded with quiet back roads lined with stunning cottages, flower-filled gardens and picturesque churches.

Next door to the tourist office is the **Gordon Russell Museum** (www.gordonrussellmuseum.org; adult/child £3.50/1; ⏰11am-5pm Tue-Sun), celebrating the work of the renowned furniture designer. Set in his

THE COTSWOLDS OLIMPICKS

The medieval sport of shin-kicking lives on in Chipping Campden, where each year the townspeople gather to compete at the **Cotswolds Olimpicks** (www.olimpickgames.co.uk), a traditional country sports day first celebrated in 1612. It is one of the most entertaining and bizarre sporting competitions in England, and many of the original events, such as welly wanging (throwing), the sack race and climbing a slippery pole, are still held. The competition was mentioned in Shakespeare's *Merry Wives of Windsor* and has even been officially sanctioned by the British Olympic Association. It is held annually at the beginning of June.

restored workshop, it features samples of his furniture, metalwork and glassware. Beyond the charm of the village itself, there are few other specific attractions.

If you're feeling energetic, the lovely, 12th-century **Church of St Eadburgha** is a signposted 1-mile walk from town. Near here, a more challenging path leads uphill for 2 miles to **Broadway Tower** (www.broadwaytower.co.uk; adult/child £4/2.50; 10.30am-5pm), a crenulated, 18th-century Gothic folly on the crest of the escarpment. It has a small William Morris exhibition on one floor and stunning views from the top.

Broadway is littered with chintzy B&Bs, but for something more modern, try **Windrush** (01386-853577; www.broadway-windrush.co.uk; Station Rd; d from £90; P), a stunning little B&B with newly refurbished rooms done in great style. Neutral colour schemes, bold patterned wallpapers and plush fabrics give it a real edge over the competition. Alternatively, try sleek and stylish **Russells** (01386-853555; www.russellsofbroadway.co.uk; 20 High St; d £95-225), where you'll find a range of slick, modern rooms with simple design and lots of little luxuries. This is also the town's best bet for food, and the award-winning modern British fare (mains £12 to £18) here is well worth a detour if you're in the area. Almost next door is the less formal **Swan** (www.theswanbroadway.co.uk; 2 The Green; mains £9-16), another swish joint with contemporary decor, wooden floors, leather seats and a tempting, modern menu.

Information

Tourist office (01386-852937; www.beautifulbroadway.com; Russell Sq; 10am-5pm Mon-Sat, 2-5pm Sun) Just off the High St.

Getting There & Away

Bus 21 goes to Moreton-in-Marsh, Chipping Campden and Stratford (50 minutes, four daily Monday to Saturday). Bus 606 goes to Cheltenham (50 minutes, four daily Monday to Saturday).

Around Broadway

About 3 miles south of Broadway is **Snowshill Manor** (NT; www.nationaltrust.org.uk; Snowshill; adult/child £8.10/4.10, garden only £4.40/2.20; noon-5pm Wed-Sun mid-Mar–Oct), a wonderful Cotswold mansion once home to the marvellously eccentric Charles Paget Wade. The house contains Wade's extraordinary collection of crafts and design, including everything from musical instruments to Victorian perambulators and Japanese armour. Outside, the lovely gardens were designed as an extension of the house, with pools, terraces and wonderful views.

Also worth visiting, nearby, is the stunning Jacobean mansion **Stanway House** (www.stanwayfountain.co.uk; Stanway; adult/child £7/2, garden only £4.50/1.50; 2-5pm Tue & Thu Jun-Aug, garden only Sat Jun-Aug). Inhabited by the same family for over 450 years, it has a delighful, lived-in charm with much of its original furniture and character intact. The house is surrounded by wonderful, baroque water gardens, home to the world's highest gravity fountain.

Winchcombe

POP 4379

Winchcombe is a sleepy Cotswold town, very much a working, living place, with butchers, bakers and small independent shops giving it a lived-in, authentic feel. It was capital of the Saxon kingdom of Mercia and one of the most important towns in the Cotswolds until the Middle Ages, and today the remnants of its illustrious past can still be seen. Winchcombe is also blessed with good accommodation and fine-dining choices, making it a great base for exploring the area.

The helpful **tourist office** (01242-602925; www.visitcotswoldsandsevernvale.gov.uk; High St; 10am-5pm Mon-Sat, 10am-4pm Sun) can help plan an itinerary.

Sights & Activities

Just wander around the town to take in its charms, but don't miss the picturesque cottages on **Vineyard St** and **Dents Tce** and look out for the fine gargoyles that adorn the lovely **St Peter's Church**.

Sudeley Castle CASTLE

(www.sudeleycastle.co.uk; adult/child £7.20/4.20; 10.30am-5pm) The town's main attraction, this magnificent castle was once a favoured retreat of Tudor and Stuart monarchs. The house is still used as a family home, and much of the interior is off limits to visitors, but you can get a glimpse of its grand proportions while visiting the exhibitions of costumes, memorabilia and paintings and the surrounding gardens. If you want an insight into real life in the castle, join one of the 'Connoisseur Tours' (£12, Tuesday, Wednesday and Thursday at 11am, 1pm and 3pm).

THROW AWAY YOUR GUIDEBOOK!

As wonderful as the Cotswolds villages may be, in the summer months they can be a nightmare of camera-wielding crowds, slow-moving pensioners and chaotic coach parking. However, most tourists stick to a well-trodden path, so it's easy to get away from the crowds and discover the rarely visited villages lurking in the hills. Stick to the B-roads and visit places like **Guiting Power** near Bourton, **Broadwell**, **Maugersbury**, **Adlestrop** and the **Swells** near Stow, **Sheepscombe** and **Slad** near Painswick, **Blockley** near Chipping Campden, **Great Tew** near Chipping Norton, **Taynton**, **Sherborne** and the **Barringtons** near Burford, **Ampney St Mary** and **Ampney Crucis** near Cirencester, or **Coln St Aldwyns** and **Hatherop** near Bibury. Better still, see the region on foot or by bike and just meander at your own pace. Alternatively, join a walking tour with **Cotswold Walking Holidays** (www.cotswoldwalks.com) or a bike tour with **Cotswold Country Cycles** (www.cotswoldcountrycycles.com).

Belas Knap BURIAL CHAMBER

If you're feeling energetic, there's easy access to the Cotswold Way from Winchcombe, and the 2½-mile hike to Belas Knap is one of the most scenic short walks in the region. Five-thousand-year-old Belas Knap is the best preserved Neolithic burial chamber in the country. Visitors are not allowed inside, but the views down to Sudeley Castle and across the surrounding countryside are breathtaking.

Hailes Abbey RUINS

(EH; www.english-heritage.org.uk; adult/child £4/2; ⏲10am-5pm) Just outside the town are the evocative ruins of this Cistercian abbey, once one of the country's main pilgrimage centres.

Sleeping & Eating

White Hart Inn HOTEL ££

(☎01242-602359; www.wineandsausage.co.uk; r £40-115) An excellent option in the centre of town. Choose the cheaper 'rambler' rooms, with shared bathrooms, or go for more luxury in a superior room. You'll also get pub staples in the bar (mains £7 to £9) and modern British fare in the 'wine and sausage' restaurant (mains £9 to £17).

Parks Farm B&B ££

(☎01242-603874; www.parksfarm.co.uk; Sudeley; s/d £45/60; P) Stay on a 17th-century Cotswold hill farm just outside the town for an insight into local life. This friendly B&B has two cosy rooms with views over the rolling hills, and guests are served breakfast in a beamed kitchen with one large table and a roaring Aga (a traditional English stove).

5 North St MODERN EUROPEAN £££

(☎01242-604566; 5 North St; 2-/3-course lunch £21.50/25.50, 3-course dinner £31-46; ⏲lunch Wed-Sun, dinner Tue-Sat) The top spot to eat for miles around, this Michelin-starred restaurant has no airs and graces, just beautifully prepared food in down-to-earth surroundings. Deep-red walls, wooden tables and friendly service make it a very unpretentious place, but the food is thoroughly ambitious with a keen mix of British ingredients and French flair.

Getting There & Away

Bus 606 runs from Broadway (65 minutes, four daily Monday to Saturday) to Cheltenham via Winchcombe.

Stow-on-the-Wold

POP 2794

A popular stop on a tour of the Cotswolds, Stow is anchored by a large market square surrounded by handsome buildings and steep-walled alleyways, originally used to funnel the sheep into the fair. The town has long held a strategic place in Cotswold history, standing as it does on the Roman Fosse Way and at the junction of six roads. Today, it's littered with antique shops, boutiques, tearooms and delis, and thronging with people from passing coach tours. On a quiet day, it's a wonderful place, but all a little artificial if you're looking for true Cotswold charm.

Go Stow (www.go-stow.co.uk; 12 Talbot Ct; ⏲10am-5pm Mon-Sat, 11am-4pm Sun) has information on local attractions, makes accommodation bookings, and rents audio tours to the town.

Sleeping & Eating

Mole End B&B ££

(☎01451-870348; www.moleendstow.co.uk; Moreton Rd; s/d from £55/80; P@) This charming

THE GOOD LIFE

The Cotswolds' mellow charms attract moneyed city folk, A-list celebrities and wealthy downsizers in equal measure, but mere mortals can get a slice of the good life at one of the numerous luxury hotels in the area. Here are just a few to whet your fancy.

Barnsley House HOTEL £££
(01285-740000; www.barnsleyhouse.com; Barnsley; d £275-495; P @) For funky chic and indulgent sophistication, this hideout for the rich and famous is just the spot for a romantic weekend.

Cowley Manor HOTEL £££
(01242-870900; www.cowleymanor.com; Cowley; d £150-475; P @) Handmade furniture and fabrics by young British designers adorn the simple but elegant rooms at this super-sleek hotel.

Lords of the Manor HOTEL £££
(01451-820243; www.lordsofthemanor.com; Upper Slaughter; d £195-370; P @) A former rectory just dripping with character, this place has a genteel air with lavishly elegant rooms.

Lygon Arms HOTEL £££
(0800 652 8413; www.barcelo-hotels.co.uk; High St, Broadway; d £123-363; P @) Choose medieval splendour or modern chic at this 16th-century inn in the heart of Broadway.

Cotswolds 88 HOTEL £££
(01452-813688; www.cotswolds88hotel.com; Painswick; d £165-515; P @) Quirky, ostentatious and opulently designed, this uberhotel aims to be rock-and-roll cool and has the tragically hip attitude to go with it.

and immaculately kept B&B on the outskirts of town is a real gem. There are three stunning rooms with acres of space, huge beds and a whiff of refined French styling. There's a large garden with bucolic views, as well as great breakfasts and amiable hosts.

Number 9 B&B ££
(01451-870333; www.number-nine.info; 9 Park St; s/d from £45/65;) Centrally located and wonderfully atmospheric, this beautiful B&B is all sloping floors and exposed beams. The three rooms are cosy but spacious and have brand-new bathrooms and subtle decor.

Stow-on-the-Wold YHA HOSTEL £
(0845 371 9540; www.yha.org.uk; The Square; dm £1; P @) Slap bang on the market square, this hostel is in a wonderful 16th-century town house and has small dorms, a children's play area and a warm welcome for families.

Old Butchers MODERN EUROPEAN ££
(01451-831700; www.theoldbutchers.com; 7 Park St; mains £13-18) Simple, smart and sophisticated, this is Stow's top spot for dining, serving robust, local ingredients whipped up into sublime dishes. For all its fanfare, there's little pretension here, just fine modern British cuisine with more than a hint of Continental European influence thrown in.

Queen's Head PUB £
(Market Sq; mains £7-10) A popular local haunt, this 17th-century inn has hops hanging from the rafters, a great atmosphere and a solid menu of traditional pub grub.

Getting There & Away

Bus 855 links Stow with Moreton, Bourton, Northleach and Cirencester (eight daily Monday to Saturday). Bus 801 runs to Cheltenham, Moreton and Bourton (four daily Monday to Friday, nine on Saturday).

The nearest train stations are 4 miles away at Kingham and Moreton-in-Marsh.

Bourton-on-the-Water

POP 3093

An undeniably picturesque town, Bourton has sold its soul to tourism, becoming a Cotswolds theme park, its handsome houses and pretty bridges overshadowed by a series of crass, commercial attractions. Take your pick from the model railway and village, bird-conservation project, perfume factory, maze or motor museum – or visit in the winter when the village's understated charm is free to reveal itself.

If you'd like to stay chic and stylish, **Dial House** (☎01451-822244; www.dialhousehotel.com; The Chestnuts; r £130-240) is unpretentious but seriously luxurious, with hand-painted wallpaper, giant beds, silky throws and a wonderful mix of period charm and designer style. The restaurant (mains £18 to £22) serves up excellent modern British cuisine.

Bus 801 runs to Cheltenham, Moreton and Stow (up to four daily Monday to Friday, nine Saturday).

The Slaughters

POP 400

An antidote to the commercialism of Bourton, the nearby picture-postcard villages of Upper and Lower Slaughter manage to maintain their unhurried medieval charm. The village names are derived from the Old English 'sloughtre', meaning slough or muddy place, but today the River Eye is contained within limestone banks and meanders peacefully through the village past the 17th-century Lower Slaughter Manor (now a top-notch hotel) to the **Old Mill** (www.oldmill-lowerslaughter.com; admission £2; ⏲10am-6pm), which houses a small museum and tea shop.

To see the Slaughters at their best, arrive on foot from Bourton (a 1-mile walk) across the fields. From here you can continue for another mile across the fields to Upper Slaughter, with its own fine manor house and glorious cottages.

Northleach

POP 1855

Little visited and underappreciated, Northleach is a lovely little market town of late-medieval cottages, imposing merchants' stores and half-timbered Tudor houses. A wonderful mix of architectural styles cluster around the market square and the narrow laneways leading off it, but the highlight is the **Church of St Peter and St Paul**, a masterpiece of Cotswold Perpendicular style. The large traceried stained-glass windows and collection of memorial brasses are unrivalled in the region.

Near the square is Oak House, a 17th-century wool house that contains **Keith Harding's World of Mechanical Music** (www.mechanicalmusic.co.uk; adult/child £8/3.50; ⏲10am-5pm), a fascinating museum of self-playing musical instruments where you can hear Rachmaninoff's works played on a reproducing piano.

Just outside town is **Chedworth Roman Villa** (NT; www.nationaltrust.org.uk; Yanworth; adult/child £6.30/3.60; ⏲10am-5pm Tue-Sun), one of the largest Roman villas in England. Built as a stately home in about AD 120, it contains some wonderful mosaics illustrating the seasons, bathhouses and, a short walk away, a temple by the River Coln. It's 3 miles northwest of Fossebridge off the A429.

For overnight stays, try the **Wheatsheaf** (☎01451-860244; www.cotswoldswheatsheaf.com; West End; d £80-100; @📶). It has eight en suite rooms that have recently been refurbished. The restaurant serves a decent menu of modern British dishes (£6 to £15).

ℹ Getting There & Away

Swanbrook runs six buses a day Monday to Saturday between Cheltenham (30 minutes) and Northleach, and three to Oxford (one hour). Bus 855 runs to Stow, Moreton, Bourton and Cirencester (eight daily Monday to Saturday)

Cirencester

POP 18,324

Refreshingly unpretentious, with narrow, winding streets and graceful town houses, charming Cirencester is an affluent, elegant kind of place. The lovely market square is surrounded by wonderful 18th-century and Victorian architecture, and the nearby streets showcase a harmonious medley of buildings from various eras.

Under the Romans, Cirencester was second only to London in terms of size and importance and, although little of this period remains, you can still see the grassed-over ruins of one of the largest amphitheatres in the country. The medieval wool trade was also good to the town, with wealthy merchants funding the building of a superb church.

Today, Cirencester is the most important town in the southern Cotswolds and retains an authentic, unaffected air, with the lively Monday and Friday markets as important as the expensive boutiques and trendy delis that line its narrow streets.

The **tourist office** (☎01285-654180; www.cotswold.gov.uk; Park St; ⏲10am-5pm Mon-Sat, 2-5pm Sun) is in the museum and has a leaflet detailing a guided walk around the town and its historic buildings.

SOMETHING FOR THE WEEKEND

Kick-start your weekend by checking into the seductively stylish **Cotswold House Hotel** in Chipping Campden, and take a sunset stroll around the village before dining at **Juliana's** or **Hick's Brasserie**. First thing the following morning, blow away the cobwebs with a short stroll and magnificent views at **Broadway Tower** and then head south to **Winchcombe** where you can loll about the lovely village or take in some history at the Tudor pile **Sudeley Castle**.

Stop for lunch at the seriously unpretentious but exceptionally good **5 North St**, before taking the cross-country route to stunning **Lower Slaughter**. If you're feeling sprightly, follow the trail over the rolling hills to Upper Slaughter, or just sit and feed the ducks before swinging back to Bourton to check into the sumptuous **Dial House** for an evening of luxury and fine food.

On Sunday, head east to **Woodstock** to ramble the grounds or the stately rooms of **Blenheim Palace**, and work up an appetite for a hearty traditional lunch at the glorious thatched **Falkland Arms** in Great Tew.

Sights & Activities

Church of St John the Baptist CHURCH
(suggested donation £3; 10am-5pm) Standing elegantly on the Market Sq, the cathedral-like St John's is one of England's largest parish churches. An outstanding Perpendicular-style tower with wild flying buttresses dominates the exterior, but it is the majestic three-storey south porch that is the real highlight. Built as an office by late 15th-century abbots, it subsequently became the medieval town hall.

Soaring arches, magnificent fan vaulting and a Tudor nave adorn the light-filled interior, where you'll also find a 15th-century painted stone pulpit and memorial brasses recording the matrimonial histories of important wool merchants. The east window contains fine medieval stained glass, and a wall safe displays the **Boleyn Cup**, made for Anne Boleyn, second wife of Henry VIII, in 1535.

Corinium Museum MUSEUM
(www.cotswold.gov.uk/go/museum; Park St; adult/child £4.50/2.25; 10am-5pm Mon-Sat, 2-5pm Sun) Modern design, innovative displays and computer reconstructions bring one of Britain's largest collections of Roman artefacts to life at the Corinium Museum. You can dress as a Roman soldier, meet an Anglo-Saxon princess and discover what Cirencester was like during its heyday as a wealthy medieval wool town. Highlights of the Roman collection include the beautiful Hunting Dogs and Four Seasons floor mosaics, and a reconstructed Roman kitchen and butcher's shop.

FREE **Brewery Arts Centre** ARTS CENTRE
(www.breweryarts.org.uk; Brewery Ct; 9am-5pm Mon-Sat, 10am-4pm Sun) Home to 12 resident craft workers and host to regular exhibitions, workshops and classes, this arts centre is set in a beautifully converted Victorian brewery.

Cirencester Park PARK
(Cecily Hill; 8am-5pm) The baroque-landscaped grounds of the Bathurst Estate, with a lovely walk along Broad Ride.

Roman Amphitheatre AMPHITHEATRE
(Cotswold Ave) The grassed-over remains of one of Britain's largest amphitheatres are worth a visit for their sheer scale.

Sleeping & Eating

No 12 B&B ££
(01285-640232; www.no12cirencester.co.uk; 12 Park St; d £95) This Georgian town house right in the centre of Cirencester has gloriously unfussy rooms kitted out with a tasteful mix of antiques and modern furnishings. Think feather pillows, merino blankets, extra-long beds, slick modern bathrooms and a host of little extras to make you smile.

Old Brewhouse B&B ££
(01285-656099; www.theoldbrewhouse.com; 7 London Rd; s/d from £56/68; P) Set in a charming 17th-century town house, this lovely B&B has bright, pretty rooms with cast-iron beds and subtle, country-style florals or patchwork quilts. The courtyard rooms are newer and larger, and the beautiful garden room even has its own patio.

Jesse's Bistro MODERN BRITISH ££
(01285-641497; www.jessesbistro.co.uk; Blackjack St; mains £12-20; lunch Tue-Sun & dinner Wed-Sat) Hidden away in a cobbled stable

yard with its own fishmonger and cheese shop, Jesse's is a great little place, with flagstone floors, wrought-iron chairs and mosaic tables. The modern menu features a selection of great dishes, but the real treat is the fresh fish and meat cooked in the wood-burning oven.

Somewhere Else FUSION ££
(☎01285-643199; www.somewhereelse.co.uk; 65 Castle St; dishes £3-9; closed Sun dinner) This 'deli bar' gives an interesting twist to the tapas concept with an extensive choice of small portions of fusion food tempting happy punters in off the street. There truly is something for everyone here, with British, Japanese, Mexican, North African and Mediterranean dishes on offer.

Getting There & Away

National Express buses run roughly hourly from Cirencester to London (£12, 2½ hours) and to Cheltenham Spa (30 minutes) and Gloucester (one hour). Stagecoach bus 51 also runs to Cheltenham Monday to Saturday (40 minutes, hourly). Bus 852 goes to Gloucester (four daily Monday to Saturday).

Bibury

POP 1235

Once described by William Morris as 'the most beautiful village in England', Bibury is another Cotswold gem with a cluster of gorgeous riverside cottages and tangle of narrow streets flanked by wayward stone buildings. It's an impossibly quaint place whose main attraction is **Arlington Row**, a stunning sweep of cottages now thought to be the most photographed street in Britain. The street was originally home to one long, 14th-century sheep house, but in the 17th century this was divided up and converted into weavers' cottages. Also worth a look is the 17th-century **Arlington Mill**, just a short stroll away across Rack Isle, a wildlife refuge once used as a cloth-drying area.

Few visitors make it past these two sights, but for a glimpse of the real Bibury, venture into the village proper behind Arlington Row, where you'll find a cluster of stunning cottages and the Saxon **Church of St Mary**. Although much altered since its original construction, many 8th-century features are still visible among the 12th- and 13th-century additions.

Despite its popularity, Bibury is seriously lacking in decent accommodation. The best place to stay is in the nearby village of Coln, where the jasmine-clad **New Inn** (☎0844-815 3434; www.new-inn.co.uk; Coln-St-Aldwyns; s/d from £120/130) offers quirky luxury in 16th-century surroundings. Look out for online deals offering rooms from £70. It's also the best bet in the area for food, with its modern British menu (mains £11 to £18.50) served in the main restaurant, bar and gorgeous garden.

Buses 860, 865, and 866 pass through Bibury en route to Cirencester (15 minutes) at least once daily from Monday to Saturday (15 minutes).

Lechlade-on-Thames

POP 4132

A quiet backwater dominated by the graceful spire of St Lawrence's Church, the attractive market town of Lechlade is temptingly close to two wonderful period houses.

Just 3 miles east, signposted off the A417, is the gorgeous Tudor pile **Kelmscott Manor** (☎01367 252486, www.kelmscottmanor.org.uk; adult/child £8.50/4.25, garden only £2; ⏲11am-5pm Wed Apr-Sep & selected Sat in summer), once the summer home of William Morris, the poet, artist and founder of the Arts and Crafts Movement. The house contains many of Morris' personal effects, as well as fabrics and furniture designed by him and his associates.

Another worthwhile trip from Lechlade is **Buscot Park** (NT; ☎01367 240932; www.buscot-park.com; adult/child £8/4, grounds only £5/2.50; ⏲2-6pm Wed-Fri & selected weekends), an ornate, Italianate country house set in gardens designed by Harold Peto. The house is now home to the Faringdon art collection, which includes paintings by Rembrandt, Reynolds, Rubens, van Dyck and Murillo. The house is 2¾ miles southeast of Lechlade on the A417.

If you're visiting either attraction, it's well worth making a detour to the pretty village of Southrop, 4 miles northwest of Lechlade, to dine at the atmospheric pub **Swan** (☎01367-850205; www.theswanatsouthrop.co.uk; mains £11-18; ⏲closed Sun dinner). This 17th-century inn has the stone floors and exposed beams you'd expect, but is refreshingly bright and uncluttered and serves extremely sophisticated food at reasonable prices.

Bus 877 runs from Lechlade to Cirencester (50 minutes, five times daily from Monday to Friday).

Tetbury

POP 5250

Once a prosperous wool-trading centre, Tetbury has managed to preserve most of its architectural heritage – its busy streets are lined with medieval cottages, sturdy old town houses and Georgian Gothic gems. It's an unspoilt place with a rather regal character: even HRH Prince Charles has a shop here – Highgrove – though it's unlikely you'll find him serving behind the counter.

Along with goodies from the Highgrove Estate, Tetbury is a great place for antique fans, with a shop of old curios on almost every corner. You'll also find plenty of chi-chi boutiques and interior-design shops, but they're tempered by the bakers, butchers and delis that ground the town and give it a sense of real identity.

The friendly **tourist office** (☎01666-503552; www.visittetbury.co.uk; 33 Church St; ⊙10am-4pm Mon-Sat) has plenty of information on the town and its history.

Sights & Activities

Just wander around the town to soak up the atmosphere, but look out for the row of gorgeous medieval weavers' cottages that line the steep hill at **Chipping Steps**, leading up to the **Chipping** (market), which is surrounded by graceful 17th- and 18th-century town houses. From here, it's a short stroll to Market Sq, where the 17th-century **Market House** stands as if on stilts. Close by, the Georgian Gothic **Church of St Mary the Virgin** has a towering spire and wonderful interior.

Just south of Tetbury is the **National Arboretum** (www.forestry.gov.uk/westonbirt; adult £6-9, child £2-4; ⊙9am-dusk) at Westonbirt. The park boasts a magnificent selection of temperate trees, with some wonderful walks and great colour throughout the year, especially in autumn.

Sleeping & Eating

Oak House No 1 B&B £££
(☎01666-505741; www.oakhouseno1.com; The Chipping; d £135-255; 📶) Indulge in the over-the-top interior design at this luxury pad in the centre of town. Set in a Georgian town house, it's all eclectic art, antique furniture and trinkets from far-off places. The rooms are suitably luxurious, with a mix of contemporary and old-school styling, all the usual high-tech gadgets and a plate of homemade cakes and scones ready for you on arrival. It's a heady mix which you may love or loathe.

Ormond HOTEL ££
(☎01666-505690; www.theormond.co.uk; 23 Long St; s/d from £59/79; P📶👪) This modern hotel has a range of individually styled rooms with subtle but striking fabrics and funky wallpapers. It's an unassuming place that offers excellent value for money. Expect duck-down duvets, flatscreen TVs, a DVD library and warm welcome for families. The modern bar and grill downstairs serve surprisingly good food (mains £10 to £14).

Lyncombe House B&B ££
(☎01666-503807; www.lyncombehouse.co.uk; 5 Silver St; s/d £50/80; P📶) Set in an 18th-century woollen store in the centre of town, the two rooms at this period town house are simply but elegantly decorated. You can also expect personal service and space to yourself as the owners only let the second room if guests are travelling together.

Chef's Table MODERN BRITISH ££
(☎01666-504466; www.thechefstable.co.uk; 49 Long St; mains £9-13; ⊙closed dinner Sun-Tue) This fantastic deli and bistro is the place to go to stock up for a picnic in the Arboretum or to sit down for a mouth-watering lunch of local organic ingredients rustled up into stunning rustic dishes. If you're feeling inspired, you can learn how to cook the dishes under the guidance of Michelin-starred chef Michael Bedford: his cookery school runs on selected days during the summer months (day course £130).

Blue Zucchini MODERN BRITISH ££
(7-9 Church St; dinner mains £8-18; ⊙closed dinner Sun & Mon) This popular cafe and bistro is a cheery place that's usually buzzing. It's great for a coffee and a look at the papers and serves a good selection of contemporary classics for lunch and dinner.

Getting There & Away

Bus 29 runs between Tetbury and Stroud (30 minutes, six daily Monday to Saturday). Bus 620 goes to Bath (1¼ hours, six daily Monday to Friday, four on Saturday), stopping at Westonbirt Arboretum en route.

Uley

POP 1100

This lovely little hamlet, with its quaint village green and jumble of pretty houses, sits below the overgrown remains of the largest Iron Age hill fort in England, **Uley Bury**. Dating from about 300 BC, the fort and its 2-mile perimeter walk provide spectacular views over the Severn Vale. To walk there, follow the steep path that runs from the village church. If you're driving, access to the car park is off the B4066, north of the village.

Just east of Uley you'll find the wonderfully romantic **Owlpen Manor** (www.owlpen.com), a Tudor mansion nestled in a wooded valley and surrounded by formal terraced gardens. The house was built between 1450 and 1616 and has a magnificent Tudor **Great Hall**. Owlpen suffered 100 years of neglect in the 19th century and was rescued and partially refurbished in 1926 by architect Norman Jewson, a follower of William Morris. The house was closed for repairs at the time of writing. Check the website for up-to-date details.

Virtually untouched since the mid-1870s, **Woodchester Mansion** (www.woodchestermansion.org.uk; adult/child £5.50/free; ⌚11am-4pm Sun Easter-Oct, plus Sat Jul & Aug) is an incredible place, abandoned before it was finished, yet amazingly grand and graceful. Doors open to nowhere, fireplaces are stuck halfway up walls, and corridors end at ledges with views of the ground below. The house also features an impressive set of gruesome gargoyles and is home to a large colony of bats and several resident ghosts. It's a mile north of Uley on the B4066.

Bus 20 runs between Uley and Stroud (55 minutes, four times daily Monday to Saturday).

Berkeley

POP 1865

An astounding relic from medieval times, **Berkeley Castle** (www.berkeley-castle.com; adult/child £7.50/4.50, grounds only £4/2; ⌚11am-5.30pm Sun-Thu) has remained virtually untouched since it was built as a sturdy fortress in Norman times. Edward II was imprisoned and then murdered here on the order of his wife, Queen Isabella, and her lover in 1327, and you can still see the King's Gallery, with its cell and dungeon. You can also visit the castle's **state rooms**, as well as the medieval **Great Hall**, **Picture Gallery** and **kitchen**. Regular jousting events and medieval banquets are held here in summer.

Berkeley is also home to the **Jenner Museum** (www.jennermuseum.com; Church Lane; adult/child £4.80/2.50; ⌚12.30-5.30pm Tue-Sat), which honours the life and works of Edward Jenner, country doctor and pioneer of vaccination. The museum is in the beautiful Queen Anne house, where the doctor performed the first smallpox vaccination in 1796. To get to the museum on foot, follow the path from the castle through St Mary's churchyard.

Bus 207 plies the route between Berkeley and Gloucester (55 minutes, three times daily Monday to Saturday).

Stroud

POP 13,058

Stroud once hummed with the sound of industry, with over 150 cloth mills operating around the town, but when the bottom fell out of the market, it fell heavily into decline and is only today recovering from the downturn in its fortunes. Although only a handful of the handsome old mills are still operating, many others have been converted into apartments or offices and the pleasant town has become a bohemian enclave littered with fair-trade and whole-foods shops, delis and organic cafes. The picturesque Shambles still holds a market three times weekly, and the Tudor town hall is also worth a look.

In the centre of town, the imposing Subscription Rooms are home to the **tourist office** (☎01453-760960; www.visitthecotswolds.org.uk; George St; ⌚10am-5pm Mon-Sat), which can provide information on visiting mills in the area.

The main attraction is the diverting FREE **Museum in the Park** (www.stroud.gov.uk/museum; Stratford Pk; ⌚10am-5pm Tue-Fri, 11am-5pm Sat & Sun), set in an 18th-century mansion surrounded by parkland. The museum tells the history of the town and its cloth-making, and there are displays of everything from dinosaurs to Victorian toys and the world's first lawn mower.

The nicest place to stay is in nearby Nailsworth at the 16th-century **Egypt Mill** (☎01453-833449; www.egyptmill.com; s/d from £80/90; P 📶), where you can fall asleep to the sound of the water gurgling over the weir. The rooms vary quite a bit and it's definitely worth paying the extra tenner for a superior option.

For food, head for **Star Anise** (www.staraniseartscafe.com; Gloucester St; mains £6-8; ⌚8am-5pm Mon-Fri, to 11pm Sat, 10am-2pm Sun), a vegetarian cafe serving fresh local produce and a popular spot for Sunday brunch.

It's also open for dinner (mains £9 to £11) on Saturday and often hosts live music.

Another good bet is **Woodruffs Organic Cafe** (www.woodruffsorganiccafe.co.uk; 24 High St; mains £5-7.80; 8.30am-5pm Mon-Sat), a small, cheerful place with a wholesome selection of salads, soups and stews.

Bus 46 runs hourly to Painswick (10 minutes) and Cheltenham (40 minutes) from Monday to Saturday. Trains run roughly hourly to London (£21, 1½ hours), Gloucester (20 minutes) and Cheltenham (40 minutes).

Painswick

POP 1666

One of the most beautiful and unspoilt towns in the Cotswolds, hilltop Painswick is an absolute gem. Largely untouched since medieval times, totally unassuming and gloriously uncommercial, it's like gaining access to an outdoor museum that is strangely lost in time. Despite its obvious charms, Painswick sees only a trickle of visitors, so you can wander the narrow winding streets and admire the picture-perfect cottages, handsome stone town houses and medieval inns in your own good time.

Sights & Activities

Running downhill beside and behind the church is a series of gorgeous streetscapes. Look out for **Bisley St**, the original main drag, which was superseded by the now ancient-looking **New St** in medieval times. Just south of the church, rare **iron stocks** stand in the street.

St Mary's Church CHURCH

The village centres on a fine, Perpendicular wool church surrounded by tabletop tombs and 99 clipped yew trees. Legend has it that if the hundredth yew tree were allowed to grow, the devil would appear and shrivel it. They planted it anyway – to celebrate the millennium – but there's been no sign of the Wicked One.

Painswick Rococo Garden ORNAMENTAL GARDEN

(www.rococogarden.co.uk; adult/child £6/3; 11am-5pm Jan-Oct;) Just a mile north of town, the ostentatious Painswick Rococo Garden is the area's biggest attraction. These flamboyant pleasure gardens were designed by Benjamin Hyett in the 1740s and have now been restored to their former glory. Winding paths soften the otherwise strict geometrical precision, bringing visitors around the central vegetable garden to the many Gothic follies dotted in the grounds. There's also a children's nature trail and maze.

Coopers Hill FESTIVAL

(www.cheese-rolling.co.uk) If you're visiting in late May, enquire about the cheese-rolling competition held on nearby Cooper's Hill in Cranham. A 200-year-old tradition sees locals running, tumbling and sliding down a local hill in pursuit of a seven-pound block of Double Gloucester cheese. For the truly committed, there is also an uphill competition.

Sleeping & Eating

St Michaels HOTEL ££

(01452-814555; www.stmichaelsrestaurant.co.uk; Victoria St; s/d £65/80; lunch & dinner Wed-Sun, dinner Sun; @) The three rooms at St Michaels are a handsome mix of luxurious fabrics, exposed stonework, rustic furniture and carved woods. Each is individual in style and has flatscreen TVs, fresh-cut flowers and a sense of tranquil calm. The restaurant downstairs serves modern British and European cuisine with a touch of Asian and Czech influence (2-/3-course dinner £28/31).

Cardynham House HOTEL ££

(01452-814006; www.cardynham.co.uk; Tibbiwell St; s/d from £55/75; lunch Tue-Sun dinner Tue-Sat;) The rooms at 15th-century Cardynham House have four-poster beds, heavy patterned fabrics and buckets of character. Choose the Shaker-style New England room, the opulent Arabian Nights room, the chintzy Old Tuscany room or for a private pool and garden, the Pool Room. Downstairs, the Bistro (mains £9 to £18) serves modern British cuisine.

St Annes B&B ££

(01452-812879; www.st-annes-painswick.co.uk; Gloucester St; s/d from £40/65; P) Set in an 18th-century wool merchant's house, this lovely B&B is a very homey place with a really warm welcome. Log fires, antique furniture and simple but elegant rooms make it a great value.

Getting There & Away

Bus 46 connects Cheltenham (30 minutes) and Stroud (10 minutes) with Painswick hourly Monday to Saturday.

GLOUCESTERSHIRE

After the crowds and coaches of the Cotswolds, Gloucestershire's languid charms are hard to beat, with its host of mellow stone villages and rustic allure. The county's greatest asset, however, is the elegant Regency town of Cheltenham, with its graceful, tree-lined terraces, upmarket boutiques and a tempting collection of accommodation and dining options.

The county capital, Gloucester, seems a dowdy cousin by comparison, but is well worth a visit for its magnificent Gothic cathedral. To the north, Tudor Tewkesbury follows the ecclesiastical splendour with a gracious Norman abbey surrounded by a town full of crooked, half-timbered houses. To the west, the picturesque Forest of Dean is a leafy backwater perfect for cycling and walking.

Activities

Gloucestershire's quiet roads, gentle gradients and numerous footpaths are ideal for walking and cycling. Tourist offices can help with route planning and stock numerous guides to the trails.

Compass Holidays (www.compass-holidays.com) offers guided cycling and walking tours of the area.

Cheltenham

POP 110,013

The shining star of the region, Cheltenham is a historic but cosmopolitan hub at the western edge of the rustic Cotswolds. The city oozes an air of gracious refinement, its streetscapes largely left intact since its heyday as a spa resort in the 18th century. At the time, it rivalled Bath as *the* place for the sick, hypochondriac and merely moneyed to go, and today it is still riddled with historic buildings, beautifully proportioned terraces and manicured squares.

Cheltenham is an affluent place, its well-heeled residents attracted by the genteel architecture, leafy crescents, wrought-iron balconies and expansive parks – all of which are kept in pristine condition. Add a slew of festivals of all persuasions and a host of fine hotels, restaurants and shops, and it's easy to conclude that it's the perfect base from which to explore the region.

History

Cheltenham languished in relative obscurity until pigeons were seen eating and thriving on salt crystals from a local spring in the early 18th century. It wasn't long before a pump was bored and Cheltenham began to establish itself as a spa town. Along with the sick, property speculators arrived in droves, and the town started to grow dramatically. Graceful terraced housing was thrown up, parks were laid out and the rich and famous followed.

By the time George III visited in 1788, the town's fate had been sealed and Cheltenham became the most fashionable holiday destination for England's upper crust. Handel, Samuel Johnson and Jane Austen all came here, and by the mid-19th century, the Victorian neo-Gothic Cheltenham College had sprung up, and, soon after, the genteel Cheltenham Ladies' College.

The town retained its period glamour and allure, and in the 20th century became known as the 'Anglo-Indians' Paradise' as so many Empire-serving, ex-military men retired here. Today, Cheltenham is the most complete Regency town in England, with millions being spent propping up the quick-buck buildings that the Regency entrepreneurs rushed to erect.

Sights

The Promenade & Montpellier BOULEVARD

Famed as one of England's most beautiful streets, the **Promenade** is a wide, tree-lined boulevard flanked by imposing period buildings. The **Municipal Offices**, built as private residences in 1825, are among the most striking on this street and they face a **statue of Edward Wilson** (1872–1912), a local man who joined Captain Scott's ill-fated second expedition to the South Pole.

Continuing on from here, you'll pass the grandiose **Imperial Gardens**, built to service the Imperial Spa (now the Queens Hotel), en route to **Montpellier**, Cheltenham's most fashionable district. Along with the handsome architecture of the area, there's a buzzing collection of bars, restaurants and boutiques. Along Montpellier Walk, **caryatids** (draped female figures based on those on the Acropolis in Athens) act as structural supports between the shops, each balancing an elaborately carved cornice on its head.

FREE **Pittville Pump Room** CONCERT HALL

(☎01242-523852; www.pittvillepumproom.org.uk; Pittville Park; ⌚9am-noon) Built in 1830 as a centrepiece to a vast estate, the Pittville Pump Room is Cheltenham's finest

Regency building. Originally used as a spa and social centre, it is now used as a concert hall and wedding venue. You can wander into the main auditorium and sample the pungent spa waters when the building is not in use for a private event, or just explore the vast parklands and the lake it overlooks. It's best to phone in advance to check the opening hours as the building is about 2 miles from the city centre.

FREE **Art Gallery & Museum** MUSEUM
(www.cheltenham.artgallery.museum; Clarence St; ⏲10am-5pm Mon-Sat) Cheltenham's excellent Art Gallery & Museum is well worth a visit for its depiction of Cheltenham life through the ages. It also has wonderful displays on William Morris and the Arts and Crafts Movement, as well as Dutch and British art, rare Chinese and English ceramics and a section on Edward Wilson's expedition to Antarctica. The museum is closed for redevelopment in 2011. Check the website for details on reopening.

Holst Birthplace Museum MUSEUM
(www.holstmuseum.org.uk; 4 Clarence Rd; adult/child £4.50/4; ⏲10am-4pm Tue-Sat) The composer Gustav Holst was born in Chelten-

Cheltenham

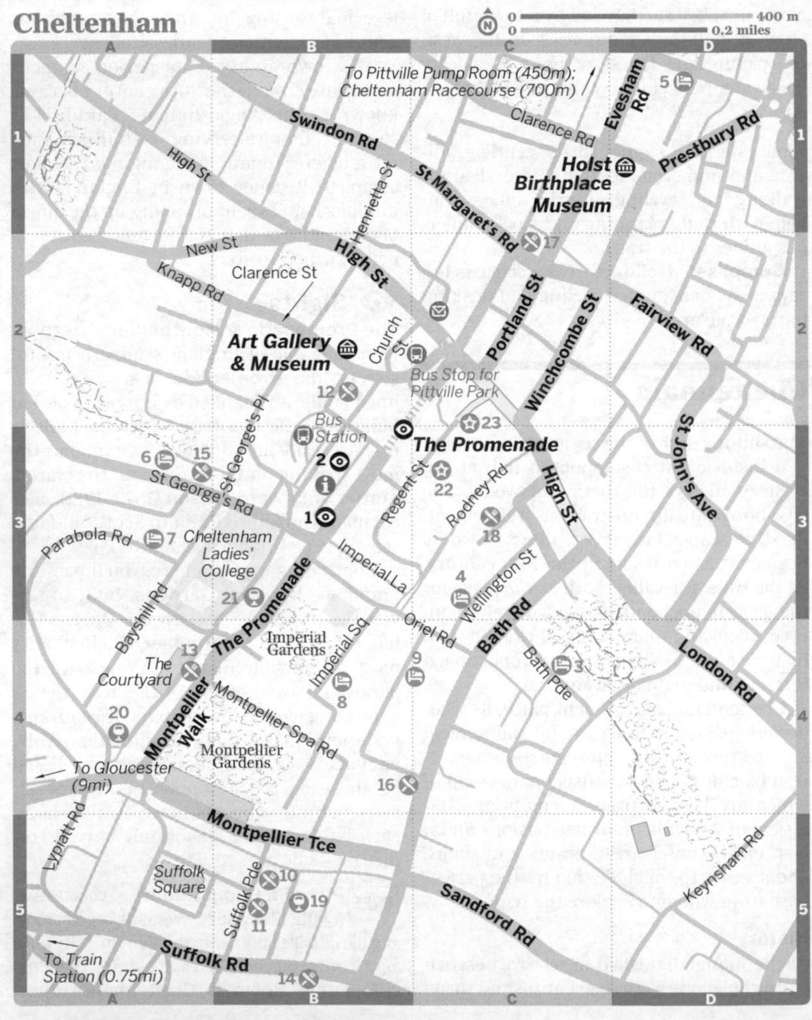

ham in 1874, and his childhood home has been turned into a museum celebrating his life and work. The rooms are laid out in typical period fashion and feature much Holst memorabilia, including the piano on which most of *The Planets* was composed. You can also visit the Victorian kitchen, which explains what life was like 'below stairs'.

Cheltenham Racecourse RACECOURSE
(www.cheltenham.co.uk) Cheltenham is more famous in some circles for its horse racing than its architecture, and its racecourse can attract up to 40,000 people a day during the **National Hunt Festival**, often simply called 'the Festival'. Held in mid-March each year, this is England's premier steeplechase event and is attended by droves of breeders, trainers, riders and spectators. The racecourse is about a mile north of the city centre via Evesham Rd.

Cheltenham

Top Sights
Art Gallery & Museum ... B2
Holst Birthplace Museum ... D1
The Promenade ... B3

Sights
1 Edward Wilson Statue ... B3
2 Municipal Offices ... B3

Sleeping
3 Abbey Hotel ... C4
4 Big Sleep ... C3
5 Cheltenham Townhouse ... D1
6 Hanover House ... A3
7 Hotel du Vin ... A3
8 Thirty Two ... B4
9 YMCA ... C4

Eating
10 Brosh ... B5
11 Daffodil ... B5
12 Dfly ... B2
13 Gusto ... A4
14 Le Champignon Sauvage ... B5
15 Monty's Brasserie ... A3
16 Spice Lodge ... B4
17 Storyteller ... C2
18 Vanilla ... C3

Drinking
19 Beehive ... B5
20 Montpellier Wine Bar ... A4
21 Subtone ... B3

Entertainment
22 21 Club ... C3
23 Everyman Theatre ... C2

Tours

Guided 1½-hour **walking tours** (£4; ⌚11.30am Sat Apr-Oct, plus Sun Jul & Aug) of Regency Cheltenham depart from the tourist office. You can also book tickets for a rolling program of daylong **coach tours** (adult/child £29/15; ⌚10.15am Thu) to various locations in the Cotswolds here.

Festivals & Events

Cheltenham is renowned as a city of festivals, and throughout the year you'll find major events going on in the city. For more information or to book tickets, visit www.cheltenhamfestivals.com.

Folk Festival A showcase of traditional and new-age folk talent in February.

Jazz Festival An imaginative program hailed as the UK's finest jazz fest, held in late April.

Science Festival Exploring the delights and intrigues of the world of science in June.

Music Festival A celebration of traditional and contemporary sounds with a geographical theme, in July.

Literature Festival A 10-day celebration of writers and the written word in October.

Sleeping

Cheltenham has an excellent choice of hotels and B&Bs, but few options in the budget range. Book as far in advance as possible during the festivals – especially for race week.

Beaumont House B&B ££
(☎01242-223311; www.bhhotel.co.uk; 56 Shurdington Rd; s/d from £68/78; P @) Set in a large garden just a short way from the centre of town, this boutique guesthouse is a memorable place with a range of carefully designed rooms with opulent decor. The cheaper standard rooms are elegant but simple, while the pricier suites are sumptuous. Go for the full-on safari look in Out of Africa, sultry boudoir in Out of Asia or more subtle design in the Prestbury Suite. To get here follow Bath Rd south from the city for about 1 mile.

Thirty Two B&B £££
(☎01242-771110; www.thirtytwoltd.com; 32 Imperial Square; s/d from £155/170; P @ wi-fi) In a league of its own, this slick boutique B&B is a rare find. It may charge hotel prices,

but it's well worth it. You get the personal service of a B&B but the luxury, style and comfort of a top-notch hotel. Expect views over the Imperial Gardens, muted colours, contemporary artwork, luxurious fabrics and rooms that could easily feature in a glossy style magazine.

Big Sleep HOTEL ££
(☎01242-696999; www.thebigsleephotel.com; Wellington St; r £55-300; P @ wifi family) A luxury budget hotel, this place is all designer looks and no-frills minimalism. The thoroughly modern rooms have playful wallpapers and simple furniture, the family rooms have their own kitchenette, and breakfast is included in the price. If you can grab one of the cheaper deals, it's an absolute steal, and a brilliant option if you're travelling with family or friends.

Hotel du Vin HOTEL £££
(☎01242-588450; www.hotelduvin.com; Parabola Rd; r from £145; P @) Sleek, stylish and very hip, this is another winning offer from the Hotel du Vin luxury hotel chain. A spiral staircase anchors the spacious public areas, which are decked out with a subtle horsey theme, while the bedrooms ooze minimalist sophistication. Some of the standard rooms are quite small so it's worth paying the extra for the superior option.

Hanover House B&B ££
(☎01242-541297; www.hanoverhouse.org; 65 St George's Rd; s/d from £70/90; P wifi) A real gem, this Victorian town house has three lovely rooms with high ceilings, big sash windows and quirky, vibrant decor. Blending period details and modern style, the rooms feel lived in, with well-stocked bookcases, colourful throws and a decanter of sherry 'to ease any stress'. Breakfast is organic and seriously good.

Cheltenham Townhouse B&B ££
(☎01242-221922; www.cheltenhamtownhouse.com; 12 Pittville Lawn; s £48-80, d £65-98; P @ wifi) Modern decor with pale, neutral colours, stylish accessories, DVD players and broadband make this central option a good bet for a midrange budget. The Townhouse is set on a quiet street just out of the centre, but the spacious rooms and sparkling bathrooms make it worth the trip.

Other options:

Abbey Hotel HOTEL ££
(☎01242-516053; www.abbeyhotel-cheltenham.com; 14-16 Bath Pde; s/d from £50/75; P) Convenient location and simple rooms.

YMCA HOSTEL £
(☎01242-524024; www.cheltenhamymca.com; 6 Victoria Walk; dm/s £14/28.50) Basic and well-worn dorms, but it's central and cheap.

Eating

Cheltenham has a great choice of top-end places to eat, but apart from the usual chains there's little choice for those on a more meagre budget. For the best range of options, head to Montpellier or the area around Suffolk Square.

Daffodil MODERN BRITISH ££
(☎01242-700055; www.thedaffodil.com; 18-20 Suffolk Pde; mains £13.50-17.50; ⏲closed Sun) A perennial favourite, the Daffodil is as loved for its top-notch modern British brasserie-style food as for its flamboyant surroundings. Set in a converted art deco cinema, it harks back to the Roaring Twenties and features live jazz and blues every Monday night. The atmosphere is suitably bubbly and the food consistently good.

Le Champignon Sauvage FRENCH £££
(☎01242-573449; www.lechampignonsauvage.co.uk; 24-26 Suffolk Rd; set menu 2-/3-course £45/55; ⏲Tue-Sat) This unpretentious but oh-so-delectable restaurant has earned two Michelin stars for its inspired cuisine. The atmosphere is refined but relaxed, the tables big and the decor simple. It's the kind of place where you can just wallow in the food, which is worth every penny. Perfect for a special occasion. Book ahead.

Brosh MEDITERRANEAN ££
(www.broshrestaurant.co.uk; 8 Suffolk Pde; mains £14-18; ⏲dinner Wed-Sat) This lovely little place serves excellent eastern Mediterranean food with everything from the *merguez* to the sourdough bread prepared on site from scratch. The menu is limited but the flavours are superb. For something lighter (£2 to £4), come for the mezedhes bar, which opens on Wednesday to Friday nights.

Dfly FUSION £
(1a Crescent Pl; dishes £3.50-8; ⏲Tue-Sat) Bar, restaurant and hip hang-out rolled into one, Dfly is a style-conscious place serving great sushi and tapas in sultry surroundings. Think deep red, oversize cushions, dark woods, liberally scattered church candles and Asian carvings. By night it's a buzzing watering hole with soulful music and monthly live gigs.

Storyteller INTERNATIONAL ££
(www.storyteller.co.uk; 11 North Pl; mains £8-16) Feel-good comfort food draws the crowds to this enduringly popular restaurant. It dishes up generous portions of barbecue ribs, seafood platters and vegetarian burritos on a menu fusing tastes from as far afield as Mexico and Asia. The place is always buzzing and is a popular spot for parties.

Gusto ITALIAN £
(www.gusto-deli.com; 12 Montpellier Walk; mains £7-10; ⏲9am-5.30pm Mon-Sat) This deli and cafe is a great place for coffee and a slab of cake, a wholesome lunch made from authentic Italian ingredients or scrumptious picnic supplies. The upstairs cafe features changing artwork from a local gallery and great big windows overlooking Montpellier Gardens.

Spice Lodge ASIAN ££
(Montpellier Dr; mains £11-15) This pan-Asian restaurant has a full menu of Indian and Thai dishes, but the real draw is the menu du jour, which features European classics cooked with an Asian twist. Set in an imposing old mansion, it's a relaxed but elegant place to dine.

Other good options:

Monty's Brasserie SEAFOOD ££
(www.montysbraz.co.uk; 41 St George's Rd, mains £12-22) Bright, buzzing brasserie with a great lunch menu.

Vanilla MODERN BRITISH ££
(www.vanillainc.co.uk; 9-10 Cambray Pl; mains £9-16; ⏲lunch Tue-Sat, dinner Mon-Sat) Relaxed basement restaurant popular with locals.

Drinking & Entertainment

Beehive PUB
(1-3 Montpellier Villas; www.thebeehivemontpellier.com) A local favourite with a mixed following, this traditional pub is always busy but still manages to feel like a great place to chill out. There's an open fire in winter, a pleasant garden in summer and a great choice of local ales and ciders on tap.

Montpellier Wine Bar WINE BAR
(www.montpellierwinebar.com; Bayshill Lodge, Montpellier St) Slick, sophisticated and self-consciously cool, this is where Cheltenham's beautiful people come to hang out, sip wine and dine on modern British food (mains £9 to £14). There's an extensive wine list, cask ales and plenty of people-watching.

Subtone NIGHTCLUB
(www.subtone.co.uk; 117 The Promenade) One of the city's most popular venues, Subtone has three floors of DJs, five bars and live music at its basement club and piano bar. Expect everything from jazz and house to funk and rock. It's a bit rough around the edges but a great spot for music-lovers.

21 Club NIGHTCLUB
(21 Regent St; ⏲Thu-Sun) A long-standing favourite, the 21 Club plays chart music to the masses. Expect little room on the dance floor and plenty of DJ banter. Arrive early to avoid the long queues.

Everyman Theatre THEATRE
(www.everymantheatre.org.uk; Regent St) Cheltenham's main stage hosts everything from Elvis impersonators to comedy and panto.

Pittville Pump Room CONCERT HALL
(☎01242-523852; www.pittvillepumproom.org.uk; Pittville Park) Cheltenham's best bet for classical music.

Information

You'll find all the major banks and the main **post office** on High St.

Cheltenham Library (Clarence St; free; ⏲9am-7pm Mon, Wed & Fri, to 5.30pm Tue & Thu, to 4pm Sat) Free web browsing.

Loft (8-9 Henrietta St; per hr £4; ⏲10am-7pm Mon-Thu, to 6pm Fri & Sat) Internet access.

Tourist Office (☎01242 522878; www.visitcheltenham.info; 77 The Promenade; ⏲9.30am-5.15pm Mon-Sat) The tourist office will move into the Cheltenham Museum & Art Gallery once it reopens.

Getting There & Away

For information on public transport to and from Cheltenham, pick up a free copy of the handy *Getting There by Public Transport* guide from the tourist office. The bus station is behind the Promenade in the town centre, but the train station is to the west of town.

Bus

National Express runs buses to **London** (£7, 2½ hours, hourly). Other bus routes:

Broadway Bus 606 (45 minutes) via **Winchcombe** (20 minutes); four times daily Monday to Friday.

Cirencester Bus 51 (40 minutes, hourly).

Gloucester Bus 94 (30 minutes, every 10 minutes Monday to Saturday, every 20 minutes on Sunday).

Moreton Bus 801 (one hour) via **Bourton** (35 minutes) and **Stow** (50 minutes); seven times daily Monday to Saturday.

Oxford Bus 853 (£7.50, 1½ hours, three daily Monday to Saturday, one Sunday).

Train

Trains run to **London** (£31, 2¼ hours), **Bristol** (£7.30, 50 minutes), **Gloucester** (£3.60, 11 minutes) and **Bath** (£11.60, 1¼ hours) roughly every half-hour.

 Getting Around

Bus D runs to Pittville Park and the train station from Clarence St every 10 minutes.

Tewkesbury

POP 10,016

Sitting at the confluence of the Rivers Avon and Severn, Tudor-heavy Tewkesbury is all crooked little half-timbered houses, buckled roof lines and narrow alleyways stuck in a medieval time warp. Throw in a few Georgian gems and the town's higgledy-piggledy charm is hard to resist. Take time to wander the ancient passageways that lead up to the main streets from the rivers, and then wander along Church St to the town's most glorious building, the magnificent medieval abbey church.

The **tourist office** (☎01684-855040; www.visitcotswoldsandsevernvale.gov.uk; 100 Church St; ⊙10am-5pm Mon-Sat, to 4pm Sun) is housed in a 17th-century hat shop that's also home to the **Out of the Hat** (www.outofthehat.org.uk; adult/child £3.50/2.50; ⊙10am-5pm Mon-Sat, to 4pm Sun) heritage centre. It explores the history of the town and the restoration of the building and has plenty of interactive games for young visitors.

Tewkesbury Abbey CHURCH

(www.tewkesburyabbey.org.uk; ⊙7.30am-6pm) This magnificent abbey is one of Britain's largest churches, far bigger than many of the country's cathedrals. The Norman abbey, built for the Benedictine monks, was consecrated in 1121 and was one of the last monasteries to be dissolved by Henry VIII. Although many of the monastery buildings were destroyed, the abbey church survived after being bought by the townspeople for the princely sum of £453 in 1542.

The church has a massive 40m-high tower and some spectacular Norman piers and arches in the nave. The Decorated-style chancel dates from the 14th century, however, and still retains much of its original stained glass. The church also features an organ dating from 1631, originally made for Magdalen College, Oxford, and an extensive collection of medieval tombs. The most interesting is that of John Wakeman, the last abbot, who is shown as a vermin-ridden skeleton.

You can take a **guided tour** (£4) of the abbey on weekdays in summer or visit an exhibition on the abbey's history at the **visitor centre** (⊙10am-5.30pm Mon-Sat Apr-Sep) by the main gate. The church also makes a wonderfully atmospheric venue for a range of summer concerts.

John Moore Countryside Museum MUSEUM

(www.johnmooremuseum.org; adult/child £1.50/1; ⊙10am-1pm & 2-5pm Tue-Sat) This small museum, set in a wonderfully atmospheric 15th-century dwelling, gives an insight into life in Tudor times and features a fully restored late-medieval home and shop.

Tewkesbury Museum MUSEUM

(www.tewkesburymuseum.org; 64 Barton St; admission £2; ⊙1-4pm Tue-Fri, 11am-4pm Sat) Displays finds from Roman and medieval times as well as a diorama on the Battle of Tewkesbury.

Sleeping & Eating

Jessop Townhouse HOTEL ££

(☎01684-292017; www.jessophousehotel.com; 65 Church St; s/d from £59/79; P 📶) A lovely little hotel set in a Georgian town house, this place has large rooms with high ceilings, big windows, old fireplaces and elegant style. The rooms are all different – some in period style, others more contemporary – but all are warm and cosy, with large TVs and new bathrooms. It's a great deal at these rates.

Ivydene House B&B ££

(☎01684-592453; www.ivydenehouse.net; Uckinghall; s/d from £67/75; P) This gorgeous B&B is well out of town but such a gem you'll be delighted you made the effort to get here. The rooms are luxuriously styled with a mix of contemporary fashion, classic furniture, soft colour schemes and gorgeous fabrics. There's an immaculately kept garden, lots of surprising little extras and the heartiest of welcomes. Uckinghall is 7 miles north of Tewkesbury off the A38.

Owens MODERN BRITISH ££

(www.eatatowens.co.uk; 73 Church St; mains £10-15; ⊙11am-10pm Tue-Sat, Sun 2-4pm) Set in a 15th-century building that's decidedly modern inside, this place is a welcome change from Tewkesbury's tearooms. The menu features big, honest flavours and a modern take on classic British and French cuisine. Try the excellent two-course set lunch for £10.

Getting There & Away

Bus 41 runs to Cheltenham (25 minutes) every 15 minutes, hourly on Sunday, and bus 71 (30 minutes) goes to Gloucester hourly. The nearest train station is 1½ miles away at Ashchurch, from where there are trains every two hours to Cheltenham (10 minutes) and Worcester (26 minutes, £6.60).

Gloucester

POP 136,203

Gloucester (*glos*-ter) began life as a settlement for retired Roman soldiers but really came into its own in medieval times, when the pious public brought wealth and prosperity to what was then a prime pilgrimage city. The faithful flocked to see the grave of Edward II and soon financed the building of what remains one of England's most beautiful cathedrals.

In more recent years, Gloucester bore the brunt of hard times and the city fell into serious decline. The centre remains a rather dowdy, workaday place with brutalist architecture and a glut of greasy-spoon cafes. But scratch the surface and you'll find a glimmer of medieval character and the beginnings of a city trying hard to transform its fortunes. The historic docks are now home to trendy apartments, lively restaurants and interesting museums and are well worth a wander. That said, Gloucester makes a better day-trip than a destination in itself.

Sights

Gloucester Cathedral CATHEDRAL
(www.gloucestercathedral.org.uk; College Green; suggested donation £3; ⌚8am-6pm) The main reason to visit Gloucester is to see its magnificent Gothic cathedral, a stunning example of English Perpendicular style. Originally the site of a Saxon abbey, a Norman church was built here by a group of Benedictine monks in the 12th century, and when Edward II was murdered in 1327, the church was chosen as his burial place. Edward's tomb proved so popular, however, that Gloucester became a centre of pilgrimage and the income generated from the pious pilgrims financed the church's conversion into the magnificent building seen today.

Inside, the cathedral skilfully combines the best of Norman and Gothic design with sturdy columns creating a sense of gracious solidity, and wonderful Norman arcading draped with beautiful mouldings. From the elaborate 14th-century wooden choir stalls, you'll get a good view of the imposing **Great East Window**, one of the largest in England.

To see the window in more detail, head for the **Tribune Gallery**, where you can also see an **exhibition** (admission £2; ⌚10.30am-4pm Mon-Fri, to 3.30pm Sat) on its creation. As you walk around the **Whispering Gallery,** you'll notice that even the quietest of murmurs reverberates across the wonderfully elaborate lierne vaulting. Beneath the window in the northern ambulatory is Edward II's magnificent tomb, and nearby is the late 15th-century **Lady Chapel**, a glorious patchwork of stained glass.

One of the cathedral's greatest treasures, however, is the exquisite **Great Cloister**. Completed in 1367, it is the first example of fan vaulting in England and is only matched in beauty by Henry VIII's Chapel at Westminster Abbey. You (or your children) might recognise the cloister from the first two Harry Potter films: it was used in the corridor scenes at Hogwart's School.

A wonderful way to take in the glory of the cathedral is to attend one of the many musical recitals and concerts held here. The stunning acoustics and breathtaking surroundings are pretty much guaranteed to make your hair stand on end.

Civic Trust volunteers provide **guided tours** (⌚10.30am-4pm Mon-Sat, noon-2.30pm Sun) of the cathedral. For more insights and a fantastic view of the town, join an hour-long guided **tower tour** (adult/child £3/1; ⌚2.30pm Mon-Fri, 1.30pm & 2.30pm Sat). Because of the steep steps it's not recommended for children under 10.

National Waterways Museum MUSEUM
(www.nwm.org.uk/gloucester; adult/child £4.25/3.25; ⌚10.30am-5pm; 👪) A major part of the city's regeneration is taking place at **Gloucester Docks**, once Britain's largest inland port. Fifteen beautiful Victorian warehouses, many now restored, surround the canal basins and house a series of museums, shops and cafes. The largest warehouse at the docks, Llanthony, is home to the National Waterways Museum, a hands-on kind of place where you can discover the history of Britain's inland waterways.

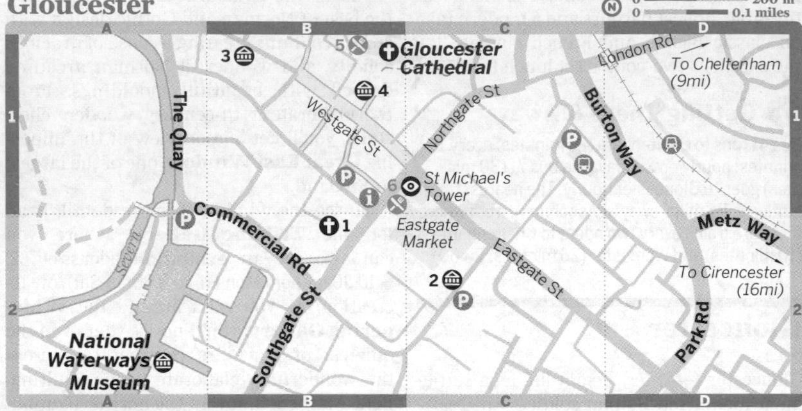

Gloucester

Exhibitions explain what it was like living, working and moving on the water, featuring plenty of historic boats and interactive exhibits that are great for children.

FREE **Gloucester Folk Museum** MUSEUM
(www.gloucester.gov.uk/folkmuseum 99-103 Westgate St; ⌚10am-5pm Tue-Sat) This folk museum examines domestic life, crafts and industries from 1500 to the present and is housed in a wonderful series of Tudor and Jacobean timber-framed buildings dating from the 16th and 17th centuries.

FREE **Gloucester City Museum & Art Gallery** MUSEUM
(www.gloucester.gov.uk/citymuseum; Brunswick Rd; ⌚10am-5pm Tue-Sat) The city museum houses everything from dinosaur fossils and Roman artefacts to paintings by the artists Turner and Gainsborough.

FREE **Blackfriars** FRIARY
(Ladybellgate St) One of Britain's best-preserved 13th-century Dominican friaries.

Tours

Civic Trust WALKING TOURS
(www.gloucestercivictrust.org; adult/child £3/free; ⌚Apr-Sep) Ninety-minute guided tours of the city's most historic buildings leave from St Michael's Tower at 11.30am Monday to Saturday. Tours of the docks depart from the National Waterways Museum at 2pm Wednesday, Saturday and Sunday.

National Waterways Museum BOATING TOURS
(www.nwm.org.uk/gloucester; adult/child £4.75/3.50; ⌚noon, 1.30 & 2.30pm Sat & Sun, daily during school holidays) This interesting 45-minute boat trip runs along the Gloucester and Sharpness Canal.

Sleeping & Eating

Gloucester's accommodation options are pretty grim. You'd be far better off staying in Cheltenham (10 minutes by train) instead.

Tigers Eye ASIAN ££
(www.theoldbell-tigerseye.co.uk; 9a Southgate St; mains £6-14; ⌚closed Sun & Mon) This place attempts to please everyone with a menu that veers from baguettes and wraps to sushi, noodles and Black Rock grills (where you cook your own meat or fish on a sizzling volcanic plate). It's a strange mix, but somehow it manages to work and the food is some of the best in town.

THE TAILOR OF GLOUCESTER

Beatrix Potter's magical tale of good-hearted mice saving a feverish Gloucester tailor from ruin was inspired by a local legend about real-life tailor John Prichard. Like the tailor in Potter's tale, Prichard had been commissioned to make a coat for the mayor, but left the garment at cutting stage on a Friday night. He returned on Monday to find it finished, save for a single button hole. A note pinned to it read: 'No more twist.'

Commercially minded Mr Prichard was soon encouraging people to come in and see his workshop where 'waistcoats are made at night by the fairies'. In reality, his two assistants had slept off a Saturday night bender at the workshop and woke to see the faithful heading to the cathedral for mass. Consumed by guilt and hoping to make amends, they had tried to finish the coat but ran out of thread.

The **House of the Tailor of Gloucester** (www.tailor-of-gloucester.org.uk; 9 College Ct; ⏲10am-5pm Mon-Sat, noon-5pm Sun), the house that Potter used in her illustrations, is now a museum and souvenir shop dedicated to the author.

Cathedral Coffee Shop CAFE £
(College Green; snacks £2-4; ⏲10am-5pm Mon-Fri, 10am-4.30pm Sat, 11am-3pm Sun) For hearty soups, diet-busting cakes and sticky buns, the cathedral coffee shop provides a wonderful setting for a quick cuppa.

Information

Tourist Office (☎01452-396572; www.visitgloucester.info; 28 Southgate St; ⏲10am-5pm Mon-Sat, 11am-3pm Sun) Pick up a free *Via Sacra* brochure to guide you around the city's most historic buildings.

Getting There & Away

National Express has buses roughly every two hours to **London** (£6, 3¼ hours). Bus 94 goes to **Cheltenham** (30 minutes) every 10 minutes Monday to Saturday, and every 20 minutes on Sunday. However, the train (11 minutes, every 20 minutes) is faster.

Forest of Dean

POP 79,982

An ancient woodland with a unique, almost magical character, the Forest of Dean is the oldest oak forest in England and a wonderfully scenic place to walk, cycle or paddle. Its steep, wooded hills, winding, tree-lined roads and glimmering lakes make it a remarkably tranquil place and an excellent spot for outdoor pursuits.

The forest was formerly a royal hunting ground and a centre of iron and coal mining, and its mysterious depths were supposedly the inspiration for Tolkien's setting of *The Lord of the Rings* and for JK Rowling's Harry Potter adventures. Numerous other writers, poets, artists and craftspeople have been inspired by the stunning scenery, designated England's first National Forest Park in 1938.

Covering 42 sq miles between Gloucester, Ross-on-Wye and Chepstow, the forest is in an isolated position, but Coleford, the main population centre, has good transport connections. You'll find information on the area at www.visitforestofdean.co.uk.

Sights & Activities

Dean Heritage Centre MUSEUM
(www.deanheritagemuseum.com; Camp Mill, Soudley; adult/child £5.40/2.75; ⏲10am-5pm) For an insight into the history of the forest since the Ice Age, this entertaining museum looks at everything from the forest's geology to Roman occupation, medieval hunting laws, free mining, cottage crafts and industrial coal mining. There's also a reconstructed forest home, adventure playground and art gallery on site.

Puzzle Wood ADVENTURE PARK
(www.puzzlewood.net;adult/child£5/3.50;⏲10am-5pm; 👪) If you're travelling with children, this wonderful forest playground is a must. An overgrown pre-Roman, open-cast ore mine, it has a maze of paths, weird rock formations, tangled vines and eerie passageways and offers a real sense of discovery. Puzzle Wood is 1 mile south of Coleford on the B4228.

Clearwell Caves CAVES
(www.clearwellcaves.com; adult/child £5.80/3.80; ⏲10am-5pm) Mined for iron ore for more than 4000 years, these caves are a warren of passageways, caverns and pools that help explain the forest's history of mining. There is also a blacksmith's workshop and the possibility of deep-level caving for

small groups. The caves are signposted off the B4228 a mile south of Coleford.

All Saints CHURCH
(www.allsaintsnewland.btik.com; ⌚9am-5pm) In Newland, you can visit the 'Cathedral of the Forest', the 13th-century All Saints church, which was restored and partially rebuilt in the 19th century and houses some fine stained-glass windows, as well as a unique brass depicting a miner with a *nelly* (tallow candle) in his mouth, a pick in his hand and a *billy* (backpack) on his back.

Sleeping & Eating

TOP CHOICE **St Briavels Castle YHA** HOSTEL £
(☎01594-530272; www.yha.org.uk; Lydney; dm from £18; P) Live like a king for a night at this unique hostel set in an imposing moated castle once used as King John's hunting lodge. Loaded with character and a snip at this price, this 13th-century castle comes complete with round towers, drawbridge and gruesome history. The dorms sleep four to six, and you can even join in the ancient spirit with full-blown medieval banquets on Wednesdays and Saturdays in August.

Three Choirs Vineyard B&B ££
(☎01531-890223; www.threechoirs.com; Newent; d from £115; P) This working vineyard has a range of extremely comfortable, classically styled rooms overlooking the sweeping fields of vines. You can also take a guided tour of the vineyard (£7.50), try the award-winning wines and then relax over lunch (mains £12.50 to £16.50) or dinner (mains £19 to £20) in the bright and airy restaurant. There's also a gift shop and microbrewery on site.

Dome Garden BOUTIQUE CAMPING ££
(☎01730-261458; www.domegarden.co.uk; Mile End, Coleford; 4-bed dome from £375, B&B d £96) For something completely different why not get back to nature in luxurious style in a cool geodesic dome? Linked by paths of recycled glass and set in glorious gardens, the domes sleep between two and eight people and have giant bean bags, wood burners and their own kitchen and showers. Yes, it's camping, just not like you know it.

Tudor Farmhouse Hotel HOTEL ££
(☎01594-833046; www.tudorfarmhousehotel.co.uk; High St, Clearwell; d from £90) You'll find oak beams, exposed stonework and old-world charm at this rustic 13th-century hotel and former farmhouse. There's a wide variety of rooms, from comfortable attic rooms to luxurious four-posters, and a popular restaurant serving modern British fare (lunch mains £6 to £15, 3-course dinner £32.50).

Garden Cafe MODERN BRITISH ££
(☎01594-860075; www.gardencafe.co.uk; Lwr Lydbrook; mains £8-13; ⌚lunch Fri-Sun, dinner Fri, Sat & Mon) An award-winning organic cafe on the banks of the River Wye, this place is set in a converted malt house and surrounded by a beautiful walled garden. The food is all seasonal and locally sourced, with vegetables from the cafe's garden. Monday night is tapas night (set menu £10).

Getting There & Around

From Gloucester, bus 31 (one hour, hourly) runs to Coleford, and there are trains to Lydney (20 minutes, hourly). The **Dean Forest Railway** (www.deanforestrailway.co.uk) runs steam trains from Lydney to Parkend (day tickets adult/child £10/5) on selected days from March to December.

You can hire bikes (£15 per day), buy maps and get advice on cycling routes at **Pedalabikeaway** (01594 860065; www.pedalabikeaway.co.uk; Cannop Valley; ⌚Tue-Sun) near Coleford.

HERTFORDSHIRE

Firmly on the commuter belt and within easy reach of the capital, Hertfordshire is a small, sleepy county liberally scattered with satellite towns that threaten to overtake the fast-disappearing countryside. However, it is also home to the historic town of St Albans, with its elegant Georgian streetscapes and Roman remains, and to Hatfield House, a spectacular stately home well worth the effort to visit.

St Albans

POP 129,005

A bustling market town with a host of crooked Tudor buildings and elegant Georgian town houses, St Albans makes a pleasant day-trip from London. The town was founded as Verulamium after the Roman invasion of AD 43 but was renamed St Albans in the 3rd century after a Roman soldier, Alban, lost his head in punishment for sheltering a Christian priest. He became England's first Christian martyr, and the small city soon became a site of pilgrimage.

(Continued on page 233)

t Paul's Cathedral (p67), London

ne cathedral was designed by Christopher Wren after the Great Fire and built between 1675 and 1710.

JULIET COOMBE

1. The Cotswolds (p200)
Its bucolic villages, country lanes and bridleways are popular cycling destinations.

2. Brighton (p162)
This bustling seaside city has a bohemian, cosmopolitan and hedonistic vibe.

3. London's parks
A vast green corridor of gardens links Westminster all the way to Kensington.

4. Windsor Castle (p237), Windsor
The largest and oldest occupied fortress in the world serves as the Queen's weekend retreat.

3

SEAN CAFFREY

GARETH MCCORMACK

1. Lavenham (p423), Suffolk
Lavenham is home to a wonderful collection of medieval, half-timbered and pargeted houses.

2. Oxford (p182), Oxfordshire
One of the world's most famous university towns, it's filled with elegant honey-coloured buildings.

3. Devon & Cornwall coastline
The South West Coast Path (p38) offers panoramic views of England's two most westerly counties.

4. Glastonbury Festival (p328)
This festival has been running for 40 years, making it the world's longest-running performing-arts festival.

5. Avebury (p298), Wessex
The stone circle here is the largest in the world. It's also one of the oldest, dating from around 2500 to 2200 BC.

ANDREW MARSHALL & LEANNE WALKER

3

RICK GERHARTER

BRINKSTOCK/ALAMY

1. Imperial War Museum North (p637), Manchester
Designed by Daniel Libeskind, the building has three distinct structures (or shards).

2. Lincoln Cathedral (p458), Lincoln
The great tower rising above the crossing is the third highest in England at 83m.

3. Northumberland castles
Isolated and desolate, Lindisfarne Castle (p774) is moulded onto a hunk of rock on Holy Island..

4. Iron Bridge (p549), Shropshire

At the time of its construction, in 1779, nobody could believe that anything so large could be built from cast iron.

5. Clifford's Tower (p602), York

This stone tower is all that's left of York Castle, with a highly unusual figure-of-eight design built into the castle's keep.

DAVID TOMLINSON

Lake District (p691)

This wonderful area of soaring peaks, endless views, deep valleys and, of course, beautiful lakes, is loved by walkers.

(Continued from page 224)

The pilgrims brought business and, subsequently, wealth to the town, and eventually the object of their affection was enshrined in what is now a magnificent cathedral. The town is also home to an excellent Roman museum, an array of chichi shops and upmarket restaurants and some wonderful pubs. The main drag, St Peter's St, is scarred by an ugly array of plastic storefronts. Head instead for the quiet back streets or follow George St into Fishpool St, a charming lane that winds its way past old-world pubs to leafy Verulamium Park.

Sights

St Albans Cathedral CATHEDRAL

(www.stalbanscathedral.org.uk; admission by donation; ⌚8am-5.45pm) Set in tranquil grounds away from the din of the main streets, St Albans' magnificent cathedral is a lesson in architectural history. The church began life as a Benedictine monastery in 793, built by King Offa of Mercia around the tomb of St Alban. In Norman times, it was completely rebuilt using material from the old Roman town of Verulamium, and then, in the 12th and 13th centuries, Gothic extensions and decorations were added.

The deceptively simple nave gives way to stunningly ornate ceilings, semi-lost wall paintings, an elaborate nave screen and, of course, the shrine of St Alban. There's also a luminescent rose window from the 20th century. The best way to appreciate the wealth of history contained in the building is to join a free **guided tour** (⌚11.30am & 2.30pm Mon-Fri, 11.30am & 2pm Sat, 2.30pm Sun). If you miss the tour you can pick up a very helpful free plan and guide at the entrance.

Verulamium Museum & Roman Ruins MUSEUM

(www.stalbansmuseums.org.uk; St Michael's St; adult/child £3.50/2; ⌚10am-5.30pm Mon-Sat, 2-5.30pm Sun) A fantastic exposé of everyday life under the Romans, the Verulamium Museum is home to a large collection of arrowheads, glassware and grave goods. Its centrepiece, however, is the **Mosaic Room**, where five superb mosaic floors, uncovered between 1930 and 1955, are laid out. You can also see re-creations of Roman rooms, and learn about life in the settlement through interactive and audiovisual displays. Every second weekend, the museum is 'invaded' by Roman soldiers who demonstrate the tactics and tools of the Roman army.

Adjacent **Verulamium Park** has remains of a basilica, bathhouse and parts of the city wall. You can pick up a map of the area with information on the site from the museum or tourist office.

Across the busy A4147 are the grassy foundations of a **Roman theatre** (☎01727-835035; www.romantheatre.co.uk; adult/child £2.50/1.50; ⌚10am-5pm), which once seated 2000 spectators.

FREE **St Alban's Museum** MUSEUM

(www.stalbansmuseums.org.uk; Hatfield Rd; ⌚10am-5pm Mon-Sat, 2-5pm Sun) For a potted history of St Albans, take a look at the local museum, which houses displays from Roman times to the present.

Clock Tower CLOCK TOWER

(High St; adult/child 80/40p; ⌚10.30am-5pm Sat & Sun) This fine flint edifice, built around 1410, is England's only medieval clock tower. 'Gabriel' (the original bell) is still there.

Sleeping & Eating

You'll find plenty of chain restaurants around the centre of town.

Fleuchary House B&B ££

(☎01727-766764; www.29stalbans.com; 29 Upper Lattimore Rd; s/d £45/60; P 📶) A beautiful Victorian house with many original features, this boutiquey B&B has elegantly stylish rooms with freshly plumped cushions, crisp, white linens, subtly patterned wallpapers and bejewelled lamps. It's about 600m from the train station: walk west down Victoria St and take the second right onto Upper Lattimore Rd.

Lussmanns Eatery MEDITERRANEAN ££

(☎01727-851941; www.lussmans.com; Waxhouse Gate; mains £11-18; ⌚11.30am-10pm Mon-Thu, to 10.30pm Fri & Sat, to 9pm Sun) This bright, modern restaurant just off the High St is enduringly popular with locals despite ample competition around town. It serves a menu of mainly Mediterranean dishes, all in a bright, modern space with oak, leather and metal decor. Ingredients are ethically sourced with plenty of information on the menu about where your food has come from. Book ahead.

Côte Brasserie FRENCH ££

(www.cote-restaurants.co.uk; 3 High St; mains £9-14) For classic French food head to this stylish but unpretentious place, which serves

ST ALBANS BEER FESTIVAL

Beer is big business in England, and to pint-swilling connoisseurs, real ale is the only brew that matters. To celebrate its key role in national culture, Camra (the Campaign for Real Ale) hosts a four-day beer festival in St Albans at the end of September. Over 9000 people converge on the Alban Arena off St Peter's St to sample and talk about the 350-odd real ales on tap and the 500 or so cask and bottled beers, ciders and perries. With food, music and good booze on offer, and tickets a mere £2 to £4, it's a great excuse for a party. For more information, see www.hertsale.org.uk/beerfest.

excellent quality traditional dishes such as *steak frites* and *moules marinières*. It's a chic but chilled-out kind of spot, with great service and simple bistro cooking.

Drinking

TOP CHOICE Ye Olde Fighting Cocks TRADITIONAL PUB

(16 Abbey Mill Lane) Reputedly the oldest pub in England, this unusual, octagon-shaped inn has oodles of charm. Oliver Cromwell spent a night here, stabling his horses in what's now the bar, and underground tunnels lead to the cathedral. Drink in this historic atmosphere while you nurse your pint.

Information

Tourist office (☎01727-864511; www.stalbans.gov.uk; Market Pl; ⏰10am-4.30pm Mon-Sat) In the grand town hall in the marketplace. Can book themed guided walks (adult/child £3/1.50) of the city.

Getting There & Away

Trains run between London St Pancras and St Albans (£9, 20 minutes) every 10 minutes. The station is on Victoria St, 800m east of St Peter's St.

Around St Albans

HATFIELD HOUSE

(www.hatfield-house.co.uk; adult/child £11.50/6, gardens only £6.50/4.50; ⏰noon-5pm Wed-Sun, gardens 11am-5.30pm Wed-Sun) For over 400 years Hatfield House has been home to the Cecils, one of England's most influential political families. This magnificent Jacobean mansion was built between 1607 and 1611 for Robert Cecil, first earl of Salisbury and secretary of state to both Elizabeth I and James I. The house is awash with grandiose portraits, tapestries, furnishings and armour. Look out for the grand marble hall, the stunning carved-oak staircase and the stained glass in the chapel.

Outside, the vast grounds were landscaped by 17th-century botanist John Tradescant, and you can see an old oak tree that marks the spot where Elizabeth I, who spent much of her childhood here, first heard of her accession to the throne.

If you'd really like to get into the character of the house, you can attend a four-course **Elizabethan banquet** (bookings ☎01707-262055; £50), complete with minstrels and court jesters, in the atmospheric Great Hall on Friday nights.

The house is opposite Hatfield train station, and there are trains from London King's Cross station (£8, 20 minutes, half-hourly).

SHAW'S CORNER

(NT; www.nationaltrust.org.uk/shawscorner; Ayot St Lawrence; adult/child £5.50/2.75; ⏰1-5pm Wed-Sun) Preserved in time and much as Shaw left it, Shaw's Corner is a tranquil Arts and Crafts building that was home to George Bernard Shaw (1856–1950) for the last 44 years of his life. His study contains his typewriter, pens, inkwell and dictionaries, and in the garden you can see his writing hut (which revolves to catch the sun) where he penned several works, including *Pygmalion,* the play on which the film *My Fair Lady* was based. The Oscar he received for the screenplay is also on display.

Ayot St Lawrence is 6 miles north of St Albans, off the B651. Bus 304 from St Albans will drop you off at Gustardwood, 1.5 miles from Ayot St Lawrence.

BEDFORDSHIRE & BUCKINGHAMSHIRE

The sweeping valleys and chalky, forested hills of Bedfordshire and Buckinghamshire once attracted the rich and famous, who used them as a rural hideaway for their majestic stately homes. Today, commuters populate the pretty villages surrounding these vast and magnificent estates and enjoy the quiet woodland walks and mountain-bike trails that criss-cross the undulating Chiltern Hills.

Woburn Abbey & Safari Park

The pretty Georgian village of Woburn is home to Bedfordshire's biggest attractions: a palatial stately home and Europe's largest conservation park.

Once a Cistercian abbey but dissolved by Henry VIII and awarded to the earl of Bedford, **Woburn Abbey** (www.woburn.co.uk; adult/child £12.50/6; ⏲11am-4pm) is a wonderful country pile set within a 1200-hectare deer park. The house is stuffed with 18th-century furniture, porcelain and silver, and displays paintings by Gainsborough, van Dyck and Canaletto. Highlights include the bedroom of Queen Victoria and Prince Albert; the beautiful wall hangings and cabinets of the Chinese Room; the mysterious story of the Flying Duchess; and the gilt-adorned dining room. An audio tour brings the history of the house and the people who lived here to life. Outside, the gardens are well worth a wander, and host theatre and music events during the summer months.

On an equally grand scale is **Woburn Safari Park** (www.woburn.co.uk/safari; adult/child £18.50/13.50; ⏲10am-5pm), the country's largest drive-through animal reserve. Rhinos, tigers, lions, zebras, bison, monkeys, elephants and giraffes roam the grounds, while in the 'foot safari' area, you can see sea lions, penguins and lemurs. Pick up a timetable on arrival for information on feeding times, keeper talks and animal demonstrations.

For both attractions, buy a **passport ticket** (adult/child £22.50/15.50), which can be used on two separate days within any 12-month period.

The abbey and safari park are easily accessible by car off the M1 motorway. First Capital Connect runs trains from King's Cross to Flitwick, the nearest station. From here it's a 15-minute taxi journey (£15 to £20) to Woburn.

Waddesdon Manor

Dripping with gilt, crystal chandeliers, tapestries, fine porcelain and elaborate furniture, **Waddesdon Manor** (☎01296-653226; www.waddesdon.org.uk; house & gardens adult/child £15/11; ⏲noon-4pm Wed-Fri, 11am-4pm Sat & Sun) is a stunning Renaissance-style chateau built by Baron Ferdinand de Rothschild to showcase his collection of French decorative arts. The baron liked to do things on a grand scale, and the ostentatious magnificence of the house, designed by French architect Destailleur and completed in 1889, is almost overwhelming.

Very little space is left unadorned – only the Bachelor's Wing stands out as being noticeably more restrained. The baron used the house for his glamorous parties, and it's not hard to imagine the great and good of the 19th century living it up in the palatial rooms. Visitors can view his outstanding collection of art, Sèvres porcelain, expensive furniture and the extensive wine cellar. The house hosts a variety of events throughout the year, from Christmas fairs to wine-tasting days, Valentine's dinners and opera and theatre events. Weekends get busy, so book tickets in advance.

The beautiful **gardens** (gardens only adult/child £7/3.50; ⏲10am-5pm Wed-Sun) boast rare

DIY WEEKEND

Buckinghamshire is littered with pretty villages with half-timbered houses, rose-clad cottages, old coaching inns and ancient parish churches. Grab a map, forget the guidebook and just take to the back roads to explore some of the lesser-known treasures lurking in London's backyard. Visit **Amersham** for half-timbered buildings and charming cottages; **Chenies** for old manor houses and an ancient parish church; **West Wycombe** for cottages and inns so quaint they're protected by the National Trust; or **Chalfont St Giles** and **Chalfont St Peter** for historic connections and picturesque settings.

Further north between Aylesbury and Buckingham, you'll find **Winslow**, home to an 18th-century hall designed by Sir Christopher Wren, and just south of Aylesbury, the quaint thatched cottages of **Wendover** and the half-timbered and Georgian shops in **Great Missenden**. To the north and west of Aylesbury, you'll find the extraordinary architecture of **Claydon House** in Middle Claydon, the duck decoy and tower at **Boarstall** and the 15th-century courthouse in **Long Crendon**.

FANTASTIC MR DAHL

One of the world's most loved children's writers, Roald Dahl, made his home at Great Missenden in Buckinghamshire. The small **Roald Dahl Museum** (www.roalddahl museum.org; 81-83 High St, Great Missenden; adult/child £6/4; ⏲10am-5pm Tue-Fri, 11am-5pm Sat & Sun; 👪) explores his writing and the inspiration behind such favourites as *Charlie and the Chocolate Factory* and *The BFG*.

Young and old are encouraged to get dressed up, make up stories, words and poems or get crafty in the art room. There are regular workshops for children, information and memorabilia on Dahl's life and a chance to explore his writing hut.

In nearby Aylesbury, the award-winning **Roald Dahl Children's Gallery** (www.bucks cc.gov.uk; Buckinghamshire County Museum, Church St, Aylesbury; adult/child £6/4; ⏲10am-5pm Mon-Sat, 2-5pm Sun during school holidays, 3-5pm Mon-Fri, 2-5pm Sun Apr-Jul; 👪) uses the characters from Dahl's children's stories to illustrate all sorts of scientific wizardry, and kids of all ages can investigate the beasts inside James' Giant Peach, explore Fantastic Mr Fox's tunnel and see the Twit's upside-down bedroom. Opening hours are complicated, particularly during term time, so please phone or check the website for details.

Trains to Great Missenden (£8, 40 minutes, hourly) and Aylesbury (£13, one hour, half-hourly) depart from London Marylebone.

flowers, divine views and a Rococo-revival aviary filled with exotic birds.

Waddesdon is 6 miles northwest of Aylesbury off the A41. Trains to Aylesbury (£13, one hour, half-hourly) depart from London Marylebone. From Aylesbury bus station take bus 16 (25 minutes), which runs roughly half-hourly Monday to Friday and every two hours on Saturday.

Bletchley Park

Once England's best-kept secret, **Bletchley Park** (www.bletchleypark.org.uk; The Manor, Bletchley; adult/child/under 12 £10/6/free; ⏲9.30am-5pm) was the scene of a huge codebreaking operation during WWII, dramatised in the film *Enigma*. Almost 8500 people worked here in total secrecy intercepting, decrypting, translating and interpreting enemy correspondence. The exhibitions are a bit dated, though, so join a guided tour (two daily Monday to Friday, hourly at weekends) to get a real insight into the complex codebreaking process and the hard work, frustration and successes that shaped this secret war effort. You can also see a collection of Churchill memorabilia, a computer museum tracing the development of computers from the early Bletchley model 'Colossus' to the modern day, and get an idea of what life was like for civilians during the war.

Bletchley is just south of Milton Keynes off the B4034. Trains run from London Euston to Bletchley (£14, 40 minutes, hourly).

Stowe

Stowe, the sort of private school so exclusive that its driveway is half a mile long, is housed in the neoclassical splendour of **Stowe House** (☎01280-818166; www.stowe.co.uk/house; adult/child £4/2.50; ⏲tours 2pm term time, noon-5pm school holidays). Mere mortals are permitted to visit the eight state rooms, which connect in a 137m enfilade, and offer stunning views of the wonderful grounds. Although the rooms are left bare (the house's contents were sold off to rescue the original owners from financial disaster), the sheer scale and ornamentation of the building is highly impressive. An interpretive centre explains the rise and fall of the family who lived here and offers a glimpse into the elaborate world of Britain's landed gentry in the 18th century. The opening hours for the house are complex, so call or check the website before travelling.

For many, the real draw at Stowe is not the house but the extraordinary **Georgian gardens** (NT; www.nationaltrust.org.uk; adult/child £6.80/3.45; ⏲10.30am-5.30pm Wed-Sun), which cover 400 hectares and were worked on by the greatest British landscape gardeners, including Charles Bridgeman, William Kent and 'Capability' Brown.

The gardens are best known for their 32 temples, created in the 18th century by the wealthy owner Sir Richard Temple, whose family motto was *Templa Quam Delecta* (How Delightful are Your Temples). There are also arches, lakes and a Palladian bridge, among other buildings.

Stowe is 3 miles northwest of Buckingham off the A422.

BERKSHIRE

Long known as the 'Royal County of Berkshire', this rather posh and prosperous part of the world acts as a country getaway for some of England's most influential figures. Within easy reach of London and yet entirely different in character, the pastoral landscape is littered with handsome villages and historic houses as well as some of the top attractions in the country. Few visitors make it past the historic towns of Windsor and Eton, home to the Queen's favourite castle and the world-renowned public school, but wander further afield and you'll be rewarded with tranquil rural countryside and exquisitely maintained villages.

READING FESTIVAL

Each August Bank Holiday weekend, about 80,000 revellers descend on the rather industrial town of Reading for one of the country's biggest music events. The **Reading Festival** (www.readingfestival.com) is a three day extravaganza that features top acts in pop, rock and dance music. Tickets will set you back about £70 per day or £175 for a three-day pass.

Windsor & Eton

POP 30,568

Dominated by the massive bulk and heavy influence of Windsor Castle, these twin towns have a rather surreal atmosphere, with the morning pomp and ceremony of the changing of the guards in Windsor and the sight of school boys dressed in formal tailcoats wandering the streets of Eton.

Windsor Castle, with its romantic architecture and superb state rooms, is an absolute must-see, while across the bridge over the Thames, England's most famous public school has an altogether different flavour. To cater for the droves of tourists that visit these star attractions, Windsor town centre is full of expensive boutiques, grand cafes and trendy restaurants. Eton, by comparison, is far quieter, its pedestrianised centre lined with antique shops and art galleries. Both towns exude an air of affluence, and if you're travelling on a tight budget, a day-trip from London is probably your best bet.

Sights

Windsor Castle CASTLE

(www.royalcollection.org.uk; adult/child £16/9.50; 9.45am-5.15pm) The largest and oldest occupied fortress in the world, Windsor Castle is a majestic vision of battlements and towers used for state occasions and as the Queen's weekend retreat.

William the Conqueror first established a royal residence in Windsor in 1070 when he built a motte and bailey here, the only naturally defendable spot in the Thames valley. Since then successive monarchs have rebuilt, remodelled and refurbished the castle complex to create the massive and sumptuous palace that stands here today. Henry II replaced the wooden stockade in 1165 with a stone round tower and built the outer walls to the north, east and south; Charles II gave the state apartments a baroque makeover; George IV swept in with his preference for Gothic style; and Queen Victoria refurbished a beautiful chapel in memory of her beloved Albert.

The castle largely escaped the bombings of WWII, but in 1992 a devastating fire tore through the building, destroying or damaging more than 100 rooms. By chance, the most important treasures were in storage at the time, and with skilled craftsmanship and painstaking restoration, the rooms were returned to their former glory.

Join a free guided tour (every half hour) or take a multilingual audio tour of the lavish state rooms and beautiful chapels. The State Apartments and St George's Chapel are closed at times during the year; check the website for details. If the Queen is in residence, you'll see the Royal Standard flying from the Round Tower.

Windsor Castle is one of England's most popular attractions. Come early and be prepared to queue.

Queen Mary's Dolls' House

Your first sight will be an incredible dolls' house, designed by Sir Edwin Lutyens for Queen Mary in 1924. The attention to detail is spellbinding – there's running water, electricity and lighting and vintage wine in the cellar! The house was intended to accurately depict households of the day, albeit on a scale of 1:12.

State Apartments

After the dolls' house, a **gallery** with drawings by Leonardo da Vinci and a **China Museum**, you'll enter the stunning State Apartments, which are home to some exquisite paintings and architecture and are still used by the Queen.

The **Grand Staircase** sets the tone for the rooms, all of which are elaborate, opulent and suitably regal. Highlights include **St George's Hall,** which incurred the most damage during the fire of 1992. The dining chairs here, dwarfed by the scale of the room, are standard size. On the ceiling, the shields of the Knights of the Garter (originally from George IV's time here) were recreated after the fire.

For intimate gatherings (just 60 people), the Queen entertains in the **Waterloo Chamber** – the super shiny table is French-polished and then dusted by someone walking over it with dusters on their feet. During large parties, this room is used for dancing and the table is tripled in size and set up in St George's Hall.

The **King's Dressing Room** has some of the most important Renaissance paintings in the royal collection. Alongside Sir Anthony van Dyck's magnificent *Triple Portrait* of Charles I, you will see works by Hans Holbein, Rembrandt, Peter Paul Rubens and Albrecht Dürer. Charles II kipped in here instead of in the **King's Bedchamber** – maybe George IV's magnificent bed (now on display) would have tempted him.

St George's Chapel

This elegant chapel, commissioned for the Order of the Garter by Edward IV in 1475, is one of Britain's finest examples of Perpendicular Gothic architecture. The nave and fan-vaulted roof were completed under

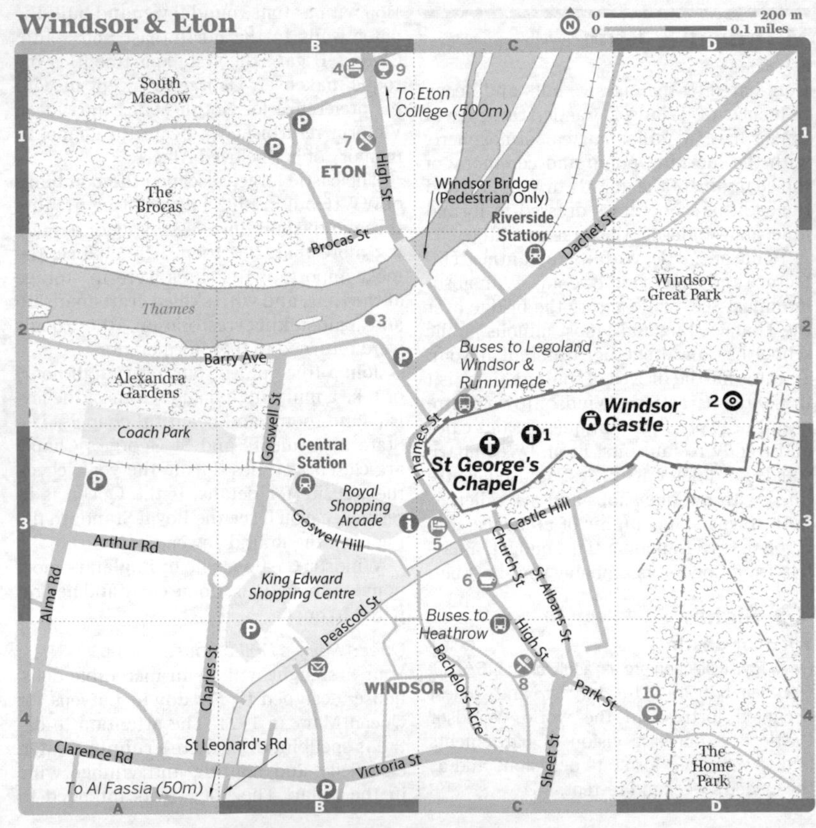

Henry VII, but the final nail was struck under Henry VIII in 1528.

The chapel – along with Westminster Abbey – serves as a **royal mausoleum**, and its tombs read like a history of the British monarchy. The most recent royal burial occurred in April 2002, when the body of George VI's widow, Queen Elizabeth, the Queen Mother (1900–2002), was transported here in a splendid and sombre procession and buried alongside her husband. And in April 2005, Prince Charles and Camilla Parker-Bowles were blessed here following their civil marriage in the town's Guildhall.

St George's Chapel closes on Sunday, but time your visit well and you can attend **Evensong** at 5.15pm daily except Wednesday.

Albert Memorial Chapel

Originally built in 1240 and dedicated to Edward the Confessor, this small chapel was the place of worship for the Order of the Garter until St George's Chapel snatched that honour. After the death of Prince Albert at Windsor Castle in 1861, Queen Victoria ordered its elaborate redecoration as a tribute to her husband. A major feature of the restoration is the magnificent vaulted roof, whose gold mosaic pieces were crafted in Venice. There's a monument to the prince, although he's actually buried with Queen Victoria in the Frogmore Royal Mausoleum in the castle grounds.

Windsor Great Park

Stretching behind Windsor Castle almost all the way to Ascot, Windsor Great Park covers about 40 sq miles and features a lake, walking tracks, a bridleway and gardens. The **Savill Garden** (www.theroyallandscape.co.uk; adult/child £8/3.75; ⏲10am-6pm) is particularly lovely and has a stunning visitor centre. The Savill Garden is about 4 miles south of Windsor Castle. Take the A308 out of town and follow the brown signs.

The **Long Walk** is a 3-mile jaunt along a tree-lined path from King George IV Gate to the Copper Horse statue (of George III) on Snow Hill, the highest point of the park. The Queen can occasionally be spotted driving down the Long Walk, accompanied only by a bodyguard. The walk is signposted from the town centre.

Changing of the guard

A fabulous spectacle of pomp, with loud commands, whispered conversations, triumphant tunes from a military band and plenty of shuffling and stamping of feet, the **changing of the guard** (11am Mon-Sat Apr-Jul, alternate days Aug-Mar) draws the crowds to the castle gates each day. It's a must for any visitor, but you'll get a better view if you stay to the right of the crowd.

Eton College BOYS' SCHOOL

Cross the bridge over the Thames to Eton and you'll enter another world, one where old-school values and traditions seem to ooze from the very walls. The streets here are surprisingly hushed as you make your way down to the most enduring and illustrious symbol of England's class system, **Eton College** (www.etoncollege.com; adult/child £6.20/5.20; ⏲guided tours 2pm & 3.15pm daily during school holidays, Wed, Fri, Sat & Sun during term time).

Those who have studied here include 18 prime ministers, countless princes, kings and maharajahs, famous explorers, authors, and economists – among them the Duke of Wellington, Princes William and Harry, George Orwell, Ian Fleming, Aldous Huxley, Sir Ranulph Fiennes and John Maynard Keynes.

Eton is the largest and most famous public (meaning very private) school in England. It was founded by Henry VI in 1440 with a view towards educating 70 highly qualified boys awarded a scholarship from a fund endowed by the king. Every year

Windsor & Eton

Top Sights

St George's Chapel ... C3
Windsor Castle ... C2

Sights

1 Albert Memorial Chapel ... C3
2 State Apartments ... D2

Activities, Courses & Tours

3 French Brothers ... B2

Sleeping

4 Christopher Hotel ... B1
5 Harte & Garter Hotel ... C3

Eating

6 Crooked House Tea Rooms ... C3
7 Gilbey's ... B1
8 Green Olive ... C4
Tower ... (see 5)

Drinking

9 Henry VI ... B1
10 Two Brewers ... D4

since then, 70 King's Scholars (aged 12 to 14) have been chosen based on the results of a highly competitive exam; these pupils are housed in separate quarters from the rest of the 1300 or so other students, who are known as Oppidans.

While the King's Scholars are chosen exclusively on the basis of exam results, Oppidans must be able to foot the bill for £28,800 per annum fees as well as passing entrance exams. All the boys are boarders and must comply with the strong traditions at Eton. The boys still wear formal tailcoats, waistcoats and white collars to lessons, the school language is full of in-house jargon, and fencing, shooting, polo and beagling are on the list of school sporting activities.

Luckily for the rest of us, the college is open to visitors taking the guided tour, which gives a fascinating insight into how this most elite of schools functions. Tours take in the **chapel** (which you can see from Windsor Castle), the **cloisters**, the **Museum of Eton Life**, the **lower school** and the **school yard**. As you wander round, you may recognise some of the buildings, as the college is often used as a film set. *Chariots of Fire*, *The Madness of King George*, *Mrs Brown* and *Shakespeare in Love* are just some of the movies that have been filmed here. To get here cross the bridge to Eton and follow the High St to its end.

Legoland Windsor THEME PARK
(www.legoland.co.uk; adult/3-15yr £38/28; ⌚hours vary) A fun-filled theme park of white-knuckle rides, Legoland is more about the thrills of scaring yourself silly than the joys of building your own make-believe castle from the eponymous bricks. The professionals have already done this for you, with almost 40 million Lego bricks transformed into some of the world's greatest landmarks. You'll also get live shows, 3-D cinema and slightly tamer activities for the less adventurous. If you prebook online, you can save about £8 off the whopping ticket prices.

The Legoland shuttle bus departs opposite the Theatre Royal from 10am, with the last bus returning 30 minutes after the park has closed.

Tours

City Sightseeing BUS TOURS
(www.city-sightseeing.com; adult/child £8/4; ⌚every 20 mins) Open-top double-decker bus tours depart from Castle Hill opposite the Harte & Garter Hotel.

French Brothers BOAT TOURS
(www.frenchbrothers.co.uk; Clewer Court Rd; ⌚11am-5pm Easter-Oct) Run a variety of boat trips to Runnymede (adult/child £5.20/2.60, 45 minutes) and around Windsor and Eton (adult/child £8.40/4.20, two hours). Boats leave from just next to Windsor Bridge. If you fancy doing the hop-on/hop-off bus plus a 35-minute boat trip, a combined boat and bus ticket costs £12.50/6 per adult/child.

Tourist Office WALKING TOURS
(☎01753-743900; www.windsor.gov.uk; adult/child £6/3; ⌚11.30am Sat & Sun) Themed guided walks of the city.

A WORLD FIRST

In June 1215, King John met his barons and bishops in a large field 3 miles southeast of Windsor, and over the next few days they hammered out an agreement on a basic charter of rights guaranteeing the liberties of the king's subjects and restricting the monarch's absolute power. The document they signed was the Magna Carta, the world's first constitution. It formed the basis for statutes and charters throughout the world's democracies. (Both the national and state constitutions of the United States, drawn up more than 500 years later, paraphrase this document.)

Runnymede (⌚9am-5pm) – from the Anglo-Saxon words *ruinige* (take council) and *moed* (meadow) – was chosen because it was the largest piece of open land between the king's residence at Windsor and the bishop's palace at Staines. Today, the field remains pretty much as it was, except that now it features two **lodges** (1930) designed by Sir Edward Lutyens. In the woods behind the field are two **memorials**, the first to the Magna Carta designed by Sir Edward Maufe (1957). The second is to John F Kennedy, and was built by Geoffrey Jellicoe in 1965 on an acre of land granted in perpetuity to the US government following Kennedy's assassination.

Runnymede is on the A308, 3 miles southeast of Windsor. Bus 71 stops near here on the Windsor–Egham route.

Sleeping

Windsor has a good selection of quality hotels and B&Bs, but few budget options.

Harte & Garter HOTEL £££
(01753-863426; www.foliohotels.com/harteandgarter; High St; d from £135;) Right opposite the castle, this Victorian hotel blends period style with modern furnishings. High ceilings, giant fireplaces, decorative cornices and dark woods seamlessly combine with contemporary fabrics, plasma-screen TVs and traditional, cast-iron baths. Some rooms enjoy wonderful views over the castle, and all guests can enjoy the luxurious spa in the converted stable block.

Frances Lodge B&B ££
(01753-832019; www.franceslodge.co.uk; 53 Frances Rd; s/d £70/90;) Set in a traditional Victorian villa, this contemporary B&B blends original period features with simple, uncluttered minimalism. Cool neutral colour schemes, stylish bathrooms, an extremely warm welcome and the relaxed atmosphere make it a great bet. Frances Lodge is 700m from High St along Sheet St.

Christopher Hotel HOTEL £££
(01753-852359; www.thechristopher.co.uk; High St, Eton; d from £120;) Set in a former coaching inn, this modern hotel offers clean-cut, uncluttered rooms with contemporary, if a little corporate, styling. The grill downstairs has big windows overlooking the street, and serves up a modern European menu (mains £9 to £15) in slick surroundings.

Eating

You'll find plenty of choice when it comes to restaurants, try Peascod St and the Windsor Royal Shopping Arcade for the old reliables.

Gilbey's MODERN BRITISH ££
(01753-854921; www.gilbeygroup.com; 82-83 High St, Eton; mains £14.50-20) Small but perfectly formed, this little restaurant with a big heart is one of the area's finest. Terracotta tiling and a sunny courtyard garden and conservatory give Gilbey's a Continental cafe feel. But the bold artwork and understated decor are reflected in a superb modern British menu, which is almost surpassed by the wide and interesting choice of wines.

Green Olive GREEK £
(01753-866655; www.green-olive.co.uk; 10 High St; mezedhes £4-10) A great spot for a light lunch or tantalising evening meal, Green Olive dishes up generous portions of traditional Greek *mezedhes* in bright, simple surroundings. You can choose from over 50 different dishes and combine a riot of flavours before rolling out the door.

Tower CLASSIC BRITISH ££
(01753-863426; High St; mains £9-16) Giant windows with views over the castle give this place an immediate allure, as do the grand chandeliers and high ceilings. The menu is brasserie style with a choice of classic British cuisine, featuring grills, fish and steaks simply and perfectly done. It's also a good spot to sample the finest of English institutions, afternoon tea.

Other options:

Al Fassia MOROCCAN ££
(27 St Leonard's Rd; mains £9.50-12.50; closed Sun) An atmospheric Moroccan restaurant with traditional decor and menu.

Crooked House Tea Rooms TEAROO £
(www.crooked-house.com; 51 High St; afternoon teas from £8; 9.30am-5.30pm) A traditional tearoom complete with sloping floors, wooden beams and royal cream teas.

Drinking

Windsor and Eton are packed with pubs, with a cluster of late-night venues situated under the railway arches of the central station.

WORTH A TRIP

ROYAL ASCOT

Get out your Sunday best and join the glitterati at **Royal Ascot** (www.ascot.co.uk) for the biggest racing meet of the year. The royal family, A-list celebrities and the rich and famous gather here to show off their Jimmy Choos and place the odd bet. The four-day festival takes place in mid-June, and it's essential to book tickets well in advance. You can soak up the atmosphere from the Silver Ring for a mere £18 per day, or head for the Grandstand and Paddock, where you can rub shoulders with the great and the good for £58 per day. Just make sure you dress to impress.

TOP CHOICE **Two Brewers** TRADITIONAL PUB
(34 Park St) This 17th-century inn perched on the edge of Windsor Great Park is close to the castle's tradesmen's entrance and supposedly frequented by staff from the castle. It's a quaint and cosy place, with dim lighting, obituaries to castle footmen and royal photographs with irreverent captions on the wall.

Henry VI PUB
(37 High St, Eton) Another old pub, but this time the low ceilings and subtle lighting are mixed with leather sofas and modern design. It's the kind of place where you can sit back with an afternoon pint and read the paper. There's a nice garden for alfresco dining and live music at weekends.

Information

Royal Windsor Information Centre (www.windsor.gov.uk; Old Booking Hall, Windsor Royal Shopping Arcade; ⌚9.30am-5pm Mon-Sat, 10am-4pm Sun) Has information on a self-guided heritage walk around town.

Getting There & Away

Bus 702 connects Windsor with **London Victoria** coach station (£8.50, one hour, hourly), and bus 77 connects Windsor with **Heathrow** airport (one hour, hourly).

Trains from Windsor Central station on Thames St go to **London Paddington** (30 to 45 minutes). Trains from Windsor Riverside station go to **London Waterloo** (one hour). Services run half-hourly from both stations and tickets cost £8.

Wessex

Includes »

Best Places to Eat

» Hix Oyster & Fish House (p282)

» Boathouse (p266)

» Truffles (p256)

» Circus (p318)

» Bordeaux Quay (p307)

Best Places to Stay

» Urban Beach (p269)

» Queensberry Hotel (p317)

» Really Green (p267)

» Beggar's Knap (p276)

» Farmer's Inn (p329)

Why Go?

With Wessex you get the cream of ancient England. This laid-back corner of the country is packed with prime prehistoric sites. They range from iconic stone circles to monumental Iron Age hillforts, and their legacy comes coupled with a cheerful counter-culture vibe. This rolling, lyrical landscape still echoes with the myths of King Arthur and Alfred the Great – and with the writings of Thomas Hardy, Jane Austen and John Fowles. And there are more riches: blockbuster stately homes, quaint thatched villages and a unique historic dockyard. Architectural eye-candy is everywhere, including Roman remains, romantic castles, serene cathedrals and Bath's sumptuous Georgian cityscape. Throw in two wildlife-rich national parks and a shoreline studded with bewitching bays and towering rock formations, and you have a bit of a dilemma. With Wessex it's not so much why go as what to do first.

When to Go

Wessex appeals at any time of year, but spring, summer and early autumn enjoy better weather; they're also when most sights are open. In April and May, cliffs, hillsides and formal gardens burst into a profusion of fragrance and blooms. June offers the chance to catch music festival fever at ultra-cool Glastonbury and on the funky Isle of Wight. In July and August, coastal areas and blockbuster city sights can get overwhelmed by visitor numbers. But early September brings the end of school summer holidays, cheaper sleeping spots, quieter beaches and warmer seas.

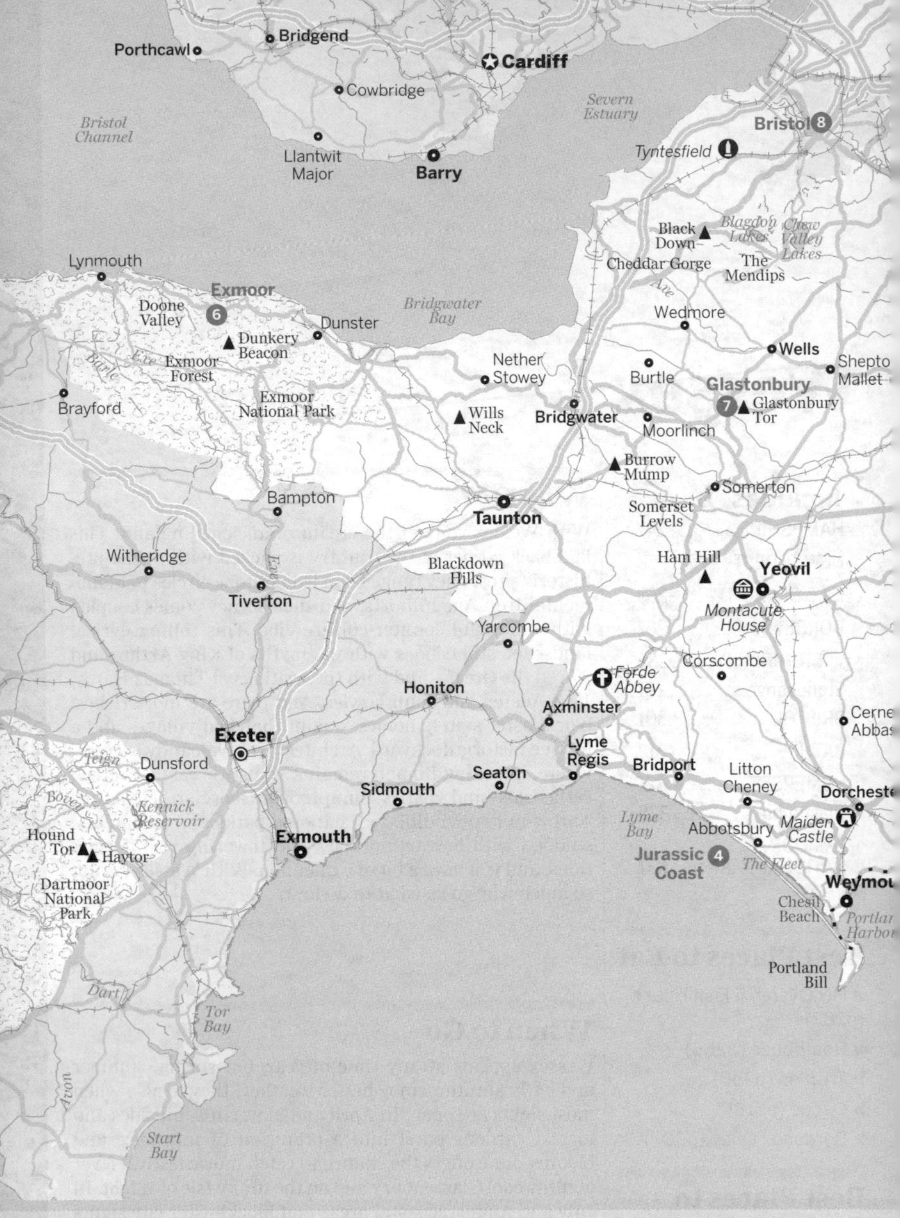

Wessex Highlights

1 Bagging a place on a memorable, early-morning walk inside the massive sarsen ring at **Stonehenge** (p291)

2 Sleeping in style inside the vast, mystical stone circle at **Avebury** (p300)

3 Cooling off (or warming up) in a flashy new spa in **Bath** (p317)

4 Foraging for 200-million-year-old fossils in Dorset's constantly crumbling **Jurassic Coast** (p282)

5 Clambering aboard the pride of Nelson's navy in the historic dockyard at **Portsmouth** (p253)

6 Taking a dawn wildlife safari on **Exmoor** (p331)

7 Having your very own happy, hippie happening at **Glastonbury** (p325)

8 Stepping onto Brunel's groundbreaking transatlantic steamer, **SS Great Britain** (p301)

9 Chilling out in the funky holiday haven that is the **Isle of Wight** (p263)

History

Wessex can trace its human history back as far as the Stone Age; a 9000-year-old skeleton was found at Cheddar Gorge. By 3000 BC a complex tribal society with clearly defined social hierarchies and shared religious beliefs had developed. This so-called Wessex culture built the magnificent stone circles of Stonehenge and Avebury, as well as the many barrows and processional avenues nearby. Centuries later, Iron Age peoples engineered massive forts at Maiden Castle (p277) and Old Sarum (p290), before being subjugated by the Romans – it is their city of Aquae Sulis that we now known as Bath.

The Anglo-Saxon kingdom of Wessex was founded by King Cerdic in the 6th century after the Romans withdrew. At the kingdom's heart was land now covered by Hampshire, Dorset, Wiltshire and Somerset, but borders shifted over the centuries, and at its height the kingdom stretched from Kent in the east to Cornwall in the west. The most famous ruler was King Alfred (r 871–99), who made Winchester his capital and ensured that Wessex was the only sizeable part of the Anglo-Saxon lands not overrun by the Danes. Wessex was officially incorporated into the kingdom of England in the mid-9th century.

Dorset novelist Thomas Hardy revived the name of Wessex 1000 years later and used it as the setting for his novels – initially in *Far from the Madding Crowd*. The old title Earl of Wessex, which had last been awarded in the 11th century, was only recently revived and presently belongs to HRH Prince Edward.

Activities

CYCLING

Gentle gradients and quiet rural lanes make Wessex ideal for cycling. In the New Forest (see boxed text, p261), hundreds of miles of cycle-paths snake through a historic, rural environment. Wiltshire is also a highlight – the 160-mile circular **Wiltshire Cycleway** is a good option for long or short rides. The Isle of Wight has 62 miles of bike-friendly routes and its own cycling festival (see p263).

The **West Country Way** (p331) is a fabulously varied 250-mile jaunt from Bristol to Padstow in Cornwall. Exmoor provides some superb, and testing, off-road cycling, as do the fields, woods and heathland of the 19km-long Quantock Hills (p328), an Area of Outstanding Natural Beauty (AONB) that peaks at 300m. The North Wessex Downs provide gentler terrain and take in the World Heritage Site of Avebury, the market towns of Marlborough and Hungerford and the western part of the Ridgeway National Trail.

WALKING

This is a fantastic region for hitting the trail. Top spots include Exmoor, the Mendips, the Quantock Hills and the Isle of Wight. The rugged **South West Coast Path** (www.southwestcoastpath.com) runs along the region's northern and southern shores, cutting through some of the main coastal towns en route.

In northeastern Wiltshire, the Ridgeway National Trail starts near Avebury and winds 44 miles through chalk hills to the River Thames at Goring in Oxfordshire. The route then continues another 41 miles (another three days' walk) through the Chiltern Hills.

OTHER ACTIVITIES

Water sports draw many to Wessex's coasts. Highlights are the Olympic venues at Weymouth and Portland (boxed text, p280), the yachting havens of the Isle of Wight (p263), and the watery playgrounds of Poole (p271), where you can try your hand at everything from kitesurfing to powerboating. Horse riding, fishing and falconry are available on Exmoor, while beachcombing takes on a whole new meaning around Lyme Regis, where the Jurassic Coast serves up superb fossil hunting (see boxed text, p282).

Information

County-specific websites are listed throughout this chapter.

www.visitsouthwest.co.uk Info on the west of the region.

www.visit-hampshire.co.uk Covers the east.

Getting Around

Traveline South West (www.travelinesw.com) Region-wide information about bus and train routes.

Bus

Local bus services are fairly comprehensive, but it pays to have your own wheels to reach the more remote spots. Route maps and timetables are available online and at tourist offices.

First (www.firstgroup.com) The region's largest bus company. The FirstDay Southwest ticket (adult/child/family £7.10/5.80/16.50) is valid for one day on most First buses.

PlusBus (www.plusbus.info) Adds local bus travel to your train ticket (from £1.60 per day).

Participating cities include Bath, Bristol, Taunton and Weymouth; buy tickets at train stations.

Stagecoach (www.stagecoachbus.com) Key provider in Hampshire; does a one-day Explorer Ticket (adult/child/family £6.50/4/16).

Wilts & Dorset (www.wdbus.co.uk) Seven-day network tickets (£20) can be used on all their buses.

Car & Motorcycle

There are plenty of car-hire companies in the region, often located around airports and mainline train stations. Rates are similar to elsewhere in the UK, starting at around £35 per day for a small hatchback (see p848).

Train

The main railway hub is Bristol, which has links to London, the southwest, the Midlands, the north and Scotland. In the south, Weymouth, Bournemouth, Southampton and Portsmouth are linked to London and Bath.

Freedom of the SouthWest Rover pass (adult/child £95/45) Allows eight days' unlimited travel over 15 days in an area that includes Salisbury, Bath, Bristol and Weymouth.

HAMPSHIRE

Hampshire is the historic heart of Wessex. Kings Alfred the Great, Knut and William the Conqueror all based their reigns in the ancient cathedral city of Winchester, whose jumble of historic buildings sits in the centre of undulating chalk downs. The county's coast is awash with heritage too – in rejuvenated Portsmouth you can clamber aboard the pride of Nelson's navy, HMS *Victory*, wonder at artefacts from the *Mary Rose* (Henry VIII's flagship), and wander wharfs buzzing with restaurants, shops and bars. Hampshire's southwestern corner claims the open heath and woods of the New Forest and, just offshore, the hip holiday hotspot that is the Isle of Wight – both areas are covered in separate sections in this chapter.

Winchester

POP 41,420

Calm, collegiate Winchester is a mellow must-see for all visitors. The past still echoes strongly around the flint-flecked walls of this ancient cathedral city. It was the capital of Saxon kings and a power base of bishops, and its statues and sights evoke two of England's mightiest myth-makers: Alfred the Great and King Arthur (he of the round table). Winchester's architecture is exquisite, from the handsome Elizabethan and Regency buildings in the narrow winding streets to the wondrous cathedral at its core. Thanks to its location, nestled in a valley of the River Itchen, there are also charming waterside trails to explore, and the city marks the beginning of the beautiful South Downs Way (see p129).

History

The Romans first put their feet under the table here, but Winchester really took off when the powerful West Saxon bishops moved their episcopal see here in AD 670. Thereafter, Winchester was the most important town in the powerful kingdom of Wessex. King Alfred the Great (r 871–99) made it his capital, and it remained so under Knut (r 1016–35) and the Danish kings. After the Norman invasion of 1066, William the Conqueror arrived here to claim the English throne. In 1086 he commissioned local monks to write the ground-breaking *Domesday Book*, an administrative survey of the entire country and the most significant clerical accomplishment of the Middle Ages. Winchester thrived until the 12th century, when a fire gutted most of the city – after this, London took its crown. A long slump lasted until the 18th century, when the town was revived as a trading centre.

Sights

Winchester Cathedral CATHEDRAL
(www.winchester-cathedral.org.uk; adult/child £6/free, combined admission & tower tour £9; 9am-5pm Mon-Sat, 12.30-3pm Sun) Almost

A COTTAGE OF YOUR OWN

After a rural bolt-hole far from the maddening crowd? Then check out these companies for self-catering cottages.

Dorset Coastal Cottages (www.dorsetcoastalcottages.com)

Dream Cottages (www.dream-cottages.co.uk)

Farm & Cottage Holidays (www.holidaycottages.co.uk)

Hideaways (www.hideaways.co.uk)

a thousand years of history are crammed into Winchester's cathedral, which is not only the city's star attraction but also one of southern England's most awe-inspiring buildings. The exterior, with a squat tower and a slightly sunken rear, isn't at first glance appealing, despite a fine Gothic facade. But the interior contains one of the longest **medieval naves** (164m) in Europe, and a fascinating jumble of features from all eras.

The cathedral sits beside foundations that mark the town's original 7th-century minster church. The cathedral was begun in 1070 and completed in 1093, and was subsequently entrusted with the bones of its patron saint, St Swithin (bishop of Winchester from 852 to 862). He is best known for the proverb that states that if it rains on St Swithin's Day (15 July) it will rain for a further 40 days and 40 nights.

Soggy ground and poor workmanship spelled disaster for the early church; the original tower collapsed in 1107 and major restructuring continued until the mid-15th century. Look out for the monument at the rear to diver William Walker, who saved the cathedral from collapse by delving repeatedly into its waterlogged underbelly from 1906 to 1912 to bolster rotting wooden foundations with vast quantities of concrete and brick.

The transepts are the most original parts of the cathedral, and the intricately carved **medieval choir stalls** are another must-see, sporting everything from mythical beasts to a mischievous green man.

Evensong is held at 5.30pm Monday to Saturday. On Sunday services take place at 8am and 10am, with evensong at 3.30pm.

The cathedral's tree-fringed lawns are a tranquil spot to take time out, especially on the quieter south side beyond the cloisters; the permanent second-hand book stall in the Deanery porch provides great bargain hunting.

Cathedral Library & Triforium Gallery
(⌚10.30am-3.30pm Tue-Sat, 2-4pm Mon Apr-Oct) Tucked away on the south side of the nave, this section provides a fine elevated view of the cathedral body and contains the dazzlingly illuminated pages of the 12th-century **Winchester Bible** – its colours as bright as if it was painted yesterday.

Jane Austen's Grave
Jane Austen, one of England's best-loved authors, is buried near the entrance in the cathedral's northern aisle. Austen died a stone's throw from the cathedral in 1817 at **Jane Austen's House** (8 College St), where

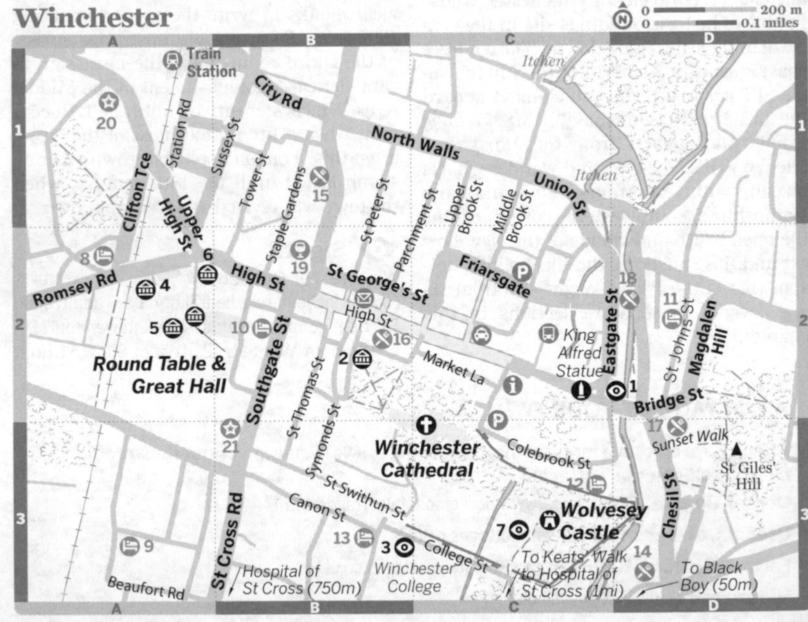

she spent her last six weeks. It's now a private residence and is marked by a slate plaque. Her former home is 18 miles away; see p251.

Tours

FREE **Cathedral body tours** (hourly 10am-3pm Mon-Sat) last one hour. **Tower and roof tours** (£6; tours at 2.15pm Wed & Sat, plus 11.30am Sat) see you clambering up narrow stairwells, and being rewarded with fine views as far as the Isle of Wight. There's an extra tour at 2.15pm Monday to Friday in July and August; tours are only open to those aged between 12 and 70, for safety reasons. FREE **Crypt Tours** (10.30am, 12.30pm & 2.30pm Mon-Sat Apr-Oct) aren't always available because of flooding. If the crypt is open, look out for the poignant solitary sculpture by Anthony Gormley called *Sound 2*.

The Round Table & Great Hall HISTORIC ARTFFACT

(Castle Ave; suggested donation adult/child £1/50p; 10am-5pm) Winchester's other showpiece sight is the cavernous Great Hall, the only part of 11th-century Winchester Castle that Oliver Cromwell spared from destruction. Crowning the wall like a giant-sized dartboard of green and cream spokes is what centuries of mythology have dubbed King Arthur's Round Table. It's actually a 700-year-old copy, but is fascinating nonetheless. It's thought to have been constructed in the late 13th century and then painted in the reign of Henry VIII (King Arthur's image is unsurprisingly reminiscent of Henry's youthful face).

This hall was also the stage for several dramatic English courtroom dramas, including the trial of adventurer Sir Walter Raleigh in 1603, who was sentenced to death but received a reprieve at the last minute.

FREE **Wolvesey Castle** CASTLE

(EH; www.english-heritage.org.uk; 10am-5pm Apr-Sep) The fantastic, crumbling remains of early 12th-century Wolvesey Castle huddle in the protective embrace of the city's walls, despite the building having been largely demolished in the 1680s. It was completed by Henry de Blois, and it served as the Bishop of Winchester's residence throughout the medieval era. Queen Mary I and Philip II of Spain celebrated their wedding feast here in 1554. According to legend, its odd name comes from a Saxon king's demand for an annual payment of 300 wolves' heads. Access is via College St. Today the bishop lives in the (private) **Wolvesey Palace** next door.

Winchester College SCHOOL

(www.winchestercollege.org; College St; tours £4; tours at 10.45am & noon Mon-Sat, plus 2.15pm & 3.30pm Fri, Sat & Sun) Winchester College gives you a rare chance to nosey around a prestigious English private school. It was set up by William Wykeham, Bishop of Winchester in 1393, 14 years after he founded Oxford's New College. Hour-long guided tours trail through the school's medieval

Winchester

Top Sights

- Round Table & Great Hall ... A2
- Winchester Cathedral ... C3
- Wolvesey Castle ... C3

Sights

- 1 City Mill ... D2
- 2 City Museum ... B2
- Gurkha Museum ... (see 5)
- 3 Jane Austen's House ... B3
- 4 Royal Green Jackets Museum ... A2
- 5 Horsepower ... A2
- 6 Westgate Museum ... A2
- 7 Wolvesey Palace ... C3

Sleeping

- 8 5 Clifton Terrace ... A2
- 9 Dolphin House ... A3
- 10 Hotel du Vin ... B2
- 11 No 21 ... D2
- 12 Wolvesey View ... C3
- 13 Wykeham Arms ... B3

Eating

- 14 Black Rat ... D3
- 15 Brasserie Blanc ... B1
- 16 Cadogan & James ... B2
- 17 Chesil Rectory ... D3
- 18 El Sabio ... D2
- Wykeham Arms ... (see 13)

Drinking

- 19 Plain & Fancy ... B2
- Wykeham Arms ... (see 13)

Entertainment

- 20 Railway Inn ... A1
- 21 Screen ... B3

core, taking in the 14th-century Gothic chapel, complete with wooden vaulted roof, the dining room (called College Hall), and a vast 17th-century open classroom (called School), where exams are still held. It's all deeply atmospheric and unshakably affluent; a revealing insight into how the other half learns. Tours start from the Porter's Lodge.

Hospital of St Cross HISTORIC HOSPITAL
(www.stcrosshospital.co.uk; St Cross Rd; adult/child £3/1; ⏲9.30am-5pm Mon-Sat, 1-5pm Sun Apr-Oct, 10.30am-3.30pm Mon-Sat Nov-Mar) Monk, bishop, knight, politician and grandson of William the Conqueror, Henry de Blois was a busy man. But he found time to establish this still-impressive hospital in 1132. As well as healing the sick and housing the needy, the hospital was built to feed and house pilgrims and crusaders en route to the Holy Land. It's the oldest charitable institution in the country, and is still roamed by 25 elderly black- or red-gowned brothers in pie-shaped trencher hats, who continue to hand out alms. Take a peek into the stumpy church, the brethren hall, the kitchen and the peaceful gardens. The best way to arrive is via the one-mile Keats' Walk (right). Upon entering, claim the centuries-old Wayfarer's Dole – a crust of bread and horn of ale (now a small swig of beer) from the Porter's Gate.

Military Museums MUSEUM
Of Winchester's clutch of army museums, the pick is the **Royal Green Jackets Museum** (The Rifles; www.winchestermilitarymuseums.co.uk; Peninsula Barracks, Romsey Rd; adult/child £3/1; ⏲10am-5pm Mon-Sat, noon-4pm Sun), which has a mini rifle-shooting range, a room of 6000 medals and an impressive blow-by-blow diorama of Napoleon's downfall, the Battle of Waterloo. The **Gurkha Museum** (www.thegurkhamuseum.co.uk; Peninsula Barracks, Romsey Rd; adult/child £2/free; ⏲10am-5pm Mon-Sat, noon-4pm Sun) features the regiment's history, combining a jungle tableau with a history of Gurkha service to the British crown.

FREE **Horsepower** (www.horsepowermuseum.co.uk; Peninsula Barracks, Romsey Rd; ⏲10am-4pm Tue-Fri, noon-4pm Sat & Sun) gallops through the combat history of the Royal Hussars, from the Charge of the Light Brigade to armour-clad vehicles.

FREE **Westgate Museum** MUSEUM
(High St; ⏲10am-5pm Mon-Sat, noon-5pm Sun Apr-Oct) This is one for fans of the grisly bit of history. Set in a medieval gateway that was once a debtors' prison, it boasts a macabre set of gibbeting irons used to display an executed criminal's body in 1777 and, scrawled crudely all over the interior walls, the 17th-century graffiti of prisoners.

FREE **City Museum** MUSEUM
(The Square; ⏲10am-5pm Mon-Sat, noon-5pm Sun Apr-Oct, 10am-4pm Tue-Sat, noon-4pm Sun Nov-Mar) Whizzes through Winchester's Roman and Saxon history, lingers on its Anglo-Norman golden age, pays homage to Jane Austen, and reconstructs several early 20th-century Winchester shops.

City Mill HISTORIC MILL
(NT; www.nationaltrust.co.uk; Bridge St; adult/child £4/2; ⏲10.30am-5pm Feb-Dec) See the city's 18th-century water-powered mill in action and buy stone-ground flour in the shop.

Activities

Winchester has a tempting range of walks. The one-mile **Keats' Walk** meanders through the water meadows to the Hospital of St Cross. Its beauty is said to have prompted the poet to pen the ode 'To Autumn' – pick up the trail near Winchester College. Alternatively, head down Wharf Hill, through the water meadows to St Catherine's Hill (1 mile). The tranquil **Riverside Walk** trails a short distance from the castle along the bank of the River Itchen to High St. The stiffer **Sunset Walk** up St Giles' Hill rewards with fine city views, especially at dusk. To get here head up East or Magdalen Hills. St Giles' Hill is also the beginning (or end) of the South Downs Way (p129).

Tours

Guided Walks HISTORY
(adult/child £4/free; ⏲11am & 2.30pm Mon-Sat Apr-Oct, 11am Sat Nov-Mar) Tourist office–

DON'T MISS

STATELY HOMES

» Osborne House (p265)
» Wilton House (p290)
» Kingston Lacy (p272)
» Longleat (p293)
» Montacute House (p330)

WORTH A TRIP

JANE AUSTEN'S HOUSE MUSEUM

There's more than a touch of the period dramas she inspired about the former home of Jane Austen (1775–1817) in Chawton village. This appealing red-brick house, where the celebrated English novelist lived with her mother and sister from 1809 to 1817, is now a **museum** (www.jane-austens-house-museum.org.uk; Chawton; adult/child £7/2; ⏲10.30am-4.30pm mid-Feb–Dec). While here she wrote *Mansfield Park, Emma* and *Persuasion*, and revised *Sense and Sensibility, Pride and Prejudice* and *Northanger Abbey*.

The interior depicts a typical well-to-do Georgian family home, complete with elegant furniture and copper pans in the kitchen. Highlights include the occasional table Austen used as a desk, first editions of her novels and the delicate handkerchief she embroidered for her sister.

The museum is 18 miles east of Winchester; take bus 64 from Winchester to Chawton roundabout (50 minutes, hourly Monday to Saturday, six on Sunday) then walk 500m to Chawton village.

run, 1½ hour, heritage-themed walks that include Jane Austen's Winchester, Ghost Walks and Canons and Courtesans.

Sleeping

Wykeham Arms HISTORIC INN ££
(☎01962-853834; www.fullershotels.com; 75 Kingsgate St; s/d/ste £70/119/150; P 📶) At 250-odd years old, the Wykeham is bursting with history – it used to be a brothel and also put up Nelson for a night (some say the two events coincided). Creaking, winding stairs lead to the cosy, traditionally styled bedrooms above the pub, while sleeker rooms (over the converted post office, opposite), look out onto a pocket-sized courtyard garden.

5 Clifton Terrace BOUTIQUE B&B ££
(☎01962-890053; cliftonterrace@hotmail.co.uk; 5 Clifton Tce; s/d/f £60/70/110; P 📶) Blending old and new, this tall Georgian town house sees plush furnishings rub shoulders with antiques and modern comforts coexist alongside claw-foot baths. The owners are utterly charming.

Dolphin House B&B ££
(☎01962-853284; www.dolphinhousestudios.co.uk; 3 Compton Rd; s/d £55/70; P 📶) At this kind of B&B-plus your continental breakfast is delivered to a compact kitchen – perfect for lazy lie-ins. The terrace, complete with cast-iron tables and chairs, overlooks a gently sloping lawn.

No 21 B&B ££
(☎01962-852989; St Johns St; s/d £45/90) Gorgeous cathedral views, a flower-filled cottage garden and rustic-chic rooms (think painted wicker and woven bedspreads) make this art-packed house a tranquil city bolt hole.

Hotel du Vin HISTORIC HOTEL £££
(☎01962-841414; www.hotelduvin.com; Southgate St; r £140-225; P @ 📶) An oh-so-stylish oasis, boasting ultracool minimalist furniture, ornate chaises longues and opulent stand-alone baths.

Wolvesey View B&B ££
(☎01962-852082; www.wintonian.com; 10 Colebrook Pl; s/d £50/75; P @) Book the simply furnished Yellow Room for grandstand views of Wolvesey Castle's fairy-tale tumblings.

Eating

TOP CHOICE **Chesil Rectory** ENGLISH ££
(☎01962-851555; www.chesilrectory.co.uk; 1 Chesil St; mains £16; ⏲lunch & dinner Mon-Sat, lunch Sun) Duck through the hobbit-sized door, settle down amid the 15th-century beams and savour perfectly prepared modern British cuisine, cooked up by the former head chef at Fortnum & Mason. New Forest rabbit, seared scallops, truffles and local watercress all feature on an assured menu. The 2-course evening menu (served 6pm to 7pm) is a snip at £15.

Black Rat ENGLISH ££
(☎01962-844465; www.theblackrat.co.uk; 88 Chesil St; mains £17-20; ⏲dinner daily, lunch Sat & Sun) Worn wooden floorboards and warm red-brick walls give this relaxed restaurant a cosy feel. Locally sourced treats such as roast venison with asparagus and Weymouth crab with marsh samphire find their way onto the sanded-down tables.

Wykeham Arms ENGLISH ££
(☎01962-853834; www.fullershotels.com; 75 Kingsgate St; mains £10-17; ⊙lunch & dinner Mon-Sat, lunch Sun; 📶) The food at this super-quirky pub (see p252) is legendary – try the pan-fried salmon, or sausages flavoured with local bitter, then finish off with some seriously addictive sticky toffee pudding.

Brasserie Blanc FRENCH ££
(☎01962-810870; www.brasserieblanc.com; 19 Jewry St; mains £13; ⊙lunch & dinner) Get a taste of French home cooking, Raymond (Blanc) style, at this super-sleek chain. The celebrity chef may not necessarily sauté your starter, but the chicken stuffed with morel mushrooms and the Toulouse sausage with onion gravy are full of Gallic charm.

El Sabio TAPAS £
(60 Eastgate St; ⊙lunch & dinner Tue-Sun, dinner Mon) Feast on the full-blooded flavours of Spain on a sunny riverside terrace.

Cadogan & James DELI £
(31A The Square; ⊙9.30am-5.30pm Mon-Sat, 10am-4pm Sun) Full of the aromas of ripe cheese, freshly baked breads, herbs and spices.

Drinking

TOP CHOICE **Wykeham Arms** PUB
(www.fullershotels.com; 75 Kingsgate St; 📶) Somehow reminiscent of an endearingly eccentric old uncle, this is just the sort of pub you'd love to have as a local: 1400 tankards, school canes and a riot of flags hang from the ceiling, while seating comes in the form of worn school desks, lending pint-supping an illicit air.

Black Boy PUB
(www.theblackboypub.com; 1 Wharf Hill; ⊙noon-11pm, to midnight Fri & Sat) This adorable old boozer is filled with obsessive and sometimes freaky collections, from pocket watches to wax facial features; bear traps to sawn-in-half paperbacks. The pumps produce five locally brewed real ales. Located just south of Black Rat.

Plain & Fancy BAR
(www.plainandfancy.co.uk; 10 Jewry St; ⊙4pm-1am Mon-Sat; 📶) A poseur's paradise: perch elegantly on a black bench seat at this shocking-pink champagne and cocktail bar.

Entertainment

For listings, pick up the free *What's On in Winchester* from the tourist office.

Railway Inn LIVE MUSIC
(☎01962-867795; www.liveattherailway.co.uk; 3 St Paul's Hill; ⊙5pm-midnight Sun-Thu, to 2am Fri, to 1am Sat) Bands ranging from acoustic to punk play at this grungy venue.

Screen MAINSTREAM CINEMA
(☎0870-0664777; www.screencinemas.co.uk; Southgate St)

Information

Discovery Centre (Jewry St; ⊙9am-7pm Mon-Fri, 9am-5pm Sat, 10am-4pm Sun) A library with free internet access.

Tourist office (☎01962-840500; www.visitwinchester.co.uk; High St; ⊙10am-5pm Mon-Sat plus 11am-4pm Sun May-Sep)

Getting There & Away

Winchester is 65 miles west of London and 14 miles north of Southampton.

Bus

Regular, direct National Express buses shuttle to **London Victoria** (£14.40, 1¾ hours). Buses run to **Southampton** (one hour, six daily Monday to Saturday). Stagecoach Explorer Tickets (adult/child £8/6) cover Winchester, Southampton and Salisbury.

Train

Trains leave every 30 minutes for **London Waterloo** (£26, 1¼ hours) and **Southampton** (£5.20, 20 minutes) and hourly for **Portsmouth** (£9.10, one hour). There are also fast links to the Midlands.

Getting Around

Bike

Bikeabout (www.winchester.gov.uk/bikeabout; membership £20) Members can borrow bikes (free) for 24 hours; pick them up from the tourist office.

Parking

The **Park & Ride** (£2 to £3 per day) is signed off junctions 10 and 11 of the M3.

Taxi

Ranks on Middle Brook St, or phone **Wintax Taxis** (☎01962-878727).

Portsmouth

POP 187,056

Prepare to splice the main brace, hoist the halyard and potter around the poop deck. Portsmouth is the principal port of Britain's Royal Navy, and its historic dockyard ranks alongside Greenwich as one of England's most fascinating centres of maritime history. Here you can jump aboard Lord Nelson's glorious warship HMS *Victory,* which led the charge at Trafalgar, and see atmospheric artefacts from Henry VIII's 16th-century flagship, the *Mary Rose*.

Regeneration at the nearby Gunwharf Quays has added fresh glitz to the city's waterfront, where a spectacular millennium-inspired structure, the Spinnaker Tower, provides jaw-dropping views. But Portsmouth is by no means noted for its beauty; it was bombed heavily during WWII and chunks of the city feature soulless postwar architecture. But the city's fine array of naval museums, a clutch of superb French restaurants and some chic places to sleep justify a longer visit. The suburb of Southsea, which begins a mile southeast of Gunwharf Quays, is rich in good hotels and eateries.

Sights & Activities

TOP CHOICE Portsmouth Historic Dockyard

HISTORIC SHIPS

(www.historicdockyard.co.uk; adult/child/family £20/14/55; ⌚10am-6pm Apr-Oct, 10am-5.30pm Nov-Mar) This is Portsmouth's blockbuster attraction. Set in the heart of one of the country's most important naval ports, it comprises two stunning ships and a cluster of museums that pay homage to the historical might of the Royal Navy. The ticket price also includes a boat trip round the harbour; together it makes for a full day's outing. The last admission is 1½ hours before closing.

The Ships

As resplendent as she is venerable, the dockyard's star sight is **HMS Victory** (www.hms-victory.com), Lord Nelson's flagship at the Battle of Trafalgar (1805) and the site of his infamous dying words 'Kiss me, Hardy' when victory over the French had been secured. This remarkable ship is topped by a forest of ropes and masts, and weighted by a swollen belly filled with cannon and paraphernalia for an 850-strong crew. Clambering through the low-beamed decks and crew's quarters is an evocative experience.

Anywhere else, the magnificent warship **HMS Warrior**, built in 1860, would grab centre stage. This stately dame was at the cutting edge of technology in her day, riding the transition from wood to iron and sail to steam. The gleaming upper deck, vast gun deck and the dimly lit cable lockers conjure up a vivid picture of life in the Victorian navy.

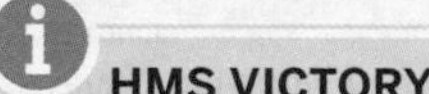

HMS VICTORY

In the summer, tours of Nelson's flagship are self-guided. But between autumn and spring, hugely popular 40-minute **guided tours** are held. Arrive early to bag a place – you can't book in advance.

Mary Rose Museum

The raising of the 16th-century warship the *Mary Rose* was an extraordinary feat of marine archaeology. This 700-tonne floating fortress and favourite of Henry VIII sank suddenly off Portsmouth while fighting the French in 1545 and was only raised from her watery grave in 1982. Of a crew of 400, it's thought 360 men died. The vessel herself currently can't be seen – a £35 million museum is being built around her, and is due to open in mid-2012.

You can still see the wealth of artefacts from the warship that fills the **Mary Rose Museum** (www.maryrose.org). Artefacts range from the military, including scores of cannons and hundreds of longbows, to the touchingly prosaic: water jugs, hair combs and even leather shoes. The museum also features a 15-minute film chronicling the delicate extraction of the still-preserved hulk from Portsmouth Harbour.

Royal Naval Museum

Expect model ships, battle dioramas, medals and paintings in this huge museum. Audiovisual displays recreate the Battle of Trafalgar and one even lets you take command of a warship – see if you can cure the scurvy and avoid mutiny. One gallery is entirely devoted to Lord Nelson.

Trafalgar Sail Exhibition

This small exhibition showcases the only HMS *Victory* sail to survive the Battle of Trafalgar. Clearly bearing the scars of conflict, it's riddled with the holes made by Napoleonic cannon – a telling illustration of the battle's ferocity.

Action Stations!

Stroll into this warehouse-based **interactive experience** (www.actionstations.org) and you'll soon be piloting a replica Merlin helicopter, controlling an aircraft carrier, upping periscope or jumping aboard a ship simulator. The whole set-up is a thinly disguised recruitment drive for the modern navy, but it's fun nonetheless.

The Point SIGNIFICANT AREA

Some 500m south of Gunwharf Quays, the Point (also known locally as Spice Island) is home to characterful cobbled streets dotted with salty sea-dog pubs; their waterside terraces are top spots to spend some time gazing at the Spinnaker Tower and the passing parade of ferries and navy ships. You can clatter up the steps of the **Round Tower** (originally built by Henry V) and stroll along the old fort walls to the **Square Tower**, which was built in 1494. Underneath, cavernous vaults frame **Sally Ports**, historic openings in the defences that give access to the sea and a strip of shingle beach.

To walk to the Point follow the chain link design set into the pavement from Gunwharf Quays.

FREE **Cathedral of St Thomas of Canterbury** CATHEDRAL

(www.portsmouthcathedral.org.uk; High St; ⌚9am-5pm) In Old Portsmouth, adjoining the Point, this airy structure retains fragments of its 12th- and 17th-century incarnations. But a striking modern makeover includes quirky statuettes by Peter Eugene

Portsmouth

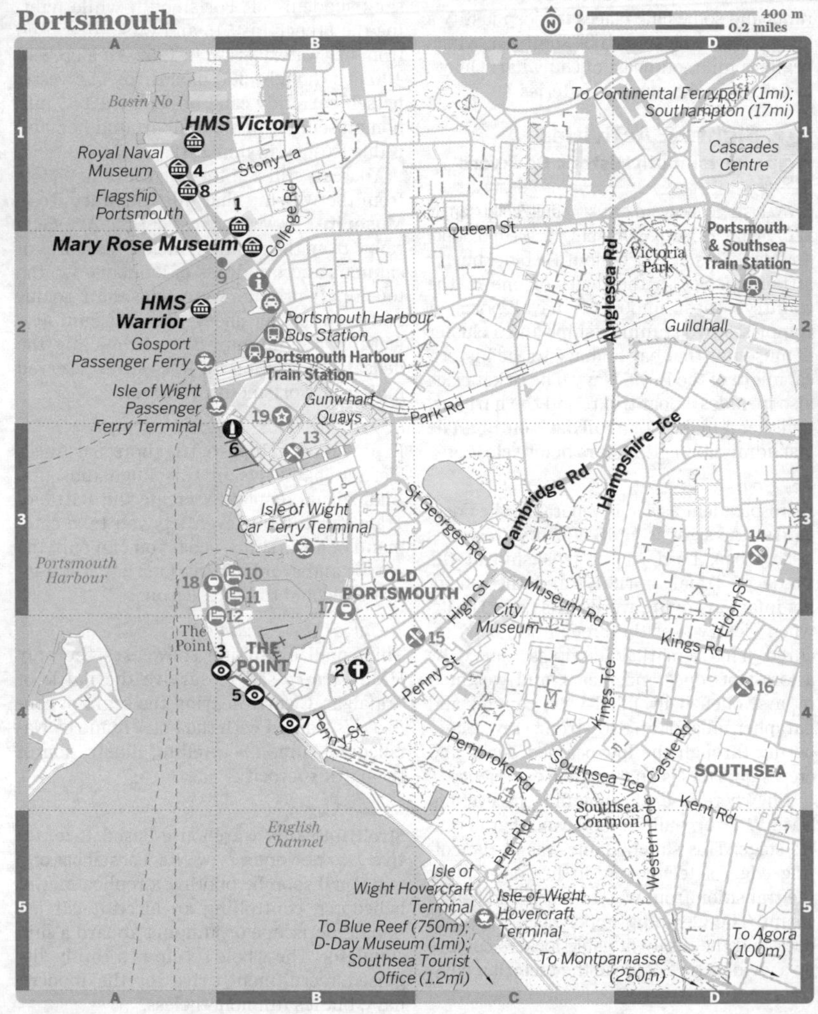

Ball; look for **Thomas Becket** with a sword through his mitred head.

Spinnaker Tower LANDMARK TOWER

(www.spinnakertower.co.uk; Gunwharf Quays; adult/child £7.25/5.75; ⌚10am-10pm) Soaring to 170m above Gunwharf Quays, the Spinnaker Tower is an unmistakable symbol of Portsmouth's new-found razzle-dazzle. Its two sweeping white arcs resemble a billowing sail from some angles, and a sharp skeletal ribcage from others.

As the UK's tallest publicly accessible structure, it offers truly extraordinary views over Portsmouth, the Isle of Wight, the South Downs and even Chichester, 23 miles to the east. **Observation Deck 1** has a hair-raising view through the glass floor, while the roofless **Crow's Nest** on Deck 3 allows you to feel the wind on your face.

Royal Navy Submarine Museum NAVY MUSEUM

(www.rnsubmus.co.uk; Haslar Jetty Rd, Gosport; adult/child £10/7; ⌚10am-4.30pm) Features a bona-fide ex-service submarine – clambering aboard provides a revealing insight into the claustrophobic conditions. The museum is in Gosport, a 20-minute ferry ride west from the Hard.

Explosion! NAVY MUSEUM

(www.explosion.org.uk; Priddy's Hard, Gosport; adult/child £10/5; ⌚10am-5pm Apr-Oct, 10am-4pm Sat & Sun Nov-Mar) A 1771 magazine full of ordinance that traces the story of naval munitions from gunpowder to Exocet missiles. In Gosport.

D-Day Museum MILITARY MUSEUM

(www.ddaymuseum.co.uk; Clarence Esplanade; adult/child £6/4.20; ⌚10am-5pm) Two miles southeast of Gunwharf Quays, exhibits here recount Portsmouth's crucial role as a departure point for Allied D-Day forces in 1944.

Royal Marines Museum COMBAT MUSEUM

(www.royalmarinesmuseum.co.uk; Barracks Rd; adult/child £6.95/4.75; ⌚10am-5pm) Tells the story of the navy's elite force, complete with jungle-warfare displays, live snakes and scorpions.

Blue Reef AQUARIUM

(www.bluereefaquarium.co.uk; Towan Promenade; adult/child £9.20/7.20; ⌚10am-5pm Mar-Oct, to 4pm Nov-Feb) Open-topped tanks, huge underwater walkways and a captivating 'seahorse ranch'.

☛ Tours

Boat Trips BOAT TRIP

(☎023-9272 8060; Historic Dockyard; ⌚11am-3pm Easter-Oct) Weather permitting, 45-minute harbour tours leave on the hour. They're free with the Dockyard ticket or can be bought separately (adult/child £5/3).

Walking Tours HERITAGE

(adult/child £3/free; ⌚2.30pm Sun Apr-Oct) Guided walk themes include Nelson, Henry VIII and Old Fortifications. Check with the tourist office for departure points.

Portsmouth

Top Sights
- HMS Victory ... A1
- HMS Warrior ... A2
- Mary Rose Museum ... B2

Sights
- 1 Action Stations! ... B1
- 2 Cathedral of St Thomas of Canterbury ... B4
- 3 Round Tower ... B4
- 4 Royal Naval Museum ... A1
- 5 Sally Ports ... B4
- 6 Spinnaker Tower ... B3
- 7 Square Tower ... B4
- 8 Trafalgar Sail Exhibition ... A1

Activities, Courses & Tours
- 9 Boat Trips ... B2

Sleeping
- 10 Cecil Cottage ... B3
- 11 Fortitude Cottage ... B3
- 12 Sailmaker's Loft ... B3

Eating
- 13 Custom House ... B3
- 14 Kitsch'n d'or ... D3
- 15 Lemon Sole ... C4
- 16 Truffles ... D4

Drinking
- 17 A Bar ... B3
- 18 Still & West ... A3

Entertainment
- 19 Vue ... B2

Sleeping

Florence House BOUTIQUE HOTEL ££
(023-9275 1666; www.florencehousehotel.co.uk; 2 Malvern Rd, Southsea; d £75-145; P @) Edwardian elegance combines beautifully with modern flourishes at this super-stylish oasis of boutique bliss. It's a winning combination of plush furnishings, sleek bathrooms, open fireplaces and the odd chaise longue – the suite, complete with spa bath, is top-notch.

Fortitude Cottage B&B ££
(023-9282 3748; www.fortitudecottage.co.uk; 51 Broad St, The Point; s £45, d £60-120; P) The ferry-port views from this fresh and airy guesthouse are interesting, while the top-floor penthouse boasts a private balcony, roof terrace and 360-degree vistas; binoculars are thoughtfully provided. The bay-windowed breakfast room is ideal for tucking into some smoked salmon and scrambled eggs.

Somerset House BOUTIQUE HOTEL £££
(023-9275 3555; www.somersethousehotel.co.uk; 10 Florence Rd, Southsea; d £95-190) At this late-Victorian sister to Florence House opposite, the same team has created another achingly tasteful haven of designer calm. Here, stained glass, dark woods and polished floors cosy up to Balinese figurines and the very latest in luxury bathrooms.

Cecil Cottage B&B ££
(078 9407 2253; www.cecilcottage.co.uk; 45 Broad St, The Point; s/d £50/70; P) Luxury smellies in the bathroom, use of a ferry-view lounge and a pot of tea and plate of biscuits on arrival make this Spice Island B&B another great option. The crisp white and soft grey colour scheme completes the soothing effect.

Sailmaker's Loft B&B ££
(023-9282 3045; www.sailmakersloft.org.uk; 5 Bath Sq, The Point; d £60-70) Traditional guesthouse with views across the water towards Gosport. Some share bathrooms.

Southsea Backpackers HOSTEL £
(023-9283 2495; www.portsmouthbackpackers.co.uk; 4 Florence Rd, Southsea; dm £15, d £33-38; P @) A well-run, old-fashioned backpackers with four- to eight-bed dorms. A pool table, patio and BBQ compensates for a low shower-to-people ratio. In Southsea.

Eating

TOP CHOICE **Truffles** FRENCH ££
(023-9273 0796; www.trufflesfrancais.co.uk; 67 Castle Rd, Southsea; 2-course lunch/dinner £7.50/22; lunch & dinner Tue-Sat, lunch Sun) The perfect marriage of Hampshire ingredients and continental gastronomy, this chic little bistro rustles up super-stylish food at bargain prices. British rump steak combines with truffle sauce, while seabass comes laced with vermouth. The painters' palettes, Eiffel Tower silhouettes and gendarme's uniform reinforce the Parisienne air.

Kitsch'n d'or FRENCH ££
(023-9286 1519; www.kitschndor.com; 37 Eldon St, Southsea; mains £13, 4-courses £18-23; lunch & dinner Mon-Sat, lunch Sun) Prepare to be transported to rural Provence. Dishes are rich with hearty rustic flavours, from venison with blackberry sauce, to mountain chorizo with baked duck eggs and Madeira. Seafood is a speciality too: mounds of lobster, steaming clams and scallops are topped off with a zingy spiced butter.

Lemon Sole ENGLISH ££
(023-928 11303; www.lemonsole.co.uk; 123 High St, Old Portsmouth; mains £9.50-18; lunch & dinner) At Lemon Sole you get to pick your own piece of fish at a counter then choose how you want it cooked. Try the seafood chowder, devilled mackerel or stunning shellfish platters (£45 for two). It's all tucked away in a lemon-yellow interior with a whole wall full of wine bottles at the end.

Montparnasse FRENCH £££
(023-9281 6754; www.bistromontparnasse.co.uk; 103 Palmerston Rd; 2-/3-courses £30/35; lunch & dinner Tue-Sat) More Gallic flavours emerge from the kitchens at this sleek Southsea eatery. This time its French classics with an English twist; seabass with white bean *cassoulet* and goats' cheese parfait with walnut and pear are among the treats.

Custom House PUB £
(Gunwharf Quays; mains £9; lunch & dinner) The best of Gunwharf Quays' numerous eateries, this smart pub occupies an 18th-century former Royal Marine hospital. Now better-than-average bar food (think glazed ham, steak and ale pie and gourmet burgers) are served up amid its raspberry-red walls and gilt-framed mirrors.

Agora TURKISH £
(9 Clarendon Rd, Southsea; mains £9, mezze £3; dinner) Expect tasty Mediterranean

food, ouzo and the occasional burst of belly-dancing at this hookah bar.

Drinking

Rows of bars and trendy balconied eateries line Gunwharf Quays.

A Bar PUB
(www.abarbistro.co.uk; 58 White Hart Rd, Old Portsmouth; ⏲11am-midnight) There's actually been a pub on this site since 1784 – these days it's home to worn floorboards, squishy leather sofas, a soundtrack of groovy tunes and a chilled, gently trendy vibe.

Still & West PUB
(2 Bath Sq, The Point) This relaxed, salty sea-dog boozer has served many a sailor and smuggler in the last 300 years. The waterside terrace is the place to down a beer to a backdrop of passing yachts and ferries.

Drift BAR
(www.driftbar.com; 78 Palmerston Rd, Southsea; ⏲11am-2am) All polka dots, pebble-coated walls and chrome lights, this hip lounge bar showcases DJs at the weekends and acoustic sets on Sundays.

☆ Entertainment

Southsea is thick with nightclubs and live-music venues.

Wedgewood Rooms NIGHTCLUB
(www.wedgewood-rooms.co.uk; Albert Rd, Southsea) One of Portsmouth's best live-music venues; also hosts DJs and comedians.

Vue CINEMA
(www.myvue.com; Gunwharf Quays)

Information

Online Café (163 Elm Grove, Southsea; per 10min/1hr 50p/£2.50; ⏲10am-10pm) Internet access.

Main tourist office (☎023-9282 6722; www.visitportsmouth.co.uk; The Hard; ⏲9.30am-5.45pm Jul & Aug, to 5.15pm Sep-Jun)

Southsea tourist office (☎023-9282 6722; Clarence Esplanade, Southsea; ⏲9.30am-5.15pm daily Mar-Aug, to 4pm Fri-Tue Sep-Feb)

Getting There & Away

Portsmouth is 100 miles southwest of London.

Boat

For details on how to reach the Isle of Wight from Portsmouth, see p264.

Prices for cross-channel routes vary wildly depending on times and dates of travel – an example fare is £300 return for a car and two adults on the Portsmouth–Cherbourg route. Book in advance, be prepared to travel off-peak and look out for special deals.

Brittany Ferries (www.brittanyferries.co.uk) Services run regularly to St Malo (10¾ hours), Caen (four hours) and Cherbourg (three hours) in France, and twice-weekly to Santander (13 hours) in Spain.

Condor Ferries (www.condorferries.co.uk) Runs a weekly car-and-passenger service to Cherbourg (6½ hours).

LD Lines (www.ldlines.co.uk) Shuttles to Le Havre (three to eight hours) in France.

Bus

There are 13 National Express buses from **London** (£18, 2¼ hours) daily; some go via **Heathrow Airport** (£17.60, 3½ hours) and continue to **Southampton** (50 minutes). Bus 700 runs to **Chichester** (one hour) and **Brighton** (four hours) half-hourly Monday to Saturday, and hourly on Sunday.

Train

Trains run every 30 minutes from **London Victoria** (£27, two hours) and **Waterloo** (£27, 1¾ hours) stations. For the Historic Dockyard get off at the final stop, Portsmouth Harbour.

Departures include:

Brighton (£14, 1½ hours, hourly)
Chichester (£6, 40 minutes, twice an hour)
Southampton (£8.30, 1¼ hours, three hourly)
Winchester (£9, one hour, hourly)

Getting Around

Bus

Bus 6 runs every 15 minutes between Portsmouth Harbour bus station and South Parade Pier in Southsea, via Old Portsmouth.

Boat

Gosport Passenger Ferry (www.gosportferry.co.uk; adult/child return £2.30/1.50, bicycle 80p; ⏲5.30am-midnight) Shuttles between the Hard and Gosport every 10 to 15 minutes.

Taxi

Ranks near the bus station. Or call **Aquacars** (☎023-9266 6666) in Southsea.

Southampton

POP 234,224

A no-nonsense port city and gateway to the Isle of Wight, Southampton lies deep in the folds of the Solent, an 8-mile inlet fed by the Rivers Itchen and Test. The city was once a flourishing medieval port but its centre was gutted by merciless bombing in WWII and only fragments of its earlier heritage survive. Southampton today is more a transport hub than an appealing place to stay. Its gritty waterfront waved the *Titanic* off on its ill-fated voyage in 1912, and larger-than-life ocean liners such as the *Queen Mary II* still dock here.

Sights & Activities

FREE **Guided Walks** HERITAGE TOUR

Southampton has the third largest section of 13th-century fortifications in the country, and free, 90-minute guided walks led by the **Southampton Tourist Guides Association** (www.stga.org.uk) see you strolling beside and on top of the towering walls. **Tours** (10.30am Jul-Sep) leave from Bargate, the city's northern medieval gate. In August walks also take place at 2.30pm.

Maritime Museum MUSEUM

(The Wool House, Town Quay; adult/child £2/1; 10am-4pm Tue-Sat, 1-4pm Sun) Set in a 14th-century waterfront warehouse, this museum tells the tragic story of the *Titanic* and the effect its sinking had on Southampton. The building was once a prison – look out for the inmates' names carved in the impressive timber roof.

Medieval Merchant's House MUSEUM

(EH; www.english-heritage.org.uk; French St; adult/child £4/2; noon-5pm Sun Apr-Sep) Brightly painted sea chests and replica period furniture dots this French merchant's home, which dates from 1290.

FREE **Southampton Art Gallery** ART GALLERY

(www.southampton.gov.uk/art; Commercial Rd; 10am-6pm Mon-Fri, 11am-6pm Sat & Sun) Features work by some of the best names in British art, including Spencer, Turner and Gainsborough.

Information

Tourist office (023-8083 3333; www.visit-southampton.co.uk; 9 Civic Centre Rd; 9.30am-5pm Mon-Sat, 10.30am-3.30pm Sun) Ten minutes' walk east of the central train station.

Getting There & Away

Air

Southampton International Airport (www.southamptonairport.com) Connects to some 40 UK and European destinations, including Amsterdam, Paris and Dublin. Five trains an hour link the airport and the main train station (seven minutes).

Boat

Red Funnel (www.redfunnel.co.uk) Operates regular passenger and car ferries to the Isle of Wight (see p264).

Passenger ferry (www.hytheferry.co.uk; adult/child return £5/3) Shuttles from the Town Quay to Hythe in the New Forest; runs half-hourly.

Bus

National Express runs 13 to 15 buses daily to **London** and **Heathrow Airport** (£12 to £15, 2½ hours), and one a day to **Lymington** (40 minutes) via **Lyndhurst** (20 minutes) in the New Forest. Buses 56 and 56A also go to **Lyndhurst**, **Brockenhurst** and **Lymington** (half hourly Monday to Saturday, six on Sunday).

Train

Three trains an hour run to **Portsmouth** (£8.30, 1¼ hours) and **Winchester** (£5.20, 20 minutes).

NEW FOREST

With typical, accidental English irony, the New Forest is anything but new – it was first proclaimed a royal hunting preserve in 1079. It's also not much of a forest, being mostly heathland ('forest' is from the Old French for 'hunting ground'). Today the forest's combined charms make it a joy to explore. Wild ponies mooch around pretty scrubland, deer flicker in the distance and rare birds flit among the foliage. Genteel villages dot the landscape, connected by a web of walking and cycling routes.

Activities

CYCLING

With all that picturesque scenery, the New Forest makes for superb cycling country, and hundreds of miles of trails link the main villages and the key railway station at Brockenhurst.

The *New Forest Cycle Map* (£2) shows the approved off-road and quieter 'on-road' routes. The *New Forest Cycle Experience RoutePack* (£4) features seven trips, ranging from a 4-mile glide through the forest to a 24-mile leg test round the cliffs of the Isle of Wight. The *Forest Leisure Cycling Route Pack* (£4) has six circular cycle routes for all abilities – all start from the village of Burley.

Maps and guides can be bought from Lyndhurst tourist office (p263) or via its website.

To rent bikes you'll need to pay a deposit (usually £20) and provide identification.

New Forest

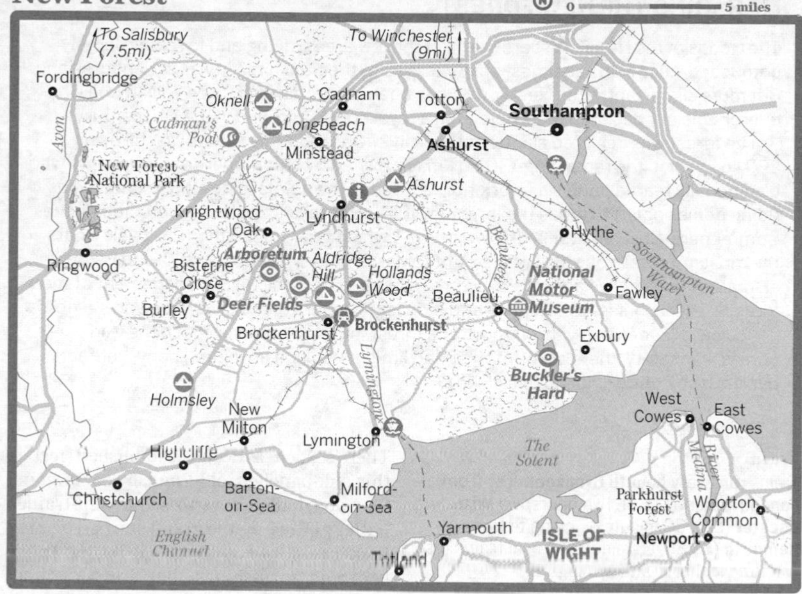

AA Bike Hire BIKE HIRE
(☎023 8028 3349; www.aabikehirenewforest.co.uk; Fern Glen, Gosport Lane, Lyndhurst; adult/child per day £10/5)

Country Lanes BIKE HIRE
(☎01590-622627; www.countrylanes.co.uk; Railway Station, Brockenhurst; bike/tandem per day £15/28; ⊙Easter-Oct)

Cyclexperience BIKE HIRE
(☎01590-624204; www.newforestcyclehire.co.uk; Brookley Rd, Brockenhurst; adult/child per day £14/7)

Forest Leisure Cycling BIKE HIRE
(☎01425-403584; www.forestleisurecycling.co.uk; The Cross, Village Centre, Burley; adult/child per day from £14/6)

HORSE RIDING

Stables that welcome beginners:

Arniss Equestrian Centre STABLE
(☎01425-654114; www.arnissequestrian.co.uk; Godshill, Fordingbridge; per hr £20)

Burley-Villa STABLE
(Western Riding; ☎01425-610278; www.burleyvilla.co.uk; New Milton; per 1/2 hr £29/49)

Forest Park STABLE
(01590-623429; www.forestparkridingstables.co.uk; Rhienfield Rd, Brockenhurst; per 1/2 hr £30/50)

OTHER ACTIVITIES

The forest is prime **hiking** territory. Ordnance Survey (OS) produces a detailed, 1:25 000 Explorer map (New Forrest; No 22, £8); Crimson Publishing's *New Forest Short Walks* (£7) features 20 day-hikes.

Rambles with a Ranger TOUR
(☎023-8028 6840; www.forestry.gov.uk; adult £6-8, child £4-5) Memorable dusk deer-watching safaris and wild-food foraging trips.

New Forest Activities WATER SPORTS
(☎01590-612377;www.newforestactivities.co.uk) Near Beaulieu. Offers canoeing (adult/child per two hours £28/22), kayaking (per two hours £28), sea kayaking (per 3 hours/day £40/70) and archery (adult/child per 1½ hours £20/15).

ℹ Getting There & Around

Bus

Regular services run to Southampton and Bournemouth.

New Forest Tour (www.thenewforesttour.info; adult/child £9/4.50; ⊙hourly 10am-5pm mid-Jun–mid-Sep) The hop-on/hop-off bus passes through Lyndhurst's main car park, Brockenhurst station, Lymington, Beaulieu and Exbury.

MANAGING THE NEW FOREST

The woods of the New Forest are some of the few areas of England to remain largely untouched since Norman times, partly thanks to their unsuitability as agricultural land. But more significantly, the New Forest has been protected ever since William the Conqueror officially declared the whole area a royal hunting ground in the 11th century.

The forest was declared a national park in 2005, and while the crown still owns 260 sq km of it, the remaining 130 sq km are owned by commoners and verderers who traditionally reared ponies as work horses. Today the animals are either schooled as riding ponies or left to graze the land at will. The verderers' status is protected by the Commoners' Charter, first laid down in 1077, which guaranteed them six basic rights, the most important of which is the right to pasture. Every year, the 300-odd verderers gather to elect five agisters, who are responsible for the daily management of the forest's 3000 ponies, 1800 cattle and smaller numbers of donkeys, pigs and sheep.

You can wander freely throughout the forest, but don't feed or touch the wild ponies. For safety, there's a 40mph speed limit. If you find an injured pony, contact **Lyndhurst Police** (☎0845 045 45 45).

Train

Trains run every hour to **Brockenhurst** from London Waterloo (£34, two hours) via **Winchester** (£10, 30 minutes) and on to **Bournemouth** (£5.80, 25 minutes). Local trains also link Brockenhurst with Lymington.

Lyndhurst

POP 2281

A good base from which to explore the national park or simply stop off for a pint, a cuppa or a map, the quaint country village of Lyndhurst is one of the New Forest's larger settlements. It boasts an evocative museum, a quintessentially English pub and an authentically Italian restaurant.

The **New Forest Centre** contains a **tourist office** (☎023-8028 2269; www.thenewforest.co.uk; High St; ⏲10am-5pm) with a wealth of information, including camping guides and walking and cycling maps. The centre is also home to the **New Forest Museum** (www.newforestcentre.org.uk; adult/child £3/2.50; ⏲10am-4pm), which features a local labourer's cottage (complete with socks drying beside the fire), potato dibbers and a cider press. Listen too for recordings of the autumn pony sales, which take place after the annual drifts (roundups).

Just across the car park, the **library** (⏲9.30am-1pm Mon, Wed & Sat, 2-5.30pm Tue & Fri) has free internet access.

Sleeping

Crown HOTEL ££

(☎023-8028 2922; www.crownhotel-lyndhurst.co.uk; 9 High St; s £70 d £80-130; P@📶) There's such a deeply established feel to this oak-panelled, old-English coaching inn that you half expect to see a well-trained butler gliding up the grand stairs. The mullioned windows and ancient beams frame bedroom furnishings that are sometimes a touch staid but sometimes surprisingly snazzy.

Whitley Ridge HOTEL £££

(☎01590-622354; www.whitleyridge.com; Beaulieu Rd; r £95-155; P) If you hanker after pure country-house atmosphere, head here. Set in 6 hectares of dappled grounds, this ivy-clad Georgian pile pampers guests amid elegant rooms finished with contemporary twists (think sleigh beds meets gilt mirrors). The classy restaurant conjures up organic, seasonal, locally sourced creations finished with Anglo-French flair. It's all tucked away 4 miles south of Lyndhurst at Brockenhurst.

Little Hayes B&B ££

(☎023-8028 3816; www.littlehayes.co.uk; 43 Romsey Rd; d £70-80; P📶) Moulded ceilings, old oak banisters and the odd chandelier speak of this Edwardian guesthouse's age. Bursts of scatter-cushion smartness liven up the good-sized rooms, while the breakfasts are full of New Forest produce.

Acorns B&B ££

(☎023-8028 4559; www.acornsoflyndhurst.co.uk; 31 Romsey Rd; d £50-80; P) One of several beside the A337 into the village from the north. Simply decked out in cream and pine.

Eating & Drinking

Fra Noi ITALIAN ££
(☎023-8028 3745; www.franoi.co.uk; 74 High St; mains £11-19; ⊙dinner Tue-Sat, lunch Sun) This swish trattoria combines techniques that are pure Tuscany with ingredients from the New Forest larder. The beef and venison are free-range, local and organic; the rich lasagne comes with black truffle and the golden ribbons of pasta are home made. Try the four-course pasta tasting menu (£30).

Waterloo Arms PUB £
(www.waterlooarmsnewforest.co.uk; Pikes Hill; mains £6-9; ⊙lunch & dinner) Cosy 17th-century thatched pub serving hearty grub and excellent ales in a snug, wood-beamed interior.

Getting There & Away

Bus

Bus 56/56A runs to **Southampton** (30 minutes twice hourly Monday to Saturday, five on Sunday).

Boat

Hythe Ferry (☎023-8084 0722; www.hythe ferry.co.uk; adult/child return £5/3) Carries foot passengers between Southampton and Hythe (12 minutes, every 30 minutes), 13 miles east of Lyndhurst.

Train

The nearest train station is at Brockenhurst, 8 miles south; see p259.

Around Lyndhurst

Petrol-heads, historians and ghost-hunters all gravitate to **Beaulieu** (www.beaulieu.co.uk; adult/child £16/8.60; ⊙10am-6pm Jun-Sep, to 5pm Oct-May) – pronounced *bew*-lee – an all-in-one vintage car museum, stately home and tourist complex based on the site of what was once England's most important 13th-century Cistercian monastery. Following Henry VIII's monastic land-grab of 1536, the abbey fell to the ancestors of current proprietors, the Montague family.

Motor-maniacs will be in raptures at Lord Montague's **National Motor Museum**, a splendid collection of vehicles that will sometimes leave you wondering if they are really are cars, or strange hybrid planes, boats or metal bubbles with wheels. It's hard to resist the romance of the early classics, or the oomph of winning F1 cars. Here, too, are several jet-powered land-speed record-breakers including *Bluebird*, which famously broke the record (403mph, or 649km/h) in 1964. There are even celebrity wheels – look out for Mr Bean's Austin Mini and James Bond's whizz-bang speed machines.

Beaulieu's grand but indefinably homely **palace** began life as a 14th-century Gothic abbey gatehouse, but received a 19th-century Scottish Baronial makeover from Baron Montague in the 1860s. Don't be surprised if you hear eerie Gregorian chanting or feel the hairs on the back of your neck quiver – the abbey is supposedly one of England's most haunted buildings.

The New Forest Tour Bus stops directly outside the complex on its circular route via Lyndhurst, Brockenhurst and Lymington. You can also get here from Lymington (35 minutes) by catching bus 112, which continues to Hythe and the ferry to Southampton.

CAMPING IN THE NEW FOREST

The New Forest is hugely popular with campers; Lyndhurst's tourist office has a free brochure detailing designated areas. For more information, go to www.thenewforest.co.uk.

THREE-DAY CYCLE TRIP

Start your woodland two-wheeled adventure with some research at Lyndhurst's **New Forest Centre** (p263). Then limber up with an 8 mile, largely off-road jaunt via Denny Wood south to Brockenhurst before checking into the pamper pad that is **Whitley Ridge** (p260). Day two is a 9-mile peddle east via copses and quiet roads to the **National Motor Museum** at Beaulieu. Next comes the 2-mile dash south to **Buckler's Hard** (p262) and the chance to soothe your weary limbs at the super-comfy digs at the **Master Builder's House Hotel** (p262). The next day it's back to Brockenhurst, via a more southerly route; from there a looping trail takes you 9 miles north and then west past pubs and through deer fields and an arboretum back to Lyndhurst, having explored some of the best cycle routes the New Forest has to offer.

Buckler's Hard

For such a tiny place, this picturesque huddle of 18th-century cottages, near the mouth of the River Beaulieu, has a big history. It started life in 1722, when one of the dukes of Montague decided to build a port to finance an expedition to the Caribbean. His dream was never realised, but when the war with France came, this embryonic village with a sheltered gravel waterfront became a secret boatyard where several of Nelson's triumphant Battle of Trafalgar warships were built. In the 20th century it played its part in more clandestine wartime manoeuvrings – the preparations for the D-Day landings.

The hamlet is now a fascinating heritage centre – **Buckler's Hard Story** (www.bucklershard.co.uk; adult/child £6/4.30; ⏲10am-5pm Mar-Oct, to 4.30pm Nov-Feb) – which features immaculately preserved 18th-century labourers' cottages. The **maritime museum** charts the inlet's shipbuilding history and its role in WWII – for a little light relief, seek out Nelson's quaint baby clothes.

The luxurious **Master Builder's House Hotel** (☎01590-616253; www.themasterbuilders.co.uk; d £105-160; P) is also part of the complex. This beautifully restored 18th-century hotel has 25 grandly chic rooms, featuring soft lighting, burnished trunks and plush fabrics. The gorgeous **restaurant** (mains £12 to £20) overlooks the river, while the wood-panelled **Yachtsman's Bar** serves classy pub grub from £5.

Swiftsure boats operate 30-minute **river cruises** (adult/child £4/2.50) from the waterfront between Easter and October.

Buckler's Hard is 2 miles downstream from Beaulieu; a picturesque riverside walking trail links the two.

Lymington

POP 14,227

Yachting haven, New Forest base and jumping-off point to the Isle of Wight – the appealing Georgian harbour town of Lymington has several strings to its tourism bow. This former smugglers' port offers great places to eat and sleep, plenty of nautical shops and, in Quay St, an utterly quaint cobbled lane.

Sights & Activities

Puffin Cruises BOAT TRIP
(☎07850 947618; www.puffincruiseslymington.com; Town Quay) Your chance to ride the waves without owning your own yacht. The best trip (adult/child £15/6, daily May to October) is an exhilarating blast down the river and across the Solent to the Isle of Wight, where the Needles lighthouse (p266) and towering chalk stacks loom from the water. They also do a two-hour sunset cruise in high summer.

St Barbe Museum MUSEUM
(www.stbarbe-museum.org.uk; New St; adult/child £4/2; ⏲10am-4pm Mon-Sat) Explores tales of boat-builders, sailing ships, contraband and farming through a mix of models and artefacts.

Sleeping

TOP CHOICE **Stanwell House** BOUTIQUE HOTEL £££
(☎01590-677123; www.stanwellhouse.com; 14 High St; s £99, d £138-175, ste £215; @ 📶) The epitome of discreet luxury, this is the place to wait for your ship to come in. Cane chairs dot the elegant conservatory, while bedrooms are an eclectic mix of stand-alone baths, rococo mirrors, gently distressed furniture and plush throws. The **seafood restaurant** (⏲noon-10pm; tapas £6, mains £17-22) rustles up bouillabaisse and seafood platters, while the chic bistro tempts you with fine dining (two-/three-courses from £22/27). There's even a vaguely decadent satin cushion–strewn bar.

Gorse Meadow B&B ££
(☎01590-673354; www.gorsemeadowguesthouse.co.uk; Sway Rd; d £80-120; P) With views from the bedrooms of fields, woods and ponies in paddocks, this rambling farmhouse eases you into the New Forest's rural vibe. Reassuringly old-fashioned rooms are packed with gilt plant stands, antique maps and velvet arm chairs, and it's all run by the indomitable Mrs Tee, a professional mushroom picker – so expect mounds of perfectly cooked King Oysters for breakfast.

Bluebird B&B ££
(☎01590-676908; www.bluebirdrestaurant.co.uk; 4 Quay St; d/f £80/120) An ancient cottage of dark beams, white walls and gleaming new bathrooms in the midst of quaintly cobbled Quay St.

Durlston House B&B ££
(☎01590-677364; www.durlstonhouse.co.uk; 61 Gosport St; s £45, d £60-70; P) Subdued furnishings, pine cabinets and neat-as-a-pin rooms.

ISLE OF WIGHT FESTIVALS

The isle's festival tradition stretches back to the early 1970s, when 600,000 hippies came to see the Doors, the Who, Joni Mitchell and rock icon Jimi Hendrix's last performance. Decades later the gatherings are still some of England's top musical events. The **Isle of Wight Festival** (www.isleofwightfestival.org), held in mid-June, has been headlined by the likes of REM, Coldplay, the Feeling, the Kaiser Chiefs and Keane, while **Bestival** (www.bestival.net), in early to mid-September, revels in an eclectic, counter-culture feel, drawing the Pet Shop Boys, Scissor Sisters, Dizzee Rascal and more.

Eating

Egan's EUROPEAN ££

(☎01590-676165; Gosport St; 2-/3-course lunch £14/16, mains £16; ⏰lunch & dinner Tue-Sat) The wooden tables here are highly polished and so is the food. Rich local ingredients are transformed by well-travelled flavours: marinated salmon combines with vodka; lobster with shellfish bisque; and beef with basil.

Vanilla Pod CAFE £

(Gosport St; snacks £5; ⏰breakfast & lunch Tue-Sun) Munch through Belgian muffins, English breakfasts and mounds of American pancakes at this top brunch spot.

Information

Library (North Close; ⏰9.30am-7pm Mon, Tue, Thu & Fri, 9.30am-1pm Wed, 9.30am-5pm Sat) Free internet access.

Tourist office (☎01590-689000; www.thenewforest.co.uk; New St; ⏰10am-5pm Mon-Sat Jul-Sep, to 4pm Mon-Sat Oct-Jun)

Getting There & Away

Bus

The New Forest Tour (p259) bus stops at Lymington.

Boat

Wightlink Ferries (☎0871 376 1000; www.wightlink.co.uk) Carries cars and passengers to Yarmouth on the Isle of Wight. Puffin Cruises (p262) take foot passengers.

Train

Lymington has two train stations: **Lymington Town** and **Lymington Pier**. Isle of Wight ferries connect with Lymington Pier. Trains run to **Southampton** (£9, 45 minutes), via Brockenhurst, every half-hour.

ISLE OF WIGHT

On the Isle of Wight these days there's something groovy in the air. For decades this slab of rock anchored off Portsmouth has been a magnet for family holidays, and it still has sea-side kitsch by the bucket and spade. But now the proms and amusement arcades are framed by pockets of pure funkiness. A brace of music festivals draws the party crowd, you can feast on just-caught seafood in cool fishermen's cafes, and 'glamping' (camping's more glamorous cousin) rules – here campsites are dotted with eco-yurts and retro camper vans. Yet still the isle's principal appeal remains: a mild climate, myriad outdoorsy activities and a 25-mile shore lined with beaches, dramatic white cliffs and tranquil sand dunes.

Activities

CYCLING

The Isle of Wight will make pedal pushers smile – there is a 62-mile cycleway, and the island has a **Cycling Festival** (☎01983-203891; www.sunseaandcycling.com) every September. The tourist office can advise and sell trail guides (£2).

Bike rentals are available all over the island for around £12 to £14 per day, or £45 per week.

Tavcycles (☎01983-812989; www.tavcycles.co.uk; 140 High St, Ryde)

Wight Cycle (☎0800 112 3751; www.thewightcycle.com; Zigzag Rd, Ventnor)

Wight Cycle Hire (☎01983-761800; www.wightcyclehire.co.uk) Brading (Station Rd, Brading); Yarmouth (Station Rd, Yarmouth) Delivers and collects across the island.

WALKING

This is one of the best spots in southern England for gentle rambling, with 500 miles of well-marked walking paths, including 67 miles of coastal routes. The island's **Walking Festival** (www.isleofwightwalkingfestival.co.uk), held over two weeks in May, is billed as the UK's largest. Tourist offices sell trail pamphlets (from £4).

OTHER ACTIVITIES

Water sports are serious business on Wight's northern shores – especially sailing but also windsurfing, sea-kayaking and surfing. Powerboat trips also run out to the Needles (p266). Wight also offers gliding lessons, paragliding, and even llama-trekking. Tourist offices can help arrange things.

Information

Main tourist office (☎01983-813813; The Guildhall, High St, Newport; ⏱9.30am-5pm Mon-Sat 10am-3pm Sun Apr-Oct, 10am-3pm Nov-Mar) The main office is in Newport; there are also branches at Cowes (p270) and Ryde (p270).

Useful websites include www.islandbreaks.co.uk and www.isleofwight.com.

Getting There & Away

Hovertravel (☎01983-811000; www.hovertravel.co.uk) Shuttles foot passengers between **Southsea** (near Portsmouth) and **Ryde** (day-return adult/child £13/6, 10 minutes, every half-hour).

Red Funnel (☎0844 844 9988; www.redfunnel.co.uk) Operates car ferries between **Southampton and East Cowes** (day-return adult/child £13/7, from £45 with car, 55 minutes) and high-speed passenger ferries between **Southampton and West Cowes** (day-return adult/child £19/10, 25 minutes).

Wightlink Ferries (☎0871 376 1000; www.wightlink.co.uk) Operates passenger ferries every half hour from **Portsmouth to Ryde** (day-return adult/child £13.50/6.50, 20 minutes). It also runs half-hourly car-and-passenger ferries from **Portsmouth to Fishbourne** (40 minutes) and from **Lymington to Yarmouth** (30 minutes). For both, an adult/child day return costs around £12/5. Car fares start at £45 for a short-break return.

Getting Around

Bus

Southern Vectis (www.islandlinetrains.co.uk) Runs buses between the eastern towns about every 30 minutes; regular services to the remoter southwest side between Blackgang Chine and Brook are less frequent. Twice daily between Easter and September, the **Island Coaster** also runs around the southern shore from Ryde to Alum Bay in the far southwest. Rover Tickets are available for a day (adult/child £10/5) or a week (adult/child £20/10).

Car

1st Call (☎01983-400055; 15 College Close, Sandown; from £30 per day) Collects and delivers island wide.

Train

Island Line (www.island-line.com) Runs trains twice-hourly from **Ryde to Shanklin**, via

Isle of Wight

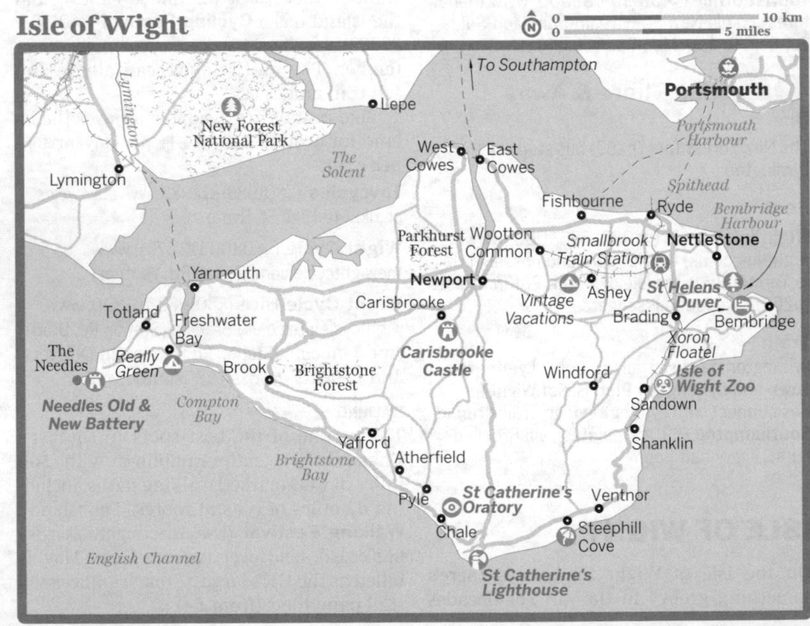

Sandown and Brading (25 minutes). Day rover tickets are available (adult/child £12/6).

Isle of Wight Steam Railway (01983-885923; www.iwsteamrailway.co.uk; May-Sep) Branches off at Smallbrook Junction and chugs to **Wootton Common** (adult/child £9.50/5, 1st class £14.50/10).

Cowes & Around

Pack your yachting cap – the hilly Georgian harbour town of Cowes is famous for **Cowes Week** (www.skandiacowesweek.co.uk), one of the longest-running and biggest annual sailing regattas in the world. Started in 1826, the regatta still sails with as much gusto as ever in late July or early August. Fibreglass playthings and vintage sailboats line Cowes' waterfronts, which are lopped into East and West Cowes by the River Medina; a chain ferry shuttles regularly between the two (foot passengers free, cars £1.80).

The **tourist office** (01983-813813; 9.30am-5pm Tue-Sat Easter-Oct, 10am-3pm Tue, Thu & Fri Nov-Easter) is at Fountain Quay in West Cowes. The island's capital, Newport, is 5 miles south.

Sights

Osborne House ROYAL HOME
(EH; www.english-heritage.org.uk; East Cowes; adult/child £10/5; 10am-6pm Apr-Sep, 10am-4pm Oct) This lemon-frosted, Italianate palace exudes the kind of pomp that defines the Victorian era. Built between 1845 and 1851 by Queen Victoria, the monarch grieved here for many years after her husband's death, and died here herself in 1901. The extravagant rooms include the stunning Durbar Room; another highlight is a carriage ride to the Swiss Cottage where the royal ankle-biters would play. Between November and March, visits are by pre-booked tours only.

Carisbrooke Castle CASTLE
(EH; www.english-heritage.org.uk; Newport; adult/child £7/3.50; 10am-5pm Apr-Sep, to 4pm Oct-Mar) Charles I was imprisoned here before his execution in 1649. Today you can clamber the sturdy ramparts and play bowls on the very green the doomed monarch used.

Sleeping & Eating

Fountain HOTEL ££
(01983-292397; www.fountaininn-cowes.com; High St, West Cowes; s £90, d £100-120) They may be in a classic old pub, but the bedrooms are all sleigh beds, leather headboards and red and gold velvet – the best have views across the Solent. Enjoy espressos and pastries in the cool **cafe,** hearty pub grub (mains £10) in the cosy **bar**; and watching the boats drifting from the seafront patio.

Anchorage B&B ££
(01983-247975; www.anchoragecowes.co.uk; 23 Mill Hill Rd, West Cowes; s £40, d £60-80; P) Unfussy cream and blue rooms combine with ecofriendly water and heating systems. Breakfasts are full of fair-trade and island foods.

CAR FERRY COSTS

The cost of car ferries to the Isle of Wight can vary enormously. Make savings by booking ahead, asking about special offers and travelling off-peak. Some deals include admission to island attractions. Booking online can be around £20 cheaper.

Ryde to Shanklin

The nippiest foot-passenger ferries between Wight and Portsmouth alight in **Ryde**, a workaday Victorian town rich in seaside kitsch and lined with amusement arcades. Next comes the cutesy village of **Brading**, with its fine Roman villa; photogenic **Bembridge Harbour**, fringed by tranquil sand dunes; and the twin resort towns of **Sandown** and **Shanklin**, boasting beaches, a zoo full of tigers, and hordes of families wielding buckets and spades. The area also features unique sleep spots including a decommissioned warship and vintage airstream trailers.

Sights

Brading Roman Villa ROMAN VILLA
(www.bradingromanvilla.co.uk; Morton Old Rd, Brading; adult/child £6.50/3; 10am-4pm) The exquisitely preserved mosaics here (including a famous cockerel-headed man) make this one of the finest Romano-British sites in the UK. Wooden walkways lead over the rubble walls and brightly painted tiles, allowing you to gaze right down onto the ruins below.

St Helens Duver NATURE RESERVE
(NT; www.nationaltrust.org.uk; 24hr) An idyllic sand and shingle spit bordering the mouth of the River Yar, where trails snake past swathes of sea pink, marram grass and

rare clovers. It's signed from the village of St Helens, near Bembridge Harbour.

Isle of Wight Zoo ZOO
(www.isleofwightzoo.com; Yaverland Rd, Sandown; adult/child £7.50/6.50; ⌚10am-6pm Apr-Sep, to 4pm Oct & Feb-Mar) One of Europe's largest collections of tigers, plus scores of cute lemurs.

Sleeping & Eating

TOP CHOICE **Xoron Floatel** FLOATING B&B ££
(☎01983-874596; www.xoronfloatel.co.uk; Bembridge Harbour; s/d £45/60) Your chance to go to sleep on a gunboat – this former WWII warship is now a cheery, bunting-draped houseboat. Comfy cabins come complete with snug bathrooms, while the views from the flower-framed sun deck are simply superb.

Vintage Vacations CAMPSITE £
(☎07802-758113; www.vintagevacations.co.uk; Ashey, near Ryde; 4-person caravans per week £390-600; ⌚Apr-Oct; P) The 10 airstream trailers from the 1960s on this farm are retro chic personified. Their gleaming aluminium shells shelter lovingly selected furnishings ranging from cheerful patchwork blankets to vivid tea cosies. Alternatively, opt for a beach-shack retreat or the Mission: a late-Victorian tin chapel.

Kasbah B&B BISTRO ££
(☎01983-810088; www.kas-bah.co.uk; 76 Union St, Ryde; s £60, d£65-85; @) More North Africa than East Wight, Kasbah brings a funky blast of the Mediterranean to Ryde. Intricate lanterns, stripy throws and furniture fresh from Marrakesh dot the chic rooms; falafel, tapas and paella (£4) are on offer in the chilled-out **bar** (⌚lunch and dinner).

Information

Ryde tourist office (☎01983-813813; 81 Union St, Ryde; ⌚9.30am-5pm Mon-Sat, 10am-3.30pm Sun Apr-Oct, 10am-3pm Nov-Mar).

Ventnor & Around

The Victorian town of **Ventnor** slaloms so steeply down the island's southern coast that you'd be forgiven for mistaking it for the south of France. The winding streets are home to a scattering of quirky boutiques, while local hotels, eateries and the atmospheric Steephill Cove (p267) are well worth a detour.

To the west, the island's southernmost point is marked by the stocky 19th-century **St Catherine's Lighthouse** and its 14th-century counterpart: **St Catherine's Oratory**. Nearby, kid-friendly **Blackgang Chine Fun Park** (www.blackgangchine.com; admission £10; ⌚10am-5pm late-Jul–Aug, 10am-5pm Apr–late-Jul, Sep & Oct), features water gardens, animated shows and a hedge maze.

Sleeping

Hambrough BOUTIQUE HOTEL £££
(☎01983-856333; www.thehambrough.com; Hambrough Rd, Ventnor; d £150-187, ste £210; P) It's hard to say which views are better: the 180-degree vistas out to sea, or those of rooms full of subtle colours, clean lines and satiny furnishings. Espresso machines, dressing gowns and heated floors keep the luxury gauge set to high.

Harbour View HOTEL ££
(☎01983-852285; www.harbourviewhotel.co.uk; Esplanade, Ventnor; d £92-108; P) Expansive sea views and crisp white linen fill this Victorian villa with bursts of period charm. The window-seated Tower Room sees light and views pour in from three sides.

Eating

TOP CHOICE **Boathouse** SEAFOOD ££
(☎01983-852747; Steephill Cove; mains £15-30; ⌚lunch Thu-Tue Jun-Sep) Arrive early enough, and you'll see the cove's fishermen (Jimmy and Mark) landing your lunch – the sanded wooden tables here are just steps from the sea. It's an idyllic spot to sip some chilled wine, sample succulent lobster and revel in Wight's new-found driftwood chic.

Crab Shed CAFE £
(Steephill Cove; snacks £4; ⌚11am-3.30pm Apr-Oct) Lobster pots and fishing boats line the slipway right outside a fisherman's shack that's a riot of sea-smoothed spas, cork floats and faded buoys. Irresistible treats include meaty crab salads, mackerel ciabatta and freshly baked crab pasties.

West Wight

Rural and remote, Wight's westerly corner is where the island really comes into its own. Sheer white cliffs rear from a surging sea and the stunning coastline peels west to Alum Bay and the most famous chunks of chalk in the region: the Needles. These jagged rocks rise shardlike out of the sea,

WORTH A TRIP

STEEPHILL COVE

You can't drive to Steephill Cove, which makes it all the more special. Its tiny, sandy beach is fringed by an eclectic mix of buildings, ranging from stone cottages to rickety-looking shacks. A cute clapper-board lighthouse presides over the scene, while beach finds festoon porches dotted with driftwood furniture and draped with fishing nets. Two great places to eat: the **Boathouse** restaurant and the **Crab Shed** cafe, add to the appeal.

Steephill Cove is 1 mile west of Ventnor; either walk down from the Botanical Gardens, or hike from the hillside car park 200m west of Ventnor Esplanade, then follow the (steep) coast path until you arrive.

forming a line like the backbone of a prehistoric sea monster.

Sights & Activities

Needles Old Battery FORT
(NT; www.nationaltrust.org.uk; adult/child £4.80/2.50; ⏲10.30am-5pm mid-Mar–Oct) Established in 1862, this remote gun emplacement was used as an observation post during WWII – today you can explore the Victorian cartridge store, trek down a 60m cliff tunnel to a searchlight lookout and drink in extraordinary views.

Also on the same site is **New Battery** (⏲11am-4pm Tue, Sat & Sun mid-Mar–Oct). Displays in its vaults outline the clandestine space-rocket testing carried out here in the 1950s.

You can hike to the battery along the cliffs from Alum Bay (1 mile) or hop on the tourist bus that runs between the bay and battery hourly (twice hourly in July and August).

Boat Trips BOAT TRIPS
(☎01983-761587; www.needlespleasurecruises.co.uk; adult/child £5/3; ⏲10.30am-4.30pm Apr-Oct) Twenty minute voyages from Alum Bay to the Needles, providing close-up views of those towering white cliffs.

FREE **Needles Park** THEME PARK
(www.theneedles.co.uk; Alum Bay; ⏲10am-5pm Easter-Nov) A happy hullabaloo of kiddies' rides, boat trips and souvenir shops; there's also a **chairlift** (£4) down to the beach.

Sleeping

TOP CHOICE **Really Green** CAMPSITE £
(☎07802 678591; www.thereallygreenholidaycompany.com; Blackbridge Rd, Freshwater Bay; yurt per week £395-490; Ⓟ) The epitome of 'glamping' (glamorous camping), the five-person, fully furnished yurts on this tree-shaded site feature four-poster beds, futons, wood-burning stoves and shabby-chic antiques. You can even have continental breakfast delivered to your tent flap – roughing it has never been so smooth.

Brighstone HOLIDAY PARK £
(☎01983-740244; www.brighstone-holidays.co.uk; tent sites per adult £4.50, B&B d £56, 2-person cabins per week from £300; Ⓟ) Perched atop cliffs looking towards the spectacular bluffs at Alum Bay. On the A3055, 6 miles east of Freshwater.

Totland Bay YHA HOSTEL £
(☎0845 371 9348; www.yha.org.uk; Hirst Hill, Totland; dm £16; Ⓟ) Family-friendly Victorian house overlooking the water, with a maximum of eight beds per room.

DORSET

For many, Dorset conjures up the kind of halcyon holiday memories you find in flickering 1970s home movies. But this county's image deserves a dramatic revamp. In party-town Bournemouth the snapshots are as likely to be of stag- and hen-party frenzies as buckets and spades on the sand; Poole provides images of the super-rich, while Dorset's Jurassic Coast would catch the eye of even the most jaded cinematographer. This stunning shoreline is studded with exquisite sea-carved bays and creamy-white rock arches around Lulworth Cove, while beaches at Lyme Regis are littered with fossils ripe for the picking. Dorchester provides a biopic of Thomas Hardy; the massive Iron Age hill fort at Maiden Castle is a battle-ground epic; and the really rather rude chalk figure at Cerne Abbas delivers a comic interlude. Then comes the regenerated resort of Weymouth, preparing to be catapulted onto TV screens worldwide as the sailing venue for England's 2012 Olympics.

Information

Jurassic Coast (www.jurassiccoast.com) Official World Heritage Site guide.

Rural Dorset (www.ruraldorset.com) Tips on inland spots.

Visit Dorset (www.visit-dorset.com) The county's official tourism website.

Getting Around

BUS

A key provider is **First** (www.firstgroup.com). **Wilts & Dorset** (www.wdbus.co.uk) connects Dorset's rural and urban areas.

TRAIN

One mainline runs from Bristol and Bath through Dorchester West to Weymouth, the other connects London and Southampton with Bournemouth and Poole.

Bournemouth

POP 163,600

In Bournemouth, four worlds collide: old folks, families and corporate delegates meet club-loads of determined drinkers. Sometimes the edges rub and on weekend evenings parts of town transform into a massive frenzy of massive party zones, full of angels with L plates and blokes in frocks, blond wigs and slingbacks. But there's also a much sunnier side to the town. A recent survey revealed Bournemouth had the happiest residents in the UK – thanks partly to its glorious 7-mile sandy beach. The town sprang up as a Victorian resort, but these days it's busy adding a much more modern attraction: it's hoped Europe's first artificial surf reef will bring even bigger barrels and more amped-up board riders to town.

Sights & Activities

Bournemouth Beach BEACH

Backed by 3000 deckchairs, Bournemouth's expansive, sandy shoreline regularly clocks up seaside awards. It stretches from Southborne in the far east to Alum Chine in the west – an immense promenade backed by ornamental gardens, cafes and toilets. The resort also prides itself on two piers (Bournemouth and Boscombe). Around **Bournemouth Pier** you can hire beach **chalets** (☎0845 0550968; per day/week from £17/55), deckchairs (£2 per day), windbreaks (£2.50) and parasols (£4).

At the **East Cliff Lift Railway** (☎01202-451781; Undercliff Dr; adult/child £1.20/80p; ⏲Easter-Oct), cable cars on rails wiz up bracken-covered slopes, cutting out the short, steep hike up the zigzag paths.

Alum Chine GARDEN

(Mountbatten Rd; ⏲24hr) This award-winning subtropical enclave dates from the 1920s, providing a taste of Bournemouth's golden age. Set 1.5 miles west from Bournemouth Pier, its plants include those from the Canary Islands, New Zealand, Mexico and the Himalayas; their bright-red bracts, silver thistles and purple flowers frame views of a glittering sea.

In the centre of Bournemouth, the **Pleasure Gardens** stretch back for 1.5 miles from behind Bournemouth Pier in three colourful sweeps.

FREE **Russell-Cotes** MUSEUM

(www.russell-cotes.bournemouth.gov.uk; Russell-Cotes Rd; ⏲10am-5pm Tue-Sun) This ostentatious mix of Italianate villa and Scottish baronial pile was built at the end of the 1800s for Merton and Annie Russell-Cotes as somewhere to showcase the remarkable range of souvenirs gathered on their world travels. Look out for a plaster version of the Parthenon frieze by the stairs, Maori woodcarvings and Persian tiles. The house also boasts fine art, including paintings by Rossetti, Edwin Landseer and William Frith.

Dorset Cruises BOAT TRIP

(☎0845 4684640; www.dorsetcruises.co.uk; Bournemouth Pier; adult/child £12.50/5; ⏲daily Apr-Sep) Dorset's extraordinary World Heritage Jurassic Coast (p268) starts some 5 miles west of Bournemouth at the chalk Old Harry Rocks. These 2½ hour cruises cross the mouth of Poole Harbour, providing up-close views of the chalky columns. The stacks used to be massive arches before erosion brought the tops tumbling down – huge scooped-out sections of cliff clearly show how the sea begins the erosion process.

Oceanarium AQUARIUM

(www.oceanarium.co.uk; adult/child £9/6.40; ⏲10am-5pm) Underwater tunnels bring you eye-to-eye with mean-looking sharks, massive moray eels and giant turtles in watery worlds ranging from Key West and the Ganges to Africa and the Med.

Sleeping

Bournemouth has huge concentrations of budget B&Bs, especially around the central

SURF REEF

Bournemouth is now home to Europe's first ever artificial surf reef. Made up of 55 immense sandbags (some 70m long), it sits submerged beneath the sea 220m offshore at **Boscombe Pier**. Despite delays and initial teething problems, the aim remains to harness and increase existing waves, push them up and form them into better breaks for surfers. The result would be a faster, more challenging ride.

The reef isn't for beginners, but you can learn nearby. The **Sorted Surf School** (☎01202-300668; www.bournemouth-surfschool.co.uk; Undercliff Drive, Boscombe Beach), 300m west of Boscombe Pier, does lessons (£30 for two hours) and hires out wetsuits (four/eight hours £10/15), surf boards (four/eight hours £10/15), bodyboards (four/eight hours £5/10) and kayaks (one/two/four hours £10/15/25).

St Michael's Rd and to the east of the train station.

TOP CHOICE **Urban Beach** BOUTIQUE HOTEL £££
(☎01202-301509; www.urbanbeachhotel.co.uk; 23 Argyll Rd; d £95-170; P @) Bournemouth's finest hipster hotel is packed with chic flourishes: oatmeal, brown leather and rippling velvet define the rooms; the hall sports brightly coloured Wellingtons for guests to borrow. There's a cool **bistro** downstairs and a heated deck for pre-dinner cocktails. It's all just a 10-minute walk from Boscombe Pier.

Balincourt B&B ££
(☎01202-552962; www.balincourt.co.uk; 58 Christchurch Rd; s £40-70, d £75-120; P) This Victorian guesthouse is a labour of love – even the china on the tea tray is hand painted to match each room's colour scheme. The decor is bright and deeply tasteful, respecting both the house's heritage and modern anti-frill sensibilities.

Langtry Manor HOTEL ££
(☎01202-553887; www.langtrymanor.com; Derby Rd; s from £100, d £105-200; P) Prepare for a delicious whiff of royal indiscretion – this minimansion was built by Edward VII for his mistress Lillie Langtry. Opulent grandeur is everywhere, from the red-carpeted entrance to immense chandeliers. Bedrooms include modern touches such as recessed lights and Jacuzzis, while the King's Suite is a real jaw-dropper: a monumental, climb-up-to-get-in four-poster bed, and a fireplace big enough to sit in.

Amarillo B&B ££
(☎01202-553884; www.amarillohotel.co.uk; 52 Frances Rd; s £25-45, d £50-90, f £80; P) Minimalist decor, beige throws and clumps of twisted willow – an inexpensive Bournemouth sleep spot with style.

Newark B&B ££
(☎01202-294989; www.thenewarkhotel.co.uk; 65 St Michael's Rd; s from £25, d £54; P) Victoriana meets modern: gold flocked wallpaper, glinting chandeliers and 21st-century curtains.

Bournemouth Backpackers HOSTEL £
(☎01202-299491; www.bournemouthbackpackers.co.uk; 3 Frances Rd; dm £14) Plain dorms in a small (19-bed), friendly suburban house. Reservations by email, or by phone between 5.30pm and 6.30pm, Sunday to Friday in summer (5pm to 7pm Sundays only in winter).

Eating

West Beach ENGLISH ££
(☎01202-587785; www.west-beach.co.uk; Pier Approach; mains £11-18; ⊙breakfast, lunch & dinner) A firm favourite with Bournemouth's foodie crowd, this buzzy eatery delivers both top-notch dishes and the best views in town. Try monkfish medallions with Parma ham or a seafood platter crammed with crab claws, lobster, razor clams and crevettes – best enjoyed on a decked dining terrace that juts out over the sand.

Print Room FRENCH ££
(☎01202-789669; Richmond Hill; mains £10-25; ⊙breakfast, lunch & dinner) This charismatic brasserie exudes Parisian chic, from the black and white tiled floors to the burnished wooden booths. Dishes are well travelled, too; try the beetroot gnocchi, grilled calves livers, or steak with black truffle potato. Or that most excellent French tradition: the *plat du jour*, including wine, for only £10.

Basilica EUROPEAN £
(73 Seamoor Rd; tapas from £3, mains £6-10; ⊙Mon-Sat) The menu tours more Mediterranean countries than your average InterRailer – expect mezze, Parma ham

parcels, grilled haloumi and pasta with chorizo.

Indian Ocean INDIAN ££
(4 West Cliff Rd; mains £9-12; ⏲lunch & dinner) Unusual karai and Bangladeshi specials as well as tried and tested Indian favourites.

Drinking & Entertainment

Most of the main entertainment venues are clustered around Firvale Rd, St Peter's Rd and Old Christchurch Rd. The gay scene kicks off around the Triangle.

Sixty Million Postcards PUB
(www.sixtymillionpostcards.com; 19 Exeter Rd; ⏲noon-midnight Sun-Wed, to 1am Thu, to 2am Fri & Sat) A hip crowd inhabits this quirky drinking den. The worn wooden floors, battered sofas and fringed lampshades are home to everything from DJ sets (including indie, synth-pop and space disco), to board games and impromptu Sunday jumble sales.

Lava Ignite NIGHTCLUB
(www.lavaignite.com; Firvale Rd) Four-room megaclub playing R&B, pop, house, hip hop and dubstep.

O2 Academy MUSIC VENUE
(www.o2academybournemouth.co.uk; Boscombe Arcade, 570 Christchurch Rd) Restored Victorian theatre lining up gigs (from jazz to rude-boy punk), DJ sets (from northern soul to drum and bass), gay nights and comedy.

Information

Cyber Place (25 St Peter's Rd; per hr £2; ⏲10am-10pm)

Tourist office (☎0845 0511700; www.bournemouth.co.uk; Westover Rd; ⏲10am-5pm Mon-Sat, plus 11am-4pm Sun Jun & Aug).

Getting There & Away

Bus

Standard routes:

Bristol (£19, four hours, daily) National Express.

London (£20, 2½ hours, hourly) National Express.

Oxford (£21, three hours, three daily) National Express.

Poole (15 minutes, every 10 minutes) Buses M1 and M2.

Salisbury (1¼ hours, half-hourly Monday to Saturday, nine on Sunday) Bus X3.

Southampton (£5.50, 50 minutes, 10 daily) National Express.

Train

Trains run every half-hour from **London Waterloo** (£35, two hours). Regular connections:

Dorchester South (£9.50, 45 minutes, hourly)

Poole (10 minutes, half-hourly)

Weymouth (£12, one hour, hourly)

Poole

POP 144,800

Just a few miles west of Bournemouth, Poole was once the preserve of hard-drinking sailors and sunburned day-trippers. But these days you're as likely to encounter super-yachts and Porsches because the town borders Sandbanks, one of the most expensive chunks of real estate in the world. But you don't have to be knee-deep in cash to enjoy Poole's quaint old harbour, excellent eateries and nautical pubs. The town is also the springboard for some irresistible boat trips and a tempting array of water sports.

Sights & Activities

Brownsea Island ISLAND
(NT; adult/child £5.50/2.70; ⏲10am-5pm late Mar–Nov) This small, wooded island in the middle of Poole harbour played a key role in a global movement famous for three-fingered salutes, shorts and toggles – Lord Baden-Powell staged the first ever scout camp here in 1907. Today trails weave through heath and woods, past peacocks, red squirrels, red deer and a wealth of birdlife.

There are free **guided walks** (⏲11am & 2pm Jul & Aug); subjects include the wartime island, smugglers and pirates.

Boats run by **Brownsea Island Ferries** (www.brownseaislandferries.com; Poole Quay) leave from **Poole Quay** (adult/child return £8.50/5.50) and **Sandbanks** (adult/child return £5/4). Services operate when the island is open only and the last boat is normally at about 4.30pm.

Poole Old Town SIGNIFICANT AREA
The attractive old buildings on Poole Quay range from the 15th to the 19th century, and include the Tudor **King Charles pub** on Thames St; the cream **Old Harbour Office** (1820s) next door; and the impressive red-brick **Custom House** (1813) opposite, complete with Union Jack and gilded coat of arms. The tourist office stocks a free heritage walking trail leaflet.

WATER SPORTS – POOLE HARBOUR

Poole Harbour's sheltered coasts may inspire you to get on the water. Operators cluster near the start of the Sandbanks peninsula. **Pool Harbour Watersports** (01202-700503; www.pooleharbour.co.uk; 284 Sandbanks Rd, Lilliput) does lessons in windsurfing (£50 for three hours) and kitesurfing (one/two/three days £99/175/240), as well as kayak tours (one/two day £35).

The nearby **FC Watersports** (01202-708283; www.fcwatersports.co.uk; 19 Banks Rd) provides similarly priced kite- and windsurfing lessons, as does **Watersports Academy** (01202-708283; www.thewatersportsacademy.com; Banks Rd), which also runs sailing courses (two hours/two days £55/165) and wakeboarding and water skiing (per 15 minutes £20).

FREE **Waterfront Museum** MUSEUM
(01202-262600; 4 High St; 10am-4pm Tue-Sat, noon-4pm Sun Apr-Oct) This beautifully restored 15th-century warehouse is home to a 2300-year old **Iron Age logboat** dredged up from Poole Harbour. At 10m long and 14 tonnes, it's the largest to be found in southern Britain and probably carried 18 people. It was hand chiselled from a single tree; centuries later you can still see the blade marks in the wood.

Sandbanks BEACH
A 2-mile, wafer-thin peninsula of land that curls around the expanse of Poole Harbour, Sandbanks is studded with some of the most expensive houses in the world. But the golden beaches that border them are free, and have some of the best water-quality standards in the country. They're also home to a host of water-sport operators (see below).

Brownsea Island Ferries (www.brownseaislandferries.com; adult/child return £8/5; 10am-5pm Apr-Oct) shuttle between Poole Quay and Sandbanks every half hour.

Sleeping

TOP CHOICE **Saltings** BOUTIQUE B&B ££
(01202-707349; www.the-saltings.com; 5 Salterns Way; d £80-90; P) You can almost hear the languid drawl of Noël Coward in this utterly delightful 1930s guesthouse. Charming art-deco flourishes include curved windows, arched doorways and decorative uplighters. Immaculate rooms feature dazzling white, spearmint and pastel blue as well as minifridges, digital radios and Lush toiletries. One room is more like a little suite, with its own seating area and pocket-sized balcony. Saltings is halfway between Poole and Sandbanks.

Milsoms B&B ££
(01202-609000; www.milsomshotel.co.uk; 47 Haven Rd; d £60-75; P) Supersleek and semi-boutique, this minihotel sits above Poole's branch of the Loch Fyne seafood restaurant chain. Bedrooms are decked out in achingly tasteful tones of chrome and cream, and finished with thoughtful extras such as cafetières and Molton Brown bath products.

Quayside B&B ££
(01202-683733; www.poolequayside.co.uk; 9 High St; s £35-50, d £55-75, f £60-80; P) Snug rooms, pine, and jazzy prints in the heart of the old harbour.

Eating & Drinking

Guildhall Tavern FRENCH ££
(01202-671717; 15 Market St; mains £15-20, 2-course lunch £15; lunch & dinner Tue-Sat) More Provence than Poole, the grub at this brasserie is Gallic gourmet charm at its best: unpretentious and top notch. Expect double-baked cheese soufflé, chargrilled sea bass flambéed with pernod, or Charolais beef with peppercorns. Exquisite aromas fill the dining room, along with the quiet murmur of people enjoying very good food.

Storm SEAFOOD ££
(01202-674970; www.stormfish.co.uk; 16 High St; mains £17; lunch & dinner Mon-Sat) The superbly cooked fish on the robust, eclectic menu here depends on what the owner's caught.

Custom House BAR-BISTRO ££
(www.customhouse.co.uk; Poole Quay; snacks £6, mains from £11; lunch & dinner) Harbourside terrace, funky eatery and fine-dining venue all rolled into one.

Information

Tourist office (01202-253253; www.pooletourism.com; Poole Quay; 10am-5pm

Apr-Oct, 10am-4pm Mon-Sat Nov-Mar) Opens longer (9.15am to 6pm) in July and August.

Getting There & Around

Bus

National Express runs hourly to **London** (£19, three hours). Buses M1 and M2 go to **Bournemouth** every 10 minutes (15 minutes). Bus 52 shuttles between **Poole** and **Sandbanks** (15 minutes, hourly).

Boat

Brittany Ferries (www.brittany-ferries. com) Sails between Poole and Cherbourg in France (2½-6½ hours, one to three daily). Expect to pay around £90 for foot passengers; £400 for a car and two adults.

Sandbanks Ferry (www.sandbanksferry.co.uk; per pedestrian/car one-way £1/3.20; 7am-11pm) Takes cars from Sandbanks to Studland every 20 minutes. It's a short-cut from Poole to Swanage, Wareham and the Isle of Purbeck, but the summer queues can be horrendous.

Taxi

Dial-a-Cab (01202-666822).

Train

Rail connections are as for Bournemouth; just add 13 minutes to times to **London Waterloo** (£30).

Wimborne

POP 14,844

Just 10 miles from Bournemouth, but half a world away, Wimborne sits in the middle of a peaceful, pastoral landscape. Its imposing minster, complete with an intriguing chained library, oversees a central array of Georgian houses, sedate tearooms and creaky old pubs. With the impressive ancestral pile of Kingston Lacy nearby, it is a soothing antidote to a sometimes cocksure coast.

Sights

TOP CHOICE **Kingston Lacy** STATELY HOME
(NT; www.nationaltrust.org.uk; house adult/child £10.50/5, grounds only £6/3; house 11am-5pm Wed-Sun mid Mar–Oct) This is Dorset's must-see stately home. Looking every inch the setting for a period drama, it overflows with rich decor, most famously in the Spanish Room, which is smothered with gold and gilt. Other highlights include the hieroglyphics in the Egyptian Room and the elegant marble staircase and loggia.

The house became the home of the aristocratic Bankes family when it was evicted from Corfe Castle (p274) by the Roundheads; look out for the bronze statue of Dame Mary Bankes in the loggia – she's shown still holding the keys to her much-loved castle in her hand. Art works include the overwhelming ceiling fresco *The Separation of Night and Day,* by Guido Reni in the library, and paintings by Rubens, Titian and Van Dyck. In the extensive landscaped grounds, hunt out the restored Japanese Tea Garden and the **Iron Age hillfort** of Badbury Rings.

Kingston Lacy is 2.5 miles west of Wimborne off the B3082.

Wimborne Minster CHURCH
(www.wimborneminster.org.uk; High St; donation requested; 9.30am-5.30pm Mon-Sat, 2-5pm Sun) St Cuthburga founded a monastery in Wimborne in around 705, but most of the present-day Wimborne Minster was built by the Normans between 1120 and 1180.

The big draw is the famous **chained library** (10.30am-12.30pm & 2-4pm Mon-Fri, 10.30am-12.30pm Sat Easter-Oct). Established in 1686, it's filled with some of the country's oldest medieval books, 12th-century manuscripts written on lambskin, and ancient recipes, including ones for making ink out of oak apples.

The west belltower has a brightly painted 14th-century **astronomical clock**; note that in this medieval depiction of the solar system, the sun and moon orbit the earth. Outside, the minster's 15th-century west tower features the **Quarter Jack**, a red-coated infantryman, complete with knee-boots and tricorne hat, who strikes the hours and quarters.

Sleeping

Percy House B&B ££
(01202-881040; e_camp@sky.com; 4 East Borough; s/d/f £70/100/110; P) A sauna, hot tub in the garden, and a river in which to fish make this gorgeously Georgian house irresistible. An impressive staircase sweeps up to rooms where the style is rustic-meets-elegant: raspberry-red walls, antique furniture and stripped woods.

Old George B&B ££
(01202-888510; www.theoldgeorge.net; 2 Corn Market; s/d £45/70; P) Hidden away in a tiny square beside the minster, this charming 18th-century house has chic bedrooms decked out in duck-egg blue and cream,

topped off by scatterings of cute cushions and elegant armchairs.

Information

Tourist office (☎01202-886116; www.ruraldorset.com; 29 High St; ⌚9am-4.30pm Mon-Sat) Sells a good town trail leaflet (£1).

Getting There & Away

Bus 3 goes to **Poole** (30 minutes, two to four per hour). Bus 13 connects with **Bournemouth** (one hour, half-hourly Monday to Saturday, five on Sunday).

Southeast Dorset

With its string of glittering bays and towering rock formations, the southeast Dorset shoreline is the most beautiful in the county. Also known as the 'Isle' of Purbeck (although it's actually a peninsula), it's also the start of the Jurassic Coast and the scenery and geology, especially around Lulworth Cove, make swimming irresistible and hiking memorable. The hinterland harbours the immense, fairy-tale ruins of Corfe Castle, while Wareham sheds light on the mysterious figure of Lawrence of Arabia.

WAREHAM & AROUND

POP 2568

Saxons established the sturdy settlement of Wareham on the banks of the River Frome in the 10th century, and their legacy lingers in the remains of their defensive walls and one of Dorset's last remaining Saxon churches. Wareham is also famous for its links to the enigmatic TE Lawrence, the British soldier immortalised in the 1962 David Lean epic *Lawrence of Arabia*.

Sights

Clouds Hill HISTORIC HOME

(NT; www.nationaltrust.org.uk; near Bovington; adult/child £4.50/2; ⌚noon-5pm Thu-Sun mid-Mar–Oct) This tiny cottage was home to **TE Lawrence** (1888–1935), the British scholar, military strategist and writer made legendary for his role in helping unite Arab tribes against Turkish forces in WWI. The house's four rooms provide a compelling insight into a complex man; they're also much as he left them – he died at the age of 46 after a motorbike accident on a nearby road.

Highlights include the deeply evocative photos Lawrence took during his desert campaign and his sketches of French crusader castles. There's also a surprisingly comfortable cork-lined bathroom, an aluminium foil-lined bunk room and a heavily beamed music room, which features the desk where Lawrence abridged *Seven Pillars of Wisdom*.

Clouds Hill is 7 miles northeast of Wareham on an unclassified road.

FREE **Wareham Museum** MUSEUM

(East St; ⌚10am-4pm Mon-Sat Easter-Oct) A good potted history of Lawrence's life, plus press cuttings on the speculation surrounding his death.

St Martin's on the Walls CHURCH

(North St; ⌚10am-4pm Mon-Sat Easter-Oct) Dating from 1020, it features a 12th-century fresco on the northern wall, and a marble effigy of Lawrence of Arabia.

Tank Museum MILITARY MUSEUM

(www.tankmuseum.org; adult/child £11/7.50; ⌚10am-5pm) Lawrence's former base is now home to 300 armoured vehicles, ranging from WWI prototypes to tanks used in the first Gulf War.

Monkey World ZOO

(www.monkeyworld.co.uk; Long-thorns, adult/child £10.75/7.50; ⌚10am-5pm Sep-Jul, to 6pm Jul & Aug) A sanctuary for rescued chimpanzees, orang-utans, gibbons, marmosets and some ridiculously cute ring-tailed lemurs.

Sleeping & Eating

Trinity B&B ££

(☎01929-556689; www.trinitybnb.co.uk; 32 South St; s/d/f £40/60/80) This 15th-century cottage oozes so much character, that you half expect to bump into a chap in doublet and hose. The staircase is a swirl of ancient timber, floors creak under plush rugs, and bathrooms gleam with yellow and green tiles and smart new fittings.

Anglebury PUB-B&B ££

(☎01929-552988; www.angleburyhouse.co.uk; 15 North St; mains £10; ⌚lunch daily, dinner Tue-Sat) Lawrence of Arabia and Thomas Hardy have, apparently, had cuppas in the coffee shop attached to this 16th-century inn. The restaurant rustles up hearty dishes such as chilli and garlic sea bass, while simple bedrooms (single/double £40/70) are done out in creams, floral fabrics and pine.

Information

Purbeck tourist office (☎01929-552740; www.purbeck.gov.uk; Holy Trinity Church, South St, Wareham; ⌚9.30am-4pm Mon-Sat, plus 10am-4pm Sun Jul & Aug)

JURASSIC COAST

The kind of massive, hands-on geology lesson you wish you had at school, the Jurassic Coast is England's first natural World Heritage Site, putting it on a par with the Great Barrier Reef and the Grand Canyon. This striking shoreline stretches from Exmouth in East Devon to Swanage in Dorset, encompassing 185 million years of the earth's history in just 95 miles. It means you can walk, in just a few hours, many millions of years in geological time.

It began when layers of rocks formed; their varying compositions determined by different climates: desert-like conditions gave way to higher then lower sea levels. Massive earth movements then tilted all the rock layers to the east. Next, erosion exposed the different strata, leaving most of the oldest formations in the west and the youngest in the east.

The differences are very tangible. Devon's rusty-red Triassic rocks are 200 to 250 million years old. Lyme Regis (see boxed text, p282) has fossil-rich, dark-clay Jurassic cliffs 190 million years old. Pockets of much younger, creamy-coloured Cretaceous rocks (a mere 140 to 65 million years old) also pop up, notably around Lulworth Cove, where erosion has sculpted a stunning display of bays, stacks and rock arches.

The coast's **website** (www.jurassiccoast.com) is a great information source; also look out locally for the highly readable *Official Guide to the Jurassic Coast* (£4.95).

Getting There & Away

Bus

Bus 40 runs hourly between **Poole** (35 minutes) and **Swanage** (30 minutes) via Wareham and Corfe Castle.

Train

Wareham is on the main railway line from **London Waterloo** (£17, 2½ hours, hourly) to **Weymouth** (£8, 30 minutes, hourly).

CORFE CASTLE

The massive, shattered ruins of Corfe Castle loom so dramatically from the landscape it's like blundering into a film set. The defensive fragments tower over an equally photogenic village, which bears the castle's name, and makes for a romantic spot for a meal or an overnight stay.

Sights & Activities

TOP CHOICE Corfe Castle CASTLE
(NT; www.nationaltrust.org.uk; adult/child £5.60/2.80; 10am-6pm Apr-Sep, 10am-4pm Oct-Mar) One of Dorset's most iconic landmarks, these towering battlements were once home to Sir John Bankes, right-hand man and attorney general to Charles I. The castle was besieged by Cromwellian forces during the Civil War – for six weeks the plucky Lady Bankes directed the defence and the castle fell only after being betrayed from within. The Bankes decamped to Kingston Lacy (p272) and the Roundheads immediately gunpowdered Corfe Castle apart, an action that's still startlingly apparent today: turrets and soaring walls sheer off at precarious angles; the gatehouse splays out as if it's just been blown up. Today you can roam over most of the site, peeping through slit windows and prowling the fractured defences.

Swanage Steam Railway RAILWAY
(www.swanagerailway.co.uk; adult/child return £9/7; Apr-Oct & many weekends in Nov, Dec, Feb & Mar) Vintage steam trains run (hourly) between Swanage and Norden (20 minutes), stopping at Corfe Castle.

Sleeping & Eating

Mortons House HOTEL £££
(01929-480988; www.mortonshouse.co.uk; East St; d £130-225; P) This is a place to break open the Bollinger: a romantic, luxurious 16th-century, mini-baronial pile. The rooms are festooned with red brocade and gold tassels; an occasional chaise longue adds to the effect.

Olivers B&B-BISTR ££
(01929-477111; www.oliverscorfecastle.co.uk; 5 West St; s/d £35/70) The spacious, simple, light-blue rooms here are finished with willow displays – for intricate beams and village views bag an upstairs one. The **bistro** (mains £8-12; lunch & dinner daily, closed Mon & Sun Oct-Easter) rustles up gourmet burgers for lunch, and some surprises for dinner: expect venison and chocolate sauce or pork terrine with onion marmalade.

Getting There & Away

Bus 40 shuttles hourly between Poole, Wareham, Corfe Castle and Swanage.

LULWORTH COVE & AROUND

South of Corfe Castle the coast steals the show. For millions of years the elements have been creating an intricate shoreline of curved bays, caves, stacks and weirdly wonderful rock formations – most notably the massive natural arch at Durdle Door.

At Lulworth Cove, a pleasing jumble of thatched cottages and fishing gear leads down to a perfect circle of white cliffs. It's a charismatic place to stay; inevitably, it draws coach party crowds in the height of summer.

Sights & Activities

Durdle Door TOP CHOICE — ROCK ARCH

This immense, 150-million-year-old Portland stone arch plunges into the sea near Lulworth Cove. Part of the Jurassic Coast (p268), it was created by a combination of massive earth movements and then erosion. Today it's framed by shimmering bays – bring a swimsuit and head down the hundreds of steps for an unforgettable dip.

There's a car park at the top of the cliffs, but it's best to hike along the coast from Lulworth Cove (1 mile), passing the delightfully named **Lulworth Crumple**, where layers of rock have been forced into dramatically zigzagging folds.

Secondwind Watersports — KAYAK TOUR

(01305-834951; www.jurassic-kayaking.com; Lulworth Cove; per person £50; up to two tours daily) This three-hour paddle offers a jaw-dropping view of Dorset's heavily eroded coast. Starting at Lulworth Cove, you glide through Stair Hole's intricate caves and stacks, across Man O'War Bay then under the massive stone arch at Durdle Door, stopping for swims and picnics along the way.

Lulworth Castle — STATELY HOME

(EH; www.lulworth.com; East Lulworth; adult/child £8.50/4; 10.30am-6pm Sun-Fri Apr-Sep, to 4pm Oct-Mar) A creamy, dreamy, white, this baronial pile looks more like a French chateau than a traditional English castle. Built in 1608 as a hunting lodge, it's survived extravagant owners, extensive remodelling and a disastrous fire in 1929. It has now been sumptuously restored. Check out the massive four-poster bed, and the suits of armour in the basement.

Sleeping & Eating

Beach House — HOTEL ££

(01929-400404; www.lulworthbeachhotel.com; Main St; d £90-120; P) At this oh-so-stylish sleep spot 200m from the beach, rooms feature blonde woods, coconut matting and flashes of leather and lime – the best has its own private sea-view deck

Bishops Cottage — B&B ££

(01929-400880; www.bishopscottage.co.uk; Main St; d £100; P) As cool as the coolest kid in the year, this shabby-chic bolt hole throws together antique furniture and sleek modern fabrics – and makes it work. Chill out on your own window seat or in the funky bar-bistro downstairs.

Fish Shack — FISH SHO £

(Lulworth Cove; Fri-Wed Easter-Oct, Sat & Sun Nov-Easter) Set right beside the path to the beach, this shed is piled with plaice, sole and brill. Settle at the tiny table outside, and tuck into crab landed at Lulworth Cove – a meal that's travelled food yards, not miles.

Durdle Door Holiday Park — CAMPSITE

(01929-400200; www.lulworth.com; sites from £15; Mar-Oct; P) Clifftop site, just metres from the famous rock arch.

Lulworth YHA — HOSTEL

(0845 371 9331; www.yha.org.uk; School Lane, West Lulworth; dm £16; Mar-Oct) A single storey, cabin-style affair.

Information

Lulworth Cove Heritage Centre (01929-400587; admission free; 10am-5pm April-Oct, till 4pm Nov-March) Has excellent displays outlining how geology and erosion have combined to shape the area's remarkable shoreline.

Dorchester

POP 16,171

With Dorchester, you get two towns in one: a real-life, bustling county town, and Thomas Hardy's fictional Casterbridge. The Victorian writer was born just outside Dorchester and clearly used it to add authenticity to his writing – so much so that his literary locations can still be found amid the town's white Georgian terraces and red-brick buildings. You can also visit his former homes here and see his original manuscripts. Add incredibly varied museums (from teddy bears to Tutankhamen) and some attractive places to eat and sleep, and you get an appealing base for a night or two.

Sights

Dorset County Museum MUSEUM
(www.dorsetcountymuseum.org; High West St; admission £6; ⏲10am-5pm Jul-Sep, closed Sun Oct-Jun) The Thomas Hardy collection here the is the biggest in the world. It offers extraordinary insights into his creative process – reading his cramped handwriting, it's often possible to spot where he's crossed out one word and substituted another. There's also a wonderful reconstruction of his study at Max Gate (see p276) and a letter from Siegfried Sassoon, asking Hardy if Sassoon can dedicate his first book of poems to him.

As well as the superb Hardy exhibits, look out for Jurassic Coast fossils, especially the huge ichthyosaur and the 6ft fore paddle of a plesiosaur. Bronze and Iron Age finds from Maiden Castle (p277) include a treasure trove of coins and neck rings, while Roman artefacts include 70 gold coins, nail cleaners and ear picks.

Max Gate HISTORIC HOME
(NT; www.nationaltrust.org.uk; Alington Ave; adult/child £3/1.50; ⏲2-5pm Mon, Wed & Sun Apr-Sep) Hardy was a trained architect and designed this house, where he lived from 1885 until his death in 1928. *Tess of the D'Urbervilles* and *Jude the Obscure* were both written here, and the house contains several pieces of original furniture, but otherwise it's a little slim on sights. The house is a mile east of Dorchester on the A352.

Hardy's Cottage HISTORIC HOME
(NT; www.nationaltrust.org.uk; admission £4; ⏲11am-5pm Sun-Thu Apr-Oct) The author was born at this picturesque cob-and-thatch house. Again it's a little short on attractions, but makes an evocative stop for Hardy completists. It's in Higher Bockhampton, 3 miles northeast of Dorchester.

FREE **Roman Town House** ROMAN VILLA
(www.romantownhouse.org; High West St; ⏲24hr) The knee-high flint walls and beautifully preserved mosaics here conjure up the Roman occupation of Dorchester (then Durnovaria). You can also peek into the summer dining room and study the underfloor heating system (hypocaust), where charcoal-warmed air circulated around pillars to produce a toasty 18°C.

Other Thomas Hardy Sites LITERARY SITES
Hardy's **statue** is at the top of High West St. **Lucetta's House**, a grand Georgian affair with ornate door posts, is near the tourist office, while in parallel South St, a red-brick mid-18th-century building (now a bank) has a plaque identifying it as the inspiration for the **Mayor of Casterbridge's house**. The tourist office sells 'location' guides to the Dorset places in Hardy's novels.

Tutankhamen MUSEUM
(www.tutankhamun-exhibition.co.uk; High West St; adult/child £7/5.50; ⏲9.30am-5.30pm) Experience the sights, sounds and smells of ancient Egypt, including a fake-gold mock-up of a pharaoh's tomb.

Terracotta Warriors MUSEUM
(www.terracottawarriors.co.uk; East Gate, East High St; adult/child £5.75/4; ⏲10am-5pm Apr-Oct, to 4.30pm Nov-Mar) Whisks you off to 8th-century China for a reconstruction of the famous figures.

Teddy Bear Museum MUSEUM
(www.teddybearmuseum.co.uk; East Gate, East High St; adult/child £5.75/4; ⏲10am-5pm Apr-Oct, to 4.30pm Nov-Mar) Populated by historical and famous bears, plus a rather disturbing family of human-sized teddies.

Sleeping

TOP CHOICE **Beggar's Knap** BOUTIQUE B&B ££
(☎01305-268191; www.beggarsknap.co.uk; 2 Weymouth Ave; s £45, d £70-90; Ⓟ) Despite the name, this utterly fabulous, vaguely decadent guesthouse is far from impoverished. Opulent raspberry-red rooms drip with chandeliers and gold brocades; beds draped in fine cottons range from French sleigh to four-poster. The breakfast room, with its towering plants and a huge harp, is gorgeous. You could pay much, much more and get something half as nice.

Slades Farm B&B ££
(☎01305-264032; www.bandbdorset.org.uk; Charminster; s/d/f £50/70/110; Ⓟ) Barn conversions don't come much more subtle and airy than this: done out in oatmeal and cream, tiny skylights dot ceilings that meet walls in gentle curves. The riverside paddock (complete with grazing alpacas) is perfect to laze in. It's 2 miles north of Dorchester.

Casterbridge HOTEL ££
(☎01305-264043; www.casterbridgehotel.co.uk; 49 High East St; s £60-70, d £100-135, f £125-160) In the 1780s this was the town jail. Now marble fireplaces, ruched furnishings and Thomas Hardy books in the rooms make it worth spending a night in an old prison. Six bedrooms are in a 1980s annexe.

WORTH A TRIP

MAIDEN CASTLE

Occupying a massive slab of horizon on the southern fringes of Dorchester, **Maiden Castle** (EH; www.english-heritage.org.uk; ⌚24hr) is the largest and most complex Iron Age hill fort in Britain. The huge, steep-sided chalk ramparts flow along the contour lines of the hill and surround 48 hectares – the equivalent of 50 football pitches. The first hill fort was built on the site around 500 BC and in its heyday was densely populated with clusters of roundhouses and a network of roads. The Romans besieged and captured it in AD 43 – an ancient Briton skeleton with a Roman crossbow bolt in the spine was found at the site. The sheer scale of the ramparts is awe-inspiring, especially from the ditches immediately below, and the winding complexity of the west entrance reveals just how hard it would be to storm. Finds from the site are displayed at **Dorset County Museum** (opposite). Maiden Castle is 1½ miles southwest of Dorchester.

Westwood B&B **££**
(☎01305-268018; www.westwoodhouse.co.uk; 29 High West St; s £60-65, d £70-90, f £85-120; 📶) Elegant Georgian town house with painted wicker chairs, cast iron bedsteads and dinky cushions.

Eating

Billy The Fish SEAFOOD **£**
(Trinity St; mains from £8; ⌚lunch Mon-Sat, dinner Thu-Sat) Former fisherman Billy doesn't catch his own any more; he's too busy cooking up a storm at this kooky bistro. The walls are hung with fabric, lobster pots and buoys; the tables are lined by locals enjoying skilfully cooked food. Try the super-fresh turbot, brill and scallops, or the intensely flavoured fish soup.

Sienna EUROPEAN **£££**
(☎01305-250022; 36 High West St; 2-course set lunch/dinner £24/35; ⌚lunch & dinner Tue-Sat) Dorchester's Michelin-starred eatery is rich in seasonal produce; look out for wild garlic and pungent white truffles; partridge might be teamed with spiced pear. The cheeseboard bears the best of the west, served with fig chutney and Bath Oliver biscuits. Booking is required.

Information

Tourist office (☎01305-267992; www.westdorset.com; Antelope Walk; ⌚9am-5pm Mon-Sat Apr-Oct, to 4pm Nov-Mar)

Getting There & Around

Bicycle

Dorchester Cycles (☎01305-268787; 31 Great Western Rd; adult/child per day £8/12).

Bus

London (£22, four hours) National Express; one direct service daily.

Lyme Regis (1¾ hours, hourly) Bus 31; runs via Weymouth (30 minutes).

Poole (1¼ hours, three daily Monday to Saturday) Bus 347/387.

Sherborne (two to three daily Monday to Friday, one hour) Bus D12; via Cerne Abbas.

Weymouth (35 minutes, three per hour Monday to Saturday, six on Sunday) Bus 10/110.

Train

Trains run twice-hourly from **Weymouth** (11 minutes) to **London Waterloo** (£30, 2¾ hours) via Dorchester South, **Bournemouth** (£9.50, 45 minutes) and **Southampton** (£20, 1¼ hours). Dorchester West has connections with **Bath** (£14, two hours) and **Bristol** (£15, 2½ hours); trains run every two hours.

Around Dorchester

CERNE ABBAS & THE CERNE GIANT

If you had to describe an archetypal sleepy Dorset village, you'd come up with something a lot like Cerne Abbas: its houses run the gamut of England's architectural styles, roses climb countless doorways, and half-timbered houses frame a honey-coloured, 12th-century church.

But this village also packs one heck of a surprise – a real nudge-nudge, wink-wink tourist attraction in the form of the **Cerne Giant**. Nude, full frontal and notoriously well endowed, this chalk figure is revealed in all his glory on a hill on the edge of town. And he's in a stage of excitement that wouldn't be allowed in most magazines. The giant is around 60m high and 51m wide and his age remains a mystery; some claim he's Roman but the first historical reference comes in 1694, when three shillings were set aside for his repair. The Victorians found it all deeply embarrassing and allowed grass to grow over his most outstanding feature. Today the hill is grazed on by sheep and cattle, though only the sheep are allowed to do their nibbling over the giant – the cows would do too much damage to his lines.

The village has the not-so-new **New Inn** (☎01300-341274; www.newinncerneabbas.co.uk; 14 Long St; mains £9-22; ⏰lunch daily, dinner Fri & Sat), a 13th-century pub with rustic, comfy rooms (doubles £100), sophisticated bar meals, such as local venison casserole, and a restaurant menu including gurnard and spiced belly pork.

Dorchester is 8 miles to the south. Bus D12 (two to three daily Monday to Friday) connects Cerne Abbas with Dorchester (20 minutes) and Sherborne.

Weymouth & Around

As the venues for the sailing events in Britain's 2012 Olympics, Weymouth and neighbouring Portland are preparing to welcome some of the world's best seafarers to their shores. But despite the waterfront spruce-up, evidence of their core characters remains. Weymouth's billowing deckchairs, candy-striped beach kiosks and Punch and Judy stands are the epitome of a faded Georgian resort, while Portland's pock-marked central plateau still proudly proclaims a rugged, quarrying past. Portland also offers jaw-dropping views down onto 17-mile Chesil Beach, which is backed by the Fleet, Britain's biggest tidal lagoon – a home to 600 nesting swans.

WEYMOUTH

POP 48,279

Weymouth has been a popular seaside spot since King George III (the one with a 'nervous disorder') took an impromptu dip here in 1789. Some 200-plus years later, the town is still popular with holidaymakers, drawn by a 3-mile sandy beach, a revitalised historic harbour and oodles of seaside kitsch.

Sights & Activities

Weymouth Beach BEACH

Weymouth's fine sandy shore is perfect for a stroll down seaside memory lane. Here you can rent a deckchair, sun-lounger or **pedalo** (each £6 per hr), watch donkey rides, and see professional sandsculptors turn the golden grains into works of art. Alternatively, go all Californian and join a volleyball game. For watersports, see the boxed text, p280.

White Motor Boats BOAT TRIP

(www.whitemotorboat.freeuk.com; adult/child return £7.50/6; ⏰Apr-Oct) This wind-blown 40-minute jaunt crosses Portland Harbour's vast Olympic sailing waters, before dropping you off at Portland Castle (p280). Boats leave from Cove Row on Weymouth Harbour (three to four daily).

Nothe Fort HISTORIC FORT

(www.nothefort.org.uk; Barrack Rd; adult/child £6/1; ⏰10.30am-5.30pm May-Oct) Crowning the headland beside Weymouth Harbour, these photogenic 19th-century defences are studded with cannons, rifles, searchlights and 12-inch coastal guns. Exhibits detail the Roman invasion of Dorset, a Victorian soldier's drill, and Weymouth in WWII. Commanding an armoured car and clambering around the magazine prove popular with regiments of children.

Timewalk & Brewers Days MUSEUM

(www.weymouth.gov.uk; Hope Sq; adult/child £4.50/3.25; ⏰10am-5.30pm) Recreates the sights, sounds and smells of Weymouth's past, from the Black Death and the Spanish Armada, to smuggling and the brewing industry; you even get to sample some ale.

Tudor House MUSEUM

(Trinity St; adult/child £3.50/1; ⏰1-3.45pm Tue-Fri May-Oct) Late 16th-century, furnished home conjuring up the atmosphere of Elizabethan England.

Sea Life AQUARIUM

(www.sealife.co.uk; Lodmoor Country Park; adult/child £17.50/15; ⏰10am-5pm) Sharks, penguins and seahorses entertain you at this 3-hectare aquatic park.

Sleeping

Harbourside APARTMENT ££

(☎01305-776757; www.mallamsrestaurant.co.uk; 5 Trinity Rd; 2-/4-person apt £100/150; P 📶) Antique chairs, brass bedsteads and fine Egyptian cotton fill two bedrooms and a lounge that looks out directly onto the bustling harbour. This bundle of elegance is often rented out as a weekly let (from £500), but the nightly rates are a bargain.

Old Harbour View B&B ££

(☎01305-774633; www.oldharbourviewweymouth.co.uk; 12 Trinity Rd; d £80-88) In this

Georgian terrace you get boating themes in the fresh, white bedrooms and boats right outside the front door – one room overlooks the bustling harbour, the other faces the back.

Chatsworth B&B ££
(☎01305-785012; www.thechatsworth.co.uk; 14 The Esplanade; s £45, d £78-108) A sunny waterside terrace lets you watch yachts cast off just metres away while you eat breakfast. Inside you'll find leather armchairs, vanilla candles, worn wood and bursts of seaside chintz.

Eating & Drinking

Clusters of bars line the old harbour; ice cream kiosks dot the prom.

Perry's EUROPEAN ££
(☎01305-785799; www.perrysrestaurant.co.uk; 4 Trinity Rd; mains £12-20; ⏰lunch Tue-Fri & Sun, dinner Tue-Sat) Effortlessly stylish, but also relaxed, this Georgian town house is a study of snowy white tablecloths and flashes of pink. The local seafood is irresistible: seabass with crushed saffron potatoes, and spiced tian of Portland crab. The cognoscenti book the 1st-floor window table (complete with fabulous harbour view) for a two-course lunch – a bargain at £15.

King Edward's CHIP SHOP £
(100 The Esplanade; mains £6; ⏰lunch & dinner) It has to be done: sit on Weymouth seafront scoffing fish 'n' chips. This classic Victorian chippy is lined with burgundy tiles and wrought iron; its menu is a feast of battered fish, chipped potatoes, mushy peas and pickled eggs.

Information

Tourist office (☎01305-785747; www.visitweymouth.co.uk; Pavilion Theatre, The Esplanade; ⏰9.30am-5pm Apr-Oct, 9.30am-4pm Nov-Mar)

Getting There & Away

Bus

National Express operates one direct coach to **London** (£21, 4¼ hours) daily. Bus 10/110 shuttles to **Dorchester** (35 minutes, three per hour Monday to Saturday, six on Sunday). Bus 31 goes hourly to **Lyme Regis** (1¾ hours) and **Axminster** (two hours). Bus X53 (two to six daily) travels from Weymouth to **Wareham** (50 minutes) and **Poole** (1½ hours), and to **Abbotsbury** (35 minutes), **Lyme Regis** (1¾ hours) and **Exeter** (2¾ hours) in the opposite direction. Bus 1 runs from Weymouth to **Fortuneswell** on the Isle of Portland every half-hour; between June and September it also goes on to **Portland Bill**.

Boat

Condor Ferries (www.condorferries.co.uk) Shuttle daily between Weymouth and the Channel Islands.

Train

Trains run twice-hourly between Weymouth and **London** (£50, three hours) via **Dorchester South** (11 minutes) and **Bournemouth**, (£10.90, one hour), and hourly to **Bath** (£15.60, two hours) and **Bristol** (£20.60, 2½ hours).

ISLE OF PORTLAND

The 'Isle' of Portland is really a hard, high comma of rock fused to the rest of Dorset by the ridge of Chesil Beach. Portland is where the pre-Olympic building boom is most apparent; chunks of waterside waste ground have been transformed into a shiny new sailing centre, a glitzy apartment block and a hotel. But inland on Portland's 500ft central plateau, a quarrying past still holds sway, evidenced by huge craters and large slabs of limestone. Proud, and at times bleak and rough around the edges, it's decidedly different from the rest of Dorset, and is all the more compelling because of it. The water sports on offer, rich birdlife and starkly beautiful cliffs make it worthy of at least a day-trip.

WORTH A TRIP

ABBOTSBURY SWANNERY

Every May some 600 free-flying swans choose to nest at the **Abbotsbury Swannery** (www.abbotsburytourism.co.uk; New Barn Rd; adult/child £9.50/6.50; ⏰10am-5pm or 6pm late-Mar–Oct), which shelters in the Fleet lagoon, protected by the ridge of Chesil Beach. The swannery was founded by local monks about 600 years ago, and feathers from the Abbotsbury swans are still used in the helmets of the Gentlemen at Arms (the Queen's official bodyguard). Wandering the network of trails that wind between the swans' nests is an awe inspiring experience that is often punctuated by occasional territorial displays (think snuffling cough and stand-up flapping), ensuring that even the liveliest children are stilled.

The swannery is at the picturesque village of Abbotsbury, 10 miles from Weymouth off the B3157.

WATER SPORTS – PORTLAND HARBOUR

Just south of Weymouth, the 890-hectare Portland Harbour is the sailing venue for the 2012 Olympics. The brand new **Weymouth & Portland National Sailing Academy** (☎0845 3373214; www.wpnsa.org.uk; Portland Harbour) runs sailing lessons (two/four days £170/325) and hires lasers (two hours/day £40/85). **Windtek** (☎01305-787900; www.windtek.co.uk; 109 Portland Rd, Wyke Regis) runs lessons in windsurfing (one/two days £90/150) and kitesurfing (per day £95).

Local waters offer super diving, with a huge variety of depths, seascapes and wrecks. Operators include **Underwater Explorers** (☎01305-824555; www.underwaterexplorers.co.uk; 15 Castletown, Portland) and **Fathom & Blues** (☎01305-766220; www.fathomandblues.co.uk; 262 Portland Rd, Wyke Regis). Lessons start at around £95 a day; some operators shuttle qualified divers to a site (around £20) and rent equipment (from £50).

Sights

TOP CHOICE Tout Quarry INDUSTRIAL ART
(⏲24hr) Portland's unique white limestone has been quarried for centuries, and has been used in some of the world's finest buildings – including the British Museum and St Paul's Cathedral. Tout Quarry is a disused working where 53 sculptures have been carved into the rock in situ. The result is a fascinating combination of the raw material, the detritus of the quarrying process and the beauty of chiselled works. Labyrinthine paths snake through hacked-out gullies and around jumbled piles of rock, revealing the half-formed bears, bison and lizards that emerge out of stone cliffs. Highlights include *Still Falling* by Antony Gormley, *Woman on Rock* by Dhruva Mistry and the well-hidden *Green Man*. Tout Quarry is signed off the main road, just south of Fortuneswell.

Portland Lighthouse LIGHTHOUSE
(adult/child £2.50/1.50; ⏲11am-5pm Sun-Fri Apr-Sep) For a real sense of the isle's remote nature, head to its southern tip, **Portland Bill**. Then climb the 13m-high, candy-striped lighthouse for breathtaking views of rugged cliffs and the Race, a surging vortex of conflicting tides.

Portland Castle CASTLE
(EH; www.english-heritage.org.uk; Castletown; adult/child £4.20/2.10; ⏲10am-5pm Apr-Sep, to 4pm Oct) A particularly fine product of Henry VIII's castle-building spree, with expansive views over Portland harbour. Open until 6pm in July and August.

Eating & Drinking

Crab House Café RESTAURANT ££
(☎01305-788867; www.crabhousecafe.co.uk; Portland Rd, Wyke Regis; mains £16; ⏲lunch & dinner Wed-Sat, lunch Sun) At this funky cabin beside the Fleet lagoon, the oyster beds are right alongside, meaning the molluscs (£8.50 per half dozen) are in your mouth minutes after leaving the water. Gutsy dishes include skate with chorizo and paprika, or get cracking on crab still in its shell (half/whole £11/19). The cafe is near the start of the road onto Portland.

Cove House PUB £
(Chiswell, Portland; mains £8; ⏲lunch & dinner) Extraordinary Chesil Beach views, memorable sunsets and great grub in a history-rich fishermen's inn.

Information

Tourist office (☎01305-861233; www.visitweymouth.co.uk; Portland Bill; ⏲11am-5pm Easter-Sep)

Getting There & Away

Bus

Bus 1 runs to Portland from Weymouth every half-hour, going on to Portland Bill between June and September.

Boat

See White Motor Boats (p278), for links to Weymouth.

CHESIL BEACH

One of the most breathtaking beaches in Britain, Chesil is 17 miles long, 15m high and moving inland at the rate of 5m a century. This mind-boggling, 100-million-tonne pebble ridge is the baby of the Jurassic Coast (see boxed text, p268); a mere 6000 years old, its stones range from pea-sized in the west to hand-sized in the east. More recently it became famous as the setting for Ian McEwan's acclaimed novel about sexual awakening, *On Chesil Beach*.

Chesil Beach Centre (www.chesilbeach.org; Ferrybridge; ⏲10am-5pm Apr-Sep, 11am-4pm Oct-Mar), just over the bridge to Portland, is a good place to get onto the beach. The pebble ridge is at its highest around this point – 15m compared to 7m at **Abbotsbury**. From the car park an energy-sapping hike up sliding pebbles leads to the constant surge and rattle of sea on stones and dazzling views of the sea, the thin pebble line and the expanse of the Fleet behind. The centre details geology, bird and plant life that includes ringed plover, redshank and oyster catchers, as well as drifts of thrift and sea campion. It also provides information, and organises talks and guided walks. Free entry.

Lyme Regis

POP 4406

Fantastically fossiliferous, Lyme Regis packs a heavyweight historical punch. Rock-hard relics of the past pop out repeatedly from the surrounding cliffs – exposed by the landslides of a retreating shoreline. Now a pivot point of the Unesco-listed Jurassic Coast (see p268), fossil fever is definitely in the air and everyone, from proper palaeontologists to those out for a bit of fun, can engage in a spot of coastal rummaging.

Lyme was also famously the setting for *The French Lieutenant's Woman,* the film version – starring Meryl Streep – immortalised the iconic Cobb harbour defences in movie history. Add sandy beaches and some delightful places to sleep and eat, and you get a charming base for explorations.

Sights & Activities

Lyme Regis Museum MUSEUM
(www.lymeregismuseum.co.uk; Bridge St; adult/child £3/free; ⏲10am-5pm Mon-Sat, 11am-5pm Sun Apr-Oct, 11am-4pm Wed-Sun Nov-Mar) In 1814 a local teenager called Mary Anning found the first full ichthyosaurus skeleton near Lyme, propelling the town onto the world stage. An incredibly famous fossilist in her day, Miss Anning did much to pioneer the science of modern-day palaeontology. The museum, on the site of her former home, exhibits her story along with spectacular fossils and other prehistoric finds.

Dinosaurland FOSSIL MUSEUM
(www.dinosaurland.co.uk; Coombe St; adult/child £5/4; ⏲10am-5pm mid-Feb–Nov) This mini, indoor Jurassic Park is packed with the remains of belemnites and the graceful plesiosaurus. Lifelike dinosaur models will thrill youngsters – the fossilised tyrannosaurus eggs and 73kg dinosaur dung will have them in raptures.

Cobb HARBOUR WALL
(⏲24hr) First built in the 13th century, this curling, protective barrier has been strengthened and extended over the years, so it doesn't present the elegant line it once did, but it's still hard to resist wandering its length for a wistful, sea-gazing Meryl moment at the tip.

Sleeping

Coombe House B&B ££
(☎01297-443849; www.coombe-house.co.uk; 41 Coombe St; s/d £36/72; P) Easygoing and stylish, this fabulous value guesthouse is full of airy rooms, bay windows, wicker and white wood. Breakfast is delivered to your door on a trolley, complete with toaster – perfect for a lazy lie-in in Lyme.

Alexandra HOTEL ££
(☎01297-442010; www.hotelalexandra.co.uk; Pound St; s £75, d £120-190; P) This grand 18th-century villa was once home to a countess; today, it's all dignified calm and murmured chatter. Rooms are scattered with antique chairs and fine drapes, and most have captivating views of the Cobb and the sea. The glorious terrace prompts urges to peruse the *Telegraph* in a panama hat.

WORTH A TRIP

FORDE ABBEY

A former Cistercian monastery, **Forde Abbey** (www.fordeabbey.co.uk; abbey adult/child £10.50/free, gardens £8.50/free; ⏲abbey noon-4pm Tue-Fri & Sun Apr-Oct, gardens 10am-4.30pm) was built in the 12th century, updated in the 17th century, and has been a private home since 1649. The building boasts magnificent plasterwork ceilings and fine tapestries but it's the gardens that are the main attraction: 12 hectares of lawns, ponds, shrubberies and flower beds with many rare and beautiful species.

It's 10 miles north of Lyme Regis; public transport is a nonstarter.

Old Lyme B&B ££
(☎01297-442929; www.oldlymeguesthouse.co.uk; 29 Coombe St; d £75; P) A 17th-century cottage featuring pastel-painted rooms, patterned curtains and china trinkets.

Eating & Drinking

TOP CHOICE **Hix Oyster & Fish House** SEAFOOD ££
(☎01297-446910; Cobb Rd; mains £8-20; ⏲lunch & dinner Wed-Sun) Expect grand-stand views of the Cobb and dazzling food at this super-stylish open-plan cabin. Cuttlefish comes with ink stew; ray with hazelnuts; and steak with baked bone marrow. Or plump for potted Morecambe Bay shrimps on toast, or oysters – choose from Brownsea Island or Falmouth – at £2 to £3 a pop.

Jurassic Seafood FUSION ££
(47 Silver St; mains £10-15; ⏲dinner) Bright and buzzy in blue and orange, this eatery revels in its prehistoric theme: fossil maps, hunting tips and replica dinosaur remains abound. A tasty, eclectic menu includes crab sushi, mussels and chips, and local mackerel, as well as salads and steaks.

Alexandra AFTERNOON TEA
(www.hotelalexandra.co.uk; Pound St, afternoon tea from £5.20; ⏲2.30-5.30pm) Head to this grand hotel's sea-view lawns for the ultimate English experience: afternoon tea, complete with scones, clotted cream and cucumber sandwiches.

Harbour Inn PUB £
(Marine Pde; mains £5-10; ⏲lunch & dinner) Stone walls, wooden settles and a harbour-side beer garden.

Information

Tourist Office (☎01297-442138; www.westdorset.com; Church St; ⏲10am-5pm Mon-Sat & 10am-4pm Sun Apr-Oct, 10am-3pm Mon-Sat Nov-Mar)

Getting There & Away

Bus 31 runs to **Dorchester** (1¼ hours) and **Weymouth** (1¾ hours) hourly (every two hours on Sunday). Bus X53 (six to nine daily, three on Sunday) goes west to **Exeter** (1¾ hours) and east to **Weymouth** (1½ hours).

Sherborne

POP 9350

Sherborne gleams with a mellow, orangey-yellow stone – it's been used to build a central cluster of 15th-century buildings and the impressive abbey church at their core. This serene town exudes wealth. The five local fee-paying schools include the famous Sherborne School, and its pupils are a frequent sight as they head off to lessons from boarding houses scattered around the town. The number of boutique shops and convertibles in the car parks reinforces the well-heeled feel. Evidence of splashing the cash 16th- and 18th-century style lies on the edge of town with two castles: one a crumbling ruin, the other a marvellous manor house, complete with a Capability Brown lake.

Sights & Activities

FREE **Sherborne Abbey** CATHEDRAL
(www.sherborneabbey.com; suggested donation £3.50; ⏲8am-6pm late Mar–late Oct, to 4pm Nov–mid-Mar) At the height of its influ-

FOSSIL HUNTING

Is catching. Lyme Regis sits in one of the most unstable sections of Britain's coast and regular landslips mean nuggets of prehistory constantly tumble from the cliffs. If you are bitten by the bug, the best cure is one of the regular fossil walks staged locally.

In the village of **Charmouth**, 3 miles east of Lyme, they're run two to four times a week by the **Charmouth Heritage Coast Centre** (☎01297-560772; www.charmouth.org; adult/child £7/5). Or, in Lyme itself, **Lyme Regis Museum** (☎01297-443370; 2-hr walks adult/child £9/5) offers four to six walks a week, and local expert **Brandon Lennon** (☎07944 664757; www.lymeregisfossilwalks.com; adult/child £7/5; ⏲Sat-Tue) also leads expeditions.

For the best chances of a find, time your trip to Lyme to within two hours of low tide; to be sure of a place on the walks, book ahead. If you choose to hunt by yourself, official advice is to check tide times, always collect on a falling tide, observe warning signs, keep away from the cliffs, stay on public paths, only pick up from the beach (never dig out from cliffs) and always leave some behind for others. Oh, and tell the experts if you find a stunner.

LOCAL KNOWLEDGE

STEVE DAVIES: OWNER OF DINOSAURLAND FOSSIL MUSEUM

Steve Davies is a man with weathered legs and a gleam in his eye. And that gleam's never brighter than when, in his trademark shorts and trainers (running shoes), he's heading off to the beach on a fossil-hunting foray.

Why's it addictive?

It's hunting and gathering, collecting booty off the beach. To look down and see a tiny, gold ammonite lying there waiting to be picked up is mind-blowing.

Best Spot

Black Ven, a mud flow between Lyme and Charmouth. The rocks tumble down, the tides wash the silt away and the fossils just drop onto the beach. Every day there's a new crop. But it's very easy to get cut off there. You must only search within 1½ hours of low tide, and take local advice on conditions first. See the boxed text opposite.

Top Tip

Don't use a fossil-hunting hammer. You'll get much better results by just looking closely at the gravel around the mudflows, then you could find bucket loads.

Don't Miss

The **Ammonite Pavement**, about 400m west of the Cobb. It has hundreds of fossilised, swirling sea creatures embedded in layers of rock. There's something to see at all stages of the tide, but for the best displays visit at low water; then it's truly extraordinary.

ence, the magnificent Abbey Church of St Mary the Virgin was the central cathedral of the 26 Saxon bishops of Wessex. Established early in the 8th century, it became a Benedictine abbey in 998 and functioned as a cathedral until 1075. The church has mesmerising fan vaulting that's the oldest in the country; a central tower supported by Saxon-Norman piers; and an 1180 Norman porch. Its tombs include the elaborate marble effigy belonging to John Lord Digby, Earl of Bristol, and those of the elder brothers of Alfred the Great, Ethelred and Ethelbert.

On the edge of the abbey lie the beautiful 15th-century **St John's Almshouses** (admission £2; ⏲2-4pm Tue & Thu-Sat May-Sep); look out, too, for the six-sided **conduit** now at the foot of Cheap St. This arched structure used to be the monks' lavatorium (washhouse), but was moved to provide the townsfolk with water when the abbey was disbanded.

Old Castle CASTLE

(EH; www.english-heritage.org.uk; adult/child £3/1.50; ⏲10am-5pm Apr-Sep, to 4pm Oct) These days the epitome of a picturesque ruin, Sherborne's Old Castle was built by Roger, Bishop of Salisbury, in around 1120. Elizabeth I gave it to her one-time favourite Sir Walter Raleigh in the late 16th century. He spent large sums of money modernising it before opting for a new-build instead – moving across the River Yeo to start work on the next Sherborne Castle. The old one became a Royalist stronghold during the English Civil War, but Cromwell reduced the 'malicious and mischievous castle' to rubble after a 16-day siege in 1645, leaving the crumbling southwest gatehouse, great tower and north range. It stays open until 6pm in July and August.

Sherborne Castle STATELY HOME

(www.sherbornecastle.com; house adult/child £9.50/free, gardens only £5/free; ⏲11am-4.30pm Tue-Thu & weekends Apr-Oct) Having had enough of the then 400-year-old Old Castle, Sir Walter Raleigh began building New Castle, really a splendid manor house, in 1594. Raleigh got as far as the central block before falling out of favour with the royals and ending up back in prison – this time at the hands of James I. In 1617 James sold the castle to Sir John Digby, Earl of Bristol, who added the wings we see today. In 1753, the grounds received a mega-makeover at the hands of landscape-gardener extraordinaire Capability Brown – visit today and marvel at the massive lake he added, along with a remarkable 12 hectares of waterside gardens.

Sherborne Museum MUSEUM
(www.sherbornemuseum.co.uk; Church Lane; adult/child £1/free; ⌚10.30am-4.30pm Tue-Sat Mar-Oct, 10.30am-12.30pm Tue & Thu Nov-Apr) Has an interactive digital version of the *Sherborne Missal,* an exquisite illuminated manuscript dating from the Middle Ages.

Walking Tours HERITAGE TOURS
(tour £3; ⌚11am Fri Jun-Sep) One and a half hour trips exploring the photogenic old town, leaving from the tourist office.

Sleeping

Cumberland House B&B ££
(☎01935-817554; www.bandbdorset.co.uk; Green Hill; s £50-55, d £65 75; Ⓟ) There are few straight lines in this 17th-century cottage; instead, walls undulate towards each other in charming rooms finished in white, beige and bursts of vivid pink. Breakfast is either continental (complete with chocolate croissants) or full English – either way, there's freshly squeezed orange juice.

Stoneleigh Barn B&B ££
(☎01935-815964; www.stoneleighbarn.com; North Wootton; s £55, d £80-90, f £80-100; Ⓟ) Outside, this gorgeous 18th-century barn delights the senses – it's smothered in bright, fragrant flowers. Inside, exposed trusses frame rooms calmly decorated in cream and gold and crammed with books and jigsaws. Stoneleigh is 3 miles southeast of Sherborne.

Eastbury HOTEL £££
(☎01935-813131; www.theeastburyhotel.co.uk; Long St; s £70, d £135-175; Ⓟ) The best rooms here have real 'wow' factor – black and gold lacquer screens frame minimalist free-standing baths, and shimmering fabrics swathe French sleigh beds. The standard rooms are much more standard, but are still elegant with stripy furnishings and pared-down wicker chairs.

Eating

Green ENGLISH ££
(☎01935-813821; 3 The Green; mains £9-17; ⌚lunch & dinner Tue-Sat) As mellow as the honey-coloured building it's set in, this intimate restaurant's menu is full of local ingredients; try the mushroom and thyme risotto with roasted butternut squash, or the guinea fowl with apples and redcurrants.

Pear Tree DELI £
(Half Moon St; snacks £4-8; ⌚9am-5pm Mon-Sat, 10am-4pm Sun) Full of mouth-watering aromas, this delectable deli is packed with gourmet picnic supplies. Spinach and feta pie, homemade soups and a wealth of local cheeses are coupled with irresistible cakes and puddings.

Information

Tourist office (☎01935-815341; www.westdorset.com; Digby Rd; ⌚9am-5pm Mon-Sat Apr-Oct, 10am-3pm Nov-Mar) Stocks the free *All About Sherborne* leaflet, which has a map and town trail.

Getting There & Away

Bus

Buses 57 and 58 shuttle hourly between Sherborne and **Yeovil** (30 minutes). National Express runs one coach a day from Sherborne to **Shaftesbury** (30 minutes). Bus D12 runs from Sherborne to **Dorchester** (two to three daily Monday to Friday), via Cerne Abbas.

Train

Hourly trains go to **Exeter** (£16, 1¼ hours), **London Waterloo** (£28, 2½ hours) and **Salisbury** (£11, 40 minutes).

Shaftesbury & Around

POP 6665

Perched on an idyllic hilltop overlooking a panorama of pastoral meadows and hog-backed hills, the village of Shaftesbury was home to the largest community of nuns in England until 1539, when Henry VIII came knocking during the Dissolution. These days its attractions are rather more prosaic; the town's best-known landmark is Gold Hill. This cobbled slope, lined by chocolate-box cottages, graces many a local postcard and also starred in a famous TV advert for Hovis bread.

Sights

Shaftesbury Abbey ECCLESIASTICAL RUINS
(www.shaftesburyabbey.org.uk; Park Walk; adult/child £4/1; ⌚10am-5pm Apr-Oct) These hilltop ruins mark the site of what was England's largest and richest nunnery. It was founded in 888 by King Alfred the Great, and was the first religious house in Britain built solely for women; Alfred's daughter, Aethelgifu, was its first abbess. St Edward is thought to have been buried here, and King Knut died at the abbey in 1035. Most of the buildings were dismantled by Henry VIII and his cronies, but you can still wander around its foundations with a well-devised audio guide, and visit the intriguing museum.

Old Wardour Castle CASTLE
(EH; adult/child £3.50/1.80; ⏲10am-5pm Apr-Sep, to 4pm Oct, 10am-4pm Sat & Sun Nov-Mar) The six-sided Old Wardour Castle was built around 1393 and suffered severe damage during the English Civil War, leaving these magnificent remains. It's an ideal spot for a picnic and there are fantastic views from the upper levels. It's open until 6pm in July and August. Bus 26 runs from Shaftesbury (four daily Monday to Friday), 4 miles west.

Gold Hill Museum MUSEUM
(Sun & Moon Cottage, Gold Hill; adult/child £4/1; ⏲10.30am-4.30pm Thu-Tue) Combines an 18th-century fire engine, a collection of decorative Dorset buttons, and the ornamental Byzant, used during the town's ancient water ceremony.

Sleeping & Eating

Fleur de Lys HOTEL-RESTAURANT £££
(☎01747 853717; Bleke St; s £80-90, d £110-135; P@) For a lovely dollop of luxury, immerse yourself in the world of Fleur de Lys. Fluffy bathrobes, minifridges and laptops ensure you click into pamper mode. The elegant **restaurant** (2/3 courses £25/30, mains £23; ⏲lunch pre-booked Wed-Sun, dinner Mon-Sat) rustles up lobster ravioli, venison in Armagnac, and lemon sole with a dash of vermouth. Lunch has to be pre-booked.

Up Down SELF-CATERING ££
(www.updowncottage.co.uk; Gold Hill; from £500 per week; P) This whitewashed, 4-bedroom cottage clinging to Gold Hill is a supremely picturesque place to sleep. Snug, beam-lined rooms, open fires and a hill-side garden make it one to remember; the boutique bathrooms make it hard to leave.

Mitre PUB ££
(23 High St; mains £6-10; ⏲lunch & dinner Mon-Sat, lunch Sun) An atmospheric old inn with drink-them-in views over Blackmore Vale from its decked terrace.

Information

Tourist office (☎01747-853514; www.shaftesburydorset.com; 8 Bell St; ⏲10am-5pm Mon-Sat Apr-Sep, to 3pm Oct-Mar)

Getting There & Away

National Express runs one bus a day to **London Victoria** (£19, four hours), via Heathrow, and one daily service to **Sherborne** (30 minutes). Buses 26 and 27 go to **Salisbury** (1¼ hours, four to five Monday to Saturday).

WILTSHIRE

Wiltshire is rich in the reminders of ritual. Its verdant landscape is littered with more ancient barrows, processional avenues and mysterious stone circles than anywhere else in Britain. It's a place that teases and tantalises the imagination – here you'll find the prehistoric majesty of Stonehenge, atmospheric Avebury and, in soaring Silbury Hill, the largest constructed earth mound in Europe. Then there's the serene 800-year-old cathedral at Salisbury – a relatively modern religious monument. Add the supremely stately homes at Stourhead and Longleat and the impossibly pretty villages of Castle Combe and Lacock, and you have a county crammed full of English charm waiting to be explored.

Activities

WALKING

Wiltshire is great walking country, much of it flat or rolling farmland, cut by steep-sided valleys, edged with grassy hills providing stunning views, and dotted with a wealth of ancient monuments.

The 87-mile **Ridgeway National Trail** (www.nationaltrail.co.uk/ridgeway) starts near Avebury, but there are plenty of shorter walks, including hikes around Stonehenge, Old Sarum and the Stourhead Estate.

The *Walking in Wiltshire* booklet (£3) details 10 easy strolls, while the *White Horse Trail* leaflet (£6) covers a 90-mile route, taking in all of Wiltshire's eight chalk horses. Both are available from tourist offices. The Visit Wiltshire website also has some useful downloadable walking routes, ranging from 2 to 10 miles.

Foot Trails (☎01747-820626; www.foottrails.co.uk) leads guided walks and can help you plan your own self-guided route.

CYCLING

Cyclists should pick up the *Wiltshire Cycleway* leaflet (£3) in tourist offices, which includes a detailed route guide and lists handy cycle shops. The waterproof *Off-Road Cycling in Wiltshire* (£6) includes trail maps for mountain-bikers. The Visit Wiltshire website has 10 downloadable cycling routes, ranging from 16 to 31 miles.

Dedicated cycling tours are offered by several operators, including **History on Your Handlebars** (☎01249-730013; www.historyonyourhandlebars.co.uk; Lacock).

CANAL TRIPS

The 87-mile-long **Kennet & Avon Canal** (www.katrust.org) runs all the way from Bristol to Reading. To get onto the water, contact **Sally Boats** (☎01225-864923; www.sallyboats.ltd.uk; Bradford-on-Avon) or **Foxhangers** (☎01380-828795; www.foxhangers.co.uk; Devizes), which both have narrow boats for hire. Weekly rates for a four-berth boat range from around £680 in the winter to £950 in high summer.

Information

Visit Wiltshire (www.visitwiltshire.co.uk)

Getting Around

BUS

The bus coverage in Wiltshire can be patchy, especially in the northwest of the county. The two main operators are:

First (www.firstgroup.com) Serves west Wiltshire.

Wilts & Dorset Buses (www.wdbus.co.uk) Covers many rural areas. It sells 1-day **Explorer tickets** (adult/child £7.50/4.50) and 7-day **Network passes** (£20).

TRAIN

Rail lines run from London to Salisbury and beyond to Exeter and Plymouth, branching off north to Bradford-on-Avon, Bath and Bristol, but most of the smaller towns and villages aren't served by trains.

Salisbury

POP 43,335

Centred on a majestic cathedral that's topped by the tallest spire in England, the gracious city of Salisbury makes a charming base from which to discover the rest of Wiltshire. It's been an important provincial city for more than 1000 years, and its streets form an architectural timeline ranging from medieval walls and half-timbered Tudor town houses to Georgian mansions and Victorian villas. Salisbury is also a lively, modern town, boasting plenty of bars, restaurants and terraced cafes, as well as a concentrated cluster of excellent museums.

Sights

Salisbury Cathedral CATHEDRAL

(www.salisburycathedral.org.uk; requested donation adult/child £5/3; ⏰7.15am-6.15pm) England is endowed with countless stunning churches, but few can hold a candle to the grandeur and sheer spectacle of Salisbury Cathedral. Built between 1220 and 1258, the cathedral bears all the hallmarks of the early English Gothic style, with an elaborate exterior decorated with pointed arches and flying buttresses, and a sombre, austere interior designed to keep its congregation suitably pious.

Beyond the highly decorative **West Front**, a small passageway leads into the 70m-long nave, lined with handsome pillars of Purbeck stone. In the north aisle look out for a fascinating **medieval clock** dating from 1386, probably the oldest working timepiece in the world. At the eastern end of the ambulatory the glorious **Prisoners of Conscience** stained-glass window (1980) hovers above the ornate tomb of Edward Seymour (1539–1621) and Lady Catherine Grey. Other monuments and tombs line the sides of the nave, including that of William Longespée, son of Henry II and half-brother of King John. When the tomb was excavated a well-preserved rat was found inside Longespée's skull.

The intensely atmospheric evensong takes place at 5.30pm Monday to Saturday and 3pm on Sunday, during term time only.

Spire

Salisbury's 123m crowning glory was added in the mid-14th century, and is the tallest spire in Britain. It represented an enormous technical challenge for its medieval builders; it weighs around 6500 tons and required an elaborate system of cross-bracing, scissor arches and supporting buttresses to keep it upright. Look closely and you'll see that the additional weight has buckled the four central piers of the nave.

Sir Christopher Wren surveyed the cathedral in 1668 and calculated that the spire was leaning by 75cm. A brass plate in the floor of the nave is used to measure any shift, but no further lean was recorded in 1951 or 1970. Despite this, reinforcement of the notoriously 'wonky spire' continues to this day.

Chapter House

(⏰10am-4.30pm Mon-Sat, 12.45-4.30pm Sun) Salisbury Cathedral is home to one of only four surviving original copies of the **Magna Carta**, the historic agreement made between King John and his barons in 1215 that acknowledged the fundamental principle that the monarch was not above the law. It's an evocative document; beautifully written and remarkably well preserved.

Tower Tours

These 1½ hour **trips** (01722-555156; adult/child £8.50/6.50; 1-4pm) climb up 332 vertigo-inducing steps to the base of the spire, revealing jaw-dropping views across the city and the surrounding countryside. Bookings are required.

Cathedral Close SIGNIFICANT AREA

Salisbury's medieval cathedral close, a tranquil enclave surrounded by beautiful houses, has an other-worldly feel. Many of the buildings date from the same period as the cathedral, although the area was heavily restored during an 18th-century clean-up by James Wyatt.

The close is encircled by a sturdy outer wall, constructed in 1333; the stout gates leading into the complex are still locked every night. Just inside narrow High St Gate is the **College of Matrons**, founded in 1682 for widows and unmarried daughters of clergymen. South of the cathedral is the **Bishop's Palace**, now the private Cathedral School, parts of which date back to 1220. The close is also home to three museums and historic buildings – Mompresson House Salisbury Museum and the Rifles (see p287).

Salisbury Museum MUSEUM

(www.salisburymuseum.org.uk; 65 Cathedral Close; adult/child £6/2; 10am 5pm Mon-Sat, plus 2-5pm Sun Jul & Aug) The hugely important archaeological finds here include the Stonehenge Archer (the bones of a man found in the ditch surrounding the stone circle – one of the arrows found alongside probably killed him). Add gold coins dating from 100 BC and a Bronze Age gold necklace, and it's a great introduction to Wiltshire's prehistory.

Mompesson House HISTORIC BUILDING

(NT; www.nationaltrust.org.uk; Cathedral Close; adult/child £5/2.50; 11am-5pm Sat-Wed Mar-Oct) Built in 1701, this fine Queen Anne building boasts magnificent plasterwork ceilings, exceptional period furnishings and a wonderful carved staircase. All that made it the perfect location for the 1995 film *Sense and Sensibility*.

St Thomas's Church CHURCH

(Minster St) This elegant church was built for cathedral workmen in 1219 and named after St Thomas Becket. Modified in the 15th century, its most famous feature is the amazing **doom painting** above the chancel arch, painted in 1475. This depicts Christ on the day of judgment, sitting astride a rainbow flanked by visions of Heaven and Hell; on the Hell side, look out for two naked kings and a nude bishop, a miser with his moneybags, and a female alehouse owner, the only person allowed to hang on to her clothes.

Market Square SIGNIFICANT AREA

Markets were first held here in 1219, and the square still bustles with traders every Tuesday and Saturday, when you can pick up anything from fresh fish to discount digital watches. The narrow lanes surrounding the square reveal their medieval specialities: Oatmeal Row, Fish Row and Silver St. The 15th-century **Poultry Cross** is the last of four market crosses that once stood on the square.

Rifles MILITARY MUSEUM

(The Wardrobe; www.thewardrobe.org.uk; 58 Cathedral Close; adult/child £3.50/1; 10am-5pm Mar-Sep, 10am-5pm Tue-Sat Oct-Nov & Feb) Collections include ranks of medals, Victorian redcoat uniforms and displays on 19th- and 21st-century conflicts in Afghanistan.

Tours

Salisbury Guides HERITAGE TOURS

(www.salisburycityguides.co.uk; adult/child £4/2; 11am Apr-Oct, 11am Sat & Sun Nov-Mar) One-and-a-half hour trips leave from the tourist office. There's an 8pm ghost walk on Fridays from May to September.

Festivals

Salisbury Festival MUSIC & ARTS

(www.salisburyA prestigious, eclectic event running from late May to early June, encompassing classical, world and pop music, plus theatre, literature and art.

Sleeping

TOP CHOICE **St Anns House** BOUTIQUE B&B ££

(01722 335657; www.stannshouse.co.uk; 32 St Ann St; s/d £60/110) For some perfectly priced indulgence head to this sumptuous town house, which overflows with antiques, fine silk and linen direct from Istanbul. Gourmet breakfasts include beef and chilli sausages, smoked salmon and Parma ham. The chef-proprietor has spent decades working for the great and the good, so ask about some past jobs and prepare for some great stories.

Salisbury

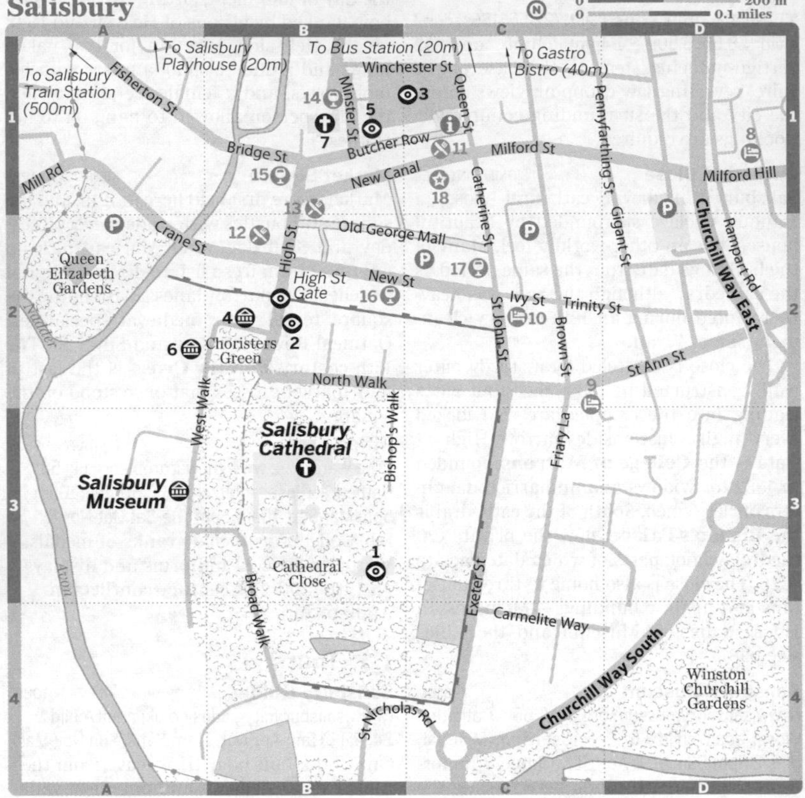

Rokeby Guesthouse B&B ££
(☎01722-329800; www.rokebyguesthouse.co.uk; 3 Wain-a-long Rd; s/d from £50/60; P@) Fancy furnishings, free-standing baths and lovely bay windows make this cheerful B&B stand out from the crowd. The decking overlooking the lawn and the minigym help, too. Rokeby is a mile northeast of the cathedral.

White Hart HOTEL ££
(☎01722-327476; www.mercure-uk.com; St John St; s from £90, d £122-142; P@) This 17th-century coaching inn is the place for a bit of pomp and pampering. Its white porticos face Cathedral Close, the service is appropriately attentive and rooms are suitably swish – the wood-rich four-poster bedrooms are positively opulent.

Websters B&B ££
(☎01722-339779; www.websters-bed-breakfast.com; 11 Hartington Rd; s £45-53, d £60-70; P@) Websters' exterior charms include quaint blue shutters and cute arched windows. Inside it's all flowery wallpaper, patterned duvets, extra tea-tray treats and a genuinely warm welcome. Websters is a mile northwest of the cathedral.

Salisbury YHA HOSTEL £
(☎0845 371 9537; www.yha.org.uk; Milford Hill; dm £18; P@) A real gem: neat rooms in a rambling, listed Victorian building. Choose from doubles or dorms – a cafe-bar, laundry and dappled gardens add to the appeal.

Old Rectory B&B ££
(☎01722-502702; www.theoldrectory-bb.co.uk; 75 Belle Vue Rd; s £40-50, d £60-80; P) Serene, airy rooms decked out in cream and shades of blue; the delightful walled garden has views of St Edmund's Church. The Old Rectory is a mile north of the cathedral.

Salisbury

Top Sights

Sights

Sleeping

Eating

Drinking

Entertainment

Eating

Gastro Bistro FRENCH ££

(☎01722-414 926; www.restaurant-salisbury.com; 19 Salt La; mains £7-16; ⏱lunch & dinner) Prepare for a Gallic, gastronomic assault on the senses. The aroma of robust French cooking fills the air, while tastebuds delight in such dishes as escargots, terrines, Toulouse sausages and confit of duck with redcurrant sauce. The three-course menu, including wine, is a bargain at £18.

Lemon Tree ENGLISH ££

(☎01722-333471; www.thelemontree.co.uk; 92 Crane St; mains £10; ⏱lunch & dinner Mon-Sat) The menu at this tiny eatery is packed with character – how about chicken laced with white wine, butternut squash with Provençal sauce, or crab claw and avocado salad? The patio-garden makes warm weather dining a delight.

Bird & Carter DELI £

(3 Fish Row, Market Sq; snacks from £4.50; ⏱8.30am-6pm Mon-Sat, 10am-4pm Sun) Nestling amid 15th-century beams, this deli-cafe blends old-world charm with a tempting array of antipasti, charcuterie and local goodies. Grab a goats' cheese and aubergine panini to go, or duck upstairs to eat alongside weathered wood, stained glass and old church pews.

One ENGLISH ££

(☎01722-411313; www.haunchofvenison.uk.com; 1 Minster St; mains £9-13; ⏱lunch & dinner) Sloping floors, slanting beams and fake pony-hide chairs surround you in this chic eatery, located above the Haunch of Venison pub (p289). The menu is equally eclectic, featuring mustard-rubbed pork chops, duck mousse with red onion marmalade and, yes: a haunch of venison (with garlic mash).

Salisbury Chocolate Bar SWEET SHOP £

(33 High St; ⏱10am-5pm Mon-Sat, 11am-4pm Sun) With a scattering of cafe tables hugging counters brimful of handmade chocs and pastries, there is no better place to blow a diet.

Drinking

Haunch of Venison HERITAGE PUB

(www.haunchofvenison.uk.com; 1 Minster St) Featuring wood-panelled snugs, spiral staircases and wonky ceilings, this 14th-century drinking den is packed with atmosphere – and ghosts. One is a cheating whist player whose hand was severed in a game – look out for his mummified bones on display inside.

Spirit BAR

(46 Catherine St; ⏱4pm-midnight Tue-Sat) Hip hang-out with a multi-coloured light-up floor, crowd-pleasing tunes on the decks and a choice of vivid cocktails.

Moloko BAR

(5 Bridge St) Red radiators, Soviet stars and flavoured vodkas create a Cold War theme.

New Inn PUB

(41 New St) Fourteenth-century boozer with a cathedral-view beer garden.

Entertainment

Salisbury Arts Centre ARTS CENTRE

(www.salisburyartscentre.co.uk; Bedwin St) Housed in the converted St Edmund's church some 800m northeast of the cathedral, this innovative arts centre showcases cutting-edge theatre, dance and live gigs; photography and arts exhibitions are held in the foyer.

Salisbury Playhouse THEATRE
(www.salisburyplayhouse.com; Malthouse Lane) Hosts top touring shows, musicals and new plays.

Goldfingers NIGHTCLUB
(www.goldfingersnightclub.com; 48 Catherine St; ⌚11pm-3am Thu-Sat) Live music on Fridays, dance-floor fillers on Saturdays, plus monthly comedy nights.

Odeon Cinema CINEMA
(www.odeon.co.uk; New Canal)

Information

Library (Market Pl; ⌚10am-7pm Mon-Wed & Fri, to 5pm Sat & Thu) Internet access; first 30 minutes free.

Tourist office (☎01722-334956; www.visitwiltshire.co.uk/salisbury; Fish Row, Market Sq; ⌚9.30am-6pm Mon-Sat, 10am-4pm Sun Jun-Sep, 9.30am-5pm Mon-Sat Oct-Apr)

Getting There & Away

Bus

National Express operates coaches to **London** via Heathrow (£16, three hours, three daily), and **Bath** (£10, 1¼ hours, one daily) and **Bristol** (£10, 2¼ hours, daily). Regular buses run to Shaftesbury, Devizes and Avebury.

Tour buses leave Salisbury for Stonehenge regularly; see p292.

Train

Trains run half-hourly from **London Waterloo** (£32, 1½ hours) and hourly to **Exeter** (£27, two hours) and the southwest. Another line provides hourly connections between Salisbury, **Portsmouth** (£15.30, 1½ hours) and **Southampton** (£7.60, 30 minutes), with hourly connections to **Bradford-on-Avon** (£9.80, 40 minutes), **Bath** (£8, one hour) and **Bristol** (£9, 1¼ hours).

Around Salisbury

OLD SARUM

The huge ramparts of **Old Sarum** (EH; www.english-heritage.org.uk; adult/child £3.50/1.80; ⌚10am-5pm Apr-Sep, 11am-3pm Oct-Mar) sit on a grassy rise about 2 miles from Salisbury. It began life as a hill fort during the Iron Age, and was later occupied by both the Romans and the Saxons. By the mid-11th century it was a town – one of the most important in the west of England; William the Conqueror convened one of his earliest councils here, with the first cathedral being built in 1092, snatching the bishopric from nearby Sherborne Abbey. But Old Sarum always had problems: it was short on water and exposed to the elements, and in 1219 the bishop was given permission to move the cathedral to a new location beside the River Avon, founding the modern-day city of Salisbury. By 1331 Old Sarum's cathedral had been demolished for building materials and the settlement was practically abandoned.

Today you can wander the grassy ramparts, see the stone foundations of the original cathedral, and look across the Wiltshire countryside to the soaring spire of Salisbury's new cathedral. Medieval tournaments, open-air plays and mock battles are held on selected days. There are free guided tours at 3pm in June, July and August. Old Sarum stays open longer in July and August: from 9am to 6pm.

Between them, buses 5, 6 and 8 run twice an hour from Salisbury to Old Sarum (hourly on Sundays).

WILTON HOUSE

Stately **Wilton House** (www.wiltonhouse.com; house & gardens adult/child £12/6.50; ⌚11.30am-4.30pm Sun-Thu May-Aug) provides an insight into the exquisite, rarefied world of the British aristocracy. One of the finest stately homes in England, the Earls of Pembroke have lived here since 1542, and it's been expanded, improved and embellished by successive generations since a devastating fire in 1647. The result is quite staggering and delivers a whistle-stop tour of the history of European art and architecture: magnificent period furniture, frescoed ceilings and elaborate plasterwork frame paintings by Van Dyck, Rembrandt and Joshua Reynolds. Highlights are the **Single** and **Double Cube Rooms**, designed by the pioneering 17th-century architect Inigo Jones. The fine landscaped **grounds** (adult/child £5/3.50; ⌚11am-5pm daily May-Aug) were largely laid out by Capability Brown.

All that architectural eye candy makes the house a favoured film location: *The Madness of King George, Sense and Sensibility* and *Pride and Prejudice* were all shot here. But Wilton was serving as an artistic haven long before the movies – famous guests include Ben Jonson, Edmund Spenser, Christopher Marlowe and John Donne. Shakespeare's *As You Like It* was performed here in 1603, shortly after the Bard had written it.

Wilton House is 2½ miles west of Salisbury; buses 3 and 13 run from Salisbury (10 minutes, three hourly Monday to Saturday, hourly on Sunday).

Stonehenge

This compelling ring of monolithic **stones** (EH; ☎01980-624715; www.english-heritage.org.uk; adult/child £6.90/3.50; ⏲9am-7pm Jun-Aug, 9.30am-6pm Mar-May & Sep-Oct, 9.30-4pm Oct-Feb) has been attracting a steady stream of pilgrims, poets and philosophers for the last 5000 years and is Britain's most iconic archaeological site.

Despite the constant flow of traffic from the main road beside the monument, and the huge numbers of visitors who traipse around the perimeter on a daily basis, Stonehenge still manages to be a mystical, ethereal place – a haunting echo from Britain's forgotten past, and a reminder of the people who once walked the many ceremonial avenues across Salisbury Plain. Even more intriguingly, it's still one of Britain's great archaeological mysteries: despite countless theories about what the site was used for, ranging from a sacrificial centre to a celestial timepiece, in truth, no one really knows what drove prehistoric Britons to expend so much time and effort on its construction.

TOP CHOICE **Stone Circle Access Visits** (☎01722-343830; www.englishheritage.org.uk; adult/child £14.50/7.50) are an unforgettable experience. Visitors normally have to stay outside the stone circle itself. But on these trips, you get to wander around the core of the site, getting up-close views of the iconic bluestones and trilithons. The walks take place in the evening or early morning so the quieter atmosphere and the slanting sunlight add to the effect. Each visit only takes 26 people; to secure a place book at least two months in advance.

THE SITE

The first phase of construction at Stonehenge started around 3000 BC, when the outer circular bank and ditch were erected. A thousand years later, an inner circle of granite stones, known as bluestones, was added. It's thought that these mammoth 4-ton blocks were hauled from the Preseli Mountains in South Wales, some 250 miles away – an almost inexplicable feat for Stone Age builders equipped with only the simplest of tools. Although no one is entirely sure how the builders transported the stones so far, it's thought they probably used a system of ropes, sledges and rollers fashioned from tree trunks – Salisbury Plain was still covered by forest during Stonehenge's construction.

Around 1500 BC, Stonehenge's main stones were dragged to the site, erected in a circle and crowned by massive lintels to make the trilithons (two vertical stones topped by a horizontal one). The sarsen (sandstone) stones were cut from an extremely hard rock found on the Marlborough Downs, 20 miles from the site. It's estimated that dragging one of these 50-ton stones across the countryside would require about 600 people.

Also around this time, the bluestones from 500 years earlier were rearranged as an inner **bluestone horseshoe** with an **altar stone** at the centre. Outside this the **trilithon horseshoe** of five massive sets of stones was erected. Three of these are intact; the other two have just a single upright. Then came the major **sarsen circle** of 30 massive vertical stones, of which 17 uprights and six lintels remain.

Much further out, another circle was delineated by the 58 **Aubrey Holes**, named after John Aubrey, who discovered them in the 1600s. Just inside this circle are the **South and North Barrows**, each originally topped by a stone. Like many stone circles in Britain (including Avebury, p298), the inner horseshoes are aligned to coincide with sunrise at the midsummer solstice, which some claim supports the theory that the site was some kind of astronomical calendar.

Prehistoric pilgrims would have entered the site via the **Avenue**, whose entrance to the circle is marked by the **Slaughter Stone** and the **Heel Stone**, located slightly further out on one side.

A marked pathway leads around the site, and although you can't walk freely in the circle itself, it's possible to see the stones fairly close up. An audio guide is included in the admission price, and can be obtained from the tourist office, which is 50m north of the main circle.

Tours

The **Stonehenge Tour** (☎01722-336855; www.thestonehengetour.info; return adult/child £11/5) leaves Salisbury's railway and bus stations half-hourly in June and August, and hourly between September and May. Tickets last all day, so you can hop off at Old Sarum (opposite) on the way back. For guided tours, try **Salisbury Guided Tours** (☎0777 567 48 16; www.salisburyguidedtours.com; from £65 per group).

Stonehenge

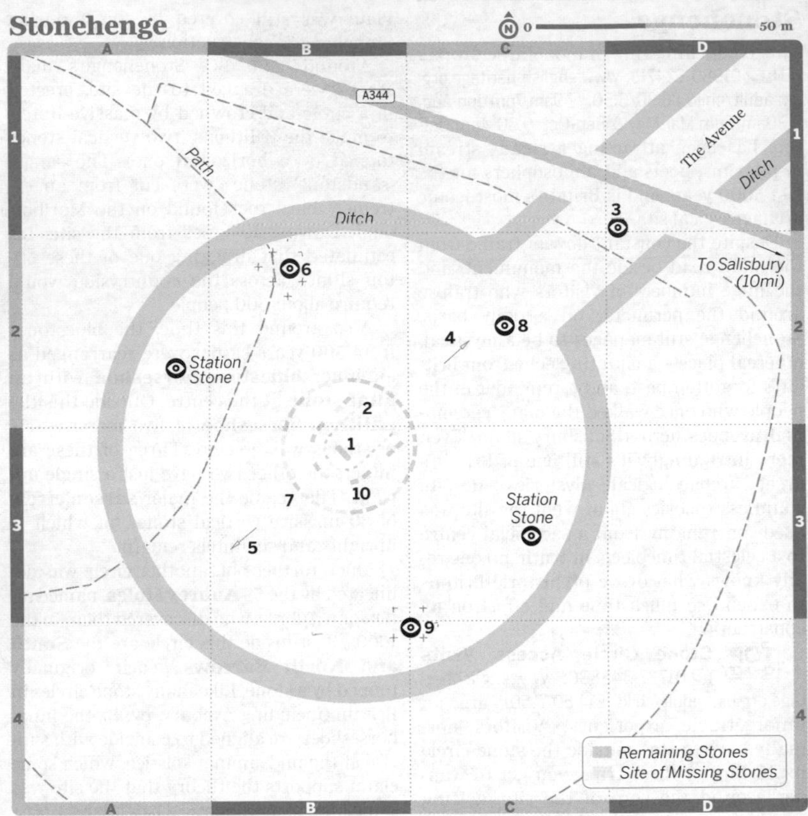

Stonehenge

Sights

Getting There & Around

Bus

No regular buses go to the site. For tours, see p291.

Taxi

Taxis charge £35 to go to the site from Salisbury, wait for an hour and come back.

Around Stonehenge

Stonehenge actually forms part of a huge complex of ancient monuments. Leaflets available from the Stonehenge visitor centre (p291) detail walking routes around the main sites; most are accessible to the public although a few are on private land.

North of Stonehenge and running roughly east–west is the **Cursus**, an elongated embanked oval; the slightly smaller **Lesser Cursus** is nearby. Theories abound as to what these sites were used for, ranging from ancient sporting arenas to processional avenues for the dead.

Other prehistoric sites around Stonehenge include a number of burial mounds, such as the **New King Barrows**, and **Vespasian's Camp**, an Iron Age hill fort.

Just north of Amesbury and 1½ miles east of Stonehenge is **Woodhenge**, a series of concentric rings that would once have been marked by wooden posts. It's thought

STONEHENGE'S FUTURE

For such a celebrated site, Stonehenge has seen a surprising amount of upheaval. While the reasons behind its creation have provoked debate, how the site is used today has proved equally controversial. The tense stand-offs between solstice-goers and police that marked the 1980s and '90s have been replaced by fresh controversy about the impact the modern world has on the jewel in Britain's archaeological crown. This World Heritage Site is framed by busy roads and wire fences; crowded with visitors throughout the summer; and underscored by the hum of traffic. For some, it's a long way from the haven of peace and spiritual tranquillity they expected to find.

Ambitious plans to tunnel the A303 under the monument and to turn the surrounding arable fields back into chalk downland came to nothing. Smaller-scale changes, involving a new visitor centre and closing part of the quieter A344, have been beset by planning and funding problems – meaning that the future of this supremely mystical site is as mysterious as its past.

there might be some correlation between the use of wood and stone in both structures, but it's unclear what the materials would have meant to ancient Britons. Excavations in the 1970s at Woodhenge revealed the skeleton of a child with a cloven skull, buried near the centre.

Stourhead

Overflowing with vistas, temples and follies, **Stourhead** (NT; www.nationaltrust.org.uk; Stourton; house or garden adult/child £7/3.80, house & garden £11.60/5.80; ⏲house 11am-5pm Fri-Tue mid-Mar–Oct) is landscape gardening at its finest. The Palladian house has some fine Chippendale furniture and paintings by Claude and Gaspard Poussin, but it's a sideshow to the magnificent 18th-century gardens, which spread out across the valley. A lovely 2-mile circuit takes you past the most ornate follies, around the lake and to the **Temple of Apollo**; a 3½-mile side trip can be made from near the Pantheon to **King Alfred's Tower** (adult/child £2.20/1.20; ⏲11.30am-4.30pm mid-Mar–Oct), a 50m-high folly with wonderful views. The garden is open, year round, from 9am to 7pm or dusk.

Stourhead is off the B3092, 8 miles south of Frome (in Somerset).

Longleat

Half ancestral mansion and half safari park, **Longleat** (www.longleat.co.uk; house & grounds adult/child £12/6, safari park £12/8, all-inclusive passport £24/17; ⏲house 10am-5pm Apr-Oct, safari park 10am-4pm Apr-Oct, other attractions 11am-5pm Apr-Oct) became the first stately home in England to open its doors to the public, in 1946. It was prompted by finance: heavy taxes and mounting bills after WWII meant the house had to earn its keep. Britain's first safari park opened on the estate in 1966, and soon Capability Brown's landscaped grounds had been transformed into an amazing drive-through zoo, populated by a menagerie of animals more at home in an African wilderness than the fields of Wiltshire. These days the zoo is backed up by a throng of touristy attractions, including a narrow-gauge railway, a Dr Who exhibit, a Postman Pat village, pets' corner and a butterfly garden.

Under all these tourist trimmings it's easy to forget the house itself, which contains fine tapestries, furniture and decorated ceilings, as well as seven libraries containing around 40,000 tomes. The highlight, though, is an extraordinary series of paintings and psychedelic murals by the present-day marquess, who was an art student in the '60s and upholds the long-standing tradition of eccentricity among the English aristocracy – check out his website at www.lordbath.co.uk.

Longleat House is just off the A362, 3 miles from both Frome and Warminster.

Bradford-on-Avon

POP 8800

Tumbling down the slopes of a wooded hillside towards the banks of the River Avon, the beautiful amber-coloured town of Bradford is one of Wiltshire's prettiest – a handsome jumble of Georgian town houses and riverside buildings that makes a pleasant day-trip from Bath, just 8 miles away.

Sights & Activities

Old Town SIGNIFICANT AREA

Bradford grew rich in the 17th and 18th centuries as a thriving centre for the weaving industry, and the town's elegant architecture is a reminder of its former wealth. To the north of the river, former warehouses line the banks, while rows of honey-yellow weavers' cottages stack up in the hills behind; some of the best examples are along **Middle Rank** and **Tory**.

Westbury House (St Margaret's St), near the river, is where a riot against the introduction of factory machinery in 1791 led to three deaths. The machinery in question was subsequently burned on **Town Bridge**.

FREE **Bradford-on-Avon Musuem** MUSUEM

(Bridge St; ⏲10.30am-12.30pm & 2-4pm Wed-Sat, 2-4pm Sun Easter-Oct) Evidence of Bradford's weaving heritage fills this tiny exhibition space above the library. As well as bobbins, reels of wool and evocative late-Victorian photos, there are some formidable ladies undergarments.

FREE **Tithe Barn** MEDIEVAL BUILDING

(EH;www.english-heritage.org.uk;⏲10.30am-4pm Apr-Mar) Tucked away 400m southwest of the town's train station, this vast 14th-century stone structure originally belonged to monks from nearby Shaftesbury Abbey (p284), and was used to store tithes (a 10% tax made on produce) during the Middle Ages. It's worth visiting for its beautiful wood-vaulted interior and stone-tiled roof.

St Laurence Church CHURCH

(Church St) One of the last surviving Saxon churches in Britain, built in the early 11th century. Look out for the twin angels carved above the chancel arch.

Sleeping & Eating

Priory Steps B&B ££

(☎01225-862230; www.priorysteps.co.uk; Newtown; s £74, d £90-104) This cosy little hillside hideaway has been created by knocking six weavers' cottages together. Now the charming rooms house antique wooden furniture and sparkling new bathrooms – the views down onto the River Avon are captivating.

Bradford Old Windmill B&B ££

(☎01225-866842; www.bradfordoldwindmill.co.uk; 4 Masons Lane; d £90-110; Ⓟ) One for the 'places-I-have-stayed' photo album: a circular, three-storey former windmill boasting eyebrow-raising features. Queen-sized waterbeds and satin sheets cosy up to conical ceilings and spiral staircases. The whole slightly saucy affair clings to a hill overlooking town.

Fat Fowl EUROPEAN ££

(☎01225-863111; Silver St; dinner mains £11-15; ⏲breakfast, lunch & dinner, closed dinner Sun) Head here for crumbly breakfast pastries, leisurely lunches (mains from £6), tasty tapas (£4) and classy Modern British cooking: expect grilled lemon sole to come with a garlic and saffron sauce. Sometimes live jazz is laid on, too.

Bradford-on-Avon

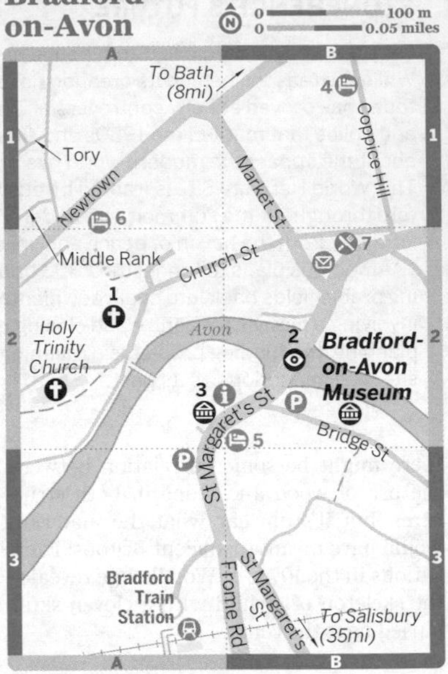

Bradford-on-Avon

Top Sights

Bradford-on-Avon Museum B2

Sights

1 St Laurence A2
2 Town Bridge B2
3 Westbury House A2

Sleeping

4 Bradford Old Windmill B1
5 Georgian Lodge B2
6 Priory Steps A1

Eating

7 Fat Fowl B2

DON'T MISS

ANCIENT SITES

» **Avebury** (p298) Bigger than Stonehenge in atmosphere and acreage, this huge stone ring encases an entire village.

» **Stonehenge** (p291) The world's most famous collection of megaliths – shame no one has a clue what it was for.

» **Maiden Castle** (p277) Massive and rampart-ringed, this is the biggest Iron Age hill fort in Britain.

» **Glastonbury Tor** (p326) Myth-rich and mighty hard to climb, this iconic mound looks down onto the Vale of Avalon.

» **Old Sarum** (p290) A stunning Iron Age stronghold on Salisbury Plain.

Georgian Lodge HOTEL ££
(☎01225-862268; www.georgianlodgehotel.com; 25 Bridge St; s/d £45/90) An old town-centre coaching inn, where rooms are dotted with shutters, ornate fireplaces and Georgian architectural plans.

Beeches Farmhouse B&B ££
(☎01225-865170; www.beeches-farmhouse.co.uk; Holt Rd; d £80-95; P) Exposed beams, rustic charm and a dollop of luxury in a honey-coloured converted barn – choose to sleep in the Milking Shed, Old Dairy or Cart House.

Information

Tourist office (☎01225-865797; www.bradfordonavon.co.uk; 50 St Margaret's St; ⏰10am-5pm Apr-Oct, 10am-4pm Mon-Sat & 11am-3pm Sun Nov-Mar)

Getting There & Away

Bus

Buses 264 and 265 run from **Bath** (30 minutes, hourly, two hourly on Sunday) en route to **Warminster** (40 minutes).

Train

Trains go roughly half-hourly to **Bath** (15 minutes), and hourly to **Warminster** (30 minutes) and **Salisbury** (£9.80, 40 minutes).

Malmesbury Abbey

The mellow hilltop town of Malmesbury is peppered with ancient buildings constructed out of honey-coloured Cotswold stone. It's the oldest borough in England, having been awarded that civic status in 880AD, and boasts one of the county's finest market crosses – a 15th-century crown-like structure built to shelter the poor from the rain.

The town's big draw is **Malmesbury Abbey** (www.malmesburyabbey.com; suggested donation £2; ⏰10am-5pm mid-Mar–Oct, 10am-4pm Nov–mid-Mar), a wonderful blend of ruin and living church, with a somewhat turbulent history. It began life as a 7th-century monastery, and was later replaced by a Norman church. By the mid-15th century the abbey had been embellished with a spire and twin towers, but in 1479 a storm toppled the east tower and spire, destroying the eastern end of the church. The west tower followed suit in 1662, destroying much of the nave. The present-day church is about a third of its original size, and is flanked by ruins at either end. Notable features include the **Norman doorway** decorated with biblical figures, the Romanesque **Apostle carvings** and a four-volume **illuminated bible** dating from 1407. A window at the western end of the church depicts Elmer the Flying Monk, who in 1010 strapped on wings and jumped from the tower. Although he broke both legs during this leap of faith, he survived and became a local hero.

Just below the abbey are the **Abbey House Gardens** (www.abbeyhousegardens.co.uk; adult/child £6.50/2.50; ⏰11am-5pm mid-Mar–Oct), which include a herb garden, river, waterfall and 2 hectares of colourful blooms.

Bus 31 runs to Swindon (45 minutes, hourly Monday to Saturday), while bus 91 heads to Chippenham (35 minutes, hourly Monday to Saturday).

Castle Combe

Proudly trumpeting itself as the 'prettiest village in England', the little hamlet of Castle Combe presents a picture-perfect image of old England – its quiet streets and stone-walled cottages doubled as the

WORTH A TRIP

WOOLLEY GRANGE

Mixing boutique style with a refreshing family-friendly attitude, **Woolley Grange** (☎01225-864705; www.woolleygrangehotel.co.uk; Woolley Green; d £130-210 f £220-460; P 📶) is one of the most welcoming country-house hotels in Wiltshire. With its designer bedrooms, laid-back attitude and quietly impressive service, it's a place whose raison d'être seems to be keeping everyone in a state of mild euphoria throughout their stay. While the little 'uns are kept lavishly entertained with everything from giant trampolines to PlayStation 2s at the Woolley Bear Den, mum and dad can relax with a truly indulgent range of spa treatments, aromatherapy massages, gourmet meals, and sparkling-wine cocktails beside the heated outdoor pool. Rooms are all individually styled, with a smattering of patchwork quilts, shiny antiques and funky fixtures. This little oasis of family fun is on the edge of Bradford-on-Avon, and is 8 miles from Bath.

fictional village of Puddleby-on-the-Marsh in the 1967 film of *Doctor Dolittle*. The village grew up around a medieval castle and later became an important centre for the local wool trade: old weavers' cottages are huddled around the medieval packhorse bridge, and the riverbanks were once lined with more than 20 clattering mills. In the centre of the village is a 13th-century **market cross**, and nearby, the medieval **church of St Andrew** contains the carved tomb of Sir Walter de Dunstanville, the 13th-century lord of the manor who fought in the Crusades and was killed in 1270.

The best place to stay in the village is the 12th-century **Castle Inn** (☎01249-783030; www.castle-inn.info; s £85-95, d £110-175), where rich fabrics cover wooden-framed beds, and soft lights illuminate worn beams and whirlpool baths. The **restaurant** (mains £9 to £20), which is open for lunch and dinner, serves up classic British fare including slow-cooked lamb shank, roast trout and a smashing Sunday lunch.

Head to the **White Hart** (mains £7-14; ⏰lunch & dinner) for real ales, cheap eats and country atmosphere.

Bus 35/35A runs from Chippenham bus station (40 minutes, one daily Monday to Saturday) to Castle Combe. There's also a direct bus to Bath on Wednesday (one hour).

Lacock

With its geranium-covered cottages, higgledy-piggledy rooftops and idyllic location beside a rushing brook, pockets of the medieval village of Lacock seem to have been preserved in aspic since the mid-19th century. The village has been in the hands of the National Trust since 1944, and in many places is remarkably free of modern development – there are no telephone poles or electric street lights, and although villagers drive around the streets, the main car park on the outskirts keeps it largely traffic-free. Unsurprisingly, it's also a popular location for costume dramas and feature films – the village and its abbey pop up in the Harry Potter films, *The Other Boleyn Girl* and BBC adaptations of *Moll Flanders* and *Pride and Prejudice*.

Sights

Lacock Abbey ABBEY

(NT; www.nationaltrust.org.uk; adult/child £10/5; ⏰11am-5pm Mar-Oct, 11am-4pm Nov-Feb) Lacock Abbey was founded as an Augustinian nunnery in 1232 by Ela, Countess of Salisbury. After the Dissolution the abbey was sold to Sir William Sharington in 1539, who converted the nunnery into a home, demolished the church, tacked a tower onto the corner of the abbey and added a brewery. Highlights are the wonderfully atmospheric medieval rooms, while the stunning Gothic entrance hall is lined with bizarre terracotta figures; spot the scapegoat with a lump of sugar on its nose. Some of the original 13th-century structure is evident in the cloisters and there are traces of medieval wall paintings. The recently restored botanic garden is also worth a visit.

On Tuesdays year-round and at winter weekends, access to the abbey is limited to the cloisters. It's possible to buy a **cheaper ticket** (adult/child £7.20/3.60), which gets you into the grounds, museum (p296) and abbey cloisters but not the abbey building itself.

Fox Talbot Museum of Photography

The ticket into the abbey also includes admission to this exhibition about the man who pioneered the photographic negative –

William Henry Fox Talbot (1800–77). A prolific inventor, he began developing the system in 1834 while working at the abbey. The museum details his ground-breaking work and displays a superb collection of his images.

Sleeping & Eating

Sign of the Angel B&B-RESTAURANT ££
(☎01249-730230; www.lacock.co.uk; 6 Church St; s £82, d £120-145; P) If you want to slumber amid a slice of history, check into this 15th-century beamed bolt-hole. Filled with antique beds, tapestries and burnished chests, comfort levels are brought up to date with free-standing sinks and slipper baths. The **restaurant** (mains from £14) revels in English classics – try the pigeon, Stilton and walnut paté, then squeeze in treacle tart with clotted cream.

King John's Hunting Lodge B&B-CAF ££
(☎01249-730313; www.kingjohnslodge.2day.ws; 21 Church St; s/d/f £65/95/115; ⏲tearooms 11am-5.30pm) Lacock's oldest building is a picturesque venue for a quintessentially English **afternoon tea** (£7 to £15): smoked salmon, cucumber sandwiches, scones, clotted cream and home-made jam. Upstairs, snug, resolutely old-fashioned rooms are crammed with creaky furniture and Tudor touches.

Lacock Pottery B&B ££
(☎01249-730266; www.lacockbedandbreakfast.com; d from £80; P) A serene, airy former workhouse graced with an oatmeal colour scheme and antiques.

George Inn PUB £
(4 West St; mains from £8; ⏲lunch & dinner) An ancient, horse brass–hung pub dispensing good grub and local ales.

Getting There & Away

Bus 234 runs hourly, Monday to Saturday, from **Chippenham** (15 minutes).

Devizes

POP 14,379

The busy market town of Devizes is famous for its grand oval marketplace, which is the largest anywhere in England. It also offers a superb collection of archaeological finds from Stonehenge and Avebury, a historic brewery and the chance to connect with slow modes of transport, ranging from shire horses to canal boats.

Sights

Wiltshire Heritage Museum MUSEUM
(www.wiltshireheritage.org.uk; 41 Long St; adult/child £4.50/3.50; ⏲10am-5pm Mon-Sat, noon-4pm Sun) The prehistoric finds here are some of Britain's finest, and include the Bush Barrow hoard – the country's richest Bronze Age burial, often dubbed the 'crown jewels of the king of Stonehenge'. This treasure trove was discovered just south of the famous stone circle and includes two exquisitely worked gold plaques, ornate belt hooks and a gold-studded dagger. Entry is free on Sundays.

Wadworth Brewery BREWERY
(☎01380-732277; www.wadworth.co.uk; New Park St; adult/child £10/4; ⏲tours 11am & 2pm Mon-Fri, booking advised) A must for ale aficionados, this Victorian brewery has been producing the tawny elixir since 1875. During a two-hour tour you get to smell the hops, see the signwriter's studio and sample the product at the end. There's also a visit to the brewery's shire horse stables. These vast creatures still stop traffic in Devizes each day, when they deliver beer to the local pubs by cart.

Old Town SIGNIFICANT AREA
Between St John's St and High St, **St John's Alley** has a wonderful collection of Elizabethan houses, their upper storeys cantilevered over the street. **St John's Church**, on Market Pl, displays elements of its original Norman construction, particularly in the solid crossing tower. Other interesting buildings include the **Corn Exchange** (topped by a figure of Ceres, goddess of agriculture), and the **Old Town Hall**, built in the 1750s. The tourist office stocks town trail leaflets.

Kennet & Avon Canal MUSEUM
(www.katrust.org.uk; The Wharf; adult/child £2/75p; ⏲10am-4pm Easter-Dec) Just west of Devizes, at Caen Hill, 29 locks raise the water level 72m in just 2½ miles. They're part of an 18th- and 19th-century inland waterway network that's brought vividly to life at this museum.

Kenavon Venture BOAT TRIPS
(☎0800 028 3707; www.katrust.org.uk; The Wharf; adult/child from £5/3; ⏲2.30pm Wed, Sat & Sun Apr-Oct) Two-hour cruises on a 60ft, wide-beam canal boat, which beautifully evoke a slower-paced past.

Sleeping & Eating

TOP CHOICE **Blounts Court** FARM B&B ££
(☎01380-727180; www.blountscourtfarm.co.uk; Coxhill La, Potterne; s £45, d £70; P)

WORTH A TRIP

CORSHAM COURT

Two miles northwest of Lacock, the Elizabethan mansion of **Corsham Court** (www.corsham-court.co.uk; adult/child £7/3; ⏲2-5.30pm Tue-Thu, Sat & Sun late Mar–Sep, 2-4.30pm Sat & Sun Oct-Nov & Jan–late Mar) dates from 1582, although the property was later improved by John Nash and Capability Brown. The sumptuous house is renowned for its superb art collection, which features works by Reynolds, Caravaggio, Rubens and Van Dyck. It's also known for its fragrance-filled formal gardens, which contain a bewitching ruined folly, stunning ornamental box hedges and a Gothic bathhouse.

In this gorgeous rural oasis the only sounds you'll hear are birdsong, whinnying horses and the bleat of the pet goats. Super-comfy bedrooms effortlessly carry off the unusual combo of old English oak beams and Ancient Greek figurines. The village cricket green is next door; it's a 5-minute walk to the local pub and Devizes is 2 miles away.

Rosemundy Cottage B&B ££
(☎01380-727122; www.rosemundycottage.co.uk; London Rd; s/d £37/65; P @ 📶 🏊) There can't be many guesthouses that can match this one's canalside terrace and heated pool. The cheerful owners delight in going the extra mile, providing plunger coffee and DVD players in the airy bedrooms, and local honey, sausages and free-range duck eggs for breakfast.

Bistro FUSION ££
(☎01380-720043; www.thebistrodevizes.co.uk; 7 Little Brittox; mains £11-16; ⏲lunch & dinner Tue-Sat) Delivering eclectic, exotic flavours to market town Devizes, this mellow eatery rustles up Moroccan lamb tagine, tofu satay skewers and aromatic duck. The chef-owner champions connecting local producers and communities, and even holds tasting sessions at nearby schools.

Bear HOTEL ££
(☎01380-734669; www.thebearhotel.net; Market Pl; s £80-85, d £105-130; P) A rambling 16th-century coaching inn with smart cream and lime candy-striped rooms, featuring the occasional oil painting and four-poster bed.

Information

Tourist office (☎01380-729408; www.visitwiltshire.co.uk; Cromwell House, Market Pl; ⏲9.30am-5pm Mon-Sat Mar-Oct, to 4.30pm Nov-Feb)

Getting There & Away

Bus 49 serves **Avebury** (25 minutes, hourly Monday to Saturday, five on Sunday), while bus 2 runs from **Salisbury** (1¼ hours, hourly Monday to Saturday). Bus 271/272/273 shuttles to **Bath** (50 minutes, hourly Monday to Saturday, seven on Sunday).

Avebury

While the tour buses usually head straight for Stonehenge, prehistoric purists make for the massive stone circle at Avebury. Though it lacks the dramatic trilithons of its sister site across the plain, Avebury is arguably a much more rewarding place to visit. A large section of the village is actually inside the ring of stones; you get much closer to the action than you do at Stonehenge; and it's bigger, older and a great deal quieter. It may also have been a more important ceremonial site, judging by its massive scale and its location at the centre of a complex of barrows, burial chambers and processional avenues.

Sights

Avebury Stone Circle STONE CIRCLE
With a diameter of about 348m, Avebury is the largest stone circle in the world. It's also one of the oldest, dating from around 2500 to 2200 BC, between the first and second phase of construction at Stonehenge. The site originally consisted of an outer circle of 98 standing stones from 3m to 6m in length, many weighing up to 20 tons, carefully selected for their size and shape. The stones were surrounded by another circle delineated by a 5.5m-high earth bank and a 6m- to 9m-deep ditch. Inside were smaller stone circles to the north (27 stones) and south (29 stones).

The present-day site represents just a fraction of the circle's original size; many of the stones were buried, removed or broken up during the Middle Ages, when Britain's pagan past became something of an embarrassment to the church. In 1934, wealthy businessman and archaeologist Alexander

RITUAL LANDSCAPE

Avebury is surrounded by a network of ancient monuments, including Silbury Hill and West Kennet Long Barrow. To the south of the village, the **West Kennet Avenue** stretched out for 1½ miles, lined by 100 pairs of stones. It linked the Avebury circle with a site called the **Sanctuary**. Post holes indicate that a wooden building surrounded by a stone circle once stood at the Sanctuary, although no one knows quite what the site was for.

The **Ridgeway National Trail** starts near Avebury and runs eastwards across Fyfield Down, where many of the sarsen stones at Avebury (and Stonehenge) were collected.

Keiller supervised the re-erection of the buried stones, and planted markers to indicate those that had disappeared; he later bought the site for posterity using funds from his family's marmalade fortune.

Self Guided Tour

Modern roads into Avebury neatly dissect the circle into four sectors. Starting at High St, near the Henge Shop, and walking round the circle in an anticlockwise direction, you'll encounter 11 standing stones in the southwest sector. They include the **Barber Surgeon Stone**, named after the skeleton of a man found under it. The equipment buried with him suggested he was a medieval travelling barber-surgeon, possibly killed when a stone accidentally fell on him.

The southeast sector starts with the huge portal stones marking the entry to the circle from the West Kennet Avenue. The **southern inner circle** stood in this sector and within this circle was the **obelisk** and a group of stones known as the **Z Feature**. Just outside this smaller circle, only the base of the **Ring Stone** remains.

In the **northern inner circle** in the northeast sector, three sarsens remain of what would have been a rectangular **cove**. The northwest sector has the most complete collection of standing stones, including the massive 65-ton **Swindon Stone**, one of the few never to have been toppled.

Silbury Hill — PREHISTORIC SITE

This huge mound rises abruptly from the surrounding fields just west of Avebury. At more than 40m high, it's the largest artificial mound in Europe, and was built in stages from around 2500 BC. No significant artefacts have been found at the site, and the reason for its construction remains unclear. A massive project to stabilise the hill took place in 2008 after a combination of erosion and damage caused by earlier excavations caused part of the top to collapse. Direct access to the hill isn't allowed, but you can view it from a car park on the A4. Hiking across the fields from Avebury (1½ miles each way) is a more atmospheric way to arrive; the tourist office sells guides (50p).

West Kennet Long Barrow — BURIAL MOUND

Set in the fields south of Silbury Hill, this is England's finest burial mound and dates from around 3500 BC. Its entrance is guarded by huge sarsens and its roof is made out of gigantic overlapping capstones. About 50 skeletons were found when it was excavated, and finds are on display at the Wiltshire

WORTH A TRIP

BOWOOD HOUSE

Stately **Bowood House** (www.bowood.org; adult/child £8.60/7; ⌚11am-5.30pm mid Mar–Oct) is a feast of extraordinary architecture. First built around 1725, it's been home to the successive earls of Shelburne (now the marquess of Lansdowne) since 1754. Colonnades, cupolas and terraces line an imposing facade, while the elaborate interiors shelter an impressive picture gallery, a wood-panelled library and the laboratory where Dr Joseph Priestly discovered oxygen in 1774. The grounds, designed by Capability Brown, are a show stopper in themselves, and include a mile-long lake, 700 types of trees and a terraced rose garden.

Bowood is 3 miles southeast of Chippenham and 6 miles northwest of Devizes.

Avebury

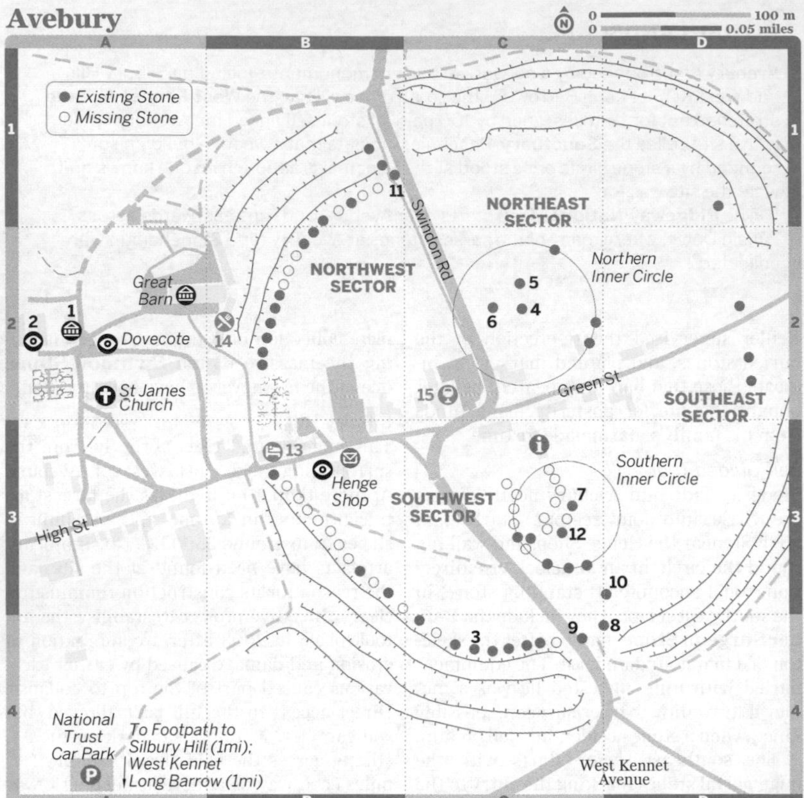

Heritage Museum (p297) in Devizes. A footpath just to the east of Silbury Hill leads to West Kennet (0.5 mile).

Avebury Manor HISTORIC HOUSE

(NT; www.nationaltrust.org.uk; Avebury Village; manor & garden adult/child £4/2, garden only £3/1.60; noon-5pm Fri-Tue Apr-Oct) Alexander Keiller bought the manor in 1939 and spent much of his later life here. The 16th-century house features Queen Anne and Edwardian era alterations, but it's the garden that's the real treat – the topiary and box hedges create a series of rooms that inspired Vita Sackville-West, creator of Sissinghurst gardens (p150) in Kent.

Alexander Keiller Museum MUSEUM

(NT; www.nationaltrust.org.uk; Avebury Village; adult/child £4.90/2.45; 10am-6pm Apr-Oct, to 4pm Nov-Mar) Explores the archaeological history of the circle and traces the story of the man who dedicated his life to unlocking the secret of the stones.

Sleeping & Eating

TOP CHOICE **Manor Farm** B&B ££

(01672-539294; www.manorfarmavebury.com; High St; d £80-90) A rare chance to sleep in style inside a stone circle – this red-brick farmhouse snuggles just inside the henge. The elegant, comfy rooms blend old woods with bright furnishings, there's a splendid free-standing claw-foot bath, and the views of the 4000-year-old standing stones provide spine-tingling views.

Circle CAFE £

(mains from £7; lunch) Veggie and wholefood cafe beside the Great Barn serving homemade quiches and cakes, chunky sandwiches and afternoon teas.

Drinking

Red Lion PUB £

(Swindon Rd; mains from £10; lunch & dinner) Having a pint here means downing a drink at the only pub in the world inside a stone

Avebury

Sights

1 Alexander Keiller Museum.................A2
2 Avebury Manor.................................A2
3 Barber Surgeon Stone.......................C4
4 Cove Stones.....................................C2
5 Cove Stones.....................................C2
6 Cove Stones.....................................C2
7 Obelisk...C3
8 Portal Stones...................................C4
9 Portal Stones...................................C4
10 Ring Stone.....................................D3
11 Swindon Stone.................................B1
12 Z Feature.......................................C3

Sleeping

13 Manor Farm....................................B3

Eating

14 Circle..B2

Drinking

15 Red Lion...C2

circle. It's also haunted by Flori, who was killed during the Civil War when her husband threw her down a well – it now forms the centrepiece of the dining room. You can stay here too (single/double £50/80).

Information

Tourist office (☎01672 539179; www.visitwiltshire.co.uk; Chapel Centre, Green St; ⌚9.30am-5pm Tue-Sun Apr-Oct, 9.30am-4.30pm Tue-Sun Nov-Mar)

Getting There & Away

Bus 5/6/96 runs to Avebury from **Salisbury** (1¾ hours, hourly Monday to Saturday, five on Sunday). Bus 49 serves **Swindon** (30 minutes) and **Devizes** (25 minutes, hourly Monday to Saturday, five on Sunday).

BRISTOL

POP 393,300

Bristol's buzzing. After decades of neglect, there's change happening everywhere you look in the southwest's biggest city these days: the historic docks have been redeveloped, the harbourside is crammed with cutting-edge galleries, designer flats and urban pieds-à-terre, and the tired old city centre is now almost unrecognisable thanks to the addition of one of Britain's largest new shopping centres at Cabot Circus and über-exclusive Quakers Friars. Long known for its industrial connections, more recently Bristol has garnered a reputation as one of the southwest's most creative corners, thanks to its thriving media industry and its lively music, theatre and art scenes. She might not be as elegant as Exeter or as beautiful as Bath, but Bristol's got plenty of life in her yet.

History

The city began as a small Saxon village and the medieval river-port of Brigstow. Bristol developed as a trading centre for cloth and wine, before 'local hero' John Cabot (actually a Genoese sailor called Giovanni Caboto) really put the city on the map, when he set sail from Bristol to discover Newfoundland in 1497. Over the following centuries, Bristol became one of Britain's major ports, and grew rich on the proceeds of the transatlantic slave trade, and from dealing in cocoa, sugar and tobacco.

By the 18th century Bristol was suffering from competition from other UK ports, especially London and Liverpool. The city repositioned itself as an industrial centre, becoming an important hub for shipbuilding and the terminus for the pioneering Great Western Railway line from London. During the 20th century Bristol also played a key role in Britain's burgeoning aeronautics industry: many key components of Concorde were developed in the nearby suburb of Filton.

During WWII the city's heavy industry became a key target for German bombing, and much of the city centre was reduced to rubble. The postwar rush for reconstruction left Bristol with plenty of concrete eyesores, but over the last decade the city has undergone extensive redevelopment, especially around the dockside.

In 2006, the city celebrated the bicentenary of the birth of Isambard Kingdom Brunel, the pioneering Victorian engineer responsible (among many other things) for developing the Great Western Railway, the Clifton Suspension Bridge and the SS *Great Britain*.

A £25-million scheme to turn the city's old Industrial Museum on the harbour into a flagship Museum of Bristol is due for completion in 2011.

Sights

TOP CHOICE **SS Great Britain** MUSEUM
(Map p302; www.ssgreatbritain.org; Great Western Dock, Gas Ferry Rd; adult/child £11.95/9.50; ⌚10am-5.30pm Apr-Oct, 10am-4.30pm Nov-Mar;) In 1843 Brunel designed

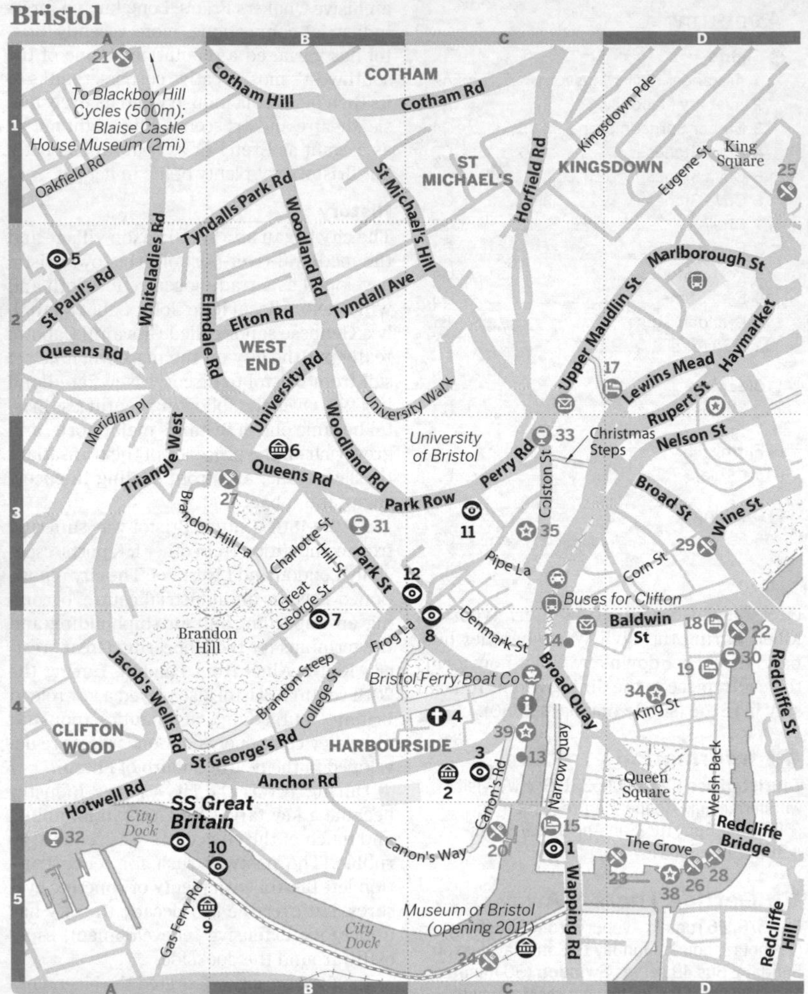

the mighty SS *Great Britain*, the first transatlantic steamship to be driven by a screw propeller. For 43 years the ship served as a luxury ocean-going liner and cargo vessel, but huge running costs and mounting debts meant she was eventually sold off to serve as a troopship and coal hulk, a sorry fate for such an important vessel. By 1937 she was no longer watertight and was abandoned near Port Stanley in the Falklands, before finally being towed back to Bristol in 1970.

Since then a massive 30-year restoration program has brought SS *Great Britain* back to stunning life. The ship's rooms have been refurbished in impeccable detail, including the galley, surgeon's quarters, mess hall and the great engine room; but the highlight is the amazing 'glass sea' on which the ship sits, enclosing an airtight dry dock that preserves the delicate hull and allows visitors to see the ground-breaking screw propeller up close. Moored nearby is a replica of John Cabot's ship **Matthew** (Map p302), which sailed from Bristol to Newfoundland in 1497.

Tickets to SS *Great Britain* also allow access to the neighbouring **Maritime Heritage Centre** (Map p302; ☎0117-927

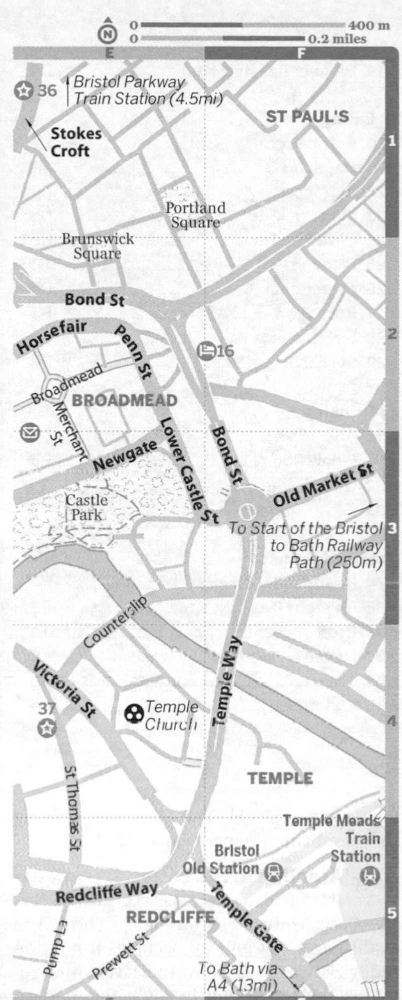

9856; Great Western Dockyard, Gas Ferry Rd; ⌚10am-5.30pm Apr-Oct, to 4.30pm Nov-Mar), which has exhibits relating to the ship's illustrious past and the city's boat-building heritage.

Clifton HISTORIC AREA

During the 18th and 19th centuries, wealthy Bristol merchants transformed the former spa resort of Clifton into an elegant hilltop suburb packed with porticoed mansions – especially around **Cornwallis Cres** and **Royal York Cres**. These days, Clifton is still the poshest postcode in Bristol, with a wealth of streetside cafes and designer shops, and a villagey atmosphere that's far removed from the rest of the city.

Clifton Suspension Bridge BRIDGE

(Map p307; www.clifton-suspension-bridge.org.uk) Clifton's most famous (and photographed) landmark is another Brunel masterpiece, the 76m-high Clifton Suspension Bridge, which spans the Avon Gorge from Clifton over to Leigh Woods in northern Somerset. Construction began in 1836, but sadly Brunel died before the bridge's completion in 1864. It was mainly designed to carry light horse-drawn traffic and foot passengers, but these days around 12,000 cars cross it every day – testament to the quality of the construction and the vision of Brunel's design.

It's free to walk or cycle across the bridge; car drivers pay a 50p toll. There's a **visitor information point** (visitinfo@clifton-suspension-bridge.org; ⌚10am-5pm) near the tower on the Leigh Woods side. Free guided tours of the bridge take place at 3pm on Saturdays and Sundays from May to October.

The Downs PARKS

Near the bridge, the grassy parks of Clifton Down and Durdham Down (often referred to as just the Downs) make a fine spot for a picnic. Nearby, a well-worn observatory houses a **camera obscura** (adult/child £2/1; ⌚10.30-5.30pm) and a tunnel leading down to the **Giant's Cave** (adult/child £1.50/0.50), a natural cavern that emerges halfway down the cliff with dizzying views across the Avon Gorge.

Bristol Lido BATHS

(☎0117-933-9530; www.lidobristol.com; Oakfield Place; pool adult/child £15/7.50; ⌚7am-10pm) Bristol's public hot tub dates back to 1849, but it's been through its fair share of trials and tribulations over the last century. Having closed in 1990, it's now been completely renovated, and the original outdoor heated pool is back to its sparkling best. Elsewhere you'll find a sauna, bar and a rather good restaurant, and needless to say there are plenty of spa treatments on offer to help you unwind after a long day's sightseeing.

Bristol Zoo ZOO

(www.bristolzoo.org.uk; Clifton; adult/child £11.81/7.27; ⌚9am-5.30pm mid-Mar–mid-Oct, 9am-5pm mid-Oct–mid-Mar) The city's award-winning zoo occupies a huge site on the north side of Clifton. Highlights include gorilla and gibbon islands, a reptile and bug house, a butterfly forest, a lion enclosure, a monkey jungle and the new **Zooropia** (adult/child

Bristol

Top Sights

SS Great Britain A5

Sights

1 Arnolfini Arts Centre C5
2 At-Bristol C4
3 Blue Reef Aquarium C4
4 Bristol Cathedral C4
5 Bristol Lido A2
6 City Museum & Art Gallery B3
7 Georgian House B4
8 Banksy's Love Triangle Stencil C4
9 Maritime Heritage Centre A5
10 Matthew B5
11 Red Lodge C3
12 Specialized (Bike Hire) C3

Activities, Courses & Tours

13 Bristol Packet Boat Trips C4
14 City Sightseeing C4

Sleeping

15 Bristol YHA C5
16 Future Inns Cabot's Circus F2
17 Hotel du Vin D2
18 Mercure Brigstow Hotel D4
19 Premier Inn, King St D4

Eating

20 Bordeaux Quay C5
21 Cowshed A1
22 Glassboat D4
23 Mud Dock D5
24 Olive Shed C5
25 Pieminister D1
26 riverstation D5
27 Rocotillo's B3
28 Severnshed D5
29 St Nicholas Market D3

Drinking

30 Apple D4
31 Elbow Room B3
32 Grain Barge A5
33 Zerodegrees C3

Entertainment

34 Bristol Old Vic D4
35 Colston Hall C3
36 Croft E1
37 Fleece & Firkin E4
38 Thekla D5
39 Watershed C4

£7.50/6), a treetop adventure park strung with net ramps, rope bridges, hanging logs and a zip-line.

At-Bristol SCIENCE MUSEUM
(Map p302; www.at-bristol.org.uk; Anchor Rd; adult/child £10.80/7; ⏲10am-5pm Mon-Fri, to 6pm Sat & Sun) Bristol's interactive science museum has several zones spanning space, technology and the human brain. In the Curiosity Zone you get to walk through a tornado, spin on a human gyroscope and strum the strings of a virtual harp. It's fun, imaginative and highly interactive, and should keep kids enthralled for a few hours.

Blue Reef Aquarium AQUARIUM
(Map p302; www.bluereefaquarium.co.uk; Harbourside; adult/child £13.50/9.20; ⏲10am-5pm Mon-Fri, to 6pm Sat & Sun) Across the square is Bristol's brand-new aquarium, with tanks recreating 40 underwater environments from tropical seas to mangrove forests and coral reefs, complete with underwater viewing tunnel. The 3D IMAX cinema shows marine-themed films.

FREE **Arnolfini Arts Centre** GALLERY
(Map p302; www.arnolfini.org.uk; 16 Narrow Quay; ⏲10am-6pm Tue-Sun) The city's avant-garde art gallery occupies a hulking redbrick warehouse by the river, and remains the top venue in town for modern art, as well as occasional exhibitions of dance, film and photography.

FREE **City Museum & Art Gallery** MUSEUM
(Map p302; Queen's Rd; ⏲10am-5pm) Housed in a stunning Edwardian baroque building, the City Museum & Art Gallery has an excellent collection of British and French art; galleries dedicated to ceramics and decorative arts; and archaeological, geological and natural-history wings.

FREE **Georgian House** ARCHITECTURE
(Map p302; 7 Great George St; ⏲10am-5pm Wed-Sat) This 18th-century house provides an atmospheric illustration of aristocratic life in Bristol during the Georgian era

– and the city's links to the slave trade. The six-storeyed house was home to West India merchant John Pinney, along with his slave Pero (after whom Pero's Bridge across the harbour is named). It's decorated throughout in period style, typified by the huge kitchen (complete with cast-iron roasting spit) and the grand drawing rooms.

FREE **Red Lodge** ARCHITECTURE
(Map p302; Park Row; admission free; ⌚10am-5pm Wed-Sat) Built in 1590 but much remodelled in 1730, this red-brick house reflects the architecture of both periods. The highlight is the Elizabethan Oak Room, which still features its original oak panelling, plasterwork ceiling and carved chimneypiece.

FREE **Ashton Court Estate** PARK
(⌚8am-9.15pm May-Aug, earlier closing rest of year) Two miles from the city centre, this huge estate is Bristol's 'green lung', with 850 sprawling acres of oak woodland, trails and public park. It hosts many of Bristol's keynote events, including the Balloon and Kite festivals, and also contains the Avon Timberland Trail, the UK's only urban mountain bike trail.

Free estate maps are available from the **visitor centre** (⌚8.30am-4.30pm Mon-Thu, 8am-4.30pm Fri).

FREE **Blaise Castle House Museum** MUSEUM
(Henbury Rd; ⌚10am-5pm Wed-Sat) In the northern suburb of Henbury is this late-18th-century house and social-history museum. Displays include vintage toys, costumes and other Victorian ephemera. Bus 43 (45 minutes, every 15 minutes) passes the castle from Colston Ave; bus 1 (20 minutes, every 10 minutes) from St Augustine's Pde doesn't stop quite as close, but is quicker and more frequent.

Bristol Cathedral CHURCH
(Map p302; ☎0117-926 4879; www.bristol-cathedral.co.uk; College Green; donations requested; ⌚8am-6pm) Originally founded as the church of an Augustinian monastery in 1140, Bristol Cathedral was remodelled during the 19th century. It's one of Britain's best examples of a 'Hall Church' (meaning the nave, chapels and choir are the same height). Although the nave and the west towers are largely 19th century, the medieval choir has some fascinating misericords depicting apes in hell, quarrelling couples and dancing bears, and the south transept shelters a rare Saxon carving of the *Harrowing of Hell*, discovered under the chapter-house floor after a 19th-century fire.

☞ Tours

Bristol Highlights Walk WALKING TOUR
(adult/under 12yr £3.50/free; ⌚11am Sat Apr-Sep) Tours the old town, city centre and Harbourside. It's run every Saturday; just turn up outside the tourist office. Themed tours exploring Clifton, Brunel and the history of Bristol traders are run on request.

FREE **MP3 Tours** WALKING TOUR
(http://visitbristol.co.uk/site/visitor-information/multimedia/mp3-audio-tours) Free MP3 guides covering Brunel, the slave trade, the harbour area and the city's heritage.

City Sightseeing SIGHTSEEING TOUR
(Map p302; www.bristolvisitor.co.uk; 24hr ticket adult/child £10/5; ⌚10am-4pm Easter-Sep) Open-topped hop-on/hop-off bus visiting all the major attractions. Buses leave Broad Quay hourly (every 30 minutes

BRISTOL IN...

Two Days

Start off your Bristol trip with a morning exploring **Clifton**. Factor in a walk across the **Suspension Bridge**, a stroll across the **Downs**, and lunch at one of the many cafés and restaurants round Clifton – we particularly like the **Clifton Sausage**, the **Primrose Café** and the **Thali Café**. Spend the afternoon at **Bristol Zoo** or lounging around the **Bristol Lido**, then overnight at the gorgeous **Hotel du Vin**.

On day two, set out for the city's historic docks. Stop off for some avant-garde art at the **Arnolfini** en route to Brunel's stately steamer, **SS Great Britain**. Enjoy lunch at the thoroughly brilliant **Bordeaux Quay**, and then in the afternoon take a cruise with the **Bristol Ferry Boat**, mosey round the shops in **Cabot Circus** or **St Nicholas Market**, or visit the city's historic houses, the **Red Lodge** and the **Georgian House**. Finish up with dinner at **riverstation**.

from July to September). Single trips adult/child £1/50p.

Bristol Packet Boat Trips BOAT TOUR
(Map p302; www.bristolpacket.co.uk; adult/child £5.25/4.75; ⏲11am-4.15pm Sat & Sun) Cruises around the harbour area (departures every 45 minutes, operates daily during school holidays). There are also weekly cruises along the Avon from May to October (adult/child £14/12), and less frequent trips to Bath and local pubs.

Festivals & Events

Bristol Shakespeare Festival THEATRE
(www.bristolshakespeare.org.uk) Britain's biggest outdoor festival devoted to the Bard, held between May and September.

St Paul's Carnival FESTIVAL
(www.stpaulscarnival.co.uk) Community knees-up on the first Saturday of July.

Bristol Harbour Festival FESTIVAL
(www.bristolharbourfestival.co.uk) Bands, events and historic ships take over the city's docks in early August.

International Balloon Fiesta FESTIVAL
(www.bristolballoonfiesta.co.uk) Hot-air balloonfest at Ashton Court in August.

International Kite Festival FESTIVAL
(www.kite-festival.org.uk) Held in September, also at Ashton Court.

Encounters FILM FESTIVAL
(www.encounters-festival.org.uk) Bristol's largest film-fest is in November.

Christmas Markets SHOPPING
Late-night shopping around St Nicholas Market in December.

Sleeping

Bristol's hotels are largely aimed at the business crowd; function rather than form is definitely the order of the day. The city also has a real shortage of quality B&Bs, but there are a couple of decent chains and a great hostel in the city centre.

TOP CHOICE **Hotel du Vin** HOTEL £££
(Map p302; ☎0117-925 5577; www.hotelduvin.com; Narrow Lewins Mead; d £150-205, ste £225; P wi-fi) For elegance and indulgence in Bristol this is the only choice. Sensitively built inside old sugar warehouses, with plenty of industrial character still in situ, this hotel is simply a treat from start to finish: giant futon beds, clawfoot baths, frying-pan showerheads and a sexy minimalist sheen. The double-height loft suites wouldn't look out of place in a Manhattan loft apartment.

Bristol YHA HOSTEL £
(Map p302; bristol@yha.org.uk; 14 Narrow Quay; dm £20, s £25-35, d £40-45; @) It's at the opposite end of the price scale, but this warehouse hostel actually has an even better location, in a renovated redbrick dockhouse overlooking the harbour. Facilities are superb: modern four-bed dorms and doubles, a cycle store, games room and the excellent Grainshed coffee lounge.

Premier Inn, King St HOTEL ££
(Map p302; ☎0117-910 0619; www.premiertravelinn.com; The Haymarket; r £59-79; ❄ wi-fi) Swallow those preconceptions – in the absence of any decent B&Bs near the city centre, this budget chain is a real find. It's literally steps from the harbour and the Old Vic, the rooms have big beds, workdesk and wi-fi, and some even have harbour glimpses. Worth considering – although the pub next door can get rowdy at weekends. The hotel offers 15% discounted parking at the NCP on Queen Charlotte Street (although it's still pretty expensive).

Future Inns Cabot Circus HOTEL ££
(Map p302; ☎0845-094 5588; reservations.bristol@futureinns.co.uk; d £59-89; P wi-fi) This hotel mini-chain has outlets in Plymouth, Cardiff and Bristol. It's modern, functional and businessy, and the concrete skin is charmless, but the rooms are clean in beige, white and pine, and the rates are pretty fantastic this close to the centre. Rates include free parking at the Cabot Circus car-park.

Mercure Brigstow Hotel HOTEL £££
(Map p302; ☎0117-929 1030; H6548@accor.com; Welsh Back; d £99-250; wi-fi) Despite the concrete-and-glass facade, this Mercure hotel's surprisingly cool inside. Bedrooms boast trendy floating beds, curved wood-panel walls and tiny TVs set into bathroom tiles (gimmicky, yes, but rather fun).

City Inn HOTEL ££
(☎0117-925 1001; bristol.reservations@cityinn.com; Temple Way; r £65-169; P @ wi-fi) Bristol's chain love-affair continues. Outside, it's about as attractive as an overpass; inside you'll find sleek furniture and wall-to-ceiling windows in every room, and luxury extras such as mist-proof mirrors, hi-fis and White Company toiletries.

Clifton

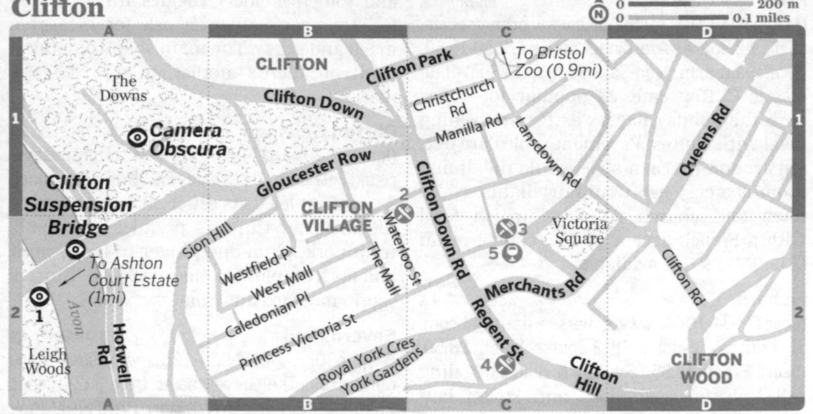

Eating

Eating out in Bristol is a real highlight – the city is jammed with restaurants of every description, ranging from classic British 'caffs' to designer dining emporiums.

TOP CHOICE riverstation RESTAURANT ££
(Map p302; ☎0117-914 4434; www.riverstation.co.uk; 2-/3-course lunch £12/14.75, dinner mains £13-19; ⊙lunch & dinner) The city's original, award winning riverside restaurant, still renowned for its super-sophisticated modern British cooking. The downstairs cafe rustles up light lunches, coffee and feather-light pastries, while up on the 1st floor it's all effortless elegance and European cuisine.

Bordeaux Quay RESTAURANT ££
(Map p302; ☎0117-943 1200; www.bordeaux-quay.co.uk; Canons Way; brasserie mains £10, restaurant mains £17-21; ⊙lunch & dinner) Top-class dining with sustainable credentials, in a fabulous converted dock warehouse overlooking the harbour. It has multiple guises: a restaurant, brasserie, bar, deli, bakery and even a cookery school if you feel like brushing up your kitchen skills. The same industrial-chic decor and continental-style food runs throughout, but it's a hot ticket: reservations recommended.

Cowshed RESTAURANT ££
(Map p302; ☎0117-973 3550; www.thecowshedbristol.com; 46 Whiteladies Rd; 3-course lunch £10, dinner mains £13.95-21.95; ⊙lunch & dinner) Country dining in a city setting. Hearty roast chicken, perfect pork chop and the house special Hot Stone steak (which you cook yourself at your table) are the order of the day, served in sophisticated surroundings blending big glass windows, wooden furniture and rough stone walls. It's a bit of a walk up the old Whiteladies Rd, but you'll be extremely glad you made the trip.

Thali Café INDIAN £
(Map p307; ☎0117-974 3793; www.thethalicafe.co.uk; 1 Regent St; set meal £6.95; ⊙lunch Tue-Sun, dinner daily) The bustle and buzz of an Indian street market comes to this much-loved ethnic café, which now has four outlets round the city, including this one in Clifton. It specialises in fresh, spicy and authentic thalis (multicourse Indian meals), and the six-course £6.95 menu is just ridiculously cheap. For big, bold flavours and dining-on-a-budget, there's nowhere better in Bristol.

Clifton

Top Sights
Camera Obscura A1
Clifton Suspension Bridge A2

Sights
1 Clifton Suspension Bridge Visitor Information A2

Eating
2 Clifton Sausage B1
3 Primrose Café C2
4 Thali Café C2

Drinking
5 Albion C2

Primrose Café BISTRO ££
(Map p307; ☎0117-946 6577; www.primrosecafe.co.uk; 1-2 Boyce's Ave; dinner mains £12.50-16.50; ⏰cafe9am-5pm Mon-Sat, 9am-3pm Sun) The classic Clifton cafe, as popular for coffee with the Sunday papers as for an evening meal with chums. Pavement tables are dotted around Parisian-style, while the dining room is a cosy grotto of fairy-lights, white linen and church candles. British food with a French accent. A 2-/3-course menu (£15.95/18.95) is available.

Fishers SEAFOOD ££
(☎0117-974 7044; www.fishers-restaurant.com; 35 Princess Victoria St; 2-course lunch £8.50, mains £14.25-18.95; ⏰lunch & dinner) Ceiling sails, porthole windows and storm lanterns conjure a shipshape atmosphere at this Clifton seafooderie, which prides itself on the freshness of its fish deliveries. The seafood is simple and superb, from bream fillets to full-blown bouillabaisse, while the hot shellfish platter (£21.50 to £36) is ideal for sharing.

Pieminister PIES £
(Map p302; 24 Stokes Croft; pies £3; ⏰10am-7pm Sat, 11am-4pm Sun) Forget boring old steak-and-kidney – the creations at Bristol's beloved pie shop range from Thai Chook (chicken with green curry sauce) to Chicken of Aragon (chicken, bacon, garlic and vermouth) and Mr Porky (pork, bacon, leeks and Somerset cider). Veggies are well cared for, too: you can even ask for meat-free mash and gravy. The main shop's on Stokes Croft, but there's another outlet in St Nick's market.

Clifton Sausage GASTROPUB ££
(Map p307; ☎0117-973 1192; www.cliftonsausage.co.uk; 7-9 Portland St; mains £8.50-16.50; ⏰lunch & dinner) At least six different bangers grace the menu at Clifton's premier gastropub, from pork, plum and ginger to lamb, mint and apricot, plus the house special 'Clifton' (pork, mustard and Somerset cider).

Severnshed RESTAURANT ££
(Map p302; ☎0117-925 1212; www.shedrestaurants.co.uk; The Grove; mains from £12, menus £18.95-22.95; ⏰lunch & dinner) Typifying 'new Bristol', this former boathouse was built by Brunel – now it's home to a designer bar, bistro and waterside cafe. The renovation is a beautiful blend of industrial trappings and contemporary chrome, while the food offers Euro-fusion flavours. Check out the cool floating bar.

St Nicholas Market MARKET
(Map p302; Corn St; ⏰9.30am-5pm Mon-Sat) The city's lively street market has a bevy of food stalls selling everything from artisan bread to cheese toasties. Look out for local **farmers markets** on Wednesdays and a **slow-food market** on the first Sunday of each month.

THE TRIANGLE TRADE

It's a sobering thought that much of Bristol's 18th-century wealth and splendour was founded on human exploitation. In the late 1600s, the first slave ship set sail from Bristol harbour, kick-starting the city's connections with the so-called 'triangular trade', in which Africans were kidnapped from their homes (or traded, usually for munitions) before being shipped across the Atlantic and sold into a life of slavery in the New World. Conditions on the boats were horrific; it was expected that one in 10 of those captured would die en route – in reality, many more did. Their human cargo unloaded, the merchants stocked their vessels with luxury goods such as sugar, rum, indigo, tobacco and cotton, and sailed back to Britain.

Bristol, London and Liverpool were the three main British ports engaged in the practice. By the time the slave trade (not slavery itself) was finally abolished in the British Empire in 1807, it's thought that 500,000 Africans had been enslaved by Bristol merchants – a fifth of all people sold into slavery by British vessels.

The financial profits for Bristol's traders were immense, and that legacy lingers. Many of the grand houses in Clifton were built on the proceeds of the 'trade', and several of the city's most elegant edifices – such as the Bristol Old Vic theatre – were partly financed by slave-trading investors.

There are many more connections – for further insights, download the MP3 audio tour from the **Visit Bristol** (www.visitbristol.co.uk) website, or pick up the *Slave Trade Trail* leaflet (£3) from the tourist office.

TYNTESFIELD

Formerly the aristocratic home of the Gibbs family, **Tyntesfield** (NT; ☎01275-461900; Wraxall; adult/child £10/5; ⊙11am-5pm Sat-Wed Mar-Oct) is an ornate Victorian pile that prickles with spiky turrets and towers. The house was built in grand Gothic Revival style by the architect John Norton, and is crammed with Victorian decorative arts, a working kitchen garden and a magnificent private chapel. The house is undergoing extensive renovation (due to finish in 2012, allowing a fascinating insight into the conservation process). Tyntesfield is 7 miles southwest of Bristol, off the B3128.

Olive Shed BISTRO ££
(Map p302; ☎0117-929 1960; www.theoliveshed.com; Princes Wharf; ⊙6.30-10pm Wed, noon-10pm Thu-Sat, noon-4pm Sun) Another popular place for waterside eating, serving mainly tapas and Med food in a bright and attractive setting.

Rocotillo's CAFE £
(Map p302; 1 Queens Row; mains £6-10; ⊙breakfast & lunch) American-style diner serving gourmet burgers, crispy fries and the best milkshakes in town.

Boston Tea Party CAFE £
(www.bostonteaparty.co.uk) Bristol's best sandwich shop has branches dotted round the city, on Princess Victoria St, Park St and Whiteladies Rd.

Chandos Deli DELI £
(www.chandosdeli.com) Popular deli chain serving gourmet goodies. Branches can be found on Whiteladies Rd, Princess Victoria St and Quaker's Friars.

Mud Dock CAFE £
(Map p302; 40 The Grove; mains £8-14; ⊙lunch & dinner Mon-Sat, 10am-4.30pm Sun) Part-bar, part-bistro, part-bike shop.

Glassboat RESTAURANT ££
(Map p302; www.glassboat.co.uk; Welsh Back; lunch menu £10, dinner mains £11-16; ⊙closed Sun) Italian flavours on a double-decked river barge.

Drinking

Apple PUB
(Map p302; Welsh Back) Bristol's legendary cider boat stocks an impressive 40 varieties of the golden elixir and specialises in organic and craft-produced varieties (try a tipple of the raspberry and strawberry varieties).

Grain Barge PUB
(Map p302; www.grainbarge.com; Mardyke Wharf, Hotwell Rd) Built in 1936, overhauled in 2007, this tow-barge near SS *Great Britain* is owned by the city's microbrewery, the Bristol Beer Factory. Boutique beers include traditional No. 7 Bitter, creamy Milk Stout, pale Sunrise Ale and dark Exhibition ale.

Albion PUB
(Map p307; Boyce's Ave) Lovely old-fashioned pub packed with evening drinkers from Clifton's well-heeled streets.

Zerodegrees PUB
(Map p302; www.zerodegrees.co.uk; 53 Colston St) Plentiful glass, chrome and steel in Bristol's boutique brewery. Options range from fruit beers and pale wheat ale to Czech-style Black and Pilsner lagers.

Elbow Room PUB
(Map p302; 64 Park St) Shoot some 8-ball at this popular outlet of the pool hall chain.

✩ Entertainment

The Bristol club scene moves fast; check the latest listings to see where the big nights are happening. The fortnightly listings magazine *Venue* (www.venue.co.uk; £1.50) contains the latest info on what's hot and what's not. The freebie mag *Folio* is published monthly.

Watershed CINEMA, MEDIA CENTRE
(Map p302; www.watershed.co.uk; 1 Canon's Rd) Bristol's digital media centre also hosts regular arthouse programs and film-related events, including the Encounters Festival in November.

Bristol Old Vic THEATRE
(Map p302; www.bristololdvic.org.uk; 103 The Cut) Bristol's stately theatre (one of England's oldest) has been through troubled times, but it's recently reopened its doors and puts on big touring productions in its famously ornate auditorium, plus more experimental work in its smaller studio.

Tobacco Factory THEATRE
(www.tobaccofactory.com; Raleigh Rd) This small-scale theatre venue is across the

BANKSY

Bristol brings you closer to a man who specialises in stencils, subverted art and stunts: the guerrilla graffiti artist **Banksy**. Banksy's true identity is a closely guarded secret, but it's rumoured he was born in 1974 in Yate (near Chipping Sodbury), 12 miles from Bristol, and cut his teeth in a city graffiti outfit. Headline-grabbing works include issuing spoof British £10 notes (with Princess Diana's head on them instead of the Queen's); replacing 500 copies of Paris Hilton's debut album in record shops with remixes (featuring tracks titled *Why Am I Famous*? and *What Have I Done*?); painting an image of a ladder going up and over the Israeli West Bank Barrier; and covertly inserting his own version of a primitive cave painting (with a human hunter-gatherer pushing a shopping trolley) into the British Museum in London. He also recently had Bristolians queuing round the block for his first official exhibition in the city at the City Museum and Art Gallery – although needless to say no-one managed to catch a glimpse of the artist himself.

Banksy's art has proved to be a divisive issue in Bristol. Most people love him, but the city authorities were initially less keen: many of his public works have long since been washed away, although the powers-that-be finally seem to have come around to Banksy's potential as a tourist magnet.

A few of his works around the city centre have survived. Look out for his notorious **love triangle** stencil (featuring an angry husband, a two-timing wife, and a naked man dangling from a window) at the bottom of Park St. Banksy's ghostly take on Charion, the River Styx boatman, graces the side of the Thekla, and there's a large mural called **Mild Mild West** featuring a Molotov cocktail-wielding teddy bear on Cheltenham Rd, opposite the junction with Jamaica St.

For more, check out www.banksy.co.uk; the tourist office has produced a free miniguide.

river in Southville. Catch bus 24 or 25 from Broadmead to the Raleigh Rd stop.

Thekla LIVE MUSIC, CLUB
(Map p302; www.thekla.co.uk; The Grove) Bristol's venerable club-boat has something to suit all moods: nights devoted to electro-punk, indie, disco and new wave, plus regular live gigs. Look out for the stencil of the River Styx boatman on the side, courtesy of the city's maverick street artist, Banksy.

Colston Hall LIVE MUSIC
(Map p302; www.colstonhall.org; Colston St) Bristol's historic concert hall hosts everything from big-name comedy to touring bands, and a recent £20-million refit has added a shiny glass-and-copper foyer to the old building.

Croft LIVE MUSIC
(Map p302; www.the-croft.com; 117-119 Stokes Croft) Chilled pub venue with a policy of supporting new names and Bristol-based artists.

Fleece & Firkin PUB, LIVE MUSIC
(Map p302; www.fleecegigs.co.uk; St Thomas St) Another gig pub much favoured by indie artists and breaking names on the local scene.

Avon Gorge Hotel PUB
(Map p302; Sion Hill) Admire stunning views of the suspension bridge from the panoramic pub terrace.

Hophouse PUB
(Map p302; 16 Kings Road) This venerable Clifton local looks fresh from a recent refit, and now serves grub too.

Shopping

The city's main shopping centres are **Broadmead** and the brand spanking new **Cabot Circus** (Map p302; www.cabotscircus.co.uk), both crammed with high street names. Luxury brands tend to favour the area around **Quakers Friars**.

Clifton has lots of smart shops selling furniture, antiques and other quirky bits-and-bobs, while the scruffy area around Gloucester Road is good for vintage clothes shops and music stores.

Information

You'll find all the main banks along Corn St, including Barclays at number 40, Lloyds at 55, and NatWest at 32.

Bristol Central Library (College Green; 9.30am-7.30pm Mon, Tue & Thu, 10am-5pm

Wed, 9am-5pm Fri & Sat, 1-5pm Sun) Free internet access.

Bristol tourist office (☎0333-321 0101; www.visitbristol.co.uk; E-Shed, 1 Canons Rd; ⏰10am-6pm) In a new purpose-built location on the harbour.

Bristol Royal Infirmary (Marlborough Street; ⏰24hr)

Police stations Nelson St (☎0845 456 7000; Nelson St); New Bridewell (☎0845-456-7000; Rupert St; ⏰9.30am-5pm Mon-Fri); Trinity Rd (☎0845-456-7000; Trinity Rd; ⏰24hr)

Post offices Baldwin St (Baldwin St); The Galleries (The Galleries, Broadmead); Upper Maudlin St (Upper Maudlin St)

This is Bristol (www.thisisbristol.com) Web edition of the *Bristol Evening Post*.

Venue (www.venue.co.uk) Online version of Bristol's listings guide.

Visit Bristol (www.visitbristol.co.uk) Official tourism website.

What's on Bristol (www.whatsonbristol.co.uk) Useful online city guide.

Dangers & Annoyances

As in any big city, it pays to keep your wits about you after dark, especially around the suburb of St Paul's, just northeast of the centre.

Getting There & Away

Air

Bristol International Airport (BRS; ☎0871-334-4344; www.bristolairport.co.uk) Eight miles southwest of the city.

Budget carriers currently include:

Air Southwest (www.airsouthwest.com) Several UK destinations including Jersey, Leeds, Manchester, Newquay and Plymouth.

easyJet (www.easyjet.com) Budget flights to UK destinations including Belfast, Edinburgh, Glasgow, Newcastle and Inverness, plus European cities.

Ryanair (www.ryanair.com) Flights to Irish airports including Derry, Dublin and Shannon, as well as European destinations.

Bus

Bristol has excellent bus and coach connections. The main bus station on Marlborough St has an **enquiry office** (⏰7.30am-6pm Mon-Fri, 10am-6pm Sat).

COACHES National Express coaches go to **Birmingham** (£17, two hours, nine daily), **London** (£18, 2½ hours, at least hourly), **Cardiff** (£7, 1¼ hours, nine daily) and **Exeter** (£12.40, two hours, four daily).

BUSES There are regular buses from Bristol to destinations across Somerset.

Bath (one hour, several per hour) Express bus X39/339.

Wells (one hour, hourly Monday to Friday) Bus 376, with onward connections to Glastonbury (1¼ hours).

Weston-super-Mare (one hour, several per hour) Bus X1/352/353.

Train

Bristol is an important rail hub, with regular services to London provided by **First Great Western** (www.firstgreatwestern.co.uk) and services to northern England and Scotland mainly covered by **Cross Country** (www.crosscountrytrains.co.uk).

DESTINATION	DETAILS		
Penzance	£37	5½ hr	hourly
Truro	£37	5 hr	hourly
Exeter	£22.50	1 hr	hourly
London	£34	1¾ hr	hourly
Birmingham	£40	1½ hr	hourly
Glasgow	£82.50	6½ hr	hourly
Edinburgh	£82.50	6½ hr	hourly

Getting Around

To/From the Airport

Bristol International Flyer (http://flyer.bristolairport.co.uk) Runs shuttle buses (one way/return £6/9, 30 minutes, every 10 minutes at peak times) from the bus station and Temple Meads.

Bicycle

Bristol to Bath Railway Path (www.bristolbathrailwaypath.org.uk) The 13-mile off-road path follows the course of an old train track between the two cities. In Bristol pick it up

DRIVING IN BRISTOL

Heavy traffic and pricey parking make driving in Bristol a bit of a nightmare. If you can, it's best to ditch the car altogether: the train station's within walking distance of the centre, and pretty much everywhere can be reached on foot or by bus. If you do drive, make sure your hotel has parking, or use the **Park & Ride buses** (☎0117-922-2910; return before 10am Mon-Fri £3.50, after 10am Mon-Fri £2.50, Sat £2.50; ⏰every 10min Mon-Sat) from Portway, Bath Rd and Long Ashton. Note that overnight parking is not permitted at the park-and-ride car-parks.

around half a mile northeast of Temple Meads Train Station.

For bike hire:

Specialized Bike Store (☎0117-929-7368; 12-14 Park St)

Blackboy Hill Cycles (☎0117-973-1420; 180 Whiteladies Rd; ⊙9am-5.30pm Mon-Sat)

Boat

Bristol Ferry Boat Co (☎0117-927-3416; www.bristolferry.com; adult/child return £3.30/2.70, day-pass £7/5) Runs two hourly commuter routes from the city centre dock, near the tourist office. The blue route goes east to Temple Meads via Millennium Sq, Welsh Back and Castle Park (for Broadmead and Cabot Circus); the red route goes west to Hotwells via Millennium Sq and SS Great Britain.

Bus

Useful city buses:

8/9 To Clifton (10 minutes), Whiteladies Rd and Bristol Zoo Gardens every 15 minutes from St Augustine's Pde. Add another 10 minutes from Temple Meads.

73 Runs from Parkway Station to the centre (30 minutes).

Taxi

The taxi rank on St Augustine's Pde is a central but rowdy place on weekend nights. There are plenty of companies; try **Streamline Taxis** (☎0117-926 4001).

BATH

POP 90,144

Ask any visitor for their ideal image of an English city, and chances are they'll come up with something pretty close to Bath – an architectural icon, cultural trendsetter and fashionable haunt for the last 300 years.

This honey-stoned city is especially renowned for its architecture: along its stately streets you'll find a celebrated set of Roman bathhouses, a grand medieval abbey and some of the finest Georgian terraces anywhere in England (in fact, Bath has so many listed buildings the entire place has been named a World Heritage Site by Unesco).

Throw in some fabulous restaurants, gorgeous hotels and top-class shopping (especially since the arrival of the new SouthGate shopping centre), and you have a city that demands your undivided attention. Just don't expect to dodge the crowds.

History

Prehistoric peoples probably knew about the hot springs; legend has it King Bladud, a Trojan refugee and father of King Lear, founded Bath some 2800 years ago when his pigs were cured of leprosy by a dip in the muddy swamps. The Romans established the town of Aquae Sulis in AD 44 and built the extensive baths complex and a temple to the goddess Sulis-Minerva.

Long after the Romans decamped, the Anglo-Saxons arrived, and in 944 a monastery was founded on the site of the present abbey. Throughout the Middle Ages, Bath was an ecclesiastical centre and a wool-trading town, but it wasn't until the early 18th century that Ralph Allen and the celebrated dandy Richard 'Beau' Nash made Bath the centre of fashionable society. Allen developed the quarries at Coombe Down, constructed Prior Park and employed the two John Woods (father and son) to create some of Bath's most glorious buildings.

During WWII, Bath was hit by the Luftwaffe during the so-called Baedeker raids, which deliberately targeted historic cities in an effort to sap British morale. Several houses on the Royal Crescent and the Circus were badly damaged, and the city's Assembly Rooms were gutted by fire, although all have since been carefully restored.

More recently, the city's futuristic (and controversial) Thermae Bath Spa has been joined by a huge new shopping centre at SouthGate, seamlessly blending in with the rest of Bath's amber-coloured buildings.

Sights & Activities

Roman Baths ARCHITECTURE, MUSEUM

(www.romanbaths.co.uk; Abbey Churchyard; adult/child £11.50/7.50, Jul & Aug £12.25/7.50; ⊙9am-8pm Jul & Aug, 9am-6pm Mar, Jun, Sep & Oct, 9.30am-5.30pm Jan, Feb, Nov & Dec, last admission one hr before closing) Ever since the Romans arrived in Bath, life in the city has revolved around the three natural springs that bubble up near the abbey. In typically ostentatious style, the Romans constructed a glorious complex of bathhouses above these thermal waters to take advantage of their natural temperature – a constant 46°C. The buildings were left to decay after the Romans departed and, apart from a few leprous souls who came looking for a cure in the Middle Ages, it wasn't until the end of the 17th century that Bath's restorative waters again became fashionable.

The 2000-year-old baths now form one of the best-preserved ancient Roman spas in the world. The site gets very, very busy in summer; you can usually dodge the worst crowds by visiting early on a midweek morning, or by avoiding July and August. Multilingual audioguides (including an optional one read by the bestselling author Bill Bryson) is included in the price.

The heart of the complex is the **Great Bath**. Head down to water level and along the raised walkway to see the Roman paving and lead base. A series of excavated passages and chambers beneath street level leads off in several directions and lets you inspect the remains of other smaller baths and hypocaust (heating) systems.

One of the most picturesque corners of the complex is the 12th-century **King's Bath**, built around the original sacred spring; 1.5 million litres of hot water still pour into the pool every day. You can see the ruins of the vast **Temple of Sulis-Minerva** under the **Pump Room**, and recent excavations of the **East Baths** give an insight into its 4th-century form.

Bath Abbey CHURCH

(www.bathabbey.org; requested donation £2.50; ⌚9am-6pm Mon-Sat Easter-Oct, to 4.30pm Nov-Easter, 1-2.30pm & 4.30-5.30pm Sun year-round) King Edgar was crowned in a church in Abbey Courtyard in 973 – though he had ruled since 959 – but the present Bath Abbey was built between 1499 and 1616, making it the last great medieval church raised in England. The nave's wonderful fan vaulting was erected in the 19th century.

Outside, the most striking feature is the west facade, where angels climb up and down stone ladders, commemorating a dream of the founder, Bishop Oliver King. Among those buried here are Sir Isaac Pitman, who devised the Pitman method of shorthand, and Beau Nash.

On the abbey's southern side, the steps lead down to the small **Heritage Vaults Museum** (admission free; ⌚10am-3.30pm Mon-Sat), which explores the abbey's history and its links with the nearby baths. It also contains fine stone bosses, archaeological artefacts and a weird model of the 10th-century monk Aelfric, dressed in his traditional black Benedictine habit.

Royal Crescent & the Circus HISTORIC AREA

Bath has so many listed buildings that the entire city has been named a World Heritage Site by Unesco. The city's crowning glory is the Royal Crescent, a semicircular terrace of majestic houses overlooking a private lawn and the green sweep of Royal Victoria Park. Designed by John Wood the Younger (1728–82) and built between 1767 and 1775, the houses would have originally been rented for the season by wealthy socialites. These days flats on the crescent are still keenly sought after, and entire houses almost never come up for sale.

For a glimpse into the splendour and razzle-dazzle of Georgian life, head for **No 1 Royal Crescent** (www.bath-preservation-trust.org.uk; adult/child £6/2.50; ⌚10.30am-5pm Tue-Sun mid-Feb–mid-Oct, 10.30am-4pm mid-Oct–Dec), given to the city by the shipping magnate Major Bernard Cayzer, and since restored using only 18th-century materials. Among the rooms on display are the drawing room, several bedrooms and the huge kitchen, complete with massive hearth, roasting spit and mousetraps.

A walk east along Brock St from the Royal Crescent leads to the **Circus**, a ring of 30 symmetrical houses divided into three terraces. Plaques on the houses commemorate famous residents such as Thomas Gainsborough, Clive of India and David Livingstone. To the south along Gravel Walk is the **Georgian Garden**, restored to resemble a typical 18th-century town house garden.

FREE **Assembly Rooms** ARCHITECTURE

(Bennett St; ⌚10.30am-5pm Mar-Oct, 10.30am-4pm Nov-Feb) Opened in 1771, the city's glorious Assembly Rooms were where fashionable Bath socialites once gathered to waltz, play cards and listen to the latest chamber music. You're free to wander around the rooms, as long as they haven't been reserved for a special function. Highlights include the card room, tearoom and the truly splendid ballroom, all of which are lit by their original 18th-century chandeliers. The Assembly Rooms were all but gutted by incendiary bombs during WWII but have since been carefully restored.

Fashion Museum MUSEUM

(www.fashionmuseum.co.uk; adult/child £7/5, joint ticket with Roman Baths £15/9; ⌚10.30am-5pm Mar-Oct, 10.30am-4pm Nov-Feb) In the basement of the Assembly Rooms, this museum displays costumes worn from the 16th to late 20th centuries, including some alarming crinolines that would have forced women to approach doorways side on.

Boat Trips CRUISES

Various cruise operators offer boat trips up and down the River Avon from the landing station underneath Pulteney Bridge. Try **Pulteney Cruisers** (☎01225-312900; www.bathboating.com; adult/child £8/4), the **Pulteney Princess** (☎07791-910650; www.pulteneypriness.co.uk; adult/child £7/3) or **Bath City Boat Trips** (☎07974-560197; www.bathcityboattrips.com; adult/child £6.95/4.95).

You can also pilot your own vessel down the Avon from the **Bathwick Boating Station** (☎01225-312900; www.bathboating.co.uk; Forrester Rd, Bathwick; first hr per adult/child

Bath

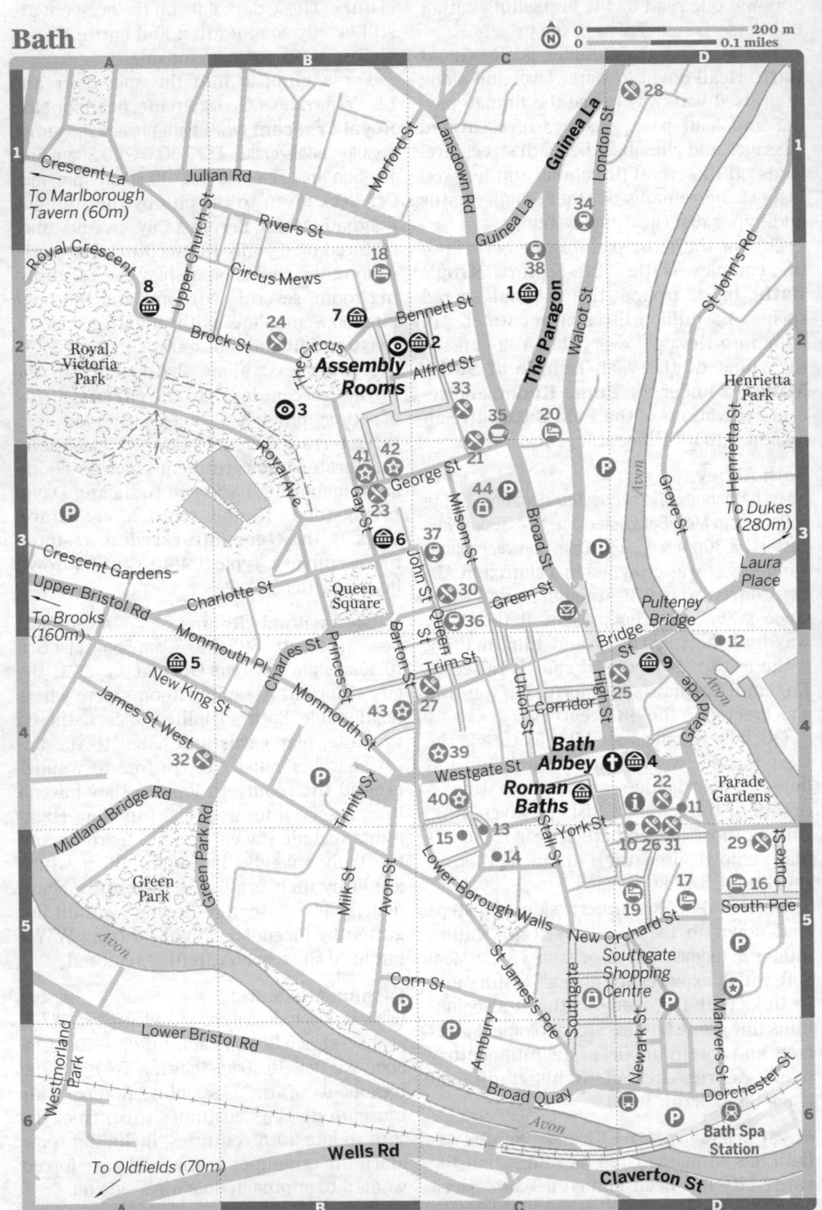

£7/3.50, subsequent hr £3/1.50; ⏲10am-6pm Easter-Oct), which rents out traditional skiffs and Canadian canoes.

Prior Park LANDSCAPED GARDEN

(NT; ☎01225-833422; priorpark@nationaltrust.org.uk; Ralph Allen Dr; adult/child £5/2.80; ⏲11am-5.30pm Wed-Mon mid-Feb–Nov, 11am-5.30pm Sat & Sun Nov-Jan) Celebrated landscape gardener Capability Brown and satirical poet Alexander Pope both had a hand in the creation of Prior Park, an 18th-century ornamental garden dreamt up by local entrepreneur Ralph Allen, who founded Britain's postal service, owned many local quarries and funded the construction of many of Bath's most notable buildings. Cascading lakes and a famous Palladian bridge can be found around the garden's winding walks, and the sweeping views of the Bath skyline are something to behold.

Prior Park is 1 mile south of Bath's centre; it can be reached on foot or by Bus 2 (every 10 minutes), as well as by the City Skyline tour.

Jane Austen Centre MUSEUM

(www.janeausten.co.uk; 40 Gay St; adult/child £6.50/3.50; ⏲9.45am-5.30pm Apr-Sep, 11am-4.30pm Oct-Mar) Bath is known to many as a location in Jane Austen's novels. *Persuasion* and *Northanger Abbey* were both largely set in the city; the writer visited it many times and lived here from 1801 to 1806. The author's connections with the city are explored at the Jane Austen Centre, where displays also include period costume and contemporary prints of Bath.

Building of Bath Museum MUSEUM

(www.bath-preservation-trust.org.uk; The Vineyards, The Paragon; adult/child £4/2; ⏲10.30am-

Bath

Top Sights

Assembly Rooms ... B2
Bath Abbey ... C4
Roman Baths ... C4

Sights

1 Building of Bath Museum ... C2
2 Fashion Museum ... C2
3 Georgian Garden ... B2
4 Heritage Vaults Museum ... D4
5 Herschel Museum of Astronomy ... A4
6 Jane Austen Centre ... B3
7 Museum of East Asian Art ... B2
8 No 1 Royal Crescent ... A2
9 Victoria Art Gallery ... D4

Activities, Courses & Tours

10 Bath Festivals ... D5
11 Bizarre Bath Comedy Walk ... D4
12 Boat Trips ... D4
13 Cross Bath ... C5
14 Hot Bath ... C5
15 Thermae Bath Spa ... C5

Sleeping

16 Halcyon ... D5
17 Henry ... D5
18 Queensberry Hotel ... B2
19 Three Abbey Green ... D5
20 YMCA ... C2

Eating

21 Adventure Cafe ... C3
22 Cafe Retro ... D4
23 Chandos Deli ... B3
24 Circus ... B2
25 Deli Shush ... D4
26 Demuth's ... D5
Firehouse Rotisserie ... (see 30)
27 Gascoyne Place ... C4
28 Hudson Steakhouse ... D1
29 Onefishtwofish ... D5
30 Paxton & Whitfield ... C3
31 Sally Lunn's ... D5
32 Thoughtful Bread Company ... A4
33 Yen Sushi ... C2

Drinking

34 Bell ... C1
35 Jika Jika ... C2
36 Raven ... C3
37 Salamander ... C3
Same Same But Different ... (see 21)
38 Star Inn ... C2

Entertainment

39 Komedia ... C4
40 Little Theatre Cinema ... C4
41 Moles ... B3
42 Porter Cellar Bar ... B3
43 Theatre Royal ... B4

Shopping

44 Milsom's Yard ... C3

5pm Tue-Sun mid-Feb–Nov) This architectural museum details how Bath's Georgian splendour came into being, tracing the city's evolution from a sleepy spa town to one of the centres of Georgian society. There are some displays on contemporary construction methods, and the museum also explores the way in which social class and interior decor were intimately linked during the Georgian era; heaven forbid should you use a wallpaper that outstripped your station...

Herschel Museum of Astronomy MUSEUM
(19 New King St; adult/child £4.50/2.50; ⏲1-5pm Mon, Tue, Thu & Fri, 11am-5pm Sat & Sun Feb-Nov) In 1781 astronomer William Herschel discovered Uranus from the garden of his home, now converted into an intriguing museum. The house is decorated as it would have been in the 18th century; an astrolabe in the garden marks where Herschel would have placed his telescope.

FREE **Victoria Art Gallery** GALLERY
(www.victoriagal.org.uk; Pulteney Bridge; ⏲10am-5pm Tue-Sat, 1.30-5pm Sun) The city's main arts collection. There are some particularly fine canvases by Gainsborough, Turner and Sickert, as well as a wonderful series of Georgian caricatures from the wicked pens of artists such as James Gillray and Thomas Rowlandson.

The 18th-century **Holburne Museum** at the end of Great Pulteney St is undergoing restoration until 2012.

Museum of East Asian Art MUSEUM
(www.meaa.org.uk; 12 Bennett St; adult/13-18yr/2-12yr £5/3.50/2; ⏲10am-5pm Tue-Sat, noon-5pm Sun) Bath's Asian arts museum contains more than 500 jade, bamboo, porcelain and bronze objects from Cambodia, Korea and Thailand, and substantial Chinese and Japanese carvings, ceramics and lacquerware.

American Museum MUSEUM
(www.americanmuseum.org; Claverton Manor; adult/child £8/4.50; ⏲noon-5pm) Britain's largest collection of American folk art, including Native American textiles, patchwork quilts and historic maps, is housed in a fine mansion a couple of miles from the city centre; catch the number 18/418/U18 from the bus station.

Tours

Bath City Sightseeing BUS TOUR
(☎01225-330444; www.city-sightseeing.com; adult/child £10/6; ⏲9.30am-5pm Mar-May, Oct & Nov, to 6.30pm Jun-Sep) Hop-on/hop-off city tour on an open-topped bus. Commentary is in seven languages. Buses stop every 20 minutes or so at various points around town. There's also a second route, the **Skyline tour**, which runs year-round and travels out to Prior Park (p315); the same tickets are valid on both routes.

Bizarre Bath Comedy Walk WALKING TOUR
(☎01225-335124; www.bizarrebath.co.uk; adult/student £8/5; ⏲8pm Mar-Oct) Daft city tour mixing street theatre and live performance. Leaves from outside the Huntsman Inn on North Parade Passage.

Jane Austen's Bath WALKING TOUR
(☎01225-443000; adult/child £5/4; ⏲11am Sat & Sun) Focuses on the Georgian city and Jane Austen sites. Tours leave from the Abbey Churchyard.

FREE **Mayor's Guide Tours** WALKING TOUR
(☎01225-477411; www.thecityofbath.co.uk; ⏲10.30am & 2pm Sun-Fri, 10.30am Sat) Excellent historical tours provided free by the Mayors Corp of Honorary guides. Leave from outside the Pump Rooms. Extra tours at 7pm on Tuesday, Friday and Saturday May to September.

Festivals & Events

Bath has lots of festivals. All bookings are handled by **Bath Festivals** (☎01225-463362; www.bathfestivals.org.uk; 2 Church St; ⏲9.30am-5.30pm Mon-Sat).

Bath Literature Festival BOOKS
(www.bathlitfest.org.uk) Annual book festival in late February or early March.

Bath International Music Festival MUSIC
(www.bathmusicfest.org.uk) Mainly classical and opera, plus smaller gigs of jazz, folk and world. Mid-May to early June.

Bath Fringe Festival THEATRE
(www.bathfringe.co.uk) Major theatre festival around mid-May to early June.

Jane Austen Festival STREET FESTIVAL
(www.janeausten.co.uk/festival) The highlight of this September festival is a costumed parade through the city's streets.

Bath Film Festival FILM
(www.bathfilmfestival.org.uk) Early November.

Sleeping

Bath gets incredibly busy, especially in the height of summer and at weekends, when prices have a tendency to skyrocket. The

THERMAE BATH SPA

Taking a dip in the Roman Baths might be off the agenda, but you can still sample the city's curative waters at **Thermae Bath Spa** (☎0844-888-0844; www.thermaebathspa.com; Hot Bath St; New Royal Bath spa session per 2hr/4hr/day £24/34/54, spa packages from £65; ⏲New Royal Bath 9am-10pm). Here the old **Cross Bath**, incorporated into an ultra-modern shell of local stone and plate glass, is now the setting for a variety of spa packages. The New Royal Bath ticket includes steam rooms, waterfall shower and a choice of bathing venues – including the jaw-dropping open-air rooftop pool, where you can swim in the thermal waters in front of a backdrop of Bath's stunning cityscape.

Across the street are treatment rooms above the old **Hot Bath**, while the Hetling Pump Room, opposite, houses a **visitor centre** (⏲10am-5pm Mon-Sat, to 4pm Sun) that explores the history of bathing in Bath.

tourist office books last-minute rooms for a £3 fee, but you're better off booking online as early as you can.

TOP CHOICE **Queensberry Hotel** HOTEL £££
(☎01225-447928; www.thequeensberry.co.uk; 4 Russell St; s £95-300, d £105-425; Wi-Fi) There's no getting away from it – the quirky Queensberry is eye-poppingly expensive – but for a right royal spoil, it's worth a splash. Four classic Georgian town houses have been combined into one seamless boutique whole, and all the rooms are different: some are sleek and zen, others indulgent and elegant, but the whole package is effortlessly chic. No parking, but give 'em your keys and they'll whisk your wheels to a private garage.

Halcyon HOTEL ££
(☎01225-444100; www.thehalcyon.com; 2/3 South Parade; d £99-125; Wi-Fi) A shabby terrace of old hotels has been knocked through, polished up and totally reinvented, and the Halcyon is now by far and away the best place in the city centre. It's style on a budget: the lobby is cool and monochrome; off-white rooms have splashes of colour, Philippe Starck bath fittings and White Company smellies; studio rooms even have kitchens. We like it a lot.

Brooks BATH ££
(☎01225-425543; www.brooksguesthouse.com; 1 & 1a Crescent Gardens; d £69-175; Wi-Fi) On the west side of Bath, this is another plush option, with heritage fixtures blending attractively with snazzy finishes. The owners have tried hard on the details: goosedown duvets, pocket-sprung mattresses, DAB radios and several breakfast spoils, including smoked salmon brioche and homemade muesli. Parking can be problematic.

Three Abbey Green B&B ££
(☎01225-428558; www.threeabbeygreen.com; 3 Abbey Green; d £85-135; Wi-Fi) Considering the location, this place is a steal – tumble out of the front door and you'll find yourself practically on the abbey's doorstep. It's on a leafy square, and though the rooms lack sparkle, the suites have adjoining singles – ideal for travellers en famille.

Appletree Guest House B&B ££
(☎01225-337642; www.appletreeguesthouse.co.uk; 7 Pulteney Gardens; s £55-66, d £85-110, f £120-132; Wi-Fi) It's absolutely tiny, but this welcoming B&B is worth recommending mainly for the sunny disposition of its husband-and-wife owners (Lynsay mainly sticks to the kitchen, while Les is a non-stop fizz of energy). Rooms are small and simple, but very cosy. Street parking is available free if you can find a space.

Henry B&B ££
(☎01225-424052; www.thehenry.com; 6 Henry St; s £50-55, d £90-130, f £90-110) Thorough renovations have removed the clutter and brought a palette of crisp whites and smooth beiges to the old Henry – unfortunately the prices have taken an upwards hike too. Still, the city-centre position is a winner.

Paradise House B&B ££
(☎01225-317723; www.paradise-house.co.uk; 88 Holloway; d £65-185; P) It's a long old slog from town, but if it's a peaceful retreat you're after, this hilltop beauty is the place. Set around a charming landscaped garden with views over Bath's rooftops, it's an old-time treat, full of half-tester beds, gilded mirrors and oils.

Bath YHA HOSTEL ££
(bath@yha.org.uk; dm £14, d from £35; P @) Hostels don't come much grander than this

BEAU NASH

While Ralph Allen and the two John Woods were responsible for moulding Bath's architectural legacy, Richard 'Beau' Nash was busily transforming the city from an inconsequential spa town to the toast of British high society.

Born in Swansea in 1674, Nash had an inauspicious start; an Oxford University drop-out, failed soldier, rubbish lawyer, inveterate gambler and insatiable womaniser, his only saving grace was his knack for organising a good knees-up. Attracted by the booming social scene, Nash became Bath's Master of Ceremonies in 1705 when his master, Captain Webster, was killed in a duel over a card game.

Over the next 50 years Nash set about reinventing fashionable Bath society, organising balls and tea dances, arranging chamber concerts and imposing strict regulations on behaviour, dress and social conduct. His rakish fashion sense – black wig, beaver-trimmed hat, ruffled shirt and florid waistcoat – earned him his dandyish nickname of 'Beau', while his 'Rules' set down the conduct of polite society. Among his dictates were a ban on swearing and the wearing of sabres (which tended to cause duels) and an eccentric fixation with male footwear (he thought calf-length boots vulgar, preferring daintier shoes). Though the rules seemed strict, snooty and frequently daft, they actually helped encourage mixing across the classes – since everyone knew how to behave, no one had any fear stepping out of line. A lifelong gambler, he was even known to bail out people's debts just to keep the social waters smooth.

But inevitably Nash fell short of his own strict standards. He financed his extravagant social life with prodigious gambling profits and, following tightened gaming rules in the mid-18th century, he fell on hard times, and eventually died in abject straits in 1761. But the city hadn't forgotten its debt to Nash; most of the fashionable city turned out for his lavish funeral at Bath Abbey, where he's now buried beneath the nave and commemorated by a surprisingly understated plaque.

Italianate mansion, a steep climb (or a short hop on bus 18) from the city centre. The refurbished rooms are surprisingly modern and many look out across the private tree-lined gardens; book early to get a double.

Dukes HOTEL £££
(☎01225-787960; www.dukesbath.co.uk; Great Pulteney St; s £99, d £139-199, ste £179; P) A Grade-I listed pile east of the centre with suitably regal rooms.

Oldfields B&B ££
(☎01225-317984; www.oldfields.co.uk; 102 Wells Rd; s £49-115, d £65-160, f £85-210; P) Luxurious B&B in a quiet area on Wells Rd.

YMCA HOSTEL £
(☎01225-325900; www.bathymca.co.uk; International House, Broad St Pl; dm £17-19, s £28-32, d & tw £46-52; @) Institutional, yes, but bright, clean and bang in the centre – it's even got a health suite and cafe.

Eating

TOP CHOICE **Circus** RESTAURANT ££
(☎01225-318918; www.thecircuscafeandrestaurant.co.uk; 34 Brock St; lunch mains £5.50-9.70, dinner mains £11-13.90; ⊙lunch & dinner) Quite simply, our favourite place to eat in Bath. In a city that's often known for its snootiness, the Circus manages to be posh but not in the slightest pretentious. The attractive town house is steps from the Royal Crescent, and you can choose to eat on the ground floor or the intimate cellar dining room: either way, expect classic modern British, beautifully presented, at bargain prices. Book now while you still can.

Marlborough Tavern GASTROPUB ££
(☎01225-423731; www.marlborough-tavern.com; 35 Marlborough Buildings; mains £10.95-15.95; ⊙lunch & dinner) Bath's best address for gastrogrub, especially if you like your flavours rich and rustic. Chef Richard Whiting's food is defined by big country dishes, and it's earned him a big following – it's not often you have to book at a pub, but we recommend you do at the Marlborough.

Demuth's RESTAURANT ££
(☎01225-446059; 2 North Parade Passage; mains £9.75-14.25; ⊙lunch & dinner)
Yes, it's vegetarian – but this place is a world away from stodgy quiches and nut roasts. For the last 20-something years this brilliant meat-free bistro has been turning

out some of Bath's most creative and imaginative food – from a chive tart made with Devon Blue cheese to a simply divine apricot and fennel tagine.

Hudson Steakhouse RESTAURANT £££
(01225-332323; www.hudsonbars.com; 14 London St; mains £15-30; dinner Mon-Sat) Steak, steak and more steak is this much-garlanded restaurant's raison d'être. Top-quality cuts take in everything from delicate *filet mignon* to cowboy rib steak, all sourced from a Staffordshire farmers' co-op.

Onefishtwofish RESTAURANT ££
(01225-330236; 10a North Pde; mains £13-18; dinner Tue-Sun) Pescatarians would do well to plump for this super seafooderie, with cute little tables crammed in under a barrel-brick roof dotted with twinkly lights. Seafood is shipped in daily: there's always a *poisson du jour,* but you'll have to order bouillabaisse ahead.

Yen Sushi JAPANESE ££
(11-12 Bartlett St; sushi £6-10; lunch & dinner) Bath has recently got its very own sushi spot, complete with colour-coded dishes and *kaiten* (conveyor belt). Take your pick from hand-rolled sushi and sashimi, or plump for a more adventurous *nigiri*: clam, turbot, eel or sweet shrimp, perhaps?

Firehouse Rotisserie RESTAURANT ££
(2 John St; pizzas £9.95-11.95, mains £13.95-21.95; lunch & dinner Mon-Sat) Stateside flavours and a Californian vibe characterise this excellent American restaurant, run by a couple of ex-LA chefs. The menu evokes Mexico and the deep South, with signature dishes including rotisserie chicken, Louisiana catfish and Texan steak, plus huge pizzas crisped in a wood-fired oven.

Café Retro CAFÉ £
(18 York St; mains £5-11; breakfast, lunch & dinner Tue-Sat, breakfast & lunch Mon) This place is a poke in the eye for the corporate coffee chains. The paint job's scruffy, the crockery's ancient and none of the furniture matches, but that's all part of the charm: this is a cafe from the old school, and there's nowhere better for a hearty burger, a crumbly cake or a good old mug of tea. Takeaways are on offer from Retro to Go next door.

Sally Lunn's TEAROOM £
(4 North Parade Passage; lunch mains £5-6, dinner mains from £8; lunch & dinner) Classic chintzy tearoom serving the trademark Sally Lunn's bun.

Adventure Cafe CAFE £
(5 Princes Bldgs, George St; mains £4-8; breakfast, lunch & dinner;) Boho cafe, equally suited to morning cappuccino, lunchtime ciabattas and late night beers.

Gascoyne Place GASTROPUB ££
(www.gascoyneplace.co.uk; 1 Sawclose; mains £8.95-16.95; lunch & dinner) Another quality gastropub opposite the Theatre Royal.

Self-Catering

Bath has the original branches of **Chandos Deli** (George St; Mon-Sat) and the **Boston Tea Party** (19 Kingsmead Sq; mains from £4; 7.30am-7pm Mon-Sat, from 8.30am Sun) both ideal for a lunchtime sarnie.

Deli Shush DELI £
(8a Guildhall Market; 8am-5.30pm Mon-Sat) Serrano ham, antipasti, samosas and 20 types of olives fill the shelves of this designer deli.

Paxton & Whitfield CHEESE SHOP £
(1 John St; Mon-Sat) Cheese connoisseurs beware – this fantastic fromagerie has enough stinky Stiltons and award-winning cheddars to send your olfactory senses into overdrive.

Thoughtful Bread Company BAKERY £
(www.thoughtfulbreadcompany.com; 9am-6pm Tue-Sat) Hand-made breads at Bath's eco-bakery, based in the old Green Park Station.

Drinking

JikaJika CAFÉ
(www.jikajika.co.uk; 4a Princes Buildings, George St; 7.30am-8pm Mon-Thu, 7.30-9pm Fri, 8.30am-9pm Sat, 10.30am-4pm Sun;) This shrine to the humble coffee bean is a must if you can't live without your lattes – beans are sourced from various rare estates and roasted by hand, ensuring that the expressos here are just about the southwest's best.

Same Same But Different CAFÉ, BAR
(7A Princes Buildings) Shabby chic hang-out for the town's trendies, stocked with mix-and-match furniture and a boho Bathonian vibe. Savour wine by the glass, snack on tapas or sip a cappuccino with the Sunday papers.

Raven PUB
(Queen St) Highly respected by real ale aficionados, this fine city drinking den com-

mands a devoted following for its well-kept beer and trad atmosphere.

Salamander PUB
(3 John St) The city's bespoke brewery, Bath Ales, owns this place, and you can sample all of their ales here. At the lighter end are amber-coloured Gem and Golden Hare, while the strongest of all is dark Rare Hare at a punchy 5.2%.

Bell PUB
(Walcot St;) Scruffily stylish pub on boho Walcot St, with a cavernous central bar and a beer garden out back which hosts visiting bands.

Star Inn PUB
(www.star-inn-bath.co.uk; 23 The Vineyards off the Paragon;) Not many pubs are registered relics, but the Star is – it still boasts many of its 19th-century bar fittings. It's the brewery tap for Bath-based Abbey Ales; some ales are served in traditional jugs, and you can ask for a pinch of snuff in the 'smaller bar'.

Entertainment

Venue magazine (www.venue.co.uk; £1.50) has comprehensive listings of Bath's theatre, music and gig scenes. Pick up a copy at any newsagency.

Moles LIVE MUSIC
(www.moles.co.uk; 14 George St; 9pm-2am Mon-Thu, to 4am Fri & Sat, 8pm-12.30am Sun) Bath's historic music club has hosted some big names down the years, and it's still the place to catch the hottest breaking acts.

Porter Cellar Bar LIVE MUSIC
(George St; 11.30am-midnight Mon-Thu, to 1am Fri & Sat, noon-11.30pm Sun) Run by the folk at Moles, this student favourite lays on the acts who aren't yet big enough to play the main venue: it's Bath's only veggie pub, too.

Theatre Royal THEATRE
(www.theatreroyal.org.uk; Sawclose) Exclusive theatre featuring major drama, opera and ballet in the main auditorium, experimental productions in the Ustinov Studio, and young people's theatre at 'the egg'.

Komedia CABARET, COMEDY
(www.komedia.co.uk; 22-23 Westgate St) The Brighton-based comedy and cabaret venue has recently extended its reach west to Bath.

Little Theatre Cinema CINEMA
(St Michael's Pl) Bath's arthouse cinema, screening a range of fringe and foreign-language flicks.

Shopping

After much comment and controversy, the multi-million-pound redevelopment of Bath's main shopping district was completed in 2010, and is now known as SouthGate (www.southgate.com). It's one of the south-west's main meccas for high street shoppers, with flagship stores for all the major retail names.

The more expensive designer stores and clothes shops are clustered around Milsom St, Milsom Place and Broad St.

For quirky shops, vintage clothes and retro furniture, head for the bohemian boutiques dotted along Walcot St.

Bath's oldest shopping landmark is Pulteney Bridge, one of only a handful in the world to be lined by shops (the most famous other example is the Ponte Vecchio in Florence). It was built in 1773 and is now Grade-I listed.

Information

Bath (enquiries 0906-711-2000, accommodation 0844-847-5256; www.visitbath.co.uk; Abbey Churchyard; 9.30am-6pm Mon-Sat & 10am-4pm Sun Jun-Sep, 9.30am-5pm Mon-Sat & 10am-4pm Sun Oct-May) Phone enquiries to the main office are charged at premium rate (50p per minute).

Main post office (27 Northgate St)

Police station (Manvers St; 7am-midnight)

Royal United Hospital (01225-428331; Combe Park)

What's On (www.whatsonbath.co.uk) City listings.

Getting There & Away

Bus

Bath's **bus and coach station** (enquiries office 9am-5pm Mon-Sat) is on Dorchester St near the train station. National Express coaches run to **London** (£21.25, 3½ hours, 10 daily) via **Heathrow** (£17.50, 2¾ hours), and to **Bristol** (45 minutes, every 30 minutes). Services to most other cities require a change at Bristol or Heathrow.

Other services:

Bristol (55 minutes, four per hour Monday to Saturday, half-hourly Sunday) Bus X39/339.

Wells (1 hour 10 minutes, hourly Monday to Saturday, seven on Sunday) Bus 173.

Frome (hourly Monday to Saturday) Bus 184.

Bradford-on-Avon (30 minutes, half-hourly, eight on Sunday) Bus 264/265.

Devizes (one hour, fifteen daily Monday to Saturday, six on Sunday) Bus 271/272/273.

Train

There are several trains per hour from Bath Spa to **Bristol** (£5.80, 11 minutes), which has connections to most major British cities. There are also direct trains to **London Paddington** and **London Waterloo** (£22 to £39, 1½ hours, at least hourly), as well as **Cardiff Central** (£15.90, one hour, six to 10 daily).

Getting Around

Bicycle

Bath's hills make getting around by bike challenging, but the canal paths along the Kennet & Avon Canal and the 13-mile **Bristol & Bath Railway Path** (www.bristolbathrailwaypath.org.uk) offer great cycling.

Bus

Bus 18 runs from the bus station, High St and Great Pulteney St up Bathwick Hill past the YHA to the university every 10 minutes. Bus 4 runs every 20 minutes to Bathampton from the same places.

Car & Motorcycle

Bath has serious traffic problems (especially at rush hour). **Park & Ride services** (01225-464446; return £2.50; 6.15am-7.30pm) operate from Lansdown to the north, Newbridge to the west and Odd Down to the south. It takes about 10 minutes to centre; buses leave every 10 to 15 minutes. If you brave the city, the best value carpark is underneath the new SouthGate shopping centre (2/8 hours £3/9.50, after 6.30pm £2).

SOMERSET

Sleepy Somerset provides the type of pleasing pastoral wanderings that are reminiscent of a simpler, calmer, kinder world. Its landscape of hedgerows, hummocks and russet-coloured fields is steeped in ancient rites and scattered with ancient sites. The cloistered calm of the cathedral city of Wells acts as a springboard for the limestone caves and gorges around Cheddar; hippie haven Glastonbury brings an ancient abbey, mud-drenched festival and masses of Arthurian myth; while the hills of the Quantocks, Mendips and Exmoor provide plenty of opportunity for hikers and bikers to stretch their legs.

Somerset hugs the coast of the Bristol Channel. The Mendip Hills (the Mendips) follow a line below Bristol, just north of Wells and Cheddar, while the Quantock Hills (the Quantocks) sit just east of Exmoor National Park. Bath makes a good base in the east; Glastonbury and Wells are more central options.

Information

Somerset Visitor Centre (01934-750833; www.visitsomerset.co.uk; Sedgemoor Services M5 South, Axbridge; 9.15am-5pm daily Easter-Oct, 9.15am-5pm Mon-Fri Nov-Easter) Provides general information.

Visit South Somerset (www.visitsouthsomerset.co.uk)

Getting Around

Most buses in Somerset are operated by **First** (0845-606-4446; www.firstgroup.com), supplemented by smaller operators. For timetables and general information contact **Traveline South West** (0871-200 2233; www.travelinesw.com).

Key train services link Bath, Bristol, Bridgwater, Taunton and Weston-Super-Mare. The M5 heads south past Bristol, to Bridgwater and Taunton, with the A39 leading west across the Quantocks to Exmoor.

Wells

POP 10,406

With Wells, small is beautiful. This tiny, picturesque metropolis is England's smallest city, and only qualifies for the 'city' title thanks to a magnificent medieval cathedral, which sits in the centre beside the grand Bishop's Palace. Wells has been the main seat of ecclesiastical power in this part of Britain since the 12th century, and is still the official residence of the Bishop of Bath and Wells. Medieval buildings and cobbled streets radiate out from the cathedral green to a marketplace that has been the bustling heart of Wells for some nine centuries (Wednesday and Saturday are market days). A quiet provincial city, Wells' excellent restaurants and busy shops help make it a good launching pad for exploring the Mendips and northern Somerset.

Sights

Wells Cathedral CHURCH

(www.wellscathedral.org.uk; Chain Gate, Cathedral Green; requested donation adult/child £5.50/2.50; 7am-7pm Apr-Sep, 7am-dusk Oct-Mar) Set in a marvellous medieval close, the Cathedral Church of St Andrew was built in stages between 1180 and 1508. The building incorporates several Gothic styles, but its most famous asset is the wonderful **west front**, an immense sculpture gallery decorated with more than 300 figures, built in the 13th century and restored to its original splendour in 1986. The facade would once have been painted in vivid colours, but has long since reverted to its original sandy hue. Apart from the figure of Christ, installed in 1985 in the uppermost niche, all the figures are original.

Inside, the most striking feature is the pair of **scissor arches** that separate the nave from the choir, designed to counter the subsidence of the central tower. High up in the north transept you'll come across a wonderful **mechanical clock** dating from 1392 – the second-oldest surviving in England after the one at Salisbury Cathedral (p286). The clock shows the position of the planets and the phases of the moon.

Other highlights are the elegant **Lady Chapel** (1326) at the eastern end and the seven effigies of Anglo-Saxon bishops ringing the choir. The 15th-century **chained library** houses books and manuscripts dating back to 1472. It's only open at certain times during the year or by prior arrangement.

From the north transept follow the worn steps to the glorious **Chapter House** (1306), with its delicate ceiling ribs sprouting like a palm from a central column. Externally, look out for the **Chain Bridge** built from the northern side of the cathedral to Vicars' Close to enable clerics to reach the cathedral without getting their robes wet. The cloisters on the southern side surround a pretty courtyard.

FREE **Guided tours** (Mon-Sat) of the cathedral are free, and usually take place every hour. Regular concerts and cathedral choir recitals are held here throughout the year. You need to buy a permit (£3) from the cathedral shop to take pictures.

Cathedral Close SIGNIFICANT AREA

Wells Cathedral forms the centrepiece of a cluster of ecclesiastical buildings dating back to (and even earlier than) the Middle Ages. Facing the west front, on the left are the 15th-century **Old Deanery** and the **Wells & Mendip Museum** (8 Cathedral Green; www.wellsmuseum.org.uk; adult/child £3/1; 10am-5.30pm Easter-Oct, 11am-4pm Wed-Mon Nov-Easter), with exhibits on local life, cathedral architecture and the infamous Witch of Wookey Hole (see p323).

Further along, **Vicars' Close** is a stunning cobbled street of uniform houses dating back to the 14th century, with a chapel at the end; members of the cathedral choir still live here. It is thought to be the oldest complete medieval street in Europe.

Penniless Porch, a corner gate leading onto Market Sq and built by Bishop Bekynton around 1450, is so-called because beggars asked for alms here.

Bishop's Palace HISTORIC BUILDING

(www.bishopspalacewells.co.uk; adult/child £5/2; 10.30am-6pm summer, 10,30-4pm winter) Beyond the cathedral, the moated 13th-century Bishop's Palace is a real delight. Purportedly the oldest inhabited building in England, ringed by water and surrounded by a huge fortified wall, the palace complex contains several fine Italian Gothic state rooms, an imposing Great Hall and beautiful tree-shaded gardens. The natural wells that gave the city its name bubble up in the palace's grounds, feeding the moat and the fountain in the market square. The swans in the moat have been trained to ring a bell outside one of the windows when they want to be fed.

Sleeping

Beryl B&B ££

(01749-678738; www.beryl-wells.co.uk; Hawkers Lane; d £75-130; P) A mile from the city centre, this tree-shaded, gabled Victorian mansion is run by an eccentric local family and is stuffed to the rafters with antique atmosphere: grandfather clocks, chaises longues and stately four-posters aplenty. The rooms have a heritage feel, and outside there are acres of private gardens and a heated pool to enjoy.

Stoberry House B&B ££

(01749-672906; www.stoberry-park.co.uk; Stoberry Park; d £70-95; P) Another extravagant Wells house has thrown open its doors to provide supremely posh B&B. Four rooms are richly furnished in silky fabrics: top of the heap are sultry Black Orchid and regal Lady Hamilton. The truly gorgeous art-filled garden is the icing on the cake. There's a £10 to £15 supplement for one-night stays.

Number Twelve B&B ££

(01749-679406; www.numbertwelve.info; 12 North Rd; d £80-95; P) Two rooms in an Arts and Crafts house on the outskirts of Wells, both finished with taste and class. The best room is number 1, which has a glass-bricked bathroom with freestanding bath and a small balcony with cathedral views. Tea and cake is served on arrival, and there's kedgeree and smoked salmon and scrambled eggs for brekkie.

BABINGTON HOUSE

You'll definitely need to save your pennies, but for out-and-out luxury this much-lauded design **hotel** (01373-812266; www.babingtonhouse.co.uk; near Frome; r £380-450;) in rolling countryside is quite simply one of the top spots in Britain. It's part of a small chain of ultra-boutique hotels that also includes the Electric House in Notting Hill, Shoreditch House in East London and various Soho Houses (in London, New York, Berlin and Hollywood).

Combining Georgian architecture with urban invention, it comes across somewhere between *Homes & Gardens* and *Wallpaper*. Heritage beds, antique dressers and period fireplaces sit side-by-side with über-minimalist furniture, sanded wood floors and retro anglepoise lamps. There's a choice of rooms in the manor house, a stable block, a twin-storeyed lodge or the mezzanine-floored coach house, but top spot goes to the lavish Playroom, with a huge canopied bed, complimentary bar and views of green grounds from every angle.

And as if all that wasn't enough, there's the Cowshed Spa for relaxing, the Log Room restaurant (dinner mains £12 to £19) for eating, the Library for reading and a 45-seat cinema for – well, watching your latest directorial magnum opus, of course.

Very expensive, very exclusive and very lovely indeed.

Eating

TOP CHOICE Old Spot BRITISH ££
(01749-689099; 12 Sadler St; 2-/3-course lunch £15/17.50, dinner £21.50/26.50; lunch Wed-Sun, dinner Tue-Sat) Little Wells conceals a culinary star in the shape of the Old Spot, run by renowned chef Ian Bates. It's a favourite with the foodie guides and the Sunday supplements, and the menu specialises in giving a modern twist to old country favourites – saddle of pork, smoked eel, rabbit stew.

Goodfellows BISTRO, BAKER ££
(01749-673866; 5 Sadler St) Two eateries rolled into one. Downstairs is a super **café-bakery** (mains £7-10; 8.30am-5pm Mon-Sat & 6-10pm Wed-Sat), which rustles up treats like goats' cheese bruschetta and handmade pastries, while upstairs is a more formal seafood **bistro** (mains £11.50-25, 3-course dinner menu £35; lunch Tue-Sat, dinner Wed-Sat). The quality of the food in both is top-drawer, and it's a favourite with Wells' ladies who lunch.

Cafe Romna INDIAN ££
(01749-670240; 13 Sadler St; mains £10-15; lunch Mon-Sat, dinner daily) More exotic flavours come to the fore at this Bangladeshi fusion restaurant, which exchanges the usual *bhuna* and *bhaji* for more unusual regional dishes such as *Thither Loboori* (chargrilled pheasant with Bangladeshi beans) and *Chingri Keemawala* (prawns and lamb cooked in a cheesy garlic sauce).

Information

Tourist office (01749-672552; www.wellstourism.com; Market Pl; 9.30am-5.30pm Apr-Oct, 10am-4pm Nov-Mar) Stocks the *Wells City Trail* leaflet (30p) and sells discount tickets to Wookey Hole and Cheddar Gorge.

Getting There & Away

The bus station is south of Cuthbert St, on Princes Rd. Useful services:

Taunton (1¼ hours, nine daily Monday to Saturday, six on Sunday) Bus 29; runs via Glastonbury.

Cheddar (25 minutes, 10 daily Monday to Saturday, seven on Sunday) Bus 126; continues on to Weston-super-Mare 1½ hours.

Bath (1 hour 10 minutes, hourly Monday to Saturday, seven on Sunday) Bus 173.

Bristol (one hour, hourly Monday to Saturday, seven on Sunday) Bus 376/377 stops in Wells en route to Glastonbury (15 minutes) and Street (25 minutes). The 377 continues to Yeovil (1¼ hours).

Wookey Hole

(www.wookey.co.uk; adult/child £16/11; 10am-5pm Apr-Oct, 10.30am-4pm Nov-Mar) On the southern edge of the Mendips, the River Axe has carved out a series of deep limestone caverns collectively known as Wookey Hole. The caves are littered with dramatic natural features, including a subterranean lake and some fascinating stalagmites and stalactites: one of which is supposedly the legendary Witch of Wookey Hole, who was turned to stone by a local priest.

The caves were inhabited by prehistoric people for some 50,000 years, but these days the deep pools and underground rivers are more often frequented by cave divers – the deepest subterranean dive ever recorded in Britain was made here in September 2004, when divers reached a depth of more than 45m.

Admission to the caves is by guided tour. Despite its natural attractions, it's very touristy: the rest of the complex is taken up by kid-friendly attractions including mirror mazes, an Edwardian penny arcade, a paper-mill and a valley stuffed with 20 giant plastic dinosaurs. Look out for Wookey's newly appointed witch, Carla Calamity (aka Carole Bonahan, an ex-estate agent who beat 300 other applicants to the job after a series of gruelling auditions in mid-2009).

Cheddar Gorge

(www.cheddarcaves.co.uk; Explorer Ticket adult/child/family £17/11/44; ⏲10am-5.30pm Jul & Aug, 10.30am-5pm Sep-Jun) If Wookey Hole is a little too touristy for your tastes, then you'd better brace yourself for Cheddar Gorge, a spectacular series of limestone caverns that's always jam-packed with coach-parties and day-trippers.

Despite the tourist throng, the natural wonders on display are genuinely impressive. The gorge itself is England's deepest, in places towering 138m above the twisting, turning road, and a network of caves extends deep into the surrounding rock on every side. Only a few are open to the public, including **Cox's Cave** and **Gough's Cave**, both decorated by an amazing gallery of stalactites and stalagmites, and subtly lit to bring out the spectrum of colours in the limestone rock. After the end of the last ice age, the caves were inhabited by prehistoric people; a 9000-year-old skeleton (imaginatively named Cheddar Man) was discovered here in 1903, and genetic tests have revealed that some of his descendants are still living in the surrounding area.

When the throngs become too much, you can clamber up the 274 steps of **Jacob's Ladder**; on a clear day you can see all the way to Glastonbury Tor and Exmoor.

Nearby, a signposted 3-mile-round walk follows the cliffs along the most spectacular parts of the gorge. Most visitors only explore the first section of the path, and you can usually escape the crowds by venturing further up the valley.

If a visit to the caves piques your interest, **Rocksport** (☎01934-742343; caves@visitcheddar.co.uk; adult/child £31/25) offers full-day subterranean trips into many of the more remote caverns, which are normally closed to the public. Needless to say, you'll get cold, wet and muddy, and if you're even vaguely claustrophobic, don't even think about it.

Mendip Hills

The Mendip Hills (often known simply as the Mendips) are a picturesque range of limestone ridges stretching from the coast near Weston-Super-Mare to Frome in eastern Somerset. Their highest point is **Black Down** (326m) to the northwest – but because they rise sharply, there are panoramic views towards Exmoor and across northwest Wiltshire.

CHEDDAR CHEESE

As well as its caves, Cheddar is also famous as the spiritual home of the nation's favourite cheese. Cheddar's strong, crumbly, tangy cheese is the essential ingredient in any self-respecting ploughman's, and has been produced in the area since at least the 12th century; Henry II boldly proclaimed cheddar to be 'the best cheese in Britain', and the king's accounts from 1170 record that he purchased 10,240lb (around 4644kg) of the stuff. In the days before refrigeration, the Cheddar caves made the ideal cool store for the cheese, with a constant temperature of around 7°C. However, the powerful smell attracted rats and the practice was eventually abandoned.

These days most cheddar cheese is made far from the village, but if you're interested in seeing how the genuine article is made, head for the **Cheddar Gorge Cheese Company** (☎01934-742810; www.cheddargorgecheeseco.co.uk; ⏲10am-4pm). You can take a guided tour of the factory from Easter to October, and pick up some tangy, whiffy souvenirs at the on-site shop.

Historically, the area has seen its share of action, and neolithic earthworks, Bronze Age barrows and Iron Age forts can be found scattered over the hills. More recently, lead and coal mining have left their mark, with the remains of mines dotting the area around Radstock and Midsomer Norton. Quarrying for stone is an important (and controversial) industry to this day, although the area has been protected as an AONB (Area of Outstanding Natural Beauty) since 1972.

Until the Middle Ages, large tracts of land lay beneath swampy meadows, and the remaining wetlands provide an important habitat for wildlife and flora. The marshland hid relics, too, including a lake village that was excavated at the turn of the 20th century (see Lake Village Museum, p327).

The landscape is peppered with pretty hamlets and isolated pubs that once served the thirsty miners. Mendip villages are also home to some delightful timbered houses, and several have fine Perpendicular church towers. The one at **Chewton Mendip** (off the A37 between Bristol and Wells) is especially striking and has an impressive medieval churchyard cross. Further west, the village of **Priddy**, the highest village in the Mendips, has a massive sheep fair on the green in mid-August, while the village of **Compton Martin** has a Norman church with a 15th-century tower. A mile to the east, **West Harptree** is prettier, with two 17th-century former manor houses. Near **East Harptree** are the remains of the Norman castle of Richmont. Local tourist offices stock leaflets with information on walking and cycling in the area.

The A371 skirts the southern side of the Mendip Hills, and any of the towns along it make good touring bases, though Wells has the best range of facilities. Buses in the Mendips are very limited – you'll really need your own transport to get around.

For information on walking, cycling and other activities, contact the **Mendips AONB** (☎01761-462338; www.mendiphillsaonb.org.uk) in Blagdon.

Glastonbury

POP 8429

If you suddenly feel the need to get your third eye cleansed or your chakras realigned, then there's really only one place in England that fits the bill: good old Glastonbury, a bohemian haven and centre for New Age culture since the days of the Summer of Love, and still a favourite hangout for hippies, mystics and countercultural types of all descriptions. The main street is more Haight Ashbury than Somerset hamlet, thronged with a bewildering assortment of crystal sellers, veggie cafés, mystical bookshops and bong emporiums, but Glastonbury has been a spiritual centre since long before the weekend Buddhists and white witches arrived. It's supposedly the birthplace of Christianity in England, and several of Britain's most important ley lines are said to converge on nearby Glastonbury Tor.

Sights

Glastonbury Abbey ABBEY

(www.glastonburyabbey.com; Magdalene St; adult/child £5.50/3.50; ⌚9.30am-6pm or dusk Sep-May, from 9am Jun-Aug) Legend has it that Joseph of Arimathea, great-uncle of Jesus, owned mines in this area and returned here with the Holy Grail (the chalice from the Last Supper) after the death of Christ. Joseph supposedly founded England's first church on the site, now occupied by the ruined abbey, but the earliest proven Christian connection dates from the 7th century, when King Ine gave a charter to a monastery in Glastonbury. In 1184 the church was destroyed by fire and reconstruction began in the reign of Henry II.

In 1191, monks claimed to have had visions confirming hints in old manuscripts that the 6th-century warrior-king Arthur and his wife Guinevere were buried in the abbey grounds. Excavations uncovered a tomb containing a skeletal couple, who were reinterred in front of the high altar of the new church in 1278. The tomb survived until 1539, when Henry VIII dissolved the monasteries and had the last abbot hung, drawn and quartered on the tor.

The remaining ruins at Glastonbury mainly date from the church that was built after the 1184 fire. It's still possible to make out some of the nave walls, the ruins of St Mary's chapel, and the remains of the crossing arches, which may have been scissor-shaped, like those in Wells Cathedral. The grounds also contain a small **museum**, cider **orchard** and **herb garden**, as well as the **Holy Thorn tree**, which supposedly sprung from Joseph's staff and mysteriously blooms twice a year, at Christmas and Easter.

Glastonbury

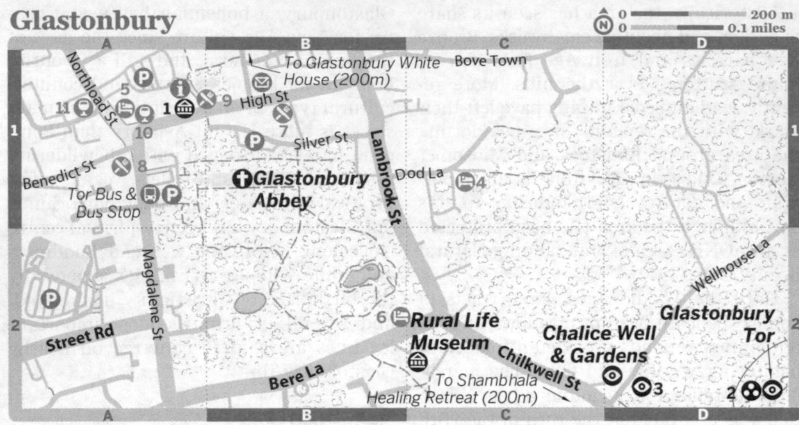

Glastonbury

Top Sights

Chalice Well & Gardens D2
Glastonbury Abbey B1
Glastonbury Tor D2
Rural Life Museum C2

Sights

1 Lake Village Museum A1
2 St Michael's Tower D2
3 White Spring D2

Sleeping

4 Chalice Hill C1
5 Glastonbury Backpackers A1
6 Parsnips B2

Eating

7 Hundred Monkeys Cafe B1
8 Mocha Berry A1
9 Rainbow's End B1

Drinking

10 George & Pilgrim A1
11 Who'd A Thought It Inn A1

FREE **Glastonbury Tor** LANDMARK

The iconic hump of Glastonbury Tor looms up from flat fields to the northwest of town. This 160m-high grassy mound provides glorious views over the surrounding countryside, and a focal point for a bewildering array of myths. According to some it's the home of a faery king, while an old Celtic legend identifies it as the stronghold of Gwyn ap Nudd (ruler of Annwyn, the Underworld) – but the most famous legend identifies the tor as the mythic Isle of Avalon, where King Arthur was taken after being mortally wounded in battle by his nephew Mordred, and where Britain's 'once and future king' sleeps until his country calls again.

Whatever the truth of the legends, the tor has been a site of pilgrimage for many years, and was once topped by the medieval church of **St Michael**, although today only the tower remains.

It takes 45 minutes to walk up and down the tor. Parking is not permitted nearby, but the **Tor Bus** (adult/child £2.50/1.50) leaves from Dunstan's car park near the abbey. The bus runs every 30 minutes from 10am to 7.30pm from April to September, and from 10am to 3.30pm from October to March. It also stops at Chalice Well and the Rural Life Museum.

Chalice Well & Gardens GARDENS

(www.chalicewell.org.uk; adult/child £3/1; 10am-5.30pm Apr-Oct, 10am-4pm Nov-Mar) Shaded by knotted yew trees and surrounded by peaceful paths, the Chalice Well and Gardens have been sites of pilgrimage since the days of the Celts. The iron-red waters from the 800-year-old well are rumoured to have healing properties, good for everything from eczema to smelly feet; some legends also identify the well as the hiding place of the Holy Grail. In fact, the reddish waters are caused by iron deposits in the soil. You can drink the water from a lion's-head spout, or rest your feet in basins surrounded by flowers.

The Chalice Well is also known as the 'Red Spring' or 'Blood Spring'; its sister, **White Spring**, surfaces across Wellhouse Lane.

FREE **Rural Life Museum** MUSEUM
(Abbey Farm, Chilkwell St; ⏲10am-5pm Tue-Fri, 2-6pm Sat & Sun Apr-Oct, 10am-5pm Tue-Sat Nov-Mar) Somerset's agricultural heritage is explored at the Rural Life Museum, which contains a varied collection of artefacts relating to traditional trades such as willow growing, peat digging, cider making and cheese making. There are often live displays of local skills, so if you fancy trying your hand at beekeeping, lace making and spinning, this is the place to do it. The late 14th-century tithe barn has fine carvings on the gables and porch, and an impressive timber roof; it now houses a collection of vintage agricultural machinery.

Lake Village Museum MUSEUM
(The Tribunal, 9 High St; adult/child £2/1.50; ⏲10am-5pm Apr-Sep, to 4pm Oct-Mar) Upstairs from Glastonbury's tourist office, in the medieval courthouse, the Lake Village Museum displays finds from a prehistoric bog village discovered in nearby Godney. The houses in the village were clustered in about six groups and were built from reeds, hazel and willow. It's thought they were occupied by summer traders who lived the rest of the year at Glastonbury Tor.

Sleeping

If you're a fan of wind chimes, organic brekkies and homemade muesli, then Glastonbury's B&Bs won't disappoint.

Chalice Hill B&B ££
(☎01458-838828; www.chalicehill.co.uk; Dod Lane; d £100; P) This grand Georgian B&B has been renovated with flair by its artistic owner Fay Hutchcroft. A sweeping staircase circles up through the house, leading to three characterful rooms: the nicest is Phoenix, with modern art, colourful fabrics and garden views. In the morning, a lavish buffet breakfast awaits in the book-lined lounge.

Shambhala Healing Retreat B&B ££
(☎01458-831797; www.shambhala.co.uk; Coursing Batch; s £44, d £76-112) If you're not in touch with your inner goddess, this spiritual sanctuary probably isn't for you. It's New Age through and through, from the meditation tent on the top floor to the reiki massage and colonic hydrotherapy on offer – you can even meet your guardian angel here. The 'clear energy' bedrooms are an appealing blend of airy fabric and snazzy designs in a choice of Tibetan and Egyptian themes.

Glastonbury White House B&B ££
(☎01458-830886; www.theglastonburywhitehouse.com; 21 Manor House Rd; d £50-60; P) Run by a London escapee, the White House only has a couple of rooms but they're both refined affairs, with extra treats including in-room fridges, fresh milk and bottles of water from the White Spring. Breakfast's extra (£5 to £7.50). It's located a couple of blocks north of the High St near the junction of Norbins Rd and Manor House Rd.

Parsnips B&B ££
(☎01458-835599; www.parsnips-glastonbury.co.uk; 99 Bere La; s/d £50/65; P @) The house is modern, but if you're looking for an escape from tie-dye and crystals, this solid B&B's a decent bet. Rooms in gingham and cream, a bright conservatory and massages.

Glastonbury Backpackers HOSTEL £
(☎01458-833353; www.glastonburybackpackers.com; 4 Market Pl; dm £14-16, tw £35-45, d £45-50; P @) A fresh lick of paint has made this basic hostel more presentable, but it's still pretty basic. Still, it's very friendly, and there's a TV lounge, kitchen and cafe-bar downstairs.

Eating & Drinking

Rainbow's End CAFE £
(17a High St; mains £4-7; ⏲10am-4pm) A Glasto classic, this charming wholefood cafe cooks up generous portions of veggie chilli, fresh quiches and hearty soups, served up in a cheery dining room dotted with potted plants and mix-and-match furniture, plus a little patio out back. The homemade cakes are particularly yummy.

Hundred Monkeys Cafe BISTRO ££
(52 High St; mains £8-15; ⏲10am-6pm Mon-Wed, to 9pm Thu-Sat, to 3.30pm Sun) Surprisingly sleek bistro, decked out with leather sofas, pine tables and a big blackboard listing fresh pastas, salads and mains. If you've a spare half-hour ask about the origin of the name – the original 100th monkey.

Who'd A Thought It Inn PUB ££
(17 Northload St; mains £8.25-16.95; ⏲lunch & dinner) In keeping with Glastonbury's outsider spirit, this town pub is brimming with wacky character, from the vintage signs and upside-down bike on the ceiling to the reclaimed red telephone box tucked in one corner. Locals pack in for its superior food and ales; Glastonbury kingpin Michael Eavis has even been known to pop in for a pint.

THE OTHER GLASTONBURY

To many people, the village of Glastonbury is synonymous with the **Glastonbury Festival of Contemporary Performing Arts** (www.glastonburyfestivals.co.uk), a majestic (and frequently mud-soaked) extravaganza of music, street theatre, dance, cabaret, carnival, ecology, spirituality and general all-round weirdness that's been held on and off on farmland in Pilton, just outside Glastonbury for the last 40 years.

The first event was held in 1970, when young dairy farmer Michael Eavis decided to stage his own British version of Woodstock on his land at Worthy Farm in Pilton, a few miles outside Glastonbury. Eavis borrowed £15,000 from the bank and invited some bands to play on a couple of makeshift stages in his field. Entry was £1, which included a pint of milk from Eavis' dairy herd; among the acts who performed at the first festival was Marc Bolan of T-Rex, who arrived in typically flamboyant style in his own velvet-covered Buick.

Forty years later, the festival has become the world's longest-running performing-arts festival, attracting some of the world's biggest acts and crowds of more than 120,000 festival-goers (actually more like 177,000 once you factor in the bands, technical staff, caterers and TV types). Glastonbury is more a way of life than a music festival, and it's a rite of passage for every self-respecting British teenager. It's even had a feature-length film made about it, directed by the renowned filmmaker Julien Temple.

More recently, Eavis' daughter Emily has stepped into her father's shoes and taken over the day-to-day running of the festival. She's also been involved in some controversial programming decisions in recent years, including a much-criticised headline slot for rapper Jay-Z in 2008. But despite inevitable grumblings that Glastonbury's lost its way and gone mainstream, in truth the festival's more stable now than it has ever been – it was recently granted its first six-year licence by Mendips District Council, which finally seems to have recognised, after years of wrangling and public disapproval, that the festival really is a national treasure after all.

Mocha Berry CAFE £
(14 Market Pl; mains £5-8; ⏲Sun-Wed) This ever-popular cafe is the top spot in Glastonbury for a frothy latte, a fresh milkshake or a stack of breakfast pancakes.

George & Pilgrim PUB ££
(1 High St; mains £7-14; ⏲lunch daily, dinner Mon-Sat) Snug pub with creaking timbers and stone arches that hint at its 15th-century inn heritage. Plenty of local ciders and ales on tap, plus a decent pub-grub menu.

ℹ Information

Glastonbury Tourist Office (☎01458-832954; www.glastonburytic.co.uk; The Tribunal, 9 High St; ⏲10am-5pm Apr-Sep, to 4pm Oct-Mar) Stocks maps and accommodation lists, and sells leaflets describing local walks and the *Glastonbury Millennium Trail* (60p).

ℹ Getting There & Away

There is no train station in Glastonbury, so buses are the only public transport option.

Bus 29 runs to **Taunton** (50 minutes, nine daily Monday to Saturday, six on Sunday), while bus 376/377 travels northwest to **Wells** (30 minutes, hourly Monday to Saturday, seven on Sundays) and **Bristol** (1¼ hours) and south to **Street** (15 minutes). The 377 runs on to **Yeovil** (one hour).

Quantock Hills

The curving, 12-mile ridge of the Quantocks forms a romantic, lyrical landscape of rolling red sandstone hills. Unsurprisingly, poet Samuel Taylor Coleridge was partial to roaming around the hills during his six-year sojourn in the village of Nether Stowey. The hills are still popular with walkers today – linking the Vale of Taunton Deane with the Somerset coast, they're only 384m at their highest point, the hummock of Wills Neck. The area is designated an AONB (Area of Outstanding Natural Beauty), and some of the most attractive country is owned by the National Trust – including the Beacon and Bicknoller Hills, which offer views of the Bristol Channel and Exmoor to the north-west. Mountain-biking is very popular in the Quantocks.

The **AONB Service** (www.quantockhills.com; ⏲9am-5pm Mon-Fri) runs an excellent program of guided walks and is based at

Fyne Court (NT; ☎01823-652400; admission free; ⌚9am-6pm or dusk), a National Trust nature reserve at Broomfield, in the south Quantocks.

Sights

Nether Stowey & Holford VILLAGE

The pretty village of Nether Stowey is best known for its association with Coleridge, who moved to the village in 1796 with his wife Sara and son Hartley. They lived at **Coleridge Cottage** (NT; ☎01278-732662; adult £4/2; ⌚2-5pm Thu-Sun Apr-Sep), where the poet composed some of his great early work, including *The Rime of the Ancient Mariner*. Wordsworth and his sister Dorothy spent 1797 at nearby Alfoxden House in Holford; during that year they all worked on the poems for *Lyrical Ballads* (1798), a short booklet that heralded the beginning of the British Romantic movement.

Crowcombe VILLAGE

One of the prettiest Quantock villages, Crowcombe is graced with a cluster of cottages made of stone and cob (a mixture of mud and straw), many with thatched roofs. The ancient **Church of the Holy Ghost** has wonderful carved 16th-century bench ends with surprisingly pagan themes (the Green Man is common). Part of its spire still stands in the churchyard where it fell when lightning struck in 1725.

Sleeping & Eating

Carew Arms PUB ££

(☎01984-618631; www.thecarewarms.co.uk; Crowcombe; mains £8.95-14.95; ⌚lunch & dinner) Plonked at the foot of the Quantocks in quaint Crowcombe, this redbrick hostelry has five centuries of experience. Classic character – inglenook fireplace, flagstone bar, grassy beer garden – plus a menu of ploughman's plates and antipasti platters, washed down with Tawny Bitter, Otter Bright and Exmoor Ale. Rooms (single £49 to £59, double £64 to £84) are small, but most have sweet country views.

Hood Arms PUB ££

(☎01278-741210; www.thehoodarms.com; Kilve; mains £8.95-14.95; ⌚lunch & dinner) The Hood in Kilve is one of the Quantocks' best grub pubs. Forget pints of prawns and scampi-in a basket – here the specials board is stocked with Exmoor trout, venison casserole and chomp of saltmarsh lamb. Hunting trophies, wooden beams and cosy rooms (single and double £95, family £115 to £125 and the standalone Stag Lodge (£250) complete the upmarket package.

Getting There & Away

Bus services around the Quantocks are very limited.

Nether Stowey, Holford, Kilve and West Quantoxhead (four daily Monday to Saturday, six on Sunday) Bus 14; runs from Bridgwater to Minehead. Sunday bus terminates at Watchet.

Crowcombe and Bicknoller (half-hourly Monday to Saturday, nine on Sunday) Bus 28; runs from Taunton to Minehead. Sunday buses only stop at Bicknoller.

Taunton

POP 58,241

There's not much to draw visitors to Somerset's main county town and administrative capital, but it's a handy transport hub and is the main gateway to the Quantocks. One of Taunton's most famous landmarks is the **Church of St Mary Magdalene**, with its 50m-high tower carved from red Quantock rock. The striking 12th-century **Taunton Castle**, on Taunton Green, is home to the Somerset County Museum, which is due to reopen in 2011, after a two year refit.

The nearby **Blackdown Hills** are a popular spot for walking, while 3 miles north in Cheddon Fitzpaine is **Hestercombe** (☎01823-413923; www.hestercombe.com; adult/child £8.90/3.30; ⌚10am-6pm), three garden designs rolled into one: a landscaped Georgian garden, a Victorian terrace and an Edwardian formal garden designed by the architect Sir Edmund Lutyens and the celebrated garden designer Gertrude Jekyll.

Sleeping & Eating

TOP CHOICE **Farmer's Inn** B&B, GASTROPUB ££

(☎01823-480480; www.farmersinnwesthatch.co.uk; West Hatch; d £125-150; P 📶) The country overcoat of this Somerset inn conceals fancy undergarments. People travel for miles around for the top-notch gastropub food (£9.95 to £15.95), and if you feel like staying overnight, there are fabulous rooms, all named after Somerset hills. Our faves are the Blackdown, with its elegant tub, mahogany furniture and exposed stone, and the Quantock, with wet-room, chaise longue and Bergère bed.

Corner House Hotel HOTEL, RESTAURANT ££

(☎01823-284683; www.cnr-house.co.uk; Park St; d £72-88; P 📶) The best option if you'd prefer

THE SOMERSET LEVELS

This huge area of native wetland – one of the largest in England – covers over 160,000 acres between the Quantock and Mendip Hills. Pan-flat, mostly sub-sea-level and dotted with pastures, cyclepaths and waterways (known locally as *rhynes*), the **Somerset Levels** are a haven for many traditional industries such as peat-digging, reed-harvesting and willow-growing. At the **Willows & Wetlands Visitor Centre** (☎01823-490249; ⌚9am-5pm Mon-Sat) near Stoke St Gregory, you can take a tour of the willow-beds before browsing the museum and shop, full of amazing willowy artefacts from pigeon panniers to picnic baskets. There are also regular willowcraft courses and demos throughout the year. It's free to browse, or you can take a guided tour for £3 per adult (children under 5 are free). Tours are run at 11.30am and 2pm Monday to Friday.

These unspoilt wetlands also harbour some of Britain's rarest wildlife and migratory birds. Several **nature reserves** have been established at Ham Wall, Shapwick Heath, Sedgemoor and Westhay, all of which are fantastic for bird-spotting. Bitterns, herons and crested grebes often put in an appearance, and Westhay is famous for the massive flocks of starlings (properly known as 'murmurations') that arrive at the reserve in October and November.

For more information, see www.isleofavalon.co.uk/avalon-moors.html or the twitching-specific site at www.avalonbirding.co.uk.

to stay in town. The old Victorian house has been much extended, and the ground floor is now occupied by the popular Wine & Sausage restaurant (mains £8.95 to £10.95), which (as the name suggests) specialises in quality British bangers and choice vintages. The upstairs rooms are on the plain side, but they're modern and good value.

Information

Taunton Tourist Office (☎01823-336344; www.heartofsomerset.com; Paul St; ⌚9.30am-5pm Mon-Sat) In the library.

Getting There & Away

Bus

Useful local services:

Minehead (1¼ hours, half-hourly Monday to Saturday, nine on Sunday) Bus 28; crosses the Quantocks.

Wells (1¼ hours, nine daily Monday to Saturday, six on Sunday) Bus 29; runs via Glastonbury (one hour).

Train

Regular services east to **London** (£41.50, two hours) and west to **Exeter** (£9.90, 30 minutes) and **Plymouth** (£15.50, 1½ hours).

Around Taunton

TOP CHOICE **Montacute House** STATELY HOME
(NT; ☎01935 823289; montacute@nationaltrust.org.uk; house adult/child £8.90/4.20, garden only £6/3; ⌚house 11am-5pm Wed-Mon mid-Mar–mid-Oct, grounds 11am-5.30pm mid-Mar–Oct, 11am-4pm Wed-Sun Nov-Mar) This stunning manor was built in the 1590s for Sir Edward Phelips, a Speaker of the House of Commons, and contains some of the finest 16th- and 17th-century interiors in the country. The house is particularly renowned for its remarkable plasterwork, fine chimneypieces and magnificent tapestries, but the highlight is the Long Gallery, decorated with Elizabethan-era portraits borrowed from the National Portrait Gallery in London. It's also surrounded by glorious parkland.

Haynes Motor Museum MUSEUM
(☎01963-440804; www.haynesmotormuseum.com; adult/child £8.95/4.25; ⌚9.30am-5.30pm Apr-Oct, 10am-4.30pm Nov-Mar) The 300-strong collection at this car museum includes an array of outstanding and outlandish motors, from Aston Martins and Ferraris to oddities such as the Sinclair C5. Don't miss the Red Room, famous for its collection of scarlet-coloured cars. And yes, it is *that* Haynes, publisher of Britain's ubiquitous car-repair manuals. The museum is near Sparkford, off the A303 northwest of Yeovil.

West Somerset Railway TRAIN TRIP
(☎01643-704996; www.west-somerset-railway.co.uk) Railway buffs will adore the vintage steam trains along this scenic railway, which chuff through the Somerset countryside from Bishops Lydeard to Minehead, 20 miles away. There are stops at Dunster and other stations, depending on

the time of year. Trains run pretty much daily from mid-March to October, otherwise occasional days only. The best value ticket is the 24-hour rover ticket (adult/child £14.80/7.40).

Bus 28 runs to Bishops Lydeard from Taunton (15 minutes, half-hourly Monday to Saturday, nine on Sunday).

Fleet Air Arm Museum MUSEUM
(☎01963-840565; www.fleetairarm.com; adult/child £10.50/7.50; ⏱10am-5.30pm Apr-Oct, 10am-4.30pm Wed-Sun Nov-Mar) This aviation museum houses a huge collection of naval aircraft, spanning the history of sea-going aviation from Sopwiths to Phantom fighters. You can walk onto the flight deck of the first British-built Concorde and take a simulated flight onto the aircraft carrier HMS *Ark Royal*. The museum is four miles north of Somerset, near Yeovilton.

EXMOOR NATIONAL PARK

Barely 21 miles across and 12 miles north to south, Exmoor might be the little sister of England's national parks, but what she lacks in scale she more than makes up in scenery. Part wilderness expanse, part rolling fields, dotted with bottle-green meadows, wooded combes and crumbling cliffs, Exmoor National Park seems to sum up everything that's green and pleasant about the English landscape. Waymarked paths criss-cross the moor, and a dramatic section of the South West Coast Path runs from Minehead (a family-fun resort just outside the park) all the way to Padstow in Cornwall.

It's a haven for ramblers, mountain-bikers and horse-riders, and it's also home to lots of rare wildlife, including some of England's largest herds of wild red deer. These skittish creatures are notoriously elusive, however, so if you want to spot them your best bet is to get up early for a dawn safari.

Activities

Active Exmoor (☎01398-324599; www.activeexmoor.com) A central contact point for all the park's outdoor activity providers, ranging from riding to rowing and sailing to surfing.

Cycling

A network of bridleways and quiet lanes makes Exmoor great cycling country, but you're not going to get away without tackling a few hills. Popular trails travel through the Brendon Hills, the Crown Estate woodland and along the old Barnstaple railway line. National Park Authority (NPA) centres sell the map *Exmoor for Off-Road Cyclists* (£10), and the *Bike It Dunster* and *Bike It Wimbleball* leaflets (75p) – both of which feature a family, beginner and explorer route. All are also available at the NPA's online shop.

Several sections of the **National Cycle Network** (NCN; www.sustrans.org.uk) cross the park, including the **West Country Way** (NCN route 3) from Bristol to Padstow, and the **Devon Coast to Coast Cycle Route** (NCN route 27) between Exmoor and Dartmoor.

Exmoor & Quantocks MTB Experiences (☎01643-705079; www.exqumtb.co.uk), runs weekend mountain-biking courses from £75 to £150.

Exmoor National Park

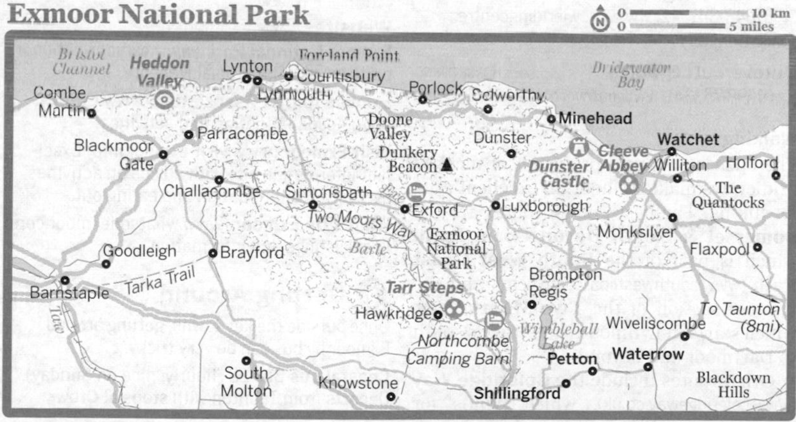

For bike hire:

Fremington Quay (☎01271-372586; www.biketrail.co.uk; Fremington; per day adult/child £16/8; ⏲10am-5pm Wed-Sun) Delivers bikes to your door.

Pompys (☎01643-704077; www.pompyscycles.co.uk; Minehead; ⏲9am-5pm Mon-Sat) Standard bikes £15 per day, full-suspension £25.

Moorland Safaris

Several companies offer 4WD 'safari' trips across the moor. If you're a nature-lover or keen photographer, bird and deer-watching safaris can be arranged. Half-day trips start at around £30.

Barle Valley Safaris SAFARI
(☎01643-851386; www.exmoorwildlifesafaris.co.uk; Dulverton & Dunster)

Discovery Safaris SAFARI
(☎]01643-863080; www.discoverysafaris.com; Porlock)

Exmoor Safari SAFARI
(☎01643-831229; www.exmoorsafari.co.uk; Exford)

Red Stag Safari SAFARI
(☎01643-841831; www.redstagsafari.co.uk)

Pony Trekking & Horse Riding

Exmoor is popular riding country and lots of stables offer pony and horse treks from around £40 for a two-hour hack – see the *Exmoor Visitor* for full details.

Brendan Manor Stables HORSE RIDING
(☎01598-741246) Near Lynton.

Burrowhayes Farm HORSE RIDING
(☎01643-862463; www.burrowhayes.co.uk; Porlock)

Knowle Riding Centre HORSE RIDING
(☎01643-841342; www.knowleridingcentre.co.uk; Dunster)

Outovercott Stables HORSE RIDING
(☎01598-753341; www.outovercott.co.uk; Lynton)

Walking

The open moors and profusion of marked bridleways make Exmoor an excellent area for hiking. The best-known routes are the **Somerset & North Devon Coast Path**, which is part of the **South West Coast Path** (www.southwestcoastpath.com), and the Exmoor section of the **Two Moors Way**, which starts in Lynmouth and travels south to Dartmoor and beyond.

Other routes include the **Coleridge Way** (www.coleridgeway.co.uk), which winds for 36 miles through Exmoor, the Brendon Hills and the Quantocks. Part of the 180-mile **Tarka Trail** also cuts through the park; join it at Combe Martin, hike along the cliffs to Lynton/Lynmouth, then head across the moor towards Barnstaple.

Organised walks run by the NPA are held throughout the year. Its autumn dawn safaris to see rutting stags are superb, as are its summertime evening deer-watching hikes. Pick up the *Exmoor Visitor* for full details – NPA walks are highlighted in green.

Sleeping

There are YHA hostels in Minehead and Ilfracombe (outside the park) and Exford within the park.

There's also YHA hostel-style accommodation at the **Pinkery Bunkhouse** (☎01643-831437; pinkery@exmoor-nationalpark.gov.uk) near Simonsbath.

The YHA also runs camping barns (often known as 'stone tents') at **Mullacott Farm** (☎01629-592700) near Ilfracombe and **Northcombe Farm** (☎01629-592700) near Dulverton. Prices start at around £8 per night, and you'll need all the usual camping supplies.

Information

Tourist Offices

There are three NPA Centres around the park – the main one is in Dulverton.

Dulverton (☎01398-323841; NPCDulverton@exmoor-nationalpark.gov.uk; 7-9 Fore St)

Dunster (☎01643-821835; NPCDunster@exmoor-nationalpark.gov.uk)

Lynmouth (☎01598-752509; NPCLynmouth@exmoor-nationalpark.gov.uk)

Websites

Exmoor National Park (www.exmoor-nationalpark.gov.uk) The official NPA site.

Exmoor Tourist Association (www.exmoor.com) Accommodation and activities.

Visit Exmoor (www.visit-exmoor.info) Excellent information site with advice on activities, events, accommodation and eating out.

What's On Exmoor (www.whatsonexmoor.com) Local listings and information.

Getting Around

Once outside the key towns, getting around Exmoor by bus can be very tricky.

Coastal bus Bus 28 (hourly, nine on Sunday). Departs from Taunton with stops at Crow-

ADVENTUROUS EXMOOR

For budding backcountry adventurers, **Mountains+Moor** (☎01643-841610; www.mountainsandmoor.co.uk) offers navigation lessons (from £80 per two days) and summer mountain-craft courses (two/five days £110/270), which include camp-craft, rope work and river crossings, and take the form of mini-expeditions. Eat your heart out, Ray Mears...

combe, Bicknoller, Williton, Watchet, Dunster and Minehead.

Cross-moor bus Bus 399 (three daily Monday to Saturday). Crosses the moor from Minehead to Tiverton via Dunster, Wheddon Cross, Exford and Dulverton.

'Coastal Link' Bus 39/300. Seasonal open-top bus from Minehead to Lynmouth via Selworthy and Porlock.

'Exmoor Explorer' Bus 401. Summer-only service that follows the coast from Porlock to Dunster and then circles inland via Wheddon Cross and Exford.

Dulverton

Dulverton is the southern gateway to Exmoor National Park, and sits at the base of the Barle Valley near the confluence of two key rivers, the Exe and Barle. It's a no-nonsense sort of country town, home to a collection of gun-sellers, fishing-tackle stores and gift shops.

There's a lovely 12-mile circular walk along the river from Dulverton to **Tarr Steps** – an ancient stone clapper bridge haphazardly placed across the River Barle and shaded by gnarled old trees. The bridge was supposedly built by the devil for sunbathing. It's a four- to five-hour trek for the average walker. You can add another three or four hours to the walk by continuing from Tarr Steps up Winsford Hill for distant views over Devon.

Eating

Woods RESTAURANT ££
(☎01398-324007; 4 Bank Sq; lunch £9.95-15, dinner £11-16.50; ⏲lunch & dinner)
This deservedly popular restaurant has built up a devoted following for its rustic dishes, quaint atmosphere and excellent service. Tummy treats include local lobster, pork belly with samphire, and Ruby Red sirloin steak.

Lewis' Tea Rooms CAFE ££
(☎01398-323850; 13 High St; mains £5-18; ⏲breakfast & lunch Mon-Sat, dinner Thu-Sat Jul & Aug) Top-class afternoon teas (including many rare estate varieties) are the main draw at this delightful town tearoom, but it's worth leaving room for the Welsh rarebits and crumbly cakes too. It's frilly and floral, but hugely friendly – and it opens late for country suppers in summer, too.

Tantivy CAFE, SHOP £
(☎01398-323465; www.tantivyexmoor.co.uk; ⏲9am-5pm Mon-Sat) Dulverton's catch-all shop (selling everything from boxes of fudge to the daily papers) has recently been refurbished and branched out into coffee and light lunch territory. Rather lovely it is, too, and the patio is one of the prettiest in town.

Sleeping

TOP CHOICE **Tarr Farm** HOTEL £
(☎01643-851507; www.tarrfarm.co.uk; s/d £90/150; P) This valley getaway is snuggled near the Tarr Steps, 5 miles from Dulverton. Despite the farmhouse appearance, it's a top-class retreat: nine rooms in rich creams and yellows, with organic bath goodies and old-fashioned bath taps, plus spoils such as home-baked cookies, in-room fridges, DVD players and a fab country **restaurant** (mains £13-18; ⏲lunch & dinner).

Town Mills B&B ££
(☎01398-323124; www.townmillsdulverton.co.uk; High St; s/d £60/85; P 📶) The nicest B&B near Dulverton's town centre, with creamy-and-beam rooms squeezed into a converted mill, livened up by bits of art and crisp fabrics. The attic rooms are a bit small, but you can hear the rush of the river from your window.

Three Acres B&B ££
(☎01398-323730; www.threeacrescountryhouse.co.uk; Brushford; s £60-75, d £90-120; P) A sweet retreat reached by narrow, twisty lanes from Dulverton. It's scooped lots of B&B awards, and with good reason: the six prim rooms overlook rolling Exmoor hills, and there's a different daily special for breakfast, from Exe trout to homemade bangers. Lovely.

Northcombe Camping Barn HOSTEL £
(☎0870 770 8868; www.yha.org.uk; per person £8) Two bunk barns about 1 mile from town, both equipped with basic kitchen goods,

plus a shower and electricity (£1 per unit). One has a wood-stove, the other an open fire.

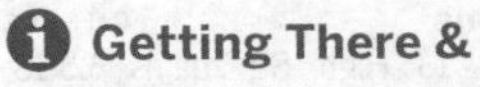

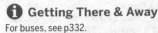

Getting There & Away

For buses, see p332.

Exford & Wheddon Cross

Nestled on the banks of the River Exe at the heart of the moor, Exford is a delightful muddle of cottages and slate-roofed houses clustered around a village green. The village is the base of Devon and Somerset Staghounds, and meets are still an important part of life here, despite the hunting ban.

Exmoor's highest point is 4 miles northeast of the village at **Dunkery Beacon** (519m). The best route up is from the village of Wheddon Cross, about 3 miles east of Exford. The round-trip is 8 miles, and steep in places; wear good boots and take a picnic.

Another popular walk from Wheddon Cross is to the local beauty spot of **Snowdrop Valley**, which as its name suggests is carpeted by snow-white blossoms in spring. A Park & Ride scheme operates during the peak season – see www.wheddoncross.org.uk/snowdropvalley.htm for details.

Sleeping & Eating

Edgcott House B&B ££
(01643-831495; info@edgcotthouse.co.uk; s £40, d £70-90; P) A 10-minute walk from Exford, this beautiful 17th-century house is set in private riverside gardens (it even has its own orchard). It's packed with period features, including a terracotta-tiled hallway and an amazing 15m 'Long Room' decorated with hand-painted murals. The best bedrooms are number 1 and number 3, which both have sofas and views over the garden.

Exford YHA HOSTEL £
(0845 371 9634; exford@yha.org.uk; Exe Mead; dm £14; P) Probably one of Exmoor's best budget bases, this brick Victorian house is just a short walk from Exford – and the pub. The dorms are small and a smidgen institutional, but the hordes of hikers and cyclists aren't too bothered.

Exmoor House RESTAURANT, B&B £
(01643-841432; www.exmoorhouse.com; Wheddon Cross; dinner, bed & breakfast £66 per person; P) This homely restaurant-and-B&B is in nearby Wheddon Cross. It's mainly worth a visit for its country specials – trout paté, homemade pies, hearty casseroles – plus a great selection of local ciders and ales (Exmoor Gold and Barn Owl). The rooms are a bit pastel-heavy, but fine for the cash.

Crown Hotel PUB ££
(01643-831554; www.crownhotelexmoor.co.uk; Chapel St; mains £13-25; lunch & dinner; P) For a taste of traditional Exmoor try the Crown, where hunting prints and stags' heads preside over leather armchairs and a colour scheme of racing-green and cream. Despite the backcountry vibe, the restaurant's surprisingly adventurous: roast wood pigeon, brill with pak choi or black cherry soufflé. You can stay here too (single £72.50, double £125 to £145).

Getting There & Away

For buses see p332.

Lynton & Lynmouth

The attractive harbour of Lynmouth is rooted at the base of a steep, tree-lined valley, where the West Lyn River empties into the sea along Exmoor's northern coastline. Its similarity to the harbour at Boscastle (p366) is striking and, in fact, the two harbours share more than just a common geography: like Boscastle, Lynmouth is famous for a devastating flash flood. A huge wave of water swept through Lynmouth in 1952 and the town paid a much heavier price than its Cornish cousin; 34 people lost their lives, and memory of the disaster remains strong in the village today.

Today Lynmouth is a busy tourist harbour town lined with pubs, souvenir sellers and fudge shops. At the top of the rocky cliffs is the more genteel Victorian resort of Lynton, which can be reached via an amazing water-operated railway, or a stiff climb up the cliff path.

Sights

Lyn & Exmoor Museum MUSEUM
(St Vincent's Cottage, Market St, Lynton; adult/child £1/20p; 10am-12.30pm & 2-5pm Mon-Fri, 2-5pm Sun Apr-Oct) The history of Lynmouth's flood is explored at this museum, which also houses some interesting archaeological finds and a collection of tools, paintings and period photos.

Cliff Railway RAILWAY
(www.cliffrailwaylynton.co.uk; single/return adult £2/3, child £1.20/1.85; 10am-6pm Easter-Oct, later at peak times) This extraordinary piece

of Victorian engineering was designed by George Marks, believed to be a pupil of Brunel. Two cars linked by a steel cable descend or ascend the slope according to the amount of water in the cars' tanks. It's been running like clockwork since 1890, and it's still the best way to commute between the two villages.

Glen Lyn Gorge GORGE

(adult/child £4/3; ⏲Easter-Oct) From the Lynmouth crossroads follow the signs 200m to the steepest of the two valleys into Lynmouth. There are several lovely gorge walks and a small exhibition centre devoted to hydroelectric power.

Activities

There are some beautiful short walks in and around the two villages, as well as access to some longer routes: the **South West Coast Path**, the **Coleridge Way** and the **Tarka Trail** all pass through Lynmouth, and it is the official starting point of the **Two Moors Way**.

The most popular hike is to the stunning **Valley of the Rocks**, described by poet laureate Robert Southey as 'rock reeling upon rock, stone piled upon stone, a huge terrifying reeling mass'. It's just over a mile west of Lynton, and is believed to mark the original course of the River Lyn. Many of the tortuous rock formations have been named over the years – look out for the **Devil's Cheesewring** and **Ragged Jack** – the valley is also home to a population of feral goats.

Other popular trails wind to the lighthouse at **Foreland Point**, east of Lynmouth, and **Watersmeet**, 2 miles upriver from Lynmouth, where a handily placed National Trust teashop is housed in a Victorian fishing lodge.

Sleeping

There are plenty of mid-price B&Bs dotted along Lee Rd in Lynton.

St Vincent House B&B ££

(☎01598-752244; www.st-vincent-hotel.co.uk; Castle Hill, Lynton; d £75-80; P) No sea view, but this classy lodge is still our favourite Lynton base. The house has history – it was built by a sea captain who sailed with Nelson – and the decor's full of cosy heritage and a rather grand central staircase.

Sea View Villa B&B ££

(☎01598-753460; www.seaviewvilla.co.uk; 6 Summer House Path, Lynmouth; d £100-150) Georgian grandeur in seaside Lynmouth. In this 1721 villa Egyptian cotton, Indian silk and suede fabrics grace rooms done out in 'Champagne', 'ginger' and 'vanilla'. Eggs Benedict, smoked salmon and cafetière coffee ensure the breakfast is classy, and they'll even pack you a picnic.

Chough's Nest B&B £

(☎01598-753315; www.choughsnesthotel.co.uk; North Walk, Lynton; d £94-110; P) For clifftop position, this Lynton B&B is unbeatable. It goes a bit overboard with the frips and floral fabrics, but if you can get a room with a sea view, you'll be a happy bunny.

Eating

St Vincent Restaurant RESTAURANT ££

(☎01598 752244; Castle Hill, Lynton; 2/3 courses £24/27; ⏲dinner Wed-Sun Easter-Oct) With the local dining scene largely limited to tearooms and seaside pubs, the St Vincent's accomplished eatery looks all the more appealing. Exmoor produce is given a Mediterranean zing by the proprietor-chef, Belgian-born Jean-Paul Salpetier: think Exmoor boar with honey, thyme and sage, or noisettes of lamb with tomatoes, capers and olives.

Rising Sun PUB ££

(☎01598-753223; Lynmouth; mains £11.25-17.70; ⏲lunch & dinner) A historic thatched pub a little walk uphill from the Lynmouth harbour. Chef Oliver Wood's food is a world way from the usual boring bar fare, and makes maximum use of ingredients on his doorstep such as lamb, game and river-fish. The Sunday roast is a real cracker too.

Information

Lynton Tourist Office (☎01598-752225; info@lyntourism.co.uk; Lynton Town Hall, Lee Rd; ⏲10am-4pm Mon-Sat, to 2pm Sun) Publishes the free newspaper *Lynton & Lynmouth Scene* (www.lyntonandlynmouthscene.co.uk), which has accommodation, eating and activities listings.

Getting There & Away

For buses see p332.

Porlock & Around

The small village of Porlock is one of the prettiest on the north Exmoor coast; the huddle of thatched cottages lining its main street is framed on one side by the sea, and on the other by a jumble of houses that cling to the steeply sloping hills behind. Winding lanes lead to the picturesque breakwater of **Porlock Weir**, a compact collection of pubs, shops and hotels, 2 miles to the west.

Coleridge's famous poem *Kubla Khan* was written during a brief sojourn in Porlock (helped along by a healthy slug of laudanum and a vicious head cold), and the villages are popular with summertime tourists, as well as walkers on the Coleridge Way and the South West Coast Path.

The village of **Selworthy**, 2½ miles southeast of Porlock, forms part of the 5060-hectare **Holnicote Estate**, the largest NT-owned area of land on Exmoor. Though its cob-and-thatch cottages look ancient, the village was almost entirely rebuilt in the 19th century by local philanthropist and landowner Thomas Acland, to provide housing for elderly workers on his estate.

Sleeping & Eating

TOP CHOICE **Andrews on the Weir** RESTAURANT £££
(☎01643-863300; www.andrewsontheweir.co.uk; Porlock Weir; 2-/3-course menu £31.50/38.50) Exmoor's starriest and starchiest restaurant is nestled behind the Porlock breakwater. Chef Andrew Dixon makes a point of sourcing all his produce from local farmers and fishing boats, so the menu is a riot of local flavours – Exmoor lamb, Withycombe pork and Devon scallops. Dinner can be pricey, but the £10 lunch menu is fab value. He also runs regular cooking courses if you fancy finding out how the magic happens.

Ship Inn PUB £
(www.shipinnporlock.co.uk; High St; mains £7.75-11.95) Coleridge and pal Robert Southey both downed pints in this venerable thatched Porlock pub – you can even sit in 'Southey's Corner'. Substantial pub food – mainly steaks, roasts and stews – are served in the wood-filled bar, and there are 10 surprisingly light **rooms** (single/double £40/60) in pine and cream.

Information

Porlock Tourist Office (☎01643-863150; www.porlock.co.uk; West End, High St; ⊙10am-5pm Mon-Sat, 10am-1pm Sun Mar-Oct, 10.30am-1pm Tue-Fri, 10am-2pm Sat Nov-Mar) Main point of contact for info on the Coleridge Way.

Getting There & Away

For buses see p332.

If you're driving, the most scenic route to Porlock is the steep, twisting **toll-road** (cars/motorbikes/bicycles £2.50/1.50/1) that hugs the coast all the way from Lynmouth. Better still, you get to avoid the 1:4 gradient on Porlock Hill.

Dunster

Centred around a scarlet-walled castle and an original medieval yarn market, Dunster is one of Exmoor's oldest villages, sprinkled with bubbling brooks, packhorse bridges and a 16th-century dovecote.

Sights

Dunster Castle CASTLE
(NT; dunster@nationaltrust.co.uk; castle adult/child £8.10/4, garden & park only £4.50/2; ⊙11am-5pm Sat-Wed Mar-Oct, 11am-4pm Nov) The castle was originally owned by the aristocratic Luttrell family whose manor encompassed much of northern Exmoor. Although it served as a fortress for around 1000 years, present-day Dunster Castle bears little resemblance to the original Norman stronghold. The 13th-century gateway is probably the only original part of the castle; the turrets, battlements and towers were all added later during a romantic remodelling at the hands of Victorian architects. Despite its 19th-century makeover, the castle is still an impressive sight, and is decorated with Tudor furnishings, gorgeous 17th-century plasterwork and ancestral portraits of the Luttrell family. The terraced gardens are also worth exploring, with fine views across Exmoor and the coastline, and an important national collection of strawberry trees.

St George's Church CHURCH
This beautiful church dates mostly from the 15th century and boasts a wonderfully carved fan-vaulted rood screen.

Watermill MILL
(Mill Lane; adult/child £3.50/2; ⊙11am-4.45pm Jun-Sep, 11am-4.45pm Sat-Thu Apr, May & Oct) Further down the road is this working 18th-century mill.

Sleeping & Eating

Dunster Castle Hotel HOTE ££
(☎01643 82 30 30; www.thedunstercastlehotel.co.uk; 5 High St; d £90-150;) Fresh from an expensive refurb, this old Dunster hostelry is now all uncluttered simplicity. The rooms are light and soothing – it's worth bumping up to one of the Superior Kingsize Rooms (£125) for more space, and we particularly liked the Grabbist and Aville rooms. Downstairs the restaurants' has the same stripped-

down feel – grey wicker chairs, crimson keynotes and modern Brit-bistro food.

Spears Cross B&B ££
(☎01643-821439; www.spearscross.co.uk; 1 West St; s £55, d £82-92) This Dunster house mostly dates back to the mid-15th-century, but if you're a sucker for inglenook grates, low ceilings and quirky crannies, you couldn't ask for a quainter sleep. The rooms are obviously small, but luxuries including Bose hifis and Penhaligons toiletries are a really welcome surprise, and the breakfast is simply fab: Quantock Mueslis, locally made jams and sausages from rare-breed pigs.

Reeve's RESTAURANT ££
(☎01643-821414; www.reevesrestaurantdunster.co.uk; lunch £4.95-14.25, dinner £12.95-24.95; ⏲lunch Thu-Sun, dinner Tue-Sat) Oak girders, worn-wood tables and twinkling candles create a bewitchingly cosy atmosphere at Reeve's, a reliable stalwart for dining in Dunster. Rich, indulgent dishes are the watchword – guineafowl, lamb's liver, venison, slow-roasted partridge – but it's refreshingly unstuffy.

Luttrell Arms PUB, HOTEL ££
(☎01643-821555; www.luttrellarms.co.uk; High St; P) In medieval times this glorious old coaching inn was the guest house of the Abbots of Cleeve. Huge flagstones, heavy armchairs and faded tapestries dot the lounge – a perfect fit for the hearty bar food. The beamed **rooms** (B&B d £116-150) might be too olde-worlde for some.

Cobblestones Cafe CAFE ££
(☎01643-821595; High St; mains £7-14; ⏲lunch Sun, Mon & Wed-Fri, dinner Sat)
Dunster's village cafe is ideal for a lunchtime treat: tuck into ham terrine, spiced potted shrimps or braised shallot and goats' cheese tart, or just sit back for the town's nicest cream tea. It's open for dinner on Saturday nights, too.

ℹ Getting There & Away

The West Somerset Railway (p330) stops at Dunster during the summer. For buses, see p332.

Devon & Cornwall

Includes »

Best Places to Eat

» Porthminster Beach Café (p376)

» Paul Ainsworth at No 6 (p368)

» Gurnard's Head (p378)

» Riverford Field Kitchen (p351)

» River Cottage Canteen (p347)

Best Places to Stay

» Scarlet (p370)

» Boskerris Hotel (p375)

» Trevalsa Court (p390)

» Cary Arms (p347)

» ABode at the Royal Clarence (p343)

Why Go?

If ever there was a region made for postcards, it's here. Coast to coast, end to end, Britain's two westermost counties are one non-stop scenic adventure from start to finish. Every twist and turn in the road seems to reveal a fresh panorama of breathtaking views: green fields criss-crossed by knotted hedgerows, rocky cliffs tumbling into pounding surf, wild moorland topped by granite tors.

But while the bewitching scenery is undoubtedly one of the region's dynamite draws, it's certainly not the only reason to visit. Long relegated to the realms of bucket-and-spade holidays, these nextdoor neighbours have definitely turned a corner: with a crackling culinary scene, a fast-growing green movement and a fascinating history stretching back over 5000 years, you could spend a lifetime exploring and still only scratch the surface. Just don't forget to pack the flip-flops.

When to Go

Padstow hosts the Obby Oss ceremony over the town's streets around May Day. The Port Eliot Festival in mid-July has music, theatre, dance and literary events and in August bursts of colour fill Plymouth's skies during the British Fireworks Championships.

DEVON

If counties were capable of emotions, those in the rest of England would envy Devon. It's all to do with a rippling landscape studded with prehistoric sites, historic homes, vibrant cities, ancient villages, intimate coves and wild, wild moors. If exhilaration is your thing, you'll be right at home: here you can get churned around by crashing surf, ride white-water rapids or hike hundreds of miles along precipitous cliffs. Landscape and lifestyle ensure food is fresh from furrow or sea – eat a Michelin-starred meal at a swanky restaurant or a fresh crab sandwich sitting on the beach – it's up to you. In Devon a day's drive can take you from Exeter's serene cathedral, via Torbay's touristy coast to the yachting haven of Dartmouth, where Agatha Christie's mysterious house waits in the wings. Totnes provides the eco-awareness, Plymouth provides the party and wilderness, Dartmoor provides the great escape, while the North Coast – rugged, remote and surf-dashed – draws you into the waves. The delights of Devon are tempting indeed.

Information

Visit Devon (www.visitdevon.co.uk)

Getting Around

Tourist offices stock timetables, the *Devon Bus Map* and the *Discovery Guide to Dartmoor*.

Traveline South West (www.travelinesw.com) Details all bus and train timetables.

Bus

First (www.firstgroup.com) The key bus operator in Dartmoor, north, south and east Devon.

Stagecoach Devon (www.stagecoachbus.com) Operates mostly local buses, especially in Exeter and Torbay.

Bus passes:

First Seven day (adult/family £32.50/49) Week-long equivalent.

Firstday Southwest (adult/child/family £7/5.70/17.20) A day's unlimited bus travel on First buses in Devon and Cornwall.

Stagecoach Explorer (adult/child/family £6.50/4/16) One day's travel on its southwest network.

Train

Devon's main line skirts southern Dartmoor, running from Exeter to Plymouth and on to Cornwall. Branch lines include the 39-mile Exeter–Barnstaple Tarka Line; the 15-mile Plymouth–Gunnislake Tamar Valley Line and the scenic Exeter–Torquay Paignton line.

The Devon and Cornwall Rover allows unlimited, off-peak train trips across Devon and Cornwall. Eight days' travel in 15 costs an adult £60; three days' travel in one week is £40.

Exeter

POP 116,393

Well heeled and comfortable, Exeter exudes evidence of its centuries-old role as the spiritual and administrative heart of Devon. The city's gloriously Gothic cathedral presides over stretches of cobbled streets, fragments of the terracotta Roman city wall and a tumbling of medieval and Georgian buildings. A snazzy new shopping centre brings bursts of the modern, thousands of university students ensure a buzzing nightlife and the vibrant quayside acts as a launch pad for cycling or kayaking trips. Throw in some stylish places to stay and eat and you have a relaxed but lively base for further explorations.

History

Exeter's past can be read in its buildings. The Romans marched in around AD 55 – their 17-hectare fortress included a 2-mile defensive wall, crumbling sections of which remain, especially in Rougemont and Northernhay Gardens. Saxon and Norman times saw growth: a castle went up in 1068, the cathedral 40 years later. The Tudor wool boom brought Exeter an export trade, riches and half-timbered houses; prosperity continued into the Georgian era when hundreds of merchants built genteel homes. The Blitz of WWII brought devastation. In just one night in 1942, 156 people died and 12 hectares of the city were flattened. In the 21st century the £220-million Princesshay shopping centre added shimmering glass and steel lines to the architectural mix.

Sights

Exeter Cathedral CATHEDRAL

(www.exeter-cathedral.org.uk; The Close; adult/child £5/free; ⌚9.30am-4.45pm Mon-Sat) Magnificent in warm, honey-coloured stone, Exeter's Cathedral Church of St Peter is framed by lawns and wonky half-timbered buildings – a quintessentially English scene often peopled by picnickers snacking to the sound of the bells.

The site has been a religious one since at least the 5th century but the Normans

Devon & Cornwall Highlights

1 Marvel at the ecological ingenuity of the **Eden Project** (p387)

2 Cracking the clues to Agatha Christie's life at her enchanting holiday home, **Greenway** (p349)

3 Discovering your very own slice of wilderness in natural breakout-zone **Dartmoor** (p356)

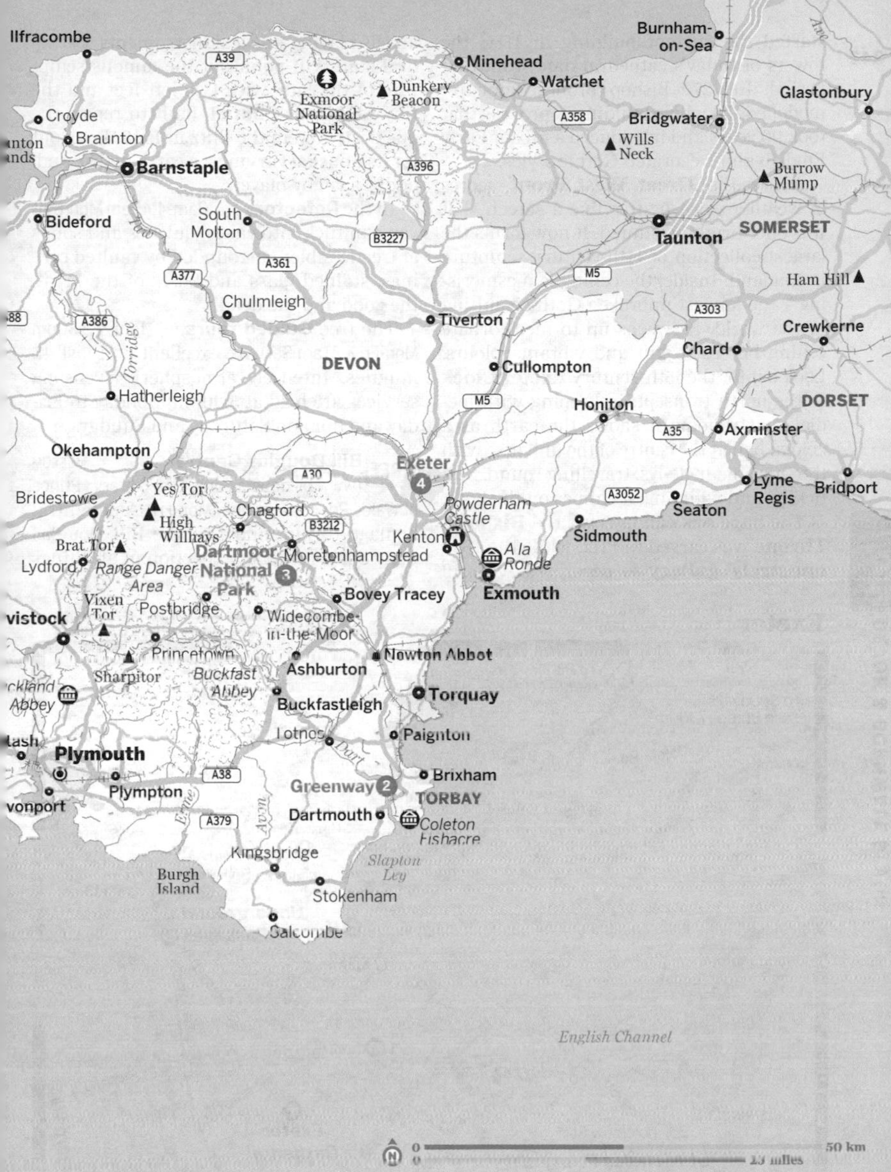

4 Goggling at the Gothic splendour of **Exeter Cathedral** (p339)

5 Escaping the 21th century on the **Isles of Scilly** (p393)

6 Hiking the wild stretch of coastline from **Sennen to Land's End** (p377)

7 Crossing the causeway to **St Michael's Mount** (p379)

8 Bringing out your inner artist around **St Ives** (p373)

started the current building in 1114; the towers of today's cathedral date from that period. In 1270 Bishop Bronescombe remodelled the whole building, a process that took 90 years and introduced a mix of Early English and Decorated Gothic styles.

Above the **Great West Front** scores of weather-worn figures line a screen that was once brightly painted. It now forms the largest collection of 14th-century sculpture in England. Inside, the ceiling is mesmerising – the longest unbroken Gothic vaulting in the world, it sweeps up to meet ornate ceiling bosses in gilt and vibrant colours. Look out for the 15th-century **Exeter Clock** in the north transept: in keeping with medieval astronomy it shows the earth as a golden ball at the centre of the universe with the sun, a fleur-de-lys, travelling round. Still ticking and whirring, it chimes on the hour.

The huge oak canopy over the **Bishop's Throne** was carved in 1312, while the 1350 **minstrels' gallery** is decorated with 12 angels playing musical instruments. Cathedral staff will point out the famous sculpture of the lady with two left feet and the tiny **St James Chapel**, built to repair the one destroyed in the Blitz in 1942. Look out for its unusual carvings: a cat, a mouse and, oddly, a rugby player.

In the **Refectory** (⏲10am-4.45pm Mon-Sat) you can tuck into cakes, quiches and soups at trestle tables surrounded by vaulted ceilings, stained glass and busts of the great, the good and the dead.

The free **Guided tours** (⏲11am & 2.30pm Mon-Fri & 11am Sat) are excellent and last 45 minutes. Intensely atmospheric evensong services are held at 5.30pm Monday to Friday and 3pm on Saturday and Sunday.

FREE **Bill Douglas Centre** MUSEUM
(www.billdouglas.org; Old Library, Prince of Wales Rd; ⏲10am-5pm Mon-Fri) A delightful homage to film and fun, the Bill Douglas Centre is a compact collection of all things

Exeter

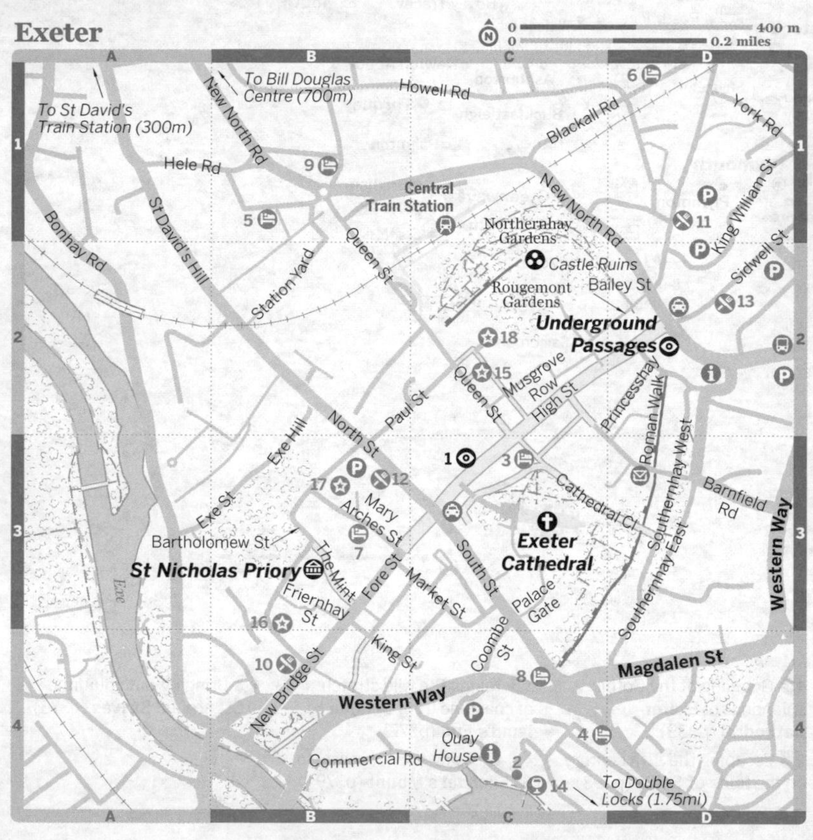

celluloid, from magic lanterns to Mickey Mouse. Inside discover just what the butler did see and why the flicks are called the flicks. In a mass of movie memorabilia Charlie Chaplin bottle stoppers mingle with Ginger Rogers playing cards, James Bond board games and Star Wars toys.

St Nicholas Priory MEDIEVAL BUILDING
(www.exeter.gov.uk/priory; Mint La; adult/child £2/free; ⏲10am-5pm Mon-Sat school holidays) This 900-year-old former Benedictine monastery is built of beautiful russet stone and vividly evokes life inside a late-Elizabethan town house. Expect brightly coloured furnishings, elaborate plaster ceilings and intricate oak panelling.

FREE **Guildhall** MEDIEVAL BUILDING
(☎01392-665500; High St) The earliest parts of the Guildhall date from 1330, making it the oldest municipal building still in use in the country. A gloriously ornate barrel roof arches above wooden benches and crests of dignitaries – the mayor still sits in the huge throne-like chair at the end. Opening hours depend on civic functions.

Activities

The River Exe and the Exeter Canal are framed by foot and cycle paths that wind south from **the Quay**, past pubs (see p345), beside an ever-broadening estuary towards the sea, 10 miles away. **Saddles & Paddles** (☎01392-424241; www.sadpad.com; 4 Kings Wharf, the Quay; ⏲9.30am-5.30pm) rents out bikes (adult per hour/day £6/15), kayaks (per hour/day £7/25) and Canadian canoes (per hour/day £15/35); the tourist office stocks maps.

Tours

FREE **Redcoat Tours** HERITAGE TOUR
(www.exeter.gov.uk/visiting; ⏲2-5 daily Apr-Oct, 2-3 daily Nov-Mar) For an informed and entertaining introduction to Exeter's history, it's hard to beat these 1½ hour tours. Themes range from murder and trade to Romans and religion – there are even torch-lit prowls through the catacombs and night-time ghost walks. Tours leave from Cathedral Yard or the Quay; pick up a program from the tourist office.

Underground Passages SUBTERRANEAN TOUR
(☎01392-665887; www.exeter.gov.uk/passages; Paris St; adult/child £5/3.50; ⏲9.30am-5.30pm Mon-Sat Jun-Sep, 11.30am-4pm Tue-Sun Oct-May) Prepare to crouch down, don a hard hat and possibly get spooked in what is the only system of its kind open to the public in England. These medieval vaulted passages were built to house pipes bringing fresh water to the city. Unlike modern utility companies, the authorities opted to have permanent access for repairs, rather than dig up the streets each time – genius. Guides lead you on a scramble through the network regaling you with tales of ghosts, escape routes and cholera. The last tour is an hour before closing; it can get busy; it's best to book.

Sleeping

ABode at the Royal Clarence HOTEL ££
(☎01392-319955; www.abodehotels.co.uk/exeter; Cathedral Yard; r £115-135, ste £175-260; wi-fi) Georgian grandeur meets minimalist chic in these, the poshest rooms in town, where

Exeter

Top Sights
- Exeter Cathedral ... C3
- St Nicholas Priory ... B3
- Underground Passages ... D2

Sights
- 1 Guildhall ... C3

Activities, Courses & Tours
- 2 Saddles & Paddles ... C4

Sleeping
- 3 ABode at the Royal Clarence Hotel ... C3
- 4 Globe Backpackers ... C4
- 5 Queen's Court ... B1
- 6 Raffles ... D1
- 7 St Olaves ... B3
- 8 White Hart ... C4
- 9 Woodbine ... B1

Eating
- 10 @Angela's ... B4
- 11 Harry's ... D1
- 12 Herbies ... B3
- Michael Caines ... (see 3)
- 13 tyepyedong ... D2

Drinking
- 14 On the Waterfront ... C4

Entertainment
- 15 Cavern Club ... C2
- 16 Exeter Picturehouse ... B3
- 17 Mamma Stone's ... B3
- 18 Phoenix ... C2

WORTH A TRIP

COMBE HOUSE

The sumptuous **Combe House** (☎01404-540400; www.thishotel.com; Gittisham; s £159-364, d £179-344, ste £384) is more like a National Trust property than a hotel. The great hall of this Elizabethan country manor is floor-to-ceiling wood panels, while ancient oak furniture and original Tudor paintings pop up everywhere. The historic splendour is matched by modern luxuries – guests are pampered with crisp cottons, monogrammed towels, rain showers and sumptuous throws. One room even has a vast copper washtub for a bath. It's all set on a massive estate near Gittisham, 14 miles east of Exeter.

wonky floors and stained glass blend with pared-down furniture and neutral tones. The top-end suite is bigger than most people's apartments; its slanted ceilings and beams frame a grandstand cathedral view.

Raffles B&B ££

(☎01392-270200; www.raffles-exeter.co.uk; 11 Blackall Rd; s/d £42/72; P) Creaking with antiques and oozing atmosphere, this late-Victorian town house is an appealing blend of old woods and tasteful modern fabrics. Plant stands and dado rails add to the turn-of-the-century feel, while the largely organic breakfasts, walled garden and much-coveted parking make it a great value choice.

Woodbine B&B ££

(☎01392-203302; www.woodbineguesthouse.co.uk; 1 Woodbine Tce; s/d £38/66;) A bit of a surprise sits behind this archetypal flower-framed terrace: fresh, contemporary rooms with low beds and flashes of burgundy – there's even underfloor heating in the showers.

White Hart HOTEL ££

(☎01392-279897; www.english-inns.co.uk; 66 South St; s £60, d £60-70; P) They've been putting people up here since the Plantagenets were on the throne in the 14th century. The courtyard is a wisteria-fringed bobble of cobbles and the bar is book-lined and beamed. Rooms are either traditional (dark woods and rich drapes) or contemporary (laminate floors and light fabrics).

St Olaves HOTEL ££

(☎01392-217736; www.olaves.co.uk; Mary Arches St; d/ste/f £125/155/165; P) This hotel's swirling spiral staircase is so gorgeous it's tempting to sleep beside it. But if you did, you'd miss out on the 18th century-with-contemporary-twist bedrooms: expect rococo mirrors, brass bedsteads and plush furnishings.

Globe Backpackers HOSTEL £

(☎01392-215521; www.exeterbackpackers.co.uk; 71 Holloway St; dm £16.50, d £42; @) A spotlessly clean, relaxed, rambling house near the Quay. There's only one double room, so book ahead.

Queen's Court HOTEL £

(☎01392-272709; www.queenscourt-hotel.co.uk; 6-8 Bystock Tce; d £110-140) Leather sofas and zebra prints spice up this sleek Victorian town house.

Eating

Michael Caines FINE DINING ££

(☎01392-223638; www.michaelcaines.com; Cathedral Yard; mains £25; breakfast, lunch & dinner) Housed in the Royal Clarence and run by a double Michelin-starred chef, the food here is a complex blend of Westcountry ingredients and full-bodied French flavours. Try the cauliflower and truffle soup with roasted scallops, or the slow-roast beef with celeriac purée and Madeira sauce. The set lunches are a bargain (per 2/3 courses £15/20), while the seven-course tasting menu (£65) really is one to linger over.

@Angela's BRITISH ££

(☎01392 499038; www.angelasrestaurant.co.uk; 38 New Bridge St; dinner mains £17; dinner Tue-Sat, lunch Wed-Sat) Dedication to sourcing local ingredients sometimes sees the chef at this smart bistro rising before dawn to bag the best fish at Brixham Market; his sea bass with caramelised ginger is worth the trip alone. The lamb and beef has grazed Devon fields, while local venison is made memorable by a rich redcurrant and chocolate sauce. Wise foodies opt for the pre-booked, 3-course lunch (£18).

Herbies VEGETARIAN £

(15 North St; mains £5-9; lunch Mon-Sat, dinner Tue-Sat) Cosy and gently groovy, Herbies has been cheerfully feeding Exeter's vegetarians

for more than 20 years. It's *the* place in town to tuck into delicious butterbean and vegetable pie, Moroccan *tagine* or cashew nut loaf. They're strong on vegan dishes, too.

Harry's EUROPEAN ££
(www.harrys-exeter.co.uk; 86 Longbrook St; mains £8-12; ⏲lunch & dinner Mon-Sat) Harry's is the kind of welcoming neighbourhood bistro you wish was on your own doorstep but rarely is. The decor is all wooden chairs, blackboards and gilt mirrors; the food includes seared tuna, Spanish ham with marinated figs, and a hearty three bean chilli.

tyepyedong NOODLE BAR £
(www.tyepyedong.com; 175 Sidwell St; mains £7-9; ⏲lunch & dinner Mon-Sat) Tucked away in an unlikely terrace of post-war shops, this minimalist eatery rustles up great value *ramen* and *udon* noodles – at lunchtime a dish and a drink will only cost you £5.40.

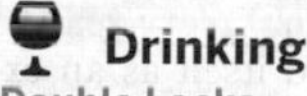

Drinking

Double Locks PUB
(www.doublelocks.com; Canal Banks) A bit of a local legend, this atmospheric former lock-house sits 2 miles south of the quay, beside the Exeter Ship Canal. Scarred floorboards, battered board games and excellent ale lend it a chilled vibe – helped by the real fires, waterside terrace and better-than-average bar food (mains £9).

On the Waterfront BAR
(www.waterfrontexeter.co.uk; The Quay) In 1835 this was a warehouse; now its red-brick, barrel-vaulted ceilings stretch back from a thoroughly modern bar. The tables outside are a popular spot for a riverside pint.

☆ Entertainment

Phoenix ARTS CENTRE
(www.exeterphoenix.org.uk; Gandy St) The city's art and soul; Phoenix is a vibrant hub of exhibitions, performance, music, dance, film, classes and workshops. There's a buzzing cafe-bar too.

Exeter Picturehouse CINEMA
(www.picture houses.co.uk; 51 Bartholomew St West) An intimate, independent cinema, screening mainstream and art-house movies.

Mamma Stone's LIVE MUSIC
(www.mamastones.com; 1 Mary Arches St; ⏲8pm-midnight, 9pm-2am when bands play) Über-cool venue showcasing everything from acoustic sets to pop, folk and jam nights. Mamma Stone's daughter, Joss (yes, *the* Joss Stone), plays sometimes too.

Cavern Club LIVE MUSIC
(www.cavernclub.co.uk; 83-84 Queen St; ⏲11am-5pm Mon-Sat, 8pm-1am Sun-Thu, 11am-2am Fri & Sat) A long-standing club and performance space, staging big-name DJs and breaking acts from the indie scene.

ℹ Information

Exeter Library (Castle St; per 30 min £2; ⏲9.30am-7pm Mon, Tue, Thu & Fri, 10am-5pm Wed, 9.30am-4pm Sat, 11am-2.30pm Sun).

Police station (☎08452 777444; Heavitree Rd; ⏲24hr)

Royal Devon & Exeter Hospital (Barrack Rd)

Tourist office Main (☎01392-665700; www.exeterandessentialdevon.com; Paris St; ⏲9am-5pm Mon-Sat, 10am-4pm Sun Jul & Aug); Quay House (☎01392-271611; The Quay; ⏲10am-5pm Easter-Oct, 11am-4pm Sat & Sun only Nov-Easter)

ℹ Getting There & Away

Air

Exeter International Airport (www.exeter-airport.co.uk) Scheduled services link with cities in Europe and the UK, including Glasgow, Manchester and Newcastle, as well as the Channel Islands and the Isles of Scilly.

FlyBe (ww.flybe.com) Key operator.

Bus

On Sundays between June and mid-September Bus 82, the Transmoor Link, makes five trips from Exeter to Plymouth via Moretonhampstead, Postbridge, Princetown and Yelverton. Standard routes:

Bude (£5.90, three hours, five Monday to Saturday) Bus X9; runs via Okehampton.

Moretonhampstead (45 minutes, seven daily Monday to Saturday) Bus 359.

Plymouth (£6, 1¼ hours, hourly Monday to Saturday, three on Sunday) Bus X38.

Sidmouth (50 minutes, one to three hourly) Bus 52.

Totnes (one hour, six daily Monday to Saturday, two on Sunday) Bus X64.

Weymouth (six to nine daily, three on Sunday) The Jurassic Coastlinx (Bus X53) runs via Beer and Lyme Regis.

Train

Main-line and branch-line trains run from Exeter St David's and Exeter Central stations:

Barnstaple (£8, 1¼ hours, hourly Monday to Saturday, four to six on Sunday) The picturesque Tarka Line.

Bristol (£18, 1¼ hours, half-hourly)
Exmouth (£4, hourly, 40 minutes)
London Paddington (£45, 2½ hours, hourly)
Paignton (£6.30, 50 minutes, half-hourly)
Penzance (£17, three hours, hourly)
Plymouth (£7.40, one hour, two or three per hour)
Torquay (£6, 45 minutes, hourly)
Totnes (£6, 35 minutes, two or three per hour)

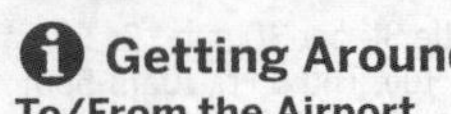

Getting Around

To/From the Airport

Buses 56 and 379 run from the bus station and Exeter St David's train station to Exeter Airport (20 to 30 minutes, hourly 7am-6pm).

Bicycle

See Saddle & Paddles (p343).

Bus

Bus H1/2 links St David's train station and the High St, passing near the bus station.

Car

Hire options include **Europcar** (www.europcar.co.uk). Park and Ride buses (adult/child £2/1.30) run from **Sowton** (near M5, junction 30), **Matford** and **Honiton Rd** (near M5, junction 29) every 10 minutes, Monday to Saturday.

Taxi

Ranks are at St David's train station and on High St. Other options:

Capital Taxis (☎01392-758472)
Club Cars (☎01392-341615)
Gemini (☎01392-342152)

Around Exeter

POWDERHAM CASTLE

The historic home of the Earl of Devon is **Powderham** (www.powderham.co.uk; adult/child £9.50/7.50; ⊙11am-4.30pm Sun-Fri Apr-Oct). A stately but still friendly place, it was built in 1391, damaged in the Civil War and remodelled in the Victorian era. A visit takes in a fine wood-panelled Great Hall, parkland with 650 deer and a glimpse of life 'below stairs' in the kitchen. The earl and family are still resident and, despite its grandeur, for charming, fleeting moments it feels like you're actually wandering through someone's sitting room.

Powderham is on the River Exe near Kenton, 8 miles south of Exeter. Bus 2 runs from Exeter (30 minutes, every 20 minutes Monday to Friday.

A LA RONDE

The delightfully quirky 16-sided **cottage** (NT; www.nationaltrust.org.uk; Summer Lane, Exmouth; adult/child £6.70/3.40; ⊙11am-5pm Sat-Wed mid-Mar–Jun & Sep-Oct, 11am-5pm Fri-Wed Jul-Aug) was built in 1796 for two spinster cousins to display a mass of curiosities acquired on a 10-year European grand tour. Its glass alcoves, low lintels and tiny doorways mean it's like clambering through a doll's house – highlights are a delicate feather frieze in the drawing room and a gallery smothered with a thousand seashells. In a fabulous collision of old and new, this can only be seen via remote control CCTV from the butler's pantry. The house is 10 miles south of Exeter, near Exmouth; bus 57 runs close by.

Torquay & Paignton

POP 110,370

For decades the bright 'n' breezy seaside resort of Torquay pitched itself as an exotic 'English Riviera' – playing on a mild microclimate, palm trees and promenades. But these days Torquay's nightclubs and bars attract a much younger crowd and the result is a sometimes bizarre clash of cultures: coach parties meet stag parties on streets lined with fudge shops and slightly saucy postcards. Chuck in some truly top-notch restaurants, a batch of good beaches and an Agatha Christie connection, and it all makes for some grand days out beside the sea. Just to the south of Torquay is Paignton with its seafront prom, multicoloured beach huts and faded 19th-century pier.

Sights & Activities

Beaches BEACHES

Torquay boasts no fewer than 20 beaches and a surprising 22 miles of coast. Holidaymakers flock to the central **Torre Abbey Sands** (covered by water at very high tides); the locals opt for the sand-and-shingle beaches beside the 240ft red-clay cliffs at **Babbacombe**. These can be accessed by a glorious 1920s **funicular railway** (Torquay; adult/child return £1.75/1.20; ⊙9.30am-5.25pm Easter-Sep); a memorable trip in a tiny wooden carriage that shuttles up and down rails set into the cliff.

Paignton Zoo ZOO

(www.paigntonzoo.org.uk; Totnes Rd, Paignton; adult/child £11.90/8.40; ⊙10am-5pm) This 80-

WORTH A TRIP

RIVER COTTAGE CANTEEN

TV chef Hugh Fearnley-Whittingstall campaigns on sustainable food, so it makes sense that his **bistro** (www.rivercottage.net; Trinity Sq, Axminster; mains £8; ⌚breakfast & lunch daily, dinner Thu-Sat) champions local, seasonal and organic ingredients. Hearty flavours include pike and parsley soup, Portland crab with fennel, and garlic mushrooms on toast with sorrel and goat's cheese shavings – a kind of deeply satisfying English crostini. Drinks include Stinger Beer, brewed from (carefully) handpicked Dorset nettles; it's spicy with just a hint of tingle. Alternatively, book a four-course gastronomic delight at the nearby **River Cottage HQ** (☎01297-630313; www.rivercottage.net; £60 4-course meal; ⌚dates vary) for a truly memorable evening.

Axminster is 30 miles east of Exeter. Trains (£8.40, 40 minutes, hourly) leave from Exeter's St David's station.

acre site is dotted with spacious enclosures re-creating habitats as varied as savannah, wetlands, tropical forest and desert. Highlights are the crocodile swamp, orang-utan island, vast glass-walled lion enclosure, and a lemur wood, where you walk over a plank suspension bridge as the primates leap around in the surrounding trees.

Living Coasts ZOO
(www.livingcoasts.org.uk; Beacon Quay, Torquay; adult/child £9.50/7.25; ⌚10am-5pm) A vast open-plan aviary bringing you up close to free-roaming penguins, punk-rocker style tufted puffins and disarmingly cute bank cormorants.

Ferry to Brixham BOAT TRIP
(www.greenwayferry.co.uk; Princess Pier; adult/child return £7/4; ⌚10 sailings daily April-Oct) Among other operators, Greenway Ferry offers grandstand views of beaches, crumbling cliffs and grand Victorian hotels.

Sleeping

Cary Arms BOUTIQUE HOTEL £££
(☎01803-327110; www.caryarms.co.uk; Babbacombe Beach, Torquay; d £150-250, ste £200-350) The great British seaside has just gone seriously stylish. At this oh so chic bolthole, neutral tones are jazzed up by candy-striped cushions; balconies directly overlook the beach and there's even a stick of rock with the hotel's name running through it on your pillow.

Headland View B&B ££
(☎01803-312612; www.headlandview.com; Babbacombe Downs, Torquay; s/d £45/70; P) Set high on the cliffs at Babbacombe, this cheery terrace is awash with nauticalia: from boat motifs on the curtains to 'welcome' lifebelts on the walls. Four rooms have tiny flower-filled balconies overlooking a cracking stretch of sea.

Lanscombe House B&B ££
(☎01803-606938; www.lanscombe house.co.uk; Cockington Lane, Torquay; s £80-100; P) Laura Ashley herself would love the lashings of tasteful fabrics, four-poster beds and free-standing slipper baths on show here. Set amid the calm of Cockington Country Park between Torquay and Paignton, it has a classic English cottage garden where you can hear owls hoot at night.

Torquay International Backpackers HOSTEL £
(☎01803-299924; www.torquaybackpackers.co.uk; 119 Abbey Rd, Torquay; dm/d £15/32; @☜) Relics of happy travels (world maps, board games and homemade wind chimes) are everywhere in this funky, friendly, laid-back hostel. The owner, Jane, hands out guitars and organise barbecues, beach trips and local pub tours.

Hillcroft BOUTIQUE B&B ££
(☎01803-297247; www.thehillcroft.co.uk; 9 St Lukes Rd, Torquay; s £65-110, d £75-85, ste £100-130; @☜) Classy rooms veer from French antique to Asian chic; the top-floor suite is gorgeous.

Eating & Drinking

Room in the Elephant FINE DINING £££
(☎01803-200044; www.elephantrestaurant.co.uk; 3 Beacon Tce, Torquay; 6 courses £45; ⌚dinner Tue-Sat) A restaurant to remember. Torbay's Michelin-starred eatery is defined by seriously good food and imaginative flavour fusions: squid and cauliflower risotto or chicken with liver and fig salad. The sumptuous cheeseboard groans under the very best Westcountry offerings.

AGATHA CHRISTIE

Torquay is the birthplace of the 'Queen of Crime', Agatha Christie (1890–1976), author of 75 novels and 33 plays, and creator of Hercule Poirot, the moustachioed, immodest Belgian detective, and Miss Marple, the surprisingly perceptive busy-body spinster. Born Agatha Miller, she grew up, courted and honeymooned in the resort town of Torquay and also worked as a hospital dispenser here during WWI, thus acquiring her famous knowledge of poisons.

The tourist office stocks the Agatha Christie Mile leaflet (free), which guides you round significant local sites, while **Torquay Museum** (529 Babbacombe Rd, Torquay; adult/child £4/2.50; ⏲10am-5pm Mon-Sat & 1.30-5pm Sun Jul-Sep) has a huge collection of photos, handwritten notes and display cases devoted to her famous detectives. The highlight, though, is **Greenway** (p349), her summer home near Dartmouth. The **Greenway Ferry** (☎01803-844010; www.greenwayferry.co.uk) sails there from Princess Pier in Torquay, and from Dartmouth and Totnes. Boats sail only when the property is open; times vary and it's best to book.

Number 7 SEAFOOD ££
(☎01803-295055; www.no7-fish.com; Beacon Tce, Torquay; mains £15; ⏲lunch Wed-Sat, dinner daily) Fabulous smells fill the air at this buzzing harbourside bistro, where the menu is packed with super-fresh crab, lobster and monkfish, often with unexpected twists. Try the king scallops with vermouth or fish and prawn tempura.

Elephant Brasserie EUROPEAN ££
(☎01803-200044; www.elephantrestaurant.co.uk; 3 Beacon Tce, Torquay; 2/3 courses £23/27; ⏲lunch & dinner Tue-Sat) The setting may be less formal, but the bistro below Torquay's Michelin-starred Room in the Elephant is still super-stylish. Treatments include lemon sole with shellfish ragout and Noilly Prat cream, and Devon duckling with spiced honey jus.

Orange Tree EUROPEAN ££
(☎01803-213936; www.orangetreerestaurant.co.uk; 14 Park Hill Rd, Torquay; mains £17; ⏲dinner Mon-Sat) This award-winning brasserie adds a dash of Continental flair to local fish, meat and game. Try to resist the Brixham crab lasagne with crab bisque or the south Devon steak with a rich blue cheese sauce. Then succumb to Chocolate Temptation, a brownie, mousse and parfait combo.

Pier Point CAFE £
(Torbay Pier, Torquay; mains £5-20; ⏲lunch & dinner) Tasty salads, pizzas and burgers overlooking Torquay marina.

Hole in the Wall PUB
(6 Park Lane, Torquay) Heavily beamed, Tardis-like boozer with a tiny terrace; an atmospheric spot for a pint.

Information

Tourist office (☎01803-211211; www.theenglishriviera.co.uk; Vaughan Pde, Torquay; ⏲9.30am-5pm Mon-Sat, daily Jun-Sep)

Getting There & Away

Bus

Bus 12 runs to Paignton from Torquay (20 minutes, every 15 minutes) and onto Brixham (40 minutes). Bus 111 goes from Torquay to Totnes (one hour, hourly Monday to Saturday, four on Sunday) and on to Dartmouth.

Ferry

Regular ferries shuttle between Torquay and Brixham; see p347.

Train

A branch train line runs from Exeter via Torquay (£5.2, 45 minutes, hourly) to Paignton (£5.40, 50 minutes).

Paignton & Dartmouth Steam Railway (Paignton Station, Paignton; www.dartmouthrailriver.co.uk; adult/child return £10/7.50; ⏲May-Sep) Puffs from Paignton to Kingswear (30 minutes, four to nine trains a day), which is linked by ferry to Dartmouth (car/pedestrian £3.50/1, six minutes).

Brixham

POP 17,460

An appealing, pastel-painted tumbling of fishermen's cottages leads down to Brixham's horseshoe harbour, signalling a very different place from Torquay. Here gently tacky arcades coexist with winding streets, brightly coloured boats and one of England's busiest fishing ports. Although picturesque, Brixham is far from a neatly packaged resort, and its brand of gritty charm offers a more accurate glimpse of life along Devon's coast.

Sights

Golden Hind SAILING SHIP
(The Quay; adult/child £4/3; ⏲10am-4pm Mar-Sep) Devon sailor and explorer Sir Francis Drake carried out a treasure-seeking circumnavigation of the globe aboard the *Golden Hind*, in the late 1500s. On this remarkably small, but full-sized, replica you get to cross the gangplank, peer into the captain's cabin and prowl around the poop deck.

Brixham Heritage Museum MUSEUM
(www.brixhamheritage.org.uk; Bolton Cross; adult/child £2/free; ⏲10am-4pm Tue-Sat Mar-Oct, 10am-1pm Tue-Fri Mar) Explores the town's salty history with exhibits on smuggling and the curious items dragged up by local trawlers.

Eating & Drinking

David Walker FISHMONGER £
(Unit B, Fish Market; ⏲9am-4pm Mon-Fri, to 1pm Sat) The place to connect with Brixham's fishing heritage, the counters here are piled high with the day's catch, plus picnic goodies such as huge, cooked shell-on prawns (per 500g £7) and dressed crab (£4.50 each).

Maritime PUB
(79 King St) Gloriously eccentric old boozer smothered in thousands of key rings, stone jugs and chamber pots, presided over by a chatty parrot called Mr Tibbs.

Information

Tourist office (☎01803-211211; www.theenglishriviera.co.uk; The Quay; ⏲9.30am-4.30pm Mon-Sat, plus 10am-4pm Sun Jun-Sep)

Getting There & Away

Bus

Bus 22 shuttles to **Kingswear** (20 minutes, one to two hourly); where you can catch the ferry to Dartmouth. Bus 12 connects **Torquay** and Brixham via Paignton (see p348).

Ferry

Regular ferries shuttle between Brixham and Torquay, see p347.

Dartmouth & Around

POP 5693

A bewitching blend of primary-coloured boats and delicately shaded houses, Dartmouth is hard to resist. Buildings cascade down steep, wooded slopes towards the River Dart while 17th-century shops with splendidly carved and gilded fronts line narrow lanes. Its popularity with a trendy sailing set risks imposing too many boutiques and upmarket restaurants, but Dartmouth is also a busy port and the constant traffic of working boats ensures an authentic tang of the sea. Agatha Christie's summer home and a captivating art-deco house are both nearby, adding to the town's appeal.

Dartmouth hugs the quay on the west side of the Dart estuary. It's linked to the village of **Kingswear** on the east bank by a string of car and foot ferries, providing a key transport link to Torbay.

Sights

TOP CHOICE **Greenway** HISTORIC HOME
(NT; ☎01803-842382; www.nationaltrust.org.uk; Greenway Rd, Galmpton; adult/child £8/4; ⏲10.30am-5pm Wed-Sun Mar-Oct, Tue-Sun mid-Jul-Aug) The enchanting summer home of crime writer Agatha Christie sits beside the River Dart near Dartmouth. Part guided tours allow you to wander between rooms where the furnishings and knick-knacks are much as she left them. You can check out her hats in the lobby, books in her library and clothes in her wardrobe, and listen to her speak (via replica radio) in the drawing room.

Woods speckled with splashes of magnolias, daffodils and hydrangeas frame the water, while the planting creates intimate, secret spaces – the boathouse and views over the river are delightful. In Christie's book *Dead Man's Folly*, Greenway doubles as Nasse House, with the boathouse making an appearance in a murder scene.

Driving to Greenway is discouraged and you have to pre-book parking spaces. The **Greenway Ferry** (☎0845 489418; www.greenwayferry.co.uk) runs regularly from Dartmouth (adult/child return £7.50/5.50), Totnes (adult/child return £11/7.50) and Torquay (adult/child return £19/12). Times vary and it's best to book. Alternatively, hike along the **Dart Valley Trail** from Kingswear (4 miles).

Coleton Fishacre HISTORIC HOME
(NT; www.nationaltrust.org.uk; Brownstone Rd, Kingswear; adult/child £7.40/3.70; ⏲10.30am-5pm Sat-Wed Mar-Oct) For an enchanting glimpse of Jazz Age glamour, drop by this former home of the D'Oyly Carte family of theatre impresarios. Built in the 1920s, its gorgeous art deco embellishments include

original Lalique tulip uplighters, comic bathroom tiles and a stunning saloon – complete with tinkling piano. The croquet terrace leads to deeply shelved subtropical gardens and suddenly revealed vistas of the sea. Hike the 4 miles along the cliffs from Kingswear, or drive.

Dartmouth Castle CASTLE
(EH; www.english-heritage.org.uk; adult/child £4.50./2.30; ⏲10am-5pm Apr-Sep, to 4pm Oct, 10am-4pm Sat & Sun Nov-Mar) Mazy passages, atmospheric guardrooms and great views from the battlements. Get there via the tiny, open-top **Castle Ferry** (return £1.40; ⏲10am-4.45pm Easter-Oct)

Sleeping

Brown's BOUTIQUE HOTEL ££
(☎01803-832572; www.brownshoteldartmouth.co.uk; 29 Victoria Rd; s £70, d £90-180; P) How do you combine leather curtains, pheasant feather-covered lampshades and animal-print chairs and still make it look classy? The owners of this sumptuous sleep spot have worked it out. Look out for the lobster and frites evenings in their tapas bar, too.

Just B ROOMS £
(☎01803-834311; www.justbdartmouth.com; reception Fosse St; r £64, apt £65) The 11 stylish options here range from bedrooms with bathrooms to mini-apartments. All feature snazzy furnishings, crisp cottons and comfy beds. They're scattered over three central properties, and the 'just B' policy (no '&B' means no breakfast) keeps the price down.

Hill View House B&B ££
(☎01803-839372; www.hillviewdartmouth.co.uk; 76 Victoria Rd; s/d £47/70) This eco-conscious house features environmentally friendly toiletries, natural cotton linen, long-life light bulbs and organic breakfasts. Rooms are tastefully decked out in cream and brown and there's a 5% discount for travellers not using cars.

Eating

TOP CHOICE **Seahorse** SEAFOOD £££
(☎01803-835147; 5 South Embankment; mains £17-23, 2-course lunch £15; ⏲lunch Wed-Sat, dinner Tue-Sat) The fish here is so fresh they change the menu twice a day. So, depending on what's been landed at Brixham (7 miles away) or Dartmouth (a few yards away), you might get cuttlefish in Chianti, sea bream with roasted garlic, or fried local squid with garlic mayonnaise. The river views are charming, the atmosphere relaxed; definitely one not to miss.

New Angel FINE DINING £££
(☎01803-839425; 2 South Embankment; mains £19-27, 2 courses £19-28; ⏲breakfast, lunch & dinner Tue-Sat) Dartmouth's Michelin-starred eatery is run by celebrity chef John Burton Race (of *French Leave* fame), so it serves up pheasant, Devon duck and local fish with more than a dash of Continental flair.

Alf Resco CAFE £
(Lower St; mains from £6; ⏲breakfast, lunch & dinner Wed-Sun) Tucked under a huge canvas awning, this cool hangout brings a dash of cosmopolitan charm to town. Rickety wooden chairs and old street signs are scattered around a front terrace, making a great place for brunch alongside the river-boat crews.

Crab Shell SANDWICH BAR £
(1 Raleigh St; sandwiches £4; ⏲lunch Apr-Dec) The shellfish gracing these sarnies has been landed on the quay a few steps away, and much of the fish has been smoked locally. Opt to fill your bread with mackerel with horseradish mayo, kiln-roast salmon with dill, or classic, delicious Dartmouth crab.

Information

Tourist office (www.discoverdartmouth.com; Mayor's Ave; ⏲9.30am-5.30pm Mon-Sat, 10am-2pm Sun Apr-Oct, 9.30am-4.30pm Mon-Sat Nov-Mar)

Getting There & Away

Boat

River Link (www.dartmouthrailriver.co.uk) Cruises along the River Dart to Totnes (1¼ hours, two to four daily April to September).

Bus

Plymouth (£5.50, two hours, three to four daily) Bus 93; runs via Kingsbridge (one hour)

Torquay (1¾ hours, hourly Monday to Saturday, four on Sunday) Bus 111; goes via Totnes.

Ferry

Dartmouth's Higher and Lower Ferries both take cars and foot passengers; they shuttle across the river to Kingswear (car/pedestrian £3.50/1) every six minutes between 6.30am and 10.45pm.

Train

For the Paignton & Dartmouth Steam Railway, see p348.

Totnes & Around

POP 8194

Totnes has such a reputation for being alternative that local jokers wrote 'twinned with Narnia' under the town sign. For decades famous as Devon's hippie haven, eco-conscious Totnes also became Britain's first 'transition town' in 2005, when it began trying to wean itself off a dependence on oil. Sustainability aside, Totnes boasts a gracious Norman castle, a mass of fine Tudor buildings and a tempting vineyard.

Sights & Activities

Sharpham Vineyard VINEYARD
(01803-732203; www.sharpham.com; Ashprington; 10am-5pm Mon-Sat Mar-Dec, daily Jun-Sep) The riverside terraces here give you the chance to wander among the vines, while a variety of **tours and tastings** (£5-50) allow you to learn about vinification and indulge in tutored slurpings; they also make cheese on the estate, so you can nibble that too. The vineyard is 3 miles south of Totnes, signed off the A381 – or walk from town along the Dart Valley Trail.

Totnes Castle CASTLE
(EH; www.english-heritage.org.uk; Castle St; adult/child £3.20/1.60; 10am-5pm Apr-Sep, to 4pm Oct) The outer keep of Totnes' Norman motte-and-bailey fortress crowns a hill at the top of town, providing captivating views. Look out for the medieval loo, too. The castle stays open until 6pm in July and August.

Devonshire Collection of Period Costume MUSEUM
(43 High St; adult/child £2/80p; 11am-5pm Tue-Fri May-Sep) Beautifully displayed garments.

Canoe Adventures CANOE TRIPS
(01803-865301; www.canoeadventures.co.uk; adult/child £20/17) Voyages in 12-seater Canadian canoes – the monthly moonlit paddles are a treat.

Sleeping

Maltsters Arms B&B ££
(01803-732350; www.tuckenhay.com; Tuckenhay; d £75-115; P) The rooms in this old creek-side pub are anything but ordinary, ranging from silky and eastern to authentically nautical – one even sports painted oil drums and real anchors. It's hidden away in the hamlet of Tuckenhay, 4 miles south of Totnes.

Steam Packet INN ££
(01803-863880; www.steampacketinn.co.uk; St Peters Quay; s/d/f £60/80/95; P) It's almost as if the minimalist bedrooms of this wharf-side former warehouse have been plucked from the pages of a design magazine; expect painted wood panels, willow arrangements and neutral tones. Ask for a riverview room, then watch the world float by.

Old Forge B&B ££
(01803-862174; www.oldforgetotnes.com; Seymour Pl; s £60, d £70-85, f £105; P) This 600-year-old B&B used to be a smithy and the town jail – thankfully comfort has now replaced incarceration: deep red and sky blue furnishings cosy up to bright throws and spa baths. The delightful family room even has its own decked sun terrace.

Eating & Drinking

TOP CHOICE **Riverford Field Kitchen** EUROPEAN ££
(01803-762074; www.riverford.co.uk; Wash Barn; 2/3 courses £18/23; lunch daily, dinner Tue-Sat) At this futuristic farm bistro vegetables are plucked to order from the fields in front of you and the meats are organic and locally sourced. Eating is a convivial affair – diners sit at trestle tables and platters laden with food are passed around. Rich flavours and imaginative treatments might include marinated, grilled Moroccan lamb and British veg transformed by cumin or saffron. Planning laws require you to book, and take a free tour of the fields. The farm is 3 miles west of Totnes.

Rumour PUB RESTAURANT ££
(01803-864682; www.rumourtotnes.com; 30 High St; mains £9-15; lunch & dinner) It's so friendly here it's almost like dining in a friend's front room. The menu is packed with pizzas, pan-fried sea trout and Salcombe ice cream; their pioneering ecopolicy includes using heat from the kitchen to warm the water.

White Hart GASTRO PUB ££
(www.dartingtonhall.com; Dartington Estate; mains £13; lunch & dinner) Lawn-side tables, real fires and a quality selection of local meats, fish and veggie options. Liquid delights include cloudy Devon cider, fragrant Sharpham wine and tangy local Otter Ale.

Willow VEGETARIAN £
(87 High St; mains £7; lunch Mon-Sat, dinner Wed, Fri & Sat) A favourite hangout

for Totnes' New Agers. Tuck into couscous, quiches, hotpots and homemade cakes – look out for their curry nights, too.

Information

Tourist office (☎01803-863168; www.totnesinformation.co.uk; Coronation Rd; ⏲9.30-5pm Mon-Fri & 10am-4pm Sat Apr-Oct, 10am-4pm Mon-Fri & 10am-1pm Sat Nov-Mar)

Getting There & Away

Boat

For river trips to Dartmouth, see p350.

Bus

Bus 111 goes to **Torquay** (30 minutes, hourly Monday to Saturday, four on Sunday) via Dartmouth.

Train

Trains shuttle at least hourly to **Exeter** (£5.40, 35 minutes) and **Plymouth** (£5, 30 minutes). The privately run **South Devon Steam Railway** (www.southdevonrailway.org) chuffs to **Buckfastleigh** (adult/child return £10/6, four or five a day, Easter to October) on the edge of Dartmoor.

Plymouth

POP 256,633

If parts of Devon are costume dramas or nature programs, Plymouth is a healthy dose of reality TV. Gritty, and certainly not always pretty, its centre has been subjected to buildings even the architects' mothers might question. But despite often being dismissed for its partying, poverty and urban problems, this is a city that's huge in spirit – and it comes with great assets. Its setting on the fringes of an impressive natural harbour and just a few miles from the wilderness expanse of Dartmoor makes it an ideal base for activities. Add a rich maritime history, a Barbican area creaking with half-timbered houses, some unusual attractions and a decidedly lively nightlife, and you have a place to reconnect with the real before another foray into the delights of Devon's chocolate-box-pretty moors and shores.

History

Plymouth's history is dominated by the sea. The first recorded cargo left the city in 1211 and by the late 16th century it was the port of choice for explorers and adventurers. It's waved off Sir Francis Drake, Sir Walter Raleigh, the fleet that defeated the Spanish Armada, the pilgrims who founded America, Charles Darwin, Captain Cook and countless boats carrying emigrants to Australia and New Zealand.

During WWII Plymouth suffered horrendously at the hands of the Luftwaffe – more than 1000 civilians died in the Blitz, which reduced the city centre to rubble. The 21st century has brought large-scale regeneration of the city's waterfront areas and the architectural mishmash of the £200-million Drake Circus shopping centre.

Sights & Activities

Plymouth Hoe HISTORIC HEADLAND

Francis Drake supposedly spied the Spanish fleet from this grassy strip overlooking Plymouth Sound; the fabled bowling green on which he finished his game was probably where his **statue** now stands. Later the Hoe became a favoured holiday spot for the Victorian aristocracy, and the wide promenade is backed by an impressive array of multi-storeyed villas and once-grand hotels.

Dominating the scene is the red-and-white-striped former lighthouse, **Smeaton's Tower** (The Hoe; adult/child £2/1; ⏲10am-noon & 1-4pm Tue-Sat Apr-Oct, 10am-noon & 1-3pm Tue-Sat Nov-Mar), which was built 14 miles offshore on the Eddystone Rocks in 1759, then moved to the Hoe in 1882. Climbing its 93 steps provides an illuminating insight into lighthouse keepers' lives and stunning views of the city, Dartmoor and the sea.

Barbican HISTORIC DISTRICT

(www.plymouthbarbican.com) To get an idea of what old Plymouth was like before the Blitz, head for the Barbican, a district of cobbled streets and Tudor and Jacobean buildings, many now converted into galleries, craft shops and restaurants.

The Pilgrim Fathers' *Mayflower* set sail for America from the Barbican on 16 September 1620. The **Mayflower Steps** mark the point of departure – track down the passenger list displayed on the side of **Island House** nearby. Scores of other famous voyages are also marked by plaques at the steps, including one led by Captain James Cook, who set out from the Barbican in 1768 in search of a southern continent.

Plymouth Gin Distillery DISTILLERY

(☎01752-665292; www.plymouthgin.com; 60 Southside St; tours £6; ⏲tours at 11.30am, 12.30pm, 2.30pm & 3.30pm) This is the oldest producer of gin in the world – they've been making it here since 1793. The Royal Navy ferried it round the world in countless officers' messes and the brand was specified in the first recorded recipe for a dry martini in the 1930s. Tours wind past the stills and take in a tutored tasting before depositing you in the heavily beamed medieval bar for a free tipple. Between Easter and October, there are extra tours at 10.30am and 4.30pm.

National Marine Aquarium AQUARIUM
(www.national-aquarium.co.uk; Rope Walk; adult/child £11/6.50; ⊙10am-6pm Apr-Oct, 10am-5pm Nov-Mar). The sharks here swim in coral seas that teem with moray eels and vividly coloured fish – there's even a loggerhead turtle called Snorkel who was rescued from a Cornish beach. Walk-through glass arches ensure huge rays glide over your head, while the immense Atlantic Reef tank reveals just what's lurking a few miles offshore.

Merchant's House HISTORIC HOME
(33 St Andrews St; adult/child £2/1; ⊙10am-5pm Tue-Sat Apr-Sep) This 17th-century building is packed with curiosities; from manacles, truncheons and a ducking stool, to a replica 19th-century school room and a Victorian pharmacy where you can try old-fashioned pill rolling.

FREE **City Museum & Art Gallery** MUSEUM
(Drake Circus; ⊙10am-5.30pm Tue-Fri, 10am-5pm Sat) Imaginative displays conjure up the history of Plymouth. Look out for Napoleonic-era bone model ships and the skis of the doomed Antarctic explorer Captain Robert Falcon Scott, a Plymouth man.

Boat Trips
Sound Cruising (www.soundcruising.com; The Barbican) offers regular cruises from the Barbican Pontoon to the huge warships at Plymouth's naval base (1½ hours, adult/child £6.25/3) and up the River Tamar to the Cornish village of Calstock (4½ hours, adult/child £10/7).

The little yellow **Mount Batten Ferry** (adult/child return £3/2, 10 minutes, half hourly) shuttles from beside the Mayflower Steps across to the Mount Batten Peninsula.

Plymouth Mayflower MUSEUM
(3 The Barbican; adult/child £2/1; ⊙10am-4pm daily May-Oct, 10am-4pm Mon-Sat Nov-Apr) Runs through Plymouth's nautical heritage, providing the background to the Pilgrim Fathers' trip via interactive gizmos and multisensory displays.

Mount Batten Centre WATERSPORTS
(☎01752-404567; www.mount-batten-centre.com; 70 Lawrence Rd, Mount Batten) Courses include kayaking (£85 for two days), sailing (£158, two days) and windsurfing (£135, two days).

Sleeping

Fertile B&B hunting grounds are just back from Hoe, especially around Citadel Rd.

St Elizabeth's House HOTEL £££
(☎01752-344840; www.stelizabeths.co.uk; Longbrook St; d £140-160 ste £180-250; P) A manor house in the 17th century, this minihotel now oozes boutique chic. Free-standing slipper baths, oak furniture and Egyptian cotton grace the rooms; the suites feature palatial bathrooms and private terraces. It's set in the suburb-village of Plympton St Maurice, 5 miles east of Plymouth city centre.

Bowling Green HOTEL ££
(☎01752-209090; www.bowlinggreenhotel.co.uk; 10 Osborne Pl; s/d/f £47/68/78; P 📶) Some of the airy cream-and-white rooms in this family-run hotel look out onto the modern incarnation of Drake's famous bowling green. If you tire of watching people throw woods after jacks you can play chess in the conservatory.

Four Seasons B&B £
☎01752-223591; www.fourseasonsguesthouse.co.uk; 207 Citadel Rd East; s £32-42, d £48-58, f £60) This place is crammed full of treats, from the big bowls of free sweets to the

TINSIDE LIDO

Tucked between the Hoe and the shore, **Tinside Lido** (Hoe Rd; adult/child £3.65/2.40; ⊙noon-6pm Mon-Fri, 10am-6pm Sat & Sun late-May–Jul, 10am-6pm daily Aug) is an outdoor, saltwater art-deco pool. During its heyday in the '40s and '50s, thousands of Plymouthians flocked to the pool on summer days, to swim to the soothing strains of a string orchestra. In the '70s and '80s the pool fell into disrepair before closing in 1992. It's since been restored to its former glory thanks to a hefty £3.4 million refurbishment and now it's packed throughout summer with school kids and sun worshippers; sadly, though, there's no sign of the string orchestra returning just yet.

mounds of Devon bacon for breakfast. They've got the basics right, too: tasteful rooms decorated in gold and cream.

Jewell's B&B £
(☎01752-254760; www.jewellsguesthouse.com; 220 Citadel Rd; s/d/f £28/50/65) Traces of the Victorian era linger in the high ceilings and ornate plasterwork of this friendly town house. Rooms are bright and modern with deep armchairs and filmy curtains; top-quality bathrooms add another layer of class.

Berkeleys of St James B&B ££
(☎01752-221654; www.onthehoe.co.uk; 4 St James Pl East; s/d/f £40/60/75) A cosy terrace, dishing up breakfasts full of local, organic goodies.

Eating

TOP CHOICE **Barbican Kitchen** BRITISH ££
(☎01752-604448; 60 Southside St; mains £11; ⏲lunch & dinner, closed Sun evening) In this bistro-style baby sister of Tanners Restaurant, the stone interior fizzes with bursts of shocking pink and lime. The food is attention grabbing, too – try the calves' liver with horseradish mash or the honey, goat's cheese and apple crostini. Their Devon beefburger, with a slab of stilton, is divine.

Tanners Restaurant FINE DINING £££
(☎01752-252001; www.tannersrestaurant.com; Finewell St; 2-/3-course dinner £32/39; ⏲lunch & dinner Tue-Sat) At Plymouth's top table reinvented British and French classics are the mainstay; expect lamb with gnocchi, char-grilled asparagus with soft poached egg, and roasted quail with pancetta. Their six-course tasting menu (£48; booking required) is a truly memorable meal.

Cap'n Jaspers CAFE £
(www.capn-jaspers.co.uk; Whitehouse Pier, Quay Rd; snacks £3-5; ⏲7.45am-11.45pm) Unique, quirky and slightly insane, this cabin-kiosk

Plymouth

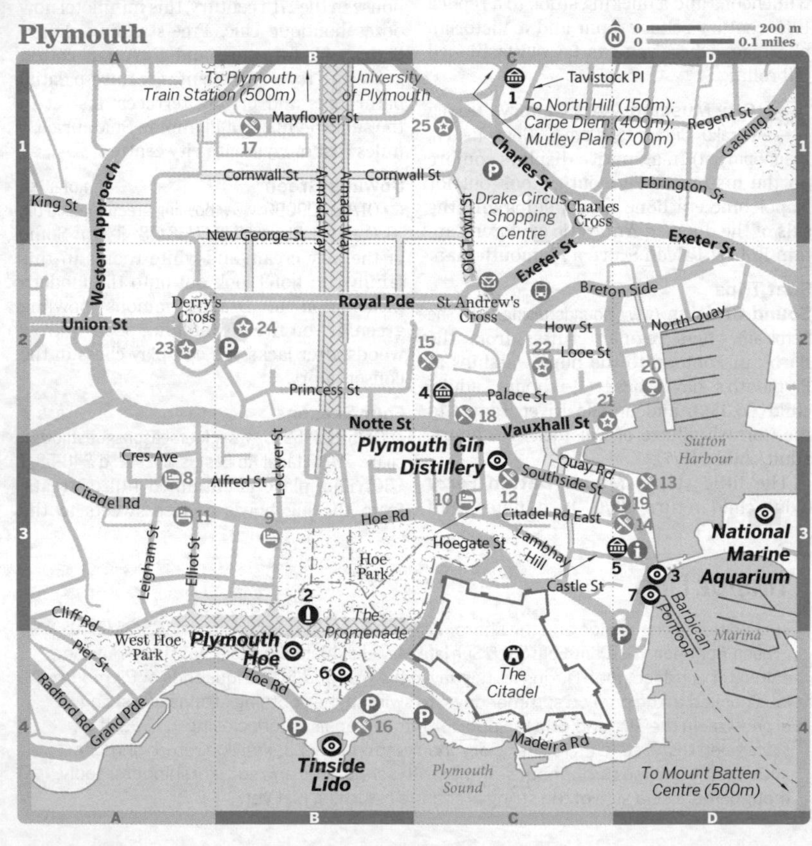

has been delighting bikers, tourists, locals and fishermen for decades with its motorised gadgets and teaspoons attached by chains. The menu is of the burger and bacon butty school – trying to eat a 'half a yard of hot dog' is a Plymouth rite of passage. Try the local crab rolls – the filling could have been caught by the bloke sitting next to you.

Terrace CAFE £
(Hoe Rd; snacks £3-6; ⏲breakfast & lunch) Tucked away beside the Tinside Lido, this bright and breezy cafe has the best location of any eatery in town, with sweeping views across Plymouth Sound complemented by a selection of sandwiches, coffees and generous jacket potatoes.

Platters SEAFOOD ££
(12 The Barbican; mains £16; ⏲lunch & dinner) A down-to-earth eatery with fish so fresh it's just stopped flapping – try the skate in butter or the locally caught sea bass.

Yukisan JAPANESE ££
(www.yukisan.co.uk; 51 Notte St; mains £15; ⏲lunch & dinner) Super-fresh sushi, light tempura and noodles worth mastering chopsticks for.

Veggie Perrin's VEGETARIAN INDIAN £
(97 Mayflower St; mains £6; ⏲lunch & dinner Mon-Sat) Excellent, authentic, flavour-filled food.

Drinking

Like any navy city, Plymouth has a more than lively nightlife. Union St is clubland; Mutley Plain and North Hill have a studenty vibe, while the Barbican has more restaurants amid the bars. All three areas get rowdy, especially at weekends.

View 2 BAR
(www.barbicanleisurebars.com; Vauxhall Quay; ⏲10am-midnight Sun-Thu, 10am-3am Fri, 10am-2am Sat) Just round from the heart of the Barbican, this cool venue's flagstone terrace is perfect for a waterside drink. Enjoy comedy, easy listening, soul, funk and R&B.

Dolphin PUB
(14 The Barbican) This wonderfully unreconstructed Barbican boozer is all scuffed tables, padded bench seats and an authentic, no-nonsense atmosphere.

Carpe Diem BAR
(www.carpediemnh.co.uk; 50 North Hill; ⏲noon-1am Tue-Sun) A beautifully lit, funky hangout done out in a kaleidoscope of colours – there's a heated, open-air chill-out room, too.

☆ Entertainment

Annabel's CABARET CLUB
(www.annabelscabaret.co.uk; 88 Vauxhall St; ⏲8.30am-2am Thu-Sat) The stage spots in this quirky venue are filled by an eclectic

Plymouth

Top Sights
National Marine Aquarium D3
Plymouth Gin Distillery C3
Plymouth Hoe B4
Tinside Lido B4

Sights
1 City Museum & Art Gallery C1
2 Drake Statue B3
Island House .... (see 14)
3 Mayflower Steps D3
4 Merchant's House C2
5 Plymouth Mayflower D3
6 Smeaton's Tower B4

Activities, Courses & Tours
7 Mount Batten Ferry D3
Sound Cruising .... (see 7)

Sleeping
8 Berkeleys of St James A3
9 Bowling Green B3
10 Four Seasons C3
11 Jewell's A3

Eating
12 Barbican Kitchen C3
13 Cap'n Jaspers D3
14 Platters D3
15 Tanners Restaurant C2
16 Terrace B4
17 Veggie Perrin's B1
18 Yukisan C2

Drinking
19 Dolphin D3
20 View 2 .... D2

Entertainment
21 Annabel's C2
22 Plymouth Arts Centre C2
23 Revolution A2
24 Theatre Royal B2
25 Voodoo Lounge C1

collection of acts (expect anything from burlesque to comedy). Crowd-pleasing tunes fill the dance floor while classy cocktails fill your glass.

Voodoo Lounge CLUB
(Drake Circus; ⏲11am-2am Sun-Thu, 11am-3am Fri & Sat) A student-friendly stalwart of Plymouth's counter-culture scene combining Hip Hop with Goth Nights and free alternative club evenings.

Revolution CLUB-BAR
(www.revolution-bars.co.uk; Derry's Cross; ⏲11.30am-2.30am Mon-Fri, 11.30am-3am Sat) A cavernous chrome-lined drinking den with a two-bar club room (open Thursday to Sunday). If you don't like the scene here the mega clubs of Union St are nearby.

Plymouth Arts Centre ARTS CENTRE
(www.plymouthac.org.uk; 38 Looe Street; ⏲10am-8.30pm Tue-Sat, 4-8.30pm Sun) This cultural hot-spot combines an independent cinema, modern-art exhibitions, and a licensed, vegetarian-friendly **cafe** (⏲11am to 8.30pm Tue-Sat).

Theatre Royal THEATRE
(www.theatreroyal.com; Royal Pde) Plymouth's main theatre stages large-scale touring and home-grown productions; its studio space, the Drum, is renowned for featuring new writing.

ℹ Information

Plymouth Library (Drake Circus; ⏲9am-7pm Mon-Fri, 9am-5pm Sat) Internet access.

Police station (Charles Cross; ⏲24hr)

Tourist office (☎01752-306330; www.visitplymouth.co.uk; Plymouth Mayflower, 3 The Barbican; ⏲9am-5pm Mon-Sat, 10am-4pm Sun Apr-Oct, 9am-5pm Mon-Fri, 10am-4pm Sat Nov-Mar)

ℹ Getting There & Away

Bus

On Sundays between June and mid-September Bus 82, the Transmoor Link, makes five trips from Plymouth to Exeter, via Yelverton, Princetown, Postbridge and Moretonhampstead.

Other services:

Birmingham (£48, 5½ hours, five daily)

Bristol (£29, three hours, five daily)

Exeter (£6, 1¼ hours, one to three daily) Bus X38.

London (£33, five to six hours, eight daily)

Penzance (£8, three hours, six daily)

Train

Bristol (£32, two hours, two or three per hour)

Exeter (£7.40, one hour, two or three per hour)

London (£40, 3¼ hours, half-hourly)

Penzance (£8, two hours, half-hourly)

Totnes (£5, 30 minutes, at least hourly)

Around Plymouth

BUCKLAND ABBEY

Stately **Buckland Abbey** (NT; www.nationaltrust.org.uk; near Yelverton; adult/child £7.80/3.90; ⏲10.30am-5.30pm daily Apr-Oct, 11am-4.30pm Fri-Sun Nov-Dec & Feb-Mar) was originally a Cistercian monastery and 13th-century abbey church, but was transformed into a family residence by Sir Richard Grenville before being purchased in 1581 by his cousin and nautical rival Sir Francis Drake. Its displays include Drake's Drum, said to beat by itself when Britain is in danger of being invaded. There's also a very fine Elizabethan garden.

Buckland Abbey is 11 miles north of Plymouth. You'll need your own transport to get here.

Dartmoor National Park

Dartmoor is an ancient, compelling landscape, so different from the rest of Devon that a visit can feel like falling straight into Tolkien's *Return of the King*. Exposed granite hills (called tors) crest on the horizon, linked by swathes of honey-tinged moors. On the fringes, streams tumble over moss-smothered boulders in woods of twisted trees. The centre of this 368-sq-mile wilderness is the higher moor; a vast, treeless expanse. Moody and utterly empty, you'll find its desolate beauty exhilarating or chilling, or quite possibly a bit of both.

Dartmoor can be picture-postcard pretty; ponies wander at will here and sheep graze beside the road, but peel back the picturesque and there's a core of hard reality – stock prices mean many farming this harsh environment struggle to make a profit. It's also a mercurial place where the urban illusion of control over our surroundings is stripped away and the elements are in charge. Dartmoor inspired Sir Arthur Conan Doyle to write *The Hound of the Baskervilles* and in sleeting rain and swirling mists you suddenly see why; the moor morphs into a bleak, wilderness where tales of a phantom hound can seem very real indeed.

But Dartmoor is also a natural breakout zone with a checklist of charms: superb walking, cycling, riding, climbing and white-water kayaking; rustic pubs and

PREHISTORIC DARTMOOR

Dartmoor is ripe for archaeological explorations. The moor has an estimated 11,000 monuments, including the largest concentration of Bronze Age (c 2300-700 BC) remains in the country. It also has around 75 stone rows (half the national total), 18 stone circles and 5000 huts.

The **Merrivale Stone Rows**, near Princetown, are a handy one-stop-shop for most monument types – the site has a parallel stone row, a stone circle, a menhir, burial chambers and dozens of hut circles. To the north east, near Chagford, the **Grey Wethers** stone circles stand side by side on a stretch of open moor; they're about a third of a mile from another stone circle near Fernworthy. Also nearby, at Gidleigh, **Scorhill** stone circle is sometimes called the Stonehenge of Dartmoor, although only half of the original stones remain. The biggest site is the Bronze Age village of **Grimspound**, just off the B3212, where you can wander inside the circular stone wall that once surrounded an entire village, and the ruins of several granite round houses.

There are a series of archaeology-themed walks (£3 to £8) all over the moor, as well as mini-guides to some sites (£4). Enquire at the tourist office.

fancy restaurants; wild camping nooks and country-house hotels – the perfect boltholes when the fog rolls in.

Activities

Walking

Some 730 miles of public footpaths snake across Dartmoor's open heaths and rocky tors. Pathfinder's *Dartmoor, Short Walks* (£5.99) is a good introduction for family day strolls, while the local tourist office can advise on all types of self-guided trails or **guided walks** (2-/6-hr £3/8). Themes include Sherlock Holmes, myths, geology, industry and archaeology. Look out for the memorable moonlit rambles amid stone rows.

Cycling

Marked cycling routes include the 11-mile **Granite Way**, which runs along a former railway line between Okehampton and Lydford. The Dartmoor Way is a 90-mile circular cycling and walking route that goes through Okehampton, Chagford, Buckfastleigh, Princetown and Tavistock.

Devon Cycle Hire BIKE HIRE
(☎01837-861141; www.devoncycle hire.co.uk; Sourton Down, near Okehampton; per full/half day £10/14; ⏲9am-5pm Apr-Sep) On the Granite Way.

Horse Riding

A half-day ride costs around £36.

Babeny Farm RIDING STABLE
(☎01364-631296; Poundsgate)

Skaigh RIDING STABLES
(☎01837-840917; www.skaighstables.co.uk; Belstone; ⏲Apr-Oct)

Shilstone Rocks RIDING STABLES
(☎01364-621281; Widecombe-in-the-Moor)

White Water

The raging River Dart makes Dartmoor a top spot for thrill seekers. Experienced kayakers can get permits from www.dart access.co.uk or the **British Canoe Union** (BCU; ☎0845 370 9500; www.bcu.org.uk). **CRS Adventures** ([0]1364-653444; www.crsadven tures.co.uk) near Ashburton runs a range of white water activities (from £35 for a half day). Rivers are only open in the winter.

Climbing

Rock Centre ROCK CLIMBING
(☎01626-852717; www.rockcentre.co.uk; Rock House, Chudleigh; 1-/2-hr lessons £40/80) Lessons.

Sleeping

From spoil-yourself-silly luxury (Gidleigh Park, p361, and 22 Mill St, p361) to snoozing under the stars, with some lovely thatched cottages in between, Dartmoor has the widest range of sleeping options around.

The **YHA** (www.yha.org.uk) has hostels at Postbridge (p360) and Okehampton (p362); the association also has three bare-bones camping barns, such as the one near Postbridge (p360). There are independent hostels and camping barns at Moretonhampstead (p361), Widecombe-in-the-Moor (p360) and Princetown (p359).

Dartmoor is also a top venue for a spot of 'wild camping' – so called by devotees to distinguished it from the 'mild camping' of official sites. Pitching a tent on some sec-

Dartmoor National Park

tions of the open moor is allowed provided you stick to some simple but strict rules – pick up a free leaflet from the tourist office then pack your pack.

Eating & Drinking

Dartmoor caters for all tastes and budgets. Chagford boasts the double-Michelin-starred Gidleigh Park (p361) and classy 22 Mill St (p361). Or try the stylish bar food at Widecombe's Rugglestone Inn (p361), the hiker-friendly grub and authentic atmosphere at the Warren House Inn (p360) near Postbridge, or some of the best cream teas in Devon at Brimpts Farm (p360).

Information

The main tourist office is in Princetown; it stocks walking guides, maps and clothes. See also the official website at www.dartmoor.co.uk. Other offices:

Haytor Vale (DNPA; ☎01364-661520; ⏲10am-5pm Easter-Oct, 10am-4pm Sat & Sun Nov & Dec)

Postbridge (DNPA; ☎01822-880272; ⏲10am-5pm Easter-Oct, 10am-4pm Sat & Sun Nov & Dec)

Getting There & Around

For environmental reasons, the local national parks authority advocates using public transport; with a bit of planning, it is a real option. The *Discovery Guide to Dartmoor*, free from most tourist offices, details bus and train services in the park.

Bus

Key routes onto the moor:

Bus 83/84/86 (hourly) From Plymouth to Tavistock, via Yelverton.

Bus 359 (two hourly Monday to Saturday) From Exeter to Moretonhampstead.

Bus 118 (one to four daily) From Barnstaple to Tavistock (2¼ hours), via Lydford and Okehampton.

Key routes around the Moor:

Haytor Hoppa (four on Saturdays April to October, plus three on Thursdays June to mid-September) A circular route taking in Haytor, Widdecombe-in-the-Moor and Bovey Tracey.

Transmoor Link/Bus 82 On Sundays between June and mid-September it makes five trips between Exeter and Plymouth (2½ hours) via Moretonhampstead, Warren House Inn, Postbridge, Two Bridges, Princetown and Yelverton. It also runs between Moretonhampstead and Yelverton (45 minutes) five times on Saturdays between April and October, and three times on Thursdays between June and mid-September.

Travel passes:

Dartmoor Sunday Rover (adult/child £6.50/4.30, Sundays June to September) Buys unlimited travel on most bus routes, and train travel on the Tamar Valley line from Plymouth to Gunnislake. Buy tickets from bus drivers or at Plymouth train station.

PRINCETOWN

Set in the heart of the remote, higher moor, Princetown is dominated by the grey, foreboding bulk of Dartmoor Prison. The jail has dictated the town's fortunes for hundreds of years. When it stopped housing French and American prisoners of war in the early 1800s, Princetown fell into decline and on bad weather days the town can still have a bleak feel. But it's also a useful insight into the harsh realities of moorland life and makes an atmospheric base for some excellent walks.

The prison reopened as a convict jail in 1850 and just up from its looming gates the **Dartmoor Prison Heritage Centre** (www.dartmoor-prison.co.uk; Princetown; adult/child £2.50/1.50; 9.30am-12.30pm & 1.30-4.30pm Mon-Thu & Sat, to 4pm Fri & Sun) provides a chilling glimpse of life (past and present) inside – look out for the straitjackets, manacles and mock-up cells, and the escape tale of Frankie 'the mad axeman' Mitchell, supposedly sprung by 1960s gangster twins the Krays. The centre also sells the bizarrely cheery garden ornaments made by the inmates.

The Moor's main **tourist office** (DNPA; 01822-890414; www.dartmoor-npa.gov.uk; 10am-5pm Apr-Oct, 10am-4pm Nov-Mar) stocks maps, guides and books. The building started life as Princetown's main hotel, where Arthur Conan Doyle began his classic Dartmoor tale *The Hound of the Baskervilles*. Ask staff to point you towards Foxtor Mires (2 to 3 miles away), the inspiration for the book's Grimpen Mire, then detect the story's other locations.

The **Plume of Feathers** (01822-890240; www.theplumeoffeathers.co.uk; Plymouth Hill; dm £14.50-17, d £34, sites £13) in the heart of town serves up typical bar food. It also offers no-nonsense rooms with shared bathrooms, as well as basic bunk-bed dorms and camping.

Getting There & Away

For details on going east along the moro, see the Transmoor Link bus. Bus 98 shuttles between Tavistock and **Princetown** (4 daily). Bus 98 runs from Princetown to **Postbridge** (one per day Monday to Friday).

POSTBRIDGE

There's not much to the quaint village of Postbridge apart from a couple of shops, pubs and whitewashed houses. It's best known for its 13th-century **clapper bridge** across the East Dart, made of large granite slabs supported by stone pillars.

There's an **information centre** (01822-880272; 10am-5pm Easter-Oct, 10am-4pm Sat & Sun Nov & Dec) in the car park, and a post office and shop in the village.

DARTMOOR HIKES

The **West Devon Way** (part of the Dartmoor Way) is a 14-mile trek between Tavistock and Okehampton, while the 18-mile **Templer Way** is a two- to three-day leg stretch from Haytor to Teignmouth. The 90-mile **Dartmoor Way** circles from Buckfastleigh in the south, through Moretonhampstead, northwest to Okehampton and south through Lydford to Tavistock. But the blockbuster route is the 103-mile **Two Moors Way**, which runs from Ivybridge, across Dartmoor and Exmoor to Lynmouth on the north Devon coast.

Be prepared for Dartmoor's notoriously fickle weather and carry a map and compass as many trails are not way-marked. The Ordnance Survey (OS) Explorer 1:25,000 map No 28, *Dartmoor* (£7.99), is the most comprehensive and shows park boundaries and MOD firing-range areas.

THE DARTMOOR GUIDE

The free *Dartmoor Guide* newspaper is packed with useful info, including details of activities, attractions, campsites and the full diary of guided walks. Pick it up at visitor centres and venues across the moor.

Sleeping

Two Bridges HOTEL £££
(01822-890581; www.twobridges.co.uk; Two Bridges; s £95-125, d £140-190; P) There's a real feel of a classy country house to this classic moorland hotel. That's no doubt down to the gently elegant rooms, huge inglenook fireplaces and squishy leather sofas; former guests Wallis Simpson, Winston Churchill and Vivien Leigh probably liked it, too. It's 3 miles southwest of Postbridge.

Runnage YHA CAMPING BARN £
(01629-592700; ww.yha.org.uk; sites per adult/child £4.50/3.50, dm £8.50; P) Set in a working farm, this converted hayloft allows you to bed down to the soundtrack of bleating sheep. It's 1½ miles from Postbridge: take the 'Widecombe' turning off the Moretonhampstead road.

Bellever YHA HOSTEL £
(0845 371 9622; www.yha.org.uk; dm £14; Mar-Oct; P) A characterful former farm on the edge of a conifer plantation, with a huge kitchen, lots of rustic stone walls and cosy dorms. It's a mile south of Postbridge.

Eating & Drinking

Warren House Inn PUB £
(www.warrenhouseinn.co.uk; mains from £7; 11am-11pm) Plonked amid miles of open moor, this former tin miners' haunt exudes the kind of hospitality you only get in a pub in the middle of nowhere. A Dartmoor institution, its stone floors, trestle tables and hearty food (served noon–8.30pm) are warmed by a fire that's reputedly been crackling since 1845. Between November and March the pub closes at 5pm on Monday and Tuesday. It's on the B3212, 2 miles northeast of Postbridge.

Brimpts Farm CAFE £
(www.brimptsfarm.co.uk; cream teas £3; 11.30am-5.30pm weekends & school holidays, 2-5.30pm weekdays) They've been serving cream teas here since 1913, and its still one of the best places to tuck in on the moor. Expect freshly baked scones, homemade jams and utterly gooey clotted cream. It's signed off the B3357, Two Bridges–Dartmeet road.

Getting There & Away

As well as being on the Transmoor Link bus 82 route (see p358), Postbridge has connections to **Princetown** via bus 98 (one per day Monday to Friday).

WIDECOMBE-IN-THE-MOOR

POP 652

This is archetypal Dartmoor, down to the ponies grazing on the village green. Widecombe's honey-grey, 15th-century buildings circle a church whose 40m tower has seen it dubbed the Cathedral of the Moor. Inside search out the boards telling the fire-and-brimstone tale of the violent storm of 1638 – it knocked a pinnacle from the roof, killing several parishioners. As ever on Dartmoor, the devil was blamed, said to be in search of souls.

The village is commemorated in the traditional English folksong of 'Widecombe Fair'; the event of the same name takes place on the second Tuesday of September.

Sleeping & Eating

Dartmoor Expedition Centre BUNK HOUSE £
(01364-621249; www.dartmoorbase.co.uk; dm £13, loft room £15; P) The real fires, hot showers and dorm beds at this 300-year-old converted barn are all best enjoyed after the

WARNING

The military uses three adjoining areas of Dartmoor as training ranges where live ammunition is used. The local tourist office can explain their locations; they're also marked on OS maps. In general you're advised to check if the route you're planning falls within a range; if it does, find out if firing is taking place when you want to walk via the **Firing Information Service** (0800 458 4868; www.dartmoor-ranges.co.uk). During the day red flags fly at the edges of in-use ranges, and red flares burn at night. Even when there's no firing, beware of unidentified metal objects lying in the grass. Don't touch anything you find: note its position and report it to the **Commandant** (01837-650010).

climbing, orienteering and caving the centre organises. It's 2 miles west of Widecombe.

Higher Venton Farm B&B ££
(☎01364-621235; www.ventonfarm.com; Widecombe; d £50-60; P) This 16th-century farmhouse could be used to define the architectural style 'picture-postcard thatch'. With low lintels and winding stone stairs, there's not a straight line in the place.

Rugglestone Inn PUB £
(www.rugglestoneinn.co.uk; mains £4-9; ⊙lunch & dinner) You'll find plenty of locals in front of this intimate old pub's wood-burning stove. Its stone floor and low beams set the scene for hearty helpings of handmade sausages and mash, or fisherman's pie.

Getting There & Away

Bus 272 goes to **Tavistock** (1¼ hours, three buses, late May to early September) via **Two Bridges** (50 minutes) and **Princetown** (55 minutes), but only on Sundays in the summer.

Bus 274 runs to **Okehampton** (1¾ hours, three on summer Sundays only) via Moretonhampstead. In the summer Widdecombe is also served by the Haytor Hoppa (see p358).

MORETONHAMPSTEAD

POP 1721

The small market town of Moretonhampstead stands at an old crossroads where two of the main routes across Dartmoor meet. It makes a handy base for exploring the eastern moor.

Sleeping & Eating

White Hart HOTEL ££
(☎01647-441340; www.whitehartdartmoor.co.uk; The Square; s £75, d £110-120) The mail coaches used to change horses here in Georgian days; today it's a smoothly comfy hotel with tartan carpets, deep terracotta walls and CD players in the rooms. The **meals** (mains from £9.50; ⊙lunch and dinner) are tasty and substantial: try the steak with port and stilton, or the chicken, mushroom and truffle lasagne.

Sparrowhawk HOSTEL £
(☎01647-440318; www.sparrowhawkbackpackers.co.uk; 45 Ford St; dm/d/f £16/36/45) The bright, light dorms in this ecofriendly hostel are set in converted stables. The central courtyard, ringed by rickety outbuildings, is a great spot to swap travellers' tales.

Cookshayes B&B £
(☎01647-440374; www.cookshayes.co.uk; Court St; s £25, d £45-70; P) Ask for a room with a view of the fields edging the moor at this tall Victorian house. Rooms are fairly plain and traditional, except the four-poster one, which is a vivid pink.

Getting There & Away

For information on the Transmoor Link bus, which goes west across the moor see p358. Bus 359 goes to **Exeter** (two hourly Monday to Saturday).

CHAGFORD

POP 1470

With its wonky thatches and cream-and-white-fronted buildings, Chagford gathers round a busy square – at first glance every inch a timeless moorland town. But the purveyors of waxed jackets and hip flasks have also been joined by health-food shops and contemporary pottery galleries. A former Stannary town (where local tin was weighed and checked), Chagford was also the first town west of London to get electric street lights.

Sleeping & Eating

Gidleigh Park HOTEL/RESTAURANT £££
(☎01647-432367; www.gidleigh.com; near Gidleigh; s £340, d £310-1155; P ᯤ) This sumptuous oasis of supreme luxury teams crests, crenellations and roaring fires with shimmering sanctuaries of blue marble, waterproof TVs and private saunas. Rates include dinner at the double-Michelin-starred **restaurant** (⊙lunch & dinner), where three courses would normally set you back a hefty £95 – crafty local foodies opt for the £35 two-course lunch instead. This dollop of utter extravagance is 2 miles west of Chagford.

22 Mill Street B&B/RESTAURANT ££
(☎01647-432244; www.22millst.com; 22 Mill St; d £110-130; P) The elegant rooms of this sleek retreat feature exposed stone walls, wooden floorboards, satin cushions and bursts of modern art. Its intimate **restaurant**

> **DRIVING ON DARTMOOR**
>
> Much of Dartmoor is unfenced grazing so you're very likely to come across Dartmoor ponies, sheep and even cows in the middle of the road. Many sections have a 40mph speed limit. Car parks on the moor can be little more than lay-bys for half a dozen cars; their surface can be rough to very rough.

(2-courses £15-36; ⏲lunch & dinner) delivers imaginative dishes packed with produce from the moors and the shores – look out for seared Exmoor venison, and rabbit with parmesan risotto.

Sandy Park INN ££

(☎01647-433267; www.sandyparkinn.co.uk; Sandy Park; s/d £55/85; P) Part pub (mains £8 to £12), part chic place to stay. At this 17th-century thatch you can sip a pint of real ale in a cosy, exposed-beam bar, sample classy Dartmoor fare in the restaurant, then totter upstairs to sleep amid plump pillows and classic furnishings.

Easton Court B&B ££

(☎01647-433369; www.easton.co.uk; Easton Cross; s £55-60, d £60-75; P) Rooms dotted with cast-iron beds and soft sofas look out onto wooded hills; breakfast options include fresh fish or soufflé omelette.

Getting There & Away

Bus 179 runs to **Okehampton** (one hour, two daily Monday to Saturday). Bus 173 travels from Moretonhampstead to **Exeter** via Chagford twice daily, Monday to Saturday.

OKEHAMPTON & AROUND

POP 7029

Okehampton has a staging post feel. The uninhabited tract of bracken-covered slopes and granite tors, huddles on the edge of the mind-expanding sweep of the higher moor. With its clusters of traditional shops and pubs, it's an agreeable place to stock up before a foray into the wilderness.

Sights & Activities

Lydford Gorge WATERFALL

(NT; www.nationaltrust.org.uk; adult/child £5.50/2.80; ⏲10am-4pm or 5pm mid-Mar–Oct) The 1½-mile rugged riverside hikes here snake past a series of bubbling whirlpools (including the fearsome 'Devil's Cauldron') to the thundering, 30m-high White Lady waterfall. Lydford is 9 miles southwest of Okehampton.

Okehampton Castle CASTLE

(EH; www.english-heritage.org.uk; adult/child £3.50/1.80; ⏲10am-5pm Apr-Jun & Sep, to 6pm Jul & Aug) Clinging to a wooded spur, the crumbling Norman motte and ruined keep of what was once Devon's largest castle allow for some picturesque rampart clambering.

Finch Foundry FORGE

(NT; www.nationaltrust.org.uk; Sticklepath; adult/child £4.40/2.20; ⏲11am-5pm Wed-Mon Apr-Oct) The last working water-powered forge in England sits at the end of a 3½-hour walk along the Tarka Trail from Okehampton.

Sleeping & Eating

Collaven Manor B&B ££

(☎01837-861522; www.collavenmanor.co.uk; Sourton; s £65, d £106-146; P) At this delightful, clematis-clad mini-manor house a wooden chandelier crowns a 16th-century hall. Restful bedrooms are lined with tapestries and window seats that provide tor-top views. Collaven Manor is 5 miles west of Okehampton.

Bracken Tor YHA HOSTEL £

(☎01837-53916; www.yha.org.uk; Saxon Gate; dm £16; P @) This 100-year-old country house sits in four acres of grounds on the fringe of the higher moor, making a perfect base for memorable hikes. It's a mile south of Okehampton and a YHA activity centre, so you can do some climbing and canoeing too.

Tors PUB ££

(☎01837-840689; www.thetors.co.uk; Belstone; mains £7-17; ⏲lunch & dinner) Tucked away in the picturesque moorland village of Belstone, this welcoming country pub offers simple, traditional **rooms** (singles/doubles £33/66), hearty food and views onto the moor. It's 2 miles east of Okehampton.

Information

Tourist office (☎01837-53020; www.okehamptondevon.co.uk; Museum Courtyard, 3 West St; ⏲10am-5pm Mon-Sat Easter-Oct, 10am-4.30pm Mon-Tue & Fri & Sat Nov-Easter)

Getting There & Away

Bus X9 runs from Exeter (50 minutes, hourly Monday to Saturday) via Okehampton to Bude (one hour). Bus 179 (two daily Monday to Saturday) goes to Chagford (30 minutes) and Moretonhampstead (50 minutes). Bus 118 (one to four daily) runs from Tavistock to Barnstaple (2¼ hours), and goes via Lydford and Okehampton.

Braunton & Croyde

POP 8319

The cheerful, chilled village of Croyde is Devon's surf central. Here olde-worlde meets new wave: thatched roofs peep out over racks of wetsuits; crowds of cool guys in board shorts sip beer outside 17th-century inns. Inland, Braunton also has surf shops, board hire and a **tourist office**

(☎01271-816400; www.brauntontic.co.uk; Caen St; ⏰10am-3pm Mon-Fri, 10am-2pm Sat).

The water's hard to resist. **Le Sport** (☎01271-890147; Hobbs Hill, Croyde; ⏰9am-5.30pm daily Mar-Oct, to 9pm Jul & Aug, 9.30am-5.30pm Sat & Sun Nov-Feb) is among those hiring wetsuits and boards (half-/full day £13/20). The British Surfing Association (BSA)-approved **Surf South West** (☎01271-890400; www.surfsouthwest.com; Croyde; per half-day £30; ⏰Mar-Nov) and **Surfing Croyde Bay** (☎01271-891200; www.surfingcroydebay.co.uk; 8 Hobbs Hill, Croyde; per half day £35) provide lessons.

Sleeping & Eating

Croyde gets very busy in the summer – book ahead, even for campsites.

Thatch B&B ££
(☎01271-890349; www.thethatchcroyde.com; 14 Hobbs Hill, Croyde; d £60-80) Set above a legendary surfer's hang out, the bedrooms in this thatched drinking-den are smart and modern, featuring delicate creams, browns and subtle checks. Some share bathrooms. It also offers a range of swish **rooms** (double £50 110, family £100–130) at neighbouring cottages and above Billy Budd's.

Chapel Farm B&B ££
(☎01271-890429, www.chapelfarmcroyde.co.uk; Hobbs Hill, Croyde; s/d £30/70; P) Walls and ceilings shoot off at atmospherically random angles in this cosy, thatched cob farmhouse, formerly a home to monks. Some of the light, pretty rooms share bathrooms. Self-catering is available, too.

Bay View Farm CAMPSITE £
(☎01271-890501; www.bayviewfarm.co.uk; Croyde; sites per adult £11) One of the area's best campsites, with laundry, showers and surf-view pitches. Often requires a week's minimum booking in summer.

Mitchum's CAMPSITE £
(☎07875 406473; www.croydebay.co.uk; Croyde; sites per adult £17-27; ⏰mid-Jun–Aug) There are two locations, one in Croyde village and one by the beach. There's often a two-night minimum booking in July and August.

Billy Budd's INTERNATIONAL £
(Hobbs Hill, Croyde; mains £6-12) Another board-rider's favourite, Billy Budd's serves jacket potatoes, chilli, nachos and huge sandwiches, along with more substantial main meals and local ales.

Getting There & Away

Bus 308 (hourly Monday to Saturday, five on Sunday) goes from Barnstaple to Braunton, Saunton Sands and Croyde (40 minutes).

Bus 3 (every 30 minutes Monday to Saturday, hourly Sunday) runs between Ilfracombe and Barnstaple, via Braunton.

Ilfracombe & Around

POP 12,430

Like a matinée idol past his prime, for years Ilfracombe had a sagging, crumpled feel. The steeply sloping streets of this Victorian watering hole are lined with town houses with cast-iron balconies; formal gardens, crazy golf and ropes of twinkling lights line the promenade. But these days there's more to Ilfracombe, as evidenced by a string of smart eateries and places to sleep, a Damien Hirst connection and the chance to go surfing or take a 'dip' in the past.

Sights & Activities

TOP CHOICE **Tunnelsbeaches** HISTORIC POOL
(www.tunnelsbeaches.co.uk; Granville Rd; adult/child £2/1.50, ⏰10am-5pm or 6pm Easter-Oct, to 7pm Jul & Aug) These Victorian tidal swimming pools beautifully evoke Ilfracombe's hey-day. Passageways hacked out of solid rock lead to a pocket-sized beach where you can still plunge into the sea. Sepia photos depict the same spot in the 19th century, conveying a world of woollen bathing suits, segregated swimming and boating etiquette ('Gentlemen who cannot swim should never take ladies upon the water').

Nick Thorn Hunter SURFING LESSONS
(☎01271-871337 www.nickthornhuntersurfacademy.com; ⏰9am-5pm Apr-Sep) Stationed at the best local surf beach, Woolacombe, 5 miles west of Ilfracombe. Lessons cost from £30 for 2½ hours.

Sleeping & Eating

Westwood BOUTIQUE B&B £
(☎01271-867443; www.west-wood.co.uk; Torrs Park Rd; d £80-110; P 📶) Modern, minimal and marvellous; this ultra-chic guesthouse is a study of neutral tones and dashes of vivid colour. It's graced by pony-skin chaises longues and stand-alone baths; some rooms have sea glimpses.

Norbury House Hotel B&B ££
(☎01271-863888; www.norburyhouse.co.uk; Torrs Park; d £8-100, f £100-135; P) This exquisite

former gentlemen's residence is now dotted with low-level beds, cool lamps and artfully placed cushions. Set on the hill overlooking Ilfracombe, there are impressive views from its terraced gardens.

11 The Quay EUROPEAN ££
(☎01271-868090; www.11thequay.com; 11 The Quay; snacks £2-9, mains £13-22; ⊙lunch & dinner Wed-Sat, dinner Sun) Full of Chelsea chic, this distinctive eatery is owned by the artist Damien Hirst, a man famous for exhibiting preserved dead cows and sharks. The menu's less controversial; sample cured ham with pickled garlic or lobster risotto with chives while admiring Hirst's artwork. It includes his *Pharmacy* installation and, with delicious irony, fish in formaldehyde. The **bistro** is open for lunch and dinner with snacks served all day.

Ocean Backpackers HOSTEL £
(☎01271-867835; www.oceanbackpackers.co.uk; 29 St James Pl; dm £10-14, d £35; P@☜) A well-run indie hostel stalwart with snug dorms and a convivial lounge. There's surfing, kayaking and archery on offer too.

Information

Tourist office (☎01271-863001; www.visitilfracombe.co.uk; Landmark Theatre, the Seafront; ⊙10am-5pm daily Easter-Sep, 10am-4pm Mon-Sat Oct-Mar)

Getting There & Away

Bus 3 (40 minutes, every half-hour Monday to Saturday, hourly Sunday) runs to Barnstaple, via Braunton. Bus 300 heads to Lynton (one hour, three daily), with connections on to Minehead (40 minutes).

Clovelly

POP 452

Clovelly is the quintessential picture-postcard pretty Devon village. Its white cottages cascade down cliffs to meet a curving crab claw of a harbour, which is lined with lobster pots and set against a deep-blue sea. Clovelly's cobbled streets are so steep that cars can't negotiate them so supplies are still brought in by sledge – you'll see these big bread baskets on runners leaning outside homes. Clovelly's tenants enjoy enviably low rents (around £400 a year) and although the village is often branded artificial, 98% of the houses are occupied – in some Westcountry villages half the properties are second homes.

Entry to the privately owned village is via the **visitor centre** (www.clovelly.co.uk; adult/child £6/4; ⊙8.45am-6.30pm Jun-Sep, 9am-5pm Apr & May, 10am-4pm Nov-Apr).

Charles Kingsley, author of the children's classic *The Water Babies,* spent much of his early life in Clovelly. You can visit his former house, as well as an old fishermen's cottage and the village's twin chapels. By the harbour, the **Red Lion** (☎01237-431237; www.clovelly.co.uk) has stylish rooms with superb views (d £120 to £136), a classy restaurant (3 courses £30), and a welcoming bar (mains £6 to £10).

Bus 319 (four to six Monday to Saturday, two on Sunday between May and September only) runs between Clovelly, Hartland Village, Bideford (40 minutes) and Barnstaple (one hour).

Hartland Abbey

This 12th-century **former monastery** (www.hartlandabbey.com; adult/child £9.50/2.50; ⊙2-4.30pm Sun-Thu Jun-Sep, Wed-Thu & Sun Apr-May) was another post-Dissolution handout, given to the sergeant of Henry VIII's wine cellar in 1539. Now a stately home, it boasts fascinating murals, ancient documents, paintings by English masters, Victorian photos, as well as bewitching **gardens** (⊙noon-5pm Sun-Fri Apr-Sep).

Hartland Abbey is 15 miles west of Bideford, off the A39 between Hartland and Hartland Quay.

CORNWALL

You can't get any further west than the ancient Celtic kingdom of Cornwall (or Kernow, as it's often referred to around these parts). Blessed with the craggiest cliffs, wildest coastline and most breathtakingly beautiful coves anywhere in England, this proud, independent corner of the Westcountry has always marched to its own tune. While the staple industries of old – mining, fishing and farming – have all but disappeared, Cornwall has picked itself up, dusted itself down and reinvented itself as one of the nation's creative and cultural corners. Whether it's exploring the space-age domes of the Eden Project, sampling the creations of a celebrity chef or chilling out on the faraway beaches of the Isles of Scilly, you're guaranteed to get inspired out west. Time to let a little Kernow into your soul.

Getting Around

Most of Cornwall's main bus, train and ferry timetables are collected into a handy brochure, available free from bus stations and tourist offices). **Traveline South West** (☎0871-200-2233; www.travelinesw.com) can also answer timetable queries.

Bus

Cornwall has two main bus operators.

First (☎timetables 0871-200-2233, customer services 0845-600-1420; www.firstgroup.com) Operates buses and trains across Cornwall.

Western Greyhound (☎01637-871871; www.westerngreyhound.com)

Train

Devon and Cornwall's main railway line follows the coast as far as Penzance, with spurs to Barnstaple, Paignton, Gunnislake, Looe, Falmouth, St Ives and Newquay.

CrossCountry (☎0844-811-0124; www.crosscountrytrains.co.uk) Shuttles between the southwest and Scotland, the north and the Midlands.

First Great Western (☎08457-000-125; www.firstgreatwestern.co.uk) Links London Paddington with Exeter, Penzance, Plymouth and Truro; plus branch lines to Exmouth, Falmouth, Newquay, St Ives and Torquay.

South West Trains (☎0845 6000 650; www.southwesttrains.co.uk) Runs services between London Waterloo and Axminster and Exeter.

Bude

POP 9242

Travelling west from Devon, the first Cornish town across the border is Bude, a popular family getaway and surfing hangout thanks to its fantastic nearby beaches.

Sights & Activities

Beaches

Closest to town is **Summerleaze**, a classic bucket-and-spade affair with bags of space at low tide, as well as a saltwater **sea pool** (10am-6pm May-Sep), built in the 1930s and fed straight from the bracing waters of the Atlantic. Just to the north is **Crooklets**, which often has decent surf, as does **Widemouth Bay** (pronounced *widmouth*) 3 miles south of town. Further along the coast, the most spectacular beach scenery is saved for are the dramatic beaches of **Crackington Haven** and the **Strangles**.

Several steps removed from the high-octane hustle of Newquay, Bude is ideal for some low-key surf lessons. Try **Big Blue Surf School** (☎01288-331764; www.bigbluesurfschool.co.uk), **BSX Surf Centre** (☎0870-777-5511; www.budesurfingexperience.co.uk) or **Raven Surf School** (☎01288-353693; www.ravensurf.co.uk). Which beach is used depends on the tide and weather conditions, but Summerleaze and Crooklets are the favourites.

Bude Castle

MUSEUM

(The Castle; adult/child £3.50/2.50; 10am-6pm Easter-Oct, 10am-4pm Nov-Easter) Other than the beaches, there's not a huge amount to keep you occupied in Bude, although it's worth taking a peek around the **Castle Heritage Centre,** which rummages through Bude's maritime, geological and social history. Look out for exhibits on local inventor Sir Goldsworthy Gurney, whose pioneering creations included theatrical limelight and steam carriages – he also built the peculiar pint-sized castle in which the museum is now housed.

Sleeping

Dylan's Guesthouse

B&B £

(☎01288-354705; www.dylansguesthouseinbude.co.uk; Downs View, s £45-50, d £50-65) This friendly, fizzy little B&B has nine rooms decked out in white linen, chocolate throws and pleasant pine, and a friendly owner full of info on the local area.

Elements Hotel

HOTEL ££

(☎01288 275066; www.elements-life.co.uk; Marine Drive; s/d/f £70/105/160; P) Smart clifftop hotel with 11 soothing rooms in whites and creams, big views from the outdoor deck, a gym and Finholme sauna, and surf lessons courtesy of nearby Raven Surf School.

Eating

Life's a Beach

CAFE ££

(www.lifesabeach.info; Summerleaze; lunch £4-6, dinner mains £16-21.50; Mon-Sat) By day it's a breezy beach caff serving the Summerleaze punters with coffees, panini and ice-creams: by night it's a snazzy candlelit restaurant specialising in seafood.

Scrummies

CAFE £

(Lansdown Rd; mains from £8; 8am-10pm) A fab fish cafe where the skate and monkfish

PUBLIC TRANSPORT PASSES

Several passes are available covering public transport in the southwest, including Devon and Cornwall.

Bus

» **FirstDay Southwest** (adult/child/family £7.10/5.80/16.50) Buys a day's unlimited bus travel on most First buses. There's also a seven-day equivalent (adult/family £32.50/49). Cheaper day and weekly passes are available for smaller zones within the region.

» **Western Greyhound Day Explorer** (adult/child £7/4.50) Covers all Western Greyhound buses in Cornwall, plus Stagecoach and Hook buses in Devon.

» **Day passes** There are usually daily bus passes (with names like Day Rover, Wayfarer or Explorer) covering travel in the region's big cities. Ask at the main bus station to see what's available.

Train

» **Freedom of the SouthWest Rover** Covers all train travel west of Bath, Bristol and Bournemouth. It allows an adult eight days' unlimited, off-peak travel in a 15-day period for £95, or three days' travel in a week for £70.

» **Devon & Cornwall Rover** Allows unlimited off-peak train travel across Devon and Cornwall. Eight days' travel in 15 costs an adult £60; three days' travel in one week is £40.

Bus & Train

» **Ride Cornwall** (adult/child £10/7.50/20) Unlimited travel on all rail and bus services within Cornwall after 9am Monday to Friday and weekends.

are caught by the owner – try their crab pasta or lobster (half/whole £12/24) and chips.

Information

Bude tourist office (☎01288-354240; www.visitbude.info; The Crescent; ⊙10am-5pm Mon-Sat, plus 10am-4pm Sun summer) In a car park at the end of town.

Getting There & Away

Boscastle (30 minutes, six daily Monday to Saturday, four on summer Sundays) Bus 594/595; runs via Widemouth and Crackington Haven. From Boscastle there are connections to Tintagel, Wadebridge, Newquay and Truro.

Boscastle

With its sturdy harbour, quaint cottages and steep valley setting, Boscastle is the perfect picture of a Cornish port, but in August 2004 the village hit the headlines for all the wrong reasons: devastating flash floods swept through the village, carrying away cars, bridges and even a couple of buildings, and forcing the emergency evacuation of many residents by naval helicopter (somewhat miraculously, not a single person lost their life).

Residents have spent the last few years piecing Boscastle back together, and most of its properties have now been completely refurbished, almost as though the floods never were. Look closely, though, and you might still be able to spot flood-marks halfway up some of the buildings, and a much-reinforced stone bridge at the centre of the village.

Elsewhere, there's plenty of fine coastal walking around Boscastle, plus a couple of woodland trails leading to local churches: ask at the tourist office for leaflets.

Sights

Museum of Witchcraft MUSEUM

(☎01840-250111; The Harbour; adult/child £3/2.50; ⊙10.30am-6pm Mon-Sat, 11.30am-6pm Sun) Among Boscastle's renovated buildings, this quirky museum rather improbably houses the world's largest collection of witchy memorabilia, from haunted skulls to hags' bridles and voodoo dolls.

Sleeping & Eating

Boscastle House B&B ££
(☎01840-250654; www.boscastlehouse.com; Tintagel Rd; d £120; P 🛜) The fanciest of Boscastle B&Bs, in a Victorian house overlooking the valley, with six rooms named after Cornish legends. Charlotte has bay window views, Nine Windows has his-and-hers sinks and a freestanding bath, Trelawney has space and its own sofa.

Orchard Lodge B&B £
(☎01840-250418; www.orchardlodgeboscastle.co.uk; Gunpool Ln; d £74-84; P 🛜) A short walk uphill from the village, this is a fine example of a thoroughly modern B&B, crisply finished in slinky fabrics and cool colours and run with efficiency by B&B newbies Geoff and Shirley Barratt. Rates get cheaper the longer you stay.

Boscastle YHA HOSTEL £
(boscastle@yha.org.uk; dm £14) Having been all but swept away by the floods, Boscastle's shoebox hostel has been polished up and now looks spanking fresh. It's in one of the village's oldest buildings by the harbour.

Boscastle's dining scene is limited almost entirely to the village pubs: try the cosy **Cobweb** (☎01840-250278; www.cobwebinn.co.uk; The Bridge; mains £5-14) and the old-time **Napoleon** (☎01840-250204; High Street; mains £6-12).

Information

Boscastle tourist office (☎01840-250010; www.visitboscastleandtintagel.com; ⏱10am 5pm Mar-Oct) In a new building by the harbour.

Getting There & Away

For buses see Tintagel, p367.

Tintagel

POP 1822

The spectre of King Arthur looms large over the village of Tintagel and its spectacular clifftop **castle** (EH; ☎01840-770328; adult/child £5.20/2.60; ⏱10am-6pm Apr-Sep, 10am 5pm Oct, 10am-4pm Nov-Mar). Though the present-day ruins mostly date from the 13th century, archaeological digs have revealed the foundations of a much earlier fortress, fuelling speculation that the legendary king may indeed have been born at the castle as local fable claims. Part of the crumbling stronghold stands on a rock tower cut off from the mainland, accessed via a bridge and steep steps, and it's still possible to make out several sturdy walls and much of the castle's interior layout.

The village is awash with touristy shops and tearooms making the most of the King Arthur connection, but there's not that much to see. The **Old Post Office** (NT; ☎01840-770024; Fore St; adult/child £3.20/1.60; ⏱11am-5.30pm mid-Mar–Sep, 11am-4pm Oct) is a beautiful example of a traditional Cornish longhouse and mostly dates from the 1500s; it was still used as the village's post office during the 19th century.

Information

Tintagel Tourist Office (☎01840-779084; www.visitboscastleandtintagel.com; Bossiney Rd; ⏱10am-5pm Mar-Oct, 10.30am-4pm Nov-Feb) Has exhibits exploring local history and the Arthur legend.

Getting There & Away

Bus 597 runs from Truro to St Columb Major where the connecting 594 goes via Wadebridge to Tintagel (two hours, seven daily Monday to Saturday) and onto Boscastle (10 minutes).

Padstow

POP 3162

If anywhere symbolises Cornwall's culinary renaissance, it's Padstow. Decades ago this was an industrious fishing village where the day's catch was battered and served up in newspaper. Today it's seared, braised or chargrilled, garnished with wasabi and dished up in some of the poshest restaurants this side of the Tamar.

The transformation is largely due to celebrity chef Rick Stein, whose property portfolio has now mushroomed to include restaurants, shops, hotels, a seafood school and even a fish and chip outlet. Inevitably, the town's much-bandied nickname of 'Padstein' raises the hackles of the locals, but there's no doubt the town has changed beyond recognition since its days as a quiet fishing harbour; while the cash has certainly swelled Padstow's coffers, it hasn't always been good for its soul.

Sights & Activities

National Lobster Hatchery MARINE CENTRE
(www.nationallobsterhatchery.co.uk; adult/child £3/1.50; ⏱10am-7.30pm Jul & Aug, 10am-5pm Apr-Jun & Sep-Oct, earlier closing Nov-Mar) In order to ensure sustainable stocks for future

THE OBBY OSS CEREMONY

Padstow's raucous May Day fertility rite, featuring the fabled Obby Oss (hobby horse), is believed to be the oldest such event in the country. The ritual begins just before midnight on 30 April, as villagers sing to the innkeeper at the Golden Lion with the news that summer is 'a-come'. Then, at 10am the next morning, the Blue Ribbon Oss – a man garbed in a huge hooped sailcloth dress and wild-looking horse headdress – dances around the town, grabbing any woman close enough and daubing her with coal (or, often, pinching her – it's believed to aid child-bearing!). He's followed at 11am by the Old Original (or Red) Oss and the madness continues until late.

generations, baby lobsters are reared in special tanks at this harbourside hatchery before being returned to the wild. It's a fascinating place to learn about the life-cycle of this tasty crustacean.

Camel Trail CYCLE PATH

The disused Padstow–Bodmin railway now forms the Camel Trail, one of Cornwall's most popular cycling tracks. Starting in Padstow, it runs east through Wadebridge (5¾ miles), Bodmin (11 miles) and beyond. Bikes can be hired from **Padstow Cycle Hire** (☎01841-533533; www.padstowcyclehire.com; ⌚9am-5pm) or **Bridge Bike Hire** (⌚01208-813050; www.bridgebikehire.co.uk), at the Wadebridge end.

Boat Trips CRUISES

Several operators leave from the harbour for scenic spins around the bay. **Padstow Boat Trips** (www.padstowboattrips.com) collects schedules and details. Operators include **Jubilee Queen** (☎07836-798457) and **Padstow Sealife Safaris** (☎01841-521613; www.padstowsealifesafaris.co.uk).

Prideaux Place HISTORIC HOME

(www.prideauxplace.co.uk; house & grounds adult £7.50, grounds only £2; ⌚1.30-4pm Sun-Thu, grounds & tearoom 12.30-5.30pm Apr-Oct) Much favoured by directors of costume dramas, this stately manor house above the village was built by the Prideaux-Brune family (who still reside here). The house can be visited on a guided tour.

Beaches

Padstow is surrounded by excellent beaches, including the so-called Seven Bays: Trevone, Harlyn, Mother Ivey's, Booby's, Constantine, Treyarnon and Porthcothan. Bus 556 runs fairly close by most of the beaches, and also stops at the surfy community of Polzeath, where you'll find plenty of outfits who can help you learn the basics of catching a break. **Animal Surf Academy** (☎01208-880617; www.animalsurfacademy.co.uk) offers options including female-only coaching and sessions with pro surfers, and **Surf's Up Surf School** (☎01208-862003; www.surfsupsurfschool.com) is a family-run outfit.

Sleeping

Treverbyn House B&B £

(☎01841-532855; www.treverbynhouse.com; Station Rd; d £80-115; P) This smart Padstow town house is topped by little turrets and has five rooms subtly themed around different colours. It's elegant and understated, and the choice of brekkies is about the best in Padstow.

Ballaminers House B&B ££

(☎01841-540933; www.ballaminershouse.co.uk; Little Petherick; d £90; P) Two miles south of Padstow, this smart stone farmhouse blends old-world atmosphere with modern elegance. Rooms feature Balinese furniture and antique chests, and boast sweeping views of the surrounding fields.

Treyarnon Bay YHA HOSTEL £

(treyarnon@yha.org.uk; Tregonnan; dm £14; P @) Settings don't get much better than this 1930s beach house on the bluffs above Treyarnon Bay. Bus 556 from Padstow stops at nearby Constantine several times a day.

Eating

TOP CHOICE **Paul Ainsworth at No 6** RESTAURANT ££

(☎01840-532093; www.number6inpadstow.co.uk; 6 Middle St; mains £13.50-15.50; ⌚lunch & dinner) You might not have heard of him yet, but take our word for it – Paul Ainsworth is the chef to watch in Padstow. He trained under some of the country's top names, and his elegant eatery is a treat. Black-and-white chequerboard tiles, besuited waiters and simple, classic decor provide the perfect setting for Ainsworth's quietly stunning food.

Rick Stein's Cafe BISTRO ££

(☎01841-532700; Middle St; mains £9-18; ⌚closed Sun) Rick Stein's original Padstow establishment, the Seafood Restaurant, is a real budget blower, but this backstreet bistro offers stripped-down samples of his trademark Med-influenced cuisine at much more reasonable prices.

Basement BISTRO ££
(☎01841-532846; 11 Broad Street; lunch mains £7.50-9, dinner mains £12.50-19.50; ⏲lunch & dinner) Newly arrived on Padstow's harbourside, this Continental cafe is a welcome addition for its breezy brasserie-style food. Plump for the smart interior or bag one of the sought-after pavement tables, sheltered under big black umbrellas.

Margot's Bistro BISTRO ££
(☎01840-533441; 11 Duke St; mains £12-15; ⏲lunch Wed-Sat, dinner Tue-Sat) Padstow's not all about big-name chefs – in fact, Margot's owner isn't even called Margot (it's now run by local boy Adrian Oliver). It's strong on seasonal food, and the decor's cosily chaotic – but there are only a few tables, so booking's a good idea.

Rojano's RESTAURANT ££
(9 Mill Sq; pizzas & pastas from £9; ⏲lunch & dinner Tue-Sun) This bright, buzzy Italian joint turns out excellent pizza and pasta, served either in the snug, sunlit dining room or on the tiny front terrace.

TOP CHOICE **St Kew Inn** GASTROPUB ££
(☎01208-841259; www.stkewinn.co.uk; mains £8-16; ⏲11am-3pm & 6-11pm) Out in the village of St Kew, 12 miles from Padstow, this inviting inn blends the warm feel of a village local with the quality grub of a bona fide gastropub. Chef and landlord Paul Ripley is a Rick Stein alumnus and former Michelin-star chef, and it shows.

Information

Padstow Tourist Office (☎01841-533449; www.padstowlive.com; North Quay; ⏲10am-5pm Mon-Sat) On the quay.

Getting There & Away

From Padstow, bus 557 (six daily Monday to Saturday) travels to St Columb Major (30 minutes) with connecting buses to Newquay (30 minutes) and Truro (1¼ hours) via the 597.

Newquay

POP 19,423

Bright, breezy and unashamedly brash: that's Newquay, Cornwall's premier party town and the undisputed capital of British surfing. Beautifully positioned above a cluster of golden beaches, a decade ago Newquay was one of Cornwall's top family resorts. But it's recently become infamous for its after-dark antics: throughout the summer, a non-stop parade of beach-blond surfers, boozed-up clubbers and cackling hen parties descends on the town in search of some high jinks beside the seashore, creating a drink-till-dawn atmosphere that's closer to the Costa del Sol than Cornwall.

Change might well be afoot in Newquay, however. The recent deaths of two teenagers after nights of heavy drinking have prompted many local residents to think again about the direction their town's taken, and perhaps contemplate a return to the family-friendly days of old. But for now the party shows no sign of slowing down, and if you're looking to learn how to brave the waves, Newquay's definitely the place.

Sights & Activities

Beaches
Newquay is set amid some of the finest beaches on the North Coast. **Fistral**, west of Towan Head, is England's best-known surfing beach and the venue for the annual Boardmasters surfing festival. Below town are **Great Western** and **Towan**; a little further up the coast you'll find **Tolcarne**, **Lusty Glaze**, **Porth** and **Watergate Bay**. All these beaches are good for swimming and supervised by lifeguards in summer.

The stately rock towers of **Bedruthan Steps**, are a few miles further east towards Padstow; **Crantock** lies 3 miles to the southwest. Further west again is family-friendly **Holywell Bay**.

Surfing SURF LESSONS
Newquay's awash with places to learn to surf, offering everything from half-day taster lessons (£25 to £30) to full-blown multiday 'surfaris' (from £130). When choosing your school, make sure it's approved by the BSA (British Surfing Association). Reputable operators include **National Surfing Centre** (☎Fistral Beach 01637-850737, Lusty Glaze 01637-851487; www.nationalsurfingcentre.com) and **Extreme Academy** (☎01637-860840; Watergate Bay; www.extreme academy.co.uk).

Adventure Sports
For those after even more thrills and spills, there are several multi-activity providers in and around Newquay specialising in outdoor sports, from kitebuggying and paddle

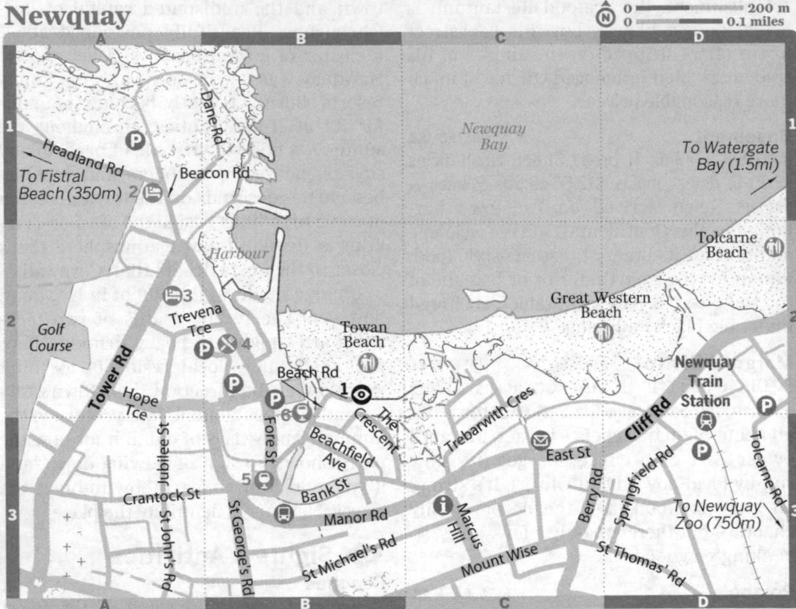

Newquay

Sights

1 Blue Reef Aquarium B2

Sleeping

2 Goofys A1
3 Pure Shores A2

Eating

4 Café Irie B2

Drinking

5 Central B3
6 Chy B2
Koola .... (see 6)

surfing to the latest Cornish craze, coasteering (pitched somewhere between rock-climbing, scrambling and wild swimming). On Lusty Glaze try **Adventure Centre** (☎01637-872444; www.adventure-centre.org), while on Holywell Bay see **EboAdventure** (☎0800-781-6861; www.penhaleadventure.com).

Blue Reef Aquarium AQUARIUM
(☎01637-878134; www.bluereefaquarium.co.uk; Towan Promenade; adult/child/family £9.20/7.20/30.80; ⏰10am-5pm) On Towan Beach, Newquay's aquarium displays a selection of weird and wonderful aquatic characters, including jellyfish, seahorses, octopi and rays. Touch-pools allow you to get up close and personal with the residents.

Newquay Zoo ZOO
(☎01637-873342; www.newquayzoo.co.uk; Trenance Gardens; adult/child/family £10.95/8.20/30.50; ⏰9:30am-6pm Apr-Sep, 10am-5pm Oct-Mar) Red pandas, sloths, penguins, great horned owls and a python called Monty (get it?) are some of the wild inhabitants at this popular zoo, ten minutes walk from the town centre.

Sleeping

Although Newquay has stacks of sleeping options, in high season prices rocket, the best get booked up, and some require a week's booking. Surf lodges seem to be on the wane in Newquay – several of the big ones have recently been sold off and redeveloped as holiday flats.

TOP CHOICE **Scarlet** HOTEL £££
(☎01637-861600; www.scarlethotel.co.uk; d £180-395; P 🛜 ≋) For out-and-out luxury, there's no topping Cornwall's newest eco-chic hotel. In a regal location above Mawgan Porth, it simply screams designer style: a stunning infinity pool, a boutique bar straight out of Soho and huge sea-view

rooms full of funky fabrics, stripped-back surfaces and ridiculously oversized TVs. 'Stunning' really doesn't do it justice.

The Hotel HOTEL ££
(01637-860543; www.watergatebay.co.uk; Watergate Bay; d £95-295, ste £205-400; P) Fresh from a multi-million-pound refit, the old Watergate has been reinvented as a beachside beauty. The rooms dazzle in slinky pinks, candy-stripes and sea-blues, partnered with wicker chairs, stripped wood and mini sea-view balconies. It's pricey, but for this kind of location it's hardly surprising.

Pure Shores B&B
(01637-878894; www.pureshoreslodge.com; 18 Tower Rd; d £50-70; P) By far the best B&B in Newquay, a Victorian town house that's been overhauled with grace and style by its globetrotting owners (look out for souvenirs collected on their travels). The four rooms are elegant and contemporary: iPod docks, Venetian blinds, shades of taupe, cream and orange.

Goofys HOSTEL £
(01637-872684; www.goofys.co.uk; 5 Headland Rd; r per person £32.50-40; P @) The town's top surf lodge bills itself as a 'boutique hostel', and it is certainly head and shoulders above the rest. There are only six rooms, so it never feels overcrowded even when it's full, and all the rooms are nicely furnished with posh cotton sheets and zip-and-link beds. There are even several doubles for those who prefer their privacy. Prices fall outside the high season.

Eating

TOP CHOICE **Fifteen Cornwall** RESTAURANT £££
(01637-861000; www.fifteencornwall.com; Watergate Bay; lunch/dinner menu £26/55; lunch & dinner) Jamie Oliver's social enterprise restaurant opened on Watergate Bay back in 2006, and it's proved enormously popular. Underprivileged youngsters learn their trade in the kitchen preparing Oliver's trademark zesty, Italian-influenced food, while diners soak up the beach views and the buzzy, beachy vibe. It's a red-hot ticket: bookings essential.

Beach Hut BISTRO ££
(01637-860877; Watergate Bay; mains £9.75-19.95; breakfast, lunch & dinner) If you can't get a table at Fifteen, head downstairs to the by-the-sand bistro at the Watergate Bay Hotel. It's similarly beachy in feel, and the menu's classic surf 'n' turf: fish curries, 'extreme' burgers and a different fresh fish dish every day.

Fistral Blu BISTRO £££
(01637-879444; Fistral Beach; mains £8-20; lunch & dinner)
Another great sundowner option, in the glass-and-steel retail complex behind Fistral Beach. Thai and Med flavours mix with Cornish ingredients in the upstairs restaurant while the ground-floor cafe turns out fish and chips and Ben & Jerry's.

Café Irie CAFE £
(01637-859200; www.cafeirie.co.uk; 38 Fore St; lunch £3-8; 9am-5.30pm Mon-Sat) Run by surfers for surfers, this cafe's famous for its coffee and hot chocolate (just the ticket after a morning in the ocean swell) plus veggie wraps, piping-hot jacket spuds and gooey cakes. The decor's cool, too: vintage vinyl on the walls, multi-coloured plates and coffee mugs, chalkboards scrawled with specials.

Drinking & Entertainment

Chy BAR
(www.thekoola.com/the-chy-bar; 12 Beach Rd) Chrome, wood and leather dominate this stylish cafe and bar overlooking Towan Beach. The patio is perfect for a gourmet breakfast or lunchtime salad, or pitch up late when the DJs take to the decks and the beers start to flow.

Koola CLUB
(www.thekoola.com; 12 Beach Rd) Underneath Chy, Koola is a world away from most of Newquay's cheese-heavy clubs. The music's eclectic – house, Latin, drum and bass, plus occasional big-name gigs.

Central PUB
(11 Central Sq) As its name suggests, this rowdy pre-club pub is right in the heart of town, and the outside patio is always overflowing on warm summer nights.

Information

Newquay tourist office (01637-854020; www.newquay.co.uk; Marcus Hill; 9.30am-5.30pm Mon-Sat, 9.30am-12.30pm Sun)

Tad & Nick's Talk'n'Surf (72 Fore St; per hr £3; 10am-6pm) Net access.

Getting There & Away

Air

Bus 556 (22 minutes, £2.80, hourly) shuttles to the airport from Newquay's bus station on Manor Rd.

TRERICE

Built in 1751, the charming Elizabethan manor of **Trerice** (NT; 01637-875404; adult/child £6.70/3.30; house 11am-5pm Sat-Thu Mar-Oct, gardens from 10.30am) is famous for the elaborate barrel-roofed ceiling of the Great Chamber, but has plenty of other intriguing features, including ornate fireplaces, original plasterwork and a fine collection of period furniture. There's also an amusing lawnmower museum in the barn, with over 100 grass-cutters going back over a century.

Trerice is 3 miles southeast of Newquay. Bus 527 runs from Newquay to Kestle Mill, about a mile from the manor house.

Newquay Airport (01637-860600; www.newquaycornwallairport.com) Regular flights to UK airports, including London, Belfast, Birmingham, Cardiff, Edinburgh and the Isles of Scilly.

Bus

The £585/586 is the fastest service to Truro (50 minutes, twice hourly Monday to Saturday), while the hourly 587 follows the coast via Crantock (14 minutes), Holywell Bay (25 minutes) and Perranporth (50 minutes).

Train

There are trains every couple of hours between Newquay and Par (£3.80, 45 minutes) on the main London–Penzance line.

Perranporth

West of Newquay, the craggy North Coast cliffs run through a string of white sandy beaches. Largest of all is Perranporth, with a huge sweep of flat sand backed by wind-whipped dunes and pounded by surf. The town itself straggles out along a single main street and is packed to bursting with holidaymakers in summer and all but deserted in the winter months.

Activities

Mobius Kite School KITE LESSONS
(08456 430630; www.mobiusonline.co.uk; Cubert) The pan-flat beach and reliable offshore winds here are perfect for kitebuggying and kitesurfing. If you fancy trying out your skills this outfit runs regular courses, as well as guided mountain-bike trips around the county.

Eating & Drinking

Tin Fin BISTRO ££
(01872-572117; 4 Beach Rd; mains £12-18; breakfast, lunch & dinner) Perran's dining scene is dominated by cheap-and-cheerful pubs and fish-and-chips shops, but if you fancy something more substantial, this bright and breezy bistro turns out the town's best food. Slate floors, multicoloured chairs and light pine tables give it a fresh seaside feel, while the menu is chalked up daily on the blackboard.

Watering Hole BEACH BAR £
(www.the-wateringhole.co.uk; Perranporth Beach) Perran's old warhorse of a beach bar makes a great spot for a sundowner, with tables spilling right onto the sand and local bands playing into the night on weekends during summer.

Getting There & Away

For buses see Porthtowan and St Agnes, p373.

Porthtowan & St Agnes

Once a centre for Cornish tin-mining, the coastline around St Agnes is littered with the remains of old minestacks and engine houses, most notably at Wheal Coates, a famously photogenic mine perched on the cliff's edge above the National Trust cove of Chapel Porth. The coast path winds out through stunning scenery on the way to Tubby's Head, or you could strike inland for the high-point panorama from St Agnes Beacon.

Sights

Blue Hills Tin Streams
(01872-553341; www.bluehillstin.com; adult/child £5.50/3; 10am-4pm Mon-Sat Jul-Aug, 10am-2pm Mon-Sat late-Mar–late-Oct) A mile or so east of St Agnes in the rocky valley of Trevellas Coombe (locally known as Blue Hills, thanks to the copious heather that cloaks the hillsides hereabouts) is one of Cornwall's last (and tiniest) tin manufacturers. Guided tours of this family-run operation take in the whole tinning process, from mining and smelting through to casting and finishing.

The site is reached via a turn-off from the St Agnes–Perranporth road, signed to Wheal Kitty. It's very steep and parking is

THE SOUTHWEST COAST PATH

Britain's longest national trail is the stunning 630-mile **South West Coast Path** (www.southwestcoastpath.com), a breathtaking route that takes in everything from dazzling bays and pretty fishing villages to craggy cliffs and wild moorland.

The route officially begins in Minehead, Somerset, and runs right the way around the peninsula before reaching journey's end at South Haven Point, near Poole Harbour. The whole trail takes about eight weeks, but the trail can be easily split into shorter day-hikes.

The trail's website has a detailed overview covering the entire route, including suggestions for day routes and details of guided walks, as well as an extremely useful distance calculator. The **South West Coast Path Association** (www.swcp.org.uk) publishes an annual guidebook.

limited, so take care when driving down. Better still, walk down.

Sleeping & Eating

Aramay B&B ££
(☎01872-553546; www.aramay.com; Quay Rd; d £95-105; P 📶) Not long on the scene, but with five fine rooms and a sweet St Agnes location, it won't stay secret for long. Try No 1, with contemporary four-poster and cream-and-crimson decor, or swanky No 3, with silky throws and views of the Stippy Stappy.

Driftwood Spars HOTEL ££
(☎01872-552428; www.driftwoodspars.com; d £86-110; P) This old warhorse by Trevaunance Cove near St Agnes has something to suit all-comers: local beers and brassy trinkets in the low-ceilinged pub, good bistro **food** (mains £10.95–16.95) in the conservatory restaurant, and nautically themed upstairs rooms, many of which overlook the cove.

Blue Bar BAR, BISTRO ££
(www.blue-bar.co.uk; Porthtowan; ⌚lunch & dinner) Porthtowan's popular surfers' hangout has a decent pub-grub menu and plenty of beachside tables, tailor-made for sinking a cold one as the sun goes down.

Getting There & Away

Western Greyhound's **bus 583** (12 daily Monday to Saturday) runs between Truro, St Agnes and Perranporth, while **bus 304** (10 to 12 Monday to Friday, six on Saturday) goes from Truro to Porthtowan. First's **bus 85** (hourly Monday to Saturday) is the most regular from Truro to St Agnes.

St Ives

POP 9870

Sitting on the fringes of a glittering arc-shaped bay, St Ives was once one of Cornwall's busiest pilchard-fishing harbours, but it's better known now as the centre of the county's arts scene. From the old harbour, cobbled alleyways and switchback lanes lead up into the jumble of buzzy galleries, cafes and brasseries that cater for thousands of summer visitors. It makes for an intriguing mix of boutique chic and traditional seaside, and while the high-season traffic can take the shine off things, St Ives is still an essential stop on any Cornish grand tour.

Sights & Activities

Tate St Ives GALLERY
(☎01736-796226; www.tate.org.uk/stives; Porthmeor Beach; adult/child £5.75/3.25; ⌚10am-5pm Mar-Oct, 10am-4pm Tue-Sun Nov-Feb) The artwork almost takes second place to the surroundings at the stunning Tate St Ives, which hovers above Porthmeor Beach. Built in 1993, the gallery contains work by celebrated local artists, including Terry Frost, Patrick Heron and Barbara Hepworth, and hosts regular special exhibitions. On the top floor there's a stylish cafe-bar with imaginative bistro food and some of the best sea views in St Ives. A joint ticket with the **Barbara Hepworth** museum can be purchased for adult/child £8.75/4.50.

There are plenty more galleries around town; at the **Sloop Craft Market** you'll find a treasure trove of tiny artists' studios selling everything from handmade jewellery to driftwood furniture.

Barbara Hepworth Museum & Sculpture Garden MUSEUM
(☎01736-796226; www.tate.org.uk/stives; Barnoon Hill; adult/child £5.75/3.25; ⌚10am-5pm Mar-Oct, 10am-4pm Tue-Sun Nov-Feb) Barbara Hepworth (1903–75) was one of the leading abstract sculptors of the 20th century, and a key figure in the St Ives art scene; fittingly, her former studio has been transformed into

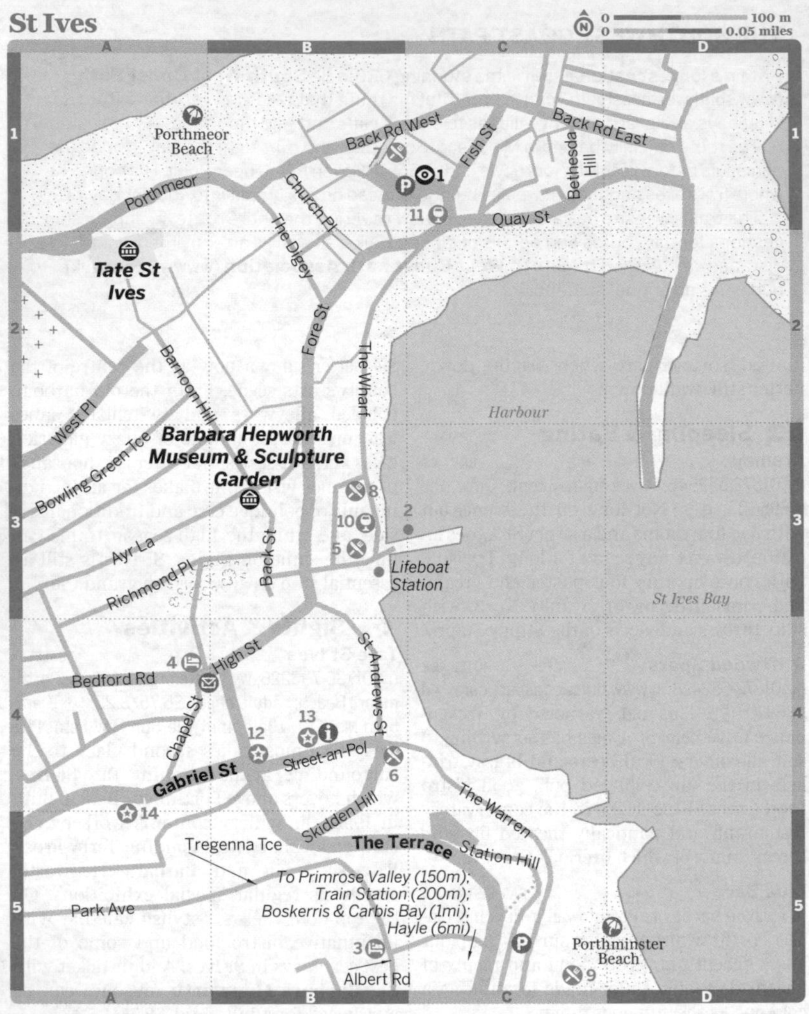

a moving archive and museum. The studio itself has remained almost untouched since her death in a fire, and the adjoining garden contains some of her most famous sculptures. A joint ticket for **Tate St Ives** can be purchased for adult/child £8.75/4.50. Hepworth's work is scattered throughout St Ives; look for her sculptures outside the Guildhall and inside the 15th-century parish church of St Ia.

Leach Pottery GALLERY

(☎01736-796398; www.leachpottery.com; adult/child £4.50/3.50; ⏰10am-5pm Mon-Sat, 11am-4pm Sun) The renowned potter Bernard Leach established his studio in upper St Ives in 1920, having spent several years studying and working in the Far East. Leach went on to develop an influential fusion of Eastern and Western ceramics based on his lifelong fascination with oriental arts, and his studio showcases many examples of his work. A recent restoration project has also added a new potter's workshop and an interesting museum exploring Leach's legacy. The gallery is about a mile uphill or 15 minutes' walk from the town centre along Higher Stennack.

St Ives

Top Sights

Barbara Hepworth Museum & Sculpture Garden........B3
Tate St Ives........A2

Sights

1 Sloop Craft Market........C1

Activities, Courses & Tours

2 Boat Trips........C3

Sleeping

3 Organic Panda........B5
4 Treliska........A4

Eating

5 Alba........B3
6 Blas Burgerworks........B4
7 Loft........B1
8 Onshore........B3
9 Porthminster Beach Café........C5

Drinking

10 Hub........B3
11 Sloop Inn........C1

Entertainment

12 Crow Rooms........B4
13 Guildhall........B4
14 Royal Cinema........A5

Beaches

The largest town beaches are **Porthmeor** and **Porthminster,** but the tiny cove of **Porthgwidden** is also popular. Nearby, on a tiny peninsula of land known locally as the Island, sits the pre-14th-century Chapel of St Nicholas. **Carbis Bay**, to the southeast, is popular with families and sun seekers.

On the opposite side of the bay from St Ives, the receding tide reveals over 3 miles of golden beach at **Gwithian** and **Godrevy Towans**, both popular spots for kiteboarders and surfers. The lighthouse just offshore at Godrevy was the inspiration for Virginia Woolf's classic stream-of-consciousness novel *To the Lighthouse*.

Gwithian boasts some of the best beach breaks in Cornwall. The **Gwithian Surf Academy** (01736-757579; www.surfacademy.co.uk) is one of only four BSA Schools of Excellence, so lessons get booked up fast.

Boat Trips

Boats heading out on sea-fishing trips and cruises to the grey seal colony on Seal Island (adult/child £9/7), include those of the **St Ives Pleasure Boat Association** (07821-774178).

Sleeping

Primrose Valley HOTEL £££
(01736-794939; www.primroseonline.co.uk; Porthminster Beach; d £105-155, ste £175-225; P wi-fi) A swash of style on the St Ives seafront. The rooms of the Edwardian house are all deliberately different: some chase a faintly maritime theme, with pale pine and soothing blues, while others plump for rich fabrics, cappuccino throws and exposed brick. It's full of spoils – therapy room, metro-modern bar, locally sourced breakfasts – and needless to say, the sea views are great.

Boskerris HOTEL ££
(01736-795295; www.boskerrishotel.co.uk; Boskerris Rd; d £130-195; P wi-fi) This Carbis Bay beauty is a favourite with the weekend supplements: a 1930s guesthouse that has had a metro-minimalist makeover. Cool monotones contrast with bespoke wallpaper, artful scatter cushions, shell-shaped chandeliers or curvy lamps; bay views extend in grandstand style from the floaty patio.

Treliska B&B ££
(01736-797678; www.treliska.com; 3 Bedford Rd; d £60-80; wi-fi) The smooth decor at this B&B is attractive – chrome taps, wooden furniture, cool sinks – but what really sells it is the fantastic position, literally steps from St Ives' centre.

Organic Panda B&B ££
(01736 793890; www.organicpanda.co.uk; 1 Pednolver Tce; d £80-120; wi-fi) Sleep with a clear conscience at this elegant B&B, run along all-organic lines. Spotty cushions, technicolour artwork and timber-salvage beds keep the funk factor high, and local artists showcase their works on the walls. The lack of parking's a pain, though.

11 Sea View Terrace B&B ££
(01736-798440; www.11stives.co.uk; 11 Sea View Tce; d £100-120; P) Creams, checks and cappuccino carpets distinguish this chic St Ives B&B. The two front rooms have lovely town and sea views, while the rear one overlooks a garden patio; for more space there's a smart holiday flat (£500 to £925 per week).

Eating

St Ives' harbourside is awash with brasseries, but the back lanes conceal plenty of tempting options too.

TOP CHOICE **Porthminster Beach Café** BISTRO ££
(☎01736-795352; www.porthminstercafe.co.uk; Porthminster Beach; lunch £10.50-16.50, dinner £10-22; ⊙9am-10pm) Fresh from scooping top prize in a recent survey to find Britain's top coastal cafe, the Porthminster boasts a sexy Riviera vibe, a suntrap patio and a seasonal menu ranging from Provençal fish soup to pan-fried scallops. The result? Cornwall's top beach cafe, bar none.

Alba RESTAURANT ££
(☎01736-797222; Old Lifeboat House; mains £11-18; ⊙lunch & dinner) Split-level sophistication next to the lifeboat house, serving some of the best seafood this side of Padstow. In-the-know locals bag tables 5, 6 or 7 for their gorgeous harbour views.

Loft RESTAURANT ££
(☎01736-794204; www.theloftrestaurantandterrace.co.uk; Norway Ln; dinner £10.95-19.95; ⊙lunch & dinner) Great new tip hidden away in a fisherman's net loft just behind the Sloop Craft Centre. The dining room's set out attic-style under A-frame beams, and window tables peep out over St Ives slate rooftops. Solid seafood, locally sourced meat, Cornish game, delivered with a minimum of fuss or frills: lovely.

Blas Burgerworks CAFE £
(The Warren; burgers £5-10; ⊙dinner Tue-Sun) This pocket-sized burger joint has a big reputation: sustainable sourcing, eco-friendly packaging and lots of wacky burger variations have earned it a loyal following. Traditionalists go for the 6oz, 100%-beef Blasburger, while veggies might plump for a halloumi stack or a ginger, coriander and chilli tofuburger.

Onshore PIZZA ££
(☎01736-796000; The Wharf; pizzas £8-16; ⊙lunch & dinner) Pizza, pizza and more pizza; woodfired and award-winning, with super harbour views from the front deck.

Drinking

Hub CAFE
(www.hub-stives.co.uk; The Wharf) As its name suggests, the open-plan Hub is the heart of St Ives' (admittedly limited) nightlife. Think frothy lattes by day, cocktails and boutique beers after-dark, plus sliding doors that open onto the harbour when the sun shines.

Sloop Inn PUB
(The Wharf) A classic fishermen's boozer, complete with low ceilings, tankards behind the bar and a comprehensive selection of Cornish ales.

Entertainment

Crow Rooms VENUE
(www.thecrowrooms.co.uk; Tregenna Hill) The old Isobar has gone under and come up again as this grungy rehearsal space and gig venue – check the website for forthcoming events.

Royal Cinema CINEMA
(www.merlincinemas.co.uk; Royal Sq) Shows new films and often has cheap matinees.

Guildhall CONCERT VENUE
(1 Street-An-Pol) Hosts music and theatre, especially during the St Ives September Festival.

Information

Library (☎01736-795377; 1 Gabriel St; per hr £3; ⊙9.30am-9.30pm Tue, to 6pm Wed-Fri, to 12.30pm Sat) Internet access.

St Ives Info (www.stives-cornwall.co.uk) Official town website with accommodation and activity guides.

Tourist office (☎01736-796297; ivtic@penwith.gov.uk; Street-an-Pol; ⊙9am-5.30pm Mon-Fri, 9am-5pm Sat, 10am-4pm Sun) Inside Guildhall.

Getting There & Away

Bus

Quickest bus to **Penzance** is bus 17 (30 minutes, twice hourly Monday to Saturday, hourly on Sunday). In summer the open-top 300 takes the scenic route via Zennor, Land's End and St Just.

Train

The gorgeous branch line from St Ives is worth taking just for the coastal views: trains terminate at **St Erth** (£3, 14 minutes, half-hourly), where you can catch connections along the Penzance–Paddington main line.

Zennor

POP 217

For one of Cornwall's most stunning drives, follow the twisting B3306 coast road all the way from St Ives to the windswept village of **Zennor** (let's be honest – the coast road's none too shabby, either). The village itself is little more than a collection of cottages collected around the medieval church of **St Senara**. Inside, a famous carved chair depicts the legendary Mermaid of Zennor, who is said to have fallen in love with the singing voice of local lad Matthew Trewhella; it's said you can still sometimes hear them singing down at nearby Pendour Cove.

The **Wayside Folk Museum** (admission £3; ⏲10.30am-5pm Sun-Fri May-Sep, 11am-5pm Sun-Fri Apr & Oct) houses a treasure trove of artefacts gathered by inveterate collector Colonel 'Freddie' Hirst in the 1930s. The displays range from blacksmiths' hammers and cobblers' tools to an 18th-century kitchen and two reclaimed watermills.

Even if you normally don't 'do' dorms, the **Old Chapel Backpackers Hostel** (☎01736-98307; dm/f £15/50; P) is a top sleeping spot. Set in a sensitively renovated former church, the smart rooms sleep four to six – ask for one with a sea view. There's a comfy, high-ceilinged cafe and lounge, too.

DH Lawrence's local while he lived at Zennor was the **Tinner's Arms** (☎01736-792697; lunch £7-10), a classic Cornish inn with a rambling main bar sheltering under a slate roof.

St Just-in-Penwith

Beyond Zennor, the Penwith landscape really starts to feel big, wild and empty. Blustery cliffs, lonely fields and heather-clad hills unfurl along the horizon en route to the stern granite mining town of **St Just** and the rocky promontory of **Cape Cornwall**, a notorious shipwreck spot in centuries past, now guarded by the blinking lighthouse at **Pendeen Watch**.

Sights

It's hard to imagine today, but the St Just area was once at the heart of Cornwall's booming tin and copper mining industry.

Geevor Tin Mine MINE
(☎01736-788662; www.geevor.com; adult/child £9.50/4.50; ⏲9am-5pm Sun-Fri Mar-Oct, 9am-4pm Sun-Fri Nov-Feb) Just north of St Just near Pendeen, this historic mine closed in 1990 and now provides an amazing insight into the dark and dangerous conditions in which Cornwall's miners worked. You can view the dressing floors and much of the original machinery used to sort the minerals and ores, before taking a tour deep into some of the underground shafts. Claustrophobes need not apply.

Levant Mine & Beam Engine MINE
(www.nationaltrust.org.uk/main/w-levantmineandbeamengine; adult/child £5.80/2.90; ⏲11am-5pm Tue-Fri & Sun Jul-Sep, Wed-Fri & Sun Jun, Wed & Fri Apr-May & Oct) More mining heritage comes to life at this National Trust–owned mine, one of the world's only working Cornish beam engines.

Botallack Mine MINE
Clinging to the cliffs near Levant Mine, one of Cornwall's most dramatic engine houses, which has abandoned mine shafts extending right out beneath the raging Atlantic waves.

Getting There & Away

St Just is 6 miles north of Land's End. Buses 17/17A/17B travel from **St Ives** (1¼ hours) via **Penzance** (half-hourly Monday to Saturday, five on Sunday).

Sennen & Land's End

Further west, the coastline peaks and plunges all the way into the sandy scoop of **Sennen**, which overlooks one of Penwith's most stunning stretches of sand on **Whitesand Bay** (pronounced Whitsand).

From here, there's a wonderful stretch of coast path that leads for about a mile-and-a-half along the clifftops all the way to **Land's End**, the westernmost point of mainland England, where the coal-black cliffs plunge dramatically down into the pounding surf, and the views stretch all the way to the Isles of Scilly on a clear day.

Unfortunately, the decision to build the **Legendary Land's End** (☎0870 458 0099; www.landsend-landmark.co.uk; adult/child £11/7; ⏲10am-4pm or 5pm Easter-Oct, 10.30am-3.30pm Nov-Easter) theme park just behind the headland in the 1980s hasn't done much to enhance the view. Take our advice: skip the tacky multimedia shows and opt for an exhilarating clifftop stroll instead.

Land's End is 9 miles from Penzance. Bus 1/1A travels from Penzance (one hour, eight daily, five on Saturday) to Land's End; half the buses go via Sennen, the other half via Treen and Porthcurno. In summer, the number 300 double-decker runs three or five times daily taking in Penzance, St Ives and all the main Penwith spots.

Mousehole

The compact harbour town Mousehole (pronounced *mowzle*) was once at the heart of Cornwall's thriving pilchard industry,

WORTH A TRIP

GURNARD'S HEAD

Pubs don't get much more remote than the gorgeous **Gurnard's Head** (☎01736-796928; www.gurnardshead.co.uk; lunch £5.50-12, dinner £12.50-16.50; ⌚12.30-2.30pm & 6.30-9.30pm). It's flung 6 miles out along the Zennor coast road, but don't worry about missing it – it's the only building for miles around, and has its name spelled out in huge white letters on the roof. Having been taken over by renowned pub–hoteliers the Inkin brothers (who previously developed the equally swish Felin Fach Griffin near Hay-on-Wye) it's become one of Cornwall's top gastropubs. Book-lined shelves, sepia prints, scruffy wood and rough stone walls create a reassuringly lived-in feel, and the menu's crammed with cockle-warming fare – haddock and mash, spring lamb and belly pork, followed by lashings of Eton Mess or sticky marmalade pudding. If you feel like overnighting, there are country-cosy rooms (doubles without dinner £90 to £160, with dinner for two £135 to £205) upstairs with views of nothing but farms and fields.

but these days it's better known for its colourful Christmas lights.

With a tightly packed knot of slate-roofed cottages gathered around the picturesque harbour, Mousehole is one of Cornwall's most appealing villages, but the picture-perfect location has its drawbacks: huge numbers of second homes means the village is practically a ghost town out of season. It's also the traditional home of 'stargazey pie', a pilchard pie in which the fish-heads are left poking up through the pie's crust. It's traditionally eaten on Tom Bawcock's Eve (23 December), named after a local lad who reputedly rescued the town from a famine by braving stormy seas to land a bumper haul of pilchards.

To stay the night, set yourself up at the **Old Coastguard Hotel** (☎01736-731222; www.oldcoastguardhotel.co.uk; d £140-210), a swish seaside hotel with jaw-dropping sea views on the edge of Mousehole. The sunlit restaurant (mains £10.50 to £16) also looks out over the glittering bay and specialises, unsurprisingly, in fantastic seafood.

Bus 6 makes the 20-minute journey to Penzance half-hourly.

Penzance

POP 21,168

Stretching along the glittering sweep of Mount's Bay, Penzance has been the last stop on the main railway line from London since the days of the Great Western Railway. With its hotchpotch of winding streets, old shopping arcades and its grand seafront promenade, Penzance is much more authentic than the polished-up, prettified towns of Padstow and St Ives, and makes an excellent base for exploring the rest of west Cornwall and Land's End.

Sights

Despite what you may have heard from Messrs Gilbert and Sullivan, Penzance was never renowned for its pirates – instead it was famous for trading in tin, grain and pilchards. The export trade brought riches and the old town is littered with elegant Georgian and Regency houses, especially around Chapel St; hunt down the 19th-century **Egyptian House**, which looks like a bizarre cross between a Georgian town house and an Egyptian sarcophagus.

Penlee House Gallery & Museum GALLERY
(www.penleehouse.org.uk; Morrab Rd; adult/child £3/2; ⌚10am-5pm Mon-Sat May-Sep, 10.30am-4.30pm Mon-Sat Oct-Apr) Penzance's historic art gallery displays a fine range of paintings by artists of the Newlyn School (including Stanhope Forbes) and hosts regular exhibitions on Cornwall's art history. Admission is free on Saturday.

Jubilee Pool SWIMMING POOL
(www.jubileepool.co.uk; adult/child/family £4/2.90/12.20; ⌚10.30am-6pm May-Sep) At the eastern end of Penzance's 19th-century promenade, the glorious 1930s lido is a fantastic place for a summer dip. Since falling into disrepair in the 1980s, it's been thoroughly spruced up and is now open to al fresco bathers throughout the summer – just don't expect the water to be warm. Entry is half-price after 3.30pm.

FREE **Newlyn Art Gallery** GALLERY
(www.newlynartgallery.co.uk; ⌚10am-5pm Mon-Sat Easter-Sep, Wed-Sat Oct-Easter) The salty old harbour of Newlyn, on the

western edge of Penzance, is known for two things: art and fishing. It's still one of the UK's busiest fishing ports, and there are plenty of shops dotted around the town where you can pick up fresh-cooked lobster, crab and seafood literally straight off the boats. During the 19th century, Newlyn was also the centre of the Newlyn School of artists, a group of figurative painters headed by Stanhope Forbes and his wife Elizabeth. The town's artistic connections live on at this contemporary art gallery.

FREE **Exchange** GALLERY
(www.theexchangegallery.co.uk; Princes Street, Penzance; ⏲10am-5pm Mon-Sat Easter-Sep, Wed-Sat Oct-Easter) Housed in Penzance's old telecoms building, this is the sister gallery to the Newlyn Art Gallery. The pulsating light installation outside is by the artist Peter Freeman, and is best seen after dark.

St Michael's Mount MONUMENT
(NT; ☎01736-710507; castle & gardens adult/child £8.75/4.25; ⏲10.30am-5.30pm Sun-Fri late-Mar–Oct) Looming up from the waters of Mount's Bay is the unmistakeable silhouette of St Michael's Mount, one of Cornwall's most iconic landmarks. Set on a craggy island connected to the mainland by a cobbled causeway, there's been a monastery here since at least the 5th century, but the present abbey largely dates from the 12th century. After the Norman conquest, the Benedictine monks of Mont St Michel in Normandy raised a new chapel on the island in 1135, and the abbey later became the family seat of the aristocratic St Aubyns (who still reside here).

It's now under the stewardship of the National Trust. Highlights include the rococo drawing room, the original armoury, the 14th-century priory church and the abbey's subtropical gardens, which teeter dramatically above the sea. You can walk across the causeway at low tide, or catch a ferry at high tide in the summer from the little town of Marazion, three miles from Penzance.

Sleeping

Penzance has lots of low-price B&Bs, especially along Alexandra Rd and Morrab Rd.

Summer House B&B ££
(☎01736-363744; www.summerhouse-cornwall.com; Cornwall Tce; d £120-150; ⏲closed Nov-Mar; P) For a touch of Chelsea-on-Sea, check into this elegant Regency house. Checks, pinstripes and cheery colours characterise the five bedrooms, and downstairs there's a Mediterranean restaurant with al fresco terrace.

Abbey Hotel HOTEL £££
(☎01736 366906; www.theabbeyonline.co.uk; Abbey St; d £130-200)
This superbly creaky sea-captain's house just off Chapel Street offers a tempting taste of Penzance in its 18th-century heyday. It's brimming with heritage touches – antique dressers, wonky corridors, canopied beds – and a couple of rooms even have their bathrooms tucked away in the cupboard. There's a divine garden out back that's perfect for an early evening tipple.

Camilla House B&B ££
(☎01736 363771; www.camillahouse.co.uk; 12 Regent Tce; s £37.50, d £75-95; P)
One of several quality B&Bs on Regent's Terrace, this old-fashioned five-starrer stands out for its classy rooms, period features

MINACK THEATRE

In terms of theatrical settings, the **Minack** (☎01736-810181; www.minack.com) really has to take top billing. Carved directly into the crags overlooking Porthcurno Bay and the azure-blue Atlantic, this amazing clifftop amphitheatre was the lifelong passion of local lady Rowena Cade, who dreamt up the idea in the 1930s and oversaw the theatre until her death in 1983. It's now a hugely popular place for al fresco theatre, with a 17-week season running from mid-May to mid-September: regulars bring wine, picnic supplies, wet-weather gear and – most importantly of all, considering the seats are carved out of granite – a very comfy cushion.

Above the theatre, the **visitor centre** (adult/child £3.50/1.40; ⏲9.30am-5.30pm Apr-Sep, 10am-4pm Oct-Mar) recounts the theatre's history; it's closed when there's a matinée.

The Minack is three miles from Land's End and 9 miles from Penzance. Bus 1/1A from Penzance stops several times daily.

Penzance

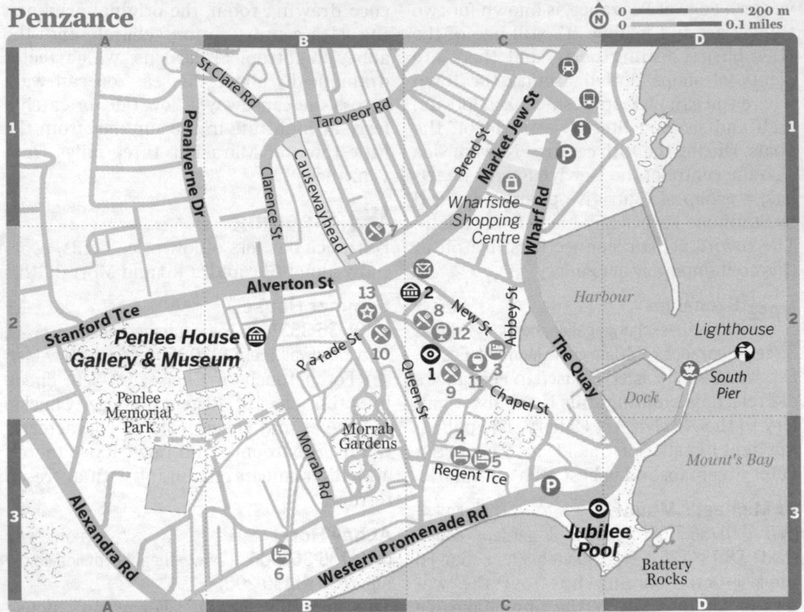

and eco-conscious stance. Fluffy bathrobes, pillow treats and views over the prom will tempt you, too.

Chy-an-Mor B&B ££

(☎01736-363441; www.chyanmor.co.uk; Regent Tce; s £40-42, d £75-88; P) The fallback option on Regent's Terrace – starting to show its age in places, but really friendly. The rooms are rather heavy on the flock and frills, but there's a lovely lounge and homemade marmalade on the breakfast table.

Penzance YHA HOSTEL £

(penzance@yha.org.uk; Castle Horneck, Alverton; dm £14; P @) Housed inside an 18th-century Georgian manor on the outskirts of town, this official hostel has an on-site cafe, laundry and four- to 10-bed dorms. Buses 5 and 6 run from the bus station to Alverton; it's a 500m walk from the bus stop.

Eating

Chapel Street Brasserie BISTR ££

(☎01736-350222; 13 Chapel St; mains £10-15; ⌚10am-11pm) Formerly Bar Coco's, this well-groomed Gallic bistro makes the perfect place for a hearty plate of French food, from steaming bowls of mussels to rich cassoulet. The 2-course *prix fixe* menu is super value at £12.50, and it's served at lunch and supper.

Bakehouse BISTRO ££

(☎01736-331331; www.bakehouserestaurant.co.uk; Chapel Str; mains £8.95-19.50; ⌚lunch Wed-Sat, dinner daily) This funky double-floored diner is tucked down an alley just down the street from the Chapel Street Brasserie. Seafood-lovers and veggies are both catered for, but it's the carnivores who do best: copious steak choices are partnered with your choice of sauce or spicy rub.

Archie Brown's CAFE £

(☎01736-362828; Bread St; mains £3-10; ⌚9.30am-5pm Mon-Sat) A cosier wholefood caff you couldn't hope to find. Archie Brown's has been serving Penzance's earth-mothers and artsy crowd for years and shows no signs of flagging, with stocked-up counters full of crispy salads, veggie quiches and carrot cake.

Honey Pot CAFE £

(☎01736-368686; 5 Parade St; mains £4-10; ⌚9am-5pm Mon-Sat) Another wonderfully friendly Penzance cafe, opposite the Acorn Arts Centre. It's a popular spot for afternoon tea and cake, but also turns out tempting fare such as jacket potatoes and homemade homity pies. Naturally, nearly everything's made on site and locally sourced, and the big glass windows keep it sunny and light-filled.

Penzance

Top Sights

Jubilee Pool C3
Penlee House Gallery & Museum B2

Sights

1 Egyptian House C2
2 Exchange C2

Sleeping

3 Abbey Hotel C2
4 Camilla House C3
5 Chy-an-Mor C3
6 Summer House B3

Eating

7 Archie Brown's B2
8 Bakehouse C2
9 Brasserie C2
10 Honey Pot B2

Drinking

11 Turk's Head C2
12 Zero Lounge C2

Entertainment

13 Acorn Arts Centre B2

Drinking & Entertainment

Turk's Head PUB
(Chapel St) They pull a fine pint of real ale at this, the oldest boozer in Penzance. It's said a smugglers' tunnel used to link the pub with the harbour – handy for sneaking in that liquid contraband – and the bar's covered in maritime memorabilia.

Zero Lounge BAR
(Chapel St) More urban chic than olde-worlde, this open-plan bar also boasts the town's best beer patio.

Acorn Arts Centre THEATRE
(www.acornartscentre.co.uk; Parade St) An excellent independent arts centre, with regular programs of film, theatre and live music.

Information

Library (Morrab Rd; per hr £3; 9.30am-6pm Mon-Fri, to 4pm Sat) Internet access.

Penzance Online (www.penzance.co.uk) Useful local guide.

Tourist office (01736-362207; penzancetic@cornwall.gov.uk; Station Approach; 9am-5pm Mon-Sat, 10am-1pm Sun) Next to the bus station.

Getting There & Away

For travel to the Isles of Scilly, see p393.

Bus

Penzance is the main local bus hub for the Penwith area.

Helston (45 minutes, six to eight daily) Buses 2/2A/2B; via Marazion and Praa Sands.

St Ives (30 minutes, twice hourly Monday to Saturday, hourly on Sunday) Buses 17/17A/17B.

Truro (one hour, four daily Monday to Saturday) Bus X18; express service.

Train

Penzance is the last stop on the main rail route from Paddington. Sample fares:

Bodmin (£8.40, 1¼ hours)
Bristol (£37, four hours)
Exeter (£11.50, three hours)
London Paddington (£57.50, hourly, 5½ hours)
St Ives (£3.30, 30 minutes)
Truro (£5.40, 30 minutes)

The Lizard

For a taste of Cornwall's stormier side, head for the ink-black cliffs, rugged coves and open heaths of the Lizard Peninsula. Windlashed in winter, in summer it bristles with wildflowers, butterflies and coves that are perfect for a secluded swim.

The Lizard used to be at the centre of Cornwall's smuggling industry and is still alive with tales of Cornish 'free-traders', contraband liquor and the government's preventive boats. The most notorious excise dodger was John Carter, the so-called King of Prussia – Prussia Cove near Marazion is named after him. It was also an ill famed graveyard for ships – more vessels have come to grief on the Lizard's treacherous reefs than almost anywhere else in Britain.

While you're exploring the Lizard, look out for the giant satellite dishes on Goonhilly Downs – they're some of the world's largest, and still play an important role in the UK's transatlantic telecommunications.

Sights & Activities

Helston & Porthleven

The Lizard's main town is **Helston**, which is famous for its annual street party, Flora Day, held on 8 May. This ancient festival is a mix of street dance, musical parade and floral pageant: the two main events are the

Hal-An-Tow, in which St Michael and the devil do battle, and the Furry Dance, which kicks off at noon and proceeds around the town's streets.

Three miles southwest of Helston is **Porthleven**, a former fishing port with a burgeoning foodie scene, epitomised by the bustling Wednesday morning market and the **Porthleven Food Festival** (www.porthlevenfoodfestival.co.uk).

The Loe

A mile south of Porthleven is the treacherous sandbank of **Loe Bar** – scene of many a shipwreck – and **Loe Pool**, Cornwall's largest freshwater lake, said by some to be the resting place of King Arthur's magical blade, Excalibur.

River Helford

The **River Helford** flows across the north of the Lizard. Lined with overhanging oaks and hidden inlets, it's the perfect smugglers' hideaway. **Frenchman's Creek**, the inspiration for Daphne du Maurier's novel of the same name, can be reached on foot from the car park in **Helford** village.

From the quayside, **Helford River Boats** (01326-250770; www.helford-river-boats.co.uk; adult/child s £4/2; ⏲9.30am-9.30pm Jun-Aug, 9.30am-5.30pm Apr-May & Sep-Oct) runs pedestrian ferries across the water to Helford Passage (near Falmouth).

National Seal Sanctuary WILDLIFE

(☎0871-423-2110; www.sealsanctuary.co.uk; adult/child £10.95/6.95; ⏲10am-5pm May-Sep, 9am-4pm Oct-Apr) Six miles from Helston at the western end of the Helford River, this sanctuary cares for sick and orphaned seals washed up along the Cornish coastline before returning them to the wild.

Lizard Lighthouse Heritage Centre LANDMARK, MUSEUM

(www.lizardlighthouse.co.uk; adult/child £4/2; ⏲Sun-Thu most of year, plus extra days in summer) Right at the tip of the peninsula is **Lizard Point**, the southernmost point in England. The vista from the surrounding cliffs is breathtaking, but it's especially worth a visit for this maritime museum, housed in a historic lighthouse built in 1751. The museum explores the Lizard's connections with smuggling, shipwrecks and nautical navigation: you even get the chance to climb up into the tower and, if you're lucky, let off a deafening blast from the foghorn.

Kynance Cove

A little way up the coast from the point is the lovely National Trust–owned Kynance Cove, sprinkled with caves and offshore islands. Much of the red-green serpentine rock fashionable during the Victorian era was mined here.

Sleeping

Chydane B&B ££

(☎01326-241232; www.chydane.co.uk; Gunwalloe; s/d £50/100; P 📶) This much-touted Lizard B&B teeters on the cliff edge right above Gunwalloe Cove, and both rooms peep over the beach and bay beyond (although the window in the Porthole Room is, as it's name suggests, tiny). Elsewhere, there are plenty of local books to browse in the lounge, and a panoramic patio where the coastal vistas truly dazzle; and the excellent Halzephron Inn is only a short walk away.

Beacon Crag B&B ££

(☎01326-573690; www.beaconcrag.com; d £85-95; P @) Built for a local artist, this Victorian villa above Porthleven is now one of the Lizard's loveliest B&Bs. Rooms are plainly furnished to make the most of the house's grandstand position: craggy coastline unfurls in abundance around the house.

Lizard YHA HOSTEL £

(lizard@yha.org.uk; dm £14; ⏲Apr-Oct) Wow – this absolutely marvellous hostel commands the kind of sea view you'd normally have to pay through the nose for. Housed in former lighthouse-keepers' cottages, it's quite simply one of the most spectacularly situated hostels anywhere in England.

Coverack YHA HOSTEL £

(coverack@yha.org.uk; Coverack; dm from £14; ⏲Mar-Oct) Set above the pretty harbour of Coverack, this was a decent hostel even before its recent refit. Five of the nine bedrooms are now en suite (making them a great B&B alternative) and the setting in a Victorian clifftop villa surrounded by private grounds is simply out of this world.

Eating

TOP CHOICE **Kota** RESTAURANT ££

(☎01326-562407; www.kotarestaurant.co.uk; Porthleven; mains £11.50-19.95; ⏲lunch Fri & Sat, dinner Mon-Sat) Not what you'd expect to find in the rural Lizard: an adventurous fusion restaurant run by a chef with Malay, Maori and Chinese roots. Hunkering under the hefty beams of an old mill on Porthleven's harbour, Jude Kereama's restaurant serves some of Cornwall's most exotic flavours, with Szechuan, Thai and Malaysian spices all finding their way into the mix. There's a two-course menu on offer for £14 from 5.30pm to 7pm. Well worth the trip.

Halzephron Inn PUB ££
(☎01326-240406; www.halzephron-inn.co.uk; mains £10.95-18.50) Hugger-mugger inn balanced on the cliffs above Gunwalloe. Forget fancy furnishings and designer food – this is a proper old Cornish local, full of old-time charm, with proper ales, filling food and a homely atmosphere.

Lizard Pasty Shop PASTIE £
(☎01326-290889; www.annspastics.co.uk; The Lizard; pasties £2.75, ⏰Tue-Sat) Looking for Cornwall's best pasties? Head for Ann Muller's shop, attached to her house near Lizard Point. The recipes are 100% authentic and the ingredients are 100% Cornish – little wonder Rick Stein's given them his seal of approval.

Getting There & Away

Buses are the only public transport option on the Lizard.

Bus 2 Penzance to Falmouth, with stops at Porthleven and Helston (eight to ten Monday to Saturday, six on Sunday).

Bus 32 Helston to Gunwalloe, Gweek, Coverack and St Keverne (two on Sundays only).

Bus 33 Helston to Poldhu, Mullion and the Lizard (three daily Monday to Friday).

Bus 82 Helston to Truro (hourly Monday to Saturday, five on Sunday).

Falmouth

POP 20,775

The maritime port of Falmouth sits on the county's south coast at the end of the Carrick Roads, a huge river estuary that empties into the third deepest natural harbour in the world. Falmouth's fortunes were made during the 18th and 19th centuries, when clippers, trading vessels and mail packets from across the world stopped off to unload their cargoes, and the town remains an important centre for shipbuilding and repairs. These days, however, it's better known for its lively nightlife and the newly built campus of the UCF (University College Falmouth), located a few miles up the road in Penryn.

Sights & Activities

National Maritime Museum MUSEUM
(www.nmmc.co.uk; Discovery Quay; adult/child £9.50/6.50; ⏰10am-5pm; 📶) This museum is home to one of the largest maritime collections in the UK, second only to its sister museum in Greenwich in London. At the heart of the complex is the Flotilla Gallery, where a collection of groundbreaking boats dangle from the ceiling on slender steel wires. Other highlights include the Nav Station, a hands-on exhibit exploring nautical navigation, the Tidal Zone, where underwater windows peer into the depths, and the Look Out, offering a 360-degree panorama of Falmouth Bay.

Pendennis Castle CASTLE
(EH; ☎01326-316594; adult/child £5.40/2.70; ⏰10am-6pm Jul & Aug, 10am-5pm Apr-Jun & Sep, 10am-4pm Oct-Mar) On the promontory of Pendennis Point, this classic Tudor castle was built by Henry VIII to defend the entrance to the Fal estuary in tandem with its sister fortress at St Mawes (p388), on the opposite side. Don't miss the superbly atmospheric Tudor gun deck (complete with cannon flashes, smoke and shouted commands), the WWI guard house and the WWII observation post.

Boat Trips
Passenger ferries make the harbour-mouth dash across to St Mawes and Flushing every hour in summer. For a longer trip, several operators run from the Prince of Wales Pier or Customs House Quay along the Fal River, making stops at National Trust–owned Trelissick Gardens, the 500-year-old Smuggler's Cottage pub and Truro. Try **Enterprise Boats** (☎01326-374241; www.enterprise-boats.co.uk) or **Newman's Cruises** (☎01872-580309; www.newmanscruises.co.uk).

Beaches
Falmouth has three main beaches. The nearest beach to town is busy **Gyllyngvase**, a short walk from the town centre, where you'll find plenty of flat sand and a decent beach cafe. Further around the headland, **Swanpool** and **Maenporth** are usually quieter. The regular Bus 500 from Falmouth stops at all three.

Trebah GARDENS
(☎01326-252200; www.trebahgarden.co.uk; adult/child £7.50/2.50 Mar-Oct, £3/1 Nov-Feb; ⏰10.30am-6.30pm, last entry 4.30pm) Two of Cornwall's great gardens sit side by side

THE FERRYBOAT INN

Having taken over the reins at the Duchy Oyster Farm along the river, the UK's leading oyster merchants, the Wright Brothers, have given the creekside **Ferryboat Inn** (☎01326-250625; Helford Passage; mains £8-18; ⏲lunch & dinner) a complete rethink. Gone are the dated furnishings of old; in comes sleek wood, glossy slate and a refreshing open-plan feel, plus a proper gastropub menu. It's expensive, but for a romantic twilight drink it's pretty unbeatable: the front patio overlooks the languid waters of the Helford, and there's even a little sandy beach that's tailor-made for a post-pint paddle.

along the northern bank of the Helford River, both of which can be visited by taking a day-trip from Falmouth. Trebah, first planted in 1840, is one of Cornwall's finest subtropical gardens, dramatically situated in a steep ravine filled with giant rhododendrons, huge Brazilian rhubarb plants and jungle ferns.

Glendurgan GARDENS
(NT; ☎01326-250906; adult/child £6/3; ⏲10.30am-5.30pm Tue-Sat Feb-Oct) Next door to Trebah, this garden was established in the 18th century by the wealthy Fox family, who imported exotic plants from the New World. Look out for the stunning views of the River Helford, the 19th-century maze and the secluded beach near Durgan village. The garden is also open on Mondays in July and August.

Sleeping

Falmouth has plenty of B&Bs and hotels, especially around Melvill Rd and Avenue Rd.

Falmouth Townhouse HOTEL ££
(☎01326-312009; www.thefalmouthtownhouse.co.uk; Grove Place; d £85-120;) The choice for the design-conscious, in an elegant mansion halfway between the high street and Discovery Quay. Despite the heritage building, the feel is studiously modernist: slate greys, retro bits and bobs and funky scatter cushions throughout, plus walk-in showers and king-size tellies in the top-of-the-line rooms.

St Michael's Hotel HOTEL £££
(☎01326-312707; www.stmichaelshotel.co.uk; r £129-333; P) One of a string of places along the Falmouth seafront, but St Michael's stands head and shoulders above the rest. Comprehensive renovations have reinvented the bedrooms in gingham checks, stripes and slatted wood, giving them a feel akin to a New England beach retreat, and the whole place is sprinkled with maritime touches, from portholes in the doors to a soothing palette of sea greens and bottle blues.

Hawthorne Dene Hotel B&B ££
(☎01326-311427; www.hawthornedenehotel.co.uk; 12 Pennance Rd; d £80-90; P) Edwardian elegance rules the roost at this family-run hotel, with its ranks of old photos and booklined gentlemen's lounge. The antique-themed bedrooms feature springy beds, polished woods and teddy bears – most also have a sea view.

Chelsea House B&B ££
(☎01326-212230; www.chelseahousehotel.com; 2 Emslie Rd; d £63-73) On a terrace of tucked-away B&Bs just off the seafront, the Chelsea's attractive rooms include a 'Ships and Castle' family suite, spacious 'Pendennis' with a sea-view bay window and a minuscule 'Captain's Cabin' in the attic.

Falmouth Backpacker's HOSTEL £
(⏲01326-319996; www.falmouthbackpackers.co.uk; 9 Gyllyngvase Terrace; dm/s £19/25, d £50-60) New owners have given this old Falmouth hostel a new lease of life, and its rooms are now much enlivened with bright colours, cosy beds and the odd funky print. There's an Aga in the kitchen and a DVD lounge, but the real asset is owner Judy, who's full of fizzy fun and often lays on BBQs and paella nights.

Greenbank HOTEL £
(☎01326-312440; www.greenbank-hotel.co.uk; Harbourside; s £95-105, d £145-185; P) It's a bit overpriced, but for harbour views the venerable Greenbank is still the choice. Inside it's old meets new: nautical knick-knacks and ships in cabinets meet beige carpets, pine furniture and cappuccino-and-cream colour combos. The cheaper rooms are looking tired, so it's worth splashing on an 'Executive Harbour' room.

Eating & Drinking

TOP CHOICE **Cove** RESTAURANT £££
(☎01326-251136; www.thecovemaenporth.co.uk; Maenporth; mains £14.25-22.50; ⏰lunch & dinner) It's a trek down to Maenporth, but you'll be more than happy you made the effort. This gorgeous and much garlanded modern fine diner has earned a big reputation thanks to the creative talents of head man Arty Williams, who imparts his own individual spin on contemporary Brit cuisine. The pièce de la resistance is the glorious beach-view deck: reserve well ahead.

Oliver's RESTAURANT ££
(☎01326-218138; 33 High St; mains £12.95-19.95; ⏰lunch & dinner Tue-Sun) There's nothing remotely fancy about the decor at this new French-style bistro – it's plain pine meets plain white walls – but here simplicity is definitely a virtue. The food is classic, unfussy and impeccably presented, with the emphasis placed on essential flavours rather than cheffy flourishes. It's particularly strong on seafood.

Gylly Beach Café CAFE ££
(☎01326-312884; www.gyllybeach.com; Gyllyngvase Beach; mains £10.95-15.95; ⏰breakfast, lunch & dinner) The decked patio over Gyllyngvase is the main draw at this lively beach restaurant. It covers all bases: fry-ups and pancakes for brekkie, platters of antipasti for lunch, quality steak, seafood and pasta after dark. It's open late for drinks, too, but gets very busy.

Indaba on the Beach RESTAURANT £££
(☎01326-311886; www.indabafish.co.uk; Swanpool; mains £10.50-37.95; ⏰lunch daily, dinner Mon-Sat) The former Three Mackerel has recently been snapped up by the folk behind Indaba Fish in Truro. It offers the same upmarket seafood menu from mussels to full-blown lobster platters, with the added benefit of a top-drawer position on the rocks above Swanpool.

Stein's Fish & Chips CAFE ££
(☎01841-532700; Discovery Quay; £6.65-10.95; ⏰12-2.30pm & 5-9pm) It had to happen – the Stein empire is spreading. Offering the same menu as his Padstow original (top-quality battered fish fried in beef dripping, or fish grilled in sunflower oil, both accompanied with hand-cut chips), Stein's Falmouth fish-and-chip shop has the addition of a snazzy **oyster bar** (mains £3.50-15.50; ⏰5-9pm) on the top floor. Pricey, mind.

Provedore CAFE £
(www.provedore.co.uk; 43 Trelawney Rd; mains £4-10; ⏰9am-4pm Tue & Wed, 9am-4pm & 6-10pm Thu & Fri, 9am-1.30pm Sat) Cool continental cafe serving Falmouth's best coffee and tapas.

Boathouse GASTROPUB ££
(Trevethan Hill; mains £6-12; ⏰lunch & dinner) Groovy gastropub with a ship's galley feel, and a deck overlooking the river to Flushing.

Harbour Lights CAFE £
(Arwenack St; ⏰11:30am-8pm Mon-Thu & Sun, 11.30am-9pm Fri & Sat) Falmouth's long-standing chippie is considerably cheaper than the Stein equivalent.

Drinking

Top spots for a pint include the **Quayside** (Arwenack St), with outside seating on the harbour, and the **Chain Locker** (Quay St), crammed with maritime atmosphere.

Information

Falmouth Tourist Office (☎01326 312300, falmouthtic@yahoo.co.uk; 11 Market Strand, Prince of Wales Pier; ⏰9.30am-5.15pm Mon-Sat) On the pier.

Getting There & Away

Bus

Falmouth is well served by buses.

Glendurgan, the Helford Passage and Gweek (nine or ten daily Monday to Saturday, two on Sunday) Bus 35. Some services continue to Helston.

Truro (hourly) Bus 88; fastest option.

WORTH A TRIP

PANDORA INN

One of Cornwall's oldest and loveliest creekside pubs, the **Pandora Inn** (☎01326-372678; www.pandorainn.com; Restronguet Creek; mains £10-16) is nestled in a beautiful river setting. Inside, blazing hearths, snug alcoves and ships in cabinets; outside, thatched roof, cob walls and a pontoon snaking out onto Restronguet Creek. The location really has the wow factor, but the food's lost some star quality since a recent change of ownership. It's a bit tricky to find if you've never been – you'll need a decent map.

Truro & Newquay (eight daily Monday to Saturday) Bus 89/90.

Helford Passage (four to six daily in summer) Western Greyhound bus 500; to the outer beaches.

Train

Falmouth is at the end of the branch line from **Truro** (£3.20, 20 minutes), which also stops at **Penryn**.

Truro

POP 17,431

Cornwall's capital city has been at the centre of the county's fortunes for over eight centuries. Truro first grew up around a now-vanished hilltop castle, and throughout the Middle Ages it was one of Cornwall's five stannary towns, where tin and copper was assayed and stamped. The 18th and 19th centuries saw it become a key industrial centre, and its wealthy merchants built swathes of elegant town houses, best seen along Lemon St and Falmouth Rd. Truro was granted its own bishop in 1877, with the city's three-spired cathedral following soon after. Today the city makes an appealing base, with a good selection of shops, galleries and restaurants and Cornwall's main museum.

Sights

FREE **Royal Cornwall Museum** MUSEUM
(01872-272205; www.royalcornwallmuseum.org.uk; River St; admission free; 10am-5pm Mon-Sat) The county's main repository for all things industrial and archaeological, with an eclectic collection taking in everything from geological specimens to Celtic torques and a ceremonial carriage. Upstairs there's a small Egyptian section and a little gallery with some surprising finds: a Turner here, a van Dyck there, and several works by Stanhope Forbes.

Truro Cathedral CHURCH
(01872-276782; www.trurocathedral.org.uk; High Cross; suggested donation £4; 7.30am-6pm Mon-Sat, 9am-7pm Sun) Built on the site of a 16th-century parish church in soaring Gothic Revival style, Truro Cathedral was finally completed in 1910, making it the first new cathedral in England since London's St Paul's. It contains a soaring high-vaulted nave, some fine Victorian stained glass and the impressive Father Willis Organ.

Lemon St Market MARKET
(Lemon St; 10.30am-5.30pm Mon-Sat) This lively covered market houses some interesting craft shops, cafes, delicatessens and an upstairs art gallery. The willow-and-paper lanterns hanging from the ceiling were built for Truro's annual Christmas street parade, the City of Lights, held in early December.

Trelissick Gardens COUNTRY ESTATE
(NT; 01872-862090; Feock; adult/child £7.40/3.70; 10.30am-5.30pm Feb-Oct, 11am-4pm Nov-Jan) At the head of the Fal estuary, 4 miles south of Truro, Trelissick is one of Cornwall's most beautiful estates, with a formal garden filled with magnolias and hydrangeas, and a huge expanse of fields and parkland criss-crossed by walking trails.

Sleeping

Mannings Hotel HOTEL ££
(01872-270345; www.manningshotels.co.uk; Lemon St; s £79, d £99-109; P) Truro's best option (formerly known as the Royal Hotel) is this efficient city-centre hotel, geared mainly towards the business crowd. Bold, bright colours, wall-mounted TVs and up-to-date furniture keep things uncluttered, and there are 'aparthotels' with all the mod cons for longer stays (£129 a night). The restaurant's none too shabby either.

Carlton Hotel HOTEL ££
(01872-223938; www.carltonhotel.co.uk; 49 Falmouth Rd; s £50-58.50, d £68.50-78.50; P) This double-fronted Victorian house is a coach-tour favourite, so it's often booked out in summer. The furnishings are pretty much bog-standard B&B (pastel colours, easy-clean carpets), but on the up side, it's only a five-minute walk down the hill into town.

Eating

Saffron RESTAURANT ££
(01872-263771; www.saffronrestauranttruro.co.uk; 5 Quay St; mains £10-16.50; lunch Mon-Fri, dinner Tue-Sat) It's been around for ages, but this titchy restaurant tucked down a Truro side-street still packs an impressive culinary punch. It's strong on seasonal Cornish produce served with a Mediterranean twist: spider-crab served bisque-style, pollock dished up with saffron mash, mutton with turnip dauphinoise.

French Bistro RESTAURANT ££
(01872-223068; www.thefrenchbistro.co.uk; 19 New Bridge St; plat du jour £5.95-7.50, mains £10-12; lunch & dinner Thu-Sat) Ooh la la – Karen

THE EDEN PROJECT

If any one thing is emblematic of Cornwall's regeneration, it's the **Eden Project** (☎01726-811911; www.edenproject.com; Bodelva; adult/child/family £16/6/39; ⏱10am-6pm Apr-Oct, 10am-4.30pm Nov-Mar). Ten years ago the site was a dusty, exhausted clay pit, a symbol of the county's industrial decline. Now, thanks to the vision of ex-record producer turned environmental pioneer Tim Smit, it's home to three giant biomes, the largest greenhouses anywhere in the world.

Inside, a huge variety of plants recreate tropical, temperate and desert habitats, from dry savannah to tropical rainforest and wild jungle, elegantly illustrating the diversity of life on earth and our own dependence on its continued survival. It's informative, educational and enormous fun, but it does get very busy: booking in advance online will allow you to dodge the worst queues, and also bag a £1 discount.

In summer the biomes also become a spectacular backdrop to a series of outdoor gigs during the **Eden Sessions** (www.edensessions.com), and in winter Eden is transformed for the seasonal **Time of Gifts** festival, complete with a full-size ice rink.

It's three miles by road from St Austell; you can catch buses from St Austell, Newquay, Helston, Falmouth and Truro, but arriving on foot or by bike snags you £3 off the admission price. Last entry is 90 minutes before the site closes.

Cairns' opulent eatery has brought a flash of French sophistication to Truro, and it's a lovely place to tuck into classic casseroles, *coq au vin* and *oeuf cocottes*. The jumble shop decor just adds to the charm. Wine is bring-your-own; corkage is £3.

Bustopher's RESTAURANT ££
(☎01872-279029; www.bustophersbarbistro.com; 62 Lemon St; mains £10-18; ⏱lunch & dinner) This longstanding Truro bistro has benefited greatly from a contemporary refit. The food is mainly British bistro standards (steaks, fish, salads) delivered simply and efficiently, and the cosy candles and wood panelling give things an intimate ambience.

Indaba Fish RESTAURANT ££
(☎01872-274700; Tabernacle St; mains £14-18; ⏱dinner) The chef here used to work for Rick Stein, and this swish fish emporium has a similar emphasis on classic, straightforward seafood, ranging from Falmouth oysters and Newlyn lobster to sea bream with garlic mash. Vegetarians and fish-phobes are catered for, too.

Ideas for a quick cafe lunch:

Archie Brown's CAFE £
(☎01872-278622; www.archiebrowns.co.uk; 105-106 Kenwyn St; mains £4-12; ⏱9am-5pm Mon-Sat) Penzance's wholefood original comes to the big city.

Duke St Sandwich Deli CAFE £
(10 Duke St; sandwiches £2.50-5; ⏱9am-5.30pm Mon-Sat) Gourmet sandwiches and handmade ciabattas.

Fodder's CAFE £
(☎01872-271384; Pannier Market, Lemon Quay; mains £6-9; ⏱9am-5.30pm Mon-Sat) Chaotic cafe hidden away above Truro's Pannier Market.

Drinking

Old Ale House PUB
(Quay St) What a relief – a city-centre pub that eschews chrome 'n' cocktails and sticks with burnished wood 'n' beer mats. The daily ales are chalked up behind the bar and there's often live jazz at weekends.

Heron PUB
(Malpas; ⏱11am-3pm & 6-10.30pm Mon-Fri, 11am-11pm Fri & Sat, noon-10.30pm Sun) Two miles along the river estuary from Truro, this Malpas pub is an idyllic place for a riverside pint.

Old Grammar School PUB
(19 St Mary St; ⏱10am-late) Open-plan drinking den with big tables and soft sofas to sink into. Lunch is served from noon to 3pm; later it's cocktails, candles and imported Belgian and Japanese beers.

Vertigo BAR
(15 St Marys St; ⏱10am-late) The pick of the bars around St Mary's St, worth a look for its quirky decor and delightful walled garden.

☆ Entertainment

Hall for Cornwall THEATRE
(☎01872-262466; www.hallforcornwall.co.uk; Lemon Quay) The county's main venue for touring theatre and music.

Plaza Cinema CINEMA
(☎01872-272894; www.wtwcinemas.co.uk; Lemon St) A four-screen cinema showing mainstream releases.

Information

Library (☎01872-279205; Union Pl; per hr £3; ⏲9am-6pm Mon-Fri, 9am-4pm Sat) Net access.

Tourist office (☎01872-274555; tic@truro.gov.uk; Boscawen St; ⏲9am-5.30pm Mon-Fri, 9am-5pm Sat)

Getting There & Away

Bus

Truro is the county's main bus terminus, with regular services all over the county and frequent National Express coaches to Exeter, Bristol, Heathrow and London Victoria. The bus station is beside Lemon Quay. Useful local lines:

St Ives (1½ hours, hourly Monday to Saturday) Bus 14/14A/14B.

Penzance (one hour, hourly Monday to Saturday, six on Sunday) Bus X18. Express service via Redruth and Camborne.

Helston (one hour, hourly, five on Sunday) Bus 82.

Newquay (hourly Mon-Sat, six on Sun) Bus 85/85A. Runs to St Agnes then along the coast via Perranporth.

Falmouth (hourly) Bus 88.

Newquay (ten daily Monday to Saturday) Bus 89/90.

Train

Truro is on the main Paddington-Penzance line and the branch line to Falmouth. Destinations:

Penzance (£5.40, 30 minutes)

Falmouth (£3.60, 30 minutes)

Bodmin (£7.40, 30 minutes)

Exeter (£15.40, 2¼ hours)

Bristol (£37, 3½ hours)

London Paddington (£57.50, five hours)

The Roseland

Stretching into the sea south of Truro, this beautiful rural peninsula gets its name not from flowers but from the Cornish word *ros,* meaning promontory. Highlights include the coastal villages of **Portloe**, a wreckers' hang out on the South West Coast Path, and **Veryan**, awash with daffodils in spring and framed by two thatched roundhouses. Nearby are the beaches of **Carne** and **Pendower**, which join at low tide to form one of the best stretches of sand on Cornwall's south coast.

St Mawes has a beautifully preserved clover-leaf **castle** (EH; ☎01326-270526; adult/child £4.20/2.10; ⏲10am-6pm Jul & Aug, 10am-5pm Apr-Jun & Sep, 10am-4pm Oct, 10am-4pm Fri-Mon Nov-Mar), commissioned by Henry VIII and designed as the sister fortress to Pendennis across the estuary.

St Just-in-Roseland boasts one of the most beautiful churchyards in the country, tumbling down to a creek filled with boats and wading birds.

St Austell & Around

While tin mining was once the staple industry for much of Cornwall, the area around St Austell was dominated by the extraction of china clay, a vital mineral used in everything from medicines to china manufacture. Though the industry is a shadow of its former self these days, you can still clearly see its legacy in the form of huge spoil heaps, mica dams and turquoise pools that loom on the horizon around St Austell (often known locally as the 'Cornish Alps').

St Austell itself is a pretty workaday place, although it's looking better since the multi-million-pound spruce-up of the town centre. Accommodation and restaurants are very thin on the ground, so this is definitely an area to visit on a day-trip.

Sights

Lost Gardens of Heligan GARDENS
(☎01726-845100; www.heligan.com; Pentewan; adult/child £8.50/5; ⏲10am-6pm Mar-Oct, 10am-5pm Nov-Feb) Cornwall's own real-life secret garden. Formerly the family estate of the Tremaynes, the gardens fell into disrepair following WWI (when many staff were killed) and have since been restored to their former splendour by Tim Smit (the man behind the Eden Project, p387) and a huge army of gardeners, horticultural specialists and volunteers. Among the treats in store at Heligan are a working kitchen garden, formal terraces, a secret grotto and a wild jungle valley – as well as the world's largest rhododendron, measuring an impressive 82 feet from root to tip.

Heligan is 7 miles from St Austell. Bus 526 (30 minutes, hourly, ten on Sunday) links Heligan with Mevagissey and St Austell train station.

CORNISH MINING SITES

Since 2006, Cornwall and West Devon's historic mining areas have formed part of the UK's newest Unesco World Heritage Site, the **Cornwall & West Devon Mining Landscape** (www.cornish-mining.org.uk).

The **Cornish Mines & Engines** (☎01209 315027; cornishmines@nationaltrust.org.uk) centre in Pool, near Redruth, makes an ideal place to get acquainted with this once-great industry. At the heart of the complex are two working beam engines, both once powered by steam boilers designed by local lad Richard Trevithick (who was born in Redruth in 1771, and whose cottage at Penponds is now open to the public). Films, photos and artefacts trace the area's rich mining history, while you can see more mining gear in action at **King Edward Mine** (☎01209-614681; www.kingedwardmine.co.uk; adult/child £5/1; ⏰10am-5pm May-Sep).

It's also well worth making a visit to the historic beam engine at Levant (p377) and the mine at Geevor (p377), where you can take an underground tour into the old mineshafts.

Charlestown Shipwreck & Heritage Centre MUSEUM
(☎01726-69897; www.shipwreckcharlestown.com; adult/child £5.95/2.95; ⏰10am-5pm Mar-Oct) The historic port of Charlestown was once a key port for shipping china clay, and is now a favourite location for film crews; several big budget blockbusters and costume dramas have used its quayside as a ready-made backdrop. The town's seagoing heritage is explored at this intriguing museum, which houses artefacts collected from 150 shipwrecks around the world, including a few choice pieces from the *Titanic* and *Lusitania*.

Restormel Castle CASTLE
(adult/child £3.20/1.60; ⏰10am-6pm Jul & Aug, 10am-5pm Apr-Jun & Sep, 10am-4pm Oct) The 13th-century Restormel Castle has one of the best-preserved circular keeps in England. The interior has largely crumbled away, but it's still possible to climb up onto the battlements and gaze over green countryside all the way to the distant Fowey River. The castle's original owner, Edward the Black Prince (for whom the title of Duke of Cornwall was created), is thought to have stayed here at least twice. The castle is 1½ miles north of Lostwithiel.

Getting Around

Bus

Western Greyhound buses from St Austell:

Truro (70 minutes, hourly Monday to Saturday) Bus 522.

Fowey (40 minutes, 10 daily) Bus 524.

Charlestown (15 minutes, 10 daily Monday to Saturday) Bus 525.

Mevagissey, Heligan and Gorran Haven (hourly Monday to Saturday, four on Sunday) Bus 526.

Newquay (hourly Monday to Saturday, five on Sunday) Bus 527 – travels from Newquay to St Austell before continuing to the Eden Project.

Train

St Austell and Lostwithiel are on the Paddington–Penzance line, with connections along the branch line to Par.

Looe

POP 5280

Looe is a pleasing mixture of breezy bucket-and-spade destination and historic fishing port. Although the industry has declined, Looe has the second-biggest fish market in Cornwall (after Newlyn), and high tide still brings the bustle of landing and ice-packing the catch. The port has been a holiday hotspot since Victorian times when bathing machines rolled up to the water's edge off Banjo Pier. Split into East and West Looe and divided by a broad estuary, inter-village rivalry is intense, with locals referring to living on the 'sunny' or the 'money' side of town.

Sights & Activities

Boat Trips

Various boat-trips set out from Buller Quay for destinations including Polperro (£19) and Fowey (£12). Check the signs on the quay for sailings, then leave your contact details in one of the books alongside.

Looe Island

Half a mile offshore is tiny St George's Island (known locally as Looe Island), a

TREVALSA COURT

Perched on the clifftops above the fishing village of Mevagissey, this Edwardian **pile** (☎01726-842468; www.trevalsa-hotel.co.uk; School Hill, Mevagissey; d £125-225; P) is one of the best places to stay on the south coast, but the word's out so you'll need to reserve well ahead. Its restoration-meets-retro approach is enormously persuasive: some rooms have sleigh beds and leather sofas, others funky fabrics and modernist lamps, while a mullion-windowed lounge opens onto coast views.

22-acre nature reserve run by the Cornwall Wildlife Trust. The boat **Islander** (☎07814-139223; adult/child return £6/4, plus £2.50/1 landing fee) runs regular summer trips depending on the weather and tides: check the board on the quay for forthcoming sailings.

Wild Futures Monkey Sanctuary WILDLIFE
(☎01503-262532; www.monkeysanctuary.org; St Martins; adult/child £7.50/3.50; ⏲11am-4.30pm Sun-Thu Easter-Sep) Half a mile west of town, this monkey centre is guaranteed to raise a few 'aaahhhhs' over its unfeasibly cute woolly and capuchin monkeys, many of which were rescued from illegal captivity.

Sleeping & Eating

Looe's B&Bs tend towards the chintzy, so choose carefully. There are plenty of cheap-and-cheerful restaurants in West Looe, but nothing that'll set your world on fire, so it's probably sensible to follow the crowd and plump for fish and chips.

Barclay House B&B ££
(☎01503-262929; www.barclayhouse.co.uk; St Martins Rd, East Looe; d £115-145; P) This gorgeous detached Victorian villa in six acres of private gardens has the best bedrooms in Looe, decorated in graceful shades of peach, pistachio and aquamarine, and some of the most glorious river views you could possibly wish for.

Beach House B&B ££
(☎01503-262598; www.thebeachhouselooe.co.uk; Hannafore Point; d £100-130; P) Smart B&B in a striking modern house overlooking Hannafore Point. The compact rooms are named after Cornish beaches: top of the pile is Kynance, with a massive bed and private balcony.

Trehaven Manor B&B ££
(☎01503-262028; www.trehavenhotel.co.uk; Station Rd; d £68-122; P) It's hardly cutting-edge, but if you like your windows gabled, your rooms spacious and your atmosphere old-fashioned, you'll be happy at the Trehaven. Owners Ella and Neil give a warm welcome and serve up a particularly tempting breakfast, and it's only a short walk into town.

Information

Looe Tourist Office (☎01503-262072; www.visit-southeastcornwall.co.uk; Fore St; ⏲10am-5pm Easter-Oct, plus occasional days Nov-Easter) In the Guildhall.

Getting There & Away

The scenic **Looe Valley Line** (every two hours Monday to Saturday, eight on Sunday, day ranger adult/child £3.40/1.70) trundles along the gorgeous stretch to Liskeard on the London–Penzance line.

Bus 572 travels to Plymouth (1¼ hours, seven daily Monday to Saturday); bus 573 goes to Polperro (30 minutes, hourly in summer).

Polperro

The ancient fishing village of Polperro is a picturesque muddle of narrow lanes and cottages set around a tiny harbour, best approached along the coastal path from Looe or Talland Bay. It's always jammed with day-trippers and coach tours in summer, so arrive in the evening or out of season if possible.

Polperro was once heavily involved in pilchard fishing by day and smuggling by night; the displays at the small **Heritage Museum** (☎01503-272423; The Warren; adult/child £1.75/50p; ⏲10am-6pm Mar-Oct) include sepia photos, pilchard barrels and fascinating smuggling memorabilia.

For buses, see p390.

Fowey

POP 2273

Nestled on the steep tree-covered hillside overlooking the River Fowey, opposite the old fishing harbour of Polruan, Fowey (pronounced Foy) is a pretty tangle of pale-shaded houses and snaking lanes. Its long maritime history includes being the base for 14th-century raids on France and Spain; to guard against reprisals Henry VIII constructed **St Catherine's Castle** above Readymoney Cove, south of town. The town later prospered by shipping china clay extracted from pits at St Austell, but the industrial trade has long declined and Fowey has now reinvented itself for summer-time tourists and second-home owners.

The **tourist office** (☎01726-833616; www.fowey.co.uk; 5 South St; ⊙9am-5.30pm Mon-Sat, 10am-5pm Sun) is also home to the compact **Daphne du Maurier Literary Centre** (☎01726-833616; www.fowey.co.uk; 5 South St; ⊙9am-5.30pm Mon-Sat, 10am-5pm Sun), which is devoted to the author of *Rebecca*, *Frenchman's Creek* and the short story that inspired Hitchcock's film *The Birds*, who spent much of her life in Fowey. Every May the town hosts the **Daphne du Maurier Literary Festival** (www.dumaurier.org) in her honour.

Sleeping

Old Quay House HOTEL £££
(☎01726-833302; 28 Fore St; www.theoldquayhouse.com; d £180-250;) The epitome of Fowey's upmarket trend, this extremely exclusive quayside hotel is all natural fabrics, rattan chairs and tasteful tones, and the rooms are a mix of estuary-view suites and attic penthouses. Very Kensington; not at all Cornish.

Coriander Cottages B&B ££
(☎01726-834998; www.foweyaccommodation.co.uk; Penventinue Ln; r £90-130, cottages £130-220; P) A delightful cottage complex on the outskirts of Fowey, with ecofriendly accommodation in a choice of B&B garden rooms or deluxe open-plan barns, all of which offer a gloriously quiet rural atmosphere far removed from Fowey's tourist fizz.

Fowey Marine Guest House B&B ££
(☎01726-833920; www.foweymarine.com; 21-27 Station Rd; s/d £50/70;) Snug room in a teeny harbour guesthouse, run by a friendly husband-and-wife team. It's especially handy for the harbour car park.

Golant YHA HOSTLE £
(golant@yha.org.uk; Penquite House; dm from £12; P @) Sheltering amid 16 hectares of tree-shaded grounds, this whitewashed Georgian manor house makes a fantastic base. There's a super kitchen and a lounge filled with leather sofas, and some rooms have estuary views. It's at the end of a long private drive – take a torch if you're venturing out at night.

Eating

Sam's BISTRO ££
(www.samsfowey.co.uk; 20 Fore St; mains £5.95-13.95; ⊙lunch & dinner) This much-loved locals' diner has long been a favourite for Fowey punters, but a recent refit has added extra space upstairs and new premises down by Polkerris Beach. Both offer a similar '60s–retro vibe, with booth seats and big specials blackboards: the Samburgers are particularly worth a mention. No bookings.

Pinky Murphy's Café CAFE £
(www.pinkymurphys.com; 19 North St; ⊙9am-5pm Mon-Sat, 9.30am-4pm Sun) Cafes don't come much quirkier than this oddbod establishment, where mismatching crockery is a virtue and seating ranges from tie-dyed beanbags to patched-up sofas. Ciabattas, panini and generous platters are washed down with Pinky's Cream Tease, mugs of Horlicks and fresh-brewed smoothies.

Dwelling House CAFE £
(6 Fore St; tea £3-6; ⊙10am-6.30pm summer, 10am-5.30pm Wed-Sun winter) Top spot for tea (20-plus varieties) and dainty cupcakes (prettily decorated with sprinkles, icing

PORT ELIOT

Stretching across the far eastern end of Cornwall is the 6000-acre estate of **Port Eliot** (☎01503 230211 www.porteliot.co.uk; house & grounds adult/child £7/free, grounds only £4/2; ⊙2-6pm Sat-Thu Mar-Jun), the family seat of the Earl of St Germans. Since March 2008 the house and grounds have been opened to the public for a hundred days every year, and the estate has also become renowned for its annual outdoor bash, the **Port Eliot Festival** (www.porteliotfestival.com), which began life as a literary festival but has now branched out into live music, theatre and outdoor art.

Occasional trains from Plymouth stop at the tiny station of St Germans; otherwise you'll need your own transport to get to the estate.

swirls and lavender sprigs, and served on their own cake stand).

King of Prussia PUB £

(www.kingofprussia.co.uk; Town Quay) The king of Fowey's many pubs takes its name from the local 'free trader' John Carter, and makes a superior spot for a quayside pint or a quick crab sandwich.

Getting There & Away

Bus

Buses to Fowey all stop at Par Station, with onward connections on the Penzance–Paddington mainline.

25 First bus to St Austell (45 minutes, hourly Monday to Saturday).

525 Western Greyhound bus to St Austell (45 minutes, 10 or 11 daily in summer).

Ferry

Bodinnick Ferry (car/pedestrian £2.20/1; last ferry 8.45pm Apr-Oct, 7pm Nov-Mar) Car ferry crossing the river to Bodinnick.

Polruan Ferry (foot passengers & bikes only; £1) Foot passenger ferry across the estuary to the village of Polruan.

Around Looe

Lanhydrock STATELY HOME

(NT; 01208-265950; house & gardens adult/child £9.90/4.90, gardens; 11am-5.30pm Tue-Sun Mar-Sep, 11am-5pm Tue-Sun Oct) Reminiscent of the classic 'upstairs-downstairs' film, *Gosford Park*. Set in 365 hectares of sweeping grounds above the River Fowey, parts date from the 17th century but the property was extensively rebuilt after a fire in 1881, creating the Victorian country house. Highlights include the gentlemen's smoking room (complete with old Etonian photos, moose heads and tiger-skin rugs), the children's toy-strewn nursery and the huge original kitchens. The **gardens** (adult/child £5.80/3.10; 10am-6pm) are open year-round.

Lanhydrock is 2½ miles southeast of Bodmin; you'll need your own transport to get here.

Cotehele STATELY HOME

(NT; 01579-351346; St Dominick; adult/child £8.70/4.35; 11am-4.30pm Sat-Thu Apr-Oct) Seven miles from Tavistock, this Tudor manor served as the family seat of the aristocratic Edgcumbe dynasty for some 400 years. It's stocked with some of Britain's finest Tudor interiors, best seen in the great hall, and dotted throughout with impressive tapestries and suits of armour. It's also notoriously haunted – several ghostly figures are said to wander through the house, accompanied by music and a peculiar herbal smell.

Outside, the lovely terraced **gardens** (adult/child £5.20/2.60) include both a me-

BODMIN MOOR

Cornwall's 'roof' is a high heath pock-marked with bogs, ancient remains and lonely granite hills, including **Rough Tor** (pronounced *row-tor,* 400m) and **Brown Willy** (419m), Cornwall's highest points. It's a desolate place that works on the imagination; for years there have been reported sightings of the Beast of Bodmin, a large, black cat-like creature, although no one's ever managed to snap a decent picture.

The wild landscape offers some superb walking, and there are some great trails suitable for hikers and mountain-bikers around **Cardinham Woods** (www.forestry.gov.uk/cardinham) on the moor's eastern edge. Other landmarks to look out for are **Dozmary Pool**, at the centre of the moor said to have been where Arthur's sword, Excalibur, was thrown after his death. Nearby is **Jamaica Inn** (01566-86250; www.jamaicainn.co.uk; s £65, d £80-110; P), made famous by Daphne du Maurier's novel of the same name (although it's sadly been modernised since du Maurier's day). It also has a small smuggling museum and a room devoted to du Maurier.

The **Bodmin & Wenford Railway** (www.bodminandwenfordrailway.co.uk; rover pass adult/child £11.50/6; Mar-Oct) is the last standard-gauge railway in Cornwall plied by steam locomotives. Trains are still decked out in original 1950s livery and chug from Bodmin Parkway and Bodmin General station to Boscarne Junction, where you can join the Camel Trail cycle route (p368). There are two to four return trips daily depending on the season.

For general information on the moor, contact **Bodmin tourist office** (01208-76616; www.bodminlive.com; Mount Folly; 10am-5pm Mon-Sat).

dieval dovecote, a working mill and a restored quay with a restored river barge moored alongside.

ISLES OF SCILLY

Twenty-eight miles southwest of mainland Cornwall lie the tiny Isles of Scilly, an archipelago of over 140 islands, five of which are inhabited. Nurtured by the Gulf Stream and blessed with a balmy sub-tropical climate, the Scillys have long survived on the traditional industries of farming, fishing and flower-growing, but these days tourism is by far the biggest moneyspinner. St Mary's is the largest and busiest island, closely followed by Tresco, while only a few hardy souls remain on Bryher, St Martin's and St Agnes.

With a laid-back island lifestyle, a strong community spirit and some of the most glorious beaches anywhere in England, it's hardly surprising that many visitors find themselves drawn back to the Scillys year after year. While life moves on at breakneck speed in the outside world, time in the Scillys seems happy to stand still.

Information

Isles of Scilly Tourist Board (01720-422536; tic@scilly.gov.uk; Hugh Town, St Mary's; 8.30am-6pm Mon-Fri, 9am-5pm Sat, 9am-2pm Sun May-Sep, shorter hrs in winter) On St Mary's.

Scilly Online (www.scillyonline.co.uk) Locally run site with lots of info on the islands.

Simply Scilly (www.simplyscilly.co.uk) Official tourist site with comprehensive listings.

Getting There & Away

Air

There are two ways to get to Scilly by air – chopper and plane – but neither's cheap.

British International (01736-363871; www.islesofscillyhelicopter.com) Helicopters run to

Isles of Scilly

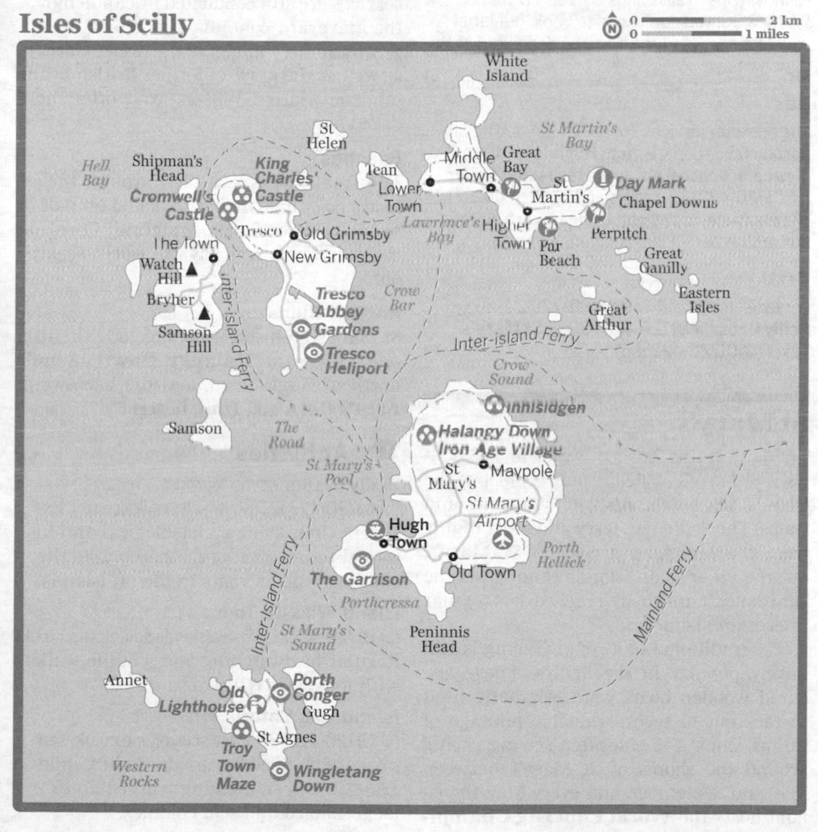

St Mary's and Tresco from Penzance heliport. Full return fares are adult/child £175/105. Saver fares (for travel Monday to Friday) and Daytrip fares are much cheaper.

Isles of Scilly Skybus (☎0845-710-5555; www.ios-travel.co.uk) Several daily flights from Land's End (adult/child return £140/89.25) and Newquay (£165/100.25), plus at least one from Exeter, Bristol and Southampton daily in summer.

Boat

Scillonian (☎0845-710-5555; www.ios-travel.co.uk; ⏲Mar-Oct) Scilly's ferry plies the choppy waters between Penzance and St Mary's (adult/child return £95/47.50). There's at least one daily crossing in summer (except on Sundays), dropping to four a week in the shoulder months.

Getting Around

Boat

Inter-island launches sail regularly from St Mary's harbour in summer to the other main islands. Trips to all islands cost adult/child £7.80/3.90; you don't need to book, but label your luggage clearly so it can be deposited at the right harbour.

Bus

The only bus services are on St Mary's. The airport bus (£3) departs from Hugh Town 40 minutes before each flight, while the **Island Rover** (☎01720-422131; www.islandrover.co.uk; £7) offers a twice-daily sightseeing trip in a vintage bus in summer.

Taxi

For taxis, try **Island Taxis** (☎01720-22126), **Scilly Cabs** (☎01720-422901) or **St Mary's Taxis** (☎01720-422555).

St Mary's

The largest and busiest island in the Scillys is St Mary's, which contains most of the islands' big hotels, B&Bs, restaurants and shops. The Scillonian ferry and most flights from the mainland arrive on St Mary's, but the other main islands (known as the 'off-islands') are easily reached via regular inter-island launches.

The traditional sport of gig racing is still hugely popular in the Scillys. These six-oared wooden boats were originally used to race out to secure valuable pilotage of sailing ships. You can often see gig racing around the shores of St Mary's between May and September, and every May the island hosts the **World Pilot Gig Championships**, which attracts teams from as far away as Holland and the USA.

Sights

Hugh Town & Old Town

About a mile west of the airport is the main settlement of **Hugh Town**, where you'll find the bulk of the island's hotels and guest houses. These islands have an absorbing, unique history, which is explored to the full in the **Isles of Scilly Museum** (Church St; adult/child £3.50/1; ⏲10am-4.30pm Mon-Fri, 10am-noon Sat Easter-Sep, 10am-noon Mon-Sat Oct-Easter or by arrangement) where exhibits include artefacts recovered from shipwrecks (including muskets, a cannon and a ship's bell), Romano-British finds and a fully rigged 1877 pilot gig.

A little way east of Hugh Town is **Old Town**, once the island's main harbour but now home to a few small cafes, a village pub and a curve of beach. Look out for the minuscule Old Town Church where evocative services are still conducted by candlelight – the graveyard contains a memorial to Augustus Smith, founder of the Abbey Garden, as well as the grave of former British prime minister Harold Wilson, who often holidayed here.

Beaches

The small inlets scattered around the island's coastline are best reached on foot or by bike. Porth Hellick, Watermill Cove and the remote Pelistry Bay are worth seeking out.

Ancient Ruins

St Mary's prehistoric sites include the Iron Age village at **Halangy Down**, a mile north of Hugh Town, and the barrows at **Bant's Carn** and **Innisidgen**.

Activities

Scilly Walks HISTORICAL TOURS
(☎01720-423326; www.scillywalks.co.uk) Excellent three-hour archaeological and historical tours, costing £5/2.50 per adult/child, as well as visits to the off-islands.

Island Wildlife Tours WILDLIFE TOURS
(☎01720-422212; www.islandwildlifetours.co.uk) Regular birdwatching and wildlife walks with local boy Will Wagstaff.

Island Sea Safaris WATER TOURS
(☎01720-422732; www.scillyonline.co.uk/seasafaris.html) Speedboat rides (adult/child £30/20) and snorkelling trips (£35) to local seabird and seal colonies.

VISITING SCILLY

Scilly gets extremely busy in summer, while many businesses shut down completely in winter. All of the islands, except Tresco, have a simple campsite, but many visitors choose to stay in self-catering accommodation as a way of keeping costs down – the two big companies are **Island Properties** (☎01720-422082; www.scillyhols.com) or **Sibley's Island Homes** (☎01720-422431; www.sibleysonscilly.co.uk).

Travelling to the islands is the major expense, although there are usually discounted fares on flights leaving Land's End after 2pm or St Mary's before 11am. Look in the local papers for discount coupons on helicopter trips and the *Scillonian* ferry, too.

Sleeping

Belmont B&B £
(☎01720-423154; www.the-belmont.co.uk; Church Rd; s £28-65, d £56-80, f £90-120) Solid St Mary's guesthouse, in a double-fronted detached house 15 minutes' walk from the quay. The six rooms are clean and bright and the price is definitely right.

Blue Carn Cottage B&B £
(☎01720-422214; Old Town; 3-night stay d £276-284; ⊙Mar-Oct) Removed from the relative bustle of Hugh Town, this whitewashed B&B near Old Town is a welcoming affair. DVD players and cosy surroundings distinguish the rooms, while there's a game-stocked guest lounge and hearty brekkies with home-reared eggs.

Star Castle Hotel HOTEL £££
(☎01720-422317; www.star-castle.co.uk; The Garrison; r incl dinner £188-312, ste incl dinner £242-362;) Shaped like an eight-pointed star, this former fort on Garrison Point is one of Scilly's star hotels, with a choice of heritage-style castle rooms or more modern garden suites. It's a bit stuffy, but prices include dinner at a choice of restaurants.

St Mary's Hall Hotel HOTEL £££
(☎01720 422316; www.stmaryshallhotel.co.uk; Church St, Hugh Town; r £180-240) Say *ciao* to this Italianate mansion, which is full of grand wooden staircases, bits of art and panelled walls. Rooms are either flowery and chintzy or candy-striped, while the super-plush designer suites have LCD TVs and a galley kitchen.

Garrison Campsite CAMPSITE
(☎01720-422670; tedmoulson@aol.com; Tower Cottage, Garrison; sites per person £6-10) This 4-hectare site sits on the garrison above Hugh Town. Fairly basic facilities, but a cut above many other sites on Scilly.

Eating

Juliet's Garden Restaurant RESTAURANT, CAFE ££
(☎01720-422228; www.julietsgardenrestaurant.co.uk; lunch £4-10, dinner £12-16; ⊙10am-5pm daily, 6pm-late Wed-Sun) Apart from a couple of pubs, cafes and a deli around Hugh Town, eating choices are pretty limited on St Mary's, which makes this converted barn 15 minutes' walk from town extra-special. Light lunches by day, candlelit fare by night, all treated with loving care and attention.

Tresco

Once owned by Tavistock Abbey, Tresco is the second-largest island, and the second most visited after St Mary's. The main attraction is the magical **Tresco Abbey Garden** (☎01720-424105; www.tresco.co.uk/stay/abbey-garden; adult/child £10/5; ⊙10am-4pm), first laid out in 1834 on the site of a 10th-century Benedictine abbey. The terraced gardens feature more than 5000 subtropical plants, including species from Brazil, New Zealand and South Africa, and the intriguing Valhalla collection made up of figureheads and nameplates salvaged from the many ships that have foundered off Tresco's shores.

Sleeping & Eating

Apart from self-catering cottages, there are now three places to stay on the island, but the two big hotels are eye-poppingly expensive. By far the most affordable choice is the **New Inn** (☎01720-422844; newinn@tresco.co.uk; d £140-230), the island's popular pub, which also has pleasant pastel rooms, some of which have views over the channel to Bryher.

Other options:

Island Hotel HOTEL £££
(☎01720-422883; www.tresco.co.uk; d incl dinner £370-720;) The island's original

luxury hotel, with regal rooms and a price-tag to match.

Flying Boat Club APARTMENT £££
(01720-422849; flyingboatclub@tresco.co.uk; apts £4500-5000;) Fabulously lavish sea-view apartments; prices drop to a mere £1375 to £1950 in winter.

Bryher & Samson

Only around 70 people live on Bryher, Scilly's smallest and wildest inhabited island. Covered by rough bracken and heather, this chunk of rock takes the full force of Atlantic storms; **Hell Bay** in a winter gale is a truly powerful sight.

Watch Hill provides cracking view over the islands, and **Rushy Bay** is one of the finest beaches in the Scillys. From the quay, occasional boats visit local seal and bird colonies and deserted **Samson Island**, where abandoned settlers' cottages tell a story of hard subsistence living.

Sleeping & Eating

Hell Bay HOTEL £££
(01720-422947; www.tresco.co.uk; d incl dinner £260-600) The island's only hotel is a real pamper pad, run by the owners of Tresco's pricey pamper pads, and offering similarly upmarket accommodation. All the rooms are huge suites, most with their own sitting rooms and private balconies. Dinner at one of the hotel's two restaurants is included in the price.

Fraggle Rock CAFE, PUB £
(01720-422222; 10.30am-4.30pm & 7-11pm;) Pretty much the only place to eat on Bryher is this relaxed cafe, which also doubles as the island pub. The menu's mainly pizzas, salads and burgers, and there are a few local ales on tap and fair-trade coffees, which help support the Cornwall Wildlife Trust.

Bryher Campsite CAMPSITE £
(01720-422886; www.bryhercampsite.co.uk; sites from £9.50) Bare-bones camping near the quay. Hot showers and transport from the boat is included in the rates.

St Martin's

The northernmost of the main islands, St Martin's is renowned for its beaches. Worth hunting out are **Lawrence's Bay** on the south coast, which becomes a broad sweep of sand at low tide; **Great Bay** on the north, arguably Scilly's finest beach; **White Island** in the northwest, which you can cross to (with care) at low tide; and the secluded cove of **Perpitch** in the southeast.

The largest settlement is **Higher Town** where you'll find a small village shop and **Scilly Diving** (01720-422848; www.scillydiving.com; Higher Town), which offers snorkelling trips and diving courses.

Sleeping

Accommodation options on the island are almost non-existent, apart from one super-expensive hotel, **St Martin's on the Isle** (01720-422090; www.stmartinshotel.co.uk; d £300-560), a campsite and a handful of B&Bs.

Polreath B&B £
(01720-422046; Higher Town; d £90-110, open all year, but weekly stays only May-Sep) This robust granite cottage is one of the few B&Bs on the island. Squeeze yourself into one of the titchy traditional rooms or sip a cool lemonade in the sunny conservatory; cream teas, baguettes and light bites are also on offer several days a week, and sometimes you'll even get a hot evening meal, too.

Campsite CAMPSITE £
(01720-422888; www.stmartinscampsite.co.uk; sites £8-10) Towards the western end of Lawrence's Bay; has a laundry, showers and fresh-water well. Eggs and veg are usually available in season.

Eating

Apart from the hotel's super-expensive restaurant, St Martin has few eating options:

Little Arthur Farm FARM £
(01720-422457; www.littlearthur.co.uk; 10.30am-4pm daily, 6.30-8.30pm Mon-Fri) Wonderful little organic farm where you can buy fresh eggs, milk, homemade cakes and other goodies.

St Martin's Bakery BAKERY £
(01720-423444; www.stmartinsbakery.co.uk; 9am-6pm Mon-Sat, 9am-2pm Sun) Fresh bread, pastries and patisseries.

St Agnes

England's southernmost community somehow transcends even the tranquillity of the other islands in the Isles of Scilly; with its cloistered coves, coastal walks and a scattering of prehistoric sites, it's an ideal spot to stroll, unwind and reflect.

Visitors disembark at Porth Conger, near the decommissioned **Old Lighthouse** – one of the oldest lighthouses in the country. Other points of interest include the 200-year-old stone **Troy Town Maze** and the inlets of Periglis Cove and St Warna's Cove (dedicated to the patron saint of shipwrecks). At low tide you can cross over to the island of **Gugh**, where you'll find intriguing standing stones and Bronze Age remains.

Sleeping & Eating

Covean Cottage B&B £

(☎01720-422620; http://st-agnes-scilly.org/covean.htm; d £60-80) A little stone-walled cottage B&B, which makes the perfect location for getting away from the crowds. It offers four pleasant, good-value rooms and serves excellent cream teas, light meals and sticky treats during the day.

Turk's Head PUB £

(☎01720-422434; mains £7-12) The most southwesterly pub in all of England is a real treat, with fine views, excellent beers, good pub grub and a hearty island atmosphere.

Troytown Farm Campsite CAMPSITE £

(☎01720-422360; www.troytown.co.uk; Troy Town Farm; sites £7-8, tents £1-7 depending on size) At the southwestern corner of the island. Originally a flower farm, it's now home to Scillys' only dairy herd.

Cambridge & East Anglia

Includes »

Best Places to Eat

» Midsummer House (p410)

» Great House (p424)

» Butley Orford Oysterage (p429)

» Alimentum (p410)

» Roger Hickman's (p435)

Best Places to Stay

» Lavenham Priory (p423)

» Cley Windmill (p442)

» Hotel du Vin (p409)

» Hotel Felix (p409)

» Swan Hotel (p423)

Why Go?

Unfurling gently eastwards to the sea, the vast flatlands of East Anglia are a rich web of lush farmland, melancholy fens and sparkling rivers. The area is justly famous for its sweeping sandy beaches, big skies and the bucolic landscape that once inspired Constable and Gainsborough.

It's not all rural idyll, though: rising out of the Fens is the world-famous university town of Cambridge, with its stunning classical architecture and earnest attitude, and to the east is the cosmopolitan city of Norwich. Around them, magnificent cathedral cities, pretty market towns and implausibly picturesque villages are testament to the enormous wealth amassed here during medieval times, when the wool and weaving industries flourished.

Meanwhile, the meandering coastline is peppered with pretty fishing villages and traditional bucket-and-spade resorts, while inland is the languid, hypnotic charm of the Norfolk Broads, an ideal location for serious relaxation.

When to Go

Aldeburgh swings into action with its classical music festival in June. You can chill out and tune in at the Latitude Festival in Southwold in July. On 24 December the King's College Chapel is at its best at the Festival of Nine Lessons and Carols.

History

East Anglia was a major Saxon kingdom, and the treasures unearthed in the Sutton Hoo burial ship proved that they enjoyed something of the good life here.

The region's heyday, however, was in the Middle Ages, during the wool and weaving boom, when Flemish weavers settled in the area and the grand churches and the world-famous university began to be established.

By the 17th century much of the region's marshland and bog had been drained and converted into arable land, and the good times rolled. The emergence of a work-happy urban bourgeoisie coupled with a strong sense of religious duty resulted in the parliamentarianism and Puritanism that would climax in the Civil War. Oliver Cromwell, the uncrowned king of the parliamentarians, was a small-time merchant residing in Ely when he answered God's call to take up arms against the fattened and corrupt monarchy of Charles I.

East Anglia's fortunes waned in the 18th century, however, when the Industrial Revolution got under way up north. The cottage industries dwindled, and today crops have replaced sheep as the rural mainstay. During WWII East Anglia became central to the fight against Nazi Germany. With plenty of flat open land and its proximity to mainland Europe, it was an ideal base for the RAF and the United States Air Force. The remains of these bases can still be seen today.

Activities

East Anglia is a great destination for walking and cycling enthusiasts, with miles of coastline to discover, vast expanses of flat land for leisurely touring and plenty of inland waterways for quiet boating. Try www.visiteastofengland.com for information, or visit local tourist offices for maps and guides.

CYCLING

East Anglia is famously flat and riddled with quiet roads; even the unfit can find vast swaths for a gentle meander on two wheels. All four counties boast networks of quiet country lanes, where the biggest natural hazard is the wind sweeping in unimpeded from the coast. When it's behind you though, you can free-wheel for miles. There's gorgeous riding to be had along the Suffolk and Norfolk coastlines and in the Fens. Finding quiet roads in Essex is a little more of a challenge. Mountain bikers should head for Thetford Forest, near Thetford, while much of the popular on- and off-road Peddars Way walking route is also open to cyclists.

WALKING

East Anglia is not everybody's idea of classic walking country; you won't find any challenging peaks here, but gentle rambles through farmland, beside rivers and lakes and along the wildlife-rich coastline are in ample supply.

The **Peddars Way and Norfolk Coast Path** (www.nationaltrail.co.uk/peddarsway) is a six-day, 93-mile national trail from Knettishall Heath near Thetford to Cromer on the coast. The first half trails along an ancient Roman road, then finishes by meandering along the beaches, sea walls, salt marshes and fishing villages of the coast. Day-trippers and weekend walkers tend to dip into its coastal stretches, which also cover some of the best birdwatching country in England.

Curving round further south, the 50-mile **Suffolk Coast Path** (www.suffolkcoastandheaths.org) wanders between Felixstowe and Lowestoft, via Snape Maltings, Aldeburgh, Dunwich and Southwold, but is also good for shorter rambles.

OTHER ACTIVITIES

With wind and water so abundant here, it's a popular destination for **sailing**, both along the coast and in the Norfolk Broads, where you can easily hire boats and arrange lessons. It's also possible to just putput your way around the Broads in **motorboats** or gently **canoe** along the slow-moving rivers. Alternatively, the wide and frequently empty beaches of the Norfolk coast make great spots for **land yachting** and **kitesurfing**.

Getting There & Around

Getting about East Anglia on public transport, both rail and coach, is straightforward. Consult **Traveline** (☎0871 200 2233; www.travelineeastanglia.org.uk) for all public transport information.

BUS **Stagecoach** (www.stagecoachbus.com) and **First Group** (www.firstgroup.com), along with a host of smaller companies, offer bus services across the region.

TRAIN **National Express East Anglia** (www.nationalexpresseastanglia.com) offers the handy **Anglia Plus Pass** (one day/three days out of seven £13.50/27), which allows you to explore Norfolk, Suffolk and parts of Cambridgeshire. The pass is valid for unlimited regional travel

Cambridge & East Anglia Highlights

1. Dreaming of your student days as you **punt** past Cambridge's historic colleges (p408)
2. Soaking up the medieval atmosphere in topsy-turvy **Lavenham** (p423)
3. Marvelling at the exquisite rib vaulting at **Norwich Cathedral** (p432)
4. Walking the prom, dining on sublime food and just chilling out in understated **Aldeburgh** (p427)
5. Wallowing in the heavenly sounds of Evensong at **King's College Chapel** (p403)
6. Canoeing your way through the tranquil waterways of the **Norfolk Broads** (p438)
7. Wandering aimlessly along the pristine sands of **Holkham beach** (p443)

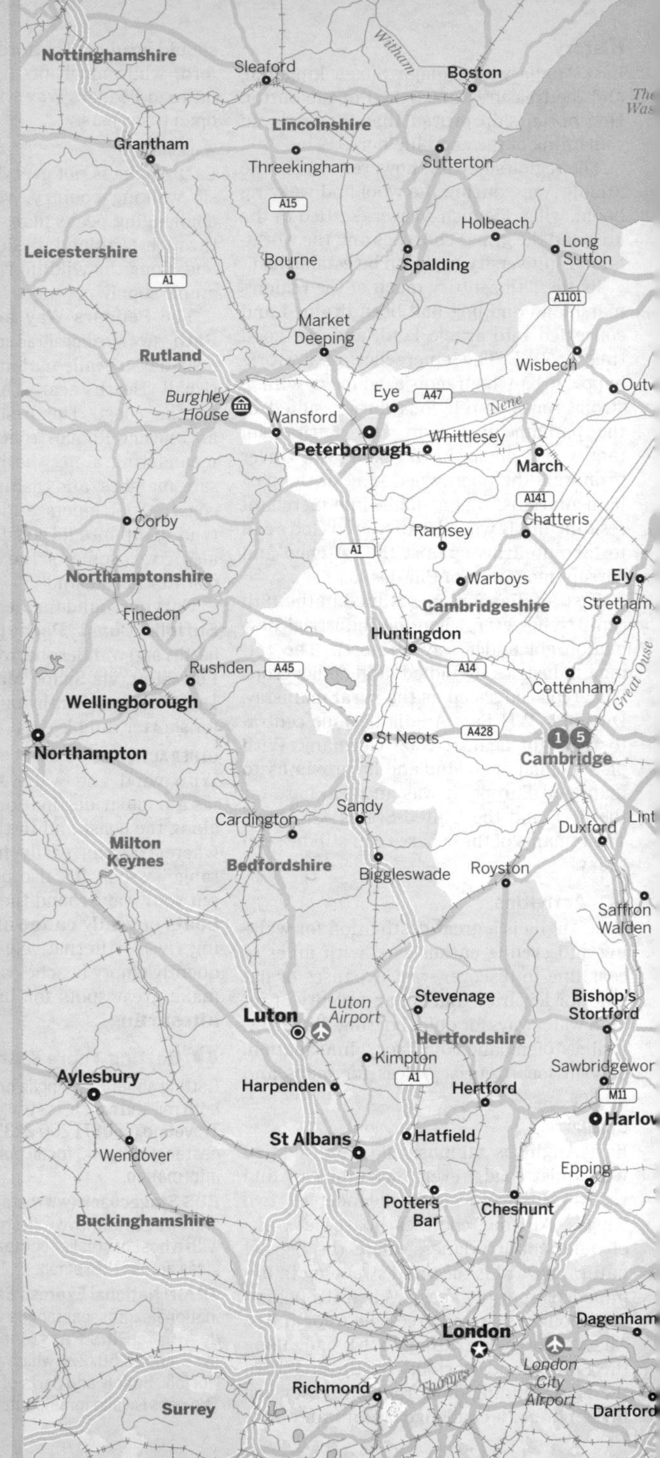

0
40 km
0
18 miles
Holkham Beach
Wells-next-the-Sea
Burnham Market
Holkham Hall
Sheringham
Blakeney
Cromer
Sustead
Ringstead
Little Walsingham
Baconsthorpe
Mundesley
Sandringham House
Houghton Hall
Fakenham
Blickling Hall
Aylsham
A149
Palling
Castle Rising
Harpley
A1067
Potter Heigham
Winterton
Wroxham
How Hill
Norfolk
Dereham
Norwich
Acle
Great Yarmouth
Norfolk Broads National Park
Swaffham
Stradsett
Wymondham
Swainsthorpe
Reedham
A1065
A134
A11
Loddon
Mundford
Attleborough
Norfolk Broads
Lowestoft
Thetford Forest
Military Camp
Bungay
Kessingland
Thetford
Scole
A143
Southwold
Suffolk Coast National Nature Reserve
A143
Ixworth
Dunwich
Bury St Edmunds
RSPB Minsmere
Newmarket
A1120
Saxmundham
Ickworth House & Park
Thorpeness
Stowmarket
A12
Aldeburgh
Suffolk
Suffolk Coast Path
A143
North Sea
Lavenham
Woodbridge
Butley
Orford
Sutton Hoo
Ipswich
Long Melford
Kersey
Hadleigh
Alderton
Sudbury
Dedham Vale
Felixstowe
Finchingfield
Halstead
Wormingford
Harwich
To Hamburg
Colchester
Baintree
Walton-on-the-Naze
Frinton-on-Sea
Layer de la Haye
Brightlingsea
Clacton-on-Sea
Witham
Tiptree
A12
Chelmsford
Essex
Brentwood
Southend-on-Sea
Canvey Island
Kent
Leysdown-on-Sea
Rochester
Chatham
Margate

WANT MORE?

Head to **Lonely Planet** (www.lonelyplanet.com/england/eastern-england/cambridge) for planning advice, author recommendations, traveller reviews and insider tips.

after 8.45am on weekdays and anytime at weekends. Up to four accompanying children can travel for £2 each.

CAMBRIDGESHIRE

Many visitors to Cambridgeshire never make it past the beautiful university town of Cambridge, where august old buildings, student cyclists in academic gowns and glorious chapels await. But beyond the breathtaking city lies a county of vast open landscapes, epic sunsets and unsullied horizons. The flat reclaimed fen, lush farmland and myriad waterways make perfect walking and cycling territory, while the extraordinary cathedrals at Peterborough and Ely, and the rip-roaring Imperial War Museum at Duxford, would be headline attractions anywhere else.

Getting Around

The region's public transport radiates from Cambridge, which is a mere 55-minute train ride from London. This line continues north through Ely to King's Lynn in Norfolk. From Ely, branch lines run east through Norwich, southeast into Suffolk and northwest to Peterborough. Local tourist offices stock bus and train timetables.

Cambridge

POP 108,863

Drowning in exquisite architecture, steeped in history and tradition and renowned for its quirky rituals, Cambridge is a university town extraordinaire. The tightly packed core of ancient colleges, the picturesque 'Backs' (college gardens) leading on to the river, and the leafy green meadows that seem to surround the city give it a far more tranquil appeal than its historic rival Oxford.

Like 'the other place', as Oxford is known, the buildings here seem unchanged for centuries, and it's possible to wander the college buildings and experience them as countless prime ministers, poets, writers and scientists have done. The sheer weight of academic achievement seems to seep from the very walls, with cyclists who are loaded down with books negotiating narrow cobbled passageways, earnest students relaxing on manicured lawns and great minds debating life-changing research in historic pubs. Meanwhile, distracted punters drift into the river banks as they soak up the breathtaking views, tills whir with brisk trade in the city's designer boutiques, and those long past their student days wonder what it would have been like to study in such auspicious surroundings.

History

First a Roman fort and then a Saxon settlement, Cambridge was little more than a rural backwater until 1209, when the university town of Oxford exploded in a riot between town and gown (see boxed text, p181).Fed up with the constant brawling between locals and students, a group of scholars upped and left to found a new university in Cambridge.

Initially students lived in halls and religious houses, but gradually a collegiate system, where tutors and students lived together in a formal community, developed. The first Cambridge college, Peterhouse, was founded in 1284. The collegiate system is still intact today in both Oxford and Cambridge.

By the 14th century, the royalty, nobility, church, trade guilds and anyone rich enough to court the prestige that their own institution offered began to found their own colleges. It was 500 years before female students were allowed into the hallowed grounds, though, and even then in women-only colleges Girton and Newnham, founded in 1869 and 1871 respectively. By 1948 Cambridge minds had broadened sufficiently to allow the women to actually graduate.

The honour roll of famous Cambridge graduates reads like an international who's who of high achievers: 87 Nobel Prize winners (more than any other institution in the world), 13 British prime ministers, nine archbishops of Canterbury, an immense number of scientists, and a healthy host of poets and authors. Crick and Watson discovered DNA here, Isaac Newton used Cambridge to work on his theory of gravity, Stephen Hawking was, until 2009, a professor of mathematics here, and Charles Darwin, William Wordsworth, Vladimir Nabokov, David Attenborough and John Cleese all studied here.

Today the university remains one of the top three for research worldwide, and international academics have polled it as the top university in the world for science. Thanks to some of the earth-shaking discoveries made here, Cambridge is inextricably linked to the history of mankind.

Sights

Cambridge University

Cambridge University comprises 31 colleges, though not all are open to the public. Most colleges close to visitors for the Easter term and all are closed for exams from mid-May to mid-June. Opening hours vary from day to day, so contact the colleges or the tourist office for information as hours given below are only a rough guide.

King's College Chapel CHAPEL
(www.kings.cam.ac.uk/chapel; King's Pde; adult/child under 12 £5/free; 9.30am-4.30pm Mon-Sat, 10am-5pm Sun) In a city crammed with show-stopping architecture, this is the show-stealer. Chances are you will already have seen it on a thousand postcards, tea towels and choral CDs before you catch your first glimpse of the grandiose King's College Chapel, but still it inspires awe. It's one of the most extraordinary examples of Gothic architecture in England, and was begun in 1446 as an act of piety by Henry VI and finished by Henry VIII around 1516.

While you can enjoy stunning front and back views of the chapel from King's Pde and the river, the real drama is within. Mouths drop open upon first glimpse of the inspirational **fan-vaulted ceiling**, its intricate tracery soaring upwards before exploding into a series of stone fireworks. This vast 80m-long canopy is the work of John Wastell and is the largest expanse of fan vaulting in the world.

The chapel is also remarkably light, its sides flanked by lofty **stained-glass windows** that retain their original glass – rare survivors of the excesses of the Civil War in this region. It's said that these windows were ordered to be spared by Cromwell himself, who knew of their beauty from his own studies in Cambridge.

The antechapel and the choir are divided by a superbly carved **wooden screen**, designed and executed by Peter Stockton for Henry VIII. The screen bears his master's initials entwined with those of Anne Boleyn. Look closely and you may find an angry human face – possibly Stockton's – amid the elaborate jungle of mythical beasts and symbolic flowers. Above is the magnificent bat-wing organ, originally constructed in 1686 though much altered since.

The thickly carved wooden stalls just beyond the screen are a stage for the chapel's world-famous **choir**. You can hear them in full voice during the magnificent **Evensong** (5.30pm Mon-Sat, 10.30am & 3.30pm Sun, term time only; admission free). If you happen to be visiting at Christmas, it is also worth queuing for admission to the incredibly popular **Festival of Nine Lessons and Carols** on Christmas Eve.

Beyond the dark-wood choir, light suffuses the **high altar**, which is framed by Rubens' masterpiece *Adoration of the Magi* (1634) and the magnificent east window. To the left of the altar in the side chapels, an **exhibition** charts the stages and methods of building the chapel.

The chapel is open for reduced hours during term time.

Trinity College COLLEGE
(www.trin.cam.ac.uk; Trinity St; adult/child £1/50p; 9am-4pm) The largest of Cambridge's colleges, Trinity, is entered through an impressive Tudor gateway first created in 1546. As you walk through, have a look at the statue of the college's founder, Henry VIII, that adorns it. His left hand holds a golden orb, while his right grips not the original sceptre but a table leg, put there by student pranksters and never replaced. It's a wonderful introduction to one of Cambridge's most venerable colleges, and a reminder of who really rules the roost.

As you enter the **Great Court**, scholastic humour gives way to wonderment, for it is the largest of its kind in the world. To the right of the entrance is a small tree, planted in the 1950s and reputed to be a descendant of the apple tree made famous by Trinity alumnus Sir Isaac Newton. Other alumni include Tennyson, Francis Bacon, Lord Byron, HRH Prince Charles and at least nine prime ministers, British and international, and a jaw-dropping 32 Nobel Prize winners.

The square is also the scene of the run made famous by the film *Chariots of Fire* – 350m in 43 seconds (the time it takes the clock to strike 12). Although many students attempt it, Harold Abrahams (the hero of the film) never actually did, and the run wasn't even filmed here. If you fancy your chances, remember that you'll need Olympian speed to even come close.

The college's vast hall has a dramatic hammerbeam roof and lantern,

Cambridge

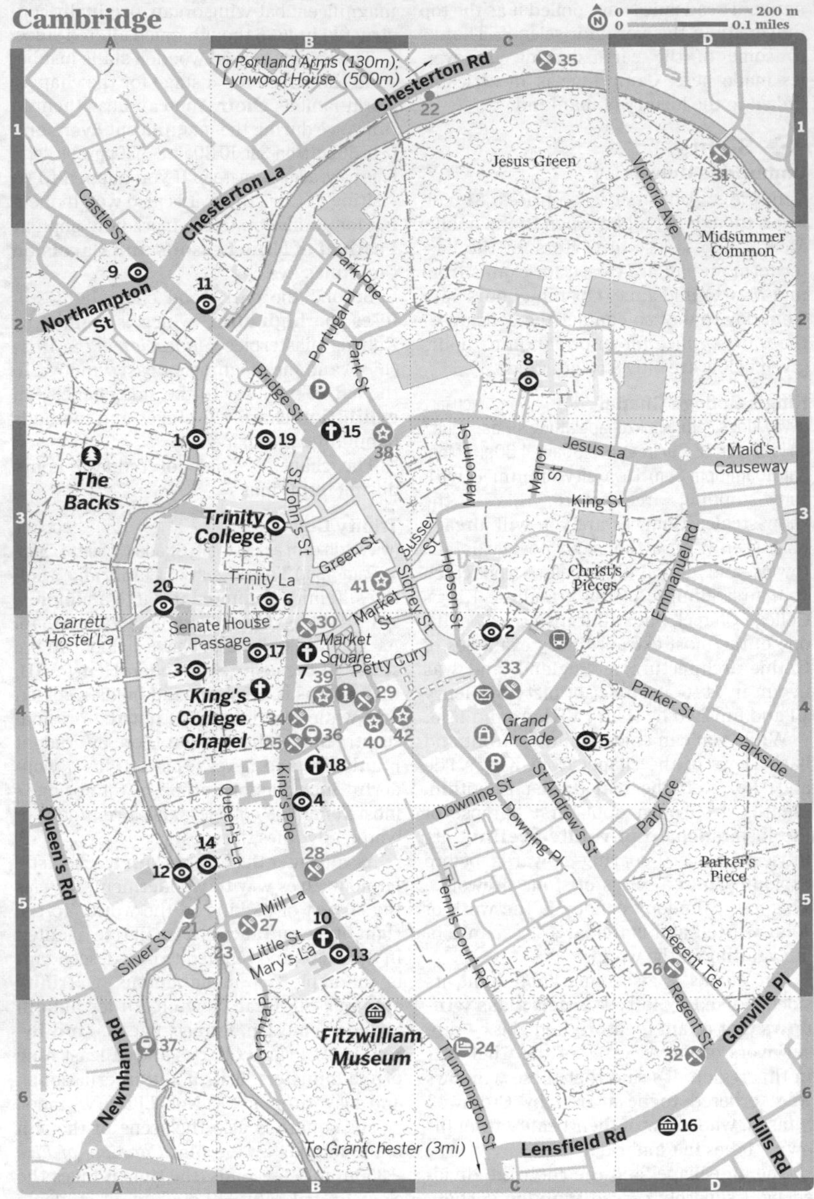

and beyond this are the dignified cloisters of Nevile's Court and the renowned **Wren Library** (⏲noon-2pm Mon-Fri). It contains 55,000 books dated before 1820 and more than 2500 manuscripts, including AA Milne's original *Winnie the Pooh*. Both Milne and his son, Christopher Robin, were graduates.

Henry VIII would have been proud to note, too, that his college would eventually come to throw the best party in town, the lavish May Ball in June.

Cambridge

Top Sights

Fitzwilliam Museum ... B6
King's College Chapel ... B4
The Backs ... A3
Trinity College ... B3

Sights

1 Bridge of Sighs ... A3
Cambridge Revisited ... (see 29)
2 Christ's College ... C4
3 Clare College ... A4
4 Corpus Christi College ... B4
5 Emmanuel College ... C4
Folk Museum ... (see 9)
6 Gonville & Caius College ... B3
7 Great St Mary's Church ... B4
8 Jesus College ... C2
9 Kettle's Yard ... A2
10 Little St Mary's Church ... B5
11 Magdalene College ... A2
12 Mathematical Bridge ... A5
13 Peterhouse ... B5
14 Queens' College ... A5
15 Round Church ... B3
16 Scott Polar Research Institute ... D6
17 Senate House ... B4
18 St Bene't's Church ... B4
19 St John's College ... B3
20 Trinity Hall College ... A3

Activities, Courses & Tours

21 Cambridge Chauffer Punts ... A5
Granta ... (see 37)
22 Riverboat Georgina ... C1
23 Scudamore's ... B5

Sleeping

24 Hotel du Vin ... C6

Eating

25 Chop House ... B4
26 De Luca ... D5
27 Dojo ... B5
28 Fitzbillies ... B5
29 Jamie's Italian ... B4
30 Michaelhouse ... B4
31 Midsummer House ... D1
32 Oak Bistro ... D6
33 Origin8 ... C4
34 Rainbow Vegetarian Bistro ... B4
35 Twenty-Two ... C1

Drinking

36 Eagle ... B4
37 Granta ... A6

Entertainment

38 ADC ... B3
39 Arts Theatre ... B4
40 Corn Exchange ... B4
41 Fez ... B3
42 Soul Tree ... B4

Corpus Christi College COLLEGE
(www.corpus.cam.ac.uk; King's Pde; admission £2) Entry to this illustrious college is via the so-called New Court, which dates back a mere 200 years. To your right is the door to the Parker Library, which holds the finest collection of Anglo-Saxon manuscripts in the world. As you enter take a look at the statue on the right, that of the eponymous Matthew Parker, who was college master in 1544 and Archbishop of Canterbury to Elizabeth I. Mr Parker was known for his curiosity, and his endless questioning gave rise to the term 'nosy parker'. Meanwhile, a monastic atmosphere still oozes from the inner Old Court, which retains its medieval form. Look out for the fascinating sundial and plaque to playwright and past student Christopher Marlowe (1564–93), author of *Dr Faustus* and *Tamburlaine*.

On the corner of Bene't St you'll find the college's new **Corpus Clock**. Made from 24-carat gold, it displays the time through a series of concentric LED lights. A hideous-looking insect 'time-eater' crawls across the top. The clock is only accurate once every five minutes. At other times it slows or stops and then speeds up, which according to its creator, JC Taylor, reflects life's irregularity.

Trinity Hall College COLLEGE
(www.trinhall.cam.ac.uk; Trinity Lane; admission by donation) Henry James once wrote of the delightfully diminutive Trinity Hall, 'If I were called upon to mention the prettiest corner of the world, I should draw a thoughtful sigh and point the way to the gardens of Trinity Hall.' Wedged cosily among the great and the famous, but unconnected to better-known Trinity, it was founded in 1350 as a refuge for lawyers and

clerics escaping the ravages of the Black Death, thus earning it the nickname, the 'Lawyers' College'. The college's 16th-century library has original Jacobean reading desks and chained books (an early antitheft device) on the shelves, while the chapel is one of the most beautiful of the colleges. You can attend **Evensong** here on Thursdays (6.30pm) and Sundays (6pm) during term time. Writer JB Priestley, astrophysicist Stephen Hawking and actor Rachel Weisz are among Trinity Hall's graduates.

Gonville & Caius College COLLEGE

(www.cai.cam.ac.uk; Trinity St; admission free) Known locally as Caius (pronounced keys), Gonville and Caius was founded twice, first by a priest called Gonville, in 1348, and then again in 1557 by Dr Caius (his given name was Keys – it was common for academics to use the Latin form of their names), a brilliant physician who supposedly spoilt his legacy by insisting the college admit no 'deaf, dumb, deformed, lame, chronic invalids, or Welshmen'! Fortunately for the college, his policy didn't last long, and the wheelchair-using megastar of astrophysics, Stephen Hawking, is now a fellow here.

The college is of particular interest thanks to its three fascinating gates: Virtue, Humility and Honour. They symbolise the progress of the good student, since the third gate (the *Porta Honoris,* a fabulous domed and sundial-sided confection) leads to the Senate House and thus graduation.

Christ's College COLLEGE

(www.christs.cam.ac.uk; St Andrew's St; admission free, Darwin room £2.50; ⌚9.30am-noon, Darwin room 10am-noon & 2-4pm) Over 500 years old and a grand old institution, Christ's is worth visiting if only for its gleaming Great Gate emblazoned with heraldic carving of spotted Beaufort yale (antelope-like creatures), Tudor roses and portcullis. Its founder, Lady Margaret Beaufort, hovers above like a guiding spirit. A stout oak door leads into First Court, which has an unusual circular lawn, magnolias and wisteria creepers. Pressing on through the Second Court there is a gate to the Fellows' Garden, which contains a mulberry tree under which 17th-century poet John Milton reputedly wrote *Lycidas.* Charles Darwin also studied here, and his room has been restored as it would have been when he lived in it. You can buy a guided-walk brochure (£1) to Darwin-related sites in the college from the porter's lodge.

Peterhouse COLLEGE

(www.pet.cam.ac.uk; Trumpington St; admission free) The oldest and smallest college, Peterhouse is a charming place founded in 1284. Much of the college was rebuilt or added to over the years, including the exceptional little chapel built in 1632, but the main hall is bona fide 13th century and has been beautifully restored. Just to the north is **Little St Mary's Church**, which has a memorial to Peterhouse student Godfrey Washington, great-uncle of George. His family coat of arms was the stars and stripes, the inspiration for the US flag.

Queens' College COLLEGE

(www.queens.cam.ac.uk; Silver St; adult/child £2.50/free; ⌚10am-4.30pm) The gorgeous 15th-century Queens' College sits elegantly astride the river and has two enchanting medieval courtyards: Old Court and Cloister Court. Here, too, is the beautiful half-timbered President's Lodge and the tower in which famous Dutch scholar and reformer Desiderius Erasmus lodged from 1510 to 1514. He had plenty to say about Cambridge: the wine tasted like vinegar, the beer was slop and the place was too expensive, but he did note that the local women were good kissers.

St John's College COLLEGE

(www.joh.cam.ac.uk; St John's St; adult/child £3.20/free; ⌚10am-5.30pm) After King's College, St John's is one of the city's most photogenic colleges, and is also the second-biggest after Trinity. Founded in 1511, it sprawls along both banks of the river, joined by the Bridge of Sighs, a masterpiece of stone tracery. Over the bridge is the 19th-century New Court, an extravagant neo-Gothic creation, and out to the left stunning views of the Backs.

Magdalene College COLLEGE

(www.magd.cam.ac.uk; Magdalene St) Originally a Benedictine hostel, riverside Magdalene has the dubious honour of being the last college to allow women students; when they were finally admitted in 1988, male students wore black armbands and flew the college flag at half-mast. Its greatest asset is the Pepys Library, housing the magnificent collection of books the famous mid-17th-century diarist bequeathed to his old college.

Emmanuel College COLLEGE

(www.emma.cam.ac.uk; St Andrew's St) The 16th-century Emmanuel College is famous for its exquisite chapel designed by Sir Christopher

Wren. Here, too, is a plaque commemorating John Harvard (BA 1632), a scholar here who later settled in New England and left his money to found his namesake university in the Massachusetts town of Cambridge.

Jesus College COLLEGE
(www.jesus.cam.ac.uk; Jesus Lane) This tranquil 15th-century college was once a nunnery before its founder, Bishop Alcock, expelled the nuns for misbehaving. Highlights include a Norman arched gallery, a 13th-century chancel and art nouveau features by Pugin, William Morris (ceilings), Burne-Jones (stained glass) and Madox Brown.

Other Sights

The Backs PARKLANDS
Behind the grandiose facades, stately courts and manicured lawns of the city's central colleges lies a series of gardens and parklands butting up against the river. Collectively known as the Backs, these tranquil green spaces and shimmering waters offer unparalleled views of the colleges and are often the most enduring image of Cambridge for visitors. The picture postcard snapshots of college life, graceful bridges and weeping willows can be seen from the pathways that cross the Backs, from the comfort of a chauffeur-driven punt or from the lovely pedestrian bridges that criss-cross the river.

The fanciful **Bridge of Sighs** (built in 1831) at St John's is best observed from the stylish bridge designed by Wren just to the south. The oldest crossing is at **Clare College**, built in 1639 and ornamented with decorative balls. Its architect was paid a grand total of 15p for his design and, feeling aggrieved at such a measly fee, it's said he cut a chunk out of one of the balls adorning the balustrade so the bridge would never be complete. Most curious of all is the flimsy looking wooden construction joining the two halves of Queen's College known as the **Mathematical Bridge**, first built in 1749. Despite what unscrupulous guides may tell you, it wasn't the handiwork of Sir Isaac Newton (he died in 1727), originally built without nails, or taken apart by students who then couldn't figure how to put it back together.

FREE **Fitzwilliam Museum** MUSEUM
(www.fitzmuseum.cam.ac.uk; Trumpington St; ⌚10am-5pm Tue-Sat, noon-5pm Sun) Fondly dubbed 'the Fitz' by locals, this colossal neoclassical pile was one of the first public art museums in Britain, built to house the fabulous treasures that the seventh Viscount Fitzwilliam had bequeathed to his old university. An unabashedly over-the-top building, it sets out to mirror its contents in an ostentatious jumble of styles that mixes mosaic with marble, Greek with Egyptian and more. It was begun by George Basevi in 1837, but he did not live to see its completion: while working on Ely Cathedral he stepped back to admire his handiwork, slipped and fell to his death.

The lower galleries are filled with priceless treasures from ancient Egyptian sarcophagi to Greek and Roman art, Chinese ceramics to English glass, and some dazzling illuminated manuscripts. The upper galleries showcase works by Leonardo da Vinci, Titian, Rubens, the Impressionists, Gainsborough and Constable, right through to Rembrandt and Picasso. You can join a one-hour **guided tour** (£3.50) of the museum on Saturdays at 2.30pm.

FREE **Kettle's Yard** ART COLLECTION
(www.kettlesyard.co.uk; cnr Northampton & Castle Sts; ⌚house 2-4pm Tue-Sun, gallery 11.30am-5pm Tue-Sun) Neither gallery nor museum, this house nonetheless oozes artistic excellence, with a collection of 20th-century art, furniture, ceramics and glass that would be the envy of many an institution. It is the former home of HS 'Jim' Ede, a former assistant keeper at the Tate Gallery in London, who opened his home to young artists, resulting in a beautiful collection by the likes of Miró, Henry Moore and others. There are also exhibitions of contemporary art in the modern **gallery** next door.

While here, take a peek in the neighbouring **Folk Museum** (www.folkmuseum.org.uk; 2/3 Castle St; adult/child £3.50/1; ⌚10.30am-5pm Tue-Sat, 2-5pm Sun), a 300-year-old former inn now cluttered with a wonderfully diverse collection of domestic tools and equipment from 1700 onwards.

FREE **Scott Polar Research Institute** MUSEUM
(www.spri.cam.ac.uk/museum; Lensfield Rd; ⌚10am-4pm Tue-Sat) For anyone interested in polar exploration or history, the Scott Polar Research Institute has a fantastic collection of artefacts, journals, paintings, photographs, clothing, equipment and maps in its museum. Reopened in 2010 after a thorough redesign, the museum is a fascinating place to learn about the great polar explorers and their harrowing expeditions, and to read the last messages left to wives, mothers and friends by Scott and his polar crew. You can

also examine Inuit carvings and scrimshaw (etched bones), sledges and snow scooters and see the scientific and domestic equipment used by various expeditions.

Great St Mary's Church CHURCH

(www.gsm.cam.ac.uk; Senate House Hill; tower adult/child £2.50/1.25; ⏲9am-5pm Mon-Sat, 12.30-5pm Sun) Cambridge's staunch university church was built between 1478 and 1519 in the late-Gothic Perpendicular style. If you're fit and fond of a view, climb the 123 steps of the tower for superb vistas of the dreamy spires, albeit marred by wire fencing.

The beautiful classical building directly across King's Pde is the **Senate House**, designed in 1730 by James Gibbs; graduations are held here in summer, when gowned and mortar-boarded students parade the streets to pick up those all-important scraps of paper.

Round Church CHURCH

(www.christianheritageuk.org.uk; Bridge St; adult/child £2/free; ⏲10am-5pm Tue-Sat, 1-5pm Sun) The beautiful Round Church is another of Cambridge's gems and one of only four such structures in England. It was built by the mysterious Knights Templar in 1130 and shelters an unusual circular nave ringed by chunky Norman pillars. It now houses an exhibition on Cambridge's Christian heritage and the city's contribution to the world.

Cambridge University Botanic Garden BOTANIC GARDEN

(www.botanic.cam.ac.uk; entrance on Bateman St; adult/child £4/free; ⏲10am-6pm) Founded by Charles Darwin's mentor, Professor John Henslow, the beautiful Botanic Garden is home to 8000 plant species, a wonderful arboretum, tropical houses, a winter garden and flamboyant herbaceous borders. You can take an hour-long **guided tour** (admission £7, includes garden) of the garden on the first Saturday of the month at 11am. The gardens are 1200m south of the city centre via Trumpington St.

Cambridge Revisited HISTORY SHOW

(Peas Hill; adult/child £3.50/2.50; ⏲10am-5.30pm Mon-Sat) Set in the former Cambridge courts, this light-hearted attraction follows the trial and punishment of fictional Mr Tymins, found guilty of using the word 'Oxford' while in Cambridge. The show aims to be a virtual educational tour of Cambridge and its colleges.

St Bene't's Church CHURCH

(http://stbenetschurch.org; Bene't St) The oldest structure in the county, the Saxon tower of this Franciscan church was built around 1025. The round holes above the belfry windows were designed to offer owls nesting privileges: they were valued as mouse killers.

Activities

Punting

Gliding a self-propelled punt along the Backs is a blissful experience once you've got the knack, though it can also be a manic challenge to begin. If you wimp out you can always opt for a relaxing chauffeured punt.

Punt hire costs £14 to £16 per hour, chauffeured trips of the Backs cost £10 to £12, and a return trip to Grantchester will set you back £20 to £30. All companies offer discounts if you pre-book tickets online. Some recommended outlets:

Cambridge Chauffer Punts (www.punting-in-cambridge.co.uk; Silver St Bridge)

Granta (www.puntingincambridge.com; Newnham Rd)

Scudamore's (www.scudamores.com; Silver St) Also hires rowboats, kayaks and canoes.

Walking & Cycling

For an easy stroll into the countryside, you won't find a prettier route than the 3-mile walk to **Grantchester** following the meandering River Cam and its punters southwest through flower-flecked meadows.

Scooting around town on a bike is easy thanks to the pancake-flat landscape, although the surrounding countryside can get a bit monotonous. The Cambridge tourist office stocks several useful guides.

Tours

Visit www.visitcambridge.org for information on self-guided walking and audio tours.

City Sightseeing BUS TOUR

(www.city-sightseeing.com; adult/child £13/7; ⏲every 20min 10am-4.40pm) Hop-on, hop-off bus tours.

Riverboat Georgina BOAT TOUR

(☎01223-307694; www.georgina.co.uk) One-/two-hour cruises £6/12) with the option of including lunch or a cream tea.

Tourist Office WALKING TOUR

(☎01223-457574; www.visitcambridge.org) Conducts two-hour city tours (adult/

HOW TO PUNT

Punting looks pretty straightforward but, believe us, it's not. As soon as we dried off and hung our clothes on the line, we thought it was a good idea to offer a couple of tips on how to move the boat and stay dry.

» 1. Standing at the end of the punt, lift the pole out of the water at the side of the punt.

» 2. Let the pole slide through your hands to touch the bottom of the river.

» 3. Tilt the pole forward (that is, in the direction of travel of the punt) and push down to propel the punt forward.

» 4. Twist the pole to free the end from the mud at the bottom of the river, and let it float up and trail behind the punt. You can then use it as a rudder to steer with.

» 5. If you haven't fallen in yet, raise the pole out of the water and into the vertical position to begin the cycle again.

child £12.50/6, 11am and 1pm Monday to Saturday, 1pm Sunday); 1½-hour city tours (adult/child £11/6, noon Monday to Friday, noon and 2pm Saturday), and ghost tours (adult/child £6/4, 6pm Friday). Book in advance.

Festivals & Events

Cambridge has a jam-packed schedule of almost continual events, from beer festivals to hippie fairs, of which the tourist office has exhaustive listings. One of the biggies is late July's **Folk Festival** (www.cambridgefolkfestival.co.uk), which has hosted the likes of Elvis Costello, Paul Simon, kd lang and Joan Armatrading.

Although you'll need to be a student to join in, the biggest event in the college year are the **May Balls** (June), when students glam up and get down after exams. Also popular are the traditional rowing races, the **Bumps** (www.cucbc.org/bumps), held in March and May, in which college boat clubs compete to collide with the crew in front.

Sleeping

Some of Cambridge's most central B&Bs use their convenient location as an excuse not to upgrade. Some of the better places are a bit of a hike from town but well worth the effort.

Hotel du Vin HOTEL £££
(☎01223-227330; www.hotelduvin.com; Trumpington St; d from £140; @) This boutique hotel chain really knows how to do things right. Its Cambridge offering has all the usual trademarks, from quirky but incredibly stylish rooms with monsoon showers and luxurious Egyptian cotton sheets to the atmospheric vaulted cellar bar and the French-style bistro (mains £14.50 to £20). The central location, character-laden building and top-notch service make it a great deal at this price.

Cambridge Rooms COLLEGE ROOMS ££
(www.cambridgerooms.co.uk; r £35-120) If you fancy experiencing life inside the hallowed college grounds, you can stay in a student room, wander the grounds, see the chapel and have breakfast in the ancient college hall. Accommodation varies from functional singles (with shared bathroom) overlooking college quads to more modern, en suite rooms in nearby annexes. There's limited availability during term time but a good choice of rooms during university holidays.

Hotel Felix HOTEL £££
(☎01223-277977; www.hotelfelix.co.uk; Whitehouse Lane, Huntingdon Rd; d £180-305; P@) This luxurious boutique hotel occupies a lovely grey-brick Victorian villa in landscaped grounds a mile from the city centre. Its 52 rooms embody designer chic with minimalist style but lots of comfort. The slick restaurant serves Mediterranean cuisine with a modern twist (mains £12.50 to £20). To get here follow Castle St and then Huntingdon Rd out of the city for about 1.5 miles.

Alexander B&B ££
(☎01223-525725; www.beesley-schuster.co.uk; 56 St Barnabas Rd; s/d from £40/65) Set in a Victorian house in a quiet residential area, the Alexander has two homey rooms with period fireplaces, big windows and lots of light. There's a two-night minimum stay, but with a convenient location and friendly atmosphere it's worth booking in advance. Continental breakfast only. The

B&B is off Mill Rd, about 1 mile from the corner of Parker's Piece.

Tenison Towers Guest House B&B ££
(01223-363924; www.cambridgecitytenisontowers.com; 148 Tenison Rd; s/d from £40/60) This exceptionally friendly and homey B&B is really handy if you're arriving by train, but well worth seeking out whatever way you arrive in town. The rooms are bright and simple, with pale colours and fresh flowers, and the aroma of freshly baked muffins greets you in the morning. The B&B is about a mile from the city centre. Follow Regent St south from the city, veer left onto Station Rd and then left onto Tension Rd just before you reach the train station.

Lynwood House B&B ££
(01223-500776; www.lynwood-house.co.uk; 217 Chesterton Rd; s/d from £40/75; P) Newly redecorated rooms with white linens, silky throws, trendy wallpapers and brocade curtains give contemporary style to this Victorian, semiclose to Midsummer Common. Breakfasts are hearty and made with organic, free-range ingredients. No children under 12 allowed.

Benson House B&B ££
(01223-311594; www.bensonhouse.co.uk; 24 Huntingdon Rd; d £85-110; P) Just a 1200m-walk from the city centre, this lovely B&B has some beautifully renovated rooms offering hotel-standard accommodation. The tasteful decor ranges from monochrome minimalism to muted classical elegance. No children. To get here follow Castle St north of the city centre into Huntingdon Rd.

Cambridge YHA HOSTEL £
(0845 371 9728; www.yha.org.uk; 97 Tenison Rd; dm/tw £16/40; @) Within walking distance of the city centre and cheap and cheerful; this well-worn hostel close to the train station fills up fast. The dorms are small and pretty basic and with lots of groups using the hostel it can be noisy. Book well ahead. To get to the hostel follow Regent St south out of the city, following signs for the train station. Veer left onto Station Rd and then left onto Tenison Rd.

Other possibilities:

Victoria Guest House B&B ££
(01223-350086; www.cambridge-accommodation.com; 55-57 Arbury Rd; s/d from £50/65; P) Tasteful rooms with contemporary decor and a hint of period character. Take bus C4 to Milton Rd.

Carolina B&B ££
(01223-247015; www.carolinaguesthouse.co.uk; 138 Perne Rd; s/d from £38/60; P) Homey B&B with cosy rooms and a large garden. It's a 30-minute walk from the city centre but bus C2 stops almost outside the door.

Warkworth House B&B ££
(01223-363682; www.warkworthhouse.co.uk; Warkworth Tce; s/d £55/75; @) Great-value, central option just off Parkside, with spacious, clean rooms. The decor is tasteful but a little dated.

Eating

Cambridge is packed with chain restaurants, particularly around the city centre. You'll find upmarket chains such as Browns and Loch Fyne on Trumpington St and plenty of Asian eateries on Regent St. If you're looking for something more independent you'll have to search a little harder.

Midsummer House MODERN BRITISH £££
(01223-369299; www.midsummerhouse.co.uk; Midsummer Common; 2-/3-course lunch £30/35, 2/3-course dinner £55/72; lunch Wed-Sat, dinner Tue-Sat) In a wonderful Victorian villa backing onto the river, but simple and modern inside, this sophisticated place is sheer gastronomic delight. It serves what is probably the best food in East Anglia, has a host of rave reviews from famous foodies and two Michelin stars, but none of the pretension you'd expect of a restaurant of its calibre. Book ahead.

Alimentum MODERN EUROPEAN £££
(01223-413001; www.restaurantalimentum.co.uk; 152-154 Hills Rd; mains £17.50-21; closed Sun dinner) Slick and stylish and eager to impress, this place aims to wow you with their ambitious menu and effortlessly casual service. The food is divine, with slow cooking and ethically sourced local produce a priority. On the down side it's way out of town (off Hills Rd) in a far-from-pretty location, and the piped music is a tad too loud.

Michaelhouse MODERN BRITISH £
(www.michaelhousecafe.co.uk; Trinity St; mains £7-9; 8am-5pm Mon-Sat) Sip fair-trade coffee and nibble focaccias among soaring medieval arches or else take a pew within reach of the altar at this stylishly converted church, which still has a working chancel. The simple lunch menu features quiche, soup and salads, as well as more substantial hot dishes, and has a good range of vegetarian options.

Origin8 DELI CAFE £
(www.origin8delicafes.com; 62 St Andrew's St; mains £4-6.50; 8am-6pm Mon-Sat, 11am-5.30pm Sun) Bright and airy, this cafe, deli and butchers shop prides itself on its local organic ingredients. It's a great place to stop for hearty soups, hog roast baps, home-cooked sausage rolls, fresh salads or luscious cakes. The shop showcases foodstuffs from East Anglia's finest producers, making it a perfect bet for picnic supplies.

Oak Bistro MODERN BRITISH ££
(01223-323361; www.theoakbistro.co.uk; 6 Lensfield Rd; mains £11-17, set 2-/3-course lunch £12/15; closed Sun) This little place on a busy corner is a great local favourite and serves up simple, classic dishes with modern flair. The atmosphere is relaxed and welcoming, the decor minimalist and the food perfectly cooked. There's even a hidden walled garden for alfresco dining. It's a popular spot so book ahead.

CB2 MODERN BRITISH ££
(www.cb2bistro.com; 5-7 Norfolk St; mains £6-13) Internet cafe, bistro, music venue and cinema all rolled into one, this lively place dishes up a great range of rustic cuisine in a relaxed and friendly atmosphere. The menu features everything from salads, pastas and wraps to heartier bistro specials. There's live music on the top floor on Wednesday nights and every other Thursday. To get here take a left off Parkside onto East Rd. Norfolk St is about 300m along on the right.

Jamie's Italian ITALIAN ££
(www.jamieoliver.com/italian; Old Library, Wheeler St; mains £8-18) Set in the city's Guildhall, the celebrity chef's 'neighbourhood Italian' is a great place to eat. The building itself has loads of character, and the funky modern design has the city's young trendsters flocking in droves. The food's great, too; simple, unpretentious dishes that leave you wanting more. Be prepared to queue.

Twenty-Two MODERN EUROPEAN £££
(01223-351880; www.restaurant22.co.uk; 22 Chesterton Rd; set dinner £28.50; 7-9.45pm Tue-Sat) Hidden away amid a row of Victorian terraced housing is this slightly odd, yet outstanding restaurant. It's an intimate kind of place, with a hushed atmosphere and old-school decor, where diners chose from a delicate set menu. Dishes are of the highest standard and the wine list is impressive. Book ahead.

Rainbow Vegetarian Bistro VEGETARIAN ££
(www.rainbowcafe.co.uk; 9a King's Pde; mains £8-10; 10am-10pm Tue-Sat, to 4pm Sun & Mon) First-rate vegetarian food and a pious glow emanate from this snug subterranean gem, accessed down a narrow passageway off King's Pde. It's decorated in funky colours and serves up organic dishes with a hint of the exotic, such as scrumptious Indonesian gado gado and Cuban peccadillo pie.

Chop House TRADITIONAL BRITISH ££
(www.chophouses.co.uk/thecambridgechophouse; 1 Kings Pde; mains £9.50-24) Set on the busy corner of Kings Pde and Bene't St, this place has wooden floors, giant windows overlooking the street, and a menu of classic English cuisine. If you're craving sausage and mash, a sizzling steak, suet pudding, fish pie or potted ham, look no further.

De Luca ITALIAN ££
(www.delucacucina.co.uk; 83 Regent St; mains £7-16, set 2-/3-course lunch £12/14; 11am-late) Contemporary style and classic Italian food collide in this lively restaurant with an open kitchen, glass ceiling and exposed brickwork. It's a much-loved spot with a great wine and cocktail list making it as popular for long lunches as it is for boozy nights out.

Dojo ASIAN £
(www.dojonoodlebar.co.uk; 1-2 Miller's Yard, Mill Lane; mains £4.50-7.50) This popular student haunt offers a great range of Chinese, Thai, Japanese, Vietnamese and Malaysian noodle and rice dishes served up in generous portions. There's outside seating for fine days and a buzzing atmosphere.

Fitzbillies BAKERY CAFE ££
(www.fitzbillies.co.uk; 52 Trumpington St; closed dinner Mon) Cambridge's oldest bakery, beloved by generations of students for its ultrasticky buns and quaint wood shopfront, makes a good stop for breakfast, while its cafe next door (mains £7 to £17) serves honest food in simple surroundings.

Drinking

Cambridge is awash with historic pubs that have the same equal mix of intellectual banter and rowdy merrymaking that they have had for centuries past.

Eagle TRADITIONAL PUB
(Bene't St) Cambridge's most famous pub has loosened the tongues and pickled the grey cells of many an illustrious academic

CAMBRIDGE FOR CHILDREN

Consider taking your little bears to meet the original Winnie the Pooh in a manuscript by ex-alumnus AA Milne at Trinity College's **Wren Library**. Or take advantage of myriad events laid on partly or wholly for kids, including the **Midsummer Fair** (late June), the **Big Weekend** (early July) and the **Children's Marquee** (early August); details for all these events can be found at www.cambridge-summer.co.uk.

Alternatively, if you're hoping a little of the university's vast reserves of knowledge will rub off, there are a host of museums on **Downing St**, covering subjects such as geology, archaeology and anthropology, zoology and the history of science.

in its day; among them are Nobel Prize-winning scientists Crick and Watson, who discussed their research into DNA here. It's a traditional 17th-century pub with five cluttered, cosy rooms, the back one once popular with WWII airmen, who left their signatures on the ceiling.

Kingston Arms PUB
(33 Kingston St; mains £8.50-13.50; food ⏲6pm-10pm Mon-Thu, all day Fri-Sun) Down to earth and full of character, this bright blue pub is tucked away off Mill Rd. Real ales, decent pub grub, a walled garden, free wi-fi and a friendly attitude make it well worth the effort to get here. You can even challenge the regulars to a game of tiddlywinks. To get here follow Parker St past Parker's Piece onto Mill Rd, turning left onto Kingston St after about 600m.

Granta PUB
(☎01223-505016; Newnham Rd) If the exterior of this picturesque waterside pub, overhanging a pretty mill pond, looks strangely familiar, it could well be because it is the darling of many a TV director. Its terrace sits directly beside the water, and when your Dutch courage has been sufficiently fuelled, there are punts for hire alongside the terrace.

Portland Arms PUB
(www.theportlandarms.co.uk; 129 Chesterton Rd) The best spot in town to catch a gig and see the pick of up-and-coming bands, the Portland is a popular student haunt and music venue. Its wood-panelled interior, honest attitude and spacious terrace make it a good bet any day of the week.

☆ Entertainment

Thanks to a steady stream of students and tourists there's always something on in Cambridge. You'll find all the railings in the city centre laden down with posters advertising classical concerts, theatre shows, academic lectures and live music. It's also worth picking up a *What's On* events guide from the tourist office or logging on to www.admin.cam.ac.uk/whatson for details of university events. Despite the huge student population, Cambridge isn't blessed with the best nightclubs in the country. Many students stick to the college bars late at night and swear that they are the best venues in town. Pity they're not open to the rest of us.

Fez NIGHTCLUB
(www.cambridgefez.com; 15 Market Passage) Hip-hop, dance, R&B, techno, funk, top-name DJs and club nights – you'll find it at Cambridge's most popular club, the Moroccan-themed Fez.

Soul Tree NIGHTCLUB
(www.soultree.co.uk; 1-6 Guildhall Chambers, Corn Exchange St; ⏲Mon, Fri & Sat) Funk, disco, '80s classics and not-so-big-name DJs at this popular club.

Corn Exchange THEATRE
(www.cornex.co.uk; Wheeler St) The city's main centre for arts and entertainment, attracting the top names in pop and rock to ballet.

Junction ARTS CENTRE
(www.junction.co.uk; Cambridge Leisure Park, Clifton Way) Theatre, dance, comedy, live music and club nights at Cambridge's youth venue near the railway station. To get here follow Regent St, then Hills Rd south out of the city for about a mile before turning left onto Clifton Way.

Arts Theatre THEATRE
(www.cambridgeartstheatre.com; 6 St Edward's Passage) Cambridge's biggest bona fide theatre puts on everything from pantomime to drama fresh from London's West End.

ADC STUDENT THEATRE
(www.adctheatre.com; Park St) Students' theatre and home to the university's Footlights comedy troupe, which jump-

started the careers of scores of England's comedy legends.

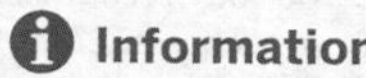

Information

You'll find all the major banks and a host of ATMs around St Andrew's St and Sidney St. The going rate for internet access is about £1 per hour.

Addenbrooke's Hospital (☎01223-245151; Hills Rd) Southeast of the centre.

Budget Internet Cafe (30 Hills Rd; ⏰10am-9pm Mon-Sat, 11am-7pm Sun)

CB2 (5-7 Norfolk St; ⏰noon-midnight) Internet access.

Jaffa Internet Cafe (22 Mill Rd; ⏰10am-10pm)

Police station (☎01223-358966; Parkside)

Post office (9-11 St Andrew's St)

Tourist office (☎0871 266 8006; www.visitcambridge.org; Old Library, Wheeler St; ⏰10am-5.30pm Mon-Fri, to 5pm Sat, 11am-3pm Sun) Pick up a guide to the Cambridge colleges (£4.99) in the gift shop or a leaflet (£1) outlining two city walks. You can also download audio tours from the website.

Getting There & Away

BUS From Parkside there are regular buses to **Stansted** (£12.40, 50 minutes), **Heathrow** (£30, 2½ to three hours) and **Gatwick** (£31, four hours) airports, while a **Luton** (£15, 1½ hours) service runs roughly every two hours. Buses to **Oxford** (£11, 3½ hours) are regular but take a very convoluted route.

TRAIN Trains run at least every 30 minutes to **London King's Cross** and Liverpool St stations (£19, 45 minutes to 1¼ hours). There are also three trains per hour to **Ely** (£4, 20 minutes) and hourly connections to **Bury St Edmunds** (£8, 45 minutes) and **King's Lynn** (£8, 50 minutes).

CAR Cambridge's centre is largely pedestrianised. Use one of the five free Park & Ride car parks on major routes into town. Buses (£2.50) serve the city centre every 10 minutes between 7am and 7pm daily, then every 20 minutes until 10pm.

Getting Around

BICYCLE Cambridge is very bike-friendly, and two wheels provide a great way of getting about town.

Cambridge Station Cycles (www.stationcycles.co.uk; Station Bldg, Station Rd; per half-day/day/week £8/12/20) Near the train station.

City Cycle Hire (www.citycyclehire.com; 61 Newnham Rd; per half-day/day/week from £6/10/20)

BUS A free gas-powered City Circle bus runs around the centre, stopping every 15 minutes from 9am to 5pm, on Downing St, King's Pde and Jesus Lane. City bus lines run around town from Drummer St bus station; C1, C3 and C7 stop at the train station. Dayrider passes (£3.30) offer unlimited travel on all buses within Cambridge for one day.

Around Cambridge

GRANTCHESTER

Old thatched cottages with gardens covered in flowers, breezy meadows and some classic cream teas aren't the only reason to make the pilgrimage along the river to the picture-postcard village of Grantchester. You'll also be following in the footsteps of some of the world's greatest minds on a 3-mile walk, cycle or punt that has changed little since Edwardian times.

The journey here is idyllic on a sunny day, and once you arrive you can flop into a deck chair under a leafy apple tree and wolf down calorific cakes or light lunches at the quintessentially English **Orchard Tea Garden** (www.orchard-grantchester.com; Mill Way; lunch mains £6-8; ⏰9.30am-7pm). This was the favourite haunt of the Bloomsbury Group and other cultural icons who came to camp, picnic, swim and discuss their work.

IMPERIAL WAR MUSEUM

The romance of the winged war machine is alive and well at Europe's biggest **aviation museum** (http://duxford.iwm.org.uk; Duxford; adult/child £16.50/free; ⏰10am-6pm) where almost 200 lovingly waxed aircraft are housed. The vast airfield, once a frontline fighter station in WWII, showcases everything from dive bombers to biplanes, Spitfire and Concorde.

Also included is the stunning **American Air Museum** hangar, designed by Norman Foster, which has the largest collection of American civil and military aircraft outside the USA, and the slick **AirSpace hangar** which houses an exhibition on British and Commonwealth aviation. WWII tanks and artillery can be seen in the **land-warfare hall**, and the regular **airshows** of modern and vintage planes are legendary.

Duxford is 9 miles south of Cambridge at Junction 10 of the M11. Bus C7 runs from Emmanuel St in Cambridge to Duxford (45 minutes, every half-hour, Monday to Saturday). The last bus back from the museum is at 5.30pm. The service is hourly on Sundays.

Ely

POP 15,102

A small but charming city steeped in history and dominated by a jaw-dropping cathedral, Ely (*ee*-lee) makes an excellent daytrip from Cambridge. Beyond the dizzying heights of the cathedral towers lie medieval streets, pretty Georgian houses and riverside walks reaching out into the eerie fens that surround the town. The abundance of eels that once inhabited the undrained fens gave the town its unusual name, and you can still sample eel stew or eel pie in local restaurants. Ely is a sleepy kind of place where traditional tearooms and antiques shops vie for attention, but it also ranks as one of the fastest-growing cities in Europe, so change is surely on the way.

Sights

Ely Cathedral CATHEDRAL

(www.elycathedral.org; adult/child £6/free; ⌚9am-5pm) Dominating the town and visible across the flat fenland for vast distances, the stunning silhouette of Ely Cathedral is locally dubbed the 'Ship of the Fens'.

Walking into the early 12th-century Romanesque nave, you're immediately struck by its clean, uncluttered lines and lofty sense of space. The cathedral is renowned for its entrancing ceilings and the masterly 14th-century octagon and lantern towers, which soar upwards in shimmering colours.

The vast 14th-century Lady Chapel is the biggest in England; it's filled with eerily empty niches that once held statues of saints and martyrs. They were hacked out unceremoniously by iconoclasts during the English Civil War. However, the astonishingly delicate tracery and carving remain.

The cathedral is a breathtaking place, its incredible architecture and light making it a popular film location. You may recognise some of its fine details from scenes in *Elizabeth: The Golden Age* or *The Other Boleyn Girl*, but wandering back to the streets it can be difficult to imagine how such a small and tranquil city ended up with such a fine monument.

Although a sleepy place today, Ely has been a place of worship and pilgrimage since at least 673, when Etheldreda, daughter of the king of East Anglia, founded a nunnery here. A colourful character, Ethel shrugged off the fact that she had been twice married in her determination to become a nun and was canonised shortly after her death. The nunnery was later sacked by the Danes, rebuilt as a monastery, demolished and then resurrected as a church after the Norman Conquest. In 1109 Ely became a cathedral, built to impress mere mortals and leave them in no doubt about the power of the church.

For more insight into the fascinating history of the cathedral join a free **guided tour**, or a **tower tour** (£4 Mon-Sat, £6 Sun, Apr-Oct) of the Octagon Tower or the West Tower. Tour times change daily and by season so check in advance. It's also worth timing a visit to attend the spine-tingling **Evensong** (⌚5.30pm Mon-Sat, 4pm Sun) or **choral service** (⌚10.30am Sun).

Near the entrance a **stained-glass museum** (www.stainedglassmuseum.com; adult/child £3.50/2.50; ⌚10.30am-5pm Mon-Fri, to 5.30pm Sat, noon-6pm Sun) tells the history of decorated glasswork from the 14th century onwards.

Historic sites cluster about the cathedral's toes. Look out for the **Bishop's Palace**, now used as a nursing home, and **King's**

SOMETHING FOR THE WEEKEND

Start your weekend in style with a night of romance and fine dining at Cambridge's **Hotel du Vin**, and venture out for a nightcap at the celebrated pub, the **Eagle**. Next morning check out the university colleges, dip into the sublime **King's College Chapel** and then reward yourself with lunch at swanky **Midsummer House**. In the afternoon, work off your excesses by **punting** along the Backs before bidding farewell to the glorious college architecture and breezing east to the **Stour Valley** and the time-transcending streets of gorgeous **Lavenham**. Install yourself in the spectacular and none-too-frugal **Lavenham Priory** and explore the town's higgledy-piggledy lanes to work up an appetite for slick French cuisine at the **Great House**. On Sunday morning roll west to check out the twin stately homes of **Long Melford**, then east for the picture-postcard hamlet of **Kersey**, where you can toast the weekend with a pint and pub lunch at the medieval **Bell Inn**.

WORTH A TRIP

PETERBOROUGH CATHEDRAL

England may be filled with fine cathedrals boasting ostentatious facades, but few can rival the instant 'wow' factor of Peterborough's unique early 13th-century western front, with its three cavernous Gothic arches.

Visitors enter the **cathedral** (www.peterborough-cathedral.org.uk; requested donation £3; ⌚9am-5.15pm Mon-Fri, to 3pm Sat, noon-3.15pm Sun), which was founded in 1118, through an odd 14th-century porch that peeks out between the arches. Inside, you'll be immediately struck by the height of the magnificent three-storeyed Norman nave and by its lightness, created by the mellow local stone and fine clerestory windows. The nave is topped by a breathtaking early 13th-century painted-timber ceiling, which is one of the earliest and most important of its kind in Europe and still sports much of its original diamond-pattern paintwork.

Press on below the Gothic tower, which was painstakingly reconstructed in the 19th century, to the northern choir aisle and you'll find the rather plain tombstone of Henry VIII's first wife, the tragic Catherine of Aragon, buried here in 1536. Her divorce, engineered by the king because she could not produce a male heir, led to the Reformation in England. Her only child (a daughter) was not even allowed to attend her funeral. Just beyond this is the cathedral's wonderful 15th-century eastern tip, which has superb fan vaulting thought to be the work of master mason John Wastell, who worked on King's College Chapel in Cambridge.

Loop around into the southern aisle, and you'll find gold lettering marking the spot where the ill-fated Mary, Queen of Scots was once buried. On the accession of her son, James, to the throne, her body was moved to Westminster Abbey.

The cathedral alone is well worth a day-trip from Cambridge or London, and the hour-long **tours** (£4; 2pm Mon, Tue & Thu-Sat, 11.30am Wed) are worth it.

The train station is an easy walk from the cathedral. Trains run to Cambridge (£6.50, 50 minutes, hourly) and London's King's Cross (£23, 45 minutes, every 15 minutes).

School, which keeps the cathedral supplied with fresh-faced choristers.

Cromwell's House MUSEUM
(☎01353-662062; adult/child £4.50/4; ⌚10am-5pm Apr-Oct, 11am-4pm Nov-Mar) A short hop from the cathedral across St Mary's Green is the attractive half-timbered house where England's warty warmonger lived with his family from 1636 to 1646, when he was the local tithe collector. The house now has Civil War exhibits, portraits, waxworks and echoes with canned commentaries of – among other things – the great man's grisly death, exhumation and posthumous decapitation.

Ely Museum MUSEUM
(www.elymuseum.org.uk; Market St; adult/child £3.50/2.50; ⌚10.30am-5pm Mon-Sat, 1-5pm Sun, closed Tue Nov-Apr) Housed in the Old Gaol House, complete with prisoners' cells and their scrawled graffiti, this place has everything from Roman remains to archive footage of eel-catching. It's the place to catch up on local history, from the formation of the Fens to the local role in the World Wars.

Waterside Antiques Centre ANTIQUES CENTRE
(www.ely.org.uk/waterside.html; The Wharf; ⌚9.30am-5.30pm Mon-Sat, 11.30am-5.30pm Sun) A great place for rummaging.

Great Ouse RIVERSIDE WALK
From the antiques centre, this charming riverside walk ambles east with the Fens stretching to the horizon.

Sleeping & Eating

You'll find a good choice of pubs serving decent food along the waterfront and the lanes off it.

Cathedral House B&B ££
(☎01353-662124; www.cathedralhouse.co.uk; 17 St Mary's St; s/d £50/80; P) Set in a lovely Georgian house bursting with antiques and curios, this elegant B&B offers three individually decorated rooms, all with period features and cast-iron baths. Outside there's a beautiful walled garden and views of the cathedral.

Riverside Inn B&B ££
(☎01353-439396; www.riversideinn-ely.co.uk; 8 Annesdale; s/d £65/90; P) You'll get great views of the river from this elegant house right on the waterfront. It has four spacious rooms with king-size beds, silky, brocade bedspreads, dark furniture and sparkling new bathrooms.

Old Fire Engine House TRADITIONAL BRITISH ££
(☎01353-662582; www.theoldfireenginehouse.co.uk; 25 St Mary's St; two-/three-course set lunch £15/20, mains £14-17; ⊙closed dinner Sun) Backed by beautiful gardens and showcasing a variety of artwork, this delightfully homey place serves classic English food and excellent afternoon teas. Expect the likes of steak-and-kidney pie or rabbit with prunes and bacon washed down with a carefully chosen wine. Book in advance.

Boathouse MODERN BRITISH ££
(☎01353-664388; www.cambscuisine.com; 5 Annesdale; two-/three-course set lunch £12/16, dinner mains £10.50-17) This sleek riverside restaurant dishes up excellent modern English food at very reasonable prices. It has wonderful patio dining overlooking the water, while the stylish interior is lined with oars. Book ahead.

Peacocks TEAROOM £
(www.peacockstearoom.co.uk; 65 Waterside; cream teas £6.50; ⊙10.30am-4.30pm Wed-Sun) Voted one of Britain's top teashops by the ladies who know at the Tea Guild, this wisteria-clad place serves a vast selection of leaf teas, as well as luscious homemade cakes and soups, salads and sandwiches.

Information

Tourist office (☎01353-662062; www.visitely.org.uk; 29 St Mary's St; ⊙10am-5pm) Stocks a leaflet on the 'Eel Trail' town walk and organises guided walking tours of the city at 2.30pm on some Sundays (£3.70).

Getting There & Away

The easiest way to get to Ely from **Cambridge** is by train (15 minutes, every 20 minutes); don't even consider the bus – it takes a roundabout route and five times as long. There are also trains to **Norwich** (£13, one hour, every 20 minutes), and hourly services to **King's Lynn** (£5.50, 30 minutes).

Following the **Fen Rivers Way** (map available from tourist offices), it's a lovely 17-mile towpath walk from Cambridge to Ely.

ESSEX

Ah, Essex; home to chavs (bling, bling youfs), bottle blonds, boy racers and brash seaside resorts – or so the stereotype goes. The county's inhabitants have been the butt of some of England's cruellest jokes and greatest snobbery for years, but beyond the fake Burberry bags and slots 'n' bumper car resorts, there's a rural idyll of sleepy medieval villages and rolling countryside. One of England's best-loved painters, Constable, found inspiration here, and the rural Essex of his time remains hidden down winding lanes little changed for centuries. Here, too, is the historic town of Colchester, Britain's oldest, with a sturdy castle and vibrant arts scene, and even Southend-on-Sea, the area's most popular resort, has a softer side in the traditional cockle-sellers and cobbled lanes of sleepy suburb Leigh.

Colchester

POP 104,390

Dominated by its sturdy castle and ancient walls, Colchester claims the title as Britain's oldest recorded city, with settlement noted here as early as the 5th century BC. Centuries later in AD 43, the Romans came, saw, conquered and constructed their northern capital Camulodunum here. So, too, the invading Normans, who saw Colchester's potential and built the monstrous war machine that is the castle.

Today the city has a rather dowdy atmosphere, but amid the maze of narrow streets in the city centre you'll find a few half-timbered gems, the fine castle and a host of new regeneration projects under way.

Sights

Colchester Castle CASTLE
(www.colchestermuseums.org.uk; adult/child £5.70/3.60; ⊙10am-5pm Mon-Sat, from 11am Sun) England's largest surviving Norman keep (bigger even than that of the Tower of London), once a hair-raising symbol of foreign invasion, now slumbers innocently amid a lush park. Built upon the foundations of a Roman fort, the castle was first established in 1076 and now houses an exceptional interactive museum, with plenty of try-on togas and sound effects to keep young curiosity alive. There are also illuminating **guided tours** (adult/child £2/1, hourly noon to 3pm) of the Roman vaults, Norman rooftop chapel and castle walls.

FREE **Hollytrees Museum** MUSEUM
(High St; www.colchestermuseums.org.uk; ⏲10am-5pm Mon-Sat, from 11am Sun) Housed in a graceful Georgian town house beside the castle, this museum trawls through 300 years of domestic life with quirky surprises that include a shipwright's baby carriage in the shape of a boat and a make-your-own Victorian silhouette feature. There are also temporary exhibitions and events throughout the year.

Dutch Quarter HISTORIC DISTRICT
The best of the city's half-timbered houses and rickety roof lines are clustered together in this Tudor enclave just a short stroll north of High St. The area remains as a testament to the 16th-century Protestant weavers who fled here from Holland.

FREE **firstsite** ARTS CENTRE
(www.firstsite.uk.net; St Botolph's) Already being promoted as a star attraction, this sparkly new arts centre was just taking shape at the time of writing. A stunning curved-glass and copper building, it will contain gallery space, a library, auditorium and conference facilities and will play host to exhibitions, workshops, lectures and performances. Check the website or tourist office for the latest information.

FREE **Clock Museum** MUSEUM
(Trinity St; www.colchestermuseums.org.uk; ⏲10am-1pm & 2-5pm Tue-Sat Apr-Oct) One of the largest clock collections in Britain housed in a magnificent 15th-century timber-framed building.

Colchester Zoo ZOO
(www.colchester-zoo.co.uk; Maldon Rd, Stanway; adult/child £17/10; ⏲9.30am-5.30pm) World-class naturalistic enclosures, 5 miles northeast of the castle. Bus 75 stops here.

Tours

Tourist Office WALKING TOUR
(☎01206-282929; www.visitcolchester.com; adult/child £3/1.50) Runs 90-minute, guided tours at 11.30am and/or 2pm daily in July and August, Saturdays only March to June and September to October.

City Sightseeing BUS TOUR
(www.city-sightseeing.com; adult/child £7.50/3; ⏲Apr-Sep) Twice daily open-top bus tours.

Sleeping & Eating

Colchester has some excellent, lovingly cared for and reasonably priced B&Bs that give the town's ancient hotels a real run for their money. Independent restaurants are in short supply, but you'll find all the usual chains along North Hill.

Charlie Browns B&B ££
(☎01206-517541; www.charliebrownsbedandbreakfast.co.uk; 60 East St; s/d £45/65; P@) A former hardware shop turned boutique B&B, this place offers incredible value, with a couple of stunning rooms blending 14th-century character with 21st-century style. Antique and modern furniture mix seamlessly with the half-timbered walls, limestone bathrooms and rich fabrics to create an intimate, luxurious feel. It's an absolute steal at these rates and should be your first port of call.

Trinity Townhouse B&B ££
(☎01206-575955; www.trinitytownhouse.co.uk; 6 Trinity St; s/d from £70/85;) This central Tudor town house has five lovely rooms, each with its own character. Go for four-poster Wilbye, cottage-style Darcy or the more modern Furley. Each has period features, king-size beds, flatscreen TV and a designer bathroom. No children under five.

Old Manse B&B ££
(☎01206-545154; www.theoldmanse.uk.com; 15 Roman Rd; s/d from £45/68; P) Hidden away on a quiet tree-lined square close to the castle, this friendly B&B is set in a Victorian house with a pretty garden. There are two spacious double rooms with large bay windows, white linens and homemade biscuits on arrival. A smaller third bedroom is also available.

Lemon Tree MODERN EUROPEAN ££
(☎01206-767337; www.the-lemon-tree.com; 48 St John's St; mains £11-16; ⏲closed Sun) This zesty little eatery serves a refreshing menu of European classics with a modern twist. The decor strikes a nice chic-to-rustic balance, with a section of knobbly Roman wall flanking the main dining area. There are tasty blackboard specials, frequent gourmet nights, a pianist on Monday nights and regular special events.

Green Room MODERN BRITISH ££
(☎01206-574001; 50-51 North Hill; lunch mains £6-8, dinner mains £13-16;) Relaxed, friendly and down to earth, this easygoing bistro has simple wooden tables, bright artwork and some of the best food in town. Locally sourced meats, fish and oysters feature heavily on the seasonal menu, and it buzzes with happy diners lapping up the superb food.

ANGLIAN ANTICS

Ah, the English; stiflingly proper, embarrassingly prudish and impeccably reserved. And just a little bit eccentric. Where else could you see laser technology employed to shoot peas, watch Elvis roll a wooden blue cheese down a village high street or find grown adults painting snails with racing stripes? Well, East Anglia of course.

Here you can enter your own pet invertebrate in the **World Snail Racing Championships** (www.snailracing.net) in Congham, about 7 miles east of King's Lynn. Each year more than 300 racing snails gather here in mid-July to battle it out for a tankard full of juicy lettuce leaves.

In Witcham, about 8 miles west of Ely, it's the **World Pea Shooting Championships** (www.witcham.org.uk) that draws contestants from far and wide. The schoolroom prank of blasting dried peas through a tube at a target (not the school master this time round) is alive and well with shooters gathering in early July on the Village Green.

And in the village of Stilton, a few miles south of Peterborough, every May Day bank holiday sees teams in fancy dress scramble along the High St to become **Stilton cheese rolling champions** (www.stilton.org).

Information

Compuccino (www.compuccino.co.uk; 17-19 Priory Walk; per hr £2.50; 9am-6.30pm Mon-Sat, 11am-5pm Sun) Internet access.

Post office (North Hill & Longe Wyre St)

Tourist office (01206-282920; www.visitcolchester.com; 1 Queen St; 9.30am-5pm Mon-Sat) Opposite the castle.

Getting There & Away

The bus station is on Queen St. There are three daily National Express buses to **London Victoria** (£13, 2½ hours).

There are two train stations, but mainline services stop at Colchester Station, about half a mile north of the centre. Trains run to **London Liverpool St** (£21, one hour, every 15 minutes).

Dedham Vale

I love every stile and stump and lane...
these scenes made me a painter

John Constable (1776–1837)

Born and bred in East Bergholt, John Constable's romantic visions of country lanes, springtime fields and babbling creeks were inspired by and painted in this serene vale. The area has hung on to its rural charm despite the intervening centuries, and although you may not see the rickety old cart pictured in his renowned painting *The Hay Wain,* the background of picturesque cottages, beautiful countryside and languid charm remains.

Now known as Constable country, Dedham Vale centres on the picturesque villages of **Dedham**, **East Bergholt** and **Flatford.** It's a glorious area to explore on foot or by bike, with leafy lanes, stunning pastoral views, graceful old churches and a wonderful choice of accommodation. There's a **tourist office** (01206-299460; www.dedhamvalestourvalley.org; Flatford Lane, East Bergholt; 10am-5pm Easter-Oct, 10.30am-4pm Sat & Sun Nov–mid-Mar) beside the vale's top attraction, a riverside mill once owned by the artist's family. **Flatford Mill** is now used as an education centre and there is no public access. Constable fans will recognise the picturesque red brick mill immediately as it features in many of his paintings and remains as idyllic a setting today.

Near the mill is thatched **Bridge Cottage** (NT; www.nationaltrust.org.uk; Flatford Lane, East Bergholt; parking £2.70; 10.30am-5.30pm May-Sep; admission free), which has an exhibition on the artist. The cottage has varied opening hours outside high season. Check the website for details.

If you'd like to base yourself here, try **Dedham Hall** (01206-323027; www.dedhamhall.co.uk; Dedham; s/d £65/110), an atmospheric 15th-century manor house where you can also take three-/seven-day **painting courses** (£220/275) if you fancy following in Constable's footsteps.

Alternatively, pamper yourself at the luxurious **Maison Talbooth** (01206-322367; www.milsomhotels.com; Stratford Rd, Dedham; r£225-325; P) or its sister hotel **Milsoms** (01206-322795; s/d from£95/115) which is next door. The **riverside restaurant** (mains £22-30) is divine.

Buses 247 and 87a run regularly from Colchester to Dedham (40 minutes); buses

93 and 93A run to East Bergholt (35 minutes). By train, come to Manningtree (eight minutes) and proceed on foot on a lovely 2-mile walk to the mill.

Saffron Walden

POP 14,313

The sleepy, higgledy-piggledy town of Saffron Walden is a delightful knot of half-timbered houses, narrow lanes, crooked roofs and ancient buildings. It's a really lovely place to wander, with some real architectural gems and a host of antique shops, galleries and second-hand bookshops to catch your eye.

The town gets its curious title from the saffron crocus, which was cultivated in the surrounding fields from the 15th century right through to the first half of the 20th century.

The **tourist office** (01799-524002; www.visitsaffronwalden.gov.uk; 1 Market Pl; 9.30am-5pm Mon-Sat) provides a useful town trail leaflet with information on the town's historic buildings.

Sights

The town's most famous building is the 14th-century **Sun Inn** (Church St), an ornate wooden structure once used as Cromwell's HQ. Don't miss the stunning 17th-century pargeting (decorative plaster work).

Nearby is the jumbo-size 15th-century **Church of St Mary the Virgin** (Church St). A symbol of the town's saffron-inspired golden age, it is one of the largest in the county and sports some impressive Gothic arches and decorative wooden ceilings.

In the little **museum** (www.saffronwaldenmuseum.org; Museum St; adult/child £1.50/free; 10am-5pm Mon-Sat, 2-5pm Sun), itself dating from 1835, you'll find an eclectic collection of artefacts covering everything from local history to costume and needlecraft, Victorian toys and ancient Egypt. The bramble-covered ruins of **Walden Castle Keep**, built about 1125, lie in the grounds.

Tucked down at the end of quiet lanes off Bridge St and Castle St is **Bridge End Garden** (www.bridgeendgarden.org; dawn to dusk; admission free), a restored Victorian garden, and on the eastern side of the town, a tiny turf **labyrinth** thought to be 800 years old.

Sleeping & Eating

Accommodation options in Saffron are limited; a day-trip from Cambridge may be a better bet.

Saffron Walden YHA HOSTEL £
(0845-371 9137; www.yha.org.uk; 1 Myddylton Pl; dm £14; mid-Apr–mid-Sep) This stunning medieval timber-framed hostel is the town's oldest inhabited building. It was once a malt house, and although facilities are relatively basic, the place just drips with character. The hostel often gets booked up with groups, so make a reservation in advance.

Saffron Hotel HOTEL ££
(01799-522676; www.saffronhotel.co.uk; 8-12 High St; s/d from £59/79;) The best of the town's lacklustre hotels, this place offers decent but instantly forgettable rooms. Some are furnished in a traditional style, others in business-like modern fashion and all could do with a little loving care.

Eight Bells PUB ££
(18 Bridge St; mains £10-18; closed dinner Sun) A warm mix of medieval character and contemporary style, this 16th-century gastropub is the top spot in town. Scrubbed wooden floors, half-timbered walls, abstract art, deep leather sofas and roaring fires make it a great place to sip on a pint or enjoy a top-notch meal from the modern European menu.

Getting There & Around

BUS The C7 bus runs into Cambridge hourly (70 minutes). Buses 301 and 59 run from Audley End station into Saffron Walden (15 minutes) regularly on weekdays, less often on weekends.

TRAIN Audley End station is 2.5 miles west of town.

London Liverpool St £15.50, one hour, twice hourly Mon-Sat, hourly Sun

Cambridge £5.60, 20 minutes, every 20 minutes

Around Saffron Walden

Positively palatial in its scale, style and the all-too-apparent ambition of its creator, the first earl of Suffolk, the fabulous early-Jacobean **Audley End House** (EH; www.english-heritage.org.uk; adult/child £11.90/6; 11am-5pm Wed-Sun Apr-Sep) eventually did become a royal palace when it was bought by Charles II in 1668.

Although hard to believe, the enormous building today is only one-third of its original size, but it's still magnificent. Its lavishly decorated rooms glitter with silverware, priceless furniture and paintings, making it one of England's grandest country homes. The sumptuous interior was remodelled in Gothic style by the third Baron Braybrooke in the 19th century, and much of his creations are what remain today. You can also visit the service wing, where a new exhibition explores the lives of those who worked in the house in Victorian times.

Outside, the house is surrounded by a dreamy landscaped **park** (⏱10am-6pm Wed-Sun Apr-Sep, earlier closing in low season) designed by Lancelot 'Capability' Brown. The grounds play host to a series of concerts throughout the summer months.

Audley End House is 1 mile west of Saffron Walden on the B1383. Audley End train station is 1¼ miles from the house. Taxis will ferry you here from the town marketplace for around £5.

Southend-On-Sea

POP 160,257

Crass, commercialised and full of flashing lights, Southend is London's lurid weekend playground, full of gaudy amusements and seedy nightclubs. But beyond the tourist tat, roller coasters and slot machines there's a glorious stretch of sandy beach, an absurdly long pier and in the suburb of Old Leigh, a traditional fishing village of cobbled streets, cockle sheds and thriving art galleries.

Sights & Activities

Other than miles upon miles of tawny imported-sand and shingle **beaches**, Southend's main attraction is its **pier** (☎01702-215620; pier train adult/child £3/1.50, pier walk & ride £2.50/1.50; ⏱8.15am-8pm Easter-Oct, to 4pm Mon-Fri, to 6pm Sat & Sun Nov-Easter), built in 1830. At a staggering 1.33 miles long – the world's longest – it's an impressive edifice and a magnet for boat crashes, storms and fires, the last of which ravaged its tip in 2005. It's a surprisingly peaceful stroll to the lifeboat station at its head, and you can hop on the **Pier Railway** to save the long slog back.

Afterwards, dip beneath the pier's entrance to see the antique slot machines at the **museum** (www.southendpiermuseum.co.uk; adult/child £1/free; ⏱11am-5pm Sun-Wed).

If the seaside tat is not your thing, swap the candyfloss for steaming cockles wrapped in newspaper in the traditional fishing village of **Old Leigh**, just west along the seafront. Wander the cobbled streets, cockle sheds, art galleries and craft shops for a taste of life before the amusement arcades took over. The **Leigh Heritage Centre** (☎01702-470834; High St, Old Leigh) offers an insight into the history and heritage of the village and its buildings. The centre is run by volunteers so call in advance to check opening times.

Sleeping & Eating

Southend is blessed with some excellent accommodation options.

Hamiltons HOTEL ££
(☎01702-332350; www.hamiltonsboutiquehotel.co.uk; 6 Royal Tce; d from £60; @) Set in a classic Georgian terrace house, this gorgeous boutique hotel offers plenty of period character yet has all your 21st-century comforts. Subtle floral wallpapers, weighty traditional fabrics, tasteful reproduction furniture and crystal chandeliers give the rooms a warm, luxurious charm without overloading the senses.

Pebbles B&B ££
(☎01702-582329; www.mypebbles.co.uk; 190 Eastern Esplanade; s/d from £45/65; @) Subtle, contemporary style is a real winner at this lovely B&B on the waterfront. The rooms here still retain their Victorian features, but the decor is modern, with funky wallpapers, plenty of cushions and big, comfy beds.

Beaches B&B ££
(☎01702-586124; www.beachesguesthouse.co.uk; 192 Eastern Esplanade; s/d from £40/70; wi-fi) A welcome respite from violent florals and heavy swag curtains, rooms at Beaches are bright, simple and tasteful, with white Egyptian-cotton bed linen, feather duvets and subtle colour schemes.

Pipe of Port BRITISH ££
(☎01702-614606; www.pipeofport.com; 84 High St; mains £10-21) A Southend institution, this subterranean wine bar and bistro is an atmospheric place, with old-world character, candlelit tables, sawdust-covered floor and its own unique charm. It's famous for its pies, casseroles and fish dishes as well as the lengthy wine list. Book ahead.

Mews FUSION ££
(☎01702-393626; www.clarencegroup.co.uk; 2 Nelson Mews; lunch mains £8-13, dinner mains £11-20) Tucked away near the train station, this relaxed, modern restaurant and bar are always buzzing with punters flocking in for the generous portions and reasonable prices for what is some of Southend's best food. There's an open kitchen, an extensive menu and good wine list.

Information

Tourist Office (01702-618747; www.visitsouthend.co.uk; Southend Pier, Western Esplanade; 8.15am-8pm high season, to 6pm low season) At the entrance to the pier.

Getting There & Around

The easiest way to arrive is by train. There are trains roughly every 15 minutes from **London Liverpool St** to Southend Victoria and from London Fenchurch St to Southend Central (£9.40, 55 minutes). The seafront is a 10- to 15-minute walk from either train station. Trains leave Southend Central for **Leigh-on-Sea** (10 minutes, every 10 to 15 minutes).

SUFFOLK

Littered with picturesque villages seemingly lost in time, and quaint seaside resorts that have doggedly refused to sell their souls to tourism, this charming county makes a delightfully tranquil destination. Suffolk built its wealth and reputation on the back of the medieval wool trade, and although the once-busy coastal ports little resemble their former selves, the inland villages remain largely untouched, with magnificent wool churches and lavish medieval homes attesting to the once-great might of the area. To the west are the picture-postcard villages of Lavenham and Long Melford; further north the languid charm and historic buildings attract visitors to Bury St Edmunds; and along the coast the genteel seaside resorts of Aldeburgh and Southwold seem miles away from their more brash neighbours to the north and south.

Information

You can whet your appetite for the region further by visiting www.visit-suffolk.org.uk.

Getting Around

Consult **Suffolk County Tourism** (www.suffolkonboard.com) or **Traveline** (www.travelineeastanglia.co.uk) for local transport information. The two main bus operators in rural areas are **Constable** (www.constablecoachesltd.co.uk) and **Chambers** (www.chamberscoaches.co.uk).

Ipswich is the main transport hub of the region but not really worth a visit in itself. Trains from Ipswich:

London Liverpool St £37.40, 1¼ hours, every 20 minutes

Norwich £12, 40 minutes, twice hourly

Bury St Edmunds £7, 40 minutes, twice hourly

Sutton Hoo

Somehow missed by plundering grave robbers and left undisturbed for 1300 years, the hull of an enormous Anglo-Saxon ship was discovered here in 1939, buried under a mound of earth. The ship was the final resting place of Raedwald, King of East Anglia until AD 625, and was stuffed with a fabulous wealth of Saxon riches. The massive effort that went into his burial gives some idea of just how important an individual he must have been.

Many of the original finds and a full-scale reconstruction of his ship and burial chamber can be seen in the **visitors centre** (NT; www.nationaltrust.org.uk/suttonhoo; Woodbridge; adult/child £7/3.50; 10.30am-5pm). The finest treasures, including the king's exquisitely crafted helmet, shields, gold ornaments and Byzantine silver, are displayed in London's British Museum, but replicas are on show here.

Access to the original burial mounds is restricted, but you can join a one-hour **guided tour** (adult/child £2.50/1.25; 11.30am & 12.30pm), which explores the area and does much to bring this fascinating site back to life. The site is open year-round but has restricted opening hours in low season. Check the website.

Sutton Hoo is 2 miles east of Woodbridge and 6 miles northeast of Ipswich off the B1083. Buses 71 and 73 go to Sutton Hoo, 10 times per day Monday to Saturday, passing through Woodbridge (10 minutes) en route to Ipswich (40 minutes).

Stour Valley

The soft, pastoral landscape and impossibly pretty villages of the Stour Valley have provided inspiration for some of England's best-loved painters. Both Constable and Gainsborough grew up or worked here, and the topsy-turvy timber-framed houses and elegant churches that date all the way back to the region's 15th-century boom in the weaving trade are still very much as they were then. This now-quiet backwater once produced more cloth than anywhere else in England, but in the 16th century production gradually shifted elsewhere and the valley reverted to a rustic idyll. Wander through the region and you'll happen on any number of picturesque villages far from the crowds.

HARVEST AT JIMMY'S

More large-scale village fete than beer-fuelled weekend binge, this wonderfully friendly **festival** (day ticket £32.50, weekend with camping £85;) in mid-September celebrates fine foods, good music and the pleasures of a simple life in the great outdoors. TV personality Jimmy Doherty opens up his Suffolk rare breeds farm for a weekend of top-name bands accompanied by demonstrations by Michelin-starred chefs, cooking master classes, gardening workshops, street theatre, den building and inspired children's events. There's lots of space, a laid-back atmosphere, a farmers market, a pop-up restaurant and food from other TV stars, including the River Cottage crew and the Hairy Bikers.

If you can't make the festival, visit the farm: it's open year-round to visitors who wish to see the animals, explore the woodland nature trail, kick up some dust in the adventure playground or pick up some goodies from the farm shop.

Jimmy's Farm is just south of Ipswich off the A137.

LONG MELFORD

POP 3675

Strung out along a winding road, the village of Long Melford is home to a clutch of historic buildings and two impressive country piles. The 2-mile High St is supposedly the longest in England; it's flanked by some stunning timber-framed houses, Georgian gems and Victorian terraces, and at one end has a sprawling village green lorded over by the magnificently pompous **Holy Trinity Church** (9am-6pm Apr-Sep, to 5pm Nov-Mar). A spectacular example of a 15th-century wool church, it has wonderful stained-glass windows and a tower dating from 1903.

From outside, the romantic Elizabethan mansion of **Melford Hall** (NT; www.nationaltrust.org.uk/melfordhall; adult/child £6.30/3.15; 1.30-5pm Wed-Sun May-Oct, 1.30-5pm Sat & Sun Apr & Oct) seems little changed since it entertained the queen in 1578. Inside, there's a panelled banqueting hall, much Regency and Victorian finery and a display on Beatrix Potter, who was related to the Parker family, which owned the house from 1786 to 1960.

There's a noticeably different atmosphere at Long Melford's other red-brick Elizabethan mansion, **Kentwell Hall** (www.kentwell.co.uk; adult/child £9.40/6.10; noon-4pm Apr-Sep;). Despite being full of Tudor pomp and centuries-old ghost stories, it is still used as a private home and has a wonderfully lived-in feel. It's surrounded by a rectangular moat, and there's a Tudor-rose maze and a rare-breeds farm that'll keep the kids happy. Kentwell hosts special events throughout the year, including several full **Tudor re-creations**, when the whole estate bristles with bodices and hose. Check the website for details.

Long Melford is also famed for its **antique shops**. Viewing appointments are required in some.

Sleeping & Eating

Black Lion Hotel & Restaurant HOTEL ££
(01787-312356; www.blacklionhotel.net; the Green; s/d from £102/157; P) Flamboyant rooms with serious swag curtains, four-poster and half-tester beds, rich fabrics and a creative combination of contemporary style and traditional elegance are on offer at this small hotel on the village green. Go for the deep red Yquem for pure, sultry passion, or try the Sancerre for something a little more restful. The hotel has two restaurants (mains £12 to £19) and a lovely walled Victorian garden.

High Street Farmhouse B&B ££
(01787-375765; www.highstreetfarmhouse.co.uk; High St; r from £60; P) This 16th-century farmhouse offers a choice of cosy but bright rooms full of rustic charm. Expect patchwork quilts, pretty florals, knotty pine and cast-iron or four-poster beds. There's a lovely mature garden outside and hearty breakfasts on offer.

Scutcher's Bistro BRITISH ££
(01787-310200; www.scutchers.com; Westgate St; mains £14-22; closed Sun & Mon) Despite the rather mismatched decor, this unpretentious place is renowned throughout the Stour Valley for its exquisite food. The menu features classic and modern English dishes that leave locals coming back regularly for more. It's just off the Green.

Getting There & Away

Buses leave from High St outside the post office:

Bury St Edmunds 50 min, hourly Mon-Sat

Sudbury 10 min, twice-hourly Mon-Sat

SUDBURY

POP 11,933

Birthplace of celebrated portrait and landscape painter Thomas Gainsborough (1727–88) and the model for Charles Dickens' fictional town Eatanswill in *The Pickwick Papers* (1836–37), Sudbury is a bustling market town that makes for a pleasant hour or two of wandering.

Most visitors come to see the birthplace of painter Thomas Gainsborough at **Gainsborough's House** (www.gainsborough.org; 46 Gainsborough St; adult/child £4.50/3.60; ⏲10am-5pm Mon-Sat), which showcases the largest collection of his work in the world. The 16th-century house and gardens feature a Georgian facade built by Thomas Gainsborough's own father in the 18th century, and a mulberry tree that features in some of his son's paintings. Inside, look for his earliest known work, *A Boy and a Girl in a Landscape,* and the exquisite *Lady Tracy,* celebrated for its delicate portrayal of drapery.

Sudbury has a train station with an hourly service to London (£23, 1¼ hours). There are regular buses to Ipswich (one hour), Long Melford, Lavenham, Bury St Edmunds and Colchester.

LAVENHAM

POP 1738

One of East Anglia's most beautiful and rewarding towns, topsy-turvy Lavenham is home to a wonderful collection of exquisitely preserved medieval buildings that lean and lurch to dramatic effect. Lavenham's 300 half-timbered and pargeted houses and thatched cottages have been left virtually untouched since the town's heyday in the 15th century when it made its fortunes on the wool trade. Curiosity shops, art galleries, quaint tearooms and ancient inns line the streets, where the predominant colour is 'Suffolk pink', a traditional finish of whitewash mixed with red ochre. On top of the medieval atmosphere and beautiful street scenery, Lavenham has an excellent choice of accommodation, making it one of the most popular spots in the area with visitors.

Sights

Many of Lavenham's most enchanting buildings cluster along High St, Water St and around Market Pl, which is dominated by the early 16th-century **guildhall** (NT; www.nationaltrust.org.uk/lavenham; adult/child £3.90/1.60; ⏲11am-5pm Apr-Oct, 11am-4pm Sat & Sun Nov, 11am-4pm Wed-Sun Mar), a superb example of a close-studded, timber-framed building. It is now a local-history museum with displays on the wool trade, and in its tranquil garden you can see dye plants that produced the typical medieval colours.

Also on Market Pl, the atmospheric 14th-century **Little Hall** (www.littlehall.org.uk; adult/child £3/free; ⏲2-5.30pm Wed, Thu, Sat & Sun Apr-Oct) was once home to a successful wool merchant. It's another medieval gem, with soft ochre plastering, timber frame and crown-post roof. Inside, the rooms are restored to period splendour.

At the village's high southern end rises the stunning **Church of St Peter & St Paul** (⏲8.30am-5.30pm Apr-Sep, to 3.30pm Oct-Mar), a late Perpendicular church that seems to lift into the sky, with its beautifully proportioned windows and soaring steeple. Built between 1485 and 1530, it was one of Suffolk's last great wool churches, completed on the eve of the Reformation, and now a lofty testament to Lavenham's past prosperity.

If you're visiting at a weekend it's well worth joining a guided village **walk** (£3, 2.30pm Sat, 11am Sun) run by the **tourist office** (☎01787-248207; lavenhamtic@babergh.gov.uk; Lady St; ⏲10am-4.45pm mid-Mar-Oct, 11am-3pm Sat & Sun Nov–mid-Mar).

Sleeping & Eating

TOP CHOICE **Lavenham Priory** B&B ££

(☎01787-247404; www.lavenhampriory.co.uk; Water St; s/d from £79/105; P) A rare treat, this sumptuously restored 15th-century B&B steals your heart as soon as you walk in the door. Every room oozes Elizabethan charm, with cavernous fireplaces, leaded windows, oak floors, original wall paintings and exquisite period features throughout. Now an upmarket six-room B&B, it must be booked well in advance.

Swan Hotel HOTEL £££

(☎01787-247477; www.theswanatlavenham.co.uk; High St; s/d from £85/170; P) A warren of stunning timber-framed 15th-century buildings now shelters one of the region's best-known hotels. Rooms are suitably spectacular, some with immense fireplaces, colossal beams and magnificent four-posters. Elsewhere the hotel cultivates a gentlefolk's country-club feel. The stunning beamed Great Hall is an atmospheric place to try the modern English cuisine (three-course set dinner £36).

Great House HOTEL ££
(☎01787-247431; www.greathouse.co.uk; Market Pl; d from £90; ⊙lunch Wed-Sat, dinner Tue-Fri; 📶) Chic design blends effortlessly with 15th-century character at this much-loved restaurant in the centre of town. The guest accommodation is decidedly contemporary, with funky wallpaper, sleek furniture and plasma-screen TVs, but there are plenty of period features and a decanter of sherry on the side. The acclaimed restaurant (three-course lunch/dinner £20/32) serves classic French dishes with a modern flourish.

Angel Hotel HOTEL ££
(☎01787-247388;www.maypolehotels.com/angel hotel; Market Pl; s/d from £80/95; P📶) Dating back to 1420, this old coaching inn has been much altered and now offers eight comfortable rooms with exposed beams or brickwork, crisp white linens and minimalist furniture. There's a busy bar and a decent restaurant serving a modern British menu (mains £10 to £16).

ℹ Getting There & Away

Regular buses connect Lavenham with Bury St Edmunds (30 minutes) and Sudbury (20 minutes) hourly until 6pm Monday to Saturday (no service on Sunday). The nearest train station is Sudbury.

KERSEY

Slithering down either side of a steep slope to a shallow ford, picture-perfect Kersey is a pocket-size hamlet lined with handsome timber-framed houses. Strolling the length of the street takes all of five minutes, after which there is little to do here save snap photos, visit the wonderful **Church of St Mary** at the top of the hill, pop into **Kersey Pottery** (www.kerseypottery.com; The Street; ⊙10am-5.30pm Tue-Sat, 11am-5pm Sun) by the ford, or grab some lunch and a pint at the 14th-century, oak-timbered **Bell Inn** (£8-13).

Kersey is 8 miles southeast of Lavenham off the A1141, though there are no direct buses connecting the two. Bus No 772 runs from Kersey to Hadleigh (every two hours), from where you can pick up hourly services to Ipswich or Sudbury.

HADLEIGH

POP 7239

Though it's hard to envisage now, the quiet country town of Hadleigh was once one of the biggest and busiest wool towns in East Anglia, and hidden just off the High St is a lovely cluster of buildings to prove it.

The town's principal jewel is its handsome three-storeyed 15th-century **guildhall** (Church St; admission free), timber framed and topped by a splendid crown-post roof. Next door, there are some fabulous original features to appreciate in 12th-century **St Mary's Church**, with its lanky spire and lofty ceiling.

Also beside the church is the high-and-mighty **Deanery Tower**, built in 1495 as a gatehouse to an archbishop's mansion that never actually got built. It's a very fanciful affair, embellished with decorous battlements and oriel windows.

Hadleigh is 2 miles southeast of Kersey. There are hourly buses from Ipswich (28 minutes) and Sudbury (28 minutes).

Bury St Edmunds

POP 36,218

Once home to one of the most powerful monasteries of medieval Europe, Bury has long attracted travellers for its powerful history, atmospheric ruins, handsome Georgian architecture and bustling agricultural markets. It's a genteel kind of place with tranquil gardens, a newly completed cathedral and a lively buzz. Bury is also home to Greene King, the famous Suffolk brewer.

History

Bury's slogan, 'Shrine of a King, Cradle of the Law' recalls two defining events in the town's history. St Edmund, last Saxon king of East Anglia, was decapitated by the Danes in 869, and in 903 the martyr's body was reburied here. Soon a series of ghostly miracles emanated from his grave, and the shrine became a centre of pilgrimage and the core of a new

A COTTAGE OF YOUR OWN

For self-catering country cottages in the area, have a browse through these sites:

Heritage Hideaways (www.heritage hideaways.com)

Farm Stay Anglia (www.farmstay anglia.co.uk)

Just Suffolk (www.justsuffolk.com)

Norfolk Cottages (www.norfolk cottages.co.uk)

Suffolk Secrets (www.suffolk-secrets.co.uk)

Benedictine monastery. In the 11th century, King Canute built a new abbey that soon became one of the wealthiest and most famous in the country. Meanwhile, the town thrived on the flocks of visiting pilgrims, and with the creation of a planned town surrounding the abbey came an influx of craftspeople.

In 1214 the English barons chose the abbey to draw up a petition that would form the basis of the Magna Carta, making it a 'Cradle of the Law' and setting the country on the road to a constitutional government. In medieval times the town grew rich on the wool trade and prospered until Henry VIII got his grubby hands on the abbey in 1539 and closed it down as part of the Dissolution.

Sights

Abbey & Park ABBEY RUINS

(dawn-dusk) Now a picturesque ruin residing in beautiful gardens behind the cathedral, the once all-powerful abbey still impresses despite the townspeople having made off with much of the stone after the Dissolution. The Reformation also meant an end to the veneration of relics, and St Edmund's grave and bones have long since disappeared.

You enter the park via one of two well-preserved old gates: opposite the tourist office, the staunch mid-14th-century **Great Gate** is intricately decorated and ominously defensive, complete with battlements, portcullis and arrow slits. The other entrance sits further up Angel Hill, where a gargoyle-studded early 12th-century **Norman Tower** looms.

Just beyond the Great Gate is a peaceful garden where the **Great Court** was once a hive of activity, and further on a dovecote marks the only remains of the **Abbot's Palace**. Most impressive, however, are the remains of the **western front**, where the original abbey walls were burrowed into in the 18th century to make way for houses. The houses are still in use and look as if they have been carved out of the stone like caves. Nearby is **Samson Tower** and in front of it a beautiful **statue of St Edmund** by Dame Elisabeth Frink (1976). The rest of the abbey spreads eastward like a ragged skeleton, with various lumps and pillars hinting at its immense size.

St Edmundsbury Cathedral CATHEDRAL

(St James; www.stedscathedral.co.uk; Angel Hill; requested donation £3; 8.30am-6pm) Completed in 2005, the 45m-high Millennium Tower of St Edmundsbury Cathedral

Bury St Edmunds

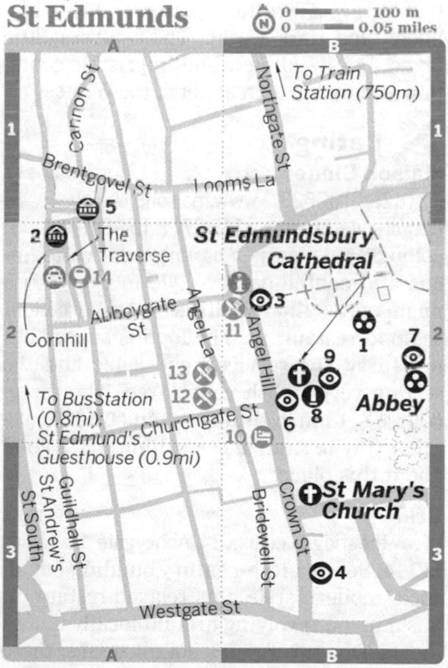

0 — 100 m
0 — 0.05 miles

Bury St Edmunds

Top Sights
- Abbey B2
- St Edmundsbury Cathedral B2
- St Mary's Church B3

Sights
- 1 Abbot's Palace B2
- 2 Art Gallery A2
- Great Court .... (see 3)
- 3 Great Gate B2
- 4 Greene King Brewery B3
- 5 Moyse's Hall Museum A1
- 6 Norman Tower B2
- 7 Samson Tower B2
- 8 Statue of St Edmund B2
- 9 Western Front B2

Sleeping
- 10 Angel Hotel B2

Eating
- 11 Grid B2
- 12 Maison Bleue A2
- 13 Zen Noodle Bar A2

Drinking
- 14 Nutshell A2

is a vision in Lincolnshire limestone, and its traditional Gothic-style construction gives a good idea of how the towers of many other English cathedrals must have looked fresh from the stonemason's chisel.

Most of the rest of the building dates from the early 16th century, though the eastern end is postwar 20th-century, and the northern side was completed in 1990. The overall effect is light and lofty, with a gorgeous hammerbeam roof and a striking sculpture of the crucified Christ by Dame Elisabeth Frink in the north transept. The impressive entrance porch has a tangible Spanish influence, a tribute to Abbot Anselm (1121–48), who opted against pilgrimage to Santiago de Compostela in favour of building a church dedicated to St James (Santiago in Spanish) right here.

For a proper insight into the church's history and heritage join one of the **guided tours** (⏲11.30am Mon-Sat Apr-Sep) of the cathedral.

St Mary's Church CHURCH

(www.stmarystpeter.net/stmaryschurch; Honey Hill; ⏲10am-4pm Mar-Oct, to 3pm Nov-Feb) One of the biggest parish churches in England, St Mary's contains the tomb of Mary Tudor (Henry VIII's sister and a one-time queen of France). Built around 1430, it also has a host of somewhat vampirelike angels swooping from its roof, and a bell is still rung to mark curfew, as it was in the Middle Ages.

Greene King Brewery BREWERY

(www.greeneking.co.uk; Crown St; tours day/evening £8/10; ⏲museum 10.30am-4.30pm Mon-Sat, tours 11am Wed-Mon, 2pm Tue-Sat, 7pm Mon-Fri) Churning out some of England's favourite booze since Victorian times, this famous brewery has a museum (admission free) and runs tours, after which you can appreciate what all the fuss is about in its brewery bar. Tours are popular so book ahead.

FREE **Art Gallery** GALLERY

(www.burystedmundsartgallery.org; Cornhill; ⏲10.30am-5pm Tue-Sat) Temporary exhibitions of contemporary art in a beautiful 18th-century theatre.

Moyse's Hall Museum MUSEUM

(www.stedmundsbury.gov.uk/moyseshall; Cornhill; adult/child £4/2; ⏲10am-4pm) Tells gruesome stories of death, burial and witchcraft in an impressive 12th-century undercroft.

Sleeping

Angel Hotel HOTEL ££

(☎01284-714000; www.theangel.co.uk; 3 Angel Hill; r from £100; P 📶) Peeking out from behind a shaggy mane of vines, this famous old coaching inn has hosted many a dignitary in its long history, including fictional celebrity Mr Pickwick, who, Dickens wrote, enjoyed an 'excellent roast dinner' here. Rooms are split between a slick contemporary wing and a traditional Georgian building. The modern restaurant has bright artwork, high ceilings and a stylish menu (mains £13 to £17).

Fox Inn HOTEL ££

(☎01284-705562; www.thefoxinnbury.co.uk; 1 Eastgate St; s/d from £84/90) Set in an old courtyard barn attached to an even older inn, the rooms here blend the warmth of exposed brick and beams with minimalist contemporary styling. You'll find trendy but subtle wallpapers, tasteful furniture and a relaxed, calming vibe. The restaurant serves a good selection of modern British food (mains £10 to £18). The Fox is about 600m from the cathedral. Head up Angel Hill, bearing right at the end into Mustow St and on to Eastgate St.

St Edmunds Guesthouse B&B ££

(☎01284-700144; www.churchgatehouse.co.uk; 35 St Andrews St Nth; s/d from £40/65; P 📶) This rather faceless modern building hides a well-run guesthouse with simple, bright rooms that have oak furniture, flatscreen TVs, white linens and dark leather chairs. It's a little bland, but it's all new and in pristine condition and makes a great bet at these rates.

Eating

Maison Bleue SEAFOOD £££

(☎01284-760623; www.maisonbleue.co.uk; 31 Churchgate St; mains £15-27; ⏲Tue-Sat) Muted colours, pale leather banquettes, white linens and contemporary style merge with a menu of imaginative dishes in this excellent seafood restaurant. The food is superb but not fussy, the service impeccable and the setting very stylish yet relaxed. The three-course set lunch/dinner menu (£19/29) is a great way to sample everything that's good about this place.

Grid BRITISH ££

(www.thegridgrill.co.uk; 34 Abbeygate St; mains £10-14) Set in a 16th-century building but all slick, modern style, this relaxed restaurant has a menu revolving around locally reared meats. Don't worry, it's not all steaks: there are fish and vegetarian choices, too, and a good range of pasta and risotto dishes. It's bright and cheery, has a relaxed atmosphere and is enduringly popular with the locals.

Zen Noodle Bar ASIAN ££
(6 Angel Lane; mains £8-10; closed Sun) Floor-to-ceiling windows bathe this sleek and contemporary Japanese restaurant in light. The menu also features Thai and Chinese rice dishes and a tempting array of starters for sharing. It's a busy place with long communal tables, but there's plenty of space and a relaxed atmosphere.

Drinking

Nutshell PUB
(The Traverse) Recognised by the *Guinness Book of Records* as Britain's smallest, this tiny timber-framed pub is an absolute gem and a tourist attraction in its own right. Mind how you knock back a pint here: in the crush you never know who you're going to elbow.

Information

Tourist Office (01284-764667; tic@stedsbc.gov.uk; 6 Angel Hill; 9.30am-5pm Mon-Sat Easter-Oct, 10am-3pm Sun May-Sep, 10am-4pm Mon-Fri, 10am-1pm Sat Nov-Easter) Has internet access and is the starting point for guided walking tours (£4, 2pm May to September).

Getting There & Around

BUS The central bus station is on St Andrew's St North.

London National Express; £14, 2½ hours, daily

Cambridge Stagecoach; bus 11, 65 minutes, hourly Monday to Saturday

TRAIN The train station is 900m north of the tourist office, with frequent buses to the centre.

Ely £8, 30 minutes, every two hours

Cambridge £8, 45 minutes, hourly

Around Bury St Edmunds

ICKWORTH HOUSE & PARK

The puffed-up pomposity of stately home **Ickworth House** (NT; www.nationaltrust.org.uk/ickworth; adult/child £8.30/3.30, park only £4.20/1; house 11am-5pm Fri-Tue Mar-Oct, gardens 10am-5pm) is palpable from the minute you catch sight of its immense oval rotunda and wide outspread wings. The building is the whimsical creation of fourth earl of Bristol and Bishop of Derry, Frederick Hervey (1730–1803), and contains fine paintings by Titian, Gainsborough and Velázquez. There's also a lovely Italian garden, parkland bearing the landscaping eye of Capability Brown, a deer enclosure and a hide to explore.

The east wing of the house now functions as the slick **Ickworth Hotel** (01284-735350; www.ickworthhotel.co.uk; d from £205; P @), where the traditional surroundings mix with designer furniture and contemporary style to create a luxurious country hideout. Despite its glam design, families are very welcome, with a play group and games room on offer.

Ickworth is 3 miles southwest of Bury on the A143. Buses 344 and 345 from Bury train station (15 minutes) to Haverhill can drop you nearby.

Aldeburgh

POP 2790

One of the region's most charming coastal towns, the small fishing and boat-building

THE ECCENTRIC EARL

The Hervey family had such a reputation for eccentricity that it was said of them that when 'God created the human race he made men, women and Herveys'. Perhaps the biggest weirdo of them all was the creator of Ickworth House, Frederick (1730–1803). As Bishop of Derry (Ireland) he was renowned not for his piety but for his agnosticism, vanity and oddity: he would force his clergymen to race each other through peat bogs in the middle of the night, sprinkle flour on the floor of his house to catch night-time adulterers, champion the cause of Catholic emancipation (he was, after all, a Protestant bishop) and earn himself the sobriquet of 'wicked prelate' from George III.

Not content with his life in Ireland, in later years Frederick took to travelling around Europe, where he indulged each and every one of his passions: women, wine, art and intrigue. He tried to pass himself off as a spy in France, horrified visiting English aristocrats with his dress sense and manners in Italy, and once chucked a bowl of pasta onto a religious procession because he hated the sound of tinkling bells.

village of Aldeburgh has an understated charm that attracts visitors back year after year. Handsome pastel-colour houses, independent shops, art galleries and ramshackle fishing huts selling fresh-from-the-nets catch line the High St, while a sweeping shingle beach stretches along the shore offering tranquil big-sky views. Although it's a popular place, the town remains defiantly unchanged, with a low-key atmosphere and a great choice of food and accommodation.

Aldeburgh also has a lively cultural scene. Composer Benjamin Britten and lesser-known poet George Crabbe both lived and worked here; Britten founded East Anglia's primary arts and music festival, the **Aldeburgh Festival** (www.aldeburgh.co.uk), which takes place in June and has been going for over 60 years. Britten's legacy is commemorated by Maggi Hambling's wonderful *Scallop* sculpture, a short stroll north along the seashore.

Aldeburgh's other photogenic gem is the intricately carved and timber-framed **Moot Hall** (www.aldeburghmuseum.org.uk; adult/child £1/free; ⏲2.30-5pm), which now houses a local history museum.

A fun way to enjoy the bracing salt air is to follow the **Suffolk Coast and Heaths Path**, which passes around half a mile north of Aldeburgh, along the coast for a few miles. Alternatively, from Aldeburgh follow the path inland for a 3-mile walk towards the village of Snape, through some pleasant wooded areas and fields.

Information can be found at the **tourist office** (☎01728-453637; atic@suffolkcoastal.gov.uk; 152 High St; ⏲9am-5.30pm Mon-Sat, 10am-4pm Sun).

Sleeping

Most places in Aldeburgh ask for a two-night minimum stay at weekends.

TOP CHOICE Ocean House B&B ££
(☎01728-452094; www.oceanhousealdeburgh.co.uk; 25 Crag Path; s/d £70/90) Right on the seafront and with only the sound of the waves to lull you to sleep at night, this beautiful Victorian guesthouse has wonderfully cosy, period-style rooms. Expect pale pastels, subtle florals and tasteful furniture, and the sound of classical music wafting from the rooms occupied by visiting music students. There's a baby grand piano on the top floor, a gaily painted rocking horse and bikes to borrow.

Number Six B&B ££
(☎01728-454226; www.numbersixaldeburgh.co.uk; 6 St Peters Rd; d £95; P) Guests can stay on the self-contained second floor of this New England–style home, where you'll find a spacious bedroom, kitchenette, and a private lounge with balcony and sea views. There's also an option of a second 'secret' adjoining room for children or friends. The decor is cosy contemporary with lots of attention to detail and loads of space.

Dunan House B&B ££
(☎01728-452486; www.dunanhouse.co.uk; 41 Park Rd; r £75-85; P 📶) Set well back off the street in lovely gardens, this charming B&B has a range of individually styled rooms mixing contemporary and traditional elements to surprisingly good effect. With friendly hosts and breakfast assembled from local, wild and home-grown produce, it's a real treat.

Toll House B&B ££
(☎01728-453239; www.tollhousealdeburgh.com; 50 Victoria Rd; s/d £65/80; P) Small but immaculate rooms with cast-iron beds and pretty florals.

Brudenell HOTEL £££
([01728-45071; www.brudenellhotel.co.uk; The Parade; s/d from £105/188) Comfortable, modern hotel with all the associated perks.

Eating

Regatta Restaurant SEAFOOD ££
(☎01728-452011; www.regattaaldeburgh.com; 171 High St; mains £11-18.50; ⏲noon-2pm & 6-10pm) Good ol' English seaside food is given star treatment at this sleek, contemporary restaurant where local fish is the main attraction. The celebrated owner-chef supplements his wonderful seafood with meat and vegetarian options and regular gourmet nights. Book ahead.

Lighthouse MODERN EUROPEAN ££
(☎01728-453377; www.lighthouserestaurant.co.uk; 77 High St; mains £10-15; 👪) This unassuming bistro-style restaurant is a fantastic place to dine, with wooden tables and floors, a menu of simple but sensational international dishes, and a relaxed and friendly atmosphere. Despite the excellent food and accolades piled upon it, children are very welcome.

Munchies CAFE £
(www.aldeburghmunchies.co.uk; 163 High St; dishes £3-7; ⏲8am-5pm) For lunch, a coffee

or picnic supplies, Munchies serves excellent locally sourced goodies such as crayfish and hot smoked-salmon sandwiches, crab salads and luscious cakes.

Fish and Chip Shop TAKE AWAY £
(226 High Street; fish & chips £4-5; ⌚noon-2pm & 5-8pm Mon-Sat, noon-7pm Sun) Aldeburgh has a reputation for the finest fish and chips in the area, and this place generally has a queue coming right out onto the street.

Getting There & Away

Aldeburgh is not well connected in terms of transport. There are frequent bus services to Ipswich (1¼ hours), where you can make connections to the rest of the country.

Around Aldeburgh

Strung along the coastline north of Aldeburgh is a poignant trail of serene and little-visited coastal heritage towns that are gradually succumbing to the sea. Most dramatically, the once-thriving port town of **Dunwich** is now a quiet village, with 12 churches and chapels and hundreds of houses washed away by the water.

The region is a favourite haunt of the binocular-wielding birdwatcher brigade, and **RSPB Minsmere** (www.rspb.org.uk; Westleton; adult/child £5/1.50; ⌚9am-dusk) flickers with airborne activity year-round. Another step south towards Aldeburgh is the odd early 20th-century 'Tudorbethan' holiday village of **Thorpeness**, which sports idiosyncratic follies, a windmill and a boating lake. And if you're wondering what the golf-ball-shaped tumour is looming just north of Thorpeness, that's **Sizewell**, the notorious nuclear-power plant.

With public transport lacking you'll need your own wheels, or the will to walk or bike this stretch of peaceful and varied coastline.

ORFORD

Secluded and seductive, the gorgeous village of Orford, 6 miles south of Snape Maltings, is well worth a detour. It's a laid-back place littered with pretty houses and dominated by the odd polygonal keep of **Orford Castle** (EH: www.english-heritage.org.uk; adult/child £5.30/2.70; ⌚10am-5pm). The 12th-century castle is remarkably intact and has an innovative, 18-sided drum design with three square turrets. You can explore right from the basement to the roof, where there are glorious views of **Orford Ness** (NT; www.nationaltrust.org.uk/orfordness; admission incl ferry crossing adult/child £7.20/3.60; ⌚10am-2pm Tue-Sat), the largest vegetated shingle spit in Europe. Once used as a secret military testing ground, it is now home to a nature reserve and many rare wading birds, animals and plants. There's a 3-mile path lined with information boards and military installations. Ferries run from Orford Quay: the last ferry departs at 2pm and returns from the reserve at 5pm.

On your return make a beeline for the **Butley Orford Oysterage** (www.butleyorfordoysterage.co.uk; mains £7-13), where you'll find fresh seafood, smoked fish and local oysters just waiting to be gobbled up. For overnight stays try the **Crown & Castle** (☎01394-450205; www.crownandcastle.co.uk; r from £125; P) which offers bright, modestly stylish rooms and excellent service from TV hotel inspector Ruth Watson. Their brasserie-style restaurant **Trinity** (mains £16-20) is renowned for its excellent food.

Southwold

POP 3858

Southwold is the kind of genteel seaside resort where beach huts cost an arm and a leg (upwards of £100,000 in some cases if local estate agents are to be believed) and the visitors are ever so posh. Its reputation as a well-heeled holiday getaway has earned it the nickname 'Kensington-on-Sea' after the upmarket London borough, and its lovely sandy beach, pebble-walled cottages, cannon-dotted clifftop and rows of beachfront bathing huts are all undeniably picturesque. Over the years the town has attracted many artists, including Turner, Charles Rennie Mackintosh, Lucian Freud and Damien Hirst.

However, this down-to-earth town also has a traditional pier, boat rides, fish and chips and its very own brewery.

Starting inland, the **Church of St Edmund** (Church St; admission free; ⌚9am-6pm Jun-Aug, to 4pm rest of year) is worth a quick peek for its fabulous medieval screen and 15th century bloodshot-eyed Jack-o-the-clock, which grumpily overlooks the church's rear. A mere stone's throw away is an old weavers' cottage that now houses the **Southwold Museum** (www.southwoldmuseum.org; 9-11 Victoria St; admission free; ⌚10.30am-noon & 2-4pm Aug, 2-4pm Apr-Oct), where you can learn about the explosive 132-ship and 50,000-men Battle of Solebay

(1672), fought just off the coast. You can also take a tour (£10) of the town's brewery **Adnams** (www.adnams.co.uk; Adnams Pl). The one-hour tours are followed by a 30-minute tutored beer tasting. They take place daily in high season but at unpredictable times, so check the website for details.

For most visitors Southwold's shorefront is the main attraction. Take time to amble along its promenade and admire the squat 19th-century **lighthouse** before ending up at the cute little **pier** (www.southwoldpier.co.uk), first built in 1899 but recently reconstructed. In the 'under the pier' show you'll find a quirky collection of handmade slot machines, a mobility masterclass for zimmerframe (walker) users, and a dog's-eye view of Southwold.

If you fancy a bit of a water jaunt, the **Coastal Voyager** (www.coastalvoyager.co.uk) offers a range of boat trips, including a 30-minute high-speed fun trip (adult/child £20/10), a leisurely river cruise (£25/12.50) to nearby Blythburgh, and a three-hour trip to Scroby Sands (£29/14.50) to see a seal colony and wind farm.

Southwold's hippest event is the **Latitude Festival** (www.latitudefestival.co.uk) held in Henham Park in mid-July. An eclectic mix of music, literature, dance, drama and comedy, its stunning location and manageable size make it popular with festival-goers fed up with fields of mud and never-ending queues.

The **tourist office** (01502-724729; www.visit-sunrisecoast.co.uk; 69 High St; 10am-5pm Mon-Sat, 11am-4pm Sun) can help with accommodation and information.

Sleeping & Eating

Despite Southwold's charm and popularity, decent accommodation is thin on the ground.

Sutherland House HOTEL £££
(01502-724544; www.sutherlandhouse.co.uk; 56 High St; d £140-220; P) Set in a beautiful 15th-century house dripping with character and period features, this small hotel has just three rooms featuring pargeted ceilings, exposed beams and elm floorboards but decked out in sleek, modern style. The top-notch restaurant (mains £10 to £17) specialises in local food, with the menu showing how many miles the principal ingredient in each dish has travelled.

Swan HOTEL £££
(01502-722186; www.adnams.co.uk; Market Sq; s/d from £95/135) There's a timeless elegance to the public rooms at the Swan, where large fireplaces, grandfather clocks and old-fashioned lamps induce a kind of soporific calm. You can choose between similarly period-style rooms or the newly refurbished lighthouse rooms with their garden views. The atmospheric restaurant serves a mainly fishy menu (mains £14 to £20).

Gorse House B&B ££
(01502-725468; www.gorsehouse.com; 19B Halesworth Rd, Reydon; d from £65; P) A 10-minute walk from the seafront but well worth the effort, this lovely B&B is one of the best in the area. The two rooms here are newly decorated in simple, contemporary style with subtle-patterned wallpapers, silky throws and flatscreen TVs.

Coasters MODERN BRITISH ££
(01502-724734; www.coastersofsouthwold.co.uk; 12 Queen St; mains £8-15; closed Mon) Right on the main drag, this unassuming restaurant has a great reputation and a loyal local following. The menu is short but sweet, and every dish is memorable. On top of the main meals there are a range of tapas for quick snacks, and sandwiches and cakes for a light lunch. Book ahead for evening meals.

Getting There & Away

Bus connections are surprisingly limited: your best bet is to catch one of the hourly services to Lowestoft (45 minutes) or Halesworth train station (30 minutes) and continue from there.

Around Southwold

WALBERSWICK

These days it requires an interstellar leap of the imagination to picture the sleepy seaside village of Walberswick as the thriving medieval port it once was. Nestled behind sandy dunes, it's a tranquil little backwater popular with well-heeled holidaymakers and home to a huddle of fresh-fish stalls.

If you've got your timing right, don't miss the chance to participate in the bizarre **British Open Crabbing Championships** (www.walberswick.ws/crabbing), held here in July or August, in which contestants compete to capture the heaviest crustacean. Anyone can take part, and competition is fierce, with baits a closely guarded secret.

Just south of the village is the largest block of freshwater reedbed in Britain, incorporated into the **Suffolk Coast National Nature Reserve** (www.naturalengland.org.uk) and home to otters, deer and rare butterflies. It's accessed by a web of public footpaths.

Oak beams, open fires and flagstone floors make the 600-year-old **Bell Inn** (☎01502-723109; www.adnams.co.uk; Ferry Rd; mains £10-15; r from £100) your best bet by far for food and bedding. The bar downstairs serves award-winning seafood but also invites hiding behind high wooden settles with a pint and newspaper. The spacious en suite rooms have pretty decor and muted colour schemes.

Walberswick is a mile south of Southwold separated by the River Blyth. Pick up the path from Southwold's High St to reach a pedestrian bridge, or catch the summer **ferry** (80p; ⏲10am-12.30pm & 2-5pm), which crosses at half-hourly intervals.

NORFOLK

Big skies, sweeping beaches, windswept marshes, meandering inland waterways and pretty flint houses make up the county of Norfolk, a handsome rural getaway with a thriving regional capital. You're never far from water here, whether it's the tranquil setting of rivers and windmills in the Norfolk Broads or the wide sandy beaches, fishing boats and nature reserves along the coast. They say the locals have 'one foot on the land, and one in the sea', and beach and boating holidays are certainly a highlight of the area. But twitchers flock here too, for some of the country's best birdwatching. Meanwhile, in Norwich, the county's bustling capital, you'll find a stunning cathedral and castle, medieval churches, a lively market and an excellent choice of pubs, clubs and restaurants.

Activities

Signposted walking trails include the well-known Peddars Way and Norfolk Coast Path. Other long-distance paths include the **Weavers Way**, a 57-mile trail from Cromer to Great Yarmouth, and the **Angles Way** (www.eastsuffolklinewalks.co.uk/anglesway), which negotiates the valleys of the Rivers Waveney and Little Ouse for 70 miles. Meanwhile the **Wherryman's Way** (www.wherrymansway.net) is a 35-mile walking and cycling route through the Broads, following the River Yare from Norwich to Great Yarmouth.

For a real challenge, the **Around Norfolk Walk** is a 220-mile circuit that combines most of the above.

If you're planning to do the Norfolk Coast Path and don't fancy carrying your bags, **Walk Free** (www.walk-free.co.uk; per bag £10) provides a bag courier service.

Information

Some handy websites:

Independent Traveller's Norfolk (www.itnorfolk.co.uk)

Norfolk Tourist Attractions (www.norfolktouristattractions.co.uk)

Tour Norfolk (www.tournorfolk.co.uk)

Visit Norfolk (www.visitnorfolk.co.uk)

Getting Around

For comprehensive travel advice and timetables, contact **Traveline East Anglia** (☎0871-200 22 33; www.travelineeastanglia.co.uk).

Norwich

POP 121,550

The affluent and easygoing city of Norwich (pronounced norritch) is a rich tapestry of meandering laneways liberally sprinkled with architectural gems – spoils of the city's heyday at the height of the medieval wool boom. A magnificent cathedral lords over it all from one end of the city centre and a sturdy Norman castle from the other. Around these two landmarks a series of leafy greens, grand squares, quiet lanes, crooked half-timbered buildings and a host of medieval churches pan out across this compact and artsy city. Meanwhile thriving markets, modern shopping centres, contemporary-art galleries and a young student population give the city a genial, debonair attitude that makes it one of the most appealing cities in East Anglia. Add easy access to the Broads and sweeping beaches along the coast and you have an excellent base to use for touring the area.

History

Though Norwich's history stretches back well over a thousand years, the city's golden age was during the Middle Ages, when it was England's most important city after London. Its relative isolation meant that it traditionally had stronger ties to the Low Countries than to London, and when Edward III encouraged Flemish weavers to settle here in the 14th century this connection was sealed. The arrival of the immigrants helped establish the wool industry that fattened the city and sustained it right through to the 18th century.

Mass immigration from the Low Countries peaked in the troubled 16th century. In 1579 more than a third of the town's citizens were foreigners of a staunch Protestant stock, which proved beneficial during the Civil War when the Protestant parliamentarians caused Norwich little strife.

Sights

Norwich is a fantastic city to see on foot, with winding laneways and narrow passageways criss-crossing the centre of town. Most radiate from the candy-stripe canopied **Market Square** (8am-4.30pm), one of the biggest and oldest markets in England, running since 1025. As you walk it's impossible to miss the huge number of **medieval churches** (www.norwich-churches.org) in the city. There are 36, to be precise – a testament to the city's wealth during the Middle Ages.

Norwich Cathedral CATHEDRAL

(www.cathedral.org.uk; admission by donation; 7.30am-6pm) Norwich's most stunning landmark is the magnificent Anglican cathedral, its barbed spire soaring higher than any in England except Salisbury, while the size of its cloisters is second to none.

Begun in 1096, the cathedral is one of the finest Anglo-Norman abbey churches in the country, rivalled only perhaps by Durham. The sheer size of its nave is impressive, but its most renowned feature is the superb **Gothic rib vaulting** added in 1463. Among the spidery stonework are 1200 sculpted roof bosses depicting Bible stories. Together they represent one of the finest achievements of English medieval masonry.

Similar bosses can be seen in closer detail in the cathedral's remarkable cloisters. Built between 1297 and 1430, the **two-storey cloisters** are unique in England today and were originally built to house a community of about 100 monks.

Outside the cathedral's eastern end is the grave of the WWI heroine Edith Cavell, a Norfolk-born nurse who was executed for helping hundreds of Allied soldiers escape from German-occupied Belgium. The **cathedral close** also contains handsome houses and the old chapel of King Edward VI School (where English hero Admiral Nelson was educated). Its current students make up the choir, which performs in at least one of the three services held daily.

The visitor entrance to the cathedral is through the stunning new **Hostry** (9.30am-4.30pm Mon-Sat) building, which rises within the walls of its original equivalent. Inside you can learn about the history and role of the Cathedral. For a deeper insight join one

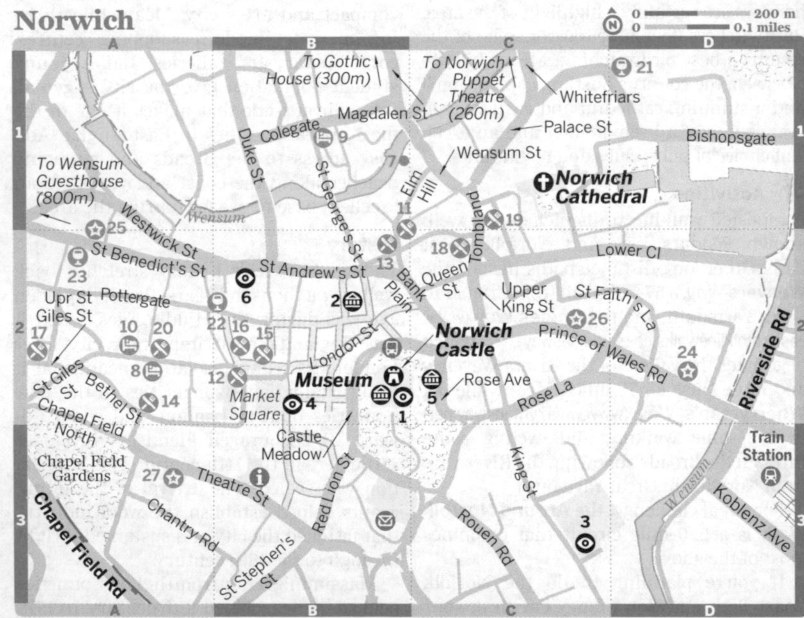

of the fascinating **guided tours** (10.45am, 12.30pm & 2.15pm); the tours are free but a donation is expected.

Tombland & Elm Hill MEDIEVAL STREETS

Leave the cathedral complex by Erpingham gate and turn left onto leafy Tombland, where the market was originally located. Despite its ominous overtones, 'tomb' is an old Norse word for empty, hence space for a market. Cross over and follow Princes St to reach Elm Hill, an utterly charming medieval cobbled street of crooked timber beams and doors, intriguing shops and snug cafes. It's one of the oldest intact streets in the city and now the centre of the local antiques business.

Norwich Castle, Museum & Art Gallery CASTLE

(www.museums.norfolk.gov.uk; castle & exhibitions adult/child £6.20/4.40, exhibitions £3.30/2.40; 10am-5pm Mon-Sat, 1-5pm Sun;) Perched on a hilltop overlooking central Norwich, this massive Norman castle keep is a sturdy example of 12th-century aristocratic living. The castle is one of the best-preserved examples of Anglo-Norman military architecture in the country, despite a 19th-century facelift and a gigantic shopping centre grafted to one side.

It's now home to an art gallery and superb interactive museum. The **museum** crams in a wealth of history, including lively exhibits on Boudicca and the Iceni, the Anglo-Saxons and Vikings, natural-history displays and even an Egyptian gallery complete with mummies. Every room is enlivened with plenty of fun for kids, but best of all is the atmospheric keep itself, which sends shivers down the spine, with graphic displays on grisly punishments meted out in its days as a medieval prison. **Guided tours** (£2.20) also run around the battlements (minimum age eight) and dungeons (minimum age five).

Meanwhile the **art gallery** houses paintings of the acclaimed 19th-century Norwich School of landscape painting founded by John Crome and – trust the English – the world's largest collection of ceramic teapots.

A claustrophobic tunnel from the castle also emerges into a reconstructed WWI trench at the **Royal Norfolk Regimental Museum** (www.rnrm.org.uk; Shirehall, Market Ave; adult/child £3/1.60; 10am-4.30pm Tue-Fri, to 5pm Sat), which details the history of the local regiment since 1830. It has another, less dramatic entrance from the road.

FREE **Sainsbury Centre for Visual Arts** GALLERY

(www.scva.org.uk; 10am-5pm Tue-Sun) Housed in the first major building by Norman Foster, now the darling of Britain's architectural set, the Sainsbury Centre is the most important centre for the arts in East Anglia. Filled with an eclectic collection of works by Picasso,

Norwich

Top Sights

- Museum B2
- Norwich Castle B2
- Norwich Cathedral C1

Sights

1 Art Gallery B2
2 Bridewell Museum B2
3 Dragon Hall C3
4 Mustard Shop B2
5 Royal Norfolk Regimental Museum C2
6 Strangers' Hall B2

Activities, Courses & Tours

7 Broads Boatrains B1

Sleeping

8 38 St Giles A2
9 By Appointment B1
10 St Giles House Hotel A2

Eating

11 Britons Arms B1
12 Caley's Cocoa Cafe B2
13 Elm Hill Brasserie B2
14 Greenhouse A2
15 Library B2
16 Pulse Cafe B2
17 Roger Hickman's A2
18 Shiki C2
19 Tatlers C1
20 Waffle House A2

Drinking

21 Adam & Eve's D1
22 Birdcage B2
23 Ten Bells A2

Entertainment

24 Mercy D2
25 Norwich Arts Centre A1
26 Optic C2
27 Theatre Royal A3

Moore, Degas and Bacon, displayed beside art from Africa, the Pacific and the Americas, it also houses changing exhibitions that cover everything from local heritage to international art movements. Even if you're not an art buff you're almost guaranteed to find something of interest going on here.

The gallery is about 2 miles west of the city centre. To get here take bus 25, 26 or 35 from Castle Meadow (20 minutes).

Strangers' Hall MEDIEVAL HOUSE
(www.museums.norfolk.gov.uk; Charing Cross; adult/child £3.50/2; ⏲10.30am-4pm Wed & Sat) A maze of atmospheric rooms furnished in different medieval styles is on view in this early 14th-century town house. You can see the Great Hall set for a banquet, examine historic toys or try your hand making a bed Tudor style. Outside is a pretty 17th-century knot garden.

Bridewell Museum MUSEUM
(www.museums.norfolk.gov.uk; Bridewell Alley) Closed for major redevelopment at the time of writing, the 14th-century bridewell or 'prison for women, beggars and tramps', is housed in a former merchant's house and is filled with fascinating paraphernalia and reconstructions of Norwich's principal shops and industries. Check the website to find out about new opening hours.

Dragon Hall MEDIEVAL HALL
(www.dragonhall.org; 115-123 King St; adult/child £4.50/3.50; ⏲10am-4pm Mon-Fri, noon-4pm Sun) Another remarkable medieval building, this magnificent trading hall dates from 1430. The first floor great hall has a stunning crown-post roof with a carved dragon figure which gave the building its name. Guided tours are available on Tuesdays at 2pm.

Mustard Shop HISTORIC SHOP
(www.colmansmustardshop.com; 15 Royal Arcade; ⏲9.30am-5pm Mon-Sat, 11am-4pm Sun) Though it's more shop than museum, this replica Victorian shop tells the 200-year story of Colman's Mustard, a famous local product. It's in the lavish art-nouveau Royal Arcade.

Tours

Tourist Office WALKING TOUR
(☎01603-213999; www.visitnorwich.co.uk; adult/child £4/1.50; ⏲11.30am or 2pm Thu-Sat Easter-Oct) The tourist office organises a dizzying array of guided tours and has free downloadable pdf and audio city tours on its website.

City Sightseeing BUS TOUR
(www.city-sightseeing.com; adult/child £8/4; ⏲hourly 10am-4pm Apr-Oct) Hop-on, hop-off bus service stopping at nine destinations around the city centre.

Broads Boatrains BOAT TOUR
(www.cityboats.co.uk; 1hr city cruise adult/child £8.50/6.50) Runs a variety of cruises from Griffin Lane, Station Quay, and Elm Hill Quay.

Tombland Tours WALKING TOUR
(www.tomblandtours.com; adult/child £4/1.50; ⏲1pm Tue-Sun) Walking tours of Norwich's medieval heart around Tombland, the cathedral and Elm Hill. Departs from the Great West Doors of the cathedral.

Ghost Walks WALKING TOUR
(www.ghostwalksnorwich.co.uk; adult/child £6/4; ⏲7.30pm Mon, Tue & Thu Jun-Nov) Tours depart from the Adam and Eve Pub.

Sleeping

Norwich has a dearth of budget-range accommodation, and battle-worn floral-patterned B&Bs are currently the only choice in this price category. You'll find most of them around the train station or outside the ring road. A new youth hostel is planned by the river in the near future; ask at the tourist office for details.

Gothic House B&B ££
(☎01603-631879; www.gothic-house-norwich.com; King's Head Yard, Magdalen St; s/d £65/95; P 📶) Step back in time at this faithfully restored Grade II Regency house hidden away in a quiet courtyard in the heart of the city. There are just two rooms here, but if period style is your thing, they are *the* place to be. From the fabrics and furnishings to the ornaments and mirrors, it just oozes great character and charm. The rooms are bright and spacious, immaculately kept and each has a private bathroom. To get here follow Wensum St north across the river into Magdalen St for 300m.

38 St Giles B&B ££
(☎01603-662944; www.38stgiles.co.uk; 38 St Giles St; s/d from £90/130; P 👪) Ideally located, beautifully styled and reassuringly friendly, this boutique B&B is a real gem. There are no airs and graces here – just handsome, homey rooms with wooden floors, hand-made rugs, original fireplaces and the odd chaise longue. The decor is restrained, with calming colour schemes

and a contemporary feel, yet the whole place seems to have oodles of character. It's a wonderful find right in the centre of town.

St Giles House Hotel HOTEL £££
(☎01603-275180; www.stgileshousehotel.com; 41-45 St Giles St; d incl breakfast £120 210;) Right in the heart of the city in a stunning 19th-century building, you'll find this large hotel with individually styled rooms. There's a grandiose air to the whole place, but the rooms range from fashionably art deco in style to less personal modern decor so check the website before booking. There's a good restaurant serving a modern British menu (mains £13.50 to £22), a spa and a lovely terrace for sipping cocktails.

By Appointment HOTEL ££
(☎01603-630730; www.byappointmentnorwich.co.uk; 25-29 St George's St; s/d incl breakfast from £90/120; @) This fabulously theatrical and delightfully eccentric B&B occupies three heavy-beamed 15th-century merchants' houses, and is also home to a labyrinthine restaurant well known for its classic English fare. Its antique furniture, creaky charm and superb breakfasts make this well worth booking in advance.

Eaton Bower B&B ££
(☎01603-462204; www.eatonbower.co.uk; 20 Mile End Rd; s/d from £50/60; P) A little out of town but worth the effort, this small B&B has a choice of cosy rooms with subtle patterns and traditional styling. En suite bathrooms, free wi-fi, private parking and a touch of period character make it one of the best bets in this price range. The B&B is about 2 miles west of the city centre just off the A11. Or take bus 25 from the railway station.

No 15 B&B ££
(☎01603-250283; www.number15bedandbreakfast.co.uk; 15 Grange Rd; s/d £45/65;) There are just two cosy but uncluttered bedrooms at this serene B&B in a leafy residential street. The rooms have period satinwood furniture, white linens and good bathrooms; breakfasts are vegetarian; holistic massage is on offer, and the whole experience is like a home away from home. No 15 is about a mile west of the city centre. Bus 25 passes nearby.

Beaufort Lodge B&B ££
(☎01603-667402; www.beaufortlodge.com; 60-62 Earlham Rd; s/d £55/70; P@) Giant windows wash the rooms in this Victorian house with light, and the spacious bedrooms have pretty fabrics and wallpapers in period style. The effect is bright and airy, with tasteful traditional touches. It's a great deal and only about a mile west of Market Sq (following Theatre St into Chapel Field North and across the roundabout to Earlham Rd).

Georgian House HOTEL ££
(☎01603-615655; www.georgian-hotel.co.uk; 32-34 Unthank Rd; s/d from £80/95; P) A rambling, elegant Victorian house turned hotel, this place has a choice of spacious, modern rooms decked out in contemporary style. There's a large tree-filled garden and a popular restaurant (mains £12 to £22). The hotel is about 700m west of Market Sq. Follow theatre St into Chapel Field North and turn left at the roundabout to reach Unthank Rd.

Wensum Guesthouse B&B ££
(☎01603-621069; www.wensumguesthouse.co.uk; 225 Dereham Rd; s/d from £45/65; P) A lovely Georgian house with spotless but impersonal modern rooms, some with shared bathroom.

Eating

Norwich has a great choice of places to eat with plenty of options for vegetarians. You'll find a cluster of good restaurants around Tombland.

Roger Hickman's MODERN BRITISH £££
(☎01603-633522; www.rogerhickmansrestaurant.com; 79 Upr St Giles St; 2/3-course set menu lunch £16/19, dinner £30/35; ⊗closed Sun) Understated, classic elegance is what this place is all about: pale floorboards, white linen, bare walls and professional, unobtrusive service. In fact, there's nothing to distract you from the glorious food. Expect top-quality dishes made with flair and imagination and a simple dedication to quality. The set lunch menu is well worth the expense. Book ahead.

Tatlers MODERN BRITISH ££
(☎01603-766670; www.butlersrestaurants.co.uk; 21 Tombland; mains £10-17; ⊗closed Sun) This converted Victorian town house is home to one of the city's best eateries, where local suppliers and ingredients are as important as the final menu. The truly divine dishes are served in a series of unpretentious dining rooms. Come for the set lunch, an excellent-value choice, but be sure to book in advance.

Elm Hill Brasserie FRENCH ££
(☎01603-624847; www.elmhillbrasserie.co.uk; 2 Elm Hill; mains £12-16; ⊗12.30-2.30pm & 5.45-10.30pm Mon-Sat, noon-6pm Sun) On the corner

of the city's most famous street, this simple and elegant restaurant is bathed in light from its giant windows. Scrubbed wooden floors, contemporary style, a relaxed atmosphere and a menu of unfussy, classic French dishes made from seasonal, local ingredients make it always busy. Book in advance.

Library MODERN EUROPEAN ££
(www.thelibraryrestaurant.co.uk; 1a Guildhall Hill; mains £10-13; ⌚closed dinner Sun) Set in a 19th-century library complete with original shelving, this chilled-out brasserie is a great spot for a good-value lunch. The menu is heavy on meats and fish, with dishes cooked in a nifty wood-fired grill, while the interior is sleek and stylish, with exhibitions of work by contemporary local artists.

Shiki JAPANESE ££
(6 Tombland; sushi £1.50-2.80, mains £9-11; ⌚closed Sun) This minimalist Japanese restaurant has a stylish, contemporary interior and a reputation for some of the best Asian food in town. From delicate sushi to superb *teppanyaki*, it's a firm local favourite with a particularly friendly vibe.

Greenhouse VEGETARIAN £
(www.greenhousetrust.co.uk; 42-48 Bethel St; snacks & mains £3.50-7; ⌚10am-5pm Tue-Sat) This organic, free-trade, vegetarian/vegan cafe is bound to leave you feeling wholesome, with a menu of simple dishes, noticeboards crammed with posters for community events, and a lovely vine-covered, herb-planted terrace.

Pulse Cafe VEGETARIAN £
(www.pulsecafebar.co.uk; Labour in Vain Yard, Guildhall Hill; mains £5-7.50;) This funky lounge-bar in the old fire station stables serves a bumper crop of hearty vegetarian dishes. There's also a great choice of sandwiches, organic ciders and beers and scrummy deserts.

Other options:

Waffle House WAFFLES £
(www.wafflehouse.co.uk; 39 St Giles St; waffles £3-9; ⌚10am-10pm Mon-Sat, from 11am Sun) Pop in for a crisp and light Belgian waffle with sweet or savoury toppings at this down-to-earth and friendly cafe beloved by Norwich families, students and professionals.

Caley's Cocoa Cafe CAFE £
(Guildhall, Market Square; snacks £3.50-6; ⌚9am-5pm Mon-Sat) Local chocolate-maker's cafe serving light meals and luscious sweets in the confection-like Guildhall's old Court of Record.

Britons Arms CAFE £
(9 Elm Hill; mains £7; ⌚9.30am-5pm Mon-Sat) Fifteenth-century thatched restaurant serving classic English dishes in a historic setting. Cash only.

Drinking

It was once said that Norwich had a pub for every day of the year, and although that may not be completely true, there's certainly plenty of choice. You'll find hip and trendy or quaint and traditional pubs all across the city centre, but start your quest in Tombland or St Benedict's St for a taste of what's on offer.

Adam & Eve's TRADITIONAL PUB
(www.adamandevenorwich.co.uk; Bishopsgate) A 13th-century brew-house built to quench the thirst of cathedral builders, this is now Norwich's oldest-surviving pub and an adorable little sunken-floored gem. It's a tiny place just loaded with character and popular with discerning locals, old timers and those in search of a quiet pint. There's a pleasant outdoor courtyard for sunny days.

Ten Bells PUB
(76 St Benedict's St) This is this kind of faded 18th-century pub where people feel instantly at ease, calmed by the real ales, mellow red velvet, battered armchairs and quirky memorabilia, including an ancient red phone booth in the corner. It also fancies itself as an intellectuals' hang-out, with poetry readings and arts-school regulars.

Birdcage BAR
(www.thebirdcagenorwich.co.uk; 22 Pottergate;) A bohemian hang-out, this is one of Norwich's quirkiest bars, with slightly kitsch decor that includes strips of bunting, mismatched furniture and a much-loved juke box. There's eclectic music in the back room, plenty of board games, free wi-fi, cabaret nights and a lovely outside deck area.

Entertainment

Norwich has a flourishing arts scene and pulsating weekend nightlife. For what's on information from ballet to boozing try www.norwichtonight.com or, for live music, www.norfolkgigs.co.uk.

Optic NIGHTCLUB
(www.optic-club.co.uk; 50 Prince of Wales Rd; ⌚Mon, Wed, Fri & Sat) Supposedly Norwich's upmarket club, this place features everything from '70s funk to chart-topping anthems.

Mercy NIGHTCLUB
(www.mercynightclub.com; 86 Prince of Wales Rd; ⏲Thu-Sat) A massive club set in a former cinema, with DJs that favour R&B and club classics.

Theatre Royal THEATRE
(www.theatreroyalnorwich.co.uk; Theatre St) Features programs by touring drama, opera and ballet companies.

Norwich Arts Centre ARTS CENTRE
(www.norwichartscentre.co.uk; St Benedict's St) A wide-ranging program of alternative drama, concerts, dance and jazz set in a medieval church.

Norwich Puppet Theatre THEATRE
(www.puppettheatre.co.uk; St James, White-friars; 👪) Set in a cute little repurposed church; goes down well with small and big kids. From the Cathedral follow Palace St east into Whitefriars.

Information

Library (The Forum; ⏲9am-8pm Mon-Fri, 9am-5pm Sat, 10.30am-4.30pm Sun) Free internet for those with ID and the patience to fill out a few forms.

Norfolk & Norwich University Hospital (☎01603-286286; Colney Lane) Four miles west of the centre.

Post office (84-85 Castle Mall)

Tourist office (☎01603-213999; www.visitnorwich.co.uk; The Forum; ⏲9.30am-6pm Mon-Sat, to 2.30pm Sun) Just inside the Forum on Millennium Plain.

Getting There & Around

Norwich has free parking at six **Park & Ride** locations. Buses (£2) run to the city centre up to every 15 minutes from 6.40am to 7.50pm.

AIR **Norwich International Airport** (www.norwichinternational.com) Four miles north of town; has cheap flights to Europe and several British destinations.

BUS The bus station is on Queen's Rd 400m south of the castle. Follow Red Lion St into Stephen's St and then turn left onto Surrey St. The bus station is on the right. **National Express** (www.nationalexpress.com) and **First Eastern Counties** (www.firstgroup.com) run several services out of Norwich.

London £16.60, three hours, seven daily
King's Lynn 1½ hours, hourly
Cromer one hour, hourly
Great Yarmouth 45 minutes, twice hourly

TRAIN The train station is off Thorpe Rd 600m east of the castle.

London Liverpool St £40.40, two hours, twice hourly
Cambridge £13.40, 1¼ hours, twice hourly
Ely £12.90, one hour, twice hourly

Around Norwich

Largely remodelled in the 17th century for Sir Henry Hobart, James I's chief justice, **Blickling Hall** (NT; www.nationaltrust.org.uk/blickling; Blickling; adult/child £9.30/4.60, garden only £6.30/3.15; ⏲house Wed-Mon late-Jul – early-Sep, Wed-Sun early-Sep & Oct & Feb-Jul, gardens 10.15am-5.15pm Mar-Oct, 11am-4pm Thu-Sun Nov-Feb) began life in the 11th century as a manor house and bishop's palace. Today it is a grand Jacobean mansion set in vast parklands and as famous for its ghostly sightings as its spectacular Long Gallery.

In 1437 the isolated house was claimed by the Boleyn family and passed through the generations to Thomas, father of Anne Boleyn. Poor old Anne was executed by her husband Henry VIII in 1533, and it's said that on the anniversary of her death a coach drives up to the house, drawn by headless horses, driven by headless coachmen and containing the queen with her head on her lap.

If you're not around to witness the spectacle that day, there's still quite a lot to see. The grand state rooms are stuffed with fine Georgian furniture, pictures and tapestries, and the Long Gallery has an impressive Jacobean plaster ceiling. There's also an

RURAL ROMANTICS

Valentine's Day forces most people into one of two camps: misty-eyed romantic or born cynic. In Norfolk, however, it seems everyone turns Cupid. Here, a mysterious character called Jack Valentine, a kind of loved-up February Father Christmas deposits a doorstep gift, rattles on the door and then promptly disappears into thin air. In Victorian times lovers went to great lengths to swap parcels on Valentine's Eve, and children rose before dawn the next day to sing valentine rhymes and beg for sweets. The tradition is carried on by many Norfolk families, though it's very rare for whole streets to wake up and find valentine's treats stuck to their doors.

ENGLAND'S FINEST SPIRITS

For 600 years the Nelstrop family have been growing and processing grain, but it was a brave decision to branch out into the ancient art of whisky-making. It's apparently such a daunting task that there has not been a whisky distillery in England for 120 years.

You can visit the **English Whisky Company** (www.englishwhisky.co.uk; Harling Rd, Roudham; ⌚tours hourly 10am-4pm) and take a guided tour (adult/child £5/2) around the distillery, which bottled its first whisky in November 2009. The tour explains the whole process, takes you through the distilling and casking room and ends with a tasting of company whiskies, liqueurs and creams. The company shop stocks a vast array of unusual and rare whiskies, and once a month there's a 'World Whisky' tour (£20), which includes a tour of the distillery with the chief whisky-maker as well as an hour-long tutored tasting of whiskies from around the world. Bring a driver to get you home.

St George's Distillery is just off the A11 between East Harling and Roudham on the B1111.

exhibition describing life below stairs, with stories from those who lived and worked at Blickling over the centuries.

Blickling Hall is 15 miles north of Norwich off the A140. Buses run twice hourly from Castle Meadow and Tombland in Norwich. Aylsham is the nearest train station, 1.5 miles away.

Norfolk Broads

A mesh of navigable slow-moving rivers, freshwater lakes, wild water meadows, fens, bogs and saltwater marshes make up the Norfolk Broads, a 125-mile stretch of lock-free waterways and the county's most beautiful attraction. The official name of the area is the 'Norfolk and Suffolk Broads', but as most of the lakes and waterways are in Norfolk, it's generally called the Norfolk Broads.

The Broads are home to some of the UK's rarest plants and animals and are protected as a national park, with flourishing nature reserves and bird sanctuaries attracting gangs of birdwatchers. But the area's appeal reaches far further, with boaters, families and those in search of scenic tranquillity all wanting a slice of the action.

Despite the Broads' popularity, it's easy to lose yourself in the hypnotic peace of the waterways. A boat is by far the best vantage point from which to spy on its myriad wildlife, and anyone fond of splashing about will undoubtedly want to linger here. Apart from the waterways and the wildlife there are restored windmills, medieval churches and glorious gardens to explore. Walkers and cyclists will also find a web of trails crossing the region, and with the Broads' highest point, How Hill, just 12m above sea level, they're accessible for all.

History

The low-lying nature of the land here was the key to its modern appearance. In the 12th century the land was dug for peat, the only local source of fuel. But dig gaping holes in low-lying land and they're bound to spring a leak. Water gradually seeped through, causing marshes and eventually lakes to develop. As water levels rose, the peat-cutting industry died out and the broads became a landscape of interconnected lakes and rivers. In no other area of England has human effort changed the natural landscape so dramatically. Around How Hill you'll find many of the picturesque wind pumps first built to drain the marshland and to return water to the rivers.

Sights & Activities

The Broads cover a meandering area that roughly follows the Rivers Wensum, Yare, Waveney, Bure, Thurne and Ant. There are more than 150 medieval churches across the area, many of which are made from flint with distinctive round towers. In addition you'll find plenty of waterside pubs, villages and market towns and stretches of river where you can feel you are the only person around.

The best way to see the Broads is to get out onto the water. Cruising is extremely popular in high season and some stretches of the most popular rivers are clogged with boats on sunny weekends. Getting away from the crowds by canoe, on foot or by bike is a far more memorable experience.

Bike and **canoe** hire are available at numerous points across the Broads from Easter to October. Bikes cost about £14 per day (you can also hire child seats and tandems), while canoe hire costs about £35 per day.

Bewilderwood ACTIVITY CENTRE
(www.bewilderwood.co.uk; Hornig Rd, Hoveton; adult/child £11.50/7; ⏲10am-5.30pm Mar-Oct;) A forest playground for children and adults alike, this place is littered with zip wires, jungle bridges, tree houses and all sorts of old-fashioned outdoor adventure. It's a magical kind of place where children can run, jump, swing and climb to their hearts' content. There are marsh walks, boat trips, mazes, den-building activities, plenty of mud and peals of laughter all over the site. You and your young ones will wish you'd found it sooner.

Bus No 12a from Norwich (hourly) drops you right at the door.

Museum of the Broads MUSEUM
(www.northnorfolk.org/museumofthebroads; Staithe, Stalham; adult/child £4/3.50; ⏲10.30am-5pm Easter-Oct) Learn about the traditional Broads' boats, the wherries, the marshmen who gathered reeds and sedge for thatching and litter, and the history and lifestyles of the area at this modest museum. There are displays on everything from early settlements to peat extraction and modern conservation. Visitors can also take a trip on a steam launch (adult/child £3.50/2.50) hourly from 11am to 3pm.

The museum is about 5 miles north of Potter Heigham off the A149.

St Helen's Church CHURCH
(Ranworth; ⏲8am-7pm) Known locally as the 'Cathedral of the Broads', this 14th-century church dominates the pretty village of Ranworth. Inside there's a magnificent painted medieval rood screen, some wonderful stained glass and in a bulletproof cabinet by the main door, a 15th-century antiphoner, a rare illustrated book of prayers. The second antiphoner from the church is in the British Library in London.

For wonderful views of the surrounding broads, climb the series of ladders to the top of the tower. There's also a small visitors centre in a converted coach house next door with displays on East Anglia's churches.

The church is next to a large nature reserve. Follow the leafy woodland path to get to the **Norfolk Wildlife Conservation Centre** (⏲10am-5pm Apr-Oct; admission free), which is set in an unusual thatched float-

LOCAL KNOWLEDGE

MARK WILKINSON: THE CANOE MAN, NORFOLK BROADS

Best paddle:

The **Buxton to Coltishall** stretch of the River Bure. It's really beautiful and you'll see kingfishers, otters, marsh harriers and a very tame barn owl here. You start in the wide open fields with their big skies and great views, then there's a tree-lined section that is like a different world – totally calm even when there's a gale howling elsewhere – the water's crystal clear and you can just meander along at a slow pace. There are no other people here – sometimes another canoeist but even this is quite unusual. At **Horstead Mill** there's a lovely open lock and weir: a great place for picnics and for families. Then you paddle on to **Coltishall Green**, where there are some lovely pubs.

Secret spot:

It's very difficult to access the **River Wensum**, but the stretches you can paddle are simply stunning.

Favourite time of year:

Late September. The holidaymakers are gone, the colours are gorgeous and there's lots of wildlife scurrying about preparing for winter.

A spot of history:

At **Bargate** you can see the remains of 14 wherries (sailing barges traditionally used on the Broads). It's known as the 'wherry graveyard' and you can see the ribs sticking up out of the water.

ing building on the edge of the broad. It has information about the area and its history.

Horsey Windpump WINDMILL
(NT; www.nationaltrust.org.uk; Horsey; adult/child £2.50/1; ⏲10am-5pm) A Grade II–listed building, this five-storey drainage windpump is typical of the area, but unlike many of its counterparts it has been faithfully restored. Built in 1912, it lies just a mile from the sea and it offers great views of the coast and Broads.

The windpump is about 15 miles north of Great Yarmouth on B115.

FREE **Toad Hole Cottage** MUSEUM
(How Hill; ⏲9.30am-6pm Jun-Sep, 10.30am-5pm Apr, May & Oct) This tiny cottage was home to a marshman and his family and is restored in period style, showing how the family lived and the tools they used to work the marshes around them. Nearby is a beautiful thatched Edwardian mansion and a picturesque nature trail.

Bure Valley Steam Railway STEAM TRAIN
(www.bvrw.co.uk; adult/child £7.50/5; ⏲Feb-Oct) This narrow-gauge steam train runs between Aylsham and Wroxham and is an ideal way to see some hidden parts of the Broads. Trains operate on different schedules depending on the month so check the website for details. For an even better experience, take the train in one direction and canoe or cruise your way back. The Canoe Man and Broads Tours both operate a connecting service.

Canoe Man CANOE TRIP
(www.thecanoeman.com; half-day trip £22.50) To see the broads at a slower pace, take to the water by canoe. Day and overnight guided trips to areas the cruisers can't reach are available, as well as canoe and kayak hire, weekend camping canoe trails (two nights £85), bushcraft courses (two/three days £125/175), geo-caching challenges, and paddle-steamer trips, which combine a canoe and steam train trip.

Canoe & Bike Hire

Broadland Cycle Hire (www.norfolkbroadscycling.co.uk; Bewilderwood, Hoveton) Bike hire.

Clippesby (www.clippesby.com; Clippesby) Bike hire.

Otney Meadow (www.outneymeadow.co.uk; Bungay) Bike and canoe hire.

Rowan Craft (www.rowancraft.com; Geldeston) Canoe hire.

Waveney River Centre (www.waveneyrivercentre.co.uk; Burgh St Peter) Bike and canoe hire.

Boat Hire

You can hire a variety of launches, from large cabin cruisers to little craft with outboards for anything from a couple of hours' gentle messing about on the water to a week-long trip. Depending on boat size, facilities and season, a boat costs from around £60 for four hours, £100 for one day, up to £600 to £1200 for a week, including fuel and insurance.

Barnes Brinkcraft (www.barnesbrinkcraft.co.uk; per half-day/day £58/102) Short-term rental from Wroxham.

Blakes (www.blakes.co.uk) Boating holidays from Wroxham and Potter Heigham.

Boats for the Broads (www.dayboathire.com) Short-term rental from Wroxham.

Hoseasons (www.hoseasons.co.uk) Boating holidays from a variety of points across the Broads.

Luxury Day Cruisers (www.daycruisers.co.uk; per half-day/day £75/110) Short-term rental from Horning and Burgh St Peter.

Boat Trips

Broads Tours (www.broads.co.uk; adult/child £7.50/6; ⏲Apr-Oct) Frequent 1½-hour pleasure trips from Potter Heigham and Wroxham.

Broads Authority (www.broads-authority.gov.uk; adult/child £7/6; Apr-Oct) Short boat trips from Beccles, Neatishead, Ranworth and How Hill.

Sleeping & Eating

Broad House HOTEL £££
(☎01603-783567; www.broadhousehotel.co.uk; The Avenue, Wroxham; d from £118-231; P @) An intimate boutique hotel with just nine rooms, this place really knows how to look after you. Set in beautiful gardens surrounding an 18th-century country house, it's a character-laden place with plenty of charm. The rooms range from full period style, with four-poster beds, swag curtains and cast-iron baths, to more modern attic rooms with contemporary design.

Recruiting Sergeant MODERN BRITISH ££
(☎01603-737077; www.recruitingsergeant.co.uk; Norwich Rd, Horstead; mains £13-22) Close to the lovely village of Coltishall is this award-

winning gastropub serving a fine selection of locally sourced meat and fish dishes. There's no contrived design style here: just honest food deftly cooked and served in hearty portions.

Information

Broads Authority (www.broads-authority.gov.uk) Has the low-down on all you could want to know about the Broads.

Enjoy the Broads (www.enjoythebroads.com) Information for visitors with accommodation, activity and event listings.

RSPB (www.rspb.org.uk) Information on birdwatching and habitats.

Getting There & Away

Wroxham, on the A1151 from Norwich, and Potter Heigham, on the A1062 from Wroxham, are the main centres. Buses leave Norwich twice hourly for **Wroxham** (40 minutes). You can get to Potter Heigham by bus from **Great Yarmouth** (40 minutes) roughly hourly.

Great Yarmouth

POP 90,810

On first glance Great Yarmouth is little more than a tatty traditional seaside resort complete with neon-lit esplanade, jingling amusement arcades, grim greasy spoons, crazy golf and cheek-by-jowl hotels. But scratch under the surface, and you'll find the old town rich in history and heritage.

Sights

Yarmouth's 'heritage quarter' looks on to the river rather than the sea and boasts a fine collection of stately period buildings.

Row Houses HISTORIC HOUSES

(EH; www.english-heritage.org.uk; South Quay; adult/child £4.20/2.10; ⏲noon-5pm Apr-Sep) You can see how life once was in Great Yarmouth in these preserved houses. One is reconstructed as it would have been in 1870, the other in 1940s style. Displays show how the 'herring girls' lived and how life was for tenants – from wealthy merchants to tenement families – over the centuries.

Time & Tide MUSEUM

(www.museums.norfolk.gov.uk; Blackfriars Rd; adult/child £4.50/3.30; ⏲10am-5pm) This is the most absorbing of Yarmouth's museums, set in a Victorian herring-curing works. It tackles everything from prehistory to penny arcades and naughty postcards, but dwells on maritime heritage with evocative reconstructions of typical fishermen's row houses.

Elizabethan House HISTORIC HOUSE

(NT; www.museums.norfolk.gov.uk; 4 South Quay; adult/child £3.50/1.90; ⏲10am-5pm Mon-Fri, noon-4pm Sat & Sun Apr-Oct) This fine 16th-century merchant's house is faithfully reconstructed to showcase Tudor and Victorian domestic life, and is home to the 'Conspiracy Room' where Cromwell and his cronies decided Charles I must be executed.

Tolhouse Museum MUSEUM

(www.museums.norfolk.gov.uk; Tolhouse St; adult/child £3.50/1.90; ⏲10am-5pm Mon-Fri, noon-4pm Sat & Sun Apr-Oct) Tales of macabre inmates, witchcraft, grisly murders and nasty punishments at this medieval jail.

Nelson Museum MUSEUM

(www.nelson-museum.co.uk; 26 South Quay; adult/child £3.20/1.90; ⏲10am-5pm Mon-Fri, 1-4pm Sat & Sun) Celebrates the life, times, romances and death of the one-eyed hero of Trafalgar.

Sleeping & Eating

B&Bs are everywhere, especially on chock-a-block Trafalgar St.

No 78 B&B ££

(☎01493-850001; www.no78.co.uk; 78 Marine Pde; d £50-85; @) A chic, modern place that bucks the chintzy local trends and offers really beautiful, bright, contemporary rooms with an eco-conscience. The toilets have water-saving devices, tea and coffee come in resealable containers and the house uses 'green' electricity.

Olive Garden MEDITERRANEAN ££

(☎01493 844641; www.olivegardenrestaurant.co.uk; 42 Regent Rd; mains £10-18; ⏲closed Mon lunch) Away from the kiss-me-quick diners and bang up to date, this vibrant, modern place serves a long and interesting menu of dishes that take the best Mediterranean ingredients and shape them into something irresistible. Lunch is a great deal, with mains costing just £5.95. Book ahead for dinner.

Information

Tourist office (☎01493-846345; www.great-yarmouth.co.uk; 25 Marine Pde; ⏲10am-5pm) On the seafront. Staff can point you towards the lovely **Weavers Way walking trail**, which cuts into the Broads from here.

Getting There & Away

There are hourly buses (40 minutes) and trains (£5.60, 33 minutes) to Norwich.

North Coast Norfolk

The north coast of Norfolk has something of a split personality, with a string of busy seaside towns with brash attractions and hordes of people clustering along the eastern end, and a collection of small villages with trendy gastropubs and boutique hotels littering the western end. In between sit stunning beaches and the marshy coast that attracts crowds of visiting seabirds.

The Coast Hoppper bus runs from Cromer to Hunstanton, serving Cley, Blakeney, Wells, Holkham, Burnham Deepdale and (with a connection) King's Lynn.

CROMER

POP 3800

Once a fashionable Victorian coastal resort, Cromer is now firmly part of the bucket-and-spade brigade, with a wonderful stretch of safe, sandy beachfront, family entertainment on the pier, a glut of fish-and-chip shops and plenty of trashy amusement arcades. The town has recently seen some major investment and may yet return to its former glory.

Stay long enough to wander off the beach and you'll find the quaint **Cromer Museum** (www.museums.norfolk.gov.uk; East Cottages, Tucker St; adult/child £3.20/1.80; 10am-5pm Mon-Sat, 1-4pm Sun), set in a Victorian fisherman's cottage. The museum depicts life in the town in the 19th century and displays a series of historic photos of the area.

Just 2 miles southwest of town off the B1436 is **Felbrigg Hall** (NT; www.nationaltrust.org.uk; adult/child £7.80/3.65; 11am-5pm Sat-Wed Mar-Oct), an elegant stately home with a fine Georgian interior. The walled gardens and orangery are particularly lovely, with access to the **Weavers Way** running through the estate.

Cromer has direct trains to Norwich hourly Monday to Saturday and services every two hours on Sunday (£5.60, 45 minutes). The Coasthopper bus runs from Cromer west along the coast roughly half-hourly in summer.

CLEY MARSHES

One of England's premier birdwatching sites, Cley (pronounced cly) Marshes, is a mecca for twitchers, with over 300 species recorded here. There's a **visitors centre** (www.norfolkwildlifetrust.org.uk; adult/child £4/free; 10am-5pm) built on high ground and a series of hides hidden amid the golden reed beds.

For food head to the lovely **Wiveton Hall Cafe** (01263-740515; www.wivetonhall.co.uk; mains £7-9; 9.30am-5pm daily, 6.30-8.30pm Fri & Sat Mar-Oct), set in the grounds of a dreamy Jacobean manor house. Sit inside in the bright converted barn or outside on pastel benches under the shady pine trees to enjoy the wholesome tarts, salads and scrummy cakes. Ingredients come from the manor farm, and if you're feeling energetic you can also pick your own fruit and veggies here. For an extraspecial experience, you can stay in the gorgeous manor house on a self-catering basis (sleeps eight, per week £850 to £2000).

Alternatively, the stunning 17th-century **Cley Windmill** (01263-740209; www.cleymill.co.uk; d £80-165) has nine bedrooms with the one at the top reached by ladder alone. It's a wonderfully quirky place to stay, with a circular living room, great views across the marshes and rooms with four-poster, half-tester or cast-iron beds.

BLAKENEY POINT

The pretty village of **Blakeney** was once a busy fishing and trading port before its harbour silted up. These days it's a good place to jump aboard boat trips out to a 500-strong colony of common and grey seals that live, bask and breed on nearby Blakeney Point. The hour-long trips (adult/child £8/4) run daily April to October, but the best time to come is between June and August when the common seals pup. Trips run either from Blakeney Harbour or nearby Morston.

Beans Boat Trips (www.beansboat trips.co.uk; Morston)

Bishop's Boats (www.norfolkseal trips.co.uk; Blakeney Harbour)

Temples Seal Trips (www.sealtrips.co.uk; Morston)

WELLS-NEXT-THE-SEA

POP 2451

Thronged with crowds on holiday weekends, this harbour town has plenty of seaside tat on the waterfront but a surprisingly tranquil old town set back from the sea. Attractive

Georgian houses and flint cottages surround a large green, while kids bounce between toy shops and ice-cream parlours, and pensioners check out the curios.

The **narrow-gauge steam train** (www.wellswalsinghamrailway.co.uk; adult/child return £6.50/5; ⏲Apr-Oct) chuffs 5 miles to **Little Walsingham**, where there are shrines and a ruined abbey that have drawn pilgrims since medieval times. The trip takes 30 minutes.

If you fancy staying overnight, the **Wells YHA** (☎0845-3719544; www.yha.org.uk; Church Plains; dm £16; P) has simple rooms in an ornately gabled early 20th-century church hall. Alternatively try **Admiral House** (☎01328-711669; www.admiralhouse-wells.co.uk; 6 Southgate Close; d £95; P 🛜) for its smart, modern rooms and clean-cut decor.

The small **tourist office** (☎01328-710885; www.visitnorthnorfolk.com; Staithe St; ⏲10am-5pm Mon-Sat, to 4pm Mar-Oct) can help with all inquiries.

The Coasthopper bus goes through Wells roughly half-hourly in summer on its way between Cromer (1 hour) and Kings Lynn (1½ hours).

HOLKHAM

The pretty village of **Holkham** is well worth a stop for its imposing stately home, incredible stretch of beach and for the pleasure of walking its picturesque streets lined with elegant buildings.

The main draw here is **Holkham Hall** (www.holkham.co.uk; adult/child £11/5.50, parking £2.50; ⏲noon-4pm Sun, Mon & Thu Apr-Oct), a grand Palladian mansion set in a vast deer park designed by Capability Brown. The slightly industrial-looking brick mansion is the ancestral seat of the Earls of Leicester and has a sumptuous interior, dripping with gilt, tapestries, fine furniture and family history. The Marble Hall (it's actually alabaster), magnificent state rooms and giant kitchen shouldn't be missed. The public entrance brings you to the rear of the building; for the best views continue along the road around the house and past the ice house to see the building as originally intended. You can also visit the **Bygones Museum** (museum only adult/child £4/2; ⏲10am-5pm Apr-Oct) in the stable block. It showcases everything from mechanical toys to agricultural equipment and vintage cars. The walled gardens are slowly being restored; if you'd like to see the work in progress, electric buggies can take you there from the courtyard from 1pm to 4pm.

For many, Holkham's true delight is not the stately home but the pristine 3-mile **beach** that meanders along the shore. Regularly voted one of England's best, it's a popular spot with walkers. The vast expanse of sand swallows people up and gives a real sense of isolation with giant skies stretching overhead. The only place to park for access to the beach is Lady Anne's Drive (parking up to £5).

Recover after a jaunt on the beach with tea or a snack at the **Marsh Larder** (Main Rd; ⏲10am-5pm) in the stunning Ancient House or a more substantial meal at the much-lauded **Victoria Arms** (☎01328-711008; www.victoriaatholkham.co.uk; Park Rd; mains £12-18; r £125-560). The menu here is modern English with an emphasis on local ingredients. The Victoria also has a choice of quirky, but extremely plush rooms, with exotic fabrics, eclectic bric-a-brac and a relaxed, colonial feel. You'd be well advised to book ahead.

The Coasthopper bus goes through Holkham roughly half-hourly in summer.

BURNHAM DEEPDALE

In-the-know backpackers and walkers flock to this lovely coastal spot, with its tiny twin villages of **Burnham Deepdale** and **Brancaster Staithe** strung along a rural road. Stroked by the beautiful Norfolk Coastal Path, surrounded by beaches and reedy marshes, alive with birdlife, criss-crossed by cycling routes and a base for a whole host of water sports, Burnham Deepdale is also home to one of the country's best backpacker hostels.

Ecofriendly **Deepdale Farm** (☎01485-210256; www.deepdalefarm.co.uk; site per adult/child £6/5, dm/tw £10.50/50, 2-/6-person tepees £80/114; P @ 🛜) is a backpackers' haven. It has spotless en suite rooms set in converted 17th-century stables as well as camping space and a collection of Native American style tepees and Mongolian yurts for extra comfort. There's a large kitchen and lounge area, picnic tables, a barbecue and a laundry and cafe next door. It's an enduring popular spot so be sure to book ahead.

The hostel also operates a **tourist office** (☎01485-210256; ⏲10am-4pm), the best place to go to organise kitesurfing or windsurfing on nearby beaches. Bike hire is also available.

Just west of the hostel is the award-winning **White Horse** (☎01485-210262; www.whitehorsebrancaster.co.uk; mains £10-14, s/d from £95/130; P @), a gastropub with a menu strong on seafood. It also has some light and fresh, New England–style guest rooms, but it lacks a little soul and some rooms have terraces overlooking the car park.

The Coasthopper bus stops outside Deepdale Farm roughly half-hourly in summer.

AROUND BURNHAM DEEPDALE

Littered with pretty little villages and a host of ancient watering holes, trendy gastropubs and boutique hotels, this part of the Norfolk coast is one of the most appealing.

At the oh-so-fashionable Georgian town of **Burnham Market**, you'll find plenty of elegant old buildings, flint cottages, delis and independent retailers. It's another excellent base, with a trio of accommodation options to suit any taste. The **Hoste Arms** (01328-738777; www.hostearms.co.uk; The Green; d £118-234; P) and its sister properties the **Vine House** (d £145-207) and the **Railway Inn** (s/d £78/94) offer everything from over-the-top classical rooms with swags and florals to trendy, contemporary suites with bold wallpaper, luscious fabrics and mountains of towels.

Just past Burnham Deepdale you come to Titchwell, home to **Titchwell Manor** (01485-210221; www.titchwellmanor.com; Titchwell; d £130-250, mains £10-18; P @), a slick contemporary hotel set in a grand Victorian house. The conservatory restaurant serves modern English cuisine, and there's a large garden loved by visiting children.

Continue west along the coast road to the village of Thornham for a choice of three more great places to eat. Right by the road is the **Orange Tree** (01485-512213; www.theorangetreethornham.co.uk; High St; mains £10-19;) an old-world pub with a modern interior. The food here is excellent and the seafood in particular is worth a detour. There's a garden with a playground for children and a selection of newly refurbished rooms (doubles from £99).

Hidden from passing traffic on the village back road is the **Lifeboat Inn** (01485-512236; www.lifeboatinn.co.uk; Ship Lane; 3-course dinner £29), a 16th-century pub laden with character and famous for its traditional food, while just west of the village is the **Yurt** (01485-525108; www.theyurt.co.uk; Drove Orchards; mains £8.50-12.50; closed dinner Sun & Mon;), a restaurant in, er, a yurt. The food is all local, with doorstep sandwiches and wholesome salads at lunch and hearty fish, meat and game dishes for dinner.

King's Lynn

POP 34,565

Once one of England's most important ports, King's Lynn was long known as 'the Warehouse on the Wash'. It was said you could cross from one side of the River Great Ouse to the other by simply stepping from boat to boat in its heyday. Something of the salty port-town tang can still be felt in old King's Lynn, with its cobbled lanes and narrow streets flanked by old merchants' houses. Unfortunately, the rest of the town is not so pretty, with modern architectural blunders and high-street chain stores blighting the landscape.

Sights

Old Lynn huddles along the eastern bank of the river. Walk between the two market places to take in the most handsome buildings in town, or pick up a heritage trail leaflet from the tourist office.

St Margaret's Church CHURCH

(www.stmargaretskingslynn.org.uk; Margaret Plain) A patchwork of architectural styles, this church is worth a look for its two extraordinarily elaborate Flemish brasses. You can also see a remarkable 17th-century moon dial, which tells the tide, not the time. You'll find historic flood-level markings by the west door.

Old Gaol House MUSEUM

(Saturday Market Pl; adult/child £3/2.15; 10am-5pm Tue-Sat Easter-Oct;) Explore the old cells and hear grisly tales of smugglers, witches and highwaymen in the town's old jail. Also here is the **Regalia Room** (admission free), which houses the town civic treasures, including the 650-year-old King John Cup, exquisitely decorated with scenes of hunting and hawking.

Lynn Museum MUSEUM

(www.museums.norfolk.gov.uk; Market St; adult/child £3.30/1.80) The town's main museum features displays on maritime life in Lynn and Norfolk history, but its highlight is the new Seahenge gallery, which showcases a 4000-year-old timber circle and explores the lives of the people who created it.

True's Yard MUSEUM

(www.truesyard.co.uk; North St; adult/child £3/1.50; 10am-4pm Tue-Sat) Housed in two restored fishermen's cottages, this museum looks at the difficult life fishermen endured and the traditions and lifestyle of the close-knit community that once lived in this part of the city.

Town House Museum MUSEUM
(www.museums.norfolk.gov.uk; 46 Queen St; adult/child £3.30/1.80; ⏲10am-5pm Mon-Sat May-Sep;) Petite museum dealing with the history of the town from the Middle Ages up to the 1950s. Next door is the magnificent flint-and-brick **town hall**, which dates from 1421.

FREE **Green Quay** MUSEUM
(www.thegreenquay.co.uk; South Quay; ⏲9am-5pm) This museum charts life in the Wash (the estuary) with exhibitions on the wildlife, flora and fauna of the area and the effects of climate change.

Festivals & Events

The July **King's Lynn Festival** (www.kingslynnfestival.org.uk) is East Anglia's most important cultural gathering. It offers a diverse program of concerts and recitals of all kinds, from medieval ballads to opera. The main festival is preceded by a free rock-and-pop bash **Festival Too** (www.festivaltoo.co.uk), now one of Europe's biggest free festivals.

Sleeping & Eating

Bank House B&B ££
(☎01553-660492; www.thebankhouse.co.uk; Kings Staithe Sq; s/d from £80/100; P) This outstanding B&B has ticks in all the right boxes: history, location, atmosphere, comfort and welcome. Overlooking the water, the 18th-century former bank is now an elegantly furnished town house with five luxurious rooms, mixing original features and modern furnishings. There's also a lovely, modern brasserie (mains £8 to £16) serving seriously good food made from locally sourced ingredients.

Bradley's MODERN BRITISH ££
(☎01553-819888; www.bradleysbytheriver.co.uk; 10 South Quay; mains £13-19; ⏲dinner Mon-Sat) Eat in the elegant Georgian dining room at this riverside restaurant, or relax in the popular wine bar with some lighter meals (£8 to £10); either way you're bound to be pleased as this is probably the finest food the city has to offer.

Information

Tourist office (☎01553-763044; www.visitwestnorfolk.com; Purfleet Quay; ⏲10am-5pm Mon-Sat, noon-5pm Sun) Housed in the lovely 17th-century Custom House, the tourist office arranges guided walks (adult/child £4/1) at 2pm on Tuesdays, Fridays and Saturdays in high season.

Getting There & Away

There are hourly trains from **Cambridge** (£8.40, 50 minutes) and **London Kings Cross** (£27.40, 1¾ hours). Bus 35 runs to **Hunstanton** (30 minutes, half hourly) and connects with the Coasthopper (www.coasthopper.co.uk) service, which runs along the north Norfolk coast.

Around King's Lynn

CASTLE RISING CASTLE

There's something bordering on ecclesiastical about the beautifully embellished keep of this **castle** (EH; www.castlerising.co.uk; adult/child £4/2.50; ⏲10am-6pm Apr-Nov), built in 1138 and set in the middle of a massive earthwork upon which pheasants scurry about like guards. So extravagant is the stonework that it's no surprise to learn that it shares stonemasons with some of East Anglia's finest cathedrals. It was once the home of Queen Isabella, who (allegedly) arranged the gruesome murder of her husband, Edward II.

It's well worth the trip 4 miles northeast of King's Lynn off the A149. Bus 41 runs here (15 minutes) hourly from the King's Lynn bus station.

SANDRINGHAM HOUSE

Royalists and those bemused by the English sovereigns will have plenty to mull over at this, the Queen's **country estate** (www.sandringhamestate.co.uk; adult/child £10/5, gardens & museum only £7/3.50; ⏲11am-4.30pm Apr-Oct), set in 25 hectares of landscaped gardens and lakes, and open to the hoi polloi when the court is not at home. (If they are in residence, the estate is closed.)

Queen Victoria bought the estate in 1862 for her son, the Prince of Wales (later Edward VII), but he promptly had it overhauled in the style later named Edwardian. Half of the surrounding 8000 hectares is leased to farm tenants, while the rest is managed by the Crown Estate as forestry.

Visitors can shuffle around the ground-floor rooms, regularly used by the royal family, then head out to the old stables, which house a flag-waving **museum** filled with diverse royal memorabilia. The superb royal **vintage-car collection** includes the very first royal motor from 1900, darling electrical toy cars driven by various princes, and the buggy in which the recently deceased Queen Mother would bounce around race tracks. For another oddity, look for the pet cemetery just outside the museum.

There are **guided tours** of the gardens on Wednesdays and Saturdays at 11am and 2pm. The **shop** is also worthy of a visit if only to browse the organic goodies produced on the sprawling estate.

Sandringham is 6 miles northeast of King's Lynn off the B1440. Bus 41 runs here from the station (30 minutes, hourly).

HOUGHTON HALL

Built for Britain's first de facto Prime Minister Sir Robert Walpole in 1730, the pompous Palladian-style **Houghton Hall** (www.houghtonhall.com; adult/child £8.80/3.50; ⌚1.30-5pm Wed, Thu & Sun Easter-Sep) is worth seeing for the ornate staterooms alone; you could build another half dozen houses with the amount of swirling decorative plasterwork here. The interiors are sumptuous and dripping with gilt, tapestries, squeaky velvets and ostentatious furniture. Six hundred deer roam the surrounding parkland, and there's an obsessive model-soldiers exhibit with over 20,000 of the little guys.

Nottingham & the East Midlands

Includes »

Best Places to Eat

- » Watson's (p474)
- » The Golden Mile (p474)
- » Restaurant Sat Bains (p453)
- » Cafe Bleu (p457)
- » Columbine Restaurant (p490)

Best Places to Stay

- » Hart's (p452)
- » Hotel Maiyango (p473)
- » Hambleton Hall (p477)
- » George Hotel (p464)
- » Old Hall Hotel (p489)

Why Go?

Apart from the postcard-perfect villages and rugged hiking trails of the Peak District, the delights of this peaceful corner of the country lie largely off the tourist radar. Away from the sprawling industrial centres of Nottingham, Leicester and Derby, the East Midlands is a rolling carpet of farmland, dotted with historic market towns, ruined castles, spellbinding cathedrals and lavish stately homes. At its best, it's the England you were expecting after reading all those Jane Austen novels. Where you go in the region will depend on your temperament. City slickers are drawn to Nottingham, with its lively nightlife and Robin Hood connections, while foodies head to Leicester to sample the imported culinary delights of the Indian subcontinent. Fans of the great outdoors make for the Peak District in their hundreds of thousands. However, you may find more peace and quiet in the backwaters of Rutland and Lincolnshire.

When to Go

The East Midlands is at its best in summer, when the countryside comes alive with village fetes and festivals. For walkers and cyclists, June through September is the high season in the Peak District. May brings flowers, parades and pagan goings-on to Castleton's Garland Festival, while February/March brings the wonderful chaos of Shrovetide football to Ashbourne.

Nottingham & the East Midlands Highlights

1 Aiming pedals or walking boots at the rugged trails of the **Peak District National Park** (p484)

2 Admiring the abundance of flamboyant architecture and leafy parks in the former spa town of **Buxton** (p487)

3 Seeing how the other half lived at the lavish Elizabethan mansion of **Hardwick Hall** (p484)

4 Being humbled by the soaring towers of Lincoln's great **cathedral** (p458)

5 Singeing your tastebuds on a fiery vegetarian curry on Leicester's **Golden Mile** (p474)

6 Stepping back into Jane Austen's England in the stone-lined streets of **Stamford** (p464)

7 Getting lost in the grandeur of **Chatsworth House** (p497), one of the nation's finest country houses.

0
40 km
0
20 miles
NORTH LINCOLNSHIRE
Grimsby
Spurn Head
Cleethorpes
North Sea
DONCASTER
Scunthorpe
M180
Doncaster
NORTHEAST LINCOLNSHIRE
A159
Saltfleetby-Theddlethorpe Dunes National Nature Reserve
A631
A1103
Market Rasen
Gainsborough
Louth
A1
A15
A16
Alford
Worksop
A158
A57
Lincoln
Sherwood Forest National Nature Reserve
A1(M1)
Horncastle
Burgh Le Marsh
Skegness
A153
A614
A16
A15
LINCOLNSHIRE
Gibraltar Point National Nature Reserve
NOTTINGHAMSHIRE
Southwell
A607
Newark-on-Trent
Witham
Sleaford
Boston
The Wash
Hunstanton
Nottingham
Grantham
A46
Belvoir Castle
A15
A16
A1
Spalding
A17
King's Lynn
Melton Mowbray
NORFOLK
A16
RUTLAND
Oakham
Wisbech
Stamford
Leicester
Rutland Water
Burghley House
Great Ouse
Peterborough
A47
A10
LEICESTERSHIRE
March
Lyddington
Kirby Hall
Fotheringhay
Market Harborough
Corby
Oundle
A427
A1
A141
Rushton Triangular Lodge
Rothwell
Ely
SUFFOLK
Kettering
A508
A6
A10
Huntingdon
Wicken Fen National Nature Reserve
NORTHAMPTONSHIRE
A45
CAMBRIDGESHIRE
Brixworth
Earls Barton
Newmarket
Althorp
A604
Northampton
Cambridge
BEDFORDSHIRE
A14
Stoke Bruerne
Bedford
A604
A10
MILTON KEYNES
A1
Haverhill
A6
Royston
M1
Milton Keynes
A10
A5
BUCKINGHAMSHIRE
HERTFORDSHIRE
ESSEX

Activities

The East Midlands calls out to fans of hiking, cycling, caving, rock climbing, and other outdoorsy activities, with the rugged hills of the Peak District as the number one spot to get in touch with nature. Famous walking trails such as the **Pennine Way** and **Limestone Way** struggle across the hills, while road cyclists pit determination and muscle against such challenging routes as the **Pennine Cycleway** (NCN Route 68) from Derby to Buxton. Sailors, windsurfers and water-babies of all ages and levels of experience flock to **Rutland Water** near Oakham and **Carsington Water** and the **Derwent Reservoirs** in the Peak District. See the Activities listings in this chapter for more details.

Information

Discover Rutland (www.discover-rutland.co.uk)

East Midlands Tourism (www.enjoyenglandseastmidlands.com)

Explore Northamptonshire (www.explorenorthamptonshire.co.uk)

Go Leicestershire (www.goleicestershire.com)

Peak District & Derbyshire (www.visitpeakdistrict.com)

Visit Lincolnshire (www.visitlincolnshire.com)

Visit Nottinghamshire (www.visitnottingham.com)

Getting There & Around

Fast and frequent trains and buses link towns across the region, but services are more sporadic in Northamptonshire and Lincolnshire, where a hire car will make life much easier. **East Midlands Airport** (☎0871 919 9000; www.eastmidlandsairport.com) near Derby is the main air hub. For public transport information, consult **Traveline East Midlands** (☎0871 200 2233; www.travelineeastmidlands.org.uk).

NOTTINGHAMSHIRE

Say Nottinghamshire and people think of one thing – Robin Hood. Whether the hero woodsman ever really existed is hotly debated, but the county makes much of its connections to the outlaw from Locksley. Story-telling seems to be in Nottinghamshire's blood – other local celebs include provocative writer DH Lawrence, of *Lady Chatterley's Lover* fame, and hedonist poet Lord Byron. The city of Nottingham is the bustling hub, but venture into the surrounding countryside and you'll find a wealth of historic towns and stately homes surrounding the green bower of Sherwood Forest.

Information

Visit Nottinghamshire (www.visitnottingham.co.uk)

Getting There & Around

Trains run frequently to most large towns, and many smaller villages in the Peak District. **National Express** (☎0871 781 8178; www.nationalexpress.com) and **Trent Barton Buses** (☎01773-712265; www.trentbarton.co.uk) provide the bulk of the bus services. See www.nottinghamshire.gov.uk/buses for timetables, or use the handy journey planner at www.itsnottingham.info.

Nottingham

POP 266,988

Forever associated with men in tights and a sheriff with anger-management issues, Nottingham is a county capital with big-city aspirations. Predictably, the Robin Hood connection is Nottingham's biggest drawcard, but look beyond the arrows and outlaws and you'll find a vibrant and historic metropolis with loads of cultural offerings and a buzzing music and club scene. Famous sons of Nottingham include fashion designer Paul Smith, and William Booth, founder of the Salvation Army, but the most impressive plinth in town is reserved for the statue of football (soccer) manager Brian Clough, who led Nottingham Forest to a cabinet full of trophies between 1976 and 1993.

Sights & Activities

Nottingham Castle Museum & Art Gallery MUSEUM

(adult/child £3.50/2; ⌚10am-5pm Tue-Sun) Set atop a sandstone outcrop worm-holed with caves and tunnels, the original Nottingham castle was founded by William the Conqueror and held by a succession of English kings before falling in the English Civil War. Its 17th-century replacement contains a diverting museum of local history, with an extensive collection of costumes, jewellery, Wedgwood jasperware and paintings, including works by Dante Gabriel Rossetti. Your ticket also gains you entry to the Museum of Nottinghamshire Life at Brewhouse Yard.

Museum of Nottingham Life at Brewhouse Yard

At the foot of the cliffs, housed in five 17th-century cottages and accessed on the same ticket as Nottingham Castle, this charming little museum will take you back through 300 years of Nottingham life using reconstructions of traditional shops and living quarters.

Mortimer's Hole

(45min tours adult/child £2.50/1.50; ⏲tours 11am, 2pm & 3pm Mon-Sat, noon, 1pm, 2pm, 3pm Sun) Burrowing through the bedrock beneath the castle, this atmospheric underground passageway emerges at Brewhouse Yard. In 1330, supporters of Edward III used this tunnel to breach the castle security and capture Roger Mortimer, the machiavellian Earl of March, who briefly appointed himself ruler of England after deposing Edward II.

City of Caves CAVE NETWORK

(☎0115-988 1955; www.cityofcaves.com; adult/child £5.75/4.25; ⏲10.30am-4pm) Over the centuries, the sandstone underneath the city of Nottingham has been carved into a veritable Swiss cheese of caverns and passageways. From the top level of the Broad marsh shopping centre, atmospheric audio tours (or guided tours at weekends) plunge into the wormholes, visiting a WWII air-raid shelter, a medieval underground tannery, several pub cellars and a mock-up of a Victorian slum dwelling.

FREE **Nottingham Contemporary** GALLERY

(www.nottinghamcontemporary.org; Weekday Cross; ⏲10am-7pm Tue-Fri, 10am-6pm Sat, 11am-5pm Sun) Housed in an eye-catching building fronted with lace-patterned concrete, this sleek gallery lives up to its name, with lots of edgy, design-oriented exhibitions of paintings, prints, photography and sculpture.

Galleries of Justice MUSEUM

(☎0115-952 0555; www.galleriesofjustice.org.uk; High Pavement; adult/child audio tour £5.75/4.25, performance tour £8.75/6.75; ⏲10.30am-5pm) Set in the grand Georgian precincts of the Shire Hall building, the Galleries of Justice offers an entertaining stroll through centuries of British justice, from medieval trials by fire and water to the controversial policing of the Miners Strike. Audio tours run on Monday and Tuesday; live-action tours with 'gaolers' run Wednesday to Sunday.

DON'T MISS

WOLLATON HALL

Built in 1588 for land owner and coal mogul, Sir Francis Willoughby, **Wollaton Hall** (Wollaton Park, Derby Rd; admission free, tours adult/child £2.50/2; ⏲11am-5pm) has more frills and ruffs than an Elizabethan banquet hall. This fabulous manor was created by architect Robert Smythson, who designed the equally avant-garde Longleat in Wessex (p293) and Doddington Hall (p463) near Lincoln. As well as extravagant rooms from the Tudor, Regency and Victorian periods, the hall boasts a natural history museum, an industrial museum and peaceful hectares of landscaped grounds and gardens.

Wollaton Hall is on the western edge of the city, 2.5 miles from the centre; get here on bus 30, 35 or 2 from Victoria bus station (15 minutes).

Tours

Original Nottingham Ghost Walk WALKING TOURS

(☎01623-721660; www.ghost-walks.co.uk; adult/child £5/3; ⏲7pm Sat Jan-Nov) Departs from Ye Olde Salutation Inn, Maid Marian Way – descend into the medieval caves if you dare…

Shaw's Heritage Services WALKING TOURS

(☎0115-925 9388; www.nottinghamtours.com) Runs various tours of the city, including popular walking tours, coach trips to Sherwood Forest and boat trips on the Trent.

Nottingham Princess CRUISES

(☎0115-910 0400; www.princessrivercruises.co.uk) Runs various lunch and dinner cruises along the River Trent.

Festivals & Events

Nottingham hosts an interesting selection of festivals – for details, use the search form at www.nottinghamcity.gov.uk. Theatre buffs will enjoy the annual **Shakespeare Festival** at the Nottingham Playhouse in July. In the same month, the Indian community get into the party mood for the annual **Mela** and the Caribbean community celebrates its **Carnival**.

Held in October in the Forest Recreation Ground, a mile north of the city centre, the medieval **Goose Fair** has evolved from a

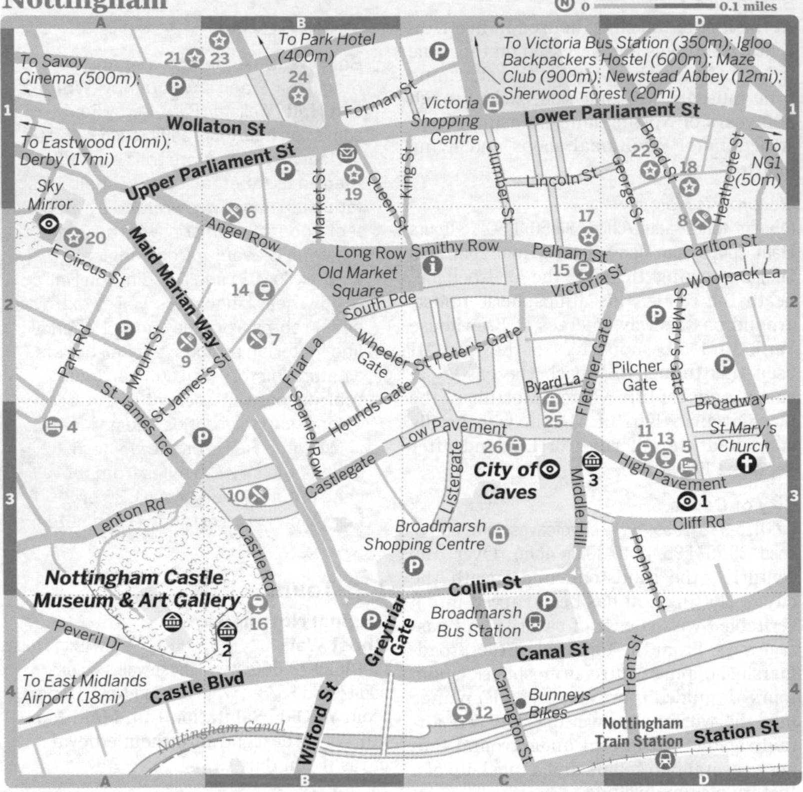

travelling market to a boisterous modern funfair. Robin Hood gets his moment in the sun during the family-friendly **Robin Hood Pageant**, held every October in Nottingham Castle.

Sleeping

Hart's HOTEL ££
(☎0115-988 1900; www.hartsnottingham.co.uk; Standard Hill, Park Row; s & d from £120; P @) In the compound of the old Nottingham General Hospital, this swish boutique hotel is a cut above the competition. The ultra-modern rooms are in a striking modernist building, while the restaurant is housed in a historic old hospital wing. Check the website for discount rates.

Lace Market Hotel HOTEL ££
(☎0115-852 3232; www.lacemarkethotel.co.uk; 29-31 High Pavement; s/d £90/115; P) In the heart of the trendy Lace Market area, this rather lovely boutique hotel is set in an elegant Georgian town house, but rooms are sleek and contemporary. Check the website for weekend promotions.

Greenwood Lodge City Guest House B&B ££
(☎0115-962 1206; www.greenwoodlodgecityguesthouse.co.uk; Third Ave, Sherwood Rise; s/d £47.50/80; P) A fantastic B&B set in a large Victorian house north of the centre. The location is quiet, the house is full of period character, there's a pretty courtyard garden and rooms are frilly but comfortable.

Park Hotel HOTEL ££
(☎0115-978 6299; www.parkhotelnottingham.co.uk; 5-7 Waverley St; s/d from £30/50; @) This imposing turn-of-the-century mansion has been transformed into a slick, modern hotel with comfortable rooms decked out in warms reds, creams and browns. Breakfast

Nottingham

Top Sights
City of Caves C3
Nottingham Castle Museum & Art Gallery A4

Sights
1 Galleries of Justice D3
2 Museum of Nottingham Life at Brewhouse Yard B4
3 Nottingham Contemporary C3

Sleeping
4 Hart's A3
5 Lace Market Hotel D3

Eating
6 Alley Cafe B2
7 Brown Betty's B2
8 Kayal D2
9 Memsaab A2
10 World Service Restaurant B3

Drinking
11 Brass Monkey D3
12 Canal Hose C4
13 Cock & Hoop D3
14 Malt Cross B2
15 Pit & Pendulum C2
16 Ye Olde Trip to Jerusalem B4

Entertainment
17 Bodega Social Club C2
18 Broadway Cinema D1
19 Gatecrasher B1
20 Nottingham Playhouse A2
21 Rock City A1
Royal Concert Hall .... (see 24)
22 Screen Room D1
23 Stealth B1
24 Theatre Royal B1

Shopping
25 Paul Smith (Byard Lane) C3
26 Paul Smith (Willoughby House) C3

is extra. To get here, follow Goldsmith St northwest from the centre.

Igloo Backpackers Hostel HOSTEL £
(☎0115-947 5250; www.igloohostel.co.uk; 110 Mansfield Rd; dm £15) A favourite with international backpackers, this independent hostel is a short walk north of Victoria bus station, opposite the Golden Fleece pub. It's always full at weekends so book ahead. Breakfast is extra.

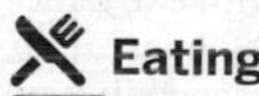

Eating

TOP CHOICE **Restaurant Sat Bains** MODERN EUROPEAN £££
(Lenton Lane; www.restaurantsatbains.com; tasting menus £55-85; ⊙dinner Tue-Sat) Tucked away on the outskirts, two miles southwest of the centre, Nottingham's only Michelin-starred restaurant delivers outstanding, inventive modern European cooking. Like the outfits worn by the clientele, the food and surroundings are exquisite, but book well in advance. To get here, follow the A52 to Wilford and turn-off near the Nottingham Trent University campus.

Alley Cafe VEGETARIAN £
(www.alleycafe.co.uk; Cannon Court; mains £5-6; ⊙lunch & dinner Mon & Tue, till late Wed-Sat) Tucked away down a hidden alleyway, this place sets out to prove that vegetarian food can be cool. The globe-trotting menu ranges from tofu and tempeh to hempseed burgers, which you can munch to a DJ soundtrack.

Memsaab INDIAN ££
(☎0115-957 0009; www.mem-saab.co.uk; 12-14 Maid Marian Way; mains £10-18; ⊙dinner) The best of the glamorous modern Indian eateries on Maid Marion Way, serving fabulous regional specialties in stylish, dinner-date friendly surroundings. Bookings recommended.

Kayal INDIAN £
(www.kayalrestaurant.com; 8 Broad St; mains £5-13) The Nottingham branch of this small Midlands chain trades the chicken tikka masala clichés for the spicy flavours of Kerala. Highlights of the menu include delicious dosas (lentil-flour pancakes) and zingy crab and kingfish curries.

World Service Restaurant MODERN BRITISH £££
(☎0115-847 5587; www.worldservicerestaurant.com; Newdigate House, Castlegate; mains £16.50-24) Set in the courtyard of a 17th-century mansion and decked out with a eclectic selection of Asian ornaments, World Service feels rather colonial, but the tantalising food is firmly modern British with plenty of local produce – come at lunchtime for cheaper set menus. Bookings recommended.

Brown Betty's CAFE £
(17b St James's St; sandwiches & salads £3-7; ⌚9am-6pm Mon-Sat) Close to the castle, this is a good choice for cheap cheerful sandwiches, bagels and ciabatta, light pasta and salads and artery-challenging fry-ups.

Drinking

Weekends in Nottingham are boisterous affairs, and the streets throng with lads on stag nights, girls on hen parties, student revellers and intoxicated grown-ups who should really know better. If you fancy something more low-key, try the bars at the Broadway Cinema or Nottingham Playhouse – see opposite.

TOP CHOICE **Ye Olde Trip to Jerusalem** PUB
(www.triptojerusalem.com; Brewhouse Yard, Castle Rd) Tucked into the cliff below the castle, this fantastically atmospheric alehouse claims to be England's oldest pub. Founded in 1189, it supposedly slaked the thirst of departing crusaders and its low-ceiling rooms and cobbled courtyards still hum with atmosphere.

Malt Cross PUB
(www.maltcross.com; 16 St James's St) A genuinely convivial drinking hole in a stately old Victorian music hall that looks like the last variety act just can-canned out the door. A fine place for a pint or a pub meal.

Pit & Pendulum PUB
(17 Victoria St) Local goths, emos and indie kids flock to this dimly lit pub for the vampire vibe and theatrical decor. For our money, it's more *Rocky Horror Picture Show* than *Hammer House of Horrors*, but it's an enjoyable spot to shake off the coffin dust.

Brass Monkey BAR
(www.brassmonkeybar.co.uk; High Pavement; ⌚4pm-1am, till midnight Sun) Small and sultry, Brass Monkey rocks the Lace Market with sets by trendy DJs and quirky takes on cocktail favourites – rum and raisin daiquiri anyone? The roof terrace gets packed out on summer evenings.

Other good places to drink:

Canal House PUB
(☎0115-955 5060; 48-52 Canal St; ⌚till midnight Thu, till 1am Fri & Sat, till 10.30pm Sun) The best of the giant waterside public houses crowding the canal, run by the independent Castle Rock Brewery and split in two by a watery inlet.

Cock & Hoop PUB
(☎0115-852 3231; 25 High Pavement) Atmospheric town-house pub with a genteel atmosphere far removed from the noisy nightspots elsewhere in the centre. Good for ales and Sunday lunches.

Entertainment

Nightclubs

Nightclub fads come and go at breakneck speed in Nottingham. Check the local press to see which venues are catching the popular imagination this week.

Stealth NIGHTCLUB
(www.stealthattack.co.uk; Masonic Pl, Goldsmith St; ⌚till 6am Fri & Sat) Around the back of Rock City, reached from Goldsmith St, this underground club caters to dancey types who like their bass heavy and their drums supercharged. The attached **Rescue Rooms** (www.rescuerooms.com) has a varied line-up of live bands and DJs.

Gatecrasher NIGHTCLUB
(www.gatecrasher.com; Elite Bldg, Queen St; ⌚10pm-4am Fri & Sat, to 3am Thu) It's mainstream all the way at this spin-off from the famous Sheffield original. Spread over numerous rooms, it throbs to the sound of house, R&B, hip hop and club classics, and there are regular slots from international guest DJs.

NG1 NIGHTCLUB
(www.ng1club.co.uk; 76-80 Lower Parliament St; ⌚10pm-4am Fri, to 6am Sat, 11pm-4am Sun) Nottingham's favourite gay club, NG1 is unpretentious, hedonistic fun, with two dance floors belting out classic funky house, pop, '80s cheese or guitar jangle depending on the night.

Live Music

TOP CHOICE **Bodega Social Club** LIVE MUSIC
(www.thebodegasocialclub.co.uk; 23 Pelham St) Agreeably grungy, the Bodega boasts a popular beer garden and a stage that attracts bands of the calibre of the Strokes, Arctic Monkeys and Coldplay.

Maze Club LIVE MUSIC
(www.themazerocks.com; 257 Mansfield Rd; ⌚6pm-midnight Sun-Thu, 6pm-2am Fri & Sat) Behind the Forest Tavern pub, this revamped venue hosts singer-songwriters and kooky stage performers.

Rock City LIVE MUSIC
(www.rock-city.co.uk; 8 Talbot St) This monster venue has hosted everything

from Goth rock and Midlands metal to Northern Soul. It shares a compound with Stealth and the Rescue Rooms.

Theatre & Classical Music

For singalong musicals, touring theatre shows and veteran music acts, try the Royal Concert Hall or the Theatre Royal, which share a **booking office** (0115-989 5555; www.royalcentre-nottingham.co.uk; Theatre Sq) and an imposing building close to the centre. Ask at the tourist office for information on smaller theatres.

Nottingham Playhouse THEATRE
(0115-941 9419; www.nottinghamplayhouse.co.uk; Wellington Circus) Beside the shining bowl of Anish Kapoor's enormous *Sky Mirror*, the Playhouse hosts serious theatre, from stage classics to the avant-garde. The attached restaurant and bar attracts plenty of arty types.

Cinema

Broadway Cinema CINEMA
(www.broadway.org.uk, 14-18 Broad St) Fans of the arty and strange head to this funky independent cinema and gallery in the cultural part of town. The Broadway bar is one of the few drinking spots downtown where you can actually hear yourself talk.

Other screens include:

Screen Room CINEMA
(www.screenroom.co.uk; 25 Broad St) Small but perfectly formed, this tiny cinema has just 21 seats, and an interesting program of arty movies.

Savoy Cinema CINEMA
(www.savoycinemas.co.uk; 233 Derby Rd) Family-friendly independent cinema west of the city.

Shopping

Shopping in Nottingham is focused on the malls and Old Market Sq, but there are lots of upmarket fashion boutiques on pedestrian Bridlesmith Gate. Fashion magpie Paul Smith has two upmarket shops in the city centre: one on **Byard Lane** (10 Byard Lane) and one in **Willoughby House** (Willoughby House, 20 Low Pavement).

Information

There are numerous banks in the streets around Old Market Sq.

Post office (Queen St; 9am-5.30pm Mon-Fri, 9am-4.30pm Sat) With bureau de change.

Tourist office (www.visitnottingham.com; The Exchange, 1-4 Smithy Row; 9am-5.30pm Mon-Fri, to 5pm Sat, 10am-4pm Sun) With internet terminals (£3 per hour), brochures and racks of Robin Hood merchandise.

Getting There & Away

Air

East Midlands Airport (0871 919 9000; www.eastmidlandsairport.com) is about 18 miles south of Nottingham; Indigo buses pass the airport (one hour, hourly) en route to Derby.

Bus

Local services run from the Victoria bus station, behind the Victoria Shopping Centre on Milton St. Bus 100 runs to Southwell (50 minutes, every 20 to 30 minutes Monday to Saturday) and bus 90 to Newark (50 minutes, every 30 minutes, six Sunday services).

Long-distance buses operate from the dingy confines of Broadmarsh bus station, south of Bridlesmith Gate. For the Peaks, the hourly Transpeak service runs to Derby (40 minutes), Matlock Bath (1¼ hours), Bakewell (two hours) and Buxton (2½ hours). Useful National Express services:

Birmingham £10, two hours, seven daily

Leicester 45 minutes, 10 daily

London £20.60, 3½ hours, 10 daily

Sheffield £8.20, one hour 20 minutes, hourly

Train

The train station is just south of the town centre. Train services include the following:

Derby £5.50, 25 minutes, three hourly

Lincoln £9.20, one hour, hourly

London £49, two hours, two hourly

Manchester £18.40, two hours, hourly

Newark-on-Trent £5.10, 30 minutes, hourly

Sheffield £10.70, one hour, half-hourly

Getting Around

For information on buses within Nottingham, call **Nottingham City Transport** (0115 950 6070, www.nctx.co.uk). The Kangaroo ticket gives you unlimited travel on buses and trams within the city for £3.40.

The single tram line operated by **Nottingham Express Transit** (www.thetram.net; single/day ticket from £1.50/£2.70) runs from Nottingham train station to Hucknall, passing close to Broadmarsh bus station, the tourist office and Theatre Royal.

Bunneys Bikes (www.bunneysbikes.com; 97 Carrington St; bike hire per day £12.99) is near the train station.

MAD, BAD & DANGEROUS TO KNOW

The Romantic poet George Gordon Byron (1788–1824) was born of eccentric stock. His father was John 'Mad Jack' Byron, a playboy army captain who married a succession of women for their money, and his great-uncle, William Byron – aka the 'Wicked Lord' – allowed the family manor of Newstead Abbey to fall into ruin to spite his son and heir. With relatives like these, it was little wonder that the sixth Lord Byron fell into a life of debauchery and scandal.

Although Byron married only once, to Anne Isabella Milbanke, he had a string of affairs with married women, including Lady Caroline Lamb, who came up with that famous 'mad, bad' description. He was also alleged to have had liaisons with numerous male lovers and with his half-sister Augusta Leigh. After the breakdown of his marriage, Byron fled to Switzerland, where he befriended the ill-fated Romantic poet Percy Bysshe Shelly and his wife-to-be Mary Godwin, who would go on to write *Frankenstein*.

In between his many affairs, Byron was an active member of the House of Lords, campaigning on behalf of Luddites who were sentenced to death for destroying the industrial machinery that was robbing them of their livelihoods. Befitting a great Romantic, Byron died pursuing another idealistic dream, succumbing to a fever while fighting against the Ottomans in the Greek War of Independence. His legacy lives on in such epic works as *Don Juan* and the revealingly autobiographical *Childe Harold's Pilgrimage*.

Around Nottingham

NEWSTEAD ABBEY

The evocative lakeside ruins of **Newstead Abbey** (www.newsteadabbey.org.uk; adult/child £8/3.50, gardens only £4/2.50; ⏲house noon-5pm Fri-Mon Apr-Sep, garden 9am-dusk year-round) are forever associated with the original tortured romantic, Lord Byron (1788–1824), who owned the house until 1817. Founded as an Augustinian priory in around 1170, the building was converted into a residence after the dissolution of the monasteries in 1539, and Byron's old living quarters are full of suitably eccentric memorabilia. The lush, landscaped grounds include a monument to Byron's yappy dog, Boatswain.

The house is 12 miles north of Nottingham, off the A60. Pronto buses run from Victoria bus station, stopping at Newstead Abbey gates (30 minutes, every 20 minutes Monday to Saturday, half-hourly on Sunday), a mile from the house and gardens. Trains run to Newstead station, about 2.5 miles from the abbey.

EASTWOOD

POP 18,000

About 10 miles northwest of Nottingham, the village of Eastwood has a handful of interesting sights linked to the author DH Lawrence (1885–1930), who rose to fame, and then notoriety, for the graphic depictions of sexuality in such novels as *Lady Chatterley's Lover,* which was only published unexpurgated in 1960.

Set in the modest terraced house where Lawrence was born, the **DH Lawrence Birthplace Museum** (8a Victoria St; joint ticket with Durban House Heritage Centre adult/child £2.50/1.75; ⏲10am-5pm) has been reconstructed as it would have been in his childhood.

Down the road, the **Durban House Heritage Centre** (Mansfield Rd; joint ticket with DH Lawrence Birthplace Museum adult/child £2.50/1.75; ⏲10am-5pm Tue-Fri & Sun) provides context for Lawrence's writing by recreating life in a Nottinghamshire mining community at the turn of the 20th century.

Rainbow bus 1 runs from Nottingham's Victoria bus station to Eastwood (20 minutes, half-hourly), or follow the A610.

SHERWOOD FOREST NATIONAL NATURE RESERVE

If Robin Hood wanted to hide out in Sherwood Forest today, he'd have to disguise himself and the Merry Men as day-trippers on mountain bikes. Covering 182 hectares of old growth forest, the park is a major destination for Nottingham city dwellers looking to fill their lungs with fresh air and chlorophyll, but there are still some peaceful corners.

On the outskirts of the forest on the B6034, the **Sherwood Forest tourist office** (www.sherwoodforest.org.uk; Swinecote Rd; parking £3; ⏲10am-5pm) has visitor information, copious quantities of Robin Hood merchandise and the lame 'Robyn Hode's Sherwode', with wooden cut-outs, murals and mannequins telling the tale of the famous woodsman.

Numerous walking trails lead through the forest, passing such Sherwood Forest landmarks as the **Major Oak**, a broad-boughed oak tree that is certainly old enough to have sheltered Robin of Locksley, if he did indeed exist. The **Robin Hood Festival** is a massive medieval re-enactment that takes place here every August.

Sherwood Forest YHA (☎0845 371 9139; www.yha.org.uk; Forest Corner, Edwinstowe; dm from £10) is a modern hostel with comfortable dorms just an arrow's flight from the tourist office.

The Sherwood Forester (bus 150) runs to the park from Sheffield on Sunday and bank holiday Mondays (May to September). From Nottingham, catch the Sherwood Arrow (bus 33, 30 minutes, four daily Monday to Saturday, two Sunday services).

Southwell

POP 6285

A graceful scattering of grand, Wisteria-draped country houses, Southwell is straight out of the pages of an English Romantic novel. In the centre, **Southwell Minster** (www.southwellminster.org; suggested donation £3, photo pass £5; 8am-7pm), is a fascinating blend of 12th- and 13th-century features, built over Saxon and Roman foundations. With its zig zag doorframes and curved arches, the minster looks almost Byzantine, and the chapter-house features some unusual stained glass and detailed carvings of faces, animals and leaves from dozens of different forest trees.

On the outskirts of town on the road to Newark, **Southwell Workhouse** (NT; Upton Rd, adult/child £5.80/3; noon-5pm Wed-Sun) is a sobering reminder of the tough life faced by paupers in the 19th century. Visitors can explore the factory floors and workers' chambers in the company of an audio guide, narrated by 'inmates' and 'officials'.

For a comfortable bed for the night, head to the **Saracen's Head Hotel** (☎01636-812701; www.saracensheadhotel.net; s/d from £75/110, meals £8-10), a rambling, timbered coaching inn by the main junction.

Bus 100 runs from Nottingham (50 minutes, every 20 minutes, four services Sunday). For Newark-on-Trent, take bus 29 (25 minutes, every 40 minutes, every two hours Sunday) or bus 3 (two daily weekdays, three services Saturday).

Newark-on-Trent

POP 25,376

Dominated by its ruined castle, Newark paid the price for backing the wrong side in the English Civil War. After surviving four sieges by Cromwell's men, the town was ransacked by Roundheads when Charles I surrendered in 1646. It's an interesting detour between Nottingham and Lincoln.

Sights

The town has a large, cobbled square overlooked by the fine, timber-framed, 14th-century **Olde White Hart Inn** (which is now a building society) and the **Clinton Arms Hotel** (now a shopping precinct), from where former prime minister Gladstone made his first political speech and where Lord Byron stayed while his first book of poems was published.

FREE **Newark Castle** CASTLE

(Castlegate; admission free, tours adult/child £2.50/1.25; till dusk) Set in a pretty park overlooking the River Trent, the ruins include an impressive Norman gate and a series of underground passages and chambers. Fans of the Robin Hood legend may be interested to learn that the real King John – who wasn't quite as villainous as legend portrays him – died here in 1216. The tourist office runs hour-long tours of the dungeon (at 11am) and tower (at 1pm) on Wednesday, Friday, Saturday and Sunday.

FREE **Millgate Museum** MUSEUM

(☎01636-655730; 48 Millgate; 10.30am-4.30pm Tue-Sun) Southwest of the castle along the river, this family-friendly place is packed with old agricultural and industrial machinery, but the highlight is the walkthrough re-creation of a Victorian shopping street.

Newark Air Museum MUSEUM

(☎01636-707170; www.newarkairmuseum.org; adult/child £6.25/4; 10am-5pm) About 2 miles east of Newark by the Winthorpe Showground, with an impressive collection of aircraft, including a fearsome Vulcan bomber.

Eating

Cafe Bleu MODERN EUROPEAN ££

(☎01636-610141; www.cafebleu.co.uk; 14 Castlegate; mains £11-19; lunch daily, dinner Mon-Sat) The riverside setting is part of the charm at this sophisticated restaurant. The chef is a keen Europhile, and a courtyard garden, a dining room painted in Provençal colours and live jazz complete the picture.

For a healthy light lunch or a well-stacked sandwich, try **Gannets Daycafe** (35 Castlegate; snacks £2-5) or arch-rival **Feeling Peckish** (33 Castlegate; snacks from £3). Both are open daily till around 4.30pm.

Information

Tourist office (☎01636-655765; gilstrap@nsdc.info; Gilstrap Centre, Castlegate; ⏰9am-5pm Apr-Sep, to 4pm Oct-Mar) Runs castle tours and has a small Civil War museum.

Getting There & Away

Newark has two stations. Trains on the East Coast Main Line between London and the north stop at Newark North Gate, while East Midlands trains between Leicester, Nottingham and Lincoln stop at Newark Castle station. Bus services include the following:

Grantham Bus 602, one hour, four daily Monday to Saturday.

Lincoln Bus 46/87, 1¼ hours, four to five daily Monday to Saturday.

Nottingham Bus 90, 55 minutes, hourly (every two hours Sunday).

LINCOLNSHIRE

One of the most sparsely populated corners of England, Lincolnshire is a blanket of farmland laid over a gently undulating landscape of low hills and pancake-flat Fens. Surrounding beguiling Lincoln are seaside resorts, scenic waterways, serene nature reserves, and stone-built towns that seem tailor-made for English period dramas. The county has also produced some rather famous 'yellowbellies' (as locals like to call themselves), including Isaac Newton, Alfred Lord Tennyson, Margaret Thatcher, Jim Broadbent and astronaut Michael Foal.

Activities

Although it lacks the drama of the Lakes or Peaks, Lincolnshire is wonderfully quiet and unpopulated, perfect for cyclists and walkers. The 140-mile **Viking Way** snakes across the gentle hills of the Lincolnshire Wolds from the banks of the River Humber to Oakham in Leicestershire.

Cyclists can find information on routes across the county in any of the local tourist offices; the **Water Rail Way** is a flat but sculpture-lined on-road cycling route that follows the River Witham through classic Fens countryside between Lincoln and Boston.

Information

South West Lincs (www.southwestlincs.com)

Visit Lincolnshire (www.visitlincolnshire.com)

Visit North Lincolnshire (www.visitnorthlincolnshire.com)

Getting There & Around

East Midlands trains connect Lincoln, Newark Castle and Nottingham, and Newark North Gate and Grantham lie on the East Coast Main Line between London and Edinburgh. Local buses connect the towns of Lincolnshire, but services are slow and infrequent. For local transport information, check the transport pages at www.lincolnshire.gov.uk. The same site offers some excellent digital pamphlets on cycle routes around the county – search for 'Cycling' and follow the links.

Lincoln

POP 85,595

A bustling metropolis by Lincolnshire standards, but a sleepy backwater compared with almost anywhere else, delightful Lincoln is a tangle of cobbled medieval streets surrounding a vast 12th-century cathedral. This is one of the Midlands' most beautiful cities – the lanes that topple over the edge of Lincoln Cliff are lined with Tudor town houses, ancient pubs and quirky independent stores. Flanking the River Witham at the base of the hill, the new town is less interesting, but the revitalised Brayford Waterfront development by the university is a pleasant place to watch the boats go by.

Sights

As well as the following sights, set aside some time to explore the achingly atmospheric medieval lanes around **Steep Hill**, which are crammed with historic buildings, including the Romanesque **Jew's House**, constructed in around 1160 (it now houses an upmarket restaurant).

The tourist office sells the Lincoln Time Travel Pass, which gives access to several heritage sites including the castle, cathedral and Bishops' Palace (single/family £10/20) and lasts three days.

Lincoln Cathedral CATHEDRAL
(www.lincolncathedral.com; Minister Yard; adult/child £6/1, audio guide £1; ⏰7.15am-8pm Mon-Fri, to 6pm Sat & Sun) Towering over Lincoln like a medieval skyscraper, Lincoln's magnificent cathedral is a breathtaking representation of divine power on earth. The great tower rising above the crossing is the third-highest in England at 83m, but in medieval

times, a lead-encased wooden spire added a further 79m to this height, topping even the great pyramids of Giza.

The first Lincoln cathedral was constructed between 1072 and 1092, but it fell in a devastating fire in 1141, and the second cathedral was destroyed by an earthquake in 1185. Putting trust in the motto 'third time lucky', Bishop Hugh of Avalon (St Hugh) rebuilt and massively expanded the cathedral, creating one of the largest Gothic buildings in Europe.

The interior of the cathedral is rich in treasures, but first pause to appreciate the fabulous exterior, with its restored Norman friezes showing Adam and Eve bringing sin into the world, and Jesus making the ultimate sacrifice to undo the damage.

The vast interior of the church is too large for modern congregations - services take place in **St Hugh's Choir**, a church within a church running east from the crossing. The choir stalls are accessed through a magnificent stone screen carved with a riot of demons and grotesque faces. Look north to see the stunning rose window known as the Dean's Eye (from 1192), mirrored to the south by the floral flourishes of the Bishop's Eye, created by master glaziers in 1330. There is more interesting stained glass in the three Services Chapels in the North Transept, recalling Lincolnshire heroes of sea, land and air.

The glory of Lincoln cathedral is in the detail. Beyond St Hugh's Choir, the **Angel Choir** is supported by 28 columns topped by carvings of angels and foliate scrollwork. Tucked away atop one of the columns is the official emblem of Lincoln, the tiny Lincoln Imp - a cheeky horned pixie, allegedly turned to stone by the angels after being sent by the devil to vandalise the church.

Other interesting details include the curious Gilbert candlesticks, the dragon-carved font, the grand mausoleums of the Bishops of Lincoln, and the 10-sided **chapterhouse** where Edward I held his parliament, and where the climax of *The Da Vinci Code* was filmed in 2005.

There are one-hour tours at least twice a day plus less frequent tours of the roof and the tower. You can hear the organ resounding through the cathedral during Evensong (daily at 5.30pm; 3.45pm on Sunday) and the Sunday Eucharist at 9.30am.

LINCOLN'S LITTLE GREEN BUS

Despite the abundance of lovely architecture, walking between the two parts of Lincoln can feel like an Everest expedition. Fortunately, the handy **Walk & Ride** (all-day pass adult/child £2.50/1.50) bus service runs every 20 minutes from the Stonebow at the corner of High St and Saltergate to the cathedral and Newport Arch, then back via Brayford Waterfront and the train station.

Lincoln Castle CASTLE
(www.lincolnshire.gov.uk/lincolncastle; adult/child £5/3.30; ⌚10am-6pm) One of the first castles thrown up by the victorious William the Conqueror to keep his new kingdom in line, Lincoln Castle offers awesome views over the city and its miles of surrounding countryside. Highlights include the chance to view one of the four surviving copies of

DON'T MISS

LINCOLN CITY GATES

Lincoln seems to have more historic city gates than there are possible directions on the compass. Starting at the north end of the city, the **Newport Arch** on Bailgate is a relic from the original Roman settlement; traffic has been passing beneath this arch for at least 1500 years. A short walk south, the 13th-century **Exchequergate** leads from Castle Hill to the courtyard of Lincoln Cathedral, marking the spot where tenant farmers gathered to pay rent to the land-owning Bishops of Lincoln.

Behind the cathedral, Pottergate is bookended by the free-standing **Priory Gate**, built in Victorian times, and the ancient **Pottergate**, part of the fortifications that once protected the Bishops' Palace. At the bottom of the hill, by the junction of High St and Saltergate, the glorious **Stonebow** marks the southern entrance to the medieval city. Constructed in 1520, this Gothic gatehouse contains the **Lincoln Guildhall**, which is periodically open to the public for guided tours.

Lincoln

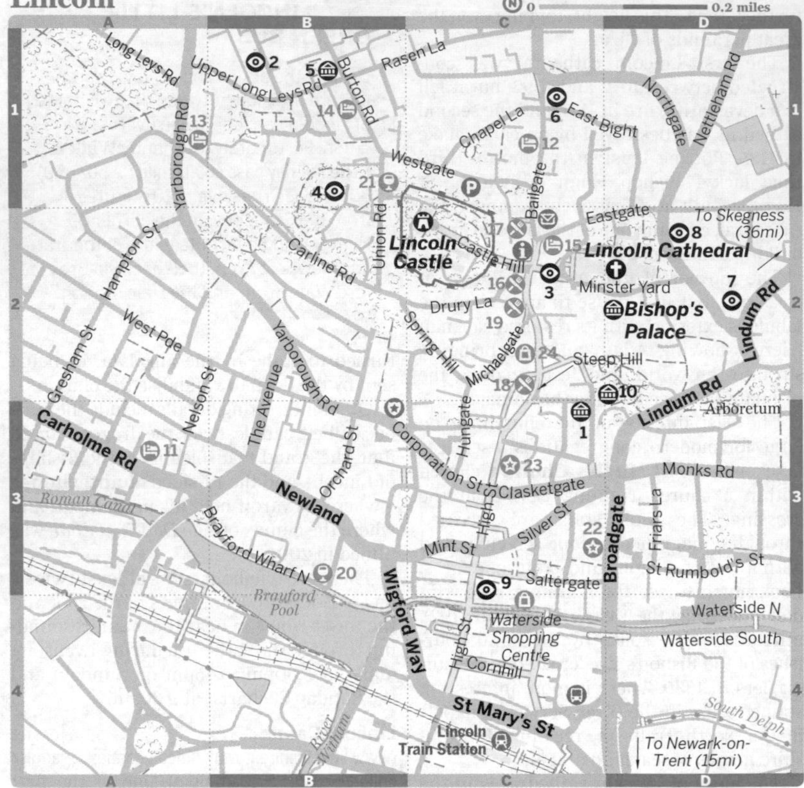

the **Magna Carta** (dated 1215), and the grim **Victorian prison chapel**, dating back to the days when this was the county jailhouse and execution ground.

Free tours of the castle run at 11am and 2pm daily from April to September and on weekends in winter.

Bishops' Palace HISTORIC RUIN

(EH; ☎01522-527468; adult/child £4.20/2.10; ⌚10am-5pm) Beside the cathedral are the time-ravaged but still imposing ruins of the 12th-century Bishops' Palace, gutted by parliamentary forces during the Civil War. From here, the local bishops once controlled a diocese stretching from the Humber to the Thames. You can roam around the ruins and undercroft in the company of an entertaining audio guide.

FREE **Collection** MUSEUM

(www.thecollection.lincoln.museum; Danes Tce; ⌚10am-5pm) An angular, modernist museum where archaeology bursts into life, with loads of hands-on displays where kids can handle artefacts and dress up in period costume. Check out the crushed skull of a 4000-year-old 'yellowbelly' (the local term for, well, the locals), pulled from a Neolithic burial site near Sleaford.

FREE **Usher Gallery** GALLERY

(Lindum Rd; ⌚10am-5pm Tue-Sat, 1-5pm Sun) Set in a handsome Edwardian building decorated with carvings of cow skulls, the town gallery has an impressive collection of works by such greats as Turner, Lowry and English watercolourist, Peter de Wint (1784–1849). The gallery is set to reopen after renovations in 2010.

FREE **Museum of Lincolnshire Life** MUSEUM

(Old Barracks, Burton Rd; ⌚10am-4pm Mon-Sat) A short trek north of the centre and set in an old Victorian barracks, this

Lincoln

community museum displays everything from Victorian farm implements to the tin-can tank built in Lincoln for WWI. Round the corner from the museum is the cute little **Ellis Mill** (Mill Rd; admission free; ⌚2-5pm Sat & Sun), the windmill that used to grind the town's flour in the 18th century.

Lawn GARDEN
(www.thelawninlincoln.co.uk; Union Rd; ⌚10am-5pm, to 5.30pm Sun) The pretty grounds of the town's former lunatic asylum contain the ornamental **Dawber Gardens** and the Sir Joseph Banks Conservatory, containing descendants of some of the plants brought back by the botanist who accompanied Captain Cook to Australia.

Tours

History-focused 1½-hour guided **walking tours** (adult/child £4/free) run from outside the tourist office in Castle Hill at 11am daily in July and August, and at weekends only from October to June. Genuinely spooky 1¼-hour **ghost walks** (adult/child £4/2) depart from outside the tourist office at 7pm Wednesday to Saturday.

Boat trips along the River Witham and Fossdyke Navigation, a canal system dating back to Roman times, start from Brayford Waterfront. The **Brayford Belle** (☎01522-881200, www.lincolnboatrips.com; adult/child £6/4) runs five times daily from Easter to September, and just at weekends in October.

Sleeping

Bail House B&B ££
(☎01522-541000; www.bailhouse.co.uk; 34 Bailgate; r from £99; P@☞≋) Stone walls, worn flagstones, secluded gardens and one room with an extraordinary timber-vaulted ceiling are just some of the charms of this lovingly restored Georgian town house in central Lincoln. There's even a heated outdoor swimming pool.

White Hart Hotel HOTEL ££
(☎01522-526222; www.whitehart-lincoln.co.uk; Bailgate; s/d from £85/99; P@☞) You can't get more venerable than this grand dame of Lincoln hotels, sandwiched between castle and cathedral. With a history dating back 600 years, the White Hart offers vast rooms with appealing country-style fabrics and tasteful trim.

Old Bakery B&B ££
(☎01522-576057; www.theold-bakery.co.uk; 26-28 Burton Rd; r from £53; P@☞) This charming guesthouse, set above the excellent restaurant of the same name, has four quaint, sunlit rooms and delicious breakfasts, as you might expect from such foodie owners. Free parking is available out front.

Carline Guest House B&B ££
(☎01522-530422; www.carlineguesthouse.co.uk; 1-3 Carline Rd; s/d from £38/58; P) An elegant brick house, in an elegant residential part of town, with big, flowery rooms.

Admiral Guest House B&B £
(☎01522-544467; www.admiralguesthouse.co.uk; 16-18 Nelson St; s/tw/d £30/45/50; P) A hike from the old town in the industrial terraces northwest of Brayford Wharf, the Admiral mainly scores points for its prices.

Eating

As well as the following restaurants, there are numerous tearooms dotted along Steep Hill. Unless otherwise stated, reservations are recommended in the evenings at the following eateries.

TOP CHOICE **Brown's Pie Shop** PIE SHOP ££
(☎01522-527330; www.brownspieshop.co.uk; 33 Steep Hill; pies £9-17) Forget Mrs Miggins and Sweeny Tod; this long-established pie shop is one of Lincoln's top restaurants, spread over a smart upstairs dining room and a cosy brick-lined basement. Come for hearty pies stuffed with locally-sourced beef, rabbit and game.

Jew's House MODERN EUROPEAN ££
(☎01522-524851; www.jewshouserestaurant.co.uk; Steep Hill; 3 courses £17.95; ⊙Tue-Sun) Set in one of England's oldest houses, this local favourite serves up gourmet Anglo-French food in atmospheric surrounds. The building was damaged by fire in 2009, but the owners plan to reopen once it is repaired.

Gino's ITALIAN £££
(☎01522-513770; www.ginoslincoln.co.uk; 7 Gordon Rd, Bailgate; mains £13-26) Run by Italian-born chef Vito Cataffo, who became famous for serving British food to Italians in Bologna, this superior restaurant serves fine dishes from northern and southern Italy.

Wig & Mitre PUB ££
(www.wigandmitre.com; 30 Steep Hill; mains £11-20; ⊙breakfast, lunch & dinner) Civilised pub-restaurant the Wig & Mitre has an excellent, upscale menu but manages to retain the mellow mood of a friendly local. Food is served throughout the day, from morning fry-ups to lunchtime sandwiches and filling evening roasts. Bookings are not necessary.

Old Bakery MODERN BRITISH £££
(☎01522-576057; www.theold-bakery.co.uk; 26-28 Burton Rd; mains £17-22; ⊙Tue-Sun) This eccentric restaurant is where visiting actors and celebs come to eat when performing in the city. The menu is built around impeccably presented local produce, and – appropriately – freshly baked bread.

Drinking

Bland chain pubs crowd the High St, but there are a few worthy independent public houses.

Victoria PUB
(6 Union Rd) A serious beer-drinker's pub with a pleasant patio looking up at the castle's western walls, the Victoria has a huge selection of guest brews, cask ales, thick stouts and superb ciders. Meals start at £7.

Royal William IV PUB
(Brayford Wharf N) Part of the regenerated Brayford Waterfront development, this student-friendly stone pub offers a more intimate drinking environment than the brash chain restaurants on all sides.

Entertainment

Ask at the tourist office about theatre venues.

Lincoln Drill Hall ARTS CENTRE
(www.lincolndrillhall.com; Freeschool Lane) Downhill near the station, this stern-looking building hosts bands, orchestras, stage shows, comedy and daytime book and beer festivals.

Sakura NIGHTCLUB
(www.sakuralincoln.com; 280-281 High St; ⊙from 10pm Mon & Wed-Sat) There's a Tokyo Underground feel at this Japanese-themed basement club, which shakes to a different beat each night. Monday is student night, with plenty of drinks deals.

Shopping

Steep Hill is packed with bijou little shops selling interesting and quirky gifts, antiques and bric-a-brac. More conventional stores fill the Waterside Shopping Centre beside the river.

Readers Rest BOOKSHOP
(13-14 Steep Hill; ⊙closed Sun) An agreeably chaotic secondhand bookshop with lots of titles on local history and stacks of books for young readers.

Information

The High St has numerous banks and ATMs. Check www.lincoln.gov.uk for events listings.

County hospital (☎01522-512512; off Greetwell Rd)

Post office (90 Bailgate; ⌚9am-5.30pm Mon-Fri, 9am-5pm Sat) With bureau de change.

Tourist office (www.visitlincolnshire.com; 9 Castle Hill; ⌚10.30am-4pm Mon-Sat) In a handsome 16th-century building by the castle.

Getting There & Away

Bus

National Express runs direct bus services from Lincoln to London (£25.20, 4¾ hours, daily) and Birmingham (£15.30, three hours, daily). Local buses mainly run Monday to Saturday; useful services include the following:

Boston Bus 5, 1½ hours, hourly (also five Sunday services)

Grantham Bus 1, 1¼ hours, half-hourly (also five Sunday services)

Louth Bus 10, one hour, six daily

Newark Bus 46, 1¼ hours, four to five daily

Skegness Bus 6, 1½ hours, hourly

Train

Getting to and from Lincoln by rail usually involves changing trains.

Boston £11, 1¼ hours, hourly, change at Sleaford

Cambridge £24, 2½ hours, hourly, change at Peterborough and Ely

Sheffield £12.40, one hour 40 minutes, hourly

Grantham

POP 34,592

Grantham would be just another country town were it not for two rather famous former inhabitants – Sir Isaac Newton and former prime minister Margaret Thatcher, the daughter of a humble Grantham greengrocer, who plied his trade at 2 North Pde. The town itself has just a few sights, but there are some interesting country houses in the surrounding countryside.

Sights

Predictably, the town **museum** (St Peter's Hill; admission free; ⌚10am-4pm Mon-Sat) focuses on Newton and Maggie memorabilia, including one of the ex-PM's famous handbags, as well as a gloriously exaggerated latex puppet from the satirical TV show *Spitting Image*.

You can easily spot the parish church of **St Wulfram's** (www.stwulframs.org.uk; ⌚9am-4pm Mon-Sat) thanks to its pin-sharp 85m spire, which provides a nesting site for peregrine falcons. Inside are an interesting crypt chapel, and a 16th-century chained library where Newton once pored over his studies.

WORTH A TRIP

DODDINGTON HALL

About 5 miles west of Lincoln on the B1190, peaceful **Doddington Hall** (www.doddingtonhall.com; adult/child £8.50/4.25, garden only £5/2.75; ⌚11am-5pm Wed, Sun & bank holidays Apr-Sep, house open from 1pm) was another creation of the talented Robert Smythson, who also designed Longleat (p293) and Hardwick Hall (p484). Completed in 1600, this handsome Elizabethan pile boasts hectares of gorgeous ornamental gardens and all the tapestries, oil paintings and heirlooms you could ask for. The easiest way to get here is by taxi from Lincoln.

Newton fans may feel the gravitational pull of the great man's former home at **Woolsthorpe Manor** (NT; Water Lane, Woolsthorpe by Colsterworth; adult/child £6.10/3.05; ⌚11am-5pm Wed-Sun), about 8 miles south of Grantham. The 17th-century house contains reconstructions of Newton's rooms; the apple that inspired the theory of gravity allegedly fell from the tree in the garden. Take Centrebus 608 from Grantham (20 minutes).

Sleeping & Eating

Red House B&B ££
(☎01476-579869; www.red-house.com; 74 North Pde; s/d from £35/59; P@☜) This handsome Georgian town house near Maggie's birthplace has large, spick-and-span rooms. The welcome is very friendly and rooms have big TVs, mini fridges and microwaves.

Angel & Royal Hotel HOTEL ££
(☎01476-565816; www.angelandroyal.com; High St; mains £9-17; s/d from £80/104.50; P@☜) Allegedly England's oldest inn, this courtyard hotel has played host to no less than seven kings of England since 1200. These days, commoners are just as welcome, and the rooms have all the anticipated olde-English touches. There's also a regal-looking restaurant with surprisingly reasonable prices.

Blue Pig PUB ££
(9 Vine St; mains from £8) A cosy nook of a pub in a half-timbered Tudor building, serving a fine selection of thirst-quenching real ales and substantial English meals.

WORTH A TRIP

BELTON HOUSE

About 3 miles northeast of Grantham, **Belton House** (NT; A607; adult/child £9.50/5.50, grounds only £7.50/4.50; ⌚11am-5pm Sat & Sun) is a dream location for English period dramas – indeed, the mansion crops up in numerous period romps from the BBC, including *Jane Eyre*, *Tom Jones* and the Colin Firth version of *Pride & Prejudice*. Built in 1688 in classic Restoration style, the house features some stunning period details, including ornate woodcarvings attributed to the master Dutch carver Grinling Gibbons, as well as elegant formal gardens. Centrebus 609 (15 minutes) and Stagecoach bus 1 run here from near Grantham train station.

Information

Tourist office (granthamtic@southkesteven.gov.uk; St Peter's Hill; ⌚9.30am-4.30pm Mon-Fri, 9.30am-1pm Sat) In the Guildhall complex; has information on local attractions.

Getting There & Away

BUS Grantham Bus 1, one hour 20 minutes, half-hourly (five services Sunday)

Stamford Bus 4, 1½ hours, five daily Monday to Saturday

TRAIN You'll need to change at Newark North Gate (£6.40, 15 minutes, two hourly), to get to Lincoln (£8.90, 1½ hours) by train. Trains also run to and from London King's Cross (£19, 1¼ hours, twice hourly).

Stamford

POP 19,525

One of England's prettiest towns, Stamford seems frozen in time, with elegant streets lined with honey-coloured limestone buildings and hidden alleyways dotted with hearty alehouses, interesting eateries and small independent boutiques. A forest of historic church spires rises overhead and the gently gurgling River Welland meanders through the town centre. Unsurprisingly, the town is a top choice for filmmakers looking for the postcard vision of England, appearing in everything from *Pride and Prejudice* to *The Da Vinci Code*.

Sights

The town's top attraction is nearby **Burghley House** (see p464), but just walking around the streets is a delight. Drop in on **St Mary's Church** (St Mary's St), with its charmingly wonky broach spire, or explore the 15th-century chapel and chambers of the **William Browne Hospital** (Broad St; adult/child £2.50/1; ⌚11am-4pm Sat & Sun).

The **Stamford Museum** (Broad St; admission free; ⌚10am-4pm Mon-Sat) has a muddle of displays on the town's history, including an exhibit on man-mountain Daniel Lambert (see boxed text, p471) who died here in 1809.

Close to pint-sized St George's Church at the Stamford Arts Centre, the **tourist office** (☎01780-755611; stamfordtic@southkesteven.gov.uk; 27 St Mary's St; ⌚9.30am-5pm Mon-Sat, 10.30am-3.30pm Sun) can arrange guided walks and boat trips.

Sleeping

TOP CHOICE **George Hotel** HOTEL £££
(☎01780-750750; www.georgehotelofstamford.com; 71 St Martin's; s/d from £93/132.50, 4-poster d £210.50; P@) Marked by a gallows sign across the road, this magnificent inn opened its doors in 1597, on the site of a former hostelry for the crusading Knights of St John of Jerusalem, but its rooms perfectly blend period charm and modern elegance. This level of luxury comes with a hefty price tag, as does the superior modern British food at the attached restaurant.

Rock Lodge B&B ££
(☎01780-481758; www.rock-lodge.co.uk; 1 Empingham Rd; s/d £72/90; P) Just a short stroll northwest of the centre, this imposing Edwardian town house sits haughtily above clipped green lawns, but the welcome is warm. The cosy country-style rooms are lovingly maintained and the breakfasts will definitely set you up for the day.

Other recommendations:

Stamford Lodge B&B ££
(☎01780-482932; www.stamfordlodge.co.uk; 66 Scotgate; s/d from £50/70) A former bakehouse with modern rooms, a friendly hostess and excellent breakfasts.

Dolphin Guest House B&B ££
(☎01780-757515; mik@mikdolphin.demon.co.uk; 12 East St; s/d £45/60; P) A rare cheap option in Stamford, with modest rooms in a modern house north of the centre.

Eating

The best meals in town are served at the George Hotel.

Tobie Norris PUB ££
(www.tobbienorris.com; 12 St Pauls St; mains £10-13; lunch daily, dinner Mon-Thu) A fine, stone-walled pub in a delightful, flagstone-floored town house serving hearty pub grub and wholesome ales from the Ufford micro-brewery.

Voujon INDIAN ££
(01780-757030; www.voujonrestaurant.co.uk; 26 Broad St; mains £7-11) Well-prepared Indian favourites are served up in stylish surroundings near the museum. Bookings recommended.

Entertainment

Stamford Arts Centre ARTS CENTRE
(01780-763203; www.stamfordartscentre.com; 27 St Mary's St) This cultured establishment hosts everything from live jazz and art-house cinema to stand-up comedy.

Getting There & Away

BUS Grantham Kimes Bus 4, 1½ hours, five daily Monday to Saturday.

London National Express, £14.30, three hours, one daily.

Peterborough Delaine Buses 201, one hour, hourly Monday to Saturday.

TRAIN Cross-country trains run to Birmingham (£31.50, 1½ hours, hourly) and Stansted Airport (£31, 1¾ hours) via Cambridge (£17.40, 1¼ hours) and Peterborough (£6.20, 15 minutes).

Boston

POP 35,124

It's hard to believe that sleepy Boston was the inspiration for its larger and more famous American cousin. Although no Boston citizens sailed on the *Mayflower,* the town became a conduit for persecuted Puritans fleeing Nottinghamshire for religious freedom in the Netherlands and America. In the 1630s, the fiery sermons of Boston vicar John Cotton inspired many locals to follow their lead, among them the ancestors of John Quincy-Adams, the sixth American president. These pioneers founded a namesake town in the new colony of Massachusetts, and the rest, as they say, is history.

Sights

Built in the early 14th-century, **St Botolph's Church** (church free, tower adult/child £3/1; 10am-4pm Mon-Sat, btwn services Sun) is known locally as the Stump - a comment on the truncated appearance of its 88m-high tower. Puff your way up the 365 steps on a clear day and you'll see to Lincoln, 32 miles away. Linguists may be interested to note that the name Boston is actually a corruption of 'St Botolph's Stone'.

Before escaping to the New World, the Pilgrim Fathers were briefly imprisoned in the 14th-century **Guildhall** (South St; adult/

DON'T MISS

BURGHLEY HOUSE

Lying just a mile south of Stamford, flamboyant **Burghley House** (www.burghley.co.uk; adult/child incl sculpture garden £11.80/5.80; 11am-5pm Sat-Thu) – pronounced bur-lee – was built by Queen Elizabeth's chief adviser William Cecil, whose descendants have lived here ever since. Needless to say, the family only use a handful of the 115 rooms, and the remainder of the house is open to the public.

Set in more than 810 hectares of grounds, landscaped by the famous Lancelot 'Capability' Brown, the house bristles with cupolas, pavilions, belvederes and chimneys, and the staterooms are a treasure-trove of ormolu clocks, priceless oil paintings, Louis XIV furniture and magnificent murals of Greco-Roman deities and Rubenesque ladies in various states of undress, painted by the 17th-century Italian master Antonio Verrio. In the aptly-titled Heaven Room, a writhing mass of deities and demons spills off the ceiling and down the walls; death is depicted in classic form as a scythe-wielding skeleton and the damned enter the Inferno through the gaping mouth of a diabolical cat.

Make time for a stroll around the lovely gardens and deer park, where an atmospheric Sculpture Garden erupts with disembodied faces and skeletal forms. The internationally famous **Burghley Horse Trials** take place here in early September. To reach Burghley, followed the marked path for 15 minutes through the park by Stamford train station.

child £3.30/1.60; ⏲10am-4.30pm Wed-Sat), one of Lincolnshire's oldest brick buildings. Inside are fun, interactive exhibits, as well as a restored 16th-century courtroom, and a mock up of a Georgian kitchen.

About 800m northeast of Market Pl, the **Maud Foster Windmill** (www.maudfoster.co.uk; adult/child £2.50/1.50; ⏲10am-5pm Wed & Sat) is the tallest working windmill in the country, with seven floors that creak and tremble with every turn of the sails.

Sleeping & Eating

Palethorpe House B&B ££

(☎01205-359000; 138 Spilsby Rd; r £60; P @) This pretty vine-covered Victorian villa has just two beautifully refurbished en suite rooms complete with living room, and it's just a 10-minute walk from Boston's centre.

White Hart PUB ££

(☎01205-311900; www.whitehartboston.com; 1-5 High St; s/d £75/95; dishes from £10; P @) Right in the middle of town, this handsome pub-hotel has tastefully modernised rooms and a decent menu of meaty mains in the modern British mold.

Information

Tourist office (South St; ticboston@boston.gov.uk; ⏲10.30am-3.30pm Wed-Fri, 10.30am-3pm Sat) Inside the Guildhall, close to the River Witham.

Getting There & Away

InterConnect bus 5 runs between Lincoln and Boston (1½ hours, hourly, five Sunday services) and bus 7 runs to Skegness (one hour, hourly, reduced service Sunday). For Lincoln, you can also take the train (£11, 1¼ hours), changing at Sleaford.

Skegness

POP 16,806

Spread out along the better-than-average yellow sand beach at Skegness ('Skeggy' to the locals) you'll find the ABC of the English seaside – amusements, bingo and candyfloss, accompanied by a constant soundtrack of tweets, klaxons and bells from the abundant slot machines and fairground rides. Culture vultures will probably run a mile, but it's all good family fun if you immerse yourself in the whole tacky spectacle.

Alternatively, you can escape the beeps and flashing lights in the National Nature Reserve at **Gibraltar Point**, a pristine area of dunes and marshes 5km south of Skegness. Plentiful birdlife includes terns, skylarks and red shanks.

There are plenty of faded seaside hotels and cheap and cheerful B&Bs start at just £18 per person – the **tourist office** (Grand Pde; ⏲9.30am-5pm) has listings and leaflets on local walks and trips to the delightful working windmills at Alford and Burgh Le Marsh. It's located inside the **Embassy Centre** (www.embassytheatre.co.uk), the centrepoint of the Skeggy cabaret scene.

From July to September, this beachfront promenade saturates the night sky with the glare of 25,000 glowing light bulbs for the annual **Skegness Illuminations**. Nothing says 'holiday' quite like leaving the lights on all night…

Trains run between Skegness and Boston (40 minutes, at least hourly Monday to Saturday, nine on Sunday). Bus services include the Interconnect 7 to Boston (one hour, hourly – reduced service Sunday) and the Interconnect 6 to Lincoln (1½ hours, hourly).

HARNESSING THE WIND

With few hills to block the breezes blowing in from the North Sea, Lincolnshire has a long history of harnessing the power of the wind. Wind-powered pumps were used to drain the Fens and the countryside is dotted with flour-grinding windmills. Many are still in operation, including Lincoln's Ellis Mill (p461), Boston's Maud Foster Windmill (p466) and the charming mills at Alford and Burgh Le Marsh near Skegness.

With growing interest in sustainable energy, Lincolnshire is now turning its attention to commercial wind power. As part of a £725 million energy project, giant wind turbines are springing up across the countryside like supersized daisies, and even appearing off the coast, providing a surreal backdrop to the seafront at Skegness.

Not everyone is happy about this development, however. A turbine north of Skegness was mysteriously wrecked in January 2009 by an unidentified flying object, on an evening when locals saw strange lights hovering in the sky. Explanations have ranged from a bird strike to a collision with a secret unmanned stealth bomber. All we know is the truth is out there…

THE FENS

One of England's most melancholy landscapes, the low-lying Fens were pulled by hand from the desolate marshlands that once lined the east coast of Norfolk, Cambridgeshire and Lincolnshire. Dutch engineer Sir Cornelius Vermuyden was commissioned to hold back the waters with giant dykes and wind-powered pumps in the 17th century, creating new tracts of farmland that could be exploited by the wealthy landowners of the day. The atmosphere of this spooky, windswept landscape is brilliantly captured in Graham Swift's haunting novel *Waterland*.

Visit while you can – with changing weather patterns and rising sea levels, it's estimated that up to 1544 sq miles could vanish beneath the still, black waters by the year 2030. The easiest way to see the Fens today is to follow the **Water Rail Way** road cycle path between Boston and Lincoln, or to swing by the sublimely quiet **Wicken Fen National Nature Reserve** (www.wicken.org.uk; Lode Lane, Wicken; adult/child £5.20/2.65; ⏲10am-5pm), 8 miles south of Ely. To find out more on the past and future of the Fens, visit the **Fenscape Discovery Centre** (☎01775-764800; www.fenscape.org; cnr A151 & A16; admission free; ⏲10am-5pm, till 4pm Sun) near Spalding.

Louth

POP 15,930

About 23 miles northeast of Lincoln, straddling the line of zero longitude, Louth was the starting point for a short-lived uprising against the dissolution of the monasteries in 1536. At the height of the revolt, 40,000 Catholic protestors marched on Lincoln and occupied the cathedral, before being driven back by the forces of Henry VIII. The leader of the revolt – Thomas Kendall, vicar of St James' Church – was hung, drawn and quartered for his troubles at Tyburn in 1537. The line of longitude is marked by a line of sculptures known as the Louth Art Trail.

Sights

Louth's big money attraction – the tallest parish church spire in England – rises atop **St James' Church** (⏲10.30am-4pm Mon-Sat), propped up by dramatic buttresses. The elbow-scraping climb to the top (£1) is rewarded by stellar views over the town and surrounding countryside. Among other parishioners, the famous New World adventurer Captain John Smith, of Pocahontas fame, once worshipped here.

Opposite the churchyard at 47 Westgate, an archway leads to Westgate Pl and a row of impossibly cute row terraced cottages, one of which bears a plaque commemorating the four years that Alfred Lord Tennyson spent here.

A short walk north from the centre, the 100-year-old **Louth Museum** (www.louthmuseum.co.uk; 4 Broadbank; adult/child £2/1.20; ⏲10am-4pm Tue-Sat) has displays on local history, including a reproduction of William Brown's *Panorama*, painted from the spire of St James' in 1844. You can view the original inside the **town hall** (admission free; ⏲2-4pm Wednesday) on Eastgate.

Sleeping & Eating

Priory HOTEL ££
(☎01507-602930; www.theprioryhotel.com; 149 Eastgate; s/d/f from £45/60/110; P) This is a glorious, whitewashed Gothic-style building from 1818, set in sprawling gardens which run down to old ruins and a lake. Rooms have beautiful period-style furnishings and dinner is available most nights.

Mad Hatter's Tearooms CAFE £
(117 Eastgate; snacks £2-5; ⏲9.30am-4pm Mon-Sat) A cute, flower-drenched place serving up a good selection of cakes, sandwiches and soups.

Chuzzlewitts SANDWICH SHOP £
(26 Upgate; sandwiches from £3) Buy gourmet sandwiches made with fresh-baked bread from this cafe, which hides behind a wonderfully bowed Georgian shopfront on the main shopping street.

Information

Tourist office (www.louth.org; cnr Eastgate & Cannon St; ⏲9am-5pm Mon-Fri, to 4pm Sat Easter-Oct) At the Town Hall.

Getting There & Around

Louth is best reached from Lincoln – take bus 10 (one hour, six daily).

Around Louth

SALTFLEETBY-THEDDLETHORPE DUNES NATIONAL NATURE RESERVE

One of the Fens' most attractive **reserves** (www.naturalengland.org.uk; admission free; ⌚dawn-dusk), Saltfleetby-Theddlethorpe erupts with orchids in early summer and attracts vast flocks of migratory wildfowl in spring and autumn, filling the grassy dunes with birdsong. There are dozens of short and long trails to keep your feet dry as you negotiate the myriad lagoons.

You'll need your own transport to get here. The reserve is 10 miles east of Louth at the end of the B1200. Turn right onto the A1031 and follow the signs.

NORTHAMPTONSHIRE

While it's hard to pin down a 'must-see' attraction, peaceful Northamptonshire has more than its fair share of stately homes, including the ancestral homes of George Washington and Lady Diana. The county capital is worth a visit for its museums and churches and the countryside is dotted with villages full of pincushion cottages with thatched roofs and Tudor timbers. As well as the towns covered below, you may find yourself changing trains or buses in Kettering or Corby, whose modest claim to fame was inventing the trouser press in 1930.

Information

Explore Northamptonshire (www.explorenorthamptonshire.co.uk)

Getting Around

Northampton is the hub for bus services around the county, but some run only a few times daily and there are fewer buses on Sundays. See the 'Transport & Streets' pages at www.northamptonshire.gov.uk for routes and timetables. Trains run by London Midlands are useful for getting to and from Northampton; Corby and Kettering are on the East Midlands line.

Northampton

POP 194,458

Rebuilt after a devastating fire in 1675, Northampton was once one of the prettiest towns in the Midlands, but WWII bombers and postwar town planners wreaked their usual havoc. Nevertheless, the heart of the town, around Market Sq and George Row, is actually rather grand, and there are some ancient monuments dotted among the pedestrian shopping arcades and concrete flyovers. Historically, the town played a significant role in the Wars of the Roses and the English Civil War, before shifting its attention to manufacturing shoes.

Sights & Activities

Constructed after the 1675 fire, **All Saints' Church** (www.allsaintsnorthampton.com; George Row; ⌚8am-6pm) owes an obvious debt to the churches built by Sir Christopher Wren after the Great Fire of London, with an ornate barrel-vaulted ceiling and dark-wood organ and reredos. For more fine architecture, take a peek at the handsome **Sessions House** (containing the tourist office) and the **Guildhall** on George Row.

Even those without a shoe fetish can get a kick out of the impressive displays at **Northampton Museum & Art Gallery** (www.northampton.gov.uk/museums; Guildhall Rd; admission free; ⌚10am-5pm Mon-Sat, 2-5pm Sun), where you can learn about the history of shoemaking and footwear fashions and faux-pas.

Northampton's oldest buildings are dotted around the inner ring road. West of Market Sq, **St Peter's Church** (Marefair; ⌚10am-4pm Wed-Sat) is a marvellous Norman edifice built in 1150 and adorned with ancient carvings. North of the centre, on the far side of the eyesore bus station, **Church of the Holy Sepulchre** (⌚2-4pm Wed & Sat) is one of the few surviving round churches in the country, founded when the first Earl of Northampton returned from the Crusades in 1100.

Sleeping & Eating

The tourist office can advise on B&Bs in the area.

Ibis Hotel HOTEL £
(☎1604-608900; www.ibishotel.com; Sol Central, Marefair; r from £45) The Ibis offers chain-hotel rooms in a chain-hotel setting, but you can't fault the location, just a few hundred yards from Market Sq in the Sol Central entertainment complex.

Church Bar & Restaurant MODERN EUROPEAN ££
(☎01604-603800; www.thechurchrestaurant.com; 67-83 Bridge St; mains £12-18; ⌚Mon-Sat) A deeply funky redevelopment of an old church, where you can feast on modern European cooking on the terrace, or sip a

cocktail under the stained-glass windows in the bar.

Drinking

Malt Shovel Tavern PUB £

(☎01604-234212; www.maltshoveltavern.com; 121 Bridge St) It's worth the hike from town to this agreeable watering hole opposite the Carlsberg brewery for the wide selection of real ales and regular live music.

Information

Tourist office (www.explorenorthamptonshire.co.uk; Sessions House, George Row; ⏲8.30am-5.30pm Mon-Fri, 10am-2pm Sat Apr-Sep)

Getting There & Away

Northampton has good rail links with Birmingham (£12.60, one hour, hourly) and London Euston (£26, one hour, three hourly). The train station is about half a mile west of town along Gold St.

Famously ugly Greyfriars bus station is on Lady's Lane, just north of the Grosvenor shopping centre. National Express coaches run services to the following places:

Birmingham £7.50, one hour 40 minutes, three daily

London £13.40, 2¼ hours, five daily

Nottingham £13.40, 2½ hours, once daily

Around Northampton

ALTHORP

The ancestral home of the Spencer family, **Althorp House** (☎bookings 01604-770107; www.althorp.com; adult/child £12.50/6, access to upper floors extra £2.50; ⏲11am-5pm Jul & Aug, last entry 4pm) – pronounced altrup – is the final resting place of Diana, Princess of Wales, who is commemorated by a memorial and museum. You don't have to be a follower of the cult of Diana to enjoy the outstanding art collection, with works by Rubens, Gainsborough and Van Dyck. Profits from ticket sales go to the charities supported by the Princess Diana Memorial Fund. The limited number of tickets available must be booked by phone or on the web.

Althorp is off the A428, 5.5 miles northwest of Northampton. Stagecoach bus 96 (hourly, not Sundays) runs from Northampton to Rugby, passing the gates to the Althorp estate, where you can call to arrange a pick up from the estate minibus.

STOKE BRUERNE

POP 395

About 8 miles south of Northampton, this charming little village nestles against the Grand Union Canal, the main drag of England's canal network. From here, you can follow the waterways all the way to Leicester, Birmingham or London. Set in a converted corn mill, the entertaining **National Waterways Museum** (www.nwm.org.uk/stoke; adult/child £4.75/2.75; ⏲10am-5pm) charts the history of the canal network and the bargemen, lock keepers and pit workers whose livelihoods depended on it.

The Grand Union Canal is still frequented by brightly-painted barges. In summer, you can cruise on the **Indian Chief** (☎01604-862428; ⏲Sun & bank holiday weekends only), run by the Boat Inn. Short trips lasting 25 minutes cost £3/2.50 per adult/child. Several other boat owners offer cruises and charters.

For overnight stays, try **Waterways Cottage** (☎01604-863865; www.waterwayscottage.co.uk; Bridge Rd; s/d incl breakfast £48/60), an adorable thatched cottage right off the front of a biscuit box.

Meals and brews are served up at the cosy **Boat Inn** (☎01604-862428; www.boatinn.co.uk; mains £5-12) alongside the canal.

Buses 86 and 87 both run between Stoke Bruerne and Northampton (30 minutes, six daily Monday to Saturday).

SULGRAVE MANOR

While **Sulgrave Manor** (www.sulgravemanor.org.uk; adult/child £6.55/3.15; ⏲noon-5.30pm Sat & Sun Apr-Oct, also 2-5.30pm Tue-Thu May-Oct, last entry 4pm) is certainly an impressively preserved Tudor mansion, the main draw for most visitors is the connection between Lawrence Washington, who built the house in 1539, and a certain George Washington of Virginia. The Washington family lived here for almost 120 years before Colonel John Washington, the great-grandfather of America's first president, sailed to Virginia in 1656.

Sulgrave Manor is southwest of Northampton, just off the B4525 near Banbury. The easiest way to get here is to take a train to Banbury, and then a taxi from there.

RUSHTON TRIANGULAR LODGE

Looking like something from *The Da Vinci Code*, this mysterious **lodge** (EH; adult/child £3.20/1.60; ⏲11am-4pm Thu-Mon) is a testament to the strength of Sir Thomas Tresham's Catholic faith. Imprisoned for 15 years

WORTH A TRIP

NORTHAMPTONSHIRE'S HISTORIC CHURCHES

Northamptonshire is dotted with ancient churches, some dating all the way back to Saxon times. The eye-catching **All Saints Church** (⏲10am-5pm Apr-Sep) in the tiny village of Brixworth, 6 miles north of Northampton, was constructed in around AD 680 and its walls are full of recycled Roman masonry. Stagecoach bus X7 runs to Brixworth from Northampton (15 minutes, hourly Monday to Saturday, five on Sunday).

There's another fine **All Saints Church** (⏲10.30am-12.30pm & 2-4pm Mon-Sat) in the village of Earls Barton, 8 miles east of Northampton. Built during the reign of Edgar the Peaceful (r 959–75), the church tower has a curious elevated doorway that may have been used during Viking raids. Stagecoach bus X4 runs from Northampton to Earls Barton (20 minutes, half-hourly Monday to Saturday, hourly on Sunday).

Jumping forwards several centuries, the **Holy Trinity Church** (⏲2-5pm Sun) in Rothwell, 13 miles north of Northampton, is a Norman construction, but the real treasure here is the crypt, where the bones of 1500 medieval parishioners are arranged in ornamental piles in one of England's only charnel houses. Bus 18 from Kettering to Market Harborough passes through Rothwell (one hour, hourly Monday to Saturday).

for refusing to convert, Tresham celebrated his release by constructing a monument to the Holy Trinity, complete with arcane geometry and esoteric inscriptions. With three of everything, from sides to floors to gables, his mysterious lodge was completed in 1597 and the silent country setting adds to the atmosphere.

The lodge is 4 miles northwest of Kettering. Stagecoach buses 18 and 19 from Kettering stop in Desborough, 2 miles away (20 minutes, every 20 to 30 minutes Monday to Saturday, hourly on Sunday). Kettering is 15 miles northeast of Northampton along the A43.

KIRBY HALL

Known as the 'Jewel of the English Renaissance', **Kirby Hall** (EH; adult/child £5.30/2.70; ⏲10am-5pm) was constructed for Christopher Hatton, Lord Chancellor to Elizabeth I, in around 1570. The house is all the more atmospheric for being partly ruined; ravens perch on the carved stone lintels and empty window frames look out over brilliantly restored parterre gardens. The Great Hall and state rooms were renovated to something of their original glory in 2004.

Kirby Hall is 4 miles northeast of Corby, which is 24 miles northeast of Northampton along the A43. Come by car or take a taxi from Corby train station.

OUNDLE & FOTHERINGHAY

A rival to Stamford, Lincolnshire, in the 'pretty village' stakes, Oundle (population 5345) is a tight tangle of streets and squares lined with 16th- and 17th-century buildings, constructed from honey-coloured Jurassic limestone and Colleyweston slate. Oundle's **tourist office** (14 West St; ⏲9am-5pm Mon-Sat, 1-4pm Sun) has plenty of leaflets to help visitors explore the picture-postcard streets.

On New St, the elegant **Talbot Hotel** (☎01832-273621; www.thetalbot-oundle.com; New St; s/d from £60/80) was built using stone and timbers from Fotheringhay Castle, birthplace of Richard III and the spot where the axe fell for Mary, Queen of Scots, in 1587. You can visit the former **castle site** in the Fotheringhay village (population 123), 4 miles north of Oundle. The hotel positively oozes history. On the way to your tastefully appointed room, you can climb the reclaimed oak staircase from the castle, walking in the very footsteps of Mary Tudor.

Bus X4 runs to Oundle from Northampton (two hours, hourly) and from Peterborough (30 minutes, hourly) in the other direction.

LEICESTERSHIRE & RUTLAND

Leicestershire was a vital creative hub during the Industrial Revolution, but its factories were a major target for German air-raids in WWII and most towns in the county still bear the scars of wartime bombing. Nevertheless, there's some impressive history among the urban chaos, from Elizabethan castles to Roman ruins, and the busy capital, Leicester, offers a taste of India with its rainbow temples and pure-veg curry houses.

Tiny Rutland was merged with Leicestershire in 1974, but in April 1997 regained its 'independence' as a county. Centred on peaceful Rutland Water, it's a hit with lovers of water sports, with some impressive country house hotels.

Information

Leicestershire Tourism (www.goleicestershire.com)

Discover Rutland (www.discover-rutland.co.uk)

Getting There & Around

Leicester is well served by buses and trains. For bus routes and timetables, visit the 'Roads & Transport' pages at www.leics.gov.uk. Regular buses connect Rutland to Leicester, Stamford and other surrounding towns.

Leicester

POP 279,923

Built over the buried ruins of two millennia of history, Leicester (*les*-ter) is another Midlands town that suffered at the hands of the Luftwaffe and postwar planners. However, a massive influx of textile workers from India and Pakistan since the 1960s has transformed the city from drab industrial workhouse to bustling global melting pot. Modern Leicester is alive with the sights, sounds and flavours of the subcontinent, creating a strange juxtaposition with the Victorian factories and eyesore concrete architecture. The city also has some surprising historical treasures, including perhaps the finest medieval guildhall in the country.

Sights

Apart from the National Space Centre, all of Leicester's **museums** (www.leicester.gov.uk/museums) are free.

FREE **New Walk Museum & Art Gallery** MUSEUM
(New Walk; ⏲10am-5pm Mon-Sat, from 11am Sun) Southeast of the centre on pedestrian New Walk, this grand Victorian museum is full of eye-catching, thought-provoking displays that show off the collection to its best advantage. Highlights include the revamped dinosaur galleries, the painting collection (with works by Francis Bacon, TS Lowry and Stanley Spencer), and the Egyptian gallery, where real mummies rub shoulders with displays on Boris Karloff's *The Mummy*.

FREE **Guildhall** HISTORIC BUILDING
(Guildhall Lane; ⏲11am-4.30pm Mon-Wed & Sat, 1-4.30pm Sun) Leicester's perfectly preserved 14th-century guildhall is reputed to be the most haunted building in Leicester. You can search for spooks in the magnificent Great Hall, the wood-panelled 'Mayor's Parlour' and the old police cells, which contain a reconstruction of a 19th-century gibbet.

National Space Centre MUSEUM
(www.spacecentre.co.uk; adult/child £12/10; ⏲10am-5pm Tue-Sun, last entry 3.30pm) Before you get too excited, British space missions usually launch from French Guyana or Kazakhstan, but Leicester's space museum is still a fascinating introduction to the mysteries of the spheres. The ill-fated Beagle 2 mission to Mars was controlled from here and fun, kiddie-friendly displays cover everything from astronomy to the status of current space missions. The centre is off the A6 about 1.5 miles north of the city centre. Take bus 54 from Charles St in the centre.

FREE **Newarke Houses Museum** MUSEUM
(The Newarke; ⏲10am-5pm Mon-Sat, from 11am Sun) Sprawling over two 16th-century mansions, this entertaining museum has exhibits detailing the lifestyles of local people through the centuries. Don't miss the displays on Daniel Lambert, the walk-through re-creation of a WWI trench, and the trophies of the Royal Leicestershire

A MAN OF MAMMOTH PROPORTIONS

An unlikely folk hero, Daniel Lambert was born a healthy baby in 1770, but he soon began to tip the scales at ever more alarming totals. Despite being an enthusiastic swimmer and eating just one meal per day, Lambert ballooned to an astounding 336kg. When he became too large to continue in his job as a prison guard, he took to the road as a professional curiosity, granting public audiences to paying onlookers who marvelled at the size of the 'Human Mammoth'. When he died in 1809, the wall of the pub where he was staying had to be dismantled to remove the coffin. Despite his fame, Lambert was a relative lightweight compared to modern levels of obesity – the world's current heaviest man, Manuel Uribe, weighs in at a ground-shaking 597kg!

Leicester

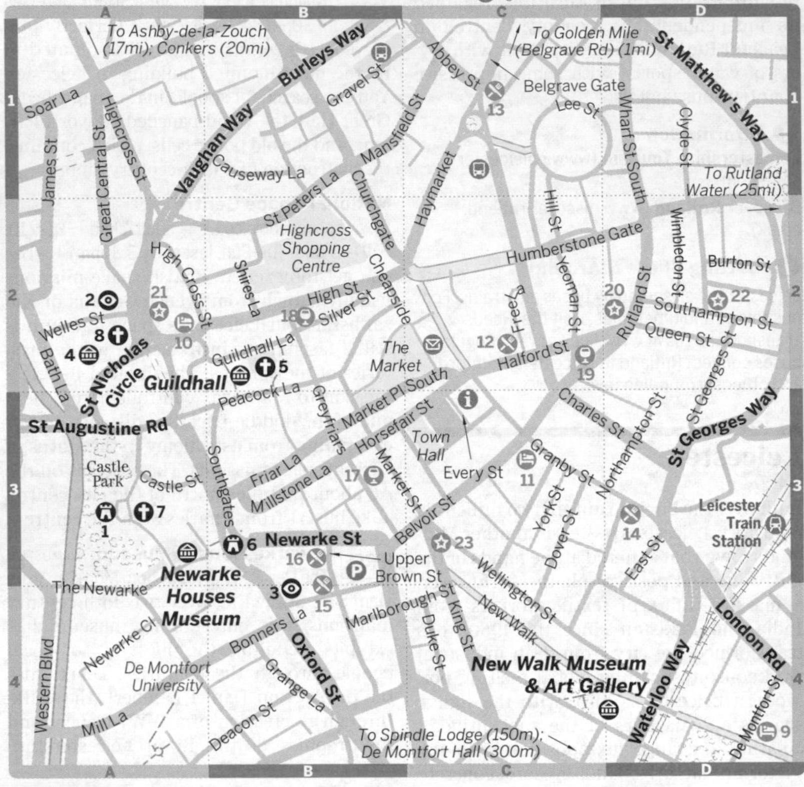

Regiment, including an outrageous snuff box made from a tiger's head.

FREE **Leicester Castle** CASTLE

Dotted around the Newarke Houses Museum are the scattered ruins of Leicester's medieval castle, where Richard III spent his final days before the Battle of Bosworth. The most impressive chunk of masonry is the monumental gateway known as the **Magazine** (Newarke St), once a storehouse for cannonballs and gunpowder. Clad in Georgian brickwork, the 12th-century **Great Hall** (Castle Yard), stands behind a 15th-century gate near the church of **St Mary de Castro** (Castle St), where Geoffrey Chaucer was married in 1336. The hall is open for tours on the first Saturday of the month – contact the tourist office for details.

Jewry Wall Museum MUSEUM

(St Nicholas Circle; ⏲11am-4.30pm) You can see fine Roman mosaics and frescoes in this museum exploring the history of Leicester from Roman times to the modern day. In front of the museum is the **Jewry Wall**, part of Leicester's Roman baths. Tiles and masonry from the baths were incorporated in the walls of neighbouring **St Nicholas' Church**.

FREE **Leicester Cathedral** CATHEDRAL

(www.cathedral.leicester.anglican.org; 21 St Martin's; ⏲8am-6pm Mon-Sat, 7am-5pm Sun) In the midst of the shopping district on Guildhall Lane, this substantial medieval church features some striking carvings on its roof supports. Inside, you can see a memorial to Richard III, who rode out from Leicester to fatal defeat at the Battle of Bosworth.

Temples TEMPLES

Leicester's Indian citizens have constructed dozens of mosques and temples, including several right in the centre.

Leicester

Top Sights
Guildhall ... B2
New Walk Museum & Art Gallery ... D4
Newarke Houses Museum ... A3

Sights
1 Great Hall ... A3
2 Guru Nanak Gurdwara ... A2
3 Jain Centre ... B4
4 Jewry Wall Museum ... A2
5 Leicester Cathedral ... B2
6 Magazine ... B3
7 St Mary de Castro ... A3
8 St Nicholas Church ... A2

Sleeping
9 Belmont House Hotel ... D4
10 Hotel Maiyango ... A2
11 Ramada Hotel ... C3

Eating
12 Good Earth ... C2
13 Haveli ... C1
14 Kayai ... D3
15 Tinseltown Diner ... B4
16 Watson's ... B3

Drinking
17 Firebug ... B3
18 Globe ... B2
Maiyango ... (see 10)
19 Quarter ... C2

Entertainment
20 Curve Theatre ... D2
21 Mosh ... A2
22 Phoenix Square ... D2
23 Superfly ... C3

Housed in a converted church, the **Jain Centre** (www.jaincentre.com; 32 Oxford St; 8.30am-8.30pm Mon-Fri, to 6.30pm Sun) caters to followers of an ancient religion that rose in India at the same time as Buddhism. Fronted with gleaming white marble, the lavish interior recalls the ancient sandstone temples at Jaisalmer in Rajasthan. Remove your shoes before entering.

Although outwardly plain, the **Guru Nanak Gurdwara** (9 Holy Bones; 1-4pm Thu, 7-8.30pm Sat) contains an engaging museum dedicated to Sikh culture and history, with an impressive model of the Golden Temple in Amritsar.

Tours

In summer, **Discover Leicester** (0844 888 5151; adult/child £7/5; 10am-4pm) runs jump-on jump-off open-topped bus tours around the city and up to Belgrave Rd, the Great Central Railway and the National Space Centre, departing from the Thomas Cook statue outside Leicester train station.

Festivals & Events

Leicester hosts numerous cultural and religious festivals throughout the year. Contact the tourist office for details.

Leicester Comedy Festival COMEDY
(0116-261 6812; www.comedy-festival.co.uk) Held in February, this is the country's longest-running comedy festival, drawing big names as well as fresh talent.

Leicester Caribbean Carnival CULTURE
(www.leicestercarnival.com) In August the city hosts the biggest Caribbean celebration in the country after London's Notting Hill Carnival, with lots of colourful costumes.

Diwali RELIGION
Held in October or November, depending on the lunar calendar, the Festival of Lights is the biggest annual festival for Leicester's Hindu community, with fire works, parades and ornate street lights on Belgrave Rd.

Sleeping

TOP CHOICE **Hotel Maiyango** HOTEL £££
(0116-251 8898; www.maiyango.com; 13-21 St Nicholas Pl; d from £148; @) A surprisingly sophisticated place to stay in a surprising setting at the end of the pedestrian High St. Attached to Leicester's funkiest bar, the hotel boasts spacious, sexy rooms, decorated with handmade Asian furniture, contemporary art and massive plasma TVs.

Belmont House Hotel HOTEL ££
(0116-254 4773; www.belmonthotel.co.uk; De Montfort St; s/d £115/120; P @) In a quiet location near De Montfort Hall, the Belmont has benefited from a hotel-wide refurbishment that has added plenty of modern style and colour to the rooms. There are great deals to be had if you book ahead.

Spindle Lodge B&B ££
(☎0116-233 8801; www.spindlelodge.com; 2 West Walk; s/d from £35/55; P@) Set in a grand Victorian house in the university quarter, this friendly place is cheaper than most, but you get what you pay for – rooms are plain and rather dated.

Ramada Hotel HOTEL ££
(☎0844 815 9012; www.ramadajarvis.co.uk; Granby St; r from £59; P@) Despite being set in a listed Victorian building, the Ramada spills out onto a noisy street that gets even noisier on weekend evenings. Rates vary day to day so check the web for the latest prices.

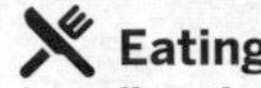

Eating

As well as the following eateries, there are numerous upscale chain restaurants in the glitzy High Cross shopping centre on Shires Lane.

Watson's MODERN EUROPEAN ££
(☎0116-255 1928; 5-9 Upper Brown St; mains £12-17; ⏲Tue-Sat) Set in a converted cotton mill south of the shopping district, this upmarket eatery is a swirl of white linen and fluted glasses. Artfully prepared and exquisitely presented modern European food is served to a jazz soundtrack. Booking is recommended.

Tinseltown Diner FAST FOOD £
(www.tinseltown.co.uk; 5-9 Upper Brown St; mains £5-11; ⏲noon-4am) Fancy a triple-decker chilli burger or an Oreo cookie and peanut butter milkshake at three in the morning? Then come on down to Tinseltown. With this being Leicester, the effect is more Bollywood than Hollywood, but kids will love the menu and razzmatazz.

Kayal INDIAN ££
(☎0116-255 4667; www.kayalrestaurant.com; 153 Granby St; dishes £5-13) This inviting restaurant offers an upmarket take on the steamy South Indian cuisine served up by the curryhouses on Belgrave Rd. Try the *kappayum meenum* – the tasty fish curry served up by Keralan toddy shops. Booking recommended.

Haveli INDIAN £
(☎0116-251 0555; 61 Belgrave Gate; mains £5-10; ⏲dinner Tue-Sun) Don't be put off by the mannequins in Indian costume and the unusual setting in a former high-street store; the balti dishes here are fiery and filling.

Good Earth VEGETARIAN £
(☎0116-262 6260; 19 Free Lane; mains £3.25-6.25; ⏲noon-3pm Mon-Fri, 10am-4pm Sat) Tucked away on a side street, this wholesome vegetarian restaurant is justifiably popular for its veggie bakes, huge, fresh salads and homemade cakes.

Drinking

Amid the rash of chain pubs in the centre, there are a few places for more discerning drinkers.

Maiyango BAR
(www.maiyango.com; 13-21 St Nicholas Pl) The Moroccan lamps, silky scatter cushions and

DON'T MISS

THE GOLDEN MILE

Lined with sari stores, jewellery emporiums, and pure-veg curry houses, Belgrave Rd – aka the Golden Mile – is *the* place to come for blisteringly authentic Indian vegetarian food. Menus are built around the spicy flavours of the south, with delicious staples such as dosas (lentil-flour pancakes), *idli* (steamed rice cakes) and huge thalis (plate meals), with a mix of vegetable curries, flatbreads, rice and condiments. Belgrave Rd is about 1 mile northeast of the centre – follow Belgrave Gate and cross Burleys Flyover.

There are more top-notch eateries on the Golden Mile than you can shake a chapatti at. Our top pick is **Bobby's** (www.eatatbobbys.com; 154-6 Belgrave Rd; mains £5-12; ⏲Tue-Sun), which has been serving pure-veg classics since 1976. As well as spicy thalis and scrumptious samosas (curry-stuffed pastries), Bobby's is famous for its *namkeen* – tongue-tingling lentil-flour snacks that come in myriad shapes and sizes.

Another recommended stop is the agreeably down-to-earth **Chaat House** (108 Belgrave Rd; mains £4-8; ⏲Wed-Mon), where the dosas are as big as rolled-up newspapers. Should you crave something sugary to finish off your meal, numerous shops along the strip sell *mithai* (Indian sweets), tooth-meltingly sweet combinations of nuts, fruit and milk curds.

smooth beats create a chilled-out atmosphere in this moody cocktail bar and restaurant attached to the Maiyango hotel.

Quarter BAR
(41 Halford St; ⏲noon-midnight) Leading the way in the city's new cultural quarter, this place has an airy bar and restaurant full of two-tone designer furniture that spills outside in summer. The funky basement lounge is all mood lighting, plush sofas and world beats.

Firebug BAR
(www.firebug.co.uk; 1 Millstone La; ⏲noon-2am, till 4am Fri & Sat, till 1am Sun) A lava lounge for the student crowd, with theme nights, stage shows, gigs and a decent selection of beers on tap.

Globe PUB
(43 Silver St; ⏲to midnight Fri & Sat) In the atmospheric Lanes – a tangle of alleys south of the High St – this old-fashioned boozer offers fine draught ales and a crowd who rate their drinks by quality rather than quantity.

Entertainment

Nightclubs & Live Music

As well as the following venues, there are numerous mainstream clubs clustered around Churchgate and Gravel St.

De Montfort Hall LIVE MUSIC
(www.demontforthall.co.uk; Granville Rd) Big-name stars, big orchestras, and big song-and-dance acts are on the bill at this huge venue near Leicester University.

Mosh NIGHTCLUB
(www.moshleicester.com; 37 St Nicholas Place) Unleash your inner indie kid at this loud and lively rock joint near the end of the High St.

Superfly NIGHTCLUB
(www.superfly-city.com; 2 King St) Behind a towering mock-Tudor facade, this place serves up four floors of diverse beats, with guest DJs and gigs appealing to Leicester party people.

Theatre & Cinema

Leicester's big cultural venues have relocated to the new Cultural Quarter development around Rutland St, just east of the centre. The tourist office has info on smaller venues.

Curve Theatre THEATRE
(www.curveonline.co.uk; Rutland St) A sleek artistic space with big-name shows and some innovative modern theatre. The bar is a sophisticated place for lunch or a sun-downer.

Phoenix Square CINEMA
(www.phoenix.org.uk; Midland St) Part of the new Cultural Quarter, this is Leicester's premier venue for art-house films and digital media.

Information

Post office (39 Gallowtree Gate; ⏲9am-5.30pm Mon-Sat) With a bureau de change.

Tourist office (www.goleicestershire.com; 7-9 Every St; ⏲10am-5.30pm Mon-Fri, 10am-5pm Sat) Brochures and information on local tours.

Getting There & Away

East Midlands trains run to London's St Pancras Station (£46.80, 1¾ hours, two to four hourly) and Birmingham (£15, one hour, twice hourly).

Buses operate from St Margaret's bus station on Gravel St, north of the centre. The useful Skylink bus runs to East Midlands airport (£6, 50 minutes, every 30 minutes, 24 hours). Bus 440 runs to Derby (£7.90, one hour, 10 daily); one bus a day continues to Buxton (£14.30, two hours). National Express services:

Coventry £6.60, 45 minutes, four daily

London £18.30, 2¾ hours, one or two hourly

Nottingham 45 minutes, two hourly

Getting Around

The centre is cut off from the suburbs by a tangle of underpasses and flyovers, but downtown Leicester is easy to get around on foot. For unlimited transport on local buses, buy a £2.70 CityDay ticket.

DON'T MISS

STEAMING AROUND LEICESTER

A fun jaunt rather than a serious way to get from A to B, the classic **Great Central Railway** (www.gcrailway.co.uk; return adult/child £14/9) operates steam locomotives from Leicester North station on Redhill Circle to Loughborough Central, following the 8-mile route along which Thomas Cook ran the original package tour in 1841. The locos chug several days a week from June to August and most weekends for the rest of the year – see the website for the latest timetable. To reach Leicester North station, take bus 70 from the Haymarket.

Around Leicester

BOSWORTH BATTLEFIELD

Given a few hundred years, every battlefield ends up just being a field, but the site of the Battle of Bosworth – where Richard III met his maker in 1485 – is livened up by an entertaining **Heritage Centre** (☎01455-290429; www.bosworthbattlefield.com; admission £6; ⏲11am-5pm) full of skeletons and musket-balls. The best time to visit is in August, when the battle is re-enacted by a legion of enthusiasts in period costume.

Although it lasted just a few hours, the Battle of Bosworth marked the end of the Plantagenet dynasty and the start of the Tudor era. This was where the mortally wounded Richard III famously proclaimed 'A horse, a horse, my kingdom for a horse'... actually, he didn't. The quote was invented by that great Tudor propagandist William Shakespeare, who also painted the able-bodied Richard as a cruel, calculating hunchback with a withered arm.

The battlefield is 16 miles southwest of Leicester at Sutton Cheny, off the A447. Arriva bus 153 runs hourly from Leicester to Market Bosworth, a 3-mile walk from the battlefield. Alternatively, book a taxi from **Bosworth Gold Cars** (☎01455-291999).

ASHBY-DE-LA-ZOUCH

POP 12,758

Named for a family of Norman nobles, sleepy Ashby-de-la-Zouch is worth a quick stop for its ruined **castle** (EH; adult/child £4.20/2.10; ⏲10am-5pm), made famous by Sir Walter Scott in his classic *Ivanhoe*. You can roam around the sundered towers and battlements in the company of an engaging audioguide – bring a torch (flashlight) to explore the underground passageway connecting the tower with the kitchen. There are displays on the rise and fall of the castle in the pocket-sized **Ashby Museum** (North St; adult/child £1/50p; ⏲11am-4pm Mon-Fri, 10am-4pm Sat).

The town is also a handy base for visits to Conkers and the National Forest – based at the town library, the **tourist office** (North St; ⏲9.30am-5pm Mon, Tue, Thu & Fri, 9.30am-4pm Sat) has more information. Ashby is on the A511 about 15 miles northwest of Leicester; Arriva bus X2 runs hourly from St Margaret's bus station in Leicester, or you can change in Coalville.

WORTH A TRIP

TWYCROSS ZOO

About 8 miles south of Ashby, **Twycross Zoo** (www.twycrosszoo.org; adult/child £13/9; ⏲10am-5.30pm) boasts the largest collection of primates in the country, from pygmy marmosets and lanky lemurs to graceful gibbons and mighty lowland gorillas. It's one of the best zoos in the country, with a successful breeding program and loads of activities for kids. Bus 7 runs here from Ashby (every 1½ hours, Monday to Saturday).

EXPLORING LEICESTERSHIRE

In summer, you can explore Ashby, Conkers and the surrounding area on an open-top, hop-on/hop-off bus tour run by **Discover Leicester** (☎0844 888 5181; adult/child £7/5; ⏲Fri mid-Jul–late Aug). Contact the Leicester or Ashby tourist offices for times.

CONKERS & THE NATIONAL FOREST

The **National Forest** (www.nationalforest.org) is an ambitious project to generate new areas of sustainable woodland by planting 30 million trees in Leicestershire, Derbyshire and Staffordshire. More than seven million saplings have already taken root, and all sorts of visitor attractions are springing up in the forest, including the fun-filled **Conkers** (www.visitconkers.com; Rawdon Rd, Moira; adult/child £7.23/5.41; ⏲10am-6pm), a family-oriented nature centre, with interactive displays, indoor and outdoor playgrounds and lots of hands-on activities. Conkers is 20 miles northwest of Leicester off the A444; bus 23 from Ashby-de-la-Zouch to Moira passes this way.

National Forest YHA hostel (☎0845 371 9672; www.yha.org.uk; beds from £14; P @), about 300m west of Conkers' entrance along Bath Lane, is packed with ecofriendly features and has a great restaurant serving local produce and organic wines.

BELVOIR CASTLE

The ancestral home of the Duke and Duchess of Rutland, **Belvoir Castle** (www.belvoircastle.com; adult/child £12/6; ⏲11am-5pm Sun-Thu) is a magnificent baroque and Gothic fantasy constructed in the 19th century over the ruins of three previous castles. Still owned by the Manners family, the home overflows with tapestries, priceless furniture, ancient oil paintings (including a magnificent portrait of Henry VIII by Holbein and works by Reynolds and Gainsborough). Being a private home, it's only open on specific dates – see the website for the latest opening times.

Belvoir is technically in Leicestershire, but the nearest town is Grantham, Lincolnshire, 6 miles east.

Rutland

Aside from the modest claim to fame of being England's smallest county, tiny Rutland is noteworthy for the outdoorsy activities that are possible on **Rutland Water**, a vast artificial reservoir created by the damming of the Gwash Valley in 1976. Covering 1255 hectares, the reservoir attracts numerous bird species, including ospreys, best viewed from the hides at the **Rutland Water Nature Reserve** (www.rutlandwater.org.uk) near Oakham.

There are tourist offices and attractions dotted around the lakeshore. At Skyes Lane near Empingham, the **Rutland Water tourist office** (☎01780-686800; www.anglianwater.co.uk; ⊙10am-4pm) has a snack kiosk, walking and cycling trails and information on the area.

A mile down the road, the **Whitwell Centre** (☎01780-460705; www.rutlandactivities.co.uk) has a vertigo-inducing high-ropes course, an outdoor climbing wall and bikes for hire (adult/child per day £21/10) for a gentle pedal around the lakeshore. In the same compound, **Rutland Watersports** (☎01780-460154; www.anglianwater.co.uk/leisure) offers a full range of watery activities, including sailing, windsurfing and kayaking. You can rent gear, take lessons or enrol in governing-body approved certification courses.

From April to October, the **Rutland Belle** (☎01572-787630; www.rutlandwatercruises.com; adult/child £7/4.50) offers afternoon cruises from Whitwell to Normanton on the southern shore of the reservoir, where a stone causeway leads out across the water to **Normanton Church** (adult/child £2/1; ⊙11am-4pm Mon-Fri, 11am-5pm Sat & Sun), saved from inundation by a limestone barrier wall. Inside are displays on the history of the reservoir.

Close to the boat jetty, the **Normanton Centre** (☎01780-720888; www.rutlandactivities.co.uk) offers bike hire at the same rates as the Whitewell Centre. Just down the road at Edith Weston, **Rutland Sailing School** (☎01780-721999; www.rutlandsailingschool.co.uk) rents out boats and runs sailing courses on dinghies and catamarans.

The nearest places to stay are in Oakham and Stamford in Lincolnshire.

OAKHAM

POP 9975

The county town of Rutland, snoozy Oakham has a famous school and winding streets dotted with historic buildings. Behind the town market place, a path leads to **Oakham Castle** (admission free; ⊙10am-5pm Tue-Fri, 10am-4pm Sat), whose unfortified Great Hall was constructed in around 1190; inside you can see a curious collection of commemorative horseshoes donated by peers of the realm. Nearby, an original set of **stocks** are displayed beneath the stone-tiled pavilion of the Buttermarket. The **tourist office** (www.discover-rutland.co.uk; museum admission free; ⊙10am-5pm Tue-Fri, 10am-4pm Sat) doubles as the Rutland County Museum.

About 7 miles south of Oakham in the village of Lyddington, lichen-encrusted **Bede House** (EH; adult/child £4.20/2.10; ⊙10am-5pm Thu-Mon) was once a palace for the Bishops of Lincoln, before being set aside for the poor of the parish, on the condition that they were free from 'lunacy, leprosy or the French pox'. The house still contains some fine 17th-century details, particularly in the Great Chamber. Rutland Flyer bus 1 runs hourly between Oakham and Lyddington from Monday to Saturday.

TOP CHOICE **Hambleton Hall** (☎01572-756991; www.hambletonhall.com; Hambleton; r from £240, mains £30-40) surveys the countryside from a peninsula jutting out into Rutland Water. One of England's finest country hotels, the hall boasts gorgeous gardens, lavishly appointed rooms and a Michelin-starred restaurant, attracting plenty of well-heeled gourmands in the Michael Winner mould.

Trains run hourly to Oakham from Leicester (£11.10, 25 minutes), Peterborough (£12.60, 30 minutes) and Birmingham (£23.50, one hour 20 minutes). Bus 19 runs from Nottingham (1¼ hours, hourly) and bus 9 runs from Stamford (20 minutes, hourly), passing along the north shore of Rutland Water.

DERBYSHIRE

Derbyshire is a country painted in two distinct tones – the lush green of rolling valleys, criss-crossed by a delicate tracery of dry stone walls, and the mottled brown of barren hilltops covered with the scrubby vegetation of the high moorlands. The big attraction here is the Peak District National Park, which preserves some of England's most evocative scenery, attracting legions of hikers, climbers, cyclists and fans of cramped dark places underground.

Activities

The **Peak District National Park** is the hub for outdoor enthusiasts – see the Activities heading in that section (p484).

Getting There & Around

East Midlands Airport (☎0871 919 9000; www.eastmidlandsairport.com) is the nearest air hub, and Derby is well served by trains, but there are few connecting services to smaller towns. In the Peak District, the Derwent Valley Line runs from Derby to Matlock. Edale and Hope lie on the Hope Valley Line from Sheffield to Manchester. For a comprehensive list of Derbyshire bus routes, visit the 'Transport' pages at www.derbyshire.gov.uk.

Derby

POP 229,407

Forever linked to football manager Brian Clough, who took Derby County to the top of the first division before his ill-fated tenure at Leeds United (a story powerfully told in the movie *The Damned United*), Derby was one of the crucibles of the Industrial Revolution. Almost overnight, a sleepy market town was transformed into a major manufacturing centre, producing everything from silk to bone china, and later locomotives and Rolls-Royce aircraft engines.

Derby suffered the ravages of industrial decline in the 1980s, but the city has bounced back with some impressive cultural developments, including the Silk Mill and Quad, a futuristic artistic space partly run by the British Film Institute. The southern half of town is dominated by the gigantic Westfield shopping centre, linked by a pedestrian crossing to the bus station.

Sights

FREE Derby Cathedral CATHEDRAL
(www.derbycathedral.org; 18 Irongate; ⏰9.30am-4.30pm Mon-Sat & during services Sun) Founded in AD 943, but extensively reconstructed in the 18th century, Derby Cathedral's vaulted ceiling towers over a fine collection of medieval tombs, including the opulent grave of the oft-married Bess of Hardwick, who at various times held court at Hardwick Hall (p484), Chatsworth House (p497) and Bolsover Castle (p484). Peregrine falcons nest in the tower – you can climb up to take a look on supervised tours (adult/child £3/2) once a month.

FREE Derby Museum of Industry & History MUSEUM
(Silk Mill Lane; ⏰11am-5pm Mon, 10am-5pm Tue-Sat, 1-4pm Sun & bank holidays) Below the cathedral, overlooking the River Derwent, this well laid-out museum is housed in a former silk mill that was one of Britain's first modern factories. Displays inside tell the story of manufacturing in Derby, from water-powered spinning wheels to the development of the Rolls-Royce aero-engine.

FREE Derby Museum & Art Gallery MUSEUM
(The Strand; ⏰11am-5pm Mon, 10am-6pm Tue-Sun, 1-4pm Sun) Attached to the town library, this nicely presented museum has more displays on local history and industry, with a focus on the fine ceramics produced by Royal Crown Derby.

FREE Quad GALLERY
(☎01332-290606; www.derbyquad.co.uk; Market Pl; ⏰gallery 11am-6pm, from noon Sun, Mediatheque 11am-8pm, from noon Sun) A striking modernist cube on Market Pl, Quad contains a futuristic art gallery, a cinema and the Mediatheque, an archive of films and TV covering decades of broadcasting, run by the British Film Institute.

Royal Crown Derby Factory POTTERY
(www.royalcrownderby.co.uk; Osmaston Rd; tour & museum adult/child £5/4.75; ⏰10am-5pm Mon-Sat, tours 11am & 1.30pm Tue-Fri) Ceramic fans will enjoy a tour around this historic pottery works, which still turns out some of the finest bone china in England, from edgy Asian-inspired designs to the kind of stuff your grandma used to collect. Only children over 10 years can join the tours.

Sleeping

Chuckles B&B ££
(☎01332-367193; www.chucklesguesthouse.co.uk; 48 Crompton St; s/d incl breakfast £30/50) The friendliest of several homely B&Bs just south of the centre, Chuckles is run by a cheerful couple with arty leanings. Rooms are simple but snug and there's a good

breakfast. To get here, take Green Lanes and turn onto Crompton St by the church.

Cathedral Quarter Hotel HOTEL ££
(01332-546080; www.thefinessecollection.com/cathedralquarter; 16 St Mary's Gate; s/d from £80/100;) Just a bell's peal from the cathedral in a grand Georgian edifice, this is the top choice for travellers with money to spend. The service is as polished as the grand marble staircase and there's an on-site spa and a lavish fine-dining restaurant.

Eating

Weekend bookings are recommended at the following eateries.

European Restaurant MODERN EUROPEAN ££
(01332-368732; 22 Irongate; mains £10-18; lunch Tue-Sat, dinner Mon-Sat) Opposite the cathedral, this trendy spot serves up good food in stylish surroundings, though 'European' generally translates to Italian when it comes to the menu.

Anoki INDIAN £££
(01332-292888; www.anoki.co.uk; 129 London Rd; mains £10-20; Mon-Sat) The best of a long line of Indian eateries on London Rd, Anoki offers an upmarket take on Midlands balti cooking. The vaulted dining room drips with baroque flourishes.

Darleys MODERN BRITISH £££
(01332-364987; www.darleys.com; Waterfront, Darley Abbey; mains £15-21; lunch & dinner Mon-Sat, lunch only Sun) Just outside of town in the village of Darley Abbey, this restaurant has a gorgeous setting in a bright converted mill overlooking the river. The modern British food's not bad either. Book ahead at weekends.

Drinking & Entertainment

Chain pubs and dance-bars abound on Wardwick, Friargate and the pedestrian lanes around Market Pl, but weekend nights can be almost Bacchanalian in their excesses.

As well as the following venues, it's worth seeing what's showing at the two theatre spaces run by **Derby Live** (01332-255800; www.derbylive.co.uk; Assembly Rooms, Market Pl & Theatre Walk, Eagle Market).

Old Bell Inn LIVE MUSIC
(01332-343701; www.myspace.com/theoldbellinnderby; Sadlergate) On a pedestrian lane just north of Market Pl, this old-school, spit-and-sawdust pub is the setting for gigs by rebel rockers and ageing punk veterans.

BUS PASSES

There are several handy bus passes covering travel in the Peak District. The Zigzag Plus ticket offers all-day travel on Trent Barton buses, including the Transpeak between Derby and Buxton, for £7.80 (one child travels free with each adult). The Derbyshire Wayfarer (adult/child £8.60/£4.30) covers buses and trains throughout the county and as far afield as Manchester and Sheffield.

Quad CINEMA
(www.derbyquad.co.uk; Market Pl) Links to the British Film Institute in London ensure that there are some interesting art-house and old-classic movies shown here among the family films and blockbusters.

Brunswick Inn PUB
(www.brunswickinn.co.uk; 1 Railway Tce) Set at the end of a working-class terrace near the station, this award-winning inn is a warren of cosy rooms where you can enjoy the nut-brown ales fermented by the house brewery.

Information

Bureau de change (Victoria St; closed Sun) At the post office.

Tourist office (www.visitderby.co.uk; Market Pl; 9.30am-5pm Mon-Sat, 10.30am-2.30pm Sun) This helpful office is under the Assembly Rooms in the main square.

Getting There & Away

Air

About 8 miles northwest of Derby, **East Midlands Airport** (www.eastmidlandsairport.com) is served by regular Skylink buses (30 minutes, half-hourly, hourly 8.20pm to 6.20am).

Bus

Local and long-distance buses run from the shiny new Derby bus station, immediately east of Westfield. From Monday to Saturday, Transpeak has hourly buses between Derby and Buxton (1½ hours), via Matlock (45 minutes) and Bakewell (one hour). Five buses continue to Manchester (three hours). Other services:

Leicester Skylink, 1½ hours, half-hourly (hourly from 8.20pm to 6.20am)

Nottingham Transpeak/Indigo, 30 minutes, half-hourly

Train

The train station is about half a mile southeast of the centre on Railway Tce. Services:

Birmingham £13.80, 45 minutes, four hourly
Leeds £33.50, 1½ hours, every 15 minutes
London £53.30, 1¾ hours, two hourly
Sheffield £17, 35 minutes, hourly

Around Derby

KEDLESTON HALL

Sitting pretty in vast landscaped grounds, the neoclassical mansion of **Kedleston Hall** (NT; house adult/child £8.58/4.27; ⏲noon-5pm Sat-Wed Feb-Nov, grounds open daily) is a must for fans of stately homes. The Curzon family has lived here since the 12th century but the current wonder was built by Sir Nathaniel Curzon in 1758. Meanwhile, the poor old peasants in Kedleston village had their humble dwellings moved a mile down the road, as they interfered with the view. Ah, the good old days…

Entering the house through a grand portico, you'll reach the breathtaking Marble Hall with its massive alabaster columns and statues of Greek deities. Other highlights include richly decorated bedrooms, a museum of Indian treasures amassed by Viceroy George Curzon, and a circular saloon with a domed roof, modelled on the Pantheon in Rome. Before you leave, take a walk around the 18th-century-style pleasure gardens, and pop into All Saints' Church to see the Curzon memorials.

Kedleston Hall is 5 miles northwest of Derby, off the A52. Arriva bus 109 between Derby and Ashbourne passes the Smithy, about 1 mile from Kedleston (25 minutes, every two hours Monday to Saturday). On summer Saturdays, the bus goes right to the hall.

CALKE ABBEY

Like an enormous, long-neglected cabinet of wonders, **Calke Abbey** (NT; ☎01332-863822; Ticknall; adult/child £9/4; ⏲12.30-5pm Sat-Wed) is not your average stately home. Built around 1703, the house was occupied by a dynasty of eccentric and reclusive baronets, who filled it with wonderful clutter, much of which can still be found in its rooms and corridors today.

The result is a ramshackle maze of rooms crammed with ancient furniture, mounted animal heads, dusty books, stuffed birds and endless piles of bric-a-brac spanning three centuries. Some rooms are in fabulous condition, while others are left much as they were found, with crumbling plaster and peeling wallpaper.

A stroll round the grounds is a similar time-warp experience – nature buffs should explore the ancient oak forests of **Calke Park**, preserved as a National Nature Reserve. You can visit the gardens at any time, but admission to the house is by timed ticket at busy times – advance bookings are recommended.

Calke is 10 miles south of Derby off the A514, close to the village of Ticknall. Arriva bus 61 from Derby to Swadlincote stops at Ticknall, a half-mile walk from the abbey.

ASHBOURNE

POP 7600

Perched at the southern edge of the Peak District National Park, Ashbourne is a pretty spread of steeply slanting stone streets, lined with cafes, pubs and antique shops. On summer weekends, the town is a magnet for walkers, cyclists and bikers bound for Matlock Bath. Try to visit on Shrove

ROYAL SHROVETIDE FOOTBALL

Some people celebrate Shrove Tuesday (the last day before Lent) by eating pancakes or dressing up in carnival finery, but Ashbourne marks the occasion with a riotous game of football where the ball is wrestled as much as kicked from one end of town to the other by vast crowds of revellers. Following rules first cooked up in the 12th century, villagers are split into two teams – those from north of the river and those living to the south – and the 'goals' are two millstones, set 3 miles apart. Participants are free to kick, carry or throw the ball, though it is usually squeezed through the crowds like a rugby ball in a scrum. Sooner or later, both players and ball end up in the river. Local shops board up their windows and the whole town comes out to watch or play – fearless visitors are welcome to participate in the melee but under a quirk of the rules, only locals are allowed to score goals.

Tuesday when Ashbourne goes football crazy – see p480.

At other times of year, the main attraction is the chance to walk or cycle along the **Tissington Trail**, part of NCN Route 68, which runs north for 13 miles to Parsley Hay, connecting with the **Pennine Cycleway** (NCN Route 68) and the **High Peak Trail** towards Buxton or Matlock. The track climbs gently along the tunnels, viaducts and cuttings of the disused railway line which once transported local milk to London, and a well-stocked cycle-hire centre rents out bikes for day-trippers.

The **tourist office** (Market Pl; ⏲10am-5pm) can provide leaflets or advice on B&Bs in the area.

Sleeping & Eating

As well as the following places, you can embrace the glory of the English sausage roll at **Spencers the Bakers** (35-39 Market Pl; ⏲till 4.30pm) on the main square.

Just B B&B ££
(☎01335-346158; www.just-b.me.uk; 6 Buxton Rd; r from £65) A modern update on a lovely old house just uphill from the main market square. Rooms range from the comfortable to the stylish, and there's a piano bar and a ritzy restaurant serving modern British cuisine.

Patrick & Brooksbank CAFE £
(☎01335-342631; 22 Market Pl; sandwiches from £3; ⏲9.30am-3pm Mon, to 4pm Tue & Wed, to 5pm Thu-Sat) A great little deli and cafe with posh light meals and sandwiches and excellent homemade pastries, cheeses, breads and cold meats.

Smith's Tavern PUB £
(36 St John's St; meals from £8) A tiny slither of a pub on the main shopping street, with a big selection of real ales and food and an old piano at the back.

Getting There & Away

Without your own transport, buses are the only way to get to/from Ashbourne. Useful services:

Buxton Bowers 42/442, 35 minutes, every one to two hours

Derby Arriva 109/Trent Barton One, 40 minutes, hourly Monday to Saturday

Leek Cowes 108, 40 minutes, six daily

Getting Around

About a mile above town along Mapleton Lane, the **Cycle Hire Centre** (☎01335-343156; half-/full day from £12/15; ⏲9am-5.30pm Mar-Oct, reduced low season hours) is right on the Tissington Trail, at the end of a huge and atmospheric old railway tunnel leading under Ashbourne. You can also rent children's bikes, bikes with baby seats, trailers for buggies and tandems. Ask for a map of pubs and teashops along the way.

WORTH A TRIP

CARSINGTON WATER

Less famous than the Derwent reservoirs to the north, but also less crowded, Carsington Water is a pretty spot to stroll, cycle or mess about on boats. The reservoir was built to store water from the River Derwent in the 1990s, but it looks almost like a natural lake, with plentiful bird life, and peaceful waterside trails for walking and cycling. Just off the B5035, **Carsington Water Sports & Cycle Hire Centre** (☎01629-540478; www.carsingtonwater.com; ⏲9.30am-dusk) rents out mountain bikes (per day £15), sailboats (per 1½ hours from £20) and windsurfing equipment (per 1½ hours £15). The 110 bus from Ashbourne to Matlock passes the centre several times a day.

DOVEDALE

About 3 miles northwest of Ashbourne, the River Dove winds through the steep-sided valley of Dovedale, where a famous set of stepping stones provides the perfect photo opportunity. Attracting hordes of visitors on summer weekends, the valley is every inch the green and pleasant land, and the final scenes of Ridley Scott's 2010 blockbuster *Robin Hood* were filmed along the riverbanks. Ashbourne's tourist office has various guides and walking pamphlets.

Dovedale was also a popular haunt for Izaak Walton, the 17th-century fisherman and author of *The Compleat Angler*. The ivy-covered **Izaak Walton Hotel** (☎01335-350555; www.izaakwaltonhotel.com; s/d from £70/80, meals from £20) at the southern end of Dovedale arranges fly-fishing on the River Dove, as well as upmarket suppers and comfortable beds for the night.

Matlock Bath

POP 2202

Unashamedly tacky, Matlock Bath looks like a seaside resort that somehow lost its way and ended up at the foot of the Peak

District National Park. Following the River Derwent through a sheer-walled gorge, the main promenade is a continuous string of amusement arcades, tacky fairground attractions, tearooms, fish and chip shops, pubs and motorcycle accessory shops, catering to the vast hordes of bikers who gather here on summer weekends. On warm, sunny days, the smell of leather and petrol can be overpowering. A few miles north is the larger village of Matlock, which offers a bit of calm when the roar of 650cc engines gets too much. Be wary of driving too far up the side of the valley – many of the lanes are too narrow for cars, with no space for turning.

Sights & Activities

To enter into the spirit of Matlock Bath, buy yourself a punnet of chips and take a turn along the promenade, then work it off by following one of the steep paths that climb the eastern side of the gorge (several pedestrian bridges run across from the A6). The tourist office has free pamphlets describing some longer, more challenging walks in the hills.

Gulliver's Kingdom THEME PARK
(www.gulliversfun.co.uk; admission £12.50; ⌚10.30am-4.30pm) A step up from the amusements on the promenade, this old-fashioned amusement park offers plenty of splashing, churning, looping attractions for anyone as tall as the signs at the start of the rides.

Heights of Abraham THEME PARK
(adult/child £11/8; ⌚10am-5pm) Further north, this long-established hilltop leisure park has profited immeasurably from the addition of a spectacular cable-car ride from the bottom of the gorge. Once you reach the top, atmospheric cave and mine tours and fossil exhibitions add extra kiddie-appeal.

Peak District Mining Museum MUSEUM
(www.peakmines.co.uk; The Pavilion; adult/child £3.50/2.50; ⌚10am-5pm) A more educational introduction to the mining history of Matlock is provided by this enthusiast-run museum, set in an old Victorian dancehall. The museum is a maze of tunnels and shafts that little ones can wriggle through, while adults browse displays on mining history. For £2.50/1.50 extra per adult/child, you can go into the workings of the **Temple Mine** by Gulliver's Kingdom and pan for 'gold' (well, shiny minerals).

Masson Mills Working Textile Museum MUSEUM
(adult/child £2.50/1.50; ⌚10am-4pm Mon-Fri, 11am-5pm Sat, to 4pm Sun) A mile south of Matlock Bath, housed in the vast brick buildings of an 18th-century mill, this museum tells the story of the textile mills that once dominated the Derwent Valley (see p483). The attached **shopping village** is full of outlet stores for big clothing brands.

> **MATLOCK ILLUMINATIONS**
>
> From the beginning of September to October, don't miss the **Matlock Illuminations** (Derwent Gardens; adult/child £4/free; ⌚from dusk Sat & Sun), with long chains of pretty lights, firework displays and a flotilla of outrageously decorated Venetian boats on the river.

Sleeping

Hodgkinson's Hotel & Restaurant HOTEL ££
(☎01629-582170; www.hodgkinsons-hotel.co.uk; 150 South Pde; s/d from £40/75; P) Right in the thick of things on the parade, this eccentric hotel has an agreeably Victorian outlook. Rooms conjure up Matlock's golden age with antique furnishings, flowery wallpaper and cast-iron fireplaces.

Ashdale Guest House B&B ££
(☎01629-57826; www.ashdaleguesthouse.co.uk; 92 North Pde; s/d from £35/60) A tall stone house just beyond the tacky part of the promenade, with smart, tasteful rooms and organic breakfasts.

Sunnybank Guesthouse B&B ££
(☎01629-584621; sunnybankmatlock@aol.com; Clifton Rd; s/d £40/64) This lovely, well-kept guesthouse is blessed with bright bedrooms, most with fine views over the surrounding countryside. The comfortable, wooden-floored breakfast room has a reassuring and lingering scent of marmalade and toast.

Temple Hotel HOTEL ££
(☎01629-583911; www.templehotel.co.uk; Temple Wk; s/d from £55/80; P) The views from this hillside inn are so lovely that Lord Byron once felt inspired to etch a poem on the restaurant window. Inside, everything is a little dated, but the rooms are comfy and the pub turns out filling meals and plenty of real ales.

DERWENT VALLEY MILLS

Unlikely as it may sound, the industrial mills that line the Derwent Valley are ranked up there with the Pyramids and the Taj Mahal on the Unesco World Heritage list. Founded in the 1770s by Richard Arkwright, the Cromford Mill near Matlock Bath was the first modern factory, producing cotton on automated machines, powered by a series of waterwheels along the River Derwent. This prototype inspired a succession of copycat mills at Derby, Matlock, Belper, Milford and Darley Abbey, ushering in the industrial age.

For an atmospheric introduction to Derbyshire's industrial history, take a tour of the original **Cromford Mill** (www.arkwrightsociety.org.uk; tour adult/child £3/2.50; ⌚9am-5pm), run by the Arkwright Society. Buses 140 and 141 run here hourly from Matlock Bath (15 minutes, no Sunday service). Another fascinating industrial relic is **Strutt's North Mill** (www.belpernorthmill; adult/child £3/2; ⌚1-5pm Wed-Sun) at Belper, accessible on the Transpeak bus between Derby and Matlock. Alternatively, you can drop into the museums housed in Derby's Silk Mill (p478) and Masson Mills near Matlock (p482).

Eating & Drinking

The official breakfast, lunch and dinner of Matlock is fish and chips, served at dozens of artery-clogging cafes along the strip. For a superior meal, head to the dining rooms at the Temple Hotel and Hodgkinson's Hotel.

Victorian Tea Shop TEAROOM £
(118 North Pde; snacks from £3; ⌚10am-5.30pm Sat-Mon, Wed & Thu Jun-Sep, reduced hours at other times) The pick of the tearooms, this cavern of chintz has the prerequisite frilly curtains, trays of iced buns and lace doilies.

Fishpond PUB
(204 South Pde) This pub gets a lively, spirited crowd, including legions of bikers. It has a mixed bag of live music and a decent selection of ales.

Information

Tourist office (www.derbyshire.gov.uk; The Pavilion; ⌚10am-5pm Mar-Oct, to 4pm Nov-Feb) Run by the helpful staff at the Mining Museum.

Getting There & Away

Trains run hourly between Matlock and Derby (30 minutes). Matlock is also a hub for buses around the Peak District.

Bakewell Bus 172, one hour, hourly, Monday to Saturday

Chesterfield Bus 17, 35 minutes, hourly

Derby Transpeak, 1¼ hours, hourly

Sheffield Bus 214, 1¼ hours, hourly

Around Matlock Bath

From a tiny platform just north of the Sainsbury's on the outskirts of Matlock village, the nostalgic steam trains run by **Peak Rail** (www.peakrail.co.uk; adult/6-15yr/under 5yr £6.50/3.50/1.50) trundle along a 4-mile length of track to the nearby village of Rowsley. Services run five times a day Saturday and Sunday (and some weekdays) from May to October, and some Sundays at other times of the year (see the website for details).

From Rowsley train station a riverside path leads to **Caudwell's Mill** (☎01629-734374; www.caudwellsmillcraftcentre.co.uk; admission free, mill tours adult/child £3.50/1.25; ⌚10am-6pm), a chugging, grinding, water-powered mill that still produces flour the old-fashioned way. There are various craft workshops and a tearoom, plus a legion of ducks and an organ-grinder to entertain tiny bakers.

You can get to Rowsley direct from Matlock by bus on the route to Bakewell.

Chesterfield

POP 100,879

The eastern gateway to the Peaks, Chesterfield is noteworthy for the bizarre crooked spire that rises atop **St Mary & All Saints Church** (☎01246-206506; www.chesterfieldparishchurch.org.uk; admission free, spire tours adult/child £3.50/1.50; ⌚9am-5pm). Dating from 1360, the 68m-high spire is twisted in a right-handed corkscrew and it leans several metres southwest – a result of warping of the green timbers used in its construction. Locals prefer the legend that the spire twisted itself to witness the unlikely event of a virgin getting married in the church. Staff run regular tours of the spire; call to confirm a time.

The Chesterfield **tourist office** (Rykneld Sq; ⌚9am-5.30pm Mon-Sat) is right opposite the crooked spire.

Chesterfield lies on the main rail line between Nottingham/Derby (20 minutes) and Sheffield (10 minutes), with hourly services in both directions. The station is just east of the centre. The Chesterfield Coach Station is on Beetwell St – useful local services include bus 170 to Bakewell (45 minutes, hourly) and bus 66 to Buxton (1½ hours, twice daily, one Sunday bus). National Express buses run to Coventry (£15.90, two hours, eight daily), Leicester (£8, 1¾ hours, five daily), Nottingham (£5.20, one hour, seven daily) and Sheffield (30 minutes, every 35 minutes).

Hardwick Hall

Perhaps the most stately of the East Midlands' stately homes, **Hardwick Hall** (NT; adult/child £9.50/4.75; ⏲11am-4.30pm Wed-Sun) is one of the most complete Elizabethan mansions in the country. It was home to the 16th century's second-most powerful woman, Elizabeth, countess of Shrewsbury – known to all as Bess of Hardwick – who amassed a staggering fortune by marrying wealthy noblemen with one foot in the grave. Hardwick Hall was constructed using the money left behind when hubby number four shuffled off his mortal coil in 1590.

Designed by eminent architect Robert Smythson, the hall featured all the latest mod-cons of the time, including fully glazed windows – a massive luxury in the 16th century, inspiring the contemporary ditty 'Hardwick Hall, more glass than wall'. The atmospheric interiors are decked out with magnificent tapestries and time-darkened oil paintings of forgotten dignitaries. Set aside some time to explore the formal gardens, or take longer walks on the peaceful trails of **Hardwick Park**. Ask at the ticket office for details of routes.

Next door to the manor is Bess' first house, **Hardwick Old Hall** (EH; adult/child £4.20/2.10, joint ticket £11/5; ⏲10am-5pm Wed-Sun), now a romantic ruin administered by English Heritage.

Offering more sophisticated meals than the National Trust kiosk, the sandstone **Hardwick Inn** (Hardwick Park, Doe Lea) by the south gate is a good place to recharge your batteries after walking the miles of corridors.

Hardwick Hall is 10 miles southeast of Chesterfield, just off the M1. The Stagecoach Chesterfield-to-Nottingham bus stops at Glapwell, from where it's a 2-mile walk to Hardwick Hall.

WORTH A TRIP

BOLSOVER CASTLE

About 6 miles east of Chesterfield on the A632, partly-ruined **Bolsover Castle** (EH; adult/child £7/3.50; ⏲10am-5pm Sun-Thu & 10am-4pm Fri & Sat) was founded in 1612 by Sir Charles Cavendish. Among other famous former residents, this was once the home of the inimitable Bess of Hardwick, and her love of extravagant interiors can be seen in the surviving frescoes and carved fireplaces.

You can get here on Stagecoach bus 83 from Chesterfield.

PEAK DISTRICT

Rolling across the southernmost hills of the Pennines, the Peak District is one of the most beautiful parts of the country. Ancient stone villages are folded into creases in the landscape and the hillsides are littered with famous stately homes and rocky outcrops that attract hordes of walkers, climbers and cavers. No one knows for certain how the Peak District got its name – certainly not from the landscape, which has hills and valleys, gorges and lakes, wild moorland and gritstone escarpments, but no peaks. The most popular theory is that the region was named for the Pecsaetan, the Anglo-Saxon tribe who once populated this part of England.

As well as being England's first national park (it was founded in 1951), the Peak District National Park is the busiest national park in Europe, but don't be put off by its popularity – there are 555 sq miles of open English countryside to play with, and escaping the crowds is easy if you avoid summer weekends. Even at the busiest times, it doesn't take much effort to find your own peaceful viewpoint to soak up the glorious scenery.

Locals divide the Peak District into the Dark Peak – dominated by exposed moorland and gritstone 'edges' – and the White Peak, made up of the limestone dales to the south.

Activities

CAVING & CLIMBING

The limestone sections of the Peak District are riddled with caves and caverns, including a series of 'showcaves' in Castleton, Buxton and Matlock Bath (described in

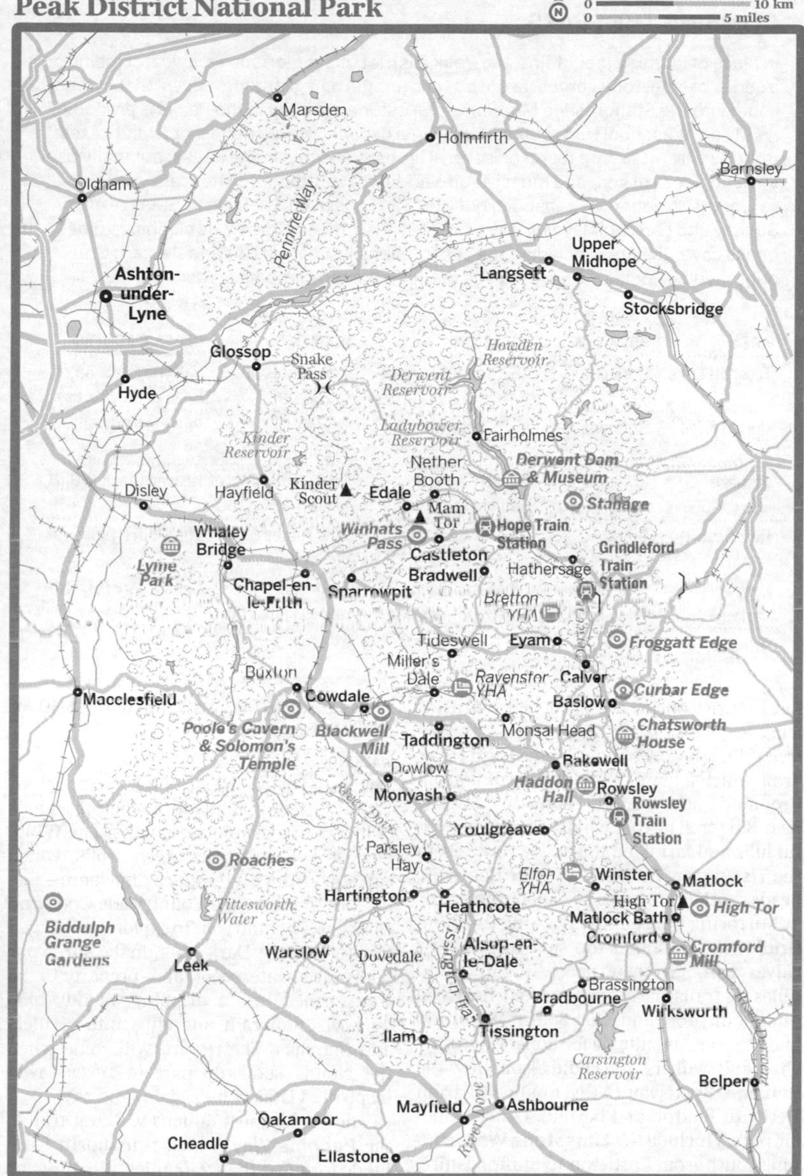

each of those sections). For serious caving (or potholing) trips, the first port of call should be the website www.peakdistrictcaving.info, run by the caving store **Hitch n Hike** (www.hitchnhike.co.uk; Mytham Bridge, Bamford), near Castleton.

If you're keen on climbing, the Peak District has long been a training ground for England's top mountaineers – see p486.

CYCLING

The plunging dales and soaring scarps are a perfect testing ground for cyclists and

CLIMBING THE PEAKS

In place of looming mountains, the Peak District offers glorious technical climbing on a series of limestone gorges, exposed tors (crags) and gritstone 'edges' that extend south into the Staffordshire Moorlands. Gritstone climbing in the Peaks is predominantly on old-school trad routes, requiring a decent rack of friends, nuts and hexes. Bolted sport routes are found on several limestone crags in the Peaks, but many use ancient pieces of gear and most require additional protection. The crags are best reached with your own transport, but bus 284 runs from Sheffield to Stanage every Sunday and bank holiday Monday from May to October. Numerous climbing guidebooks cover the area, including the comprehensive *Eastern Grit* and *Western Grit* published by Rockfax. Here's a quick guide to the top climbing areas:

AREA	ROCK TYPE	LOCATION	ROUTES	CLASSIC ROUTES
Froggatt Edge	Gritstone	A625, near Froggatt	Trad routes up to 20m	Valkyrie (HVS, 5a), Beau Geste (E6, 6c)
Curbar Edge	Gritstone	A625, near Calver	Trad routes up to 23m	Peapod (HVS, 5b)
Stanage	Gritstone	Off A6187, near Hathersage	Trad routes up to 30m	Heaven Crack (VDiff)
Roaches	Gritstone	Off A53, near Leek	Trad routes & bouldering	The Sloth (HVS, 5a)
High Tor	Limestone	Off A6, between Matlock & Matlock Bath	Trad/sport routes up to 60m	Debauchery (E1, 5b)

local tourist offices are piled high with cycling maps and pamphlets. For easy traffic-free riding, head for the 17.5-mile **High Peak Trail**, which follows the old railway line from Cromford, near Matlock Bath, to Dowlow near Buxton. The trail winds through beautiful hills and farmland to Parsley Hay, where the **Tissington Trail**, part of NCN Route 68, heads south for 13 miles to Ashbourne.

Mirroring the Pennine Way, the **Pennine Bridleway** is another top spot to put your calves through their paces. Around 120 miles of trails have been created between Middleton Top and the South Pennines, and the route is suitable for horse riders, cyclists and walkers. You could also follow the **Pennine Cycleway** (NCN Route 68) from Derby to Buxton and beyond. Other popular routes include the **Limestone Way**, running south from Castleton to Staffordshire, and the **Monsal Trail** between Bakewall and Buxton.

Peak Tours (www.peak-tours.com; mountain bike per day £18) will deliver its rental bikes to anywhere in the Peak District, and it also offers guided cycling tours. Derbyshire council operates several cycle-hire centres in the Peak District charging standard rates of £12/15 for a half-/full day (£8/10 for a child's bike).

WALKING

The Peak District is one of the most popular walking areas in England, attracting legions of hikers in the summer months. The White Peak is perfect for leisurely strolls, which can start from pretty much anywhere – just be sure to follow the Countryside Code and close gates behind you. To explore the rugged territory of the Dark Peak, make sure your boots are waterproof and prepare to be transformed into a dripping, muddy blob by horizontal rain and slips into rivulets and marshes. The reward will come when the clouds suddenly part to reveal awe-inspiring vistas of hills, dales and sky.

The Peak's most famous walking trail is the **Pennine Way**, which runs north from Edale for more than 250 miles, finishing far north in the Scottish Borders. If you don't have three weeks to spare, you can reach the pretty town of Hebden Bridge in Yorkshire in three comfortable days.

The 46-mile **Limestone Way** winds through the Derbyshire countryside from Castleton to Rocester in Staffordshire, following a mix of footpaths, tracks and quiet lanes. Plenty of people walk the 26-mile section between Castleton and Matlock in one long, tiring day, but two days is better – the Ravenstor YHA at Miller's Dale (p491) is a handy place to break the hike. Tourist offices have a detailed leaflet.

Other popular routes include the **High Peak Trail**, **Tissington Trail**, and **Monsal Trail**, described under Cycling (opposite). Most of the towns and villages in the Peaks are well set up for visiting walkers with pubs, B&Bs and tearooms that welcome muddy boots. Numerous short walks are described in the following sections.

Information

There are tourist offices or national park visitor centres in Buxton, Bakewell, Castleton, Edale and other major stops for tourists, and the official park website at www.peakdistrict.org is a goldmine of information on transport, activities and local events.

Getting There & Away

Trains run to Matlock Bath, Buxton, Edale and several other towns and villages, and buses run from regional centres like Sheffield and Derby to destinations across the Peak District. Be aware that buses are much more frequent at weekends, and many services close down completely in winter. Timetables are available from all the tourist offices, or online at www.derbyshire.gov.uk/buses.

Buxton

POP 24,112

Imagine Bath or Brighton, transported to the rolling hills of the Derbyshire dales. That's Buxton, a picturesque sprawl of Georgian terraces, Victorian amusements and pretty parks, set at the very heart of the Peak District National Park. The town built its fortunes on its natural warm-water springs, which attracted hordes of health tourists in Buxton's heyday. Today, visitors are drawn here by the flamboyant Regency architecture, the cute shops and cafes and the abundant natural wonders waiting in the surrounding countryside. Tuesday and Saturday are market days, bringing an extra dash of colour to the grey limestone market place.

Sights

Victoriana

At the foot of the Slopes, the historic centre of Buxton is a riot of Victorian pavilions, concert halls and glasshouse domes. The most famous building in town is the flamboyant, turreted **Opera House** (Water St), which hosts an impressive variety of stage shows, with a notable preference for Gilbert & Sullivan.

The Opera House shares an entrance with the equally flamboyant **Pavilion Gardens** (www.paviliongardens.co.uk; 10am-4.30pm), where a series of domed pavilions sprawl across a pretty park like a seaside pier, dropped into the middle of the Derbyshire Dales. The main building contains a tropical greenhouse, a nostalgic cafe and the tourist office.

Uphill from the Pavilion Gardens is another glorious piece of Victoriana, the **Devonshire Hospital**, whose enormous dome contains part of the campus for the University of Derby and – surprisingly – an opulent **spa** (01332-594408; www.devonshire-spa.co.uk) offering a full range of pampering treatments.

Buxton Spa ARCHITECTURE

In Victorian times, spa activities were centred on the extravagant Buxton Baths complex, built in grand Regency style in 1854. The various bath buildings are fronted by a grand, curving facade, known as **the Crescent**, inspired by the Royal Crescent in Bath. Today it sits empty, awaiting a developer with enough money to restore the town spa. For a taste of what the baths looked like in their heyday, pop around the corner to **Cavendish Arcade**, whose walls retain their original eggshell-blue art-deco tiles.

Across from the Crescent at the base of the Slopes is the empty **Pump Room**, which dispensed Buxton's spring water for nearly a century. Modern day health-tourists queue up to fill plastic bottles from a small spout known as **St Ann's Well**, immediately west of the Pump Room. It's worth climbing the green terraces of the Slopes for the definitive view over Buxton's grand Victorian rooftops.

HOSTELS FOR HIKERS

Hikers, outdoors types and shoestring travellers can take advantage of some useful YHA hostels, including the phenomenally popular properties at Edale, Castleton, Tideswell and Eyam, plus a series of rudimentary 'camping barns' (beds per person from £6) in remote locations around the peak. Contact the **YHA** (01629-592700; www.yha.org.uk) for details and locations.

Buxton

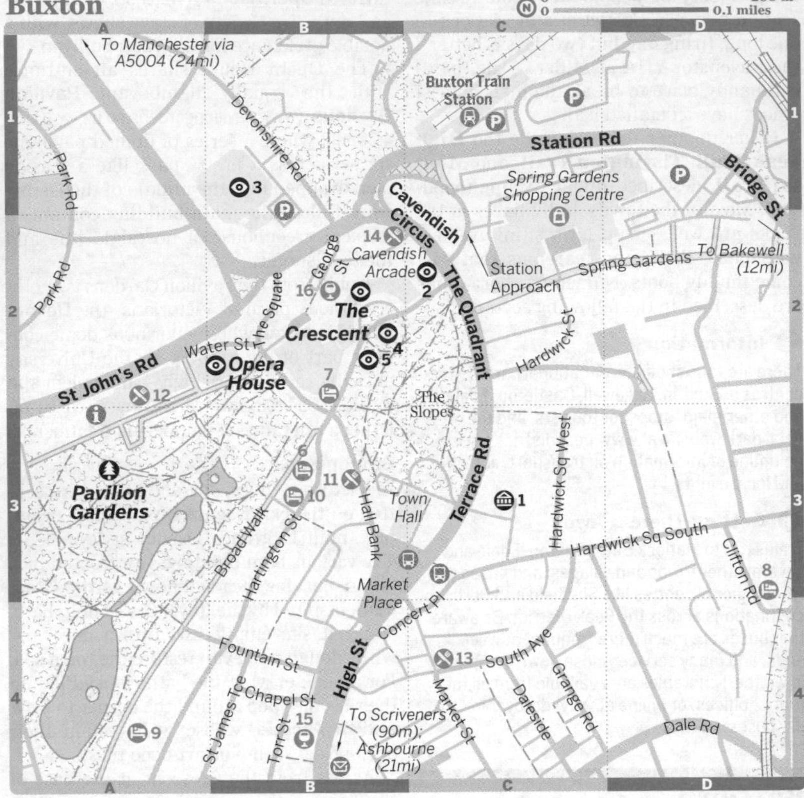

FREE **Buxton Museum & Art Gallery** MUSEUM
(Terrace Rd; ⌚9.30am-5.30pm Tue-Sat year-round, 10.30am-5pm Sun Apr-Sep) Just downhill from the Town Hall in a handsome Victorian building, the town museum displays local historical bric-a-brac and curiosities from Castleton's Victorian-era 'House of Wonders', including Harry Houdini's handcuffs.

Activities

Walking & Cycling

There are some pleasant local walks and cycle rides, as well as the more challenging cross-country routes. A pleasant mile stroll southwest from the centre will take you to **Poole's Cavern** (www.poolescavern.co.uk; adult/child £8/4.75; ⌚9.30am-5pm), a magnificent natural limestone cavern, replete with toothlike stalactites, and distinctive 'poached egg' formation stalagmites.

From the cavern's car park, a 20-minute walk leads up through Grin Low Wood to **Solomon's Temple**, a ruined tower with fine views over the town. If you need to burn off some serious calories, set your sights on the **Monsal Trail**, beginning 3 miles east of the town and running all the way to Bakewell.

Good-quality bikes (both road and mountain bikes) can be rented from **Parsley Hay Cycle Hire** (☎01298-84493), about 8 miles south of Buxton at the junction of the High Peak and Tissington Trails (half-/full day £11/14).

Festivals & Events

All the big events in Buxton revolve around the beautifully restored Opera House.

Four Four Time MUSIC
An annual live-music festival staged each February, featuring a medley of jazz, blues, folk and world-music acts.

Buxton

Top Sights

The Crescent ... B2
Opera House ... B2
Pavilion Gardens ... A3

Sights

1 Buxton Museum & Art Gallery ... C3
2 Cavendish Arcade ... C2
3 Devonshire Hospital ... B1
4 Pump Room ... B2
Spa ... (see 3)
5 St Ann's Well ... B2

Sleeping

6 Grosvenor House ... B3
7 Old Hall Hotel ... B2
8 Old Manse Hotel ... D3
Nat's Kitchen ... (see 13)
9 Roseleigh Hotel ... A4
10 Victorian Guest House ... B3

Eating

11 Columbine Restaurant ... B3
12 Pavilion Cafe ... A2
13 Nat's Kitchen ... C4
14 Simply Thai ... B2

Drinking

15 Old Sun Inn ... B4
16 Project X ... B2

Buxton Festival CULTURE
(www.buxtonfestival.co.uk) This renowned July festival is one of the largest cultural festivals in the country, attracting top names in literature, music and opera.

Buxton Fringe CULTURE
(www.buxtonfringe.org.uk) A more contemporary festival that spans film, music, dance, theatre and comedy. Held in July.

International Gilbert & Sullivan Festival MUSICAL THEATRE
(www.gs-festival.co.uk) This very popular festival is held at the end of July/start of August.

Sleeping

The nearest hostel is the Ravenstor YHA near Tideswell (p491).

TOP CHOICE **Old Hall Hotel** HOTEL ££
(01298-22841; www.oldhallhotelbuxton.co.uk; The Square; s/d incl breakfast from £65/100; @) There is a tale to go with every creak of the floorboards at this history-soaked establishment, supposedly the oldest hotel in England. Among other esteemed residents, Mary, Queen of Scots, stayed here from 1576 to 1578, albeit against her will. The rooms are still the grandest in town.

Roseleigh Hotel B&B ££
(01298-24904; www.roseleighhotel.co.uk; 19 Broad Walk; s/d incl breakfast from £38/72; P@) This gorgeous family-run B&B in a roomy old Victorian house has lovingly decorated rooms, many with fine views out over the Pavilion Gardens. The owners are a welcoming couple, both seasoned travellers, with plenty of interesting tales to tell.

Victorian Guest House B&B ££
(01298-78759; www.buxtonvictorian.co.uk; 3a Broad Walk; d incl breakfast from £78; P) Overlooking the park, this elegant house has eight individually decorated bedrooms furnished with Victorian and Edwardian antiques, and the home-cooked breakfasts are renowned.

Nat's Kitchen B&B ££
(01298-214642; www.natskitchen.co.uk; 9-11 Market St; r £60-85) Upstairs above a trendy eatery near Market Pl, Nat's offers five tasteful rooms with interesting pieces of antique furniture. There's a minimum two-night stay at weekends.

Grosvenor House B&B ££
(01298-72439; www.grosvenorbuxton.co.uk; 1 Broad Walk; s/d incl breakfast from £45/60; P@) Overlooking the Pavilion Gardens, the Grosvenor is another venerable Victorian guesthouse that benefits from a huge parlour overlooking the park. The rooms come with flowery upholstery, flowery drapes and, well, flowery everything else, really.

Old Manse Hotel B&B ££
(01298-25638; www.oldmanse.co.uk; 6 Clifton Rd, Silverlands; s/d from £35/70; P@) A Victorian stone building full of cream-coloured rooms with a decent selection of mod-cons. The guesthouse is a short walk east of Terrace Rd and the helpful hosts are happy to provide maps and info about the area.

Eating

As well as the following restaurants, there are several simple Italian places around Market Pl that offer inexpensive and filling, though not exactly authentic, pizzas and pasta.

Columbine Restaurant MODERN BRITISH ££
(☎01298-78752; 7 Hall Bank; mains £11-17; ⊙dinner Mon-Sat, closed Tue Nov-Apr) On the lane leading down beside the Town Hall, this understated restaurant is the top choice among Buxtonites in the know. The chef conjures up imaginative dishes using mainly local produce and there's a sinful list of fattening puddings. Bookings recommended.

Pavilion Cafe CAFE £
(snacks £3-7; ⊙9.30am-5pm Apr-Sep) Set in a renovated wing of the Pavilion, these tearooms conjure up images of jazz-fuelled tea-dances sometime between the wars.

Nat's Kitchen MODERN BRITISH ££
(☎01298-214642; www.natskitchen.co.uk; 9-11 Market St; mains £9.50-17) A relaxing dining room full of natural wood tones provides the backdrop to some inventive modern British cooking at this cosmopolitan option near Market Pl. Ingredients are sourced from local suppliers and there are some smart B&B rooms upstairs. Bookings recommended.

Simply Thai THAI £
(2-3 Cavendish Circus; mains £7.50-13.50) This uptown Thai – all polished wood floors, Siamese sculptures and silk-attired staff – is a great place to enjoy a bit of Asian spice.

Drinking & Entertainment

Nightlife in Buxton is centred on the pubs and restaurants around Market Pl and along the High St.

Project X BAR
(www.project-x-cafe.com; The Old Court House, George St; ⊙8am-midnight) Young folk in Buxton thank their lucky stars for this sultry cafe and bar at the back of the baths complex. Moroccan tables, hanging lanterns and deep violet walls create a casbah vibe. By day, people sip lattes and munch on paninis (snacks £5 to £10); after dark, drinkers move on to beers and cocktails.

Old Sun Inn PUB
(33 High St) The cosiest of the High St pubs, with a warren of rooms full of original features and a lively crowd that spans the generations. The pub grub (mains £6 to £9.50), while predictable, is inexpensive and tasty.

Opera House OPERA
(www.buxtonoperahouse.org.uk; Water St) Buxton's gorgeously restored Victorian Opera House hosts a full program of drama, dance, concerts and comedy as well as some renowned festivals and events.

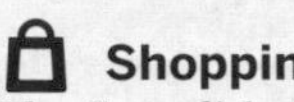

Shopping

The Cavendish Arcade is full of boutiques selling upmarket gifts.

Scriveners BOOKSHOP
(☎01298-73100; 42 High St; ⊙9am-5pm Mon-Sat, noon-4pm Sun) A delightfully chaotic bookshop, sprawling over three floors, where books are filed in piles and the Dewey system has yet to be discovered.

Information

There are several banks with ATMs along Spring Gardens and opposite Cavendish Arcade.

Grove Movie Centre (2 Eagle Pde; per 30min £2; ⊙11am-9pm Mon-Fri, 10am-9pm Sat, noon-9pm Sun; @) Video shop with several internet terminals.

Post office (High St) With a bureau de change.

Tourist office (www.visitpeakdistrict.com; Pavilion Gardens; ⊙9.30am-5pm Oct-Mar, 10am-4pm Apr-Sep)

Getting There & Away

Northern Rail has trains to and from Manchester (£9.20, one hour, hourly). Buses stop on both sides of the road at Market Pl. The hourly Transpeak runs to Derby (1¾ hours) and Nottingham (2½ hours), via Bakewell (one hour) and Matlock Bath (1½ hours). There are also six daily Transpeak buses to Manchester (one hour). Other services:

Chesterfield Bus 66, 1¼ hours, two daily

Sheffield Bus 65, one hour, five daily (three services Sunday)

Around Buxton

TIDESWELL

POP 2000

About 8 miles east of Buxton, deep in the Derbyshire countryside, the former lead-mining village of Tideswell makes a good base for walking and cycling around the White Peak. As well as the popular **Limestone Way** and **Monsal Trail**, there are numerous short local circuits, including the 6-mile round trip to Litton Mill, which became notorious during the Industrial Revolution for exploiting the children of impoverished families as cheap labour.

Tideswell's centrepiece is the massive parish church of St John the Baptist – known as the **Cathedral of the Peak** (⌚daylight hours) – which has stood here virtually unchanged for 600 years. Look out for the wooden panels inscribed with the Ten Commandments and the grand 14th-century tomb of local landowner Thurston de Bower, depicted in full medieval armour.

For accommodation, **Poppies** (☎01298-871083; www.poppiesbandb.co.uk; Bank Sq; s/d from £23/46) is frequently recommended by walkers for its cosy welcome and hearty evening meals.

About 2 miles from Tideswell at Miller's Dale, the **Ravenstor YHA** (☎0845 371 9655; www.yha.org.uk; dm from £16) is a great base for walkers, set in a huge, rambling country house with a cafe and bar.

Bus 65 from Buxton to Sheffield and bus 66 from Buxton to Chesterfield both pass through Tideswell and Miller's Dale.

Castleton

POP 1200

Guarding the entrance to the forbidding gorge known as Winnats Pass, Castleton is blessed with more than its fair share of visitor attractions. The streets are lined with leaning stone houses, walking trails criss-cross the surrounding hills, a wonderfully atmospheric castle crowns the ridge above town, and the bedrock under Castleton is riddled with caves which were once mined for Blue John Stone, a vivid violet form of fluorspar. On summer weekends, it can seem like the entire population of the East Midlands has descended on the town, so come in the week to enjoy the sights in relative peace and quiet.

Sights

Peveril Castle CASTLE

(EH; adult/child £4.20/2.10; ⌚10am-5pm Apr-Oct, 10am-4pm Nov-Mar) Topping the ridge to the south of Castleton, this evocative castle has been so ravaged by the centuries that it almost looks like a crag itself. Constructed by William Peveril, son of William the Conqueror, the castle was used as a hunting lodge by Henry II, King John and Henry III, and the crumbling ruins offer swoon-inducing views over the Hope Valley.

Castleton Caves CAVES

The limestone caves around town have been mined for lead, silver and the semi-precious Blue John Stone for centuries and four are open to the public on guided tours.

Peak Cavern

(☎01433-620285; www.devilsarse.com; adult/child £7.75/5.75; ⌚10am-5pm, tours hourly till 4pm) A short walk from the castle tourist office is the largest natural cave entrance in England, known locally as the Devil's Arse. Should you choose to enter Beelzebub's rocky crevasse, you'll see some dramatic limestone formations, lit with fibreoptic cables.

Speedwell Cavern

(☎01433-621888; www.speedwellcavern.co.uk; adult/child £8.25/6.25; ⌚10am-5pm, tours hourly till 4pm) About half a mile west of Castleton at the mouth of Winnats Pass, this cave is reached via an eerie boat ride through flooded tunnels, emerging by a huge subterranean lake called the Bottomless Pit. New chambers are being discovered here all the time by potholing expeditions.

FLOWERY KINGS & QUEENS

Every 29 May – or on the 28th if the 29th is a Sunday – Castleton celebrates **Oak Apple Day** with a flamboyant village festival that can trace its origins back to at least the 17th century, and possibly all the way back to Celtic times. Every year, two residents of the village are chosen to be Garland King and Queen and paraded through the village on horseback, with the Garland King buried under an enormous headdress woven with flowers. It's all very *Wicker Man*, and the strange behaviour of the Nettle Man, who whips anyone not wearing a sprig of oak leaves with a bunch of stinging nettles, only adds to the surreal mood. In fact, the tradition of wearing oak leaves dates back to the English Civil War, when it served as a badge of identification for supporters of Charles II, who escaped capture at the Battle of Worcester by hiding in an oak tree. However, scholars believe the festival may have its ultimate roots in the worship of the pagan fertility goddess Brigantia. Needless to say, if anyone asks for help looking for a mysterious child, be very afraid...

CASTLETON WALKS

Serious walkers are lured to Castleton by the Limestone Way, but there plenty of easier walks in the area. For a scenic **6-mile circuit** (three to four hours), follow the Limestone Way up **Cave Dale** and then loop round on paths and tracks to the west of **Rowter Farm** to meet the Buxton Rd. Go straight (north) across fields and cross another road to reach **Mam Nick**, where the Edale road passes through a gap in the ridge. From here, steps climb to the summit of **Mam Tor**, offering spectacular views along the Hope Valley. The path then strikes northwest along the ridge to another gap called **Hollins Cross**, where several tracks lead back down to Castleton.

A shorter option from Castleton is to take the path direct to **Hollins Cross**, then go to **Mam Tor**, and return by the same route (about 4 miles, two to three hours). From Hollins Cross, you can extend any walk by dropping down to **Edale**. For an easier leg-stretch, follow the **Chapel-en-le-Frith road** northwest along the narrow, spectacular gorge of **Winnats Pass**, or trace the path of the **old Edale road**, which was destroyed in a landslide in 1977, cresting the ridge at Mam Tor. Maps and leaflets on these and other walking trails are available at the Castleton tourist office.

Treak Cliff Cavern
(☎01433-620571; www.bluejohnstone.com; adult/child £7.95/4; ⏰10am-5pm, last tour 4.20pm) A short walk across the fields from Speedwell Cavern, Treak Cliff is notable for its forest of stalactites and exposed seams of colourful Blue John Stone, which is still mined to supply the jewellery trade. Tours focus on the history of mining, and kids can polish their own piece of Blue John Stone on school holidays.

Blue John Cavern
(☎01433-620638; www.bluejohn-cavern.co.uk; adult/child £9/4.50; ⏰10am-5.30pm) Up the side of Mam Tor, Blue John is a maze of natural caverns with rich seams of Blue John Stone that are still mined every winter. You can get here on foot up the closed section of the Mam Tor road.

FREE **Castleton Museum** MUSEUM
(☎01433-620679; Castleton tourist office, Buxton Rd; ⏰9.30am-5.30pm) Attached to the tourist office, the cute town museum has displays on everything from mining and geology to rock climbing, hang-gliding and the curious Garland Festival (see boxed text, p491).

Activities

Set at the base of 517m Mam Tor, Castleton is the northern terminus of the **Limestone Way**, which follows narrow, rocky Cave Dale, far below the east wall of the castle. The tourist office has maps and walk leaflets – see p492 for shorter walks in the area.

Sleeping

Most visitors to Castleton are weekenders – ask about cheaper deals on weekdays.

Castleton YHA HOSTEL £
(☎0845 371 9628; www.yha.org.uk; Castle St; dm members/non-members from £14/17; P @) The inviting town hostel scores extra points for being in the middle of Castleton, rather than out in the sticks. Set in a rambling stone house, the hostel has tidy rooms, knowledgeable staff and – good news for thirsty walkers – a licensed bar.

Causeway House B&B ££
(☎01433-623921; www.causewayhouse.co.uk; Back St; s/d £33/65) The floors within this ancient character-soaked stone cottage are worn and warped with age, but the quaint bedrooms are bright and welcoming.

Ye Olde Nag's Head Hotel HOTEL ££
(☎01433-620248; www.yeoldenagshead.co.uk; Cross St; r from £50) The cosiest of a long line of 'residential' pubs along the main road, offering comfortable, well-appointed rooms, some with luxuries such as four-poster beds and Jacuzzis. There's also a quality restaurant.

Rowter Farm CAMPSITE £
(☎01433-620271; sites per person £5; ⏰Easter-Sep) A simple campsite about 1 mile west of Castleton in a stunning location up in the hills. Drivers should approach via Winnats Pass; on foot, follow the Cave Dale path.

Eating & Drinking

Castle Inn PUB £
(Castle St; mains £5-10) On the road up to the castle, unsurprisingly, with a cosy flagstone

lounge bar, an open fire and a decent selection of hearty meals including good Sunday roasts.

Ye Olde Cheshire Cheese Inn PUB ££
(☎01433-620330; www.cheshirecheeseinn.co.uk; How Lane; mains £5 14) Tradition is everything at this well-known alehouse, set in a fine old timbered building on the main road. The pub menu is more exotic than most (try the rabbit hot pot) and there are also comfy rooms for rent (singles/doubles £35/65).

Teashops abound in Castleton – probably the most popular purveyor of cream teas and light meals is **Three Roofs Cafe** (The Island; light meals £5-9; ⏲10am-5pm), opposite the turn-off to the tourist office.

The village shop has limited stocks of provisions for walkers and it's open seven days.

Information

Tourist office (Buxton Rd; ⏲9.30am-5.30pm Mar-Oct, 10am-5pm Nov-Feb) With a snack kiosk, museum and lots of leaflets on local walks.

Getting There & Away

The nearest train station is at Hope, about 3 miles east of Castleton on the line between Sheffield and Manchester. On summer weekends, a bus runs between Hope station and Castleton to meet the trains, but it's an easy walk.

Bus 272 runs to Sheffield (1¼ hours, hourly) and bus 173 to Bakewell (50 minutes, three daily) via Hope (10 minutes) and Tideswell (25 minutes). From Monday to Saturday, bus 68 goes from Castleton to Buxton (one hour) in the morning, returning in the afternoon. On Sundays only, bus 260 runs between Castleton and Edale (25 minutes, six services).

Around Castleton

DERWENT RESERVOIRS

North of the Hope Valley, the upper reaches of the Derwent Valley were flooded between 1916 and 1935 to create three huge reservoirs to supply Sheffield, Leicester, Nottingham and Derby with water. These man-made lakes soon proved their worth – the Dambusters squadron carried out practice runs over Derwent Reservoir before unleashing their 'bouncing bombs' on the Ruhr Valley in Germany in WWII. One of the towers atop the Derwent Dam contains a small **museum** (admission free; ⏲10am-4pm Sun) detailing their exploits.

These days, the Ladybower, Derwent and Howden Reservoirs are popular destinations for walkers, cyclists and mountain-bikers – and ducks, lots of ducks, so drive slowly! The focal point for visitors is **Fairholmes**, near the Derwent Dam, which has a **tourist office** (⏲9.30am-5.30pm), a car park, a snack bar and a good **cycle hire centre** (☎01433-651261; ⏲9.30am-5.30pm), charging the standard Peak rates.

Numerous walks start here, from gentle strolls along the lakeside to serious expeditions into the moors above the valley. For casual **cycling**, a lane leads up the west side of Derwent and Howden reservoirs, meeting the dirt track that traces the east shore, a rewarding 12-mile circuit. Off-road routes for mountain-biking climb high into the hills – the tourist office stocks maps and guidebooks.

Fairholmes is 2 miles north of the A57, the main road between Sheffield and Manchester. Bus 273 from Sheffield Interchange runs out to Fairholmes in the morning, returning in the afternoon.

Edale

POP 316

Surrounded by majestic Peak District countryside, this cluster of stone houses set around a pretty parish church is an enchanting place to pass the time. Edale lies between the White and Dark Peak areas, and is the southern terminus of the Pennine Way – despite the remote location, the Manchester–Sheffield line passes through the village, bringing legions of outdoorsy types on summer weekends.

Activities

Predictably, walking is the number one drawcard, and the **Pennine Way** – running north for 268 miles to the Scottish Borders – is the number one choice for hardcore hikers. However, there are plenty of diverting strolls for less committed hill walkers.

As well as trips to Hollins Cross and Mam Tor, on the ridge dividing Edale from Castleton, you can walk north onto the **Kinder Plateau**, dark and brooding in the mist, gloriously high and open when the sun's out. This was the setting for a famous act of civil disobedience by ramblers in 1932 that paved the way for the legal 'right to roam' and the creation of England's national parks.

Weather permitting, a fine circular walk starts by following the Pennine Way through fields to **Upper Booth**, then up a path called Jacobs Ladder and along the southern edge of Kinder, before dropping down to Edale via the steep rocky valley of Grindsbrook Clough, or the ridge of Ringing Roger.

About 1.5 miles east of Edale, **Ladybrook Equestrian Centre** (01433-670205; www.ladybooth.co.uk; Nether Booth) offers horseback trips around the Peaks, lasting anything from one hour to a full day.

Sleeping

Upper Booth Farm CAMPSITE £
(01433-670250; www.upperboothcamping.co.uk; sites per person/car £5/2; Feb-Nov; P) Located along the Pennine Way about a mile from Edale, this peaceful campsite is set on a working farm and is surrounded by spectacular scenery. For hikers, there's a camping barn and small shop.

Edale YHA HOSTEL £
(0845 371 9514; www.yha.org.uk; Nether Booth; dm from £16; P@) This substantial hostel is set in a slightly austere-looking country house 1.5 miles east of Edale, with spectacular views across to Back Tor. The attached activity centre is very popular with student groups. To get here, follow the signed road past a rather fragrant farm from the Hope road.

Stonecroft B&B ££
(01433-670262; www.stonecroftguesthouse.co.uk; Grindsbrook; r from £75; P) This handsomely fitted-out stone house, built in the 1900s, has two comfortable bedrooms. Vegetarians and vegans are well catered for – the organic breakfast is excellent. The owner also runs landscape-photography courses.

Cooper's Camp CAMPSITE £
(01433-670372; sites per person/car £4.50/2; P) This simple campsite is situated at the far end of the village on a farm. Caravans are also welcome at Cooper's and there is a shop, post office and cafe by the entrance.

Fieldhead Campsite CAMPSITE £
(01433-670386; www.fieldhead-campsite.co.uk; sites per person/car £5/2; P) Right next to the Moorland Centre, this pretty and well-equipped campsite spreads over six fields, with some pitches right by the river.

Eating

To stock up on carbs for hiking, head to **Cooper's Cafe** (01433-670401; Cooper's Camp; sandwiches & burgers £2-5; 8am-4pm; @), a cheerful greasy spoon with wi-fi internet, close to the village school.

Old Nag's Head PUB ££
(Grindsbrook; meals £8-15) Refurbished, warm and welcoming walker-friendly pub.

Rambler Inn PUB ££
(01433-670268; www.theramblerinn.com; Grindsbrook; mains £8-16) Ales, B&B rooms (per person from £38) and a petting zoo for the kids.

Information

Moorland tourist office (01433-670207; www.edale-valley.co.uk; Grindsbrook; 9.30am-5pm Mon-Fri, to 5.30pm Sat & Sun, shorter hours in low season) With brochures, maps, displays on the moors, a kiosk and a campsite.

Getting There & Away

Trains run from Edale to Manchester (£8.90, every two hours, 45 minutes) and Sheffield (£5.50, every two hours, 30 minutes) via Hope. From Monday to Friday, bus 200 runs between Edale and Castleton (20 minutes, three daily) via Hope. On Sunday and on bank holidays, take bus 260 (six services) via Winnats Pass.

Eyam

POP 926

Quaint little Eyam (ee-em), a former lead-mining village, has a tragic and touching history. In 1665, the town was infected by the dreaded Black Death plague, carried here by fleas on a consignment of cloth from London, and the village rector, William Mompesson, convinced villagers to quarantine themselves rather than transmit the disease further. Some 270 of the village's 800 inhabitants succumbed, while surrounding villages remained relatively unscathed. Even independently of this poignant story, Eyam is a delightful place to wander around, with its sloping streets of old cottages backed by rows of green hills.

Sights

Eyam Parish Church CHURCH
(9am-6pm Mon-Sat) Inside this church, where many of the plague victims were

buried, you can view stained-glass panels and moving displays telling the story of the outbreak, and a plague register, recording those who died, name by name, day by day. Note the morbid skeleton mural on the tower wall, painted to illustrate a bible story, but extremely apt to the Eyam tale. The churchyard contains a fantastically well-preserved **Celtic cross**, carved in the 8th century.

Eyam Hall HISTORIC HOUSE
(www.eyamhall.co.uk; adult/child £6.25/4; ⊙noon-4pm Sun-Fri) This solid-looking 17th-century manor house with stone windows and doorframes is home to a **craft centre** (admission free; ⊙10.30am-5pm, closed Mon) and several eateries, surrounding a traditional English walled garden.

Eyam Museum MUSEUM
(www.eyammuseum.demon.co.uk; Hawkhill Rd; adult/child £2/1.50; ⊙10am-4.30pm Tue-Sun) The town's museum has some vivid displays on the Eyam plague, plus exhibits on the village's history of lead-mining and silk-weaving.

Activities

Eyam makes a great base for walking and cycling in the White Peak area. For an interesting short walk, follow Water Lane out of the village from the main square, then turn right and climb the hill to reach **Mompesson's Well**, where food and other supplies were left during the plague time for Eyam folk by friends from other villages. The goods were paid for using coins sterilised in vinegar. To return to Eyam, retrace your steps back down the lane, then take a path which leads directly to the church. This 2-mile circuit takes about 1½ hours; the village shop has picnic supplies.

Sleeping

Eyam YHA HOSTEL £
(☎0845 371 9738; www.yha.org.uk; Hawkhill Rd; dm £18) A simple place in a dignified old Victorian house with a folly tower, perched up a hill overlooking the village.

Bretton YHA HOSTEL £
(☎0845 371 9626; www.yha.org.uk; Bretton, Hope Valley; dm £14) If the Eyam YHA is full, this basic place, the smallest hostel in the Peaks, is only 1.5 miles away.

Miner's Arms HOTEL ££
(☎01433-630853; Water Lane; s/d £45/70) Although its age isn't immediately obvious, this traditional village inn was built shortly before the plague hit Eyam. Inside you'll find beamed ceilings, affable staff, a cosy stone fireplace, comfy en suite rooms and decent pub food (meals £8 to £12).

Crown Cottage B&B ££
(☎01433-630858; www.crown-cottage.co.uk; Main Rd; s/d from £45/64) Very walker- and cyclist-friendly, this stone house full of pottery ornaments is crammed to the rafters most weekends. Book ahead to be sure of a spot.

Eating

As well as the Miner's Arms pub, Eyam has several tearooms serving meals.

Peak Pantry TEAROOM £
(The Square; snacks £3-5; ⊙9am-5pm Mon-Sat, 10am-5pm Sun) This unpretentious place on the village square has a mouth-watering array of slices and decent coffee.

Eyam Tea Rooms TEAROOM £
(The Square; snacks from £2; ⊙till 4pm, closed Tue) All chintz and doilies, this tearoom serves delicious homemade cakes and pastries as well as hearty lunches.

Getting There & Away

Bus services from Eyam:

Bakewell Bus 175, 25 minutes, five daily Monday to Saturday

Buxton Bus 65/66, 40 minutes, seven daily (four Sunday)

Chesterfield Bus 66/66A, 40 minutes, 10 daily (four Sunday)

Sheffield Bus 65, 40 minutes, seven daily (three Sunday)

Bakewell

POP 3979

The second-largest town in the Peak District, Bakewell lacks the spa-town grandeur of Buxton, but it's still a pretty place to explore and a great base for exploring the White Peak. The town is ring-fenced by famous walking trails and stately homes, but it's probably best known for its famous pudding (of which the Bakewell Tart is just a poor imitation). Like other Peak towns, Bakewell is mobbed during the summer months – expect traffic jams and cut-throat competition for hotel rooms at weekends. The centre of town is Rutland Sq, the meeting point of the roads from Matlock, Buxton and Chesterfield.

Sights

Up on the hill above Rutland Sq, **All Saints Church** (9am-4.30pm) is packed with ancient features, including a 14th-century font, a pair of Norman arches, some fine heraldic tombs and a collection of crude stone gravestones and crosses dating back to the 12th century.

Set in a time-worn stone house near the church, the **Old House Museum** (Cunningham Pl; adult/child £3/1.50; 11am-4pm) explores local history. Check out the Tudor loo and the displays on wattle and daub, a traditional technique for building walls using woven twigs and cow dung.

Activities

Unsurprisingly, walking and cycling are the main attractions, and the popular and scenic **Monsal Trail** follows the path of a disused railway line from Combs Viaduct on the outskirts of Bakewell to Topley Pike in Wye Dale, about 3 miles east of Buxton. A number of old railway tunnels are set to be opened to visitors in 2011, extending the route all the way from Bakewell to Buxton.

For a rewarding shorter walk, follow the Monsal Trail for 3 miles to the dramatic viewpoint at **Monsal Head**, where you can pause for refreshment at the **Monsal Head Hotel** (www.monsalhead.com; mains from £8). With more time to kill, continue to **Miller's Dale**, where viaducts give a spectacular vista across the steep-sided valley. The tourist offices at Bakewell and Buxton have a *Monsal Trail* leaflet with all the details.

Other walking routes go to the stately homes of Haddon Hall (p496) and Chatsworth House (p497).

Sleeping

Melbourne House B&B ££
(01629-815357; Buxton Rd; r from £55; P) Located in a picturesque, creeper-covered building dating back more than three centuries, this is an inviting B&B situated on the main road leading to Buxton.

Rutland Arms Hotel HOTEL ££
(01629-812812; www.rutlandarmsbakewell.co.uk; The Square; s/d £50/125; P) Aristocratic but slightly careworn, this hotel is the most refined offering in Bakewell. It's a substantial stone coaching inn, and the more expensive rooms have lots of flowery Victorian flourishes.

PUDDING OF CHAMPIONS

The Peak District's most famous dessert is – as any Bakewell resident will tell you – a pudding, not a tart. Invented following an accidental misreading of a recipe in around 1820, the Bakewell Pudding is a pastry shell, spread with jam and topped with frangipane, a mixture of egg and ground almonds. If you've only ever seen the glazed version produced by commercial bakeries, the Bakewell original can look crude and misshapen, but we can confirm from experience that it's delicious. Numerous shops in Bakewell, all claiming to be the 'original' progenitor of the Bakewell Pudding, serve this tasty Derbyshire treat.

Eating & Drinking

Bakewell's streets are lined with cute tearooms and bakeries, most with 'pudding' in the name.

Piedaniels FRENCH ££
(01629-812687; www.piedaniels-restaurant.co.uk; Bath St; mains £12; Tue-Sat) The toast of the local restaurants, serving exquisitely presented modern-French cuisine in exquisite surroundings. Weekday lunch menus (three courses for £12) are fantastic value.

Castle Inn PUB ££
(Bridge St; mains from £8) The ivy-draped Castle Inn is one of the better pubs in Bakewell, with four centuries' practice in warming the cockles of hamstrung hikers.

Information

Tourist office (01629-813227; Bridge St; 9.30am-5pm, from 10am Nov-Mar) Helpful place with racks of leaflets and books; can help book accommodation. In the old Market Hall.

Getting There & Away

Bakewell lies on the popular Transpeak bus route. Buses run hourly to Nottingham (1¾ hours), Derby (1¼ hours), Matlock Bath (30 minutes) and Buxton (50 minutes). Five services a day continue to Manchester (1¾ hours).

Around Bakewell

HADDON HALL

Glorious **Haddon Hall** (www.haddonhall.co.uk; adult/child £8.95/4.95; noon-5pm, last entry

4pm) looks exactly like a medieval manor house should look – all stone turrets, time-worn timbers and walled gardens. The house was founded in the 12th century, and then expanded and remodelled throughout the medieval period. The 'modernisation' stopped when the house was abandoned in the 18th century, saving Haddon Hall from the more florid excesses of the Victorian period. If the house looks familiar, it was used as a location for the period blockbusters *Jane Eyre* (1996), *Elizabeth* (1998) and *Pride and Prejudice* (2005).

The house is 2 miles south of Bakewell on the A6. You can get here on the Transpeak bus from Bakewell to Matlock and Derby (hourly) or walk along the footpath through the fields, mostly on the east side of the river.

CHATSWORTH HOUSE

It's easy to get stately home fatigue with all the grand manors dotted around the Midlands, but sumptuous **Chatsworth House** (www.chatsworth.org; adult/child house & garden £10.50/6.25, garden only £7.50/4.50; ⏲11am-5.30pm) is really something else. Known as the 'Palace of the Peak', this vast edifice has been occupied by the earls and dukes of Devonshire for centuries. The manor was founded in 1552 by the formidable Bess of Hardwick and her second husband, William Cavendish, who earned grace and favour by helping Henry VIII dissolve the English monasteries. Bess was onto her fourth husband, George Talbot, Earl of Shrewsbury, by the time Mary, Queen of Scots was imprisoned at Chatsworth on the orders of Elizabeth I in 1569.

While the core of the house dates from the 16th century, Chatsworth was altered and enlarged repeatedly over the centuries, and the current building has a Georgian feel, dating back to the last overhaul in 1820. Inside, the lavish apartments and mural-painted staterooms are packed with paintings and priceless items of period furniture. Among the historic treasures, look out for the portraits of the current generation of Devonshires by Lucian Freud.

The house sits in 25 sq miles of grounds and ornamental gardens, some landscaped by Lancelot 'Capability' Brown. When the kids tire of playing hide-and-seek around the fountains, take them to the **farmyard adventure playground** (admission £5.25) with loads of ropes, swings and slides, and farmyard critters.

Chatsworth is 3 miles northeast of Bakewell. Bus 214 from Sheffield Interchange to Matlock goes right to Chatsworth (hourly, 50 minutes) and bus 215 runs from Bakewell (20 minutes, hourly) on Sunday. On other days, take the Transpeak bus towards Derby and change to the 214 at Darley Dale.

Coming from Bakewell, walkers can take footpaths through Chatsworth park via the mock-Venetian village of Edensor (en-sor), while cyclists can pedal via Pilsley.

Birmingham, the West Midlands & the Marches

Includes »

Best Places to Eat

» The Balti Triangle (p509)
» Simpsons (p508)
» Lambs (p523)
» Drapers Hall (p547)
» La Bécasse (p558)

Best Places to Stay

» Hotel du Vin (p507)
» Castle House (p538)
» The Start (p540)
» Library House (p551)
» Feathers Hotel (p558)

Why Go?

Because few other places in the country come so close to the dream of England. If you are searching for chocolate-box villages of wonky timbered houses and ancient stone churches, or stately homes that look like the last lord of the manor just clip-clopped out of the stables, or the chance to walk in thc footsteps of William Shakespeare, you'll find it here.

You'll also find the dust and grime of centuries of industrial history – exemplified by the World Heritage–listed mills of Ironbridge – and tumbling hills where the air is so clean you can taste it. Walkers and cyclists flock to the Marches, the long line of hills that marks out the border between England and Wales, only to vanish into the vastness of the landscape. Then there's the city of Birmingham, an industrial crucible reinvented as cultural melting pot, with the best food and nightlife in the Midlands.

When to Go

Literary buffs take note: Shakespeare takes a back seat to contemporary wordsmiths at Stratford's Literary Festival in April/May, and in May/June bookworms descend on Hay-on-Wye for the annual book festival. If you're up for a belt-loosening, belly-stretching good time, head to Ludlow's famous Food & Drink Festival in September.

On weekends from April to September, shuttle buses provide access to wonderful walking trails on the Long Mynd and the Shropshire Hills.

History

This region has seen its share of action over the centuries, much of it centred on the Marches, where a succession of kingdoms and empires struggled to gain a foothold in the homelands of the Welsh tribes. Cross-border skirmishes became so problematic that 8th-century Anglo-Saxon king Offa of Mercia built an earthwork barricade along the border to keep the warring factions apart, and this border is now the route of a popular walking trail.

In an effort to subdue the Welsh and secure his new kingdom, William the Conqueror installed powerful, feudal barons – called Lords Marcher, from the Anglo-Saxon word *mearc* (meaning 'boundary') – in castles all along the border. Over the following centuries, these warlords staged repeated raids into Wales, taking as much territory as possible under their control.

Things continued in a similar vein until the 18th century, when the inventive locals discovered that industry was an easier way of making money than squabbling over land. The invention of modern iron-smelting in the Shropshire village of Ironbridge in 1709 gave birth to the Industrial Revolution, while the visionary Birmingham-based Lunar Society spawned factory owners, canal-builders, scientists and engineers who transformed the world.

Activities

Outdoorsy types make a beeline for the lush green hills of the **Marches**. The tumbling landscape is scattered with ruined castles, and the exposed summits of the highest hills offer views to match anything in the Peaks and Lakes. As well as the famous **Offa's Dyke Path**, there are numerous waymarked trails and long-distance paths. Top spots for walking and cycling include the Long Mynd and Stiperstones in Shropshire, the Malvern Hills in Worcestershire and the area around Symonds Yat in Herefordshire.

Canoeing and **kayaking** are popular diversions at Hereford, Hay-on-Wye, and Symonds Yat in Herefordshire and Ironbridge in Shropshire, and **hang-gliders** and **paragliders** launch from the hills above Church Stretton in Shropshire. See the Activities sections in this chapter for more information.

Information

Heart of England Tourist Board (☎01905-761100; www.visitheartofengland.com)

Getting Around

There are excellent rail connections to towns across the West Midlands, and **National Express** (☎08718 818181; www.nationalexpress.com) and local bus companies connect larger towns and villages, though services are reduced in the low season. Ask locally about discounted all-day tickets. **Birmingham Airport** (www.birminghamairport.co.uk) near Derby is the main air hub. For general route information, consult **Traveline** (☎0871 200 2233; www.travelinemidlands.co.uk) or visit www.networkwestmidlands.com.

BIRMINGHAM

POP 977,087

Once a byword for bad town-planning, England's second-largest city – known to locals as 'Brum' – is shaking off the legacy of industrial decline, and spending some serious money replacing its drab 1960s concrete architecture with gleaming glass and steel. The town centre looks better than it has done in decades, helped in no small part by the revitalised Bullring centre, and the iconic Selfridges building, which looks out over the city like the compound eye of a giant robot insect.

With its industrial legacy and chaotic road network, Birmingham might not leap out as a tourist attraction, but there's a lot to see, including some fine museums and galleries, and the nightlife and food are the best in the Midlands. Sleek Modern British restaurants dominate in the centre, while the 'burbs were the birthplace of the balti – England's unique contribution to the world of curry, invented by Pakistani workers who moved here in the 1970s.

History

Birmingham was first mentioned in the Domesday Book of 1086, where it was described as a small village, home to a handful of villagers and two ploughs, with a total value of £1. From these humble beginnings, Brum exploded into a bustling industrial and mercantile hub, building its fortunes first on the wool trade, and then on metalworking from the 16th century.

In the mid-18th century, the Lunar Society brought together the leading geologists, chemists, scientists, engineers and theorists of the age – see boxed text, p508 – and Birmingham became the world's first industrialised town, attracting a tide of workers from across the nation. Overcrowding,

Birmingham, the West Midlands & the Marches Highlights

1. Enjoying England's great contribution to the world of curry in the balti restaurants of **Birmingham** (p499)
2. Walking in the footsteps of the Bard in Shakespeare-obsessed **Stratford-upon-Avon** (p519)
3. Forging a path across the Shropshire Hills at the Long Mynd and Stiperstones near **Church Stretton** (p554)
4. Eating up a storm at the foodie mecca that is **Ludlow** (p557)
5. Leafing through worthy tomes in the eccentric secondhand bookstores of **Hay-on-Wye** (p539)

6 Admiring the dragon-infested medieval map of the world in gorgeous **Hereford Cathedral** (p536)

7 Strolling around lovely **Lichfield** (p526), home to a fine cathedral, Dr Johnson and Darwin's grandad

poverty and pollution soon became major social ills.

A degree of salvation came in the mid-1800s, when enlightened mayors such as Joseph Chamberlain (1836–1914) cleaned out the slums and filled the centre with grand civic buildings. Sadly, little evidence of this golden age remains today thanks to WWII bombers and overzealous town-planning. Vast swaths of the centre were demolished in a bid to transform Birmingham into 'Britain's Motor City'.

Whatever the mistakes of the past, recent years have seen a series of successful regeneration projects as part of the 'Big City Plan', with 21st-century landmarks appearing all over the city.

One thing that has endured through all this is the distinctive Brummie accent – in a controversial nationwide survey in 2008, it was rated worse than silence, to the outrage of locals. Oh, and for any rock fans out there, Birmingham was also the birthplace of the original Prince of Darkness, Ozzy Osbourne. Bat lovers look away now...

Sights & Activities

For information on all of Birmingham's museums, visit www.bmag.org.uk.

CITY CENTRE

Birmingham's grandest civic buildings are clustered around pedestrianised **Victoria Sq**, at the western end of New St, dominated by the stately facade of **Council House**, erected in 1874–9. The square was given a facelift in 1993, with modernist sphinxes and a **fountain** topped by a naked female figure, nicknamed 'the floozy in the Jacuzzi' by locals, overlooked by a disapproving **statue of Queen Victoria**. Nearby is the armless **Iron Man**, by Antony Gormley, of *Angel of the North* fame (p747).

Housed in the annexe at the back of Council House, the delightful **Birmingham Museum & Art Gallery** (☎0121-303 2834;

Birmingham

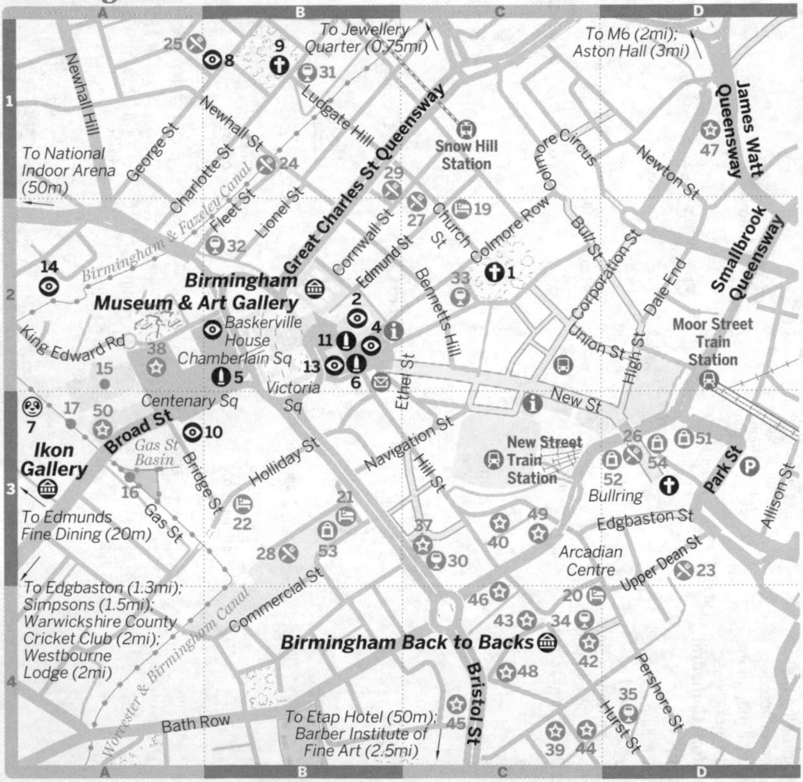

www.bmag.org.uk; Chamberlain Sq; admission free; ⏲10am-5pm Mon-Thu & Sat, 10.30am-5pm Fri, 12.30-5pm Sun) houses an impressive collection of ancient treasures and Victorian art, including an important collection of major Pre-Raphaelite works by Rossetti, Edward Burne-Jones and others. The museum's latest arrival is part of the Staffordshire Hoard, a treasure trove of 7th-century Anglo-Saxon gold, unearthed in a field near Lichfield in 2009. To keep young minds engaged, objects from the collection are used to ask interesting cultural questions.

The west side of the square is marked out by the neo-classical **Town Hall** (☎0121-780 3333; www.thsh.co.uk), constructed in 1834 and styled after the Temple of Castor and Pollux in Rome, and now used as a venue for classical concerts and stage performances.

Further west, Centenary Sq is book-ended by the art deco **Hall of Memory War Memorial** and the **International Convention Centre** (ICC) and **Symphony Hall**. Across the road is a gilded **statue of Boulton, Watt and Murdoch**, who were three of the brightest lights of the Lunar Society. In 2013, the Birmingham Library will be relocated to a ritzy new building on the north side of the square as part of the Big City Plan.

North of the New St shopping precinct, the small but perfectly formed **Cathedral Church of St Philip** (☎0121-262 1840; Colmore Row; donations requested; ⏲7.30am-6.30pm Mon-Fri, 8.30am-5pm Sat & Sun) was constructed in a neoclassical style between 1709 and 1715. The Pre-Raphaelite artist Edward Burne-Jones was responsible for the magnificent stained-glass windows.

On the other side of the Bullring, **Birmingham Back to Backs** (NT; ☎0121-666 7671; 55-63 Hurst St; adult/child £5.45/2.70; ⏲10am-5pm Tue-Sun, guided tour only) is a cluster of restored back-to-back terraced houses – a quirky tour takes you through four working-class homes, telling the stories of the people who lived here from the 1840s to the 1970s.

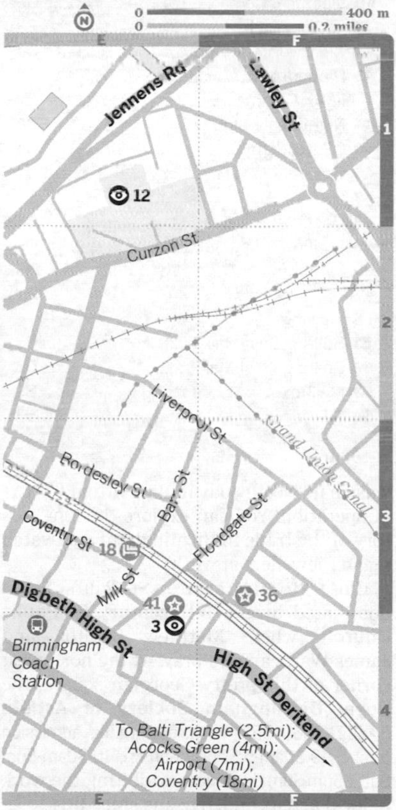

BIRMINGHAM CANALS

During the industrial age, Birmingham was a major hub on the English canal network (the city technically has more miles of canals than Venice), and visiting narrow boats still float into Gas St Basin in the heart of the city, passing a string of swanky wharf-side developments.

Across the canal from the International Convention Centre and Symphony Hall, the sleek Brindley Pl development contains banking offices, designer restaurants and the sleek **Ikon Gallery** (☎0121-248 0708; www.ikon-gallery.co.uk; 1 Oozells Sq; admission free; ⏲11am-6pm Tue-Sun). This cutting-edge art gallery is housed in a stylishly converted Gothic schoolhouse. Prepare to be thrilled, bemused or outraged, depending on your take on conceptual art.

Nearby, the Sir Norman Foster–designed **National Sea Life Centre** (☎0121-643 6777; www.sealifeeurope.com; 3a Brindley Pl; adult/child £17.50/14; ⏲10am-4pm Mon-Fri, to 5pm Sat & Sun) is the largest inland aquarium in England, and the tanks teem with exotic marine life including razor-jawed hammerhead sharks, turtles and otters. During the school holidays, the queues can stretch around several blocks – buy tickets online ahead of time for fast-track entry.

JEWELLERY QUARTER

Birmingham has been a major player on the British jewellery scene ever since Charles II

Birmingham

Top Sights
Birmingham Back to Backs ... C4
Birmingham Museum & Art Gallery ... B2
Ikon Gallery ... A3

Sights
1 Cathedral Church of St Philip ... C2
2 Council House ... B2
3 Custard Factory ... E4
4 Fountain ... B2
5 Hall of Memory War Memorial ... B2
6 Iron Man ... B2
7 National Sea Life Centre ... A3
Planetarium ... (see 12)
8 Royal Birmingham Society of Artists ... B1
9 St Paul's Church ... B1
10 Statue of Boulton, Watt & Murdoch ... A3
11 Statue of Queen Victoria ... B2
12 Thinktank ... E1
13 Town Hall ... B2
14 West Midlands Waterways ... A2

Activities, Courses & Tours
15 International Convention Centre ... A2
16 Second City Canal Cruises ... A3
17 Sherborne Wharf ... A3

Sleeping
18 Birmingham Central Backpackers ... E3
19 Hotel du Vin ... C2
20 Ibis Hotel ... C4
21 Malmaison ... B3
22 Nitenite ... B3

Eating
23 Cafe Soya ... D3
24 Itihaas ... B1
25 Lasan ... A1
26 Mount Fuji ... D3
27 Opus ... C2
28 Oriental ... B3
29 Purnells ... B1

Drinking
30 Island Bar ... C3
31 Jam House ... B1
32 Mechu ... B2
33 Old Joint Stock ... C2
34 Sobar ... C4
35 Village Inn ... D4

Entertainment
36 Air ... F3
37 Alexandra Theatre ... C3
38 Birmingham Repertory Theatre ... A2
39 Club DV8 ... C4
40 Electric Cinema ... C3
41 Factory Club ... E3
42 Glee Club ... C4
43 Hippodrome ... C4
IMAX Cinema ... (see 12)
44 Nightingale Club ... C4
45 O2 Academy ... C4
46 Oceana ... C4
47 Q Club ... D1
48 Queens Tavern ... C4
49 Sunflower Lounge ... C3
50 Symphony Hall ... A3

Shopping
51 Bullring East Mall ... D3
52 Bullring West Mall ... D3
53 Mailbox ... B3
54 Selfridges ... D3

brought back a taste for fancy buckles and sparkly brocade from France in the 17th century. Stretching north from the last Georgian square in Birmingham, the Jewellery Quarter still produces 40% of the jewellery manufactured in the UK, and dozens of workshops are open to the public. The tourist office provides a free booklet, *Jewellery Quarter: The Essential Guide*, or you can take a virtual tour at www.jewelleryquarter.net.

In the **Museum of the Jewellery Quarter** (☎0121-554 3598; 75-79 Vyse St; admission free; ⏲10.30am-4pm Tue-Sun), the Smith & Pepper jewellery factory is preserved as it was on its closing day in 1981, after 80 years of operation. You can explore the long history of the trade in Birmingham and watch master jewellers at work.

Closer to the centre, St Paul's Sq is dominated by the 18th-century **St Paul's Church**, where Matthew Boulton and James Watt came to pray. At the northwest corner of this pretty Georgian square, the **Royal Birmingham Society of Artists** (☎0121-236 4353; www.rbsa.org.uk; admission free; ⏲10.30am-5.30pm Mon-Fri, 10.30am-5pm Sat, 1-5pm Sun) has been exhibiting the work of local artists and artisans since 1814.

THE MIDLANDS OR MIDDLE-EARTH?

Unlikely as it may sound, Birmingham was part of the inspiration for *The Lord of the Rings*. Author JR Tolkien spent his childhood in and around the suburb of Edgbaston, where he encountered such sights as the twin towers of Perrott's Folly and the Edgbaston Waterworks, said to have inspired the Two Towers. He was also influenced by **Sarehole Mill** (☎0121-777 6612; www.bmag.org.uk/sarehole-mill; Cole Bank Rd; admission free; ⊙noon-4pm Tue-Sun Apr-Oct), which was reinvented as the Old Mill in the Shire. For the fire-blackened landscape of Mordor, Tolkien only had to look as far as the soot-choked iron foundries of the Black Country. For more on the Tolkien connection, search for the author's name at www.birmingham.gov.uk.

About 1.5 miles northwest of the Jewellery Quarter is **Soho House** (☎0121-554 9122; Soho Ave, Handsworth; admission free; ⊙11.30am-4pm Tue-Sun Apr-Oct), where industrialist Matthew Boulton lived from 1766 to 1809. Among the restored 18th-century chambers is the dining room where Boulton and members of the Lunar Society met to discuss their world-changing ideas (see boxed text, p508).

The Jewellery Quarter is three-quarters of a mile northwest of the centre; take bus 101 or ride the metro from Snow Hill or the train from Moor St to Jewellery Quarter station. Buses 74 and 79 pass close to Soho House.

OUTLYING AREAS

A 10-minute walk northeast of the centre, surrounded by the footprints of vanished factories, the Millennium Point development contains the entertaining **Thinktank** (☎0121-202 2222; www.thinktank.ac; Curzon St; adult/child £11.75/7.95; ⊙10am-5pm, last admission 4pm), an ambitious attempt to make science accessible to children (and anyone else with an interest in levers, pulleys and bubbling test tubes). There's also a **Planetarium**, covered by the same ticket, and an **IMAX cinema**.

Around 2.5 miles south of the centre at the University of Birmingham, the **Barber Institute of Fine Art** (☎0121-414 7333; www.barber.org.uk; admission free; ⊙10am-5pm Mon-Sat, noon-5pm Sun) takes in Renaissance masterpieces, European masters such as Rubens and Van Dyck, British greats including Gainsborough, Reynolds and Turner, and modern classics by the likes of Picasso and Schiele. To get here, take the train from New St to University station, or catch bus 61, 62 or 63 from Corporation St.

In Edgbaston, the **Birmingham Botanical Gardens** (☎0121-454 1860; www.birminghambotanicalgardens.org.uk; Westbourne Rd; adult/child £7.50/4.75; ⊙9am-7pm Mon-Sat Apr-Sep, to dusk low season, from 10am Sun) are the Midlands' answer to Kew, with grand Victorian glasshouses full of flowers, cacti and palms. Take bus 10, 22 or 23 from near the cathedral.

The next best thing to Willy Wonka's Chocolate Factory, **Cadbury World** (☎0844 880 7667; www.cadburyworld.co.uk; Linden Rd; adult/child £13.90/10.10, under 3yr free; ⊙opening hrs vary, see website) is about 4 miles south of Birmingham in the village of Bournville. This sweet-toothed attraction aims to educate visitors about the history of cocoa and the Cadbury family, but sweetens the deal with free samples, displays of chocolate-making machines, and chocolate-themed rides. Opening hours vary through the year and bookings are essential in July and August. The easiest way to get to Bournville is by train from Birmingham New St (11 minutes).

Surrounding the chocolate works, pretty **Bournville Village** was built by the philanthropic Cadbury family to accommodate early-20th-century factory workers. In the centre of the village, **Selly Manor** (☎0121-472 0199; www.bvt.org.uk/sellymanor; Maple Rd; adult/child £3.50/1.50; ⊙10am-5pm Tue-Fri year-round, plus 2-5pm Sat & Sun Apr-Sep) is a bona fide 14th-century manor house, shifted brick and mortar from its original location by George Cadbury to save it from destruction.

BIRMINGHAM'S HISTORY BUS

Every Sunday from May to October, a free bus runs around Birmingham's museums, stopping at the Birmingham Museum & Art Gallery, Soho House, Aston Hall and Sarehole Mill, as well as several smaller museums. Contact any of the museums for details.

BIRMINGHAM IN...

Two Days

Start off in the centre, dropping into Victoria Sq and the eclectic **Birmingham Museum & Art Gallery**. Go west through Centenary Sq to reach the Birmingham Canals, where you can while away an afternoon at the **National Sea Life Centre** or **Ikon gallery**, before an evening of rock and cocktails at the Island Bar or Sunflower Lounge. On day two, indulge your inner shopaholic at the gleaming malls of the **Bullring** and **Mailbox**, which both have good options for lunch. In the afternoon, catch up on some social history at the **Birmingham Back to Backs**. After dark, roam south to the **Balti Triangle** to sample Birmingham's unique contribution to the world of curry.

Four Days

Follow the two-day itinerary, but add a **canal cruise**. On day three, head north from the centre to **Aston Hall** and **Soho House**, or south to the famous **Barber Institute**, then take in a show at the **Repertory Theatre** or a concert at **Symphony Hall**. Use day four to explore the fascinating **Jewellery Quarter**, with an upmarket Indian lunch at Itihaas or Lasan, and spend the afternoon reliving *Charlie and the Chocolate Factory* fantasies at **Cadbury World**.

About 3 miles north of the centre in Aston (of Aston Villa fame), well-preserved **Aston Hall** (☎0121-675 4722; Trinity Rd, Aston; ⊙noon-4pm Tue-Sun Apr-Oct) was built in extravagant Jacobean style between 1618 and 1635. The lush grounds are a wonderful retreat from the city streets, and the sumptuous interiors are full of friezes, moulded ceilings and tapestries. To get here, take a train to Aston station from New St station, or jump on bus 65 from Corporation St, north of the Old Sq junction.

Tours

The tourist office has a number of free themed walking tour pamphlets.

Birmingham Tours WALKING/BUS TOUR
(☎0121-427 2555; www.birmingham-tours.co.uk; prices vary) Runs popular walking tours and the hop-on/hop-off **Big Brum Buz** (all day ticket adult/child £10/5, Saturdays from May to September).

Second City Canal Cruises CANAL CRUISE
(☎0121-236 9811; www.secondcityboats.co.uk; fares vary) Narrow-boat tours of Birmingham's canals lasting anything from one hour to two days, leaving from the Gas St Basin.

Sherborne Wharf NARROW-BOAT CRUISE
(☎0121-455 6163; www.sherbornewharf.co.uk; Sherborne St; adult/child £6.50/5; ⊙11.30am, 1pm, 2.30pm & 4pm daily mid-Apr–Oct, Sat & Sun Nov–mid-Apr) Nostalgic narrow-boat cruises from the quayside by the International Convention Centre.

West Midlands Waterways CANAL CRUISE
(☎0121-200 7400; www.britishwaterways.co.uk/west-midlands; Cambrian House, 2 Canalside; ⊙noon-2pm Mon-Fri) Provides information on hiring canal boats; a short walk along the canal from the National Indoor Arena.

Festivals & Events

Crufts Dog Show DOG SHOW
(www.crufts.org.uk) The world's greatest collection of pooches on parade, held every March at the National Exhibition Centre.

Birmingham Pride GAY FESTIVAL
(www.birminghampride.com) One of the largest and most colourful celebrations of gay and lesbian culture in the country, held in May.

Artsfest ARTS FESTIVAL
(www.artsfest.org.uk) The UK's largest free arts festival features visual arts, dance and musical performances in venues across the city in September.

Horse of the Year Show HORSE SHOW
(www.hoys.co.uk) Held in October, the UK's biggest annual equestrian event, with jumping, mounted sports and dressage.

Sleeping

Most Birmingham hotels are aimed at business travellers, ensuring high prices during the week. Look out for cheap deals at weekends or for longer stays. B&Bs are concentrated outside the centre in Acocks Green (to the southeast) or Edgbaston and Selly Oak (to the southwest). The tourist office has a long accommodation list.

TOP CHOICE **Hotel du Vin** HOTEL £££
(☎0121-200 0600; www.hotelduvin.com; Church St; d from £160; P@🛜) Housed in the handsome Victorian precincts of the former Birmingham Eye Hospital, this upmarket hotel has real class. Polished communal areas give way to art deco–inspired rooms with spectacular bathrooms, and the hotel boasts a pampering spa and a bistro with a stellar wine list.

Malmaison HOTEL £££
(☎0121-246 5000; www.malmaison-birmingham.com; 1 Wharfside St; d from £160; P@🛜) Within tickling distance of Harvey Nichols and the posh eateries of the Mailbox, there is nothing 'mal' about this sleek hotel. Mood lighting and Regency tones set the scene in the stylish rooms, which offer floor-to-ceiling views. Indulgences include a brasserie, champagne bar and miniature spa. Wheelchair accessible.

Birmingham Central Backpackers HOSTEL £
(☎0121-643 0033; www.birminghamcentralbackpackers.com; 58 Coventry St; dm from £13; @🛜) Despite the setting in down-at-heel Digbeth, Birmingham's backpacker hostel is handy for the bus station, and guests have a choice of standard dorms or funky Japanese-style pods. The excellent facilities include a lounge with DVD movies, a guest kitchen and a bar.

Nitenite HOTEL ££
(☎0121-631 5550; www.nitenite.com; 18 Holliday St; r from £56; P@🛜) Taking the chain hotel concept to another level, Nitenite offers catwalk style on a shoestring budget. The compact rooms feel a little like yacht cabins, with panelled walls, floating double beds, and giant plasma TV screens with webcam images of the city streets. Wheelchair accessible.

Etap Hotel HOTEL £
(☎0121-622 7575; www.etaphotel.com; 1 Great Colmore St; r from £38; P@🛜) The Birmingham branch of this cost-effective European chain has a breakfast room and net-cafe and a handy location for the O2 Academy and the clubs around Bristol St. Rooms are simple but good value and the hotel attracts plenty of party-minded young folk.

Westbourne Lodge B&B ££
(☎0121-429 1003; www.westbournelodge.co.uk; Fountain Rd; s/d from £49.50/69; P@🛜) Removed from the bustle of the city centre, this B&B is still conveniently located, about 2 miles out in the suburb of Edgbaston (follow the A456). Rooms are a little chintzy but spacious, and there's a pleasant terrace to enjoy in summer.

Ibis Hotel HOTEL £
(☎0121-622 6010; www.ibishotel.com; Arcadian Centre, Ladywell Walk; d from £43; P@🛜) You won't find any surprises at the Ibis – the

BIRMINGHAM FOR CHILDREN

Despite the trials of finding somewhere to park, it's easy to keep the kids amused in Birmingham. Start with the shark-infested National Sea Life Centre, followed by a cruise on the Birmingham canals, then stop for lunch at the revamped Bullring (teens will love the chance to shop for posh brands). For some educational fun, wobble the levers at Thinktank, and scan the stars in the Planetarium, or walk with dinosaurs at the IMAX cinema. Regrettably, the biggest kid-friendly attraction in town is the one that sends dentists into apoplexies. Out on the outskirts in Bournville, Cadbury World is actually quite educational, but the pill is sugar-wrapped with free samples and chocolate-themed fun rides.

WORTH A TRIP

THE CUSTARD FACTORY

If you happen to find yourself in Digbeth, drop into the **Custard Factory** (☎0121-224 7777; www.custardfactory.com; Gibb St), a trendy art and design enclave set in the converted buildings of the factory that once churned out Britain's favourite custard. It's full of small galleries, quirky design boutiques, offbeat cafes, and grown men on skateboards.

Fans of techno and drum and bass may know the Custard Factory as the location of the legendary **Factory Club** (www.factoryclub.co.uk), but the future of this cult venue is up in the air after four people were shot here in June, 2010 – check the website for the latest.

clean rooms look exactly the same as the rooms in any other Ibis anywhere. However, look at the location, right on the doorstep of the Bullring, and next to a handy public car park. Wheelchair accessible.

Eating

Birmingham is best known for its brilliant baltis (see boxed text, p509) but the city has a growing reputation for fine dining and gastronomy. For cheap eats, look to the myriad Asian eateries in Chinatown, just south of the centre.

Lasan INDIAN ££
(www.lasangroup.com; 3-4 Dakota Buildings, James St; mains £12-18; ⏲lunch Sun-Fri, dinner daily) Expletive-loving chef Gordon Ramsay gave his endorsement to this elegant and upscale Indian as Britain's best local restaurant. From our experience, the service and style are spot on and the North and South Indian dishes are ****ing masterpieces.

Simpsons MODERN BRITISH £££
(☎0121-454 3434; www.simpsonsrestaurant.co.uk; 20 Highfield Rd, Edgbaston; 3-course set lunch/dinner £30/32.50; ⏲closed dinner Sun) Simpsons is far from the centre in a gorgeous Victorian house, but it's worth making the journey for the imaginative creations sliced and diced by Michelin-starred chef Andreas Antona. You could even stay the night in one of the four luxurious bedrooms upstairs. Reservations recommended.

Purnells MODERN BRITISH £££
(☎0121-212 9799; www.purnellsrestaurant.com; 55 Cornwall St; 2/3 courses £36/42; ⏲lunch Tue-Fri, dinner Tue-Sat) Exquisite, inventive dishes (such as ox cheek with lentils cooked in toffee) are served in an airy Victorian red-brick building with a striking modern interior. Run by celebrated chef Glynn Purnell.

Itihaas INDIAN ££
(☎0121-212 3383; www.itihaas.co.uk; 18 Fleet St; mains £11-17; ⏲lunch Mon-Fri, dinner daily) Voted best Indian restaurant in the UK by drinkers of Cobra beer, Itihaas does everything right – presentation, decor, service, flavours. It's a big hit with Birmingham's wealthy Indian expats.

Edmunds Fine Dining MODERN BRITISH £££
(☎0121-633 4944; www.edmundsbirmingham.com; 6 Central Sq, Brindley Pl; 2/3 courses from £19/21; ⏲lunch Mon-Fri, dinner Mon-Sat) The latest venture for Michelin-starred chef Andy Waters, this sleek place is where traders from the surrounding banking houses come to spend their bonuses. Expect lots of locally sourced meats, fish and farm-fresh produce. The restaurant is just back from the river in the Brindley Place precinct.

Oriental PAN-ASIAN ££
(☎0121-633 9988; www.theoriental.uk.com; 4 The Mailbox, 128–130 Wharfside St; mains £8-13) The most glamorous of the eateries around the Mailbox wharf, with wok-tastic dishes from China, Thailand and Malaysia, served in a funky dining room full of designer wallpaper and prints of Asian celebs.

Other options:

Mount Fuji JAPANESE ££
(☎0121-633 9853; www.mountfuji.co.uk/bullring.htm; Bullring; mains £7-14) When you tire of retail therapy, sashay to this minimalist Japanese sushi cafe under the West Mall for raw fish, bento boxes and sake.

Opus MODERN BRITISH £££
(☎0121-200 2323; www.opusrestaurant.co.uk; 54 Cornwall St; mains £14-24; ⏲lunch Mon-Fri, dinner Mon-Sat) Fronted by a window shaped like the letters of its name, this sleek modernist place is all starched linen,

BIRMINGHAM BRAINS

The Industrial Revolution was a great time for entrepreneurs, and nowhere more so than in Birmingham, where the industrialists, philosophers and intellectuals of the Lunar Society came together to swap ideas for the greatest technological leap forward since the invention of wheel. As well as engineers like Matthew Boulton, James Watt and gaslight mogul William Murdoch, the society drew in such great thinkers as philosopher and naturalist Erasmus Darwin, oxygen-discoverer Joseph Priestley, pottery boss Josiah Wedgwood, botanist Joseph Banks (who sailed to Australia with Captain Cook) and founding father Benjamin Franklin. Between 1765 and 1813, this esteemed company held regular meetings at Soho House (now an engaging museum) to thrash out their groundbreaking ideas. If you don't feel like dragging yourself out to the 'burbs, there's a gleaming golden statue of Boulton, Watt and Murdoch near Centenary Sq.

THE BEAUTIFUL BALTI

If curry is the unofficial national dish of England, then the balti is its finest interpretation. First cooked up in the curry-houses of Sparkbrook in southern Birmingham, this one-pot curry is prepared in a cast-iron wok with plenty of onion and chilli. Tracing its origins back to Baltistan in northern Pakistan, the balti is traditionally served with a giant *karack* naan bread that's big enough to feed the whole table.

The best place to sample this Brummie delicacy is in the so-called Balti Triangle about 2.5 miles southeast of the centre, formed by Ladypool Rd, Stoney Lane and Stratford Rd. Reflecting the religious sensibilities of local residents, restaurants serve soft drinks, fruit juices and *lassis* (yoghurt shakes) instead of alcohol, but diners are welcome to bring their own beer and wine. Expect to pay £7 to £9 for a balti and rice or naan bread. To get here, take bus 2, 5, 5A or 6 from Corporation St and ask the driver for Ladypool Rd.

Here are our picks of the Birmingham baltis:

Grameen Khana (☎0121-449 9994; www.grameenkhana.com; 310-12 Ladypool Rd) Multicoloured lights and Bollywood movies provide a backdrop to Birmingham's best balti – according to a city-wide poll in 2009.

Saleem's Restaurant & Sweet House (☎0121-449 1861; 256-8 Ladypool Rd) Long established and understandably popular for its tasty milk-based Indian sweets and generous portions of balti.

Desi Express (☎0121-446 5068; 225 Ladypool Rd) Tasty Pakistani fast food, kebabs and juices, served in a fun, family-friendly environment.

Al Faisal's (☎0121-449 5695; www.alfaisal.co.uk; 136-140 Stoney Lane) Come here for delicious dishes from the mountains of Kashmir, as well for as classic Birmingham baltis.

silver cutlery and upmarket ingredients from famous-name farms.

Cafe Soya ASIAN £
(☎0121 622 3888; Upper Dean St; mains £5-9) Excellent cafe dishing up tasty dim sum and filling bowls of *pho* (Vietnamese noodle soup). There's also a branch in the Arcadian Centre (closed Wednesday).

Drinking

The pub scene in the centre is dominated by bland commercial chains, but there are a few gems if you know where to look.

Island Bar BAR
(☎0121-632 5296; www.bar-island.co.uk; 14-16 Suffolk St; ⏰5pm-late Mon-Sat) Locals rave about the cocktails at this funky nightspot, where you can sit in Perspex chairs in front of giant blow-ups of Hawaiian beaches and groove to rock and roll.

Old Joint Stock PUB
(☎0121-200 1892; www.oldjointstocktheatre.co.uk; 4 Temple Row West; ⏰noon-5pm Sun) A vast, high-ceilinged temple of a pub, housed in a former bank and appealing to a high-spirited after-work crowd. There's an 80-seat theatre upstairs that puts on plays and comedy shows.

Sobar BAR
(☎0121-693 5084; Arcadian Centre, Hurst St; ⏰5pm-late Tue & Wed, noon-2am Thu, noon-3am Fri & Sat) A glammed-up, shirted and booted crowd packs out this black-and-red bar to the strains of mainstream dance and house.

Mechu BAR
(☎0121-710 4233; www.summerrow.com/mechu; 47-59 Summer Row; ⏰noon-1am Mon-Wed, noon-3am Fri, 5pm-3am Sat) Work-eat-drink-play is the motto at this slick bistro and club northwest of the centre. Accordingly, most patrons come straight from the office to sup, sip and sway.

Entertainment

Tickets for most events can be purchased via the entertainment megacorp **TicketWeb** (☎0870 060 0100; www.ticketweb.co.uk). Also check the free Birmingham listings mags for what's going on.

Nightclubs

The main party district is south of New St station, where a series of defunct pubs and warehouses have found new life as bars and clubs. Chinatown's **Arcadian Centre** (www.thearcadian.co.uk; Hurst St) is the gateway to this hedonistic quarter, with numerous party bars and dancing spots.

Air CLUB
(www.airbirmingham.com; Heath Mill Lane) Don't be put off by the grungy Digbeth location; this superclub is home to the renowned Godskitchen night (www.godskitchen.com), where some of the country's top DJs whip the crowd into a frenzy.

Q Club CLUB
(www.qclub.co.uk; 212 Corporation St; from 8.30pm or 10pm) The old brick Central Hall that houses this legendary club is on its last legs, but the 'Q' is still going strong. DJs pump out boisterous electro, house, jungle and old-school club classics.

Oceana CLUB
(www.oceanaclubs.com; Hurst St; to 3.30am Thu-Sat) Huge and unashamedly commercial, Oceana offers multiple rooms, multiple dance floors and more drinks promotions than you can shake a shot glass at.

Glee Club COMEDY
(www.glee.co.uk; Arcadian Centre; tickets £9.50-17.50; from 7.30pm Thu-Sat) No connection to the hit TV show, this rib-tickler is Birmingham's favourite comedy club, attracting local talent and big names on tour.

Live Music

As well as the following venues, the **National Indoor Arena** (0121-767 2937; www.thenia.co.uk; King Edwards Rd), north of Brindley Pl, and the giant **National Exhibition Centre Arena** (0121-780 4141; www.thenec.co.uk; off the M42), near Birmingham International Airport, host stadium-fillers from the world of rock and pop.

Sunflower Lounge LIVE MUSIC
(0121-632 6756; www.thesunflowerlounge.co.uk; 76 Smallbrook Queensway; to 2am Fri & Sat) A quirky little mod bar tucked away on the dual carriageway near New St train station, with a great alternative soundtrack and a regular program of live gigs and DJ nights.

Jam House BAR
(www.thejamhouse.com; 1 St Paul's Sq; noon-midnight Tue & Wed, noon-1am Thu, noon-2am Fri & Sat) Nasal-toned piano-meister Jools Holland was the brains behind this moody music venue in posh St Paul's Sq. Acts range from jazz big bands to famous soul crooners. Over 21s only.

O2 Academy LIVE MUSIC
(www.birmingham-academy.co.uk; 16-18 Horsefair, Bristol St) Replacing the defunct Carling Academy at Dale End, this is Birmingham's leading venue for big-name rockers and tribute bands.

Symphony Hall ARTS CENTRE
(www.symphonyhall.co.uk; Broad St) To hear top talent from the world of classical music, head to the ultramodern Symphony Hall, the official home of the City of Birmingham Symphony Orchestra. Shows also take place in the handsome auditorium at the Town Hall (p502).

Theatre & Cinema

Birmingham Repertory Theatre THEATRE
(www.birmingham-rep.co.uk; Centenary Sq, Broad St) With two performances spaces – the Main House and the more experimental Door – 'the Rep' presents edgy drama and musicals, with an emphasis on contemporary work.

Electric Cinema CINEMA
(www.theelectric.co.uk; 47-49 Station St; deluxe seats £12) At the oldest working cinema in the UK (the projectors have been rolling since 1909), you can enjoy a mix of mainstream and art-house cinema, while sitting in plush two-seater sofas.

IMAX CINEMA
(www.imax.ac; Curzon St; tickets adult/child £9.60/7.75) Coming into its own in the age of the 3-D blockbuster, Birmingham's five-storey IMAX cinema is housed in the same building as the Thinktank.

Other venues:

Hippodrome THEATRE
(www.birminghamhippodrome.com; Hurst St) The place to come to see stars off the telly, plus highbrow entertainment from the Birmingham Royal Ballet.

Alexandra Theatre THEATRE
(www.alexandratheatre.org.uk; Suffolk St Queensway) This Brummie institution has been around even longer than the veteran comedians and touring stage shows that grace its stage.

Sport

Villa Park FOOTBALL
(www.avfc.co.uk; Aston) The fourth most successful British football club of all time, Aston Villa Football Club packs out its ground

GAY & LESBIAN BIRMINGHAM

Birmingham's loud and lively gay scene is centred on the streets south of the Bullring, which throng with the bold, bright and beautiful on weekend nights. For up-to-the-minute information on the Brummie scene visit www.gaybrum.com and www.visit-gaybrum.com, or ask the crowds during the bustling Pride march (www.birmingham-pride.com) in May.

Top gay nightspots:

Nightingale Club (☎0121-622 1718; www.nightingaleclub.co.uk; Kent St) Birmingham's most established gay nightclub, the Nightingale rocks on three levels, with mainstream pop on the bottom floor and hardcore techno upstairs.

Village Inn (☎0121-622 4742; www.villagebirmingham.co.uk; 152 Hurst St; ⏰noon-2am Sun-Thu, to 4am Fri & Sat) A lively late bar with a sideline in drag nights and camp cabaret.

Queens Tavern (☎0121-622 7091; www.queenstavern.co.uk; 23 Essex St) This bustling, unpretentious corner pub switches to risqué stage shows at weekends.

Club DV8 (☎0121-666 6366; www.clubdv8.co.uk; 16 Lower Essex St) Dance tunes dominate at this animated dance spot, where the focus is on frolics and flirting.

with loyal fans on match days. General sale tickets for Premiership matches can be purchased from the **Premier League website** (www.premierleague.com). The ground is northwest of the centre, a five minute walk from Witton train station.

Warwickshire County Cricket Club CRICKET
(www.edgbaston.com; County Ground, Edgbaston) Tickets for tests and one-day internationals sell out early, but seats are often available for county matches and fast-paced Twenty20 games.

Shopping

The workshops of the Jewellery Quarter are well worth a browse – see p503 – and there are several bustling markets selling cheap imported clothes in the pedestrian precincts surrounding the Bullring.

Downtown Birmingham is mall central. You won't find many small, independent boutiques in these cathedrals to consumerism, but you probably won't leave empty-handed, either.

Bullring MALL
(www.bullring.co.uk; St Martin's Circus; ⏰9.30am-8pm Mon-Fri, 9am-8pm Sat, 11am-5pm Sun) Split into two vast retail spaces – the East Mall and West Mall – the Bullring has all the international brands and chain cafes you could ask for, plus the architectural wonder that is the **Selfridges** department store.

Mailbox MALL
(www.mailboxlife.com; Wharfside St; ⏰10am-6pm Mon-Wed, to 7pm Thu-Sat, 11am-5pm Sun) Birmingham's newest 'shopping experience' could hold its own on Madison Ave, with a designer hotel, a fleet of upmarket restaurants, a branch of posh department store Harvey Nichols, and a new extension in a metallic cube that resembles a prop from the *Transformers* movie.

Information

Bookshops

Waterstone's High St (☎0121-633 4353; 24 High St); New St (☎0121-631 4333, 128 New St)

Dangers & Annoyances

As in most large cities, it's wise to avoid walking alone late at night in unlit areas. The area around Digbeth bus station can be quite rough after dark – stick to the High St if you are walking to central Birmingham.

Emergency

Police station (☎0845 113 5000; Steelhouse Lane)

Internet Access

Internet Lounge (loft level, Pavilions Shopping Centre; per 30min £2; ⏰9.30am-6pm Mon-Wed, Fri & Sat, to 7pm Thu, 11am-5pm Sun) Internet lounge and coffee bar.

Left Luggage

New St train station has left luggage facilities, but there are cheaper bag lockers in the East and West malls at the Bullring (£2 to £4 per 24 hours).

Media

Numerous free listings magazines are available in hotel lobbies, bars and restaurants, including

THE SHAKESPEARE EXPRESS

In July and August, this nostalgic **steam train** (0121-708 4960; http://www.shakespeareexpress.com; adult/child £10/5) chugs its way south-west from Birmingham Snow Hill to Stratford-upon-Avon, blowing out clouds of vapour as it goes. The train runs twice each Sunday and the journey takes one hour.

the fortnightly *What's On* and the monthly *Birmingham 24seven* magazine, which cover everything from exhibitions to club nights.

Medical Services

Birmingham Children's Hospital (0121-333 9999; www.bch.nhs.uk; Steelhouse Lane)

Heartlands Hospital (0121-424 2000; www.heartofengland.nhs.uk; Bordesley) Catch bus 15, 17, 97 or 97A.

Money

You can't walk more than a block in the town centre without coming across a bank or an ATM, particularly around Brindley Pl and New St.

Thomas Cook (0121-643 5057; Middle Mall, Bullring; 10am-8pm Mon-Fri, 9am-8pm Sat, 11am-5pm Sun) Bureau de change.

Post

Central post office (1 Pinfold St, Victoria Sq; 9am-5.30pm Mon-Sat) With bureau de change.

Tourist Information

Tourist office Main Office (0121-202 5115; www.visitbirmingham.com; The Rotunda, 150 New St; 9.30am-5.30pm Mon & Wed-Sat, 10am-5.30pm Tue, 10.30am-4.30pm Sun); Welcome Centre (cnr New & Stephenson Sts; 9am-5pm Mon-Sat, 10am-6pm Sun) With racks of brochures, maps and info on activities, transport and sights.

Getting There & Away

Air

Birmingham's **international airport** (0844 576 6000; www.birminghamairport.co.uk) is about 8 miles east of the centre, with flights to destinations around the UK and Europe, plus a few long-haul connections to America and Dubai.

Bus

Most intercity buses run from the Birmingham Coach Station on Digbeth High Street, but the X20 to Stratford-upon-Avon (1¼ hours, hourly, every two hours at weekends) leaves from a stop on Moor St, just north of the Pavilions mall.

National Express (08717 81 81 81; www.nationalexpress.com) runs coaches between Birmingham and major cities across the country, including:

Oxford £11.60, 1½ to two hours, five daily

London £15.70, 2¾ hours, every 30 minutes

Manchester £12.60, 2½ hours, 12 daily

Train

Most long-distance trains leave from New St station, beneath the Pallasades shopping centre, but Chiltern Railways runs to London Marylebone (£31.90; 2½ hours, two per hourly) from Birmingham Snow Hill, and London Midland runs to Stratford-upon-Avon (£6.30, one hour, hourly) from Snow Hill and Moor St station.

Useful services from New St:

Derby £13.80, 45 minutes, four per hour

Leicester £13.10, one hour, two per hour

London Euston £40.90, 1½ hours, every 30 minutes

Manchester £30.50, 1¾ hours, every 15 minutes

Shrewsbury £11.70, one hour, two per hour

WORTH A TRIP

THE BLACK COUNTRY

The industrial region west of Birmingham is known as the Black Country, after the soot that once rained down on the landscape from the factory chimneys of Dudley, Walsall and Wolverhampton. The heavy industry is now a distant memory, but it's worth swinging by to see the **Black Country Living Museum** (0121-557 9643; www.bclm.co.uk; Tipton Rd, Dudley; adult/child £13.20/7; 10am-5pm Mar-Oct, to 4pm Nov-Feb), a perfect recreation of a 19th-century mining village, inhabited by a complete cast of characters in period costume. Trams and trolleybuses run between the various buildings, where kids and history buffs can enjoy mine trips, narrow-boat rides, silent movie shows and recreations of crafts and industries of the time (the confectioners making traditional sweets always draw in a crowd).

Getting Around

To/From the Airport

Fast and convenient trains run regularly between New St and Birmingham International station (20 minutes, every 10 minutes), or take bus 58 or 900 (45 minutes, every 20 minutes) from Moor St Queensway. A taxi from the airport to the centre costs about £20.

Car

All the big car-hire companies have town offices:

Avis (0844 544 6038; www.avis.co.uk; 17 Horse Fair)

Enterprise Rent-a-Car (0121-782 5158; www.enterprise.co.uk; 9-10 Suffolk St Queensway)

Public Transport

Local buses run from a convenient hub on Corporation St, just north of the New St junction. For routes, pick up a free copy of the *Network Birmingham Map & Guide* from the tourist office. Commuter trains to destinations in the north of Birmingham (including Aston) operate from Moor St station, close to Selfridges. Birmingham's single tram line, the **Metro** (www.travelmetro.co.uk), runs from Snow Hill to Wolverhampton via the Jewellery Quarter, West Bromwich and Dudley.

Special saver tickets covering all the buses and trains are available from **Network West Midlands** (0121-214 7214; www.networkwestmidlands.com; 9am-5.30pm Mon-Fri, to 5pm Sat) on the lower ground floor of the Pavilions mall.

TOA Taxis (0121-427 8888; www.toataxis.net) are a reliable black-cab taxi firm.

NAVIGATING BRUM

The endless ringroads, roundabouts and underpasses make driving in Birmingham a descent into madness. Do as the locals do and ditch your wheels in one of the car parks around the Bullring, then explore the city on foot. For a downloadable map of car park locations, search for 'car park' at www.birmingham.gov.uk.

WARWICKSHIRE

Warwickshire could have been just another picturesque English county of rolling hills and market towns were it not for the birth of a rather well-known wordsmith. William Shakespeare was born in, and died in, Stratford-upon-Avon, and the sights linked to his life are a magnet for tourists from around the globe. Famous Warwick Castle attracts similar crowds. Visitor numbers dwindle away from these tourist hubs, but Kenilworth boasts atmospheric castle ruins and Coventry has two fine cathedrals and an excellent motoring museum.

Information

Shakespeare Country (www.shakespeare-country.co.uk)

Getting There & Around

The Warwickshire transport site (www.warwickshire.gov.uk/transport) covers all aspects of travel in the county, including bus and train timetables. Coventry is the main transport hub, with frequent rail connections to London Euston and Birmingham New St.

Coventry

POP 300,848

Over the centuries, Coventry has been a bustling hub for the production of cloth, clocks, bicycles, automobiles and munitions. It was this last industry that attracted the attention of the German Luftwaffe in WWII. The city was blitzed so badly that the Nazis coined a new verb, 'Coventrieren', meaning 'to flatten'. Postwar planners filled in the gaps with dull concrete developments, and the city faced a further setback with the collapse of the British motor industry in the 1980s.

However, it's not all doom and gloom – a handful of medieval streets escaped the bombers, offering a taste of what the city must have been like in its heyday. It's well worth taking a day here to explore the fantastic motoring museum, and the dramatic modernist cathedral, built alongside the ruins of its bombed out predecessor.

Sights

Coventry Cathedrals CATHEDRAL

The evocative ruins of **St Michael's Cathedral** (Priory Row), built around 1300 but destroyed by Nazi incendiary bombs in the blitz of 14 November 1940, still stand as a permanent memorial to Coventry's darkest hour. You can climb the 180 steps of its **Gothic spire** (adult/child £2.50/1) for panoramic views.

Symbolically adjoining the old cathedral's sandstone walls is the Sir Basil Spence-designed **Coventry Cathedral** (024-7652 1200; www.coventrycathedral.org.uk; Priory Row; adult/child under 7 £4.50/3.50; 9.30am-4.30pm). This cathedral is a modernist architectural masterpiece, with a futuristic organ, stained glass, a Jacob Epstein statue of the devil and St Michael, and ghostlike angels etched into its glass facade.

FREE **Coventry Transport Museum** MUSEUM
(☎024-7623 4270; www.transport-museum.com; Hales St; ⏲10am-5pm) Down by the bus station, this stupendous museum is every schoolboy's dream. Inside you can view hundreds of motor cars from across the ages, from the earliest 'horseless carriages' produced by Daimler in the 1890s to the jet-powered car that broke the land speed record (and the sound barrier) in 1997. Also on display are motorcycles, buses, tractors and early pushbikes and the car that Field Marshall Montgomery drove to Berlin in WWII. Kids will love the atmospheric 'Coventry Blitz Experience' and the Thrust speed simulator.

FREE **Herbert Art Gallery & Museum** GALLERY
(☎024-76832386;www.theherbert.org.uk;⏲10am-4pm Mon-Sat, noon-4pm Sun) Behind the twin cathedrals, the Herbert has an eclectic collection of paintings and sculptures (including work by TS Lowry and Stanley Spencer), a delightful cafe, and lots of exhibitions and activities aimed at kids. Don't miss the room dedicated to Lady Godiva, the Anglo-Saxon princess who rode through town naked on a white horse to protest the taxes imposed by her tyrannical husband, the Earl of Mercia.

Other Sights

Near the Transport Museum, **Holy Trinity Church** (☎024-7622 0418; www.holy trinitycoventry.org.uk; Priory Row; admission free; ⏲9.30am-4pm Mon-Sat) has a sinister mural of the Last Judgement, dating from the early 1400s. The graveyard backs onto the ruins of the Benedictine priory of St Mary's, whose history is explored at the **Priory Visitor Centre** (☎024-7655 2242; Priory Row; ⏲10am-5pm Mon-Sat, noon-4pm Sun); tours of the undercrofts leave at 12.30pm (£1 per person).

On the other side of the cathedral ruins is **St Mary's Guildhall** (☎024-7683 3328; Bayley Lane; admission free; ⏲10am-4pm), one of the country's finest medieval guildhalls. Inside rooms that once imprisoned Mary Queen of Scots, you can view arms and armour, ancient oil paintings and 15th-century tapestries.

On the other side of town, past the ghastly shopping precincts, **Medieval Spon St** is lined with creaky Tudor buildings that now house cute cafes and boutiques.

Sleeping

Spire View Guest House B&B ££
(☎024-7625 1602; www.spireviewguesthouse.co.uk; 36 Park Rd; s/d from £25/51; P) Crisp, clean rooms in a quiet residential street a few minutes' walk from the train station. The hosts are eager to please and there's a guest lounge with plenty of books for browsing.

Ramada Coventry HOTE ££
(☎024-7623 8110; www.ramadacoventry.co.uk; The Butts; r incl breakfast from £81; P @) Chain hotels are chain hotels, but this tall tower overlooking the city from just outside the ringroad has cosier rooms than most. Views and stylish bathrooms add to the appeal. Wheelchair accessible.

Eating & Drinking

As well as the following options, the cafe at the Herbert Art Gallery & Museum (p514) is a great spot for a healthy light lunch.

Playwrights CAFE ££
(☎024-7623 1441; www.playwrightsrestaurant.co.uk; 4-6 Hay Lane; mains £10-14; ⏲closed Sun) On the cobbled lane leading from Earl St to the cathedral, this bright, inviting cafe, bar

CATCH THE THRUST WAVE

Coventry's excellent transport museum houses not one but two of the fastest motor vehicles ever driven. As well as Thrust SCC, the current holder of the World Land Speed Record, which reached a staggering 763.035 mph in the Nevada desert in 1997, you can view the Thrust 2, the previous record holder, which clocked up an impressive 633.468 mph in 1983. These rocket-powered racers were created by aviation entrepreneur Richard Noble, who is now at work on an even faster machine, the Bloodhound SCC, designed to exceed 1000 mph – or to put it another way, four times the take-off speed of a Boeing 747. The speed trials are set to be held in Nevada in 2011 – see www.bloodhoundssc.com for the latest updates.

and bistro is as good for breakfast as it is for a working lunch or an intimate dinner.

Golden Cross PUB
(8 Hay Lane) The beer is warm and so is the atmosphere at this historic ale-house, set in a jettied timber-framed building from 1583.

Tin Angel BAR
(www.thetinangel.co.uk; Medieval Spon St) Looking like something you'd find in an arty part of Berlin or Barcelona, Tin Angel is where local hipsters come to sip, chat and groove. There are regular live gigs, film screenings and comedy nights.

Information

Tourist office (024-7622 5616; www visitcoventry.co.uk; 9.30am-4.30pm Mon-Fri, 10am-4.30pm Sat, 10am-noon & 1-4.30pm Sun) Housed in the restored tower of St Michael's.

PA's Word Internet Cafe (Pool Meadow Bus Station; per hr £1; 10am-8pm Mon-Fri, to 7pm Sat, to 4pm Sun) Check your email here.

Getting There & Away

Trains go south to London Euston (£37.80; 1¼ hours, every 20 minutes) and you will rarely have to wait for a train to Birmingham (30 minutes, every 10 minutes).

From the main bus station, National Express buses serve most parts of the country. Bus X17 (every 20 minutes) goes to Kenilworth (25 minutes), Leamington Spa (40 minutes) and Warwick (1¼ hours).

Warwick

POP 25,434

Regularly name-checked by Shakespeare, Warwick was the ancestral seat of the Earls of Warwick, who played a pivotal role in the Wars of the Roses, ousting Henry VI and installing the young Edward IV on the English throne. Despite a devastating fire in 1694, Warwick remains a treasure-house of medieval architecture, dominated by the soaring turrets of Warwick Castle, which has been transformed into a major tourist attraction by the team behind Madame Tussauds. Unfortunately, the summer queues at the castle can resemble a medieval siege – you can escape the melee in the surrounding streets, which are jammed with interesting buildings and museums.

Sights

Warwick Castle CASTLE
(0870 442 2000; www.warwick-castle.co.uk; castle adult/child £19.95/11.95, castle & dungeon adult/child £27.45/19.45; 10am-6pm Apr-Sep, to 5pm Oct-Mar; P) Founded in 1068 by William the Conqueror, the stunningly preserved Warwick Castle is the biggest show in town. The ancestral home of the Earls of Warwick, the castle remains impressively intact, and The Tussauds Group has filled the interior with noisy attractions that bring the castle's rich history to life in a flamboyant but undeniably family-friendly way.

With waxwork-populated private apartments, sumptuous interiors, landscaped gardens, towering ramparts, displays of arms and armour, medieval jousting and a theme-park dungeon (complete with torture chamber and ham actors in grisly make-up), there's plenty to keep the family busy for a whole day. Tickets are discounted if you buy online.

Collegiate Church of St Mary CHURCH
(01926-492909; Old Sq; suggested donation £2; 10am-6pm Apr-Oct, to 4.30pm Nov-Mar) Drag yourself away from the castle ramparts to explore this magnificent Norman church, founded in 1123 and packed with 16th- and 17th-century tombs. Highlights include the Norman crypt, the Beauchamp Chapel (built between 1442 and 1464 to enshrine the mortal remains of the Earls of Warwick), and the **clock tower** (admission adult/child £2.50/1), which offers supreme views over town.

Lord Leycester Hospital HISTORIC BUILDING
(01926-491422; www.lordleycester.com; High St; adult/child £4.90/3.90; 10am-5pm Tue-Sun Apr-Sep, to 4.30pm Oct-Mar) Leaning against the Westgate like a rest home for Hobbits, the wonderfully wonky Lord Leycester Hospital has been used as a retirement home for soldiers (but not as a hospital) since 1571. Visitors can wander around the courtyard, chapel, guildhall and regimental museum.

Other Sights

Housed in Warwick's striking 17th-century market hall, the **Warwickshire Museum** (01926-412501; Market Pl; admission free; 10am-5pm Tue-Sat year-round, plus 11.30am-5pm Sun Apr-Sep) has some entertaining displays on local history and the Warwick

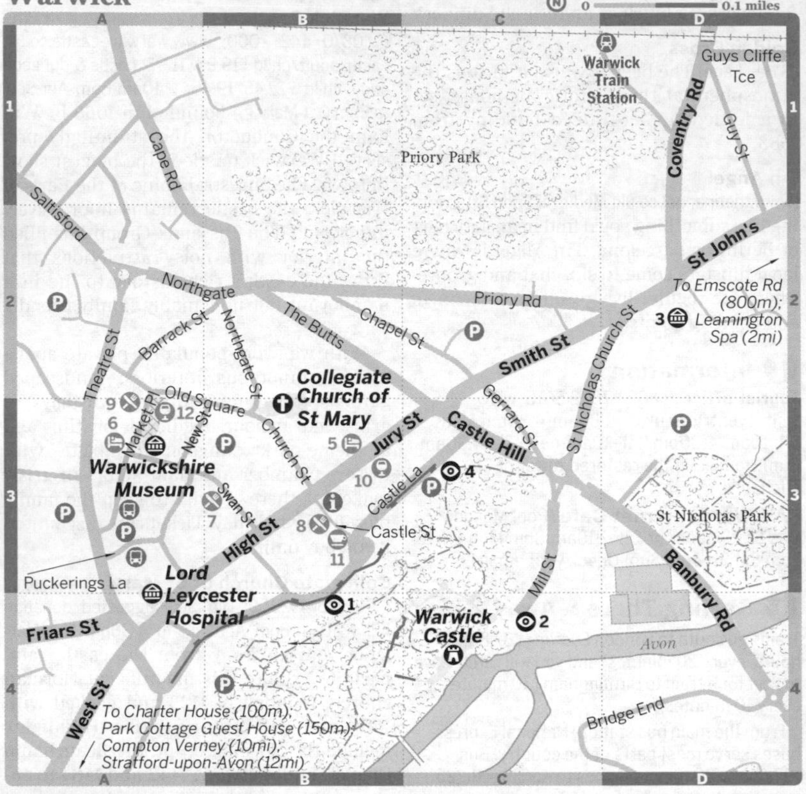

Warwick

Top Sights

Collegiate Church of St Mary B3
Lord Leycester Hospital A3
Warwick Castle C4
Warwickshire Museum A3

Sights

1 Warwick Castle Ticket Office B4
2 Mill Garden C4
3 St John's House D2
4 Warwick Castle Pedestrian Entrance C3

Sleeping

5 Lord Leycester Hotel B3
6 Rose & Crown A3

Eating

7 Art Kitchen & Gallery B3
8 Lane's Bar & Restaurant B3
9 Tailors A3

Drinking

10 Aqua Food & Mood B3
11 Thomas Oken Tea Rooms B3
12 Tilted Wig A3

Sea Dragons (ancient dinosaurs that once roamed the Jurassic seas).

For a fragrant perspective of the castle, head for the **Mill Garden** (01926-492877; 55 Mill St; admission £1.50; 9am-6pm Apr-Oct), an explosion of flowers and plants within splashing distance of the weir that powered the castle mill.

Handsome **St John's House** (01926-412132; St John's; admission free; 10am-5pm

Tue-Sat year-round, plus 2.30-5pm Sun Apr-Sep) has displays of Victoriana downstairs and a regimental museum upstairs, with uniforms, weaponry, and relics captured from the dervishes of Sudan.

Sleeping

The nearest YHA (Youth Hostels Association) hostel is in Stratford-upon-Avon (see p522), but reasonably priced B&Bs line Emscote Rd, which runs northeast towards Leamington Spa.

Rose & Crown GASTROPUB ££
(01926-411117; www.roseandcrownwarwick.co.uk; 30 Market Pl; mains from £8; r incl breakfast from £70; P @) Warwick's finest, this convivial gastropub has five appealing rooms with tasteful modern trim (some with views of the town square), as well as good beer and superior food.

Charter House B&B ££
(01926 496965; sheila@penon.gotadsl.co.uk; 87-91 West St; s/d from £65/85; P @) Found southwest of the centre, this cute little timbered cottage has three rooms convincingly decorated in medieval period styles, and a long list of options for breakfast. Book well ahead.

Park Cottage Guest House B&B ££
(01926-410319; www.parkcottagewarwick.co.uk; 113 West St; s/d £50/68; P) Also southwest of the centre, this 16th-century timbered building hides six spacious rooms decked out with Victoriana, each with a teddy bear for company.

Lord Leycester Hotel HOTEL ££
(01926-491481; www.lord-leycester.co.uk; 17 Jury St; r from £79.50; P) This rambling stone town house, built in 1726, has helpful staff but dated rooms.

Eating

Tailors MODERN BRITISH £££
(01926-410590; www.tailorsrestaurant.co.uk; 22 Market Pl; 2-/3-course dinner £28/32.50; Tue-Sat) Set in a former gentlemen's tailor shop, this elegant eatery serves prime ingredients – guinea fowl, pork belly and lamb from named farms – presented oh-so-delicately in neat little towers.

Art Kitchen & Gallery THAI ££
(01926-494303; www.theartkitchen.com; 7 Swan St; mains £7-13) Come for zingy Thai dishes prepared with lots of local produce, served up in a snug dining room that doubles as a gallery. All of the art on display is for sale.

Lane's Bar & Restaurant MODERN BRITISH ££
(01926-403030; 6 Castle St; mains £10-16; lunch Tue-Sun, dinner Tue-Sat) Handy for the castle, this is a good choice for an upmarket lunch – expect farm-fresh meats and lots of unusual side dishes.

Drinking

Tilted Wig PUB
(11 Market Pl) This large, lively pub on the main square spills out onto the streets in summer, provides a cosy haven in winter, and serves some great beers.

Aqua Food & Mood BAR/RESTAURANT
(01926-495491; www.aqua-food-mood.co.uk; 12-14 Jury St; mains £9-13; dinner Tue-Sat) Bringing a kasbah vibe to historic Warwick, this swish Lebanese place serves cocktails and tasty kebabs. In the post-smoking-ban era, the sheesha pipes are reserved for the garden.

Thomas Oken Tea Rooms TEAROOM £
(01926-499307; 20 Castle St; snacks from £3; 10am-6pm) Just an arrow's flight away from the castle, this tearoom is set in the former home of a local nobleman who became famous for his charitable works in the 16th century.

Information

Tourist office (01926-492212; www.warwick-uk.co.uk; Court House, Jury St; 9.30am-4.30pm Mon-Fri, from 10am Sat, 10am-3.30pm Sun) Found near the junction with Castle St, the tourist office sells the informative *Warwick Town Trail* leaflet (45p).

Getting There & Away

National Express coaches operate from Puckerings Lane. Stagecoach X17 runs to Coventry (1¼ hours, every 15 minutes Monday to Saturday), via Kenilworth (30 minutes). Stagecoach bus 16 goes to Stratford-upon-Avon (40 minutes, hourly) in one direction, and Coventry in the other. The main bus stops are on Market St.

Trains run to Birmingham (£7.40, 45 minutes, half-hourly), Stratford-upon-Avon (£5.20, 30 minutes, hourly) and London (£30, 1¾ hours, every 20 minutes), from the station northeast of the centre.

Around Warwick

LEAMINGTON SPA

Trading on the alleged healing qualities of its natural mineral waters, this pretty spa town is almost a suburb of Warwick, 2 miles to the east. As well as being a favourite destination for Victorian health tourists, the town was also the birthplace of lawn tennis, invented here in 1872 by tweaking the rules of rackets (the forerunner to squash) so it could be played outdoors on the croquet lawn. Cucumber sandwiches, anyone?

Today, the **Royal Pump Rooms** (01926-742700; www.warwickdc.gov.uk/royalpumprooms; admission free; 10.30am-5pm Tue, Wed, Fri & Sat, 1.30-8pm Thu, 11am-4pm Sun) contains tearooms, a small gallery and a diverting museum on the history of the spa. To get here, jump on bus X17 from Warwick (five minutes, every 15 minutes Monday to Saturday).

BADDESLEY CLINTON

Boasting Elizabethan interiors that have barely changed since the 17th century, **Baddesley Clinton** (NT; 01564-783294; adult/child £8.40/4.20, grounds only £4.20/2.10; 11am-5pm Mar-Oct, Wed-Sun low season) is a beguiling medieval moated house. It was a haven for persecuted Catholics in the 16th century, as demonstrated by the three cramped priest-holes. Some of these men of the cloth had other reasons to hide – in the 15th-century, the parish priest was murdered by the owner of Baddesley Clinton after being caught taking liberties with the lady of the house.

Baddesley Clinton is 7.5 miles northwest of Warwick, just off the A4141. It is a pleasant 2-mile walk from Lapworth train station, served by hourly trains from Warwick (15 minutes) and Birmingham (30 minutes).

Kenilworth

POP 23,219

It's well worth deviating from the A46 between Warwick and Coventry to visit the spine-tinglingly atmospheric ruins of Kenilworth Castle. A refreshing counterpoint to the commercialism of Warwick's royal ruin, the castle was the inspiration for Walter Scott's *Kenilworth,* and it still feels pretty inspiring today.

Sights & Activities

Kenilworth Castle CASTLE

(EH; 01926-852078; adult/child £7.60/3.80; 10am-5pm Mar-Oct, to 4pm Nov-Feb) This wonderful ruin sprawls among fields and hedges on the outskirts of Kenilworth. Built in the 1120s, the castle survived the longest siege in English history in 1266, when the forces of Lord Edward (later Edward I) threw themselves at the moat and battlements for six solid months. The fortress was dramatically extended in Tudor times, but it fell in the English Civil War and its walls were breached and water defences drained.

The excellent audio guide will tell you all about the relationship between former owner Robert Dudley and the 'Virgin Queen', who was wined and dined here at tremendous expense, almost bankrupting the castle. The magnificent Elizabethan gardens were restored in 2009.

Stoneleigh Abbey STATELY HOME

(01926-858535; www.stoneleighabbey.org; adult/child £7/3; tours 11am, 1pm & 3pm Tue-Thu & Sun Easter-Oct) The kind of stately home that makes movie directors go weak at the knees, this 850-year-old country house has hosted some celebrities in its time, from Charles I to Jane Austen. The original abbey was founded by Cistercian monks in 1154, but the house was massively expanded by the wealthy Leigh family (distant cousins of the Austens) in the 16th century. The splendid Palladian west wing, completed in 1726, contains richly detailed plasterwork ceilings and wood-panelled rooms, and the landscaped grounds are fine picnic territory. Stoneleigh is 2 miles east of Kenilworth, off the B4115.

Sleeping & Eating

As well as the following choices, there are numerous pubs and eateries along the High St (just north of the castle) and Warwick Rd (just south).

Loweridge Guest House B&B ££

(01926-859522; www.loweridgeguesthouse.co.uk; Hawkesworth Dr; s/d from £75/90; P @) This handsome Victorian house has a grand staircase and elegant guest lounge straight out of *Country Life* magazine. There are four huge rooms with swish, modern bathrooms, and three have their own private sun-trap patio. The guesthouse is a short walk northeast from the High St, off Coventry road.

Castle Laurels Hotel B&B ££

(01926-856179; www.castlelaurels.co.uk; 22 Castle Rd; s/d £45/60; P @) A stately guesthouse opposite the castle, where the owners pride themselves on the spotless rooms and the warmth of the welcome. The home-cooked breakfasts (with free-range eggs) are lovely.

Clarendon Arms PUB £

(01926-852017; www.clarendonarmspub.co.uk; 44 Castle Hill; mains £8-13) Almost opposite the castle, this bright and homely alehouse has home-cooked food, a warm ambience and a cosy little beer garden.

Information

For tourist information, browse the brochures at the town **library** (☎01926-852595; 11 Smalley Pl; ⊙9am-7pm Mon & Thu, to 5.30pm Tue & Fri, 10.30am-5.30pm Wed, 9.30am-4pm Sat).

Getting There & Away

From Monday to Saturday, bus X17 runs every 15 minutes from Coventry to Kenilworth (25 minutes) and on to Leamington Spa (from Kenilworth, 15 minutes) and Warwick (20 minutes). On Sunday, take bus U17 (half-hourly) for Coventry or bus 18A (hourly) for Warwick.

Stratford-upon-Avon

POP 22,187

It's hard to believe that one man could spark so much interest – and so much merchandise – as Stratford's most famous son. The author of some of the most quoted lines ever written in the English language, William Shakespeare was born in Stratford in 1564 and died here in 1616, and the five houses linked to his life form the centrepiece of a tourist attraction that verges on a cult of personality.

Experiences in this unmistakably Tudor town range from the touristy (medieval recreations and Bard-themed tearooms) to the humbling (Shakespeare's modest grave in Holy Trinity Church) and the sublime (taking in a play by the world famous Royal Shakespeare Company). Nevertheless, if you can leave without buying at least a Shakespeare novelty pencil, you'll have resisted one of the most keenly honed marketing machines in the nation.

Sights & Activities

The Shakespeare Houses MUSEUMS

Five of the most important buildings associated with Shakespeare contain museums that form the core of the visitor experience at Stratford, run by the **Shakespeare Birthplace Trust** (☎01789-204016; www.shakespeare.org.uk; adult/child all five properties £19/12, three in-town houses £12.50/8; ⊙9am-5pm Apr-Oct, see website for low-season hrs). You can buy individual tickets, but it's more cost-effective to buy a combination ticket covering the three houses in town, or all five properties. Expect long queues throughout the summer.

Shakespeare's Birthplace

(Henley St) Start your Shakespeare tour at the house where the world's most famous playwright supposedly spent his childhood days. In fact, the jury is still out on whether this really was Shakespeare's birthplace, but devotees of the Bard have been dropping in since at least the 19th century, leaving their signatures scratched onto the windows. Set behind a modern facade, the house contains restored Tudor rooms, live presentations from famous Shakespearean characters, and an engaging exhibition on Stratford's favourite son.

Nash's House & New Place

(☎01789-292325; cnr Chapel St & Chapel Lane) When Shakespeare retired, he swapped the bright lights of London for a comfortable town house at New Pl, where he died of unknown causes in April 1616. The house was demolished in 1759, but an attractive Elizabethan **knot garden** occupies part of the grounds. Archaeologists are digging beneath the plot in search of Shakespearean treasures – see www.digforshakespeare.com for the latest finds.

Displays in the adjacent **Nash's House**, where Shakespeare's granddaughter Elizabeth lived, describe the town's history, and there's a collection of 17th-century furniture and tapestries.

Hall's Croft

(☎01789-292107; Old Town) Shakespeare's daughter Susanna married respected doctor John Hall, and their fine Elizabethan town house is south of the centre on the way to Holy Trinity Church. Deviating from the main Shakespearean theme, the exhibition offers fascinating insights into medicine in the 16th century.

Anne Hathaway's Cottage

(☎01789-292100; Cottage La, Shottery) Before marrying Shakespeare, Anne Hathaway lived in Shottery, a mile west of the centre, in this pretty thatched farmhouse. As well as period furniture, there's an orchard and arboretum, with examples of all the trees mentioned in Shakespeare's plays. A footpath (no bikes allowed) leads to Shottery from Evesham Pl.

Mary Arden's Farm

(☎01789-293455; Station Rd, Wilmcote) If you fancy going back even further, you can visit the childhood home of Shakespeare's mum at Wilmcote, 3 miles west of Stratford. Aimed firmly at families, the farm has

Stratford-upon-Avon

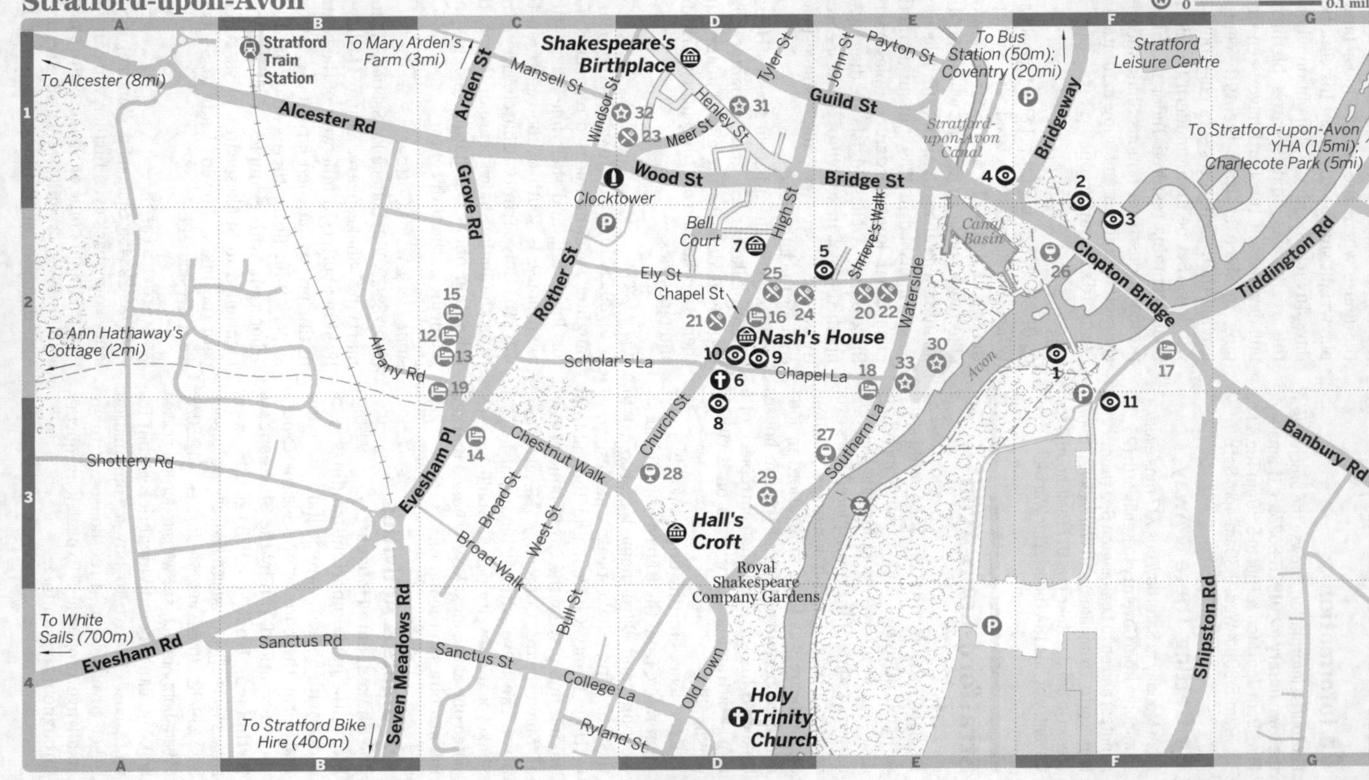

Stratford-upon-Avon

Top Sights
Hall's Croft ... D3
Holy Trinity Church ... D4
Nash's House ... D2
Shakespeare's Birthplace ... D1

Sights
1 Avon Boating River Cruises ... F2
2 Avon Boating River Cruises ... F1
3 Bancroft Cruisers ... F2
4 City Sightseeing Bus Tours ... E1
5 Falstaff's Experience ... E2
6 Guild Chapel ... D2
7 Harvard House ... D2
8 King Edward VI School ... D3
9 Knot Garden ... D2
10 New Place ... D2
11 Stratford-upon-Avon Butterfly Farm ... F3

Sleeping
12 Ambleside Guest House ... C2
13 Ashgrove Guest House ... C2
14 Broadlands Guest House ... C3
15 Salamander Guest House ... C2
16 Shakespeare Hotel ... D2
17 Swan's Nest Hotel ... F2
18 Arden Hotel ... E2
19 Woodstock Guest House ... C2

Eating
20 Coconut Lagoon ... E2
21 Edward Moon's ... D2
22 Georgetown ... E2
23 Oscar's ... D1
24 Lambs ... D2
25 Vintner Wine Bar ... D2

Drinking
26 Cox's Yard ... F2
27 Dirty Duck (Black Swan) ... E3
28 Windmill Inn ... D3

Entertainment
29 Courtyard Theatre ... D3
30 Royal Shakespeare Theatre ... E2
31 Saint Club ... D1
32 Stratford Picture House ... D1
33 Swan Theatre ... E2

exhibits tracing country life over the centuries, with nature trails, falconry displays and a collection of rare-breed farm animals. You can get here on the City Sightseeing bus, or cycle via Anne Hathaway's Cottage, following the Stratford-upon-Avon Canal towpath.

Holy Trinity Church CHURCH
(☎01789-266316; www.stratford-upon-avon.org; Old Town; admission to church free, Shakespeare's grave adult/child £1.50/50p; ⏲8.30am-6pm Mon-Sat, 12.30-5pm Sun Apr-Sep, reduced low season hrs) The final resting place of the Bard is said to be the most visited parish church in England. Inside are handsome 16th- and 17th-century tombs (particularly in the Clopton Chapel), some fabulous carvings on the choir stalls and, of course, the grave of William Shakespeare, with its ominous epitaph: 'cvrst be he yt moves my bones'.

Other Sights
Tucked in beside the lavishly carved Garrick Inn pub, **Harvard House** (☎01789-204507; High St; adult/child £3.50/free, admission free with Shakespeare Houses ticket; ⏲call for current opening times) was home to the mother of John Harvard, who lent his name to Boston's Harvard University. It now houses a museum of British pewter. Opening hours are under review so call for details.

The **Stratford-upon-Avon Butterfly Farm** (☎01789-299288; www.butterflyfarm.co.uk; Swan's Nest Lane; adult/child £5.95/4.95; ⏲10am-6pm summer, 10am-dusk winter) is a large greenhouse with hundreds of species of exotic butterflies, plus giant scorpions and spiders for the shudder factor.

Set in an old timbered building, **Falstaff's Experience** (☎01789-298070; www.falstaffsexperience.co.uk; 40 Sheep St; adult/child £4.80/1.30; ⏲10.30am-5.30pm) offers a ghost-train take on Shakespeare's tales, with olde-worlde walk-throughs, mannequins of Tudor celebs and live actors hamming it up like Olivier. Night-time ghost tours (adults only) are led by famous mediums.

Also at this end of town is the **Guild Chapel** (cnr Chapel Lane & Church St), founded in 1269 and painted with motivational frescoes showing the fate of the damned in the 15th century. It's only open to the public for services (10am Wednesday and noon on the first Saturday of the month, April to September).

Next door is **King Edward VI School**, which Shakespeare almost certainly

DON'T MISS

STRATFORD LITERARY FESTIVAL

Although Shakespeare is the biggest show in town, the top event on the cultural calendar is the **Stratford Literary Festival** (☎01789-207100; www.stratfordliteraryfestival.co.uk) in April/May, which attracts literary big-hitters of the calibre of John Simpson and Jonathan Miller.

attended, housed in a vast timbered building that used to be the guildhall.

Tours

Popular and informative two-hour **guided town walks** (☎01789-292478; adult/child £5/2; ⏲11am Mon-Wed, 2pm Thu-Sun) depart from Waterside, opposite Sheep St, which is also the starting point for the spooky **Stratford Town Ghost Walk** (adult/child £6/3; ⏲7.30pm Mon, Thu, Fri & Sat).

Other options:

City Sightseeing BUS TOURS
(☎01789-412680; www.citysightseeing-stratford.com; adult/child £11.50/6; ⏲every 20min Apr-Sep, less frequently in low season) Open-top, hop-on/hop-off bus tours leave from the tourist office and go to each of the Shakespeare properties. Tickets are valid for 24 hours.

Avon Boating RIVER CRUISES
(☎01789-267073; www.avon-boating.co.uk; The Boathouse, Swan's Nest Lane; 30min river cruises adult/child £4.50/3) Runs river cruises that depart every 20 minutes from either side of the main bridge.

Bancroft Cruisers RIVER CRUISES
(☎01789-269669; www.bancroftcruisers.co.uk; 45min river cruises adult/child £5/3.50; ⏲daily departures Apr-Oct) These fun trips leave from the riverbank by the Holiday Inn, off Bridgeway.

Sleeping

B&Bs are plentiful, particularly along Grove Rd and Evesham Pl, but vacancies can be hard to find during the high season – the tourist office can help with bookings, for a fee.

Stratford-upon-Avon YHA HOSTEL £
(☎0845 371 9661; www.yha.org.uk; Hemmingford House, Alveston; dm from £16; P @) Set in a large, 200-year-old mansion 1.5 miles east of the town centre along Tiddington Rd, this superior hostel attracts travellers of all ages. There's a canteen, bar and kitchen, and buses 18 and 18a run here from Bridge St.

Shakespeare Hotel HOTEL £££
(☎01789-294997; www.mercure.com; Chapel St; s/d £135/150; P @) For the full Tudor inn experience, head to this atmospheric Mercure property in a timbered medieval charmer on the main street. As well as a perfect location, you get tasteful rooms – some with four-poster beds and wood panels – and a sense of history that's missing from the competition.

Arden Hotel HOTEL £££
(☎01789-298682; www.theardenhotelstratford.com; Waterside; r incl breakfast from £125; P @) Formerly the Thistle, this elegant property facing the Swan Theatre has been stylishly revamped, with a sleek brasserie and champagne bar, and rooms featuring designer fabrics and bathrooms full of polished stone.

White Sails B&B ££
☎01789-264326; www.white-sails.co.uk; 85 Evesham Rd; r from £95; P @ 📶) Plush fabrics, framed prints, brass bedsteads and shabby-chic tables and lamps set the scene at this gorgeous, intimate guesthouse. The four individually furnished rooms come with flatscreen TVs, climate control and glamorous bathrooms.

Swan's Nest Hotel HOTEL ££
(☎0844 879 9140; www.macdonaldhotels.co.uk/swansnest; Swan's Nest Lane; d incl breakfast from £82; P @) In a 17th-century red-brick house near the banks of the Avon, this hotel has airy rooms in shades of brown and cream, many overlooking the hotel gardens. Other perks include a wood-panelled pub, a bistro and a sun terrace.

Eating

Sheep St is clustered with upmarket eating options, mostly aimed at theatregoers (look out for good-value pre-theatre menus).

ASK A LOCAL

For local information, turn to the helpful Town Hosts, who stroll around Stratford in yellow jerseys helping confused tourists find their way to sights, hotels and restaurants.

STRATFORD BED & BREAKFASTS

Stratford is well-stocked with old-fashioned B&Bs, to the level that some streets are a continuous line of almost identical guesthouses, offering almost identical facilities at almost identical prices.

With so much choice, it pays to be selective – here are our top five beds (and breakfasts):

Ambleside Guest House (☎01789-297239; www.amblesideguesthouse.co.uk; 41 Grove Rd; s/d from £25/50; P @) Lovely, nonfrilly B&B, with spotless rooms, amiable, well-informed hosts and big organic breakfasts.

Ashgrove Guest House (☎01789-297278; www.ashgrovehousestratford.co.uk; 37 Grove Rd; s/d from £25/50; P) Tidy, airy rooms decked out in varying degrees of burgundy. Look for the wooden bear sculpture outside.

Broadlands Guest House (☎01789-299181; www.broadlandsguesthouse.co.uk; 23 Evesham Pl; s/d from £48/80; P) Prim and blue, with classic English B&B rooms and filling breakfasts served in a pretty breakfast room.

Salamander Guest House (☎01789-205728; www.salamanderguesthouse.co.uk; 40 Grove Rd; s/d incl breakfast from £20/40; P @ wi-fi) Comfortable and homely, with the added appeal of wi-fi.

Woodstock Guest House (☎01789-299881; www.woodstock-house.co.uk; 30 Grove Rd; s/d from £30/55; P) Agreeable flowery rooms, soft carpets and a warm welcome in a house with a tidy garden and gravel drive.

Lambs MODERN EUROPEAN ££
(☎01789-292554; www.lambsrestaurant.co.uk; 12 Sheep St; mains £12-16; ⏰lunch Tue-Sun, dinner daily) The classiest joint in town – Lambs skips the Shakespeare chintz in favour of Venetian blinds and modern elegance. The menu includes slow cooked lamb, Gressingham duck and the like, and the wine list is excellent.

Edward Moon's MODERN BRITISH ££
(☎01789-267069; www.edwardmoon.com/moonsrestaurant; 9 Chapel St; mains £10-15) Named after a famous travelling chef, who cooked up the flavours of home for the British colonial service, this snug eatery serves delicious, hearty English dishes, many livened up with herbs and spices from the East.

Vintner Wine Bar MODERN BRITISH ££
(☎01789-297259; www.the-vintner.co.uk; 5 Sheep St; mains £10-20; ⏰breakfast, lunch & dinner) Set in a town house from 1600, this quirky place is full of beams, exposed brickwork, and low ceilings on which to bang your head. Locals as well as out-of-towners come here for good food (mostly steaks, salads and roasts) and lively conversation.

Other recommendations:

Oscar's CAFE £
(13/14 Meer St; sandwiches & lunches £4-7; ⏰11.30am-late) A casual cafe serving appetising breakfasts, lunches and afternoon teas; it turns into a bar after hours.

Georgetown MALAYSIAN ££
(☎01789-204445; www.georgetownrestaurants.co.uk; 23 Sheep St; mains £12-26) This classy Malaysian restaurant serves classic Straits cuisine at tables with starched white linen and wicker chairs.

Coconut Lagoon INDIAN ££
(☎01789-293546; www.coconutlagoon.com; 21 Sheep St; mains £10-14) Breaking away from the usual Indian standards, this swish eatery draws in influences from as far afield as Kerala and Hyderabad.

Drinking

Dirty Duck PUB
(Waterside) Officially called the 'Black Swan', this enchanting riverside alehouse is a favourite thespian watering hole, and has a roll-call of former regulars (Olivier, Attenborough etc) that reads like an actors' *Who's Who*. Just be sure not to mention Macbeth...

Windmill Inn PUB
(Church St) Ale was flowing here at the same time as rhyming couplets flowed from Shakespeare's quill – this pub has been around a while. Despite its age it's still one of the liveliest places in town, and slightly removed from the tourist hubbub.

Cox's Yard PUB

(www.coxsyard.co.uk; Bridgefoot; ⏲10am-late) Set in a converted factory, complete with chimney stack, this tourist-oriented riverside complex has a pub, cafe and music venue. It's a bit commercial, but kids are welcome and the riverside setting is dreamy.

☆ Entertainment

Royal Shakespeare Company THEATRE

(RSC; ☎0844 800 1110; www.rsc.org.uk; tickets £8-38) Coming to Stratford without seeing a production of Shakespeare would be like going to Rome and not visiting the Vatican. The three theatre spaces run by the world-renowned Royal Shakespeare Company have witnessed performances by such legends as Lawrence Olivier, Richard Burton, Judi Dench, Helen Mirren, Ian McKellan, Patrick Stewart (of Star Trek fame) and former Dr Who, David Tennant.

There are three grand stages in Stratford – **Royal Shakespeare Theatre** and **Swan Theatre** on Waterside and the **Courtyard Theatre** on Southern La. The first two properties were extensively redeveloped between 2007 and 2010 – contact the RSC for the latest news on performance times at the three venues. There are often special deals for under 25-year-olds, students and seniors and a few tickets are held back for sale on the day of the performance, but eager backpackers tend to snap these up fast. Wise theatregoers book well ahead.

Stratford Picture House CINEMA

(www.picturehouses.co.uk; Windsor St) This cinema, tucked away just off the main drag, shows Hollywood blockbusters as well as art-house films.

Saint Club CLUB

(www.worshipsaint.com; 4-5 Henley St; ⏲events Mon, Fri & Sat) Another night of Shakespeare is pretty low on the list of must-dos for young folk in Stratford – instead, they bop to '80s classics and mainstream dance at this nightclub on the main street.

Information

Cyber Junction (www.thecyberjunction.co.uk; 28 Greenhill St; per 30min £2; ⏲10.30am-8pm Mon-Fri, to 5.30pm Sat)

Tourist office (☎0870 160 7930; www.shakespeare-country.co.uk; Bridgefoot; ⏲call for opening times) Under refurbishment at the time of writing, but due to re-open on same site.

> ### STEAMING TO BIRMINGHAM
>
> Offering a chance to relive the golden age of rail travel, the **Shakespeare Express steam train** (☎0121-708 4960; www.shakespeareexpress.com; one-way adult/child £10/5) runs twice every Sunday in July and August between Stratford and Birmingham Snow Hill.

Getting There & Away

If you drive to Stratford, be warned that town car parks charge high fees, 24 hours a day. From Stratford train station, London Midland runs to Birmingham (£6.30, one hour, hourly) and Chiltern Railways runs to London Marylebone (£49.50, 2¼ hours, four daily).

National Express coaches and other bus companies run from Stratford's Riverside bus station (behind the Stratford Leisure Centre on Bridgeway). Destinations served:

Birmingham National Express, £7.70, one hour, twice daily

London Victoria National Express, £17.10, three to four hours, five daily

Moreton-in-Marsh Bus 21/22, one hour, hourly

Oxford National Express, £9.90, one hour, twice daily

Warwick Bus 16, 40 minutes, hourly

Getting Around

Bicycle

A bicycle is handy for getting out to the outlying Shakespeare properties, and **Stratford Bike Hire** (☎07711-776340; www.stratfordbikehire.com; 7 Seven Meadows Rd; per half-/full-day from £7/13) will deliver to your accommodation.

Boat

Punts, canoes and rowing boats are available for hire from **Avon Boating** (☎01789-267073; www.avon-boating.co.uk; The Boathouse, Swan's Nest Lane) near Clopton Bridge.

Around Stratford-upon-Avon

CHARLECOTE PARK

A youthful Shakespeare is said to have poached deer in the grounds of **Charlecote Park** (NT; ☎01789-470277; Wellesbourne; adult/child £8.15/4.05; ⏲noon-5pm Fri-Tue Mar-Oct, noon-4pm Sat & Sun Dec), a lavish Elizabethan pile which backs onto the River

Avon. Fallow deer still roam the grounds today, and the interiors were restored from Georgian chintz to Tudor splendour in 1823. Highlights include culinary-mould-filled Victorian kitchens and an original Tudor gatehouse, unaltered since 1551. Charlecote is around 5 miles east of Stratford-upon-Avon. Bus 18 (18A on Sunday) runs to Charlecote hourly from Stratford (30 minutes), continuing to Leamington Spa (30 minutes).

RAGLEY HALL

In a region crammed with stately homes, **Ragley Hall** (☎01789-762090; www.ragleyhall.com; adult/child £8.50/5; ⏱house noon-4pm, grounds 10am-6pm Sat & Sun Feb-Oct) stands out as a testament to the extravagance of inherited wealth. The family home of the Marquess and Marchioness of Hertford, this grand Palladian mansion was built between 1679 and 1683, and it features some truly opulent interior design, from the scarlet damask walls of the Red Saloon, to the astonishing *trompe l'oeil* murals in the South Staircase, showing the temptation of Christ in a garden full of toucans and marmosets. Youngsters can run wild in the attached **adventure playground**.

The house and grounds are open most weekends plus additional weekdays in summer – see the website for details. The mansion is about 10 miles west of Stratford-upon-Avon, easily accessible by taxi. With your own vehicle, follow the A46 and look for the signs.

COMPTON VERNEY

The once-decrepit 18th-century mansion of **Compton Verney** (☎01926-645500; www.comptonverney.org.uk, adult/child £8/2; ⏱11am-5pm Tue-Sun mid-Mar–mid-Dec) opened to the public in 2004 after a multimillion-pound overhaul. It now houses a grand art gallery, with an impressive collection of British folk art, Neapolitan masterpieces, Germanic medieval art, and Chinese bronzes, as well as visiting exhibitions. If it gets too packed, retreat to the lovely grounds, landscaped by Lancelot 'Capability' Brown. Bus 269 runs directly here from Stratford-upon-Avon (except on Sunday). You can also reach Compton Verney on the **City Sight-Seeing bus** (adult/child £9.50/5; half-hourly; May–October) known as the 'Heart of Warwickshire' from Stratford.

STAFFORDSHIRE

Despite being wedged between the ever-expanding conurbations of Birmingham and Manchester, Staffordshire is surprisingly green and pleasant, and the northern half of the county rises to meet the rugged hills of the Peak District. Highlights of this under-explored neck of the woods include cathedral-crowned Lichfield, the famous theme parks at Drayton Manor and Alton Towers, and the outstanding walking country around Cannock Chase and the Roaches.

ℹ Information

Staffordshire Tourism (www.enjoystaffordshire.co.uk)

ℹ Getting There & Around

Regular trains and National Express buses serve Stafford and other major towns. The main local bus operator is **First Group** (☎0870 850 0868; www.firstgroup.com). For details of services, browse the public transport pages at www.staffordshire.gov.uk/transport.

Stafford

POP 63,681

The capital of Staffordshire is a quiet little place that seems somewhat overshadowed by Lichfield and other towns around the county. The main shopping street has some handsome Georgian and medieval buildings, but little evidence remains that this was once the capital of the Anglo-Saxon kingdom of Mercia. For local info, drop into the **tourist office** (☎01785-619619; www.visitstafford.org; Eastgate St; ⏱9.30am-5pm Mon-Fri, 10am-4pm Sat) at the Stafford Gatehouse Theatre.

Surrounded by high-street shops, the **Ancient High House** (☎01785-619131; Greengate St; admission free; ⏱10am-4pm Tue-Sat) is the largest timber-framed town house in the country, artistically assembled in 1595. Creaking stairways lead to carefully restored rooms, and to displays on the history of the town and medieval construction techniques.

The hilltop remains of **Stafford Castle** (☎01785-257698; Newport Rd; admission free; ⏱visitor centre 11am-4pm Wed-Sun Apr-Oct, 11am-4pm Sat & Sun Nov-Mar), a classic Norman moat and bailey, sit romantically in a forest glade about 1 mile southwest of town, just off the A518.

Buses X1 and 101 run between Stafford and Hanley (Stoke-on-Trent; £6.90, 1¼ hours, hourly). Trains run to Birmingham (£8.70,

40 minutes, every 20 minutes), Manchester (£17.40, one hour, every 30 minutes) and London Euston (£48.90, 1½ hours, hourly).

Around Stafford

On the edge of Cannock Chase, the regal, neoclassical mansion of **Shugborough** (☎01889-881388; www.shugborough.org.uk; adult/child £12/7, parking £3; ⏲11am-5pm Tue-Sun Mar-Oct) is the ancestral home of renowned royal photographer Lord Lichfield and, accordingly, a good proportion of the wall space is devoted to his work. Unless you're an ardent monarchist, a more compelling reason to visit is the collection of exquisite Louis XV and XVI furniture in the state rooms. Kids may get more out of the grounds, where costumed actors demonstrate what life was like for landowners and the hoi polloi in the 19th century.

Shugborough is 6 miles east of Stafford on the A513; bus 825 from Stafford to Lichfield runs nearby (20 minutes, half-hourly Monday to Saturday).

Lichfield

POP 27,900

Even without its magnificent Gothic cathedral (one of the most spectacular in the country) this quaintly cobbled market town would be worth a visit to tread in the footsteps of lexicographer and wit Samuel Johnson, and natural philosopher Erasmus Darwin, grandfather of Charles. Johnson once described Lichfield folk as 'the most sober, decent people in England,' which was rather generous considering that this was the last place in the country to stop burning people at the stake!

Sights & Activities

Lichfield Cathedral CATHEDRAL

(☎01543-306100; donation requested; ⏲7.30am-6.15pm, to 5pm Sun low season) Crowned by three dramatic towers, Lichfield Cathedral is a stunning Gothic fantasy, constructed in stages from 1200 to 1350. The enormous vaulted nave is set slightly off line from the choir, creating a bizarre perspective when viewed from the west door, and carvings inside the cathedral still bear signs of damage caused by soldiers sharpening their swords during the English Civil War.

In the octagonal Chapter House, you can view the illuminated *Chad Gospels,* created around AD730, and an ornate Anglo-Saxon bas-relief known as the Lichfield Angel. The Lady Chapel features 16th-century Flemish stained glass, and along the north and south aisles are memorials to generations of Lichfield bishops.

For all its grandeur, the interior is nothing compared to the grand west facade, which positively bows under the weight of 113 statues of bishops, saints and kings of England. Before you move on, take a stroll around tranquil **Cathedral Close**, which is ringed with imposing 17th- and 18th-century houses.

Erasmus Darwin House MUSEUM

(☎01543-306260; www.erasmusdarwin.org; Beacon St; adult/child £3/1; ⏲noon-5pm Tue-Sun, last admission 4.15pm) After turning down the job of royal physician to King George III – perhaps a lucky escape, considering the monarch's descent into madness – Erasmus Darwin became a leading light in the Lunar Society, debating the origins of life with such luminaries as Wedgwood, Boulton and Watt, decades before his grandson Charles came up with the theory of evolution. His former house contains some intriguing personal effects, and at the back is a fragrant herb garden leading to Cathedral Close.

FREE **Samuel Johnson Birthplace Museum** MUSEUM

(☎01543-264972; www.samueljohnsonbirthplace.org.uk; Breadmarket St; ⏲10.30am-4.30pm Apr-Sep, 11am-3.30pm Oct-Mar) A short walk south of Erasmus Darwin House, this small but absorbing museum charts the life of the pioneering lexicographer Samuel Johnson, who moved to London from his native Lichfield and devoted nine years to producing the first dictionary of the English language. Johnson was later immortalised in James Boswell's famous biography *The Life of Samuel Johnson*.

Lichfield Heritage Centre HERITAGE CENTRE

(☎01543-256611; www.lichfieldheritage.org.uk; Market Sq; adult/child £3.50/1; ⏲9.30am-4pm Mon-Sat, from 10am Sun) A nicely presented series of exhibits covering 1300 years of Lichfield history, set in the old St Mary's Church. Climb the **tower** (adult/child £2.75/1.25) for sweeping city views.

Sleeping

No 8 The Close B&B ££

(☎01543-418483; www.ldb.co.uk/accommodation.htm; 8 The Close; s/d from £38/58) Right on

WORTH A TRIP

CANNOCK CHASE

Designated as an Area of Outstanding Natural Beauty, Cannock Chase is a pretty swath of natural forest, managed conifer plantations and heathland, home to wild deer and rare birdlife. It's a popular destination for walkers and mountain bikers, who are lured here by a series of rugged cross-country circuits. Quality mountain bikes (from £30 per day) can be rented from the bike-hire depot at **Birches Valley Forest Centre** (01889-586593; www.visitcanncockchase.co.uk; 10am-sunset Mon-Fri, from 9am Sat & Sun) off the A51 near Rugeley. Buses run from Stafford to Rugeley but you need your own transport to reach the visitor centre.

Cathedral Close (so, in a prime location), this family-run B&B is set in a listed 19th-century town house. There are three comfortable rooms; book in advance.

George Hotel HOTEL ££
(01543-414822; www.thegeorgelichfield.co.uk; 12-14 Bird St; r from £80; P @) Now part of the Best Western chain, this old Georgian pub has been upgraded into a comfortable midrange hotel, but it scores points for location rather than atmosphere.

Eating & Drinking

Chandlers' Grande Brasserie MODERN EUROPEAN ££
(01543-416688; Bore St; mains £10-23; closed lunch Sun) Set in the old Corn Exchange and decked out with natural wood and polished brass, this is where locals go for a big night out, as much for the ambience as for the Mediterranean-inspired main courses.

Ma Ma Thai THAI ££
(01543-411911; 7 Bird St; mains £7.50-15; lunch Tue-Sat, dinner Mon-Sat) A glamorous new arrival, this posh Thai eatery is decked out with violet upholstery and murals from the doors of Thai monasteries. Food perfectly complements the elegant surroundings.

Chapters Cathedral Coffee Shop CAFE £
(01543-306125; 19 The Close; sandwiches & salads £3-6; breakfast & lunch) A charming 18th-century house with a view onto a 13th-century walled garden, serving morning and afternoon tea and Sunday lunches.

Information

The **tourist office** (01543-412112; www.visitlichfield.com; Lichfield Garrick, Castle Dyke; 9am-5pm Mon-Sat) doubles as the box office for the Lichfield Garrick theatre.

Getting There & Away

The bus station is opposite the main train station on Birmingham Rd. Bus 112 runs to Birmingham (1¼ hours, hourly), while the 825 serves Stafford (1¼ hours, hourly).

Lichfield has two stations. Trains to Birmingham (40 minutes, every 20 minutes) leave from Lichfield City station in the centre. To reach London Euston (£36.50, 2¼ hours), travel from Lichfield Trent Valley station to Rugby and change.

Stoke-on-Trent

POP 240,636

At the heart of the Potteries – the famous pottery-producing region of Staffordshire –Stoke-on-Trent is famed for its ceramics, but don't expect cute little artisanal producers. This was where pottery shifted to mass production during the Industrial Revolution, and Stoke is a sprawl of industrial townships tied together by flyovers and bypasses. There are dozens of active potteries that you can visit, including the famous Wedgwood factory, but the town museum presents a good overview for less-ceramic-obsessed visitors. Hanley is the official 'city centre' with the main bus station, surrounded by the suburbs of Tunstall, Burslem, Fenton, Longton and Stoke (with the train station).

Sights & Activities

Wedgwood Visitor Centre POTTERY
(0870 606 1759; www.wedgwoodvisitorcentre.com; Barlaston; adult/child £9.50/7; 9am-5pm Mon-Fri, 10am-5pm Sat & Sun) Set in attractive parkland, the modern production centre for Josiah Wedgwood's porcelain empire displays an extensive collection of historic pieces, including plenty of Wedgwood's delicate, neo-classical blue-and-white jasperware. You can observe the fascinating industrial process and there's an interesting film on

POTTERY IN THE POTTERIES

Stoke-on-Trent lies at the hub of England's ceramic heartland, thanks to the pioneering work of the famous Wedgwood pottery, established by Josiah Wedgwood in 1759. A founding member of the Lunar Society, Wedgwood was one of the great creative thinkers of his age, inventing new industrial techniques and machines, funding the construction of canals and factories, campaigning for the abolition of slavery, and devising such marketing mainstays as the money-back guarantee and buy-one-get-one-free offers.

The Wedgwood factory moved from its original location in 1950, but the visitor centre (p527) still offers a fascinating insight into porcelain production techniques. The tourist office in Stoke-on-Trent has leaflets on other historic potteries that are open to the public.

Top picks:

Gladstone Pottery Museum (01782-237777; stoke.gov.uk/museum; Uttoxeter Rd, Longton; adult/child £5.95/4.50; 10am-5pm) One of the more traditional potteries; an atmospheric sprawl of brick buildings and bottle kilns, with an unusual display on ceramic toilets.

Dudson Museum (01782-285286; www.dudson.com; Hope St, Hanley; admission free; 10am-3pm Mon-Fri) Set inside one of the aptly-named bottle kilns, with displays on all the famous styles of Stoke porcelain.

Moorcroft Heritage Visitor Centre (01782-207943; www.moorcroft.com; Sandbach Rd, Burslem; tours adult/child £4.50/2.50; 10am-5pm Mon-Fri, 9.30am-4.30pm Sat) Looking like a giant milk-bottle holder, this historic factory offers tours at 11am and 2pm (11am only on Friday).

Josiah's life, and his work in the fields of pottery, canal-building and the abolishment of slavery.

FREE **Potteries Museum & Art Gallery** MUSEUM
(01782-232323; Bethesda St, Hanley; 10am-5pm Mon-Sat & 1-2pm Sun Nov-Feb) This museum houses an extensive ceramics display, from Toby jugs and jasperware to outrageous ornamental pieces like the Minton Peacock. You can also see treasures from the Staffordshire hoard, displays on the Spitfire fighter plane (created by the Stoke-born aviator Reginald Mitchell) and artworks by TS Lowry and Sir Henry Moore.

Sleeping & Eating

Hanley is well-stocked with chain eateries and pubs.

Verdon Guest House B&B £
(01782-264244; www.verdonguesthouse.co.uk; 44 Charles St, Hanley; s/d from £26/40; P @) Set in an unlovely area but central and lovingly kept, this B&B offers comfy rooms a few short steps from the bus station.

Victoria on the Square PUB £
(www.victoriaonthesquare.co.uk; Victoria Sq, Hanley; mains £6-13) Part pub, part cabaret, this reliable local serves decent steaks and other pub staples. It's a popular venue for speed-dating so watch whose eye you catch!

Information

Tourist office (01782-236000; www.visitstoke.co.uk; Victoria Hall, Bagnall St, Hanley; 9am-5pm Mon-Fri, 10am-2pm Sat) Ask for a map with the locations of the various potteries.

Getting There & Away

From Stoke-on-Trent station in Stoke, trains run to Stafford (20 minutes, half-hourly) and London (£53.50, 1½ hours, two hourly). The Hanley bus station is on Lichfield St:

Alton Towers Bus 32A, one hour, every two hours

London National Express, £23.80, four hours, seven daily

Manchester National Express, £6.50, 1½ hours, eight daily

Stafford First Bus 101, 1¼ hours, hourly

Around Stoke-on-Trent

LITTLE MORETON HALL

About 10 miles north of Stoke-on-Trent, wonderfully wonky **Little Moreton Hall** (NT; 01260-272018; adult/child £6.40/3.20; 11am-5pm Wed-Sun late Mar-Oct, weekends only Feb &

Nov-mid Dec) is a gem of medieval architecture. A stack of time-worn timbers, warped gables and leaded windows, dating back to the 16th-century, this moated mansion is a bona fide museum piece, with original frescoes and a charming knot garden. Little Moreton is off the A34 south of Congleton but you'll need your own transport to get here.

BIDDULPH GRANGE GARDENS

Assembled by Victorian horticulturalist James Bateman, the superbly landscaped **Biddulph Grange Gardens** (NT; ☎01782-517999; adult/child £6.35/3.15; ⏲11am-5pm Apr-Oct; reduced hours winter) present a botanical-world tour, including Chinese, Egyptian and Italian gardens and a huge bank of Himalayan rhododendrons that flower simultaneously in spring. The gardens are 7 miles north of Stoke; take bus 6A from Hanley bus station (40 minutes, every 20 minutes) and walk the last few hundred yards.

Leek

POP 18,768

Northeast of Stoke-on-Trent, the attractive market town of Leek is the gateway to the rugged Staffordshire Moorlands, which form part of the Peak District National Park. Topped by a line of gritstone crags known as the **Roaches**, this is prime walking and climbing country (see boxed text, p486) and the crags are home to curlews, peregrine falcons, buzzards and owls – and supposedly, a colony of wallabies who escaped from a private zoo in the 1940s.

The **tourist office** (☎01538-483741; tourism.services@staffsmoorlands.gov.uk; 1 Market Pl; ⏲9.30am-5pm Mon-Fri, 10am-4pm Sat) has loads of information on walks in the area, including the useful *The Roaches* and *Leek to Peak* booklets. Ask about shuttle buses to Alton Towers.

Sights & Activities

Leek was a major centre for the production of textiles during the Industrial Revolution, and there are several interesting sights in town. Almost across from the tourist office, the 14th-century **St Edward's Church** (☎01538-388134; Church St; ⏲10am-3pm) has a ruined Saxon cross and beautiful Pre-Raphaelite stained-glass windows by Arts and Crafts icon Edward Burne-Jones.

Walk down St Edward St and Compton to reach the squat, Victorian **All Saints Church** (☎01538-382588; Compton; ⏲9-11am Mon-Thu & Sat), which is decorated inside with winsome Pre-Raphaelite murals and more Edward Burne-Jones stained glass.

Downhill from St Edward's on the road to Macclesfield, historic **Brindley Mill** (www.brindleymill.net; Mill St; adult/child £2/1.50; ⏲2-5pm Mon-Wed mid-Jul–Aug, 2-5pm Sat & Sun Easter-Sep) was built in 1752, and its restored waterwheel still grinds flour for sale in Leek.

About 3 miles north of Leek at Tittesworth Water, **Peak Pursuits** (☎01782-722226; www.peakpursuits.co.uk; ⏲10am-7pm Mar-Nov) offers family-friendly outdoor activities like kayaking and rock climbing on the Roaches. It's off the A53 near Meerbrook.

Sleeping

Peak Weavers (☎01538-383729; www.peakweavershotel.co.uk; 21 King St; s/d incl breakfast from £35/85; P @) is a delightfully restored mill owner's mansion, decked out with ornamental tiles and other original Georgian features. Rooms are light and airy and there's a great restaurant.

Getting There & Away

Leek's bus station is on Haywood St. Services:

Alton Towers Bus 10/10A, 25 minutes, six daily

Ashbourne Bus 108, 40 minutes, six daily (no Sunday service)

WORTH A TRIP

PUGIN'S MASTERPIECE

About 11 miles from Stoke-on-Trent, the sleepy market town of Cheadle is worth a detour for the fabulous **St Giles Church** (☎01538-753130; www.stgilescatholicchurch.co.uk; 18 Charles St; ⏲8am-3pm), created by the Gothic-revivalist Augustus Welby Pugin (1812–52). Famous for adding the Gothic flourishes to London's Houses of Parliament, Pugin filled St Giles with extravagant gilded murals of angels and medieval motifs that cover every inch of the walls and ceiling. Visiting feels a bit like stepping into an illuminated manuscript. The church is a 10-minute walk south from Cheadle High St; buses 32 and 32a run to Cheadle every 20 minutes from the Hanley bus stand (30 minutes).

THEME PARK SHENANIGANS

Staffordshire is rightly famous for its theme parks, which resound with the screams of adrenaline junkies lured here by fast and furious thrill rides like Thirteen, the world's first vertical drop roller coaster. As with anywhere, the rattle-and-shake rides are bundled together with costume parades, gentle merry-go-rounds for youngsters, and lots of junk food, and the queues can be horrendous, particularly during school holidays. Buckle up, it's going to be a bumpy ride...

Alton Towers

The phenomenally popular **Alton Towers** (☎0870 444 4455; www.altontowers.com; adult/under 12yr £38/29; ⏲main hrs 10am-5.30pm, open later for school holidays, weekends & high season) offers maximum G-forces for your buck. Roller coaster fans are well catered for – as well as Thirteen, you can ride lying down, sitting down or suspended from the rails on the Nemesis, Oblivion, Air and Rita. Gentler thrills include log flumes, carousels, stage shows, a pirate-themed aquarium and a splashtastic water park (adult/child £14/10). For discounted entry fees, book online.

The attached resort has two hotels, but many people prefer to retreat from the action to one of the surrounding villages. The **Dimmingsdale YHA** (☎0845 371 9513; www.yha.org.uk; Oakamoor; dm from £14) is a miniature hostel 2 miles northwest of the park, set in pleasant walking country.

Alton Towers is east of Cheadle off the B5032. Most large towns in the area offer package coach tours (inquire at tourist offices), or you can ride the Alton Towers bus from Leek, Stoke-on-Trent, Uttoxeter, Nottingham and Derby (see the Alton Towers website for details).

Drayton Manor

Alton Towers' closest rival, **Drayton Manor** (☎0844 472 1950; www.draytonmanor.co.uk; adult/child £23/19; ⏲10.30am-5pm Easter-Oct, longer hrs May-Sep) has been serving up screams since 1949. Crowd-pleasers include the Apocalypse free-fall tower, voted Britain's scariest ride, and Shockwave, Europe's only stand-up roller-coaster. Younger kids will be just as thrilled by Thomas Land, dedicated to the animated steam-train character.

The park currently has no on-site accommodation, but Tamworth is just 2 miles away, with plenty of B&Bs and hotels – contact **Tamworth Tourist Information** (☎01827-709581; Market St) for recommendations. Drayton Manor is on the A4091, between junctions 9 and 10 of the M42. Package coach tours run from Birmingham, or you can take bus 110 from Birmingham Bull St to Fazeley (one hour, every 20 minutes), and walk the last 15 minutes.

Buxton Bus 118, 30 minutes, four daily (three on Sunday)

Hanley (Stoke-on-Trent) Bus 18/118, 45 minutes, every 20 minutes

WORCESTERSHIRE

Probably best known for its famous condiment, invented by two Worcester chemists in 1837, Worcestershire marks the transition from the industrial heart of the Midlands to the peaceful countryside of the Welsh Marches. The southern and western fringes of the county burst with lush countryside and sleepy market towns, while the capital is a classic English county town, whose magnificent cathedral inspired the composer Elgar to write some of his greatest works. Further south, the elegant Victorian resort of Great Malvern sits regally at the heart of the rumpled Malvern Hills, one of England's great 'edges' and a mecca for walkers.

Activities

The longest riverside walk in the UK, the 210-mile **Severn Way** (www.severnway.com) winds its way through Worcestershire en route from Plynlimon in Wales to the sea at Bristol. A shorter challenge is the 100-mile **Three Choirs Way**, linking Worcester to Hereford and Gloucester. The Malvern Hills are also prime country for walking, cycling and paragliding, though are no official cycling routes.

ℹ Information

Visit Worcestershire (www.visitworcestershire.org)

ℹ Getting Around

Worcester is a convenient rail hub, and Kidderminster is the southern railhead of the quaint Severn Valley Railway. Buses connect larger towns, but services to rural areas can be frustratingly infrequent – search the transport pages at www.worcestershire.gov.uk for bus companies and timetables.

Worcester

POP 94,029

Worcester – pronounced *woos*-ter, as in 'Jeeves and' – has enough historic treasures to forgive the architectural eyesores thrown up during the postwar love affair with all things concrete. The home of Lea & Perrins and that famous sauce (an unlikely combination of fermented tamarinds and anchovies), this ancient cathedral city was the site of the last battle of the Civil War. The defeated Charles II only narrowly escaped the pursuing Roundheads by hiding in an oak tree, an event still celebrated in Worcester every 29 May, when government buildings are decked out with oak sprigs.

Sights

Worcester Cathedral CATHEDRAL

(☎01905-732900; www.worcestercathedral.org.uk; suggested donation £5; ⏲7.30am-6pm) Rising above the River Severn, Worcester's majestic cathedral is best known as the final resting place of Magna Carta signatory King John, damned by history for attempting to seize the throne while his brother Richard the Lionheart was fighting in the Crusades. At least that's what the Robin Hood version of history would have you believe – the real King John was no worse than his father, Henry II, and certainly no worse than his brother Richard, who spoke little English, lived in France, and was responsible for massacres across England and the Middle East.

John's tomb is just one of many grand memorials dotted around the cathedral, from the ostentatious mausoleums of bishops and earls to the worn graves of forgotten Crusader knights. Beneath it all is an atmospheric Norman crypt, constructed in 1084 by St Wulfstan, the only Saxon bishop to hang on to his seat after the Norman invasion. Other highlights include a charming cloister and a 12th-century circular chapterhouse.

The strong-legged can tackle the 249 steps to the top of the **tower** (adult/child £4/2; ⏲11am-5pm Sat & school holidays Easter-Sep), where Charles II surveyed his troops during the disastrous Battle of Worcester. Hour-long **cathedral tours** (adult/child £3/free; ⏲11am & 2.30pm Mon-Sat Apr-Sep, Sat Oct-Mar) run from the gift shop. Composer Edward Elgar was a local lad, and several of his works had their first public outings at the cathedral – to appreciate the acoustics, come for **evensong**, (5.30pm Mon–Wed, Fri& Sat, 4pm Sun).

Commandery MUSEUM

(☎01905-361821; www.worcestercitymuseums.org.uk; College St; adult/child £5.40/2.30; ⏲10am-5pm Mon-Sat, 1.30-5pm Sun) The town's history museum is housed in a splendid Tudor building that served as King Charles II's headquarters during the battle of Worcester. Engaging audio guides and interactive exhibits tell the story of Worcester during key periods in its history. Be sure to visit the 'painted chamber', covered with intriguing 15th-century religious frescos.

Royal Worcester Porcelain Works MUSEUM

(☎01905-21247; www.worcesterporcelainmuseum.org.uk; Severn St; adult/concession £6/5; ⏲10am-5pm Mon-Sat Easter-Oct, 10.30am-4pm Tue-Sat low season) Up there with Crown Derby and Wedgwood, the Royal Worcester porcelain factory gained an edge over its rivals by picking up the contract to provide fine crockery to the English monarchy. Today, the crocks displayed in the museum on the site of the old Royal Worcester factory are worth staggering sums to collectors. An entertaining audio tour reveals some quirkier sides to the Royal Worcester story, including its brief foray into porcelain dentures and 'portable fonts' designed for cholera outbreaks.

Ancient Houses HISTORIC BUILDINGS

Saved in the nick of time by the National Trust, **Greyfriars** (NT; ☎01905-23571; Friar St; adult/child £4.15/2.05; ⏲1-5pm Wed-Sun Mar-Dec) offers the chance to poke around a timber-framed merchant's house from 1480. The house is full of atmospheric wood-panelled rooms and backed by a pretty walled garden.

A few doors down, the mid-16th-century **Tudor House** (☎01905-426402; www.tudorhouse.org.uk; ⏲10am-4pm Wed & Sat, plus 1-4pm Fri in summer) is wonderfully warped; inside is a heritage centre run by local volunteers.

Also peek into the flamboyant **Guildhall** (High St; admission free; ⏲8.30am-4.30pm Mon-Sat), created in 1722 by a pupil of Sir Christopher Wren who died in poverty while waiting for the city to pay him his dues.

Tours

Worcester Walks (☎01905-726331; www.worcesterwalks.co.uk; adult £4; ⊙11am Mon-Fri) Offers popular half-hour walking tours.

Worcester River Cruises (☎01905-611060; www.worcesterrivercruises.co.uk; adult/child £5/3; ⊙hourly 11am-5pm) Runs 45-minute cruises on the Severn.

Discover History Walking Tours (☎07949 222137; www.discover-history.co.uk; adult £5) Offers a variety of themed historic tours.

Sleeping

Diglis House Hotel HOTEL ££
(☎01905-353518; www.diglishousehotel.co.uk; Severn St; s/d from £75/95; P) This rambling Georgian house has an idyllic setting, right by the water, a short stroll from the cathedral. The best rooms have four posters, luxe bathrooms and river views.

Barrington House B&B ££
(☎01905-422965; www.barringtonhouse.eu; 204 Henwick Rd; r £80-90; P@) A lovely Georgian house by the river with wonderful views, a pretty walled garden, three plush bedrooms full of brocade and trim, and hearty breakfasts served with eggs from the owners' hens.

Ye Olde Talbot Hotel PUB/HOTEL ££
(☎01905-235730; www.oldenglishinns.co.uk; Friar St; mains s/d from £50/70) Attached to a popular bar and bistro right in the centre, this tasteful inn dates back to the 13th century, but many of the rooms are housed in a modern extension. Rooms have modern gadgets but period touches. Discounted parking is available nearby.

Eating

Phat Nancy's CAFE £
(☎01905-612658; www.phatnancys.co.uk; 16 New St; sandwiches from £3; ⊙9am-4pm Mon-Sat) A sandwich shop for the Facebook generation, Nancy's has a punk diner vibe and quirky sandwich fillings chalked up on the walls. It's takeaway only, and busy, busy at lunchtime.

Little Ginger Pig CAFE £
(☎01905-338913; www.littlegingerpig.co.uk; 9-11 Copenhagen St; dishes from £6; ⊙8am-3pm Mon-Wed, to 11pm Thu-Sat) The focus is on local produce and independent labels at this airy cafe. Locally sourced meats crop up in everything from the steak dinners to the lunchtime BLTs.

Glasshouse MODERN BRITISH ££
(☎01905-611120; www.theglasshouse.co.uk; Danesbury House, College St; mains £13-19, 2-/3-course set lunch £10-14; ⊙closed dinner Sun) Designer details abound at this magenta-hued restaurant near the Commandery. The Mediterranean-inspired food is as flawless as the decor, but staff are friendly and the mood is unpretentious.

Drinking & Entertainment

Cardinal's Hat PUB
(31 Friar St) Despite looking as English as Tudor ruffs, this atmospheric Worcester institution sells Austrian beers in traditional steins and serves authentic Austrian delicacies at lunchtime.

Marr's Bar LIVE MUSIC
(www.marrsbar.co.uk; 12 Pierpoint St; ⊙from 8pm) The best live-music venue for miles around, Marr's still has its original sprung dance floors from its days as a dance studio. You can bounce on them to your heart's content most nights, thanks to a lively schedule of gigs and shows.

Information

The **tourist office** (☎01905-726311; www.visitworcester.com; Guildhall, High St; ⊙9.30am-5pm Mon-Sat) has stacks of brochures.

Getting There & Around

Worcester Foregate is the main rail hub, but services also run from Worcester Shrub Hill. Regular trains run to London Paddington (£31, 2½ hours, twice hourly) and Hereford (£9.80, 50 minutes, hourly).

The bus station is inside the Crowngate Centre on Friary Walk. Services:

Birmingham Bus 144, 1¾ hours, every 20 minutes (hourly Sunday)

Great Malvern Bus 44, 30 minutes, twice hourly

London National Express, £21.10, four hours, two daily

Ledbury Bus 417, 50 minutes, five daily Mon–Sat

Upton-upon-Severn Bus 363, 30 minutes, hourly

Around Worcester

WITLEY COURT

One of the country's most romantic ruins, **Witley Court** (EH; ☎01299-896636; Great

WORTH A TRIP

ELGAR BIRTHPLACE MUSEUM

England's most popular classical composer is celebrated with appropriate pomp and circumstance at **Elgar Birthplace Museum** (☎01905-333224; www.elgarmuseum.org; Lower Broadheath; adult/child £7/3; ⊙11am-5pm, closed late-Dec–Jan), housed in the humble cottage where Edward Elgar was born in 1857. Admission includes an audio tour with musical interludes so that you can appreciate what all the fuss is about.

Next to the museum, **Oldbury Farm** (☎01905-421357; Lower Broadheath; s/d £35/55; P) has airy, country-style rooms, beautiful views and easy access to local walking routes. Buses 308 and 310 go from Worcester to Broadheath Common (15 minutes, three daily Monday to Saturday), a short walk from the museum.

Witley; adult/5-15yr/under 5yr £6/3/free; ⊙10am-5pm Mar-Oct, 10am-4pm Wed-Sun Nov-Feb) was a lavish Italianate mid-19th-century home until a devastating fire swept through the state rooms while the owner was away in 1937. Today, the house is an empty shell, but the 19th-century formal gardens and spectacular fountains have been brilliantly restored. Don't miss the gilded-plaster interior at the nearby **Great Witley Church** (www.greatwitleychurch.org.uk), the finest baroque church in England. It's home to paintings by Bellucci and a glorious organ once played by the composer Handel.

Bus 758 from Worcester to Tenbury Wells passes eight times daily (25 minutes).

HANBURY HALL

Close to the sleepy former spa town of Droitwich, about 10 miles northeast of Worcester, the early-18th-century mansion of **Hanbury Hall** (NT; ☎01527-821214; School Rd; adult/child £7.25/3.60; ⊙11am-5pm Sat-Thu Feb-Oct, also Thu summer, Sat & Sun only winter) offers a typical stately home experience with the added bonus of baroque murals and painted ceilings by Sir John Thornhill, who also decorated the cupola of St Paul's in London.

Buses 144 and 244 run from Worcester to Droitwich Spa (30 minutes, every 10 minutes Monday to Saturday), passing within a few miles of Hanbury Hall – or you can take a taxi.

KIDDERMINSTER

Divided from Birmingham's urban sprawl by open fields, Kidderminster was a busy carpet-weaving centre during the Industrial Revolution. However, the main reason to visit today is to jump aboard the **Severn Valley Railway** (☎01299-403816; www.svr.co.uk; ⊙daily May-Sep, weekends in low season), a restored steam loco that chugs and puffs along 32 miles of track between Kidderminster and Bridgnorth in Shropshire (p554). One-way/return tickets cost £15.50/11 (half-price for children) and the journey takes one hour.

Bus 192 runs between Birmingham and Kidderminster (one hour, hourly, every two hours Sunday); from Worcester, take bus 303 (40 minutes, hourly, take bus 300 Sunday).

Great Malvern

POP 35,558

Tumbling down the side of a forested ridge about 7 miles southwest of Worcester, the picturesque spa town of Great Malvern is the gateway to the Malverns, a soaring range of volcanic hills that rise unexpectedly from the surrounding meadows. In Victorian times, the medicinal waters were prescribed as a panacea for everything from gout to 'sore eyes' – should you wish to test the theory, you can sample Malvern water straight from the ground at a series of public wells dotted around the town. In June, classical musicians flock to town for the biannual **Elgar Festival** (www.elgar-festival.com). This festival celebrates the life and works of great English composer Edward Elgar, who lived nearby at Malvern Link.

Sights & Activities

Great Malvern Priory PRIORY

(☎01684-561020; www.greatmalvernpriory.org.uk; Church St; suggested donation £3; ⊙9am-5pm Apr-Oct, reduced hrs low season) The 11th-century Great Malvern Priory is packed with remarkable features, from original Norman pillars to surreal modernist stained glass. The choir is enclosed by a screen of 15th-century tiles and the monks' stalls are

WALKING IN THE MALVERN HILLS

The jack-in-the-box Malvern Hills, which dramatically pop up out of the Severn plains on the boundary between Worcestershire and Herefordshire, rise to the lofty peak of the Worcester Beacon (419m), reached by a steep 3-mile climb above Great Malvern. More than 100 miles of trails traipse over the various summits, which are mostly capped by exposed grassland, offering the kind of views that inspire orchestral movements. The tourist office has racks of pamphlets covering popular hikes, including a map of the mineral water springs, wells and fountains dotted around the town and the surrounding hills. The enthusiast-run website www.malverntrail.co.uk is also a goldmine of useful walking information.

decorated with delightfully irreverent 14th-century misericords, depicting everything from three rats hanging a cat to the mythological basilisk.

Malvern Museum of Local History MUSEUM
(☎01684-567811; Priory Gatehouse, Abbey Rd; adult/child £2/50p; ⊙10.30am-5pm Mar-Oct, except Wed during school terms) Straddling Abbey Rd in the grand Priory Gatehouse (from 1470), the town museum offers a thorough exploration of the things for which Great Malvern is renowned, including spring waters, medieval monasteries, the Malvern Hills and Morgan Motors.

FREE **Morgan Motor Company** MUSEUM
(☎01684-584580; www.morgan-motor.co.uk; Pickersleigh Rd, Malvern Link; museum admission free, tours £10; ⊙8.30am-5pm Mon-Thu) The Morgan Motor Company has been hand-crafting elegant and beautiful sports cars since 1909, and you can still see the mechanics at work on guided tours of the factory (pre-booking essential). The museum has a fine fleet of vintage classics. Bus 44 from Church St runs past the factory.

Tours

Walking tours (adult/child £3/1.50) leave from the tourist office at 10.30am Saturday and 2.30pm Sunday, exploring the town's medieval and Victorian history.

Sleeping

Bredon House HOTEL ££
(☎01684-566990; www.bredonhouse.co.uk; 34 Worcester Rd; s/d from £50/80; P @) A short saunter from the centre, this genteel family- and pet-friendly Victorian hotel backs onto a stunning vista. Rooms are decorated in a quirky but tasteful mix of new and old, and the books, magazines and family photographs dotted around the place make it feel like staying with family.

Como House B&B ££
(☎01684-561486; www.comohouse.co.uk; Como Rd; s/d £40/62; P @) This handsome Malvern-stone house benefits from a quiet location away from the central bustle. Rooms are snug, the garden is a delight and the mood is restoratively calm. The owners will pick you up from the station and drop you off by the walking trails.

Abbey Hotel HOTEL £££
(☎01684-892332; www.savora.co.uk; Abbey Rd; s/d from £130/140; P @) Cloaked by a crazy tangle of vines, like a Brother's Grimm fairy-tale castle, this stately property offers Great Malvern's grandest bedrooms, in a prime location by the museum and priory.

Eating

St Ann's Well Cafe CAFE £
(www.hillsarts.co.uk/stannswell; snacks from £4; ⊙10am-4pm daily Easter-Sep, Fri-Sun low season) A steep climb above St Ann's Rd, this quaint cafe is set in a handsome early-19th-century villa. You can wash back its cakes and vegetarian snacks with mountain-fresh spring water that bubbles into a carved basin by the door. Check the latest opening times with the tourist office before you start the climb.

Pepper and Oz MODERN EUROPEAN ££
(☎01684-562676; www.pepperandoz.co.uk; 23 Abbey Rd; mains £8-18.50; ⊙closed Sun & Mon) Wedged in beside the museum, this bijou brasserie has a lovely alfresco terrace and a superior wine list. The menu is full of locally sourced classics like smoked duck and Herefordshire steaks, with special promos for pre-theatre diners.

Anupam INDIAN ££
(☎01684-573814; www.anupam.co.uk; 85 Church St; mains £9-14) Hidden in an arcade just off the main road, this stylish place has a menu that roams the subcontinent, from hearty

Mughlai curries to Keralan treats such as tandoori kingfish.

Priors Croft MODERN BRITISH ££
(☎01684-891369; Grange Rd; mains £9-16) A grand folly opposite the theatre, offering quality pub-style food that you can eat inside or out in the sunny garden.

☆ Entertainment

Malvern Theatres THEATRE
(www.malvern-theatres.co.uk; Grange Rd) One of the country's best provincial theatres, this long-established cultural hub packs in a lively program of classical music, dance, comedy, drama and cinema. Several nearby restaurants offer good value pre-theatre menus.

Theatre of Small Convenience THEATRE
(www.wctheatre.co.uk; Edith Walk) This curious place is set in a converted Victorian public lavatory decked out with theatrical Italianate flourishes. With just 12 seats, and a program that runs from puppet shows to opera, it feels like something cooked up by Monty Python's Terry Gilliam.

Information

The **tourist office** (☎01684-892289; www.malvernhills.gov.uk; 21 Church St; ⏲10am-5pm) is a mine of walking and cycling information. The post office on the square has a bureau de change. The **library** (☎01684-566553; Graham Rd; ⏲9.30am-5.30pm Mon, Fri & Sat, to 8pm Tue-Thu) has free internet access.

Getting There & Around

The train station is east of the centre, off Ave Rd. Trains run to Hereford (£6.90, 35 minutes, hourly), Worcester (15 to 20 minutes, two or three hourly) and Ledbury (13 minutes, hourly).

National Express runs one bus daily to London (£21.70, 3½ hours). For Worcester (30 minutes, twice hourly), take bus 44 or 362/363 (the Malvern Link).

Upton-upon-Severn

POP 1789

A pretty little town with an eclectic mix of Tudor and Georgian buildings lining its meandering streets, Upton makes for a pleasant detour if you're travelling between Great Malvern and Ledbury. In June, Upton awakes from its slumbers for the **Oliver Cromwell Jazz Festival** (www.uptonjazz.co.uk).

Sights & Activities

The town's oldest building is the copper-domed **tower** known as the 'Pepperpot' – all that remains of the 13th-century Church of St Peter & St Paul. Looking like something from a small town in Massachusetts, the building contains a **Heritage Centre** (☎01684-592679; Church St; admission free; ⏲10.30am-4.30pm mid-Apr–Sep), devoted to local history.

Across the road, **Tudor House** (☎01684-592447; 16 Church St; adult/child £1.50/1; ⏲2-5pm Apr-Oct) displays a haphazard collection of objects relating to Upton, from Victorian crocks to carved wooden spoons.

Boats offer cruises along the tranquil River Severn, including the glass-topped **Avon Belle** (☎01684-592708; www.avonbelle riverboattrips.co.uk; adult/child £3.50/2.50, ⏲hourly 10am-5pm), which departs from near the King's Head pub.

Sleeping & Eating

White Lion HOTEL ££
(☎01684-592551; www.whitelionhotel.biz; 21 High St; s/d £70/99, mains £11-19; P) This 16th-century coaching inn, famous for its Civil War connections and its place in Henry Fielding's *Tom Jones,* is now known just as well for its richly furnished classic rooms and romantic oak-beamed and candlelit restaurant. Wheelchair accessible.

Tiltridge Vineyard B&B ££
(☎01684-592906; www.tiltridge.com; Upper Hook Rd; s/d £45/70; P) A home-from-home farmhouse B&B 1 mile west of town, connected to a thriving vineyard. As well as comfy rooms, Tiltridge offers little treats such as wine-tasting on the terrace.

Drinking

Founded in 1601, **Ye Olde Anchor Inn** (High St) is the oldest pub in town, but the **King's Head** (www.kingsheadupton.co.uk; Riverside; mains £5-16) has the best location, perched on the riverbank with a wooden deck overlooking the water. It also serves hearty, inexpensive meals.

Information

Tourist office (☎01684-594200; upton-info@visitthemalverns.org; 4 High St; ⏲10am-5pm Mon-Wed, Fri & Sat) Has local information and brochures.

Map Shop (☎01684-593146; www.themapshop.co.uk; 15 High St; ⏲9am-5.30pm Mon-Sat) Walkers and map enthusiasts should head to this impressively well-stocked shop.

Getting There & Away

The 362/363 Malvern Link bus runs between Upton and Worcester (30 minutes, twice hourly) from Monday to Saturday.

HEREFORDSHIRE

Slumbering quietly in the English countryside, Herefordshire is a patchwork of fields, hills and cute little black-and-white villages, many dating back to the Tudor era and beyond. Getting around is complicated by infrequent bus services and meandering country lanes, but taking the scenic route is part of the appeal of this laid-back rural idyll. The scenic River Wye provides a watery highway for canoeists, and there's plenty to see, including Hereford's glorious cathedral and literature-mad Hay-on-Wye, setting for the country's biggest book fair.

Activities

As well as the famous Offa's Dyke Path – see boxed text, p499 – walkers can follow the **Herefordshire Trail** (www.herefordshiretrail.com) on a 150-mile circular loop through Leominster, Ledbury, Ross-on-Wye and Kington. Only slightly less ambitious is the 107-mile **Wye Valley Walk** (www.wyevalleywalk.org), which runs from Chepstow in Wales through Herefordshire and back out again to Rhayader. Then there's the **Three Choirs Way**, a 100-mile route connecting the cathedrals of Hereford, Worcester and Gloucester. Cyclists can trace the **Six Castles Cycleway** (NCN Route 44) from Hereford to Leominster and Shrewsbury, or NCN Route 68 to Great Malvern and Worcester.

Information

Visit Herefordshire (www.visitherefordshire.co.uk)

Getting Around

Trains run frequently to Hereford, Leominster and Ledbury, with regular bus connections on to the rest of the county. For bus timetables, search for 'bus' at www.herefordshire.gov.uk. Alternatively, pick up the chunky *Bus and Train Timetable* from any tourist office (50p).

BLACK-AND-WHITE VILLAGES

A triangle of Tudor England survives almost untouched in northwest Herefordshire, where higgledy-piggledy black-and-white houses cluster round idyllic village greens, seemingly oblivious to the modern world. A delightful 40-mile circular drive follows the **Black-and-White-Village Trail**, meandering past the most handsome timber-framed buildings, starting at Leominster and looping round through Eardisland and Kington (the southern terminus of the Mortimer Trail from Ludlow). You can pick up guides to exploring the villages by car, bus or bicycle from any tourist office.

Hereford

POP 56,353

Best known for prime steaks, cider and the Pretenders (three of the original band members were local boys), Hereford dozes in the midst of apple orchards and rolling cow pastures at the heart of the Marches. Straddling the River Wye, the town seems more preoccupied with agriculture than tourism, but there are some interesting things to see, including a vast Norman cathedral whose organist, George Sinclair, was a mentor to the young Edward Elgar.

Sights

Hereford Cathedral CATHEDRAL

(☎01432-374200; www.herefordcathedral.org; 5 College Cloisters; suggested donation £4) After Welsh marauders torched the original Saxon cathedral, the Norman rulers of Hereford erected a larger, grander cathedral on the same site, which was subsequently remodelled in a succession of medieval architectural styles. The Hereford bishops were a colourful company – Peter of Aquablanca (1240–68) was a close ally of Henry III and a notorious tax fraudster, while the pious St Thomas de Cantilupe (1275–82) was excommunicated for forcing members of the nobility to perform humiliating acts of penance at the cathedral. Memorials to past bishops – some worn smooth with age – are dotted around the nave and transept.

However, all fades into insignificance compared to the magnificent **Mappa Mundi** (adult/child £4.50/3.50; ⏲10am-5pm Mon-Sat May-Sep, to 4pm Mon-Sat Oct-Apr), a piece of calfskin vellum intricately painted with some rather fantastical assumptions about the layout of the globe in around 1290 – see boxed text, p538 for more about this glorious piece of cartography. The same wing contains the world's largest surviving chained library,

Hereford

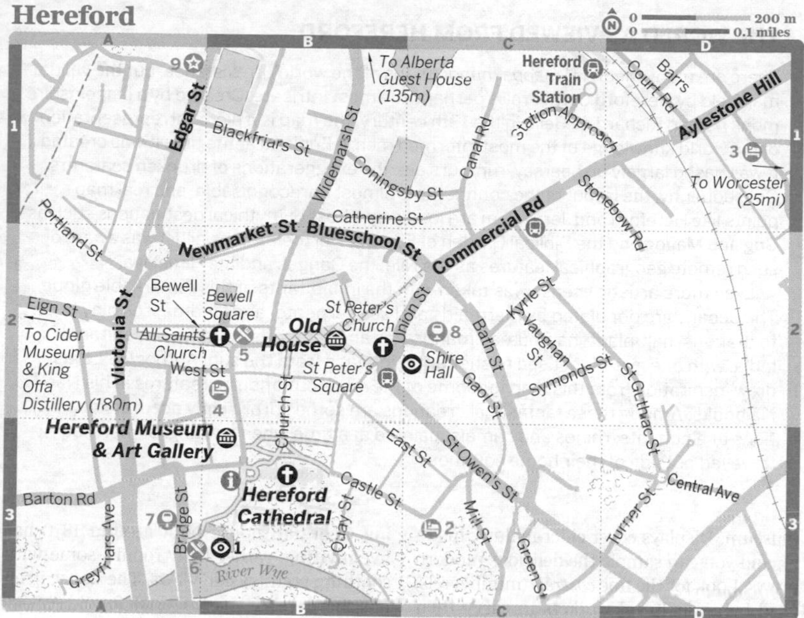

Hereford

Top Sights

- Hereford Cathedral B3
- Hereford Museum & Art Gallery B3
- Old House B2

Sights

- 1 Ultimate Left Bank B3

Sleeping

- 2 Castle House C3
- 3 Charades D1
- 4 Green Dragon Hotel B2

Eating

- 5 Cafe@All Saints B2
- 6 Floodgates Brasserie A3

Drinking

- 7 Black Lion A3
- 8 Jailhouse C2

Entertainment

- 9 Courtyard Centre for the Arts A1

with rare manuscripts manacled to the shelves. The collection includes an AD1217 copy of the revised *Magna Carta* and the illuminated 8th-century *Hereford Gospels.*

The cathedral comes alive with **Evensong** (5.30pm Mon–Sat, 3.30pm Sun) and every three years in August it holds the famous **Three Choirs Festival** (www.3choirs.org), shared with Gloucester and Worcester Cathedrals.

FREE **Old House** MUSEUM

(☎01432-260694; ⏰10am-5pm Tue-Sat year-round, to 4pm Sun Apr-Sep) Marooned in a sea of shops, this wonderfully creaky black-and-white, three-storey wooden house was built in 1621. Inside you can see a series of medieval rooms full of period furniture and carved wood panelling.

FREE **Hereford Museum & Art Gallery** MUSEUM

(☎01432-260692; Broad St; ⏰10am-5pm Tue-Sat year-round, to 4pm Sun Apr-Sep) The quirky collection at the town museum has displays on just about everything from 19th-century witches' curses to Roman antiquities. There's also some dressing-up gear to keep kids entertained.

Cider Museum & King Offa Distillery BREWERY

(☎01432-354207; www.cidermuseum.co.uk; 21 Ryelands St; adult/child £4/2.50; ⏰10am-5pm Tue-Sat Apr-Oct, 11am-3pm Tue-Sat Nov-Mar) The name is the giveaway at this brewery and

THE WORLD AS VIEWED FROM HEREFORD

There are many medieval *mappa mundi* (maps of the world) in existence, but the vellum map held by Hereford Cathedral is perhaps the most intricate. Created by a Lincolnshire monk named Richard de Bello in the 13th century, the map is a pictorial representation of the world knowledge of the most informed men in England at the time it was created. It was based largely on hearsay, rumours and the exaggerations of drunken seafarers. Consequently, the layout of the continents is almost unrecognisable, and real map-points like Hereford and Jerusalem are joined by a host of mythical destinations such as Gog and Magog and the Biblical Garden of Eden. Nevertheless, the artist was aware of such remote geographical features as the Nile, the Ganges and the Himalaya.

Even more artistic license was taken with the inhabitants of this remarkable globe. The oceans are populated by mermaids and sea serpents, and landmasses play host to dragons, half-plant–half-human mandrakes and sciapods, mythical inhabitants of India, with one giant foot used to shelter their heads from the sun. Author CS Lewis drew inspiration from this map for some of the more outlandish creatures in his Narnia books. Among these fantastical creations are some surprisingly accurate depictions of elephants, rhinos and camels, painted at a time when few Englishmen had travelled outside of their home counties.

museum. Displays cover cider-making history, and you can sample the delicious modern brews. Look for the fine *costrels* (minibarrels) used by agricultural workers to carry their wages, which were partially paid in cider. To reach the brewery, follow Eign St west from the centre and turn south along Ryelands St.

Tours

Guided walks (adult/child £3/free; 11am Mon-Sat, 2.30pm Sun May-Oct) start from the tourist office, exploring less-well-known historic sights in the centre.

If you fancy guiding yourself along the River Wye, you can rent open canoes from **Ultimate Left Bank** (01432-360057; www.leftbankcanoehire.com; Bridge St; half-/full day £15/20) at the Left Bank centre.

Sleeping

Castle House — TOP CHOICE — HOTEL £££
(01432-356321; www.castlehse.co.uk; Castle St; s/d from £125/185; P @ wi-fi) This award-winning boutique hotel is set in a regal Georgian town house that was once the luxurious digs of the Bishop of Hereford. There's a seriously sophisticated restaurant, the sun-kissed garden spills down to the river, and the sumptuous fabrics and furnishings in the rooms become ever more refined as you move up the price scale. Wheelchair accessible.

Charades — B&B ££
(01432-269444; www.charadeshereford.co.uk; 34 Southbank Rd; s/d £45/65; P @) This imposing Georgian house built around 1870 has five inviting, rather frilly rooms, some with soothing countryside views. The house itself has character in spades – look for old service bells in the hall. It's handy for the bus station, but a 1km walk from the cathedral.

Other possibilities:

Green Dragon Hotel — HOTEL ££
(01432-252506; www.greendragon-hereford.co.uk; Broad St; d £55-110; P) Offering a certain faded Regency charm, this substantial hotel has cavernous rooms with flowery curtains and bedspreads.

Alberta Guest House — B&B £
(01432-270313; www.thealbertaguesthouse.co.uk; 5-13 Newtown Rd; s/d £30/45; P) Simple but warm and welcoming; in the north of town.

Eating

Three Crowns Inn — GASTROPUB ££
(01432-820279; www.threecrownsinn.com; Ullingswick; mains £15, s/d £80/95; closed Mon) Burrow into the countryside, 5 miles northeast of Hereford, to find this gorgeous 16th-century half-timbered gastropub. As well as delicious organic dishes made with rare-breed meats and homemade cheese, you can stay in classy rooms. Ullingswick is just off the A417.

Floodgates Brasserie — MODERN EUROPEAN ££
(01432-349000; www.leftbank.co.uk; Left Bank, 20-22 Bridge St; mains £12.50-18; closed Mon) You can watch the swans glide by as you eat at this swish, modern place in the posh Left

Bank development. The menu is upscale modern European.

Cafe@All Saints CAFE £
(☎01432-370414; www.cafeatallsaints.co.uk; High St; mains £6-9; ⏰8am-5pm Mon-Sat) A surprisingly modern and trendy offering inside the renovated nave of All Saint's Church. The menu is wholesome and mostly vegetarian, and you can even enjoy a beer or glass of wine – just remember, God's watching.

Drinking & Entertainment

Black Lion PUB
(31 Bridge St) The more real ales and local ciders you knock back in this traditional pub, the more you may believe the tales that there are resident ghosts from the site's history as a monastery, an orphanage, a brothel and even a Chinese restaurant.

Jailhouse CLUB
(thejailhouse.wordpress.com; Gaol St; ⏰to 3am Wed, Fri & Sat) Edgy, underground DJs are coming out of the woodwork at Hereford's leading club. Look out for secret sets by big-name spinners.

Courtyard Centre for the Arts ART CENTRE
(www.courtyard.org.uk; Edgar St) This lively arts centre has two venues staging a busy schedule of comedy, theatre, film and poetry.

Information

Tourist office (☎01432-268430; www.visitherefordshire.co.uk; 1 King St; ⏰10am-5pm Mon-Sat) Opposite the cathedral.

Library (Broad St; ⏰9.30am-7.30pm Tue, Wed & Fri, to 5.30pm Thu, to 4pm Sat) There's free internet access at the library, which is in the same building as the Hereford Museum & Art Gallery.

Getting There & Around

The bus station is on Commercial Rd, northeast of the town centre. National Express goes to London (£21.70, 4½ hours, three daily) and Gloucester (£6.20, 1¼ hours, five daily). Local services:

Hay-on-Wye Bus 39/39A, one hour, twice hourly (three Sunday services)

Ledbury Bus 476, 30 minutes, hourly (five Sunday services)

Ludlow Bus 492, 1¼ hours, twice hourly (three Sunday services)

Ross-on-Wye Bus 38, 45 minutes, hourly (six Sunday services)

Worcester Bus 420, one hour, twice hourly (four services Sunday)

The train station is northeast of the centre, with hourly trains to Birmingham (£13.20, 1½ hours) and London Paddington (£56.70, three hours), either direct or with a change in Newport, South Wales.

Around Hereford

AYMESTREY & AROUND

About 15 miles north of Hereford, off the B4362 near the village of Aymestrey, the fanciful 14th-century **Croft Castle** (NT; ☎01568-780246; adult/child £6.80/3.25; ⏰11am-5pm daily Apr-Aug, closed Mon & Tue Mar, Sep & Oct, to 4pm Sat & Sun Nov & Dec) was just another country house until the owners adorned it with castlelike trim in the 18th century. Surrounded by groves of ancient oaks and chestnuts, it's worth the trip if you're turned on by flamboyant interiors and forest walks. Without a car, the only way to get here is to take bus 492 from Ludlow or Hereford and disembark at Gorbett Bank, a 2.5 mile walk from the castle.

TOP CHOICE **Riverside Inn** (☎01568-708440; www.theriversideinn.org; Aymestrey; s/d from £45/70; P) is a classic 16th-century black-and-white coaching inn resting alongside the River Lugg in the diminutive village of Aymestrey. It isn't on the way to anywhere, but gourmands are lured here by the locally-sourced Modern British food, cooked up by award-winning chefs. The **Mortimer Trail** passes close by.

KILPECK CHURCH

Deep in the Herefordshire countryside is the tiny hamlet of Kilpeck, home to the beguiling Norman **Church of St Mary & St David**. The church is encircled by pagan carvings, from cartoonlike pigs and bunnies to a famous sheila-na-gig (Celtic fertility figure). It's an extraordinary sight, well worth the 9-mile trip south from Hereford; just follow the A465 and turn off at Kilpeck.

Hay-On-Wye

POP 1450

This tiny border town has totally submitted itself to the secondhand book trade, attracting idle browsers, eagle-eyed collectors, and serious academics from around the world. Book couriers buzz up and down the narrow streets, and locals and visitors spend their days leafing through well-thumbed tomes in cafes, restaurants, pubs and even on the edge of the pavement.

WORTH A TRIP

GOLDEN VALLEY

Nudging the foot of the Black Mountains, this lush valley was made famous by children's author CS Lewis, of Narnia acclaim. Following the meandering River Dore, the valley is peppered with historical relics, including **Arthur's Stone**, a 5000-year-old Neolithic chamber-tomb near the village of Dorestone, and the handsome 12th-century **Dore Abbey** (www.doreabbey.org.uk) in the appropriately named village of Abbey Dore. Bus 39 between Hereford and Hay-on-Wye (five daily, Monday to Saturday) follows the valley, stopping at Dorestone and Peterchurch. For accommodation and dining ideas, visit www.herefordholidays.co.uk.

It's an eccentric spot (locals even declared themselves independent from Britain in 1977, in a famous publicity stunt) and every year for a week in May/June, the town becomes the centre of the literary universe for the **Hay Festival of Literature** (www.hayfestival.com). The festival attracts big shots from the worlds of literature, art and politics, from Salman Rushdie and Martin Amis to Desmond Tutu and Bill Clinton.

Sights & Activities

Books (hundreds of thousands of them) are the main thing to see in Hay-on-Wye, but it's also worth taking a peek at the crumbling remains of the 13th-century town **castle**, home to a succession of Lords Marcher. Unfortunately, heritage regulations mean nothing can be done to stabilise the ruin – it's 'a listed building that's listing,' as one local quipped.

Hay sits on the northeastern corner of Brecon Beacons National Park and makes an excellent base for rambles into the Welsh Black Mountains, or tramps along **Offa's Dyke Path** (see boxed text, p499). The Offa's Dyke Flyer minibus runs three times on summer Sundays and bank holidays to help you along the way. Alternatively, just explore the local area – there are trails along both banks of the river, connecting with the **Wye Valley Walk**.

For fun on the river, hire kayaks and Canadian canoes from **Paddles & Pedals** (01497-820604; www.canoehire.co.uk; 15 Castle St; kayaks per half-/full day £15/25; Easter-Oct), which, despite the name, doesn't do bikes. Rental prices include transport to pick-up/drop-off points along the Wye.

Sleeping

Don't bet on a bed *anywhere* nearby while the festival is on.

Start B&B ££
(01497-821391; www.the-start.net; Hay Bridge; s/d £40/70; P) Simply a delight, this 18th-century stone cottage stands alone on a grassy bank on the northwest side of the river, giving it a blissful feeling of space and solitude. Patchwork quilts adorn the pleasant country-style rooms – some of which have a view of the river – and there are useful lock-up and drying facilities for hikers and bikers.

Old Black Lion HOTEL/PUB ££
(01497-820841; www.oldblacklion.co.uk; Lion St; s/d £45/70; P) An atmospheric 17th-century inn full of blackened oak beams and moody lighting. The spacious bedrooms are full of sturdy country furniture and colourful fabrics, and each has a resident teddy.

Old Post Office B&B ££
(01497-820008; www.oldpost-office.co.uk; Llanigon; d from £70; P) Two miles southwest of Hay off the B4350, this gorgeous converted post office is all polished-oak floors, exposed beams and rural idyll. Breakfast is vegetarian: no meat feasts here.

Eating & Drinking

Three Tuns PUB £
(01497-821855; www.three-tuns.com; Broad St; mains £10-19; lunch & dinner Wed-Sun) The chef at this cosy stone pub is making quite a name for himself with his inventive cooking, using only sustainable and locally sourced ingredients. The courtyard tables are also a great place for an evening pint.

For a quick lunchtime sandwich, soup or quiche, head to **Oscars Bistro** (High Town; dishes from £5; 10.30am-5pm) or the **Granary** (Broad St; mains £6-10; 10am-5.30pm; @). Both offer quick service and tables that spill out onto the street.

There are also good meals at the **Old Black Lion** (Lion St, mains £12-16).

Shopping

Ask at the tourist office for the handy *Booksellers* map and pamphlet, marking the town's three dozen bookshops, from crime-specialists **Murder and Mayhem** (☎01497-821613; 5 Lion St) to **Mostly Maps** (☎01497-820539; www.mostlymaps.com; 2 Castle St) with antique prints and cartography.

The most famous bookseller in town is the delightful, column-fronted **Richard Booth's Bookshop** (☎01497-820322; www.richardbooth.demon.co.uk; 44 Lion St; ⏲9am-5.30pm Mon-Sat, 11am-5pm Sun), which allegedly has the highest turnover of secondhand books of any bookshop in the world. A smaller branch is housed in a Jacobean mansion built into the walls of the battered 13th-century town castle.

Information

Tourist office (☎01497-820144; www.hay-on-wye.co.uk; Oxford Rd; ⏲10am-1pm & 2-5pm Easter-Oct, 11am-1pm & 2-4pm Nov-Easter) Beside the main car park.

Getting There & Away

Bus 39/39A runs to Hay from Hereford (one hour, twice hourly, three Sunday services), continuing to Brecon (45 minutes).

Near the tourist office, **Drover Holidays** (☎01497-821134; www.droverholidays.co.uk; 3 Oxford Rd) rents out good-quality road and mountain bikes from £25 per day.

Ross-On-Wye

POP 10,085

Laid-back Ross-on-Wye, which sits pretty on a red sandstone bluff over a kink in the River Wye, is an easy paddle from Symonds Yat, but there are enough sights to warrant a trip by road. The town was propelled to fame in the 18th century by Alexander Pope and Samuel Taylor Coleridge, who penned tributes to philanthropist John Kyrle, Man of Ross, who dedicated his life and fortune to the poor of the parish.

Sights & Activities

The 17th-century **Market House** (☎01989-260675; ⏲10am-5pm Mon-Sat & 10.30am-4pm Sun Apr-Oct, 10.30am-4pm Tue-Sun Nov-Mar) sits atop weathered sandstone columns in the Market Pl; inside the salmon-pink building is an agreeably hand-crafted heritage centre with local history displays.

About 1 mile west of town, beside the River Wye, **Wilton Castle** (☎01989-565759; www.wiltoncastle.eclipse.co.uk; Wilton; adult/child £4/2; ⏲11am-5pm Wed & Sun Jun-Aug) is a delightful 12th-century ruin, scattered through the pretty gardens of a vine-covered private home.

Crowning the hilltop, pin-straight **St Mary's Church** (Church St; ⏲9am-5pm) is a 13th-century construction with a fine east window and grand alabaster memorials, including the grave of John Kyrle and the outrageously ostentatious tombs of the noble Rudhall family. Behind the church, Royal Parade runs to the edge of the bluff, lined with realistic-looking but ersatz **castle ruins**, constructed in 1833.

Sleeping & Eating

White House Guest House B&B ££
(☎01989-763572; www.whitehouseross.com; Wye St; s/d £45/65; P @ T) This 18th-century stone house has a great location across the road from the River Wye. Vivid window boxes give it a splash of colour, and the rooms, decorated in shades of burgundy and crisp white, are quiet and comfortable.

Bridge at Wilton B&B ££
(☎01989-562655; www.bridge-house-hotel.com; Wilton; s/d from £80/98; P) A distinguished Georgian country-house restaurant a mile west of Ross, with smart rooms and a highly praised menu of Modern British food.

Pots and Pieces CAFE £
(40 High St; mains from £5; ⏲breakfast & lunch) The best of the tearooms around the market place, with ceramics and crafts to browse while you sip a coffee or munch on a cupcake or sandwich.

Drinking

Hope & Anchor PUB
(Wye St; mains £6-17) At the foot of the bluff on the riverside, this friendly pub is a great place to while away the time; tables spread right down to the water's edge, attracting lots of visiting canoeists in summer.

Information

Tourist office (☎01989-562768; tic-ross@herefordshire.gov.uk; Edde Cross St; ⏲9am-5pm Mon-Sat, to 4pm low season) Has information on sights and walks – ask for the *Ross-on-Wye Heritage Trail* booklet (50p).

Getting There & Around

The bus stand is on Cantilupe Rd. From Monday to Saturday, bus 38 runs hourly to Hereford (45 minutes), and bus 33 runs hourly to Gloucester (40 minutes). For Monmouth, take bus 34 (45 minutes, every two hours Monday to Saturday).

For local exploring, you can hire bikes from **Revolutions** (01989-562639; www.revolutionsatross.co.uk; 48 Broad St; per day from £10).

Forest of Dean

The Forest of Dean spills over the Gloucestershire border near the village of Goodrich, just off the A40 between Ross-on-Wye and Monmouth. The River Wye skirts the edge of the forest, offering glorious views to canoeists who paddle out from the delightful village of Symonds Yat.

GOODRICH

Seemingly part of its craggy bedrock, **Goodrich Castle** (EH; 01600-890538; adult/child £5.50/2.80; 10am-5pm Apr-Oct, to 6pm Jul & Aug, 10am-4pm Wed-Sun Nov-Mar) is an exceptionally complete medieval castle, topped by a superb 12th-century keep that affords spectacular views. A small exhibition tells the story of the castle from its 11th-century origins to its demise in the 1600s.

Welsh Bicknor YHA (0845 371 9666; www.yha.org.uk; dm from £10; Apr-Oct; P) is an austere-looking former Victorian rectory surveying a grand sweep of countryside from its lovely riverside grounds. It's on the Wye Valley Walk, 1½ miles from Goodrich; follow the signed road near Goodrich Castle and take the right fork where the road splits.

Goodrich is five miles south of Ross off the A40. Bus 34 stops here every two hours on its way between Ross (20 minutes) and Monmouth (20 minutes), except on Sundays.

SYMONDS YAT

Right on the edge of the forest, squeezed between the River Wye and the towering limestone outcrop known as **Symonds Yat Rock**, Symonds Yat East is an endearing tangle of pubs and guesthouses, with great walks and an excellent canoeing centre and campsite right in the middle of the village.

An ancient hand-hauled **ferry** (adult/child/bicycle £1/50p/50p) crosses the Wye to Symonds Yat West on the other side of the valley, where you'll find a riverside caravan park and some family-friendly amusements for campers. Travelling between the two villages by road involves a convoluted detour via the A40.

Activities

This area is renowned for canoeing and rock climbing and there's also good hiking and cycling in the nearby Forest of Dean – the scenic **Peregrine Path** follows the riverbanks from Symonds Yat East to Monmouth.

The most popular walk from Symonds Yat East picks its way up the side of the 504m **Symonds Yat Rock**, affording fabulous views of river and valley. In July and August, you may be lucky enough to spot peregrine falcons soaring by the drop-off. A **kiosk** (10am-4pm summer) atop the rock sells drinks and snacks, and peaceful walking trails continue east through the forest into Gloucestershire.

Rock climbers follow a series of mainly trad routes directly up the face of the cliff, but routes in the easier grades tend to be very polished, and rock falls are common – bring a varied rack and wear your helmet. *Symonds Yat* by John Willson is the definitive guidebook.

The **Wyedean Canoe Centre** (01594-833238; www.wyedean.co.uk; half-day hire from £28; 8.30am-8.30pm) hires out canoes and kayaks, and also organises multiday kayak trips, white-water trips, caving and climbing. Several companies offer a similar service in Symonds Yat West. Strong currents make the river dangerous for swimming.

Fair-weather water-babies can enjoy the Wye without the hard work on a sedate, 40-minute gorge cruise run by **Kingfisher Cruises** (01600-891063; adult/child £5.50/3), leaving from beside the ferry crossing.

Sleeping & Eating

Garth Cottage B&B ££
(01600-890364; www.garthcottage-symondsyat.com; Symonds Yat East; B&B per person £37.50; Apr-Oct; P) The pick of accommodation on the east side, this friendly, family-run B&B sits by the riverside near the ferry crossing, and has spotlessly maintained, bright rooms with river views.

Old Court Hotel HOTEL £££
(01600-890367; www.oldcourthotel.co.uk; Symonds Yat West; r £80-200; P) A striking 16th-century manor house set in lovely gardens on the outskirts of Symonds Yat West, complete with heated pool. You can choose from spic-and-span contemporary rooms or timbered charmers with four-posters.

Wyedean Canoe Centre Campsite CAMPSITE £

(01594-833238; www.wyedean.co.uk; sites per adult/child £9.50/6) This popular canoe centre has a lovely campsite with a clean bathroom block, set right by the river – perfect for a weekend of splashing around in the Wye. Rates drop by 30% from Monday to Thursday.

Royal Lodge HOTEL ££

(01600-890238; www.royallodgesymondsyat.co.uk; Symonds Yat East; mains £5-17, s/d from £35/80) With a pretty tree-sheltered garden, neat modern rooms and a fine restaurant, the Royal Lodge is great value. It's worth swinging by for a drink in the pretty gardens, even if you don't stay here.

Getting There & Away

There is no direct public transport, but bus 34 between Ross-on-Wye and Monmouth can drop you off on the main road 1.5 miles from the village (services run every two hours). Bikes are available for hire from the Royal Hotel (Symonds Yat East) for £15 per day.

Ledbury

POP 8491

An atmospheric little town creaking with history and dotted with antique shops, Ledbury is a favourite destination for day-trippers. The best way to pass the time is to wander the crooked black-and-white streets, which zero in on a delightfully leggy medieval market house.

Sights

Markets still take place in Ledbury's delicate black-and-white **Market House**, as they have since the 17th century. The timber-framed structure is precariously balanced atop a series of wooden posts supposedly taken from the wrecked ships of the Spanish Armada. Nearby at the corner with Church St, the **Painted Room** (admission free; 11am-1pm & 2-4pm Mon-Fri Easter-Sep, plus 2-5pm Sun Jul-Sep) is adorned with 16th-century floral frescos, from the days before wallpaper.

Almost impossibly cute Church Lane runs its cobbled way from the High St to the town church, crowded with tilting timber-framed buildings, like JK Rowling's Diagon Alley. **Butcher's Row House** (01531-632942; Church Lane; admission free; 11am-5pm Easter-Sep) contains a pocket-sized folk museum stuffed with local curios, including an 18th-century communal bath that used to be carted from door to door for the poor to scrub up in. The **Heritage Centre** (01531-635680; admission free; 10.30am-4.30pm Easter-Oct) sits in another half-timbered treasure across the street, and has more displays on local history.

At the top of the lane lies the 12th-century church of **St Michael and All Angels** (www.ledburyparishchurch.org.uk; 8.30am-6pm, to 4pm low season) with a splendid 18th-century spire and tower divided from its medieval knave. The floor and walls are embedded with memorials to late medieval lords and ladies.

Sleeping & Eating

The town pubs offer reasonably priced meals, but budget travellers will struggle to find cheap accommodation.

Verzon House Hotel HOTEL £££

(01531-670381; www.verzonhouse.com; Trumpet; s/d from £105/155; P @) The ultimate country-chic retreat, this lovely Georgian farmhouse has undergone a rather debonair makeover without sacrificing its rustic charm. Its eight rooms are luxuriously appointed with tactile fabrics, free-standing baths, goose-down pillows, and toe-tickling deep-pile carpets, and there's a very posh brasserie. Verzon House is 3 miles west of Ledbury on the A438.

Feathers Hotel HOTEL £££

(01531-635266; www.feathers-ledbury.co.uk; High St; mains £10-17, s/d from £89.50/135; P) This charming black-and-white Tudor hotel looms over the main road. Rooms in the oldest part of the building come with slanting floorboards, painted beams, and much more character than the modern rooms. There's an atmospheric wood-panelled restaurant and a swimming pool.

Cameron & Swan DELI-CAFE £

(01531-636791; www.cameronandswan.co.uk; 15 The Homend; mains £6-7; breakfast & lunch Mon-Sat) A bustling cafe serving tasty deli sandwiches, giant meringues and other tasty homemade treats in a bright, airy dining room.

Information

Tourist office (01531-636147; www.visitledbury.co.uk; 3 The Homend; 10am-5pm Mon-Sat Apr-Oct, to 4pm Nov-Mar) Just off the High St, behind St Katherine's Chapel, this helpful office has information on tours of the town.

OFFA'S DYKE PATH

Tracing the route of the mighty earthworks raised by the Saxon king Offa to keep the Welsh tribes out of England, the **Offa's Dyke Path** runs for 177 miles through Wales, Herefordshire and Shropshire, creating one of England's most scenic coast-to-coast walks. This is one of 15 designated national trails, rivalling the Pennine Way and Hadrian's Wall Path for natural beauty but without as many day-trippers.

The route starts at Sedbury near Chepstow and runs north through Monmouth, Hay-on-Wye, Kington and Knighton on its way to Prestatyn in North Wales. Most hikers complete the walk in two weeks, staying at pubs, hotels and guesthouses all along the route. The **Offa's Dyke Association** (www.offasdyke.demon.co.uk) is an excellent source of information, or you can drop into the **Offa's Dyke Centre** (01547-528753; 10am-5pm daily, to 4pm Mon-Sat low season) in Knighton, 17 miles west of Ludlow (buses 738/740 run here five times daily, except Sunday).

 Getting There & Away

Trains run to Great Malvern (15 minutes, hourly), Hereford (£5, 20 minutes, hourly), Worcester (£5.40, 30 minutes, hourly) and further afield. Bus 476 runs to Hereford hourly (40 minutes, hourly, every two hours on Sunday); bus 132 runs to Gloucester (one hour, hourly Monday to Saturday).

Around Ledbury

EASTNOR CASTLE

Built more for fancy than fortification, the extravagant medieval-revival folly of **Eastnor Castle** (01531-633160; www.eastnorcastle.com; adult/child £8.50/5.50, grounds only £5.50/3.50; 11am-4.30pm Sun-Thu Jul & Aug, Sun only Jun & Sep) is still the family home of the grandchildren of the first Earl Somers, who constructed this elaborate confection in 1810. The grounds are delightful and the opulent interior continues the romantic theme, with Gothic and Italianate flourishes and the kinds of antiques that make collectors weak at the knees. Glam-rockers Slade filmed the video for *Run Runaway* here in 1984, and the grounds still host big rock acts every August as part of the **Big Chill** (www.bigchill.net).

The castle is just over 2 miles east of Ledbury on the A438; a taxi from Ledbury station will cost around £10.

MUCH MARCLE

Not much more than a blip on the map, the tiny village of Much Marcle is home to one of England's oldest and most fascinating houses. Built in the 12th century, **Hellens** (01531-660504; www.hellensmanor.com; adult/child £6/4.50; tours 2pm, 3pm & 4pm Wed, Thu, Sun & bank holidays Apr-Sep) is crammed with priceless tapestries, heirlooms and oils, including pieces formerly owned by Mary, Queen of Scots, Charles I and Ann Boleyn. As this is still a family home, you can only enter on guided tours, but the sense of history is tangible, both inside, and outside in the restored medieval garden.

You can see the brightly painted tomb of the former owner, Walter de Helyon, nearby at **St Bartholomew's Church** (9am-dusk), along with other fine alabaster memorials from the 14th and 17th centuries.

Bus 45 from Ledbury goes to Much Marcle (40 minutes, four daily Monday to Friday, five services Saturday).

SHROPSHIRE

Travellers in search of England as it was before the arrival of the chain stores and out-of-town shopping centres will find their dreams fulfilled in peaceful Shropshire, a glorious scattering of hills, castles and timber-framed villages tucked against the Welsh border. In this sleepy neck of the woods, traditions like folk singing and Morris dancing are just business as usual on a Saturday night. Highlights include food-obsessed Ludlow, industrial Ironbridge and the beautiful Shropshire Hills, which offer the best walking and cycling in the Marches.

Activities

WALKING

The towering Shropshire Hills call out to walkers like a siren. Between Shrewsbury and Ludlow, the landscape rucks up into dramatic folds, with spectacular trails climbing the flanks of **Wenlock Edge** and the **Long Mynd** near Church Stretton – see those sections for details. The county is also crossed by long-distance trails, including the famous **Offa's Dyke Path** and the popular **Shropshire Way**, which meanders around Ludlow, Craven Arms and Church Stretton. For general information on walking in the county, visit www.shropshire walking.co.uk.

CYCLING

Mountain bikers head for the muddy tracks that scramble over the Long Mynd near Church Stretton, or the rugged forest trails of **Hopton Wood**, near Craven Arms, while road riders aim for the **Six Castles Cycleway** (NCN 44), which runs for 58 miles from Shrewsbury to Leominster – see boxed text, p560, for more about the route.

Tourists offices sell copies of *Cycling for Pleasure in the Marches,* a pack of five maps and guides covering the entire county. Alternatively, you can download cycling pamphlets for free from www.shropshire cycling.co.uk.

Information

For online information:

North Shropshire (www.northshropshire co.uk)

Secret Shropshire (www.secretshropshire. org.uk)

Shropshire Tourism (www.shropshiretourism. co.uk)

Virtual Shropshire (www.virtual-shropshire. co.uk)

Visit South Shropshire (www.visitsouthshrop shire.co.uk)

Getting Around

Shrewsbury is the local transport hub, and handy rail services go to Church Stretton, Craven Arms and Ludlow. The invaluable *Shropshire Bus & Train Map,* available free from tourist offices, shows useful routes. **Shropshire Hills Shuttles** (www.shropshirehillsshuttles.co.uk) runs useful bus services along popular hiking routes on weekends and bank holidays.

Shrewsbury

POP 67,126

A delightful jumble of winding medieval streets and timbered Tudor houses leaning at precarious angles, Shrewsbury (*shroos-*bree) was a crucial front in the conflict between English and Welsh in medieval times. Even today, the road bridge running east towards London is known as the English Bridge to mark it out from the Welsh Bridge leading northwest towards Holyhead. Shrewsbury was once an important centre for the wool trade, but its biggest claim to fame is being the birthplace of Charles Darwin (1809–82), who went on to rock the world with his theory of evolution.

Sights

Shrewsbury Abbey ABBEY

(☎01743-232723; www.shrewsburyabbey.com; Abbey Foregate; suggested donation adult/child £2/1; ⏰10.30am-3pm Mon-Sat, 11.30am-2.30pm Sun) Famous as the setting for Ellis Peters' *Chronicles of Brother Cadfael,* the lovely red-sandstone Shrewsbury Abbey is all that remains of a vast, cruciform Benedictine monastery founded in 1083. Twice the setting for meetings of the English parliament, the Abbey church lost its spire and two wings when the monastery was dissolved in 1540. It sustained further damage in 1826 when engineer Thomas Telford ran the London–Holyhead road right through the grounds. Nevertheless, you can still see some impressive Norman, Early English and Victorian features, including an exceptional 14th-century west window.

FREE **Shrewsbury Museum & Art Gallery** MUSEUM

(☎01743-281205; www.shrewsburymuseums. com; Barker St; ⏰10am-5pm Mon-Sat, to 4pm Sun May-Sep) The town museum is currently

SIPPING YOUR WAY AROUND CIDER COUNTRY

Crisp, dry ciders have been produced in Herefordshire since medieval times. The **Herefordshire Cider Route** (www.ciderroute.co.uk) drops in on numerous local cider producers, where you can try before you buy, and then totter off to the next cidery. Putting road safety first, tourist offices have maps and guide booklets to help you explore by bus or bicycle.

If you only have time to visit one cider-maker, make it **Westons Cider Mills** (☎01531-660233; www.westons-cider.co.uk; The Bounds; ⏰9am-4.30pm Mon-Fri, 10am-4pm Sat & Sun), whose house brew is even served in the Houses of Parliament! Informative tours (adult/child £6/3.25, 1¼ hours) start at 11am, 12.30pm and 2.30pm, with free tastings for the grown-ups. Westons is just under a mile west of Much Marcle.

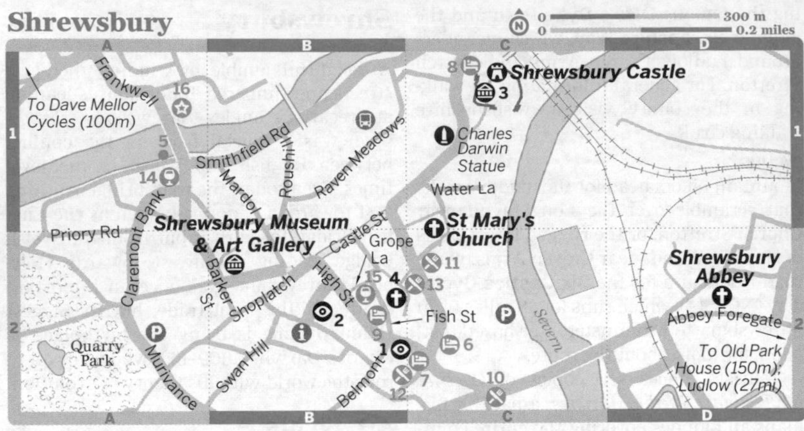

Shrewsbury

Top Sights
Shrewsbury Abbey ... D2
Shrewsbury Castle ... C1
Shrewsbury Museum & Art Gallery ... B2
St Mary's Church ... C1

Sights
1 Henry Tudor House ... B2
2 Old Market Hall ... B2
3 Shropshire Regimental Museum ... C1
4 St Alkmond's Church ... B2

Activities
5 Sabrina boat trips ... A1

Sleeping
6 Catherine of Aragon Suite ... C2
7 Lion Hotel ... C2
8 Lucroft Guest House ... C1
9 Tudor House ... B2

Eating
10 Cornhouse ... C2
11 Drapers Hall ... C2
12 Good Life Wholefood Restaurant ... B2
13 Mad Jack's ... C2

Drinking
14 Armoury ... A1
15 Three Fishes ... B2

Entertainment
Old Market Hall Film & Digital Media Centre ... (see 2)
16 Theatre Severn ... A1

housed in the timbered, Tudor-era Rowley's House, with an eclectic selection of exhibits, from Roman treasures to Darwin memorabilia. In 2012, the museum and tourist office will move to the Music Hall on the Square – visit the website for the latest news.

Shrewsbury Castle CASTLE
(☎01743-358516; adult/child £2.50/1.50; ⊙10.30am-5pm Fri-Wed Jun-Sep, 10.30am-4pm Mon-Wed & Fri-Sat Feb-May & Sep-Dec) Hewn from sunset-red Shropshire sandstone, the town castle contains the **Shropshire Regimental Museum**, plus fine views from its battlements.

St Mary's Church CHURCH
(St Mary's St; ⊙10am-4pm Mon-Sat) The magnificent spire of this roughly hewn medieval church is one of the highest in England, and the interior is graced with an impressive collection of stained glass, including a 14th-century window depicting the Tree of Jesse, a Biblical representation of the lineage of Jesus.

Other Sights
Shrewsbury is studded with two-tone timbered beauties, many dating back to the Tudor era and beyond. The most handsome buildings can be found on the narrow lanes surrounding **St Alkmond's**

Church, particularly along **Fish St** and amorously named **Grope Lane**. At the bottom of the High St on Wyle Cop, the seriously overhanging **Henry Tudor House** was where Henry VII stayed before the Battle of Bosworth.

At the other end of the High St in a cute cobbled square is Shrewsbury's 16th-century **Old Market Hall** (www.oldmarkethall.co.uk), whose upper levels contain the town's pocket-sized cinema. This was once the hub of Shrewsbury's wool trade – look for the holes in the pillars, used to count how many fleeces were sold.

Tours

Guided **walking tours** (adult/child £4/2.50) leave the tourist office at 2.30pm from Monday to Saturday, and at 11am on Sunday. Tours only run on Saturday from November to April.

Alternatively, enjoy Shrewsbury from the water on board the **Sabrina** (01743-369741; www.sabrinaboat.co.uk; from £5), which cruises the River Severn. Trips leave roughly hourly between 10am and 4pm (March to October).

Sleeping

As well as the following choices, pretty Abbey Foregate is lined with B&Bs.

Lion Hotel HOTEL ££
(01753-353107; www.thelionhotelshrewsbury.co.uk; Wyle Cop; s/d from £80/98; P) A gilded wooden lion crowns the doorway of this famous coaching inn, decked out inside with portraits of lords and ladies in powdered wigs. The guest lounge is warmed by a grand stone fireplace and the rooms are note-perfect, down to the period-pattern fabrics and ceramic water jugs.

Old Park House HOTEL ££
(01743-289750; 37 Abbey Foregate; s/d £60/75; P @ wi-fi) Despite the age of this fine old building you won't find any faux Tudor interiors here. Fifteenth-century timbered rooms have received a tasteful modern makeover, with bright contemporary fabrics and quirky artwork.

Tudor House B&B ££
(01743-351735; www.tudorhouseshrewsbury.com; 2 Fish St; s/d from £69/79; @ wi-fi) A bowing frontage festooned with hanging baskets and window boxes sets the scene at this delightful Tudor cottage on a delightful Tudor lane. It's handy for everything in the centre, and rooms are adorned with shimmery fabrics and flowery trim. Not all rooms have an en suite.

Albright Hussey Manor HOTEL ££
(01743-362421; www.lucrofthotel.com; Castle Gates; s/d from £28/44) The price is the main appeal at this cheap and cheerful guesthouse, and you can't fault the location between station and castle.

Albright Hussey Manor HOTEL ££
(01939-290523; www.albrighthussey.co.uk; Ellesmere Rd; s/d from £79/120; P @ wi-fi) A charmingly mismatched medieval manor with an excellent restaurant, surrounded by a moat. Found 2 miles north of town.

Eating

Drapers Hall FRENCH £££
(01743-344679; St Mary's Pl; mains £14-25, s/d from £100/120) The sense of history is palpable in this beautifully preserved 16th-century hall, fronted by an elegant Elizabethan facade. Award-wining Anglo-French haute cuisine is served in rooms adorned with wood panelling and artwork, and upstairs are spectacular, heirloom-filled rooms.

Mad Jack's MODERN EUROPEAN ££
(01743-358870; www.madjacksuk.com; 15 St Mary's St; mains £11-16, s/d from £70/80) A classy place that straddles the boundary between cafe, restaurant and bar, with an elegant dining room and a plant-filled courtyard. The menu features inventive Modern European cuisine prepared with ingredients

DON'T MISS

SLEEP LIKE A QUEEN

Shrewsbury's most eccentric place to stay, the **Catherine of Aragon Suite** (01743-271092; www.aragonsuite.co.uk; the Old House, 20 Dogpole; s/d £85/125; P @) is a lavish suite of rooms in a gloriously crooked timbered Tudor town house that was once owned by one of Catherine's courtiers. Looking like a medieval oil painting brought to life, the bedroom and drawing room are decked out with ancient wood panelling and heirloom pieces of furniture, with the added bonus of broadband internet and Sky TV.

from local farms and suppliers. There are swish contemporary bedrooms upstairs.

 **Good Life Wholefood Restaurant** VEGETARIAN £

(01743-350455; Barracks Passage; mains £3.50-7; lunch Mon-Sat) Healthy, freshly prepared vegetarian food is the name of the game AT this cute little refuge off Wyle Cop. Favourites include quiches, nut loaf, salads, soups and veggie lasagne.

Cornhouse MODERN BRITISH ££

(01743-231991; www.cornhouse.co.uk; 59a Wyle Cop; mains £10-15; closed dinner Sun) A relaxed wine bar and restaurant in a handsome old town house, laid out with white linen and wicker chairs. The menu of inventive modern British food features occasional nods to North Africa.

Drinking

Armoury PUB

(www.armoury-shrewsbury.co.uk; Victoria Ave) Despite being a modern invention, the Armoury still manages to feel like it has been here for generations. Inside this inviting pub are long wooden tables, dotted around among floor-to-ceiling bookshelves and assorted collectibles.

Three Fishes PUB

(4 Fish St) The quintessential creaky Tudor alehouse, with a jolly publican, mellow regulars and hops hanging from the 15th-century beamed ceiling.

Entertainment

To view mainstream and art-house movies in a charming Elizabethan setting, visit the **Old Market Hall Film & Digital Media Centre** (www.oldmarkethall.co.uk; The Square).

Theatre Severn THEATRE

(www.theatresevern.co.uk; Frankwell Quay) This expansive riverside theatre and music venue opened in 2009 to great acclaim, hosting everything from pop gigs and comedy nights to plays and classical concerts.

Information

Reference Library (Castle Gates; 9.30am-5pm Mon, Wed, Fri & Sat, to 8pm Tue & Thu, 1-4pm Sun) Free internet access.

Royal Shrewsbury Hospital (01743-261000; Mytton Oak Rd)

Tourist office (01743-281200; www.visitshrewsbury.com; Shrewsbury Museum & Art Gallery, Barker St; 9.30am-5.30pm Mon-Sat, 10am-4pm Sun May-Sep, 10am-5pm Mon-Sat Oct-Apr) Come for walking tours and stacks of brochures.

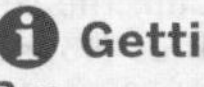

Getting There & Away

Bus

The bus station is beside the river on Smithfield Rd. Bus 435 runs to Ludlow (1½ hours, hourly Monday to Saturday), via Church Stretton. Other useful services:

Birmingham National Express, £6.80, 1½ hours, twice daily

Ironbridge Bus 96, 35 minutes, every two hours Monday to Saturday

London National Express, £21.30, 4½ hours, twice daily

Train

From the train station at the bottom of Castle Foregate, trains run half-hourly to Ludlow (£9.60, 30 minutes, hourly at weekends). Trains also go direct to London Marylebone (£52, 2¾ hours, four daily Monday to Saturday, two Sunday services). Alternatively, take one of the regular trains to Birmingham or Crewe and change.

If you're bound for Wales, **Arriva Trains Wales** (0845 606 1660; www.arrivatrainswales.co.uk) runs to Swansea (£33.80, 3¾ hours, hourly) and Holyhead (£34.80, three hours, hourly).

Getting Around

You can hire bikes at **Dave Mellor Cycles** (www.davemellorcycles.com; 9 New St).

Around Shrewsbury

ATTINGHAM PARK

The most impressive of Shropshire's stately homes, **Attingham Park** (NT; 01743-708123; house & grounds adult/child £8.50/5.15, grounds only £3.80/2; house 11am-5.30pm Thu-Tue mid-Mar–early-Nov, grounds 9am-6am daily) was built in imposing neoclassical style in 1785. With its grand columned facade and manicured lawns, and a stagecoach turning-circle in the courtyard, the house could have been plucked straight from a bodice-ripping period drama. Inside you can see an elegant picture gallery by John Nash, and two wings, decorated in very different Regency styles – highlights include the cherub-filled ladies' boudoir and the grand dining room, laid out as if the banquet guests could arrive any minute. Home to some 300 fallow deer, the landscaped grounds swirl around an ornamental lake.

Attingham Park is 4 miles southeast of Shrewsbury at Atcham – take bus 81 or 96 (18 minutes, six daily Monday to Friday, less frequently at weekends).

Ironbridge Gorge

Strolling or cycling through the woods, hills and villages of this peaceful river gorge, it's hard to believe such a sleepy enclave could really have been the birthplace of the Industrial Revolution. Nevertheless, it was here that Abraham Darby perfected the art of smelting iron-ore with coke in 1709, making it possible to mass-produce cast iron for the first time. Before long, the valley was dotted with factories churning out iron components for newly invented steam engines, pumps and turbines.

Abraham Darby's son, Abraham Darby II, invented a new forging process for producing single beams of iron, allowing Abraham Darby III to astound the world with the first ever iron bridge, constructed in 1779. The bridge remains the focal point of this World Heritage Site, and 10 very different museums tell the story of the Industrial Revolution in the very buildings where it took place.

The Ironbridge museums are spread out along both sides of the River Severn near the village of Coalbrookdale. The best way to explore is on foot, or by rented bicycle or the special tourist bus.

Sights & Activities

The Ironbridge museums are administered by the **Ironbridge Gorge Museum Trust** (☎01952-884391; www.ironbridge.org.uk), and all are open from 10am to 5pm from late March to early November, unless stated otherwise. You can buy tickets as you go, but the good-value **passport ticket** (adult/child £21.95/14.25) allows year-round entry to all of the sites.

Museum of the Gorge MUSEUM
(The Wharfage; adult/child £3.60/2.35) Kick off your visit at the Museum of the Gorge, which offers an overview of the World Heritage Site using film, photos and 3-D models. Housed in a Gothic warehouse by the river, it's filled with entertaining, hands-on exhibits.

Coalbrookdale Museum of Iron MUSEUM
(Wellington Rd; adult/child, £7.40/4.95) Set in the brooding buildings of Abraham Darby's original iron foundry, the Museum of Iron contains some excellent interactive exhibits. As well as producing the girders for the Ironbridge, the factory became famous for heavy machinery and extravagant ornamental castings, including the gates for London's Hyde Park. Combined tickets with Darby Houses also available.

Darby Houses MUSEUM
(☎01952-433522; adult/child £4.60/3; ⊙Apr-Oct) Just uphill from the Museum of Iron are these beautifully restored 18th-century homes, which housed generations of the Darby family in gracious but modest Quaker comfort.

Iron Bridge & Tollhouse BRIDGE
The flamboyant, arching **Iron Bridge** that gives the area its name was constructed to flaunt the new technology invented by the inventive Darby family. At the time of its construction in 1779, nobody could believe that anything so large could be built from cast iron without collapsing under its own weight. There's a small exhibition on the bridge's history at the former **tollhouse** (admission free).

Blists Hill Victorian Town MUSEUM
(☎01952-433522; Legges Way, Madeley; adult/child £14.60/9.35) Set at the top of the Hay Inclined Plane (a cable lift that once transported coal barges uphill from the Shropshire Canal), Blists Hill is a lovingly restored Victorian village that has been repopulated with townsfolk in period costume, carrying out day-to-day activities like washing clothes, mending hobnail boots and working the village iron foundry. Some buildings are original, while others have been convincingly re-created or moved here from other villages. There's even a bank, where you can exchange your modern pounds for shillings to use at the village shops.

Coalport China Museum & Tar Tunnel MUSEUM
As ironmaking fell into decline, Ironbridge turned its attention to manufacturing chi na pots, using the fine clay mined around Blists Hill. Dominated by a pair of towering bottle kilns, the atmospheric old china works now contains an absorbing **museum** (adult/child £7.40/4.95) tracing the history of the industry, with demonstrations of traditional pottery techniques.

A short stroll along the canal brings you to the 200-year-old **Tar Tunnel** (adult/child £2.50/1.95; ⊙Apr-Sep), an artificial

Ironbridge Gorge

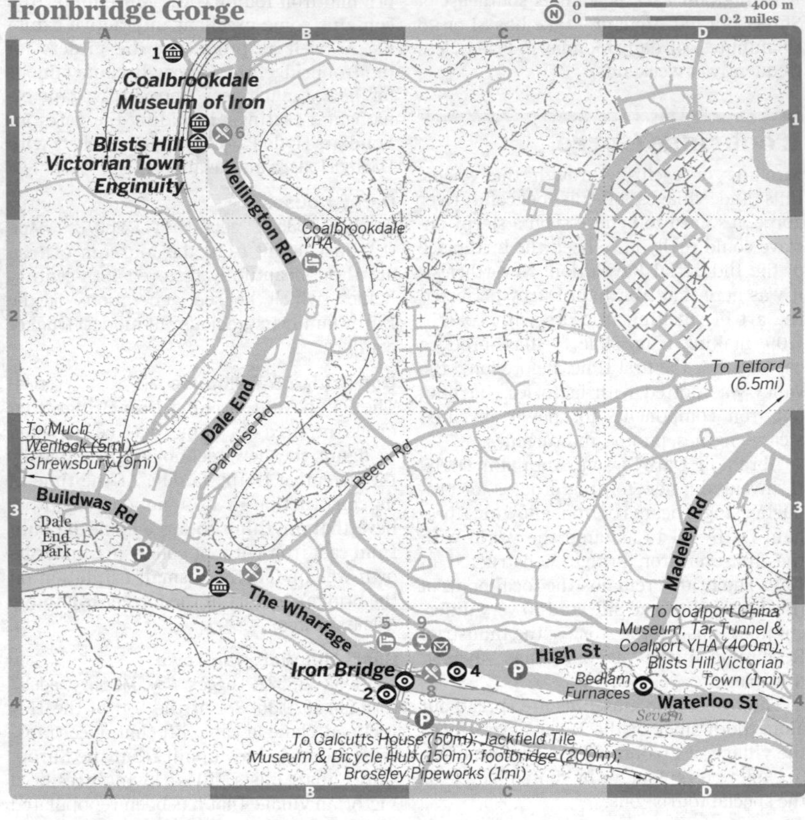

Ironbridge Gorge

Top Sights

Coalbrookdale Museum of Iron ... A1
Blists Hill Victorian Town Enginuity ... A1
Iron Bridge ... B4

Sights

1 Darby Houses ... A1
2 Iron Bridge Tollhouse ... B4
3 Museum of the Gorge ... B3
4 Ironbridge Canoe Hire & Sales ... C4

Sleeping

5 Library House ... B4

Eating

6 Fat Frog ... B1
7 Malthouse ... B3
8 Restaurant Severn ... C4

Drinking

9 Front Cafe Bar ... C4

watercourse that was abandoned when natural bitumen started trickling from its walls. You can don a hard hat and stoop in deep enough to see the black stuff ooze.

Jackfield Tile Museum MUSEUM
(Jackfield; adult/child £7.40/4.95) Once the largest tile factory in the world, Jackfield was famous for its encaustic tiles, with ornate designs produced using layers of different coloured clay (the tiles are still produced here today for period restorations). Gas-lit galleries re-create ornately tiled rooms from past centuries, from Victorian public conveniences to fairy-tale friezes from children's hospital wards. The museum is on the south bank of the Severn, near the footbridge to the Coalport China Museum.

Broseley Pipeworks MUSEUM
(adult/child £4.55/3; ⌚1-5pm mid-May–Sep) This was once the biggest clay tobacco

pipe-maker in the country, but the industry took a nose-dive after the introduction of pre-rolled cigarettes in the 1880s, and the factory was preserved much as the last worker left it when the doors finally closed in 1957. The pipeworks is a 1-mile walk south of the river, on a winding lane that passes the old workers' cottages (ask the tourist office for the *Jitties* leaflet).

Enginuity MUSEUM
(Wellington Rd; adult/child £7.65/6.55) If the kids are tired of fusty historical displays, recharge their batteries at this levers-and-pulleys science centre beside the Museum of Iron, where you can control robots, move a steam locomotive with your bare hands (and a little engineering know-how) and power up a vacuum cleaner with self-generated electricity.

Ironbridge Canoe Hire & Sales CANOEING
(☎01952 433040; www.ironbridgecanoes.com; High St; from £20 per canoe) In summer, when the river is at a safe level, you can rent canoes with which to paddle along the Severn. Longer trips run upstream to Shrewsbury or downstream to Bridgnorth via the Jackfield rapids.

Sleeping

There are two YHA hostels at Ironbridge, but the Coalbrookdale hostel is reserved for groups.

TOP CHOICE **Library House** B&B ££
(☎01952-432299; www.libraryhouse.com; 11 Severn Bank; s/d from £60/70; P @ ᯤ) Up an alley off the main street, this lovingly restored Georgian library building is hugged by vines, backed by a beautiful garden and decked out with stacks of vintage books, curios, prints and lithographs. There are three charming, individually decorated rooms, each of them named after a famous writer.

Coalport YHA HOSTEL £
(☎0845 371 9325; www.yha.org.uk; High St, Coalport; dm from £16, f from £50; P) This superior hostel is set in a converted china factory next to the China Museum and canal. Rooms are modern and functional; the big drawcards are the facilities, including a laundry, kitchen and licensed cafe, and its location in the quietest, prettiest corner of Ironbridge.

Calcutts House B&B ££
(☎01952-882631; www.calcuttshouse.co.uk; Calcutts Rd; s/d/tr from £45/53/90; P) This former ironmaster's pad, built in the 18th century, is tucked away on the south bank, a few paces from the Jackfield Tile Museum. Its traditionally decorated rooms have heaps of character, and each is named after a famous former resident or guest at the house.

Eating & Drinking

Most places to eat are along the High St, but there are old-fashioned pubs scattered along both banks of the River Severn.

Restaurant Severn ANGLO-FRENCH £££
(☎01952-432233; www.restaurantseven.co.uk; 33 High St; 2-/3-course dinner from £23/25; ⊙dinner Wed-Sat, lunch Sun) The highly praised food is a hybrid of English and French at this elegant fine-dining waterfront restaurant. The simple decor and laid-back service attests to the fact that the real star here is the food, and the delectable, locally sourced menu changes weekly.

Fat Frog FRENCH ££
(☎01952-432240; www.fat-frog.co.uk; Wellington Rd; mains £10-17; ⊙closed dinner Sun) The quirky French bar-bistro at the Grove Hotel is cluttered with toy frogs and showbiz memorabilia, amassed by its Gallic proprietor. The food is excellent, and, as you'd expect, there's a great wine list with plenty of half-bottles.

WORTH A TRIP

WESTON PARK

About 10 miles northeast of Ironbridge Gorge on the Staffordshire border, the sprawling stately home of **Weston Park** (☎01952-852100; www.weston-park.com; house & gardens adult/child £8/5.50, grounds only £5/3; ⊙May-Sep, hours change every year so see website for exact times) is one of the two venues for the annual **V Festival** (www.vfestival.com) in August, attracting more than 40,000 revellers. If state rooms and gardens are more your cup of tea, Weston Park has all the oil paintings, chandeliers and fountains you could ask for, plus grounds landscaped by Lancelot 'Capability' Brown. You'll need your own transport to get here.

WORTH A TRIP

COSFORD ROYAL AIR FORCE MUSEUM

About 13 miles east of Ironbridge, this famous aerospace **museum** (☎01902-376200; www.rafmuseum.org; Shifnal; ⊙10am-6pm, closed 2nd week Jan) is run by the Royal Air Force, whose pilots once steered many of these winged wonders across the skies. Aircraft on display range from fearsome war machines like the Vulcan bomber (which once carried Britain's nuclear deterrent) to strange experimental aircraft like the FA330 Bachstelze, a tiny helicopterlike glider towed behind German U-boats to warn them of approaching enemy ships. The museum is a half-mile walk from Cosford train station, on the Birmingham–Shrewsbury line. Visit in June for the annual **Cosford Air Show** (www.cosfordairshow.co.uk), when the Red Arrows stunt team paint the sky with coloured smoke.

Malthouse PUB ££
(☎01952-433712; www.themalthouseironbridge.com; The Wharfage; mains £10-15, s/d £60/70) Facing the river, this former malting house is the best of several similar pubs strung out along the Wharfage. Food comes in generous portions and there's live music nightly from Thursday to Saturday. Tasteful contemporary rooms are also available.

Font Cafe Bar CAFE BAR £
(High St; snacks from £3; ⊙9.30am-6.30pm Sun-Thu, to midnight Fri & Sat; @ wi-fi) Travellers with mobile devices can take advantage of free wi-fi at this watering hole on the main road.

Information

Tourist office (☎01952-884391; www.visitironbridge.co.uk; The Wharfage; ⊙10am-5pm) Located at the Museum of the Gorge.

Getting There & Away

The nearest train station is 6 miles away at Telford, but you can continue on to Ironbridge on bus 96 (20 minutes, every two hours Monday to Saturday). The same bus continues from the Visitor Centre to Shrewsbury (40 minutes). Bus 9 runs from Bridgnorth (30 minutes, four daily, no Sunday service) and bus 39 runs to Much Wenlock (30 minutes, four daily, no Sunday service).

Getting Around

At weekends and on bank holidays from Easter to October, the Gorge Connect bus (free to Museum Passport holders) runs from Telford bus station to all of the museums on the north bank of the Severn. A Day Rover pass costs £2.50/1.50 per adult/child. To reach the Jackfield Tile Museum, cross the footbridge at the bottom of the Hay Inclined Plane; to reach the Broseley Pipeworks, cross the Ironbridge and follow the signs.

Bikes can be rented from **Bicycle Hub** (☎01952-883249; Jackfield; rental per day from £15; ⊙10am-5pm Mon-Sat) in the Fusion centre, behind the Jackfield Tile Museum.

Much Wenlock

POP 1959

With one of those quirky names that abound in the English countryside, Much Wenlock is as charming as it sounds. Surrounding the time-worn ruins of Wenlock Priory, the streets are studded with Tudor, Jacobean and Georgian houses, and locals say hello to everyone. As well as being a perfect English village, Much Wenlock also claims to have jump-started the modern Olympics (see the boxed text, p553).

The **tourist office** (☎01952-727679; www.muchwenlockguide.info; The Square; ⊙10.30am-1pm & 1.30-5pm Apr-Oct, 10.30am-1pm & 1.30-5pm Tue, Fri & Sat morning Nov-Mar) has stacks of brochures on local sights and walks, and a modest **museum** (admission free) of local history.

Sights & Activities

Wenlock Priory RUINS
(EH; ☎01952-727466; adult/child incl audio tour £3.80/1.90; ⊙10am-5pm May-Aug, 10am-5pm Wed-Sun Mar, Apr, Sep & Oct, 10am-4pm Thu-Sun Nov-Feb) The atmospheric ruins of Wenlock Priory rise up from vivid green lawns, sprinkled with animal-shaped topiary. Raised by Norman monks over the ruins of a Saxon monastery from AD680, the hallowed ruins include a finely decorated chapterhouse and an unusual carved lavabo, where monks came to ceremonially wash before eating.

Across from the tourist office, the wonky **Guildhall** (☎01952-727509; admission £1;

⏲10.30am-1pm & 2-4.30pm Mon-Sat & 2-4.30pm Sun Apr-Oct), built in classic Tudor style in 1540, features some splendidly ornate woodcarving. One of the pillars supporting it was used for public floggings in medieval times.

A short walk north, the ancient, eroded **Holy Trinity Church** (www.muchwenlockchurch.co.uk; ⏲9am-5pm) was built in 1150 over Saxon foundations.

Sleeping & Eating

Raven Hotel HOTEL £££
(☎01952-727251; www.ravenhotel.com; Barrow St; mains from £10-20; s/d £85/130; P) Much Wenlock's finest, this 17th-century coaching inn and converted stables has oodles of historical charm and rich country-chic styling throughout. The excellent restaurant overlooks a flowery courtyard and serves up classic Mediterranean and British fare.

Fox PUB ££
(☎01952-727292; www.the-fox-inn.co.uk; 46 High St; mains £8-17, s/d from £65/85; @) Warm yourself by the massive fireplace, then settle down in the dining room to enjoy locally sourced venison, pheasant and beef, swished down with a pint of Shropshire ale. It also has some surprisingly contemporary rooms.

The closest hostel is Wilderhope Manor YHA on Wenlock Edge.

Getting There & Away

Buses 436 and 437 run from Shrewsbury to Much Wenlock (35 minutes, hourly, every two hours Sunday) and on to Bridgnorth (20 minutes).

Bus 39 runs to Ironbridge (30 minutes, four daily, no Sunday service).

Around Much Wenlock

The spectacular limestone escarpment of **Wenlock Edge** swells up like an immense petrified wave, breaking over the Shropshire countryside. Formed from limestone that once lined the bottom of Silurian seas, the ridge sprawls for 15 miles from Much Wenlock to Craven Arms, providing a fantastic **hiking** back-route from Ludlow and Ironbridge. The National Trust (NT) owns much of the ridge, and there are many marked trails starting from car parks dotted along the B4371. However, there are no convenient buses along this route.

For a bite, a beer or a bed, point your hiking boots towards the 17th-century **Wenlock Edge Inn** (☎01746-785678; Hilltop, Easthope; s/d £50/75; P), perched atop the Edge about 4.5 miles southwest of Much Wenlock. It's a down-to-earth place with above-average pub grub (mains £9 to £15) and five chintzy but cosy rooms.

Alternatively, ramble out to the remote **Wilderhope Manor YHA** (☎0845 371 9149; www.yha.org.uk; Longville-in-the-Dale; dm £13.95, f £44.95; ⏲Fri, Sat & school holidays; P), a gloriously atmospheric gabled greystone Elizabethan manor, with spiral staircases, wood-panelled walls, an impressive stone-floored dining hall and spacious, oak-beamed rooms. This is hostelling for royalty!

Bus 155 from Ludlow and buses 153 and 154 from Bridgnorth run infrequently to

GRANDADDY OF THE MODERN OLYMPICS

All eyes will be on London when the Olympic Games arrive in 2012, but tiny Much Wenlock will be holding its own Olympic Games in July the same year, as it has every year since 1850. The idea of holding a sporting tournament based on the games of ancient Greece was the brainchild of local doctor William Penny Brookes, who was looking for a healthy diversion for bored local youths. Accordingly, he created a tournament for 'every kind of man', with running races, high and long jumps, tilting, hammer throwing and wheelbarrow races – plus glee singing, knitting and sewing so every kind of woman didn't feel left out!

The games soon piqued the interest of Baron Pierre Coubertin, who visited Much Wenlock in 1890 and consulted Brookes extensively before launching the modern Olympic Games in Athens in 1896. Unfortunately, Brookes was effectively airbrushed out of the Olympic story until 1994, when International Olympic Committee President Juan Antonio Samaranch visited Much Wenlock to pay his respects to 'the founder of the Modern Olympic Games'.

The Much Wenlock Olympics are still held every July, with events that range from the triathlon to volleyball. You can find details at www.wenlock-olympian-society.org.uk.

AN ABUNDANCE OF ABBEYS

Ravaged by Henry VIII's battle between church and state, Shropshire is dotted with ruined medieval monasteries, most bearing the scars of this tumultuous time in history. **Wenlock Priory** (see p552) and **Shrewsbury Abbey** (see p545) are rightly famous, and you'll find more atmospheric ruins dating back to the 12th century at delightful **Buildwas Abbey** (EH; Buildwas; adult/child £3.20/1.60; ⏲10am-5pm Wed-Sun Apr-Sep) on the A1469, 2 miles west of Ironbridge, and peaceful **Haughmond Abbey** (EH; nr Shrewsbury; adult/child £3.20/1.60; ⏲10am-5pm Wed-Sun Apr-Sep), 3 miles north-east of Shrewsbury on the B5092.

Shipton, a half-mile walk from Wilderhope – call the hostel for the latest timetable.

Bridgnorth & Around

POP 11,891

Cleaved into two by a dramatic sandstone bluff that tumbles down to the River Severn, Bridgnorth is worth a trip for a nostalgic ride on the **Bridgnorth Cliff Railway** (☎01746-762052; www.bridgnorthcliffrailway.co.uk; return £1; ⏲8am-8pm Mon-Sat & noon-8pm Sun May-Sep, to 6.30pm Oct-Apr), the steepest inland railway in Britain. Looking like a Victorian omnibus jacked up on girders, the train has been trundling its way up the cliff since 1892. At the top of the route, a pedestrian walkway curves around the bluff to a pretty park dotted with scattered masonry – all that remains of **Bridgnorth Castle** – passing the Thomas Telford–designed **St Mary's Church**.

Bridgnorth is also the northern terminus of the **Severn Valley Railway** (☎01299-403816; www.svr.co.uk; one-way/return £15.50/11, children half-price; ⏲daily May-Sep, weekends winter), whose trains chug down the valley to Kidderminster (one hour), starting from the station on Hollybush Rd. Cyclists can follow a beautiful 20-mile section of the **Mercian Way** (NCN Route 45) beside the railway line towards the Wyre Forest.

Just south of town, **Daniels Mill** (☎01746-762753; www.danielsmill.co.uk; Eardington; adult/child £3/2.50; ⏲11am-5pm Easter-Oct) is the largest working water-powered mill in the country, and it still produces flour for local bakers. Visitors get a personal tour of the working machinery from the resident miller.

Several narrow lanes drop down from the High Town to the Low Town, including the pedestrian Cartway, where the **Cinnamon Cafe** (☎01746-762944; Waterloo House, Cartway; mains £5-8; ⏲9am-6pm Mon-Wed & Fri, 10am-4pm Sat & Sun) serves up savoury bakes (many vegetarian and vegan) plus quiches and homemade cakes, which you can munch indoors or in front of the views from the terrace.

Based at the town library, the **tourist office** (☎01746-763257; www.visitbridgnorth.co.uk; ⏲9.30am-5pm Mon-Sat Apr-Oct, closed Thu Nov-Mar) can advise on local B&Bs.

Getting There & Away

Buses 436 and 437 run hourly from Shrewsbury to Bridgnorth (one hour, five Sunday services), via Much Wenlock (25 minutes). Bus 9 runs to Ironbridge (30 minutes, four daily, no Sunday service).

Church Stretton & Around

POP 3841

Set in a deep valley formed by the Long Mynd and the Caradoc Hills, Church Stretton is an ideal base for walks or cycle tours through the Shropshire Hills. Although black-and-white timbers are heavily in evidence, most of the buildings in town are 19th-century fakes, built by the Victorians who flocked here to take the country air. The surrounding hills are the main attraction, but the village is a pleasant place to explore. The Norman-era **St Laurence's Church** features an exhibitionist sheila-na-gig over its north door.

The **tourist office** (☎01694-723133; www.churchstretton.co.uk; Church St, Church Stretton; ⏲9.30am-5pm Mon-Sat, closed 12.30-1.30pm winter), adjoining the library, has abundant walking information as well as free internet access.

Activities

Walking

Church Stretton clings to the steeply sloping sides of the **Long Mynd**, Shropshire's most famous hill, which rises to 517m. Dubbed 'Little Switzerland' by the Victorians, this desolate but dramatic bluff is girdled by walking trails that offer soaring views over the surrounding countryside. Most people start walking from the National Trust car park at the end of the **Carding Mill Valley** (www.cardingmillvalley.org.uk), half a mile west of Shrewsbury Rd – a small **tea-room** (⏲11am-5pm) provides refreshments. To escape the summer weekend crowds, head east across the A49 and climb the 459m summit of **Caer Caradoc**.

A maze of single-track roads climbs over the Long Mynd to the adjacent ridge of **Stiperstones**, which is crowned by a line of spooky-looking crags where Satan is said to hold court. You can continue right over the ridge to the village of **Snailbeach**, with its intriguing mining relics (see boxed text, p556), passing the **Bog** (www.bogcentre.co.uk; 10am-5pm Wed-Sun Easter-Oct), a cosy cafe and information centre next to the ruins of an abandoned mining village.

Other Activities

The tourist office has maps of local mountain-biking circuits and details of local riding stables. To soar above the Long Mynd like a bird of prey, contact **Beyond Extreme** (☎01691-682640; www.beyondextreme.co.uk; 2 Burway Rd, Church Stretton) for hill-launch paragliding lessons and tandem flights.

Sleeping

Bridges Long Mynd YHA HOSTEL £
(☎01588-650656; www.yha.org.uk; Bridges; dm from £13; P) On the far side of the Long Mynd, this superior YHA property is housed in a former school in the tiny hamlet of Bridges near Ratlinghope. Popular with hikers, the hostel is wonderfully isolated, but meals and liquid refreshment are available at the nearby Horseshoe Inn pub. To get here, cross the Mynd to Ratlinghope, or take the Long Mynd shuttle bus.

Jinlye Guest House B&B ££
(☎01694-723243; www.jinlye.co.uk; Castle Hill, All Stretton; s/d £60/80; P) High above the village of All Stretton on the top of the Mynd, Jinlye is a beautifully restored crofter's cottage. In contrast to the rugged terrain on all sides, the interior is warm and cosy, with old beams, log fires and bright bedrooms full of historic odds and ends. Wheelchair accessible.

Mynd House B&B ££
(☎01694-722212; www.myndhouse.com; Ludlow Rd, Little Stretton; s/d from £40/75; P @ ☎). South of Church Stretton in Little Stretton, this inviting, family-friendly guesthouse has splendid views across the valley, and it backs directly onto the Mynd. The tastefully furnished rooms are bright and airy, there's a small bar and lounge stocked with local books, and the owners are full of hiking advice.

Longmynd Hotel HOTEL ££
(☎01694-722244; www.longmynd.co.uk; Cunnery Rd, Church Stretton; s/d £60/120; P @ ☎) Above town on the edge of the Mynd, this long-established Victorian hotel has neoclassical airs. Rooms are cosy and facilities include a drying room for your hiking boots, a swimming pool, a sculpture trail and excellent food.

Eating & Drinking

As well as the following places, there are several cosy pubs along the High St.

Berry's Coffee House CAFE £
(☎01694-724452; www.berryscoffeehouse.co.uk; 17 High St, Church Stretton; meals £6-8; ⏲10am-5pm) A sociable cafe in an 18th-century house with a pretty conservatory, just off the main street. Berry's is proud of its organic, free-range, fair-trade, wholesome menu, but makes up for all that goodness with wicked desserts.

Studio MODERN EUROPEAN £££
(☎01694-722672; www.thestudiorestaurant.net; 59 High St, Church Stretton; 2/3 courses £24/26.50; ⏲dinner Wed-Sat) A former artist's studio (still littered with interesting works) sets the scene for the town's most intimate restaurant, which features an award-winning menu of modern English and traditional French food.

Van Doesburg's DELI £
(www.vandoesburgs.co.uk; sandwiches from £3; 3 High St, Church Stretton; ⏲9am-5pm Mon-Sat) You'll find everything you need for a posh picnic at this excellent patisserie-delicatessen, which sources its ingredients from local farms and small producers.

Getting There & Around

Trains between Ludlow and Shrewsbury stop here every hour, taking 20 minutes from either end. Alternatively, take bus 435 from Shrewsbury or Ludlow (40 minutes, hourly, Monday to Saturday).

From April to September, the **Long Mynd & Stiperstones Shuttle** (www.shropshirehillsshuttles.co.uk; all-day adult/child £7/2.50, seven daily Sat, Sun & bank holiday Mon) runs from the Carding Mill Valley in Church Stretton to the villages atop the Long Mynd, passing the YHA at Bridges, the Stiperstones and the Snailbeach mine.

You can hire good-quality road and mountain bikes from **Shropshire Hills Bike Hire**

(☎01694-723302; 6 Castle Hill, All Stretton; per day from £12.50).

Bishop's Castle

POP 1630

Set amid blissfully peaceful Shropshire countryside, Bishop's Castle is a higgledy-piggledy tangle of timbered town houses and Old Mother Hubbard cottages. No trace remains of the eponymous castle, but the village is a fine base for hiking or cycling, with several historic pubs where you can find liquid refreshment at the end of an energetic day. Lined with surprisingly posh boutiques, the High St climbs from the town church to the adorable Georgian **town hall** abutting the crooked 16th-century **House on Crutches** (☎01588 630007; admission free; ⊙2-5pm Sat & Sun Apr-Sep), which also houses the town **museum**.

The pleasingly potty **Old Time** (☎01588-638467; www.oldtime.co.uk; 29 High St; ⊙10am-6pm Mon-Sat, to 2pm Sun) is part furniture workshop and part tourist information office.

Activities

Walkers can hike from north Bishops Castle along the **Shropshire Way**, which joins up with the long-distance **Offa's Dyke Path** and **Kerry Ridgeway** to the west. The northern sections of the Shropshire Way climb to the high country of the Stiperstones and the Long Mynd near Church Stretton. The tourist office sells a series of *Walking for Pleasure* pamphlets covering local walks. Bishops Castle also lies on the popular **Six Castles Cycleway** (NCN Route 44) between Shrewsbury and Leominster.

Sleeping & Eating

Poppy House B&B ££
(☎01588-638443; www.poppyhouse.co.uk; 20 Market Sq; s/d from £30/60, dishes from £6; ⊙10am-5pm Wed-Sun, to 10pm Sat) An artistic air pervades this sweet guesthouse, attached to a friendly cafe that upgrades to fine dining on Saturday nights. Rooms are bright and welcoming and the Saturday menu runs to braised lamb shanks and cod mornay.

Castle Hotel HOTEL ££
(☎01588-638403; www.thecastlehotelbishopscastle.co.uk; The Square; s/d £45/90; P) Boasting a delightful pergola and water-feature-filled garden, this solid-looking 18th-century coaching inn was allegedly built from the ruins of the vanished Bishop's Castle. The wood-panelled rooms are great value and the pub kitchen serves up hearty English meals.

Other possibilities:

Porch House B&B ££
(☎01588-638854; www.theporchhouse.com; High St; s/d from £45/70; P @ ᯤ) Part of a terrace of timbered 16th-century buildings, this stylish place has imaginatively modernised rooms full of family ornaments and tasteful little details.

Yarborough House CAFE £
(www.yarboroughhouse.com; The Square; ⊙10am-5pm Tue-Sun) Excellent coffee and cakes in a quirky classical music shop and secondhand bookshop.

SOFT GOLD

The rich lead deposits on the western flank of the Long Mynd have been mined since Roman times, when that soft, pliable metal was almost as sought after as gold. Despite being highly toxic, lead was highly valued as a material for serving-dishes, water pipes and cosmetics and – bizarrely – as a food additive. Defrutum, a combination of grape juice and lead acetate, was used to sweeten food well into the medieval period, leading to horrifying levels of lead poisoning.

Lead mining really took off in Shropshire in the 18th century, and the relics of this time are scattered along the route of the A488 between Bishops Castle and Shrewsbury.

In the tiny village of Snailbeach, you can explore the atmospheric ruins of the largest lead mine in Europe on a self-guiding trail. On Sundays from May to October, staff run informative tours, including eerie trips deep into the old **mine workings** (☎01743-790613; www.snailbeachmine.org.uk; tours adult/child £2/1) – advance booking are essential. Snailbeach can also be reached via the Long Mynd & Stiperstone Shuttle from Church Stretton.

Drinking

Three Tuns PUB

(www.thethreetunsinn.co.uk; Salop St) Bishop's Castle's finest watering hole is attached to the tiny **Three Tuns Brewery** (www.threetunsbrewery.co.uk), which has been rolling barrels of nut-brown ale across the courtyard since 1642. It's a cosy local and the ales are delicious – we recommend the Cleric's Cure.

Six Bells Inn PUB

(Church St; mains £8-13; ⏲lunch Tue-Sun, dinner Wed-Sat) This historic 17th-century coaching inn is alive with loyal locals and ramblers who come to sample ales from its adjoining brewery. The pub also has a reputation for traditional English comfort food such as homemade pies and Big Nev's bangers made with local ale.

Getting There & Away

Bus 553 runs to and from Shrewsbury (one hour, six daily). On Saturdays and bank holiday weekends, you can jump on the Secret Hills Shuttle from Craven Arms (40 minutes, four per day).

Ludlow

POP 9548

Fanning out from the rambling ruins of a fine Norman castle, beautiful Ludlow's muddle of narrow streets are a mecca for foodies from across the country. Quite why this genteel market town became a national gastronomic phenomenon is not entirely clear, but the centre is crammed with independent butchers, bakers, grocers, cheesemongers and exceptional restaurants. Factor in bustling markets and a scattering of leaning Jacobean and Georgian buildings and it's easy to see the appeal.

Sights & Activities

Ludlow Castle CASTLE

(☎01584-873355; www.ludlowcastle.com; Castle Sq; adult/child £4.50/2.50; ⏲10am-7pm Aug, to 5pm Apr-Jul & Sep, to 4pm Oct-Mar, Sat & Sun only Dec & Jan). Perched in an ideal defensive location atop a cliff above a crook in the river, the town castle was built to ward off the marauding Welsh – or to enforce the English expansion into Wales, according to those west of the border. Founded after the Norman conquest, the castle was dramatically expanded in the 14th century by the notorious Roger Mortimer, the first Earl of March, who conspired to cause the

Ludlow

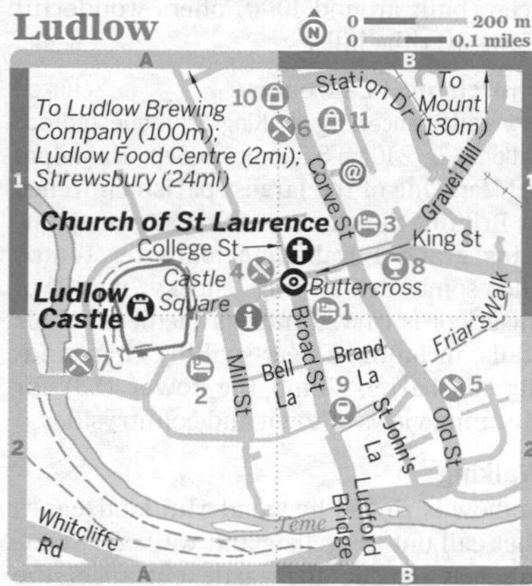

Ludlow

Top Sights

Church of St Laurence B1
Ludlow Castle A1

Sights

Holloways of Ludlow .... (see 11)

Sleeping

1 De Grey's B1
2 Dinham Hall Hotel A2
3 Feathers Hotel B1

Eating

4 Courtyard A1
5 Koo B2
6 La Bécasse B1
7 Mr Underhill's A2

Drinking

8 Church Inn B1
9 Wheatsheaf Inn B2

Shopping

10 Myriad Organics A1
11 Period House Shop B1

grisly death of Edward II and was the de facto ruler of England for three years (before getting his comeuppance at the hands of Edward III).

Despite the passing centuries, the ruins are in impressive shape, with a tangle of secret passageways, ruined rooms and timeworn stairways. The Norman chapel in the inner bailey is one of the few surviving round chapels in England, and the sturdy keep (built around 1090) offers wonderful views over the hills.

Church of St Laurence CHURCH
(www.stlaurences.org.uk; King St; requested donation £2; ⏲10am-5.30pm Apr-Sep, 11am-4pm Oct-Mar) One of the largest parish churches in Britain, the church of St Laurence contains grand Elizabethan alabaster tombs and some delightfully cheeky medieval misericords carved into its medieval choir stalls, including a beer-swilling chap raiding his barrel. Climb the **tower** (£3) for stunning views of town and countryside.

Walking

Ludlow is ringed by wonderful landscapes that call out to cyclists and walkers. Starting just outside the castle entrance, the waymarked **Mortimer Trail** runs for 30 miles through idyllic English countryside to Kington in Herefordshire. The tourist office has various leaflets describing the route, or visit www.mortimercountry.co.uk.

Another fine walking or cycling route is the **Shropshire Way**, which runs northwest to Craven Arms, or northeast to Wenlock Edge over the dramatic summit of **Clee Hill** (540m), the highest point in the county. The hill affords awe-inspiring views south to Worcestershire's Malvern Hills.

For something more leisurely, just take a stroll around town. A scenic path drops behind Ludlow Castle and crosses the River Teme via the Dinham Bridge, following the south bank east to Ludford Bridge. Climbing the hill, duck through the narrow **Broadgate**, which marks the medieval town limits, and stroll past the Georgian town houses of Broad St to reach the **Buttercross**, Ludlow's medieval butter market.

Tours

Popular **town tours** (www.ludlowhistory.co.uk; per person £2.50) run at weekends from April to October, leaving the Cannon in Castle Sq at 2.30pm on Saturday and Sunday. Alternatively, search for spooks on the **ghost walk** (www.shropshireghostwalks.co.uk; adult/child £4/3; ⏲8pm Fri) from outside the Church Inn on the Buttercross.

Festivals & Events

The town's busy calendar peaks with the **Ludlow Festival** (www.ludlowfestival.co.uk), a fortnight of theatre and music in June and July that uses the castle as its dramatic backdrop. The **Ludlow Food & Drink Festival** (www.foodfestival.co.uk) is one of Britain's best foodie celebrations, spanning a long weekend in September.

Sleeping

TOP CHOICE **Feathers Hotel** HOTEL ££
(☎01584-875261; www.feathersatludlow.co.uk; Bull Ring; s/d from £75/95, 2/3 courses £32/39.50; P) Stepping through the almost impossibly ornate timbered Jacobean facade of the Feathers, you can almost hear the cavaliers toasting the health of King Charles. The best rooms are in the old building – rooms in the newer wing lack the character and romance. The restaurant is also highly recommended.

De Grey's B&B ££
(☎01584-872764; www.degreys.co.uk; 73 Broad St; s/d from £60/80) Above the tearooms of the same name, this classy B&B has nine luxurious rooms with low ceilings, beams, leaded windows and reassuringly solid oak beds. The balance of period features and modern luxury is spot on.

Mount B&B ££
(☎01584-874084; www.themountludlow.co.uk; 61 Gravel Hill; s/d from £30/55; P) On the hill northeast of the centre, this agreeable Victorian house offers lovely valley views and a warm welcome for walkers and cyclists. Rooms have crisp white linen and the hostess offers lifts from the railway station.

Dinham Hall Hotel HOTEL ££
(☎01584-876464; www.dinhamhall.co.uk; s/d from £95/125; P) A resplendent 18th-century country manor on the edge of the Mortimer Forest, with gorgeous rooms full of heirloom furniture and posh branded toiletries, plus a superb fine-dining restaurant.

Eating

Almost every pub and restaurant in town has caught the local-produce-and-deli-ingredients bug.

La Bécasse MODERN FRENCH £££
(☎01584-872325; www.labecasse.co.uk; 17 Corve St; 2/3 courses £49/55; ⏲lunch Wed-Sun, dinner Tue-Sat) Artistically presented Modern French cuisine bursting with inventive flavours is served in an oak-panelled, brick walled dining room in a 17th-century coach house. Michelin-starred chef Will Holland has created some remarkable dishes – try the pigeon ballotine with wasabi and mango salsa.

Mr Underhill's MODERN BRITISH £££
(☎01584-874431; www.mr-underhills.co.uk; Dinham Weir; 9-course set menu from £49.50, s/d from £120/130; ⊙dinner Wed-Sun) This dignified and award-winning restaurant is set in a converted corn mill that dips its toes in the river, and the Modern British food is exquisitely prepared, using market-fresh ingredients. Should you be too full to walk home, it has some extremely elegant rooms decked out with designer fabrics and all mod cons.

De Grey's TEAROOM £
(www.degreys.co.uk; 73 Broad St; light meals from £4; ⊙breakfast & lunch) A swooningly nostalgic tearoom that easily could be plucked from an Agatha Christie mystery, serving excellent breakfasts, lunches and afternoon teas, and superior cakes and patisserie throughout the day.

Courtyard CAFE £
(www.thecourtyard.uk.com; 2 Quality Sq; mains £5.50-10; ⊙lunch Mon-Sat, dinner Fri & Sat) Offering light relief from too much gastronomic extravagance, this simple cafe, tucked away in a tranquil courtyard near the market square, has a faithful local following for its lightning service and tasty seasonal food.

Koo JAPANESE ££
(☎01584-878462; 127 Old St; mains £11-15; ⊙dinner Tue-Sat) Cute and kooky, this bright green cubby hole is run by a friendly Japanese chef who's always eager to chat with diners about Japanese etiquette.

Drinking & Entertainment

Real ales are the order of the day in flavour-obsessed Ludlow. The **Ludlow Brewing Company** (www.theludlowbrewingcompany.co.uk; 105 Corve St; ⊙10am-5pm Mon-Fri, to 1pm Sun) produces award-winning brews, and sells directly from the brewery.

Of the many pubs, the hop-strewn **Church Inn** (Buttercross) is a cosy little escape, tucked away on the narrow lane beside the old butter market. The quiet little **Wheatsheaf Inn** (Lower Broad St), under the medieval Broadgate, has a good choice of local ales.

Overlooking the market square, **Ludlow Assembly Rooms** (☎01584-878141; www.ludlowassemblyrooms.co.uk; adult/child £5/3) also double as the town cinema, with an intriguing program of mainstream features and challenging documentaries, vintage classics and world cinema, appealing to the cultured tastes of the locals.

Shopping

The best of the delis, independent butchers and artisanal bakers are clustered around the market square and the surrounding lanes, and small producers crowd the markets held in Castle Sq every Monday, Wednesday, Friday and Saturday.

If you can't wait till market day, try **Myriad Organics** (☎01584-872665; 22 Corve St; ⊙8.30am-6pm Mon-Sat) or the **Ludlow Food Centre** (☎01584-856000; Bromfield; ⊙9.30am-5.30pm Mon-Sat, 10.30am-4.30pm Sun), a handy one-stop-shop for wholefoods and gourmet ingredients, about 2 miles northwest of Ludlow on the A49.

In the town centre, elegant Corve St is lined with quirky interiors stores, including famous **Holloways of Ludlow** (☎01584-876207; www.hollowaysofludlow.com; 140 Corve St; ⊙9.30am-5pm Tue-Sat), with reclaimed Victorian treasures, and the **Period House Shop** (☎01584-877276; www.periodhouseshops.com; 141 Corve St; ⊙9.30am-5pm Mon-Sat) with reproduction brass knobs and knockers.

Information

Tourist office (☎01584-875053; www.ludlow.org.uk; Castle Sq; ⊙10am-5pm Mon-Sat, 10.30am-5pm Sun) This office contains an inside-out **museum** (☎01584-813666, admission free, open 10am to 5pm Monday to Saturday, plus Sunday from June to August) featuring the town and surrounding area.

Library (☎01584-813600; 7-9 Parkway; ⊙9.30am-5pm Mon-Wed & Sat, to 7.30pm Fri) Internet can be tracked down here.

Getting There & Around

Trains run frequently from the station on the north edge of town to Hereford (£7.40, 25 minutes, every half-hour) and Shrewsbury (£9.60, 30 minutes, every half-hour) via Church Stretton (16 minutes). You can also reach Shrewsbury on bus 435 (1½ hours, hourly Monday to Saturday), which runs via Craven Arms (20 minutes) and Church Stretton (40 minutes).

You can hire bikes from **Wheely Wonderful** (☎01568-770755; www.wheelywonderfulcycling.co.uk; Petchfield Farm, Elton; bike per day from £24), 5 miles west of Ludlow.

Around Ludlow

Just 7 miles northwest of Ludlow, **Craven Arms** bills itself as the gateway to the Shropshire Hills, by virtue of its train station and its position near the southern end of

THE CASTLES OF MARCH

The hills between Shrewsbury and Leominster are crowned by a series of dramatic castles, constructed by the Lords Marcher to protect their territory from the marauding Welsh. Some are impressively intact, while others, like Richard's Castle near Ludlow, have been almost entirely reclaimed by nature. Many of these time-worn fortresses can be visited on the **Shropshire Way** walking trail or the 58-mile **Six Castles Cycleway** (NCN Route 44), which runs south from Shrewsbury to Leominster and Hereford, via Bishop's Castle, Craven Arms and Ludlow.

Top stops on the castle trail:

» Shrewsbury Castle (p546): russet-sandstone walls enclosing a military museum

» Bishop's Castle (p556): the castle is gone, but its stones prop up the hilltop pub

» Clun Castle (p560): a classic moat and bailey ruin overlooking the river, in Clun

» Stokesay Castle (p560): a Lord-of-the-Rings fantasy south of Craven Arms

» Ludlow Castle (p557): a ruin and round chapel in the middle of Shropshire's most charming town

» Croft Castle (p539): not medieval, but suitably grand and turreted; near Aymestrey

Wenlock Edge. It's worth deviating west along the B4368 to the quaint village of **Clun**, with its stone bridge and ruined **castle**, and **Clunton**, where a forest trail leads to the Bury Ditches, a huge Iron-Age hill fort.

Craven Arms is also the central point on the **Shropshire Way** – from here, you can hike west to Bishop's Castle, north to the Long Mynd, or east to the summit of Clee Hill (540m) and Wenlock Edge. Eight miles west of Craven Arms, **Hopton Wood** is a favourite destination for mountain-bikers, with some challenging waymarked trails.

Housed in a striking turf-roofed building on the A49, the **Shropshire Hills Discovery Centre** (☎01588-676000; adult/child £4.50/3; ⏲10am-5.30pm Apr-Oct, to 4.30pm Nov-Mar) provides local information and has a great family-friendly museum on the geology and natural history of the Shropshire Hills. A reconstructed mammoth and simulated balloon flight are the highlights.

Trains on the Shrewsbury–Ludlow line pass through every 30 minutes; you can also get here on bus 435 from Shrewsbury or Ludlow (hourly Monday to Saturday). On weekends from April to September, the **Shropshire Hills Shuttles** (www.shropshirehillsshuttles.co.uk; all-day adult/child £7/2.50; ⏲Sat & Sun Apr-Sep) run to Clun, Bishop's Castle, Church Stretton and the villages of the Long Mynd.

Just 1 mile south of Craven Arms, Tolkeinesque **Stokesay Castle** (EH; ☎01588-672544; adult/child £5.50/2.80; ⏲10am-5pm Apr-Sep, 10am-5pm Wed-Sun Mar & Oct, 10am-4pm Thu-Sun Nov-Feb) was built by Lawrence of Ludlow, Britain's most successful wool merchant, in 1291. The formidable fortifications were largely built for show, as the Anglo-Welsh wars were effectively over when it was constructed, but the wooden staircase in the great hall once creaked with the footsteps of knights and lords.

To really escape from it all, head to the secluded **Waterdine Inn** (☎01547-528214; www.waterdine.com; Llanfair Waterdine; s/d incl dinner & breakfast £85/170; Ⓟ), a timbered and ivy-clad 16th-century longhouse set right against the border with Wales. As well as offering comfortable cottage-style rooms, this foodie retreat serves some of the best Modern British food in Shropshire, with plenty of organic meats and wild game. Llanfair Waterdine is about 12 miles west of Ludlow.

North Shropshire

North of Shrewsbury, the hills are lower and the landscape less dramatic, but there are several worthwhile diversions set among the rolling green pastures. With a market dating back 750 years, **Market Drayton** was once home to Clive of India, founder of Britain's Indian Empire. The town church contains the medieval tomb of Thomas and Elizabeth Bulkley, distant ancestors of George W Bush. The **tourist office** (☎01584-653114; 49 Cheshire St; ⏲9.30am-4pm Mon-Sat) can point you towards the sights.

Five miles southwest of Market Drayton, **Wollerton Old Hall** (☎01630-685760; www.

wollertonoldhallgarden.com; Wollerton; adult/child £5.50/1; ⌚Fri, Sun & bank holidays noon-5pm Apr-Sep) is a treat for gardeners, with its beautifully manicured lawns and flowers surrounding a 16th-century house.

Heading 4 miles west of Wollerton Old Hall, you'll find the ideal energy-burning spot for kids, **Hawkstone Park** (☎01939-200611; www.hawkstone.co.uk; Weston-under-Redcastle; adult/child £6.95/4; ⌚10am-4pm Apr-Aug, see website for winter opening times). This is a grand country house whose grounds contain the **Follies**, which is a magical complex of fantasy towers, deep ravines and spooky rock-hewn grottoes that were created in the 18th century.

Another leap westwards will bring you to the beautiful countryside around **Ellesmere**. The six glacial lakes surrounding the town are ideal for gentle walking, with well-signposted circular routes.

So close to Wales you can almost hear the male-voice choirs, **Oswestry** is famous for its Iron Age hill fort and the community-owned **Whittington Castle** (☎01691-662397; Whittington; admission free; ⌚10am-4pm Wed-Sun Mar-Oct, 10am-4pm Fri-Sun Nov-Feb), whose romantic turrets are built around a 12th-century keep.

About 3 miles northwest of Oswestry, the elegant **Pen-y-Dyffryn Hotel** (☎01691-653700; www.peny.co.uk; Rhydycroesau, Oswestry; s/d from £60/120; P) offers calm comfort in a wonderful setting among steep green hills. Inside this Georgian rectory, you'll find comfy lounges around open fires, and a restaurant serving the best organic cuisine.

Yorkshire

Includes »

Best Places to Eat

- J Baker's Bistro Moderne (p606)
- The Stone Trough (p609)
- Star Inn (p621)

Best Places to Stay

- Devonshire Fell (p584)
- Beiderbecke's Hotel (p617)
- Holme House (p579)

Why Go?

With a population as big as Scotland's and an area half the size of Belgium, Yorkshire is almost a country in itself. It has its own flag, its own dialect and its own Yorkshire Day celebration (1 August). While local folk are proud to be English, they're even prouder to be natives of 'God's Own Country'.

What makes Yorkshire so special? First there's the landscape – from the brooding moors and green dales that roll their way to the dramatic coastline, Yorkshire has some of England's finest scenery. Second, there's the sheer breadth of history – every facet of the English experience is represented here, from Roman times to the 20th century.

But Yorkshire's greatest appeal is its people. Industrious and opinionated, they have a wry wit and a shrewd friendliness. Stay here for a while and you'll come away believing, like the locals, that God is indeed a Yorkshirewoman.

When to Go

In February the week-long Jorvik Festival sees York taken over by a Viking invasion.

In July, the Great Yorkshire Show happens in Harrogate, and Yorkshire's coastal sea-cliffs become a frenzy of nesting seabirds.

The ideal time for hiking in the Yorkshire Dales is September; the Walking Festival in Richmond also happens in September.

History

As you drive through Yorkshire on the main A1 road, you're following in the footsteps of the Roman legions who conquered northern Britain in the 1st century AD. In fact, many Yorkshire towns – including York, Catterick and Malton – were founded by the Romans, and many modern roads (including the A1, A59, A166 and A1079) follow the lines of Roman roads.

When the Romans departed in the 5th century, native Britons battled for supremacy with invading Angles and, for a while, Yorkshire was part of the Kingdom of Northumbria. In the 9th century the Vikings arrived and conquered most of northern Britain. They divided the territory that is now Yorkshire into *thridings* (thirds), which all met at Jorvik (York), their thriving commercial capital.

In 1066 Yorkshire was the scene of a pivotal showdown in the struggle for the English crown, when the Anglo-Saxon king Harold II rode north to defeat the forces of the Norwegian king Harold Hardrada at the Battle of Stamford Bridge, before returning south to meet his appointment with William the Conqueror – and a fatal arrow – at the Battle of Hastings.

The inhabitants of northern England did not take the subsequent Norman invasion lying down. The Norman nobles built a chain of formidable castles throughout Yorkshire, including those at York, Richmond, Scarborough, Pickering and Helmsley. They also oversaw the establishment of the great abbeys of Rievaulx, Fountains and Whitby.

The Norman land grab formed the basis of the great estates that supported England's medieval aristocrats. By the 15th century, the duchies of York and Lancaster had become so wealthy and powerful that they ended up battling for the English throne – known as the Wars of the Roses (1455–87), it was a recurring conflict between the supporters of King Henry VI of the House of Lancaster (the red rose) and Richard, Duke of York (the white rose). They ended with the defeat of the Yorkist king Richard III by the earl of Richmond, Henry Tudor, at the Battle of Bosworth Field.

Yorkshire prospered quietly, with fertile farms in the north and the cutlery business of Sheffield in the south, until the big bang of the Industrial Revolution transformed the landscape: south Yorkshire became a centre of coal mining and steel works, while west Yorkshire was home to a massive textile industry, and the cities of Leeds, Bradford, Sheffield and Rotherham flourished. By the late 20th century another revolution was taking place. The heavy industries had died out, and the cities of Yorkshire were re-inventing themselves as shiny, high-tech centres of finance, higher education and tourism.

Activities

Yorkshire's varied landscape of wild hills, tranquil valleys, high moors and spectacular coastline offers plenty of opportunities for outdoor activities. See www.outdooryorkshire.com for more details.

CYCLING

Yorkshire has a vast network of country lanes, although the most scenic areas also attract lots of motorists so even minor roads can be busy at weekends. Options include:

North York Moors
(www.mtb-routes.co.uk/northyorkmoors) Off-road bikers can avail themselves of the networks of bridleways, former railways and disused mining tracks now converted to two-wheel use.

Moor to Sea Cycle Route
(www.moortoseacycle.net) Network of routes between Pickering, Danby and the coast, including a 20-mile traffic-free route that follows a disused railway line between Whitby and Scarborough.

White Rose Cycle Route
(NCN route 65; www.sustrans.org.uk) A 120-mile cruise from Hull to York and on to Middlesbrough, via the rolling Yorkshire Wolds and the dramatic western scarp of the North York Moors, with a traffic-free section on the old railway between Selby and York.

Yorkshire Dales Cycleway
(www.cyclethedales.org.uk) An exhilarating 130-mile loop, taking in the best of the national park. There's also lots of scope for off road riding, with around 500 miles of bridleways and trails – check out www.mtbthedales.org.uk for inspiration.

WALKING

For shorter walks and rambles the best area is the **Yorkshire Dales**, with a great selection of walks through scenic valleys or over wild hilltops, with a few higher summits thrown in for good measure. The East Riding's **Yorkshire Wolds** hold hidden delights, while the quiet valleys and dramatic

Yorkshire Highlights

1 Exploring the medieval streets of **York** (p597) and its awe-inspiring cathedral

2 Pulling on your hiking boots and striding out across the moors of the **Yorkshire Dales** (p582)

3 Chilling out in **Leeds** (p570): shopping, eating, drinking, dancing

4 Being beside the seaside at **Scarborough** (p615) with its traditional bucket-and-spade atmosphere

5 Riding on the **North Yorkshire Moors Railway** (p623), one of England's most scenic railway lines

6 Discovering mining's dark side at the **National Coal Mining Museum for England** (p578)

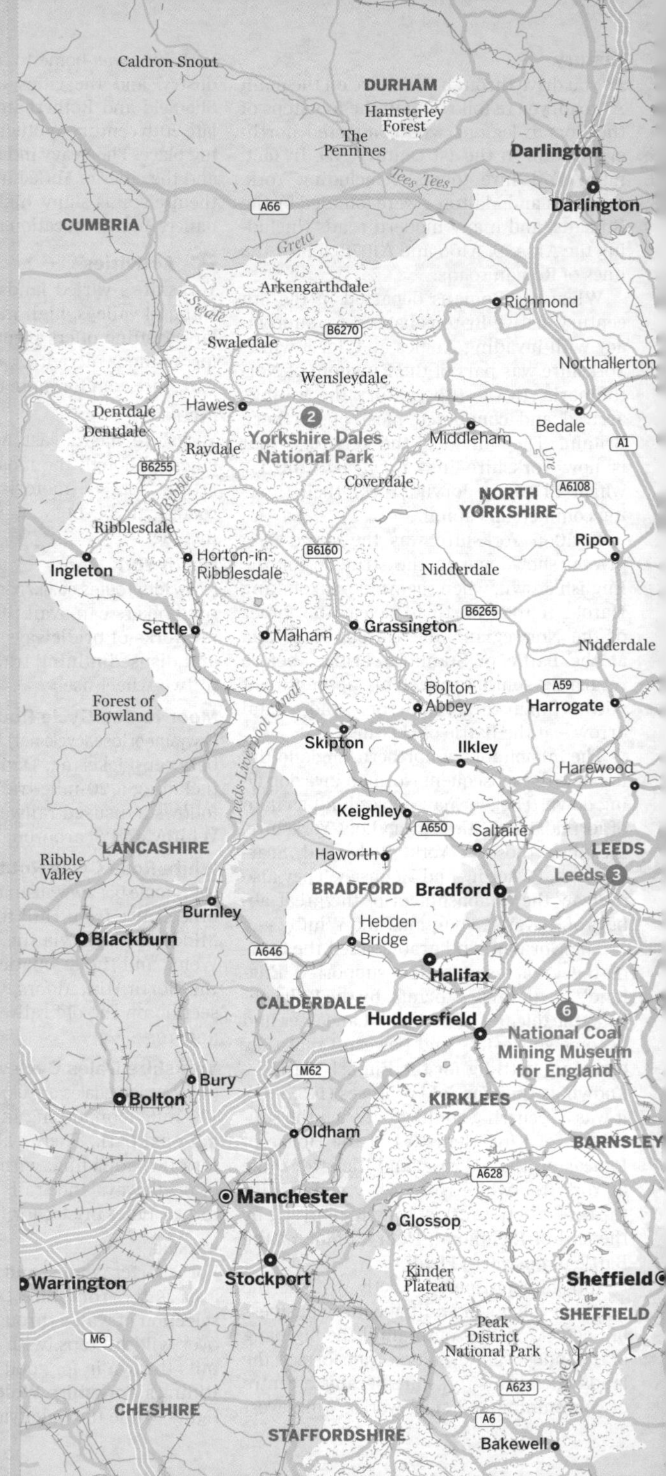

0 20 km
0 10 miles
North Sea
Billingham
Middlesbrough
Stockton-on-Tees
Egglescliffe
Stokesley
Danby
Grosmont
Whitby
Robin Hood's Bay
A174
A171
A19
North York Moors National Park
5 North Yorkshire Moors Railway
Hambleton Hills
Hutton-le-Hole
4 Scarborough
Helmsley
Pickering
Thirsk
Bempton Cliffs Nature Reserve
Flamborough Head
Malton
Cleveland Hills
Derwent
Rye
Hertford
Bridlington
Boroughbridge
B1363
A64
Great Driffield
A166
A59
1 York
YORK
A1079
EAST RIDING OF YORKSHIRE
A1
Beverley
A164
Hull
Hull Ferry Terminal
Ouse
Patrington
Easington
Kilnsea
Humber
Trent
WAKEFIELD
NORTH LINCOLNSHIRE
A15
Grimsby
Spurn Head
Scunthorpe
Cleethorpes
DONCASTER
To Rotterdam & Zeebrugge
Doncaster
NORTHEAST LINCOLNSHIRE
A1031
A18
Rotherham
Market Rasen
A631
Gainsborough
Louth
ROTHERHAM
A46
LINCOLNSHIRE
Worksop
A153
A158
NOTTINGHAMSHIRE
A57
Lincoln
Chesterfield
DERBYSHIRE
Sherwood Forest
Horncastle

coast of the **North York Moors** also have many good opportunities.

Long-distance trails include:

Cleveland Way
(www.nationaltrail.co.uk/clevelandway) A venerable moor-and-coast classic that circles the North York Moors National Park on its 109-mile, nine-day route from Helmsley to Filey.

Coast to Coast Walk
(www.wainwright.org.uk/coasttocoast.html) England's number one walk, 190 miles across northern England from the Lake District across the Yorkshire Dales and North York Moors. The Yorkshire section takes a week to 10 days and offers some of the finest walking of its kind in England.

Dales Way
(www.dalesway.org.uk) A charming and not-too-strenuous amble from the Yorkshire Dales to the Lake District, following the River Wharfe through the heart of the Dales, and finishing at Bowness-on-Windermere.

Pennine Way
(www.nationaltrail.co.uk/pennineway) The Yorkshire section of England's most famous walk runs for over 100 miles via Hebden Bridge, Malham, Horton-in-Ribblesdale and Hawes, passing near Haworth and Skipton.

Wolds Way
(www.nationaltrail.co.uk/yorkshirewoldsway) A beautiful but oft-overlooked walk that winds through the most scenic part of the East Riding of Yorkshire.

ℹ Information

Yorkshire Tourist Board (www.yorkshire.com; 312 Tadcaster Rd, York, YO24 1GS) Has plenty of general leaflets and brochures (postal and email enquiries only). For more detailed information contact the local tourist offices listed throughout this chapter.

ℹ Getting There & Around

The major north-south transport routes – the M1 and A1 motorways and the main London-to-Edinburgh railway line – run through the middle of Yorkshire, serving the key cities of Sheffield, Leeds and York.

If you're arriving by sea from northern Europe, Hull (in the East Riding) is the region's main port. More specific details for each area are given under Getting There & Away sections throughout this chapter. **Traveline Yorkshire** (☎0871 200 22 33; www.yorkshiretravel.net) provides public transport information for the whole of Yorkshire.

BUS Long-distances coaches run by **National Express** (☎08717 81 81 78; www.nationalexpress.com) serve most cities and large towns in Yorkshire from London, the south of England, the Midlands and Scotland. More details are given under Getting There & Away in the individual town and city sections.

Bus transport around Yorkshire is frequent and efficient, especially between major towns. Services are more sporadic in the national parks but still adequate for reaching most places, particularly in the summer months (June to September).

TRAIN The main line between London and Edinburgh runs through Yorkshire, with at least 10 trains per day calling at York and Doncaster, where you can change trains for other Yorkshire destinations. There are also direct services between the major towns and cities of Yorkshire and other northern cities such as Manchester and Newcastle. For timetable information contact **National Rail Enquiries** (☎08457 48 49 50; www.nationalrail.co.uk).

SOUTH YORKSHIRE

As in the valleys of South Wales, it was a confluence of natural resources – coal, iron ore and ample water – that made South Yorkshire a crucible of the British iron, steel and mining industries. From the 18th century to the 20th, the region was the industrial powerhouse of northern England.

Sheffield's and Rotherham's blast furnaces and the coal pits of Barnsley and Doncaster may have closed long ago, but the hulking reminders of that irrepressible Victorian dynamism remain, not only in the old steel works and pit-heads – some of which have been converted into enthralling museums and exhibition spaces – but also in the grand civic buildings that grace Sheffield's city centre, fitting testaments to the untrammelled ambitions of their 19th-century patrons.

Sheffield

POP 525,800

Steel is everywhere in Sheffield. Today, however, it's not the steel of the foundries, mills and forges that made the city's fortune, nor the canteens of cutlery that made 'Sheffield steel' a household name, but the steel of scaffolding and cranes, of modern sculptures and supertrams, and of new steel-framed buildings rising against the skyline.

The steel industry that made the city famous is long since gone, but after many years of decline Sheffield is on the up again –

like many of northern England's cities it has grabbed the opportunities presented by urban renewal with both hands and is working hard to reinvent itself. The new economy is based on services, shopping and the 'knowledge industry' that flows from the city's universities.

This renaissance got off to a shaky start in 2000 when the city's signature millennium project, the National Centre for Popular Music, closed down due to lack of visitors only 15 months after it opened. An eye-catching and controversial piece of modern architecture shaped like four giant, stainless-steel kettles, it now houses Sheffield Hallam University's student union.

But the city's redevelopment seems to be hitting its stride now, with attractive new public spaces and a clutch of interesting museums and galleries. And there's a lively nightlife fuelled by the large student population – the city's two universities support around 24,000 potential pubbers and clubbers – and Sheffield's long-standing reputation as a top spot for music (the birthplace of Pulp, Arctic Monkeys and the up-and-coming Mabel Love).

The most interesting parts of Sheffield are clustered in the 'Heart of the City' district about 300m northwest of the train station (and immediately west of the bus station), a compact area outlined by Arundel Gate, Furnival St, Carver St, West St, Church St and High St. Stretching west from here, Division St and Devonshire St have hip clothes and record shops, popular restaurants and trendy bars.

Sights

Since 2000 the city centre has been in the throes of a massive redevelopment that will continue into 2020 and beyond, so expect building sites and road works for several years to come.

Of the parts that are already complete, pride of place goes to the **Winter Gardens** (admission free; ⌚8am-6pm), a wonderfully ambitious public space with a soaring glass roof supported by graceful arches of laminated timber. The 21st-century architecture contrasts sharply with the Victorian **town hall** nearby, and is further enhanced by the **Peace Gardens** – complete with fountains, sculptures and lawns full of lunching office workers whenever there's a bit of sun.

Sheffield's cultural revival is spearheaded by the **Millennium Gallery** (www.museums-sheffield.org.uk; Arundel Gate; admission free; ⌚10am-5pm Mon-Sat, 11am-5pm Sun), a collection of four galleries under one roof. Inside, the **Ruskin Gallery** houses an eclectic collection of paintings, drawings and manuscripts established and inspired by Victorian artist, writer, critic and philosopher John Ruskin, while the **Metalwork Gallery** charts the transformation of Sheffield's steel industry into craft and design – the 'Sheffield Steel' stamp on locally made cutlery and tableware now has the cachet of designer chic.

The nearby **Graves Gallery** (Surrey St; admission free; ⌚10am-5pm Mon-Sat) has a neat and accessible display of British and European modern art; the big names represented include Cézanne, Gauguin, Miró, Klee and Picasso.

In the days before steel mills, metalworking was a cottage industry (just like wool and cotton). For a glimpse of that earlier, more innocent era, explore the restored 18th-century forges, workshops and machines at the **Abbeydale Industrial Hamlet** (www.simt.co.uk; admission free; ⌚10am-4pm Mon-Thu, 11am-4.45pm Sun, closed early Oct-early Apr), 4 miles southwest of the centre on the A621 (towards the Peak District).

Festivals & Events

The hugely popular **World Snooker Championship** (www.worldsnooker.com) is staged at the Crucible Theatre in April. Accommodation is at a premium.

Sleeping & Eating

Tourism has not quite taken off yet in Sheffield, and most of the city-centre hotels cater primarily to business travellers. New restaurants are springing up – there are several in the Leopold Square development on Leopold St – but the main restaurant areas are outside the centre.

There's a mile-long strip of bars, restaurants, cafes and take-aways on Ecclesall Rd, a mile to the southwest of the city centre, while London Rd, a mile south of the city centre, has a concentration of good-value ethnic restaurants ranging from Turkish to Thai. To find student bars and eateries head along Division St and Devonshire St just west of the city centre.

Leopold Hotel BOUTIQUE HOTEL **££**
(☎0845 078 0067; www.leopoldhotel.co.uk; 2 Leopold St; r £70-90; 📶) Housed in a former grammar school building, Sheffield's first boutique hotel brings some much-needed

style and sophistication to the city's accommodation scene (but without a London-sized price tag). Can suffer late-night noise from the bars on Leopold Square – ask for a quiet room at the back.

Houseboat Hotels HOUSEBOAT ££
(01909-569393; www.houseboathotels.com; Victoria Quays, Wharfe St; s/d/q from £59/69/95; P) Here's something a bit different: kick off your shoes and relax on board your very own permanently moored houseboat, complete with self-catering kitchen and patio area. Guests are entitled to use the gym and pool facilities at the Hilton across the road.

TOP CHOICE **Gusto Italiano** ITALIAN £
(18 Church St; lunch mains £6-10; breakfast & lunch Mon-Sat) A *real* Italian cafe, from the Italian owners serving homemade Italian food to the genuine Italian coffee being enjoyed by Italian customers reading the Italian newspapers... you get the idea. Daily lunch specials include dishes such as fennel sausage casserole, and vegetable lasagne with mushrooms and rosemary.

22a CAFE £
(22a Norfolk Row; mains £4-8; breakfast & lunch Mon-Sat) Nice music, nice people, nice place – this homely cafe serves hearty breakfasts and offers a mean wrap at lunchtime (hummus and roasted veggie is our favourite) and serves it with a decent cup of java.

Blue Moon Cafe VEGETARIAN £
(2 St James St; mains £5-7; breakfast, lunch & dinner Mon-Sat) Tasty veggie and vegan creations, soups and other healthy dishes, all served with the ubiquitous salad, in a very pleasant atmosphere – perfect for a spot of Saturday afternoon lounging.

Drinking

Lots of bars in a relatively small area plus 24,000 students = a wild night out – a pretty straightforward formula, really! The main concentrations of bars are around Division St/Devonshire St and West St in the city centre, and Ecclesall Rd to the southwest. Virtually every bar does pub grub until about 7pm.

Showroom Bar CAFE, BAR
(www.showroomworkstation.org.uk; 7 Paternoster Row;) Originally aimed at film fans, this stylish bar with its arty, hip clientele is one of the best night-time destinations in town. The ambience is good, and so is the food (served from noon to 9pm), and Sunday afternoons have live jazz.

Fat Cat PUB
(www.thefatcat.co.uk; 23 Alma St) One of Sheffield's finest pubs, the Fat Cat serves a wide range of real ales (including Kelham Island, brewed nearby by the pub's owner) in a wonderfully unreconstructed interior. There are three bars, good pub grub, a roaring fire in winter and – in the men's toilets – a fascinating exhibit on local sanitation.

Frog & Parrot PUB
(94 Division St) Home to the world's strongest beer (allegedly), the 12% ABV 'Roger & Out'. Unsuspecting ale-heads saunter in looking to down a pint of something as strong as your average wine, which is why they only serve this particular brew in half-pint glasses (...so that you have at least a 50/50 chance of walking out under your own steam).

Entertainment

Sheffield has a good selection of nightclubs, a couple of top-notch theatres, and venues that attract the big names in music – both classical and popular. The weekly *Sheffield Telegraph* (out on Friday) has the lowdown on Sheffield's entertainment scene, as does the freebie *Exposed,* available almost everywhere, and the e-zine www.sheffieldmusicscene.info.

Clubs & Live Music

Boardwalk LIVE MUSIC
(www.theboardwalklive.co.uk; 39 Snig Hill) A Sheffield institution, the Boardwalk provides a stage for local bands, old rockers, up-and-coming stars, world music, the obscure, the novel and the downright weird – they all play here. No real music fan should miss the chance to catch a gig here.

Leadmill LIVE MUSIC, CLUB
(www.leadmill.co.uk; 6-7 Leadmill Rd) Every touring band has played the dark and dingy Leadmill on the way up (or on the way down), and it remains the best place in town to hear live rock and alternative music. There are club nights too, but they tend to be cheesy 1970s and '80s disco classics.

University of Sheffield Student Union LIVE MUSIC, CLUB
(www.sheffieldunion.com; Western Bank) A varied and generally good program of rock gigs and club nights – including appearances by some pretty classy DJs – make this a good spot to spend an evening, plus there's the Last Laugh Comedy Club on Sunday nights. The Union is about a mile west of the city centre.

Theatre & Cinemas

The **Crucible Theatre** and **Lyceum Theatre** on Tudor Sq share the same **box office** (☎0114-249 6000; www.sheffieldtheatres.co.uk). Both are home to excellent regional drama as wells as Shakespeare, musicals and children's theatre.

The **Showroom Cinema** (www.showroomworkstation.org.uk; Paternoster Row) is the largest independent cinema in England, screening a great mix of art-house, off-beat and not-quite-mainstream films. For everything else, there's the **Odeon** (www.odeon.co.uk; 45-47 Arundel Gate).

Information

Post office (Norfolk Row; ⊙8.30am-5.30pm Mon-Fri, to 3pm Sat)

Tourist office (☎0114-221 1900; www.sheffieldcitycentre.com; 14 Norfolk Row; ⊙10am-5pm Mon-Fri, 10am-4pm Sat)

Getting There & Away

For all travel-related info in Sheffield and South Yorkshire, call ☎01709-51 51 51 or consult www.travelsouthyorkshire.com.

BUS The bus station – called the Interchange – is just east of the centre, about 250m north of the train station. National Express services link Sheffield with most major centres in the north; there are frequent buses linking Sheffield with Leeds (£5.20, one hour, hourly), Manchester (£8, 1½ hours, four daily) and London (£18, 4½ hours, eight daily).

TRAIN Sheffield is served by trains from all directions: Leeds (£8.70, one hour, twice hourly); London St Pancras (£70, 2½ hours, hourly) via Derby or Nottingham; Manchester Piccadilly (£16, one hour, twice hourly); and York (£15, 1¼ hours, twice hourly).

Getting Around

BUS Buses run every 10 minutes during the day (Monday to Saturday, less frequently on Sundays).

SIGHTSEEING For a day of sightseeing, a **South Yorkshire Day Tripper Pass** (£5.80) is valid for one day on all bus and tram services in South Yorkshire. Buy a pass at the **transport information centre** (⊙8am-6pm Mon-Fri, 9am-5pm Sat & Sun) in Sheffield bus station, from the bus driver or at a train station.

TRAM Sheffield also boasts a modern **Supertram** (www.supertram.com; tickets £1.20-2.70; ⊙6am-midnight Mon-Sat, 8am-midnight Sun) that links the train station to the city centre and outer suburbs.

Around Sheffield

Magna INDUSTRIAL MUSEUM

(www.visitmagna.co.uk; Sheffield Rd, Rotherham; adult/child £9.95/7.95; ⊙10am-5pm Feb-Aug, closed Mon Sep-Jan) At its peak, the Templeborough steelworks was the world's most productive steel smelter, with six 3000°C, electric-arc furnaces producing 1.8 million tonnes of metal a year. The mile-long works, which once had a 10,000-strong workforce, is now a 'science adventure centre' called Magna.

An unashamed celebration of heavy industry, this vast, dimly lit shed smelling vaguely of machine oil, hot metal and past glory, is a hands-on paradise for kids of all ages, with a huge range of science and technology exhibits based around the themes of earth, air, water and fire. The latter section is especially impressive, with a towering tornado of flame as a centrepiece and the chance to use a real electric arc to create your own tiny puddle of molten steel (if only for a moment or two). The hourly 'Big Melt' – a massive sound, light and fireworks show – re-enacts the firing up of one of the original arc furnaces.

Magna is 4 miles northeast of Sheffield, just off the M1 motorway near Rotherham. Takes bus 69 from Sheffield bus station (30 minutes, every 20 minutes Monday to Friday, half-hourly Saturday, hourly Sunday) towards Rotherham; it'll drop you at the door.

WEST YORKSHIRE

What steel was to South Yorkshire, so wool was to West Yorkshire. It was the tough and unforgiving textile industry that drove the county's economy from the 18th century on. The woollen mills, factories and canals that were built to transport raw materials and finished products defined much of this landscape. But that's all in the past, and recent years have seen the transformation of this once hard-bitten area into quite the picture postcard.

Leeds and Bradford, two adjoining cities so big that they've virtually become one, are the perfect case in point. Though both were founded amid the dark, satanic mills of the Industrial Revolution, both are undergoing radical redevelopment and reinvention, prettifying their town centres and trying to tempt the more adventurous tourist with a slew of new museums, galleries, restaurants and bars.

Beyond the cities, West Yorkshire is a landscape of bleak moorland dissected by deep valleys dotted with old mill towns and villages. The relics of the wool and cloth industries are still visible in the rows of weavers' cottages and workers' houses built along ridges overlooking the towering chimneys of the mills in the valleys – landscapes that were so vividly described by the Brontë sisters, West Yorkshire's most renowned literary export and biggest tourist draw.

Getting Around

The Metro is West Yorkshire's highly efficient train and bus network, centred on Leeds and Bradford – which are also the main gateways to the county. For transport information call **Metroline** (☎0113-245 7676; www.wymetro.com).

Day Rover (£6.20) tickets are good for travel on buses and trains after 9.30am on weekdays and all day at weekends. There's a range of additional Rover tickets covering buses and/or trains, plus heaps of useful Metro maps and timetables, available from bus and train stations and most tourist offices in West Yorkshire.

Leeds

POP 750,200

One of the fastest growing cities in the UK, Leeds is the glitzy embodiment of newly rediscovered northern self-confidence. More than a decade of redevelopment has seen the city centre transform from near-derelict mill town into a vision of 21st-century urban chic, with skyscraping office blocks, glass and steel waterfront apartment complexes and renovated Victorian shopping arcades. However, the financial crisis of 2008–2010 saw many flagship development projects grind to a halt.

Known as the 'Knightsbridge of the North', Leeds has made itself into a shopping mecca, its streets lined with bustling malls sporting the top names in fashion. And when you've shopped 'til you've dropped there's a plethora of pubs, clubs and excellent restaurants to relax in. From cutting-edge couture to contemporary cuisine, Leeds will serve it to you on a plate (or more likely in a stylishly designed bag). Amid all this cutting-edge style, it seems fitting that the network of city bus routes includes peach, mauve and magenta lines as well as the more humdrum red, orange and blue.

Sights

FREE **Royal Armouries** MUSEUM
(www.royalarmouries.org; Armouries Dr; ⏰10am-5pm) Leeds' most interesting museum is undoubtedly the Royal Armouries, beside the snazzy Clarence Dock residential development. It was originally built to house the armour and weapons from the Tower of London but was subsequently expanded to cover 3000-years'-worth of fighting and self-defence. It all sounds a bit macho, but the exhibits are as varied as they are fascinating: films, live-action demonstrations and hands-on technology can awaken interests you never thought you had, from jousting to Indian elephant armour – we dare you not to learn something! To get here, walk east along the river from Centenary Footbridge (10 minutes), or take bus 28 from Albion St.

Leeds Industrial Museum MUSEUM
(www.leeds.gov.uk/armleymills; Canal Rd; adult/child £3.10/1.10; ⏰10am-5pm Tue-Sat, 1-5pm Sun) One of the world's largest textile mills has been transformed into the Leeds Industrial Museum, telling the story of Leeds' industrial past, both glorious and ignominious. The city became rich off the sheep's back, but at some cost in human terms – working conditions were, well, Dickensian. As well as a selection of working machinery, there's a particularly informative display on how cloth is made. Take bus 5 from the train station to get here.

FREE **Kirkstall Abbey** MEDIEVAL ABBEY
(www.leeds.gov.uk/kirkstallabbey; Abbey Rd; ⏰10am-5pm Tue-Thu, Sat & Sun Apr-Sep, to 4pm Oct-Mar) Leeds' most impressive medieval structure is the beautiful Kirkstall Abbey, founded in 1152 by Cistercian monks from Fountains Abbey in North Yorkshire, and one of the best-preserved medieval abbeys in Britain. Across the road, the **Abbey House Museum** (www.leeds.gov.uk/abbeyhouse; Abbey Rd; adult/child £3.60/1.60; ⏰10am-5pm Tue-Fri & Sun, noon-5pm Sat; 👪), once the Great Gate House to the abbey, contains meticulously reconstructed shops and houses that evoke Victorian Leeds, and displays that give an interesting insight into monastic life.

The abbey and museum are off the A65, 3 miles northwest of the centre; take bus 33, 33A or 757.

FREE **Leeds Art Gallery** ART GALLERY (www.leeds.gov.uk/artgallery; The Headrow; ⏲10am-5pm Mon, Tue & Thu-Sat, noon-5pm Wed, 1-5pm Sun) The municipal gallery is packed with 19th- and 20th-century British heavyweights – Turner, Constable, Stanley Spencer, Wyndham Lewis et al – along with contemporary pieces by more recent arrivals such as Antony Gormley, sculptor of the *Angel of the North* (p747).

FREE **Henry Moore Institute** ART GALLERY (www.henry-moore-fdn.co.uk; The Headrow; ⏲10am-5.30pm Thu-Mon, 10am-9pm Wed) Housed in a converted Victorian warehouse in the city centre, this gallery showcases the work of 20th-century sculptors, but not, despite the name, anything by Henry Moore (1898–1986), who graduated from the Leeds School of Art. To see works by Moore, head to the Yorkshire Sculpture Park (p578).

Festivals

The August Bank Holiday (the weekend preceding the last Monday in August) sees 50,000-plus music fans converge on Bramham Park, 10 miles outside the city centre, for the **Leeds Festival** (www.leedsfestival.com), one of England's biggest rock music extravaganzas, spread across four stages.

Sleeping

There are no budget options in the city centre, and the midrange choices here are either chain hotels or places we wouldn't recommend. If you want somewhere cheapish you'll be forced to head for the 'burbs, where there are plenty of decent B&Bs and smallish hotels.

TOP CHOICE **Quebecs** BOUTIQUE HOTEL £££ (0113-244 8989; www.theetoncollection.com; 9 Quebec St; s/d/ste from £170/190/325; @ wi-fi) Victorian grace at its opulent best is the theme of our favourite hotel in town, a conversion of the former Leeds & County Liberal Club. The elaborate wood panelling and heraldic stained-glass windows in the public areas are matched by the contemporary design of the bedrooms. Booking online can get you a room for as little as half price.

42 The Calls BOUTIQUE HOTEL £££ (0113-244 0099; www.42thecalls.co.uk; 42 The Calls; r/ste from £150/280; @ wi-fi) This snazzy boutique hotel in what was once a 19th-century grain mill overlooking the river is a big hit with the trendy business crowd, who love its sharp, polished lines and designer aesthetic. The smaller 'study' rooms are pretty compact, and breakfast is not included; it'll cost you an extra £15 for the full English.

Bewleys Hotel HOTEL ££ (0113-234 2340; www.bewleyshotels.com/leeds; City Walk, Sweet St; r from £69; P @ wi-fi) Bewleys is super-convenient for motorists, just off Junction 3 on the M621 but also just 10 minutes' walk from the city centre, and with secure basement parking. Rooms are stylish and well appointed, with soundproofed walls and windows. The flat rate accommodates up to two adults plus two kids under 12.

Roomzzz Central APARTMENTS ££ (0113-233 0400; www.roomzzz.co.uk; 10 Swinegate & 2 Burley Rd; 2-person apt from £89; P @ wi-fi) This outfit offers bright and modern luxury apartments complete with fitted kitchen, with the added advantage of a 24-hour hotel reception. Roomzzz City is at 10 Swinegate, right in the city centre; Roomzzz Central is half a mile west on Burley Rd.

Malmaison BOUTIQUE HOTEL £££ (0113-398 1000; www.malmaison.com; 1 Swinegate; s/d/ste from £160/190/369; wi-fi) Self-consciously stylish, this typical Malmaison property is set in a former bus and tram company HQ with a fabulous waterfront location and all of the trademark touches: huge, comfy beds, sexy lighting and all the latest designer gear.

Jury's Inn HOTEL ££ (0113-283 8800; www.jurysinns.com; Kendell St, Brewery Pl; r £69-115; P @ wi-fi) The successful Irish hotel chain has another hit with its Leeds hotel: large, functional rooms, plenty of personal charm and few complaints. If you're walking, it's just across the Centenary footbridge from the city centre, in the heart of the fashionable Brewery Wharf district.

Radisson Blu HOTEL ££ (0113-236 6000; www.radissonblu.co.uk/hotel-leeds; 1 The Light, Cookridge St; r £90-130; P @) An extraordinary conversion of the former HQ of the Leeds Permanent Building Society, the Radisson inhabits a listed building dating from 1930, with 'standard' rooms that are anything but. You have a choice of three styles: high-tech, art deco and Italian, while the business-class rooms are truly luxurious.

The following places outside the city centre are also recommended:

Moorlea B&B £
(☎0113-243 2653; www.moorleahotel.co.uk; 146 Woodsley Rd; s/d from £40/50;) Gay-friendly hotel northwest of the centre, near the University of Leeds.

Boundary Hotel Express HOTEL £
(☎0113-275 7700; www.boundaryhotel.co.uk; 42 Cardigan Rd; s/d £42/54; @) Basic but welcoming; 1.5 miles northwest of centre, near Headingley cricket ground.

Headingley Lodge HOTEL £
(☎0113-278 5323; www.headingleylodge.co.uk; Headingley Stadium, St Michael's La; d/f £50/60; P @) Smart, comfortable rooms with views of Headingley cricket ground; part of the stadium complex.

Eating

The Leeds restaurant scene is constantly evolving, with new places springing up in the wake of new shopping and residential developments. The newly refurbished **Corn Exchange** (www.cornx.net), a beautiful Victorian building with a spectacular domed roof, now houses a new branch of Anthony's, while celebrity chef Jamie Oliver's new restaurant – **Jamie's Italian** (www.jamieoliver.com/italian/leeds; 35 Park Row; lunch & dinner) – opened in 2010, just too late to be reviewed here.

Brasserie Blanc FRENCH ££
(☎0113-220 6060; www.brasserieblanc.com; Victoria Mill, Sovereign St; mains £11-20; lunch & dinner;) Raymond Blanc manages to create a surprisingly intimate and romantic space amid the cast-iron pillars and red brick of an old Victorian warehouse, with a scatter of outdoor tables for sunny lunchtimes beside the river. The menu is unerr-

Leeds

Top Sights

Sleeping

Eating

Drinking

Entertainment

Shopping

ingly French, from escargots (edible snails) to Toulouse sausage. The pre-7pm menu (6.30pm Saturday) offers three courses plus a glass of wine for £15.

Livebait SEAFOOD ££
(www.livebaitrestaurants.co.uk; 11-15 Wharf St, High Court; mains £12-20; ⊙breakfast Mon-Thu, lunch & dinner Mon Sat) Quality seafood – from Whitby crab and Canadian lobster to fresh oysters and langoustines – is the order of the day in this friendly and welcoming restaurant. Classic fish and chips is done with a light and crispy batter and served with homemade tartare sauce and deliciously minty mushy peas.

Hansa's Gujarati INDIAN £
(www.hansasrestaurant.com; 72-74 North St; mains £6-8; ⊙lunch Sun, dinner Mon-Sat) A Leeds institution, Hansa's has been dishing up wholesome Gujarati vegetarian cuisine for 20 years. The restaurant is plain and unassuming (save for a Hindu shrine), but the food is exquisite – specialities of the house include *samosa chaat*, a mix of spiced potato and chickpea samosas with a yogurt and tamarind sauce.

Piazza by Anthony INTERNATIONAL ££
(www.anthonysrestaurant.co.uk; Corn Exchange, Call La; mains £7-12; ⊙lunch & dinner;) Leeds' landmark new development is the refurbished Corn Exchange, with this cool-and-contemporary restaurant taking pride of place. The all-day menu ranges from gourmet salads and sandwiches to pasta, meat and fish dishes such as bouillabaisse (Mediterranean fish stew) with confit potatoes and rouille (sauce of olive oil, breadcrumbs, garlic, saffron and chilli).

Pickles & Potter DELI, CAFE £
(18-20 Queens Arcade; mains £3-5; ⊙breakfast & lunch) This rustic cafe is famous for its superb sandwiches, especially the sumptuous roast-beef version compete with mustard, onion marmalade and fresh salad. There's also homemade soup, delicious cakes, and a meat or vegetarian main course of the day.

Akbar's INDIAN £
(www.akbars.co.uk; 15 Eastgate; mains £7-9; ⊙dinner) Bit of an Egyptian theme going on at this exceptionally popular Indian restaurant – sarcophagi and cat-gods watch over the cutting-edge decor beneath a 'night-in-

the-desert' ceiling. The traditional curry dishes come in pyramid-size portions, and they don't take bookings – expect to wait 30 minutes for a table on weekend nights.

Art's Cafe Bar & Restaurant INTERNATIONAL ££
(www.artscafebar.co.uk; 42 Call Lane; mains lunch £5-7, dinner £10-15; ⊙lunch & dinner) Local art on the walls and a Bohemian vibe throughout make this a popular place for quiet reflection, a chat and a really good cup of coffee. The dinner menu offers a half-dozen classic dishes, including tarragon-crusted chicken, and roast butternut squash risotto.

Anthony's MODERN BRITISH £££
(☎0113-245 5922; www.anthonysrestaurant.co.uk; 19 Boar Lane; 2-/3-course dinner £36/45; ⊙lunch & dinner Tue-Sat) Probably the most talked-about restaurant in town, Anthony's serves top-notch Modern British cuisine (try sea bream with smoked potatoes, peas and mint jelly) to a clientele so eager that they'll think nothing of booking a month in advance. If you go at any other time except Saturday evening, you'll get away with making your reservations a day or so earlier.

Little Tokyo JAPANESE ££
(24 Central Rd; mains £8-16; ⊙lunch & dinner) Fans of genuine Japanese food should go no further than this superb restaurant, which serves a wide array of quality sushi and sashimi (including half-portions) and Bento boxes – those handy trays that serve the Japanese equivalent of a four-course meal.

Salt's Deli DELI £
(www.saltsdeli.co.uk; 14 Swinegate; mains £3-6; ⊙breakfast & lunch Mon-Sat) One of Leeds' best delis also has a takeaway counter, offering superb, freshly made soups, salads and sandwiches (Yorkshire pork-and-leek sausage with caramelised red onion and chilli jam is our favourite), plus hot lunch specials that include spinach-and-mushroom lasagne, cous cous with roasted veg, and lamb-and-chickpea curry.

Anthony's at Flannel's FRENCH ££
(www.anthonysatflannels.co.uk; 3rd floor, Flannel's Fashion Centre, 68-78 Vicar Lane; mains £8-12, 2-/3-course lunch £18/22; ⊙breakfast Tue-Sat, lunch Tue-Sun, dinner Fri & Sat) The brasserie-style brother of award-winning Anthony's, this bright and cheerful modern restaurant set amid white walls and timber beams features much of Anthony's style stuffed into its excellent sandwiches, salads, lunches and luxurious afternoon teas (£13). If you want to see and be seen, there's also **Anthony's Patisserie** in the classy setting of the Victoria Quarter arcade across the street.

Drinking

Leeds is justifiably renowned for its selection of pubs and bars. Glammed-up hordes of party animals crawl the cluster of venues around Boar and Call Lanes, where bars are opening (and closing) all the time. Most bars open till 2am; many turn into clubs after 11pm or midnight, with an admission charge.

Northbar BAR
(www.northbar.com; 24 New Briggate) There's a continental feel to this long, narrow, minimalist bar that's enhanced by the unfamiliar beer labels, from Dortmunder and Duvel to Schneider and Snake Dog. In fact, Northbar is dedicated to introducing Leeds to the best of world beers, with more than a dozen ales on tap and dozens more in bottles.

Duck & Drake PUB
(www.duckndrake.co.uk; 43 Kirkgate) A down-to-earth, traditional boozer with a well-worn atmosphere, a cast of regular pub characters and no fewer than 16 hand-pulled real ales to choose from. The Duck also provides a stage for local rock and blues bands from Wednesday to Sunday nights.

Whitelocks PUB
(www.whitelocks.co.uk; 6-8 Turk's Head Yard) There's lots of polished wood, gleaming brass and colourful stained glass in this popular, traditional pub dating from 1715. Theakstons, Deuchars IPA and several other real ales are on tap, and in summer the crowds spill out into the courtyard.

Baby Jupiter BAR
(11 York Pl) A retro gem with lots of purple velvet, hanging fishbowls and images from old sci-fi films, this basement bar sports a cool soundtrack that ranges from indie, funk and soul to punk, new wave and electro.

Sandinista COCKTAIL BAR
(www.sandinistaleeds.co.uk; 5/5a Cross Belgrave St) This laid-back bar has a Latin look but a unifying theme, attracting an eclectic clientele with its mixed bag of music and unpretentious atmosphere. If you enjoy a well-mixed cocktail but aren't too fussed about looking glam, this is the spot for you.

Bar Fibre BAR
(www.barfibre.com; 168 Lower Briggate) Leeds' most popular gay bar, which spills out onto the cleverly named Queen's Court, is where

the beautiful set congregates. There's another cluster of gay bars downhill at the junction of Lower Briggate and The Calls.

Oracle COCKTAIL BAR
(www.oraclebar.com; 3 Brewery Pl) *The* place to be seen on a summer afternoon, Oracle has a huge outdoor terrace overlooking the River Aire. It serves gourmet burgers, cocktails and a great selection of international beers just made to be served cold, from Guinness to Grolsch to Tsingtao.

Other tips for a tipple:

Adelphi PUB
(www.theadelphi.co.uk; 3-5 Hunslet Rd) Built in 1898 and hardly changed since.

Aire Bar BAR
(www.airebar.co.uk; 32 The Calls) Red-brick vaults, leather sofas, Timothy Taylor's Landlord real ale and a terrace overhanging the river.

Elbow Room BAR
(www.theelbowroom.co.uk/leeds; 64 Call Lane) Pop art, purple pool tables and laid-back music.

☆ Entertainment

In order to make sense of the ever-evolving scene, get your hands on the fortnightly *Leeds Guide* (www.leedsguide.co.uk; £1.50).

Clubs

The tremendous Leeds club scene attracts people from miles around. In true northern tradition people brave the cold wearing next to nothing, even in winter, which is a spectacle in itself. Clubs charge a variety of admission prices, ranging from as little as £1 on a slow weeknight to £10 or more on Saturday.

HiFi Club CLUB
(www.thehificlub.co.uk; 2 Central Rd) This intimate club is a good break from the hardcore sound of four-to-the-floor: if it's Tamla Motown or the percussive beats of dancefloor jazz that shake your booty, this is the spot for you.

Cockpit LIVE MUSIC
(www.thecockpit.co.uk; Swinegate) Snugly ensconced in a series of railway arches, the legendary Cockpit is the antidote to dance clubs. A live music venue of note (Coldplay, The White Stripes, The Flaming Lips and Amy Winehouse have all cut their teeth here), it also hosts The Session on Friday nights, a superb indie/electro/guitar club night.

Mission CLUB
(www.clubmission.com; 8-13 Heaton's Ct) A massive club that redefines the term 'up-for-it'. Thursday sees the 'Full Moon Thai Beach Party' student night, while Saturdays offer a range of house, dance and classic-anthem club nights.

Wire CLUB
(www.wireclub.co.uk; 2-8 Call Lane) This small, atmospheric basement club, set in a forest of Victorian cast-iron pillars, throbs to a different beat every night, from rock 'n' roll to drum and bass. Popular with local students.

Theatre & Opera

Grand Theatre & Opera House MUSICALS, THEATRE
(www.leedsgrandtheatre.com; 46 New Briggate) Hosts musicals, plays and opera, including performances by the acclaimed **Opera North** (www.operanorth.co.uk).

West Yorkshire Playhouse THEATRE
(www.wyp.org.uk; Quarry Hill Mount) The Playhouse has a reputation for excellent live drama, from the classics to cutting-edge new writing.

City Varieties MUSIC HALL
(www.cityvarieties.co.uk; Swan St) This old-fashioned music hall features anything from clairvoyants to comedy acts to country music. Closed for major refurbishment at time of research.

Cinema

Hyde Park Picture House ART HOUSE
(www.hydeparkpicturehouse.co.uk; Brudenell Rd) This Edwardian cinema shows a meaty range of art-house and mainstream choices. Take bus 56 from the city centre to get here.

Vue Cinema MULTIPLEX
(www.myvue.com; 22 The Light, The Headrow) For mainstream, first-run films, head for the Vue on the second floor of The Light entertainment complex.

Sport

Leeds United Football Club SOCCER
(www.leedsunited.com; Elland Rd) Leeds supporters know all about pain: the team was relegated from the Premiership in 2004, and then from the Championship to League One in 2007. Loyal fans were rewarded with promotion back to the Championship in 2010, and continue to pack the Elland Rd stadium in their masses. Take bus 93 or 96 from City Sq.

Yorkshire County Cricket Club CRICKET (www.yorkshireccc.com; Headingley Carnegie Cricket Ground, St Michael's Lane) Headingley, the spiritual home of Yorkshire cricket, has been hosting cricket matches since 1890 and is still used for test matches. To get to the ground, take bus 18 or 56 from the city centre.

Shopping

Leeds' city centre has so many shopping arcades that they all seem to blend into one giant mall. The latest development – **Trinity Leeds** (www.trinityleeds.com) between Commercial St and Boar Lane, still under construction at the time of research – will be the city's biggest.

The mosaic-paved, stained-glass-roofed Victorian arcades of **Victoria Quarter** (www.v-q.co.uk), between Briggate and Vicar Lane, are well worth visiting for aesthetic reasons alone. Dedicated shoppers can join the footballers' wives browsing boutiques by Louis Vuitton, Vivienne Westwood and Swarovski. The flagship store here, of course, is **Harvey Nichols** (www.harveynichols.com; 107-111 Briggate).

Just across the street to the east you'll find the opposite end of the retail spectrum in **Leeds City Market** (www.leedsmarket.com; Kirkgate; ⌚9am-5pm Mon-Sat, to 1pm Wed, open-air market Thu-Tue). Once the home of Michael Marks, who later joined Spencer, this is Britain's largest covered market, selling fresh meat, fish, fruit and vegetables, as well as household goods.

Information

Gateway Yorkshire/Leeds tourist office (☎0113-242 5242; www.visitleeds.co.uk; The Arcade, Leeds City Train Station; ⌚9am-5.30pm Mon-Sat, 10am-4pm Sun)

Leeds General Infirmary (☎0113-243 2799; Great George St)

Post office (St John's Centre, 116 Albion St; ⌚9am-5.30pm Mon-Sat)

Getting There & Away

AIR Eleven miles northwest of the city via the A65, **Leeds Bradford International Airport** (www.lbia.co.uk) offers flights to a range of domestic and international destinations. The Metroconnect 757 bus (£2.50, 40 minutes, every 30 minutes, hourly on Sunday) runs between Leeds bus station and the airport. A taxi costs about £20.

BUS **National Express** (www.nationalexpress.com) serves most major cities, including services from London (£22, 4½ hours, hourly) and Manchester (£9.20, 1¼ hours, every 30 minutes).

Yorkshire Coastliner (www.coastliner.co.uk) has useful services from Leeds to York, Castle Howard, Goathland and Whitby (840 and 842); to York and Scarborough (843); and to Filey and Bridlington (845 and X45). A Freedom Ticket (£13) gives unlimited bus travel for a day.

TRAIN Leeds City Station has hourly services from London King's Cross (£85, 2½ hours), Sheffield (£12, one hour), Manchester (£16, one hour) and York (£11, 30 minutes).

Leeds is also the starting point for services on the famous Settle-Carlisle railway line; for details see p587.

Getting Around

Metro's **FreeCityBus** (www.wymetro.com) service runs every few minutes from 6.30am to 7.30pm Monday to Saturday, linking the bus and train stations to all the main shopping areas in the city centre.

The various Day Rover passes (see p576) covering trains and/or buses are good for reaching Bradford, Haworth and Hebden Bridge.

Around Leeds

A day-trip from Leeds opens up a fascinating range of options: stately splendour at Harewood, dust and darkness at the National Coal Mining Museum for England, or technology and poppadums at Bradford, to name but a few. Places are listed roughly in order of distance from Leeds, first to the west and north, then to the south.

BRADFORD

POP 293,700

Their suburbs may have merged into one sprawling urban conurbation, but Bradford remains far removed from its much more glamorous neighbour, Leeds. Thanks to its role as a major player in the wool trade, Bradford attracted large numbers of Bangladeshi and Pakistani immigrants throughout the 20th century, who – despite occasional racial tensions – have helped reinvigorate the city and give it new energy (plus a reputation for superb curry restaurants). A high point of the year is the colourful **Bradford Mela** (www.bradfordmela.org.uk), a two-day celebration of Asian music, dance, arts, crafts and food in mid-June.

Bradford's top attraction is the **National Media Museum** (www.nationalmediamuseum.org.uk; admission free; ⌚10am-6pm Tue-Sun), an impressive, glass-fronted building that chronicles the story of photography, film,

TV, radio and the web from 19th-century cameras and early animation to digital technology and the psychology of advertising. There's lots of hands-on stuff too; you can film yourself in a bedroom scene or play at being a TV newsreader. The **IMAX cinema** (adult/child £9/7) here shows the usual combination of in-your-face nature films, space documentaries and 3-D animation.

Bradford is famous for its curries, so if you're still here in the evening don't miss trying one of the city's hundred or so restaurants. A great help is the **Bradford Curry Guide** (http://website.lineone.net/~bradfordcurryguide), which sorts out the rogan josh from the rotten nosh.

Top recommendations include Bradford's oldest curry house, the **Kashmir** (27 Morley St; mains £4-6; ⌚dinner), for top Asian tucker, served with no frills in very basic surroundings. At the opposite end of the spectrum is **Zouk Tea Bar** (www.zoukteabar.co.uk; 1312 Leeds Rd; mains £7-15; ⌚breakfast, lunch & dinner), a modern and stylish cafe-restaurant staffed by chefs from Lahore, and serving everything from *chana puri* (curried chickpeas) for breakfast to *gwadari khas* (curried lobster) for dinner.

Bradford is on the Metro train line from Leeds (£2.85, 20 minutes), with very frequent services every day.

SALTAIRE

A Victorian-era landmark, Saltaire was a model industrial village built in 1851 by philanthropic wool-baron and teetotaller Titus Salt. The rows of neat, honey-coloured cottages – now a Unesco World Heritage Site – overlook what was once the largest factory in the world.

The factory is now **Salt's Mill** (www.saltsmill.org.uk; admission free; ⌚10am-5.30pm Mon-Fri, 10am-6pm Sat & Sun), a splendidly bright and airy building where the main draw is a permanent exhibition of art by local boy David Hockney (1937–). In a fitting metaphor for the shift in the British economy from making things to selling them, this former engine of industry is now a shrine to retail therapy, housing shops selling books, crafts and outdoor equipment, and a cafe and restaurant.

Saltaire's **tourist office** (www.saltairevillage.info; 2 Victoria Rd; ⌚10am-5pm) has maps of the village and runs hour-long guided walks (adult/child £3.50/2.50) through the town throughout the year.

Saltaire is 9 miles west of Leeds centre, and 3 miles north of Bradford centre. It's easily reached by Metro rail from either.

HAREWOOD

The great park, sumptuous gardens and mighty edifice of **Harewood House** (www.harewood.org; adult/child £14.30/7.25; ⌚grounds 10am-6pm, house noon-4.30pm Apr-Oct; 👪) could easily fill an entire day-trip from Leeds, and also makes a good port of call on the way to Harrogate.

A classic example of a stately English pile, the house was built between 1759 and 1772 by the era's superstar designers: John Carr designed the exterior, Lancelot 'Capability' Brown laid out the grounds, Thomas Chippendale supplied the furniture (the largest commission he ever received, costing the unheard of amount of £10,000), Robert Adams designed the interior, and Italy was raided to create an appropriate art collection. The superb terrace was added 100 years later by yet another top name, Sir Charles Barry – he of the Houses of Parliament.

Many locals come to Harewood just to relax or saunter through the **grounds** (grounds-only ticket £10/6.10), without even thinking of going inside the house. Hours of entertainment can be had in the **Bird Garden**, with many exotic species including penguins (feeding time at 2pm is a highlight), and there's also a boating lake, cafe and adventure playground. For more activity, there's a network of walking trails around the lake or through the parkland.

Harewood is about 7 miles north of Leeds on the A61. Take bus 36 (20 minutes, at least half-hourly Monday to Saturday, hourly on Sunday) which continues to Harrogate. Visitors coming by bus get half-price admission, so hang on to your ticket. From the main gate, it's a 2-mile walk through the grounds to the house and gardens, or you can use the free shuttle service.

NATIONAL COAL MINING MUSEUM FOR ENGLAND

For close to three centuries, West and South Yorkshire were synonymous with coal production; the collieries shaped and scarred the landscape, while entire villages grew up around the pits, each male inhabitant and their descendants destined to spend their working lives underground. The industry came to a shuddering halt in the 1980s, but the imprint of coal is still very much in evidence, even if there's only a handful of collieries left. One of these, at Claphouse, is now the **National Coal Mining Museum for England** (www.ncm.org.uk; Overton, near Wakefield; admission free; ⌚10am-5pm, last tour 3.15pm), a superb testament to the inner workings of a coal mine.

The highlight of a visit is the underground tour (departing every 10 minutes): equipped with helmet and head-torch you descend almost 150m in the 'cage' then follow subterranean passages to the coal seam where massive drilling machines now stand idle. Former miners work as guides, and explain the details – sometimes with a suitably authentic and almost impenetrable mix of local dialect (known in Yorkshire as Tyke) and technical terminology.

Up on top, there are audiovisual displays, some fascinating memorabilia (including sketches by Henry Moore), and exhibits about trade unions, strikes and the wider mining communities – only a bit over-romanticised in parts. You can also stroll round the pit-pony stables (their equine inhabitants also now retired) or the slightly eerie bathhouse, unchanged since the miners scrubbed off the coal dust for the last time and emptied their lockers.

The museum is about 10 miles south of Leeds on the A642 between Wakefield and Huddersfield, which drivers can reach via Junction 40 on the M1. By public transport, take a train from Leeds to Wakefield (15 minutes, at least hourly), and then bus 232 towards Huddersfield (25 minutes, hourly).

YORKSHIRE SCULPTURE PARK

One of England's most impressive collections of sculpture is scattered across the formidable 18th-century estate of Bretton Park, 200-odd hectares of lawns, fields and trees. A bit like the art world's equivalent of a safari park, the **Yorkshire Sculpture Park** (www.ysp.co.uk; Bretton, near Wakefield; admission free, parking £4; ⌚10am-6pm Apr-Sep, to 5pm Oct-Mar) showcases the work of dozens of sculptors both national and international. But the main focus of this outdoor gallery is the work of local kids Barbara Hepworth (1903–75), who was born in nearby Wakefield, and Henry Moore (1898–1986).

The rural setting is especially fitting for Moore's work, as the artist was hugely influenced by the outdoors and preferred his art to be sited in the landscape rather than indoors. Other highlights include pieces by Andy Goldsworthy and Eduardo Paolozzi. There's also a program of temporary exhibitions and installations by visiting artists, plus a bookshop and cafe.

The park is 12 miles south of Leeds and 18 miles north of Sheffield, just off Junction 38 on the M1 motorway. If you're on public transport, take a train from Leeds to Wakefield (15 minutes, at least hourly), or from Sheffield to Barnsley (20 minutes, at least hourly); then take bus 444 which runs between Wakefield and Barnsley via Bretton Park (30 minutes, hourly Monday to Saturday).

Hebden Bridge

POP 4086

Tucked tightly into the fold of a steep-sided valley, Yorkshire's funkiest little town is a former mill town that refused to go gently into that good night with the dying of industry's light. Instead it raged a bit and then morphed into an attractive little tourist trap with a distinctly bohemian atmosphere. Besides the honest-to-God Yorkshire folk who have lived here for years, the town is home to university academics, artists, die-hard hippies and a substantial gay community (it allegedly boasts the highest proportion of lesbians per head of population in the UK) – all of which explains the abundance of craft shops, organic cafes and secondhand bookstores.

From the town centre, a short stroll along the attractive waterfront of the Rochdale Canal leads to the **Alternative Technology Centre** (www.alternativetechnology.org.uk; Hebble End Mill; admission free; ⌚10am-5pm Mon-Fri, noon-4pm Sat, 1-4pm Sun), which promotes renewable energy, recycling and sustainable lifestyles through a series of intriguing exhibits and workshops.

Above the town is the much older village of **Heptonstall**, its narrow cobbled street lined with 500-year-old cottages and the ruins of a beautiful 13th-century church. But it is the churchyard of the newer St Thomas' Church that draws literary pilgrims, for here is buried the poet Sylvia Plath (1932–63), wife of another famous poet, Ted Hughes (1930–98), who was born in nearby Mytholmroyd.

The **Hebden Bridge tourist office & Canal Centre** (☎01422-843831; Butlers Wharf, New Rd; ⌚9.30am-5.30pm Mon-Fri & 10.30am-5pm Sat & Sun mid-Mar–mid-Oct, shorter hours rest of year) has a good stock of maps and leaflets on local walks, including a saunter to **Hardcastle Crags**, the local beauty spot, and nearby **Gibson Mill** (NT; adult/child £3.60/1.80; 11am-4pm Tue-Thu, Sat & Sun Mar-Oct, 11am-3pm Sat & Sun Nov-Feb), a renovated 19th-century cotton mill. The mill houses a visitor centre with exhibitions covering the industrial and social history of the mill and its former workers.

Sleeping & Eating

Holme House B&B ££
(01422-847588; www.holmehousehebdenbridge.co.uk; New Rd; s/d from £60/75;) Holme House is an elegant Victorian villa right in the heart of town, with stylish and spacious bedrooms and fluffy robes and towels in the bathrooms. At breakfast you can choose from smoked haddock with poached egg, fresh fruit and yoghurt, or a fry-up prepared using local produce.

Mankinholes YHA HOSTEL £
(0845 371 9751; www.yha.org.uk; Todmorden; dm £16; P) A converted 17th-century manor house 4 miles southwest of Hebden Bridge, this hostel has limited facilities (no TV room) but is very popular with walkers (the Pennine Way passes only half a mile away). There are buses from New Rd in Hebden to Todmorden every 10 minutes; from there, bus T6/T8 goes to the hostel.

Mooch CAFE, BAR £
(www.moochcafe.co.uk; 24 Market St; mains £5-7; 9am-8pm Mon & Tue-Sat, 10am-7pm Sun) This chilled-out little cafe-bar exemplifies Hebden's alternative atmosphere, with a menu that includes a full-vegan breakfast, brie-and-grape ciabatta, and Mediterranean lunch platters of olives, hummus, stuffed vine leaves, tabouleh and more. There's also Krombacher beer on draught, and excellent espresso.

Relish VEGETARIAN ££
(01422-843587; www.relishhebden.co.uk; Old Oxford House, Albert St; mains £10-11; dinner Thu-Sat) Voted one of the UK's Top Five vegetarian restaurants in 2008, Relish adopts a gourmet attitude towards veggie and vegan cuisine, serving dishes such as leek, sage and walnut risotto with Parmesan shavings, and Sri Lankan red curry with plantain, lemongrass and black bean cakes. Best book a table to avoid disappointment.

Organic House CAFE £
(www.organic-house.co.uk; 2 Market St; mains £6-11; breakfast & lunch;) Practically everything on the menu at this busy local caff is organic, locally produced or fair trade, from the veggie breakfast to the paté *du jour* (served with toast and chutney). There are outdoor tables in the garden, and a shiatsu and reflexology studio upstairs.

Getting There & Away

Hebden Bridge is on the Leeds–Manchester train line (£4.05, 50 minutes, every 20 minutes Monday to Saturday, hourly on Sunday). Get off at Todmorden for the Mankinholes YHA.

Haworth

POP 6100

It seems that only Shakespeare himself is held in higher esteem than the beloved Brontë sisters – Emily, Anne and Charlotte – at least, judging by the 8 million visitors a year who trudge up the hill from the train station to pay their respects at the handsome parsonage where the literary classics *Jane Eyre* and *Wuthering Heights* were born.

Not surprisingly, the whole village is given over to Brontë-linked tourism, but even without the literary associations Haworth is still worth a visit, though you'll be hard pushed not to be overwhelmed by the cottage industry that has grown up around the Brontës and their wonderful creations.

Sights

FREE **Haworth Parish Church** CHURCH
(Church St; 9am-5.30pm) Your first stop should be Haworth Parish Church, a lovely old place of worship built in the late 19th century on the site of the older church that the Brontë sisters knew, which was demolished in 1879. In the surrounding churchyard, gravestones are covered in moss or thrust to one side by gnarled tree roots, giving the place a tremendous feeling of age.

Brontë Parsonage Museum MUSEUM
(www.bronte.info; Church St; adult/child £6.50/3.50; 10am-5.30pm Apr-Sep, 11am-5pm Oct-Mar) Set in a pretty garden overlooking the church and graveyard, the house where the Brontë family lived from 1820 till 1861 is now a museum. The rooms are meticulously furnished and decorated exactly as they were in the Brontë era, with many personal possessions on display. There's also a neat and informative exhibition, which

Haworth

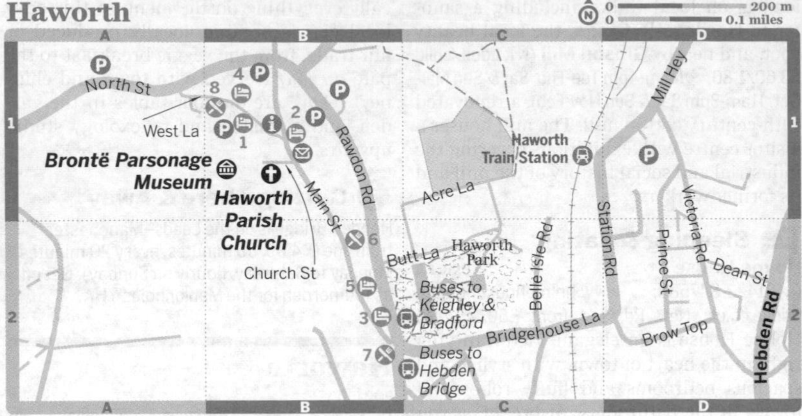

Haworth

Top Sights

Brontë Parsonage Museum B1
Haworth Parish Church B1

Sleeping

1 Aitches B1
2 Apothecary Guest House B1
3 Old Registry B2
4 Old White Lion Hotel B1
5 Ye Sleeping House B2

Eating

6 Cobbles and Clay B2
7 Haworth Old Hall B2
8 Weaver's Restaurant with Rooms B1

includes the fascinating miniature books the Brontës wrote as children.

Activities

Above Haworth stretch the bleak moors of the South Pennines – immediately familiar to Brontë fans – and the tourist office has leaflets on local **walks** to endless Brontë-related places. A 6.5-mile favourite leads to Top Withins, a ruined farm thought to have inspired *Wuthering Heights*, even though a plaque clearly states that the farmhouse bore no resemblance to the one Emily wrote about.

Other walks can be worked around the **Brontë Way**, a longer route linking Bradford and Colne via Haworth. Alternatively, you can walk or cycle the 8 miles south to Hebden Bridge via the scenic valley of Hardcastle Crags.

Sleeping & Eating

Virtually every second house on Main St offers B&B; they're mostly indistinguishable from each other but some are just that little bit cuter. There are a couple of good restaurants in town, and many of the B&Bs also have small cafes that are good for a spot of lunch.

Old Registry B&B ££

(01535-646503; www.theoldregistryhaworth.co.uk; 2-4 Main St; r £75-120;) This place is a bit special. It's an elegantly rustic guesthouse where each of the carefully themed rooms has a four-poster bed, whirlpool bath or valley view. The Blue Heaven room is just that – at least for fans of Laura Ashley's delphinium blue.

Ye Sleeping House B&B ££

(01535-546992; www.yesleepinghouse.co.uk; 8 Main St; s/d from £29/58) There's a cosy, country cottage atmosphere at this welcoming B&B, with just three small rooms and two friendly resident cats. Try to get the one en suite room, which can sleep a family of four and has great views over the valley.

Aitches B&B ££

(01535-642501; www.aitches.co.uk; 11 West Lane; s/d from £40/58) A very classy, stone-built Victorian house with four en suite rooms, each differently decorated with a pleasantly olde-worlde atmosphere. There's a residents' dining room where a three-course meal will cost £16 (prebooked, minimum four persons).

Cobbles and Clay CAFE £

(www.cobblesandclay.co.uk; 60 Main St; mains £4-8;) This attractive, child-friendly cafe not only offers fair-trade coffee and healthy salads and snacks – Tuscan bean stew, or hummus with pita bread and raw veggie sticks – but also the opportunity to indulge in a bit of pottery painting.

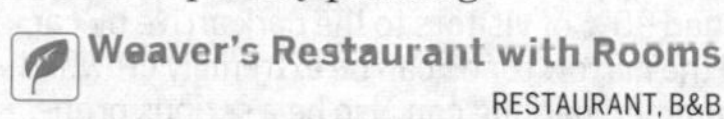

Weaver's Restaurant with Rooms RESTAURANT, B&B ££
(01535-643822; www.weaversmallhotel.co.uk; 15 West Lane; s/d £65/110, mains £13-19; lunch Wed-Fri, dinner Tue-Sat) A stylish and atmospheric restaurant, Weaver's offers a menu featuring local produce (such as slow-cooked shoulder of Pennine lamb with fennel seed and coriander stuffing), or simple lunches like an Ellison's pork pie with mushy peas and mint sauce. Upstairs are three comfy bedrooms, two of which have views towards the moors.

Apothecary Guest House B&B ££
(01535-643642; www.theapothecaryguesthouse.co.uk; 86 Main St; s/d £35/55;) Oak beams and narrow, slanted passageways lead to smallish rooms with cheerful decor.

Old White Lion Hotel HOTEL ££
(01535-642313; www.oldwhitelionhotel.com; West Lane; s/d from £63/88;) Pub-style accommodation – comfortable if not spectacular – above an oak-panelled bar and highly rated restaurant (mains £8 to £13).

Haworth YHA HOSTEL £
(0845 371 9520; www.yha.org.uk; Longlands Dr; dm £16; P @) A big old house with a games room, lounge, cycle store and laundry. It's on the northeastern edge of town, off Lees Lane.

Haworth Old Hall PUB ££
(01535-642709; www.hawortholdhall.co.uk; Sun St; mains £9-15) A 16th-century pub serving real ale and decent food. If you want to linger longer, two comfortable doubles cost £65 each.

Information

Post office (98 Main St; 9am-5.30pm Mon-Fri, to 12.30pm Sat)

Tourist office (01535-642329, www.haworth-village.org.uk; 2-4 West Lane; 9am-5.30pm Apr-Sep, to 5pm Oct-Mar)

Venables & Bainbridge (111 Main St; 11am-5pm daily) Secondhand books including many vintage Brontë volumes.

Getting There & Away

From Leeds, the easiest approach is via Keighley, which is on the Metro rail network. Bus 500 runs from Keighley bus station to Haworth (15 minutes, hourly) and continues to Todmorden and Hebden Bridge. However, the most interesting way to get from Keighley to Haworth is via

BAD-LUCK BRONTËS

The Rev Patrick Brontë, his wife Maria and six children moved to Haworth Parsonage in 1820. Within four years Maria and the two eldest daughters had died from cancer and tuberculosis. The treble tragedy led the good reverend to keep his remaining family close to him, and for the next few years the children were home-schooled in a highly creative environment.

The children conjured up mythical heroes and fantasy lands, and produced miniature homemade books. It was an auspicious start, at least for the three girls, Charlotte, Emily and Anne; the lone boy, Branwell, was more of a painter but lacked his sisters' drive and discipline. After a short stint as a professional artist, he ended up spending most of his days in the Black Bull pub, drunk and stoned on laudanum obtained across the street at Rose & Co Apothecary.

While the three sisters were setting the London literary world alight with the publication of three superb novels – *Jane Eyre*, *Wuthering Heights* and *Agnes Grey* – in one extraordinary year (1847), Branwell was fading quickly and died of tuberculosis in 1848. The family was devastated, but things quickly got worse. Emily fell ill with tuberculosis soon after her brother's funeral; she never left the house again and died on 19 December. Anne, who had also been sick, was next; Charlotte took her to Scarborough to seek a sea cure but she died on 28 May 1849.

The remaining family never recovered. Despite her growing fame, Charlotte struggled with depression and never quite adapted to her high position in literary society. Despite her misgivings she eventually married, but she too died, in the early stages of pregnancy, on 31 March 1855. All things considered, it's hardly surprising that poor old Patrick Brontë spent the remaining years of his life going increasingly insane.

STEAM ENGINES & RAILWAY CHILDREN

Haworth is on the **Keighley & Worth Valley Railway** (www.kwvr.co.uk; adult/child return £9.40/4.70, adult/child Day Rover £14/7), which runs steam and classic diesel engines between Keighley and Oxenhope. It was here, in 1969, that the classic movie *The Railway Children* was shot: Mr Perks was stationmaster at Oakworth, where the Edwardian look has been meticulously maintained. Trains operate about hourly at weekends all year; in holiday periods they run hourly every day.

the Keighley & Worth Valley Railway (see boxed text, p582).

YORKSHIRE DALES NATIONAL PARK

The Yorkshire Dales – named from the old Norse word *dalr*, meaning 'valleys' – is the central jewel in the necklace of three national parks strung across the neck of northern England, with the dramatic fells of the Lake District to the west and the brooding heaths of the North York Moors to the east.

From well-known names such as Wensleydale and Ribblesdale, to obscure and evocative Langstrothdale and Arkengarthdale, these glacial valleys are characterised by a distinctive landscape of high heather moorland, stepped skylines and flat-topped hills. Down in the green valleys, patchworked with drystone dykes, are picture-postcard towns and hamlets, where sheep and cattle still graze on village greens. And in the limestone country in the southern Dales you'll find England's best examples of karst scenery.

The Dales have been protected as a national park since the 1950s, assuring their status as a walker's and cyclist's paradise. But there's plenty for non-walkers as well, from exploring the legacy of literary vet James Herriot of *All Creatures Great and Small* fame, to sampling Wallace and Gromit's favourite teatime snack at the Wensleydale Creamery.

The *Visitor* newspaper, available from tourist offices, lists local events and walks guided by park rangers, as well as many places to stay and eat. The official park website (www.yorkshiredales.org.uk) is also useful.

Getting There & Around

Around 90% of visitors to the park arrive by car, and the narrow roads can be extremely crowded in summer; parking can also be a serious problem. If you can, try to use public transport as much as possible.

Pick up a *Dales Bus Timetable* from tourist offices, or consult the **Traveldales** (www.traveldales.org.uk) and **Dalesbus** (www.dalesbus.org) websites.

By train, the best and most interesting access to the Dales is via the famous **Settle-Carlisle Line** (p587). Trains run between Leeds and Carlisle, stopping at Skipton, Settle, and numerous small villages, offering unrivalled access to the hills straight from the station platform.

Skipton

POP 14,300

This busy market town on the southern edge of the Dales takes its name from the Anglo-Saxon *sceape ton* (sheep town) – no prizes for guessing how it made its money. Monday, Wednesday, Friday and Saturday are market days on High St, bringing crowds from all over and giving the town something of a festive atmosphere. The **tourist office** (☎01756-792809; www.skiptononline.co.uk; 35 Coach St; ⏲10am-5pm Mon-Fri, 9am-5pm Sat) is on the northern edge of the town centre.

Sights & Activities

A pleasant stroll from the tourist office along the canal path leads to **Skipton Castle** (www.skiptoncastle.co.uk; High St; adult/child £6.20/3.70; ⏲10am-6pm Mon-Sat & noon-6pm Sun Mar-Sep, to 4pm Oct-Feb), one of the best-preserved medieval castles in England – a fascinating contrast to the ruins you'll see elsewhere.

From the castle, wander along Skipton's pride and joy – the broad and bustling **High St**, one of the most attractive shopping streets in Yorkshire. On the first Sunday of the month it hosts the **Northern Dales Farmers Market** (www.ndfm.co.uk).

No trip to Skipton is complete without a cruise along the Leeds-Liverpool Canal that runs through the middle of town. **Pennine Cruisers** (www.penninecruisers.com; The Wharf, Coach St; adult/child £3/2; ⏲10.30am-dusk Mar-Oct) runs half-hour trips to Skipton Castle and back.

Sleeping & Eating

There's a strip of B&Bs just outside the centre on Keighley Rd. All those between Nos 46 and 57 are worth trying.

Carlton House B&B ££

(☎01756-700921; www.carltonhouse.rapidial.co.uk; 46 Keighley Rd; s/d from £30/60) A handsome house with five pretty, comfortable rooms – no frills but lots of floral prints. The house is deservedly popular on account of the friendly welcome.

Le Caveau FRENCH ££

(☎01756-794274; www.lecaveau.co.uk; 86 High St; mains £13-18; lunch Tue-Fri, dinner Tue-Sat) Set in a stylishly decorated 16th-century cellar with barrel-vaulted ceilings, this friendly bistro offers a seasonal menu built lovingly around fresh local produce. Daily specials include dishes such as a light and flavourful quiche made with black pudding, bacon and mushrooms, and a succulent fish pie topped with mashed potato. On weekdays you can get a two-course lunch for £10.

Bojangles CAFE, BAR £

(20 Newmarket St; mains £3-6) The best coffee in town. American-style breakfasts and burgers by day; tapas and cocktails in the evening.

Bizzie Lizzies FISH & CHIPS £

(www.bizzielizzies.co.uk; 36 Swadford St; mains £6-8; lunch & dinner) An award-winning, sit-down fish-and-chip restaurant overlooking the canal. There's also a takeaway counter (mains £3 to £5, open to 11.15pm).

Narrow Boat PUB £

(38 Victoria St; mains £5-8) A traditionally styled pub with a great selection of local ales and foreign beers, friendly service and bar food.

Yorkshire Dales National Park

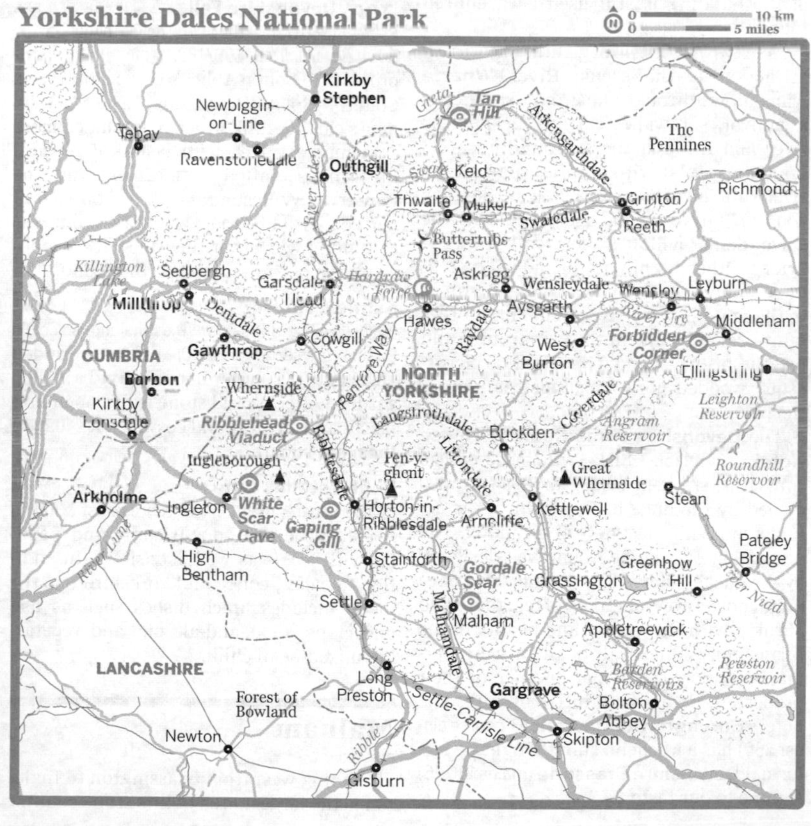

Getting There & Away

Skipton is the last stop on the Metro rail network from Leeds and Bradford (£7.50, 40 minutes, half-hourly, hourly on Sunday). For heading into the Dales, see the boxed text on p587.

For Grassington, take bus 72 (30 minutes, hourly Monday to Saturday, no Sunday service) from Skipton train station, or 66A (hourly on Sunday) from the Market Pl.

Bolton Abbey

The tiny village and country estate of Bolton Abbey, owned by the duke of Devonshire, is about 5 miles east of Skipton. The big draw here is the ruined church of **Bolton Priory** (www.boltonabbey.com; admission free, parking £6; 9am-7pm Apr-Oct, last admission 5.30pm, shorter hours Nov-Mar), an evocative and beautiful 12th-century ruin. Its soaring arches and huge windows silhouetted against the sky have inspired artists such as Wordsworth and Turner. Part of the building is still used as a church today.

Apart from the priory ruins, the main attraction is the scenic **River Wharfe** which flows through the grounds – there's a network of walking trails beside the river and through the surrounding area. It's very popular with families (part of the riverbank looks like a beach at weekends); you can buy teas and ice creams in the **Cavendish Pavilion**, a short walk from the priory. Other highlights include the stepping stones – a large gap between stones in the middle of the river frequently forces faint-hearted walkers to turn around and use the bridge – and **The Strid**, a picturesque wooded gorge just upstream from the pavilion.

The **Devonshire Arms Country House Hotel** (01756-718111; www.thedevonshirearms.co.uk; s/d from £198/238; P @) – also owned by the duke of Devonshire – is actually more like a 'stately home' hotel. The decoration of each bedroom was designed by the duchess herself, and while her tastes might not be everyone's cup of tea, there's no arguing with the quality and beauty of the furnishings; almost all of them were permanently borrowed from another of their properties, Chatsworth in Derbyshire. The hotel's **Burlington Restaurant** (3-course dinner £60) has a Michelin star, though the less formal **Devonshire Brasserie** (mains £10-16) is more to our taste.

There are half-hourly buses here from Skipton and Grassington Monday to Saturday; on Sunday there's only an hourly service from Skipton.

Grassington

POP 1120

The perfect base for jaunts around the south Dales, Grassington's handsome Georgian centre teems with walkers and visitors throughout the summer months, soaking up an atmosphere that – despite the odd touch of faux rusticity – is as attractive and traditional as you'll find in these parts.

The **tourist office** (01756-751690; Hebden Rd; 9.30am-5pm Apr-Oct, Fri-Sun only Nov-Mar) is beside the big car park on the edge of town.

Sleeping & Eating

There are several B&Bs along and just off Main St.

TOP CHOICE Devonshire Fell HOTEL £££
(01756-718111; www.devonshirefell.co.uk; Burnsall; s/d from £99/138; P @) A sister property to Bolton Abbey's Devonshire Arms Country House Hotel, this former gentleman's club for mill owners has a much more contemporary feel, with beautiful modern furnishings crafted by local experts. The Conservatory Restaurant (three-course dinner £32; also used as a breakfast room) has a stunning view over the valley. It's 3 miles southeast of Grassington on the B6160.

Ashfield House B&B ££
(01756-752584; www.ashfieldhouse.co.uk; Summers Fold; r from £90; P @) A secluded 17th-century country house behind a walled garden with exposed stone walls, open fireplaces and an all-round cosy feel. It's just off the main square.

Cobblestones Café CAFE £
(3 The Square; mains £4-6; breakfast & lunch) A cute little cafe, dog-friendly and popular with locals as well as visitors. In addition to cakes, coffee and Yorkshire tea, the menu includes lunch dishes such as fish and chips, steak-and-ale pie, and vegetarian mixed-bean chilli.

Malham

POP 120

Stretching west from Grassington to Ingleton is the largest area of limestone country in England, which has created a distinctive landscape dotted with dry valleys, potholes, limestone pavements and gorges. Two of the most spectacular features – Malham Cove and Gordale Scar – lie near the pretty village of Malham.

The **national park centre** (☎01969-652380; www.yorkshiredales.org.uk; ⏲10am-5pm daily Apr-Oct, 10am-4pm Sat & Sun Nov-Mar) at the southern edge of the village has the usual wealth of information. Note that Malham can only be reached via narrow roads that can be very congested in summer; leave your car at the national park centre and walk into the village.

Sights & Activities

A half mile walk north from Malham village leads to **Malham Cove**, a huge rock amphitheatre lined with 80m-high vertical cliffs. You can hike steeply up the left-hand end of the cove (on the Pennine Way footpath) to see the extensive limestone pavement above the cliffs. Another 1.5 miles further north is **Malham Tarn**, a glacial lake and nature reserve.

A mile east of Malham along a narrow road (very limited parking) is spectacular **Gordale Scar**, a deep limestone canyon with scenic cascades and the remains of an Iron-Age settlement. The national park centre has a leaflet describing the **Malham Landscape Trail**, a 5-mile circular walk that takes in Malham Cove, Gordale Scar and the Janet's Foss waterfall.

The **Pennine Way** passes through Malham; Horton-in-Ribblesdale lies a day's hike away to the northwest.

Sleeping & Eating

Beck Hall HOTEL ££
(☎01729-830332; www.beckhallmalham.com; s/d from £36/54; P 📶) This rambling 17th century country house on the edge of the village has 15 individually decorated rooms – we recommend the Green Room, with its old-style furnishings and four-poster bed. There's a gurgling stream flowing through the garden and a nice tearoom (mains £3 to £5, open lunch Tuesday to Sunday).

Malham YHA HOSTEL £
(☎0845 371 9529; www.yha.org.uk; dm £18; P 👪) In the village centre you will find this purpose-built hostel; the facilities are top-notch and young children are well catered for.

Ribblesdale & the Three Peaks

Scenic Ribblesdale cuts through the south-western corner of the Yorkshire Dales National Park, where the skyline is dominated by a trio of distinctive hills known as the **Three Peaks** – Whernside (735m), Ingleborough (724m) and Pen-y-ghent (694m). Easily accessible via the Settle-Carlisle railway line, this is one of England's most popular areas for outdoor activities, attracting thousands of hikers, cyclists and cavers each weekend.

SETTLE

POP 3621

The busy market town of Settle, dominated by its grand neo-Gothic town hall, is the gateway to Ribblesdale and marks the beginning of the scenic part of the famous Settle-Carlisle railway line. Narrow cobbled streets lined with shops and pubs lead out from the central market square (Tuesday is market day), and the town offers plenty of accommodation options.

The **tourist office** (☎01729 825192; Town Hall, Cheapside; ⏲9.30am-4.30pm Apr-Oct, to 4pm Nov-Mar) has maps and guidebooks.

Around the main square there are several good cafes, including **Ye Olde Naked Man** (Market Pl; mains £4-7), formerly an undertakers (look for the 'naked man' on the outside wall, dated 1663); and the excellent **Shambles** (Market Pl; fish & chips £5-7).

Trains from Leeds or Skipton heading to Carlisle stop at the station near the town centre; those heading for Morecambe (on the west coast) stop at Giggleswick, about 1.5 miles outside town.

HORTON-IN-RIBBLESDALE

POP 560

A favourite with outdoor enthusiasts, the little village of Horton and its railway station is 5 miles north of Settle. Everything centres on the Pen-y-ghent Cafe which acts as the village tourist office, wet-weather retreat and hikers' information centre.

Horton is the starting point for climbing Pen-y-ghent and for doing the **Three Peaks Walk** (see the boxed text, p586); it's also a stop on the Pennine Way. At the head of the valley, 5 miles north of Horton, is the spectacular **Ribblehead Viaduct**, built in 1874 and the longest on the Settle-Carlisle Line – more than 30m high and 400m long. You can hike there along the Pennine Way

THREE PEAKS CHALLENGES

Since 1968 more than 200,000 hikers have taken up the challenge of climbing Yorkshire's Three Peaks in less than 12 hours. The circular 25-mile route begins and ends at the Pen-y-ghent Café in Horton-in-Ribblesdale – where you clock-in and clock-out to verify your time – and takes in the summits of Pen-y-ghent, Whernside and Ingleborough. Succeed, and you're a member of the cafe's Three Peaks of Yorkshire Club. You can find details of the route at www.merseyventure.com/yorks and download a guide (£4) at www.walkingworld.com (walk ID 4228 and 4229).

Fancy a more gruelling test of your endurance? Then join the fell-runners in the annual **Three Peaks Race** (www.threepeaksrace.org.uk) on the last Saturday in April, and run the route instead of walking it. First held in 1954 when six people competed, it now attracts around 900 entries; the course record is two hours, 43 minutes and three seconds.

In the last week of September, cyclists get their chance too in the **Three Peaks Cyclo-Cross** (www.3peakscyclocross.org.uk) which covers 38 miles of rough country and 1524m of ascent.

and travel back by train from Ribblehead station.

Sleeping & Eating

Horton is popular, so it's wise to book accommodation in advance.

Golden Lion B&B/BUNKHOUSE £

(01729-860206; www.goldenlionhotel.co.uk; s/d from £40/60, bunkhouse per person £12) The Golden Lion is a lively pub that offers comfortable B&B bedrooms, a brand new 40-bed bunkhouse, and three public bars where you can tuck into a bit of grub washed down with a pint of hand-pulled ale.

Holme Farm Campsite CAMPSITE £

(01729-860281; per person £2, per tent £1) Basic, no-frills campsite right next door to the Golden Lion pub, much used by Pennine Way hikers.

Pen-y-ghent Cafe CAFE £

(mains £2-6; breakfast & lunch) A traditional caff run by the same family since 1965, the Pen-y-ghent fills walkers' fuel tanks with fried egg and chips, homemade scones and pint-sized mugs of tea. It also sells maps, guidebooks and walking gear.

INGLETON

POP 2000

The village of Ingleton, perched precariously above a river gorge, is the caving capital of England. It sits at the foot of one of the country's most extensive areas of limestone upland, crowned by the dominating peak of Ingleborough and riddled with countless potholes and cave systems.

The **tourist office** (01524-241049; www.visitingleton.co.uk; 10am-4pm Apr-Sep) is beside the main car park, while **Bernie's Cafe** (4 Main St; 9am-4pm Mon, Wed & Thu, 9am-6pm Fri-Sun) is the centre of the local caving scene.

Ingleton is the starting point for two famous Dales hikes. The shorter and easier of the two is the circular, 4.5-mile **Waterfalls Walk** (www.ingletonwaterfallswalk.co.uk), which passes through native oak woodland on its way past a series of spectacular waterfalls on the River Twiss and River Doe. The more strenuous option is **Ingleborough** (724m). Around 120,000 people climb this hill every year, but that doesn't make the 6-mile round trip any less of an effort; this is a proper hill walk, so pack waterproofs, food, water, a map and a compass.

Although most of the local caves are accessible only to experienced potholers, some are open to the general public. **White Scar Cave** (www.whitescarcave.co.uk; 80-min guided tour adult/child £7.95/4.95; 10am-4.30pm Feb-Oct, Sat & Sun only Nov-Jan) is the longest show cave in England, with a series of underground waterfalls and impressive dripstone formations leading to the 100m-long Battlefield Cavern, one of the largest cave chambers in the country. The cave is 1.5 miles northeast of the village on the B6255 road.

Gaping Gill, on the southeastern flank of Ingleborough, is one of the most famous caves in England. A huge vertical pothole 105m deep, it was the largest known cave shaft in the UK until the discovery of Titan in Derbyshire in 1999. Gaping Gill is normally off-limits to non-cavers but, twice a year on the May and August bank holiday weekends, local caving clubs set up a winch so that members of the public can descend into the depths in a special chair (£10 per person). For details see www.bpc-cave.org.uk and www.cravenpotholeclub.org, and click on the Gaping Gill link.

Ingleton is 10 miles northwest of Settle; take bus 581 from Settle train station (25 minutes, two daily).

Hawes

POP 700

The beating heart of Wensleydale is Hawes, a thriving and picturesque market town (market day is Tuesday) that has the added attraction of its own waterfall in the village centre. On busy summer weekends, however, Hawes' narrow arteries can get seriously clogged with traffic – leave the car in the parking area beside the **national park centre** (☎01969-666210; Station Yard; ⏲10am-5pm year round) at the eastern entrance to the village.

Sights & Activities

Sharing a building with the park centre is the **Dales Countryside Museum** (☎01969-666210; Station Yard; adult/child £3/free), a beautifully presented social history of the area that explains the forces that shaped the landscape, from geology to lead mining to land enclosure.

At the other end of the village lies the **Wensleydale Creamery** (www.wensleydale.co.uk; ⏲9.30am-5pm Mon-Sat, 10am-4.30pm Sun), devoted to the production of Wallace and Gromit's favourite crumbly, white cheese. You can visit the cheese museum and then try-before-you-buy in the shop, which is free to enter. There are one-hour tours of the creamery (adult/child £2.50/1.50) between 10am and 3pm.

About 1.5 miles north of Hawes is 30m-high **Hardraw Force**, the highest unbroken waterfall in England. By international standards it's not that impressive (except after heavy rain); access is through the Green Dragon pub, which levies a £2 admission fee.

Sleeping & Eating

Herriot's Guest House B&B ££

(☎01969-667536; www.herriotsinhawes.co.uk; Main St; r per person from £38; 📶) A delightful guesthouse set in an old stone building close to the bridge by the waterfall, Herriot's has seven comfy, en-suite bedrooms set above an art gallery and coffee shop.

Green Dragon Inn B&B ££

(☎01969-667392; www.greendragonhardraw.co.uk; Hardraw; s/d from £26/50) A fine old pub with flagstone floors, low timber beams, ancient oak furniture and Theakstons on draught, the Dragon serves up a tasty steak-and-ale pie and offers B&B accommodation in plain but adequate rooms.

THE SETTLE-CARLISLE LINE

The 72-mile Settle-Carlisle Line (SCL), built between 1869 and 1875, offers one of England's most scenic railway journeys. The line's construction was one of the great engineering achievements of the Victorian era: 5000 navvies armed with picks and shovels built 325 bridges, 21 viaducts and blasted 14 tunnels in horrific conditions – nearly 200 of them died in the process.

Trains run between Leeds and Carlisle via Settle about eight times per day. The first section of the journey from Leeds is along the Aire Valley, stopping at **Keighley**, where the Keighley & Worth Valley Railway branches off to **Haworth**, **Skipton** (gateway to the southern Dales) and **Settle**. The train then labours up the valley beside the River Ribble, through **Horton-in-Ribblesdale**, across the spectacular **Ribblehead Viaduct** and then through Blea Moor Tunnel to reach remote **Dent station**, at 350m the highest main-line station in the country.

The line reaches its highest point (356m) at Ais Gill where it leaves the Dales behind before easing down to **Kirkby Stephen**. The last halts are **Appleby** and **Langwathby**, just northwest of Penrith (a jumping-off point for the Lake District), before the train finally pulls into **Carlisle**.

The entire journey from Leeds to Carlisle takes two hours and 40 minutes and costs £23.10/27.80 for a single/day return. Various hop-on/hop-off passes for one or three days are also available. You can pick up a free SCL timetable – which includes a colour map of the line and brief details about places of interest – from most Yorkshire stations. For more information contact **National Rail Enquiries** (☎08457 48 49 50) or see www.settle-carlisle.co.uk.

Bainbridge Ings Caravan & Camp Site CAMPSITE £
(☎01969-667354; www.bainbridge-ings.co.uk; hikers & cyclists per person £5, car, tent & 2 adults £13) An attractive site set in stone-walled fields around a spacious farmhouse about half a mile east of town. Gas, milk and eggs are sold on site.

Hawes YHA HOSTEL £
(☎0845 371 9120; www.yha.org.uk; Lancaster Tce; dm £16; P 👪) A modern place on the western edge of town, at the junction of the main A684 (Aysgarth Rd) and B6255, this is a family-friendly hostel with great views of Wensleydale.

Chaste BISTRO ££
(www.chaste-food.co.uk; Market Pl; mains lunch £4-8, dinner £13-15; 📶) An unusual name for a bistro, but this place is far from coy when it comes to promoting Yorkshire produce – almost everything on the menu, from the all-day breakfast to the vegetable burger to the lamb chops with peppercorn-and-strawberry gravy, is either homemade or locally sourced.

Cart House TEAROOM £
(☎01969-667691; www.hardrawforce.co.uk; Hardraw; mains £6; ⊙Mar-Nov) Across the bridge from the Green Dragon, this craft shop and tearoom offers a healthier diet of homemade soup, organic bread, and a 'Fellman's Lunch' of Wensleydale cheese, pickle and salad. There's a basic campsite at the back (£11 for two adults, tent and car).

Getting There & Away

Dales & District buses 156 and 157 run from Bedale to Hawes (1¼ hours, eight daily Monday to Saturday, four on Sunday) via Leyburn, where you can connect with transport to/from Richmond. To get to Bedale from Northallerton train station on the main York–Newcastle line, take bus 73 (25 minutes, half-hourly Monday to Saturday, every two hours Sunday).

From Garsdale station on the Settle-Carlisle Line, bus 113 runs to Hawes (20 minutes, three daily Monday to Saturday); on Sundays and bank holidays bus 808 goes to Hawes from Ribblehead station (50 minutes, two daily). Check the bus times at www.yorkshiretravel.net or a tourist office before using these routes.

WORTH A TRIP

WEST BURTON

Hidden away at the foot of a valley leading off Wensleydale, West Burton is easy to miss. But this picturesque hamlet is often voted 'Most beautiful Village in England', and beautiful it most certainly is. There are no real sights as such, just a necklace of sandstone cottages, including a pub, tearoom, village shop and butcher shop, strung around a vast village green complete with ancient market cross and punishment stocks. There's not much to do except soak up the view, or perhaps take a stroll to Cauldron Falls, the local beauty spot. By then, it'll be time for a pint…

To find West Burton, turn south off the A684 Leyburn to Hawes road, a few miles east of Aysgarth, on the B6160 (signposted West Burton, Kettlewell and Grassington).

Richmond

POP 8200

The handsome market town of Richmond is one of England's best-kept secrets, perched on a rocky outcrop overlooking the River Swale and guarded by the ruins of a massive castle. A maze of cobbled streets radiates from the broad, sloping market square (market day is Saturday), lined with elegant Georgian buildings and photogenic stone cottages, with glimpses of the surrounding hills and dales peeking through the gaps.

Sights

Top of the pile is the impressive heap that is **Richmond Castle** (EH; www.english-heritage.org.uk; Market Pl; adult/child £4.50/2.30; ⊙10am-6pm Apr-Sep, to 4pm Oct-Mar), founded in 1070 and one of the first castles in England since Roman times to be built of stone. It's had many uses through the years, including a stint as a prison for conscientious objectors during WWI (there's a small and sobering exhibition about their part in the castle's history). The best part is the view from the top of the remarkably well-preserved 30m-high keep which towers over the River Swale.

Military buffs will enjoy the **Green Howards Museum** (www.greenhowards.org.uk; Trinity Church Sq; adult/child £3.50/free; ⊙10am-4.30pm Mon-Sat, closed 24 Dec-31 Jan), which pays tribute to the famous Yorkshire regiment. In a different vein, the **Richmondshire Museum** (www.richmondshiremuseum.org.uk; Ryder's Wynd; adult/child £2.50/2;

⊙10.30am-4.30pm Apr-Oct) is a delight, with local history exhibits including an early Yorkshire cave-dweller and displays on lead mining, which forever altered the Swaledale landscape a century ago. You can also see the original set that served as James Herriot's surgery in the TV series *All Creatures Great and Small*.

Built in 1788, the **Georgian Theatre Royal** (www.georgiantheatreroyal.co.uk; Victoria Rd; tours per person £3.50; ⊙tours hourly 10am-4pm Mon-Sat mid-Feb–mid-Dec) is the most complete Georgian playhouse in Britain. Tours include a look at the country's oldest surviving stage scenery, painted between 1818 and 1836.

Activities

Walkers can follow paths along the River Swale, both upstream and downstream from the town. A longer option is to follow part of the famous long-distance **Coast to Coast Walk** all the way to Reeth (11 miles) and take the bus back (see www.dalesbus.info/richmond).

In September/October the town hosts the **Richmond Walking & Book Festival** (www.booksandboots.org), 10 days of guided walks, talks, films and other events.

Cyclists can also follow Swaledale – as far as Reeth may be enough, while a trip along Arkengarthdale and then over the high wild moors to Kirkby Stephen via the Tan Hill Inn is a more serious (but very rewarding) 40-mile undertaking.

Sleeping

TOP CHOICE **Millgate House** B&B £££

(☎01748-823571; www.millgatehouse.com; Market Pl; r £110-145; P @) Behind an unassuming green door lies the unexpected pleasure of one of the most attractive guesthouses in England. While the house itself is a Georgian gem crammed with period details, it is overshadowed by the multi-award-winning garden at the back, which has superb views over the River Swale and the Cleveland Hills – if possible, book the Garden Suite.

Frenchgate Hotel HOTEL ££

(☎01748-822087; www.thefrenchgate.co.uk; 59-61 Frenchgate; s/d from £88/118; P) Nine elegant bedrooms occupy the upper floors of this converted Georgian town house, now a boutique hotel decorated with local art. The rooms have cool designer fittings that set off a period fireplace here, a Victorian roll-top bath there; downstairs there's an excellent restaurant (three-course dinner £34) and a hospitable lounge with oak beams and an open fire.

Willance House B&B ££

(☎01748-824467; www.willancehouse.com; 24 Frenchgate; s/d £50/70; wi-fi) This is an oak-beamed house, built in 1600, with three immaculate rooms (one with a four-poster bed) that combine old-fashioned charm and all mod cons.

There's also a batch of pleasant places to stay along Frenchgate, and a couple more on Pottergate (the road into town from the east). These include:

66 Frenchgate B&B ££

(☎01748 823421; www.66frenchgate.co.uk; 66 Frenchgate; s/d from £40/60; wi-fi) One of the three rooms has a superb river view.

Pottergate Guesthouse B&B ££

(☎01748 823826; 4 Pottergate; d from £50) Compact and chintzy, with a friendly and helpful landlady.

Eating & Drinking

Rustique FRENCH ££

(☎01748-821565; Chantry Wynd, Finkle St; mains £10-16; ⊙lunch & dinner Mon-Sat) Newly opened and hard to find (tucked away in an arcade), this cosy bistro has consistently impressed with its mastery of French country cooking, from *confit de canard* (duck slow roasted in its own fat) to *paupiette de poulet* (chicken breast stuffed with brie and sun-dried tomatoes). Booking recommended.

Cross View Tearoom CAFE £

(38 Market Pl; mains £4-9; ⊙9am-5.50pm Mon-Sat) So popular with locals that you might have to queue for a table at lunchtime, the Cross View is the place to go for a hearty breakfast, homemade cakes, a hot lunch, or just a nice cup of tea.

Seasons Restaurant & Cafe INTERNATIONAL ££

(www.restaurant-seasons.co.uk; Richmond Station, Station Rd; mains £8-11; ⊙breakfast, lunch & dinner) Housed in the restored Victorian station building, this attractive, open-plan eatery shares space with a boutique brewery, artisan bakery, ice-cream factory and cheesemonger – and yes, all this local produce is on the menu.

Barkers FISH & CHIPS £

(Trinity Church Sq; mains £6-10; ⊙lunch & dinner) The best fish and chips in town, sit-down or takeaway.

Richmond

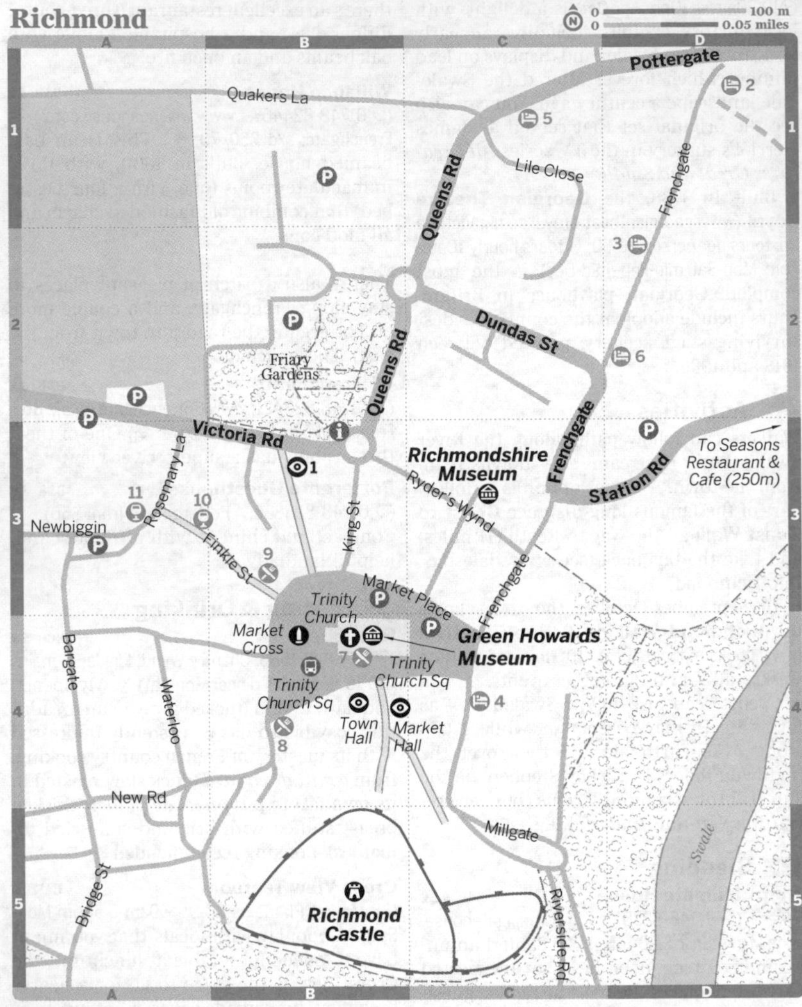

Black Lion Hotel PUB
(Finkle St) Cosy bars, low beams and good beer and food.

Unicorn Inn PUB
(2 Newbiggin) A determinedly old-fashioned free house serving Theakstons and Old Speckled Hen.

Information

The **tourist office** (☎01748-828742; www.richmond.org; Friary Gardens, Victoria Rd; ⊙9.30am-5.30pm Apr-Oct, to 4.30pm Nov-Mar) has the usual maps and guides, plus several leaflets showing walks in town and the surrounding countryside.

Getting There & Away

From Darlington (on the railway between London and Edinburgh) it's easy to reach Richmond on bus X26 or X27 (35 minutes, every 15 minutes, every 30 minutes on Sunday). All buses stop in Market Pl.

On Sundays and bank holiday Mondays only, from late May to late October, the Eastern Dalesman bus 820 runs from Leeds to Richmond (3½ hours, one daily) via Fountains Abbey, Ripon, Masham and Middleham.

Richmond

Top Sights
Green Howards Museum........B4
Richmond Castle........B5
Richmondshire Museum........C3

Sights
1 Georgian Theatre Royal........B3

Sleeping
2 66 Frenchgate........D1
3 Frenchgate Hotel........D2
4 Millgate House........C4
5 Pottergate Guesthouse........C1
6 Willance House........D2

Eating
7 Barkers........B4
8 Cross View Tearoom........B4
9 Rustique........B3

Drinking
10 Black Lion Hotel........A3
11 Unicorn Inn........A3

Swaledale & Arkengarthdale

The quietest and least-visited of the Dales stretch west from Richmond, their wild and rugged beauty in sharp contrast to the softer, greener dales to the south. It's hard to imagine that only a century ago this was a major lead-mining area. When the price of ore fell in the 19th century, many people left to find work in England's burgeoning industrial cities, while others emigrated – especially to Wisconsin in the USA – leaving the valley almost empty, with just a few lonely villages scattered along its length.

Where the two dales meet is the pretty village of **Reeth**, home to some art-and-craft shops, cafes and a few good pubs dotted around a large sloping green (Friday is market day). There is a **national park centre** (☎01748-884059) and the dusty little **Swaledale Museum** (www.swaledalemuseum.org; admission £1.50; ⊙10.30am-5.30pm Sun-Fri Apr-Oct), which tells the story of the Dales' fascinating history.

The best way to explore the dales is by bike, which you can hire from the **Dales Bike Centre** (www.dalesbikecentre.co.uk), just east of Reeth (road bikes/full-suspension mountain bikes for £18/40 per day).

There are many B&B options here, including the **Arkleside Hotel** (☎01748-884418; www.arklesidehotel.co.uk; s/d from £45/80; P), made up of a converted row of old cottages just by the green.

For lunch or dinner, the excellent **Overton House Café** (www.overtonhousecafe.co.uk; High Row; mains £5-15; ⊙lunch Wed-Sat, dinner Thu-Sat) has a menu ranging from a simple bacon sandwich (on ciabatta with onion relish) to expertly prepared fish dishes such as omelette Arnold Bennet, scallops with cheddar and leeks, and even lobster thermidor!

EAST RIDING OF YORKSHIRE

In command of the East Riding of Yorkshire is the tough old sea dog known as Hull, a no-nonsense port that looks to the North Sea and the broad horizons of the Humber estuary for its livelihood. Just to its north, and in complete contrast to Hull's salt and grit, is East Riding's most attractive town, Beverley, with lots of Georgian character and one of England's finest churches.

Stretching north from Hull and Beverley are the Yorkshire Wolds, an area of gently rolling, chalky hills that reaches the coast in a splash of white sea cliffs at Flamborough Head. Close by there are some classic seaside towns – bucket-and-spade Bridlington and the rather more upmarket Filey – while further south the coastline tapers away into the strange and other-wordly landscape of sand dunes and tussock grass that is Spurn Head.

Hull

POP 256,200

Tough and uncompromising, Hull is a curmudgeonly English seaport with a proud seafaring tradition. It has long been the principal cargo port of England's east coast, with an economy that grew up around carrying wool out and bringing wine in. It was also a major whaling and fishing port until the trawling industry died out, but it remains a busy cargo terminal and departure point for ferries to the Continent.

Hull too has climbed aboard the regeneration bandwagon, although the recession has called a halt to some projects including the Fruit Market redevelopment on the waterfront. Meanwhile, the city's attractions include a fine collection of Victorian and Edwardian architecture, several good museums and a world-class aquarium. It's

WORTH A TRIP

TAN HILL INN

From Reeth, a narrow, twisting road leads northwest through scenic Arkengarthdale before climbing up to the vast, bleak expanses of the north Pennine moors. About 11 miles from Reeth, sitting in the middle of nowhere at an elevation of 328m (1732ft) is Britain's highest pub.

Despite its isolation the **Tan Hill Inn** (☎01833-628246; www.tanhillinn.com; Tan Hill) is an unexpectedly comfortable and welcoming hostelry, with an ancient fireplace in the atmospheric, stone-flagged public bar and leather sofas in the lounge, and an assorted menagerie of dogs, cats and sheep wandering in and out of the building. An important watering hole on the Pennine Way, the inn offers real ale on tap, a decent pub-grub menu (mains £6 to £9), live music in the evenings, B&B accommodation (from £70 a double), a bunkhouse (£20 per person) and basic camping (£2 per person).

also home to the famous Hull Truck Theatre company, and counts among its famous former residents William Wilberforce (1759–1833), the Yorkshire politician who led the movement to abolish the slave trade; and the quintessentially English poet Philip Larkin (1922–85), who presided over Hull's university library for many years.

A distinctive feature of the city and surrounding area is its old-fashioned telephone boxes, which are cream-coloured rather than red. Hull was the only place in the UK to retain its own municipal phone system after all others were taken over by the Post Office in 1913; the company, now known as Kingston Communications, still provides the local phone service independently of British Telecom.

The train and bus stations – collectively known as Hull Paragon Interchange – sit on the western edge of the city centre; all the main sights are within 20 minutes' walk from here.

Sights

The Deep AQUARIUM

(www.thedeep.co.uk; Tower St; adult/child £9.50/7.50; 10am-6pm, last entry 5pm;) Hull's biggest tourist attraction is The Deep, a vast aquarium housed in a colossal, angular building that appears to lunge above the muddy waters of the Humber like a giant shark's head. Inside it's just as dramatic, with echoing commentaries and computer-generated interactive displays that guide you through the formation of the oceans and the evolution of sea life. The largest aquarium is 10m deep, filled with sharks, stingrays and colourful coral fishes, with moray eels draped over rocks like scarves of iridescent slime. A glass elevator plies up and down inside the tank, though you'll get a better view by taking the stairs. Don't miss the cafe on the very top floor, which has a great view of the Humber estuary.

FREE **Museum Quarter** MUSEUMS

Hull has several city-run **museums** (www.hullcc.gov.uk/museums; 36 High St; 10am-5pm Mon-Sat, 1.30-4.30pm Sun) concentrated in an area promoted as the Museum Quarter. All share the same contact details and opening hours, and all are free.

The fascinating **Streetlife Museum** contains re-created street scenes from Georgian and Victorian times and from the 1930s, with all sorts of historic vehicles to explore, from stagecoaches to bicycles to buses and trams. Behind the museum, marooned in the mud of the River Hull, is the **Arctic Corsair** (tours 10am-4.30pm Wed & Sat, 1.30-4.30pm Sun). Tours of this Atlantic trawler, a veteran of the 1970s 'Cod Wars', demonstrate the hardships of fishing north of the Arctic Circle.

Nearby you'll find the **Hull & East Riding Museum** (local history and archaeology), and **Wilberforce House** (the birthplace of William Wilberforce, now a museum about the slave trade and its abolition).

FREE **Old Town** ARCHITECTURE

Hull's Old Town, whose grand public buildings retain a sense of the prosperity the town once knew, occupies the thumb of land between the River Hull to the east and Princes Quay to the west. The most impressive legacy is the **Guildhall** (☎01482-300300; Low Gate; 8.30am-4.30pm Mon-Thu, to 3.30pm Fri), a huge neoclassical building that dates from 1916 and houses acres of polished marble, and oak and walnut panelling, plus a small collection of sculpture and art. Phone to arrange a free guided tour.

FREE **Ferens Art Gallery** ART GALLERY
(Queen Victoria Sq; ⏲10am-5pm Mon-Sat, 1.30-4.30pm Sun) Has works by Stanley Spencer and Peter Blake.

Maritime Museum MUSEUM
(Queen Victoria Sq; ⏲10am-5pm Mon-Sat, 1.30-4.30pm Sun) Housed in the former dock offices (1871), the Maritime Museum celebrates Hull's long association with the sea.

Spurn Lightship MUSEUM
(Castle St) Built in 1927, Hull's lighthouse-ship once served as a navigation mark for ships entering the notorious Humber estuary. Now safely retired in the marina undergoing renovation, it's not yet open to public.

Festivals

Hull Literature Festival LITERATURE
(www.humbermouth.org.uk) Besides the Larkin connection, poets Andrew Marvell, Stevie Smith and playwrights Alan Plater and John Godber all hail from Hull. Last two weeks of June.

Hull Jazz Festival JAZZ
(www.hulljazz.org.uk) This week-long July festival brings an impressive line-up of great jazz musicians to the city.

Sleeping & Eating

Good accommodation in the city centre is pretty thin on the ground – mostly business-oriented chain hotels and a few mediocre guesthouses. The tourist office will help book accommodation for free.

The best concentration of eating places is to be found along Princes Ave, from Welbeck St to Blenheim St, a mile northwest of the centre.

Kingston Theatre Hotel HOTEL ££
(☎01482-225828; www.kingstontheatrehotel.com; 1-2 Kingston Sq; s/d/ste from £50/65/90,) Overlooking leafy Kingston Sq, close to the New Theatre, this recently refurbished hotel is one of the best options in the city centre, with elegant bedrooms, friendly service and an excellent breakfast.

Fudge CAFE, BRASSERIE ££
(www.fudgecafe-restaurant.com; 93 Princes Ave; mains £9-15; ⏲breakfast & lunch Tue-Sun, dinner Tue-Sat;) This funky cafe serves hearty breakfasts, cakes and coffee all day, but also offers a tempting brasserie menu at lunch and dinner times, with dishes that include juicy burgers (beef or veggie), seafood gumbo and chickpea casserole with chilli and coriander.

Boar's Nest MODERN BRITISH ££
(☎01482-445577; www.theboarsnesthull.com; 22-24 Princes Ave; mains £14-19; ⏲lunch & dinner) Set in a former butcher's shop with quirky Edwardian decor, the Boar's Nest has built its reputation on sourcing quality British produce and serving it in a straightforward fashion: from Bridlington crab (on granary toast with a quail's egg on top) to roast rib of beef (with mashed potato and cauliflower cheese). Booking recommended at weekends.

Hitchcock's Vegetarian Restaurant VEGETARIAN ££
(☎01482-320233; www.hitchcocksrestaurant.co.uk; 1 Bishop Lane, High St; per person £15; ⏲dinner Tue-Sat) The word 'quirky' could have been invented to describe this place – an atmospheric maze of small rooms, and an all-you-can-eat vegetarian buffet whose theme – Thai, Indian, Spanish, whatever – is chosen by the first person to book that evening. But hey – the food is excellent and the welcome is warm. Bookings necessary.

Drinking & Entertainment

Come nightfall – especially at weekends – Hull can be raucous and often rowdy, especially in the streets around Trinity Sq in the Old Town, and on the strip of pubs along Beverley Rd to the north of the city centre.

Hull Truck Theatre THEATRE
(www.hulltruck.co.uk; Spring St) Home to acclaimed playwright John Godber, who made his name with gritty comedies *Bouncers* and *Up'n'Under* (he is one of the most-performed playwrights in the English-speaking world), Hull Truck presents a lively program of drama, comedy and Sunday jazz. It's just northwest of the Old Town.

Welly Club CLUB
(www.giveitsomewelly.com; 105-107 Beverley Rd; admission £5-12; ⏲10pm-3am Thu-Sat) The East Riding's top nightclub offers two venues – the mainstream Welly:One (which hosts Shuffle, the regular Saturday night dance club) and the more alternative Welly:Two (more house, techno, drum and bass). First Friday of the month is the famed Déjà vu house night, while Thursday is indie rock.

Minerva PUB
(Nelson St) If you're more into pubbing than clubbing, try a pint of Black Sheep

at this lovely, 200-year-old pub down by the waterfront; on a sunny day you can sit outdoors and watch the ships go by.

Hull New Theatre THEATRE
(www.hullcc.gov.uk; Kingston Sq) A traditional regional theatre hosting popular drama, concerts and musicals.

Information

Post office (63 Market Pl; ⌚9am-5.30pm Mon-Sat)

Tourist office (☎0844 811 2070; www.realyorkshire.co.uk; 1 Paragon St; ⌚10am-5pm Mon-Sat, 11am-3pm Sun)

Getting There & Away

BOAT The ferry port is 3 miles east of the centre at King George Dock; a bus connects the train station with the ferries. For details of ferry services to Zeebrugge and Rotterdam see p847.

BUS There are buses direct from London (£26, 6½ hours, one daily), Leeds (£7, 1¾ hours, six daily Monday to Friday, eight Saturday, two Sunday) and York (£7.60, 1¾ hours, one daily).

TRAIN Hull has good rail links north and south to Newcastle (£30, 2½ hours, hourly, change at York or Doncaster) and London King's Cross (£50, 2¾ hours, every two hours), and west to York (£18, 1¼ hours, every two hours) and Leeds (£16, one hour, hourly).

Around Hull

HUMBER BRIDGE

Opened in 1981, the **Humber Bridge** (www.humberbridge.co.uk) swoops gracefully across the broad estuary of the River Humber. Its 1410m span made it the world's longest single-span suspension bridge – until 1998 when it lost the title to Japan's Akashi Kaikyo bridge. It links Yorkshire to Lincolnshire, opening up what was once an often-overlooked corner of the country.

The best way to appreciate the scale of the bridge, and the vastness of the estuary, is to walk or cycle out along the footway from the **Humber Bridge tourist office** (☎01482-640852; ⌚9am-5pm May-Sep, 10am-3pm Nov-Feb, to 4pm Mar, Apr & Oct, to 3pm Nov-Feb) at the north end of the bridge (follow road signs for Humber Bridge Country Park). The car park here hosts a popular **farmers market** on the first Sunday in the month.

The bridge is a mile west of the small riverside town of Hessle, about 4 miles west of Hull. Bus 350 runs from Hull Paragon Interchange to Ferriby Rd in Hessle (15 minutes, every two hours), from where it's a 300m walk to the tourist office.

SPURN HEAD

About 3½ miles long and less than 100m wide, Spurn Head (also called Spurn Point) is the front line in a constant battle between the River Humber and the North Sea. A series of sand and shingle banks tenuously held together by tussocks of marram grass, this fragile and unusual environment is a paradise for birdwatchers and fossil hunters. It is also under threat – as the fastest-eroding stretch of coastline in Britain, it is only ever a storm away from destruction.

Most of the land is now part of the **Spurn National Nature Reserve** (www.ywt.org.uk; admission per car £3) which is managed by the Yorkshire Wildlife Trust; the tidal mud flats on the west side of the headland are a haven for wading birds and migrating water fowl. You can park for free at the **Blue Bell Tea Room & tourist office** (⌚11am-4.30pm Sat & 11am-5pm Sun Apr-Oct) and walk out along the Spurn Footpath to the tip of the headland (7 miles round trip), or pay the admission fee and drive along the very narrow road to a parking area at the old lighthouse. There are sandy beaches on either side, where the shingle is littered with fossil ammonites, and the very end of the headland is home to a remote community of lifeboat personnel and harbour pilots.

In 1804 gun batteries were built here to repel a possible French invasion, and during WWII guns of all sizes mounted in heavy concrete emplacements were added – the shattered concrete blocks and sandy scarps near the Blue Bell are a graphic illustration of how fast this coast is being lost to the sea.

There are a couple of pubs and tearooms in **Kilnsea**, the last village before the Blue Bell, and at **Easington**, two miles to the north.

Spurn Head is about 28 miles southeast of Hull city centre, on mostly minor roads – it's about an hour's drive. On Sundays and bank holidays from Easter to October, you can take bus 75 from Hull to Patrington (one hour, hourly), then the 73 Spurn Ranger to Spurn Head (one hour, four a day).

Beverley

POP 29,110

Handsome, unspoilt Beverley is one of the most attractive towns in Yorkshire, largely on account of its magnificent minster – a rival to any cathedral in England – and the tangle of streets that lie beneath it, each brimming with exquisite Georgian and Victorian buildings.

All the sights are a short walk from either train or bus station. There's a large market in the main square on Saturday, and a smaller one on Wednesday on the square called...Wednesday Market.

Sights

Beverley Minster CHURCH

(www.beverleyminster.org; admission by donation; 9am-4pm Mon-Sat & noon-4pm Sun, till 5pm Mon-Sat May-Aug) One of the great glories of English religious architecture, Beverley Minster is the most impressive church in the country that is not a cathedral. Construction began in 1220 – it was the third church to be built on this site, the first dating from the 7th century – and continued for two centuries, spanning the Early English, Decorated and Perpendicular periods of the Gothic style.

The soaring lines of the exterior are imposing, but it is inside that the charm and beauty lie. The 14th-century **north aisle** is lined with original stone carvings, mostly of musicians. Indeed, much of our knowledge of early musical instruments comes from these images. You'll also see goblins, devils and grotesque figures. Look out for the bagpipe player.

Close to the altar, the elaborate and intricate **Percy Canopy** (1340), a decorative frill above the tomb of local aristocrat Lady Eleanor Percy, is a testament to the skill of the sculptor, and the finest example of Gothic stone carving in England. In complete contrast, in the nearby chancel, is the 10th-century Saxon **frith stool**, a plain and polished stone chair that once gave sanctuary to anyone escaping the law.

In the roof of the tower is a restored **treadwheel crane** (guided tours £5; 11.15am, 2.15pm & 3.30pm Mon-Sat), where workers ground around like hapless hamsters to lift the huge loads necessary to build a medieval church. Access is by guided tour only.

FREE **St Mary's Church** CHURCH

(9.30am-4.30pm Mon-Fri, 10am-4pm Sat & 2-4pm Sun Apr-Sep, shorter hours Oct-Mar) Doomed to play second fiddle to Beverley Minster, St Mary's Church at the other end of town was built between 1120 and 1530. The west front (early 15th century) is considered one of the finest of any parish church in England. In the north choir aisle there is a **carving** (c 1330) of a rabbit dressed as a pilgrim that is said to have inspired Lewis Carroll's White Rabbit.

Sleeping & Eating

Friary YHA HOSTEL £

(0845 371 9004; www.yha.org.uk; Friar's Lane; dm from £14; P) In Beverley, the cheapest accommodation also has the best setting and location. This hostel is housed in a beautifully restored 14th-century Dominican friary mentioned in Chaucer's *The Canterbury Tales*, and is only 100m from the minster and a short walk from the train station.

Kings Head B&B ££

(01482-868103; www.kingsheadpubbeverley.co.uk; 38 Saturday Market; r from £73; @) A Georgian coaching inn that has been given a modern makeover, the Kings Head is a lively, family-friendly pub with 12 bright and cheerful rooms above the bar. The pub opens late on weekend nights, but earplugs are supplied for those who don't want to join the revelry!

Dine on the Rowe BRASSERIE ££

(01482-502269; www.dineontherowe.com; 12-14 Butcher Row; mains £16-18; lunch daily, dinner Wed-Sat) This new kid on the block rivals Grant's Bistro in its dedication to local produce, but offers a rather less formal atmosphere. Try the roast duck from Leven farm (just northeast of Beverley) with a sweet-and-sour Yorkshire rhubarb jus. Lunch dishes such as sausage and mash are available noon to 7.30pm, and a sharing platter for two, including two glasses of wine, costs £25.

Grant's Bistro MODERN BRITISH ££

(01482-887624; www.grantsbistro.co.uk; 22 North Bar Within; mains £15-21; lunch Fri & Sat, dinner Mon Sat) Grant's is a great place for a romantic dinner *à deux*, with darkwood tables, fresh flowers and candlelight. The menu makes the most of fresh local beef, game and especially seafood, with dishes such as pan-fried scallops with black pudding. From Monday to Thursday you can get a two-course dinner including a glass of wine for £15.

Eastgate Guest House B&B ££

(01482-868464; www.eastgateguesthouse.com; 7 Eastgate; s/d £50/80) A red-brick Victorian town house with comfortable rooms in a central location.

Boutique du Café Lempicka CAFE £

(13 Wednesday Market; mains £5-7) Stylish and sepia-toned little cafe with a 1930s

art deco atmosphere. Serves fair-trade coffee and tea, wicked hot chocolate, homemade cakes and daily lunch specials.

Information

Post office (Register Sq; 9am-5.30pm Mon-Fri, to 12.30pm Sat)

Tourist office (01482-391672; www.beverley.gov.uk; 34 Butcher Row; 9.30am-5.15pm Mon-Fri & 10am-4.45pm Sat year-round, 11am-3pm Sun Jul & Aug)

Getting There & Away

BUS There are frequent bus services from Hull including numbers 121, 122, 246 and X46/X47 (30 minutes, every 20 minutes). Bus X46/X47 links Beverley with York (1¼ hours, hourly).

TRAIN There are regular trains to Scarborough via Filey (£11.40, 1½ hours, every two hours) and Hull (£5.50, 15 minutes, twice hourly).

Bridlington

POP 33,600

Bridlington is one of those sleepy seaside resorts that seems to have been bypassed by the 21st century, pulling in a crowd of contented regulars who return year after year to enjoy the neatly groomed beaches of golden sand, the minigolf and paddling pool, the deckchairs and donkey rides.

So the reopening of **Bridlington Spa** (01262-401400; South Marine Dr;) in 2007, and the transfer of the **Musicport Festival** (www.musicportfestival.com) – a weekend-long festival of world music in mid-October – from Whitby to here were both a bit of a shot in the arm. The renovated building, which retains its Edwardian theatre and 1930s art deco ballroom, stages a lively program of music and entertainment events that has livened things up down by the South Beach, and has a decent **cafe-bar** with a panoramic sea view.

Food wise, Bridlington is famous for **Audrey's Fish & Chips** (2 Queen St; mains £4-6; lunch), an old-school fish-and-chip restaurant that serves superbly crisp battered haddock fried in beef dripping – the real deal.

For something more contemporary try **Seasalt and Passion** (www.seasaltandpassion.co.uk; 22 West St; mains £5-6; breakfast & lunch Tue-Sat), a health-food cafe offering dishes such as chestnut and cashew fritters with salad and yoghurt dressing.

The **tourist office** (01262-673474; 25 Prince St; 9.30am-5.30pm Mon-Sat, 11am-3pm Sun) is near the North Beach and has short-term parking at the front.

Bridlington is on the railway line between Hull (£10.20, 50 minutes, every 30 minutes) and Scarborough (£5.90, 40 minutes, every two hours).

Around Bridlington

Northeast of Bridlington, the 120m-high chalk cliffs of **Flamborough Head** thrust out into the North Sea, providing nesting sites for England's largest seabird colony. The headland is also home to the country's oldest-surviving **lighthouse tower**, dating from around 1670 – it stands in the golf course about 300m before the car park beside the modern lighthouse.

On the northern side of the headland, about 4 miles north of Bridlington, is the RSPB's **Bempton Cliffs Nature Reserve** (www.rspb.org.uk; pedestrian/car free/£3.50; tourist office 10am-5pm Mar-Oct, 9.30am-4pm Nov-Feb). From April to August these cliffs are home to more than 200,000 nesting seabirds, including guillemots, razorbills, fulmars, a rare colony of gannets, and those supermodels of the seagull world, the delicate and elegant kittiwakes, with their fat and fluffy chicks. The big crowd-pullers, though, are the comical and colourful puffins. There is a good tourist office at the car park and the reserve has 3 miles of well-maintained paths along the cliffs. Binoculars can be rented for £3; there are helpful volunteers on hand to offer guidance.

To get here take a train from Bridlington to Bempton village (seven minutes, every 1½ hours), from where it's a 1½-mile walk to the reserve.

NORTH YORKSHIRE

The largest of Yorkshire's four counties – and the largest county in England – is also the most beautiful. Unlike the rest of northern England, it has survived almost unscarred by the Industrial Revolution. On the contrary, North Yorkshire has always, since the Middle Ages, been about sheep and the woolly wealth that they produce.

Instead of closed-down factories, mills and mines, the man-made monuments that dot the landscape round these parts are of the magnificent variety – the great houses and wealthy abbeys that sit ruined or restored, a reminder that there was plenty of money to be made off the sheep's back.

All the same, North Yorkshire's biggest attraction is an urban one. Sure, the genteel spa town of Harrogate and the bright and breezy seaside resorts of Scarborough and Whitby have many fans, but nothing compares to the unparalleled splendour of York, England's most-visited city outside London.

York

POP 181,100

Nowhere in northern England says 'medieval' quite like York, a city of extraordinary cultural and historical wealth that has lost little of its pre-industrial lustre. Its medieval spider's web of narrow streets is enclosed by a magnificent circuit of 13th-century walls. At the heart of the city lies the immense, awe-inspiring minster, one of the most beautiful Gothic cathedrals in the world. The city's long history and rich heritage is woven into virtually every brick and beam, and modern, tourist-oriented York – with its myriad museums, restaurants, cafes and traditional pubs – is a carefully maintained heir to that heritage.

Just to avoid the inevitable confusion, remember that round these parts *gate* means street and *bar* means gate.

Sights

York Minster CATHEDRAL

(www.yorkminster.org; adult/child £8/free; ⌚9am-5.30pm Mon-Sat, noon-3.45pm Sun) Not content with being Yorkshire's most important historic building, the awe-inspiring York Minster is also the largest medieval cathedral in all of Northern Europe. Seat of the archbishop of York, primate of England, it is second in importance only to Canterbury, home of the primate of *all* England – the separate titles were created to settle a debate over whether York or Canterbury was the true centre of the English church. But that's where Canterbury's superiority ends, for this is without doubt one of the world's most beautiful Gothic buildings. If this is the only cathedral you visit in England, you'll still walk away satisfied – so long as you have the patience to deal with the constant flow of school groups and organised tours that will invariably clog up your camera's viewfinder.

The first church on this spot was a wooden chapel built for the baptism of King Edwin of Northumbria on Easter Day 627; its location is marked in the crypt. It was replaced with a stone church that was built on the site of a Roman basilica, parts of which can be seen in the foundations. The first Norman minster was built in the 11th century; again, you can see surviving fragments in the foundations and crypt.

The present minster, built mainly from 1220 to 1480, manages to encompass all the major stages of Gothic architectural development. The transepts (1220–55) were built in Early English style; the octagonal chapter house (1260–90) and the nave (1291–1340) in the Decorated style; and the west towers, west front and central (or lantern) tower (1470–72) in Perpendicular style.

Choir, Chapter House & Nave

You enter via the south transept, which was badly damaged by fire in 1984 but has now been fully restored. To your right is the 15th-century **choir screen** depicting the 15 kings from William I to Henry VI. Facing you is the magnificent **Five Sisters Window**, with five lancets over 15m high. This is the minster's oldest complete window; most of its tangle of coloured glass dates from around 1250. Just beyond it to the right is the 13th-century **chapter house**, a fine example of the Decorated style. Sinuous and intricately carved stonework – there are more than 200 expressive carved heads and figures – surrounds an airy, uninterrupted space.

Back in the main church, take note of the unusually tall and wide **nave**, the aisles of which (to the sides) are roofed in stone in contrast to the central roof, which is wood painted to look like stone. On both sides of the nave are painted stone shields of the nobles who met with Edward II at a parliament in York. Also note the **dragon's head** projecting from the gallery – it's a crane believed to have been used to lift a font cover. There are several fine windows dating from the early 14th century, but the most impressive is the **Great West Window** (1338), with its beautiful stone tracery.

Beyond the screen and the choir is the **lady chapel** and, behind it, the **high altar**,

WANT MORE?

Head to **Lonely Planet** (www.lonelyplanet.com/england/yorkshire/york) for planning advice, author recommendations, traveller reviews and insider tips.

York

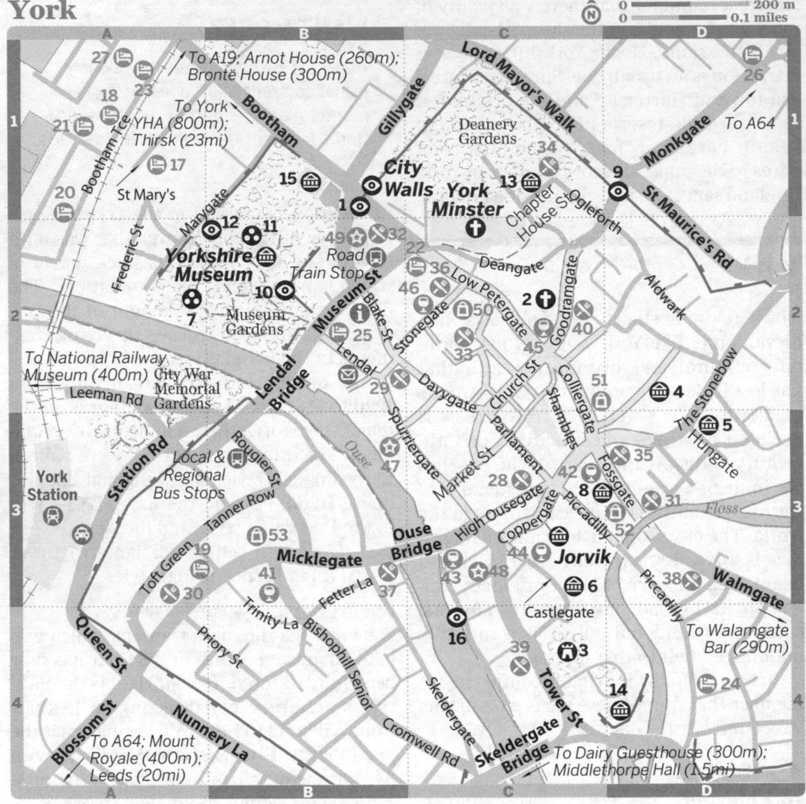

which is dominated by the huge **Great East Window** (1405). At 23.7m by 9.4m – roughly the size of a tennis court – it is the world's largest medieval stained-glass window and the cathedral's single most important treasure. Needless to say, its epic size matches the epic theme depicted within: the beginning and end of the world as described in Genesis and the Book of Revelations.

Undercroft, Treasury & Crypt

A set of stairs in the south transept leads down to the undercroft, where you'll also find the treasury and crypt – these should on no account be missed. In 1967 the foundations were shored up when the central tower threatened to collapse; while engineers worked frantically to save the building, archaeologists uncovered Roman and Norman remains that attest to the site's ancient history – one of the most extraordinary finds is a **Roman culvert**, still carrying water to the Ouse. The **treasury** houses 11th-century artefacts including relics from the graves of medieval archbishops.

The **crypt** contains fragments from the Norman cathedral, including the font showing King Edwin's baptism that also marks the site of the original wooden chapel. Look out for the **Doomstone**, a 12th-century carving showing a scene from the Last Judgement with demons casting doomed souls into Hell.

Tower

At the heart of the minster is the massive tower (extra admission adult/child £5/3), which is well worth climbing for the unparalleled **views of York**. You'll have to tackle a fairly claustrophobic climb of 275 steps and, most probably, a queue of people with cameras in hand. Access to the tower is near the entrance in the south transept, dominated by the exquisite **Rose Window**, commemorating the union of the royal houses of Lancaster and York through the

York

Top Sights

Sights

Sleeping

Eating

Drinking

Entertainment

Shopping

marriage of Henry VII and Elizabeth of York, which ended the Wars of the Roses and began the Tudor dynasty.

FREE **National Railway Museum** MUSEUM (www.nrm.org.uk; Leeman Rd; ⏲10am-6pm daily, closed 24-26 Dec) Many railway museums are the sole preserve of lone men in anoraks comparing dog-eared notebooks and getting high on the smell of machine oil, coal smoke and nostalgia. But this place is different. York's National Railway Museum – the biggest in the world, with more than 100 locomotives – is so well presented and full of fascinating stuff that it's interesting even to folk whose eyes don't mist over at the thought of a 4-6-2 A1 Pacific class chuffing into a tunnel.

Highlights for the trainspotters among us include a replica of George Stephenson's *Rocket* (1829), the world's first 'modern' steam locomotive; the sleek and streamlined *Mallard,* which set the world speed record for a steam locomotive in 1938 (126mph); a 1960s Japanese *Shinkansen* bullet train; and the world-famous *Flying Scotsman,* the first steam engine to break the 100mph barrier (currently undergoing restoration; should be in full working order by 2011). There's also a massive 4-6-2 loco

YORK: FROM THE BEGINNING

York – or the marshy area that preceded the first settlement – has been coveted by pretty much everyone that has ever set foot on this island. In the beginning there were the Brigantes, a local tribe that minded their own business. In AD 71 the Romans – who were spectacularly successful at minding everyone else's business – built their first garrison here for the troops fighting the poor old Brigantes. They called it Eboracum, and in time a civilian settlement prospered around what became a large fort. Hadrian used it as the base for his northern campaign, while Constantine the Great was proclaimed emperor here in AD 306 after the death of his father. When the Roman Empire collapsed, the town was taken by the Anglo-Saxons who renamed it Eoforwic and made it the capital of the independent kingdom of Northumbria.

Enter the Christians. In 625 a Roman priest, Paulinus, arrived and managed to convert King Edwin and all his nobles. Two years later, they built the first wooden church; for most of the next century the city was a major centre of learning, attracting students from all over Europe.

The student party lasted until 866, when the next wave of invaders arrived. This time it was those marauding Vikings, who chucked everybody out and gave the town a more tongue-friendly name, Jorvik. It was to be their capital for the next 100 years, and during that time they reined in their pillaging ways and turned the city into an important trading port.

The next arrival was King Eadred of Wessex, who drove out the last Viking ruler in 954 and reunited Danelaw with the south, but trouble quickly followed. In 1066 King Harold II managed to fend off a Norwegian invasion/rebellion at Stamford Bridge, east of York, but his turn came at the hands of William the Conqueror a few months later at the Battle of Hastings.

Willie exercised his own brand of tough love in York. After his two wooden castles were captured by an Anglo-Scandinavian army, he torched the whole city (and Durham) and the surrounding countryside so that the rebels knew who was boss – the 'harrying of the north'. The Normans then set about rebuilding the city, including a new minster. From that moment, everything in York was rosy – except for a blip in 1137 when the whole city caught fire – and over the next 300 years it prospered through royal patronage, textiles, trade and the church.

No sooner did the church finally get built, though, than the city went into full recession. In the 15th century Hull took over as the region's main port and the textile industry moved elsewhere. Henry VIII's inability to keep a wife and the ensuing brouhaha with the church that resulted in the Reformation also hit York pretty hard. Henry did establish a branch of the King's Council here to help govern the north, and this contributed to the city's recovery under Elizabeth I and James I.

The council was abolished during Charles I's reign, but the king established his court here during the Civil War, which drew the devastating attentions of the Parliamentarians. They besieged the rabidly pro-monarchist York for three months in 1644, but by a fortunate accident of history their leader was a local chap called Sir Thomas Fairfax, who prevented his troops from setting York alight, thereby preserving the city and the minster.

Not much happened after that. Throughout the 18th century the city was a fashionable social centre dominated by the aristocracy, who were drawn by its culture and new racecourse. When the railway was built in 1839 thousands of people were employed in the new industries that sprung up around it, such as confectionery. These industries went into decline in the latter half of the 20th century, but by then a new invader was asking for directions at the city gates, armed only with a guidebook.

from 1949 that's been cut in half so you can see how it works.

But even if you're not a rail nerd you'll enjoy looking around the gleaming, silk-lined carriages of the royal trains used by Queen Victoria and Edward VII, or having a *Brief Encounter* moment over tea and scones at the museum's station platform cafe called, erm, Brief Encounter. Allow at least two hours to do the museum justice.

The museum is about 400m west of the train station; if you don't fancy walking you can ride the road train (adult/child £2/1) that runs every 30 minutes from 11am to 4pm between the minster and the museum.

Jorvik MUSEUM
(www.vikingjorvik.com; Coppergate; adult/child £8.95/6, Jorvik & Dig combined £13/9.75; ⏲10am-5pm Apr-Oct, to 4pm Nov-Mar) Interactive multimedia exhibits aimed at 'bringing history to life' often achieve exactly the opposite, but the much-hyped Jorvik – the most visited attraction in town after the minster – manages to pull it off with admirable aplomb. It's a smells-and-all reconstruction of the Viking settlement that was unearthed here during excavations in the late 1970s, brought to you courtesy of a 'time-car' monorail that transports you through 9th-century Jorvik (the Viking name for York). While some of the 'you will now travel back in time' malarkey is a bit naff, it's all done with a sense of humour tied to a historical authenticity that will leave you with a pretty good idea of what life must have been like in Viking-era York. In the exhibition at the end of the monorail, look out for the **Lloyds Bank Turd** – a fossilised human stool that measures an eye-watering nine inches long and half a pound in weight, and must be the only jobbie in the world to have its own Wikipedia entry.

You can cut time spent waiting in the queue by booking your tickets online and choosing the time you want to visit – it only costs £1 extra.

FREE **City Walls** CITY WALLS
(⏲8am-dusk) If the weather's good, don't miss the chance to walk the City Walls, which follow the line of the original Roman walls – it gives a whole new perspective on the city. The full circuit is 4.5 miles (allow 1½ to two hours); if you're pushed for time, the short stretch from Bootham Bar to Monk Bar is worth doing for the views of the minster.

Start and finish in the Museum Gardens or at **Bootham Bar** (on the site of a Roman gate), where a multimedia exhibit provides some historical context, and go clockwise. Highlights include **Monk Bar**, the best-preserved medieval gate, which still has a working portcullis, and **Walmgate Bar**, England's only city gate with an intact barbican (an extended gateway to ward off uninvited guests).

At Monk Bar you'll find the **Richard III Museum** (www.richardiiimuseum.co.uk; adult/child £2.50/free; ⏲9am-5pm Mar-Oct, 9.30am-4pm Nov-Feb). The museum sets out the case of the murdered 'Princes in the Tower' and invites visitors to judge whether their uncle, Richard III, killed them.

You can download a free guide to the wall walk from www.visityork.org/explore/walls.html.

Yorkshire Museum MUSEUM
(www.yorkshiremuseum.org.uk; Museum St; adult/child £7/free; ⏲10am-5pm) Most of York's Roman archaeology is hidden beneath the medieval city, so the displays in the Yorkshire Museum are invaluable if you want to get an idea of what Eboracum was like. There are excellent exhibits on Viking and medieval York too, including priceless artefacts such as the 8th-century Coppergate helmet; a 9th-century Anglian sword decorated with silver; and the 15th-century Middleham Jewel, an engraved gold pendant adorned with a giant sapphire.

In the grounds of the peaceful **Museum Gardens** (⏲dawn-dusk) you can see the **Multangular Tower**, a part of the city walls that was once the western tower of the Roman garrison's defensive ramparts. The Roman stonework at the base has been built over with 13th-century additions.

On the other side of the Museum Gardens are the ruins of **St Mary's Abbey** (founded 1089), dating from 1270–1294. The ruined **Gatehall** was its main entrance, providing access from the abbey to the river. The adjacent **Hospitium** dates from the 14th century, although the timber-framed upper storey is a much-restored survivor from the 15th century; it was used as the abbey guesthouse. **St Mary's Lodge** was built around 1470 to provide VIP accommodation.

Shambles MEDIEVAL STREET
(www.yorkshambles.com) The narrow, cobbled lane known as the Shambles, lined with 15th-century Tudor buildings that overhang so much they seem to meet above your head, is the most visited street in Europe. Quaint and picturesque it most certainly is, and it hints at what a medieval street may have looked like – even if it's now overrun with people told they have to buy a tacky souvenir and be back on the tour bus in 15 minutes. It takes its name from the Saxon word *shamel*, meaning 'slaughterhouse' – in 1862 there were 26 butcher shops on this one street.

York Castle Museum MUSEUM
(www.yorkcastlemuseum.org.uk; Tower St; adult/child £8/free; ⌚9.30am-5pm) This excellent museum contains displays of everyday life through the centuries, with reconstructed domestic interiors, a Victorian street, and a less-than-homely prison cell where you can try out a condemned man's bed – in this case the highwayman Dick Turpin's (he was imprisoned here before being hanged in 1739). There's a bewildering array of evocative objects from the past 400 years, gathered together by a certain Dr Kirk from the 1920s onwards for fear that the items would become obsolete and disappear completely. He wasn't far wrong, which makes this place all the more interesting.

Treasurer's House HISTORIC BUILDING
(NT; www.nationaltrust.org.uk; Minster Yard; adult/child £6/3; ⌚11am-4.30pm Sat-Thu Apr-Oct, 11am-3pm Sat-Thu Nov) The Treasurer's House was home to the York Minster's medieval treasurers. Substantially rebuilt in the 17th and 18th centuries, the 13 rooms here house a fine collection of furniture and provide a good insight into 18th-century life. The house is also the setting for one of the city's most enduring ghost stories: during the 1950s a plumber working in the basement swore he saw a band of Roman soldiers walking *through* the walls. His story remains popular if unproven – but you can explore the cellar to find out.

Dig MUSEUM
(www.digyork.co.uk; St Saviour's Church, St Saviourgate; adult/child £5.50/5, Dig & Jorvik £13/9.75; ⌚10am-5pm, closed 24-26 Dec; 👪) Under the same management as Jorvik, Dig cashes in on the popularity of archaeology programs on TV by giving you the chance to be an 'archaeological detective', unearthing the secrets of York's distant past as well as learning something of the archaeologist's world – what they do, how they do it and so on. Aimed mainly at kids, it's much more hands-on than Jorvik, and a lot depends on how good – and entertaining – your guide is.

Up to the end of 2011 you can go also visit a real live archaeological dig at **Dig Hungate** (www.dighungate.com; tours per person £1); ask at Dig or check the website for times and details.

Clifford's Tower CASTLE
(EH; www.english-heritage.org.uk; Tower St; adult/child £3.50/1.80; ⌚10am-6pm Apr-Sep, to 5pm Oct, to 4pm Nov-Mar) There's precious little left of York Castle except for this evocative stone tower, a highly unusual figure-of-eight design built into the castle's keep after the original one was destroyed in 1190 during anti-Jewish riots. An angry mob forced 150 Jews to be locked inside the tower and the hapless victims took their own lives rather than be killed. There's not much to see inside but the views over the city are excellent.

FREE **Church of the Holy Trinity** CHURCH
(Goodramgate; ⌚10am-5pm Tue-Sat May-Sep, 10am-4pm Oct-Apr) Tucked away behind an inconspicuous gate and seemingly cut off from the rest of the town, the Church of the Holy Trinity is a fantastically atmospheric old building, having survived almost unchanged for the last 200 years. Inside are rare 17th- to 18th-century box pews, 15th-century stained glass, and wonky walls that seem to have been built without plumb line or spirit level.

FREE **York City Art Gallery** ART GALLERY
(www.yorkartgallery.org.uk; Exhibition Sq; ⌚10am-5pm) Includes works by Reynolds, Nash, Boudin, LS Lowry and controversial York artist William Etty, who, back in the 1820s, was the first major British artist to specialise in nude painting.

Merchant Adventurers' Hall HISTORIC BUILDING
(www.theyorkcompany.co.uk; Fossgate; adult/child £5/free; ⌚9am-5pm Mon-Thu, 9am-3.30pm Fri & Sat, noon-4pm Sun Apr-Sep, 9am-3.30pm Mon-Sat Oct-Mar) One of the most handsome timber-framed buildings in Europe, built between 1357 and 1361. Displays include oil paintings and antique silver, but the building itself is the star.

Fairfax House HISTORIC BUILDING
(www.fairfaxhouse.co.uk; Castlegate; adult/child £6/free; ⌚11am-4.30pm Mon-Thu & Sat, 1.30-5pm Sun, guided tours 11am & 2pm Fri) Built in 1762 by John Carr (of Harewood House fame), Fairfax House contains a superb collection of Georgian furniture.

Tours

There's a bewildering range of tours on offer, from historic walking tours to a host of ever more competitive night-time ghost tours (York is reputed to be England's most haunted city). For starters, check the tourist office's own suggestions for walking itineraries at www.visityork.org/explore.

Ghost Hunt of York WALKING TOURS
(www.ghosthunt.co.uk; adult/child £5/3; ⌚tours 7.30pm) Award-winning and highly entertaining 75-minute tour laced with

authentic ghost stories; the kids will just love this one. Begins at the Shambles, whatever the weather (they never cancel). No need to book, just turn up.

Yorkwalk WALKING TOURS
(www.yorkwalk.co.uk; adult/child £5.50/3.50; tours 10.30am & 2.15pm) Offers a series of two-hour themed walks on an ever-growing list of themes, from the classics – Roman York, the snickelways (alleys) and City Walls – to specialised walks on chocolates and sweets, women in York, secret York and the inevitable graveyard, coffin and plague tour. Walks depart from Museum Gardens Gate on Museum St; no need to book.

YorkBoat BOAT TOURS
(www.yorkboat.co.uk; King's Staith; adult/child £7.50/3.50; ⌚tours 10.30am, noon, 1.30pm & 3pm Feb-Nov) Runs one-hour cruises on the River Ouse departing from King's Staith (and Lendal Bridge 10 minutes later). Also special lunch, dinner and evening cruises.

Original Ghost Walk of York WALKING TOURS
(www.theoriginalghostwalkofyork.co.uk; adult/child £4.50/3; ⌚tours 8pm) An evening of ghouls, ghosts, mystery and history courtesy of a well-established group departing from the King's Arms pub by Ouse Bridge.

York City Sightseeing BUS TOURS
(www.city-sightseeing.com; day tickets adult/child £10/4; ⌚9am-5pm) Hop-on/hop-off route with 16 stops, calling at all the main sights. Buses leave every 10 minutes from Exhibition Sq near York Minster.

FREE **Association of Voluntary Guides** WALKING TOURS
(www.visityork.org; ⌚tours 10.15am, also 2.15pm Apr-Sep & 6.45pm Jun-Aug) Two-hour walking tours of the city starting from Exhibition Sq in front of York City Art Gallery.

Festivals & Events

Check out a full calendar of events at www.yorkfestivals.com.

Jorvik Viking Festival HISTORY
(www.vikingjorvik.com) For a week in mid-February, York is invaded by Vikings once again as part of this festival, which features battle re-enactments, themed walks, markets and other bits of Viking-themed fun.

York Food Festival FOOD & DRINK
(www.yorkfoodfestival.com) Ten days in September of all that's good to eat and drink in Yorkshire – food stalls, tastings, beer tent, cookery demonstrations etc.

York Christmas SHOPPING
(www.visityork.org/christmas) Kicking off with St Nicholas Fayre market in late November, the run-up to Christmas is an extravaganza of street decorations, market stalls, carol singers and mulled wine.

Sleeping

Beds are tough to find midsummer, even with the inflated prices of the high season. The tourist office's accommodation booking service charges £4, which might be the best four quid you spend if you arrive without a booking.

Needless to say, prices get higher the closer to the city centre you are. However, there are plenty of decent B&Bs on the streets north and south of Bootham. Southwest of the town centre, there are B&Bs clustered around Scarcroft Rd, Southlands Rd and Bishopthorpe Rd.

It's also worth looking at serviced apartments if you're planning to stay two or three nights. **City Lets** (☎01904-652729; www.citylets york.co.uk) offers a good selection of places from around £90 a night for a two-person apartment – we particularly like the stylish, modern flats in the peaceful courtyard at Talbot Court on Low Petergate.

Abbeyfields B&B ££
(☎01904-636471; www.abbeyfields.co.uk; 19 Bootham Tce; s/d from £49/78; 📶) Expect a warm welcome and thoughtfully arranged bedrooms here, with chairs and bedside lamps for comfortable reading. Breakfasts are among the best in town, with sausage and bacon from the local butcher, freshly laid eggs from a nearby farm, and the smell of newly baked bread.

Elliotts B&B B&B ££
(☎01904-623333; www.elliottshotel.co.uk; 2 Sycamore Pl; s/d from £55/80; P@📶) A beautifully converted 'gentleman's residence', Elliotts leans towards the boutique end of the guesthouse market with stylish and elegant rooms, and high-tech touches such as flatscreen TVs and free wi-fi. Excellent location, both quiet and central.

Hedley House Hotel B&B ££
(☎01904-637404; www.hedleyhouse.com; 3 Bootham Tce; s/d/f from £50/80/90; P📶👪) Run by a couple with young children, this smart red-brick terrace-house hotel could hardly be more family-friendly – plus it has private

THE YORKSHIRE PASS

If you plan on visiting a lot of sights, you can save yourself some money by using a **Yorkshire Pass** (www.yorkshirepass.com; 1/2/3/6 days adult £28/38/44/68, child £18/22/26/44). It grants you free access to more than 70 pay-to-visit sights in Yorkshire, including all the major attractions in York. It's available at York tourist office, or you can buy online.

parking at the back, and is barely five minutes' walk from the city centre through the Museum Gardens.

Arnot House B&B ££
(☎01904-641966; www.arnothouseyork.co.uk; 17 Grosvenor Tce; r £70-85; P) With three beautifully decorated rooms (provided you're a fan of Victorian floral patterns), including two with impressive four-poster beds, Arnot House sports an authentically old-fashioned look that appeals to a more mature clientele. No children allowed.

Brontë House B&B ££
(☎01904-621066; www.bronte-guesthouse.com; 22 Grosvenor Tce; s/d from £40/76; wi-fi) The Brontë offers five homely en-suite rooms, each decorated differently; our favourite is the double with a carved, 19th-century canopied bed, William Morris wallpaper and assorted bits and pieces from another era.

23 St Mary's B&B ££
(☎01904-622738; www.23stmarys.co.uk; 23 St Mary's; s/d £55/90; P @) A smart and stately town house with nine chintzy, country house-style rooms, some with hand-painted furniture for that rustic look, while others are decorated with antiques, lace and polished mahogany.

Dairy Guesthouse B&B ££
(☎01904-639367; www.dairyguesthouse.co.uk; 3 Scarcroft Rd; s/d from £55/75; wi-fi) A lovely Victorian home that has retained many of its original features, including pine doors, stained glass and cast-iron fireplaces. But the real treat is the flower- and plant-filled courtyard that leads to the cottage-style rooms. Minimum two-night stay at weekends.

Guy Fawkes Inn HOTEL ££
(☎0845 460 2020; www.guy-fawkes-hotel.co.uk; 25 High Petergate; s/d/ste from £65/90/200; wi-fi) Directly opposite the minster is this comfortable and atmospheric hotel complete with gas lamps and log fires. The premises include a cottage that is reputed to be the birthplace of Guy Fawkes himself. We're not convinced, but the cottage is still the handsomest room in the building, complete with a four-poster and lots of red velvet.

York YHA HOSTEL £
(☎0845 371 9051; www.yha.org.uk; 42 Water End, Clifton; dm £18-20; P @ wi-fi family) Originally the Rowntree (Quaker confectioners) mansion, this handsome Victorian house makes a spacious and child-friendly youth hostel, with most of the rooms being four-bed dorms. It's about a mile northwest of the city centre; there's a riverside footpath from Lendal Bridge (poorly lit so avoid after dark). Alternatively, take bus 2 from Station Ave or Museum St.

Judges Lodgings Hotel HOTEL £££
(☎01904-638733; www.judgeslodgings.com; 9 Lendal; s/d from £120/185; P) Despite being housed in an elegant Georgian mansion that was built for a wealthy physician, this is really a place for the party crowd to crash – it's within easy reach of city centre pubs, and the hotel's own lively courtyard bar rocks late into the night.

Mount Royale HOTEL £££
(☎01904-628856; www.mountroyale.co.uk; The Mount; r £100-210; P wi-fi) A grand, early 19th-century listed building that has been converted into a superb luxury hotel, complete with a solarium, beauty spa and outdoor heated tub and swimming pool. The rooms in the main house are gorgeous, but the best of the lot are the open-plan garden suites, reached via a corridor of tropical fruit trees and bougainvillea.

Middlethorpe Hall HOTEL £££
(☎01904-641241; www.middlethorpe.com; Bishopsthorpe Rd; s/d from £130/200; P wi-fi) York's top spot is this breathtaking 17th-century country house set in 20 acres of parkland that was once the home of diarist Lady Mary Wortley Montagu. The rooms are spread between the main house, the restored courtyard buildings and three cottage suites. Although we preferred the grandeur of the rooms in the main house, every room is beautifully decorated with original antiques and oil paintings carefully collected so as to best reflect the period.

Ace Hotel HOSTEL £
(☎01904-627720; www.acehotelyork.co.uk; 88-90 Micklegate; dm/tw from £20/60; @) Housed in a Grade I Georgian building that was once home to the High Sheriff of Yorkshire, this is a large and well-equipped hostel that is popular with school groups and stag and hen parties – don't come here looking for peace and quiet!

York Yurts YURTS ££
(☎01759-380901; www.yorkyurts.com; Tadpole Cottage, Sutton Lane, Barmby Moor; d £65-75; P) Only a 15-minute drive from York, but half a world away in ambience, York Yurts offers the chance to sleep under canvas without having to rough it. There are four yurts (circular, wood-framed tents originating from Mongolia) in a three-acre field, complete with double beds, candles (no electricity), wood-burning stoves, cooking tents and barbecues (though you can order breakfast brought to you in bed if you want). There's also a communal bathroom tent with rolltop bath and hot tub.

Briar Lea Guest House B&B ££
(☎01904-635061; www.briarlea.co.uk; 8 Longfield Tce; s/d from £37/62;) Clean, simple rooms and a friendly welcome in a central location.

St Raphael B&B ££
(☎01904-645028; www.straphaelguesthouse.co.uk; 44 Queen Annes Rd; s/d from £65/76;) Historic house with that half-timbered look, great central location and home baked bread for breakfast.

Monkgate Guesthouse B&B ££
(☎01904-655947; www.monkgateguesthouse.com; 65 Monkgate; s/d from £42/70; P) Attractive guesthouse with special family suite with separate bedroom for two kids.

Hotel 53 HOTEL ££
(☎01904-559000; www.hotel53.com; 53 Piccadilly; r from £86; P) Modern and minimalist, but very central with secure parking just across the street.

Eating

TOP CHOICE **J Baker's Bistro Moderne** MODERN BRITISH ££
(☎01904-622688; www.jbakers.co.uk; 7 Fossgate; lunch mains £10, 2-/3-course dinner £25/29.50; ⊙lunch & dinner Tue-Sat) Superstar chef Jeff Baker left a Michelin star in Leeds to pursue his own vision of Modern British cuisine here. The ironic '70s-style decor (think chocolate/oatmeal/tango) with moo-cow paintings is echoed in the unusual menu, which offers witty, gourmet interpretations of retro classics – try Tongue 'n' Cheek (a crisp pie containing ox tongue, beef cheeks and beef jelly), or Whitby crab cocktail with apple and avocado. And don't miss his signature dessert, Lemon Tops.

Gray's Court CAFE ££
(www.grayscourtyork.com; Chapter House St; mains £6-7; ⊙breakfast & lunch) An unexpected find right in the very heart of York, this 16th-century house has more of a country atmosphere. Enjoy gourmet coffee and cake in the sunny garden, or indulge in a light lunch in the historic setting of the oak-panelled Jacobean gallery (extra points if you grab the alcove table above the main door). The menu runs from smoked salmon and scrambled eggs to roast butternut squash, red pepper and goat's cheese tart, and from lavender shortbread to lemon drizzle cake.

Blake Head Vegetarian Cafe VEGETARIAN £
(104 Micklegate; mains £5-7; ⊙breakfast & lunch) A bright and airy space at the back of a bookshop, filled with modern oak furniture and funky art, the Blake Head offers a tempting menu of daily lunch specials such as spicy bean burger with salsa, or hummus and roast red pepper open sandwich. Great ginger and lemon cake, too. Veggie breakfasts served until 11.30am.

Ate O'Clock BISTRO ££
(☎01904-644080; www.ateoclock.co.uk; 13a High Ousegate; mains £14-17; ⊙lunch & dinner Tue-Sat) A tempting menu of classic bistro dishes (fillet of beef with mushrooms, pork-and-chive sausage with mash and onion gravy) made with fresh Yorkshire produce has made this place hugely popular with locals – best book a table to avoid disappointment. Three-course dinner for £16.75 from 6pm to 7.55pm Tuesday to Thursday.

Olive Tree MEDITERRANEAN ££
(☎01904-624433; www.theolivetreeyork.co.uk; 10 Tower St; mains £9-18; ⊙lunch & dinner) Local produce gets a Mediterranean makeover at this bright and breezy bistro with a view across the street to Clifford's Tower. Classic pizza and pasta dishes are complemented by more ambitious recipes such as seared scallops with chorizo, and sea bass with asparagus, cherry tomatoes and saffron cream sauce. The lunchtime and early evening menu offers two courses for £13.

Café Concerto CAFE, BISTRO ££

(☎01904-610478; www.cafeconcerto.biz; 21 High Petergate; snacks £3-8, mains £10-17; ⏲8.30am-10pm) Walls papered with sheet music, chilled jazz on the stereo and battered, mismatched tables and chairs set the bohemian tone in this comforting coffee shop. During the day expect breakfasts, bagels and cappuccinos big enough to float a boat in, and a sophisticated bistro menu in the evening.

Betty's TEAROOM ££

(www.bettys.co.uk; St Helen's Sq; mains £6-11, afternoon tea £16; ⏲breakfast, lunch & dinner) Afternoon tea, old-school style, with white-aproned waitresses, linen tablecloths and a teapot collection ranged along the walls. House speciality is the Yorkshire Fat Rascal – a huge fruit scone smothered in melted butter – but the smoked haddock with poached egg and Hollandaise sauce is our favourite lunch dish.

El Piano VEGAN £

(www.elpiano.com; 15 Grape Lane; mains £4-7; ⏲lunch daily, dinner Mon-Sat;) With a menu that is 100% vegan, nut-free and gluten-free, this colourful, Hispanic-style spot is a vegetarian haven. There's a lovely cafe downstairs and three themed rooms upstairs. The menu offers dishes such as falafel, onion bhaji, corn fritters and mushroom-and-basil salad, either in tapas-size portions or as mixed platters. There's also a takeaway counter.

Melton's Too BAR, BISTRO ££

(www.meltonstoo.co.uk; 25 Walmgate; mains £9-12; ⏲breakfast, lunch & dinner) A comfortable, chilled-out cafe-bar and bistro, Melton's Too serves everything from cake and cappuccino (or Bombay Sapphire gin and tonic), to tapas-style snacks or a three-course dinner of smoked mackerel and watercress salad, duck confit with apple salad, and Yorkshire rhubarb crumble.

Blue Bicycle FRENCH, FUSION ££

(☎01904-673990; www.thebluebicycle.com; 34 Fossgate; mains £15-24; ⏲lunch Thu-Sun, dinner daily) Once upon a time, this building was a well-frequented brothel; these days it's a romantic, candlelit restaurant that makes for a top-notch dining experience.

Little Betty's TEAROOM ££

(www.bettys.co.uk; 46 Stonegate; mains £8-10; ⏲10am-5.30pm) Betty's younger sister is more demure and less frequented, but just as good.

Living Room INTERNATIONAL ££

(www.thelivingroom.co.uk; 1 Bridge St; mains £10-17; ⏲breakfast, lunch & dinner) Balcony tables overlooking the river and a menu focused on quality versions of classic dishes from around the world. Sunday brunch served noon to 6pm.

Siam House THAI ££

(63a Goodramgate; mains £9-15; ⏲dinner Mon-Sat) Delicious, authentic Thai food in about as authentic an atmosphere as you could muster up 6000km from Bangkok.

Drinking

With only a couple of exceptions, the best drinking holes in town are the older, traditional pubs. In recent years, the area around Ousegate and Micklegate has gone from moribund to mental, especially at weekends.

TOP CHOICE **Blue Bell** PUB

(53 Fossgate) This is what a real English pub looks like – a tiny, wood-panelled room with a smouldering fireplace, decor (and beer and smoke stains) dating from c 1798, a pile of ancient board games in the corner, friendly and efficient bar staff, and Timothy Taylor and Black Sheep ales on tap. Bliss, with froth on top.

Ye Olde Starre PUB

(40 Stonegate) Licensed since 1644, this is York's oldest pub – a warren of small rooms and a small beer garden, with a half-dozen real ales on tap. It was used as a morgue by the Roundheads during the Civil War, but the atmosphere's improved a lot since then.

Ackhorne PUB

(9 St Martin's La) Tucked away off beery, sloppy Micklegate, this locals' inn is as comfortable as old slippers – some of the old guys here look like they've merged with the furniture. There's a pleasant beer garden at the back, and an open-mic night for local musicians on the first Tuesday of the month.

Little John PUB

(5 Castlegate) This historic pub – the third oldest in York – is the city's top gay venue, with regular club nights and other events. In 1739 the corpse of executed highwayman Dick Turpin was laid out in the cellar here for the public to view at a penny a head; the pub is said to be haunted by his ghost. Not sure what's scarier though – the ghost story, or the Thursday night karaoke session...

Old White Swan PUB
(80 Goodramgate) Popular and atmospheric old pub with small beer garden and a good range of guest real ales. And it's haunted...

King's Arms PUB
(King's Staith) York's best-known pub in a fabulous riverside location, with tables spilling out onto the quayside – a perfect spot for a summer's evening, but be prepared to share it with a few hundred other people.

☆ Entertainment

There are a couple of good theatres in York, and an interesting art-house cinema, but as far as clubs are concerned, forget it: historic York is best enjoyed without them anyway.

York Theatre Royal THEATRE
(www.yorktheatreroyal.co.uk; St Leonard's Pl) Stages well-regarded productions of theatre, opera and dance.

Grand Opera House MUSIC, COMEDY
(www.grandoperahouseyork.org.uk; Clifford St) Despite the name there's no opera here, but a wide range of productions from live bands and popular musicals to stand-up comics and pantomime.

City Screen CINEMA
(www.picturehouses.co.uk; 13-17 Coney St) Appealing modern building in a converted printing works, screening both mainstream and art-house films. There's also a nice cafe-bar on the terrace overlooking the river.

Shopping

Coney St, Davygate and the adjoining streets are the hub of York's high-street shopping scene, but the real treat for visitors are the antique, bric-a-brac and secondhand book shops, which are concentrated in Colliergate, Micklegate and Fossgate.

Ken Spelman Booksellers BOOKS
(www.kenspelman.com; 70 Micklegate) This fascinating shop has been selling rare, antiquarian and secondhand books since 1910. With an open fire crackling in the grate in winter, it's a browser's paradise.

Antiques Centre ANTIQUES
(www.antiquescentreyorkeshop.co.uk; 41 Stonegate) A Georgian town house with a veritable maze of rooms and corridors, showcasing the wares of around 120 dealers: everything from lapel pins and snuff boxes to oil paintings and longcase clocks. And the house is haunted, too...

Barbican Books BOOKS
(www.barbicanbookshop.co.uk; 24 Fossgate) Wide range of secondhand titles, with special subjects that include railways, aviation, walking and mountaineering.

Azendi JEWELLERY
(www.azendi.com; 20 Colliergate) This jewellery boutique sells a range of beautiful contemporary designs in silver, white gold and platinum.

Information

American Express (6 Stonegate; ⌚9am-5.30pm Mon-Fri, 9am-5pm Sat) With foreign exchange service.

Post office (22 Lendal; ⌚8.30am-5.30pm Mon & Tue, 9am-5.30pm Wed-Sat)

York District Hospital (☎01904-631313; Wigginton Rd) A mile north of the centre.

York tourist office (☎01904-550099; www.visityork.org; 1 Museum St; ⌚9am-6pm Mon-Sat, 10am-5pm Sun Apr-Sep, shorter hours Oct-Mar; @) Brand new tourist office with visitor and transport info for all of Yorkshire, accommodation booking, ticket sales and internet access.

Getting There & Away

Bus

For timetable information call **Traveline Yorkshire** (☎0871 200 2233; www.yorkshiretravel.net), or check the computerised 24-hour information points at the train station and Rougier St. All local and regional buses stop on Rougier St, about 200m northeast of the train station.

There are National Express coaches to London (£26, 5½ hours, four daily), Birmingham (£26, 3¼ hours, one daily) and Newcastle (£15, 2¾ hours, four daily).

Car

A car is more of a hindrance than a help in the city centre; use one of the Park & Ride car parks on the edge of the city. If you want to explore the surrounding area, rental options include **Europcar** (☎01904-654040; www.europcar.co.uk), by platform 1 in the train station (which also rents bicycles and stores luggage for £4 per bag); and **Hertz** (☎01904-612586; www.hertz.co.uk) near platform 3 in the train station.

Train

York is a major railway hub with frequent direct services to Birmingham (£45, 2¼ hours), Newcastle (£15, one hour), Leeds (£11, 30 minutes), London's King's Cross (£80, two hours), Manchester (£15, 1½ hours) and Scarborough (£10, 50 minutes).

LOCAL KNOWLEDGE

ANDY DEXTROUS: GHOST TOUR GUIDE, YORK

Things I love about York include its outstanding architecture, the maze of 'snickelways' (narrow alleys), the array of small independent shops, the street entertainment and festivals, and central, green spaces like **Museum Gardens** (p602). All year round the streets are full of appreciative visitors from all over the world enjoying the city, relaxing and adding to the atmosphere.

York's Spookiest Spots

Haunted pubs like the **Old White Swan** (p607). Plus the **Antiques Centre** (p608) on Stonegate, which is also haunted. In the streets around the Minster you're always within a breath of a ghost tale.

Best of York

For beer and atmosphere, the **Blue Bell** (p607). For veggie and vegan food and a place that welcomes children, **El Piano** (p606). And for sheer ambience, **Gray's Court** (p606).

Best of Yorkshire

The **Forbidden Corner** (p612) near Leyburn. Or take the **North Yorkshire Moors Railway** (p623) to Goathland, then walk to Mallyan Spout waterfall. Include a drink at the Birch Hall Inn at Beck Hole.

For a special meal there's the **Star Inn** (p621) at Harome or the **Stone Trough** (p609) at Kirkham; stroll down to the abbey ruins before or after your meal.

There are also trains to Cambridge (£70, 2¾ hours), changing at Peterborough.

Getting Around

York is easy to get around on foot – you're never really more than 20 minutes from any of the major sights.

Bicycle

The tourist office has a useful free map showing York's cycle routes. If you're energetic you could pedal out to Castle Howard (15 miles), Helmsley and Rievaulx Abbey (12 miles) and Thirsk (a further 12 miles), and then catch a train back to York. There's also a section of the Trans-Pennine Trail cycle path from Bishopthorpe in York to Selby (15 miles) along the old railway line.

You can rent bikes from **Bob Trotter** (13 Lord Mayor's Walk; ⌚9am-5.30pm Mon-Sat, 10am-4pm Sun), outside Monk Bar; and **Europcar** (⌚8am-8.30pm Mon-Sat, 9am-8.30pm Sun), by platform 1 in the train station; both charge around £15 per day.

Bus

Local bus services are operated by **First York** (www.firstgroup.com); single fares range from £1 to £2.70, and a day pass valid on all local buses is £3.70 (available at Park & Ride car parks).

Taxi

Station Taxis (☎01904-623332) has a kiosk outside the train station.

Around York

CASTLE HOWARD

Stately homes may be two a penny in England, but you'll have to try pretty damn hard to find one as breathtakingly stately as **Castle Howard** (www.castlehoward.co.uk; house & grounds adult/child £12.50/7.50, grounds only £8.50/6; ⌚house 11am-4.30pm, grounds 10am-6.30pm Mar-Oct & 1st 3 weeks of Dec), a work of theatrical grandeur and audacity set in the rolling Howardian Hills. This is one of the world's most beautiful buildings, instantly recognisable from its starring role in the 1980s TV series *Brideshead Revisited* and more recently in the 2008 film of the same name (both based on Evelyn Waugh's 1945 novel of nostalgia for the English aristocracy).

When the earl of Carlisle hired his pal Sir John Vanbrugh to design his new home in 1699, he was hiring a bloke who had no formal training and was best known as a playwright. Luckily, Vanbrugh hired Nicholas Hawksmoor who had worked for Christopher Wren as his clerk of works – not only would Hawksmoor have a big part to play in the house's design but the two would later work wonders with Blenheim Palace. Today, the house is still home to the Hon Simon Howard and his family; he can often be seen around the place.

If you can, try to visit on a weekday, when it's easier to find the space to appreciate this hedonistic marriage of art, architecture, landscaping and natural beauty. As you wander about the peacock-haunted grounds, views open up over the hills, Vanbrugh's playful Temple of the Four Winds and Hawksmoor's stately mausoleum, but the great baroque house with its magnificent central cupola is an irresistible visual magnet. Inside, it is full of treasures – the breathtaking Great Hall with its soaring Corinthian pilasters, Pre-Raphaelite stained glass in the chapel, and corridors lined with classical antiquities.

Castle Howard is 15 miles northeast of York, off the A64. There are several organised tours from York – check with the tourist office for up-to-date schedules. Yorkshire Coastliner bus 840 (40 minutes from York, one daily) links Leeds, York, Castle Howard, Pickering and Whitby.

Thirsk

POP 9100

Monday and Saturday are market days in handsome Thirsk, which has been trading on its tidy, attractive streets and cobbled square since the Middle Ages. Thirsk's brisk business was always helped by its key position on two medieval trading routes: the old drove road between Scotland and York, and the route linking the Yorkshire Dales with the coast. That's all in the past, though: today, the town is all about the legacy of James Herriot, the wry Yorkshire vet adored by millions of fans of *All Creatures Great and Small*.

Thirsk does a good job as the real-life Darrowby of the books and TV series, and it should, as the real-life Herriot was in fact local vet Alf Wight, whose house and surgery has been dipped in 1940s aspic and turned into the incredibly popular **World of James Herriot** (www.worldofjamesherriot.org; 23 Kirkgate; adult/child £6/4.20; ⏲10am-5pm Apr-Oct, 11am-4pm Nov-Mar), an excellent museum full of Wight-related artefacts, a video documentary of his life and a re-creation of the TV-show set (the original set can be seen in the Richmondshire Museum in Richmond, p588).

Thirsk is also a major horse-racing venue, and **Thirsk Racecourse** (www.thirskracecourse.net) hosts regular race meetings from April to September.

If you arrive in time for breakfast or just fancy a quick snack, head for the **Arabica Coffee Shop** (87 Market Pl; mains £3-6; ⏲7.30am-5.30pm Mon-Sat, 10am-4.30pm Sun) on the main square. This smart chrome-and-black diner is the opposite of chintz, and serves excellent freshly ground coffee, croissants, fry-ups, panini and wraps.

Thirsk's **tourist office** (☎01845-522755; www.thirsk.org.uk; 49 Market Pl; ⏲10am-5pm Apr-Nov, 10am-4pm Dec-Mar) is on the main square.

Thirsk is well served by trains on the line between York and Middlesbrough; however, the train station is a mile west of town and the only way to cover that distance is on foot or by **taxi** (☎01845-522473). There are also frequent daily buses from York (45 minutes).

Ripon

POP 16,468

Small town, huge cathedral: Ripon – all winding streets and a broad, symmetrical marketplace lined with Georgian houses – is mostly about its elegant church, but tourists also seem quite taken by the **Ripon Hornblower**, who 'sets the watch' every evening at 9pm in a tradition that supposedly dates back to 886, when Alfred the

WORTH A TRIP

KIRKHAM PRIORY & STONE TROUGH INN

While the crowds queue up to get into Castle Howard, you could turn off on the other side of the A64 along the minor road to the hamlet of Kirkham. Here, the picturesque ruins of **Kirkham Priory** (EH; www.english-heritage.org.uk; adult/child £3.20/1.60; ⏲10am-5pm Thu-Mon Apr-Sep, daily Aug) rise gracefully above the banks of the River Derwent, sporting an impressive 13th-century gatehouse encrusted with heraldic symbols.

After a stroll by the river, head up the hill on the far side to the **Stone Trough Inn** (www.stonetroughinn.co.uk; mains £8-16; ⏲lunch & dinner Tue-Sun; 📶) for a spot of lunch. This traditional country inn serves gourmet-style pub grub (try the roast cod with creamed leek sauce), and has an outdoor terrace with a great view over the valley.

BLACK SHEEP OF THE BREWING FAMILY

The village of Masham is a place of pilgrimage for connoisseurs of real ale – it's the frothing fountainhead of Theakston's beers, which have been brewed here since 1827. The company's most famous brew, Old Peculier, takes its name from the Peculier of Masham, a parish court established in medieval times to deal with religious offences, including drunkenness, brawling, and 'taking a skull from the churchyard and placing it under a person's head to charm them to sleep'. The court seal is used as the emblem of Theakston Ales.

To the horror of real-ale fans, and after much falling out among members of the Theakston family, the Theakston Brewery was taken over by much-hated megabrewer Scottish & Newcastle in 1987. Five years later, Paul Theakston – who had refused to go and work for S&N, and was determined to keep small-scale, artisan brewing alive – bought an old maltings building in Masham and set up his own brewery, which he called Black Sheep. He managed to salvage all kinds of traditional brewing equipment, including six Yorkshire 'stone square' brewing vessels, and was soon running a successful enterprise.

History came full circle in 2004 when Paul's four brothers took the Theakston brewery back into family ownership. Both breweries now have tourist offices – the **Black Sheep Brewery** (www.blacksheepbrewery.com; ⏲10.30am-4.30pm Sun-Thu, 10.30am-11pm Fri & Sat) and the **Theakston's Brewery** (www.theakstons.co.uk; ⏲10.30am-5.30pm Jul & Aug, to 4.30pm May, Jun, Sep & Oct) both offer guided tours (best booked in advance).

Masham (pronounced 'Massam') is 9 miles northwest of Ripon on the A6108 to Leyburn. Bus 159 from Ripon (25 minutes, every two hours Monday to Saturday) and the Eastern Dalesman bus 820 from Leeds (2¾ hours, one daily, Sunday and bank holidays only, late May to late September) stop at Masham.

Great gave the locals a horn to sound the changing of the guard.

Ripon Cathedral (www.riponcathedral.org.uk; suggested donation £3, treasury £1; ⏲7.30am-6.15pm, evensong 5.30pm) is well worth exploring. The first church on this site was built in 660 by St Wilfred, and its rough, humble crypt lies intact beneath today's soaring edifice. Above ground, the building was begun in the 11th century, with its harmonious Early-English west front clocking in at 1220. Medieval additions have resulted in a medley of Gothic styles throughout, culminating in the rebuilding of the central tower – work that was never completed. It was not until 1836 that this impressive parish church got cathedral status. Look out for the fantastical creatures (including a pig playing bagpipes) decorating the medieval misericords, which are believed to have inspired Lewis Carroll – his father was canon here from 1852 to 1868.

Until 1888 Ripon was responsible for its own law enforcement, and this has resulted in a grand array of punishing attractions. The **Law & Order Museums** (www.riponmuseums.co.uk; adult/child £7/free; ⏲1-4pm Apr-Oct, 10am-4pm during school holidays, closed Nov-Mar) include the **Courthouse Museum** (Minster Rd), a 19th-century courthouse (recognisable from sappy TV series *Heartbeat*), the **Prison & Police Museum** (St Marygate), which includes the medieval punishment yard and the clammy cells where no-good Victorians were banged up, and the **Workhouse Museum** (Allhallowgate), which shows the grim treatment meted out to poor vagrants from the 19th century to WWII.

The **tourist office** (☎01765-604625; Minster Rd; ⏲10am-1pm & 1.30-5.30pm Mon-Sat, 1-4pm Sun) is near the cathedral and has information on local walks, and will book accommodation. Market day is Thursday.

Bus 36 runs from Leeds via Harrogate to Ripon (one hour 20 minutes, every 20 minutes). From York, take the train to Harrogate, then bus 36 to Ripon. Bus 159 runs between Ripon and Richmond (1½ hours, every two hours Monday to Saturday) via Masham and Middleham.

Around Ripon

Nestled in the secluded valley of the River Skell lie two of Yorkshire's most beautiful attractions – an absolute must on any northern itinerary. The beautiful and strangely obsessive water gardens of the **Studley Royal** estate were built in the 18th century to enhance the picturesque ruins of 12th-century **Fountains Abbey** (NT; www.fountainsabbey.org.uk; adult/child £8.50/4.55; ⏲10am-5pm Apr-Sep, to 4pm Oct-Mar). Together they present a breathtaking picture of pastoral elegance and tranquillity that have made them a Unesco World Heritage Site, and the most visited of all the National Trust's pay-to-enter properties.

After falling out with the Benedictines of York in 1132, a band of rebel monks came here to what was then a desolate and unyielding patch of land to establish their own monastery. Struggling to make it on their own, they were formally adopted by the Cistercians in 1135; by the middle of the 13th century the new abbey had become the most successful Cistercian venture in the country. It was during this time that most of the abbey was built, including the church's nave, transepts and eastern end, and the outlying buildings (the church tower was added in the late 15th century).

After the Dissolution (p790) the abbey's estate was sold into private hands, and between 1598 and 1611 Fountains Hall was built using stone from the abbey ruins. The hall and ruins were united with the Studley Royal estate in 1768.

Studley Royal was owned by John Aislabie (once Chancellor of the Exchequer), who dedicated his life to creating the park after a financial scandal saw him expelled from parliament. The main house of Studley Royal burnt down in 1946 but the superb landscaping, with its serene artificial lakes, survives almost unchanged from the 18th century.

Fountains Abbey is 4 miles west of Ripon off the B6265. Public transport is limited to shuttle bus 139 from Ripon on Sunday and bank holidays only (10 to 20 minutes, eight daily), from April to October.

Harrogate

POP 85,128

The quintessential Victorian spa town, prim, pretty Harrogate has long been associated with a certain kind of old-fashioned Englishness, the kind that seems to be the preserve of retired army chaps and formidable dowagers who always vote Tory. They come to Harrogate to enjoy the flower shows and gardens that fill the town with magnificent displays of colour, especially in spring and autumn. It is fitting that the town's most famous visitor was Agatha Christie, who fled here incognito in 1926 to escape her broken marriage.

Yet this picture of Victoriana redux is not quite complete. While it's undoubtedly true that Harrogate remains a firm favourite of visitors in their golden years, the New Britain makeover has left its mark in the shape of smart new hotels and trendy eateries catering to the boom in Harrogate's newest trade – conferences. All those dynamic young sales-and-marketing guns have to eat and sleep somewhere...

Sights & Activities

Royal Pump Room Museum MUSEUM

(www.harrogate.gov.uk/harrogate-987; Crown Pl; adult/child £3.30/1.90; ⏲10am-5pm Mon-Sat & 2-5pm Sun Apr-Oct, to 4pm Nov-Mar) The ritual of visiting a spa town to 'take the waters' as a health cure became fashionable in the 19th century and peaked during the Edwardian era in the years before WWI. Charles Dickens visited Harrogate in 1858 and described it as 'the queerest place, with the strangest people in it, leading the oddest lives of dancing, newspaper-reading and dining'; sounds quite pleasant, really.

You can learn all about the history of Harrogate as a spa town in the ornate Royal Pump Room, built in 1842 over the most famous of the sulphur springs. It gives an insight into how the phenomenon shaped the town and records the illustrious visitors that it attracted; at the end you get the chance to sample the spa water, if you dare.

Montpellier Quarter DISTRICT

(www.montpellierharrogate.com) The most attractive part of town is the Montpellier Quarter, overlooking Prospect Gardens between Crescent Rd and Montpellier Hill. It's an area of pedestrianised streets lined with restored 19th-century buildings that are now home to art galleries, antique shops, fashion boutiques, cafes and restaurants – an upmarket annex to the main shopping area around Oxford St and Cambridge St.

Turkish Baths HISTORIC BUILDING

(☎01423 556746; www.harrogate.gov.uk/harrogate-1100; Parliament St; admission £13-19; ⏲9.30am-9pm Mon-Fri, 9am-8.30pm Sat & Sun) If drinking the water isn't enough, you can immerse yourself in it at Harrogate's fabulously tiled Turkish Baths. This mock-Moorish facility is gloriously Victorian

Harrogate

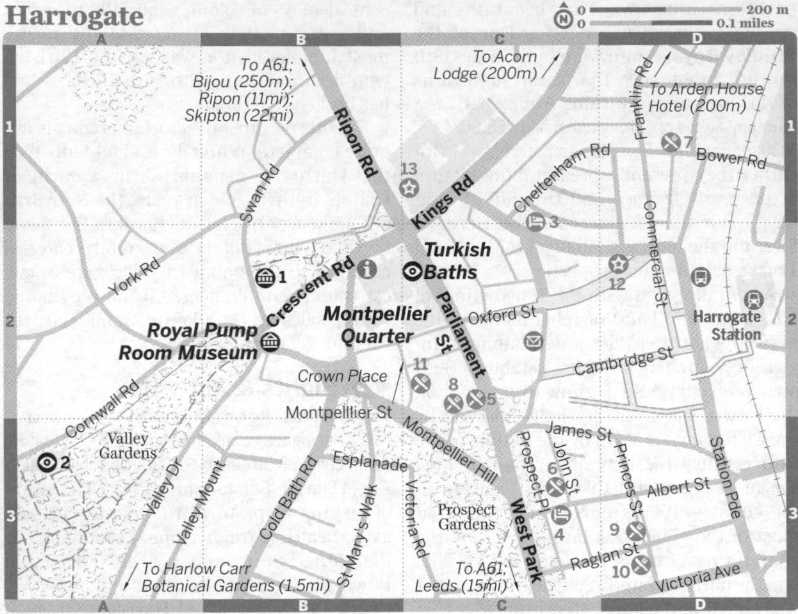

and offers a range of watery delights – hot rooms, steam rooms, plunge pools and so on; a visit should last around 1½ hours. There's a complicated schedule of opening hours that are by turns single-sex and mixed – call or check online for details.

Gardens GARDENS

A huge green thumbs-up to Harrogate's gardeners; the town has some of the most beautiful public gardens in England. Flower fanatics should make for the **Harlow Carr Botanical Gardens** (www.rhs.org.uk; Crag Lane, Beckwithshaw; adult/child £7/2.50; ⏲9.30am-6pm Mar-Oct, to 4pm Nov-Feb), the northern showpiece of the Royal Horticultural Society. The gardens are 1.5 miles southwest of town; take the B6162 Otley Rd, or walk through the Pine Woods southwest of the Valley Gardens.

Much closer to the town centre are the **Valley Gardens**, overlooked by the vast, glass-domed **Sun Pavilion**, built in 1933. The nearby bandstand houses concerts on Sunday afternoons from June to August.

FREE **Mercer Art Gallery** ART GALLERY

(Swan Rd; ⏲10am-5pm Tue-Sat, 2-5pm Sun) Another surviving spa building, the Promenade Room, is now home to this elegant gallery, a stately space that hosts constantly changing exhibitions of visual arts.

Festivals & Events

All three of Harrogate's major events are held at the Great Yorkshire Showground, just off the A661 on the southeastern edge of town.

Spring Flower Show HORTICULTURE

(www.flowershow.org.uk; admission £12-13) The year's main event, held in late April. A colourful three-day extravaganza of blooms and blossoms, flower competitions, gardening demonstrations, market stalls, crafts and gardening shops.

Great Yorkshire Show AGRICULTURE

(www.greatyorkshireshow.co.uk; adult/child £21/10) Staged over three days in mid-July by the Yorkshire Agricultural Society. Expect all manner of primped and prettified farm animals competing for prizes, and entertainment ranging from show-jumping and falconry to cookery demonstrations and hot-air balloon rides.

Autumn Flower Show HORTICULTURE

(www.flowershow.org.uk; admission £12-13) Held in late September. Vegetable- and fruit-growing championships, heaviest-onion competition, cookery demonstrations, children's events...

Harrogate

Top Sights

Montpellier Quarter B2
Royal Pump Room Museum B2
Turkish Baths C2

Sights

1 Mercer Art Gallery B2
2 Sun Pavilion A3

Sleeping

3 Harrogate Brasserie & Hotel C1
4 Hotel du Vin C3

Eating

5 Betty's C2
6 Fodder C3
7 Le D2 .... D1
8 Le Jardin C2
9 Sasso D3
10 Tannin Level D3
11 Van Zeller C2

Entertainment

12 Harrogate Theatre D2
13 Royal Hall C1

Sleeping

There are lots of excellent B&Bs and guesthouses just north of Harrogate town centre on and around Franklin Rd and Ripon Rd.

Bijou B&B ££

(01423-567974; www.thebijou.co.uk; 17 Ripon Rd; s/d from £65/85; P @) Bijou by name and bijou by nature, this Victorian villa sits firmly at the boutique end of the B&B spectrum – you can tell that a lot of thought and care has gone into the design of the place. The husband-and-wife team who own the place make fantastic hosts, warm and helpful but unobtrusive.

Acorn Lodge B&B ££

(01423-525630; www.acornlodgeharrogate.co.uk; 1 Studley Rd; s/d from £47/80; P) Attention to detail makes the difference between an average and an excellent B&B, and the details at Acorn Lodge are spot on – stylish decor, crisp cotton sheets, powerful showers, and perfect poached eggs for breakfast. Location is good too, just 10 minutes' walk from the town centre.

Harrogate Brasserie & Hotel BOUTIQUE HOTEL ££

(01423-505041; www.harrogatebrasserie.co.uk; 26-30 Cheltenham Pde; s/d from £60/80; P) Stripped pine, leather armchairs and subtle colour combinations make this one of Harrogate's most appealing places to stay. The cheerful and cosy accommodation is complemented by an excellent restaurant and bar, with live jazz every evening except Monday.

Arden House Hotel B&B ££

(01423-509224; www.ardenhousehotel.co.uk; 69-71 Franklin Rd; s/d from £50/80; P) This grand old Edwardian house has been given a modern makeover with stylish contemporary furniture, Egyptian cotton bed linen and posh toiletries, but still retains some lovely period details including tiled, cast-iron fireplaces. Attentive service, good breakfasts and a central location are the icing on the cake.

Hotel du Vin BOUTIQUE HOTEL £££

(01423-856800; www.hotelduvin.com; Prospect Pl; r/ste from £110/170; P @) An extremely stylish boutique hotel that has made the other lodgings in town sit up and take notice. The loft suites (from £280) with their exposed

WORTH A TRIP

DETOUR: FORBIDDEN CORNER

Hidden away in the eastern foothills of the Yorkshire Dales, 2 miles west of the village of Middleham, is one of Yorkshire's most bizarre tourist attractions. Built around 20 years ago as a private 'folly' for a local landowner, the **Forbidden Corner** (01969-640638; www.theforbiddencorner.co.uk; Tupgill Park, Middleham; adult/child/family £10/8/34; noon-6pm Mon-Sat, 10am-6pm Sun Apr-Oct) is a labyrinth of miniature castles, caves, temples and gardens decorated with all manner of weird and wonderful sculptures. Enter through a gateway in the shape of a fanged mouth and follow the 'clues' in rhyming couplets to reach a 'temple of the underworld'. It's great fun for kids, and some of the jokes will make adults smile. And watch out for the sign *cave aquae* ('beware of the water').

Admission is through bookings only – online, by phone at the number above, or in person at the **tourist office** (4 Central Chambers, Railway St) in Leyburn.

oak beams, hardwood floors and designer bathrooms are the nicest rooms we've seen in town, but even the standard rooms are spacious and very comfortable (though they can be noisy), each with a trademark huge bed draped in soft Egyptian cotton.

Eating

Tannin Level BISTRO ££
(☎01423-560595; 5 Raglan St; mains £10-15; ⏲lunch & dinner Tue-Sat) Old terracotta floor tiles, polished mahogany tables and gilt-framed mirrors and paintings create a relaxed yet elegant atmosphere at this hugely popular neighbourhood bistro. A competitively priced menu based on seasonal local produce – shank of lamb with honey-roasted carrots, fish pie with mustard mash and smoked-cheese crust – means that you'd best book a table or face being turned away.

Betty's TEAROOM ££
(www.bettys.co.uk; 1 Parliament St; mains £8-11, afternoon tea £16; ⏲breakfast, lunch & dinner) A classic tearoom in a classic location with views across the park, Betty's is a local institution. It was established in 1919 by a Swiss immigrant confectioner who took the wrong train, ended up in Yorkshire and decided to stay. Exquisite home-baked breads, scones and cakes, quality tea and coffee, and a downstairs gallery lined with art nouveau marquetry designs of Yorkshire scenes commissioned by the founder in the 1930s.

Le Jardin BISTRO £
(☎01423-507323; www.lejardin-harrogate.com; 7 Montpellier Pde; mains £5-8; ⏲lunch Tue-Fri & Sun, dinner Tue-Sat) This cool little bistro has a snug, intimate atmosphere, especially in the evening when candlelight adds a romantic glow. During the day locals throng to the tables, enjoying great salads, sandwiches and homemade ice cream. A two-/three-course dinner is £9/13.

Le D2 BISTRO ££
(www.led2.co.uk; 7 Bower Rd; 2-course lunch/dinner £10/15; ⏲lunch & dinner Tue-Sat) This bright and airy bistro is always busy, with diners drawn back again and again by the relaxed atmosphere, warm and friendly service, and a menu that takes fresh local produce and adds a twist of French sophistication.

Fodder CAFE £
(www.fodderweb.co.uk; 4 John St; mains £3-5; ⏲9.30am-5.30pm Mon-Sat, 10am-4pm Sun) Owned by the Yorkshire Agricultural Society (there's a bigger branch at the Great Yorkshire Showground), this cafe serves fresh, healthy salads, sandwiches and lunch specials such as mung beans, chorizo and roast veg.

Van Zeller FRENCH £££
(☎01423-508762; www.vanzellerrestaurants.co.uk; 8 Montpellier St; mains £18-29; ⏲lunch Tue-Sun, dinner Tue-Sat) New fine-dining restaurant from Michelin-trained Yorkshire chef Tom van Zeller. Lunch and pre-theatre menu: four courses for £20.

Sasso ITALIAN ££
(☎01423-508838; 8-10 Princes Sq; mains £14-22; ⏲lunch & dinner Mon-Sat) A top-class basement trattoria where homemade pasta is served in a variety of traditional and authentic ways, along with a host of other Italian specialties.

Entertainment

Harrogate Theatre VARIETY
(www.harrogatetheatre.co.uk; Oxford St) An historic Victorian building that dates from 1900, staging variety, comedy, musicals and dancing.

Royal Hall MUSIC
(www.royalhall.co.uk; Ripon Rd) A gorgeous Edwardian theatre that is now a part of the Harrogate International conference centre. The musical program covers orchestral and choral performances, piano recitals, jazz etc.

Information

Post office (11 Cambridge Rd; ⏲9.30am-5.30pm Mon-Sat)

Tourist office (☎0845 389 3223; www.harrogate.gov.uk/tourism; Crescent Rd; ⏲9am-6pm Mon-Sat & 10am-1pm Sun Apr-Sep, 9am-5pm Mon-Fri & 9am-4pm Sat Oct-Mar)

Getting There & Away

BUS National Express coaches run from Leeds (£3.60, 40 minutes, five daily). Bus 36 comes from Ripon (30 minutes, every 20 minutes), continuing to Leeds.

TRAIN Trains run to Harrogate from Leeds (£6.60, 40 minutes, about half-hourly) and York (£6.60, 45 minutes, hourly).

Scarborough

POP 57,649

Scarborough is where the whole tradition of English seaside holidays began. And it began earlier than you might think – it was in the 1660s that a book promoting the medicinal properties of a local spring (now the site of Scarborough Spa) pulled in the first flood of visitors. A belief in the health-giving effects of sea-bathing saw wheeled bathing carriages appear on the beach in the 1730s, and with the arrival of the railway in 1845 Scarborough's fate was sealed. By the time the 20th century rolled in, it was all donkey rides, fish and chips, seaside rock and boat trips round the bay, with saucy postcards, kiss-me-quick hats and blokes from Leeds with knotted hankies on their heads just a decade or two away.

Like all British seaside towns, Scarborough suffered a downturn in recent decades as people jetted off to the Costa Blanca on newly affordable foreign holidays, but things are looking up again. The town retains all the trappings of the classic seaside resort, but is in the process of reinventing itself as a centre for the creative arts and digital industries – the Victorian spa is being redeveloped as a conference and entertainment centre, a former museum has been converted into studio space for artists, and there's free, open-access wi-fi along the promenade beside the harbour – an area being developed as the town's bar, cafe and restaurant quarter.

As well as the usual seaside attractions, Scarborough offers excellent coastal walking, a new geology museum, one of Yorkshire's most impressively sited castles, and a renowned theatre that is the home base of popular playwright Alan Ayckbourn, whose plays always premier here.

Sights

Scarborough Castle CASTLE
(EH; www.english-heritage.org.uk; adult/child £4.70/2.40; ⌚10am-6pm Apr-Sep, 10am-4pm Thu-Mon Oct-Mar) Scarborough is not exclusively about sandcastles, seaside rock and walks along the prom. The massive medieval keep of Scarborough Castle occupies a commanding position atop its headland – legend has it that Richard I loved the views so much that his ghost just keeps coming back. Take a walk out to the edge of the cliffs where you can see the 2000-year-old remains of a **Roman signal station** – the Romans appreciated this viewpoint too.

Rotunda Museum MUSEUM
(www.rotundamuseum.co.uk; Vernon Rd; adult/child £4.50/free; ⌚10am-5pm Tue-Sun;) The newly restored Rotunda Museum is dedicated to seaside rock of a different kind – the coastal geology of northeast Yorkshire, which has yielded many of Britain's most important dinosaur fossils. The strata in the local cliffs here were also important in deciphering the geological history of England. Founded by William Smith, the 'father of English geology', who lived in Scarborough in the 1820s, the museum displays original Victorian exhibits, as well as having a hands-on gallery for kids.

Sea Life Centre & Marine Sanctuary AQUARIUM
(www.sealife.co.uk; Scalby Mills; adult/child £14.50/10.95; ⌚10am-6pm) Of all the family-oriented attractions on the waterfront, the best of the lot is the Sea Life Centre overlooking North Bay. You can see coral reefs, turtles, octopuses, seahorses, otters and many other fascinating creatures, though the biggest draw is the **Seal Rescue Centre** (feeding times 11.30am and 2.30pm). It's at the far north end of North Beach; the miniature **North Bay Railway** (www.nbr.org.uk; return adult/child £3/2.40; ⌚10.30am-4.45pm Apr-Sep) runs the 0.75-mile route.

FREE **St Mary's Church** CHURCH
(Castle Rd; ⌚10am-4pm Mon-Fri, 1-4pm Sun May-Sep) This church dates from 1180. In the little cemetery across the lane from the church is the **grave of Anne Brontë**.

Activities

There are some decent waves on England's northeast coast, which support a growing surfing scene. A top spot is **Cayton Bay**, 4 miles south of town, where you'll find **Scarborough Surf School** (www.scarboroughsurfschool.co.uk) offering full-day lessons for £45 per person, and equipment hire.

Back in town, you can get information and advice from the **Secretspot Surf Shop** (www.secretspot.co.uk; 4 Pavilion Tce) near the train station.

Sleeping

In Scarborough, if a house has four walls and a roof it'll offer B&B. Competition is intense, and in such a tough market multinight-stay special offers are two a penny, which means that single-night rates are the highest of all.

TOP CHOICE **Hotel Helaina** B&B ££
(☎01723-375191; www.hotelhelaina.co.uk; 14 Blenheim Tce; r £54-92;) Location, location, location – you'd be hard pushed to find a place with a better sea view than this elegant guesthouse perched on the clifftop

Scarborough

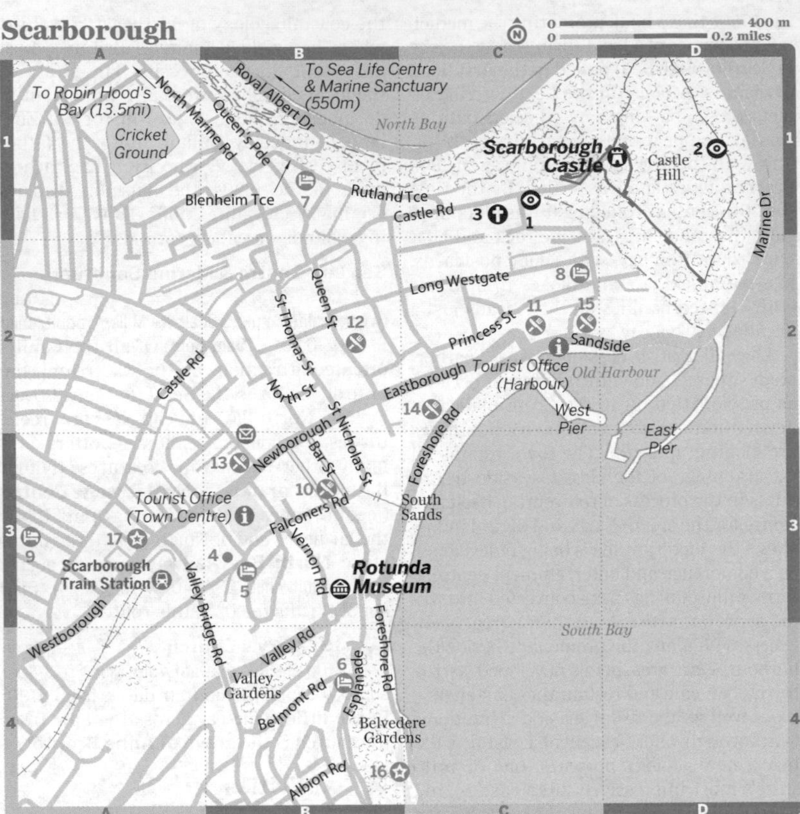

overlooking North Beach. And the view inside the rooms is pretty good too, with sharply styled contemporary furniture and cool colours. The standard rooms are a touch on the small side – it's well worth splashing out on the deluxe sea-view room with the bay window.

Beiderbecke's Hotel HOTEL ££
(☎01723-365766; www.beiderbeckes.com; 1-3 The Crescent; s/d from £85/115; P wi-fi) Set in an elegant Georgian terrace in the middle of town, on a quiet street overlooking gardens, this hotel combines stylish and spacious rooms with attentive but friendly and informal service. It's not quite boutique, but with its intriguing modern art on the walls and snazzily coloured toilet seats it's heading in that direction.

Windmill B&B ££
(☎01723-372735; www.windmill-hotel.co.uk; Mill St; tw/d from £75/85; P) Quirky doesn't begin to describe this place – a beautifully converted 18th-century windmill in the middle of town. There are tight-fitting but comfortable doubles around a cobbled courtyard, but try to get the balcony suite (£120 a night) in the upper floors of the windmill itself, with great views from the wrap-around balcony.

Interludes B&B ££
(☎01723-360513; www.interludeshotel.co.uk; 32 Princess St; s/d £36/66; wi-fi) Owners Ian and Bob have a flair for the theatrical and have brought it to bear with visible success on this lovely, gay-friendly Georgian home plastered with old theatre posters, prints and other thespian mementos. The individually decorated rooms are given to colourful flights of fancy that can't but put a smile on your face. Children, alas, are not welcome.

Wrea Head Country House Hotel HOTEL £££
(☎01723-378211; www.englishrosehotels.co.uk; Barmoor Lane, Scalby; s/d from £110/180; P)

Scarborough

Top Sights
Rotunda Museum B3
Scarborough Castle D1

Sights
1 Grave of Anne Brontë C1
2 Roman Signal Station D1
3 St Mary's Church C1

Activities, Courses & Tours
4 Secret Spot Surf Shop B3

Sleeping
5 Beiderbecke's Hotel B3
6 Crown Spa Hotel B4
7 Hotel Helaina B1
8 Interludes C2
9 Windmill A3

Eating
10 Bonnet's B3
11 Golden Grid C2
12 Lanterna B2
Marmalade's .... (see 5)
13 Roasters B3
14 Roasters C2
15 Tunny Club C2

Entertainment
16 Scarborough Spa B4
17 Stephen Joseph Theatre A3

This fabulous country house about 2 miles north of the centre is straight out of *Remains of the Day*. The 20 individually styled bedrooms have canopied four-poster beds, plush fabrics and delicate furnishings, while the leather couches in the book-cased, wood-heavy lounges are tailor-made for important discussions over cigars and expensive brandy. Check website for special rates that can be as low as half the rack rate.

Scarborough YHA HOSTEL £
(01845 371 9657; www.yha.org.uk; Burniston Rd; dm £18; P) An idyllic hostel set in a converted 17th-century water mill. It's 2 miles north of town along the A166 to Whitby; take bus 3, 12 or 21.

Crown Spa Hotel HOTEL ££
(0800 072 6134; www.crownspahotel.com; Esplanade; s/d from £58/99; P) This grand old hotel opened its doors in 1845 and has been going strong ever since, offering superb sea views and a luxurious spa.

Eating

Marmalade's BRASSERIE ££
(01723-365766; 1-3 The Crescent; mains £11-17; lunch & dinner) The stylish brasserie in Beiderbecke's Hotel – cream and chocolate colours, art with a musical theme, and cool jazz in the background – has a menu that adds a gourmet twist to traditional dishes such as cider-braised belly pork with mustard mash and onion gravy, lavender-crusted rack of lamb, and smoked fish pie with sautéed greens.

Glass House CAFE, BISTRO £
(01723 368791; www.glasshousebistro.co.uk, Burniston Rd; mains £4-8; cafe breakfast & lunch daily, bistro dinner Fri & Sat;) Homemade lasagne, steak-and ale pie, and filled baked potatoes pull in the crowds at this appealing (and always busy) cafe beside the start of the North Bay Railway. The bistro menu (mains £11 to £16) ranges from sesame-crusted tuna steak with soy and lime dressing, to pan-fried venison with red-wine gravy. Reservations recommended for dinner.

Roasters CAFE £
(www.roasterscoffee.co.uk; 8 Aberdeen Walk; mains £5-6; breakfast & lunch) A funky coffee shop with chunky pine tables, brown leather chairs, and an excellent range of freshly ground coffees. There's a juice and smoothie bar too, and the lunch menu includes ciabatta sandwiches, salads and jacket potatoes.

Lanterna ITALIAN £££
(01723-363616, www.lanterna-ristorante.co.uk; 33 Queen St; mains £15-21; dinner Mon-Sat) A snug, old-fashioned Italian trattoria that specialises in fresh local seafood (including lobster, from £32), and classic dishes from the old country such as *stufato de ceci* (old-style chickpea stew with oxtail), and white-truffle dishes in season (October to December). As well as sourcing Yorkshire produce, the chef imports delicacies direct from Italy, including truffles, olive oil, prosciutto and a range of cheeses.

Golden Grid SEAFOOD ££
(www.goldengrid.co.uk; 4 Sandside; mains £7-18; lunch & dinner) Whoever said fish and chips

THE TUNNY CLUB

Strange but true: in the 1930s Atlantic bluefin tuna (also known as tunny) started to follow the herring shoals into the North Sea, and Yorkshire became the hub of a US-style big-game fishery. Professional hunter Lorenzo Mitchell-Henry set the record for a rod-caught fish in British waters when he landed a 386kg monster in 1933, and Scarborough was soon home to the Tunny Club of Great Britain. Visiting millionaires and movie stars chartered local boats and vied with each other to smash the record.

Overfishing led to the disappearance of the herring shoals in the 1950s, and with them the tunny. However, in recent years the ocean giants have returned, attracted by warmer waters (a result of climate change) and recovering herring stocks. Meanwhile, all that remains in Scarborough is the former premises of the Tunny Club at 1 Sandgate, now a fish-and-chip shop; the upstairs dining room is filled with big-game fishing memorabilia.

can't be eaten with dignity hasn't tried the Golden Grid, a sit-down fish restaurant that has been serving the best cod in Scarborough since 1883. It's staunchly traditional, with starched white tablecloths and starched white aprons, as is the menu – as well as fish and chips there's freshly landed crab, lobster, prawns and oysters, plus sausage and mash, liver and bacon, and steak and chips.

Bonnet's TEAROOM £
(38-40 Huntriss Row; mains £5-10; ⏲breakfast Mon-Sat, lunch daily) One of the oldest cafes in town (open since 1880), Bonnet's serves delicious cakes and light meals in a quiet courtyard.

Roasters CAFE £
(www.roasterscoffee.co.uk; 24 Foreshore Rd; ⏲breakfast & lunch) Seaside branch of the excellent coffee shop, with outdoor tables.

Tunny Club FISH & CHIPS £
(1 Sandgate; mains £3-5; ⏲lunch & dinner) Decent chippie whose upstairs dining room is a shrine to Scarborough's history of big-game fishing.

☆ Entertainment

Stephen Joseph Theatre THEATRE
(www.sjt.uk.com; Westborough) Stages a good range of drama – renowned chronicler of middle-class mores Alan Ayckbourn premieres his plays here.

Scarborough Spa VARIETY
(www.scarboroughspa.co.uk; South Bay) The revitalised spa complex stages a wide range of entertainment, especially in the summer months – orchestral performances, variety shows, popular musicals and old-fashioned afternoon-tea dances.

Information

FreeBay Wifi Free wi-fi internet access along harbourfront from West Pier to East Pier.

Post office (11-15 Aberdeen Walk; ⏲9am-5.30pm Mon-Fri, to 12.30pm Sat)

Tourist office Town Centre (☎01723-383637; www.discoveryorkshirecoast.com; Brunswick Shopping Centre, Westborough; ⏲9.30am-5.30pm daily Apr-Oct, 10am-4.30pm Mon-Sat Nov-Mar) Harbour (Sandside; ⏲10am-5.30pm Apr-Oct, to 9pm Jul & Aug)

Getting There & Away

BUS Bus 128 goes along the A170 from Helmsley to Scarborough (1½ hours, hourly) via Pickering, while buses 93 and X93 come from Whitby (one hour, every 30 minutes) via Robin Hood's Bay (hourly). Bus 843 arrives from Leeds (£12, 2¾ hours, hourly) via York.

TRAIN There are regular trains from Hull (£12.50, 1½ hours, hourly), Leeds (£22, one hour 20 minutes, hourly) and York (£16, 50 minutes, hourly).

Getting Around

Tiny, Victorian-era **funicular railways** rattle up and down Scarborough's steep cliffs between town and beach daily from February until the end of October (70p). Local buses leave from the western end of Westborough and outside the train station.

For a taxi call ☎01723-361009; £5 should get you to most places in town.

NORTH YORK MOORS NATIONAL PARK

Inland from the north Yorkshire coast, the wild and windswept North York Moors rise in desolate splendour. Three-quarters of all the world's heather moorland is to be found in Britain, and this is the largest expanse in all of England. Ridge-top roads climb up from lush green valleys to the bleak open moors where weather-beaten stone crosses mark the line of ancient drove roads. In summer the heather blooms in billowing drifts of purple haze.

This is classic walking country, and the moors are criss-crossed with footpaths old and new, and dotted with pretty, flower-bedecked villages. The national park is also home to one of England's most picturesque steam railways.

The park produces the very useful *Moors & Coast* visitor guide, available at tourist offices, hotels etc, with information on things to see and do. See also www.northyork moors.org.uk.

Getting Around

The **Moorsbus** (www.northyorkmoors.org.uk/moorsbus) operates on Sundays and bank holiday Mondays from May to October, plus Wednesdays in July and September, and daily from late July to early September. Pick up a timetable and route map from tourist offices or download one from the website. A standard day pass costs £5. Family tickets and one-off fares for short journeys are also available.

There's also a free public transport map, the *Moors Explorer Travel Guide*, available from tourist offices.

If you're planning to drive on the minor roads over the moors, beware of wandering sheep and lambs – hundreds are killed by careless drivers every year.

Helmsley

POP 1620

Helmsley is a classic North-Yorkshire market town, a handsome place full of old houses, historic coaching inns and – inevitably – a cobbled market square (market day Friday), all basking under the watchful gaze of a sturdy Norman castle. Nearby are the romantic ruins of Rievaulx Abbey and a fistful of country walks.

Sights & Activities

The impressive ruins of 12th-century **Helmsley Castle** (EH; www.english-heritage.org.uk; adult/child £4.70/2.40; ⏲10am-6pm Apr-Sep, 10am-5pm Mar & Oct, 10am-4pm Thu-Mon Nov-Feb) are defended by a striking series of deep ditches and banks to which later rulers added the thick stone walls and defensive towers – only one tooth-shaped tower survives today following the dismantling of the fortress by Sir Thomas Fairfax after the Civil War. The castle's tumultuous history is well explained in the tourist office.

North York Moors National Park

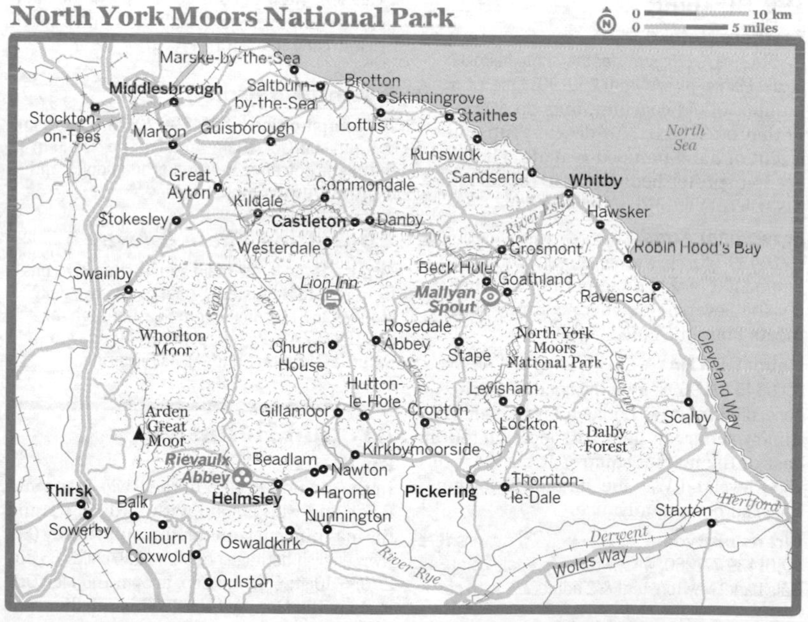

Located just outside the castle, **Helmsley Walled Garden** (www.helmsleywalledgarden.org.uk; adult/child £4/free; ⏲10.30am-5pm daily Apr-Oct, Mon-Fri Nov-Mar) would be just another plant-and-produce centre were it not for its dramatic position and fabulous selection of flowers, fruits and vegetables – some of which are rare – not to mention the herbs, including 40 varieties of mint. If you're into horticulture with a historical twist, this is Eden.

South of the castle stretches the superb landscape of Duncombe Park estate with the stately home of **Duncombe Park House** (www.duncombepark.com; adult/child house & gardens £8.25/3.75, gardens only £5/3; ⏲11am-5.30pm Sun-Thu Apr-Oct) at its heart. From the house (guided tours depart hourly 12.30pm to 3.30pm) and formal gardens, wide grassy walkways and terraces lead through woodland to mock-classical temples, while longer walking trails are set out in the parkland, now protected as a nature reserve. The house is 1.5 miles south of town, an easy walk through the park.

You could easily spend a day here, especially if you take in one of the many **walks**. Cream of the crop is the 3.5-mile route to **Rievaulx Abbey** – the tourist office can provide route leaflets and advise on buses if you don't want to walk both ways. This route is also the opening section of the **Cleveland Way**.

Sleeping

Feathers Hotel B&B ££
(☎01439-770275; www.feathershotelhelmsley.co.uk; Market Pl; s/d from £50/90) One of a number of old coaching inns on Market Pl that offer B&B, half-decent grub and a pint of hand-pumped real ale. There are four-poster beds in some rooms and historical trimmings throughout.

Feversham Arms B&B £££
(☎01439-770766; www.fevershamarms.com; r from £155; P 📶) For something plusher try the Feversham, where country charm meets boutique chic.

Helmsley YHA HOSTEL £
(☎0845 371 9638; www.yha.org.uk; Carlton Lane; dm £18; P 👪) Looks a bit like an ordinary suburban home; its location (400m east of the market square) at the start of the Cleveland Way means that it's often busy, so book in advance.

Wrens of Rydale CAMPSITE £
(☎01439-771260; www.wrensofryedale.co.uk; Gale Lane, Nawton; tent & 2 adults £9, with car £15; ⏲Apr-Oct) Sheltered campsite with three acres of pristine parkland 3 miles east of Helmsley, just south of Beadlam.

Eating

Helmsley is a bit of a foodie town, sporting a couple of quality delicatessens on the main square. There's **Perns** (18 Market Pl; ⏲7.30am-5.30pm Mon-Sat, 10am-4pm Sun), a butcher, deli and wine merchant under the same ownership as the Star Inn at Harome; and flower-bedecked **Hunters of Helmsley** (www.huntersofhelmsley.com; 13 Market Pl; ⏲8am-5.30pm daily), a cornucopia of locally made chutneys, jams, beers, cheeses, bacon, humbugs and ice cream – a great place to stock up for a gourmet picnic.

TOP CHOICE **Star Inn** GASTROPUB £££
(☎01439-770397; www.thestaratharome.co.uk; Harome; mains £15-24; ⏲lunch Tue-Sun, dinner Mon-Sat) This thatch-roofed country pub is home to one of Yorkshire's best restaurants, with a Michelin-starred menu that revels in top quality produce from the surrounding farms – slow-roasted belly pork with black pudding, apple salad and a fried duck egg, or roast roe deer venison with mushrooms and tarragon jus. It's the sort of place you won't want to leave, and the good news is you don't have to: the adjacent lodge has eight magnificent bedrooms (£150 to £240), each decorated in classic but luxurious country style. It's about 2 miles south of Helmsley just off the A170.

Information

The **tourist office** (☎01439-770173; ⏲9.30am-5.30pm Mar-Oct, 10am-4pm Fri-Sun Nov-Feb) at the castle entrance sells maps and books, and helps with accommodation.

Getting There & Away

All buses stop in the main square. Bus 31X runs from York to Helmsley (£7, 1¼ hours, two daily Monday to Saturday). From Scarborough take bus 128 (£7.40, 1½ hours, hourly Monday to Saturday, four on Sunday) via Pickering.

Around Helmsley

RIEVAULX

In the secluded valley of the River Rye, amid fields and woods loud with birdsong, stand the magnificent ruins of **Rievaulx Abbey** (EH; www.english-heritage.org.uk; adult/child £5.30/2.70; ⏲10am-6pm Apr-Sep, to 5pm Thu-Mon Oct, to 4pm Thu-Mon Nov-Mar). This idyllic spot was chosen by Cistercian monks in 1132 as a base for missionary activity in northern Britain. St Aelred, the third abbot, famously described the abbey's setting as 'everywhere peace, everywhere serenity, and a marvellous freedom from the tumult of the world'. But the monks of Rievaulx (pronounced 'Ree-voh') were far from unworldly, and soon created a network of commercial interests ranging from sheep farms to lead mines that formed the backbone of the local economy. The extensive ruins give a wonderful feel for the size and complexity of the community that once lived here – their story is fleshed out in a series of fascinating exhibits in the neighbouring tourist office.

In the 1750s landscape gardening fashion favoured a Gothic look, and many aristocrats had mock ruins built in their parks. The Duncombe family went one better, as their lands contained a real medieval ruin – Rievaulx Abbey. They built **Rievaulx Terrace & Temples** (NT; www.nationaltrust.org.uk; adult/child £5.25/2.90; ⏱11am-5pm Mar-Oct) so that lords and ladies could stroll effortlessly in the 'wilderness' and admire the abbey in the valley below. Today, we can do the same, with views over Ryedale and the Hambleton Hills forming a perfect backdrop.

Rievaulx is about 3 miles west of Helmsley. Note that there's no direct access between the abbey and the terrace – their entrance gates are about a mile apart, though easily reached along a lane – steeply uphill if you're going from the abbey to the terrace.

Hutton-le-Hole

POP 210

With a scatter of gorgeous stone cottages, a gurgling brook and a flock of sheep grazing contentedly on the village green, Hutton-le-Hole must be a contender for the best-looking village in Yorkshire. The dips and hollows on the green may have given the place its name – it was once called simply Hutton Hole but wannabe posh Victorians added the Frenchified 'le', which the locals defiantly pronounce 'lee'.

The **tourist office** (☎01751-417367; ⏱10am-5.30pm mid-Mar–early Nov) has leaflets on walks in the area, including a 5-mile circuit to the nearby village of Lastingham.

Attached to the tourist office is the largely open-air **Ryedale Folk Museum** (☎01751-417367; www.ryedalefolkmuseum.co.uk; adult/child £5.50/4; ⏱10am-5.30pm mid-Mar–Oct, 10am-dusk Nov–mid-Mar, closed mid-Dec–mid-Jan), a constantly expanding collection of North York Moors buildings from different eras, including a medieval manor house, simple farmers' houses, a blacksmith's forge and a row of 1930s village shops. Demonstrations and displays throughout the season give a fascinating insight into local life as it was in the past.

The **Daffodil Walk** is a 2½-mile circular walk following the banks of the River Dove. As the name suggests, the main draws are the daffs, usually at their best in the last couple of weeks in April.

Sleeping & Eating

Lion Inn PUB, B&B ££
(☎01751-417320; www.lionblakey.co.uk; Blakey Ridge; s/d from £42/64; mains £10-18; Ⓟ) From Hutton, the Blakey Ridge road climbs over the moors to Danby and, after 6 miles, passes one of the highest and most remote pubs in England (altitude 404m). With its low-beamed ceilings and cosy fireplaces, hearty grub and range of real ales, the Lion is a firm favourite with hikers and bikers.

Burnley House B&B ££
(☎01751-417548; www.burnleyhouse.co.uk; d £75-90; Ⓟ) This elegant Georgian home offers comfortable bedrooms and a hearty breakfast, but the best features are the lovely sitting room and garden where you can relax with a cup of tea and a book.

Getting There & Away

Hutton-le-Hole is 2½ miles north of the main A170 road, about halfway between Helmsley and Pickering. Moorsbus services (p620) through Hutton-le-Hole include the M3 between Helmsley and Danby (seven per day) and the M1 and M2 between Pickering and Danby (eight per day) via the Lion Inn. Outside times when the Moorsbus runs, you'll need your own transport to get here.

Pickering

POP 6600

Pickering is a lively market town with an imposing Norman castle that advertises itself as the 'Gateway to the North York Moors'. That gateway is the terminus of the wonderful North Yorkshire Moors Railway, a picturesque survivor from the great days of steam.

The **tourist office** (☎01751-473791; www.yorkshiremoorsandcoast.com; The Ropery; ⏱9.30am-5.30pm Mon-Sat & 9.30am-4pm Sun Mar-Oct, 10am-4pm Mon-Sat Nov-Feb) has the usual details as well as plenty of NYMR-related info.

Sights

The privately owned **North Yorkshire Moors Railway** (NYMR; www.nymr.co.uk; Pickering-Whitby Day Rover ticket adult/child £21/10.50) runs for 18 miles through beautiful countryside to the village of Grosmont, with connections to Whitby. Lovingly restored steam locos pull period carriages, resplendent in polished brass and bright paintwork. For visitors without wheels, it's ideal for reaching out-of-the-way villages in the middle of the moors. Grosmont is also on the main railway line between Middlesbrough and Whitby, opening up yet more possibilities for walking and sightseeing. Check the website for the latest on hours of operation.

Dating mostly from the 13th and 14th centuries, **Pickering Castle** (EH; www.english-heritage.org.uk; adult/child £3.70/1.90; 10am-6pm Apr-Sep, 10am-4pm Thu-Mon Oct) is a lot like the castles we drew as kids: thick stone walls around a central keep, perched atop a high motte (mound) with great views of the surrounding countryside.

Sleeping & Eating

White Swan Hotel PUB, HOTEL **£££**
(01751-472288; www.white-swan.co.uk; Market Pl; s/d from £115/150, mains £11-20; P) The top spot in town successfully combines a smart pub, a superb restaurant serving local dishes with a Continental twist, and a luxurious boutique hotel. Nine modern rooms in the converted coach house up the ante with flatscreen TVs and other stylish paraphernalia that add to the luxury found throughout the hotel.

There's a strip of B&Bs on tree-lined Eastgate (the A170 to Scarborough), and a few more on Westgate (heading towards Helmsley). Decent options include **Eleven Westgate** (01751-475111; www.elevenwestgate.co.uk; 11 Westgate; s/d £50/70; P), a pretty house with patio and garden; and the elegant Georgian town house at **17 Burgate** (01751-473463; www.17burgate.co.uk; 17 Burgate; s/d from £79/89; P @).

There are several cafes and teashops on Market Pl, but don't overlook the **tearoom** (Pickering Station; mains £2-6) at Pickering station, which serves excellent home-baked goodies and does a tasty roast-pork roll with apple sauce, crackling and stuffing.

Getting There & Away

In addition to the NYMR trains, bus 128 between Helmsley (40 minutes) and Scarborough (50 minutes) runs hourly via Pickering. Yorkshire Coastliner service 840 between Leeds and Whitby links Pickering with York (£12, 70 minutes, hourly).

Danby

POP 290

The Blakey Ridge road from Hutton-le-Hole swoops steeply down to Danby, a compact, stone-built village set deep amid the moors at the head of Eskdale. It's home to the **Moors Centre** (www.visitthemoors.co.uk; 10am-5pm Apr-Oct, 10.30am-3.30pm Nov, Dec & Mar, 10.30am-3.30pm Sat & Sun Jan-Feb), the national park's HQ, which has interesting exhibits on the natural history of the moors as well as a cafe, an accommodation booking service and a huge range of local guidebooks, maps and leaflets.

You can reach Danby on the delightful **Esk Valley Railway** (www.eskvalleyrailway.co.uk) – Whitby is 20 minutes east, Middlesbrough 45 minutes west. There are four departures daily Monday to Saturday, and two on Sunday.

Whitby

POP 13,600

Whitby is a town of two halves, split down the middle by the mouth of the River Esk. It's also a town with two personalities – on the one hand a busy commercial and fishing port with a bustling quayside fishmarket; on the other a traditional seaside resort, complete with sandy beach, amusement arcades and promenading holidaymakers slurping ice-cream cones in the sun.

It's the combination of these two facets that makes Whitby more interesting than your average resort. The town has managed to retain much of its 18th-century character, recalling the time when James Cook – Whitby's most famous adopted son – was making his first forays at sea on his way towards becoming one of the best-known explorers in history. The narrow streets and alleys of the old town hug the riverside, now lined with restaurants, pubs and cute little shops, all with views across the handsome harbour where colourful fishing boats ply to and fro. Keeping a watchful eye over the whole scene is the atmospheric ruined abbey atop the East Cliff.

But Whitby also has a darker side. Most famously, it was the inspiration and setting for part of Bram Stoker's Gothic horror story *Dracula*. Less well known is the fact that Whitby is famous for the jet (fossilised wood) that has been mined from the local sea cliffs for centuries; this smooth, black substance was popularised in the 19th century when Queen Victoria took to wearing mourning jewellery made from Whitby jet. In recent years these morbid associations have seen the rise of a series of hugely popular Goth festivals.

Sights

Whitby Abbey ABBEY RUINS
(EH; www.english-heritage.org.uk; adult/child £5.80/2.90; ⏲10am-6pm Apr-Sep, 10am-4pm Thu-Mon Oct-Mar) There are ruined abbeys and there are picturesque ruined abbeys, and then there's **Whitby Abbey**, dominating the skyline above the East Cliff like a great Gothic tombstone silhouetted against the sky. Looking more like it was built as an atmospheric film set than as a monastic establishment, it is hardly surprising that this medieval hulk inspired the Victorian novelist Bram Stoker – who holidayed in Whitby – to make it the setting for Count Dracula's dramatic landfall.

From the end of **Church St**, which has many shops selling jet jewellery, the 199 steps of **Church Stairs** lead steeply up to Whitby Abbey passing the equally atmospheric **St Mary's Church** (admission free; ⏲10am-5pm Apr-Oct, to 4pm Nov-Mar) and its spooky graveyard, a favourite haunt of courting Goth couples.

Captain Cook Memorial Museum MUSEUM
(www.cookmuseumwhitby.co.uk; Grape Lane; adult/child £4.50/3; ⏲9.45am-5pm Apr-Oct, 11am-3pm Mar) This fascinating museum occupies the house of the ship owner with whom Cook began his seafaring career. Highlights include the attic where Cook lodged as a young apprentice, Cook's own maps and letters, etchings from the South Seas and a wonderful model of the *Endeavour*, with all the crew and stores laid out for inspection.

Whitby Sands BEACH
Whitby's days as a seaside resort continue with donkey rides, ice cream and bucket-and-spade escapades on Whitby Sands, stretching west from the harbour mouth. Atop the cliff on the harbour's west side, the **Captain Cook Monument** shows the great man looking out to sea, often with a seagull perched on his head. Nearby is the **Whalebone Arch**, which recalls Whitby's days as a whaling port. Whitby Sands can be reached from West Cliff via the **cliff lift** (rides 70p; ⏲May-Sep only), an elevator that has been running since 1931.

WORTH A TRIP

GOATHLAND

This picture-postcard halt on the North Yorkshire Moors Railway stars as Hogsmeade train station in the Harry Potter films, and the village appears as Aidensfield in the British TV series *Heartbeat*. It's also the starting point for lots of easy and enjoyable walks, often with the chuff-chuff-chuff of passing steam engines in the background.

One of the most popular hikes is to head northwest from the station (via a gate on the platform on the far side from the village) to the hamlet of Beck Hole, where you can stop for a pork pie and a pint of Black Sheep at the wonderfully atmospheric **Birch Hall Inn** (www.beckhole.info) – like stepping into the past. Return to Goathland via the waterfall at **Mallyan Spout**.

Whitby Museum MUSEUM
(www.whitbymuseum.org.uk; Pannett Park; adult/child £3/1; ⏲9.30am-4.30pm Tue-Sun) Set in a park to the west of the town centre is the wonderfully eclectic Whitby Museum with its displays of fossil plesiosaurs and dinosaur footprints, Cook memorabilia, ships in bottles, jet jewellery and even the 'Hand of Glory' – a preserved human hand reputedly cut from the corpse of an executed criminal.

Activities

For a cracking day out, take a bus to Robin Hood's Bay, explore the village, have lunch, then hike the 6-mile **clifftop footpath** back to Whitby (allow three hours).

First choice for a bike ride is the excellent 20-mile Whitby-to-Scarborough **Coastal Cycle Trail**, which starts a mile south of the town centre and follows the route of an old railway line via Robin Hood's Bay. Bikes can be hired from **Dr Crank's Bike Shack** (20 Skinner St; ⏲10am-5pm Mon, Tue & Thu-Sat) in Whitby, or **Trailways** (www.trailways.info) at Hawsker for £12 to £20 a day.

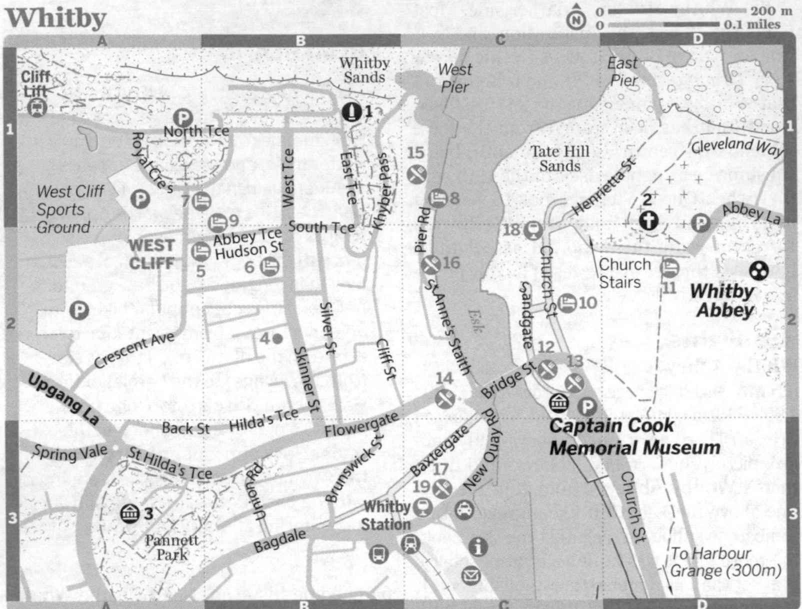

Festivals & Events

Whitby Gothic Weekends COUNTER CULTURE
(www.wgw.topmum.co.uk; tickets £40) Goth heaven, with gigs, events and the Bizarre Bazaar – dozens of traders selling Goth gear, jewellery, art and music. Twice yearly on the last weekends of April and October.

Whitby Spring Session MUSIC & ARTS
(www.moorandcoast.co.uk; tickets from £35) Beards, sandals and real ale galore at this traditional festival of folk music, dance and dubious Celtic art. May Bank Holiday weekend.

Sleeping

B&Bs are concentrated in West Cliff in the streets to the south and east of Royal Cres; if a house here ain't offering B&B, chances are it's derelict. Accommodation can be tough to find at festival times; it's wise to book ahead.

TOP CHOICE **Marine Hotel** HOTEL £££
(☎01947-605022; www.the-marine-hotel.co.uk; 13 Marine Pde; r £150) Feeling more like mini-suites than ordinary hotel accommodation, the four bedrooms at the Marine are quirky, stylish and comfortable – the sort of place that makes you want to stay in rather than go out. Ask for one of the two rooms that have a balcony – they have great views across the harbour.

Langley Hotel B&B ££
(☎01947-604250; www.langleyhotel.com; 16 Royal Cres; s/d from £70/100; P 📶) With a cream-and-crimson colour scheme, and a gilt four-poster bed in one room, this grand old guesthouse exudes a whiff of Victorian splendour. Go for room 1 or 2, if possible, to make the most of the panoramic views from West Cliff.

Shepherd's Purse B&B ££
(☎01947-820228; www.theshepherdspurse.com; 95 Church St; r £55-70) This place combines a beads-and-baubles boutique with a wholefood shop and guesthouse accommodation in the courtyard at the back. The plainer rooms share a bathroom and are perfectly adequate, but we recommend the rustic en-suite bedrooms situated around the courtyard; the four-poster beds feel a bit like they've been shoehorned in, but the atmosphere is cute rather than cramped. (Breakfast is not provided.)

Whitby YHA HOSTEL £
(☎0845 371 9049; www.yha.org.uk; Church Lane; dm £18-22; P @ 📶) With an unbeatable position next to the abbey, this hostel doesn't

Whitby

Top Sights
Captain Cook Memorial Museum C2
Whitby Abbey D2

Sights
1 Captain Cook Monument B1
2 St Mary's Church D1
Whalebone Arch .... (see 1)
3 Whitby Museum A3

Activities, Courses & Tours
4 Dr Crank's Bike Shack B2

Sleeping
5 Argyle House A2
6 Bramblewick B2
7 Langley Hotel A1
8 Marine Hotel C1
9 Rosslyn House B1
10 Shepherd's Purse C2
11 Whitby YHA D2

Eating
12 Green's C2
13 Humble Pie'n'Mash C2
14 Java Cafe-Bar C2
15 Magpie Café C1
16 Moon & Sixpence C2
17 Trenchers C3

Drinking
18 Duke of York C2
19 Station Inn C3

have to try too hard, and it doesn't. You'll have to book well in advance to get your body into one of the basic bunks. Hike up from the station, or take bus 97 (hourly Monday to Saturday).

Harbour Grange HOSTEL £
(☎01947-600817; www.whitbybackpackers.co.uk; Spital Bridge, dm £17) Overlooking the harbour and less than 10 minutes' walk from the train station, this tidy hostel is conveniently located but has an 11.30pm curfew – good thing we're all teetotalling early-to-bedders, right?

Trailways HOTEL ££
(☎01947-820207; www.trailways.info; from £290 for 3 nights; P) If travelling on the North Yorkshire Moors Railway has given you a taste for trains, how about sleeping in one? Trailways has a beautifully converted InterCity125 coach parked at the old Hawsker train station on the Whitby–Scarborough cycle route, offering luxurious self-catering accommodation with all mod cons for two to seven people.

Rosslyn House B&B ££
(☎01947-604086; www.guesthousewhitby.co.uk; 11 Abbey Tce; s/d £35/55) Bright and cheerful with a friendly welcome.

Bramblewick B&B ££
(☎01947-604504; www.bramblewickwhitby.com; 3 Havelock Pl; s/d £32/66; P 📶) Friendly owners, hearty breakfasts and abbey views from the top floor room.

Argyle House B&B ££
(☎01947-602733; www.argyle-house.co.uk; 18 Hudson St; s/d £40/66; 📶) Comfortable as old slippers, with kippers for breakfast.

WHITBY'S DARK SIDE

The famous story of *Dracula*, inspiration for a thousand lurid movies, was written by Bram Stoker while staying at a B&B in Whitby in 1897. Although most Hollywood versions of the tale concentrate on deepest, darkest Transylvania, much of the original book was set in Whitby, and many sites can still be seen today. The tourist office sells an excellent *Dracula Trail* leaflet.

Eating & Drinking

Green's SEAFOOD, BRITISH ££
(☎01947-600284; www.greensofwhitby.com; 13 Bridge St; bistro mains £10-19, restaurant 2-/3-course dinner £34/41; ⏱lunch & dinner Mon-Fri) The classiest eatery in town is ideally situated to take its pick of the fish and shellfish freshly landed at the harbour. Grab a hearty lunch in the ground floor bistro (*moules-frites*, sausage and mash, fish and chips) or head to the upstairs restaurant for a sophisticated dinner date.

Moon & Sixpence BRASSERIE ££
(☎01947-604416; 5 Marine Pde; mains £10-18; ⏲breakfast, lunch & dinner) This brand-new brasserie and cocktail bar has a prime position, with views across the harbour to the abbey ruins. The seafood-dominated menu ranges from hearty winter warmers such as chunky vegetable soup and fish pie, to more sophisticated dishes like a half-dozen oysters *au naturel* and seared scallops with black pudding.

Magpie Café SEAFOOD ££
(www.magpiecafe.co.uk; 14 Pier Rd; mains £9-18; ⏲lunch & dinner) The Magpie flaunts its reputation for serving the 'World's Best Fish and Chips'. Damn fine they are too, but the world and his dog knows about it, and summertime queues can stretch along the street. Fish and chips from the takeaway counter cost £5; the sit-down restaurant is dearer, but offers a wide range of seafood dishes, from grilled sea bass to paella.

Java Cafe-Bar CAFE £
(2 Flowergate; mains £4-6; ⏲8am-6pm; 📶) A cool little diner with stainless-steel counters and retro decor, with internet access, music vids on the flatscreen and a menu of healthy salads, sandwiches and wraps washed down with excellent coffee.

Humble Pie'n'Mash PIES £
(www.humblepienmash.com; 163 Church St; mains £5; ⏲lunch daily, dinner Mon-Sat) Superb homemade pies with fillings ranging from lamb, leek and rosemary to roast veg and goat's cheese, served in a cosy, timber-framed cottage.

Trenchers FISH & CHIPS ££
(www.trenchersrestaurant.co.uk; New Quay Rd; mains £10-15; ⏲lunch & dinner) Top-notch fish and chips minus the 'World's Best' tagline – this place is your best bet if you want to avoid the queues at the Magpie (don't be put off by the modern look).

Station Inn PUB
(New Quay Rd) Best place in town for atmosphere and real ale with an impressive range of cask-conditioned beers including Theakston's Black Bull and Black Dog Abbey Ale.

Duke of York PUB
(Church St) Popular watering hole at the bottom of the Church Stairs, with great views over the harbour. Serves Timothy Taylor ales.

Information

Post office (⏲8.30am-5.30pm Mon-Sat) Inside the Co-op supermarket.

Tourist office (☎01947-602674; www.visitwhitby.com; Langborne Rd; ⏲10am-6pm May-Sep, 10am-4.30pm Oct-Apr)

Getting There & Away

BUS Buses 93 and X93 run south to Scarborough (one hour, every 30 minutes) via Robin Hood's Bay (15 minutes, hourly), and north to Middlesbrough (hourly), with fewer services on Sunday. See p576 for details of the Yorkshire Coastliner service from Leeds to Whitby.

TRAIN Coming from the north, you can get to Whitby by train along the Esk Valley Railway from Middlesbrough (£4.70, 1½ hours, four per day), with connections from Durham and Newcastle. From the south, it's easier to get a train from York to Scarborough, then a bus from Scarborough to Whitby.

Around Whitby

ROBIN HOOD'S BAY

Picturesque Robin Hood's Bay (www.robin-hoods-bay.co.uk) has nothing to do with

CAPTAIN COOK – WHITBY'S ADOPTED SON

Although he was born in Marton (now a suburb of Middlesbrough), Whitby has adopted the famous explorer Captain James Cook, and ever since the first tourists got off the train in Victorian times local entrepreneurs have mercilessly cashed in on his memory, as endless 'Endeavour Cafes' and 'Captain Cook Chip Shops' testify.

Still, Whitby played a key role in Cook's eventual success as a world-famous explorer. It was here that he first went to sea, serving his apprenticeship with local ship owners, and the design of the ships used for his voyages of discovery – including the famous *Endeavour* – were based on the design of Whitby 'cats', flat-bottomed ships that carried coal from Newcastle to London.

the hero of Sherwood Forest – the origin of the name is a mystery, and the locals call it Bay Town, or just Bay. But there's no denying that this fishing village is one of the prettiest spots on the Yorkshire coast.

Leave your car at the parking area in the upper village, where 19th-century ship's captains built comfortable Victorian villas, and walk downhill to **Old Bay**, the oldest part of the village (don't even think about driving down). This maze of narrow lanes and passages is dotted with tearooms, pubs, craft shops and artists' studios – there's even a tiny cinema – and at low tide you can go down onto the beach and fossick around in the rock pools.

There are several pubs and cafes – best pub for ambience and real ale is **Ye Dolphin** (King St), while the **Swell Cafe** (www.swell.org.uk; Chapel St; mains £4-7; ⏲breakfast & lunch) does great coffee and has a terrace with a view over the beach.

Robin Hood's Bay is 6 miles south of Whitby; you can walk here along the coastal path in two or three hours, or bike it along the cycle trail in 40 minutes. Also, bus 93 runs hourly between Whitby and Scarborough via Robin Hood's Bay – the bus stop is at the top of the hill, in the new part of town.

Manchester, Liverpool & the Northwest

Includes »

Best Places to Eat

» Lime Tree (p643)
» Italian Club (p664)
» Mark Addy (p643)
» Upstairs at the Grill (p653)
» Tanroagan (p685)

Best Places to Stay

» Green Bough (p651)
» Eleven Didsbury Park (p642)
» Hope St Hotel (p662)
» Velvet Hotel (p640)
» Number One (p678)

Why Go?

Music, history and hedonism. Three great reasons to venture into England's once-mighty industrial heartland, the cradle of capitalism and the Industrial Revolution. Among the hulking relics of the region's industrial past are two of the most exciting cities in the country, a picture-postcard town dripping with Tudor charm and the most stomach-turning roller coaster we've ever been on. If you fancy a bit of respite from the concrete paw-print of humankind, there's some of the most beautiful countryside in England. Oh, and a rich musical tradition that defines your MP3 playlists as much as anywhere else in the world.

The northwest helped define the progress of the last two centuries, but these days it's all about making an imprint on the 21st. A tall order, but the region knows a thing or two about mighty achievements, urban redesign and bloody good music: look and listen for yourself.

When to Go

Steeplechase lovers should head to the world-famous Aintree Grand National, run just outside Liverpool, on the first weekend of April, while petrol heads should make a beeline to the Isle of Man's TT Festival, held for two weeks in May/June. For fans of the region's most important sport, football (soccer), August/September is a good time to visit as it's the start of the season.

Those with an appreciation of culture shouldn't miss the Manchester International Arts Festival, a biennial showstopper held in July. To appreciate the area's rich musical past visit Liverpool in the last week of August for madness at Creamfields (dance) and Matthew St Festival, an ode to all things Beatles.

Activities

Although predominantly an urban area, the northwest does have some decent walking and cycling options, most notably in the Ribble Valley in northern Lancashire, home to plenty of good walks including the 70-mile **Ribble Way**. The historic village of Whalley, in the heart of the Ribble Valley, is the meeting point of the two circular routes that make up the 260-mile **Lancashire Cycle Way**.

The Isle of Man has top-notch walking and cycling opportunities. Regional tourism websites contain walking and cycling information, and tourist offices stock free leaflets as well as maps and guides (usually £1 to £5) that cover walking, cycling and other activities.

Information

Discover England's Northwest (www.visitnorthwest.com) is the centralised tourist authority; for the Isle of Man, check out the main **Isle of Man Government** (www.gov.im) site.

Getting Around

The towns and cities covered in this chapter are all within easy reach of each other, and are well linked by public transport. The two main cities, Manchester and Liverpool, are only 34 miles apart and are linked by hourly bus and train services. Chester is 18 miles south of Liverpool, but is also easily accessible from Manchester by train or via the M56. Blackpool is 50 miles to the north of both cities, and is also well connected. Try the following for transport information:

Greater Manchester Passenger Transport Authority (www.gmpte.com) Extensive info on Manchester and its environs.

Merseytravel (www.merseytravel.gov.uk) Taking care of all travel in Merseyside.

National Express (www.nationalexpress.com) Extensive coach services in the northwest; Manchester and Liverpool are major hubs.

MANCHESTER

POP 394,270

'Manchester has everything but a beach.' Former Stone Roses' frontman Ian Brown's description of his native city has become Manchester's unofficial motto – and even accounting for a bit of northern bluster Brown isn't far wrong. The uncrowned capital of the north was the world's first modern city and the birthplace of capitalism; it is where the Industrial Revolution blossomed; where communism and feminism were given theoretical legs; and where the first computer beeped into life.

WANT MORE?

For in-depth information, reviews and recommendations at your fingertips, head to the Apple App Store to purchase Lonely Planet's *Manchester City Guide* iPhone app.

Alternatively, head to **Lonely Planet** (http://www.lonelyplanet.com/england/northwest-england/manchester) for planning advice, author recommendations, traveller reviews and insider tips.

Manchester was raised on lofty ambition, so it stands to reason that it likes to plan on an impressive scale. Its world-class museums and heavyweight art galleries – spread across the city centre and west in Salford Quays – are noteworthy, but what makes this city truly special are its distractions of pure pleasure: you can dine, drink and dance yourself into happy oblivion in the swirl of nightlife that once made the city a key stop on the global party tour, from the boho Northern Quarter to the elegant eateries of the southern suburb of Didsbury.

The future looks very bright indeed for Manchester, beginning with the arrival in 2011 of five departments of the BBC to the purpose-built Media City in Salford – proof that when it comes to representing the national interest, Manchester is the obvious choice.

History

Canals and steam-powered cotton mills were what transformed Manchester from a small disease-infested provincial town into a big disease-infested industrial city. It all happened in the 1760s, with the opening of the Bridgewater Canal between Manchester and the coal mines at Worsley in 1763, and with Richard Arkwright patenting his super cotton mill in 1769. Thereafter, Manchester and the world would never be the same again. When the canal was extended to Liverpool and the open sea in 1776, Manchester – dubbed 'Cottonopolis' – kicked into high gear and took off on the coal-fuelled, steam-powered gravy train.

There was plenty of gravy to go around, but the good burghers of 19th-century Manchester made sure that the vast majority of

Liverpool, Manchester & the Northwest Highlights

1. Learning a valuable history lesson at the outstanding **International Slavery Museum** (p661) in Liverpool
2. Having your insides churned and twisted at Blackpool's **Pleasure Beach** (p677)
3. Learning exactly what kind of hell war is in the **Imperial War Museum North** (p637) in Manchester
4. Sampling Manchester culinary delights at one (or more!) of the city's superb **restaurants** (p642)

5 Getting to grips with the **Isle of Man** (p683) – about as exotic as England gets

6 Walking in Frodo's footsteps in and around **Hurst Green** (p683)

7 Tramping Chester's **city walls** (p650), like the Romans did 2000 years ago

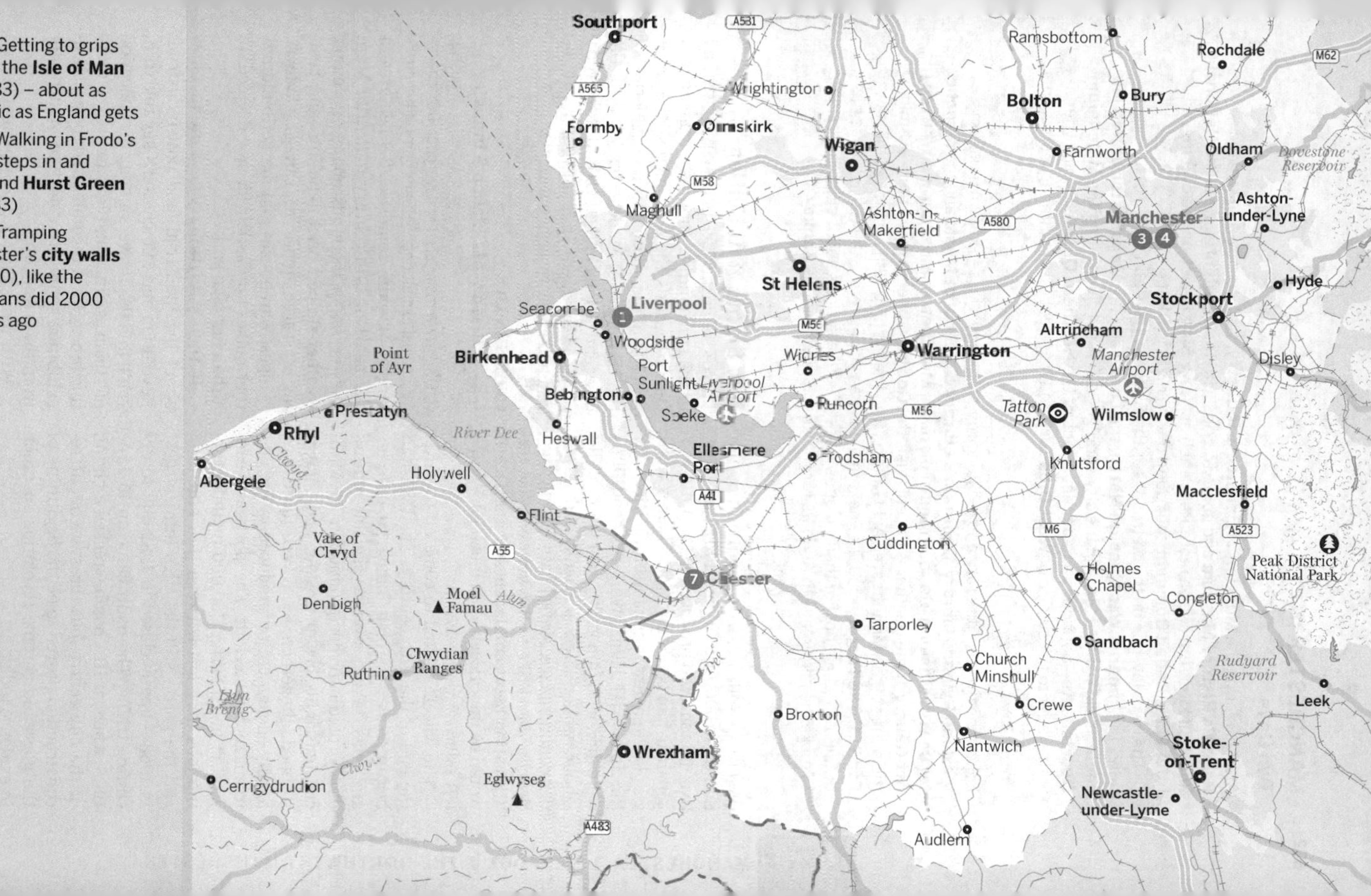

MANCHESTER IN...

Two Days

After exploring the **Museum of Science & Industry**, visit the newly renovated **People's History Museum** and come to grips with the beautiful game at the **National Football Museum**. Pick a restaurant such as **Yang Sing** to kick off the evening, then try **A Place Called Common** and round off the night in **Bluu**.

The next day, hop on the Metrolink for the Salford Quays and its trio of top attractions: the **Imperial War Museum North**, the **Lowry** and the **Manchester United Museum** at Old Trafford. Back in the city, indulge your retail chi in either the **Millennium Quarter** or the boutiques and offbeat shops of the **Northern Quarter**. Finish your day with a jaunt to the suburb of **West Didsbury** and its selection of fantastic restaurants.

Four Days

Follow the two-day itinerary and tackle some of the city's lesser-known museums – the **John Rylands Library**, **Chetham's Library & School of Music** and the **Manchester Jewish Museum**. Go south and explore the **Manchester Museum** and **Whitworth Art Gallery**. If the weather is decent, visit the **Godlee Observatory** before examining the riches of the **Manchester Art Gallery**. End the evening with a dance at the new **Fac 251: The Factory** club. The next day, take a walking tour – the tourist office has details of a whole host of themed ones – and if you're serious about clubbing, be sure to make the pilgrimage to Ancoats for the absolutely fabulous **Sankey's**.

the city's swollen citizenry (with a population of 90,000 in 1801, and 100 years later, two million) who produced most of it never got their hands on any of it. Their reward was life in a new kind of urban settlement: the industrial slum. Working conditions were dire, with impossibly long hours, child labour, work-related accidents and fatalities commonplace. Mark Twain commented that he would like to live here because the 'transition between Manchester and Death would be unnoticeable'. So much for Victorian values.

The wheels started to come off towards the end of the 19th century. The USA had begun to flex its own industrial muscles and was taking over a sizeable chunk of the textile trade; production in Manchester's mills began to slow, and then it stopped altogether. By WWII there was hardly enough cotton produced in the city to make a tablecloth. The postwar years weren't much better: 150,000 manufacturing jobs were lost between 1961 and 1983 and the port – still the UK's third largest in 1963 – finally closed in 1982 due to declining traffic. The nadir came on 15 June 1996, when an IRA bomb wrecked a chunk of the city centre, but the subsequent reconstruction proved to be the beginning of the glass-and-chrome revolution so much in evidence today.

Sights & Activities

There's so much to see in the city centre and in the surrounding suburbs – from Salford Quays towards the west (across the River Irwell) to the museums and galleries of the University of Manchester (south of the city centre along and off Oxford Rd). Pretty much everywhere in Manchester can be reached easily by public transport.

CITY CENTRE

FREE **Museum of Science & Industry** MUSEUM

(MOSI; www.msim.org.uk; Liverpool Rd; charge for special exhibitions; ⏲10am-5pm) The city's largest museum comprises 2.8 hectares in the heart of 19th-century industrial Manchester. It's in the landscape of enormous, weather-stained brick buildings and rusting cast-iron relics of canals, viaducts, bridges, warehouses and market buildings that makes up Castlefield, now deemed an 'urban heritage park'.

If there's anything you want to know about the Industrial (and post-Industrial) Revolution and Manchester's key role in it, you'll find the answers among the collection of steam engines and locomotives, factory machinery from the mills, and the excellent exhibition telling the story of Manchester from the sewers up.

With more than a dozen permanent exhibits, you could spend a whole day poking about the place, testing early electric-shock machines here and trying out a printing press there. A unifying theme (besides the fact that science and industry were pretty handy to the development of society) is that Manchester and Mancunians had a key role to play: did you know that Manchester was home to the world's first computer (a giant contraption called 'the baby'), in 1948, or that the world's first submarine was built to the designs of local curate Reverend George Garrett, in 1880? Nope, neither did we.

FREE **People's History Museum** MUSEUM
(www.phm.org.uk; Left Bank, Bridge St; 10am-5pm daily) A major refurb of an Edwardian pumping station – including the construction of a striking new annexe – has resulted in the expansion of one of the city's best museums, which is devoted to British social history and the labour movement. You clock in on the 1st floor (literally: punch your card in an old mill clock, which managers would infamously fiddle so as to make employees work longer) and plunge into the heart of Britain's struggle for basic democratic rights, labour reform and fair pay. Amid displays like the (tiny) desk at which Thomas Paine (1737–1809) wrote *Rights of Man* (1791) and an array of beautifully made and colourful union banners are compelling interactive displays, including a screen where you can trace the effects of all the events covered in the museum on five generations of the same family. The 2nd floor takes up the struggle for equal rights from WWII to the current day, touching on gay rights, antiracism initiatives and the defining British socio-political landmarks of the last 50 years, including the founding of the National Health Service (NHS), the Miners' Strike and the widespread protests against the Poll Tax. It's compelling stuff, and a marvellous example of a museum's relevance to our everyday lives.

National Football Museum MUSEUM
(www.nationalfootballmuseum.com; Urbis, Cathedral Gardens, Corporation St) It's the world's most popular game and Manchester is home to the world's most popular team, so when this museum went looking for a new home (from its previous location in the stand of Preston North End Football Club [FC], winners of the first professional league championship in 1889), it made sense that it would find its way to the stunning glass triangle that is Urbis. Slated to open in 2011, the museum will be a major stop in the football fan's Manchester pilgrimage and promises a major revamp of the displays exhibited in Preston. There'll be the usual array of footy memorabilia as well as a host of interactive, multimedia displays that will (hopefully) explain the game's overwhelming popularity even to those who grin and bear their way through their loved ones' frothing fanaticism.

FREE **Manchester Art Gallery** GALLERY
(www.manchestergalleries.org; Mosley St; 10am-5pm Tue-Sun) A superb collection of British art and a hefty number of European masters are on display at the city's top gallery. The older wing, designed by Charles Barry (of Houses of Parliament fame) in 1834, has an impressive collection that includes 37 Turner watercolours, as well as the

IN THE RED

The tide has turned in Manchester. In 2008, down-at-heel Manchester City Football Club were spectacularly bought out by the Abu Dhabi United Group, who proceeded to throw more than £150 million into the club in the hope of buying the kind of success their cross town neighbours at Old Trafford treat as their birthright. It'll be many years before City can even hold a candle to United's array of domestic and international trophies, but the newly crowned richest club in the world will be able to afford the outlandish transfer fees and exorbitant salaries commanded by the top tier players in the world game.

Just as City's fortunes are on the rise, so United's have begun to wane. Their US owners, the Glazer family, who bought the club in 2005, did so by taking out mortgages on 63 of 64 shopping malls that make up the bulk of the family business (which also includes the Tampa Bay Buccaneers), which saddled the club with £700 million of debt (in 2010). While the Glazers' financial situation worsens, so do the potential fortunes of Manchester United, who have all the clout in the world but no money to buy new players, especially the expensive ones that give the best sides the edge. Although it is far to early to say that United's reign at the top is over, there is little doubt that Manchester City will challenge them more fiercely than ever.

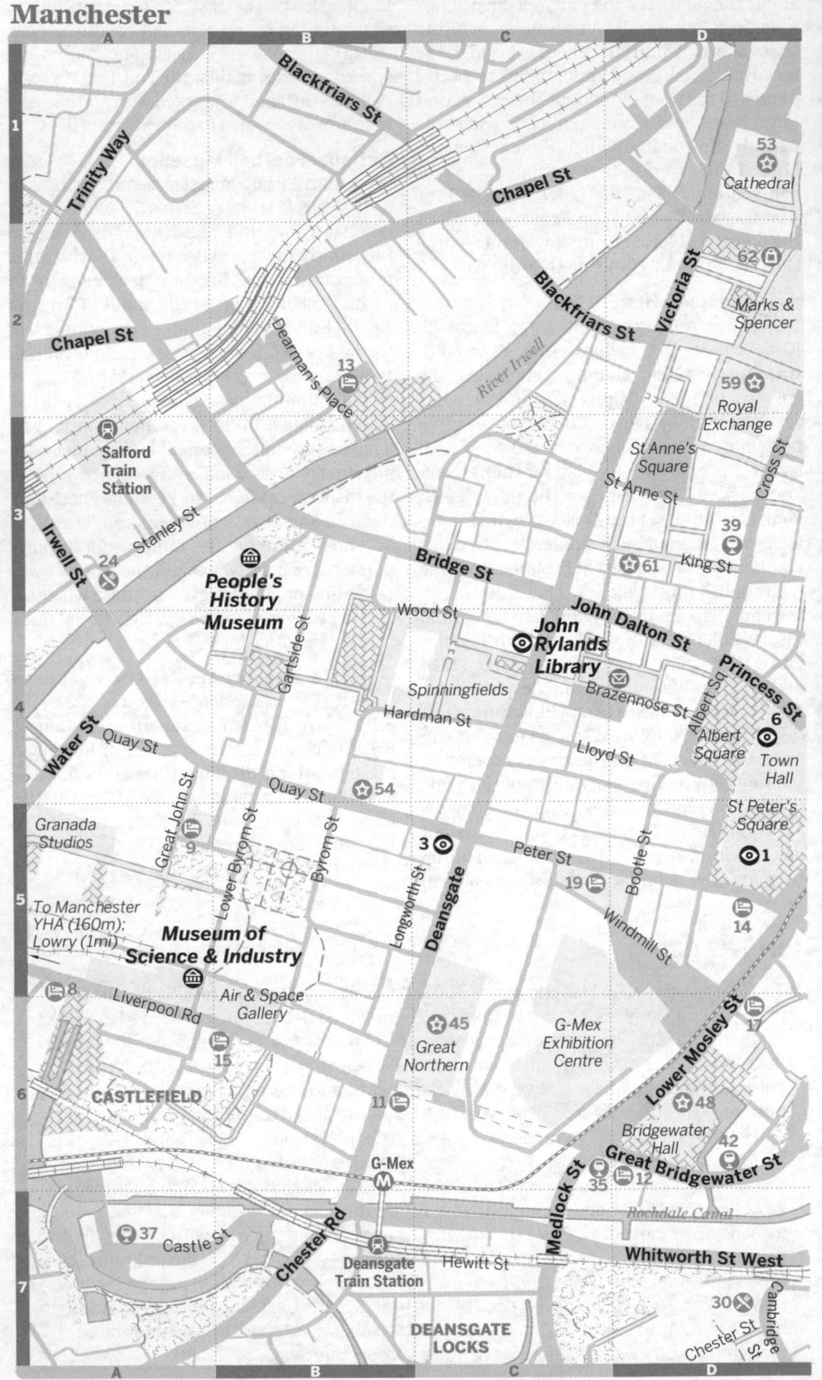
Blackfriars St
Trinity Way
Chapel St
Cathedral
53
62
Marks & Spencer
Victoria St
River Irwell
13
Dearman's Place
59
Royal Exchange
Salford Train Station
St Anne's Square
St Anne St
Cross St
Irwell St
Stanley St
39
King St
24
Bridge St
61
People's History Museum
Wood St
John Rylands Library
John Dalton St
Princess St
Gartside St
Spinningfields
Brazennose St
Albert Sq
6
Hardman St
Albert Square
Town Hall
Water St
Quay St
Lloyd St
Great John St
54
St Peter's Square
Granada Studios
9
Lower Byrom St
Byrom St
3
Peter St
1
Longworth St
Deansgate
19
Bootle St
14
To Manchester YHA (160m); Lowry (1mi)
Museum of Science & Industry
Windmill St
8
Air & Space Gallery
Liverpool Rd
45
Great Northern
G-Mex Exhibition Centre
Lower Mosley St
17
15
CASTLEFIELD
11
48
Bridgewater Hall
42
G-Mex
Medlock St
Great Bridgewater St
35
12
Rochdale Canal
37
Castle St
Chester Rd
Deansgate Train Station
Hewitt St
Whitworth St West
30
Cambridge St
Chester St
DEANSGATE LOCKS

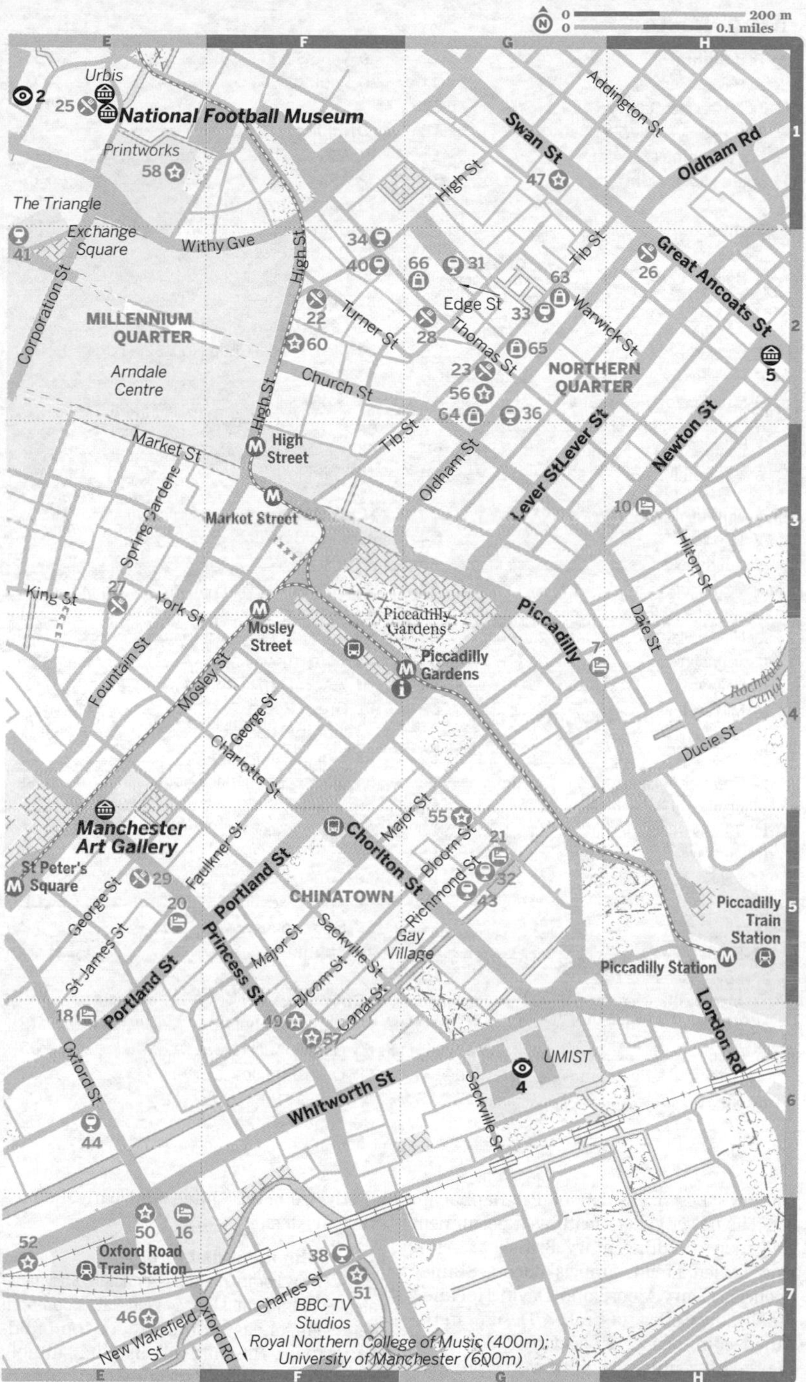
0 200 m
0 0.1 miles
Urbis
National Football Museum
Printworks
The Triangle
Exchange Square
Withy Gve
Corporation St
MILLENNIUM QUARTER
Arndale Centre
High St
Market St
High Street
Market Street
Spring Gardens
King St
York St
Mosley Street
Fountain St
Mosley St
George St
Charlotte St
Piccadilly Gardens
Manchester Art Gallery
St Peter's Square
Faulkner St
Portland St
Chorlton St
CHINATOWN
Princess St
Major St
Sackville St
Bloom St
Canal St
Richmond St
Gay Village
St James St
Oxford St
Whitworth St
UMIST
Sackville St
Oxford Road Train Station
Charles St
BBC TV Studios
New Wakefield St
Oxford Rd
Royal Northern College of Music (400m); University of Manchester (600m)
Swan St
Addington St
Oldham Rd
Turner St
Edge St
Thomas St
Tib St
Warwick St
Great Ancoats St
Church St
NORTHERN QUARTER
Oldham St
Lever St
Newton St
Hilton St
Dale St
Piccadilly
Rochdale Canal
Ducie St
Piccadilly Train Station
Piccadilly Station
London Rd

Manchester

Top Sights

John Rylands Library C4
Manchester Art Gallery E5
Museum of Science & Industry A5
National Football Museum E1
People's History Museum B3

Sights

Beetham Tower .... (see 11)
1 Central Library D5
2 Chetham's Library & School of Music E1
3 Early Years & Play C5
4 Godlee Observatory G6
5 Museum of the Greater Manchester Police H2
Lesbian & Gay Foundation .... (see 49)
6 Town Hall D4

Sleeping

7 ABode G4
8 Castlefield A5
9 Great John Street Hotel A5
10 Hatters H3
11 Hilton Manchester Deansgate B6
12 Jury's Inn D6
13 Lowry B2
14 Midland D5
15 Ox B6
16 Palace Hotel E7
17 Premier Travel Inn D6
18 Premier Travel Inn E6
19 Radisson Edwardian C5
20 Roomzzz E5
21 Velvet Hotel G5

Eating

22 Earth Cafe F2
23 Love Saves the Day G2
24 Mark Addy A3
25 Modern E1
26 Ning H2
River Bar & Restaurant .... (see 13)
27 Rosso E3
28 Trof G2
29 Yang Sing E5
30 Zouk D7

Drinking

31 A Place Called Common G2
32 AXM G5
33 Bar Centro G2
34 Bluu F2
35 Britons Protection C6
36 Dry Bar G2
37 Dukes 92 .... A7
38 Lass O'Gowrie F7
39 Mr Thomas' Chop House D3
40 Odd F2
41 Old Wellington Inn E2
42 Peveril of the Peak D6
43 Taurus G5
44 Temple E6

Entertainment

45 AMC Cinemas C6
46 Attic E7
47 Band on the Wall G1
48 Bridgewater Hall D6
49 Club Alter Ego F6
50 Cornerhouse E7
51 Fac 251: The Factory F7
52 Green Room E7
Library Theatre .... (see 1)
53 Manchester Cathedral D1
54 Manchester Opera House B4
55 Mancunia G5
56 Moho Live G2
57 New Union Hotel F6
58 Odeon Cinema E1
59 Royal Exchange D2
60 Ruby Lounge F2
61 South D3

Shopping

62 Harvey Nichols D2
63 Oi Polloi G2
64 Oxfam Originals G2
65 Rags to Bitches G2
66 Thomas St Post Office G2

country's best collection of Pre-Raphaelite art. The newer gallery features a permanent collection of 20th-century British art starring Lucien Freud, Francis Bacon, Stanley Spencer, Henry Moore and David Hockney. Finally, the Gallery of Craft & Design, in the Athenaeum, houses a permanent collection of pre-17th-century art, with works predominantly from the Dutch and early Renaissance masters.

FREE **John Rylands Library** LIBRARY
(www.library.manchester.ac.uk; 35 Deansgate; 10am-5pm Mon & Wed-Sat, noon-5pm Tue & Sun) An easy candidate for top building in town, this marvellous (and suitably ominous looking) Victorian Gothic library

was one hell of a way for Rylands' widow to remember her husband, John. Less a library and more a cathedral to books, Basil Champneys' stunning building is arguably the most beautiful library in Britain – although there's not much argument when you're standing in the simply exquisite Gothic 'Reading Room', complete with high-vaulted ceilings and stained-glass windows. It's such a breathtaking building that you could easily ignore the magnificent collection of early printed books and rare manuscripts. A £16 million refit has resulted in the addition of a surprisingly tasteful modern annexe with a cafe and a bookshop.

FREE **Museum of the Greater Manchester Police** MUSEUM
(57a Newton St; ⏲10.30am-3.30pm Tue) One of the city's best-kept secrets is this superb museum housed within a former Victorian police station. The original building has been magnificently – if a little creepily – brought back to life, and you can wander in and out of 19th-century cells where prisoners rested their heads on wooden (!!) pillows; visit a restored magistrates' court from 1895; and examine the case histories (complete with mugshots and photos of weapons) of some of the more notorious names to have passed through its doors.

Other city centre highlights:

Town Hall SIGNIFICANT BUILDING
(☎0161-234 5000; www.manchester.gov.uk; Albert Sq; tours adult/child £5/4; ⏲tours 2pm Sat Mar-Sep) The city's main administrative centre is this superb Victorian Gothic building. The interior is rich in sculpture and ornate decoration, while the exterior is crowned by an impressive 85m-high tower.

FREE **Central Library** LIBRARY
(☎0161-234 1900; St Peter's Sq; ⏲10am-8pm Mon-Thu, 10am-6pm Fri & Sat) Just behind the town hall, the elegant Roman Pantheon lookalike was built in 1934. It is the country's largest municipal library, with more than 20 miles of shelves.

SALFORD QUAYS

It seems that no 21st-century urban plan is complete without a docklands development; in Manchester's case, the docks are at the southern end of the Salford Quays, west of the city centre along the Ship Canal. Three major attractions draw in the punters, and a shopping centre makes sure they have outlets at which to spend their money. It's a cinch to get here from the city centre via Metrolink (£2); for the Imperial War Museum North and the Lowry, look for the Harbour City stop; get off at Old Trafford for the eponymous stadium.

FREE **Imperial War Museum North** MUSEUM
(www.iwm.org.uk/north; Trafford Wharf Rd; ⏲10am-6pm) War museums generally appeal to those with a fascination for military hardware and battle strategy (toy soldiers optional), but Daniel Libeskind's visually stunning Imperial War Museum North takes a radically different approach. War is hell, it tells us, but it's a hell we revisit with tragic regularity.

The exhibits cover the main conflicts of the 20th century through a broad selection of displays, but the really effective bit comes every half-hour when the entire exhibition hall goes dark and one of three 15-minute films *(Children and War, The War at Home* or *Weapons of War)* is projected throughout. Visitors are encouraged to walk around the darkened room so as to get the most out of the sensory bombardment.

Although the audiovisuals and displays are quite compelling, the extraordinary aluminium-clad building itself is a huge part of the attraction, and the exhibition spaces are genuinely breathtaking. Libeskind designed three distinct structures (or

WORTH A TRIP

ELIZABETH GASKELL HOUSE

About 3 miles south of the city centre is **Elizabeth Gaskell House** (www.elizabethgaskellhouse.org; 84 Plymouth Grove, Ardwick; admission free; ⏲noon-4pm 1st Sun of month Mar-Dec), a Grade II detached Regency-style villa that was the home of novelist Elizabeth Gaskell, who lived here from 1850 to 1865 (and whose family continued to live here until 1913). It is a rare property: besides its unique literary associations (Charlotte Brontë and Charles Dickens were regular visitors), it is one of the few homes in Manchester whose interior has been carefully maintained and restored to its original elegance. The house has limited opening hours; to get here, take bus 50, 113, 130, 147, 191 or 197 from Piccadilly Gardens, or take the train to Ardwick.

shards) that represent the three main theatres of war: air, land and sea.

FREE **Lowry** ARTS CENTRE
(www.thelowry.com; Pier 8, Salford Quays; ⏲11am-8pm Tue-Fri, 10am-8pm Sat, 11am-6pm Sun & Mon) Looking more like a shiny steel ship than an arts centre, the Lowry is the quays' most notable success. It attracts more than one million visitors a year to its myriad functions, which include everything from art exhibits and performances to bars, restaurants and, inevitably, shops. You can even get married in the place.

The complex is home to more than 300 paintings and drawings by northern England's favourite artist, LS Lowry (1887–1976), who was born in nearby Stretford. He became famous for his humanistic depictions of industrial landscapes and northern towns, and gave his name to the complex.

Old Trafford (Manchester United Museum & Tour) STADIUM
(☎0870 442 1994; www.manutd.com; Sir Matt Busby Way; ⏲9.30am-5pm) Home of the world's most famous club, the Old Trafford stadium is both a theatre and a temple for its millions of fans worldwide, many of whom come in pilgrimage to the ground to pay tribute to the minor deities disguised as highly paid footballers that play there. Ironically, Manchester United are not as popular in Manchester as their cross-town rivals Manchester City, whose fans have traditionally regarded United's enormous wealth and success in strictly Faustian terms. United fans snigger and dismiss this as small-minded jealousy, but they too have become disillusioned with the price of success and during the 2009–10 season protested vehemently against the club's owners, the Glazer family, whom they hold responsible for the club's parlous financial state (see boxed text, p633).

Still, a visit to the stadium is one of the more memorable things you'll do here. We strongly recommend that you take the **tour** (adult/child £12.50/8.50; ⏲every 10min except match days 9.40am-4.30pm), which includes a seat in the stands, a stop in the changing rooms, a peek at the players' lounge (from which the manager is banned unless invited by the players) and a walk down the tunnel to the pitchside dugout, which is as close to ecstasy as many of the club's fans will ever get. It's pretty impressive stuff. The **museum** (adult/child £9/7; ⏲9.30am-5pm), which is part of the tour but can be visited independently, has a comprehensive history of the club, and a state-of-the-art call-up system that means you can view your favourite goals – as well as a holographic 'chat' with Sir Alex Ferguson.

University of Manchester UNIVERSITY
About a mile south of the city, the University of Manchester is one of England's most extraordinary institutions, and not just because it is a top-class university with a remarkable academic pedigree and a great place to party. It is also home to a world-class museum and a superb art gallery. Take bus 11, 16, 41 or 42 from Piccadilly Gardens or bus 47, 190 or 191 from Victoria station.

Manchester Museum
(www.museum.manchester.ac.uk; University of Manchester, Oxford Rd; ⏲10am-5pm Tue-Sat, 11am-4pm Sun & Mon) If you're into natural history and social science, this extraordinary museum is the place for you. It has galleries devoted to archaeology, archery, botany, ethnology, geology, numismatics and zoology. The real treat here, though, is the Egyptology section and its collection of mummies. One particularly interesting part is devoted to the work of Dr Richard Neave, who has rebuilt faces of people who have been dead for more than 3000 years; his pioneering techniques are now used in criminal forensics.

SKY'S THE LIMIT

Maybe it's the vertiginous spiral staircase, but hardly anyone ever visits the fabulous **Godlee Observatory** (☎0161-200 4977; www.manastro.co.uk; ground fl, Sackville Bldg, UMIST, Sackville St; admission free; ⏲by appointment only), one of the most interesting places in town. Built in 1902, it is a fully functioning observatory with its original Grubb telescope in place; even the rope and wheels that move the telescope are original. Not only can you glimpse the heavens (if the weather allows), but the views of the city from the balcony are exceptional. It's located at the University of Manchester Institute of Science and Technology (UMIST).

Alternatively, you'll get great views of the city from the Hilton bar atop the city's tallest skyscraper, the Beetham Tower.

MORE MUSEUMS

If you can't get enough of annotated exhibits, Manchester has a number of other museums worth checking out.

The **Manchester Jewish Museum** (www.manchesterjewishmuseum.com; 190 Cheetham Hill Rd; adult/child £3.95/2.95; ⏲10.30am-4pm Mon-Thu, 1-5pm Sun), in a Moorish-style former synagogue, tells the story of the city's Jewish community in fascinating detail, including the story of Polish refugee Michael Marks, who opened his first shop with partner Tom Spencer at 20 Cheetham Hill Rd in 1894. From Piccadilly Gardens, take bus 59, 89, 135 or 167.

Nearby, the wonderful **Museum of Transport** (www.gmts.co.uk; Boyle St, Cheetham Hill; adult/child £4/free; ⏲10am-4.30pm Wed, Sat & Sun) is packed with old buses, fire engines and lorries (trucks) built in the last 100 years.

FREE **Chetham's Library & School of Music** (☎0161-834 7861; www.chethams.org.uk; Long Millgate; ⏲9am-12.30pm & 1.30-4.30pm Mon-Fri), built in 1421, is the city's oldest structure that's still completely intact – and was where Messrs Marx and Engels used to study (by the big bay window in the main reading room). It is only open by prearranged visit, as it is part of a national school for young musicians.

FREE **Pankhurst Centre** (www.thepankhurstcentre.org.uk; 60-62 Nelson St; ⏲10am-4pm Mon-Fri) is the converted childhood home of Emmeline Pankhurst (1858–1928), a leading light of the British suffragette movement. It has displays on her remarkable life and political struggles. The museum is on Nelson St, which marks the southern boundary of the University of Manchester and the northern side of the Manchester Infirmary.

Immensely popular with plane spotters, the **Runway Visitor Park** (www.manchesterairport.co.uk; Sunbank Lane, Altrincham; admission free, Concorde tour £13; ⏲8am-dusk) is also the only place in Britain where you can climb aboard Concorde (by separate tour) and explore the inside of a DC-10, an Avro RJX-100 (the last civilian airliner built in the UK) and an RAF Nimrod, which was in active service in Afghanistan as recently as 2010. The park is signposted off the A538 between Junction 6 of the M56 and the airport tunnels, but can also be reached via bus transfer from the airport itself.

Whitworth Art Gallery
(www.whitworth.manchester.ac.uk; University of Manchester, Oxford Rd; ⏲10am-5pm Mon-Sat, noon-4pm Sun) Manchester's second most important art gallery has a wonderful collection of British watercolours. It also houses the best selection of historic textiles outside London, and has a number of galleries devoted to the work of artists from Dürer and Rembrandt to Lucien Freud and David Hockney.

All this high art aside, you may find that the most interesting part of the gallery is the group of rooms dedicated to wallpaper – proof that bland pastels and horrible flowery patterns are not the final word in home decoration.

Tours

The tourist office sells tickets for guided walks on all aspects of the city, from architecture to radical history, which operate almost daily year-round and cost £6/5 per adult/child.

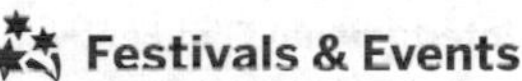

Festivals & Events

Queer Up North LGBT
(www.queerupnorth.com) This biennial festival is the country's biggest gay and lesbian arts festival – the next will be in spring 2011.

FutureEverything CONTEMPORARY ARTS
(www.futureeverything.org) Superb music and media arts festival that takes place in various venues over a week in mid-May.

Manchester Day PARADE
(www.themanchesterdayparade.co.uk) Inaugurated in 2010, a parade to celebrate all things Manchester, with music, performances and fireworks. In June.

Manchester International Festival ARTS
(www.manchesterinternationalfestival.com) With its exciting showcase of only new, commissioned work, this largely musical biennial festival (held in July) is already the city's most popular.

Manchester Jazz Festival MUSIC
(www.manchesterjazz.com) Takes place in 50

GAY & LESBIAN MANCHESTER

The city's gay scene is unrivalled outside London, and caters to every taste. Its healthy heart beats loudest in the Gay Village, centred on handsome Canal St. Here you'll find bars, clubs, restaurants and – crucially – karaoke joints that cater almost exclusively to the pink pound.

The country's biggest gay and lesbian arts festival, **Queer Up North** (☎0161-833 2288; www.queerupnorth.com), takes place every two years – the next in spring 2011. **Manchester Pride** (www.manchesterpride.com) is a 10-day festival from the middle of August each year and attracts more than 500,000 people.

There are bars to suit every taste, but you won't go far wrong in **AXM** (www.axm-bar.co.uk; 10 Canal St), which is more of a cocktail lounge for the city's flash crowd; or **Taurus** (www.taurus-bar.co.uk; 1 Canal St), which is a little shabbier but equally good fun.

For your clubbing needs, look no further than **Club Alter Ego** (www.clubalterego.co.uk; 105-107 Princess St; ⏲11pm-5am Thu-Sat) and **Mancunia** (www.mancuniaclub.co.uk; 8 Minshull St; ⏲11pm-5am Thu-Sat), which is just as popular.

And then there's karaoke, the ultimate choice for midweek fun. The best of the lot is at the **New Union Hotel** (www.newunionhotel.com; 111 Princess St; ⏲9pm-2am), where you can find your inner Madonna and Cyndi Lauper every Tuesday and Thursday – for a top prize of £50.

For more information, check with the **Lesbian & Gay Foundation** (☎0161-235 8035; www.lgf.org.uk; 105-107 Princess St; ⏲4-10pm). The city's best pink website is www.visitgaymanchester.co.uk.

venues throughout the city over the last week in July.

Manchester Pride LGBT
(www.manchesterpride.com) One of England's biggest celebrations of gay, bisexual and transgender life, held in late August.

Manchester International Film Festival FILM
(www.kinofilm.org.uk) A biennial late-October film festival that was launched in 2007.

Sleeping

Manchester's hotels recognise that the business traveller is their best bet, but in keeping with their capital of cool status, they like to throw in more than a bit of style, so you'll find plenty of designer digs around town. The popularity of serviced apartments has spread, offering a little more versatility than the standard hotel room. Remember that during the football season (August to May), rooms can be almost impossible to find if either of the city's football clubs are playing at home (especially United). If you are having difficulty finding a bed, the tourist office's free accommodation service can help.

CITY CENTRE

TOP CHOICE **Velvet Hotel** BOUTIQUE HOTEL ££
(☎0161-236 9003; www.velvetmanchester.com; 2 Canal St; r from £99; 📶) Nineteen beautiful bespoke rooms, each decorated with exquisite taste and style, make this a real contender for best in the city. We ooh'd and aah'd over every element of this gorgeous new hotel – the sleigh bed in Room 24, the double bath of Room 34, the saucy framed photographs of a stripped-down David Beckham (this is Gay Village, after all!) – and were impressed with the DVD library, iPod docking stations in every room and the free wi-fi. Despite the tantalising decor and location, this is not an exclusive hotel and is as popular with straight visitors as it is with the same-sex crowd.

Great John Street Hotel HOTEL £££
(☎0161-831 3211; www.greatjohnstreet.co.uk; Great John St; r £85-345; @📶) Elegant, designer luxury? Present. Fabulous rooms with all the usual delights (Egyptian cotton sheets, fabulous toiletries, free-standing baths and lots of high-tech electronics)? Present. A butler to run your bath in the Opus Grand Suite? Present. This former schoolhouse (ah, now you get it) is small and sumptuous – and just across the street from Granada TV studios. A rare treat: the rooftop garden has a hot tub and views of the *Coronation Street* set. Now that's something you don't see every day.

Roomzzz SERVICED ACCOMMODATION ££
(☎0161-236 2121; www.roomzzz.co.uk; 36 Princess St; r £89-199; @📶) The short-lived Yang

Sing Oriental Hotel was just a little bit too luxurious for the changing times; enter the Roomzzz group who converted this superb hotel in a Grade II building into equally elegant serviced apartments – at a fraction of the price. Every room is equipped with a kitchen (there's a small pantry with food for sale downstairs) and a Mac computer (there's also free wi-fi throughout). Highly recommended if you're planning a longer stay.

Hatters HOSTEL £
(☎0161-236 9500; www.hattersgroup.com; 50 Newton St; dm/s/d/tr from £14.50/27.50/50/67.50; P@wi-fi) The old-style lift and porcelain sinks are the only leftovers of this former milliner's factory, now one of the best hostels in town, with location to boot – smack in the heart of the Northern Quarter, you won't have to go far to get the best of alternative Manchester.

ABode HOTEL ££
(☎0161-247 7744; www.abodehotels.co.uk; 107 Piccadilly St; r from £80; @wi-fi) Modern British style is the catchphrase at this converted textile factory. The original fittings have been combined successfully with 61 bedrooms divided into four categories of ever-increasing luxury: Comfortable, Desirable, Enviable and Fabulous, the latter being five seriously swanky top-floor suites. Vi-Spring beds, Monsoon showers, LCD-screen TVs and stacks of Aqua Sulis toiletries are standard throughout. In the basement, star chef Michael Caines has a champagne and cocktail bar adjacent to his very own restaurant.

Radisson Edwardian HOTEL ££
(☎0161-835 9929; www.radissonedwardian.com/manchester; Peter St; r from £90; P@wi-fi) The Free Trade Hall saw it all, from Emmeline Pankhurst's suffragette campaign to the Sex Pistols' legendary 1976 gig. Today, those rabble-rousing noisemakers wouldn't be allowed to set foot in the door of what is now a sumptuous five-star hotel, all minimalist Zen and luxury. Unless, of course, they were *famous* rabble-rousing noisemakers, and then they would probably be headed straight for one of the four penthouse suites, one of which is named after Bob Dylan, who went electric at the Free Trade Hall in 1965.

Ox B&B ££
(☎0161-839 7740; www.theox.co.uk; 71 Liverpool Rd; d/tr from £49/79; wi-fi) Not quite your traditional B&B (breakfast is extra), but an excellent choice, nonetheless: nine ox-blood-red rooms with tidy amenities above a fine gastropub in the heart of Castlefield. It's the best deal in town for the location.

Manchester YHA HOSTEL £
(☎0845 371 9647; www.yha.org.uk; Potato Wharf; dm incl breakfast from £16; P@wi-fi) This purpose-built canalside hostel in the Castlefield area is one of the best in the country. It's a top-class option with four- and six-bed dorms, all with bathroom, as well as three doubles and a host of good facilities. Potato Wharf is just left off Liverpool Rd.

New Union Hotel HOTEL ££
(☎0161-228 1492; www.newunionhotel.com; 111 Princess St; d/tr/q from £50/60/70) In the heart of the Gay Village but not exclusively pink, this terrific little hotel is all about affordable fun – the rooms are functional, but the karaoke machine downstairs works just fine. Not recommended for a quiet layover.

Palace Hotel BOUTIQUE HOTEL ££
(☎0161-288 1111; www.principal-hotels.com; Oxford St; s/d from £85/105; wi-fi) An elegant refurbishment of one of Manchester's most magnificent Victorian palaces resulted in a special boutique hotel, combining the grandeur of the public areas with the modern look of the bedrooms.

Castlefield HOTEL ££
(☎0161-832 7073; www.castlefield-hotel.co.uk; 3 Liverpool Rd; s/d from £60/90; P wi-fi pool) This is another successful warehouse conversion that has resulted in a thoroughly modern business hotel. Overlooking the canal basin, it has spacious, comfortable rooms and excellent amenities, including a fitness centre and pool that are free to guests.

Hilton Manchester Deansgate HOTEL ££
(☎0161-870 1600; www.hilton.co.uk; Beetham Tower, 303 Deansgate; r from £99; wi-fi) This no-surprises Hilton occupies the lower 23 floors of the city's tallest landmark, the Beetham Tower. The tower is growing on even the most reluctant Mancunians; the hotel has been a hit with the business crowd since the day it opened.

Other options worth considering:

Jury's Inn HOTEL ££
(☎0161-953 8888; www.jurysdoyle.com; 56 Great Bridgewater St; r from £55) Comfortable Irish chain hotel a few doors down from the Bridgewater Hall.

Park Inn Hotel HOTEL ££
(☎0161-832 6565; www.sasparkinn.com; 4 Cheetham Hill Rd; r from £99; wi-fi pool) Spacious, modern rooms (with floor-to-ceiling

windows) in a massive hotel overlooking the MEN Arena; perfect if you're going to a gig. The hotel is about 300m north of Victoria Station along Cheetham Hill Rd.

Premier Travel Inn HOTEL ££
(☎0870 990 6444; www.premiertravelinn.com; r from £60) G-Max (Bishopsgate, 11 Lower Mosley St); Portland St (The Circus, 112 Portland St) Two convenient city-centre locations for this tidy chain.

Midland HOTEL ££
(☎0161-236 3333; www.themidland.co.uk; Peter St; r from £104; @) Mr Rolls and Mr Royce sealed the deal in the elegant lobby of this fancy business hotel.

SALFORD QUAYS

Lowry HOTEL £££
(☎0161-827 4000; www.roccofortecollection.com; 50 Dearman's Pl, Chapel Wharf; r £120-950; P 📶 @) Simply dripping with designer luxury and five-star comfort, Manchester's top hotel (not to be confused with the arts centre in the Salford Quays) has fabulous rooms with enormous beds, ergonomically designed furniture, walk-in wardrobes, and bathrooms finished with Italian porcelain tiles and glass mosaic. You can soothe yourself with a skin-brightening treatment or an aromatherapy head-massage at the health spa.

Old Trafford Lodge HOTEL ££
(☎0161-874 3333; www.lccc.co.uk; Talbot Rd; d Mon-Fri £59, d Sat & Sun £49; @ P 📶) Cricket fans will salivate at the thought of watching a first-class match from the comfort of their bedroom balcony; for the rest of us, this is a pretty good business hotel with decent amenities. Take the Metrolink to Old Trafford.

DIDSBURY

Eleven Didsbury Park HOTEL ££
(☎0161-448 7711; www.elevendidsburypark.com; 11 Didsbury Park, Didsbury; r £99-185; P 📶) Tucked away in fashionably bohemian Didsbury, this utterly wonderful boutique hotel (part of the Eclectic group) is as romantic and stylish a place as you'll find in the city. Avoid, if you can, the smaller doubles. Although it's about 5 miles south of the city centre, it's easily reached by train from Piccadilly (to East Didsbury station) or by buses 43 and 143 from Oxford Rd.

Eating

The choice of restaurants in Manchester is unrivalled outside of London with something for every palate and every budget. There are good restaurants throughout the city, including a superb selection in Chinatown and the organic havens of the Northern Quarter, where you'll also find some excellent veggie spots. If you want to dine like an in-the-know Mancunian, you'll have to go to suburbs such as Didsbury (divided into East and West), about 5 miles south of the city centre. The best way to get there is by buses 43 or 143 from Oxford Rd. Along the way, you'll pass by Rusholme, home to the nationally renowned Curry Mile, on account of the 70 or so Indian and Pakistani restaurants that line Wilmslow Rd. Following is but a small starter course.

CITY CENTRE

Yang Sing CHINESE ££
(☎0161-236 2200; 34 Princess St; mains £9-17) A serious contender for best Chinese restaurant in England, Yang Sing attracts diners from all over with its exceptional Cantonese cuisine. From a dim-sum lunch to a full evening banquet, the food is superb, and the waiters will patiently explain the intricacies of each item to punters who can barely pronounce the dishes' names. Bookings suggested for evening meals.

Earth Cafe VEGETARIAN £
(www.earthcafe.co.uk; 16-20 Turner St; chef's special £3.20; ⏲10am-5pm Tue-Sat) Below the Manchester Buddhist Centre, this gourmet vegetarian cafe's motto is 'right food, right place, right time', which is reflected in its overriding commitment to ensuring that it serves as much local seasonable produce as possible. The result is wonderful: here you'll eat well in the knowledge that you're eating right. The chef's special – a main dish, side and two salad portions – is generally excellent and always filling.

Modern MODERN BRITISH ££
(☎0161-605 8282; Urbis, Cathedral Gardens, Corporation St; 2-/3-course lunch £12/15, dinner mains £11-21) Top fare on top of the world, or an excellent meal atop Manchester's most distinctive landmark, Urbis (soon to be home to the National Football Museum), is one of the city's most enjoyable dining experiences. The food – mostly modern British cuisine – will not disappoint, but being able to sit at a table close to the floor-to-ceiling windows makes this place worthwhile; book a table in advance.

Ning MALAYSIAN ££
(www.ningcatering.com; 92-94 Oldham St; mains £9.50-11.50; dinner Tue-Sun) Head chef Norman Musa has become one of the Northern Quarter's biggest draws, thanks to his exquisite presentations of Malaysian dishes such as *ikan goreng masam manis* (pan-fried sea bass fillets with sweet and sour chilli gravy) and *sambal udang* (prawns with onions and vegetables, coated with spicy chilli gravy) and a handful of Thai selections, all served in a beautiful room that has the informal feeling of a canteen.

Love Saves the Day CAFE £
(0161-832 0777; Tib St; lunch £6-8; 8am-7pm Mon-Wed, to 9pm Thu, to 8pm Fri, 10am-6pm Sat, 10am-4pm Sun) The Northern Quarter's most popular cafe is a New York–style deli, small supermarket and sit-down eatery in one large, airy room. Everybody comes here – from crusties to corporate types – to sit around over a spot of (locally sourced) lunch and discuss the day's goings on. A wonderful spot. The house salad is £5.50.

Rosso ITALIAN ££
(0161-832 1400; www.rossorestaurants.com; 43-45 Spring Gardens; mains £11.95-21.95) A Grade II–listed building with two restored domes, an ornate plaster ceiling, stained glass and polished-marble columns is the setting for this new restaurant owned by Manchester United's Rio Ferdinand (hence the name, Italian for 'red'). Whatever possibilities for hubristic disaster (famous footballer owns fancy restaurant?) are averted by the excellent menu, which features well-made Italian classics, and the all-round top-notch atmosphere, which is classy but unfussy.

Trof CAFE £
(0161-832 1870; 5-8 Thomas St; sandwiches £4, mains £8; breakfast, lunch & dinner) Great music, top staff and a fab selection of sandwiches, roasts and other dishes (the huge breakfast is a proper hangover cure), as well as a broad selection of beers and tunes (Tuesday night is acoustic night), have made this hang-out a firm favourite with students.

Zouk INDIAN ££
(0161-233 1090; www.zoukteabar.co.uk; Unit 5 Quadrangle, Chester St; mains £8-14) Huge, fancy and totally contemporary, this is the best of a new breed of Indian restaurants, dishing out revamped versions of classic dishes to an enthusiastic clientele that are as mindful of their health as they are of a bloody good curry.

SALFORD QUAYS

Mark Addy MODERN BRITISH ££
(0161-832 4080; www.markaddy.co.uk; Stanley St; mains £8.90-12.50; lunch & dinner Wed-Fri, dinner Sat) A contender for best pub grub in town, the Mark Addy owes its culinary success to Robert Owen Brown, whose loving interpretations of standard British classics – pork hop with honey-roasted bramley, pan-friend Dab with cockles and spring onion et al (all locally sourced) – has them queuing at the door for a taste. It recently opened a riverside deck, so you can eat by the river where, during the 19th century, local publican Mark Addy rescued 50 people from drowning.

River Bar & Restaurant MODERN BRITISH £££
(0161-832 1000; www.theriverrestaurant.com; Lowry Hotel, 50 Dearman's Pl, Chapel Wharf; mains £18-39; Mon-Sat) Head chef Oliver Thomas won the 'Taste of Manchester' award in 2010 for his outstanding British cuisine, which emphasises the use of local produce and traditional cooking methods. The result is terrific: how about grilled native lobster with garlic butter and chips, or Welsh Salt Marsh lamb with sweet potato, apricots and sugar-snap peas? Floor-to-ceiling glass panels flood the room with light during the day, and make for romantic evening dining, with the twinkle of the city lights.

DIDSBURY & SOUTHERN SUBURBS

TOP CHOICE **Lime Tree** MODERN BRITISH £££
(0161-445 1217; www.thelimetreerestaurant.co.uk; 8 Lapwing Lane, West Didsbury; mains £15-23; lunch & dinner Tue-Fri & Sun, dinner Mon & Sat) The ambience is refined without being stuffy; the service is relaxed but spot on; and the food is divine – this is as good a restaurant as you'll find anywhere in the northwest. The fillet steak in peppercorn sauce (£21.50) is to die for; the second time we visited we opted for the pan-fried Goosnargh duck with a cranberry and ginger compote (£15.95). We'll be back. And back again.

Cachumba Cafe INTERNATIONAL £
0161-445 2479; www.cachumba.co.uk; 220 Burton Rd; mains £4-9; dinner Tue-Sat) Cachumba does for food what the 'global beats' section in a record shop does for music: it brings together flavours from all over the world (Southeast Asia, India and a selection from Africa) and serves them up in small, tapas-style portions. Friendly, relaxed,

LOCAL KNOWLEDGE

OLIVER THOMAS: CHEF, THE RIVER RESTAURANT

Tell us about the food scene in Manchester.

It's been pretty well established since Marco Pierre White first started this restaurant about 10 years ago.

Secrets to its success?

Manchester's best restaurants are committed to discovering their own locality, and using produce from local farms, especially from the Goosnargh area north of Preston, which is fabulous for all kinds of produce, from cheese to geese.

Where would you go for a good meal?

I'm a big fan of Robert Owen Brown's food at the **Mark Addy** (p643); really good renditions of classic British dishes. I also rate the food in **Harvey Nichols** (p648) and the **Fat Loaf** in Didsbury.

informal and exactly the kind of cafe we like to linger in. Recommended.

Fat Loaf MODERN BRITISH ££
(0161-438 0319; www.thefatloaf.co.uk; 846 Wilmslow Rd; mains £10.95-15.95; lunch & dinner Mon-Sat, noon-7pm Sun) This increasingly popular restaurant is in a Grade II–listed building on Didsbury Green. Dishes are sourced locally (slow braised English lamb shank, roast Gressingham duck) and are done to perfection.

Frankie's Fish Bar MODERN BRITISH £
(0161-445 3300; www.frankiesfishbar.co.uk; 178 Burton Rd; mains £5-9.50; 4.30-9.30pm Mon-Thu, 11.30am-10.30pm Fri & Sat, noon-9.30pm Sun) This is best described as a posh chipper – you can get a take-out (£4.80), but the best way to appreciate the quality in store is to pick from the more extensive eat-in menu, which features a lovely lemon sole and gorgeous homemade fish cakes.

Al Bilal INDIAN ££
(0161-257 0006; 87-81 Wilmslow Rd; mains £7-14; Sun-Fri) It's a given that you cannot leave Manchester without tucking into a curry along Wilmslow Rd, which is as famous as Bradford or Birmingham for its Indian cuisine. There are so many great restaurants to pick from – and some pretty awful ones, too – but Al Bilal's tandoori sizzler will treat you and your tummy right. Like everywhere else along here the service is chaotic and hurried, but what else would you expect?

Drinking

There's every kind of drinking hole in Manchester, from the really grungy ones that smell but have plenty of character to the ones that were designed by a team of architects but have the atmosphere of a freezer. Every neighbourhood in town has its favourites; here's a few to get you going.

Temple BAR
(Great Bridgewater St; noon-midnight Mon-Thu, to 1am Fri & Sat, noon-11pm Sun) This tiny basement bar with a capacity of about 30 has a great jukebox and a fine selection of spirits, all crammed into a converted public toilet. If you want to get up close and personal, this is the perfect spot to do it in. Hardly your bog-standard pub.

Britons Protection PUB
(50 Great Bridgewater St) Whisky – 200 different kinds of it – is the beverage of choice at this liver-threatening, proper English pub that also does Tudor-style meals (boar, venison and the like; mains £8). An old-fashioned boozer with open fires in the back rooms, a cosy atmosphere…perfect on a cold evening.

Bluu BAR
(www.bluu.co.uk; Unit 1, Smithfield Market, Thomas St; noon-midnight Sun-Mon, to 1am Tue-Thu, to 2am Fri & Sat) Our favourite of the Northern Quarter's collection of great bars. Bluu is cool, comfortable and comes with a great terrace on which to enjoy a pint and listen to music selected by folks with really good taste.

Lass O'Gowrie PUB
(36 Charles St) A Victorian classic off Princess St that brews its own beer in the basement. It's a favourite with students, old-timers and a clique of BBC employees who work just across the street in the Beeb's Manchester HQ. It also does good-value bar meals (£6).

A Place Called Common BAR
(www.aplacecalledcommon.co.uk; 39-41 Edge St; ⏲noon-midnight Mon-Wed, to 1am Thu, to 2am Fri & Sat, 2pm-midnight Sun) Common by name but great by nature, this is a terrific boozer favoured by an unpretentious crowd who like the changing artwork on the walls and the DJs who play nightly.

Odd BAR
(www.oddbar.co.uk; 30-32 Thomas St; ⏲11am-11pm Mon-Sat, to 10.30pm Sun) This eclectic little bar – with its oddball furnishings, wacky tunes and anti-establishment crew of customers – is the perfect antidote to the increasingly similar look of so many modern bars. A slice of Mancuniana to be treasured.

Bar Centro BAR
(72-74 Tib St; ⏲noon-midnight Mon-Wed, to 1am Thu, to 2am Fri & Sat, 2pm-midnight Sun) A Northern Quarter stalwart, very popular with the bohemian crowd precisely because it doesn't try to be. Great beer, nice staff and a better-than average bar menu (mains £6 to £9) make this one of the choice spots in the area.

Dry Bar BAR
(28-30 Oldham Rd; ⏲noon-midnight Mon-Wed, noon-2am Thu-Sat, 6pm-midnight Sun) The former HQ of Madchester's maddest protagonists (legend has it Shaun Ryder once pulled a gun on Tony Wilson here), Dry has remained cool long after the scene froze over, and it's still one of the best bars in the Northern Quarter.

Dukes 92 PUB
(www.dukes92.com; 2 Castle St) Castlefield's best pub, housed in converted stables that once belonged to the duke of Bridgewater, has comfy, deep sofas inside and plenty of seating outside, overlooking Lock 92 of the Rochdale Canal – hence the name. If it's sunny, there's no better spot to enjoy a pint of ale.

Other decent boozers:

Mr Thomas' Chop House PUB
(52 Cross St) An old-style boozer that is very popular for a pint as well as for food (mains £10).

Old Wellington Inn PUB
(4 Cathedral Gates) One of the oldest buildings in the city and a lovely spot for a pint of genuine ale.

Peveril of the Peak PUB
(127 Great Bridgewater St) An unpretentious pub with wonderful Victorian glazed tilework outside.

★ Entertainment

Nightclubs

A handy tip: if you want to thrive in Manchester's excellent nightlife, drop all mention of Madchester and keep talk of being 'up for it' to strict irony. Otherwise, you'll risk being labelled a saddo nostalgic or, worse, someone who should have gone home and grown up a decade ago. But fear not: there is still a terrific club scene and Manchester remains at the vanguard of dance-floor culture. There's a constantly changing mixture of club nights, so check the *Manchester Evening News* for details of what's on. Following are our favourite places.

TOP CHOICE **Sankey's** NIGHTCLUB
(www.sankeys.info; Radium St, Ancoats; ⏲10pm-3am Thu & Fri, 10pm-4am Sat) If you're a fan of techno, electro or any kind of non-mainstream house music, then a pilgrimage to Manchester's best nightclub should on no account be missed. Sankey's has earned itself legendary status for being at the vanguard of dance music (Chemical Brothers, Daft Punk and others got their start here) and its commitment to top-class DJs is unwavering: these days, you'll hear the likes of Timo Maas, Seb Leger and Thomas Schumacher mix it up with the absolutely superb residents. Choon! The best way to get here is to board the free Disco Bus that picks up at locations throughout the city from 10.30pm to 2am Friday and Saturday, and between 10.10pm and 1am the rest of the week. See the website for details.

FAC 251: The Factory NIGHTCLUB
(www.factorymanchester.com; 112-118 Princess St; ⏲9.30pm-3am Mon-Sat) Tony Wilson's legendary Factory Records label HQ has been converted into a brand new club and live-music venue part-owned by Peter Hook, ex-bass player of Joy Division and New Order. The club nights have a pretty broad appeal, from Monday's Hit & Run (drum 'n' bass, hip hop and dubstep) to Stoned Love on Saturday, which features the music of the ribald days of the late '80s and early '90s. Ex-Stone Roses bass player Mani is on the decks for Wednesday's Fuel.

South NIGHTCLUB
(4a South King St; ⏲10pm-3am Fri & Sat) An excellent basement club to kick off the weekend: Friday night is CWord with Strangerways, featuring everything from Ibrahim Ferrer to Northern Soul, and

THE MADCHESTER SOUND

It is often claimed that Manchester is the engine room of British pop. If this is indeed the case, then the chief engineer was TV presenter and music impresario Tony Wilson (1950–2007), founder of Factory Records. This is the label that in 1983 released New Order's ground-breaking 'Blue Monday', to this day the best-selling 12in in British history, which successfully fused the guitar-driven sound of punk with a pulsating dance beat.

When the money started pouring in, Wilson took the next, all-important step: he opened his own nightclub that would provide a platform for local bands to perform. The Haçienda opened its doors with plenty of fanfare but just wouldn't take off. Things started to turn around when the club embraced a brand new sound coming out of Chicago and Detroit: house. DJs Mike Pickering, Graeme Park and Jon Da Silva were the music's most important apostles, and when ecstasy hit the scene late in the decade, it seemed that every kid in town was 'mad for it'.

Heavily influenced by these new arrivals, the city's guitar bands took notice and began shaping their sounds to suit the clubbers' needs. The most successful was the Stone Roses, who in 1989 released 'Fools Gold', a pulsating hit with the rapid shuffle of James Brown's 'Funky Drummer' and a druggie guitar sound that drove dancers wild. Around the same time, Happy Mondays, fronted by the laddish Shaun Ryder and the wacked-out Bez (whose only job was to lead the dancing from the stage), hit the scene with the infectious 'Hallelujah'. The other big anthems of the day were 'The One I Love' by the Charlatans, 'Voodoo Ray' by A Guy Called Gerald, and 'Pacific' by 808 State – all local bands and producers. The party known as Madchester was officially opened.

The party ended in 1992. Overdanced and overdrugged, the city woke up with a terrible hangover. The Haçienda went bust, Shaun Ryder's legendary drug intake stymied his musical creativity and the Stone Roses withdrew in a haze of postparty depression. The latter were not to be heard of again until 1994 when they released *Second Coming,* which just couldn't match their eponymous debut album. They lasted another two years before breaking up. The fertile crossover scene, which had seen clubbers go mad at rock gigs, and rock bands play the kind of dance sounds that kept the floor thumping until the early hours, virtually disappeared and the two genres withdrew into a more familiar isolation.

The next five years saw the rise of Manchester's most successful band, Oasis, whose *(What's the Story) Morning Glory* hit the shelves in 1995, selling more copies than all of the Manchester bands that preceded them. Despite their success and the in-your-face posturing of the Gallagher brothers, they were doomed to a limited run because they relied too much on the chord structures and infectious melodic lines created by the Beatles 25 years earlier. They're still going, but their one-time claim of being the most famous band in the world is sadly out of date.

Madchester is legendary precisely because it is no more, but it was exciting. If you missed the party, you can get a terrific sense of what it was like by watching Michael Winterbottom's *24-Hour Party People* (2002), which captures the hedonism, extravagance and genius of Madchester's cast of characters; and the superb *Control* (2007) by Anton Corbijn, which tells the story of Ian Curtis, Joy Division's tragic lead singer.

Saturday is the always excellent Disco Rescue with Clint Boon (once of the Inspiral Carpets), which is more of the same eclectic mix of alternative and dance.

FREE **Attic** NIGHTCLUB
(www.thirstyscholar.co.uk; New Wakefield St; ⌚11pm-2am Thu & Fri, to 3am Sat) This superb venue is at the top of a flight of stairs, in a building beneath a railway arch. Northern Soul nights share space with techno, alt grunge and live-music nights. A student favourite and a great night out.

Cinemas

Cornerhouse ART HOUSE
(www.cornerhouse.org; 70 Oxford St) Your only destination for good art-house

releases; also has a gallery, bookshop and cafe.

Odeon Cinema MULTIPLEX
(www.odeon.co.uk; The Printworks, Exchange Sq) An ultramodern 20-screen complex in the middle of the Printworks centre.

AMC Cinemas MULTIPLEX
(www.amccinemas.co.uk; The Great Northern, 235 Deansgate) A 16-screen multiplex in a retail centre that was formerly a goods warehouse for the Northern Railway Company.

Theatre

Green Room THEATRE
(☎0161-236 1677; 54 Whitworth St W) The premiere fringe venue in town.

Manchester Opera House MUSIC VENUE
(☎0161-242 2509; www.manchestertheatres.co.uk; Quay St) West End shows and lavish musicals make up the bulk of the program.

Library Theatre THEATRE
(☎0161-236 7110; Central Library, St Peter's Sq) Old plays and new work in a small theatre beneath the Central Library.

Royal Exchange THEATRE
(☎0161-833 9833; St Anne's Sq) Interesting contemporary plays are standard at this magnificent, modern theatre-in-the-round.

Live Music

ROCK MUSIC

Band on the Wall BAR
(www.bandonthewall.org; 25 Swan St) A top-notch venue that hosts everything from rock to world music, with splashes of jazz, blues and folk thrown in for good measure.

FAC 251: The Factory NIGHTCLUB
(www.factorymanchester.com; 112-118 Princess St; ⏲9.30pm-3am Mon-Sat) Indie rock is the mainstay of the live-music gigs at the former HQ of the legendary Factory Records. Gigs usually go from 9pm to 10.30pm.

TOP FIVE MANCHESTER ALBUMS

» *Some Friendly* Charlatans

» *Pills 'n' Thrills & Bellyaches* Happy Mondays

» *Stone Roses* The Stone Roses

» *Strangeways Here We Come* The Smiths

» *Permanent* Joy Division

THE FOLK TRAIN

One of the more offbeat ways to enjoy live music is to ride the **Folk Train** (☎0161-244 1880; www.hvhptp.org.uk/folktran.htm; ticket £9; ⏲11.45am Sat Jul-Sep), a one-hour journey between Manchester and Hathersage in the Peak District. On-board entertainment is blues, folk, Irish and old-style country music, played by a rotating list of terrific local bands. There's nothing formal about it: just get on board and enjoy the music. The train departs from Manchester Piccadilly.

MEN Arena VENUE
(Great Ducie St) A giant arena north of the centre that hosts large-scale rock concerts (as well as being the home of the city's ice-hockey and basketball teams). It's about 300m north of Victoria Station.

Moho Live VENUE
(www.moholive.com; 21-31 Oldham St) A new 500-capacity live-music venue that has already proven incredibly popular with its line-up of live music and club nights.

Ruby Lounge BAR
(☎0161-834 1392; 26-28 High St) Terrific live music venue in the Northern Quarter that features mostly rock bands.

CLASSICAL MUSIC

Bridgewater Hall CONCERT HALL
(☎0161-907 9000; www.bridgewater-hall.co.uk; Lower Mosley St) The world-renowned Hallé Orchestra has its home at this enormous and impressive concert hall, which hosts up to 250 concerts and events a year. It has a widespread program that includes opera, folk music, children's shows, comedy and contemporary music.

Lowry THEATRE
(☎0161-876 2000; www.thelowry.com; Pier 8, Salford Quays) The Lowry has two theatres – the 1750-capacity Lyric and 460-capacity Quays – hosting a diverse range of performances, from dance to comedy.

Manchester Cathedral CATHEDRAL
(☎0161-833 2220; www.manchestercathedral.org; Victoria St) Hosts a summer season of concerts by the Cantata Choir and ensemble groups.

Royal Northern College of Music COLLEGE
(☎0161-907 5555; www.rncm.ac.uk; 124 Oxford Rd) Presents a full program of extremely high-quality classical music and other contemporary offerings.

Sport

For most people, Manchester plus sport equals football, and football means Manchester United. This is why United is covered in the Sights & Activities section. Manchester United's reign may be about to end as the scrappy underdog with the big heart that is Manchester City is poised to establish itself as a major presence in world football thanks to the arrival of a consortium of oil-rich sheiks.

Manchester City FOOTBALL
Manchester's best-loved team is the perennial underachiever, Manchester City. But the 2008 takeover of the club by the Abu Dhabi United Group, who proceeded to invest £210 million (and counting) in new players and a new manager (out went scrappy Welshman Mark Hughes, in came suave Italian Roberto Mancini), all with the stated intent of becoming the most successful club in Britain. It won't be easy: despite offering astronomical wages, the club has yet to attract any of the world's truly outstanding players (Brazilian magician Robinho arrived for £32.5 million, stayed a year and then sulked his way out of the club) and its failure to finish in the top four in 2010, thereby guaranteeing all-important Champion's League football in 2010–11, are major setbacks, but the new owners are confident that the future is bright and so keep throwing money into the club. In the meantime, you can enjoy the **Manchester City Experience** (☎0870 062 1894; www.mcfc.co.uk; tours adult/child £7.50/6; ⊙tours 11am, 1.30pm & 3.30pm Mon-Sat, 11.45am, 1.45pm & 3.30pm Sun except match days) – a tour of the ground, dressing rooms and museum before the inevitable steer into the kit shop. Tours must be booked in advance. Take bus 53, 54, 185, 186, 216, 217, 230, 231, 232, 233, 234, 235, 236, 237, X36 or X37 from Piccadilly Gardens.

Lancashire County Cricket Club CRICKET
Cricket is a big deal here, and **Lancashire** (☎0161-282 4000; www.lccc.co.uk; Warwick Rd), founded in 1816 as the Aurora before changing its name in 1864, is one of the most beloved of England's county teams, despite the fact that it hasn't won the county championship since 1934. Matches are played at Old Trafford (same name, different but adjacent ground to the football stadium) and the key fixture in Lancashire's calendar is the Roses match against Yorkshire, but if you're not around for that, the other games in the county season (admission £11 to £17) are a great day out. The season runs throughout the summer. International test matches are also played here occasionally. Take the Metrolink to Old Trafford.

Shopping

The huge selection of shops here will send a shopper's pulse into orbit; every taste and budget is catered for. The huge Millennium Quarter in the heart of the city centre encompasses the newly refurbed Arndale Centre and a host of high-street stores as well the upmarket boutiques of New Cathedral St. Otherwise, King St is full of lovely boutiques, while for all things boho just head to the Northern Quarter.

Oi Polloi BOUTIQUE
(www.oipolloi.com; 70 Tib St) Besides the impressive range of casual footwear, this trendy boutique also stocks a range of designers including APC, Lyle & Scott, Nudie Jeans and Fjallraven.

Thomas St Post Office BOUTIQUE
(www.thomasstpostoffice.com; 61 Thomas St) Carhartt, Edwin, Pointer and Undefeated are just some of the trendy labels represented on the racks of this lovely boutique housed in a converted post office.

Harvey Nichols DEPARTMENT STORE
(21 New Cathedral St) The king of British department stores has an elegant presence on fashionista row. The 2nd-floor **restaurant** (mains £8-16; ⊙lunch daily, dinner Tue-Sat) is excellent and even has a wine list of more than 400 different wines.

Tib Street Market MARKET
(Tib St; ⊙10am-5pm Sat) Up-and-coming local designers get a chance to display their wares at this relatively new weekly market where you can pick up everything from purses to lingerie and hats to jewellery.

Oxfam Originals VINTAGE
(Unit 8, Smithfield Bldg, Oldham St) If you're into retro, this terrific store has high-quality gear from the 1960s and '70s. Shop in the knowledge that it's for a good cause.

Rags to Bitches VINTAGE
(www.rags-to-bitches.co.uk; 60 Tib St) Award-winning vintage boutique with fashions

from the 1930s to the '80s. This is the place to go to pick up unusual, individual pieces or that outfit for the fancy-dress ball.

Cornerhouse BOOKS
(www.cornerhouse.org; 70 Oxford St) Art and film books, specialist magazines and kitschy cards.

Waterstone's BOOKS
(www.waterstones.com) Biggest bookstore in town, with branches on Deansgate and St Anne's Sq.

Information

Emergency

Ambulance (0161-436 3999)

Police station (0161-872 5050; Bootle St)

Rape Crisis Centre (0161-273 4500)

Samaritans (0161-236 8000)

Internet Access

Loops Computer (83 Princess St; per 30min £2; 9am-10pm Mon-Fri, 9am-9pm Sat & Sun)

L2K Internet Gaming Cafe (32 Princess St; per 30min £2; 9am-10pm Mon-Fri, 9am-9pm Sat & Sun)

Internet Resources

Manchester After Dark (www.manchesterad.com) Reviews and descriptions of the best places to be when the sun goes down.

Manchester City Council (www.manchester.gov.uk) The council's official website, which includes a visitors' section.

Manchester Evening News (www.menmedia.co.uk) The city's evening paper in electronic form.

Manchester Online (www.manchesteronline.co.uk) Local online newspaper.

Real Manchester (www.realmanchester.com) Online guide to nightlife.

Restaurants of Manchester (www.restaurantsofmanchester.com) Thorough, reliable and up-to-date reviews of restaurants in the city and suburbs.

Virtual Manchester (www.manchester.com) Restaurants, pubs, clubs and where to sleep.

Visit Manchester (www.visitmanchester.com) The official website for Greater Manchester.

Medical Services

Cameolord Chemist (St Peter's Sq; 10am-10pm)

Manchester Royal Infirmary (Oxford Rd)

Post

Post office (Brazennose St; 9am-5.30pm Mon-Fri)

Tourist Information

Tourist office (www.visitmanchester.com; Piccadilly Plaza, Portland St; 10am-5.15pm Mon-Sat, 10am-4.30pm Sun)

Getting There & Away

Air

Manchester Airport (0161-489 3000; www.manchesterairport.co.uk), south of the city, is the largest airport outside London and is served by 13 locations throughout Britain as well as more than 50 international destinations.

Bus

National Express (www.nationalexpress.com) serves most major cities almost hourly from Chorlton St coach station in the city centre. Sample destinations:

Leeds £8.40, one hour, hourly.

Liverpool £6.30, 1¼ hours, hourly.

London £24.40, 3¾ hours, hourly.

Train

Manchester Piccadilly (east of the Gay Village) is the main station for trains to and from the rest of the country, although Victoria station (north of the National Football Museum) serves Halifax and Bradford. The two stations are linked by Metrolink. Off-peak fares are considerably cheaper.

Blackpool £13.50, 1¼ hours, half-hourly.

Liverpool Lime St £9.80, 45 minutes, half-hourly.

London Euston £131, three hours, seven daily.

Newcastle £51.20, three hours, six daily.

Getting Around

To/From the Airport

The airport is 12 miles south of the city. A train to or from Victoria station costs £2, and a coach is £3. A taxi is nearly four times as much in light traffic.

Public Transport

The excellent public transport system can be used with a variety of **Day Saver tickets** (bus £3.70, train £4, Metrolink £6, bus, train and Metrolink £10). For inquiries about local transport, including night buses, contact **Travelshop** (0161-228 7811; www.gmpte.com; 9 Portland St, Piccadilly Gardens; 8am-8pm).

BUS Centreline bus 4 provides a free service around the heart of Manchester every 10 minutes. Pick up a route map from the tourist office. Most local buses start from Piccadilly Gardens.

METROLINK There are frequent **Metrolink** (www.metrolink.co.uk) trams between Victoria and Piccadilly train stations and G-Mex (for Castlefield) as well as further afield to Salford Quays. Buy your tickets from the platform machine.

TRAIN Castlefield is served by Deansgate station with rail links to Piccadilly, Oxford Rd and Salford stations.

CHESHIRE

Generally overshadowed by the loud, busy conurbations of Liverpool and Manchester, Cheshire gets on with life in a quiet, usually pastoral kind of way, happy enough with its reputation as a contemporary version of ye olde Englande. Fields full of Friesian cows are interspersed with clusters of half-timbered Tudor houses and working farmyards, an idyll that in recent decades has attracted the soccerati millionaires from nearby cities, whose blinged up mansions remain largely unseen behind tall security walls. For the rest of us mere mortals, however, Cheshire is really just about Chester.

Chester

POP 80,130

Marvellous Chester is one of English history's greatest gifts to the contemporary visitor. Its red-sandstone wall, which today gift-wraps a tidy collection of Tudor and Victorian buildings, was built during Roman times. The town was then called Castra Devana, and was the largest Roman fortress in Britain.

It's hard to believe today, but throughout the Middle Ages Chester made its money as the most important port in the northwest. However, the River Dee silted up over time and Chester fell behind Liverpool in importance.

Besides its obvious elegance and grace, Chester ekes out a fairly substantial living as a major retail centre and tourist hot spot: visitors come, see and shop.

Sights & Activities

City Walls ARCHITECTURE

A good way to get a sense of Chester's unique character is to walk the 2-mile circuit along the walls that surround the historic centre. Originally built by the Romans around AD 70, the walls were altered substantially over the following centuries but have retained their current position since around 1200. The tourist office's *Walk Around Chester Walls* leaflet is an excellent guide.

Of the many features along the walls, the most eye-catching is the prominent **Eastgate**, where you can see the most famous **clock** in England after London's Big Ben, built for Queen Victoria's Diamond Jubilee in 1897.

At the southeastern corner of the walls are the **wishing steps**, added in 1785; local legend claims that if you can run up and down these uneven steps while holding your breath your wish will come true. We question the veracity of this claim because our wish was not to twist an ankle.

Just inside Southgate, known here as **Bridgegate** (as it is located at the northern end of the Old Dee Bridge), is the 1664 **Bear & Billet** pub, Chester's oldest timber-framed building and once a tollgate into the city.

Rows ARCHITECTURE

Chester's other great draw is the **Rows**, a series of two-level galleried arcades along the four streets that fan out in each direction from the **Central Cross**. The architecture is a handsome mix of Victorian and Tudor (original and mock) buildings that house a fantastic collection of individually owned shops. The origin of the Rows is a little unclear, but it is believed that as the Roman walls slowly crumbled, medieval traders built their shops against the resulting rubble banks, while later arrivals built theirs on top.

Chester Cathedral CATHEDRAL

(www.chestercathedral.com; Northgate St; adult/child £5/2.50; ⌚9am-5pm Mon-Sat, 1-4pm Sun) Originally a Benedictine abbey built on the remains of an earlier Saxon church dedicated to St Werburgh (the city's patron saint), it was shut down in 1540 as part of Henry VIII's dissolution frenzy but reconsecrated as a cathedral the following year. Although the cathedral itself was given a substantial Victorian facelift, the 12th-century cloister and its surrounding buildings are essentially unaltered and retain much of the structure from the early monastic years. There are 1¼-hour **guided tours** (free; ⌚9.30am-4pm Mon-Sat) to really get to grips with the building and its history.

FREE **Grosvenor Museum** MUSEUM

(www.grosvenormuseum.co.uk; Grosvenor St; ⌚10.30am-5pm Mon-Sat, 2-5pm Sun) Excellent museum with the country's most comprehensive collection of Roman tombstones. At the back of the museum is a preserved Georgian house, complete with kitchen, drawing room, bedroom and bathroom.

Dewa Roman Experience MUSEUM
(www.dewaromanexperience.co.uk; Pierpoint Lane; adult/child £4.95/3.25; ⏲9am-5pm Mon-Sat, 10am-5pm Sun) Walk through a reconstructed Roman street to reveal what Roman life was like. It's just off Bridge St.

FREE **Roman Amphitheatre** RUINS
Just outside the city walls is what was once an arena that seated 7000 spectators (making it the country's largest); now it's little more than steps buried in grass.

St John the Baptist Church CHURCH
(Vicar's Lane; ⏲9.15am-6pm) Built on the site of an older Saxon church in 1075, it's been a peaceful ruin since 1581. It includes the remains of a Norman choir and medieval chapels.

Tours

The tourist office and Chester Visitors' Centre offer a broad range of walking tours departing from both centres. Each tour lasts between 1½ and two hours.

City Sightseeing Chester BUS TOURS
(☎01244-347452; www.city-sightseeing.com; adult/child £8.50/3; ⏲every 15-20min) Offers open-top bus tours of the city, picking up from the tourist office and Chester Visitors' Centre.

Bithell Boats BOAT TOURS
(☎01244-325394; www.chesterboats.co.uk) Runs 30-minute and hour-long cruises up and down the Dee, including a foray into the gorgeous Eaton Estate, home of the duke and duchess of Westminster. All departures are from the riverside along the promenade known as the Groves and cost from £6.50 to £14.

Chester Rows: The Inside Story WALKING TOURS
(adult/child £5/4; ⏲2pm) The fascinating history of Chester's most outstanding architectural feature.

Ghosthunter Trail WALKING TOURS
(adult/child £5/4; ⏲7.30pm Thu-Sat Jul-Oct) The ubiquitous ghost tour, looking for things that go bump in the night.

History Hunter WALKING TOURS
(adult/child £5/4; ⏲10.30am) Two thousand years of Chester history.

Roman Soldier Patrol WALKING TOURS
(adult/child £5/4; ⏲2pm Thu, Fri & Sat, Jul & Aug) Patrol Fortress Deva in the company of Caius Julius Quartus.

Taste of Chester WALKING TOURS
(adult/child £5/4; ⏲2pm Thu & Sat May-Oct) Two thousand years of Chester history and samples of local produce.

Secret Chester WALKING TOURS
(adult/child £5/4; ⏲2pm Tue, Thu, Sat & Sun May-Oct) Exactly what it says on the tin.

Festivals & Events

Chestival ARTS & MUSIC
(www.chesterfestivals.co.uk) A brand new festival to kick off the summer, June sees all kinds of events, from show jumping to bike riding.

Summer Music Festival MUSIC
(www.chesterfestivals.co.uk) A season highlight is this three-week festival (held mid-July to August) featuring performances by all manner of stars both big and small.

Chester Jazz Festival MUSIC
(www.chesterjazz.co.uk; admission free-£12) A two-week showcase of national and international jazz talent held in August/September.

Sleeping

If you're visiting between Easter and September, you'd better book early if you want to avoid going over budget or settling for far less than you bargained for. Except for a handful of options most of the accommodation is outside the city walls but within easy walking distance of the centre. Hoole Rd, just under a mile's walk northeast from the centre and leading beyond the railway tracks to the M53/M56, is lined with budget to midrange B&Bs.

TOP CHOICE **Green Bough** BOUTIQUE HOTEL £££
(☎01244-326241; www.chestergreenboughhotel.co.uk; 60 Hoole Rd; r from £150; P @ ᯤ) The epitome of the boutique hotel, this exclusive, award-winning Victorian town house has individually styled rooms dressed in the best Italian fabrics. The rooms come adorned with wall coverings, superb antique furniture and period cast-iron and wooden beds, including a handful of elegant four-posters. Modern touches include plasma-screen TVs, mini stereos and a range of fancy toiletries.

Chester

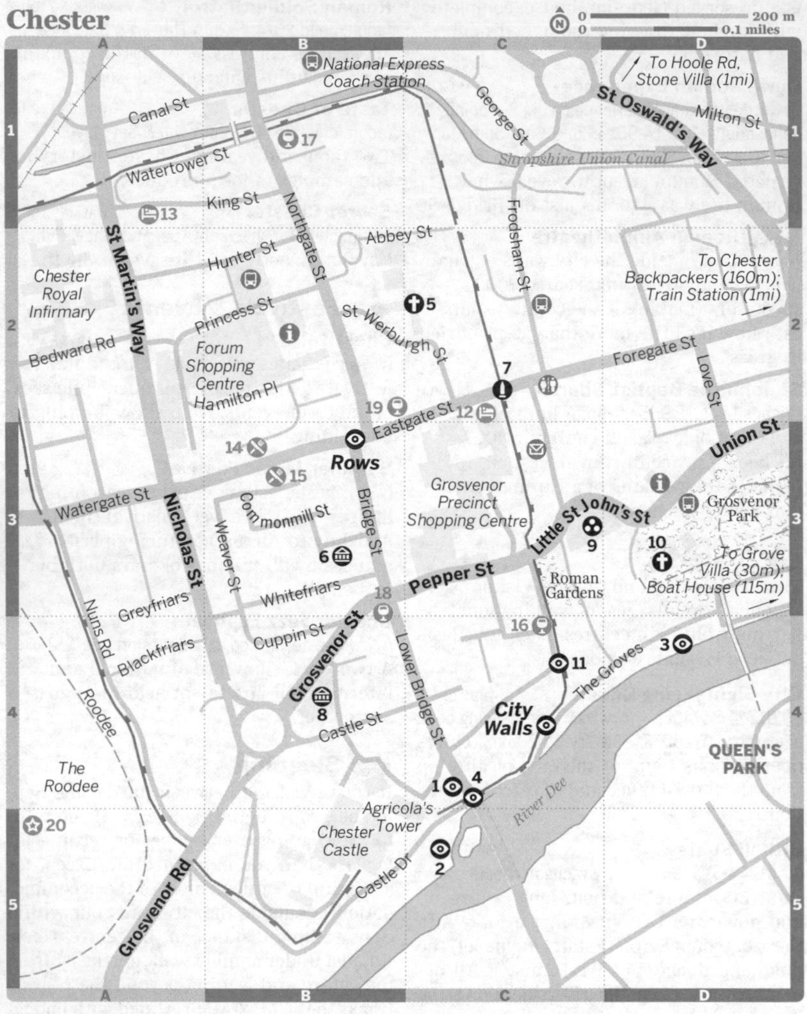

Stone Villa B&B ££

(☎01244-345014; www.stonevillachester.co.uk; 3 Stone Pl, Hoole Rd; s/d from £45/75) Twice winner of Chester's B&B of the Year in the last 10 years, this beautiful villa has everything you need for a memorable stay. Elegant bedrooms (from standard to executive, which have flatscreen TVs), a fabulous breakfast and welcoming, friendly owners all add up to one of the best lodgings in town.

Chester Grosvenor Hotel & Spa HOTEL £££

(☎01244-324024; www.chestergrosvenor.com; 58 Eastgate St; r from £180; P @) This hotel is perfectly located, has huge, sprawling rooms with exquisite period furnishings and all mod cons. The spa (which is open to nonguests) offers a range of body treatments, including reiki, LaStone therapy, Indian head massage and four-handed massage. There's also a Michelin-starred restaurant downstairs.

Chester Backpackers HOSTEL £

(☎01244-400185; www.chesterbackpackers.co.uk; 67 Boughton; dm from £13.50;) Comfortable dorm rooms with nice pine beds in a typically Tudor white-and-black building.

Chester

It's just a short walk from the city walls and there's also a pleasant garden.

Other good options:

Bawn Lodge B&B ££
(☎01244-324971; www.bawnlodge.co.uk; 10 Hoole Rd; r from £75; P 🛜) Spotless rooms with plenty of colour make this charming guesthouse a very pleasant option. Rates go up during the Chester Races.

Chester Townhouse B&B ££
(☎01244-350021; www.chestertownhouse.co.uk; 23 King St; s/d £45/75; P) Five beautifully decorated rooms in a handsome 17th-century house within the city walls make Chester Townhouse a terrific option – you're close to the action and you'll sleep in relative luxury.

Grove Villa B&B ££
(☎01244-349713; www.grovevillachester.com; 18 The Groves; r from £65; P) A wonderfully positioned Victorian home overlooking the Dee. The rooms have antique beds and great river views.

Eating

Chester has great food – it's just not in any of the tourist-oriented restaurants that line the Rows. Besides the better restaurants, you'll find the best grub in some of the pubs (see p654).

Upstairs at the Grill STEAKHOUSE £££
(☎01244-344883; www.upstairsatthegrill.co.uk; 70 Watergate St; mains £15-25; ⊙dinner Mon-Sat, lunch & dinner Sun) A Manhattan-style steakhouse almost hidden on the 2nd floor, this is the place to devour every cut of meat from American-style porterhouse to a sauce-sodden chateaubriand. All of the cuts are locally sourced and dry aged five weeks to guarantee succulence; most cuts are available in 225g or 340g except for the Bone-in Rib Eye, which comes in a daunting 680g, racket-sized hunk of meat.

Simon Radley at the Chester Grosvenor FRENCH £££
(☎01244-895618; www.chestergrosvenor.com; Chester Grosvenor Hotel & Spa, 58 Eastgate St; 3-course à la carte £89; ⊙dinner Tue-Sat) Formerly the Arkle, the hotel opted to rename the Michelin-starred restaurant in recognition of their brilliant head chef, whose French-influenced cuisine continues to earn rave reviews. The menu has some exquisite creations – how about roast cushion of veal sweetbread, lobster knuckles, almond milk and chickpea? – that are complemented by an extraordinary wine list. Needless to say, it's elegant (gentlemen in jackets, please) and bookings are most definitely required.

Katie's Tea Rooms TEAROOM £
(38 Watergate St; tea & scones £4, restaurant 2-course dinner £13; ⊙tearoom 9am-5pm Tue-Sat, restaurant dinner Tue-Sat) This stone-walled tearoom inside an historic building is the place to go for a light lunch. After

5pm it turns into **MD's Restaurant**, a Continental eatery with a pretty tasty menu.

Old Harker's Arms PUB ££

(www.harkersarms-chester.co.uk; 1 Russell St; mains £9-14; ⏲11am-late) An old-style boozer with a gourmet kitchen, this is the perfect place to tuck into Cumberland sausages or a Creole rice salad with sweet potatoes, and then rinse your palate with a pint of local ale, such as Cheshire Cat. It also serves bar snacks and sandwiches. To get here, follow Eastgate St east for 100m and take a left onto Russell St.

Drinking

Albion PUB

(4 Albion St) No children, no music, and no machines or big screens (but plenty of Union Jacks). This 'family hostile' Edwardian classic pub is a throwback to a time when ale-drinking still had its own rituals. Still, this is one of the finest pubs in northwest England precisely because it doggedly refuses to modernise.

Falcon PUB

(Lower Bridge St) This is an old-fashioned boozer with a lovely atmosphere; the surprisingly adventurous menu offers up dishes such as Jamaican peppered beef or spicy Italian sausage casserole. Great for both a pint and a bite (mains from £5.50).

Other good options:

Ye Olde Boot Inn PUB

(Eastgate St) Dating from 1643, it is where 14 Roundheads were killed during the Civil War; these days its known for serving decent ale at rock-bottom prices.

Alexander's BAR

(Rufus Ct; ⏲8pm-2am Mon-Sat, 7.30pm-12.30am Sun) A combination wine bar, coffee bar and tapas bar. It also does live music at night.

Boat House BAR

(The Groves) A nice bar with great views overlooking the river.

Entertainment

Roodee HORSE RACING

(www.chester-races.co.uk; ⏲May-Sep) Chester's ancient and very beautiful racetrack is on the western side of the walls, which has been hosting races since the 16th century. Highlights of the summer flat season include the two-day July Festival and the August equivalent.

Information

Cheshire Constabulary (☎01244-350000; Town Hall, Northgate St)

Chester Visitors' Centre (www.visitchester.com; Vicar's Lane; ⏲9.30am-5.30pm Mon-Sat & 10am-4pm Sun)

Countess of Chester Hospital (☎01244-365000; Health Park, Liverpool Rd)

Post office (2 St John St; ⏲9am-5.30pm Mon-Sat)

Tourist office (www.chester.gov.uk; Town Hall, Northgate St; ⏲9am-5.30pm Mon-Sat & 10am-4pm Sun)

Getting There & Away

Bus

National Express (www.nationalexpress.com) coaches stop on Vicar's Lane, just opposite the tourist office by the Roman amphitheatre. Destinations include the following:

Birmingham £12.40, 2¼ hours, four daily.

Liverpool £7.20, one hour, four daily.

London £24.60, 5½ hours, three daily.

Manchester £6.80, 1¼ hours, three daily.

For information on local bus services, ring the **Cheshire Bus Line** (☎01244-602666). Local buses leave from the Town Hall Bus Exchange on Princess St.

Train

The train station is about a mile from the city centre via Foregate St and City Rd, or Brook St. City-Rail Link buses are free for people with rail tickets, and operate between the station and Bus Stop A on Frodsham St. Destinations:

Liverpool £4.35, 45 minutes, hourly.

London Euston £65.20, 2½ hours, hourly.

Manchester £12.60, one hour, hourly.

Getting Around

Much of the city centre is closed to traffic from 10.30am to 4.30pm, so a car is likely to be a hindrance. Anyway, the city is easy to walk around and most places of interest are close to the wall.

City buses depart from the Town Hall Bus Exchange.

Around Chester

Chester Zoo ZOO

(www.chesterzoo.org; adult/child £16.90/12.45; ⏲10am-dusk, last admission 4pm Mon-Fri, till 5pm Sat & Sun) The largest of its kind in the country, Chester Zoo is about as pleasant a place as caged animals in artificial renditions of their natural habitats could ever expect to live. It's so big that there's even a **monorail** (adult/child £2/1.50) and a **waterbus** (adult/child £2/1.50) on which to get around. The zoo is on the A41, 3 miles north of Chester's city centre. Buses 11C and 12C (every 15 minutes Monday to Saturday, half-hourly Sunday) run between Chester's Town Hall Bus Exchange and the zoo.

Blue Planet Aquarium AQUARIUM
(www.blueplanetaquarium.com; adult/child £14.75/10.75; ⌚10am-5pm Mon-Fri, 10am-6pm Sat & Sun) Things aren't done by halves around Chester: you'll also find the country's largest aquarium, Blue Planet. It's home to 10 different kinds of shark, which are able to be viewed from a 70m-long moving walkway that lets you eye them up close. It's 9 miles north of Chester at junction 10 of the M53 to Liverpool. Buses 1 and 4 run there every half-hour from the Town Hall Bus Exchange in Chester.

Ellesmere Port Boat Museum MUSEUM
(www.nwm.org.uk; South Pier Rd; adult/child £6/4, ⌚10am-5pm) Near the aquarium, on the Shropshire Union Canal about 8 miles north of Chester, is the superb Ellesmere Port Boat Museum, which has a large collection of canal boats as well as indoor exhibits. Take bus 4 from the Town Hall Bus Exchange in Chester, or it's a 10-minute walk from Ellesmere Port train station.

Knutsford

POP 12,660

An increasingly popular commuter town for the Manchester middle classes, Knutsford's appeal is largely the result of the eccentric philanthropy of Richard Watt (1842–1913), a millionaire glove manufacturer whose love of Mediterranean architecture resulted in the commissioning of a group of weird and wonderful buildings that make the town centre one of the most interesting places in Cheshire.

Knutsford's *other* celebrity link is with author Elizabeth Cleghorn Gaskell (1810–65), who used the town as the model for *Cranford* (1853), her most noteworthy novel, which she wrote in her home in the Manchester suburb of Ardwick, which has been converted into a museum (see p637).

Knutsford Heritage Centre (90a King St; admission free; ⌚1.30-4pm Mon-Fri, noon-4pm Sat, 2-4.30pm Sun) is a reconstructed former smithy that has plenty of information on Gaskell, including the *Cranford Walk Around Knutsford*, a leaflet about her local haunts. The most interesting displays, though, are on Watt and his quirky contributions to English architecture.

ROYAL MAY DAY

Since 1864 Knutsford has liked to go a bit wild on Royal May Day. The main festivities take place on the Heath, a large area of common land, and include Morris dancing, brass bands and a pageant of historical characters from fiction and fact. Perhaps the most interesting tradition is that of 'sanding', whereby the streets are covered in colourful messages written in sand. Legend has it that the Danish King Knut, while crossing the marsh between Over and Nether Knutsford, scrawled a message in the sand wishing happiness to a young couple who were on the way to their wedding. The custom is also practised on weddings and feast days.

You can see the best of these along King St, which is a fine example of the splendidly haphazard harmony of English urban architecture. See in particular the **King's Coffee House** (meant to lure the men from the pubs) and the **Ruskin Reading Room** (Drury Lane).

The **Gaskell Memorial Tower** incorporates the swanky **Belle Epoque Brasserie** (☎01565-633060; www.thebelleepoque.com; 60 King St; mains £9-16, s/d £95/110; ⌚Mon-Sat), a fin-de-siècle-style restaurant that Oscar Wilde would look perfectly at home in. Upstairs are seven gorgeous rooms styled in accordance with the overall late-19th-century theme of the building.

Information

Tourist office (Toft Rd; ⌚9am-5pm Mon-Fri, 9am-1pm Sat) In the council offices opposite the train station.

Getting There & Away

Knutsford is 15 miles southwest of Manchester and is on the Manchester–Chester train line (Chester £10, 45 minutes, hourly; Manchester £4.90, 30 minutes, hourly). The train station is on Adams Hill, at the southern end of King St.

Around Knutsford

The northern end of King St marks the entrance to the 400-hectare **Tatton Park** (NT; www.tattonpark.org.uk; admission free, individual attractions adult/child £4.50/2.50; ⏲10am-7pm, last entry 6pm). At the heart is a Regency **mansion** (guided tours £3; ⏲1-5pm Tue-Sun); a wonderful Tudor **Old Hall** that is open only on select days (see the website for details); a 1930s-style **working farm** (⏲noon-5pm Tue-Sun); and a series of superb Victorian **gardens** (⏲10am-6pm Tue-Sun). The **Totally Tatton Ticket** (adult/child £7/3.50) allows you entry to all attractions over two days. Car admission to the park costs £5.

On Sunday bus X2 links Tatton Park with Chester (one hour). At other times you'll need your own wheels.

Nantwich

POP 13,450

If it wasn't for salt, Cheshire's second-best example of black-and-white Tudor architecture might never have been rebuilt after a devastating fire in 1583. The town produced the stuff, and Elizabeth I thought it so important that she interceded and donated £1000 of her (well, England's) money for the reconstruction. The town thanked her for her largesse with a handsome plaque on the appropriately named **Queen's Aid House** (High St), itself a striking Tudor building.

The rest of the largely pedestrianised centre has plenty of fine examples of the black-and-white style, although it's a wonder how so many of them stay standing, such is their off-kilter shape and design.

Very few buildings survived the fire; the most important of those that did is the 14th-century **Church of St Mary** (⏲9am-5pm), a fine example of medieval architecture.

Apart from salt, the town grew up around the production of cheese and leather, and all three are depicted in the **Nantwich Museum** (Pillory St; admission free; ⏲10am-4.30pm Mon-Sat Apr-Sep, Tue-Sat Oct-Mar).

Sleeping & Eating

Crown Hotel HOTEL ££
(☎01565-625283; www.crownhotelnantwich.com; High St; s/d from £40/74) There is barely a straight line in the place, but this gorgeous Tudor half-timbered hotel (part of the Best Western group) is easily top choice in town. The ground-floor **Casa Italiana** (mains £8.25-14.95; ⏲lunch & dinner Mon-Sat, dinner only Sun) is a decent and popular brasserie with an unsurprising but generally tasty selection of Italian dishes.

Pillory House & Coffee Shop TEAROOM £
(18 Pillory St; sandwiches £3.50-5) An old-style tearoom that serves sandwiches and inexpensive hot dishes – perfect for that quick lunch.

Information

Tourist office (Church Walk; ⏲9.30am-5pm Mon-Fri, 10am-4pm Sat, 11am-3pm Sun) Near the main square.

Getting There & Away

The **bus station** (Beam St) is 300m north of the tourist office; Arriva bus 84 serves the town from Chester (£5.40, one hour).

To get to Manchester, Chester or Liverpool by train, you'll have to change in Crewe (15 minutes, half-hourly). The train station is about half a mile south of the centre.

LIVERPOOL

POP 469,020

Beleaguered by a history of hard times and chronic misfortune, Liverpool's luck has changed dramatically in recent years. The city centre, which for decades was an unattractive mix of ugly retail outlets and depressing dereliction, is in the process of being transformed, largely on the back of a substantial program of urban regeneration.

Besides giving us a host of new buildings such as the impressive, ultraswish Liverpool ONE shopping district, the city's rebirth has breathed new life into its magnificent cultural heritage, established more than 200 years ago when the city was a thriving trading port and one of the empire's most important cities. This legacy of power is best exemplified by the magnificent waterfront around Albert Dock, which has more listed buildings than any city in England except London and is now a Unesco World Heritage Site. Now home to some of the best museums and galleries north of the Watford Gap, Albert Dock is proof that Liverpool doesn't want to celebrate its glorious past as much as create an exciting, contemporary equivalent of it.

Whatever the weather, Scousers are one of the city's great constants, and while over-the-top tributes to their great character and legendary sense of humour smack a little of patronising hyperbole, there's little doubt that the city's reputation for merriment is well-deserved.

The main attractions are Albert Dock (west of the city centre), and the trendy Ropewalks area (south of Hanover St and west of the two cathedrals). Lime St station, the Paradise St bus station, the 08 Place tourist office and the Cavern Quarter – a mecca for Beatles fans – lie just to the north.

History

Liverpool grew wealthy on the back of the triangular trading of slaves, raw materials and finished goods. From 1700 ships carried cotton goods and hardware from Liverpool to West Africa, where they were exchanged for slaves, who in turn were carried to the West Indies and Virginia, where they were exchanged for sugar, rum, tobacco and raw cotton.

As a great port, the city drew thousands of Irish and Scottish immigrants, and its Celtic influences are still apparent; however, between 1830 and 1930 nine million emigrants – mainly English, Scots and Irish, but also Swedes, Norwegians and Russian Jews – sailed from here for the New World.

The start of WWII led to a resurgence of Liverpool's importance. More than one million American GIs disembarked here before D-Day and the port was, once again, hugely important as the western gateway for transatlantic supplies. The GIs brought with them the latest American records, and Liverpool was thus the first European port of call for the new rhythm and blues that would eventually become rock and roll. Within 20 years, the Mersey Beat was *the* sound of British pop, and four mop-topped Scousers had formed a skiffle band…

Sights

The wonderful Albert Dock is the city's biggest tourist attraction, and the key to understanding the city's history, but the city centre is where you'll find most of Liverpool's real day-to-day life.

CITY CENTRE

FREE **World Museum Liverpool** MUSEUM
(www.liverpoolmuseums.org.uk/wml; William Brown St; ⌚10am-5pm) Natural history, science and technology are the themes of this sprawling museum, whose exhibits range from birds of prey to space exploration. It also includes the country's only free planetarium. This vastly entertaining and educational museum is divided into four major sections: the Human World, one of the top anthropological collections in the country; the Natural World, which includes a new aquarium as well as live insect colonies; Earth, a geological treasure trove; and Space & Time, which includes the planetarium. Highly recommended.

FREE **Walker Art Gallery** GALLERY
(www.liverpoolmuseums.org.uk/walker; William Brown St; ⌚10am-5pm) Touted as the 'National Gallery of the North', the city's

LIVERPOOL IN...

Two Days

Head to the waterfront and explore the Albert Dock museums – the **Tate Liverpool**, the **Merseyside Maritime Museum** and the unmissable **International Slavery Museum** – before paying tribute to the Fab Four at the **Beatles Story**. Keep to the Beatles theme and head north towards the Cavern Quarter around Mathew St before surrendering to the retail giant that is **Liverpool ONE**, with its hundreds of shops. Round off your evening with dinner at **London Carriage Works** and a pint at the marvellous **Philharmonic**, and wrap yourself in the crisp linen sheets of the **Hope Street Hotel**. Night hawks can tear it up in the bars and clubs of the hip **Ropewalks** area. The next day, explore the city's two **cathedrals** and check out the twin delights of the **World Museum Liverpool** and the **Walker Art Gallery**.

Four Days

Follow the two-day itinerary but add in a **Yellow Duckmarine Tour** to experience the docks from the water. On day three, make a pilgrimage to **Mendips** and **20 Forthlin Rd**, the childhood homes of John Lennon and Paul McCartney respectively. That evening, get some good Italian food at the **Italian Club**. The next day, walk on holy ground at Anfield, home of **Liverpool Football Club**. Race junkies can head to the visitor centre at **Aintree racecourse**, which hosts England's beloved race, the Grand National.

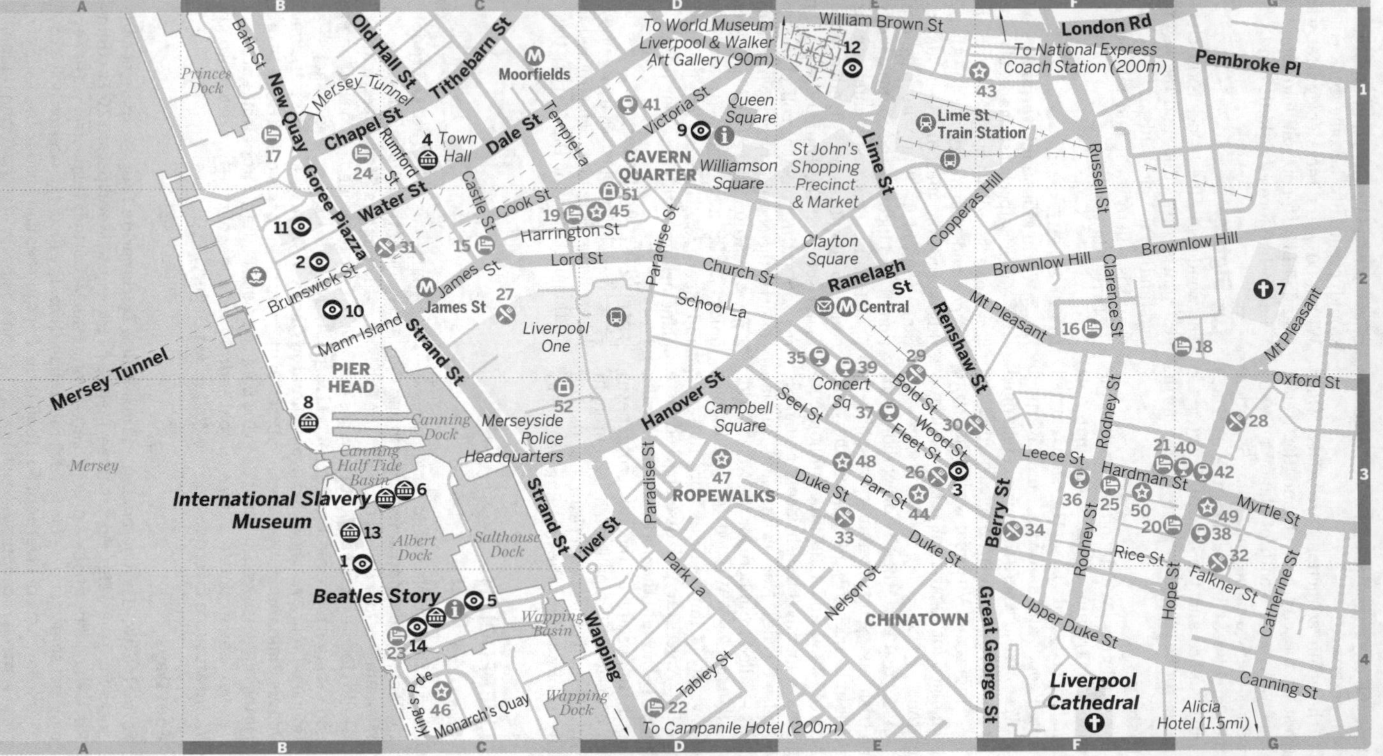
Liverpool
400 m
0.2 miles
Bath St
Princes Dock
New Quay
Mersey Tunnel
Old Hall St
Tithebarn St
Moorfields
To World Museum Liverpool & Walker Art Gallery (90m)
William Brown St
London Rd
To National Express Coach Station (200m)
Pembroke Pl
Chapel St
Rumford St
Town Hall
Dale St
Temple La
Victoria St
Queen Square
Lime St Train Station
Russell St
CAVERN QUARTER
Williamson Square
St John's Shopping Precinct & Market
Lime St
Goree Piazza
Water St
Castle St
Cook St
Harrington St
Paradise St
Copperas Hill
Clayton Square
Brownlow Hill
Brunswick St
Lord St
Church St
Ranelagh St
Clarence St
James St
Central
Mt Pleasant
School La
Mann Island
Liverpool One
Renshaw St
Oxford St
PIER HEAD
Strand St
Concert Sq
Bold St
Seel St
Campbell Square
Wood St
Fleet St
Hanover St
Canning Dock
Merseyside Police Headquarters
Rodney St
Leece St
Hardman St
Canning Half Tide Basin
Mersey
ROPEWALKS
Duke St
Parr St
Myrtle St
International Slavery Museum
Berry St
Albert Dock
Salthouse Dock
Liver St
Rice St
Park La
Falkner St
Hope St
Catherine St
Nelson St
Beatles Story
CHINATOWN
Wapping Basin
Wapping
Upper Duke St
Great George St
King's Pde
Tabley St
Monarch's Quay
Wapping Dock
Liverpool Cathedral
Alicia Hotel (1.5mi)
Canning St
To Campanile Hotel (200m)

Liverpool

Top Sights
Beatles Story C4
International Slavery Museum C3
Liverpool Cathedral F4

Sights
1 Bugworld Experience B3
2 Cunard Building B2
3 FACT E3
4 Liverpool War Museum C1
5 Magical Mystery Tour Bus Stop C4
6 Merseyside Maritime Museum C3
7 Metropolitan Cathedral of Christ the King G2
8 Museum of Liverpool B3
9 National Conservation Centre D1
10 Port of Liverpool Building B2
11 Royal Liver Building B2
12 St George's Hall F1
13 Tate Liverpool B3
14 Yellow Duckmarine Tour Bus Stop C4

Sleeping
15 62 Castle St C2
16 Aachen Hotel F2
17 Crowne Plaza Liverpool B1
18 Feathers Hotel G2
19 Hard Days Night Hotel C2
20 Hope Street Hotel F3
21 International Inn F3
22 Liverpool YHA D4
23 Premier Inn C4
24 Racquet Club B1
25 Roscoe House F3

Eating
26 Alma de Cuba E3
27 Chaophraya C2
28 Everyman Bistro G3
29 Italian Club E2
30 Italian Club Fish E3
London Carriage Works .... (see 20)
31 Meet Argentinean C2
32 Quarter G3
33 Sapporo Teppanyaki E3
34 Tokyou F3

Drinking
35 Bar Ça Va E2
36 Hannah's F3
37 Jacaranda E3
38 Korova G3
39 Lime Kiln (Loyd's Bar) E2
40 Magnet G3
41 Masquerade Bar D1
42 Philharmonic G3

Entertainment
43 Academy F1
44 Masque E3
45 Cavern Club D2
46 ECHO Arena C4
Everyman Theatre .... (see 28)
47 Le Bateau D3
48 Nation E3
49 Philharmonic Hall G3
50 Unity Theatre F3

Shopping
51 Beatles Shop D2
52 Liverpool ONE C3

foremost gallery is the national gallery for northern England, housing an outstanding collection of art from the 14th to the 21st centuries. Its strong suits are Pre-Raphaelite art, modern British art and sculpture – not to mention the rotating exhibits of contemporary expression. It's a family-friendly place, too: the ground-floor Big Art for Little People gallery is designed especially for under-eights and features interactive exhibits and games that will (hopefully) result in a life-long love affair with art.

Liverpool Cathedral CATHEDRAL
(www.liverpoolcathedral.org.uk; Hope St; ⌚8am-6pm) Liverpool's Anglican cathedral is a building of superlatives. Not only is it Britain's largest church; it's also the world's largest Anglican cathedral, and it's all thanks to Sir Giles Gilbert Scott, who made its construction his life's work. Sir Scott also gave us the red telephone box and the Southwark Power Station in London, now the Tate Modern. The central bell is the world's third-largest (with the world's highest and heaviest peal), while the organ, with its 9765 pipes, is likely the world's largest operational model.

The visitor centre features the **Great Space** (adult/child £5/3.50; ⌚9am-4pm Mon-Sat, noon-2.30pm Sun), a 10-minute, panoramic high-definition movie about the history of the cathedral. It's followed by your own audiovisual tour, courtesy of a headset.

Your ticket also gives you access to the cathedral's 101m tower, from which there are terrific views of the city and beyond – on a clear day you can see Blackpool Tower.

FREE **St George's Hall** CULTURAL CENTRE
(www.stgeorgesliverpool.co.uk; William Brown St; ⌚10am-5pm Tue-Sat, 1-5pm Sun) Arguably Liverpool's most impressive building is the Grade I–listed St George's Hall, a magnificent example of neoclassical architecture that is as imposing today as it was when it was completed in 1854. Curiously, it was built as law courts *and* a concert hall – presumably a judge could pass sentence and then relax to a string quartet. Today it serves as an all-purpose cultural and civic centre, hosting concerts, corporate gigs and a host of other civic get-togethers; it is also the focal point of any city-wide celebration. **Tours** (☎0151-225 6909; £3.50; ⌚2pm Wed, 11am & 2pm Sat & Sun) of the hall are run in conjunction with the tourist office; the tour route can vary depending on what's going on in the building.

Metropolitan Cathedral of Christ the King CATHEDRAL
(www.liverpoolmetrocathedral.org.uk; Mt Pleasant; ⌚8am-6pm Mon-Sat, 8am-5pm Sun Oct-Mar) Known colloquially as Paddy's Wigwam, Liverpool's Catholic cathedral is a mightily impressive modern building that looks like a soaring concrete teepee, hence its nickname. It was completed in 1967 according to the design of Sir Frederick Gibberd, and after the original plans by Sir Edwin Lutyens, whose crypt is inside. The central tower frames the world's largest stained-glass window, created by John Piper and Patrick Reyntiens.

Liverpool War Museum MUSEUM
(www.liverpoolwarmuseum.co.uk; 1 Rumford St; adult/child £5.50/3.75; ⌚10.30am-4.30pm Mon-Thu & Sat) The secret command centre for the Battle of the Atlantic, the Western Approaches, was abandoned at the end of the war with virtually everything left intact. You can get a good glimpse of the labyrinthine nerve centre of Allied operations, including the all-important map room, where you can imagine playing a real-life, full-scale version of Risk.

FREE **National Conservation Centre** MUSEUM
(www.liverpoolmuseums.org.uk/conservation; Whitechapel; ⌚10am-5pm) Ever wonder how art actually gets restored? Find out at this terrific conservation centre, housed in a converted railway goods depot. Hand-held audio wands help tell the story, but the real fun is actually attempting a restoration technique with your own hands. Sadly, our trembling paws weren't allowed near anything of value – that was left to the real experts, whose skills are pretty amazing.

FACT GALLERY
(Foundation for Art & Creative Technology; www.fact.co.uk; 88 Wood St; ⌚galleries 11am-6pm Tue & Wed, 11am-8pm Thu-Sat, noon-5pm Sun, cinemas noon-10pm) Proof that Ropewalks isn't all about booze and bars, this media centre is all about film and new media such as digital art. Two galleries feature constantly changing exhibitions and three screens show the latest art-house releases, although we've noticed that the odd mainstream release has crept into the schedule – financial pressures overriding creative intent? There's also a bar and cafe.

ALBERT DOCK

Liverpool's biggest tourist attraction is **Albert Dock** (admission free), 2.75 hectares of water ringed by enormous cast-iron columns and impressive five-storey warehouses; these make up the country's largest collection of protected buildings and are a World Heritage Site. A fabulous development program has really brought the dock to life; here you'll find several outstanding museums and an extension of London's Tate Gallery, as well as a couple of top-class restaurants and bars.

TOP CHOICE **International Slavery Museum** MUSEUM
(www.liverpoolmuseums.org.uk/ism; Albert Dock; admission free; ⌚10am-5pm) Museums are, by their very nature, like a still of the past, but the extraordinary International Slavery Museum resonates very much in the present. It reveals slavery's unimaginable horrors – including Liverpool's own role in the triangular slave trade – in a clear and uncompromising manner. It does this through a remarkable series of multimedia and other displays, and it doesn't baulk at confronting racism, slavery's shadowy ideological justification for this inhumane practice.

The history of slavery is made real through a series of personal experiences, including a carefully kept ship's log and captain's diary. These tell the story of one slaver's experience on a typical trip, departing Liverpool for West Africa. The ship then purchased or captured as many slaves as it could carry before embarking on the gruesome 'middle passage' across the Atlantic to the West Indies. The slaves that survived the torturous journey were sold for sugar, rum and molasses, which were then brought back to England for profit. Exhibits include original shackles, chains and instruments used to punish rebellious slaves – each piece of metal is more horrendous than the next.

It's heady, disturbing stuff, but as well as providing an insightful history lesson, we are reminded of our own obligations to humanity and justice throughout the museum, not least in the Legacies of Slavery exhibit, which explores the continuing fight for freedom and equality. A visit to this magnificent museum is unmissable.

Beatles Story MUSEUM
(www.beatlesstory.com; Albert Dock; adult/child £12.95/6.50; ⏲9am-7pm, last admission 5pm) Liverpool's most popular museum won't illuminate any dark, juicy corners in the turbulent history of the world's most famous foursome – there's ne'er a mention of internal discord, drugs or Yoko Ono – but there's plenty of genuine memorabilia to keep a Beatles fan happy. Particularly impressive is the full-size replica Cavern Club (which was actually tiny) and the Abbey Rd studio where the lads recorded their first singles, while George Harrison's crappy first guitar (now worth half a million quid) should inspire budding, penniless musicians to keep the faith. The museum is also the departure point for the Yellow Duckmarine Tour (see p662).

FREE **Merseyside Maritime Museum** MUSEUM
(www.liverpoolmuseums.org.uk/maritime; Albert Dock; ⏲10am-5pm) The story of one of the world's great ports is the theme of this excellent museum and, believe us, it's a graphic and compelling page-turner. One of the many great exhibits is Emigration to a New World, which tells the story of nine million emigrants and their efforts to get to North America and Australia; the walk-through model of a typical ship shows just how tough conditions on board really were.

FREE **Tate Liverpool** GALLERY
(www.tate.org.uk/liverpool; Albert Dock; special exhibitions adult/child from £5/4; ⏲10am-5.50pm) Touted as the home of modern art in the north, this gallery features a substantial checklist of 20th-century artists across its four floors, as well as touring exhibitions from the mother ship on London's Bankside. But it's all a little sparse, with none of the energy we'd expect from the world-famous Tate.

FREE **Bugworld Experience** MUSEUM
(www.bugworldexperience.co.uk; Grand Hall, Colonnades, Albert Dock; ⏲10am-5pm) Get up close and personal with 36 different species of bug and insect by clambering around six distinctive habitats; see the world from their eyes; and, for an extra special treat, sample some oven-baked tarantula, chilli locusts or a meal worm pancake. This is just part of the fun at this brand new interactive museum, which will surely have the kids pestering you to buy a book on insects and their funny habits when you're done.

NORTH OF ALBERT DOCK

The area to the north of Albert Dock is known as **Pier Head**, after a stone pier built in the 1760s. This is still the departure point for ferries across the River Mersey, and was, for millions of migrants, their final contact with European soil.

Their story – and that of the city in general both past and present – will be told in the eye-catching, giant-X-shaped **Museum of Liverpool** (Mann Island) currently being built on an area known as Mann Island and not slated to open until sometime in 2011. Until then, this part of the dock will continue to be dominated by a trio of Edwardian buildings known as the 'Three Graces', dating from the days when Liverpool's star was still ascending. The southernmost, with the dome mimicking St Paul's Cathedral, is the **Port of Liverpool Building**, completed in 1907. Next to it is the **Cunard Building**, in the style of an Italian palazzo, once HQ to the Cunard Steamship Line. Finally, the **Royal Liver Building** (pronounced *lie*-ver) was opened in 1911 as the head office of the Royal Liver Friendly Society. It's crowned by Liverpool's symbol, the famous 5.5m copper Liver Bird.

☞ Tours

Beatles Fab Four Taxi Tour MUSIC TOURS
(☎0151-601 2111; www.thebeatlesfabfourtaxitour.co.uk; per tour £50) Get your own personalised 2½-hour tour of the city's mop-top landmarks. Pick-ups arranged when booking. Up to five people per tour.

Liverpool Beatles Tour MUSIC TOURS
(☎0151-281 7738; www.beatlestours.co.uk; tours from £45) Your own personalised tour of every bit of Beatles minutiae, from cradle to grave. Tours range from the two-hour Helter Skelter excursion to the all-day

LIVERPOOL FOR CHILDREN

The museums on Albert Dock are extremely popular with kids, especially the brand-new **Bugworld Experience** (p661) and the **Merseyside Maritime Museum** (p661) – which has a couple of boats for kids to mess about on. The **Yellow Duckmarine Tour** (p662) is a sure-fire winner, as is the **National Conservation Centre** (p660), which gets everyone involved in the drama of restoration. The Big Art for Little People gallery at the **Walker Art Gallery** (p657) is perfect for kids who want to find out that art is more than just something adults stare at.

Need a break from the tots? Drop them off at **Zoe's Childminding Service** (☎0151-228 2685; 15 Woodbourne Rd), 2 miles east of the city centre.

There Are Places I Remember, by the end of which, presumably, you'll be convinced you were actually in the band. Pick-ups are arranged upon booking.

Magical Mystery Tour MUSIC TOURS
(☎0151-709 3285; www.beatlestour.org; per person £14.95; ⌚2.30pm year-round, plus noon Sat Jul & Aug) Two-hour tour that takes in all Beatles-related landmarks – their birthplaces, childhood homes, schools and places such as Penny Lane and Strawberry Field – before finishing up in the Cavern Club (which isn't the original). Departs from outside the tourist office at the 08 Place.

River Explorer Cruise WATER TOURS
(☎0151-639 0609; www.merseyferries.co.uk; adult/child return £6.50/4; ⌚hourly 10am-3pm Mon-Fri, 10am-5pm Sat & Sun) Do as Gerry & the Pacemakers wanted and take a ferry 'cross the Mersey, exploring the bay and all its attractions as you go. Departs from Pier Head.

Yellow Duckmarine Tour WATER TOURS
(☎0151-708 7799; www.theyellowduckmarine.co.uk; adult/child £11.95/9.95; ⌚from 11am) Take to the dock waters in a WWII amphibious vehicle after a quickie tour of the city centre's main points of interest. It's not especially educational, but it is a bit of fun. Departs from Albert Dock, near the Beatles Story.

Festivals & Events

Aintree Festival HORSE RACING
(www.aintree.co.uk) A three-day race meeting culminating in the world-famous Grand National steeplechase, held on the first Saturday in April.

Africa Oye MUSIC
(www.africaoye.com) The UK's largest free festival celebrating African music and culture takes place in the suburb of Sefton Park in the second half of June.

Liverpool Comedy Festival COMEDY
(☎0870 787 1866; www.liverpoolcomedyfestival.com) A fortnight of comedy with the best of local and international talent in venues throughout the city. Usually kicks off in mid-July.

Merseyside International Street Festival CULTURE
(www.brouhaha.uk.com) A three-week extravaganza of world culture beginning in mid-July and featuring indoor and outdoor performances by artists and musicians from pretty much everywhere.

Creamfields MUSIC
(www.cream.co.uk) An alfresco dance-fest that brings together some of the world's best DJs and dance acts during the last weekend in August. It takes place at the Daresbury Estate near Halton, Cheshire.

Mathew St Festival MUSIC
(☎0151-239 9091; www.mathewstreetfestival.org) The world's biggest tribute to the Beatles features six days of music, a convention and a memorabilia auction during the last week of August.

Sleeping

There are some pretty fancy pillows upon which to lay your head, from sexy boutique hotels to stylish upmarket properties. For the rest, it's all about standard business hotels and midrange chains. Beds are rarer than hen's teeth when Liverpool FC are playing at home (it's less of an issue with Everton) and during the mobbed out Beatles convention in the last week of August. If you fancy self-catering options, the tourist office has all the information you need.

CITY CENTRE

Hope Street Hotel BOUTIQUE HOTEL £££
(☎0151-709 3000; www.hopestreethotel.co.uk; 40 Hope St; r/ste from £120/180; @📶) Luxurious Liverpool's pre-eminent flag-waver is this stunning boutique hotel, on the city's

most elegant street. King-sized beds draped in Egyptian cotton; oak floors with underfloor heating; LCD wide-screen TVs; and sleek modern bathrooms (with REN bath and beauty products) are but the most obvious touches of class at this supremely cool address. Breakfast, taken in the marvellous London Carriage Works, is not included.

Racquet Club BOUTIQUE HOTEL ££
(☎0151-236 6676; www.racquetclub.org.uk; Hargreaves Bldg, 5 Chapel St; r £110; 📶) Eight individually styled rooms with influences that range from French country house to Japanese minimalist chic (often in the same room) make this boutique hotel one of the most elegant choices in town. Antique beds, sumptuous Frette linen, free-standing baths and exclusive toiletries are all teasers to a pretty classy stay.

International Inn HOSTEL £
(☎0151 709 8135; www.internationalinn.co.uk; 4 South Hunter St; dm/d from £15/36; 📶) A superb converted warehouse in the middle of uni land: heated rooms with tidy wooden beds and bunks accommodate from two to 10 people. Facilities include a lounge, baggage storage, laundry and 24-hour front desk. The staff is terrific and CafeLatte.net internet cafe is next door.

62 Castle St BOUTIQUE HOTEL ££
(☎0151 702 7898; www.62castlest.com; 62 Castle St; r from £79; P@📶) This elegant property – voted one of Britain's top 100 lodgings in 2010 by the *Sunday Times* – successfully blends the traditional Victorian features of the building with a sleek, contemporary style. The 20 fabulously different suites come with HD plasma screen TVs, drench showers and Elemis toiletries as standard.

Hard Days Night Hotel HOTEL £££
(☎0151-236 1964; www.harddaysnighthotel.com; Central Bldgs, North John St; r £110-160, ste £750; @📶) You don't have to be a fan to stay here, but it helps: unquestionably luxurious, the 110 ultramodern, fully equipped rooms are decorated with specially commissioned drawings of the Beatles. And if you opt for one of the suites, named after Lennon and McCartney, you'll get a white baby grand piano in the style of 'Imagine' and a bottle of fancy bubbly on arrival.

Roscoe House BOUTIQUE HOTEL ££
(☎0151-709 0286; www.hotelliverpool.net; 27 Rodney St; r from £50; 📶) A handsome Georgian home once owned by Liverpool-born writer and historian William Roscoe (1753–1831) has been given the once-over and is now a chic boutique hotel. The elegant rooms combine period touches (original coving, fireplaces and furnishings) with contemporary comforts such as flatscreen TVs and fancy Egyptian cotton linen.

Alicia Hotel HOTEL ££
(☎0151-727 4411; www.feathers.uk.com; 3 Aigburth Dr, Sefton Park; r from £84; P📶) Once a wealthy cotton merchant's home, Alicia is a sister hotel to Feathers, but it's a far more handsome place. Most of the rooms have extra luxuries, such as CD players and PlayStations. There's also a nice park on the grounds. The hotel is southeast of the city centre.

Other midrange options in town:

Aachen Hotel HOTEL ££
(☎0151-709 3477; www.aachenhotel.co.uk; 89-91 Mt Pleasant; s/d from £50/70; 📶) A funky listed building with a mix of rooms (some with attached bathroom, some shared). The decor has lots of flower patterns and crazy colour schemes.

Feathers Hotel HOTEL ££
(☎0151-709 9655; www.feathers.uk.com; 119-125 Mt Pleasant; s/d from £52/74) The newly refurbished rooms are well-appointed and all feature nice touches such as full-package satellite TV. The all-you-can-eat buffet breakfast is a welcome morning treat.

AROUND ALBERT DOCK

Crowne Plaza Liverpool HOTEL ££
(☎0151-243 8000; www.cpliverpool.com; St Nicholas Pl, Princes Dock, Pier Head; r from £79; P@📶🏊) The paragon of the modern and luxurious business hotel, the Crowne Plaza has a marvellous waterfront location and plenty of facilities including a health club and swimming pool.

Liverpool YHA HOSTEL £
(☎0845 371 9527; www.yha.org.uk; 25 Tabley St; dm incl breakfast from £16; P📶) It may have the look of an Eastern European apartment complex, but this award-winning hostel, adorned with plenty of Beatles memorabilia, is one of the most comfortable you'll find anywhere in the country. The dorms with attached bathroom even have heated towel rails.

Other dockside options:

Campanile Hotel HOTEL ££
(☎0151-709 8104; www.campanile-liverpool-queens-dock.co.uk; Chaloner St, Queen's Dock;

r from £50; **P** **wi-fi**) Functional, motel-style rooms in a purpose-built hotel. Great location and perfect for families – children under 12 stay for free.

Premier Inn HOTEL ££
(☎0870 990 6432; www.premierinn.co.uk; Albert Dock; r from £49; **P** **wi-fi**) Decent chain hotel about two steps away from the Beatles Story museum on Albert Dock.

Eating

Top grade international cuisine, the best of British and the greasy spoon…you'll find plenty of choices to satisfy every taste. Best spots include Ropewalks, along Hardman St and Hope St or along Nelson St in the heart of Chinatown.

Italian Club ITALIAN £
(85 Bold St; mains £6-10; ⏲10am-7pm Mon-Sat) The Crolla family must have been homesick for southern Italy, so they opened this fabulous spot, adorned it with family pictures and began serving the kind of food relatives visiting from the home country would be glad to tuck into. They've been so successful that they recently opened **Italian Club Fish** (☎0151-707 2110; 128 Bold St; mains £8-14; ⏲Tue-Sun) just down the street, specialising in, erm, fish.

London Carriage Works MODERN BRITISH £££
(☎0151-705 2222; www.thelondoncarriageworks.co.uk; 40 Hope St; 2-/3-course meals £15/20, mains £14-33) Liverpool's dining revolution is being led by Paul Askew's award-winning restaurant, which successfully blends ethnic influences from around the globe with staunch British favourites and serves up the result in a beautiful dining room – actually more of a bright glass box divided only by a series of sculpted glass shards. Reservations are recommended.

Everyman Bistro CAFE £
(☎0151-708 9545; www.everyman.co.uk; 13 Hope St; mains £5-8; ⏲noon-2am Mon-Fri, 11am-2am Sat, 7-10.30pm Sun) Out-of-work actors and other creative types on a budget make this great cafe-restaurant (beneath the Everyman Theatre) their second home – with good reason. Great tucker and a terrific atmosphere.

Alma de Cuba CUBAN £££
(www.alma-de-cuba.com; St Peter's Church, Seel St; mains £16-24) This extraordinary venture has seen the transformation of a Polish church into a Miami-style Cuban extravaganza, a bar and restaurant where you can feast on a suckling pig (the menu heavily favours meat) or clink a perfectly made mojito at the long bar. *¡Salud!*

Meet Argentinean STEAKHOUSE ££
(☎0151-258 1816; www.meetrestaurant.co.uk; 2 Brunswick St; mains £11-26) Liverpool's first Argentine restaurant is really an elegant tribute to grilled beef served the size of a small wheel – just as any self-respecting gaucho would demand. Thankfully, there are some cuts that are smaller but just as good; the 450g grilled fillet steak was plenty for us.

Other dining options:

Sapporo Teppanyaki JAPANESE £££
(☎0151-705 3005; www.sapporo.co.uk; 134 Duke St; teppanyaki sets £25-40, mains £15-25) As good a teppan-yaki (food that is grilled on a hot plate in front of you) experience as you'll have outside of Japan. Also decent sushi and sashimi.

Quarter BISTRO ££
(☎0151-707 1965; 7-11 Falkner St; mains £9-13) A gorgeous little wine bar and bistro with outdoor seating for that elusive summer's day.

Chaophraya THAI ££
(☎0151-707 6323; www.chaophraya.co.uk; Liverpool ONE; mains £9-17; ⏲11am-late) New restaurant on the upper deck of Liverpool ONE has an exhaustive menu of fabulous dishes from the Land of Smiles and a commanding view of the city centre.

Tokyou ASIAN ££
(☎0151-445 1023; 7 Berry St; mains £8-13.95; ⏲dinner) Cheap, healthy Asian cuisine from Japan, China, Taiwan and Korea; whether takeaway or eat-in (at long picnic-style benches), the food is terrific.

Drinking

There's no doubt that Scousers like the odd drink. The first, the fifth, the 11th… health officials may despair, but Liverpool's wealth of pubs and bars of every hue only exist to satisfy a seemingly inexhaustible desire to get loaded, especially in the 'party zone' that is Ropewalks. Unless specified, all the bars included here open 11am until 2am Monday to Saturday, although most have a nominal entry charge after 11pm.

(Continued on page 673)

Iconic England

Tower of London »
The River Thames »
Hadrian's Wall »

» The clock tower of Big Ben (p50) is actually the moniker of its 13-ton bell, named after Benjamin Hall

Tower of London

TACKLING THE TOWER

Although it's usually less busy in the late afternoon, don't leave your assault on the Tower until too late in the day. You could easily spend hours here and not see it all. Start by getting your bearings with the hour-long Yeoman Warder (Beefeater) tours; they're included in the cost of admission, entertaining and the only way to access the Chapel Royal of St Peter ad Vincula **1** which is where they finish up.

When you leave the chapel, the Tower Green scaffold site **2** is directly in front. The building immediately to your left is Waterloo Barracks , where the Crown Jewels **3** are housed. These are the absolute highlight of a Tower visit, so keep an eye on the entrance and pick a time to visit when it looks relatively quiet. Once inside, take things at your own pace. Slow-moving travelators shunt you past the dozen or so crowns that are the treasury's centrepiece, but feel free to double-back for a second or even third pass – particularly if you ended up on the rear travelator the first time around. Allow plenty of time for the White Tower **4**, the core of the whole complex, starting with the exhibition of royal armour. As you continue onto the 2nd floor, keep an eye out for St John's Chapel **5**. The famous ravens **6** can be seen in the courtyard around the White Tower. Head next through the towers that formed the Medieval Palace **7**, then take the East Wall Walk **8** to get a feel for the castle's mighty battlements. Spend the rest of your time poking around the many, many other fascinating nooks and crannies of the Tower complex.

BEAT THE QUEUES

» **Buy** your fast-track ticket in advance online or at the City of London Information Centre in St Paul's Churchyard.

» **Palacepalooza** An annual Historic Royal Palaces membership allows you to jump the queues and visit the Tower (and four other London palaces) as often as you like.

MIKE BOOTH/ALAMY

Chapel Royal of St Peter ad Vincula
The chapel serves as the resting place for the royals and other members of the aristocracy who were executed on the small green out front. Several notable identities are buried under the chapel's altar.

Tower Green scaffold site
Seven people, including three queens (Anne Boleyn, Catherine Howard and Jane Grey), lost their heads here during Tudor times, saving the monarch the embarrassment of the usual public execution on Tower Hill.

Main Entrance

White Tower
Much of the White Tower is taken up with this exhibition of 500 years of royal armour. Look for the virtually cuboid suit made to match Henry VIII's bloated body, complete with an oversized armoured pouch to protect his, ahem, crown jewels.

PAWEL LIBERA IMAGES/ALAMY

St John's Chapel
Kept as plain and unadorned as it would have been in Norman times, the White Tower's 2nd-floor chapel is the oldest surviving church in London, dating from 1080.

TOM HANLEY/ALAMY

Crown Jewels
When they're not being worn for affairs of state, Her Majesty's bling is kept here. Among the 23,578 gems, look out for the 530-carat Cullinan diamond at the top of the Royal Sceptre, the largest part of what was (until 1985) the largest diamond ever found.

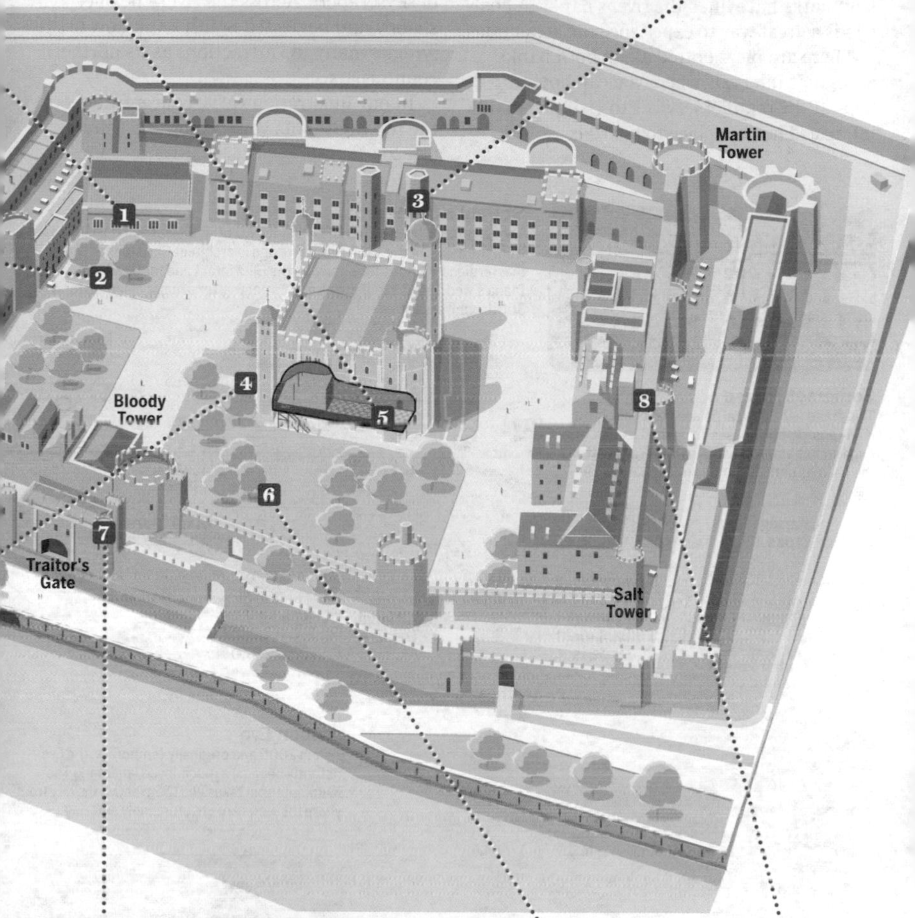

Martin Tower

1

2

3

4

5

6

7

8

Bloody Tower

Traitor's Gate

Salt Tower

Medieval Palace
This part of the Tower complex was commenced around 1220 and was home to England's medieval monarchs. Look for the recreations of the bedchamber of Edward I (1272–1307) in St Thomas's Tower and the throne room on the upper floor of the Wakefield Tower.

ENIGMA/ALAMY

Ravens
This stretch of green is where the Tower's famous ravens are kept, fed on raw meat and blood-soaked bird biscuits. According to legend, if the birds were to leave the Tower, the kingdom would fall.

East Wall Walk
Follow the inner ramparts, starting from the 13th-century Salt Tower, passing through the Broad Arrow and Constable Towers, and ending at the Martin Tower, where the Crown Jewels were once stored.

The River Thames

A FLOATING TOUR

London's history has always been determined by the Thames. The city was founded as a Roman port nearly 2000 years ago and over the centuries since then many of the capital's landmarks have lined the river's banks. A boat trip is a great way to experience the attractions.

There are piers dotted along both banks at regular intervals where you can hop-on/hop-off the regular services to visit places of interest. The best place to board is Westminster Pier, from where boats head downstream, taking you from the City of Westminster, the seat of government, to the original City of London, now the financial district and dominated by a growing band of skyscrapers. Across the river, the once shabby and neglected South Bank now bristles with as many top attractions as its northern counterpart.

In our illustration we've concentrated on the top highlights you'll enjoy at a fish's-eye

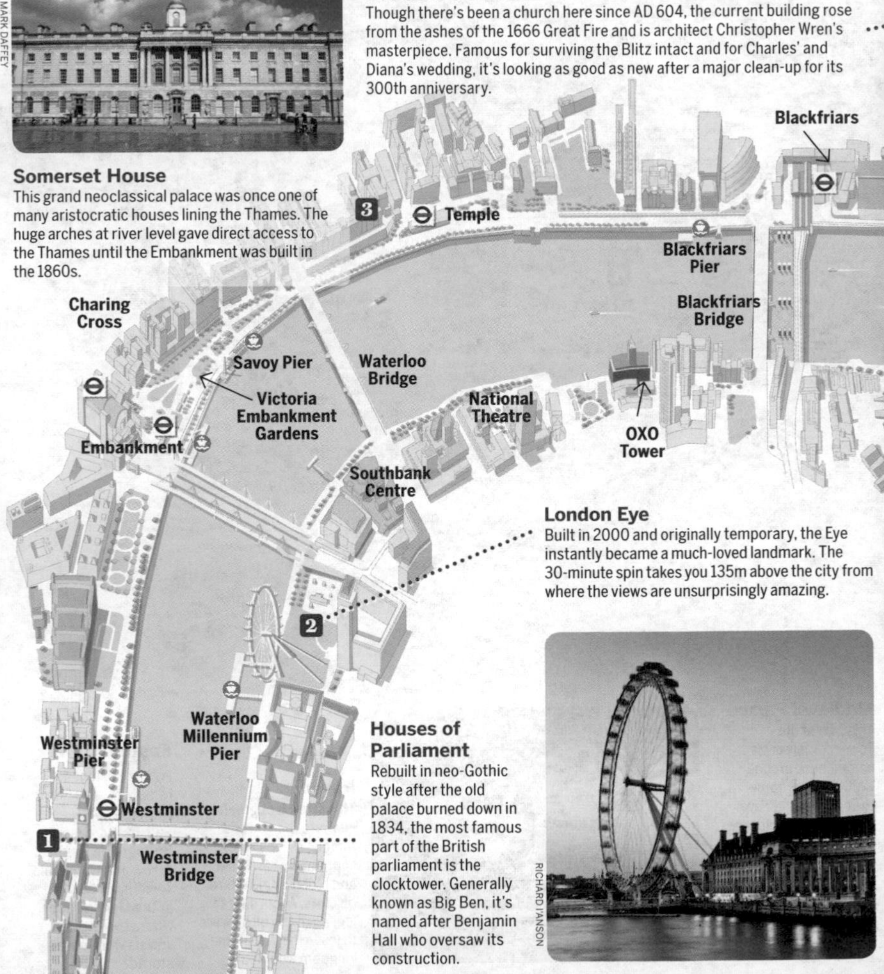

St Paul's Cathedral

Though there's been a church here since AD 604, the current building rose from the ashes of the 1666 Great Fire and is architect Christopher Wren's masterpiece. Famous for surviving the Blitz intact and for Charles' and Diana's wedding, it's looking as good as new after a major clean-up for its 300th anniversary.

Somerset House

This grand neoclassical palace was once one of many aristocratic houses lining the Thames. The huge arches at river level gave direct access to the Thames until the Embankment was built in the 1860s.

London Eye

Built in 2000 and originally temporary, the Eye instantly became a much-loved landmark. The 30-minute spin takes you 135m above the city from where the views are unsurprisingly amazing.

Houses of Parliament

Rebuilt in neo-Gothic style after the old palace burned down in 1834, the most famous part of the British parliament is the clocktower. Generally known as Big Ben, it's named after Benjamin Hall who oversaw its construction.

view as you sail along. These are, from west to east, the Houses of Parliament 1, the London Eye 2, Somerset House 3, St Paul's Cathedral 4, Tate Modern 5, Shakespeare's Globe 6, the Tower of London 7 and Tower Bridge 8.

Apart from covering this central section of the river, boats can also be taken upstream as far as Kew Gardens and Hampton Court Palace, and downstream to Greenwich and the Thames Barrier.

BOAT HOPPING

Thames Clippers hop-on/hop-off services are aimed at commuters but are equally useful for visitors, operating every 15 minutes on a loop from piers at Embankment, Waterloo, Blackfriars, Bankside, London Bridge and the Tower. Other services also go from Westminster. Oyster cardholders get a discount off the boat ticket price.

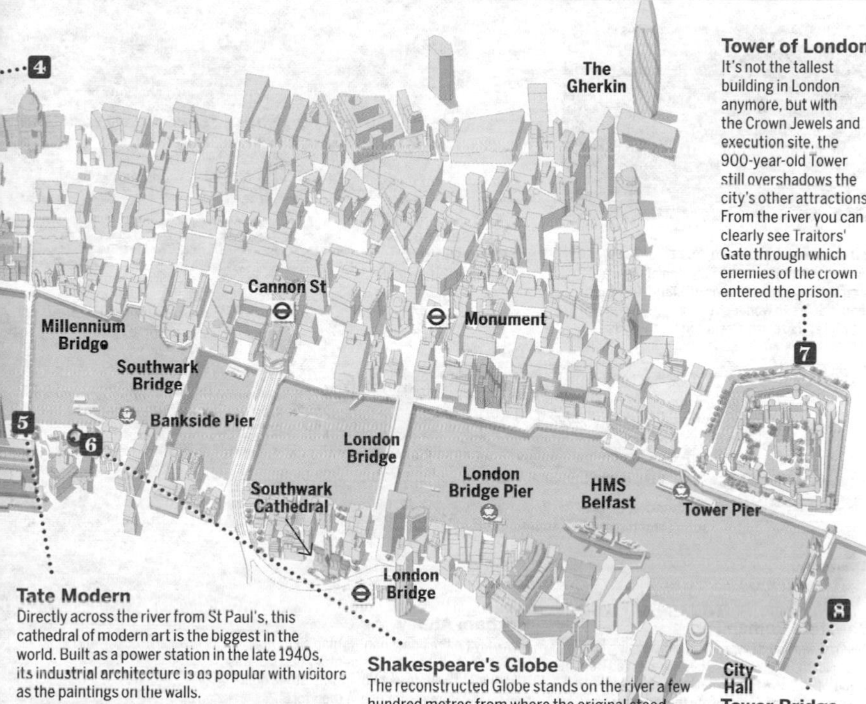

Tower of London

It's not the tallest building in London anymore, but with the Crown Jewels and execution site, the 900-year-old Tower still overshadows the city's other attractions. From the river you can clearly see Traitors' Gate through which enemies of the crown entered the prison.

Tate Modern

Directly across the river from St Paul's, this cathedral of modern art is the biggest in the world. Built as a power station in the late 1940s, its industrial architecture is as popular with visitors as the paintings on the walls.

Shakespeare's Globe

The reconstructed Globe stands on the river a few hundred metres from where the original stood (and burnt down in 1613 during a performance). The life's work of American actor Sam Wanamaker, the theatre runs a hugely popular season from April to October each year.

Tower Bridge

It might look as old as its namesake neighbour but one of the world's most iconic bridges was only completed in 1894. Not to be confused with London Bridge upstream, this one's famous raising bascules allowed tall ships to dock at the old wharves to the west and are still lifted up to 1000 times a year.

DOUG MCKINLAY

DOUG MCKINLAY

Hadrian's Wall

ROME'S FINAL FRONTIER

Of all Britain's Roman ruins, Emperor Hadrian's 2nd-century wall, cutting across northern England from the Irish Sea to the North Sea, is by far the most spectacular; Unesco awarded it world cultural heritage status in 1987.

We've picked out the highlights, one of which is the prime remaining Roman fort on the wall, Housesteads, which we've reconstructed here.

GEOGPHOTOS/ALAMY

Housesteads' granaries
Nothing like the clever underground ventilation system, which kept vital supplies of grain dry in Northumberland's damp and drizzly climate, would be seen again in these parts for 1500 years.

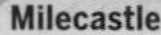

North Gate

JASON SMALLEY/ALAMY

Birdoswald Roman Fort
Explore the longest intact stretch of the wall, scramble over the remains of a large fort then head indoors to wonder at a full-scale model of the wall at its zenith. Great fun for the kids.

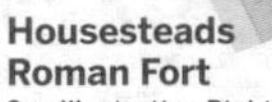

Housesteads Roman Fort
See Illustration Right

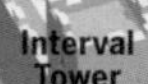

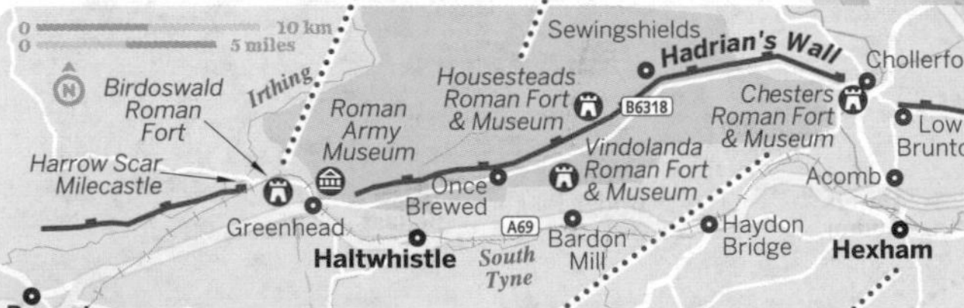

Chesters Roman Fort
Built to keep watch over a bridge spanning the River North Tyne, Britain's best-preserved Roman cavalry fort has a terrific bathhouse, essential if you have months of nippy northern winter ahead.

Hexham Abbey
This may be the finest non-Roman sight near Hadrian's Wall, but the 7th-century parts of this magnificent church were built with stone quarried by the Romans for use in their forts.

Housesteads' hospital
Operations performed at the hospital would have been surprisingly effective, even without anaesthetics; religious rituals and prayers to Aesculapius, the Roman god of healing, were possibly less helpful for a hernia or appendicitis.

NEIL HOLMES/ALAMY

REALIMAGE/ALAMY

GLYN THOMAS/ALAMY

Housesteads' latrines
Communal toilets were the norm in Roman times and Housesteads' are remarkably well preserved – fortunately no traces remain of the vinegar-soaked sponges that were used instead of toilet paper.

QUICK WALL FACTS & FIGURES

» **Latin name** Vallum Aelium
» **Length** 73.5 miles (80 Roman miles)
» **Construction date** AD 122–128
» **Manpower for construction** Three legions (around 16,000 men)
» **Features** at least 16 forts, 80 milecastles, 160 turrets.
» **Did you know** Hadrian's wasn't the only wall in Britain – the Antonine Wall was built across what is now central Scotland in the AD 140s, but it was abandoned soon after

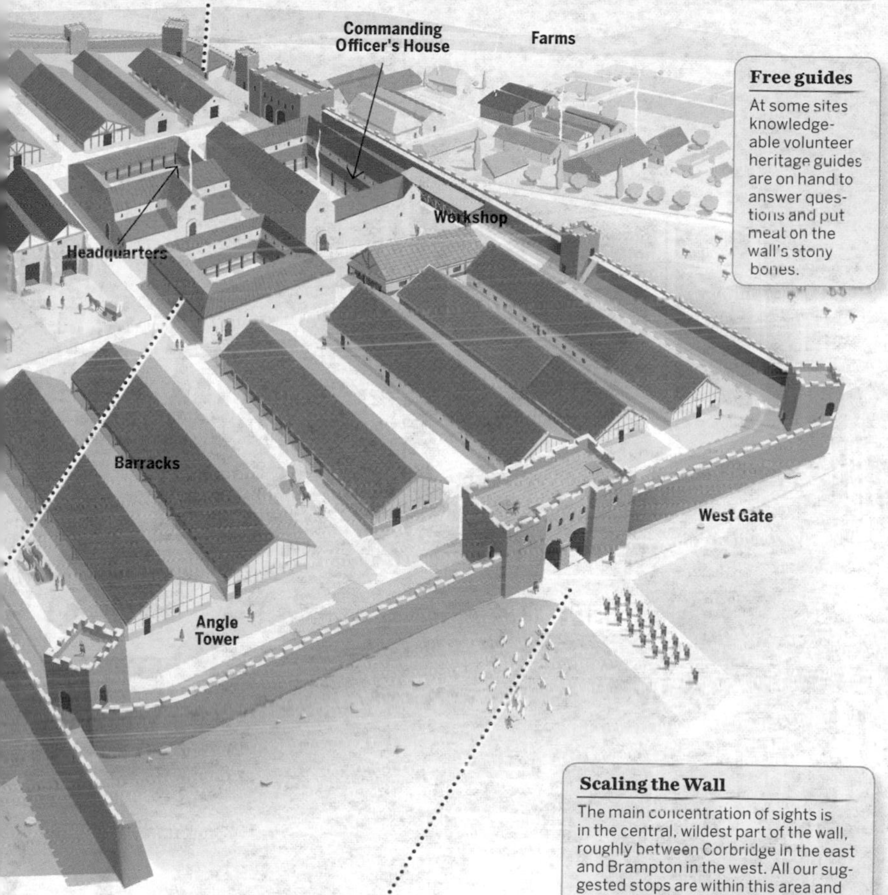

Free guides

At some sites knowledgeable volunteer heritage guides are on hand to answer questions and put meat on the wall's stony bones.

Housesteads' gatehouses
Unusually at Housesteads neither of the gates faces the enemy, as was the norm at a Roman fort – builders aligned them east-west. Ruts worn by cart wheels are still visible in the stone.

Scaling the Wall

The main concentration of sights is in the central, wildest part of the wall, roughly between Corbridge in the east and Brampton in the west. All our suggested stops are within this area and follow an east-west route. The easiest way to travel is by car, scooting along the B6318, but special bus AD122 will also get you there. Hiking along the designated Hadrian's Wall Path (84 miles) allows you to appreciate the achievement up close.

» Trams trundle past the 150m-high Blackpool Tower (p677), built in 1894.

(Continued from page 664)

Magnet DJ BAR
(39 Hardman St; ⏲11am-2am Mon-Sat) Red leather booths, plenty of velvet and a suitably seedy New York–dive atmosphere where Iggy Pop or Tom Waits would feel right at home. The upstairs bar is very cool but totally chilled out, while downstairs the dance floor shakes to the best music in town, spun by up-and-comers and supported with guest slots by some of England's most established DJs.

Philharmonic PUB
(36 Hope St; ⏲11am-11.30pm) This extraordinary bar, designed by the shipwrights who built the *Lusitania,* is one of the most beautiful bars in all of England. The interior is resplendent with etched and stained glass, wrought iron, mosaics and ceramic tiling – and if you think that's good, just wait until you see inside the marble men's toilets, the only heritage-listed lav in the country.

Korova MUSIC BAR
(32 Hope St; ⏲11am-2am Mon-Sat) A new, supercool bar that takes its name from the Russian for 'cow' (fans of *A Clockwork Orange* take note), it is a great place to drink, hang out and hear some decent live music from a range of up-and-coming bands. Very trendy, but not at all stuck up.

Bar Ça Va BAR
(4a Wood St; ⏲11am-2am Mon-Sat) Our favourite of the Ropewalks bars, this place has more of an indie vibe than the others that surround it. You can still get coloured jello shots and cheap bottles of alcopops, but the crowd here is a little more discerning, meaning it takes a lot more booze than usual to start a conga line.

Jacaranda PUB
(21-23 Slater St; ⏲11am-2am Mon-Sat) The Beatles used to play in this cellar bar – the clue is in the murals on the walls (one is apparently the joint efforts of two art students called Stuart Sutcliffe and John Lennon) and the constant playing of their albums – but this is a great, no-nonsense boozer in its own right.

Hannah's BAR
(2 Leece St; ⏲11am-2am Mon-Sat) One of the top student bars in town. Try to land yourself a table on the outdoor patio, which is covered in the event of rain. Staying open late, a friendly, easygoing crowd and some pretty decent music make this one of the better places in which to have a drink.

TOP FIVE PUBS FOR PINT IN THE NORTHWEST

- » Philharmonic (p665; Liverpool)
- » Temple (p644; Manchester)
- » Britons Protection (p644; Manchester)
- » Albion (p654; Chester)
- » Magnet (p673; Liverpool)

Lime Kiln (Lloyd's Bar) BAR
(26 Fleet St; ⏲11am-2am Mon-Sat) It's a chain bar, but it's immensely popular with revellers in Ropewalks, who come for the cheap drinks, charty music and the surprisingly pleasant covered outdoor area where you can smoke and observe the carnage on Concert Sq.

☆ Entertainment

The schedule is pretty full these days, whether it's excellent fringe theatre, a performance by the superb Philharmonic or an all-day rock concert. And then there's the constant backbeat provided by the city's club scene, which pulses and throbs to the wee hours, six nights out of seven. For all information, consult the *Liverpool Echo.*

Nightclubs

Most of the city's clubs are concentrated in Ropewalks, where they compete for customers with a ton of late-night bars; considering the number of punters in the area on a Friday or Saturday night, we're guessing there's plenty of business for everyone.

Masque NIGHTCLUB
(90 Seel St; ⏲11pm-3am Mon-Sat) This converted theatre is home to our favourite club in town. The fortnightly Saturday **Chibuku** (www.chibuku.com) is one of the best club nights in all of England, led by a mix of superb DJs including Yousef (formerly of Cream nightclub) and superstars such as Dmitri from Paris and Gilles Peterson. The music ranges from hip hop to deep house – if you're in town, get in line. Other nights feature a superb mixed bag of music, from trash to techno.

Nation NIGHTCLUB
(40 Slater St, Wolstenholme Sq; ⏲11pm-3am) It looks like an air-raid shelter, but it's the big-name DJs dropping the bombs at the city's premier dance club, formerly the home of

DOING THE BEATLES TO DEATH

They broke up more than 40 years ago. Half the band is no longer alive. Yet the Beatles phenomenon lives on, fuelled by re-releases (the *Beatles Remastered* in 2009 is just the latest) and their hometown's commitment to…er…keeping their memory alive (*and* generating a healthy revenue from Fab Four Tourism).

It doesn't matter that two of them are dead, that the much-visited Cavern Club is a reconstruction of the original club that was the scene of their earliest gigs, or that, if he were alive, John Lennon would have devoted much of his cynical energy to mocking the 'Cavern Quarter' that has grown up around Mathew St. No, it doesn't matter at all, because the phenomenon lives on and a huge chunk of the city's visitors come to visit, see and touch anything – and we mean anything – even vaguely associated with the Beatles.

Which isn't to say that a wander around Mathew St isn't fun: from shucking oysters in the Rubber Soul Oyster Bar to buying a Ringo pillowcase in the From Me to You shop, virtually all of your Beatles needs can be taken care of. For decent memorabilia, check out the **Beatles Shop** (www.thebeatleshop.co.uk; 31 Mathew St).

True fans will undoubtedly want to visit the National Trust–owned **Mendips**, the home where John lived with his Aunt Mimi from 1945 to 1963 (which is also the time period covered by Sam Taylor-Wood's superb 2009 biopic of the young Lennon, *Nowhere Boy*) and **20 Forthlin Road**, the plain terraced home where Paul grew up; you can only do so by prebooked **tour** (☎0151-427 7231; adult/child £16.80/3.15; ⏲10.30am & 11.20am Wed-Sun Easter-Oct) from outside the National Conservation Centre (p660). Visitors to Speke Hall (see p677) can also visit both from there.

If you'd rather do it yourself, the tourist offices stock the *Discover Lennon's Liverpool* guide and map, and *Robin Jones' Beatles Liverpool*.

Cream. These days, it also hosts live bands as well as pumping techno nights.

Le Bateau NIGHTCLUB
(62 Duke St; ⏲11pm-3am Thu-Sat) This oddly named club – there's nothing boatlike about this building – is home to a superb indie club, where 500 punters cram the dance floor and shake it to sounds that have nothing to do with the charts – you'll hear everything from techno to hard rock. Friday night is the excellent Indiecation.

Theatre

Most of Liverpool's theatres feature a mixed bag of revues, musicals and stage successes that are as easy on the eye as they are on the mind, but there is also more interesting work on offer.

Everyman Theatre THEATRE
(☎0151-709 4776; 13 Hope St) This is one of England's most famous repertory theatres, and it's an avid supporter of local talent, which has included the likes of Alan Bleasdale.

Unity Theatre THEATRE
(☎0151-709 4988; Hope Pl) Fringe theatre for those keen on the unusual and challenging. There's also a great bar on the premises.

Music

Philharmonic Hall CLASSICAL MUSIC
(☎0151-709 3789; Hope St) One of Liverpool's most beautiful buildings, the art deco Phil is home to the city's main classical orchestra, but it also stages the work of avant-garde musicians such as John Cage and Nick Cave.

Academy LIVE MUSIC
(Liverpool University, 11-13 Hotham St) Good spot to see midsize bands on tour.

Cavern Club LIVE MUSIC
(8-10 Mathew St) Reconstruction of 'world's most famous club'; good selection of local bands.

ECHO Arena LIVE MUSIC
(☎0844 800 0400; Monarch's Quay) Brand new mega venue that hosts the city's pop shows, from top artists to Broadway extravaganzas.

Sport

Liverpool's two football teams – the reds of Liverpool FC and the blues of Everton – are pretty much the alpha and the omega of sporting interest in the city. There is no other city in England where the fortunes of its home football clubs are so inextricably linked with those of its inhabitants. It's almost easy to forget Liverpool is also home to the Grand National – the world's most famous steeplechase event – which is run on the first weekend in April at Aintree, north of the city.

LIVERPOOL FC

Doff o' the cap to Evertonians and Beatlemaniacs, but no single institution represents the Mersey spirit and strong sense of identity more powerfully than **Liverpool FC** (0151-263 9199, ticket office 220 2345; www.liverpoolfc.tv; Anfield Rd), England's most successful football club. Virtually unbeatable for much of the 1970s and '80s, they haven't won the league championship since 1990, but they did bag the European Champions' League in 2005 for the fifth time under the tenure of Spanish manager Rafael Benitez, who left the club in 2010 after yet another disappointing season.

The fans' disaffection is aimed primarily at George Gillett and Tom Hicks, the US owners who bought the club in 2007 with the promise of a new stadium and plenty of funds to restore the club to its former glories. Neither happened and in 2010 the two owners put the club up for sale: at the time of writing there were no appropriate buyers and the club's fortunes remain unchanged.

But the fans' love of their club remains undiminished, as does their affection for the utterly marvellous **Anfield Road** (0151-260 6677; www.liverpoolfc.tv; Anfield Rd; tour & museum adult/child £14/8, museum only adult/child £6/4; hourly 10am-3pm except match days), where the experience of a live match is one of the sporting highlights of an English visit, especially the sound of 40,000 fans singing the club's anthem, 'You'll Never Walk Alone', before cheering their heroes, which include local lad and Liverpool legend Steven Gerrard. Take bus 26 or 27 from Paradise St Interchange or 17 or 217 from the Queen St Bus Station.

EVERTON FOOTBALL CLUB

Liverpool's 'other' team are the blues of **Everton Football Club** (0151-330 2400, ticket office 330 2300; www.evertonfc.com; Goodison Park), who may not have their rivals' winning pedigree but are just as popular locally.

Tours (0151-330 2277; adult/child £8.50/5; 11am & 2pm Sun-Wed & Fri) of Goodison Park run throughout the year, except on the Friday before home matches. Take bus 19, 20 or 21 from Paradise St Interchange or Queen St Bus Station.

Shopping

In 2008, Liverpool's city centre was transformed by the opening of the simply enormous **Liverpool ONE** (www.liverpool-one.com) shopping district ('centre' just feels too small), 17 hectares of retail and restaurant pleasure between Hanover St to the south, Paradise St to the east, James and Lord Sts to the north and Albert Dock to the west.

For books, there's alwasy the ubiquitous **Waterstone's** (14-16 Bold St).

Information

Emergency

Merseyside police headquarters (0151-709 6010; Canning Pl) Opposite Albert Dock.

Internet Access

CafeLatte.net (4 South Hunter St; per 30min £2; 9am-6pm)

Planet Electra (36 London Rd; per 30min £2; 9am-5pm)

Internet Resources

Clubbing Liverpool (www.clubbingliverpool.co.uk) Everything you need to know about what goes on when the sun goes down.

Itchy Liverpool (www.itchyliverpool.co.uk) Irreverent guide to the city.

Liverpool Magazine (www.liverpool.com) Insiders' guide to the city, including lots of great recommendations for food and nights out.

THE GRAND NATIONAL

The world's most famous steeplechase – and one of England's most cherished events – takes place on the first Saturday in April across 4.5 miles, over the most difficult fences in world racing. Its protagonists are 40 odd veteran stalwarts of the jumps, ageing bruisers full of the oh-so-English qualities of grit and derring-do.

You can book **tickets** (0151-522 2929; www.aintree.co.uk) for the Grand National, or visit the **Grand National Experience** (0151-523 2600; www.aintree.co.uk; adult/child with tour £10/6, without tour £5/4), a visitor centre that includes a race simulator – those jumps are very steep indeed. Redevelopment work on the centre means you have to book the tour in advance – call to make sure.

Mersey Guide (www.merseyguide.co.uk) Guide to the Greater Mersey area.

Tourist office (www.visitliverpool.com)

Medical Services

Mars Pharmacy (68 London Rd) Open until 10pm every night.

Royal Liverpool University Hospital (☎0151-706 2000; Prescot St)

Post

Post office (Ranelagh St; ⊙9am-5.30pm Mon-Sat)

Tourist Information

Liverpool's tourist office has three branches in the city. It also offers an **accommodation hotline** (☎0845 601 1125; ⊙9am-5.30pm Mon-Fri, 10am-4pm Sat).

08 Place tourist office (☎0151-233 2008; Whitechapel; ⊙9am-8pm Mon-Sat, 11am-4pm Sun) The main branch of the tourist office.

Albert Dock tourist office (☎0151-478 4599; ⊙10am-6pm) Two branches: Anchor Courtyard and Merseyside Maritime Museum.

Getting There & Away

Air

Liverpool John Lennon Airport (☎0870 750 8484; www.liverpoolairport.com) serves a variety of international destinations as well as destinations in the UK (Belfast, London and the Isle of Man).

Bus

The **National Express Coach Station** (Norton St) is 300m north of Lime St station. There are services to/from most major towns:

Birmingham £12.40, 2¾ hours, five daily.

London £25.60, five to six hours, six daily.

Manchester £6.30, 1¼ hours, hourly.

Newcastle £21.60, 6½ hours, three daily.

Train

Liverpool's main station is Lime St. It has hourly services to almost everywhere, including the following:

Chester £4.35, 45 minutes.

London Euston £65.20, 3¼ hours.

Manchester £9.80, 45 minutes.

Wigan £5.40, 50 minutes.

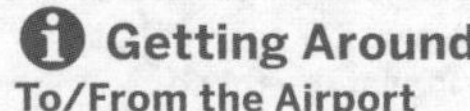

Getting Around

To/From the Airport

The airport is 8 miles south of the centre. **Arriva Airlink** (per person £1.90; ⊙6am-11pm) buses 80A and 180 depart from Paradise St bus station, and **Airportxpress 500** (per person £2.90; ⊙5.15am-12.15am) buses leave from outside Lime St station. Buses from both stations take half an hour and run every 20 minutes. A taxi to the city centre should cost no more than £18.

Boat

The famous cross-Mersey **ferry** (adult/child £1.55/1.25) for Woodside and Seacombe departs from Pier Head Ferry Terminal, next to the Royal Liver Building (to the north of Albert Dock).

Car & Motorcycle

You won't really have much use for a car in Liverpool, and it'll no doubt end up costing you plenty in parking fees. If you have to drive, there are parking meters around the city and a number of open and sheltered car parks. Car break-ins are a significant problem, so leave absolutely nothing of value in the car.

Public Transport

Local public transport is coordinated by **Merseytravel** (www.merseytravel.gov.uk). Highly recommended is the **Saveaway ticket** (adult/child £4.50/2.30), which allows for one day's off-peak (after 9.30am) travel on all bus, train and ferry services throughout Merseyside. Tickets are available at shops and post offices throughout the city. Paradise St bus station is in the city centre.

TRAIN **Merseyrail** (www.merseyrail.org) is an extensive suburban rail service linking Liverpool with the Greater Merseyside area. There are four stops in the city centre: Lime St, Central (handy for Ropewalks), James St (close to Albert Dock) and Moorfields (for the Liverpool War Museum).

Taxi

Mersey Cabs (☎0151-298 2222) operates tourist taxi services and also has some wheelchair-accessible cabs.

AROUND LIVERPOOL

Port Sunlight

Southwest of Liverpool, across the River Mersey on the Wirral Peninsula, picturesque Port Sunlight is a 19th-century village created by the philanthropic Lever family to house workers from their soap factory. The main reason to come here is the wonderful **Lady Lever Art Gallery** (www.liverpoolmuseums.org.uk/ladylever; admission free; ⊙10am-5pm), off Greendale Rd, where you can see some of the greatest works of the Pre-Raphaelite Brotherhood, as well as some fine Wedgwood pottery.

Take the Merseyrail to Bebington on the Wirral line; the gallery is a five-minute walk from the station. Alternatively, bus 51 from Woodside will get you here.

Speke

A marvellous example of a black-and-white half-timbered hall can be visited at **Speke Hall** (NT; www.nationaltrust.org.uk; house & gardens adult/child £8.40/4.20, gardens only adult/child £5/2.60; ⏲11am-5.30pm Wed-Sun), 6 miles south of Liverpool in the plain suburb of Speke. It contains several priests' holes where 16th-century Roman Catholic priests could hide when they were forbidden to hold Masses. Any airport bus from Paradise St will drop you within a half-mile of the entrance. Speke Hall can also be combined with a National Trust 1½-hour **tour** (☎0151-486 4006; with Speke Hall adult/child £16.80/3.15) to the childhood homes of both Lennon and McCartney (see the boxed text, p674) – you can book at Speke Hall or at the tourist offices in Liverpool.

LANCASHIRE

As isolated as it is industrious, not all of Lancashire is an endless stretch of urban jungle. Its southern half has its fair share of concrete – no part of England is so heavily urbanised – and it includes both Liverpool and Manchester, who are so big that they've been administered separately since 1974. But as you travel north, beyond Blackpool – the belle of the beach holiday – you'll arrive at the undulating folds of the Ribble Valley, a gentle warm-up for the Lake District that lies just beyond Lancashire's northern border. North of the Ribble Valley is the county's handsome Georgian capital, Lancaster.

Blackpool

POP 142,290

The queen bee of England's fun-by-the-sea-type resorts is unquestionably Blackpool. It's bold and brazen in its efforts to cement its position as the country's second-most-visited town after London. Tacky, trashy and, in recent years, just a little bit tawdry, Blackpool doesn't care because 16 million annual visitors don't either.

Blackpool works so well because it has mastered the time-tested, traditional British holiday-by-the-sea formula with high-tech, 21st-century amusements that thrill even the most cynical observer. Basically, a holiday here is all about pure, unadulterated fun.

The town is famous for its tower, its three piers, its Pleasure Beach and its Illuminations, the latter being a successful ploy to extend the brief summer holiday season. From early September to early November, 5 miles of the Promenade are illuminated with thousands of electric and neon lights.

Sights

Pleasure Beach AMUSEMENT PARK
(www.blackpoolpleasurebeach.com; Central Promenade; Pleasure Beach Pass £5; ⏲from 10am Feb-Oct, Sat & Sun only Nov) The main reason for Blackpool's immense popularity is the Pleasure Beach, a 16-hectare collection of more than 145 rides that attracts some seven million visitors annually, and, as amusement parks go, is easily the best in Britain.

The park's major rides include the Big One, the tallest and fastest roller coaster in Europe, reaching a top speed of 85mph before hitting a near-vertical descent of 75m; the Ice Blast, which delivers you up a 65m steel tower before returning to earth at 80mph; and the vertiginous Infusion, which features five loops, a double-line twist and a suspended looping coaster – which should help bring up that lunch just nicely.

The high-tech, modern rides draw the biggest queues, but spare a moment to check out the marvellous collection of old-style wooden roller coasters, known as 'woodies'. You can see the world's first Big Dipper (1923), but be sure to have a go on the Grand National (1935), whose carriages trundle along a 1⅛-mile track in an experience that is typically Blackpool – complete with riders waving their hands (despite the sombre-toned announcement not to).

Rides are divided into categories, and once you've gained entry to the park with your Freedom Ticket you can buy tickets for individual categories or for a mixture of them all. Alternatively, an Unlimited Ride **wristband** (1-day adult/child £30/25, 2-day £40/32) includes the £5 entrance fee; there are great discounts if you book your tickets online in advance.

There are no set times for closing; it depends how busy it is.

Blackpool Tower ENTERTAINMENT COMPLEX
(www.theblackpooltower.co.uk; adult/child £17/14; ⏲10am-6pm) Built in 1894, this

STAYING IN THE BLACK

A visit to all of Blackpool's attractions – including those dreaded words 'again, Daddy, again!' – can put a strain on the budget. Consider booking all of your tickets online – try www.blackpool pleasurebeach.com, where you can benefit from substantial discounts on standard prices. It all adds up!

150m-high tower is Blackpool's most recognisable landmark. Inside is a vast entertainment complex including a dinosaur ride, Europe's largest indoor jungle gym and a Moorish circus.

The highlight of the tower is the magnificent rococo **ballroom** (⏲10am-6pm Mon-Fri & Sun, to 11pm Sat), with extraordinary sculptured and gilded plasterwork, murals, chandeliers and couples gliding across the beautifully polished wooden floor to the melodramatic tones of a huge Wurlitzer organ.

Sandcastle Waterpark WATERPARK
(www.sandcastle-waterpark.co.uk; adult/child £15/13; ⏲from 10am May-Oct, from 10am Sat & Sun Nov-Feb) Across from the Pleasure Beach is this indoor water complex with 15 different slides and rides, including the Master Blaster, the world's largest indoor waterslide.

Sealife Centre AQUARIUM
(www.sealifeeurope.com; New Bonny St; adult/child £13.95/10.95; ⏲10am-8pm) State-of-the-art sealife centre which features 2.5m-long sharks and a giant octopus.

FREE **North Pier** ARCHITECTURAL LANDMARK
(Promenade) Built in 1862 and opening a year later, the most famous of the three Victorian piers once charged a penny for admission; its plethora of unexciting rides are now free.

Sleeping

With so many visitors, it's hardly surprising that every second building in town seems to be a hotel, B&B or self-catering unit. Most of them are fairly unremarkable, and you're advised to book ahead if you want to get a decent room between July and September. If you want to stay close to the waterfront, prepare for a noisy, boisterous night; accommodation along Albert and Hornby Rds, 300m back from the sea, is that little bit quieter. The tourist office will assist you in finding a bed.

Number One BOUTIQUE HOTEL ££
(☎01253-343901; www.numberoneblackpool.com; 1 St Lukes Rd; s/d from £70/120; P wifi) Far fancier than anything else around, this stunning boutique guesthouse is all luxury and contemporary style. Everything exudes a kind of discreet elegance, from the darkwood furniture and high-end mod cons to the top-notch breakfast. It's on a quiet road just set back from the South Promenade near the Pleasure Beach.

Big Blue Hotel HOTEL ££
(☎0845 367 3333; www.bigbluehotel.com; Blackpool Pleasure Beach; s/d/ste from £69/89/119; P @ wifi) A handsome family hotel with smartly kitted-out rooms. Kids' needs are met with DVD players and computer games, while its location at the southern entrance to the Pleasure Beach should ensure that everyone has something to do.

Other options you can try:

New President Hotel HOTEL ££
(☎01253-624460; www.thepresidenthotel.co.uk; 320-324 North Promenade; s/d from £42/65; P) Decent choice with 65 comfortable rooms. Also serves meals (£8 to £12) in the fancy-ish Atlanta restaurant.

Ruskin Hotel HOTEL ££
(☎01253-624063; www.ruskinhotel.com; Albert Rd; s/d £45/80) Victorian-style hotel at the prom end of Albert Rd, near Blackpool Tower.

Eating

Forget gourmet meals – the Blackpool experience is all about stuffing your face with burgers, doughnuts, and fish and chips. Most people eat at their hotels, where roast and three vegetables often costs just £5 per head.

There are a few restaurants around Talbot Sq (near the tourist office) on Queen St, Talbot Rd and Clifton St. Our favourite meal in town is at the Mediterranean **Kwizeen** (www.kwizeenrestaurant.co.uk; 49 King St; mains £13), which serves a delicious suckling pig in a Sardinian style, topped with a bacon roulade.

Information

Tourist office (☎01253-478222; www.visitblackpool.com; 1 Clifton St; ⏲9am-5pm Mon-Sat)

Getting There & Away

Bus

The central coach station is on Talbot Rd, near the town centre.

London £29, 6½ hours, four daily.

Manchester £7.30, 1¾ hours, four daily.

Train

The main train station is Blackpool North, about five blocks east of the North Pier on Talbot Rd. There is a direct service from Manchester (£13.50, 1¼ hours, half-hourly) and Liverpool (£14.60, 1½ hours, seven daily), but most other arrivals change in Preston (£6.70, 30 minutes, half-hourly).

Getting Around

A host of travel-card options for trams and buses ranging from one day to a week are available at the tourist office and most newsagents. With more than 14,000 car-parking spaces in Blackpool, you'll have no problem parking. The **land train service** (one way/return £2/3; ⌚from 10.30am Apr-Oct) shuttles funsters between the central corridor car parks and the main entrance to the Pleasure Beach every five minutes or so throughout the day. Otherwise, the town has recently introduced a **bike hire scheme** (www.hourbike.com/blackpool; 3hr for £6) with bikes available for hire from stations along the Promenade and in Stanley Park.

Lancaster

POP 45,960

Lancashire's county seat is genteel, austere and much, much quieter than it was in its 18th-century heyday, when it served as an important trading port for all manner of goods, including people. The city's handsome Georgian architecture was one of the slave trade's ancillary benefits.

Sights

Lancaster Castle & Priory CASTLE

(☎01524-64998; www.lancastercastle.com; Castle Park; adult/child £5/4; ⌚10am-5pm) Lancaster's imposing castle was originally built in 1150. Later additions include the **Well Tower**, more commonly known as the Witches' Tower because it was used to incarcerate the accused of the famous Pendle Witches Trial of 1612, and the impressive twin-towered **gatehouse**, both of which were added in the 14th century. However, most of what you see today dates from the 18th and 19th centuries, when the castle was substantially altered to suit its new, and still current, role as a prison. Consequently, you can only visit the castle as part of a 45-minute **guided tour** (⌚every 30min 10.30am-4pm), but you do get a chance to experience what it was like to be locked up in the dungeon.

Immediately next to the castle is the equally fine **priory church** (Priory Cl; admission free; ⌚9.30am-5pm), founded in 1094 but extensively remodelled in the Middle Ages.

Judges' Lodgings MUSEUM

(Church St; adult/child £3/2; ⌚10am-4pm Mon-Fri & noon-4pm Sat & Sun) Once the home of witch-hunter Thomas Covell (he who 'caught' the poor Pendle women), Lancaster's oldest town house, a Grade I-listed Georgian building, is now home to a Museum of Furnishings by master builders Gillows of Lancaster, whose work graces the Houses of Parliament. It also houses a Museum of Childhood, which has memorabilia from the turn of the 20th century.

Williamson Park & Tropical Butterfly House GARDENS

(www.williamsonpark.com; ⌚10am-5pm) Lancaster's highest point is the 22-hectare spread of this elegant park, from which there are great views of the town, Morecambe Bay and the Cumbrian fells to the north. In the middle is the **Ashton Memorial**, a 67m-high baroque folly built by Lord Ashton (the son of the park's founder, James Williamson) for his wife.

More beautiful, however, is the Edwardian Palm House, now the **Tropical Butterfly House** (adult/child £4.50/3.50), full of exotic and stunning species. Take bus 25 or 25A from the station, or else it's a steep short walk up Moor Lane.

A trio of other museums complete the picture:

Maritime Museum MUSEUM

(St George's Quay; adult/child £3/2; ⌚11am-5pm) The 18th-century Custom House recalls the days when Lancaster was a flourishing port at the centre of the slave trade.

Cottage Museum MUSEUM

(15 Castle Hill; adult/child £1/free; ⌚2-5pm Easter-Sep) Gives us a peep into life in early Victorian times.

FREE **City Museum** MUSEUM

(Market Sq; ⌚10am-5pm Mon-Sat) A mixed bag of local historical and archaeological exhibits.

Lancaster

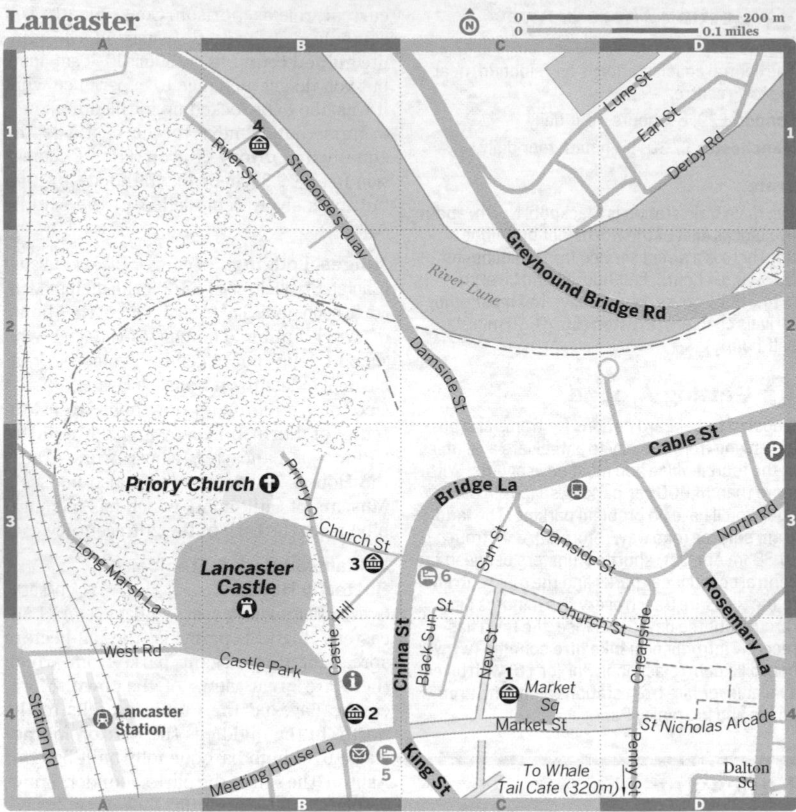

Lancaster

Sleeping & Eating

Sun Hotel & Bar HOTEL ££
(☎01524-66006; www.thesunhotelandbar.co.uk; 63 Church St; s/d from £72/82; P 📶) An excellent hotel in a 300-year-old building with a rustic, old-world look that stops at the bedroom door; a recent renovation has resulted in 16 pretty snazzy rooms. The pub downstairs is one of the best in town and a top spot for a bit of grub; the two-course roast of the day (£9.95) is excellent.

Royal King's Arms Hotel HOTEL ££
(☎01524-32451; www.oxfordhotelsandinns.com; Market St; s/d from £59/79; P 📶) Lancaster's swankiest hotel is a period house with modern, comfortable rooms and an all-round businesslike interior. Look out for the beautiful stained-glass windows, one of the only leftovers from the mid-19th century when Charles Dickens frequented the place. The hotel restaurant is an excellent dining choice, with mains around £11.

Whale Tail Cafe VEGETARIAN £
(www.whaletailcafe.co.uk; 78a Penny St; mains £6-8; ⏰10am-4pm Mon-Fri, to 5pm Sat, to 3pm Sun) This gorgeous 1st-floor veggie res-

taurant has an elegant dining room and a more informal plant-filled yard for lunch on a sunny day. The spicy bean burger (£6) is particularly good. Food here is locally produced and, when possible, organic.

Information

Post office (85 Market St; ⌚9am-5.30pm Mon-Fri, 9am-12.30pm Sat)

Tourist office (☎01524-841656; www.citycoastcountryside.co.uk; 29 Castle Hill; ⌚9am-5pm Mon-Sat)

Getting There & Away

Lancaster is on the main west-coast railway line and on the Cumbrian coast line. Destinations include Carlisle (£17.40, one hour, hourly), Manchester (£13.90, one hour, hourly) and Morecambe (£2.10, 15 minutes, half-hourly).

Morecambe

POP 49,570

Blackpool is tough enough competition for traditional seaside resorts in *other* parts of England, so imagine what it must be like for Morecambe. It was a minding-its-own-business fishing village until the middle of the 19th century, when the railway brought trains packed with mill workers and their families to its shores. Its popularity with the bucket-and-spade brigade fell away dramatically after WWII, when bolder and brasher Blackpool to the south really began to flex its muscles.

The **tourist office** (☎01524-582808; Old Station Bldgs; ⌚9.30am-5pm Mon-Sat year-round, plus 10am-4pm Sun Jun-Sep) is on Central Promenade and runs a free accommodation service.

The town is in the middle of a regeneration project that will bring new life to the crumbling arcades that line the glorious bay. The bay is considered the country's most important wintering site for birds, and sunsets here can be quite spectacular.

Further down the promenade is the town's most famous statue: Graham Ibbeson's tribute to Ernie Bartholomew, better known as Eric Morecambe, one half of comic duo Morecambe and Wise.

There are plenty of hotels in the town, none more inviting than the **Midland Hotel** (☎01524-424000; www.midlandmorecambe.co.uk; Marine Rd West; r £45-90, with sea view £63-126; P@☎), an art deco masterpiece with 44 thoroughly modern rooms that have retained the essence of their 1930s style.

Trains run half-hourly from Lancaster (15 minutes), only 5 miles to the southeast.

Ribble Valley

Lancashire's most attractive landscapes lie east of the brash tackiness of Blackpool and north of the sprawling conurbations of Preston and Blackburn.

The northern half of the valley is dominated by the sparsely populated moorland of the Forest of Bowland, which is a fantastic place for walks, while the southern half features rolling hills, attractive market towns and ruins, with the River Ribble flowing between them.

Activities

WALKING & CYCLING

The **Ribble Way**, a 70-mile footpath that follows the River Ribble from its source at Ribblehead (in the Yorkshire Dales) to the estuary at Preston, is one of the more popular walks in the area and passes through Clitheroe. For online information check out www.visitlancashire.com.

The valley is also well covered by the northern loop of the **Lancashire Cycle**

WORTH A TRIP

HELMSHORE MILLS TEXTILE MUSEUM

If you're on your way to the Ribble Valley from Manchester, or if, like us, you have an insatiable curiosity about the Industrial Revolution's early years, then a visit to this **museum** (Holcombe Rd, Helmshore, Rossendale; adult/child £4/free; ⌚noon-4pm Mon-Fri, noon-5pm Sat & Sun Mar Oct) is a must. Two of Lancashire's original textile mills – Higher Mill and Whitaker's Mill – house exhibits which tell the story of how cotton and wool became cloth, including a version of Richard Arkwright's Water Frame and a working water wheel. These fabrics made the fortunes of many an 18th-century industrialist, and helped determine the course of human history, which is no mean boast. The museum is in Helmshore (on the outskirts of Haslingden), about 16 miles north of Manchester.

Way; for more information about routes, safety and so on contact **Blazing Saddles** (☎01442-844435; www.blazingsaddles.co.uk), a Yorkshire-based bike store.

The tourist office in Clitheroe has three useful publications: *Bowlands by Bike* (£1), *Mountain Bike Ribble Valley Circular Routes* (£2.50) and *Mountain Bike Rides in Gisburn Forest* (£2).

CLITHEROE

POP 14,700

Located northeast of Preston, the Ribble Valley's largest market town is best known for its impressive **Norman keep** (admission free; ⏰dawn-dusk), built in the 12th century and now, sadly, standing empty; from it there are great views of the river valley below.

The extensive grounds are home to the newly refurbished **castle museum** (Castle Hill; adult/child £3.50/free; ⏰11am-5pm Apr-Oct, noon-4pm Nov-Mar), which explores 350 *million* years of local history.

Sleeping & Eating

Old Post House Hotel HOTEL ££
(☎01200-422025; www.posthousehotel.co.uk; 44-48 King St; s/d from £40/65; P ☎) A former post office is now Clitheroe's most handsome hotel, with 11 superbly decorated rooms.

Eaves Hall Hotel HOTEL ££
(☎01200-425271; www.eaveshall.co.uk; Eaves Hall Lane, West Bradford; s/d from £50/90; ☎) Just north of the village, this is the archetypal country house hotel with 34 well-appointed rooms in a beautiful building surrounded by 5 hectares of lush, landscaped gardens.

Halpenny's of Clitheroe TEAROOM £
(Old Toll House, 1-5 Parson Lane; mains £6) A traditional teashop that serves sandwiches, and dishes such as Lancashire hotpot.

Information

Tourist office (☎01200-425566; www.visitribblevalley.co.uk; Church Walk; ⏰9am-5pm Mon-Sat) Information on the town and surrounding area.

PENDLE HILL

The valley's top attraction is Pendle Hill (558m), made famous in 1612 as the stomping ground of the Pendle Witches. These were 10 women who, allegedly, practised all kinds of malefic doings until they were convicted on the sole testimony of a child, and hanged. The tourist authority makes a big deal of the mythology surrounding the unfortunate women, and every Halloween a pseudomystical ceremony is performed here to commemorate their 'activities'.

If that isn't enough, the hill is also renowned as the spot where George Fox had a vision in 1652 that led him to found the Quakers. Whatever your thoughts on witchcraft and religious visions, the hill, a couple of miles east of Clitheroe, is a great spot for a walk.

FOREST OF BOWLAND

This vast, grouse-ridden moorland is somewhat of a misnomer. The use of 'forest' is a throwback to an earlier definition, when it served as a royal hunting ground. Today it is an Area of Outstanding Natural Beauty (AONB), which makes for good walking and cycling. The **Pendle Witch Way**, a 45-mile walk from Pendle Hill to northeast of Lancaster, cuts right through the area, and the **Lancashire Cycle Way** runs along the eastern border. The forest's main town is **Slaidburn**, about 9 miles north of Clitheroe on the B6478.

Other villages worth exploring are **Newton**, **Whitewell** and **Dunsop Bridge**.

Sleeping & Eating

Inn at Whitewell INN ££
(☎01200-448222; www.innatwhitewell.com; Whitewell Village; s/d from £70/96) Once the home of Bowland's forest keeper, this is now a superb guesthouse with antique furniture, peat fires and Victorian claw-foot baths. The restaurant (mains £10 to £16) specialises in traditional English game dishes.

Hark to Bounty Inn INN ££
(☎01200-446246; www.harktobounty.co.uk; Slaidburn; s/d £42/85) This marvellous 13th-century inn has atmospheric rooms with exposed oak beams. An excellent restaurant (mains £8 to £13) downstairs specialises in homemade herb breads.

Slaidburn YHA HOSTEL £
(☎0845 371 9343; www.yha.org.uk; King's House, Slaidburn; dm £16; ⏰Apr-Oct) A converted 17th-century village inn that is especially popular with walkers and cyclists.

Getting There & Away

Clitheroe is served by regular buses from Preston and Blackburn as well as by hourly train from

A WALK THROUGH MIDDLE EARTH

Ever wondered what it would be like to walk in Frodo Baggins' beloved Shire...without the aid of hallucinogens? JRR Tolkien's descriptions of Hobbiton and the Shire in *The Lord of the Rings* were inspired by the countryside around Hurst Green, about 5 miles southwest of Clitheroe. Tolkien was a regular guest in the grounds of Stonyhurst College during the years in which he wrote the epic novel, a favourite of fantasy nerds all over the world (including this author).

A 5.5-mile circular walk has been created, following Tolkien's own footsteps – it begins at Shireburn Arms (where he was partial to the ale) and includes the crossing of the Rivers Ribble and Hodder (Rivers Shirebourne and Brandywine in the book). The Ribble Valley official website (www.ribblevalley.gov.uk) has details of the walk; Hurst Green is on the Clitheroe–Preston bus line (the bus trip takes about 10 minutes).

Manchester (£8.70, 75 minutes) and Preston (£5.90, 50 minutes). Once here, you're better off if you have your own transport, as there is only a Sunday bus service between Clitheroe and the rest of the valley villages.

ISLE OF MAN

It pays to be different. Best known as a tax haven, petrol-head heaven and the home of the tailless cat, the Isle of Man (Ellan Vannin in Manx, the local lingo) doggedly refuses to relinquish its quasi-independent status, which gives rise to the oft-quoted mainland prejudice that the islanders' rejection of England's warm embrace must mean there's something odd about them.

We've noticed nothing of the kind, but the island undoubtedly has a different feel about it, as though it has deliberately avoided efforts to hurry up and modernise. Crass commercialism and mass tourism have no place here, except of course for the world-famous summer season of Tourist Trophy (TT) motorbike racing, which attracts around 50,000 punters and bike freaks every May and June, bringing noise and mayhem to otherwise lush valleys, barren hills and rugged coastlines of this beautiful island. Needless to say, if you want a slice of silence, be sure to avoid the high-rev bike fest.

Home to the world's oldest continuous parliament, the Isle of Man enjoys special status in Britain, and its annual parliamentary ceremony honours the thousand-year history of the Tynwald (a Scandinavian word meaning 'meeting field'). Douglas, the capital, is a run-down relic of Victorian tourism with fading B&Bs.

Activities

WALKING & CYCLING

With plenty of great marked trails, the Isle of Man is a firm favourite with walkers and is regularly voted one of the best walking destinations in Britain. Ordnance Survey (OS) Landranger Map 95 (£6.99) covers the whole island, while the free *Walks on the Isle of Man* is available from the tourist office in Douglas. The **Millennium Way** is a walking path that runs the length of the island amid some spectacular scenery. The most demanding of all the island's walks is the 95-mile **Raad ny Foillan** (Road of the Gull), a well-marked path that makes a complete circuit of the island and normally takes about five days to complete. The **Isle of Man Walking Festival** (www.isleofmanwalking.com) takes place over five days in June.

There are six off-road mountain-biking trails on the island, each with varying ranges of difficulty. See www.gov.im/tourism/activities/events/mountainbiking.xml for details.

Information

Most of the island's historic sites are operated by Manx Heritage, which offers free admission for National Trust or English Heritage members. Unless otherwise indicated, **Manx Heritage** (MH; www.gov.im/mnh) sites are open 10am to 5pm daily, from Easter to October. The Manx Heritage **5 Site Pass** (adult/child £16/8) grants you entry into five of the island's heritage attractions; pick it up at any of the tourist offices or online.

Getting There & Away

AIR Ronaldsway Airport (www.iom-airport.com; Ballasalla) is 10 miles south of Douglas near Castletown.

Airline contacts:

Aer Arann (www.aerarann.com; from £10) From Dublin and London City.

Isle of Man

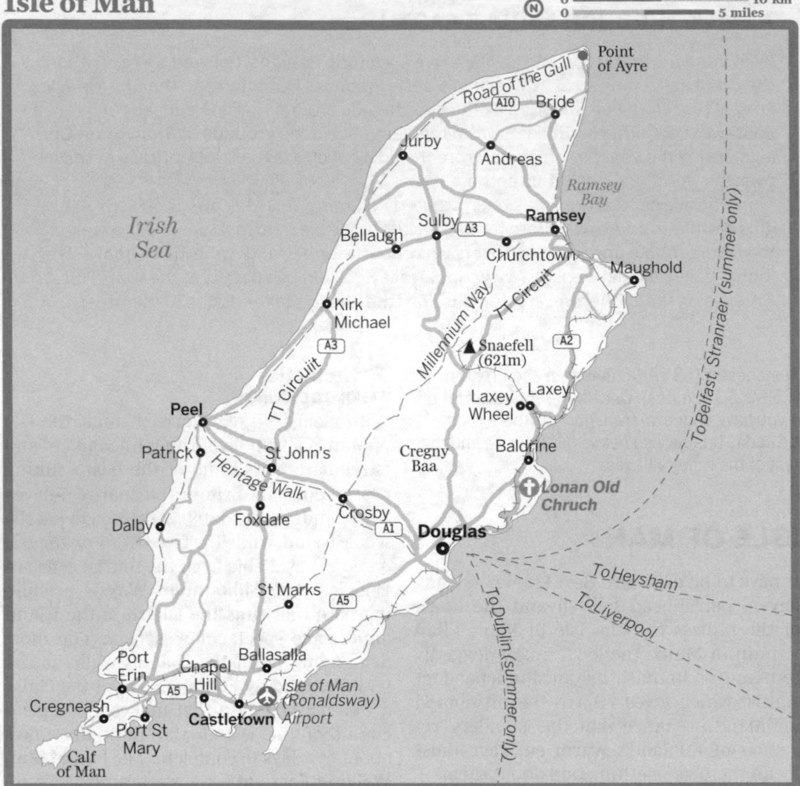

Blue Islands (www.blueislands.com; from £157) From Guernsey and Jersey.

easyJet (www.easyjet; from £19) From Liverpool.

Flybe (www.flybe.com; from £21) From Birmingham, Bristol, London Gatwick, Luton, Liverpool, Manchester, Glasgow and Edinburgh.

Manx2 (www.manx2.com; from £20) From Belfast, Blackpool, Leeds-Bradford, Gloucester M5, Newcastle and East Midlands.

BOAT Isle of Man Steam Packet (www.steam-packet.com; foot passenger single/return £19/30.50, car & 2 passengers single/return £154/145) is a car ferry and high-speed catamaran service from Liverpool and Heysham to Douglas. There is also a summer service (mid-April to mid-September) to Dublin (three hours) and Belfast (three hours). It's usually cheaper to buy a return ticket than to pay the single fare.

ℹ Getting Around

Buses link the airport with Douglas every 30 minutes between 7am and 11pm; a taxi should cost you no more than £18.

The island has a comprehensive **bus service** (www.iombusandrail.info); the tourist office in Douglas has timetables and sells tickets. It also sells the **Island Explorer** (1-day adult/child £15/7, 3-day £30/14), which gives you free rides on all public transport, including the tram to Snaefell and Douglas' horse-trams.

Bikes can be hired from **Eurocycles** (www.eurocycles.iofm.net; 8a Victoria Rd; per day £14-20; ⏲Mon-Sat).

Petrol-heads will love the scenic, sweeping bends that make for some exciting driving – and the fact that outside of Douglas town there's no speed limit. Naturally, the most popular drive is along the TT route. Car-hire operators have desks at the airport, and charge from around £38 per day.

The 19th-century electric and steam **rail services** (☎01624-663366; ⏲Easter-Sep) are a thoroughly satisfying way of getting from A to B:

Douglas–Castletown–Port Erin Steam Train (return £10.80)

Douglas–Laxey–Ramsey Electric Tramway (return £10.80)

Laxey–Summit Snaefell Mountain Railway (return £10.80)

Douglas

POP 26,218

Much like Blackpool across the water, Douglas' heyday was in the middle of the 19th century, when it was a favourite destination for Victorian mass tourism. It's not nearly as popular – or as pretty – today, but it still has the best of the island's hotels and restaurants – as well as the bulk of the finance houses that are frequented so regularly by tax-allergic Brits.

The **Manx Museum** (MH; www.gov.im/mnh; Kingswood Grove; admission free; 10am-5pm Mon-Sat) gives an introduction to everything from the island's prehistoric past to the latest TT race winners.

Sleeping

The seafront promenade is crammed with B&Bs. Unless you booked back at the beginning of the millennium, however, there's little chance of finding accommodation during TT week and the weeks either side of it. The tourist office's camping information sheet lists sites all around the island.

Sefton Hotel HOTEL ££

(01624-645500; www.seftonhotel.co.im; Harris Promenade; r from £95; P) Douglas' best hotel is an upmarket oasis with its own indoor water garden and rooms that range from plain and comfy to elegant and very luxurious. The rooms overlooking the water garden are superb, even better than the ones with sea views. You save up to 10% if you book online.

Admiral House B&B ££

(01624-629551; www.admiralhouse.com; Loch Promenade; r from £55; P) This elegant guesthouse overlooks the harbour near the ferry port. The 23 spotless and modern rooms are a cheerful alternative to the worn look of a lot of other seafront B&Bs.

Other decent options:

Ascot Hotel HOTEL ££

(01624-675081; www.hotel-ascot.co.uk; 7 Empire Tce; s/d from £40/80; P@) Although a little worn around the edges, this is one of the friendliest hotels in town. First-rate service and a top breakfast – but get a room with a harbour view.

Hilton Hotel HOTEL ££

(01624-662662; www.hilton.co.uk/isleofman; Central Promenade; r from £75; P@) Tidy, modern rooms, a small gym and a casino – the Hilton takes care of your every need.

Eating & Drinking

Tanroagan SEAFOOD ££

(01624-472411; www.tanroagan.co.uk; 9 Ridgeway St; mains £9-18; lunch & dinner Tue-Fri, dinner Sat) The place for all things from the sea, this elegant eatery is the trendiest in Douglas. It serves fresh fish straight off the boats, giving them the merest of Continental twists or just a spell on the hot grill. Reservations are recommended.

Cacio e Pepe ITALIAN ££

(6 Victoria St; mains £8-13; Mon-Sat) Authentic Italian cuisine served in warm, friendly surroundings. The pasta with parma ham is divine, the side salads as fresh and crisp as you'd like.

There are a few good pubs around, including the trendy **Bar George** (St George's Chambers, 3 Hill St), and **Rover's Return** (11 Church St), which specialises in the local brew, Bushy Ales.

Information

Tourist office (01624-686766; www.visitisleofman.com; Sea Terminal Bldg; 9.15am-7pm) Makes accommodation bookings for free.

Around Douglas

You can follow the TT circuit up and over the mountain or wind around the coast. The mountain route goes close to the summit of **Snaefell** (621m), the island's highest point. It's an easy walk up to the summit, or you can take the electric tram from Laxey, near the coast.

On the edge of Ramsey, on the north of the island, is the **Grove Rural Life Museum** (MH; Andreas Rd; admission £3.50; 10am-5pm Apr-Oct). The church in the small village of **Maughold** is on the site of an ancient monastery; a small shelter houses quite a good selection of stone crosses and ancient inscriptions.

It's no exaggeration to describe the **Lady Isabella Laxey Wheel** (MH; Mines Rd, Laxey; admission £3.50; 10am-5pm Apr-Oct), built in 1854 to pump water from a mine, as a 'great' wheel; it measures 22m across and can draw 1140L of water per minute from a depth of 550m. It is named after the wife of the then lieutenant-governor and is the largest wheel of its kind in the world.

The wheel-headed cross at **Lonan Old Church**, just north of Douglas, is the island's most impressive early Christian cross.

Castletown & Around

At the southern end of the island is Castletown, a quiet harbour town that was originally the capital of the Isle of Man. The town is dominated by the impressive 13th-century **Castle Rushen** (MH; Castletown Sq; admission £5; 10am-5pm Apr-Oct). The flag tower affords fine views of the town and coast. There's also a small **Nautical Museum** (MH; Bridge St; admission £4; 10am-5pm Easter-Oct) displaying, among other things, its pride and joy, *Peggy*, a boat built in 1791 and still housed in its original boathouse. There is a school dating back to 1570 in **St Mary's church** (MH; admission free), behind the castle.

Between Castletown and Cregneash, the Iron Age hillfort at **Chapel Hill** encloses a Viking ship burial site.

On the southern tip of the island, the **Cregneash Village Folk Museum** (MH; admission £4; 10am-5pm Apr-Oct) recalls traditional Manx rural life. The **Calf of Man**, the small island just off Cregneash, is a bird sanctuary. **Calf Island Cruises** (01624-832339; adult/child £12/6; 10.15am, 11.30am & 1.30pm Apr-Oct, weather permitting) run between Port Erin and the island.

For a decent bit of grub, the **Garrison Tapas Bar** (5 Castle St; tapas £5-8; lunch & dinner Mon-Sat, lunch Sun) brings Iberian flavour to a handsome 17th-century building in the centre of town. The paella (£26.50) is fantastic, but it feeds four.

PORT ERIN & PORT ST MARY

Port Erin, another Victorian seaside resort, plays host to the small **Railway Museum** (Station Rd; adult/child £1/50p; 10am-5pm Apr-Oct), which reveals the history of steam railway on the island.

Port Erin has a good range of accommodation, as does Port St Mary, across the headland and linked by steam train.

Our Port Erin accommodation choice would be the Victorian **Falcon's Nest Hotel** (01624-834077; falconsnest@enterprise.net; Station Rd; r from £42;), once supremely elegant, now just handsome in a nostalgic sort of way. The rooms are not particularly special, but the views over the water are superb.

The slightly more splendid Victorian-style **Aaron House** (01624-835702; www.aaronhouse.co.uk; The Promenade, Port St Mary; s/d from £35/70) is a B&B that has fussed over every detail, from the gorgeous brass beds and claw-foot baths to the old-fashioned photographs on the walls. The sea views are also sensational.

Peel & Around

The west coast's most appealing town, Peel has a fine sandy beach, but its real attraction is the 11th-century **Peel Castle** (MH; admission £3.80; 10am-5pm Apr-Oct), stunningly positioned atop St Patrick's Island and joined to Peel by a causeway.

The excellent **House of Manannan** (MH; admission £6; 10am-5pm Apr-Oct) museum uses interactive displays to explain Manx history and its seafaring traditions. A combined ticket for both the castle and museum costs £7.70.

Three miles east of Peel is **Tynwald Hill** at St John's, where the annual parliamentary ceremony takes place on 5 July.

Peel has several B&Bs, including the **Fernleigh Hotel** (01624-842435; www.isleofman.com/Business/f/fernleigh; Marine Pde; r per person incl breakfast from £26; Feb-Nov), which has 12 decent bedrooms. For a better-than-average bite, head for the **Creek Inn** (01624-842216; East Quay; mains around £8), opposite the House of Manannan, which serves Manx queenies (scallops served with white cheese sauce) and has self-catering rooms from £35.

The Lake District & Cumbria

Includes »

Best Places to Eat

- » Punch Bowl Inn (p701)
- » Jumble Room (p705)
- » Rogan & Company (p723)
- » Drunken Duck (p707)
- » Wasdale Head Inn (p712)

Best Places to Stay

- » Moss Grove Organic (p704)
- » Waterhead Hotel (p701)
- » Yewfield (p706)
- » Howe Keld (p716)
- » Summer Hill Country House (p709)

Why Go?

If it's grandstand views you're looking for, nowhere in England can match Cumbria. It's a place where the superlatives simply run dry – home to the nation's longest and deepest lakes, as well as its smallest church, steepest road, highest town and loftiest peak. The glaciers that carved out this landscape during the last ice age have long since melted, leaving behind a string of crags, fells and sparkling tarns that form the core of one of England's oldest national parks – the stunning Lake District, founded in 1951 and still considered by many to be the spiritual heartland of English hiking.

But there's much more to this region than just fine views. With a wealth of literary and artistic connections, a history stretching back over 5000 years and some of the halest and heartiest cooking anywhere in England, it's packed with more natural appeal than almost anywhere else in Britain.

When to Go

Cumbria's largest mountain festival is held in Keswick in mid May, while the Beer Festival in June welcomes ale aficionados from across the globe. Ambleside's traditional sports day on the last Saturday in July features events such as houndtrailing and Cumbrian wrestling; Grasmere's annual sports day takes place on the August Bank Holiday. In November, the world's greatest liars congregate on Santon Bridge for their annual fibbing contest.

The Lake District & Cumbria Highlights

1. Slogging to the top of England's highest mountain, **Scaféll Pike** (p712)
2. Cruising across the silvery waters of **Coniston Water** (p708)
3. Visiting the former homes of WIlliam Wordsworth at **Dove Cottage** (p704) and **Rydal Mount** (p703)
4. Drinking in the dramatic fell views from **Wasdale** (p711)
5. Spotting England's only resident ospreys on **Bassenthwaite Lake** (p718)
6. Exploring the outdoor art and wooded trails of **Grizedale Forest** (p707)
7. Staring out from the red-brick battlements of **Carlisle Castle** (p727)
8. Hopping aboard the miniature steam trains of **La'al Ratty** (p725) in Ravenglass

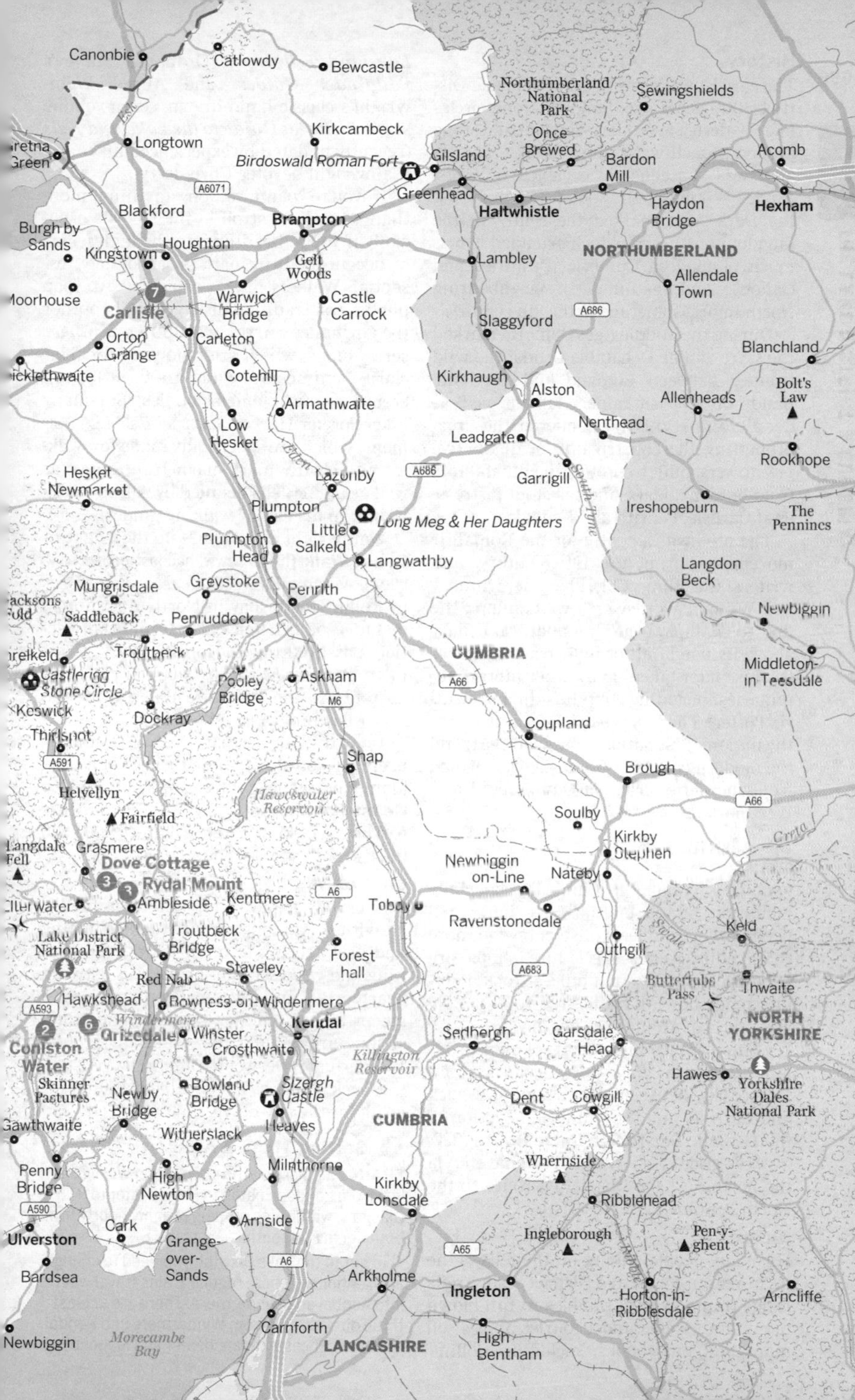

Canonbie
Catlowdy
Bewcastle
Northumberland National Park
Sewingshields
Kirkcambeck
Longtown
Once Brewed
Acomb
Gilsland
Birdoswald Roman Fort
Bardon Mill
Greenhead
Haltwhistle
Haydon Bridge
Hexham
Blackford
Brampton
Burgh by Sands
Houghton
Kingstown
Gelt Woods
Lambley
NORTHUMBERLAND
Allendale Town
Warwick Bridge
Castle Carrock
Carlisle
Slaggyford
Orton Grange
Carleton
Blanchland
Cotehill
Kirkhaugh
Alston
Bolt's Law
Allenheads
Armathwaite
Low Hesket
Nenthead
Leadgate
Rookhope
Hesket Newmarket
Lazonby
Garrigill
South Tyne
Eden
Plumpton
Ireshopeburn
The Pennines
Long Meg & Her Daughters
Little Salkeld
Plumpton Head
Langwathby
Langdon Beck
Mungrisdale
Greystoke
Penrith
Newbiggin
Saddleback
Penruddock
Troutbeck
CUMBRIA
Middleton-in-Teesdale
Castlerigg Stone Circle
Pooley Bridge
Askham
Keswick
Dockray
Coupland
Thirlspot
Shap
Brough
Helvellyn
Haweswater Reservoir
Fairfield
Soulby
Kirkby Stephen
Grasmere
Dove Cottage
Newbiggin on-Line
Nateby
Rydal Mount
Ambleside
Kentmere
Tebay
Ravenstonedale
Keld
Lake District National Park
Troutbeck Bridge
Forest hall
Outhgill
Red Nab
Staveley
Buttertubs Pass
Thwaite
Hawkshead
Bowness-on-Windermere
Windermere
NORTH YORKSHIRE
Kendal
Grizedale
Winster
Sedbergh
Garsdale Head
Coniston Water
Crosthwaite
Killington Reservoir
Hawes
Skinner Pastures
Bowland Bridge
Sizergh Castle
Yorkshire Dales National Park
Newby Bridge
Heaves
Dent
Cowgill
CUMBRIA
Witherslack
Whernside
Penny Bridge
High Newton
Milnthorpe
Kirkby Lonsdale
Ribblehead
Cark
Arnside
Ingleborough
Pen-y-ghent
Ulverston
Grange-over-Sands
Ribble
Bardsea
Arkholme
Ingleton
Horton-in-Ribblesdale
Arncliffe
Carnforth
Newbiggin
Morecambe Bay
LANCASHIRE
High Bentham
A6071
A686
A66
M6
A591
A6
A683
A593
A590
A65
Esk
Swale
Creta

History

The earliest settlers arrived in the Lake District 5000 years ago, building stone circles like Castlerigg and quarrying flint and stone around Stonethwaite and Seatoller. The region was subsequently occupied by Celts, Angles, Vikings and Romans, and during the Dark Ages marked the centre of the kingdom of Rheged, which extended across much of modern Cumbria, Dumfries and Galloway, and was annexed by neighbouring Northumbria sometime in the 8th century.

During the Middle Ages Cumbria marked the start of 'The Debatable Lands', the wild frontier between England and Scotland. Bands of Scottish raiders known as Border Reivers regularly plundered the area, prompting the construction of distinctive *pele* towers, built to protect the inhabitants from border raiders, and the stout fortresses at Carlisle, Penrith and Kendal.

The area was a centre for the Romantic movement during the 19th century, and writers including Coleridge, de Quincey and William Wordsworth were among the first to champion the area's natural beauty above its potential for industrial resources (a cause later taken up by other literary luminaries, including John Ruskin and Beatrix Potter). The Lake District became one of the nation's first national parks in 1951, and the modern county of Cumbria was formed from the old districts of Cumberland and Westmorland in 1974.

Activities

CYCLING

Cycling is popular in Cumbria, especially mountain biking on the fells, but you'll need nerves (and legs) of steel on the more challenging routes. Cycle-hire shops are widespread, and tourist offices stock a cycling map showing traffic-free routes. Bike hire starts at around £15 per day.

Long-distance bikers can follow the 72-mile **Cumbria Way** (www.cumbriawaycycleroute.co.uk) between Ulverston, Keswick and Carlisle, and the Cumbrian section of the 140-mile **Sea to Sea Cycle Route** (C2C; www.c2c-guide.co.uk) from Whitehaven via the northern Lake District en route to the North Pennines and Newcastle.

WALKING

For many people, hiking on the fells is the main reason for a Lake District visit. Trails range from low-level rambles to full-blown mountain ascents; most tourist offices sell maps and guidebooks, including Collins' *Lakeland Fellranger*, Ordnance Survey's *Pathfinder Guides*, and Alfred Wainwright's classic hand-drawn, seven-volume set, *A Pictorial Guide to the Lakeland Fells* (recently updated by experienced hiker and Wainwright devotee Chris Jesty).

If you're planning on anything more than a low-level stroll in the Lakes – especially if you're heading into the high fells – a decent-quality map is absolutely essential. Walkers have a choice of two map publishers: traditionalists generally opt for the Ordnance Survey 1:25,000 *Landranger* series maps, which are renowned for their clarity and accuracy and are used for reference by most official bodies. But many hikers prefer Harvey *Superwalker* 1:25,000 maps, which are specifically made for walkers and clearly mark major trail routes (as well as all 214 fells detailed by Alfred Wainwright in his classic walking guides).

Wainwright also dreamt up the **Coast to Coast Walk** (http://www.thecoasttocoastwalk.info/), which cuts west to east from St Bees to Robin Hood's Bay in North Yorkshire, a distance of 191 miles. The Cumbrian section passes through Honister Pass, Grasmere, Patterdale, Kirkby Stephen and Shap en route to the Yorkshire Dales, a five- to seven-day hike of 82 miles.

Door-to-door baggage services can be useful if you don't want to lug your pack along the whole route. Contact **Coast to Coast Packhorse** (☎017683-71777; www.c2cpackhorse.co.uk) or **Sherpa Van** (☎0871 520 0124; www.sherpavan.com).

OTHER ACTIVITIES

Cumbria is a haven for adrenalin-fuelled activities, ranging from rock climbing and orienteering to quad biking, fell running and *ghyll* scrambling (a cross between coasteering and river canyoning along a steep ravine). Sailing, kayaking and windsurfing are popular too, especially around Windermere, Derwent Water and Coniston.

Check out www.lakedistrictoutdoors.co.uk for the low-down.

Getting There & Away

TRAIN Carlisle is on the main Virgin West Coast line from London Euston to Manchester to Glasgow, with trains running roughly hourly from both north and south.

To get to the Lake District, you need to change at Oxenholme, where regular trains travel west into Kendal and Windermere. There are at least three direct trains from Windermere and Kendal south to Lancaster, Manchester and Manchester airport. Call ☎08457-484950 for information on Day Ranger passes covering the Cumbrian rail network.

For something more soulful, Carlisle sits along some of the UK's most scenic railways:

Cumbrian Coast Line via Ulverston and Ravenglass (see p730)

Settle-Carlisle Line across the Yorkshire Dales (see p587)

Lakeside & Haverthwaite Steam Railway from Bowness/Ambleside to Windermere (p696)

Ravenglass & Eskdale Railway (p725), often known as La'al Ratty

BUS National Express coaches run direct from London and Glasgow to Windermere, Carlisle and Kendal. Count on seven hours between London Victoria and Windermere.

Getting Around

Traveline (☎0871-200 22 33; www.travelinenortheast.info) provides travel information. Tourist offices stock the free *Getting Around Cumbria* booklet, with timetables for buses, trains and ferries.

BOAT Windermere, Coniston Water, Ullswater and Derwent Water all offer ferry services, providing time-saving links for walkers. Boats on Coniston and Windermere also tie in with the Cross-Lakes Experience (p693).

BUS The main bus operator is **Stagecoach** (www.stagecoachbus.com). Bus suggestions in this chapter are based on summer timetables; most routes run a reduced winter service. You can download timetables from the Stagecoach website or the **Cumbria County Council** (www.cumbria.gov.uk) site.

Useful bus routes:

555 (Lakeslink): between Lancaster and Carlisle, stopping at all the main towns.

505 (Coniston Rambler): linking Kendal, Windermere, Ambleside and Coniston.

X4/X5: Penrith to Workington via Troutbeck, Keswick and Cockermouth.

CAR Driving in the Lake District can be a headache, especially on holiday weekends; you might find it easier to leave the car wherever you're staying and get around using local buses.

Many Cumbrian towns use a timed parking permit for on-street parking, which you can pick up for free from local shops and tourist offices.

CUMBRIAN BUS PASSES

Cumbria has a really good bus network, and several useful bus passes are available, all of which can be purchased from the driver or any Stagecoach office.

North West Explorer (one-/four-day pass adult £9.75/22, child £6.50/15.50) The best-value ticket, allowing unlimited travel on services in Cumbria and Lancashire.

Borrowdale Day Rider (adult/child £5.60/4.20) Valid on Bus 79 between Keswick and Seatoller.

Carlisle Day Rider (£3.30) Unlimited travel in Carlisle.

Central Lakes Dayrider (adult/child £6.30/4.70) Covers Bowness, Ambleside, Grasmere, Langdale and Coniston; includes the 599, 505 and 516.

Honister Dayrider (adult/child £6.50/4.75) Valid on Bus 77 between Keswick and Borrowdale.

THE LAKE DISTRICT

If you're a lover of the great outdoors, the Lake District is one corner of England where you'll want to linger. This sweeping panorama of slate-capped fells, craggy hilltops, misty mountain tarns and glittering lakes has been pulling in the crowds ever since the Romantics pitched up in the early 19th century, and it remains one of the country's most popular beauty spots. Literary landmarks abound, from Wordsworth's boyhood school to the lavish country estate of John Ruskin at Brantwood, and there are enough hilltop trails, hidden pubs and historic country hotels to fill a lifetime of visits.

Information

The Lake District's tourist offices are among the best in England, crammed with information on local hikes, activities and accommodation, and stocked with trail books, maps and hiking supplies. The main offices are in Windermere, Ambleside, Keswick and Carlisle, and there's a fantastic visitor centre at Brockhole (p699).

Kendal

POP 28,398

Technically Kendal isn't in the Lake District, but it's a major gateway town. Often known as the 'Auld Grey Town' thanks to the sombre grey stone used for many of its buildings, Kendal is a bustling shopping centre with some good restaurants, a funky arts centre and intriguing museums.

The Lake District

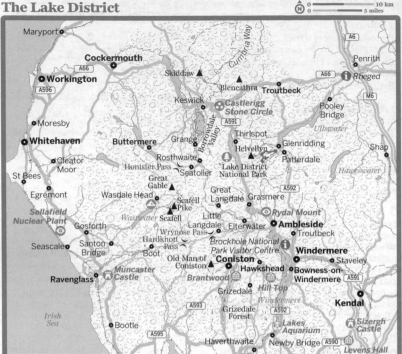

But it'll forever be synonymous in many people's minds with its famous mint cake, a staple item in the nation's hiking packs ever since Edmund Hillary and Tensing Norgay munched it during their ascent of Everest in 1953.

Sights

Kendal Museum MUSEUM

(☎01539-721374; www.kendalmuseum.org.uk; Station Rd; adult/child £2.80/free; ⊙noon-5pm Thu-Sat) Founded in 1796 by the inveterate Victorian collector William Todhunter, this mixed-bag museum features everything from stuffed beasts to medieval coin hoards (look out for the Alethiometer, from Philip Pullman's *His Dark Materials* trilogy). There's also a reconstruction of the office of Alfred Wainwright, the famous hill-walker and author of the classic *Pictorial Guides*, who served as honorary curator at the museum from 1945 to 1974.

Abbot Hall Art Gallery GALLERY

(☎01539-722464; www.abbothall.org.uk; adult/child £5.75/free; ⊙10.30am-5pm Mon-Sat Apr-Oct, to 4pm Nov-Mar) Kendal's gallery houses one of the northwest's best collections of 18th- and 19th-century art; it's especially strong on portraiture and Lakeland landscapes. Look out for works by Constable, Varley and Turner, as well as portraits by John Ruskin and local boy George Romney, born in Dalton-in-Furness in 1734, and a key figure in the 'Kendal School'.

Museum of Lakeland Life & Industry MUSEUM

(☎01539-722464; www.lakelandmuseum.org.uk; adult/child £4.75/3.40; ⊙10.30am-5pm Mon-Sat Apr-Oct, to 4pm Nov-Mar) Opposite Abbot Hall, this museum recreates various scenes from Lakeland life during the 18th and 19th centuries, including a farmhouse parlour, a Lakeland kitchen, an apothecary and the study of Arthur Ransome, author of *Swallows and Amazons.*

Festivals & Events

Kendal Mountain Festival OUTDOOR ACTIVITIES
(www.mountainfest.co.uk) Annual mountain-themed celebration encompassing books, film and live talks in November.

Sleeping

Beech House B&B ££
(☎01539-720385; www.beechhouse-kendal.co.uk; 40 Greenside; s £60-75, d £80-100; P) Top Kendal honours go to this thoroughly marvellous B&B with a dash of designer style inside a creeper-clad house in central Kendal. Some rooms have velour bedspreads and fluffy cushions, others roll-top tubs and minifridges; Sebergh Soap Company goodies are standard throughout. The 'Penthouse' and 'Serpentine' rooms are particularly swish.

Hillside B&B ££
(☎01539-722836; www.hillside-kendal.co.uk; 4 Beast Banks; s £33-41, d £66-82;) Another decent guesthouse option in Kendal, in a Victorian town house dating from the late 19th century. Rooms are small and quite traditional but comfy nonetheless; parking permits are available for the street outside.

Heaves Hotel B&B ££
(☎01539-560396; www.heavesthotel.com; Heaves; s £45, d £60-80; P) It's a way out of Kendal – 4 miles out, in fact, along the A591 – but for a *Homes and Gardens* setting, this fine old 19th-century mansion is tough to beat. The old-fashioned rooms are cluttered with antiques, old rugs and gilded mirrors, and most have bucolic views à la *Gosford Park.*

Kendal YHA HOSTEL ££
(☎0845-371 9641; kendal@yha.org.uk; 118 Highgate; dm from £16; reception 7.30-10am & 1-11.30pm; @) It's definitely not on the level of some of the Lakeland hostels, but this Georgian house next door to the Brewery Arts Centre is decent enough, in a functional YHA way. Dorms are mostly small five- or six bed rooms, and there's a kitchen, lounge and pool room on the ground floor. No kitchen.

Eating

1657 Chocolate House CAFE £
(54 Branthwaite Brow; lunches £2-8) Got a sweet tooth? Then dip into this chocaholic honeypot, brimming with handmade candies and umpteen varieties of mint cake. Upstairs, waitresses in bonnets serve up 18 types of hot chocolate, including almondy 'Old Noll's Potion' and the bitter-choc 'Dungeon'. Take that, Willy Wonka...

THE CROSS-LAKES EXPERIENCE

To help cut down on summer traffic jams, the **Cross-Lakes Experience** (Map p696; mid-Mar–Oct) is an integrated transport service that allows you to cross from Windermere to Coniston without needing to get behind the wheel.

Windermere cruise boats operate from Bowness to Ferry House, from where the Mountain Goat minibus travels to Hill Top and Hawkshead. From Hawkshead, you can catch the X30 bus to Moor Top, Grizedale and Haverthwaite, or catch the 505 bus to High Cross and Coniston Water.

The route operates 10 times daily from Bowness to Coniston (roughly hourly from 10am to 5pm). The only drawback is that the buses get very crowded in summer, and if they're full you'll have to wait for the next one (you can't prebook). Cyclists should note there's only space for five bikes on the minibuses. Current prices for one-way fares from Bowness:

Coniston (adult/child £10.60/5.65)

Ferry House (£2.45/1.40)

Grizedale (£7.65/4.25)

Hawkshead (£6/3.25)

Hill Top (£5.10/2.80)

For info and timetables, contact **Mountain Goat** (Map p696; ☎015394-45161; www.mountain-goat.com; Victoria Rd, Windermere) or ask at any tourist office.

New Moon RESTAURANT ££
(☎01539-729254; 129 Highgate; 2-course lunch £9, mains £10-17; ⏲Tue-Sat) Kendal's best food is served at the fresh and funky New Moon, which takes the best Lakeland produce and gives it a zippy Mediterranean spin – roast duck breast in a five-spice-and-honey marinade, pork with Parma ham, hake with a pesto crust. The two-course Early Supper menu, served before 7pm, is great value at £9.95.

Waterside Wholefoods CAFE £
(Kent View, Waterside; light meals £4-10; ⏲8.30am-4.30pm Mon-Sat) Kendal's veggies make a beeline for this lovely riverside cafe, a longstanding staple for chunky doorstep sandwiches, soups and naughty-but-nice cakes.

Grain Store BISTRO £
(pizzas £6.50-9, mains £9-16.50; ⏲10am-11pm Mon-Sat) The buzzy bistro at the Brewery Arts centre is great for stone-baked pizzas and swish fish after dark, but it's just as good for a lunchtime wrap or a pre-show coffee.

Drinking & Entertainment

Burgundy's Wine Bar WINE BAR
(19 Lowther St, closed Mon) Don't be put off by the wine bar tag – this is one of Kendal's cosiest places for a drink, whether you're after a quality Pinot noir or just a pint of ale.

Ring O' Bells PUB
(Kirkland Ave) Another reliable town boozer where even the beer is blessed: the pub stands on consecrated ground next to the parish church.

Brewery Arts Centre THEATRE, CINEMA
(☎01539-725133; Highgate; www.breweryarts.co.uk) Excellent arts complex with two cinemas, gallery space, cafe and a theatre hosting dance, performance and live music.

Information

Library (75 Stricklandgate; per hr £2; ⏲9.30am-5.30pm Mon & Tue, 9.30am-7pm Wed & Fri, 9.30am-1pm Thu, 9am-4pm Sat, noon-4pm Sun)Internet access.

Tourist office (☎01539-725758; kendaltic@southlakeland.gov.uk; Highgate; ⏲10am-5pm Mon-Sat)

Getting There & Around

BUSUseful buses from Kendal:

555/556 Lakeslink (hourly Monday to Saturday, 10 on Sunday) Hits Kendal en route to Windermere (30 minutes), Ambleside (40 minutes) and Grasmere (1¼ hours), or Lancaster (one hour) in the opposite direction.

505 Coniston (one hour, 10 daily Monday to Saturday, six on Sunday) via Windermere, Ambleside and Hawkshead.

X35 Travels south to Grange (30 minutes) before returning via Haverthwaite Station, Ulverston and Barrow (hourly Monday to Saturday, four on Sunday).

TRAIN The train line from Windermere runs to Kendal (£3.80, 15 minutes, hourly) en route to Oxenholme.

Around Kendal

Sizergh Castle CASTLE
(NT; ☎015395-60070; adult/child £7.15/3.60, gardens only £4.65/2.40; ⏲gardens 11am-5pm, castle noon-5pm Sun-Thu mid-Mar–Nov) Three and half miles south of Kendal along the A591, this impressive castle is the feudal seat of the Strickland family. The castle is renowned for its *pele* tower and for the lavish wood panelling on display in the Great Hall.

Levens Hall HISTORIC HOME
(☎015395-60321; www.levenshall.co.uk; adult/child £11/4.50, gardens only £8/3.50; ⏲gardens 10am-5pm, house noon-5pm Sun-Thu mid-Mar–mid-Oct) Two miles further south along the A6 is another Elizabethan manor built around a mid 13th-century *pele* tower. Fine Jacobean furniture is on display throughout the house, but the real draw is the 17th-century topiary garden: a surreal riot of pyramids, swirls, curls, pom-poms and peacocks straight out of *Alice in Wonderland*. Rather peculiarly, it holds a chilli festival in August.

The 555/556 bus (hourly Monday to Saturday, 10 on Sunday) from Grasmere, Ambleside, Windermere and Kendal runs past the castle gates.

Windermere & Bowness

POP 8432

Of all England's lakes, none carries quite the cachet of regal Windermere. Stretching for 10.5 silvery miles from Ambleside to Newby Bridge, it's one of the classic Lake District vistas, and has been a centre for Lakeland tourism since the first steam trains chugged into town in 1847 (much to the chagrin of the local gentry, including William Wordsworth). The town itself is split between Windermere, 1.5 miles uphill from the lake, and bustling Bowness – officially 'Bowness-on-Windermere' – where a bevy of boat trips, ice-cream booths and frilly teashops jostle for space around the

LOW SIZERGH BARN

Food shop (☎015395-60426; www.lowsizerghbarn.co.uk; ⏲shop 9am-5.30pm, tearoom 9.30am-5.30pm), this fantastic farm shop spot near Sizergh Castle is the place to go when you want to be sure your goodies are 100% food-mile free. Nearly everything in the shop is sourced from the Lakeland area, from homemade chutneys to farm-reared hams and traditional Cumbrian puddings (look out for the award-winning flapjacks from Kendal Jacksmiths and organic wines from Mansergh Hall).

Once you've filled up your picnic basket, you could plump for a cuppa in the tearoom, follow the farm trail or stick around to watch the cows being milked at 1.15pm – don't worry if you don't want to get muddy, as the action's beamed live to TV screens. If you've ever wondered what life down on the farm is really like, this is a fantastic place to find out.

The shop is off the A590 from Kendal. Follow the brown signs to Sizergh Castle and look out for signs to Low Sizergh Barn. Bus 555/6 also stops nearby.

shoreline. It's busy, brash and a touch tatty in places, but the lake itself is still a stunner, especially when viewed from one of Windermere's historic cruise boats.

The A592 travels into Bowness from southern Cumbria, tracking the lakeshore before joining the A591 northwest of town. The train and bus stations are in Windermere town. Most of the hotels and B&Bs are dotted around Lake Rd, which leads downhill to Bowness and the lakeshore.

Sights

Lakes Aquarium AQUARIUM

(☎015395-30153; www.lakesaquarium.co.uk; Lakeside, Newby Bridge; adult/child £8.95/5.95; ⏲9am-6pm Apr-Oct; 👪) At the southern end of the lake near Newby Bridge, this small aquarium explores underwater habitats from tropical Africa through to Morecambe Bay. Highlights include a simulated diving bell and an underwater tunnel beneath Windermere's lake bed, complete with pike, char and diving ducks. You could arrive by ferry from Bowness or Ambleside, aboard the Lakeside & Haverthwaite Railway, or via bus 618 from Windermere. Last admission is at 5pm.

Discounts are available for buying tickets in advance online.

World of Beatrix Potter CHILDREN'S MUSEUM

(Map p698; www.hop-skip-jump.com; adult/child £6.75/3.50; ⏲10am-5.30pm Apr-Sep, 10am-4.30pm Oct-Mar; 👪) This decidedly odd theme attraction brings to life scenes from Beatrix Potter's books (including Peter Rabbit's garden and Mr McGregor's greenhouse) using a combination of life-size models and themed rooms.

Seeing a human-size Mrs Tiggywinkle is quite a weird experience; seek refuge in the Tailor of Gloucester tearoom if it all gets a bit much, or pick up a Potter-themed souvenir from the on-site shop.

Be prepared for queues: for some reason, Japanese visitors are obsessed with all things Beatrix Potter, and this place is number one on their list after Hill Top.

Activities

Boat Trips

Windermere Lake Cruises

(Map p698; ☎015395-31188; www.windermere-lakecruises.co.uk) Top on the list of things to do in Windermere is to take a lake cruise. The first passenger ferry was launched back in 1845, and cruising on the lake is still a hugely popular pastime: some of the vessels are modern, but there are a couple of period beauties dating back to the 1930s. Cruises allow you to jump off at one of the ferry landings (Waterhead/Ambleside, Wray Castle, Brockhole, Bowness, Ferry Landing, Fell Foot Ferry and Lakeside) and catch a later boat back.

Blue Cruise (adult/child/family £6.75/3.40/18.50) 45-minute cruise around Windermere's islands and bays.

Green Cruise (adult/child/family £6.20/3.10/17) 45-minute cruise from Waterhead/Ambleside via Wray Castle and Brockhole Visitor Centre.

Red Cruise (adult/child/family £9.15/5.30/26) North lake cruise from Bowness to Ambleside.

Yellow Cruise (adult/child/family £9.45/5.50/27) South cruise from Bowness to Lakeside and the Lakes Aquarium.

Bowness to Ferry House (single adult/child/family £2.45/1.50/7) Ferry service

Windermere

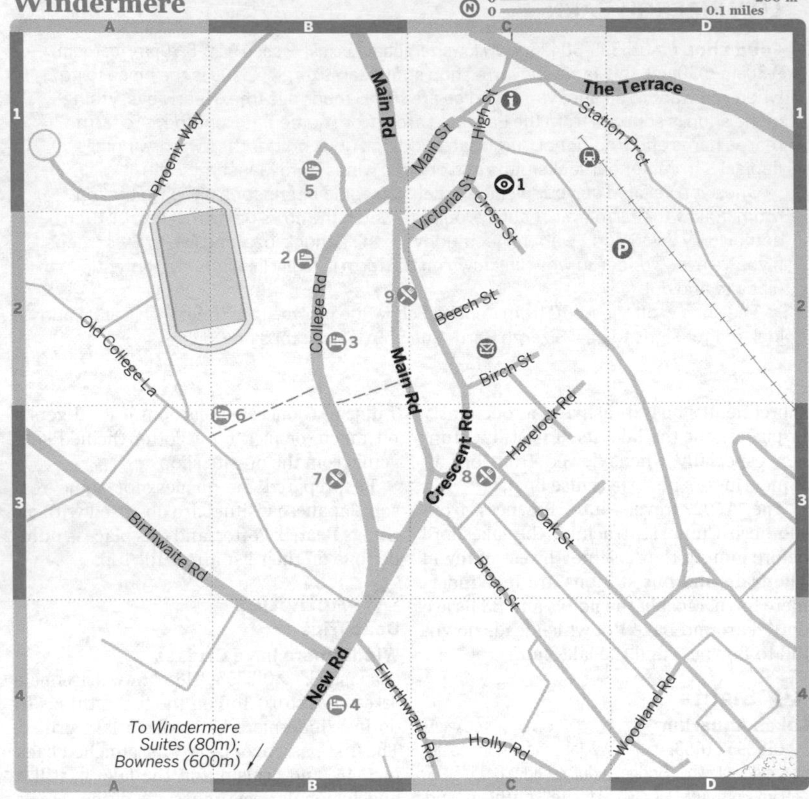

that links up with the Cross-Lakes shuttle to Hill Top and Hawkshead.

If you'd rather explore under your own steam, from April to October rowing boats can be hired along the waterfront for £5/2.50 per adult/child. Open-top motorboats cost £15 per hour, or there's a closed-cabin version for £18. There's a 10mph speed limit on Windermere, much to the dismay of local power-boaters and water-skiers.

Train Rides

Lakeside & Haverthwaite Railway STEAM RAILWAY

Classic standard-gauge steam trains puff their way along this vintage **railway** (☎015395-31594; www.lakesiderailway.co.uk; Haverthwaite Station; ⏲mid-Mar–Oct) from Haverthwaite, near Ulverston, to Newby Bridge and Lakeside. There are five to seven daily trains in season, timed to correspond with the Windermere cruise boats. There are various combo tickets available for local attractions – see the boxed text or ask at the ticket office. Standard fares from Haverthwaite:

Lakeside (adult/child £5.90/2.95)

Bowness (adult/child £14.00/7.50)

Ambleside (adult/child £19.40/9.70)

Sleeping

Windermere's popularity means accommodation tends to be pricier than elsewhere around the Lakes. The main road down to Bowness is stacked with wall-to-wall guesthouses.

TOP CHOICE **Wheatlands Lodge** B&B ££

(Map p696; ☎015394-43789; www.wheatlandslodge-windermere.co.uk; Old College Lane; d £70-150; P ☎) Set back from the hustle of Windermere town, this elegant detached residence looks venerably Victorian,

Windermere

Sights

1 Mountain Goat / Cross-Lakes Experience C1

Sleeping

2 Applegarth Hotel B2
3 Archway B2
4 Howbeck B4
5 Lake District Backpackers Lodge B1
6 Wheatlands Lodge B3

Eating

7 Jericho's B3
8 Lazy Daisy's Lakeland Kitchen C3
9 Lighthouse B2

but inside it reveals some contemporary surprises: lovely, large rooms each with their own keynote colour (maroon, coffee, pistachio), big bathrooms with a choice of walk-in shower or jacuzzi hot tub, and an extremely upmarket dining room serving one of the best breakfasts we had in Windermere. Really rather good.

Cranleigh HOTEL ££
(Map p698; ☎015394-43293; www.thecranleigh.com; Kendal Rd; d £85-148, ste £240-325; P 📶) They certainly haven't spared any expense at this pimped-up pamper-palace. The rooms simply ooze invention: for an out-and-out spoil, the newly opened Sanctuary bungalow is the one to go for, with a remote-controlled fire, huge headboard and a glass bath that's straight out of *Blade Runner*. The rest of the rooms are less starry, but still a distinct cut above most places in town.

Windermere Suites B&B £££
(Map p696; ☎01539-444739; www.windermeresuites.co.uk; New Rd; d £140-280, P 📶) Newly renovated by the owners of the Howbeck, the rooms here are simply enormous: all are named after different Lakeland locations but share a similar taste for soothing whites, gloss-wood floors, enormous flatscreen TVs and the odd touch of boutique wallpaper or funky artwork. In fact, it might all be a bit much for some, and it is a little on the pricey side.

Aphrodite's Themed Lodge HOTEL ££
(☎015394-45052; www.aphroditesthemedlodge.co.uk; Longtail Hill; d £90-160; P 📶 🏊) Something must have got into the water around Windermere – this is another wildly over-the-top design project, where every suite takes on a different theatrical theme: a Tarzan and Jane room with bamboo walls and jungle plants, an Austin Powers pop art room, or a Flintstones suite – complete with faux furs and mock-rock plaster walls. It's completely insane, but you've got to give them an A for effort. The lodge is about 0.8 miles south of Bowness.

Applegarth Hotel HOTEL £££
(Map p696; ☎015394 43206; www.lakesapplegarth.co.uk; College Rd; s £57-62, d £100-196; P) Traditional in style, undoubtedly, but then this is one of the loveliest Arts & Crafts houses in Windermere, built in the 19th century by industrial bigwig John Riggs. Polished panels, burnished furniture and the odd bit of stained glass conjure up the restrained Victorian vibe, although cheaper rooms are a tad bland.

Howbeck B&B ££
(Map p696; ☎015394-44739; www.howbeck.co.uk; New Rd; d £100-160; P 📶) Not quite as spangly as Windermere Suites, its sister business up the road, the Howbeck is still a top B&B choice, with 10 rooms, crisply finished in up-to-date fabrics and a minimum of clutter. A bit more cash buys plusher furnishings, but you won't completely dodge the road noise.

LAKE CRUISE TICKETS

Various combination tickets are available covering lake cruises and admission to local attractions.

Freedom of the Lake ticket (adult/child/family £15/7.50/40) A day's unlimited travel on the lake boats.

Boat & Train (return from Bowness; adult/child/family £14/8.50/39.50) Cruise and travel on the Lakeside & Haverthwaite Steam Railway.

Boat & Aquarium (return from Bowness; adult/child/family £15.90/8.95/46.80). Cruise and entry to the Lakes Aquarium.

Bowness

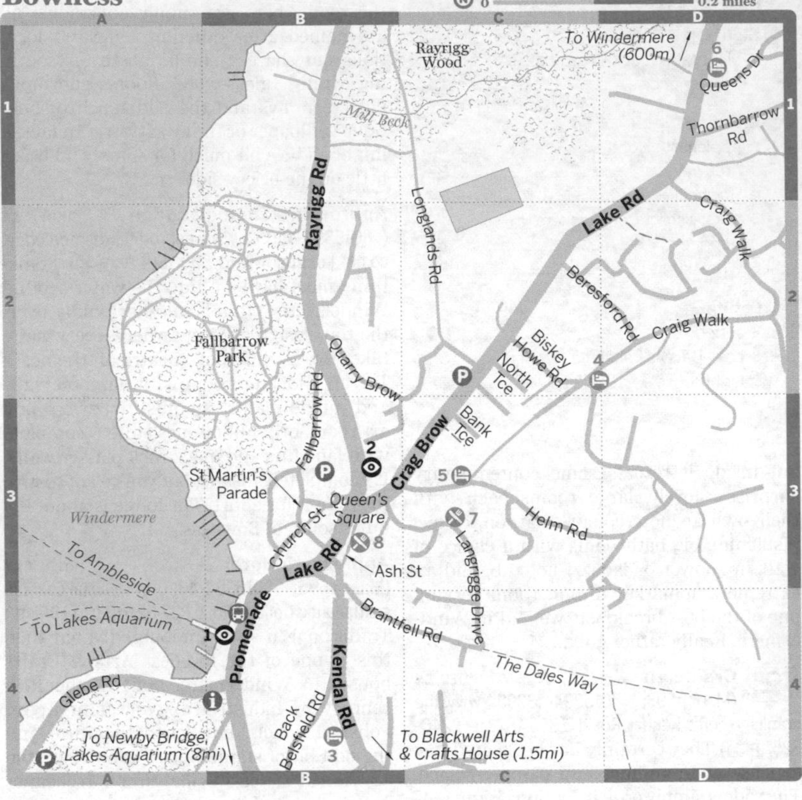

Bowness

Sights

1 Windermere Lake Cruises B4
2 World of Beatrix Potter B3

Sleeping

3 Cranleigh B4
4 Number 80 Bed Then Breakfast C2
5 Oakbank House C3
6 Windermere Boutique Hotel D1

Eating

7 Angel Inn C3
8 Lucy 4 at the Porthole B3

Archway B&B ££
(Map p696; ☎015394-45613; www.the-archway.com; 13 College Rd; d £50-55) There's nothing particularly fancy about this stone-fronted B&B (although there are spanking fell views from the front rooms), but it's worth a mention for its breakfast: Manx kippers, smoked haddock and American-style pancakes are all on offer.

Number 80 Bed Then Breakfast B&B ££
(Map p698; ☎015394-43584; www.number80bed.co.uk; 80 Craig Walk; d £80-90; Ⓦ) This Bowness refuge is still off the radar, so keep it under your hats. Just four rooms, but each one has its own decorative ticks: room 1 feels traditional with a pine four-poster, but the other three are more modern.

Fair Rigg B&B ££
(☎015394-43941; www.fairrigg.co.uk; Ferry View; d £66-84; Ⓟ) If all you're after in Windermere is a plain, unpretentious B&B with nary a flounce or frill in sight, then this is a sound choice. Rooms are pleasant in cream and pine, and the rates are great. It's about 0.8 miles southeast of Bowness.

Lake District Backpackers Lodge HOSTEL £ (Map p696; ☎015394-46374; www.lakedistrictbackpackers.co.uk; High St; dm £15-17; @) The only hostel in Windermere proper, and it's a little underwhelming, with cramped bunk-bed dorms squeezed into a slate-roofed house down a cul-de-sac near the station. Still, the beds are cheap, there's a cosy lounge (with Sky TV) and the managers organise biking and hiking trips.

Other options:

Windermere Boutique Hotel B&B £££ (Map p696; ☎015394-45052; www.21thelakes.co.uk; Lake Rd; d £70-180; P) Run by the owners of Aphrodite's Theme Lodge, with a similarly extravagant approach.

Gilpin Lodge HOTEL £££ (☎015394-88818; www.gilpinlodge.co.uk; Crook Rd; ste £290-550; P) Much lauded country house–hotel in private grounds 2 miles from the lakeshore. It's just off the B5284 towards Kendal.

Oakbank House B&B ££ (Map p698; ☎015394-43386; www.oakbankhousehotel.co.uk; Helm Rd; s/d £47/94; P) Reliable if unspectacular Bowness B&B in a slate topped house along Helm Rd.

Eating & Drinking

Lazy Daisy's Lakeland Kitchen CAFE £ (Map p696; ☎015394-43877; 31-33 Crescent Rd; lunch £4-10, dinner £10-16; ⏲Mon-Sat 10am-9pm) Cute as they come, and chock-full of Lakeland goodness, this little Windermere cafe has something to suit regardless of the hour of the day: morning coffee, lunchtime sandwiches, afternoon tea and cakes, and rich dinner dishes along the lines of buttered trout and steak-and-merlot pie.

Jericho's RESTAURANT £££ (Map p696; ☎015394-42522; www.jerichos.co.uk; Waverly Hotel, College Rd; dinner mains £15-24; ⏲dinner Tue-Sun) Now installed at the Waverley Hotel, the town's most upmarket restaurant is a favourite with the foodie guides, and head chef Chris Blaydes has acquired a deserved name as one of the Lake District's most talented chefs. The town house setting is an ideal counterpoint for the modern Brit bistro food.

Lucy 4 at the Porthole BISTRO ££ (3 Ash St; tapas £5-10; ⏲lunch Sat & Sun, dinner daily) The homey old Porthole has been overhauled courtesy of Lucy Nicholson, of Lucy's of Ambleside fame (see p702). It boasts the same laid-back atmosphere, pick-and-mix tapas menu and wine-bar feel as the original Lucy 4, only this time steps from the Windermere shoreline.

Angel Inn GASTROPUB ££ (Map p698; ☎015394-44080; www.the-angelinn.com; Helm Rd; mains £11-16) The Lake District isn't just about cosy country inns – it has its fair share of gastropubs too, like this one on a grassy hump beside the Bowness shoreline. Stripped wood, banquette seats and leather sofas conjure an urban-chic ambiance, and the menu's stocked with solid gastropub stuff – mussels, beer-battered haddock and seared sea bass.

Lighthouse CAFE £ (Map p696; Main Rd; mains £8-15; ⏲breakfast, lunch & dinner) This triple-floored cafe at the top of Windermere offers a continental-style menu, quality cappuccino and fresh-baked pastries.

Information

Brockhole National Park Visitor Centre (☎015394-46601; www.lake-district.gov.uk; ⏲10am-5pm Easter-Oct) The Lake District's flagship visitor centre is 3 miles north of Windermere on the A591, with a teashop, adventure playground and gardens.

Library (☎015394-62400; Broad St; per 30min £1; ⏲9am-7pm Mon, to 5pm Tue, Thu & Fri, to 1pm Sat, closed Wed & Sun) Internet access.

Tourist office Bowness (☎015394-42895; bownesstic@lake-district.gov.uk; Glebe Rd; ⏲9.30am-5.30pm Easter-Oct, 10am-4pm Fri-Sun Nov-Easter); Windermere (☎015394-46499; windermeretic@southlakeland.gov.uk; Victoria St; ⏲9am-5.30pm Mon-Sat, 9.30am-5.30pm Sun Apr-Oct, shorter hours in winter) The latter branch is opposite NatWest Bank.

Getting There & Away

BOAT The **Windermere Ferry** (car/bike/foot passenger £4/1/50p; ⏲6.50am-9.50pm Mon-Fri, 9.10am-9.50pm Sat & Sun Mar-Oct, last ferry one hour earlier in winter) carries vehicles and foot passengers roughly every 20 minutes from Ferry Nab, just south of Bowness, across the lake to Ferry House on the lake's west side. Ferries can be cancelled at short notice due to bad weather, and summer queues can be long.

BUS There's one daily National Express coach from London (£37, eight hours) via Lancaster and Kendal. Local buses:

555/556 Lakeslink Tracks the lake to Brockhole Visitor Centre (seven minutes, at least hourly), Ambleside (15 minutes) and Grasmere (30 minutes), or Kendal in the opposite direction.

505 Coniston Rambler To Coniston (50 minutes, 10 daily Monday to Saturday, six on Sunday) via Brockhole, Ambleside and Hawkshead.

599 Lakes Rider (three times hourly Monday to Saturday, hourly on Sunday, reduced service in winter) To Bowness, Windermere, Troutbeck, Brockhole, Rydal Church (for Rydal Mount, p703), Dove Cottage and Grasmere.

TRAINWindermere is the only town inside the national park accessible by train. It's on the branch line to Kendal and Oxenholme, from where there are frequent connections north and south.

Train services:

DESTINATION	FARE (ONE WAY)	DURATION (HR)
Oxenholme	£4.30	20min
Kendal	£3.80	15min
Manchester	£28.40	1½-2
Lancaster	£11	45min
London	£82	3¼
Glasgow	£42	2¾
Edinburgh	£46.50	2½

Around Bowness

Blackwell Arts & Crafts House

HISTORIC HOME

(www.blackwell.org.uk; adult/child £6.50/4.20; ⏲10.30am-5pm Apr-Oct, to 4pm Feb-Mar & Nov-Dec) Two miles south of Bowness on the B5360, Blackwell House is one of the finest examples of the 19th-century Arts and Crafts Movement. Inspired by the aesthetic principles of John Ruskin and William Morris, Arts and Crafts was a reaction against the machine-driven mentality of the Industrial Revolution, placing emphasis on simple architecture, high-quality craftsmanship and natural light. Designed by Mackay Hugh Baillie Scott, the house has all the hallmarks of classic Arts and Crafts: light, airy rooms, serene decor, and bespoke craftwork ranging from Delft tiles to handmade doorknobs and wood panelling. There's a tearoom and gift shop for when you've finished moseying round the house.

Townend

HISTORIC HOME

(NT; ☎01539-432628; adult/child £4.20/2.10; ⏲1-5pm Wed-Sun Mar-Oct, earlier guided tours by arrangement) Hidden on a hilltop in the tiny hamlet of Troutbeck, a mile from Windermere, this Lakeland farmhouse was built for a wealthy yeoman farmer in the 17th century. Topped by cylindrical chimneys and grey slate tiles, the house contains rustic artefacts, books and vintage farming tools, plus original wooden furniture carved by the Browne family, who owned the house until 1943.

Sleeping & Eating

TOP CHOICE Queen's Head

PUB, HOTEL ££

(☎015394-32174; www.queensheadhotel.com; mains £12-16, d £110-130; P) This fancy Troutbeck pub conceals a modern soul under a historic skin. The upstairs rooms have bags of charms, ranging from standard doubles to posh four-posters, but the real draw here is the gastrogrub: belly pork, rabbit-and-chicken hotpot and crispy duck leg, delivered with flashes of real flair.

Windermere YHA

HOSTEL £

(☎0845-371 9352; www.yha.org.uk; Bridge Lane, Troutbeck; dm £14; ⏲reception 7.30-11.30am & 1-11pm; P @) The closest YHA to Windermere, in a superb Lakeland house. The rooms are modern, and facilities include a well-stocked shop, a canteen and a gear-drying room. Buses stop at Troutbeck Bridge, from where it's an uphill walk of about a mile to the hostel; minibus pick-ups can be arranged between April and October.

Getting There & Away

Bus 517, the Kirkstone Rambler, travels through Troutbeck en route to Ullswater (one hour, three daily mid-July to August, weekends only other times of year).

Ambleside

POP 3382

Tucked at the northern head of Windermere and backed by a cluster of dramatic fells, Ambleside feels a lot less commercialised than its sister towns further to the south, but that doesn't stop it getting jam-packed throughout the summer months. It's a favourite base for hikers, with plenty of quality outdoors shops dotted round town, and it marks the start of several classic fell hikes. It's also handily positioned for forays west towards Grasmere and the lakes beyond, and cruise boats from Bowness dock regularly down at the Waterhead dock, just south of town.

Sights & Activities

Ambleside hasn't really got any must-see sights, but its stout broad granite streets are made for wandering. The town's best-known landmark is **Bridge House**, a tiny cottage that spans the clattering brook of Stock Ghyll; now occupied by a National Trust shop, it's thought to have originally been built as an apple store.

Armitt Museum MUSEUM
(www.armitt.com; Rydal Rd; adult £2.50; ⏲10am-5pm) Artefacts at Ambleside's modest town museum include a lock of John Ruskin's hair, a collection of botanical watercolours by Beatrix Potter, and prints by the pharmacist-turned-photographer Herbert Bell.

Fell Hikes WALKING
Ambleside marks the start of several well-known walks, including the wooded trail up to the 60ft waterfall of **Stock Ghyll Force**, or the three-hour round trip via **Wansfell** and **Jenkins Crag**, with views across to Coniston and the Langdale Pikes. Serious hikers can tackle the 10-mile **Fairfield Horseshoe** via Nab Scar, Heron Pike, Fairfield and Dove Crag.

Low Wood Watersports BOAT HIRE
(☎015394-39441; watersports@elhmail.co.uk) If you feel like getting out on the lake, this watersports centre rents row boats (one/four hours £12/34), kayaks (two/four hours £16/21), canoes (two/four hours £20/30) and motor boats (one/four hours £20/45).

Sleeping

Waterhead Hotel HOTEL £££
(☎08458-504503; www.elh.co.uk/hotels/waterhead; r £106-256; P 📶) Outside, it's quintessential Lakeland: stone, slate, watery views. Inside, it's bespoke and boutique: cream-and-beige rooms, leather chairs, LCD TVs, flashy fabrics. The lakeside patio-bar's a beauty, too and the upmarket Bay Restaurant serves some of Ambleside's best bistro food (mains £12.95 to £19.95).

 **Cote How Organic Guest House** B&B £££
(☎015394-32765; www.bedbreakfastlakedistrict.com; Rydal, near Ambleside; s £98-£108, d £120-160; P 📶) If it's an eco-conscious sleep you're after, Cote How's the place – it's one of only three UK B&Bs licensed by the Soil Association. Food is 100% local and organic, power's sourced from a green supplier, and they'll even lend you wind-up torches and candles (5% discount if you arrive by bus, too). The three rooms are elegantly Edwardian, with cast-iron beds, roll-top baths and fireplaces. The house is in Rydal, 1.5 miles north of Ambleside.

WORTH A TRIP

PUNCH BOWL INN

Having scooped oodles of awards over the last couple of years, this cracking **country pub** (☎015395-68237; www.the-punchbowl.co.uk; Crosthwaite; mains £14-28; r £160-310; P) is unfortunately no longer the secret tip it used to be. Even so, it's still an essential stop for gastropub connoisseurs, and serves up some of the finest food in Lakeland.

We're a long world away from scampi-and-chips here – you might feel like tucking into roast veal blanquette, skate wing with shrimp butter or home-smoked duck, washed down perhaps with a choice ale from the in-house Barngates Brewery. Indulged too much? No problem: upstairs rooms dazzle, with reclaimed beams, Roberts Revival radios and underfloor heating.

The pub's in the hamlet of Crosthwaite, about 6 miles southeast of Windermere along the A5074.

Riverside B&B ££
(☎015394-32395; www.riverside-at-ambleside.co.uk; Under Loughrigg; d £92-108; P) Lodged beside the clattering River Rothay half a mile from town, this detached Victorian villa is distinguished by lots of little luxuries that make it special: walking guides, ethical bath products, fresh chutneys from the Hawkshead Relish Company. Two rooms have spa baths, one a pine four-poster.

Lakes Lodge B&B ££
(☎015394-33240; www.lakeslodge.co.uk; Lake Rd; r £89-129; 📶) Trendy cross between a minihotel and a modern guesthouse: the rooms are all clean lines, stark walls and zero clutter, and there are several extra-big rooms that are ideal for families.

Compston House Hotel B&B ££
(☎015394-32305; www.compstonhouse.co.uk; Compston Rd; d from £76) Quirky Stateside-style B&B, run by expat New Yorkers. Every room is themed after a different state: sunny Hawaii, airy Florida, maritime Maine – you get the idea. Needless to say, there are muffins and maple pancakes for breakfast.

The Gables B&B ££
(☎015394-33272; www.thegables-ambleside.co.uk; Church Walk; s £40-50, d £60-80; P) Gabled

NATIONAL TRUST CAMPSITE BOOKINGS

The NT's three Lake District campsites at Low Wray, Wasdale and Great Langdale have recently started to accept **bookings**, much to the delight of regular Lakeland campers. Pitches can be reserved up to 24 hours before your stay for periods of two nights or longer. There's an online booking fee of £5, or £7.50 for telephone and email bookings. Discounts are also available if you arrive by 'green transport' (eg by showing a train or bus ticket).

Contact the **Bookings Coordinator** (015394-63862; campsite.bookings@nationaltrust.org.uk; 1-5pm Mon-Fri), or search for the relevant campsite with the **National Trust** (www.nationaltrust.org.uk) online.

by name, gabled by nature, this double-fronted house is in a quiet spot overlooking the recreation ground. The 14 rooms vary in size – ask for the largest that's available. The owners run Sheila's Cottage restaurant, and guests receive a discount when they dine.

Low Wray CAMPSITE £
(lowwraycampsite@nationaltrust.org.uk; tent sites for 1 adult, car and small tent £8-11, per extra adult £5, extra child £2.50, lake view supplement £7.50-10; campsite arrivals 3-7pm Sat-Thu, 3-9pm Fri) Lovely lakeside campsite run by the National Trust, recently supplemented by the addition of yurts, ecopods and tepees. The site is 3 miles from town along the B5286; bus 505 stops nearby. For ecopod and tent bookings, contact the National Trust, but for yurt and tepee hire, try **4Winds Lakeland Tipis** (01539-821227; www.4windslakelandtipis.co.uk; tipi per week £270-440), **Long Valley** (01539-731089; www.long-valley-yurts.co.uk; yurts per week £385-460), or **Wild in Style** (07909-446381; www.wildinstyle.co.uk; yurts per week £350-450), which has more-luxurious yurts.

Ambleside YHA HOSTEL £
(0845-371 9620; ambleside@yha.org.uk; Windermere Rd; dm from £14; P) Fresh from a refit, this flagship YHA is open for business again with fresh rooms (including plenty of doubles), lake views and a host of organised activities (from kayaking to ghyll-scrambling). Great facilities (kitchen, bike rental, boat jetty and bar) mean it's heavily subscribed in high season.

Ambleside Backpackers HOSTEL ££
(015394-32340; www.englishlakesbackpackers.co.uk; Old Lake Rd; dm £16; P @) Cottage hostel a short walk south from Ambleside's centre.

Full Circle CAMPSITE £££
(07975-671928; www.lake-district-yurts.co.uk; yurts £295-440; P) Yurt camping in the grounds of Rydal Hall, near Rydal Mount.

Eating

It's wise to book the following places.

TOP CHOICE **Lucy's on a Plate** RESTAURANT ££
(015394-31191; www.lucysofambleside.co.uk; Church St; mains lunch £6-15, dinner £15-25; 10am-9pm) Lucy's started life in 1989 as a specialist grocery, but over the last decade it's mushroomed into a full-blown gastronomic empire, with premises dotted all over Ambleside, as well as a Windermere outpost and even a cookery school in Staveley. The original bistro is still the best of the bunch, though: a light and inviting space with pine tables and a sweet conservatory, serving Lucy's trademark quirkily named food, such as 'fruity porker', 'fell-walker filler' or 'pruned piggy-wig'. It gets very busy, so bookings are essential at busy times and weekends.

Glass House RESTAURANT ££
(015394-32137; Rydal Rd; mains lunch £8-14, dinner £13-19) Ritzy restaurant in a converted watermill (with the original mill wheel and machinery still on site), serving some of the most accomplished Med and French food in the Lakes, underpinned by top-quality local ingredients – Herdwick lamb, Lakeland chicken, and fish from the north coast ports.

Fellini's VEGETARIAN ££
(015394-32487; Church St; mains £10.95; dinner only, closed Mon in winter) Fear not, vegetarians: you might be in the land of the Cumberland sausage and the tattie hotpot, but thanks to this new veggie venture you won't have to go without a good meal. It's a long way from tired old nut roasts: think grilled courgette towers, potato filo baskets and walnut and pear cannelloni. It's run by the owners of Ambleside's cinema and Zeffirelli's restaurant (as well as the lovely Yewfield B&B, see p706). The movie-meal combo costs £19.95.

Zeffirelli's BISTRO £
(☎015394 33845; Compston Rd; pizzas & mains £8-10; ⏲until 10pm) Affectionately known as Zeff's by the locals, this buzzy pizza and pasta joint doubles as Ambleside's jazz club after dark. Artful lighting and big curvy seats conjure a cool vibe. The movie-meal combo costs £17.95, including a two-course meal and a ticket to the flicks.

Tarantella RESTAURANT ££
(10 Lake Rd; mains £10-16) Snazzy Italian served in elegant surroundings, with wood-fired pizzas and authentic pastas partnered by unusual regional fare such as duck-and-chilli sausage and roast tuna.

Lucy 4 TAPAS £
(Map p698; 2 St Mary's Lane; tapas £4-10; ⏲5-11pm Mon-Sat, to 10.30pm Sun) Tapas and wine-bar offshoot of Lucy's eating empire.

Apple Pie CAFE £
(Rydal Rd; lunches £4-10; ⏲breakfast & lunch) Sunny cafe popular for its cakes, sandwiches, Bath buns and hearty pies.

Lucy's Specialist Grocery DELI £
(Compston Rd) The deli that started it all, now relocated to Compston Rd. Shelves stocked with chutneys, chocs and other tempting treats, plus chiller cabinets full of Lakeland produce.

Drinking & Entertainment

Ambleside has plenty of pubs: locals favour the **Golden Rule** (Smithy Brow) for its ale selection, while the **Royal Oak** (Market Pl) packs in the post-hike punters.

Ambleside's two-screen **Zeffirelli's Cinema** (☎015394-33100; Compston Rd) is next to Zeff's, with extra screens in a converted church down the road.

Shopping

Compston Rd has enough equipment shops to launch an assault on Everest, with branches of **Rohan** and **Gaymer Sports** on Market Cross. Also on Compston Rd, **Black's** is a favourite with hikers, and the **Climber's Shop** specialises in rock-climbing gear.

Information

Library (Kelsick Rd; per hr £3; ⏲10am-5pm Mon & Wed, to 7pm Tue & Fri, to 1pm Sat) Internet access.

Tourist office (☎015394 32582; tic@thehubofambleside.com; Central Buildings, Market Cross; ⏲9am-5pm)

Getting There & Around

BICYCLE For mountain-bike hire, including maps, pump, helmet and lock:

Biketreks (☎015394-31505; www.biketreks.net; Compston Rd; per day £20) **Ghyllside Cycles** (☎015394-33592; www.ghyllside.co.uk; The Slack; per day £18)

BUS Lots of buses run through Ambleside.

555 to Grasmere and Windermere (hourly, 10 buses on Sunday).

505 to Hawkshead and Coniston (10 a day Monday to Saturday, six on Sunday, mid-March to October).

516 (six daily, five on Sunday) to Elterwater and Langdale.

Around Ambleside

TOP CHOICE **Rydal Mount** HISTORIC HOME
(www.rydalmount.co.uk; adult/child £6/2.50, gardens only adults £4; ⏲9.30am-5pm daily Mar-Oct, 11am-4pm Wed-Mon Nov & Feb) While most people flock to Dove Cottage in search of William Wordsworth, those in the know head for Rydal Mount, the Wordsworth family home from 1813 until his death in 1850.

Still owned by the poet's distant descendants, the house is a treasure trove of Wordsworth memorabilia. Downstairs you can wander around the book-lined drawing room (look out for William's pen, inkstand and picnic box, and a celebrated portrait of the poet by the American painter Henry Inman). Upstairs you can nose around the family bedrooms (including one belonging to Wordsworth's sister Dorothy, who never married and remained with the family until her death in 1855). On the top floor is Wordsworth's attic study, containing his encyclopedia and a sword belonging to his younger brother John, who was killed in a shipwreck in 1805.

Most of the gardens around the house were laid out according to Wordsworth's own designs; you can even rest your legs in the little summer house where the poet liked to try out his latest verse. Below the house is **Dora's Field**, which Wordsworth planted with daffodils in memory of his eldest daughter, who succumbed to tuberculosis in 1847.

The house is 1.5 miles northwest of Ambleside, off the A591. Bus 555 (and bus 599 from April to October), between Grasmere, Ambleside, Windermere and Kendal, stops at the end of the drive.

Grasmere

POP 1458

Even without its Romantic connections, gorgeous Grasmere would still be one of the Lakes' biggest draws. It's one of the prettiest of the Lakeland hamlets, huddled at the base of a sweeping valley dotted with woods, pastures and slate-coloured hills, but most of the thousands of trippers come in search of its famous former residents: opium-eating Thomas de Quincey, unruly Coleridge and grand old man William Wordsworth. With such a rich literary heritage, Grasmere unsurprisingly gets crammed; avoid high summer if you can.

Sights

Dove Cottage HISTORIC HOME

(015394-35544; www.wordsworth.org.uk; adult/child £7.50/4.50; 9.30am-5.30pm, last admission 4pm winter) Originally an inn called The Dove and Olive, this tiny cottage just outside Grasmere is the most famous former home of William Wordsworth. He arrived here with his sister Dorothy in 1799 before being joined in 1802 by his new wife, Mary, and soon after, three children – John, Dora and Thomas – who were born here in 1803, 1804 and 1806.

The tiny cottage was a cramped but happy home for the growing family – a time memorably recounted in Dorothy's diary, later published as the *Grasmere Journal* – and after they were eventually forced to seek more space at nearby Allan House in 1808, the cottage was leased by Wordsworth's young friend Thomas de Quincey (author of *Confessions of an English Opium Eater*).

Covered with climbing roses, honeysuckle and tiny latticed windows, the cottage contains some fascinating artefacts – keep your eyes peeled for some fine portraits of Wordsworth, a cabinet containing his spectacles, shaving case and razor, and a set of scales used by de Quincey to weigh out his opium. Entry is by timed ticket to prevent overcrowding, and includes a half-hour tour.

Next door is the **Wordsworth Museum & Art Gallery**, which houses a collection of letters, portraits and manuscripts relating to the Romantic movement, and regularly hosts events and poetry readings.

St Oswald's Church CHURCH

Parts of Grasmere's delightful village church date back to the 13th century. The Wordsworth family regularly came here to worship: inside you'll see a memorial to the poet alongside his own prayer book, and in the churchyard you'll find the graves of William, Mary and Dorothy; the Wordsworth children Dora, Catherine and Thomas; and Samuel Taylor Coleridge's son Hartley.

Activities

Popular **fell hikes** starting from Grasmere include Helm Crag (1328ft), often known as the 'Lion and the Lamb', thanks to its distinctive shape, Silver Howe (1292ft), Loughrigg Fell (1099ft) and the multi-peak circuit known as the Easedale Round (five to six hours, 8.5 to 9 miles).

Sleeping

TOP CHOICE **Moss Grove Organic** HOTEL £££

(015394-35251; www.mossgrove.com; r £225-325; P) This Victorian villa has been lavishly redeveloped as Lakeland's loveliest eco-chic hotel, second to none in terms of green credentials: sheep-fleece insulation, natural-ink wallpapers, organic paints, reclaimed-timber beds. The rooms are mostly enormous, and luxury touches, such as duck-down duvets, underfloor-heated bathrooms and a organic buffet breakfast, really make it stand out from the crowd. It's expensive, but definitely one to remember.

How Foot Lodge B&B ££

(015394-35366; www.howfoot.co.uk; Town End; d £70-78; P) Wordsworth groupies will adore this stone cottage just a stroll from William's digs at Dove Cottage. The six rooms are light and contemporary, finished in fawns and beiges; ask for the one with the private sun lounge for that indulgent edge. The rates are fantastic, too, especially considering the heritage and location.

Harwood Hotel B&B ££

(015394-35248; www.harwoodhotel.co.uk; Red Lion Square; d £95-135;) Despite the 'hotel' in the name, this is a really a B&B – but a very classy one. Nestled right in the middle of Grasmere above Heidi's cafe, the six rooms are chocolate-box cute – expect plenty of Cath Kidston–style patterns and frilly heart-shape cushions. Ask for room 1 for its fell views and spacious layout, or room 3, with its Tardis-like jacuzzi-shower.

Raise View House B&B ££

(015394-35215; www.raiseviewhouse.co.uk; White Bridge; s/d £90/110; P) For that all-essential fell view, you can't really top this excellent B&B. All the rooms have a different outlook (the ones from Helm Crag, Easedale and Stone Arthur are particularly impressive), and the rest of the house is beautifully appointed: Farrow & Ball paints, Gilchrist & Soames bathstuffs, and Wedgwood china on the breakfast table.

Lancrigg B&B £££
(☎015394-35317; www.lancrigg.co.uk; Easedale; r £110-170; P) This all-vegetarian country house once owned by Arctic adventurer John Richardson, is half a mile outside Grasmere along Easedale Rd. It's very traditional in feel – heavy on the swags, ruches and flock papers – but it's very comfortable, and the views of gardens and mountains are grand.

Grasmere Hostel HOSTEL £
(☎015394-35055; www.grasmerehostel.co.uk; Broadrayne Farm; dm £18.50; P @) When was the last time you stayed at a hostel with a Nordic sauna? It might be pricier than Grasmere's two YHAs, but you'll be treating yourself to a superior sleep: bathrooms en suite for every room, a mountain-view lounge and two kitchens. The hostel's just off the A591 near the Traveller's Rest pub. Bus 555 stops nearby.

Butharlyp How YHA HOSTEL £
(☎0845-371 9319; www.yha.org.uk; Easedale Rd; dm £15.50; ⏲reception 7am-10pm Feb-Nov, weekends only Dec & Jan; P @) The biggest of Grasmere's two YHA hostels is in a fine Victorian house plonked amidst grassy grounds. The dorms are starting to show their age, but the idyllic setting and decent bar-restaurant make this another superior YHA. The hostel also handles bookings for Thorney How.

Thorney How YHA HOSTEL £
(☎0845-371 9319; grasmere@yha.org.uk; Easedale Rd; dm from £14; ⏲reception 7.30-10am & 5-11pm Apr-Oct) For rustic character, try this old farmhouse tucked away on a back lane 15 minutes from Grasmere. The rooms are spartan and the facilities basic, but you'll be staying in a historic spot – Thorney How was the first property purchased by the YHA back in 1931.

Eating & Drinking

TOP CHOICE **Jumble Room** RESTAURANT £££
(☎015394-35188; Langdale Rd; mains £13-24; ⏲lunch weekends, dinner Wed-Mon) Husband-and-wife team Andy and Crissy Hill have turned this tiny boho bistro into a real gastronomic heavy-hitter. Mixing quality Lakeland produce with Mediterranean influences (particularly from Spain and Italy), it attracts diners from far and wide, and the decor oozes oddball appeal, from the jumble-shop-chic furniture and polka dot plates to the colourful cow pictures on the downstairs walls. Reserve ahead.

Sara's Bistro BISTRO ££
(Broadgate; mains £10-16) Hearty homespun cooking is Sarah's raison d'être – big portions of roast chicken, lamb shanks and apple crumble, served without the faintest hint of fuss.

Heidi's of Grasmere CAFE £
(Red Lion Sq; lunch mains £4-8; ⏲9am-5.30pm) Yummy little sandwich shop and cafe beneath the Harwood Hotel. Pull up a pine table for some piping-hot soup, a toasted sandwich or the house special, 'cheese smokey'.

Sarah Nelson's Gingerbread Shop CONFECTIONERY SHOP
(www.grasmeregingerbread.co.uk; Church Stile; 12 pieces of gingerbread £3.50; ⏲9.15am-5.30pm Mon-Sat, 12.30-5pm Sun) Don't think about leaving Grasmere without sampling Sarah Nelson's legendary gingerbread, produced to the same secret recipe for the last 150 years and still served by ladies in frilly pinnies and starched bonnets.

Traveller's Rest PUB ££
(A591; mains £8-20; ⏲noon-11pm Mon-Sat, noon-10.30pm Sun) With its sputtering fires, deep seats and inglenook bar, Grasmere's 16th-century coaching inn still makes a fine place for a steak pie or a hotpot, accompanied (of course) by a pint of Jennings Bitter or Cockerhoop.

Other options:

Rowan Tree CAFE £
(Stocks Lane; mains £3-10, pizzas £6-9) Riverside cafe good for lunchtime ciabattas, fish dishes and veggie plates.

Villa Colombina BISTRO ££
(Townend; lunch mains £4-10, dinner from £12) Italian dishes a hop and a skip from Dove Cottage.

Miller Howe Cafe CAFE ££
(Red Lion Sq; mains £5-14) Chic cafe on the main village square.

Getting There & Away

The hourly 555 runs from Windermere to Grasmere (15 minutes), via Ambleside, Rydal Church and Dove Cottage. The open-top 599 (two or three per hour March to August) runs from Grasmere south via Ambleside, Troutbeck Bridge, Windermere and Bowness.

Hawkshead

POP 1640

Lakeland villages don't come much more postcard-perfect than Hawkshead, a muddle of whitewashed cottages, cobbled lanes and old pubs lost amongst bottle-green countryside between Ambleside and Coniston. Chuck in connections to both Wordsworth and Beatrix Potter, and you won't be surprised to find Hawkshead awash with visitors in the high summer – although the fact that cars are banned in the village centre keeps things a bit more tranquil.

Sights

Hawkshead Grammar School HISTORIC BUILDING

(www.hawksheadgrammar.org.uk; admission £2; 10am-1pm & 2-5pm Mon-Sat, 1-5pm Sun Apr-Sep, 10am-1pm & 2-3.30pm Mon-Sat, 1-3.30pm Sun Oct) In centuries past, promising young Lakeland gentleman were sent to Hawkshead's village school for their educational foundations, including a young William Wordsworth, who attended the school from 1779 to 1787. The curriculum was punishing: 10 hours' study a day, covering weighty subjects such as Latin, Greek, geometry, science and rhetoric. Hardly surprising young Willie (amongst others) felt the urge to carve his name into one of the desks.

Upstairs is a small exhibition exploring the history of the school.

Beatrix Potter Gallery GALLERY

(NT; Red Lion Sq; adult/child £4.40/2.10; 10.30am-4.30pm Sat-Thu mid-Mar–Oct) Beatrix Potter's husband, the solicitor William Heelis, was based in Hawkshead. His former office is now owned by the National Trust and contains a selection of delicate wildlife watercolours by Beatrix Potter, illustrating her considerable skills as a botanical painter and amateur naturalist.

Discounted admission is available if you keep hold of your ticket from Hill Top.

Sleeping & Eating

Accommodation in Hawkshead proper is fairly limited, but there are some good options further afield.

TOP CHOICE **Yewfield** B&B ££

(015394-36765; www.yewfield.co.uk; Hawkshead Hill; d £96-120; P) Run by the owners of Zeff's in Ambleside, the rooms at this all-veggie house combine oriental fabrics, slinky finishes and Edwardian features (although the Tower Room has a more classic feel). Breakfast is organic, vegetarian and sourced from the kitchen garden, and the gardens are gorgeous: there are also self-catering apartments in the Swallows Nest (£280 to £550 per week). The house is 2 miles west of Hawkshead on the B5285.

Ivy House Hotel B&B ££

(015394-36204; Main St; d £90-110; P) A great village location and Grade II heritage listing make this a tempting option in Hawkshead. A circular staircase swirls up through the house to six pleasant, slightly prissy rooms; the ones in the annexe are more mundane.

Hawkshead YHA HOSTEL £

(0845-371 9321; hawkshead@yha.org.uk; dm from £14; P @) This hostel occupies a Regency house a mile along the Newby Bridge road. Like many Lakeland YHAs, the period architecture is impressive – cornicing, panelled doors, a veranda – and the big dorms boast big views. There's bike rental and a kitchen, and buses stop outside the door.

Queen's Head Hotel PUB, B&B ££

(015394-36271; Main St; mains £14-22, d £40-90) Hawkshead has several decent pubs, but our pick is the old Queen's Head, which fairly brims with oak-panelled appeal. Hale and hearty country food (Esthwaite trout, Winster pork, Gressingham duck) in the low-ceilinged bar, partnered by small, prim rooms upstairs and a less appealing lodge out back.

Hawkshead Relish Company DELI £

(015394-36614; www.hawksheadrelish.com; The Square; 9.30am-5pm Mon-Fri, from 10am Sun) Award-winning chutneys, relishes and mustards, from classic piccalilli to damson jam.

Getting There & Away

Hawkshead is linked with Windermere, Ambleside and Coniston by bus 505 (10 Monday to Saturday, six on Sunday mid-March to October), and to Hill Top and Coniston by the Cross-Lakes Shuttle.

Around Hawkshead

TARN HOWS

About 2 miles off the B5285 from Hawkshead, a windy country lane wends its way to **Tarn Hows**, a famously photogenic artificial lake built on land donated to the National Trust by Beatrix Potter in 1930. Trails wind their way around the lakeshore – keep you eyes peeled for rare red squirrels frolicking in the treetops.

Parking can be difficult in summer and on weekends, so you might prefer to catch the bus. Several services, including the 505, the X31/32 and the Cross-Lakes Experience, stop nearby.

GRIZEDALE FOREST

Stretching across the hills between Coniston Water and Esthwaite Water is Grizedale (from the Old Norse for 'wild boar'), a dense woodland of oak, larch and pine that has been almost entirely replanted over the last hundred years after extensive logging during the 19th century.

The forest is now a hugely popular spot with mountain bikers and walkers; eight marked walking paths and five mountain bike routes wind their way through the trees. On your way around, look out for some of the 90-odd outdoor sculptures that have been created in the forest by local and international artists over the course of the last 30 years.

Budding 'Gorillas' (adults) and 'Baboons' (children) can also test their skills at **Go Ape** (www.goape.co.uk; adult/child £30/25; 9-5pm Mar-Oct, plus winter weekends), a gravity-defying assault course along rope ladders, bridges, platforms and hair-raising zip-slides.

For general information on the forest, the new **Grizedale Visitors Centre** (01229-860010; www.forestry.gov.uk/grizedaleforestpark; 10am-5pm, 11am-4pm winter) provides trail leaflets and forest maps. It's also home to the small **Café in the Forest** (10am-5pm) and **Grizedale Mountain Bike Hire** (www.grizedalemountainbikes.co.uk; per day adult/child from £25/10; 9am-5.30pm Mar-Oct, last hire 2pm).

HILL TOP

(NT; 015394-36269; hilltop@nationaltrust.org.uk; adult/child £6.60/3.10; 10am-4.30pm mid-May-Aug, 10.30am-4.30pm mid-Mar–mid-May & Sep-Oct, 11.30am-3.30pm mid-Feb–mid-Mar) In the tiny village of Near Sawrey, 2 miles south of Hawkshead, this idyllic farmhouse is a must for Beatrix Potter buffs: it was the first house she lived in after moving to the Lake District, and it's also where she wrote and illustrated many of her famous tales.

Purchased in 1905 (largely on the proceeds of her first bestseller, *The Tale of Peter Rabbit*), Hill Top is crammed with decorative details that fans will recognise from the author's illustrations. The house features directly in *Samuel Whiskers*, *Tom Kitten* and *Jemima Puddleduck*, and you might recognise the cast-iron kitchen range from many of Potter's underground burrows.

DON'T MISS

THE DRUNKEN DUCK

TOP CHOICE **Drunken Duck** (015394-36347; www.drunkenduckinn.co.uk; Barngates, Hawkeshead; mains £13-25, r £95-275; P) This designer place is much, much more than a bog-standard gastropub – it's a brewery, boutique B&B, historic boozer and lip-smacking bistro rolled into one indulgent bundle. Inside the 400-year-old inn, vintage architecture marries up with modern touches. Slate fireplaces and old signs sit alongside leather chairs and neutral shades, and while the rooms are small, they're all fresh and inviting, with Roberts radios, enamel baths and rolling rural views (some even overlook a private tarn). The real treat, though, is the pub itself, where home-brewed ales from the Barngates Brewery accompany a menu oozing with sophisticated flavours – crab-claw salad, venison loin, pan-fried turbot. Simply super.

Thanks to its worldwide fame (helped along by the 2006 biopic *Miss Potter*), Hill Top is one of the Lakes' most popular spots. Entry is by timed ticket, and the queues can be seriously daunting during the summer holidays.

Getting There & Away

For details on the Cross-Lakes Experience, see p693.

X30 Grizedale Wanderer (four daily March to November) Runs from Haverthwaite to Grizedale via Hawkshead and Moor Top.

505 Stops at Hawkshead en route between Coniston and Windermere.

Coniston

POP 1948

Hunkered beneath the pockmarked peak of the Old Man (803m), the lakeside village of Coniston was originally established as a centre for the copper-mining industry, but the only remnants of the industry left are the many abandoned quarries and mine shafts that now litter the surrounding hilltops.

Coniston's main claim to fame is as the location for a string of world-record speed attempts made here by Sir Malcolm Campbell and his son, Donald, between the 1930s and 1960s. Tragically, after beating the record several times, Donald was killed during an attempt in 1967, when his futuristic jet-boat *Bluebird* flipped at around 320mph. The boat and its pilot were recovered in 2001, and Campbell was buried in the cemetery near St Andrew's church.

Coniston is a fairly quiet village these days, mainly worth a visit for its lovely lake cruises and a trip to the former house of John Ruskin at Brantwood.

Sights

Brantwood HISTORIC HOME

(015394-41396; www.brantwood.org.uk; adult/child£6.30/1.35,gardensonly£4.50/1.35; 11am-5.30pm mid-Mar–mid-Nov, to 4.30pm Wed-Sun mid-Nov–mid-Mar) John Ruskin (1819–1900), the Victorian polymath, philosopher and critic, was one of the great thinkers of 19th-century society, expounding views on everything from Venetian architecture to the finer points of traditional lace-making. In 1871 he purchased Brantwood and spent the next 20 years expanding and modifying the house and grounds, championing the value of traditional 'Arts and Crafts' over soulless factory-made materials.

The result is a living monument to Ruskin's aesthetic principles. Every inch of the house, from the handmade furniture through to the formal gardens, was designed according to his painstaking instructions (he even dreamt up some of the wallpaper designs).

Upstairs you can view a collection of his watercolours before stopping for lunch at the excellent **Jumping Jenny** (lunches £4-8) cafe and catching a leisurely boat back to Coniston. The boat trip from Brantwood back to Coniston takes about half an hour. Alternatively you can drive to the house – take the B5285 towards Hawkshead and follow the brown signs to Brantwood.

Ruskin Museum MUSEUM

(www.ruskinmuseum.com; adult/child £5.25/2.50; 10am-5.30pm Easter–mid-Nov, 10.30am-3.30pm Wed-Sun mid-Nov–Easter) Coniston's museum explores the village's history, touching on copper mining, Arthur Ransome and the Campbell story. There's also an extensive section on John Ruskin, with displays of his writings, watercolours and sketchbooks. An extension is currently being built to house Campbell's K7 boat: if it's not finished by the time you get here, you can see the boat's tail fin, air intake and engine. The museum also arranges **guided walks** (adult/child £7/3.50) exploring the Campbell story and the area's John Ruskin connections.

Activities

Boating

Lake Coniston famously inspired Arthur Ransome's classic children's tale *Swallows & Amazons*. Peel Island, towards the southern end of Coniston Water, doubles in the book as 'Wild Cat Island', while the Gondola steam yacht allegedly gave Ransome the idea for Captain Flint's houseboat. **Coniston Boating Centre** (015394-41366; Coniston Jetty) hires out rowing boats, Canadian canoes and motorboats, or you can take one of the two cruise services which glide out across the glassy waters.

Steam Yacht Gondola LAKE CRUISE

(015394-63850; adult/child £8.50/4.50) Built in 1859 and restored in the 1980s by the National Trust, this wonderful steam yacht looks like a cross between a Venetian *vaporetto* and an English houseboat, complete with cushioned saloons and polished wood seats. It's a stately way of seeing the lake, especially if you're visiting Brantwood. There are five trips daily from mid-March to October, plus less frequent commentated Explorer cruises covering Ransome, the Campbells and Ruskin. Reduced fares are available to other points round the lake.

And don't fret about carbon emissions; since 2008 the Gondola's been running on ecofriendly waste-wood logs, cutting her carbon footprint by 90%.

Coniston Launch LAKE CRUISE

(015394-36216; www.conistonlaunch.co.uk) A more contemporary way to get around the lake is aboard Coniston's two modern launches, which have run on solar panels since 2005. There are two routes: the **Northern service** (adult/child return £8.90/4.95) calls at the Waterhead Hotel, Torver and Brantwood, while the **Southern service** (adult/child return £12.50/6.25) sails to the jetties at Torver, Water Park, Lake Bank, Sunny Bank and Brantwood via Peel Island. You can break your journey and walk to the next jetty. There are between five and nine daily trips depending on the time of year.

As with the Gondola, commentated cruises on the Campbells (adult/child £11.70/5.75) and *Swallows & Amazons* (£12/6) are available throughout the year. Ask at the ticket office for details.

Walking

If you're in Coniston to hike, chances are you've come to conquer the **Old Man** (7.5 miles, four to five hours). It's a steep but rewarding climb past Coniston's abandoned copper mines to the summit, from where the views stretch to the Cumbrian Coast on a clear day.

The tourist office has leaflets on possible routes up the Old Man and other walks, as well as the annual **Coniston Walking Festival** (www.conistonwalkingfestival.org), held in September.

Sleeping

TOP CHOICE **Yew Tree Farm** B&B ££
(☎015394-41433; www.yewtree-farm.com; d £100-124; P) Farmhouses don't come finer than this whitewashed, slate-roofed beauty, which doubled for Hill Top in *Miss Potter* (fittingly, since Beatrix Potter owned Yew Tree in the 1930s). It's still a working farm, but these days it offers luxurious lodgings alongside the cowsheds. Cream of the crop is 'Tarn Hows', with its wood-frame rafters, slate-floor bathroom and regal four-poster bed. If it's fully booked, console yourself with a nutty flapjack or a Hot Herdwick sandwich at the delightful Yew Tree Tea Room next door.

Bank Ground Farm B&B ££
(☎015394-41264; www.bankground.com; East of the Lake; d £70-80; P) This lakeside farmhouse has literary clout: Arthur Ransome used it as the model for Holly Howe Farm in *Swallows & Amazons*. Parts of the house date back to the 15th century, so the rooms are obviously snug, but they're all smartly done, some with sleigh beds, others with exposed beams. The **tearoom** (⏲noon-5pm Fri-Sun Easter-Oct) is a beauty, too, and there are several pretty cottages if you can't bear to tear yourself away.

Summer Hill Country House HOTEL ££
(☎015394-36180; www.summerhillcountryhouse.com; Hawkshead Hill; d £70-104; P @ ᯤ) You'll need a car to get to this elegant house-hotel, as it's halfway between Coniston and Hawkshead, but it's really worth the drive. There are only five rooms, but each has its own feel: we particularly recommend the monochrome No 4 and crimson No 5. Plenty of treats, too: posh bath products, sculptures in the garden, and Mac minis for getting online or watching DVDs.

Crown Inn Coniston B&B ££
(☎015394-41243; Tilberthwaite Ave; www.crowninnconiston.com; s/d £60/90; P) This village inn offers more than the usual pub rooms: careful refurbishment have given all 12 rooms an attractive and contemporary spin, although some are still on the small side.

Holly How YHA HOSTEL £
(☎0845-371 9511; conistonhh@yha.org.uk; Far End; dm £16) Coniston's main hostel occupies a slate-fronted period house along the road towards Ambleside, and offers the usual YHA facilities: kitchens, evening meals and bike hire, with a choice of four-, eight- or 10-bed dorms. It's a school-trip favourite, so book ahead.

Coppermines YHA HOSTEL £
(☎0845-371 9630; coppermines@yha.org.uk; dm £16; ⏲Easter-Oct) Mountain hostel popular with hikers setting out for the Old Man. It's 1.5 miles from Coniston; no car access.

Coniston Hall Campsite CAMPSITE £
(☎015394-41223; sites from £12; ⏲Easter-Oct) Busy lakeside campsite a mile from town.

Eating & Drinking

There are several cafes dotted round Coniston, but your best bet for filling food is one of the village pubs.

Black Bull PUB ££
(www.conistonbrewery.com; Yewdale Rd; mains £6-14) Quality pub grub right in the middle of Coniston village: the Cumberland sausage is particularly noteworthy, as are the house-brewed ales, including Bluebird Bitter, Old Man Ale and Winter Warmer Blacksmiths.

Sun Hotel PUB ££
(www.thesunconiston.com; mains £12-20) Dine under hefty beams or in a fell-view conservatory at the Sun, perched on a little hill just behind the village and famously used as an HQ by Donald Campbell during his final fateful campaign.

Harry's CAFE £
(4 Yewdale Rd; mains £6-12) Part wine bar, part cafe, part bistro, serving solid (if rather unstarry) steaks, pizzas, pastas and club sandwiches, along with the prodigious Harry's Big Breakfast.

Bluebird Cafe CAFE £
(Lake Rd; lunch mains £4-8; ⏲breakfast & lunch) Perfectly placed by the Coniston jetty, the Bluebird is a fine spot for tea and cakes or a quick ice cream before hopping aboard the cross-lake launch.

Information

Coniston Tourist Office (☎015394-41533; www.conistontic.org; Ruskin Ave; ⏲9.30am-5.30pm Easter-Oct, till 4pm Nov-Easter) The Coniston Loyalty Card (£2) offers local discounts. The Ruskin Explorer ticket (adult/child £14.95/6.50) includes Windermere bus fare, a Coniston launch ticket and entrance to Brantwood; pick it up here or from the bus driver.

Hollands Cafe (☎015394-41303; Tilberthwaite Ave; per hr £5; ⏲9am-4pm or 5pm Mon-Sat) Internet access.

Getting There & Away

Bus 505 runs from Windermere (10 Monday to Saturday, six on Sunday mid-March to October), via Ambleside, with a couple of daily connections to Kendal (1¼ hours).

Langdale

Travelling north from Coniston, the road passes into increasingly wild, empty countryside. Barren hilltops loom as you travel north past the old Viking settlement of Elterwater en route to Great Langdale, where the main road comes to an end and many of the Lakes' greatest trails begin – including the stomp up the Langdale Pikes past Harrison Stickle (736m) and Pike o' Stickle (709m), and the spectacular ascent of Crinkle Crags (819m). An old road (now sealed with tarmac, although still one of the steepest and twistiest in the entire country) leads through Little Langdale over Wrynose and Hardknott Passes to the coast, passing a ruined Roman fort en route.

Getting There & Away

Bus 516 (the Langdale Rambler, six daily, five on Sunday) is the only scheduled bus service to the valley, with stops at Ambleside, Skelwith Bridge, Elterwater, and the Old Dungeon Ghyll Hotel in Great Langdale.

ELTERWATER

Ringed by trees and fields, the small, charming lake of Elterwater derives its name from the Old Norse for 'swan', after the colonies of whooper swans that winter here. With its maple-shaded village green and quiet country setting, it's a popular base for exploring the Langdale fells.

Langdale YHA (☎0845-371 9748; langdale@yha.org.uk; High Close, Loughrigg; dm £14; ⏲reception 7.30-10am & 5-11pm Mar-Oct; Ⓟ@), halfway between Grasmere and Elterwater, has an impressive Victorian facade, but the rooms are fairly standard YHA. Lots of dorm-size choice though, and good amenities, including laundry, shop and games room.

Elterwater YHA (☎0845-371 9017; elterwater@yha.org.uk; dm £14; ⏲reception 7.30am-10am & 5-10.30pm Easter-Oct; @) is lodged inside an old barn and farmhouse opposite the village pub. It's institutional – easy-clean fabrics, boarding-school bunk beds and a functional kitchen – but dead handy for local trails.

The lovely old **Britannia Inn** (☎015394-37210; www.britinn.net; d £90-118; Ⓟ) is a long-standing walkers' favourite. All the rooms have been redone with fresh fabrics and shiny en suites, and hikers cram into the downstairs bar (mains £8 to £14) for hearty steaks, pints and pies. The Sunday roast is rather fine, too.

GREAT LANGDALE

Hemmed in by hills, this hamlet is one of the Lake District's classic walking centres. Some of the most famous (and challenging) Lakeland fells are within reach, including **Pike o' Blisco** (705m), the five summits of the **Crinkle Crags** and the chain of peaks known as the **Langdale Pikes**: Pike O' Stickle (709m), Loft Crag (682m), Harrison Stickle (736m) and Pavey Ark (700m). It's a full-day, strenuous hike if you choose to take it on, and it's best left for good weather – after all that effort, you'll at the least want to be rewarded with a good view.

The classic place stay in Great Langdale is the **Old Dungeon Ghyll** (☎015394-37272; www.odg.co.uk; d £102-112; Ⓟ), backed by soaring fells and built from sturdy Lakeland stone. It's been the getaway of choice for many well-known walkers and it's still endearingly old-fashioned: country chintz and venerable furniture in the rooms; oak beams, wood tables and a crackling fire in the walkers' bar; and more history per square inch than practically anywhere in the Lakes. For more contemporary trappings, try the **New Dungeon Ghyll** (☎015394-37213; www.dungeon-ghyll.co.uk; d £98-120; Ⓟ) next door.

The **Stickle Barn** (☎015394-37356; mains £4-12) is a popular choice for a posthike dinner, with curries, casseroles and stews to warm those weary bones. There's basic dorm accommodation in the bunkhouse out back.

Many hikers choose to kip at the **Great Langdale Campsite** (langdalecamp@nationaltrust.org.uk; tent sites 1 adult with car £8-11, extra adult/child £5/2.50; arrivals 3-7pm Sat-Thu, 3-9pm Fri), a typically well-run NT campground a mile up the valley, with glorious mountain views and the recent addition of eco-pods (£20 to £40 per night) and Long Valley yurts (£285 to £460 per week).

LITTLE LANGDALE

Separated from Great Langdale by Lingmoor Fell (459m), Little Langdale is a quiet village on the road to Wrynose Pass. There are many little-known walks nearby, and at the head of the valley is the Three Shire Stone, marking the traditional meeting point of Cumberland, Westmoreland and Lancashire.

The only place to stay is the **Three Shires Inn** (www.threeshiresinn.co.uk; lunch mains £8-12, dinner £10-16, d £99-115; P), ideally placed for walkers on the route to Lingmoor Fell via Blea Tarn. There's a great selection of local ales behind the bar, including Jennings Best, Black Sheep and Hawkshead Bitters.

Eskdale

Strap yourself in: the road west from Little Langdale into the Eskdale Valley is a roller coaster, snaking across glacial valleys and empty hills all the way to the Cumbrian coast, traversing two of the country's steepest roads, Wrynose Pass (1 in 4 – 1m up for every 4m forward) and Hardknott Pass (1 in 3) en route. If you don't feel up the challenge of the twin passes (a seriously wise decision on busy summer weekends and icy winter days), you can also reach Eskdale from the west via the turn-off near Gosforth, or via the Ravenglass & Eskdale Railway (p725).

Perched above Eskdale are the ruins of **Hardknott Roman Fort**, which once guarded the old pack route from the Roman harbour at Ravenglass. You can still make out the foundations of the commandant's house, watchtowers and parade ground and the views are eye-popping, but you can't help feeling sympathy for the legionaries stationed here – it's hard to think of a lonelier spot in the Roman Empire.

Three miles further down the valley is shoebox-size **Boot**, which hosts a hearty **beer festival** (www.bootbeer.co.uk) every June. It's also handy for **Dalegarth**, the eastern terminus of the Ravenglass & Eskdale Railway.

Sleeping & Eating

Stanley House B&B ££

(019467-23327; www.stanleyghyll-eskdale.co.uk; Eskdale; d/f from £100/140; P) Recently taken over by new owners, this detached house halfway down the valley near Beckfoot station is by far the nicest place to kip in Eskdale. The 12 thoroughly refurbed rooms err towards the classic rather than the contemporary, but they're very comfy and have surprising spoils such as high-def TVs and a complementary DVD library. Half are dog-friendly too.

Boot Inn PUB ££

(019467-23224; www.bootinn.co.uk; Boot; mains £7-12; P) As the venue for the annual Boot Beer Festival, you can probably imagine what's most important to this lovely old pub: ale, and lots of it. There's a comprehensive selection behind the bar, simple food and even simpler rooms (single/double £45/90).

Eskdale YHA HOSTEL £

(0845 371 9317; eskdale@yha.org.uk; Boot; dm £16; reception 7.30-10am & 5-10.30pm Easter-Oct) Many's the walker who's welcomed the site of this excellent back-country hostel, in a stone house livened up with a zingy interior colour palette. There's a good kitchen, bike rental on site and plenty of walks at your doorstep.

Woolpack Inn PUB £

(019467-23230; www.woolpack.co.uk; Boot; mains £8-15; P) This cosy pub has its own microbrewery concocting homemade ales for the two hugger-mugger 'baas', both covered in sporting prints and country memorabilia. The grub's good and there's often live music (think fiddles and guitars).

Wasdale

Hunkered down amidst a dramatic amphitheatre of brooding peaks, Wasdale feels considerably wilder and more remote than many of the Lake District's gentler valleys. Overlooked by the snow-flecked summits of Scafell Pike and Great Gable, it's a famously scenic corner of the Lakes – in fact, it topped a recent TV poll to find the nation's favourite view. With so many summits circled around the valley, it's unsurprisingly a favourite area for hikers who like their views big, wild and empty.

THE ROOF OF ENGLAND

In Scotland it's Ben Nevis (1344m, 4409ft), in Wales it's Snowdon (1085m, 3560ft), and in England the highest peak is **Scaféll Pike** (978m, 3210ft). While they might not be on quite the same scale as the French Alps or the Canadian Rockies, many a hiker has set out to conquer this sky-topping trio, the ultimate goal for British peak-baggers (especially for hardy souls attempting the Three Peaks Challenge, in which all three mountains are conquered in 24 hours).

The classic ascent up Scaféll Pike is from Wasdale Head; there's also a more scenic route that starts near Seathwaite in Borrowdale. Either way, you're looking at around six hours out on the mountain; don't even think about tackling it without proper supplies (rucksack, OS map, compass, food and water, and decent hiking boots) and a favourable weather forecast.

Pretty much the only place for supplies is the **Barn Door Shop** (☎019467-26384; www.wasdaleweb.com) at Wasdale Head, right next to the Wasdale Head Inn.

Sleeping & Eating

TOP CHOICE **Wasdale Head Inn** B&B, PUB ££
(☎019467-26229; www.wasdale.com; d £118, mains £4-12, menus £28; P) This historic inn can stake a claim as the spiritual home of English mountain climbing: one of the inn's early owners, Will Ritson, was among the adventurous gaggle of Victorian gents who pioneered the techniques of early mountaineering in the late 19th century. Dog-eared photos and climbing memorabilia are dotted around the inn, and upstairs you'll find simple, snug rooms crammed with character – and a refreshing absence of TVs. For more space, ask for one of the barn-conversion rooms across the way. Home-brewed ales, hearty food and a genuine slice of Lakeland history – what more could you ask for?

TOP CHOICE **Wasdale Head Campsite** CAMPSITE £
(www.wasdalecampsite.org.uk; sites for 1 adult with car £8-11, extra adult/child £5/2.50; arrivals 8-11am & 5-8pm) This NT campsite is in a fantastically wild spot, nestled beneath the Scaféll range a mile from Wastwater. Facilities are basic (laundry room, showers and not much else), but the views are simply out of this world. A new barrier system has been installed; if you've prebooked you'll have an access card, otherwise you need to arrive between 8am and 11am or 5pm and 8pm.

Low Wood Hall HOTEL ££
(☎019467-26100; www.lowwoodhall.co.uk; Nether Wasdale; s £60-85, d £75-120; P) The only hotel worth the name in the valley is this converted country house, with pleasant rooms split between the main house or a separate lodge. Some are a little flouncy, but with views as good as this, you won't really care.

Wastwater YHA HOSTEL £
(☎0845-371 9350; wasdale@yha.org.uk; Wasdale Hall, Nether Wasdale; dm £14) Nestled beside the green-grey waters of Wastwater, this is yet another stunningly situated hostel in a half-timbered 19th-century mansion in Nether Wasdale, at the lake's western end. There's a restaurant serving Cumbrian nosh and real ales, and many dorms have outlooks across the water.

Rainors Farm B&B ££
(☎019467-25934; www.rainorsfarm.co.uk; Gosforth; s/d £45/65) Three sweet rooms in a whitewashed farmhouse cottage, prettied up with checks, crimson spreads and country views. There's a choice of traditional or veggie breakfasts, and campers can bunk down in a couple of back-garden yurts (£340 to £595 per week). Gosforth is about 5 miles west of Nether Wasdale.

Lingmell House B&B ££
(☎019467-26261; www.lingmellhouse.co.uk; Wasdale Head; s/d £35/70; P) Tucked up at the far end of the valley, this farmhouse B&B is just about as far removed as you can get in Wasdale. The rooms are sparse – don't expect creature comforts, or even much furniture – but at least traffic noise won't be a problem.

Getting There & Away

The **Wasdale Taxibus** (☎019467-25308) runs between Gosforth and Wasdale twice daily on Thursday, Saturday and Sunday, but only if there are enough people to make it worthwhile – you need to ring and book a seat.

Cockermouth

POP 8225

Plonked in flat fields beyond the northerly fells, the Georgian town of Cockermouth was hitherto best known as the birthplace of William Wordsworth and the home base of one of Cumbria's largest beer makers, Jenning's Brewery. But in November 2009 the town hit the national headlines after flash floods inundated the town centre, causing millions of pounds of damage and forcing the emergency evacuation of many residents by RAF helicopter.

Despite its recent trials and tribulations, Cockermouth is slowly picking itself up, and is determined to show the rest of the world it's very much open for business, although the havoc and destruction wreaked by the floods are still plain to see as you wander along Main St.

Sights

Wordsworth House HISTORIC HOME
(NT; ☎01900-824805; Main St; adult/child £5.60/2.80; ⏲11am-4.30pm Mon-Sat mid-Mar–Oct) At the eastern end of Main St, this elegant Georgian mansion is the celebrated birthplace of all five Wordsworth children (William was the second to arrive, born on 7 April 1770, followed a year later by Dorothy). Built around 1745, the house had been painstakingly restored using authentic materials based on family accounts from the Wordsworth archive.

Happily, the house narrowly escaped devastation during the 2009 floods: the floodwaters stopped just inches short of the ground floor, although one of the exterior walls and the back garden (famously mentioned in Wordsworth's epic biographical poem *The Prelude*) were badly damaged. Since the floods, the house has been thoroughly dried out, dehumidified and given a fresh lick of paint, and it's now (almost) back to its former self – don't miss the flagstoned kitchen, the grand 1st-floor drawing room and the bedroom thought to have belonged to wee Willie himself.

Jenning's Brewery BREWERY
(☎01900-821011; www.jenningsbrewery.co.uk; adult/child £6/3) The town's historic brewer, in business since 1874, fared rather less well. The floods left the brewery's main site under around five feet of water, and production at the plant was halted until January 2010. Once again, however, Cockermouth's fighting spirit kicked in, and the brewery is now back up and running. **Guided tours** (⏲11am & 2pm Mon-Sat Mar-Oct, plus Sun Jul & Aug) include a tasting session in the Cooperage Bar. Admirably, since November 2009 Jenning's has donated 10p from every pint of its beer sold in British pubs to the Cumbria Flood Recovery Fund.

Sleeping

TOP CHOICE **Old Homestead** B&B ££
(☎01900-822223; www.byresteads.co.uk; Byresteads Farm; d £76-96; P) This spankingly good farm conversion is 2 miles west of Cockermouth. The farmhouse clutter has been cleared to leave light, airy rooms with

THE COCKERMOUTH FLOODS

On the night of 19 November 2009, some of the heaviest rain ever seen in Britain fell across northwest England. It's estimated that over 314mm (12.4 inches) fell in just over 24 hours, topping the previously held record of 279.4mm (11in) recorded in Martinstown, Dorset, in July 1955. Bridges, roads, walls and buildings across much of Cumbria were swept away as the region's rivers swelled and burst their banks, but the town of Cockermouth was by far the worst affected. The town's position at the confluence of two major rivers, the Cocker and Derwent, meant that the floods rose higher and faster here than anywhere else: at their peak, it's thought that the floodwaters reached a height of 2.5m. Key bridges in the town were destroyed, the entire town centre and Main St were flooded, and thousands of businesses and homes were left without electricity, water and other essential supplies – in some cases for several weeks.

Cockermouth has since rallied in impressive fashion, although it's thought that it could take several years before the town has fully recovered. In the meantime, local businesses have banded together to try to make the most out of their harrowing experience. Demonstrating typical Cumbrian gumption, two enterprising residents have recently developed a **Cockermouth Flood Trail** to help visitors learn more about the nature and extent of the floods. The trail leaflets cost £1 and can be picked up at the tourist office, Wordsworth House and several other locations around town. All proceeds go towards the ongoing reconstruction effort.

just a few rustic touches for character (a wood rafter here, a stone tile or hardwood mirror there). Top choices are the Cruck rooms (with burnished leather sofas) and the Master's Room (with handcrafted four-poster bed), both with vistas across the working sheep farm.

Six Castlegate B&B ££
(☎01900-826749; www.sixcastlegate.co.uk; 6 Castlegate; s/d £48/65;) Saved from the floods by its fortunate position on a slight rise at the far end of Main St, this Grade II–listed town house offers Georgian heritage with a modern twist. Feathery pillows, lofty ceilings and shiny showers make this one of Cockermouth's top sleeps.

Cockermouth YHA HOSTEL £
(☎0845-371 9313; www.yha.org.uk; Double Mills; dm £14; ⏲reception 7.30-10am & 5-10.30pm Apr-Oct) A simple hostel in a converted 17th-century watermill, about half a mile's walk from town. Camping space and cycle storage are available.

Eating & Drinking

Quince & Medlar RESTAURANT ££
(13 Castlegate; www.quinceandmedlar.co.uk; mains £12-16; ⏲dinner Tue-Sat) This renowned veggie establishment was another fortunate flood escapee, and it's a good thing too: it serves some of the fanciest meat-free food you could ever hope to taste. Burnished panels, candles and squeaky leather chairs give it the atmosphere of a private drawing room.

Merienda CAFE £
(7a Station St; mains £4-8; ⏲breakfast & lunch, to 10pm Fri) Savour light bites, authentic tapas and open-face sandwiches at this sunny Med-style diner with an admirable penchant for fair-trade goods, local produce and specialist coffees.

Bitter End PUB ££
(Kirkgate) Much-loved pub/microbrewery, which produces its own beers – Cockermouth Pride, Lakeland Honey Beer and the fantastically named Cuddy Lugs.

Information

Cockermouth (www.cockermouth.org.uk) Useful town guide.

Tourist office (☎01900-822634; cockermouthtic@co-net.com; ⏲9.30am-5pm Mon-Sat, 10am-2pm Sun Jul-Aug, 9.30am-4.30pm Mon-Sat Apr-Jun & Sep-Oct, 9.30am-4pm Mon-Fri, 10am-2pm Sat Jan-Mar & Nov-Dec) Inside the town hall.

Getting There & Away

The X4/X5 (13 to 15 Monday to Saturday, six on Sunday) travels from Workington via Cockermouth on to Keswick (35 minutes) and Penrith (1¼ hours).

Keswick

POP 5257

The sturdy slate town of Keswick is nestled alongside one of the region's most idyllic lakes, Derwent Water, a silvery curve studded by wooded islands and criss-crossed by puttering cruise boats. Keswick makes a less frantic Lakeland base than Ambleside or Windermere, but there's plenty to keep you occupied: classic trails rove the hilltops, and the town is home to a clutch of odd attractions, including an original Batmobile and the world's largest pencil.

Sights

The heart of Keswick is the old Market Pl, in the shadow of the town's former prison and meeting rooms at the **Moot Hall** (now occupied by the tourist office).

FREE **Keswick Museum & Art Gallery** MUSEUM
(☎017687-73263; Station Rd; ⏲10am-4pm Tue-Sat Feb-Oct) Hardly anything has changed since Keswick's municipal museum opened its doors in 1898. Dusty cases fill the halls: the most famous exhibits are a centuries-old mummified cat and the celebrated Musical Stones of Skiddaw, a truly weird instrument made from hornsfel rock that was once played for Queen Victoria.

FREE **Castlerigg Stone Circle** MONUMENT
Set on a fabulously wild hilltop a mile east of town, this famous stone circle consists of 48 stones between 3000 and 4000 years old, surrounded by a dramatic circle of mountain peaks.

Cars of the Stars Motor Museum MUSEUM
(☎017687-73757; www.carsofthestars.com; Standish St; adult/child £5/3; ⏲10am-5pm) This museum houses a fleet of celebrity vehicles: Chitty Chitty Bang Bang, Mr Bean's Mini, a Batmobile, KITT from *Knight Rider,* the A-Team van and the Delorean from *Back to the Future,* as well as lots of Bond cars.

Pencil Museum MUSEUM
(☎017687-73626; www.pencilmuseum.co.uk; Southy Works; adult/child £3.25/1.75; ⏲9.30am-5pm) For over 350 years, Keswick was a

Keswick

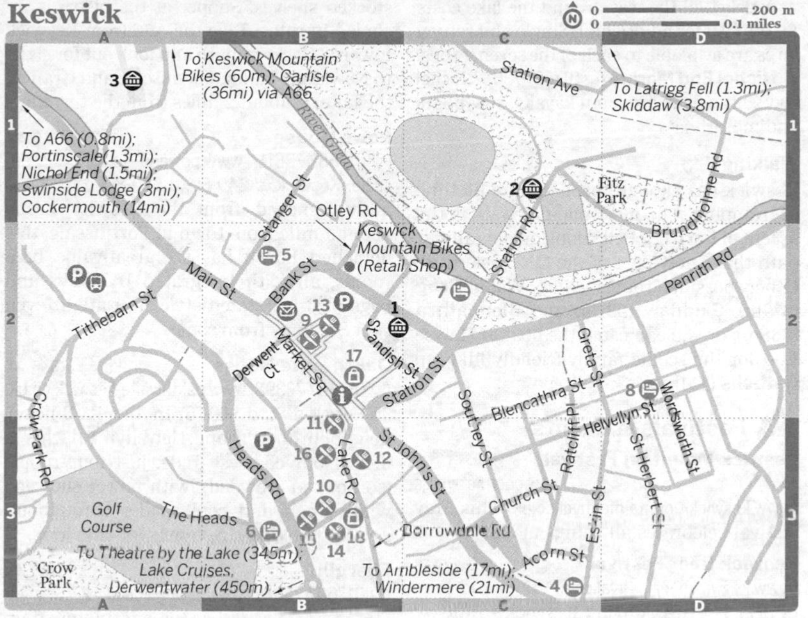

Keswick

Sights

1 Cars of the Stars Motor Museum........B2
2 Keswick Museum & Art Gallery..........C1
3 Pencil Museum..............................A1

Sleeping

4 Allerdale House............................C3
5 Ellergill..B2
6 Howe Keld....................................B3
7 Keswick YHA.................................C2
8 Oakthwaite House..........................D2

Eating

9 Bryson's.......................................B2
10 Cafe-Bar 26.................................B3
11 Dog & Gun...................................B3
12 Good Taste..................................B3
13 Lakeland Pedlar Wholefood Cafe.......B2
14 Mayson's.....................................B3
15 Morrel's......................................B3
16 Sweeney's Bar Restaurant & Rooms.....B3

Shopping

17 Cotswold Outdoor..........................B2
18 George Fisher...............................B3

centre for graphite mining and pencil manufacture (Derwent colouring pencils are still a favourite amongst discerning artists). At the southern end of Main St, the former Cumberland Pencil Factory now houses various exhibits exploring the industry, including a reconstruction of the old Borrowdale slate mine and the world's longest pencil (measuring 8m end to end).

Activities

Boating

Studded with wooded islands and ringed by high fells, **Derwentwater** is unquestionably one of the most beautiful of all the Lakeland lakes (it's also supposed to have been Beatrix Potter's favourite).

From the jetty near Crow Park, a short walk south of the town centre, **Keswick Launch Company** (☎017687-72263; www.keswick-launch.co.uk) runs cruise boats to seven landing stages around the lake shore: Ashness Gate, Lodore Falls, High Brandlehow, Low Brandlehow, Hawse End, Nichol End and back to Keswick.

There are at least eight daily boats in summer, dropping to around three in winter. Summer twilight cruises run at 6.30pm and 7.30pm (adult/child £9/4.50, one hour, July and August).

A ticket all the way around the lake costs £9.00/4.50 for adult/child. Single and return fares are available to each of the seven jetties.

Nichol End Marine (☎017687-73082; Nichol End; ⏰9am-5pm) hires out kayaks, row boats and motorboats.

Walking

Keswick has enough hikes to fill a lifetime of tramping. The most popular walk is the ascent of **Lattrigg Fell**, along an old railway path that's now part of the C2C cycle trail. Other possible routes climb **Walla Crag** (379m), **Skiddaw** (931m) and **Blencathra** (868m), or you can catch the boat to Hawse End for the scenic family-friendly hike up **Catbells** (451m).

Festivals & Events

Keswick Mountain Festival OUTDOOR ACTIVITIES
(www.keswickmountainfestival.co.uk) This May festival celebrates all things mountainous.

Keswick Beer Festival BEER
(www.keswickbeerfestival.co.uk) Lots and lots of beer is drunk during Keswick's June real ale fest.

Keswick Agricultural Show FARMING
(www.keswickshow.co.uk) Held every year since 1860 on the August Bank Holiday.

Sleeping

Keswick is crammed with B&Bs, especially around Stanger St and Helvellyn Rd.

TOP CHOICE **Howe Keld** B&B ££
(☎017687-72417; www.howekeld.co.uk; 5-7 The Heads; s £50, d £90-100; 📶) This revamped Crow Park B&B pulls out all the stops. The kitsch clutter has been jettisoned for goose-down duvets, slate-floored bathrooms and handmade furniture courtesy of a local joiner; TVs are flatscreen, the decor's sleek, and the key-fobs are fashioned from local slate. The breakfast's even up for a national award: homemade smoothies, vegetarian rissoles, French pancakes and a smorgasbord of nuts, seeds and grains. Mmmmm.

TOP CHOICE **Swinside Lodge** HOTEL ££
(☎017687-72948; www.swinsidelodge-hotel.co.uk; Newlands; d incl dinner £92-136; 🅿) Tucked below Catbells, this fancy number has scooped awards for its gourmet food and Georgian finery. It's classy without being chichi: rooms are furnished in country style, and the house is a reassuring mix of creaky floorboards, cosy lounges and book-stocked shelves. Supper at the bistro is included in rates. Take the A66 from Keswick towards Cockermouth and look out for signs to Newlands Valley, Portinscale and Grange; the hotel is about 2 miles from the turning.

Powe House B&B ££
(☎017687-73611; www.powehouse.com; Portinscale, Keswick; s £40-50, d £60-80; 📶) Pleasantly removed from the Keswick crush about a mile from town in Portinscale, this detached house has six great-value bedrooms, all with integrated DVD/TVs and bags of understated style. You might even spot Skiddaw from some.

Oakthwaite House B&B ££
(☎017687-72398; www.oakthwaite-keswick.co.uk; 35 Helvellyn St; d £60-76) In the B&B-heavy neighbourhood round Helvellyn Rd, this is one of our choicest finds: just four rooms (so not too crowded), with power showers, white linen and cool shades throughout. Ask for the king-size rooms for fell views.

Ellergill B&B ££
(☎017687-73347; www.ellergill.co.uk; 22 Stanger St; d £64-72) Velour bedspreads, plumped-up cushions and either regal purples or fiery reds give this B&B an opulent edge, marrying well with the house's Victorian features (including tiled hearths and a lovely hallway floor).

Allerdale House B&B ££
(☎017687-73891; www.allerdale-house.co.uk; 1 Eskin St; s £38, d £76-90; 📶) There's space to spare around this solid house, constructed from typical granite-grey Keswick stone. The rooms are fairly bog-standard in style, but they're extra spacious, and nice touches such as fair-trade tea trays and wi-fi are a bonus.

Keswick YHA HOSTEL £
(☎0845-371 9746; www.yha.org.uk; Station Rd; dm from £14; @) In a converted wool mill beside the clattering river, this efficient hostel offers roomy dorms, doubles and triples, some with balconies overlooking Fitz Park.

Eating

Morrel's RESTAURANT ££
(☎017687-72666; Lake Rd; 2/3-course menu £13.50/16; ⏰dinner Tue-Sun) Keswick's top table is this glossy restaurant, smoothly done in shades of cappuccino, cream and chocolate and enlivened by pop art movie prints. Expect quality bistro food spiced by the occasional Spanish, Catalan or Italian influence.

WHINLATTER FOREST PARK

Encompassing 1200 hectares of pine, larch and spruce, **Whinlatter** is England's only true area of mountain forest, rising sharply to 790m around the Whinlatter Pass, about 5 miles from Keswick. The forest is a designated red squirrel reserve; you can check out live video feeds from squirrel cams at the **Whinlatter visitor centre** (☎017687-78469; Braithwaite; ⏲10am-5pm).

Thrill-junkies can monkey about in the trees at **Go Ape** (☎017687-78469; adult/10-17yr £30/25; ⏲9am-5pm mid-Mar–Oct, closed Mon in term time) or mountain bike along the **Altura** and **Quercus** trails.

You can hire bikes at **Cyclewise** (☎017687-78711; www.cyclewisetraining.co.uk), next to the visitor centre.

Bus 77 (four daily) goes to Whinlatter from Keswick.

Good Taste CAFE £
(www.simplygoodtaste.co.uk; 19 Lake Rd; lunches £3-6; ⏲8.30am-4.30pm Mon-Sat) Peter Sidwell's snazzy cafe is one of the town's most popular places for lunch, and it's not really surprising. Tuck into gourmet sandwiches, fresh-made smoothies and more-filling mains shot through with Italian and French flavours. Best coffee in Keswick, too.

Mayson's DINER £
(33 Lake Rd; mains £6-10) Buffet dining in a cosy space sprinkled with potted plants and bench seating. Select your daily special from one of the woks on the counter, choose a drink and wait for your grub to arrive in double-quick time.

Lakeland Pedlar Wholefood Cafe CAFE £
(www.lakelandpedlar.co.uk; Hendersons Yard; mains £3-10; ⏲9am-5pm) You'll be hard-pressed to find a heartier lunch in the Lakes than the ones served up at this long-standing establishment, noted for its chunky sandwiches, homemade soups, veggie chillis and inch-thick cakes. There's a bike shop upstairs.

Sweeney's Bar Restaurant & Rooms BISTRO ££
(☎017687-772990; 18-20 Lake Rd; mains £7-12) Count on decent Brit cooking in comfortable surrounds at Sweeney's. It's half chic wine bar, half restaurant-with-rooms: leather sofas and polished tables spread over two floors, with a beer garden for soaking up the rays.

Dog & Gun PUB £
(2 Lake Rd; mains from £8) Plenty of pubs in Keswick, but this is the pick: deep booths, flickering hearths, a well-worn wooden bar and proper pub grub and ale, including 'Thirst rescue', which helps fund the Keswick Mountain Rescue Team.

Bryson's CAFE £
(42 Main St; cakes £2-5) Much-loved bakery known for its fruit cakes, Battenburgs and florentines.

Cafe-Bar 26 CAFE £
(26 Lake Rd; mains £3-10) Smart cafe and wine bar that also turns out snacky tapas, burgers and bruschetta.

☆ Entertainment

Theatre by the Lake THEATRE
(www.theatrebythelake.com; Lakeside) Lakeside theatre showing drama, music and other live events.

Shopping

Keswick has plenty of outdoor shops. There's a huge branch of **Cotswold Outdoor** (16 Main St), but the traditionalists' choice is **George Fisher** (2 Borrowdale Rd).

Information

Keswick & the North Lakes (www.keswick.org) Comprehensive guide to all things Keswick.

Tourist office (☎017687-72645; keswicktic@lake-district.gov.uk; Moot Hall, Market Pl; ⏲9.30am-5.30pm Apr-Oct, to 4.30pm Nov-Mar) Sells discounted launch tickets.

U Compute (48 Main St; ⏲9am-5.30pm; per hr £3) Net access above the post office.

Getting There & Away

Buses from Keswick:

555/556 Lakeslink Hourly to Ambleside (40 minutes), Windermere (50 minutes) and Kendal (1½ hours).

X4/X5 Penrith to Workington via Keswick (hourly Monday to Friday, six on Sunday).

77/77A Honister Rambler (Four daily) The main Buttermere bus, including stops at Seathwaite, Lorton and Whinlatter. The bus then crosses Honister Pass and travels through Borrowdale back to Keswick.

78 Borrowdale Rambler Regular bus to the Borrowdale valley (hourly Monday to Saturday, seven on Sunday).

Getting Around

Hire full-suspension bikes, hard tails and hybrids at **Keswick Mountain Bikes** (017687-75202; 1 Daleston Ct) from £20 per day. They have a second branch on Otley Rd.

Borrowdale & Buttermere

Views don't get any more breathtaking than the one from the B5289 into Borrowdale. Historically, the valley was an important centre for two crucial local industries – farming and slate-mining – but these days Borrowdale is walkers' country, with countless paths crossing the surrounding fells, including landmark routes up to the summits of Great Gable and Scafell Pike, and an idyllic panorama of tree-clad fells, patchwork pastures and rickety barns.

Getting There & Away

Buses 77/77A and 78 connect Borrowdale and Buttermere with Keswick.

BORROWDALE TO SEATOLLER

The B5289 tracks Derwent Water into the heart of Borrowdale Valley, overlooked by the impressive peaks of Scafell and Scafell Pike. Past the small village of **Grange-in-Borrowdale**, the valley winds into the jagged ravine of the **Jaws of Borrowdale**, a well-known hiking spot with wonderful views, notably from the summit of **Castle Crag** (290m) at the southern end of Derwentwater.

A mile or so further south from Grange, a turn-off leads up to a National Trust car park and the geological curiosity of the **Bowder Stone**, a 1870-ton lump of rock thought to have been left behind by a retreating glacier. A small stepladder leads up to the top of the rock.

From here, the road curls into the stout hamlet of **Rosthwaithe**, which marks the starting point for the annual **Borrowdale Fell Race**. Held on the first Saturday in August, this muscle-shredding 17-mile slog makes the Iron Man Challenge look like child's play; you can see a list of previous winners in the bar at the Scafell Hotel.

Past the tiny cluster of houses that make up **Seathwaite**, the road rumbles on to the foot of Honister Pass and titchy **Seatoller**, originally a settlement for workers employed in the local slate quarries, and even now a long way from the outside world.

Sleeping & Eating

TOP CHOICE **Langstrath Inn** B&B ££
(017687-77239; www.thelangstrath.com; Stonethwaite; d £99-108; P) Borrowdale digs are on the pricey side, which makes this whitewashed inn in Stonethwaite a doubly welcome discovery. The slate-topped building surrounded by valley views is attractive enough: throw in elegant rooms finished in crimsons and cool whites, and a rustic pub-restaurant downstairs serving classic Cumbrian dishes, and you have a very tempting Borrowdale option indeed. The house even once featured in a novel by Ian McEwan – and you can't say that every day, now can you?

Seatoller House B&B ££
(017687-77218; www.seatollerhouse.co.uk; s/d £55/122; P) Another tiny hideaway with an air of a Beatrix Potter burrow, tucked be-

THE BASSENTHWAITE OSPREYS

In 2001 the first wild ospreys to breed in England for 150 years set up home at Bassenthwaite Lake, near Keswick. These magnificent birds of prey were once widespread, but were driven to extinction by hunting, environmental degradation and egg collectors. The last wild breeding pair was destroyed in Scotland in 1916, but following years of careful conservation, the ospreys have slowly recolonised several areas of the British Isles.

Over the last few years, the birds have usually arrived at Bassenthwaite in April, spending the summer at the lake before heading for Africa in late August or early September. There are two official viewpoints, both in **Dodd Wood**, about 3 miles north of Keswick on the A591 (follow signs for Dodd Wood and Cattle Inn). The **lower hide** (10am-5pm) is about 15 minutes' walk from the car park at Mirehouse, and the new **upper hide** (10.30am-4.30pm) is half an hour further. There's an informative osprey display and live video feed at the **Whinlatter Forest Park visitor centre** (p717).

From Keswick, the 73/73A bus stops at nearby Mirehouse, or there's a special 47/74A Osprey Bus (six on weekends April to mid-July, daily July and August).

Find out more at www.ospreywatch.co.uk.

neath the climb up to Honister Pass. All the rooms are named after animals – attic Osprey has sky views through a Velux window, Rabbit is pleasantly pine-filled and Badger has views over the garden.

Scaféll Hotel HOTEL £££
(☎017687-77208; www.scafell.co.uk; Rosthwaite; d £125-185; P) Rosthwaite's former coaching inn makes for a cosy stay. Period furniture and well-worn rugs conjure up an antique air (the newer annexe is more contemporary). En suite bathrooms and country views are (nearly) universal, and the fire-lit Riverside Bar makes the ideal place to sink a brew.

Yew Tree Farm B&B ££
(☎017687-77675; www.borrowdaleherdwick.co.uk; Rosthwaite; d from £75; P) Cottage style rules the roost at this button-cute farmhouse, with three rooms snuggled in under low ceilings, and the lovely Flock In tearoom across the way serving sticky toffee pud, giant flapjacks and piping-hot tea. Rumour has it that Prince Charles once stayed here during an incognito walking holiday.

Derwentwater YHA HOSTEL £
(☎0845-371 9314; derwentwater@yha.org.uk; Barrow House; dm £16; ⊙Feb-Nov, weekends Nov-Jan; P @) The first of Borrowdale's two hostels is in an impressive mansion built for the 19th-century notable Joseph Pocklington, who built an artificial waterfall in the back garden that now runs the hostel's hydro-electric turbine. The rooms are fairly old-time YHA, but there's a billiard room and a big lounge for post-trek chilling.

Borrowdale YHA HOSTEL £
(☎0845-371 9624; borrowdale@yha.org.uk; Longthwaite; dm from £16; ⊙Feb-Dec) Purpose-built chalet-style hostel further up the valley, specialising in walking and activity trips. The facilities are great, but it's often booked out throughout the summer.

Hazel Bank HOTEL ££
(☎017687-77248; www.hazelbankhotel.co.uk; Rosthwaite; d £112-124, incl dinner £158-164; P) This detached mansion is one of Borrowdale's cosiest country hotels, set in sweeping private grounds and reached via its own humpback bridge. Minimal it certainly isn't, but it's a fine option if you like your boudoir furnished with swags, swooshy curtains and canopied beds. The four-course dinner for nonguests is £30.

HONISTER PASS

From Borrowdale, a narrow, winding and perilously steep road snakes up the fellside to Honister Pass and the Buttermere valley beyond. This was once the most productive quarrying area in the Lake District, and is still the source of much of the region's iconic grey-green Westmorland slate. Overlooking the top of the pass is the **Honister Slate Mine** (☎017687-77230; www.honister-slate-mine.co.uk; adult/child £9.75/4.75; ⊙tours 10.30am, 12.30pm & 3.30pm Mar-Oct), where underground tours venture deep into the bowels of the old 'Edge' and 'Kimberley' mines (a tour into the 'Cathedral' mine runs on Friday by request, but you'll need eight people and it costs £19.75). If you fancy taking home a souvenir, you can pick up knick-knacks in the mine shop or fill up your boot with slate – just be careful on the brakes on the way down.

Honister's latest attraction is the UK's first **Via Ferrata** (Iron Way; adult/10-15yr £25/20). Modelled on the century-old routes across the Italian Dolomites, this vertiginous clamber follows the cliff trail once used by the Honister slate miners, using a system of fixed ropes and iron ladders. It's exhilarating and great fun, but unsurprisingly you'll need a head for heights.

Right beside the pass, former mine-workers' lodgings have been converted into the **Honister Hause YHA** (☎0845-371 9522; www.yha.org.uk; Seatoller; dm from £14; ⊙Easter-Oct, weekends Nov), a bare-bones hostel mainly used by hikers.

Even more remote is **Black Sail YHA** (☎07711-108450; www.yha.org.uk; Ennerdale, Cleator; dm £14; ⊙Easter-Oct), a gloriously isolated shepherd's bothy that's only accessible on foot 2.5 miles west of Honister Pass en route to the wild Ennerdale Valley. You definitely don't come here for the luxury – there's no mains electricity, the cooking facilities are extremely basic and the dorms are cramped, but the mountain setting is absolutely unforgettable.

BUTTERMERE

From the high point of Honister, the road drops sharply into the deep bowl of Buttermere, skirting the lakeshore to Buttermere village, 4 miles from Honister and 9 miles from Keswick. From here, the B5289 cuts past Crummock Water (once joined with its neighbour) before exiting the valley's northern edge.

Buttermere marks the start of Alfred Wainwright's all-time favourite circuit: up

Red Pike (755m), and along **High Stile**, **High Crag** and **Haystacks** (597m). In fact, the great man liked it so much he decided to stay here for good: after his death in 1991, his ashes were scattered across the top of Haystacks as was requested in his will.

Buttermere has limited accommodation. Walkers bunk down at the **Buttermere YHA** (☎0845-371 9508; buttermere@yha.org.uk; dm £16), a slate-stone house above Buttermere Lake, while those looking for more luxury try one of the valley's two hotels, the upmarket **Bridge Hotel** (☎017687-70252; www.bridge-hotel.com; r £130-150, incl dinner £185-210; P) or the **Fish Hotel** (☎017687-70253; 2-night minimum stay d £200; P).

Better still, if you're up for a night under canvas there's one of the Lake District's best rural campsites, **Syke Farm** (☎01768-770222; sites adult/child £7/3.50; ⏲Feb-Nov). Facilities are limited to basic loos and his-and-hers showers, but pick your spot and you'll wake up to views of Red Pike, High Stile and Haystacks. There's a river to chill your booze in, and the farmer makes ice cream with milk straight from his dairy herd (the marzipan and vanilla are to die for).

Ullswater & Around

After Windermere, the second-largest lake in the Lake District is Ullswater, a silvery slash that stretches for 7.5 miles between Pooley Bridge, and Glenridding and Patterdale in the south. Carved out by a long-extinct glacier, the deep valley in which the lake sits is flanked by an impressive string of fells, most notably the razor ridge of **Helvellyn**, Cumbria's third-highest mountain. Historic steamers have sputtered around the lake since 1859, and there are lovely woods and gardens to explore nearby if the summer crowds are too much.

POOLEY BRIDGE

ELEVATION 301M

Tucked into the northern corner of Ullswater, this pint-size village is mainly worth a visit as the starting point for the **Ullswater 'Steamers'** (☎017684-82229; www.ullswater-steamers.co.uk), which putter south along the lake, making stops at Howtown and Glenridding before looping back to Pooley Bridge. Up to 12 daily ferries run in summer, dropping to three in winter. Round trips are adult/child £9.00/4.50 to Howtown, or £12.30/6.15 for an all-day pass.

Sleeping & Eating

Rampsbeck Country House Hotel HOTEL £££
(☎017684-86442; www.rampsbeck.co.uk; Watermillock; d £140-188, ste £250-290; P) Surrounded by lovingly tended lawns and landscaped gardens, this lakeside hotel boasts some of the best views of Ullswater from its classy rooms. It's a winning mix of past and present: antique clocks, roll-top baths and four-poster beds contrast with Bose radios and the odd contemporary fabric, and the restaurant serves fine Cumbrian fare. Sit back and soak it up.

Brackenrigg Inn B&B ££
(☎017684-86206; www.brackenrigginn.co.uk; Watermillock; d £79, incl dinner £119) Near the Rampsbeck, this roadside coaching inn is a slightly more affordable option. The lake-view rooms are obviously the choicest, but you'll have to put up with the buzz of traffic from the A592. The pub offers quality beer and nosh options.

Sun Inn PUB £
(Pooley Bridge; mains £5-14) Right in the middle of Pooley Bridge, this Jenning's pub is a longstanding stop-off for punters waiting for the Ullswater ferries. Solid chicken pies, pork chops and bangers-and-mash are the menu's mainstays, and there's the full range of Jenning's beers on tap, best appreciated in the grassy garden while the kids lark about on the miniature wooden fort.

There's plenty of choice for campers:

TOP CHOICE **The Quiet Site** CAMPSITE £
(☎07768-727016; www.thequietsite.co.uk; sites £17-30, pods £35-50; 📶) Swanky eco-camping on a hill halfway between Pooley Bridge and Gowbarrow Park.

Waterside House CAMPSITE £
(☎017684-86332; www.watersidefarm-campsite.co.uk; Howtown Rd; sites £14-22) Lakeside tent-and-caravan camping with canoes, kayaks and sea-cycles for hire.

Park Foot CAMPSITE £
(☎017684-86309; www.parkfootullswater.co.uk; Howtown Rd; sites £13-26) Facility-packed site on the lake's east side, with tennis courts, bike hire and pony trekking.

GLENRIDDING & PATTERDALE

ELEVATION 253M

Seven miles south as the crow files from Pooley Bridge are the neighbouring villages of **Patterdale** and **Glenridding**, the favoured starting point for the challenging ascent of Helvellyn. If your legs won't stretch to the main event, you can tackle lower-level trails nearby: the easy amble to **Lanty's Tarn** starts just south of Glenridding, while the popular walks up to **High Force** and **Aira Force** start in the wooded surroundings of **Gowbarrow Park**, a couple of miles north.

Famously, it was the prodigious spring daffodil displays around the shores of Ullswater that moved Wordsworth to compose one of his most popular (and oft-quoted) poems, beginning with the immortal lines: 'I wandered lonely as a cloud/That floats on high over hills and dales/When all at once I saw a crowd/A host, of golden daffodils...'

Sleeping & Eating

Old Water View B&B ££
(017684-82175; www.oldwaterview.co.uk; Patterdale; d £84) Frilly B&B with something to cover all bases: split-level 'Bothy' is ideal for families with attic beds for the kids, while 'Little Gem' overlooks the tinkling stream and 'Place Fell' is reputed to be have been a favourite of Alfred Wainwright.

Cherry Holme B&B ££
(017684-82512; www.cherryholme.co.uk; Glenridding; s £60, d £80-120;) There are plenty of luxury extras at this roomy house on the edge of Glenridding, including a Nordic-style sauna that makes a perfect place to soothe those bones post-Helvellyn – although the fairly standard rooms are underwhelming considering the price.

Inn on the Lake HOTEL £££
(017684-82444; http://lakedistricthotels.net/innonthelake; Patterdale; d £150-242; P@) Apart from the Glenridding Hotel (now owned by Best Western), this is the only passable hotel in the village. It's more corporate than characterful, but as long as you can look past the generic decor, you'll be treated to fancy facilities: jacuzzi baths, tennis courts, sauna and gym, plus a choice of mountain or lake views from the rooms.

Patterdale YHA HOSTEL £
(0845-371 9337; patterdale@yha.org.uk; Patterdale; dm £14; reception 7.30-10am & 5-10.30am Easter-Oct) This modern hostel makes a nice change from the heritage settings enjoyed by some of the other Lakeland YHAs. It's got a whiff of the '70s around it – a patch of timber cladding here, some pop-art colours there – but the facilities are good (cafe-bar, bike hire, spacious kitchen).

Helvellyn YHA HOSTEL £
(0845-371 9742; www.yha.org.uk; Greenside; dm £12; Easter-Oct, rest of year by reservation) Formerly occupied by high-mountain miners, this basic hostel-in-the-wilds sits 274m above Glenridding along a rocky mountain track. It's miles from anything, but if you're after a solitude hit and don't mind the ¾-mile trek, you'll be in for a treat. The hostel's mainly used by hikers looking for an early start on Helvellyn; guided walks can be arranged through the hostel staff.

Traveller's Rest PUB ££
(Glenridding; mains £5.50-15) Typically friendly Cumbrian pub known for its 'Traveller's Mixed Grill' (£14.70) of steak, lamb chop, gammon, black pudding and Cumberland sausage, all crowned with a fried egg.

Fellbites CAFE ££
(Glenridding; lunch mains £6-12; evening menus £17.50-21.50; lunch daily, dinner Thu-Sat) Attractive village cafe good for soups and sarnies (sandwiches) at lunch, plus more sophisticated stuff after dark.

Information

Ullswater Information Centre (017684-82414; ullswatertic@lake-district.gov.uk; Beckside car park; 9am-5.30pm Apr-Oct)

Getting There & Away

The Ullswater Bus-and-Boat Combo ticket (£13.60) includes a day's travel on the 108 with a return trip on an Ullswater Steamer; buy the ticket on the bus. Useful buses:

108 Penrith to Patterdale via Pooley Bridge and Glenridding (six Monday to Friday, five on Saturday, four on Sunday).

517 (Kirkstone Rambler; three daily July and August, otherwise weekends only) Over the Kirkstone Pass from Bowness and Troutbeck, stopping at Glenridding and Patterdale.

CUMBRIAN COAST

While the central lakes and fells pull in a never-ending stream of visitors, surprisingly few ever make the trek west to explore Cumbria's coastline. And that's a shame: while it might not compare to the wild grandeur of Northumberland or the rugged splendour of Scotland's shores, Cumbria's coast is well worth exploring, with a cluster of sandy bays and a gaggle of seaside towns, including the old port of Whitehaven, the Edwardian resort of Grange-over-Sands and the Roman harbour at Ravenglass, starting point for the La'al Ratty steam railway. Less attractive is the nuclear plant of Sellafield, still stirring up controversy some 50 years after its construction.

Getting Around

The railway line loops 120 miles from Lancaster to Carlisle, stopping at the coastal resorts of Grange, Ulverston, Ravenglass, Whitehaven and Workington.

Grange-over-Sands

POP 4098

Teashops, manicured gardens and Victorian villas line the winding streets of Grange, which established itself as a seaside getaway for Edwardian day-trippers following the 19th-century arrival of the railway. The town's heyday has long since passed, but as long as you don't mind your sea air stiff and bracing, Grange makes a fine spot to sample the peculiar charms of the English seaside, stroll the elegant seafront and drink in the sweeping views over Morecambe Bay.

Sleeping & Eating

Grange has two or three huge hotels dating from its days as a Victorian resort, but they're a lot more corporate these days and generally chronically overpriced.

TOP CHOICE No 43 B&B £££
(01524-762761; www.no43.org.uk; The Promenade, Arnside; r £110-180; P) Across the sands of Morecambe in the pleasantly faded resort of Arnside, this brilliant boutique B&B comes as a shock – with its bespoke wallpapers, Belfast sinks and metro-chic trappings, it'd feel more at home in Soho than the Cumbrian seaside. Some rooms have Bose hi-fis, others picture-frame fires: ask for No 2 or 7 if you're after an estuary view.

Lymehurst Hotel B&B ££
(015395-33076; www.lymehurst.co.uk; Kents Bank Rd; s £40, d £90-120; P) Despite the classic Grange architecture, inside this guesthouse is a model of contemporariness. Light, bright rooms feature simple pine furniture, buttermilk walls and digi-TVs, and there's a shiny brass bed in the Premier room.

Hampsfell House B&B ££
(015393-33076; www.hampsfellhouse.co.uk; Hampsfell Rd; s £45, d £60-85) The traditionalists' choice, dominated by fallback B&B shades of china blue and candy mauve, with views over shrub-filled gardens. Nothing to set your world on fire, perhaps, but cosy all the same.

Hazelmere Cafe CAFE £
(1-2 Yewbarrow Tce; sandwiches £4-6, mains £6-10; 10am-5pm) The English passion for afternoon tea is alive and well at this delightfully doily-clad tearoom near Grange's public gardens. Sponge cakes, sticky buns and egg-and-cress sandwiches are served in the old-fashioned way, or you could tuck into Cumbrian delicacies such as potted shrimps, rabbit pie and Venison sausage. For tea, take your pick from 30-odd varieties.

Information

Tourist office (015395-34026; grangetic@southlakeland.gov.uk; Victoria Hall, Main St; 10am-5pm Easter-Oct)

Getting There & Away

Both the train station and bus stop are downhill from the tourist office.

BUS Bus X35 from Kendal stops at Grange (30 minutes, hourly) on its way to Ulverston (one hour). Bus 532 serves Cartmel and other local villages.

TRAIN Grange is on the coast line, with frequent connections south to Arnside, Lancaster, and beyond, and west to Cark-in-Cartmel and the Cumbrian coast.

Around Grange

CARTMEL

POP 1798

Tucked away in the countryside near Grange, tiny Cartmel is known for three things: its 12th-century priory, its miniature racecourse and its world-famous sticky toffee pudding, on sale at the **Cartmel Village Shop** (www.stickytoffeepudding.co.uk; The Square; 9am-5pm Mon-Sat, 10am-4.30pm Sun).

The heart of the village is the medieval market square, from where a winding lane leads to **Cartmel Priory** (9am-5.30pm May-Oct, to 3.30pm Nov-Apr), one of the few priories to escape demolition during the dissolution. Light pours in through the 15th-century **east window**, illuminating the tombs set into the flagstoned floor; note the memento mori of skulls and hourglasses, intended to remind the pious of their own inescapable mortality.

THE MORECAMBE BAY CROSSING

Before the coming of the railway, the sandy expanse of **Morecambe Bay** provided the quickest route into the Lake District from the south of England. The traditional crossing is made from Arnside on the eastern side of the bay over to Kents Bank, near Grange-over-Sands. It's always been a risky journey. Morecambe Bay is notorious for its fast-rising tide and treacherous sands; even experienced locals have been known to lose carts, horses and tractors, and there have been numerous strandings, most recently in 2004, when at least 21 Chinese cockle-pickers were caught by the tide and drowned (an incident that inspired Nick Broomfield's 2006 film *Ghosts*).

It's possible to walk across the flats at low tide, but only in the company of the official **Queen's Guide**, a role established in 1536. Cedric Robinson, a local fisherman, is the 25th official Queen's Guide, and leads walks across the sands throughout the year. You'll need to register a fortnight in advance; ask at the Grange tourist office for details of the next crossing. The 8-mile crossing takes around 3½ hours.

Find out more about this unique waterway at www.morecambebay.org.uk.

Sleeping & Eating

TOP CHOICE **Rogan & Company** RESTAURANT ££
(015395-35917; The Square; mains £15-18.50) Renowned chef Simon Rogan is one of Cumbria's top culinary stars. He made his name at the fantastically fancy L'Enclume, but you don't necessarily need a second mortgage to sample his food: his Cartmel bistro showcases the same culinary flair at a much more affordable price. The food is modern Brit dining at its best, the restaurant mixes old beams with trendy fabrics, and there's even a sweet garden for alfresco dining. Definitely one not to miss.

Howbarrow Organic Farm FARM SHOP, B&B ££
(015395-36330; www.howbarroworganic.co.uk; farm shop 10am-5pm Wed-Sat) Food-miles are a distant dream at this wonderful little pocket of sustainability just outside Cartmel. Practically everything on sale comes straight from the working farm, supplemented by choice chutneys, cheeses and other goodies hand picked from Cumbrian suppliers.

Prior's Yeat B&B ££
(015395-35178; priorsyeat@hotmail.com; Aynsome Rd; s/d £35/70; P) The village is short on really good B&Bs, but this red-brick Edwardian house is smarter than most. Three rooms: one's sky blue with twin beds, the other two are doubles with flower prints and pine.

L'Enclume RESTAURANT £££
(015395-36362; www.lenclume.co.uk; Cavendish St; 2-/3-course lunches £18/25, dinner menus £65; lunch Thu-Sun, dinner Tue-Sun) Michelin-starred and much-touted, Simon Rogan's original gastronomic venture is one of Cumbria's most adventurous, exciting and expensive restaurants. It's dining as art, where the presentation's almost as important as the food. Unsurprisingly, it features in all the top food guides, and the upstairs rooms showcase the same flamboyant class. Reservations essential.

Cavendish Arms PUB £
(www.thecavendisharms.co.uk; mains £10-15; d £65) Snug coaching inn just off the village square, serving good beer, filling food and a great Sunday roast.

King's Arms PUB £
(The Square; mains £8-14; d £60-80) Another lovely village pub, dotted with hunting prints and country curios. Barngates and Hawkshead ales are on tap, and simple rooms overlook the market square or the garden.

Getting There & Away

Bus 530/532 travels from Cartmel to Grange (40 minutes) 10 to 12 times daily from Monday to Saturday.

HOLKER HALL

Holker Hall (015395-58328; www.holker-hall.co.uk; adult/child £10/5.50, grounds only £6.50/3.50; house 10.30am-4.30pm Sun-Fri, grounds 10am-6pm Mar-Oct) has been the family seat of the Cavendish family for nigh on 400 years. Though parts of the house date from the 16th century, the house was almost entirely rebuilt following a devastating fire in 1871. It's a typically ostentatious Victorian affair, covered with mullioned windows, gables and copper-topped turrets. Among its wealth of grand rooms are the drawing room (packed with antique furniture, including a choice few Chippendales), the library (stocked with over 3500 tomes) and the lavish Long Gallery (renowned for its elaborate plasterwork).

Outside, Holker's grounds sprawl for over 10 hectares, encompassing a rose garden, woodland, ornamental fountains and a 22m-high lime tree. There's also a fantastic **food hall** (☎015395-59084; www.holderfoodhall.co.uk) stocking produce from the estate.

Ulverston

POP 11,670

It's not the prettiest town in Cumbria, but at least Ulverston has an excuse for its workmanlike appearance: the town was once an important industrial centre for leather, copper and iron ore.

With a network of streets radiating out from the main market square, Ulverston makes a cheap, quiet launch pad for exploring the Cumbrian coast and the western Lakes, but it's perhaps best-known as the birthplace of Stan Laurel, the spindlier half of Laurel & Hardy. A new statue of the bumbling duo was unveiled with great fanfare outside Coronation Hall in 2009. Costing around £60,000, it was created by artist Graham Ibbeson, who also designed the statue of Eric Morecambe on the seafront in Morecambe.

Sights

Laurel & Hardy Museum MUSEUM

(www.laurel-and-hardy.co.uk; Brogden St; adult/child £4/2; ⏲10am-4.30pm Feb-Dec) Founded by avid Laurel & Hardy collector Bill Cubin back in 1983, this eclectic cinematic museum now has new premises in the town's old Roxy cinema. The museum still houses all the old floor-to-ceiling memorabilia relating to the duo, but presented in a rather less chaotic fashion than at the former site; happily, the much-loved little 15-seat cinema has been retained, and still shows back-to-back Laurel & Hardy classics.

Hoad Monument VIEWPOINT

(Hoad Hill) This tower commemorates the explorer, author and Secretary to the Admiralty Sir John Barrow (1764–1848), who helped map much of the Northwest Passage. The views east to the fells and west to the coast are wonderful. The monument is usually open on summer Sundays and bank holidays, but you can walk up the hill at any time of year.

Sleeping

Lonsdale House Hotel HOTEL ££

(☎01229-581260; www.lonsdalehousehotel.co.uk; 11 Daltongate; s £65-70, d £85-105; P) The most convenient option for the town centre is this pleasant Georgian town house just a few steps from the market square. The 20-odd rooms are cheerily furnished, but it's worth bumping up the price bracket for a private jacuzzi bath or a view over the walled garden.

St Mary's Mount Manor House B&B ££

(☎01229-849005; www.stmarysmount.co.uk; Belmont; s £45, d £50-75; P) Cosy B&B nestled on the hilltop above Ulverston. Half-testers and other frilly touches might be a bit feminine for some, but it still boasts lots of Georgian features and the welcome's warm.

Bay Horse Hotel HOTEL ££

(☎01229-583972; www.thebayhorsehotel.co.uk; Canal Foot; s/d from £80/100; P Wi-Fi) It's a bit behind the times in terms of decor, but if you're after a view, this is the place in Ulverston. It sits on the pebbly sands of the Levens Estuary, and is well known locally for its country restaurant. Follow signs to Canal Foot from the A590.

Eating & Drinking

Ulverston's lively **market** fills the town's streets every Thursday, with a smaller market on Saturday and a local **food fair** every third Saturday of the month.

Farmer's Arms PUB ££

(3 Market Place; mains £6-14) Top stop for evening food in Ulverston is this venerable pub on the market square. The trappings are traditional (whitewashed frontage, wood beams, beer-stocked bar), but the menu's bold, encompassing duck steak, pan-cooked mussels and crispy-skinned chicken.

Gillams CAFE £

(64 Market St; lunches £3-10; ⏲Mon-Sat) With a century of tea service behind it, this place should know how to pour a perfect cuppa by now – and it surely does. These days it's run along sustainable, organic lines and serves a tempting selection of lunchtime salads, sandwiches and cakes in well-worn surroundings.

World Peace Cafe CAFE £

(www.worldpeacecafe.org; 5 Cavendish St; mains £3-8; ⏲10am-4.30pm Tue-Sat) This cross between a cafe and a meditation centre is co-run by the Conishead Priory: organic food and fair-trade coffee are downstairs, meditation sessions and chill-out rooms upstairs.

Hot Mango CAFE £
(27 King St; lunches £5-8; ⏰lunch Tue-Sat) A good lunchtime bet, sunnily decorated in pine, oranges and yellows and matched by no-nonsense comfort food – fish-finger sandwiches, piping-hot jacket potatoes, generous burgers served with thick chips and homemade salsa.

Information

Library (Kings Rd; per 30 min £1) Internet access.

Tourist office (☎01229-587120; ulverstontic@south lakeland.gov.uk; County Sq; ⏰9am-5pm Mon-Sat)

Ulverston Online (www.ulverston.net) Town website.

 Getting There & Away

The hourly X35 bus travels from Ulverston via Haverthwaite, Newby Bridge, Grange and Kendal from Monday to Saturday (three times on Sunday).

Regular trains from Carlisle (£33.50, two hours) and Lancaster (£8, 40 minutes) stop at Ulverston station, five minutes' walk south of the centre.

Around Ulverston

CONISHEAD PRIORY

Two miles south of Ulverston, **Conishead Priory** (www.manjushri.org.uk; admission free; ⏰2-5pm Mon-Fri, noon-5pm Sat, Sun & bank holidays Easter-Oct, 2-4pm Nov-Easter) is one of the UK's main Manjushri Buddhist centres and the site of Europe's only Kadampa Temple. There are weekend tours at 2.15pm and 3.30pm, and meditation retreats are available.

FURNESS ABBEY

Eight and a half miles southwest of Ulverston, the rosy ruins of **Furness Abbey** (EH; www.english-heritage.org.uk/daysout/properties/furness-abbey; adult/child £3.70/1.90; ⏰10am-6pm Apr-Sep, to 5pm Oct, to 4pm Wed-Sun Nov-Mar) are all that remains of one of northern England's most powerful monasteries. Founded in the 12th century, the abbey's lands and properties once stretched across southern Cumbria and the Lakes, but like many of England's monasteries, it met an ignominious end in 1537 during the dissolution. You can still make out the abbey's basic footprint; various arches, windows and the north and south transept walls are still standing, alongside the remains of the abbey bell tower. An informative audio guide is included in the admission price.

Several buses, including the hourly X35 from Ulverston, stop nearby.

Ravenglass & Around

West of Ulverston, the coastline curves through a string of quiet seaside towns past the green hump of **Black Combe**, the highest fell to lie outside the boundaries of the national park. Further north is **Ravenglass**, famous as the starting station for the miniature steam trains of La'al Ratty, and the gloomy chimney stacks of **Sellafield**, Britain's largest nuclear reprocessing plant. Just before Whitehaven, the dune-backed headland of **St Bees Head** marks the start of Wainwright's official cross-country Coast to Coast trail, which ends 190 miles to the east at Robin Hood's Bay.

Ravenglass & Eskdale Railway STEAM RAILWAY
(☎01229-717171; www.ravenglass-railway.co.uk; single fares adult/child £6.60/3.30, day tickets £11.20/5.60), built in 1875 to ferry iron ore from the Eskdale mines to the coast. Affectionately known as **La'al Ratty**, the pocket-size choo-choos chug for 7 miles into Eskdale and the Lake District foothills, terminating at Dalegarth Station, near Boot. There are up to 17 trips daily in summer, dropping to two in winter.

While you wait for your train, there's an interesting **museum** exploring the railway's history, and good grub and ales at the **Ratty Arms** (mains £8-15), which is covered with memorabilia from the railway's heyday.

Muncaster Castle CASTLE
(www.muncaster.co.uk; adult/child £11/7.50, gardens only £8.50/6; ⏰gardens 10.30am-dusk, castle noon-4.30pm Sun-Fri Feb-Nov) Like many Cumbrian castles, Muncaster was originally built around a 14th-century *pele* tower, constructed to resist Reiver raids from across the Scottish border. Home to the Pennington family for the last seven centuries, the castle's celebrated features include its majestic great hall and octagonal library, and on its grounds you'll find an ornamental maze and an owl centre. The castle is also known for its many ghosts: keep your eyes peeled for the Muncaster Boggle

and a malevolent jester known as Tom Fool (hence 'tomfoolery'). Brave souls can even arrange their own overnight 'ghost sit' (for £405 to £475).

Getting There & Away

Bus 6 from Whitehaven stops at Ravenglass and terminates at Muncaster (70 minutes, five daily). Bus X6 travels the same route on Sunday (four daily).

Ravenglass has frequent rail links north to Whitehaven (£4.20, 30 minutes) and, in the other direction, Ulverston (£7.40, 1¼ hours), Grange-over-Sands (£10.70, 1½ hours) and beyond.

Whitehaven

POP 23,795

During its heyday in the 18th century, Whitehaven was the largest harbour on the Cumbrian coast (and the third largest in England), with a fortune founded on the lucrative trade in coal, iron, spices and slaves. It was also the first English town to be redeveloped from scratch along an orderly grid system – an idea dreamt up by the 17th-century landowner Sir James Lowther, who replaced the town's haphazard medieval alleys with long, straight streets lined with smart Georgian houses.

Sadly, Whitehaven is still reeling from the shocking events of 2 June 2010, when local taxi driver Derrick Bird embarked on a shooting spree, killing 12 local residents and wounding 25 others before committing suicide. The events (thankfully rare in the UK) have obviously left an enormous impression on a rural community that was only just recovering from the devastating floods of late 2009. But despite these events, Whitehaven remains one of Cumbria's most attractive coastal towns, and makes an ideal day-trip when you feel like a break from the fells.

Sights

The Beacon MUSEUM

(www.thebeacon-whitehaven.co.uk; West Strand; adult/child £5.40/free; 10am-4.30pm Tue-Sun) This intriguing museum is housed in Whitehaven's old lighthouse and explores the town's history as well as its connections with smuggling and the sugar, rum and slave trades. It's split into four levels: Work and Play on the second floor, Time & Tides on the third, and the Viewing Gallery and Weather Zone on the fourth, where you can gaze across the harbour with a high-powered telescope and present your own weather forecast.

Look out for displays on the infamous raid of John Paul Jones, an US naval commander (actually born in Scotland) who attacked the town during the American War of Independence, hoping to strike a decisive blow against a key British port. Unfortunately, the raid was a flop: of the 200-odd ships stationed in Whitehaven's harbour, Jones sank just a single coal barge.

The Rum Story WAXWORK MUSEUM

(www.rumstory.co.uk; Lowther St; adult/child £5.45/3.45; 10am-4.30pm) This family-orientated attraction explores Whitehaven's rum-running history. It's fun, if slightly tacky – look out for an 18th-century sugar workshop and a debauched re-creation of an 18th-century 'punch tavern'.

St Nicholas Church CHURCH

(Lowther St) Built in the 17th century and redeveloped in the 19th, this red-brick church was burned to the ground during a huge fire in 1971. Only the clock tower remains, but the former church nave has been turned into a pleasant public garden – look out for a memorial commemorating the many miners killed in Ulverston's coal pits.

Sleeping & Eating

Georgian House Hotel HOTEL ££

(01946-696611; www.thegeorgianhousehotel.net; 9-11 Church St; s/d from £79/89; P) Comfy and central, this former merchant's house has the town's best rooms, decked out in shipshape fashion with modern touches mixed with Georgian features.

Moresby Hall HOTEL ££

(01946-696317; www.moresbyhall.co.uk; Moresby; s £80-100, d £100-140; P) Dig deep and treat yourself to a night in a bona fide stately home, 2 miles north along the A595. It's straight out of *The Remains of the Day*: the Grade I–listed house has enormous rooms and one of the grandest staircases you'll ever see. 'De Asby' and 'Copeland' have hydro-massage showers, four-posters and views across the grounds.

Zest BISTRO ££

(www.zestwhitehaven.com) West St (mains £4.50-8.25; 10am-9pm Sun-Thu, 10am-9.30pm Fri & Sat) Low Rd (mains £14-20; dinner Wed-Sat) Ignore the pubs, pie shops and fish-and-chip shops, and head straight for the town's zingiest food at this Whitehaven twinset. There are two branches: the funky harbourside cafe on West St opens daily for salads, risottos and 'blinding butties', and the classier bistro on Low Rd serves top-notch British cooking.

Lowther House B&B £

(☎01946-63169; www.lowtherhouse-whitehaven.com; s/d £65/80; 📶) Newly refreshed B&B, with boutiquey touches evoking Whitehaven's past.

Glenfield B&B ££

(☎01946-691911; www.glenfield-whitehaven.co.uk; Back Corkickle; s £35, d £55-65; Ⓟ) Heritage B&B with six Victoriana-stocked rooms.

Getting There & Away

Whitehaven is on the Cumbrian Coast Line with hourly trains in each direction. Bus 6/X6 travels to Ravenglass (one hour, four daily).

NORTHERN & EASTERN CUMBRIA

Many visitors speed through the northern and eastern reaches of Cumbria in a headlong dash for the Lake District, but this is an area that's worth exploring – a bleakly beautiful landscape of isolated farms, barren heaths and solid hilltop towns, cut through by the Roman barrier of Hadrian's Wall.

Carlisle

POP 69,527

Precariously perched on the tempestuous border between England and Scotland, in the area once ominously dubbed the 'Debatable Lands', Carlisle is a city with a notoriously stormy past. Sacked by the Vikings, pillaged by the Scots, and plundered by the Border Reivers, Carlisle has stood on the frontline of England's defences for the last 1000 years. The battlements and keeps of the stout medieval castle still stand watch, built from the same rosy red sandstone as the city's cathedral and terraced houses. But Cumbria's only city is a more peaceful place these days, with a buzzy student population that keeps this old city young at heart.

History

A Celtic camp (or *caer*) provided an early military station for the Romans, and Carlisle became the northwest's main administrative centre following the construction of Hadrian's Wall. After centuries of intermittent conflict between Picts, Saxons and Viking raiders, the Normans seized Carlisle from the Scots in 1092.

The English developed Carlisle as a military stronghold throughout the Middle Ages, enlarging the walls, citadels and the great gates, and the city became an important strategic base for Royalist forces during the Civil War.

Peace came to the city with the Restoration, and the city developed as an industrial centre for cotton and textiles after the arrival of the railway in the mid-19th century.

Sights & Activities

Carlisle Castle CASTLE

(☎01228-591922; www.english-heritage.org.uk/daysout/properties/carlisle-castle/; adult/child £4.50/2.30; ⌚9.30am-5pm Apr-Sep, 10am-4pm Oct-Mar) Carlisle's brooding, rust-red castle lurks dramatically on the north side of the city. Founded around a Celtic and Roman stronghold, the Norman keep was added in 1092 by William Rufus, followed by successive refortifications by Henry II, Edward I and Henry VIII (who added the supposedly cannon-proof towers).

The castle has witnessed some dramatic events over the centuries: Mary, Queen of Scots was imprisoned here in 1568, and the castle was the site of a notorious eight-month siege during the English Civil War, when the Royalist garrison survived by eating rats, mice and the castle dogs before finally surrendering in 1645. Look out for the 'licking stones' in the dungeon, which Jacobite prisoners supposedly lapped for moisture.

Admission includes entry to the **Kings Own Royal Border Regiment Museum**, which explores the history of Cumbria's Infantry Regiment. There are guided tours from April to September.

Carlisle Cathedral CHURCH

(www.carlislecathedral.org.uk; 7 The Abbey; donation £2; ⌚7.30am-6.15pm Mon-Sat, to 5pm Sun) Built from the same rosy stone as many of the city's buildings, Carlisle's cathedral began life as a priory church in 1122, before later being raised to cathedral status when its first abbot, Athelwold, became the first Bishop of Carlisle. Among its notable features are the 15th-century choir stalls, the impressive barrel-vaulted roof and the wonderful 14th-century East Window, one of the largest Gothic windows in England. Surrounding the cathedral are other priory relics, including the 16th-century **Fratry** (see Prior's Kitchen Restaurant) and the **Prior's Tower**.

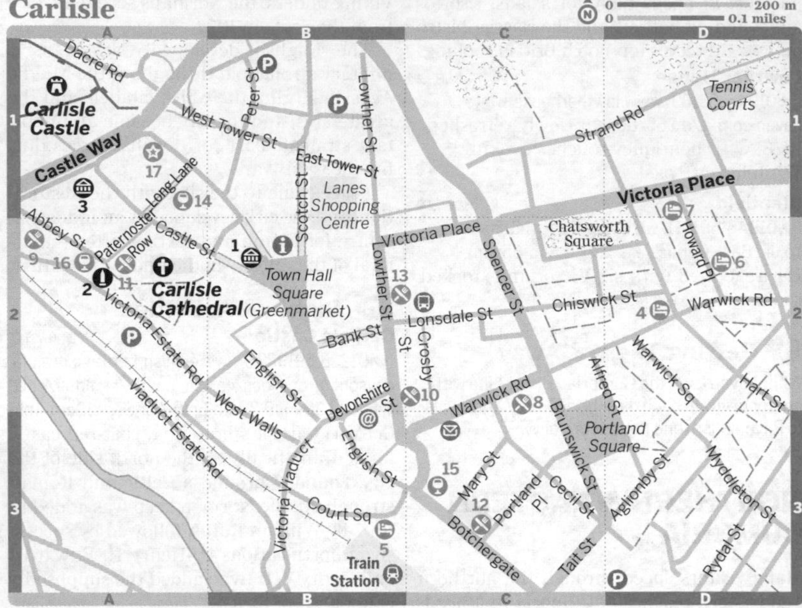

Carlisle

Top Sights

Carlisle Castle A1
Carlisle Cathedral A2

Sights

Fratry .... (see 11)
1 Guildhall Museum B2
2 Prior's Tower A2
3 Tullie House Museum A1

Sleeping

4 Cornerways D2
5 Hallmark Hotel B3
6 Langleigh Guest House D2
7 Number Thirty One D1

Eating

8 David's C2
9 Foxes Cafe Lounge A2
10 Gilded Lily C2
11 Prior's Kitchen Restaurant A2
12 Teza Indian Canteen C3
13 Townhouse B2

Drinking

14 Alcoves Cafe Bar A1
15 Cafe Solo C3
16 Fats A2

Entertainment

17 Brickyard A1

Tullie House Museum MUSEUM
(www.tulliehouse.co.uk; Castle St; adult/child £5.20/free; 10am-5pm Mon-Sat, 11am-5pm Sun Jul & Aug, 10am-5pm Mon-Sat, noon-5pm Sun Apr-Jun & Sep-Oct, earlier closing at other times) The city museum ranges through Carlisle's turbulent history, starting from its Celtic foundation through to the development of modern Carlisle. The museum has a strong archaeology collection, including a Bronze Age spear-mould, Roman tablets collected from Hadrian's Wall, and artefacts recovered from Viking burial sites in nearby Ormside and Hesket.

Guildhall Museum MUSEUM
(Greenmarket; admission free; noon-4.30pm Tue-Sun Apr-Oct) This tiny museum is housed in a wonky 15th-century town house built for Carlisle's trade guilds. Among the modest exhibits are a ceremonial mace, the city's stocks and a section of exposed wall showing the building's wattle-and-daub construction.

Tours

Open Book Visitor Guiding SIGHTSEEING TOURS
(☎01228-670578; www.greatguidedtours.co.uk) Tours of Carlisle and the surrounding area, including visits to Carlisle Castle and Hadrian's Wall. Tours leave from the tourist office.

Sleeping

Hallmark Hotel HOTEL ££
(☎01228-531951; carlisle.reception@hallmarkhotels.co.uk; Court Sq; d from £75; P wi-fi) Chain it may be, but the reborn Lakes Court Hotel is now a superior Carlisle sleep. It's certainly not 'boutique' (despite what the brochure says), but it's perfectly comfortable: rooms in golds and yellows (all with big beds, wi-fi and flatscreen tellies), posh function rooms, and a handy location steps from the station. Rates vary depending on dates of stay.

Willowbeck Lodge B&B ££
(☎01228-513607; www.willowbeck-lodge.com; Lambley Bank, Scotby; d £100-120; P wi-fi) Escape the city hustle at this superb modern house, 3 miles from the centre. Six deluxe rooms are closer to hotel standard than B&B, offering lovely fabrics, fancy bath stuff, oodles of space and views of a private pond. The easiest route to get here is to take Warwick Rd onto the A69, but it might be worth phoning for directions.

Number Thirty One B&B ££
(☎01228-597080;www.number31.freeservers.com; 31 Howard Pl; s/d from £70/100; P) Stylish B&B digs a short walk from the centre. There are only three rooms, but all have something different to recommend them, from a Zen-print headboard in the Red room to a half-tester in the Yellow room.

Langleigh Guest House B&B ££
(☎01228-530440; www.langleighhouse.co.uk; 6 Howard Pl; s/d £45/80; P) Completely chaotic, but with lots of period charm, this pleasant city B&B is decorated throughout in well-to-do Edwardian fashion – think brass lamps, antique clocks and watercolour prints. Be prepared for the dogs.

Carlisle YHA HOSTEL £
(☎0870-770 5752; carlisle@yha.org.uk; Bridge Lane; dm £21; ⏰Jul-Sep) In the summer hols, Carlisle's student digs offer YHA accommodation just west of the centre.

Cornerways B&B ££
(☎01228-521733; www.cornerwaysguest house.co.uk; 107 Warwick Rd; s £30-35, d £55-65; P @ wi-fi) This rambling red-brick is basic as they come, but offers some of the cheapest B&B rooms in the city.

Eating

Teza Indian Canteen INDIAN ££
(4a English Gate Plaza; mains £8-14; ⏰lunch & dinner Mon-Sat) After a disappointing dip in form, Teza's groundbreaking Indian is back in vogue, especially since the return of head chef Dinesh Rawat (who helped launch the restaurant back in 2005). This award-winning Indian does the usual bhunas (medium-hot dry curries) and bhajis, but it's the regionally influenced cuisine that fires things up: flavours from Kerala, Goa and Kashmir all make it into the mix.

Holme Bistro RESTAURANT ££
(56-58 Denton St; mains £11-15; ⏰lunch & dinner Mon-Sat) A little stroll southwards from the train station brings you to this little-known local gem, where the British bistro food is streets ahead of the competition. There's nary a whiff of pretension here, either in the simply done dining room or the simply done food. Tuck into confit duck or pan-fried pork chop, or pitch up on Friday for steak night.

David's BISTRO ££
(☎01228-523578; 62 Warwick Rd; lunch mains £8-12, dinner £14-24; ⏰lunch & dinner Tue-Sat) Town house dining with a gentlemanly air. David's has been a big name on the Carlisle scene for some years, and it's still up there with the best. Expect original mantelpieces and overhead chandeliers partnered with suave country dishes.

Foxes Cafe Lounge CAFE £
(18 Abbey St; mains £4-10; ⏰9.30am-4.30pm Tue-Sat, plus 7.30-11.30pm Fri & Sat) Lively, much-loved cafe-gallery displaying local art on the walls and providing an outlet for all kinds of creative happenings, from open mic nights to photo exhibitions. Serves continental cafe food during the day, with more sophisticated mains as the sun goes down.

Townhouse CAFE £
(34 Lowther St; lunches £3.95-5.15; ⏰9am-5pm) This cafe makes a handsome hideaway from the hustle of Lowther St. It's full of fairy lights, chalkboard menus and primary colours. Check out the double porridge choice and decide whether you're a northerner or a southerner…

Prior's Kitchen Restaurant CAFE £
(Carlisle Cathedral; lunches £4-6; ⏲9.45am-4pm Mon-Sat) Afternoon tea in this stone-vaulted cafe (formerly a monk's mess hall) has been a tradition in Carlisle for as long as anyone cares to remember. The cream teas are cracking, or there are quiches, cakes and rounds of sandwiches for something more filling.

Drinking

Botchergate's the place for late-night action, but it gets notoriously rowdy so watch your step.

Gilded Lily PUB
(6 Lowther St; ⏲9am-midnight Mon-Thu, 9am-2am Fri & Sat, noon-midnight Sun) Former bank turned sprawling city pub. Indulge in Continental beers and bespoke cocktails beneath the original skylight, and be prepared for plenty of dolled-up drinkers come the weekend.

Fats PUB
(48 Abbey St; ⏲11am-11pm) Slate, steel and an open fireplace attract a classy clientele to Fats. There are world beers behind the bar, while open-mic nights, scratch sessions and hot-tip DJs pull in the crowds.

Alcoves Cafe Bar BAR
(Up Long Lane, 18 Fisher St; ⏲6pm-late Tue-Sat) Easy to miss, but this alleyway hang-out near the cathedral is a popular spot for late-night drinks and DJs when you're wanting to evade the Botchergate hullabaloo. Look out for the lane off Fisher St.

Cafe Solo BAR
(1 Botchergate) Spanish-themed cocktails, late-night tapas and Sol beers at a tiny corner-bar on the edge of Botchergate.

Brickyard CONCERT HALL
(www.thebrickyardonline.com; 14 Fisher St) Carlisle's main (read: only) regular gig venue, housed in the former Memorial Hall.

Information

@Cybercafe (www.atcybercafe.co.uk; 8-10 Devonshire St; per hr £3; ⏲10am-10pm Mon-Sat, 1-10pm Sun)

Cumberland Infirmary (☎01228-523444; Newtown Rd) Half a mile west of the city centre.

Police station (☎0845-330 0247; English St; ⏲8am-midnight)

Tourist office (☎01228-625600; www.historic-carlisle.org.uk; Greenmarket; ⏲9.30am-5pm Mon-Sat, 10.30am-4pm Sun)

Getting There & Away

BUS Carlisle is Cumbria's main transport hub. National Express coaches depart from the bus station on Lonsdale St. Popular routes:

London £35, 7½ hours, three direct daily, with extra buses via Birmingham

Glasgow £20.70, two hours, 14 daily

Manchester £28, 3¼ hours, eight daily

Useful links to the Lakes:

104 (40 minutes, hourly Monday to Saturday, nine on Sunday) Penrith.

554 (70 minutes, three daily) Keswick.

555/556 (at least hourly) Windermere and Ambleside.

600 (one hour, seven daily Monday to Saturday) Cockermouth and towns in between.

AD 122 (Hadrian's Wall bus; six daily late May to late September) Connects Hexham and Carlisle.

TRAIN Carlisle is on the London Euston (£91, 3¼ to 4¼ hours) to Glasgow (£22, 1¼ to 1½ hours) line. It's also the terminus for several regional railways:

Cumbrian Coast Line Loops round the coastline all the way to Lancaster (£26, three to four hours via the coast, 45 minutes direct).

Settle-Carlisle Line (www.settle-carlisle.co.uk) Cuts southeast across the Yorkshire Dales (£23 return, 1½ hours); see also p587.

Tyne Valley Line Follows Hadrian's Wall to Newcastle-upon-Tyne (£13, 1½ hours).

Getting Around

To book a taxi, call **Radio Taxis** (☎01228-527575), **Citadel Station Taxis** (☎01228-523971) or **County Cabs** (☎01228-596789).

Alston

POP 2227

Surrounded by the bleak hilltops of the Pennines, isolated Alston's main claim to fame is its elevation: at 305m above sea level, it's thought to be the highest market town in England (despite no longer having a market). It's also famous among steam enthusiasts thanks to the **South Tynedale Railway** (☎01434-381696, timetable 01434-382828; www.strps.org.uk; adult/child return £6/3; ⏲Apr-Oct), which puffs and clatters through the hilly country between Alston and Kirkhaugh, along a route that originally operated from 1852 to 1976. The return trip takes about an hour; there are up to five daily trains in midsummer.

Penrith

POP 14,882

Traditional butchers, greengrocers and quaint little teashops line the streets of Penrith, a stout, red-brick town that feels closer to the no-nonsense villages of the Yorkshire Dales than to the chocolate-box villages of the Central Lakes. Once the region's capital, Penrith remains a busy commercial centre for eastern Cumbria; life still revolves around the centuries-old market square, from where a tight warren of colonnaded alleyways and cobbled streets radiate out towards Beacon Fell, where warning fires were once lit to warn of impending border raids.

Penrith Castle RUINS

(⏲7.30am-9pm Easter-Oct, to 4.30pm Oct-Easter) Opposite the station are the ruins of Penrith's 14th-century castle, built by William Strickland (later Bishop of Carlisle and Archbishop of Canterbury) and expanded by Richard III to resist Scottish raids, one of which razed the town in 1345.

St Andrews Church CHURCH

Penrith's name derives from an old Celtic word meaning 'red fell', and the area's crimson sandstone can be seen in many town buildings, including the town's 19th-century church. A legendary giant (the 'rightful king of all Cumbria') is said to be buried in the churchyard, but the stone pillars supposedly marking his grave are actually the weathered remains of Celtic crosses.

Rheged VISITOR CENTRE

(www.rheged.com; ⏲10am-6pm) Cunningly disguised as a Lakeland hill 2 miles west of Penrith, this visitor centre houses a large-screen Imax cinema and an exhibition on the history and geology of Cumbria, as well as a retail hall selling Cumbrian goods from handmade paper to chocolate and chutneys. The frequent X4/X5 bus stops at the centre.

Sleeping

Penrith's nicest B&Bs are clustered around Portland Pl; the ones on Victoria Rd are much more basic.

Brooklands B&B ££

(☎01768-863395; www.brooklandsguesthouse.com; 2 Portland Pl; s £38, d £75-85; wi-fi) The town's most elegant B&B is this Victorian red-brick on Portland Place. Rich furnishings and posh extras (such as White Company toiletries, fridges and chocs on the tea tray) keep it a cut above the crowd.

Brandelhow B&B ££

(☎01768-864470; www.brandelhowguesthouse.co.uk; 1 Portland Pl; s/d £35/70; wi-fi) Bang next door to Brooklands, things are more staid at this friendly, family-run guesthouse. Nothing remarkable about the rooms, but the little treats make it worth considering – such as the sit-down welcome tea accompanied by Bootle Gingerbread or Lanic's Expedition Flapjack.

George Hotel HOTEL ££

(☎01768-862696; www.lakedistricthotels.net/georgehotel; d £108-180; P wi-fi) You won't find a better location in Penrith than the one belonging to this scarlet-bricked stalwart right on the market square. Once the town's main coaching inn, it's now mainly frequented by business travellers – expect efficient service and corporate rooms in creams, taupes and beiges, plus a rather quaint bar and country restaurant.

Hornby Hall HOTEL ££

(☎01768-891114; www.hornbyhall.co.uk; Brougham; d £80-100; P) Aspiring aristocrats should head for this amber-stone manor-house, 3 miles south of Penrith in Brougham. The five sunny rooms overlook the manicured grounds; two are reached via a Hogwartsesque spiral staircase, and breakfast is served in the 16th-century dining hall with its original stone hearth and Victorian range. Two- and three-course

BIRDOSWALD ROMAN FORT

Though most of the forts along Hadrian's Wall have long since been plundered for building materials, you can still visit **Birdoswald Roman Fort** (EH; ☎01697-747602; adult/child £4.80/2.40; ⏲10am-5.30pm mid-Mar–Sep, 10am-4pm Oct–mid-Mar). Built to replace an earlier timber-and-turf fort, Birdoswald would have been the operating base for around 1000 Roman soldiers; excavations have revealed three of the four gateways, as well as granary stores, workshops, exterior walls and a military drill hall. A visitors centre explores the fort's history and the background behind the wall's construction. The AD 122 bus connecting Carlisle with Hexham passes by the fort.

dinners are available for £20 and £30, respectively.

Bank House B&B ££
(☎01768-868714; www.bankhousepenrith.co.uk; Graham St; s £49, d £70-112; 📶) Four cosy, chintzy rooms and a stonking Cumbrian breakfast, including local jams and bread from the nearby Watermill organic bakery.

Eating

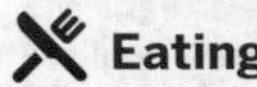

Yanwath Gate Inn GASTROPUB ££
(☎01768-862886; Yanwath; mains £16-19) Gastropub gorgeousness is at the order of the day at the Yat, 2 miles south of town. It's been named Cumbria's Top Dining Pub three times by the *Good Pub Guide*, and the grub puts many of the county's gastronomic restaurants to shame: wild venison, salt-marsh lamb, Brougham Hall chicken and crispy pork belly, chased down by Cumbrian cheeses and beers from three local breweries.

No 15 CAFE ££
(15 Victoria Rd; lunches £6-10; ⏲9am-5pm Mon-Sat) Our tip for the town's top lunch is this groovy cafe-gallery, proffering tempting pies, salads and wraps accompanied by first-rate coffee and freshly-mixed smoothies. Look out for art and photography exhibitions in the annexe, and late-night music sessions.

Magic Bean CAFE ££
(Poet's Walk; mains £6-14; ⏲lunch & dinner Mon-Sat) Light lunches and coffees during the day, backed up by curries and other global fare after dark.

Grants of Castlegate BISTRO ££
(Castlegate) Swish wine bar a short uphill walk from the market square.

JJ Graham DELI £
(6-7 Market Sq) Wonderful old-world grocer selling crusty breads, cakes, jams, biscuits, cheeses, meats and practically every other Cumbrian treat you can think of.

Information

Tourist office (☎01768-867466; pen.tic@eden.gov.uk; Middlegate; ⏲9.30am-5pm Mon-Sat, 1-4.45pm Sun) Also houses Penrith's little local museum.

Getting There & Away

BUS The bus station is northeast of the centre, off Sandgate. There are regular services to eastern Cumbria and the Eden Valley.

104 Penrith to Carlisle (45 minutes, hourly Monday to Saturday, nine on Sunday).

X4/X5 Travels via Rheged, Keswick and Cockermouth en route to the Cumbrian coast (hourly Monday to Saturday, six on Sunday).

TRAIN Penrith has frequent connections to Carlisle (£5.70, 15 minutes, hourly) and Lancaster (£13.70, one hour, hourly).

Newcastle & the Northeast

Includes »

Best Places to Eat

» Oldfields (p743)

» Jesmond Dene House (p744)

» Bouchon Bistrot (p763)

Best Places to Stay

» Ashcroft (p764)

» No 1 Sallyport (p775)

» Fallen Angel (p752)

Why Go?

Ask a Kentish farmer or Cornish fisherman about northeast England and they may describe a forbidding industrial wasteland inhabited by soccer-mad folk with impenetrable accents. What they won't mention are the untamed landscapes, Newcastle's cultural renaissance, the wealth of Roman sites and the no-nonsense likeability of the locals. Some post-industrial gloom remains, but there's so much more to this frontier country than slag heaps and silenced steelworks.

In fact, if it's silence you are looking for, the northeast is ideal for flits into unpeopled backcountry – from the rounded Cheviot Hills, to the brooding Northumberland National Park to the harsh remoteness of the North Pennines, you're spoilt for choice when it comes to fleeing the urban hullabaloo. Spectacular Hadrian's Wall cuts a lonely path through this wild landscape dotted with dramatic castle ruins, haunting reminders of a long and bloody struggle with the Scots to the north.

When to Go

The best time to discover Northumberland's miles of wide sandy beaches is during the June to August season. September through October is great for losing yourself in the autumnal landscapes of the North Pennines. A good place to celebrate New Year's Eve is in Allendale at the Baal Fire procession.

Newcastle & the Northeast Highlights

1 Viewing cutting-edge contemporary art and the River Tyne at the **BALTIC Centre for Contemporary Art** (p741)

2 Enjoying a thumping **night out** on the tiles in Newcastle's raucous city centre (p745)

3 Hugging the XXL ankles of the **Angel of the North** (p747)

4 Gazing in awe at **Durham Cathedral** (p749), a spectacular Unesco World Heritage Site

5 Getting all hands-on with the northeast's industrial past at **Beamish Open-Air Museum** (p753)

6 Walking like a Roman – by taking a hike along **Hadrian's Wall** (p760)

7 Clambering to the top of the **Cheviot** (p768) the highest peak in the Northumberland National Park.

History

Violent history has shaped the region more than any other in England, primarily because of its frontier position. Although Hadrian's Wall didn't serve as a defensive barrier, it nevertheless marked the northern limit of Roman Britain and was the Empire's most heavily fortified line. Following the Romans' departure, the region became part of the Anglian kingdom of Bernicia, which united with the kingdom of Deira (encompassing much of modern-day Yorkshire) to form Northumbria in 604.

The kingdom changed hands and borders shifted several times over the next 500 years as Anglo-Saxons and Danes struggled to seize it. The land north of the River Tweed was finally ceded to Scotland in 1018, while the nascent kingdom of England kept everything below it.

The arrival of the Normans in 1066 added new spice to the mix, as William I was eager to secure his northern borders against the Scots. He commissioned most of the castles you see along the coast, and cut deals with the prince bishops of Durham to ensure their loyalty. The new lords of Northumberland became very powerful because, as Marcher Lords (from the use of 'march' as a synonym of 'border'), they kept the Scots at bay.

Northumberland's reputation as a hotbed of rebellion intensified during the Tudor years, when the largely Catholic north, led by the seventh duke of Northumberland, Thomas Percy, rose up against Elizabeth I in the defeated Rising of the North in 1569. The Border Reivers, raiders from both sides of the border in the 16th century kept the region in a perpetual state of lawlessness, which only subsided after the Act of Union between England and Scotland in 1707.

The 19th century saw County Durham play a central role in the Industrial Revolution. The region's coalmines were the key to the industrialisation of the Northeast, powering steelworks, shipyards and armament works that grew up along the Tyne and Tees. In 1825 the mines also spawned the world's first steam railway, the Stockton & Darlington built by local engineer George Stephenson. However, social strife emerged in the 20th century, the locals' plight most vividly depicted by the Jarrow Crusade in October 1936, which saw 200 men from the shipbuilding town of Jarrow march to London to demand aid for their community devastated by the Great Depression. Decline was the watchword of the postwar years with mines, shipbuilding, steel production and the railway industry all winding down. Reinventing the Northeast has been a mammoth task but regeneration is just beginning to bear fruit.

Activities

With the rugged moors of the Pennines and stunning seascape of the Northumberland coast, there's some good walking and cycling in this region. The scenery is beautiful in a wild and untouched way – quite different from the picture-postcard landscape of areas such as Devon or the Cotswolds. When out in the open, be prepared for wind and rain at any time of year and for very harsh conditions in winter. Regional tourism websites all contain walking and cycling information, and tourist offices all stock free leaflets plus maps and guides (usually £1 to £5) covering walking, cycling and other activities. Recommendations for shorter routes are given throughout this chapter.

CYCLING

The northeast has some of the most inspiring cycle routes in England. Part of the National Cycle Network (NCN), a long-time favourite is the **Coast & Castles Cycle Route** (NCN Route 1), which runs south–north along the glorious Northumberland coast between Newcastle-upon-Tyne and Berwick-upon-Tweed, before swinging inland into Scotland to finish at Edinburgh. Of course you can also do it north–south, or just do the northeast England section. The coast is exposed, though, so check the weather and try to time your ride so that the wind is behind you.

The 140-mile **Sea to Sea Cycle Route** (C2C; www.c2c-guide.co.uk) runs across northern England from Whitehaven or Workington on the Cumbrian coast, through the northern part of the Lake District, and then over the wild hills of the North Pennines to finish at Newcastle-upon-Tyne or Sunderland. This popular route is fast becoming a classic, and most people go west–east to take advantage of prevailing winds. You'll need five days to complete the whole route; the northeast England section, from Penrith (in Cumbria) to the east coast is a good three-day trip. If you wanted to cut the urban sections, Penrith to Consett is perfect in a weekend. The C2C is aimed at road bikes, but there are several optional off-road sections.

The other option is the **Hadrian's Cycleway** (www.cycle-routes.org), a 191-mile route opened in July 2006 that runs from South Shields in Tyneside, west along the wall and down to Ravenglass in Cumbria.

The **Wheels to the Wild** is a 70-mile circular cycle route that explores the dales of the North Pennines. From Wolsingham, it weaves a paved route through Weardale, Allendale and Teesdale on mostly quiet country lanes.

For dedicated off-road riding, good places to aim for in northeast England include Kielder Forest in Northumberland and Hamsterley Forest in County Durham, which both have a network of sylvan tracks and options for all abilities.

WALKING

The North Pennines are billed as 'England's last wilderness', and if you like to walk in quiet and fairly remote areas, these hills – along with the Cheviots further north – are the best in England. Long routes through this area include the famous **Pennine Way**, which keeps mainly to the high ground as it crosses the region between the Yorkshire Dales and the Scottish border, but also goes through sections of river valley and some tedious patches of plantation. The whole route is over 250 miles, but the 70-mile section between Bowes and Hadrian's Wall would be a fine four-day taster. If you prefer to go walking just for the day, good bases for circular walks in the North Pennines include the towns of Alston and Middleton-in-Teesdale.

Elsewhere in the area, the great Roman ruin of **Hadrian's Wall** is an ideal focus for walking. There's a huge range of easy loops taking in forts and other historical highlights. A very popular walk is the long-distance route from end to end, providing good options for anything from one to four days (see p761).

The Northumberland coast has endless miles of open beaches, and little in the way of resort towns, so walkers can often enjoy this wild, windswept shore in virtual solitude. One of the finest walks is between the villages of Craster and Bamburgh via Dunstanburgh, which includes two of the county's most spectacular castles.

ℹ Getting There & Around

BUS

Bus transport around the region can be difficult, particularly around the more remote reaches of western Northumberland. Contact **Traveline** (☎0871-2002233; www.travelinenortheast.info) for information on connections, timetables and prices.

Several one-day Explorer tickets are available; always ask if one might be appropriate. The Explorer North East (adult/child £8/7), available on buses, covers from Berwick down to Scarborough, and allows unlimited travel for one day, as well as numerous admission discounts.

Train

The main lines run north to Edinburgh via Durham, Newcastle and Berwick, and west to Carlisle roughly following Hadrian's Wall.

There are numerous Rover tickets for single-day travel and longer periods, so ask if one might be worthwhile. For example, the North Country Rover (adult/child £72/36) allows unlimited travel throughout the north (not including Northumberland) any four days out of eight.

NEWCASTLE-UPON-TYNE

POP 189,863

Of all of northern England's cities, Newcastle is perhaps the most surprising to the first-time visitor, especially if they come armed with the preconceived notions that have dogged the city's reputation since, well, always. A sooty, industrial wasteland for salt-of-the-earth toughies whose favourite hobby is drinking and braving the elements bare-chested. Coal slags and cold slags? You may be in for a pleasant surprise.

Welcome to the hipster capital of the northeast, a cool urban centre that knows how to take care of itself and anyone else who comes to visit with an unexpected mix of culture, heritage and sophistication, best exemplified not just by its excellent new art galleries and magnificent concert hall, but by its growing number of fine restaurants, choice hotels and interesting bars. It's not just about the Tyne bridges – although the eclectic, cluttered array of Newcastle's most recognisable feature is pretty impressive.

Thankfully, Newcastle's hip rep is built on a set of deep-rooted traditions embodied by the city's greatest strength: the locals. Raised and subsequently abandoned by coal and steel, Geordies are a fiercely independent bunch, tied together by history, adversity and that impenetrable dialect, the closest language to 1500-year-old Anglo-Saxon left in England. They are also proud, independently minded and surprisingly positive – perhaps their greatest quality considering how tough life has been.

And then of course there's the nightlife, source of so many of the city's most brazen stereotypes. Of course you can go mad here – there's an irrepressible energy that borders on the irresponsible – but you don't have to, and there are plenty of options that don't involve draining blue-coloured vodka or running unclad through the streets.

Sights

QUAYSIDE

Newcastle's most recognisable attractions are the seven bridges that span the Tyne and some of the striking buildings that line it. Along the Quayside, on the river's northern side, is a handsome boardwalk that makes for a pleasant stroll during the day but really comes to life at night, when the bars, clubs and restaurants that line it are full to bursting. A really great way of experiencing the river and its sights is by boat.

FREE **Bessie Surtee's House**
MERCHANT'S HOUSE

(EH; 41-44 Sandhill; ⏲10am-4pm Mon-Fri) The Tyne's northern bank was the hub of commercial Newcastle in the 16th century and on Sandhill a row of leaning merchant houses has survived from that era. One of them is the Bessie Surtee's House where three rooms are open to the public. The daughter of a wealthy banker, feisty Bessie annoyed Daddy by falling in love with John Scott (1751–1838), a pauper. It all ended in smiles as John went on to become Lord Chancellor.

CITY CENTRE

Newcastle's Victorian centre, a compact area bordered roughly by Grainger St to the west and Pilgrim St to the east, is supremely elegant and one of the most compelling examples of urban rejuvenation in England. At its heart is the extraordinarily handsome Grey St, lined with fine classical buildings – undoubtedly one of the coun-

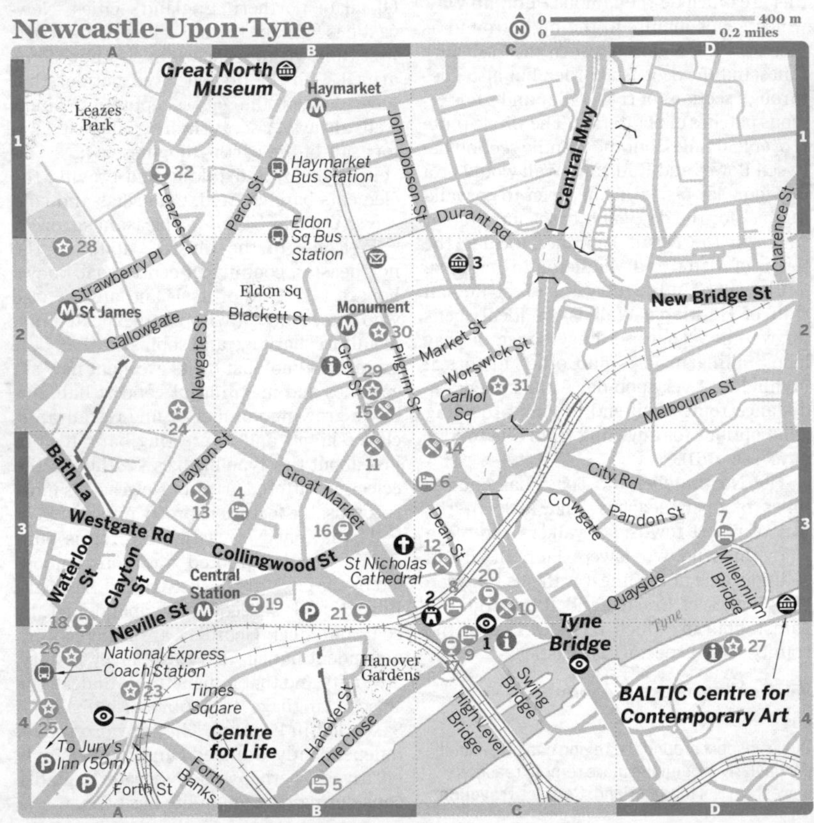

try's finest thoroughfares: it was even voted the UK's 3rd prettiest street in the Google Street View Awards 2010.

FREE Great North Museum MUSEUM
(www.greatnorthmuseum.org; Barras Bridge; ⏲10am-5pm Mon-Sat, 2-5pm Sun) This outstanding new museum has been created by bringing together the contents of Newcastle University's museums and adding them to the natural history exhibits of the prestigious Hancock Museum in the latter's renovated neoclassical building. The result is a fascinating jumble of dinosaurs, Roman altar stones, Egyptian mummies, Samurai warriors and some impressive taxidermy, all presented in an engaging and easily digestible way. The indisputable highlights are a life-size model of a *Tyrannosaurus rex* and an interactive model of Hadrian's Wall showing every milecastle and fortress. There's also lots of hands-on stuff for the kids, a planetarium with screenings throughout the day and a decent snack bar.

Centre for Life SCIENCE VILLAGE
(www.life.org.uk; Times Sq; adult/child £9.95/6.95; ⏲10am-6pm Mon-Sat, 11am-6pm Sun, last admission 4pm) This excellent science village, part of the sober-minded complex of institutes devoted to the study of genetic science, is one of the more interesting attractions in town. Through a series of hands-on exhibits and the latest technology you (or your kids) can discover the incredible secrets of life. The highlight is the Motion Ride, a motion simulator that lets you 'feel' what it's like to experience things like bungee jumping and other extreme sports (the 3-D film changes every year). There's lots of thought-provoking arcade-style games, and if the information sometimes gets lost on the way, never mind, kids will love it.

FREE Discovery Museum MUSEUM
(www.twmuseums.org.uk; Blandford Sq; ⏲10am-5pm Mon-Sat, 2-5pm Sun) Tyneside's rich history is uncovered through a fascinating series of exhibits at this unmissable museum. The exhibitions, spread across three floors of the former Co-operative Wholesale Society building, surround the mightily impressive 30m-long *Turbinia*, the fastest ship in the world in 1897. There's an absorbing section dedicated to shipbuilding on the Tyne including a scale model of the river as it was in 1929, a buzzers-and-bells science maze for the kids and a 'Story

Newcastle-Upon-Tyne

Top Sights
- BALTIC Centre for Contemporary Art ... D3
- Centre for Life ... A4
- Great North Museum ... B1
- Tyne Bridge ... C4

Sights
- 1 Bessie Surtee's House ... C4
- 2 Castle Garth Keep ... C3
- 3 Laing Art Gallery ... C2

Sleeping
- 4 Albatross Backpackers Inn ... B3
- 5 Copthorne ... B4
- 6 Greystreethotel ... C3
- 7 Malmaison ... D3
- 8 Vermont ... C3
- 9 Waterside Hotel ... C4

Eating
- 10 Big Mussel ... C3
- 11 Blake's Coffee House ... B3
- Buee ... (see 10)
- 12 Oldfields ... C3
- 13 Scrumpy Willow & Singing Kettle ... A3
- 14 Secco Ristorante Salentino ... C3
- 15 Starters & Puds ... B2

Drinking
- 16 Blackie Boy ... B3
- 17 Bridge Hotel ... C4
- 18 Camp David ... A3
- 19 Centurion Bar ... B3
- 20 Crown Posada ... C3
- 21 Tokyo ... B3
- 22 Trent House ... A1

Entertainment
- Beyond Bar & Grill ... (see 24)
- 23 Digital ... A4
- 24 Gate ... A2
- 25 Loft ... A4
- 26 Powerhouse Nightclub ... A4
- 27 Sage Gateshead ... D4
- 28 St James' Park ... A2
- 29 Theatre Royal ... B2
- 30 Tyneside Cinema ... B2
- 31 World Headquarters ... C2

BRIDGING THE TYNE

The most famous view in Newcastle is the cluster of Tyne bridges, the most famous of these being the **Tyne Bridge** (1925–28). Its resemblance to Australia's Sydney Harbour Bridge is no coincidence as both were built by the same company (Dorman Long of Middlesbrough) around the same time. The quaint little **Swing Bridge** pivots in the middle to let ships through. Nearby, **High Level Bridge**, designed by Robert Stephenson, was the world's first combined road and railway bridge (1849). The most recent addition is the multiple-award-winning **Millennium Bridge** (aka Blinking Bridge; 2002), which opens like an eyelid to let ships pass.

of Newcastle' section giving the low-down on the city's history from Pons Aelius (Newcastle's Roman name) to Cheryl Cole.

The museum is about a 10 minute walk west of Central Station along Neville St and Westmorland Rd.

Castle Garth Keep CASTLE
(adult/child £4/free; ⏲10am-5pm Mon-Sat, from noon Sun) The stronghold that put both the 'new' and 'castle' into Newcastle has been largely swallowed up by the train station, leaving only the square Norman keep as one of the few remaining fragments. Inside you'll discover a fine chevron-covered chapel and an exhibition of architectural models ranging from Hadrian's Wall to 20th-century eyesores. The 360-degree city views from the rooftop are much better than from the BALTIC's 'Viewing Box' across the water.

FREE **Laing Art Gallery** GALLERY
(www.twmuseums.org.uk; New Bridge St; ⏲10am-5pm Mon-Sat, 2-5pm Sun) The exceptional collection at the Laing includes works by Gainsborough, Gauguin and Henry Moore, and an important collection of paintings by Northumberland-born artist John Martin (1789–1854). Free guided tours run Saturdays at 11am.

OUSEBURN VALLEY

About a mile east of the city centre is the much-touted Ouseburn Valley, the 19th-century industrial heartland of Newcastle and now an up-and-coming, semi-regenerated district, dotted with potteries, glass-blowing studios and other skilled craftspeople, as well as a handful of great bars, clubs and a superb cinema (though much of the area is still an unsightly industrial estate). Yellow Quayside Q2 bus loops through the valley from the city centre. For more info, check out www.ouseburntrust.org.uk.

Biscuit Factory COMMERCIAL GALLERY
(www.thebiscuitfactory.com; 16 Stoddart St; ⏲11am-5pm Sun & Mon, 10am-6pm Tue-Sat, to 8pm Thu) No prizes for guessing what this commercial art gallery used to be. What it is now, though, is the country's biggest art shop, where you can peruse and buy work by artists from near and far in a variety of mediums, including painting, sculpture, glassware and furniture, much of which has a northeast theme. Even if you don't buy, the art is excellent and there's a top-class restaurant too (Brasserie Black Door).

Seven Stories – the Centre for Children's Books LITERATURE MUSEUM
(www.sevenstories.org.uk; 30 Lime St; adult/child £6/5; ⏲10am-5pm Mon-Sat, to 4pm Sun) A marvellous conversion of a handsome Victorian mill has resulted in Seven Stories, a very hands-on museum dedicated to the wondrous world of children's literature. Across the seven floors you'll find original manuscripts, a growing collection of artwork from the 1930s onwards, and a constantly changing program of exhibitions, activities and events designed to encourage the AA Milnes of the new millennium.

WHY A GEORDIE?

Truth is, no one really knows for sure, not even the Geordies themselves. The most attractive explanation, at least here, is that the name was coined to disparage the townspeople who chose to side with the German Protestant George I ('Geordie' being a diminutive of George) against the 'Old Pretender', the Catholic James Stuart, during the Jacobite Rebellion of 1715. But a whole other school contends that the origins are a little less dramatic, and stem from Northumberland miners opting to use a lamp pioneered by George 'Geordie' Stephenson over one invented by Sir Humphrey Davy.

36 Lime Street ARTISTS COOPERATIVE
(www.36limestreet.co.uk; Ouseburn Warehouse, 36 Lime St) The artistic, independent spirit of Ouseburn is particularly well represented in this artists cooperative, the largest of its kind in the northeast, featuring an interesting mix of artists, performers, designers and musicians. They all share a historic building designed by Newcastle's most important architect, John Dobson (1787–1865), who also designed Grey St and Central Station in the neoclassical style. As it's a working studio you can't just wander in, but there are regular exhibitions and open days; check the website for details.

GATESHEAD

You probably didn't realise that that bit of Newcastle south of the Tyne is the 'town' of Gateshead, but local authorities are going to great lengths to put it right, even promoting the whole kit-and-caboodle-on-Tyne as 'NewcastleGateshead', a clumsy piece of marketing indeed. To date, the ambitious program of development has seen the impressive transformation of the southern banks of the Tyne, but as yet there's little to make you travel further than the water's edge.

FREE **BALTIC Centre for Contemporary Art** GALLERY
(www.balticmill.com; Gateshead Quays; ⏲10am-6pm Wed-Mon, from 10.30 Tue) Once a huge, dirty, yellow grain store overlooking the Tyne, BALTIC is now a huge, dirty, yellow art gallery to rival London's Tate Modern. Unlike the Tate, there are no permanent exhibitions here, but the constantly rotating shows feature the work and installations of some of contemporary art's biggest show stoppers. The complex has artists in residence, a performance space, a cinema, a bar, a spectacular rooftop restaurant (you'll need to book) and a ground-floor restaurant with riverside tables. There's also a viewing box for a fine Tyne vista.

Tours

Newcastle City Tours WALKING TOURS
(☎07780-958679; www.newcastlecitytours.co.uk; per tour from £40) Tailored tours of the city as well as heritage tours of the surrounding region.

River Escapes RIVER CRUISES
(☎01670-785 666; www.riverescapes.co.uk; adult/child £6/4; ⏲noon, 1.30pm & 3.30pm Sat & Sun Jun-Sep) One-hour river cruises departing from Quayside pier at the Millennium Bridge, opposite the BALTIC.

Ghost Tours WALKING TOURS
(☎0191-400078; www.aloneinthedarkentertainment.com; per person £8; ⏲7pm & 8.30pm Fri & Sat, 7pm Sun) People swear unexplainable things occur on these fascinating but spine-chilling walks. Groups meet at the entrance to the Castle Garth Keep.

Tom Keating Tours WALKING TOURS
(☎0191-488 5115; www.tomkeating.net) Expert, tailor-made tours of the city by a well-respected blue-badge guide. Tours of surrounding region also available.

NEWCASTLE FOR CHILDREN

Although at first glance the bonhomie mightn't seem to extend past buying rounds in the pub, on closer inspection there's plenty to keep the young 'uns entertained.

The utterly wonderful **Seven Stories** is the perfect destination for any kid who has an imagination, while closer to the centre the **Centre for Life** and the **Discovery Museum** are brilliant and should keep the kids busy for the guts of a day. The most popular park in town is **Leazes Park**, just north of St James' Park, which has a rowing lake, but the nicest of all is **Saltwell Park** (⏲dawn-dusk), an elegant Victorian space behind Gateshead College and easily accessible by bus 53 and 54 from the Gateshead Interchange. Pedestrians can get in through entrances on East Park Rd, West Rd, Saltwell Rd South, Saltwell View and Joicey Rd.

Sleeping

Although the number of city-centre options is on the increase, they are still generally restricted to the chain variety – either budget or business – that caters conveniently to the party people and business folk that make up the majority of Newcastle's overnight guests. Most of the other accommodations are in the handsome northern suburb of Jesmond, where the forces of gentrification and student power fight it out for territory; Jesmond's main drag, Osborne Rd, is lined with all kinds of bed types as well as bars and restaurants – making it a strong rival with the city centre for the late-night party scene. As the city is a major business destination, weekend arrivals will find that most places drop their prices for Friday and Saturday nights.

CITY CENTRE

As you'd expect, bedrooms in the city centre are pricier than almost anywhere else, but there are some good budget and midrange options that don't involve too much of a hike.

Malmaison HOTEL £££
(☎0191-245 5000; www.malmaison-newcastle.com; Quayside; r from £125, ste from £195; P @) The affectedly stylish Malmaison touch has been applied to this former warehouse with considerable success, even down to the French-speaking lifts. Big beds, sleek lighting and designer furniture embellish the bouncy boudoirs and slick chambers.

Backpackers Newcastle HOSTEL £
(☎0191-340 7334; www.backpackersnewcastle.com; 262 Westgate Rd; dm from £17.95;) This clean, well-run budget flophouse has just 26 beds lending it a bit more of a backpacker vibe than its competitors in the city. Bike storage, kitchen, a big games room, power-showers and a mildly design feel make this a great kip on the Tyne.

Waterside Hotel HOTEL ££
(☎0191-230 0111; www.watersidehotel.com; 48-52 Sandhill, Quayside; s/d £75/85;) The rooms are a tad small, but they're among the most elegant in town: lavish furnishings and heavy velvet drapes in a heritage-listed building. The location is excellent.

Greystreethotel HOTEL ££
(☎0191-230 6777; www.greystreethotel.com; 2-12 Grey St; d from £109; P) A bit of designer class along the classiest street in the city centre has been long overdue: the rooms are gorgeous if a tad poky, all cluttered up with flatscreen TVs, big beds and handsome modern furnishings.

Copthorne HOTEL ££
(☎0191-222 0333; www.millenniumhotels.com; The Close, Quayside; s/d from £93/112; P) A superb waterside location makes this modern hotel a perfect choice – especially if you pick a room overlooking the water (the Connoisseur rooms, for instance). You may even bump into the odd celebrity performing at the nearby Newcastle Arena. Book online for the best rates.

Vermont HOTEL £££
(☎0191-233 1010; www.vermont-hotel.com; Castle Garth; r £130; P) Mid-1930s Manhattan with new-millennium facilities, the Vermont was the top dog in town, until the arrival of the Mal and Greystreet. The location is good, but a view of the castle keep just isn't enough of a sales pitch; the iPod docking stations are a decent contemporary touch.

Jury's Inn HOTEL ££
(☎0191-201 4400; www.jurysinn.com; St James' Gate, Scotswood Rd; r from £49) A short walk from Central Station and the Newcastle Arena, this edition of the popular Irish chain has rooms, a restaurant, and a bar best described as big, bland and absolutely inoffensive. And at these prices, who cares? The difference here is the friendliness of the staff, which is genuine.

Albatross Backpackers In! HOSTEL £
(☎0191-233 1330; www.albatrossnewcastle.com; 51 Grainger St; dm/d from £16.50/45; P @) Clean, fully equipped hostel with decent-sized dorms, a self-catering kitchen, top-notch bathroom facilities, CCTV, electronic key cards and an internet station. There's even a small car park.

JESMOND

The shabby chic suburb of Jesmond is the place to head for budget and midrange accommodation. Catch the Metro to Jesmond or West Jesmond, bus 80A from near Central Station, or the 38 from Westgate Rd.

Jesmond Dene House HOTEL £££
(☎0191-212 3000; www.jesmonddenehouse.co.uk; Jesmond Dene Rd; s £165, d £175-250, ste £295-375; P @) As elegant a hotel as you'll find anywhere, this exquisite property is the perfect marriage between traditional styles and modern luxury. The large, gorgeous bedrooms are furnished in a modern interpretation of the Arts and Crafts style and are bedecked with all manner of technological goodies (flatscreen digital TVs, digital radios) and wonderful bathrooms complete with underfloor heating. The restaurant is not bad either.

Adelphi Hotel HOTEL ££
(☎0191-281 3109; www.adelphihotelnewcastle.co.uk; 63 Fern Ave; s/d £40/60) Just off Osborne Rd, the Adelphi is more B&B than hotel but has nice floral rooms that are clean and very neat – a rare thing around here for this price range.

LET THERE BE LIGHT

Mosley St, which runs on an east–west axis across the bottom of Grey St, was the first street in the world to be lit by electricity, all thanks to the genius of Sir Joseph Wilson Swan (1828–1914), the inventor of the incandescent light bulb, for which he received a patent in 1878 – a year before Thomas Edison got his. Swan, who had a business on Mosley St, hung the first light outside his shop in February 1879.

The two inventors worked in tandem to improve on Swan's original design, and in 1883 the two formed the Edison & Swan Electric Light Company (better known as Ediswan, the forerunner to US giant General Electric), changing the world forever.

Avenue B&B ££
(☎0191-281 1396; 2 Manor House Rd; s/d £39.50/60) Buried in a sleepy residential area but just a couple of blocks' walk from the action on Osborne Rd, this well-run, family-friendly B&B goes big on busy floral flounce and faux country style.

Newcastle YHA YOUTH HOSTEL £
(☎0845 371 9335; www.yha.org.uk; 107 Jesmond Rd; dm from £18) This nice, rambling place has small dorms that are generally full, so book in advance. It's close to the Jesmond Metro stop.

Eating

The Geordie palate is pretty refined these days and there are a host of fine dining options in all price categories that make their mark. Of course for many locals, Geordies plus food equals the legendary **Greggs** (15 locations throughout the city centre; ⏲8am-5pm), Newcastle's very own fast food chain serving cheap and filling cakes, sandwiches, pastries and drinks since 1951.

CITY CENTRE

TOP CHOICE Oldfields BRITISH ££
(Milburn House, Dean St; www.oldfieldsrealfood.co.uk; mains £12-19; ⏲Mon-Sat, lunch Sun) Top-notch, no-nonsense British gourmet fare, using locally sourced ingredients wherever possible, is Oldfields' tasty trade. Tuck into rich and satisfying dishes such as Durham rabbit and crayfish pie, mutton hotpot and Eccles cake with custard in the circular, wood-panelled dining room, before finishing off with a shot of Wylam gin or locally microbrewed ale.

Blake's Coffee House CAFE £
(☎0191-261 5463; 53 Grey St; breakfast £1.95-8.95, sandwiches £3-4; ⏲9am-6pm) There is nowhere better than this high-ceilinged cafe for a Sunday-morning cure on any day of the week. It's friendly, relaxed and serves up the biggest selection of coffees in town. Every second Thursday is Acoustic Night, which has featured big names such as Katie Tunstall as well as lesser known local strummers.

Starters & Puds RESTAURANT ££
(www.startersandpuds.com; 2-6 Shakespeare St; starters £3.50-7, puddings £4.70; ⏲Mon-Sat) Situated in a low-lit cellar next to the Theatre Royal, the idea here is to come for a pre-theatre starter, cross the road for a thespian main course then head back for a post-performance dessert (and drink). However, word has got round about the award-winning fare served up here so now there's a lunch menu (£10).

Scrumpy Willow & Singing Kettle ORGANIC RESTAURANT ££
(☎0191-221 2323; 89 Clayton St; mains £5-10; ⏲Mon-Sat, lunch Sun) Voted one of the UK's top organic eateries by Guardian readers, this incredibly popular place bursts at the seams at mealtimes, and one mouthful is enough to understand why. Vegans, veggies and gluten-freers are all catered for with an eclectic menu featuring everything from peanut butter sarnies to Irish stew. All the art on the walls is for sale. Booking recommended.

Buee FRENCH ££
(1-3 The Side; mains £8-16; ⏲9.30am-10pm Tue-Sat, to 6pm Sun & Mon) Local and not-so-local ingredients are given a simple Gallic twist at this brand-new bistro just off the Quayside. A great light lunch spot with big-window people-watching possibilities downstairs or a more substantial dinner in the upstairs dining room with Tyne views – whenever you come the food, plated up by a real French cook, is first rate.

Big Mussel BELGIAN DINER ££
(www.bigmussel.co.uk; 15 The Side; mains £5-15) This informal diner specialises in one of Europe's oddest national dishes – mussels and chips – the favourite nosh of the Belgians, ideally washed down with a fruity Flemish ale. There are ample pasta and

vegetarian options and live jazz on weekday evenings (from 7pm).

Secco Ristorante Salentino ITALIAN ££
(0191-230 0444; www.seccouk.com; 86 Pilgrim St; mains £10-16; Mon-Sat) Top-notch local ingredients such as Northumberland lamb and North Sea red mullet are infused with southern Italian essence by chefs from Salento in the Italian heel of Puglia. Surely a contender for the northeast's best Italian restaurant so reserve in advance.

OUSEBURN VALLEY

Brasserie Black Door BRASSERIE ££
(Biscuit Factory, 16 Stoddard St; mains £10-16; Mon-Sat, lunch Sun) Less a gallery restaurant and more a restaurant in a gallery, the Black Door serves up excellent modern English fare – which generally involves a twist from pretty much any other part of the world – in a bright, elegant dining space. A great spot for lunch even if you're not visiting the gallery.

JESMOND

TOP CHOICE **Jesmond Dene House** REGIONAL CUISINE £££
(0191-212 5555; www.jesmonddenehouse.co.uk; Jesmond Dene Rd; mains £13-40) Head chef Pierre Rigothier is the architect of an exquisite menu heavily influenced by the northeast – venison from County Durham, oysters from Lindisfarne and the freshest herbs plucked straight from the garden – all infused with a touch of French sophistication. The result is a gourmet delight and one of the best dining experiences in the city.

Pizzeria Francesca PIZZERIA ££
(134 Manor House Rd, Jesmond; pizzas & pastas £5, other mains £7-15; Mon-Sat) One of the northeast's best pizza and pasta joints, this chaotic, friendly place is how all Italian restaurants should be. Excitable, happy waiters and huge portions of pizza and pasta keep them queuing at the door – get in line and wait because you can't book in advance.

Drinking

It's no secret that Geordies like a good night on the razzle but you may be surprised to know that not only is there nightlife beyond the coloured cocktails of the Bigg Market, but that it is infinitely more interesting and satisfying than the sloppy boozefest that defines the stereotype. The Ouseburn attracts a mellower crowd, and the western end of Neville St has a decent mix of great bars and is also home to the best of the gay scene.

CITY CENTRE

Centurion Bar BAR
(Central Station) Voted Newcastle's best bar in 2008, the former first-class waiting room at Central Station is ideal for a pre-club drink in style or a pre-train brew on the hop. The exquisitely ornate Victorian tile decoration reaching from floor to ceiling is said to be worth four million pounds. There's an adjoining cafe and deli platform-side.

Crown Posada PUB
(31 The Side) An unspoilt, real-ale pub that is a favourite with more seasoned drinkers, be they the after-work or instead-of-work crowd.

Trent House PUB
(1-2 Leazes Lane) The wall has a simple message: 'Drink Beer. Be Sincere.' This simply unique place is one of the best bars in town because it is all about an ethos rather than a look. Totally relaxed and utterly devoid of pretentiousness, it is an old-school boozer that out-cools every other bar because it isn't trying to. Run by the same folks behind the superb World Headquarters.

Bridge Hotel PUB
(Castle Sq) Next to the High-Level Bridge, this is one of the city centre's more traditional taverns with dark-wood Victorian snugs, kaleidoscope stained glass and a very long bar of real ales.

Blackie Boy PUB
(11 Groat Market) Locals grumble that this darkened boozer, one of the city's original taverns, has gone too upmarket but it's still a popular place to drink even if the decor has gone all weird. Visitors from the US may have trouble deciphering the novel toilet door signage.

Tokyo COCKTAIL BAR
(17 Westgate Rd) Tokyo has a suitably darkened atmosphere for what the cognoscenti consider the best cocktail bar in town, but we loved the upstairs garden bar where you can drink, smoke and chat with a view.

OUSEBURN VALLEY

Ship Inn PUB
(Stepney Bank) A firm fixture on the valley's pub crawl, the Ouseburn's oldest surviving pub (early 19th century) is a traditional boozer popular with locals and incoming fun seekers. On busy days the elbow-bending spills out onto the small green in front.

Cumberland Arms PUB
(off Byker Bank, Ouseburn) Sitting on a hill at the top of the Ouseburn, this 19th-century bar has a sensational selection of ales and ciders as well as a range of Northumberland meads. There's a terrace outside, where you can read a book from the Bring One, Borrow One library inside.

Cluny BAR, MUSIC VENUE
(36 Lime St) Cool bar by day, even cooler music venue by night, this superpopular spot defines the independent spirit of the Ouseburn Valley.

JESMOND

Mr Lynch BAR
(Archbold Tce) Newcastle goes shabby chic with this '60s-style retro bar at the southernmost edge of Jesmond. Ignore the appearance and focus on the crowd, a knowledgeable mix of students and local trendies. There's live music Friday and Saturday.

☆ Entertainment

Are you up for it? You'd better be, because Newcastle's nightlife doesn't mess about. There is action beyond the club scene – you'll just have to wade through a sea of staggering, glassy-eyed clubbers to get to it.

Love it or hate it, the **Gate** (www.thegatenewcastle.co.uk; Newgate St) adds another tier to Newcastle's entertainment scene, albeit one that smells of new plastic and pizza. Behind the shimmering glass edifice there are countless chain eateries, a nightclub, bars, a casino and a 12-screen cinema.

The Crack (www.thecrackmagazine.com) is a free monthly magazine available from clubs, tourist offices and some hotels containing comprehensive club, theatre, music and cinema listings for the northeast's nightlife hotspots.

GAY & LESBIAN NEWCASTLE

Newcastle's gay scene is pretty dynamic, with its hub at the 'Pink Triangle' formed by Waterloo, Neville and Collingwood Sts, but stretching as far south as Scotswood Rd. There are plenty of gay bars in the area and a few great clubs.

Camp David (www.campdavidnewcastle.com; 8-10 Westmorland Rd) Mixed bar as trendy with straights as it is with the gay community.

Loft (10A Scotswood Rd) Loud, proud and completely cheesy, this 1st-floor club is open seven nights a week from 11pm.

Powerhouse Nightclub (www.clubph.co.uk; 9-19 Westmorland Rd) Newcastle's brashest queer nightclub, with flashing lights, video screens and lots of suggestive posing.

Cinema

Tyneside Cinema CINEMA
(www.tynesidecinema.co.uk; Pilgrim St) Opened in 1937 as Newcastle's first newsreel cinema, this period picture house, all plush red-velvet seats and swish art deco design, screens a blend of mainstream and offbeat movies as well as archive Newsreel films (11.30am; free). Free guided tours of the building (one hour) run on Tuesday, Wednesday, Friday and Saturday at 11.15am.

Star and Shadow CINEMA
(www.starandshadow.org.uk; Stepney Bank, Ouseburn Valley; membership £1, admission £4) This unlikely looking cine-club is based in an old warehouse once used to store props for Tyne-Tees TV. It is the best movie experience in town, and the place to go for your art-house, cult, black and white, and gay and lesbian film needs. Asylum seekers get in free.

Live Music

Sage Gateshead MUSIC VENUE
(☎0191-443 4666; www.thesagegateshead.org; Gateshead Quays) Few contemporary pieces of architecture will stand the test of time, but Norman Foster's magnificent chrome-and-glass horizontal bottle might just be one that does. Most come to gape and wander, some to hear live music, from folk to classical orchestras, or engage in educational or research activities. It is the home of the Northern Sinfonia and Folkworks.

Head of Steam@The Cluny MUSIC VENUE
(☎0191-230 4474; www.headofsteam.co.uk; 36 Lime St, Ouseburn Valley) This is one of the best-known spots in town to hear live music, attracting all kinds of performers, from experimental prog-rock heads to up-and-coming pop goddesses. Touring acts and local talent fill the bill every night of the week.

Newcastle Arena MUSIC VENUE
(☎0844-493 6666; www.metroradioarena.co.uk) The biggest concert venue in the northeast attracts some of the most glitter-sprinkled

names of the international pop and rock world as well as musical productions and TV talent show spin-offs. Gigs share the multipurpose auditorium with basketball, ice-hockey and other events.

Nightclubs

Digital NIGHTCLUB
(www.yourfutureisdigital.com; Times Sq) A two-floored cathedral to dance music, this megaclub was voted one of the top 20 clubs in the world by *DJ Magazine* – thanks to the best sound system you're ever likely to hear. Mondays are 'Born in the '80s' nights, Thursdays 'Stonelove' Indie nights are unmissable and Saturdays are pure 'Love'.

World Headquarters NIGHTCLUB
(www.welovewhq.com; Curtis Mayfield House, Carliol Sq) Dedicated to the genius of black music in all its guises – funk, rare groove, dance-floor jazz, northern soul, genuine R&B, lush disco, proper house and reggae – this fabulous club is strictly for true believers, and judging from the numbers, there are thousands of them.

Beyond Bar & Grill NIGHTCLUB
(www.beyondbar.co.uk; The Gate, Newgate St) Cheapo student nights, sexy urban R&B events, and Saturday mash-ups – with slabs of vinyl from the '60s to Brit pop going under the needle – fill this popular venue at the Gate.

Theatre

Northern Stage THEATRE
(☎0191-230 5151; www.northernstage.co.uk; Barras Bridge, Haymarket) The original Newcastle Playhouse has been transformed into this marvellous new performance space (three stages and a high-tech, movable acoustic wall) that attracts touring international and national shows.

Theatre Royal THEATRE
(☎08448-112121; www.theatreroyal.co.uk; 100 Grey St) The winter home of the Royal Shakespeare Company is full of Victorian splendour and has an excellent program of drama.

Sport

Newcastle United Football Club FOOTBALL CLUB
(www.nufc.co.uk) NUFC is more than just a football team: it is the collective expression of Geordie hope and pride as well as the release for decades of economic, social and sporting frustration. The club's fabulous ground, **St James' Park** (Strawberry Pl), is always packed, but you can get a **stadium tour** (☎0844-372 1892; adult/child £10/7; ⏲11am, 1.30pm daily & 4hr before kick-off on match days) of the place, including the dugout and changing rooms. Match tickets go on public sale about two weeks before a game or you can try the stadium on the day, but there's no chance for big matches, such as those against arch-rivals Sunderland.

THE GREAT NORTH RUN

First held in 1981, the world's biggest half-marathon sees over 50,000 runners grunt and sweat a gruelling 13.1 miles from just north of the city centre, along the central motorway, across the Tyne Bridge and east along the Tyne to slump on the seafront at South Shields. Held in early autumn, it's one of the largest annual occasions in the city's sporting calendar and brings out the Geordie crowds, who line the route egging on the athletes with applause and, less appropriately, plastic cups of Newkie Brown beer. Bands pump out Geordie anthems at strategic points, adding to the festival atmosphere.

Information

City Library (33 New Bridge St W; ⏲8.30am-8pm Mon-Thu, to 5.30 Fri & Sat) Free internet access at Newcastle's stomping new library building. Bring ID.

Police station (☎03456-043043; cnr Pilgrim & Market Sts)

Post office (36 Northumberland St; ⏲9am-5.30pm Mon-Sat) On the second floor of WH Smith. Has a bureau de change.

Newcastle General Hospital (☎0191-233 6161; Westgate Rd) Has an Accident and Emergency unit.

Tourist offices (www.visitnewcastlegateshead.com) Main branch (☎0191-277 8000; Central Arcade, Market St; ⏲9.30am-5.30pm Mon-Fri, from 9.30 Sat); Gateshead Library (☎0191-433 8420; Prince Consort Rd; ⏲9am-7pm Mon, Tue, Thu & Fri, to 5pm Wed, to 1pm Sat); Guildhall (☎0191-277 8000; Newcastle Quayside; ⏲10am-5pm Mon-Fri, 9am-5pm Sat, 9am-4pm Sun); Sage Gateshead (☎0191-478 4222; Gateshead Quays; ⏲10am-5pm) All offices listed here provide a booking service as well as other assorted tourist sundries.

Getting There & Away

Air

Newcastle International Airport (☎0871-882 1121; www.newcastleairport.com) Seven miles north of the city off the A696. It has direct services to many UK and European cities as well as long-haul flights to Dubai. Tour operators fly charters to the Americas and Africa.

Boat

DFDS Seaways (☎0870 522 9955; www.dfdsseaways.co.uk) Operates ferries to Newcastle from the Dutch port of Ijmuiden, near Amsterdam. No-frills flights have put paid to all the ferries to and from Norway and Sweden.

Bus

Local and regional buses leave from Haymarket or Eldon Sq bus stations. National Express buses arrive and depart from the coach station on St James Blvd. For local buses around the northeast, the excellent-value Explorer North East ticket (£8) is valid on most services.

Berwick-upon-Tweed Bus 501/505; two hours, five daily.

Edinburgh National Express; £17.50, three hours, three daily.

London National Express/Megabus; £10 to £27, seven hours, nine daily.

Manchester National Express; £19.50, five hours, five daily.

Train

Newcastle is on the main rail line between London and Edinburgh and is the starting point of the scenic Tyne Valley Line west to Carlisle.

Alnmouth (for bus connections to Alnwick) £7.70, 25 minutes, hourly.

Berwick £21.50, 45 minutes, hourly.

Carlisle £14.50, 1½ hours, hourly.

Edinburgh £32, 1½ hours, half-hourly.

London King's Cross £103.60, three hours, half-hourly.

York £23.50, one hour, every 20 minutes.

Getting Around

To/From the Airport

The airport is linked to town by the Metro (£2.90, 20 minutes, every 15 minutes).

Car

Driving around Newcastle isn't fun thanks to the web of roads, bridges and one-way systems, but there are plenty of car parks.

Public Transport

There's a large bus network, but the best means of getting around is the excellent Metro, with fares from £1.40. Several saver passes are also available. The tourist office can supply you with route plans for the bus and Metro networks.

The DaySaver (£4.80, £3.90 after 9am) gives unlimited Metro travel for one day, and the DayRover (adult/child £6.50/3.50) gives unlimited travel on all modes of transport in Tyne and Wear for one day.

Taxi

On weekend nights taxis can be as rare as covered flesh; try **Noda Taxis** (☎0191-222 1888), which has a kiosk outside the entrance to Central Station.

AROUND NEWCASTLE

If you're in town for a longer stretch there's plenty to keep you entertained even beyond the city limits. All of the following are easily reached on the city's superb public transport system.

Angel of the North

Nicknamed the Gateshead Flasher, this extraordinary 200-tonne, rust-coloured human frame with wings, more soberly known as the *Angel of the North,* has been looming over A1 (M) about 5 miles south of Newcastle for almost a decade and a half. At 20m high and with a wingspan wider than a Boeing 767, Antony Gormley's most successful work is the UK's largest sculpture and the most viewed piece of public art in the country, though Mark Wallinger's *White Horse* in Kent (see the boxed text, p140) may pinch both titles over the next decade. Buses 21 and 22 from Eldon Sq will take you there.

Tynemouth

One of the most popular Geordie days out is to this handsome seaside resort 6 miles east of the city centre. Besides being the mouth of the Tyne, this is one of the best surf spots in all England, with great all-year breaks off the immense, crescent-shaped Blue Flag beach. The town even occasionally hosts the **National Surfing Championships** (www.britsurf.co.uk).

For all your surfing needs, including lessons, call into the **Tynemouth Surf Company** (☎0191-258 2496; www.tynemouthsurf.co.uk; Grand Pde), which provides two-hour group lessons for £25 or one-hour individual lesson for the same price.

NORTHUMBERLANDIA

Surely set to become one of the northeast's greatest and most bizarre attractions, and a rival to the *Angel of the North*, **Northumberlandia** (www.northumberlandia.com) between the A1 and the town of Cramlington, around 7 miles north of Newcastle city centre, will be the world's largest human form sculpted into the landscape. Using 1.5 million tons of slag (nicknames already abound) from Shotton surface mine, artist Charles Jencks (or more like a gang of Geordies with excavators) will fashion a 400m-long female nude, whose breasts will reach a perky height of 34m. Northumberlandia will be draped slinkily next to an artificial lake, one arm apparently floating on the water. Though new and innovative, Jencks has described Northumberlandia as just another in a long line of effigies man has scraped into the landscape over the millennia.

If riding nippy surf is not your thing, the town's other main draw is the 11th-century ruins of **Tynemouth Priory** (EH; adult/child £4.20/2.10; ⏲10am-5pm Apr-Sep), built by Benedictine monks on a strategic bluff above the mouth of the Tyne, but ransacked during the Dissolution in 1539. The military took over for four centuries, only leaving in 1960, and today the skeletal remains of the priory church sit alongside old military installations, their guns aimed out to sea at an enemy that never came.

Every weekend Tynemouth's beautiful Victorian Metro station hosts **Tynemouth Market** (www.tynemouthmarket.co.uk), one of Tyneside's best secondhand bazaars.

From Newcastle city centre take the Metro to Tynemouth or bus 306 from the Haymarket.

Segedunum

The last strong post of Hadrian's Wall was the fort of **Segedunum** (www.twmuseums.org.uk; adult/child £4.35/free; ⏲10am-5pm Apr-Oct), 6 miles east of Newcastle at Wallsend. Beneath the 35m-high tower, which you can climb for some terrific views, is an absorbing site that includes a reconstructed Roman bathhouse (with steaming pools and frescoes) and a fascinating museum that gives visitors a well-rounded picture of life during Roman times.

Take the Metro to Wallsend.

COUNTY DURHAM

Best known for its strikingly beautiful capital that is one of England's star attractions, County Durham spreads itself across the lonely, rabbit-inhabited North Pennines and the gentle ochre hills of Teesdale, each dotted with picturesque, peaceful villages and traditional market towns.

Ironically, this pastoral image, so resonant of its rich medieval history, has only been reclaimed in recent years; it took the final demise of the coal industry, all-pervasive for the guts of 300 years, to render the county back to some kind of pre-industrial look. A brutal and dangerous business, coal mining was the lifeblood of entire communities and its sudden end in 1984 by the stroke of a Conservative pen has left some purposeless towns and an evocatively scarred landscape.

Durham has had a turbulent history, though it pales in comparison with its troublesome northern neighbour. To keep the Scots and local Saxon tribes quiet, William the Conqueror created the title of prince bishop in 1081 and gave them viceregal power over an area known as the Palatinate of Durham, which became almost a separate country. It raised its own armies, collected taxes and administered a separate legal system that – incredibly – wasn't fully incorporated into the greater English structure until 1971.

Durham

POP 42,940

The sheer magnificence of Durham is best appreciated if arriving by train on a clear morning: emerging from the train station, the view across the River Wear to the hilltop peninsula will confirm your reason for coming. England's most beautiful Romanesque cathedral, a masterpiece of Norman architecture and a resplendent monument to the country's ecclesiastical history, rates pretty highly in any Best of Britain list. Consider the setting: a huge castle, the aforementioned cathedral and, surrounding them both, a cobweb of cobbled streets usually full of upper-crust students attending Durham's other big pull, England's third university of choice (after Oxford and Cambridge).

Durham is unquestionably beautiful, but once you've visited the cathedral and walked the old town looking for the best views there isn't much else to do; a day-trip from Newcastle or an overnight stop on your way to explore the rest of the county is the best way to see the city of the Prince Bishops.

Sights

Durham Cathedral CATHEDRAL

(www.durham cathedral.co.uk; donation requested; ⏲7.30am-6pm, to 5.30pm Sun) Durham's most famous building – and the main reason for visiting unless someone you know is at university here – has earned superlative praise for so long that to add more would be redundant; how can you do better than the 19th-century novelist Nathaniel Hawthorne, who wrote fawningly: 'I never saw so lovely and magnificent a scene, nor (being content with this) do I care to see better'. This may be overstating things a bit but no one can deny that as the definitive structure of the Anglo-Norman Romanesque style, Durham Cathedral is one of the world's greatest places of worship. Unesco certainly thought so when they declared it a World Heritage Site in 1986.

The cathedral is enormous and has a pretty fortified look; this is due to the fact that although it may have been built to pay tribute to God and to house the holy bones of St Cuthbert, it also needed to withstand any potential attack by the pesky Scots and Northumberland tribes who weren't too thrilled by the arrival of the Normans a few years before. Times have changed, but the cathedral remains an overwhelming presence, and modern-day visitors will hardly fail to be impressed by its visual impact.

First up is the main door and the famous (and much-reproduced) **Sanctuary Knocker,** which medieval felons would strike to gain 37 days asylum within the cathedral before standing trial or leaving the country.

Once inside, things get genuinely spectacular. The superb nave is dominated by massive, powerful piers – every second one round, with an equal height and circumference of 6.6m, and carved with geometric designs. Durham was the first European cathedral to be roofed with stone-ribbed vaulting, which upheld the heavy stone roof and made it possible to build pointed transverse arches – the first in England, and a great architectural achievement. The central tower dates from 1262, but was damaged in a fire caused by lightning in 1429, and was unsatisfactorily patched up until it was entirely rebuilt in 1470. The western towers were added in 1217–26.

Built in 1175 and renovated 300 years later, the **Galilee Chapel** is one of the most beautiful parts. The northern side's **paintings** are rare surviving examples of 12th-century wall painting and are thought to feature Sts Cuthbert and Oswald. The chapel also contains the **Venerable Bede's tomb**. Bede was an 8th-century Northumbrian monk, a great historian and polymath whose work *The Ecclesiastical History of the English People* is still the prime source of information on the development of early Christian Britain. Among other things, he introduced the numbering of years from the birth of Jesus. He was first buried at Jarrow (see boxed text, p749), but in 1022 a miscreant monk stole his remains and brought them here.

The **Bishop's Throne**, built over the tomb of Bishop Thomas Hatfield, dates from the mid-14th century. Hatfield's effigy is the only one to have survived another turbulent time: the Reformation. The **high altar** is separated from **St Cuthbert's tomb** by the beautiful stone **Neville Screen**, made around 1372–80. Until the Reformation, the screen included 107 statues of saints.

The cathedral has worthwhile **guided tours** (adult/child £4/free; ⏲10.30am, 11am & 2pm Mon & Sat). Evensong is at 5.15pm from

WORTH A TRIP

BEDE'S WORLD

The fairly grim southeastern suburb of Jarrow is embedded in labour history for the 1936 Jarrow Crusade, when 200 men walked from here to London to protest against the appalling conditions brought about by unemployment.

But it is also famous as the home of the Venerable Bede, author of the *Ecclesiastical History of the English People*. **Bede's World** (www.bedesworld.co.uk; Church Bank, Jarrow; admission £5.50; ⏲10am-5pm Mon-Sat, noon-5pm Sun) comprises St Paul's Church, which dates back to the 7th century; a museum; and many reconstructed medieval buildings. It's accessible via the Metro.

Durham

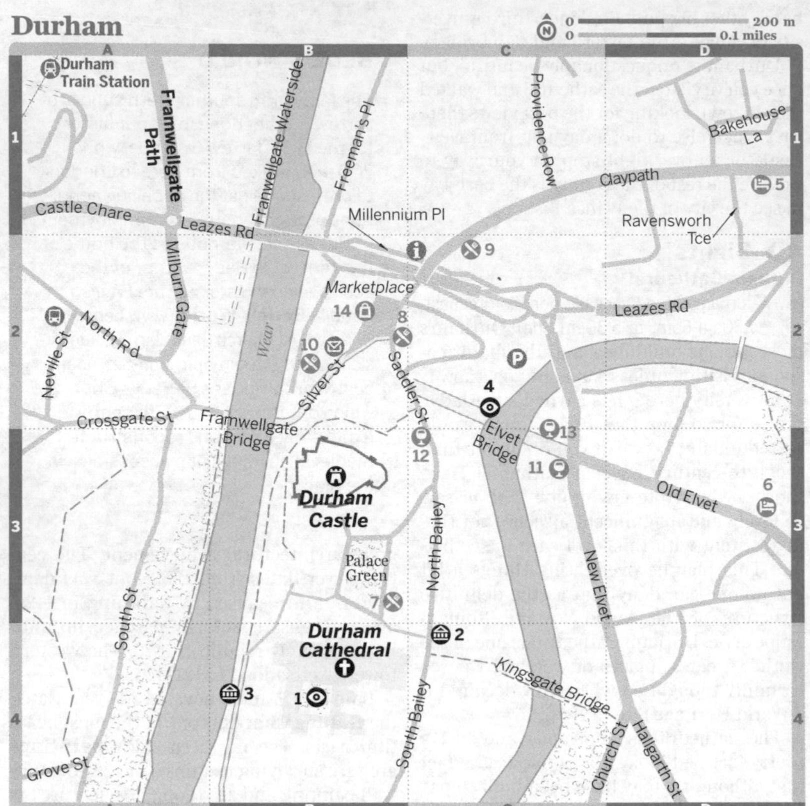

Monday to Saturday and at 3.30pm on Sunday.

The **tower** (adult/child £5/2.50; 10am-4pm Mon-Sat Apr-Sep, to 3pm Oct-Mar) provides show-stopping vistas, but you've got to climb 325 steps (and part with a hefty £5) to enjoy them.

Other attractions include the mostly 19th-century **Cloisters** where you'll find the **Monk's Domitory** (adult/child £1/30p; 10am-4pm Mon-Sat, 12.30-4pm Sun Apr-Sep), now a library of 30,000 books and displaying Anglo-Saxon carved stones. There are also **audiovisual displays** (adult/child £1/30p; 10am-3pm Mon-Sat) on the building of the cathedral and the life of St Cuthbert.

The **Treasures** (adult/child £2.50/70p; 10am-4.30pm Mon-Sat, 2-4.30pm Sun) refer to the relics of St Cuthbert, but besides his cross and coffin, there's very little here related to the saint, the collection consisting mostly of religious paraphernalia from later centuries. This exhibition may be moving to another site in coming years.

Durham Castle CASTLE
(www.dur.ac.uk;adult/concession£5/3.50; tours 2pm, 3pm, 4pm term time, 10am, 11am & noon during university vacations) Built as a standard motte-and-bailey fort in 1072, Durham Castle was the prince bishops' home until 1837, when it became the first college of the new university. It remains a university hall, and you can stay here.

The castle has been much altered over the centuries, as each successive prince bishop sought to put his particular imprint on the place, but heavy restoration and reconstruction were necessary anyway as the castle is built of soft stone on soft ground. Highlights of the 45-minute tour include the groaning 17th-century **Black Staircase**, the

Durham

Top Sights

Durham Castle ... B3
Durham Cathedral ... B4

Sights

1 Cloisters & Treasures ... B4
2 Durham Heritage Centre ... C4
3 Museum of Archaeology ... B4

Activities, Courses & Tours

Browns Boathouse ... (see 4)
4 Prince Bishop River Cruiser ... C2

Sleeping

5 Cathedral View ... D1
6 Fallen Angel ... D3

Eating

7 Almshouse ... B3
8 Greggs ... B2
9 Oldfields ... C2
10 Rumbletums ... B2

Drinking

11 Half Moon Inn ... C3
12 Shakespeare ... C3
13 Swan & Three Cygnets ... C3

Shopping

14 Durham Indoor Market ... B2

16th-century **chapel** and the beautifully preserved **Norman chapel** (1080).

Durham Heritage Centre MUSEUM
(www.durhamheritagecentre.org.uk; North Bailey; admission £2; 2pm-4.30pm Easter-Oct) Near the cathedral, in what was the St Mary-le-Bow Church, this museum has a pretty crowded collection of displays on Durham's history from the Middle Ages to mining. It's all suitably grim, especially the reconstructed Victorian prison cell.

Museum of Archaeology MUSEUM
(Old Fulling Mill, Prebend's Walk; admission £1; 11am-4pm Apr-Oct) Occupying a converted riverside mill, this small university museum has collections ranging from prehistory to medieval times via the Romans and Anglo-Saxons.

Oriental Museum MUSEUM
(Elvet Hill; admission £1.50; 10am-5pm Mon-Fri, noon-5pm Sat & Sun) Another university museum, located on campus 3 miles south of the city centre, with surprisingly good collections ranging from fine Egyptian artefacts to a monster of a Chinese bed. Take bus 5 or 5a.

Crook Hall GARDENS
(www.crookhallgardens.co.uk; Frankland Lane, Sidegate; adult/child £6/5; 11am-5pm Sun-Thu Apr-Sep) This medieval hall with 1.6 hectares of charming small gardens is about 200m north of the city centre. From the tourist office, cross the main road bridge across the Wear then follow the river north.

Durham Light Infantry Museum MUSEUM
(Aykley Heads; admission £4.50; 10am-5pm Apr-Oct) The history of Durham's County Regiment and its part in various wars from 1758 to 1968 is brought to life at this museum 500m northwest of city centre; there's a small art gallery with changing exhibitions.

Activities

There are superb views back to the cathedral and castle from the leafy riverbanks; walk around the bend between Elvet and Framwellgate Bridges, or hire a boat at Elvet Bridge.

Prince Bishop River Cruiser RIVER TRIPS
(0191-386 9525; www.princebishoprc.co.uk; Elvet Bridge; adult/child £6/3; cruises 2pm & 3pm Jun-Sep) One-hour cruises on the Wear.

Browns Boathouse BOAT HIRE
(per hr per person £5) Rowing boats can be hired from below Elvet Bridge.

Guided Walks WALKS
(adult/child £3.50/free; 2pm Sat & Sun May-Sep) Walks lasting 1½ hours leave from Millennium Pl. Contact the tourist office for details.

Ghost Walks THEMED WALKS
(adult/child £4/1; 7.30pm Mon Jul-Sep) Ghost walks also drift around town. Contact the tourist office for details.

Sleeping

There's only one view that counts – a cathedral view. But when you consider that it's visible from pretty much everywhere, it's quality, not quantity, that counts. The tourist office makes local bookings free of charge, which is a good thing considering that Durham is always busy with visitors; graduation week in late June results in accommodation gridlock.

ENGLAND'S WONDER WORKER

St Cuthbert (c 634–87) is one of Britain's most venerated saints as much for an eventful afterlife as for a pious life. A kick-arse monk who fought under arms, nurtured the poor and succeeded in the thankless task of bringing the independent monastic settlements of the northeast to Roman heel following the Synod of Whitby (664), which laid down the law on when exactly Easter should be observed, Cuthbert spent the last years of his life in contemplative solitude on Inner Farne, dying on 20 March 687. And then things got really interesting.

According to legend, his burial casket was opened a few years after his death and his body was found to be perfectly preserved, or incorrupt, which quickly made him the most popular British saint in the country. When the Vikings invaded Lindisfarne in 875, a group of monks took his body on a seven-year journey across the northeast, but another Danish invasion in 995 led to another prolonged period of wandering. He eventually found a permanent home in a stone church that preceded the current cathedral. In 1104 his body and relics were transferred to a shrine inside the new cathedral, which itself was desecrated during the Reformation, although his relics surprisingly survived.

TOP CHOICE **Fallen Angel** BOUTIQUE HOTEL £££
(☎0191-384 1037; www.fallenangelhotel.com; 34 Old Elvet; d from £150) Possibly the northeast's most bizarre digs, the 10 rooms at this fun place leave few indifferent. Each room has a theme with the 'Le Jardin' featuring a shed and garden furniture, the 'Sci-fi' room containing a *Doctor Who* Tardis and the 'Premiere' boasting a huge projection screen and popcorn machine, while the 'Edwardian Express' recreates a night in a yesteryear sleeper compartment. The most 'normal' room is the Library though even here military uniforms hang from the bookcases as if their owners could return any moment. The restaurant is superb and some rooms have cathedral views. Pricey, but worth every penny.

Cathedral View B&B ££
(☎0191-386 9566; www.cathedralview.com; 212 Gilesgate; s/d from £60/80) This anonymous Georgian house has no sign, but inside it does exactly what it says on the tin. Six large rooms decorated with lots of cushions and coordinated bed linen and window dressings make up the numbers, but it's the two at the back that are worth the fuss: the views of the cathedral are fantastic. Breakfast is cooked to order and served out on the vista-rich terrace or in the dining room lined with Beryl Cook prints.

Farnley Tower B&B ££
(☎0191-375 0011; www.farnley-tower.co.uk; The Ave; s/d from £65/85; P) A beautiful Victorian stone building that looks more like a small manor house than a family-run B&B, this place has 13 large rooms, none better than the superior class, which are not just spacious but have excellent views of the cathedral and castle. The service is impeccable. It's situated around 1km southwest of the train station.

Victorian Town House B&B ££
(☎05601-459168; www.durhambedandbreakfast.co.uk; 2 Victoria Tce; s/d £60/80; wi-fi) This three-room B&B occupying an 1850s town house near the train station comfortably combines period fireplaces and fancy ceiling roses with flatscreen TVs and DVD libraries. Two rooms have cathedral views and there's a peaceful terraced garden out back.

Eating

Cheap eats aren't a problem in Durham thanks to the students, but quality is a little thin on the ground. Some pubs do good bar food and if you're really desperate, there's always bakers **Greggs** (14 Saddler St) to fall back on for some good old northern stodge.

Oldfields BRITISH ££
(18 Claypath; mains £12-19) With its strictly seasonal menus that use only local or organic ingredients sourced within a 60-mile radius of Durham, this award-winning restaurant is one of the county's finest, though it's not quite as good as its Newcastle sister. With dishes such as smoked haddock pan haggerty and wild boar pie on the menu, all served in the old boardroom of the former

HQ of the Durham Gas Company (1881), it's still the best meal in town.

Almshouse CAFE ££
(Palace Green; dishes £5-9; ⌚9am-5pm, to 8pm Jul & Aug) Fancy imaginative and satisfying snacks served in a genuine 17th-century house right on Palace Green? It's a shame about the interior, which has been restored to look like any old museum canteen. All the artwork on the walls is for sale.

Rumbletums CAFE £
(32 Silver St; snacks £2.50-5; ⌚9.30am-5.30pm Mon-Sat, 11am-4.30 Sun) Down an inconspicuous flight of steps two doors along from the post office, this junk shop/art gallery/tearoom hides in a brick-and-stone cellar where a range of teas plus sandwiches, jacket potatoes and cakes are served to in-the-know punters. New owners have promised to leave things just the way they are.

Drinking

Durham may be a big student town, but most scholars seem to take the whole study thing really seriously, and the nightlife here isn't as boisterous as you might expect from a university town. There is, however, a fistful of lovely old bars.

Half Moon Inn PUB
(New Elvet) Sports fans love this old-style bar for its devotion to the mixed pleasures of Sky Sports; we like it for its wonderful collection of whiskies and ales. There's a summer beer garden if you want to avoid the whoops and hollers of the armchair jocks.

Shakespeare PUB
(63 Saddler St) As authentic a traditional bar as you're likely to find in these parts, this is the perfect locals' boozer, complete with dartboard, cosy snugs and a small corner TV to show the racing. Needless to say, the selection of beers and spirits is terrific. Not surprisingly, students love it too.

Swan & Three Cygnets PUB
(Elvet Bridge) This high-ceilinged riverside pub with courtyard tables overlooks the river. It also serves some pretty good food (mains around £8) – usually fancy versions of standard bar fare such as bangers and mash.

Shopping

Durham Indoor Market MARKET
(Market Pl; ⌚9am-4.30pm Mon-Sat) This 150-year-old covered market building is less about what you might buy and more about the Victorian cast-iron architecture.

Information

Post office (Silver St)

Public library (Millennium Pl; ⌚9.30am-7pm Mon-Fri, 9am-5pm Sat, 10.30am-4pm Sun) Bring ID to surf the web.

Tourist office (☎0191-384 3720; www.thisisdurham.com; 2 Millennium Pl; ⌚9.30am-5.30pm Mon-Sat, 10am-4pm Sun) In the Gala complex, which includes a theatre and cinema.

Getting There & Away

Bus

Darlington Buses 5 and 7; one hour, four hourly.

Leeds National Express; £16.10, 2½ hours, four daily.

London National Express; £29.80, 6½ hours, four daily.

Newcastle Buses 21, 44, X41, X2; one hour to 1¾ hours, several per hour.

Train

The East Coast mainline arches over Durham meaning speedy connections to many destinations across the country:

Edinburgh £50.30, two hours, hourly.

London £103.60, three hours, hourly.

Newcastle £5.20, 15 minutes, five hourly.

York £21.90, one hour, four hourly.

Getting Around

Cycle Force (29 Claypath) Charges £10/16 per half-/full day for mountain-bike hire.

Pratt's (☎0191-386 0700) A trustworthy taxi company.

Around Durham

BEAMISH OPEN-AIR MUSEUM

County Durham's greatest attraction is **Beamish** (www.beamish.org.uk; adult/child £16/10; ⌚10am-5pm Apr-Oct), a living, breathing, working museum that offers a fabulous, warts-and-all portrait of industrial life in the northeast during the 19th and 20th centuries. Instructive and lots of fun to boot, this huge museum spread over 121 hectares will appeal to all ages.

You can go underground, explore mine heads, a working farm, a school, a dentist and a pub, and marvel at how every cramped pit cottage seemed to find room for a piano. Don't miss a ride behind an 1815

WORTH A TRIP

LOCOMOTION

If steam gets you and your kids hot under the collar, then a half-day trip to the National Railway Museum at Shildon, now known as **Locomotion** (www.nrm.org.uk; Shildon; admission free; ⌚10am-5pm Apr-Oct) is a must. Shildon is best known as the starting point for Stephenson's *No 1 Locomotion* in 1825, finishing up in Stockton-on-Tees. Less museum and more hands-on experience, this regional extension of the National Railway Museum in York (see p599) has all manner of railway paraphernalia spread out over a half-mile area that all leads to a huge hanger containing 70-odd locomotives from all eras. Shildon is on the Darlington to Bishop Auckland rail line; alternatively take buses 1 and 1B from Darlington.

Steam Elephant locomotive or a replica of Stephenson's *Locomotion No 1.*

Allow at least three hours to do the place justice. Many elements (such as the railway) aren't open in the winter (when the admission price is lower); check the web for details.

Beamish is about 8 miles northwest of Durham. Buses 28 from Newcastle (one hour, half hourly) and 720 from Durham (30 minutes, hourly) operate to the museum.

BISHOP AUCKLAND

The name's a giveaway, but this friendly, midsized market town 11 miles southwest of Durham has been the country residence of the bishops of Durham since the 12th century and their official home for over 100 years. The castle is just next to the large, attractive market square; leading off it are small-town streets lined with high-street shops and a sense that anything exciting is happening elsewhere.

The imposing gates of **Auckland Castle** (www.auckland-castle.co.uk; adult/child £4/free; ⌚2-5pm Sun-Mon Easter-Jul & Sep, plus Wed Aug), just off Market Pl behind the town hall, lead to the official home of the bishop of Durham. It's palatial – each successive bishop extended the building. Underneath the spiky Restoration Gothic exterior, the buildings are mainly medieval. The outstanding attraction of the castle is the striking 17th-century chapel, which thrusts up into the sky. It has a remarkable partially 12th-century interior, converted from the former great hall. Admission is by guided tour only.

Around the castle is a hilly and wooded 324-hectare **deer park** (admission free; ⌚7am-sunset) with an 18th-century deer shelter.

Ever noticed that Stan Laurel had a bit of a north country accent? He spent much of his childhood in Bishop Auckland where ma and pa ran the Theatre Royal. The tourist office has free maps of the **Stan Laurel walk** for fans.

The **tourist office** (☎01388-604922; Market Pl; ⌚10am-5pm Mon-Fri, 9am-4pm Sat) is in the town hall on the main square.

Bus 1/1B (three hourly) run to Darlington, Durham is served hourly by bus X24 and to and from Newcastle take bus 21 (half hourly). Change at Darlington for regular trains to Bishop Auckland.

BINCHESTER ROMAN FORT

One and a half miles north of Bishop Auckland are the ruins of **Binchester Roman Fort** (www.durham.gov.uk/binchester; admission £2.50; ⌚11am-5pm Easter-Jun & Sep, 10am-5pm Jul & Aug), or Vinovia as it was originally called. The fort, first built in wood around AD 80 and refashioned in stone early in the 2nd century, was the largest in County Durham, covering 4 hectares. Excavations show the remains of Dere St, the main high road from York to Hadrian's Wall, and the best-preserved example of a heating system in the country – part of the commandant's private bath suite. Findings from the site are displayed at the Bowes Museum in Barnard Castle.

ESCOMB CHURCH

The stones of the abandoned Binchester Fort were often reused, and Roman inscriptions can be spotted in the walls of the hauntingly beautiful **Escomb Church** (www.escombsaxonchurch.com; Saxon Green, Escomb; admission free; ⌚9am-8pm Apr-Sep). The church dates from the 7th century – it's one of only three complete surviving Saxon churches in Britain. The whitewashed cell, striking and moving in its simplicity is incongruously encircled by 20th-century housing. If no one's about, the keys sometimes hang on a hook outside a nearby house. Escomb is 3 miles west of Bishop Auckland (bus 86, hourly).

Darlington

POP 97,838

The old Quaker market town of Darlington may be best known these days as a shopping mecca, but its main claim to fame came in 1825, when it found itself at one end of the world's first passenger railway, the Stockton & Darlington. The first train was pulled by George Stephenson's aptly named *Locomotion No 1,* which rumbled along the new cast-iron rail link to docks on the Tees at the breakneck speed of 10mph to 13mph, carrying 350 people – mostly in coal trucks.

The event – and the subsequent effect on transport history – is the subject of the town's top attraction, the excellent **Head of Steam** (www.head-of-steam.co.uk; North Rd; adult/child £4.95/3; ⏲10am-4pm Tue-Sun Apr-Sep), aka Darlington Railway Museum, which is actually situated on the original 1825 route, in 19th-century Stockton & Darlington railway buildings attached to North Rd Station, one of the oldest in the world. Pride of place goes to the surprisingly small and fragile-looking *Locomotion,* but railway buffs will also enjoy a close look at other engines, such as the *Derwent,* the earliest surviving Darlington-built locomotive. Railway memorabilia is complemented by an impressive range of audiovisuals that tell the story of the railway, Darlington's locomotive building industry (and its demise in the 1960s) and the impacts of these events on the town. There's also a 19th-century ticket office that seems to have been dunked in formaldehyde and an original Victorian Gents toilets. The museum is about a mile north of the centre.

There aren't many other reasons to linger, but you should definitely pop your head into Our Lady of the North, better known as **St Cuthbert's Church** (www.stcuthbertsdarlington.net; Market Pl; ⏲11am-1pm Mon-Sat Easter-Sep plus during services), founded in 1183 and one of the finest examples of the Early English Perpendicular style, topped with a 14th-century tower. Guided tours of the church can be arranged through the tourist office.

Eating

The town has some decent restaurants around the centre; **Crombies** (36-44 Tubwell Row; mains £4.70-6) must be doing something right as it's been serving simple filling fare for over 70 years. **Oven** (30 Duke St; mains £8-17; ⏲Mon-Sat, noon-8pm Sun) is a classy French spot that was voted the northeast's best Sunday lunch by *Observer* readers.

Information

Tourist office (☎01325-388666; www.visitdarlington.com; Dolphin Centre, Horsemarket; ⏲9am-5pm Mon-Fri, to 3pm Sat)

Getting There & Away

Most buses arrive and depart opposite the Town Hall on Feethams, just off Market Pl. There are no direct bus services to Newcastle.

Darlington Bus 7/7A; 50 minutes, hourly.

Richmond (North Yorkshire) X26 and X27; 40 minutes, twice hourly.

Darlington is on the east coast main line with connections to **York** (£16.10, 30 minutes, three hourly), **Newcastle** (£8.90, 30 minutes, three hourly) and **London** (£99.40, two hours 40 minutes, hourly).

Barnard Castle

POP 6720

Barnard Castle, or just plain Barney, is anything but: this thoroughly charming market town is a traditionalist's dream, full of antiquarian shops and atmospheric old pubs that serve as a wonderful setting for the town's twin-starred attractions, a daunting ruined castle at its edge and an extraordinary French chateau on its outskirts. If you can drag yourself away, it is also a terrific base for exploring Teesdale and the North Pennines.

Sights

Barnard Castle CASTLE RUINS
(EH; adult/child £4.20/2.10; ⏲10am-6pm Easter-Sep) Partly dismantled during the 16th century, one of northern England's largest castles built on a cliff above the Tees still manages to cover more than two very impressive hectares. Founded by Guy de Bailleul and rebuilt around 1150, its occupants spent their time suppressing the locals and fighting off the Scots – on their days off they sat around enjoying the wonderful river views.

Bowes Museum MUSEUM
(www.thebowesmuseum.org.uk; adult/child £8/free; ⏲10am-5pm) About half a mile east of town stands a Louvre-inspired French chateau containing an extraordinary and wholly unexpected museum. Funded by 19th-century industrialist John Bowes, but largely the brainchild of his Parisienne actress wife Josephine, the museum was

WORTH A TRIP

MIDDLESBROUGH INSTITUTE OF MODERN ART (MIMA)

Middlesbrough, 15 miles east of Darlington, and Teeside's largest town, is something of a post-industrial mess, an unattractive urban centre that does little to entice visitors. However the town's one redeeming attraction is the boldly modern **Middlesbrough Institute of Modern Art** (www.visitmima.com; Centre Sq, Middlesbrough; admission free; ⌚10am-5pm Tue, Wed, Fri & Sat, 10am-7pm Thu, noon-4pm Sun), which has gathered the city's municipal art collections under one impressive roof. The 1500 or so pieces include work by some of Britain's most important 20th-century artists, including Duncan Grant, Vanessa Bell (sister of Virginia Woolf), Henri Gaudier-Brzeska and Frank Auerbach. There's also a good collection of ceramics and jewellery.

Middlesbrough is served by hourly buses from Darlington (£4.90, 30 minutes). The bus station is about 500m from MIMA.

built by French architect Jules Pellechet to display a collection the Bowes had travelled the world to assemble. Opened in 1892, this spectacular museum has lavish furniture and paintings by Canaletto, El Greco and Goya as well as 15,000 other objets d'art including 55 paintings by Josephine herself. A new section examines textiles through the ages, with some incredible dresses from the 17th century to the 1970s, while the precious metals exhibition displays clocks, watches and tableware in gold and silver. The museum's star attraction, however, is the marvellous mechanical , which performs every day at 2pm. If you miss it or arrive too early, there's now a film showing it in action.

Sleeping & Eating

Marwood House B&B ££
(☎01833-637493; www.marwoodhouse.co.uk; 98 Galgate; s/d from £29/58) A handsome Victorian property with tastefully appointed rooms (the owner's tapestries feature in the decor and her homemade biscuits sit on a tray), Marwood House's standout feature is the small fitness room in the basement, complete with a sauna that fits up to four people.

Jersey Farm Country Hotel HOTEL ££
(☎01833-638223; www.jerseyfarm.co.uk; Darlington Rd; s/d from £72/99; P 📶) Another genteel farmhouse conversion, right? Wrong. From the moment you step into the funky reception you know you're not in for the usual frills-and-flowers B&B experience. Although the owners haven't gone the whole design-boutique hog, rooms sport cool retro colour schemes, ultra sleek bathrooms in several shades of black and gadgets galore. The restaurant is a clean-cut affair. It's a mile east of the town just off the A67.

Old Well Inn HOTEL ££
(☎01833-690130; www.theoldwellinn.co.uk; 21 The Bank; r from £69; 📶) You won't find larger bedrooms in town than at this old coaching inn, built over a huge well (not visible). Of the 10 rooms, No 9 is the most impressive with its own private entrance, flagstone floors and a bath. The pub has a reputation for excellent, filling pub grub and real ales from Darlington and Yorkshire. The amateur Castle Players, who perform a different Shakespeare play at the castle every summer, were formed here during an early '80s power cut.

Information

Tourist office (☎01833- 696356; www.teesdalediscovery.com; Woodleigh, Flatts Rd; ⌚9.30am-5pm Mon-Sat, 10am-4pm Sun Easter-Oct) Has information on all the sights, a small cafe and internet access for £1.50 per half hour.

Getting There & Away

Darlington Buses 75 and 76; 40 minutes, twice hourly.

Middleton-in-Teesdale Buses 95 and 96; hourly.

Around Barnard Castle

EGGLESTONE ABBEY

The ransacked, spectral ruins of **Egglestone Abbey** (EH; ⌚dawn-dusk), dating from the 1190s, overlook a lovely bend of the Tees. You can envisage the abbey's one-time grandeur despite the gaunt remains. They're a pleasant 1.5-mile-long walk southeast of Barnard Castle.

RABY CASTLE

About 7 miles northeast of Barnard Castle is the sprawling, romantic **Raby Castle** (www.rabycastle.com; adult/child £9.50/4; ⌚1-

5pm Sun-Wed May, Jun & Sep, Sun-Fri Jul & Aug), a stronghold of the Catholic Neville family until it engaged in some ill-judged plotting (the 'Rising of the North') against the oh-so Protestant Queen Elizabeth in 1569. Most of the interior dates from the 18th and 19th centuries, but the exterior remains true to the original design, built around a courtyard and surrounded by a moat. There are beautiful formal gardens and a deer park. Bus 8 zips between Barnard Castle and Raby (15 minutes, eight daily).

NORTH PENNINES

The North Pennines stretch from western Durham to just short of Hadrian's Wall in the north. In the south is Teesdale, the gently undulating valley of the River Tees; to the north is the much wilder Weardale, carved through by the River Wear. Both dales are marked by ancient quarries and mines – industries that date back to Roman times. The wilds of the North Pennines are also home to the picturesque Derwent and Allen Valleys, north of Weardale.

For online information, check out www.northpennines.org.uk and www.exploreteesdale.co.uk.

Teesdale

A patchwork quilt of sheep-dotted green, sewn with dry-stone thread, Teesdale, stretching from the confluence of the Rivers Greta and Tees to Caldron Snout waterfall at the eastern end of Cow Green Reservoir (the source of the Tees), is a relaxing introduction to the North Pennines. The landscapes get wilder as you travel northward into the Pennines; the Pennine Way snakes along the dale.

MIDDLETON-IN-TEESDALE

This tranquil, pretty village of white and stone houses among soft green hills was from 1753 a 'company town', the entire kit and caboodle being the property of the London Lead Company, a Quaker concern. The upshot was that the lead miners worked the same hours in the same appalling conditions as everyone else, but couldn't benefit from a Sunday pint to let off steam.

For information on local walks, go to the volunteer-run **tourist office** (☎01833-641001; 10 Market Sq; ⏲10am-1pm).

MIDDLETON TO LANGDON BECK

As you travel up the valley past Middleton towards Langdon Beck, you'll find the Durham Wildlife Trust's **Bowlees Visitor Centre** (☎01833-622292; ⏲10.30am-5pm Apr-Sep) 3 miles on, with plenty of walking and wildlife leaflets, a small natural-history display and a basic cafe. A number of easy-going trails spread out from here, including a five-minute stroll to **Low Force**, a series of tumbling rapids and steps urging the otherwise slow-moving waters of the Tees along a scenic stretch of river. Around 1.5 miles further on (along the B2677) is the much more compelling **High Force** (adult/child £1.50/1, car park £2), England's largest waterfall – 21m of almighty roar that shatters the general tranquillity of the surroundings. If you follow the Pennine Way along the south bank of the Tees you'll hear High Force a long time before it comes into sight (and there's no admission fee).

The B6277 leaves the River Tees at High Force and continues up to the hamlet of **Langdon Beck**, where the scenery quickly turns from green rounded hills to the lonely landscape of the North Pennines. You can either continue on the B6277 over the Pennines to Alston and Cumbria or turn right and take an amazingly scenic minor road over the moors to St John's Chapel in Weardale.

Sleeping & Eating

Langdon Beck YHA YOUTH HOSTEL £
(☎0845 371 9027; www.yha.org.uk; Forest-in-Teesdale; dm £10) Walkers on the Pennine Way are avid fans of this remote hostel between High Force and Langdon Beck. With its own wind turbine, recycling bins and lots of other green facilities, you'll not find a more ecofriendly hostel in the UK. The food's good too.

Brunswick House B&B ££
(☎01833-640393; www.brunswickhouse.net; 55 Market Pl, Middleton in-Teesdale; s/d £45/70) This pretty Georgian house has smart en suite rooms, real coal fires heating a cosy lounge and a scrumptious optional dinner – just the ticket after a day in the Pennine's bracing, appetite-inducing air.

High Force Hotel HOTEL ££
(☎01833-622222; www.highforcehotel.com; Forest-in-Teesdale; s/d £40/80) This former brewery by the High Force waterfall has six decent enough bedrooms and the bar serves food.

Getting There & Away

Bus 73 connects Middleton and Langdon Beck, via Bowlees and High Force three times a day. Bus 95 serves Middleton from Barnard Castle at least three times daily.

Weardale

A one-time hunting ground of the prince bishops, Weardale's 19th-century legacy as a lead-mining centre has left rust- and olive-coloured patchwork moors pitted with mining scars. Mining relics notwithstanding, there are some splendid walks in and around the surrounding valley, which is sheltered by the Pennines.

STANHOPE & IRESHOPEBURN

Peaceful Stanhope is a honey-coloured town with a cobbled marketplace – a good base for windswept walks across the moors. Its interesting church is Norman at the base, but mostly dates from the 12th century. There's a great farmers market on the last Saturday of every month.

In Ireshopeburn, 8 miles west of Stanhope, the **Weardale Museum** (01388-537433; www.weardalemuseum.co.uk; adult/child £2/50p; 2-5pm Wed-Sun May-Jul & Sep, daily Aug) allows a glimpse into local history, including a spotless lead-mining family kitchen and information on preacher John Wesley. It's next to **High House Chapel**, the oldest Methodist chapel (1760) in the country to have held weekly services since it was established and one of Wesley's old stomping grounds.

Sleeping & Eating

Fossil Tree B&B ££

(01388-527851; www.weardale-accommodation.co.uk; 2 Market Pl, Stanhope; s/d £35/58) This new B&B near the tourist office has three modern, fresh, light rooms but you may have to queue for your morning shower as facilities are shared. Two-wheelers stay free of charge (the town is the last stop on the C2C route before cyclists push on to Sunderland).

Queen's Head PUB £

(89 Front St, Stanhope; mains £5-7) This handsome pub in the middle of Stanhope is a good spot for hearty pub grub.

KILLHOPE

At the top of the valley, about 13 miles from Stanhope, is a good example of just how bleak miners' lives really were. At the **Killhope Lead Mining Museum** (01388-537505; www.killhope.org.uk; adult/child £4.50/1.50, with mine trip £12/6.50; 10.30am-5pm Apr-Oct), the blackened machinery of the old works is dominated by an imposing 10m-high water wheel that drove a crushing mechanism (most northeasterners still refer to the museum as the 'Killhope Wheel').

In one of those unfortunate linguistic ironies, 'hope' actually means 'side valley', but once you get a look inside the place you'll understand the miners' black humour about the name. An absorbing exhibition demonstrates the backbreaking work involved in separating the gravel from the lead ore and you can also take a peek into a mock-up of the living quarters where miners slept four to a bed. Miners were on piece work (unlike pampered coal miners) hence the range of ingenious contraptions they designed to eke out every speck of ore – nothing went to waste. Most were also farmers, tending flocks in the surrounding hills on their days off. The mine closed in 1910 but you can still visit its atmospheric underground network as it was in 1878, on a fascinating hour-long guided tour, the highlight of any visit; wear warm clothes. There's also a brand-new visitors centre housing a collection of miners' 'spar boxes' blinged up with local minerals.

Information

Tourist office (01388-527650; www.durhamdalescentre.co.uk; Market Pl; 10am-5pm Apr-Oct) Has lots of information on walks in the area, and there's a large tearoom.

Getting There & Away

Bus 101 makes the regular trip up the valley from Bishop Auckland to Stanhope (11 daily). If you ring ahead, it will go on to Killhope mid-morning and pick you up in the afternoon. Call **Wearhead Motor Services** (01388-528235) to arrange the service.

Derwent Valley

The cute little villages of Blanchland and Edmundbyers lie south of the drinkably-pure expanse of **Derwent Reservoir**, surrounded by wind-tussled moorland and forests. The 3.5-mile-long reservoir has been here since 1967, and the county border separating Durham and Northumberland runs right through it. The valley's a good spot for walking and cycling, as well as sailing, which can be arranged through the

LOCAL KNOWLEDGE

GEOFF LEE: EXPERT GUIDE AT KILLHOPE LEAD MINING MUSEUM

I've lived and worked in this beautiful area for most of my life but I still see new and wonderful things. That's why I always carry a camera with me – I never know when I'll spot something amazing to snap! Here are my reasons why you should head into the wild and remote North Pennines, with or without your camera:

Must-see

Killhope Lead Mining Museum is an opportunity to see what life was like here over a century ago. Try your hand at a washer boy's work and take home a small piece of galena or rare green Weardale fluorspar. Our red squirrels are also a big draw.

Top tip

The Weardale Museum at Ireshopeburn adds more to the social history of the area and is particularly interesting for anyone researching family history. As the mines closed in Weardale in the late 19th century many emigrated to Australasia and America, so visitors hail from all over the world.

Off the Beaten Track

The North Pennines Area of Outstanding Natural Beauty (AONB) is a stunning landscape of open heather moors, dramatic dales, and close knit communities. Get out there to discover glorious waterfalls, rare plant life, stone-built villages and reminders of our mining and industrial past, as well as many species of bird and insect inhabiting the heather-carpeted moors.

Derwent Reservoir Sailing Club (☎01434-675033; www.drsc.co.uk).

Nestling among trees, and surrounded by wild mauve and mustard moors, **Blanchland** is an unexpected surprise. It's a charming, golden-stoned grouping of small cottages arranged around an L-shaped square, framed by a medieval gateway. The village was named after the white cassocks of local monks – there was a Premonstratensian abbey here from the 12th century. Around 1721 the prince bishop of the time, Lord Crewe, seeing the village and abbey falling into disrepair, bequeathed the buildings to trustees on the condition that they be protected and looked after.

Another inviting, quiet village, **Edmundbyers** is 4 miles east of Blanchland on the B6306 along the southern edge of Derwent Reservoir.

Edmundbyers is 12 miles north of Stanhope and 10 miles south of Hexham on the B6306. Bus 773 runs from Consett to Townfield via Blanchland and Edmundbyers four times a day, Monday to Saturday.

Sleeping & Eating

Edmundbyers YHA YOUTH HOSTEL £
(☎0845-371 9633; www.yha.org.uk; Low House, Edmundbyers; dm £14) This beautiful hostel is in a converted 17th-century former inn. The hostel is a welcome halt for walkers in the area and cyclists on the C2C route.

Lord Crewe Arms Hotel HOTEL ££
(☎01434-675251; www.lordcrewehotel.co.uk; Blanchland; s/d from £60/100) This glorious hotel was built as the abbot's lodge. It's a mainly 17th century building, with a 12th-century crypt that makes a cosy bar. If you're looking for a bit of atmosphere – open fires, hidden corners, tall windows and superb food (lunch £6 to £12) – you won't find better, but make sure to ask for a garden room, which has its own sitting room.

Allen Valley

The Allen Valley is in the heart of the North Pennines, with individual, remote villages huddled high up, surrounded by bumpy hills and heather- and gorse-covered moors. It's fantastic walking country, speckled with the legacy of the lead-mining industry.

Tiny **Allendale** is a hamlet around a big open square. The quiet rural community hots up on New Year's Eve when the distinctly pagan and magical 'Tar Barrels' ceremony is performed. It's 7 miles from Hexham on the B6295.

FLAMING ALLENDALE

Thought to be Viking or pagan in origin, the **Baal Fire** (aka Tar Barrels) on New Year's Eve – a procession of flaming whisky barrels through Allendale – has certainly been taking place for centuries. The 45 barrels are filled with tar and carried on the heads of a team of 'guisers' with blackened or painted faces – this hot and hereditary honour gets passed from generation to generation. The mesmerising procession, accompanied by pounding music, leads to a pile of branches, where the guisers chuck the scorching barrels to fire up an enormous pyre at midnight, doing their best not to set themselves alight.

Four miles further south towards the Wear Valley is **Allenheads**, England's highest village nestled at the head of Allen Valley. No more than a few houses and a marvellously eccentric hotel, it's also a major stop on the C2C cycling route. There's a tiny **heritage centre** (admission £1; 9am-5pm Apr-Oct) with some displays on the history of the village and surroundings, occasional access to a blacksmith's cottage, and a cafe.

An attraction in its own right, **Allenheads Inn** (01434-685200; www.theallenheadsinn.co.uk; Allenheads; s/d £39/60), an 18th-century low-beamed pub, has a quite extraordinary and bizarre collection of assorted bric-a-brac and ephemera, from ancient skis to Queen Mum plates. However, the one-star rooms above are the haunt of sweaty cyclists and the service here isn't always as friendly as you might like.

Bus 688 runs up and down the Allen Valley from Hexham to Allenheads (stopping at Allendale town; 45 minutes, five daily).

HADRIAN'S WALL

What exactly have the Romans ever done for us? The aqueducts. Law and order. And this enormous wall, built between AD 122 and 128 to keep 'us' (Romans, subdued Brits) in and 'them' (hairy Pictish barbarians from Scotland) out. Or so the story goes. Hadrian's Wall, named in honour of the emperor who ordered it built, was one of Rome's greatest engineering projects, a spectacular 73-mile testament to ambition and the practical Roman mind. Even today, almost 2000 years after the first stone was laid, the sections that are still standing remain an awe-inspiring sight, proof that when the Romans wanted something done, they just knuckled down and did it.

It wasn't easy. When completed, the mammoth structure ran across the narrow neck of the island, from the Solway Firth in the west almost to the mouth of the Tyne in the east. Every Roman mile (0.95 miles) there was a gateway guarded by a small fort (milecastle) and between each milecastle were two observation turrets. Milecastles are numbered right across the country, starting with Milecastle 0 at Wallsend and ending with Milecastle 80 at Bowness-on-Solway.

A series of forts was developed as bases some distance south (and may predate the wall), and 16 lie astride it. The prime remaining forts on the wall are Cilurnum (Chesters), Vercovicium (Housesteads) and Banna (Birdoswald). The best forts behind the wall are Corstopitum at Corbridge, and Vindolanda, north of Bardon Mill.

Carlisle, in the west, and Newcastle, in the east, are obviously good starting points, but Brampton, Haltwhistle, Hexham and Corbridge all make good bases. The B6318 follows the course of the wall from the outskirts of Newcastle to Birdoswald; from Birdoswald to Carlisle it pays to have a detailed map. The main A69 road and the railway line follow 3 or 4 miles to the south.

History

Emperor Hadrian didn't order the wall built from fear of a northern invasion. Truth is no part of the wall was impenetrable – a concentrated attack at any single point would have surely breached it – but it was meant to mark the border as though to say that the Roman Empire would extend no further. By drawing a physical boundary, the Romans were also tightening their grip on the population to the south – for the first time in history, passports were issued to citizens of the Empire, marking them out not just as citizens but, more importantly, as taxpayers.

But all good things come to an end. It's likely that around 409, as the Roman administration collapsed, the frontier garrisons ceased receiving Roman pay. The wall communities had to then rely on their own resources and were gradually reabsorbed into the local population. Most of the foreign soldiers posted to Hadrian's Wall at

Hadrian's Wall & Northumberland National Park

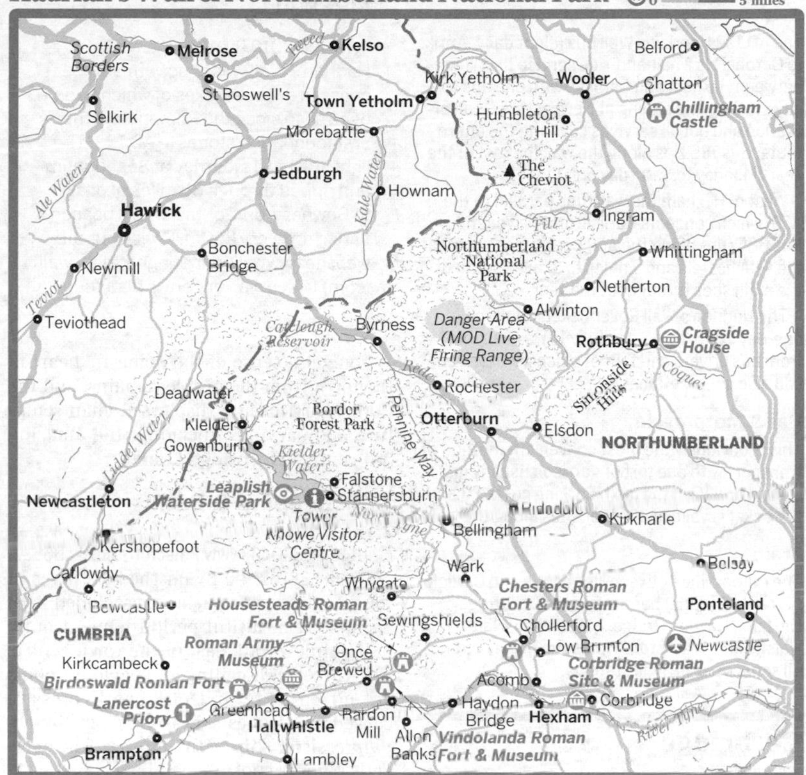

the zenith of the Roman Empire had long since returned home.

Activities

The **Hadrian's Wall Path** (www.nationaltrail.co.uk/hadrianswall) is an 84-mile National Trail that runs the length of the wall from Wallsend in the east to Bowness-on-Solway in the west. The entire route should take about seven days on foot, giving plenty of time to explore the rich archaeological heritage along the way. Anthony Burton's *Hadrian's Wall Path – National Trail Guide* (Aurum Press, £12.99) available at most bookshops and tourist offices in the region, is good for history, archaeology and the like, while the *Essential Guide to Hadrian's Wall Path National Trail* (Hadrian's Wall Heritage Ltd, £3.95) by David McGlade is a guide to everyday facilities and services along the walk.

If you're planning to cycle along the wall, tourist offices sell the *Hadrian's Wall Country Cycle Map* (£3.50); you'll be cycling along part of Hadrian's Cycleway.

Information

Carlisle and Newcastle tourist offices are good places to start gathering information, but there are also tourist offices in Hexham, Haltwhistle, Corbridge and Brampton.

Hadrian's Wall (www.hadrians-wall.org) The official portal for the whole of Hadrian's Wall Country. An excellent, easily navigable site.

Hadrian's Wall information line (01434-322002)

Northumberland National Park Visitor Centre (01434-344396; Once Brewed; 9.30am-5pm Apr-Oct) Off the B6318.

May sees a **spring festival**, with lots of re-creations of Roman life along the wall (contact tourist offices for details).

Getting There & Around

Bus

The AD 122 Hadrian's Wall bus (eight daily, April to October) is a hail-and-ride service that runs between Hexham and Carlisle, with one bus a day starting and ending at Newcastle's Central Station and not all services covering the entire route. Bus 185 zips along the wall the rest of the year (Monday to Saturday only).

West of Hexham the wall runs parallel to the A69, which connects Carlisle and Newcastle. Bus 685 runs along the A69 hourly, passing near the YHA hostels and 2 miles to 3 miles south of the main sites throughout the year.

The Hadrian's Wall Rover ticket (adult/child one-day £8/5, three-day £16/10) is available from bus drivers and tourist offices, where you can also get timetables.

Car & Motorcycle

This is obviously the most convenient method of transport with one fort or garrison usually just a short hop from the next. Parking costs £3 and the ticket is valid at all other sites along the wall.

Train

The railway line between Newcastle and Carlisle (Tyne Valley Line) has stations at Corbridge, Hexham, Haydon Bridge, Bardon Mill, Haltwhistle and Brampton. Trains run hourly but not all services stop at all stations.

Corbridge

POP 2800

The mellow commuter town of Corbridge is a handsome spot above a green-banked curve in the Tyne, its shady, cobbled streets lined with old-fashioned shops. Folks have lived here since Saxon times when there was a substantial monastery, while many of the buildings feature stones nicked from nearby Corstopitum.

Corbridge Roman Site & Museum ROMAN GARRISON

(EH; adult/child £4.80/2.40; ⏲10am-5.30pm Apr-Sep) What's left of the Roman garrison town of Corstopitum lies about a half a mile west of Market Pl on Dere St, once the main road from York to Scotland. It is the oldest fortified site in the area, predating the wall itself by some 40 years, when it was used by troops launching retaliation raids into Scotland. Most of what you see here, though, dates from around AD 200, when the fort had developed into a civilian settlement and was the main base along the wall.

FIREWALL

In March 2010 the entire length of Hadrian's Wall was lit up with 500 beacons, an event the likes of which hadn't been seen since the Romans laid the first foundation stones in AD 122. The light started its journey at Segedunum and ripped through 85 miles of dusk to Bowness-on-Solway, with a beacon flaring up every 250m. Check out the website (www.illuminatinghadrianswall.com) to see if an encore is planned.

You get a sense of the domestic heart of the town from the visible remains, and the Corbridge Museum displays Roman sculpture and carvings, including the amazing 3rd-century **Corbridge Lion**.

Sleeping & Eating

2 The Crofts B&B ££

(☎01434-633046; www.2thecrofts.co.uk; B6530; s/d from £38/62; P) By far the best place in town to drop your pack, this secluded B&B occupies a beautiful period home around half a mile's walk east of the town centre. The three high-ceilinged, spacious rooms are all en suite and one has impressive carved wardrobes said to be from the *Olympic,* sister ship to the *Titanic.* The energetic owners cook a mean breakfast.

The Black Bull BRITISH ££

(Middle St; mains £7-16) A menu of British comfort food, such as beef burgers, fish in beer batter and slow-cooked New Zealand lamb, and a series of low-ceilinged, atmospheric dining rooms, make this restaurant/tavern a fine spot to fill the hole.

Valley Restaurant INDIAN ££

(Station Rd; mains £8-12; ⏲dinner Mon-Sat) Taking up the entire train station building, this temple to spice was declared 'best Indian in the north' by the Curry Club, and they're a bunch who know good subcontinental grub when they taste it. A group of 10 or more diners from Newcastle can catch the 'Passage to India' train to Corbridge accompanied by a waiter, who will supply snacks and phone ahead to have the meal ready when the train arrives!

Information

Tourist office (☎01434-632815; www.thisiscorbridge.co.uk; Hill St; ⏲10am-5pm Mon-

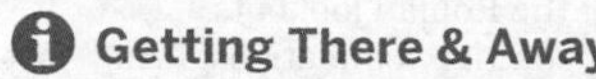
Sat, 1-5pm Sun Easter-Oct) Occupies a corner of the library.

Getting There & Away

Bus 685 between Newcastle and Carlisle comes through Corbridge, as does the half-hourly bus 602 from Newcastle to Hexham, where you can connect with the Hadrian's Wall bus AD 122. Corbridge is also on the Newcastle–Carlisle railway line.

Hexham

POP 10,690

Bustling Hexham is a handsome if somewhat scuffed little market town long famed for its grand Augustinian abbey. Its cobbled alleyways boast more shops and amenities than any other wall town between Carlisle and Newcastle, making it a good place to take on provisions if you're heading out into the windswept wilds beyond.

Sights

Hexham Abbey ABBEY
(www.hexhamabbey.org.uk; 9.30am-5pm) Dominating tiny Market Pl, Hexham's stately abbey is a marvellous example of Early English architecture. It cleverly escaped the Dissolution of 1537 by rebranding as Hexham's parish church, a role it still has today. The highlight is the 7th-century **Saxon crypt** (11am & 3.30pm), the only surviving element of St Wilifrid's Church, built with inscribed stones from Corstopitum in 674.

Old Gaol HISTORICAL JAIL
(adult/child £4/2.10; 11am-4.30pm Tue-Sat) This strapping stone structure was completed in 1333 as England's first purpose-built prison; today its four floors tell the history of the jail in all its gruesome glory. The history of the Border Reivers – a group of clans who fought, kidnapped, blackmailed and killed each other in an effort to exercise control over a lawless tract of land along the Anglo-Scottish border throughout the 16th century – is also retold, along with tales of the punishments handed out in the prison.

Sleeping & Eating

Hexham has few accommodation options and some of the tourist office's recommendations are unashamedly grotty. There are several bakeries on Fore St (including two branches of Greggs).

Hallbank Guest House B&B ££
(01434-605567; www.hallbankguesthouse.com; Hallgate; s/d from £60/80; P) Behind the Old Gaol is this fine Edwardian house with eight stylishly furnished rooms, which combine period elegance with flatscreen TVs and huge beds. Very popular so book ahead.

County Hotel HOTEL ££
(01434-603601; www.thecountyhexham.co.uk; Priestpopple; s/d from £49.50/70) Located on the delightfully named Priestpopple, this hotel has clean, well-maintained, if unimaginative rooms, a passable restaurant and quirky collections of bric-a-brac gathering dust throughout.

TOP CHOICE **Bouchon Bistrot** FRENCH ££
(www.bouchonbistrot.co.uk; 4-6 Gilesgate; mains £12-19; Tue-Sat) Hexham may be an unlikely setting for some true fine dining, but this Gallic affair has such an enviable reputation and was voted the UK's best local French restaurant in 2010 by Channel 4 viewers. Country-style menus are reassuringly brief, ingredients as fresh as nature can provide and the wine list an elite selection of champagnes, reds and whites. The owners have also created a cosy, understated interior in which to enjoy all of the above.

Dipton Mill PUB £
(Dipton Mill Rd; mains around £6-10) This superb country pub 2 miles out on the road to Blanchland, among woodland and by a river, offers real ploughman's lunches and real ale by real fires – really.

Information

Tourist office (01434-652220; Wentworth Car Park; 9am-6pm Mon-Sat, 10am-5pm Sun) Northeast of the town centre.

Getting There & Away

Bus 685 between Newcastle and Carlisle comes through Hexham hourly. The AD 122 and the winter-service bus 185 connect with other towns along the wall, and the town is on the scenic railway line between Newcastle (twice hourly) and Carlisle (hourly).

Chesters Roman Fort & Museum

The best-preserved remains of a Roman cavalry fort in England are at **Chesters** (EH; 01434-681379; Chollerford; adult/child £4.80/2.40; 10am-6pm Apr-Sep), set among idyllic green woods and meadows near the village of Chollerford and originally constructed to house a unit of troops from Asturias in northern Spain. They include part of a bridge (beautifully constructed and best appreciated from the eastern bank) across the River North Tyne, four well-preserved gatehouses, an extraordinary bathhouse and an underfloor heating system. The museum has a large collection of Roman sculpture. Take bus 880 or 882 from Hexham (5.5 miles away); it is also on the route of Hadrian's Wall bus AD 122.

Haltwhistle & Around

POP 3810

It's one of the more important debates in contemporary Britain: where exactly is the centre of the country? The residents of Haltwhistle, basically one long street just north of the A69, claim that they're the ones. But then so do the folks in Dunsop Bridge, 71 miles to the south. Will we ever know the truth? In the meantime, Haltwhistle is the spot to get some cash and load up on gear and groceries. Thursday is market day.

Sights

Vindolanda Roman Fort & Museum ROMAN FORT

(www.vindolanda.com; adult/child £5.90/3.50, with Roman Army Museum £9/5; ⌚10am-6pm Apr-Sep, to 5pm Feb-Mar & Oct) The extensive site of Vindolanda offers a fascinating glimpse into the daily life of a Roman garrison town. The time-capsule museum displays leather sandals, signature Roman toothbrush-flourish helmet decorations, and a new exhibition featuring numerous writing tablets recently returned from the British Library. These include a student's marked work ('sloppy'), and a parent's note with a present of socks and underpants (things haven't changed – in this climate you can never have too many).

The museum is just one part of this large, extensively excavated site, which includes impressive parts of the fort and town (excavations continue) and reconstructed turrets and temple.

It's 1.5 miles north of Bardon Mill between the A69 and B6318 and a mile from Once Brewed.

Housesteads Roman Fort & Museum ROMAN FORT

(EH; adult/child £4.80/2.40; ⌚10am-6pm Apr-Sep) The wall's most dramatic site – and the best-preserved Roman fort in the whole country – is at Housesteads. From here, high on a ridge and covering 2 hectares, you can survey the moors of Northumberland National Park, and the snaking wall, with a sense of awe at the landscape and the aura of the Roman lookouts.

The substantial foundations bring fort life alive. The remains include an impressive hospital, granaries with a carefully worked-out ventilation system and barrack blocks. Most memorable are the spectacularly situated communal flushable latrines, which summon up Romans at their most mundane. Information boards show what the individual buildings would have looked like in their heyday and there's a scale model of the entire fort in the small museum at the ticket office.

Housesteads is 2.5 miles north of Bardon Mill on the B6318, and about 6 miles from Haltwhistle.

Roman Army Museum MUSEUM

(www.vindolanda.com; adult/child £4.50/2.50, with Vindolanda £9/5; ⌚10am-6pm) A mile north-west of Greenhead, near Walltown Crags, this kid-pleasing museum provides lots of colourful background detail to wall life, such as how the soldiers spent their R&R time in this lonely outpost of the empire.

Birdoswald Roman Fort ROMAN FORT

(EH; adult/child £4.80/2.40; ⌚10am-5.30pm Mar-Oct) *Technically* in Cumbria (we won't tell if you don't), the remains of this once-formidable fort on an escarpment overlooking the beautiful Irthing Gorge are on a minor road off the B6318, about 3 miles west of Greenhead; a fine stretch of wall extends from here to Harrow's Scar Milecastle.

Lanercost Priory PRIORY

(EH; adult/child £3.20/1.60; ⌚10am-5pm Apr-Sep, to 4pm Thu-Mon Oct) About 3 miles further west along the A69 from Birdoswald, these peaceful raspberry-coloured ruins are all that remain of a priory founded in 1166 by Augustinian canons. Post-dissolution it became a private house and a priory church was created from the Early English nave. The AD 122 bus drops off at the gate.

Sleeping

TOP CHOICE **Ashcroft** B&B ££

(☎01434-320213; www.ashcroftguesthouse.co.uk; Lanty's Lonnen, Haltwhistle; s/d from £48/78;) In the world of British B&Bs, things don't get better than this. Picture a large, elegant Edwardian vicarage surrounded by two acres of beautifully manicured, layered lawns and gardens from which there are stunning views. Inside, the nine rooms, some with private balconies and terraces, hoist preposterously high ceilings and are fitted out in an understated style but also contain every gadget 21st-century man needs for survival. The dining room is grander than some snooty hotels and the welcome certainly more genuine. Highly recommended.

Centre of Britain HOTEL ££
(☎01434-322422; www.centre-of-britain.org.uk; Haltwhistle; s/d from £59/70) Just across from where locals claim the 'Centre of Britain' to be, this Norwegian-owned hotel (hence the slightly Scandinavian feel) incorporates a sturdy 15th-century *pele* (fortified) tower, one of the oldest chunks of architecture in town. The most spacious rooms (two have their own full-blown sauna!) are located in the historical main building, there are smaller, quite oddly designed two-level rooms in the courtyard and a separate annex almost next door takes the spill-over. Ask staff to see the smuggler's tunnel and secret staircase if you dare.

Holmhead Guest House B&B ££
(☎01697-747402; www.bandbhadrianswall.com; Greenhead; dm/s/d from £12.50/42.50/65) Built using recycled bits of the wall on whose foundations its stands, this superb farmhouse B&B offers everything from comfy rooms to a basic bunk barn to camping pitches. Both the Pennine Way and the Hadrian's Wall Path pass through the grounds and the jagged ruins of Thirwall Castle loom above the scene. The owners will gladly show you their piece of 3rd-century Roman graffiti. Half a mile north of Greenhead.

Hadrian's Wall Camp Site CAMPSITE £
(☎01434-320495; www.romanwallcamping.co.uk; Melkridge Tilery, near Haltwhistle; pitch/dm from £10/15) Small, secluded camping ground with a bunk barn for when the weather turns particularly cruel. Signposted just south of the B6318.

There are three hostels in the area:

Once Brewed YHA YOUTH HOSTEL £
(☎0845 371 9753; www.yha.org.uk; Military Rd, Bardon Mill; dm £12; ⏲Feb-Nov) This modern and well-equipped hostel is central for visiting both Housesteads Fort, 3 miles away, and Vindolanda, 1 mile away. The Hadrian's Wall bus drops you at the door.

Greenhead YOUTH HOSTEL £
(☎016977-47411; Greenhead; dm £15) No longer affiliated to the YHA, this hostel occupies a converted Methodist chapel by a trickling stream and a pleasant garden, 3 miles west of Haltwhistle. Served by bus AD 122 or 685.

Birdoswald YHA YOUTH HOSTEL £
(☎0845 371 9551; www.yha.org.uk; dm £14; ⏲Jul-Sep, call to check other times) Within the grounds of the Birdoswald complex this hostel has basic facilities, including a self-service kitchen and laundry. The price includes a visit to the fort.

ℹ Information

Tourist office (☎01434-322002; ⏲9.30am-1pm & 2-5.30pm Mon-Sat, 1-5pm Sun) Haltwhistle's tourist office is in the train station, but may soon be moving to the library in Main St.

NORTHUMBERLAND NATIONAL PARK

England's last great wilderness is the 405 sq miles of natural wonderland that make up Northumberland National Park, spread about the soft swells of the Cheviot Hills, the spiky moors of autumn-coloured heather and gorse, and the endless acres of forest guarding the deep, colossal Kielder Water. Even the negligible human influence (this is England's least populated national park with only 2000 inhabitants) has been benevolent: the finest sections of Hadrian's Wall run along the park's southern edge and the landscape is dotted with prehistoric remains and fortified houses – the thick-walled *peles* were the only solid buildings built here until the mid-18th century.

Activities

The most spectacular stretch of the Hadrian's Wall Path is between Sewingshields and Greenhead in the south of the park.

There are many fine walks through the Cheviots, frequently passing by prehistoric remnants; the towns of Ingram, Wooler and Rothbury make good bases, and their tourist offices can provide maps, guides and route information.

Though at times strenuous, cycling in the park is a pleasure; the roads are good and the traffic is light here. There's off-road cycling in Border Forest Park.

ℹ Information

For information, contact **Northumberland National Park** (☎01434-605555; www.northumberland-national-park.org.uk; Eastburn, South Park, Hexham). Besides the tourist offices listed in each town, there are national park offices in **Once Brewed** (☎01434-344396; ⌚9.30am-5pm Apr-Oct) and **Ingram** (☎01665-578890; ⌚10am-5pm Apr-Oct). All the tourist offices handle accommodation bookings.

Getting There & Around

Public transport options are limited, aside from buses on the A69. See the Hadrian's Wall section for access to the south. Bus 808 (55 minutes, two daily Monday to Saturday) runs between Otterburn and Newcastle. Bus 880 (50 minutes, twice daily Tuesday, Friday & Saturday) run between Hexham and Bellingham (and on to Kielder). A National Express service calls at Otterburn (£5.70, 50 minutes, daily) on its way from Newcastle to Edinburgh.

Rothbury

POP 1740

The one-time prosperous Victorian resort of Rothbury is an attractive, restful market town on the River Coquet that makes a convenient base for the Cheviots.

Visitors flock to Rothbury to see **Cragside House, Garden and Estate** (NT; ☎01669-620333; admission £13.90, gardens & estate only £9; ⌚house 1-5pm or 11am-5pm Tue-Sun depending on the month, gardens 10.30am-5pm Tue-Sun mid-Mar–Oct), the quite incredible country retreat of the first Lord Armstrong. In the 1880s the house had hot and cold running water, a telephone and alarm system, and was the first in the world to be lit by electricity, generated through hydropower – the original system has been restored and can be observed in the Power House. The Victorian gardens are also well worth exploring: huge and remarkably varied, they feature lakes, moors and one of Europe's largest rock gardens. Visit late May to mid-June to see Cragside's famous rhododendrons in bloom.

The estate is 1 mile northeast of town just off the B6341; there's no public transport to the front gates from Rothbury; try **Rothbury Motors** (☎01669-620516) if you need a taxi.

High St is a good area to look for a place to stay. Beamed ceilings, stone fireplaces and canopied four-poster beds make **Katerina's Guest House** (☎01669-620691; Sun Buildings, High St; www.katerinasguesthouse.co.uk; r £74; 📶) one of the town's better choices, though the three rooms are a little small for the price. Alternatively, the **Haven** (☎01669-620577; Back Crofts; www.thehavenrothbury.co.uk; s/d/ste £40/80/130; 🅿) is a beautiful Edwardian home up on a hill with six comfy bedrooms and one elegant suite.

There's plenty of pub grub available along High St or you could try **Sun Kitchen** (High St; snacks & meals £3.60-6.50) where they've been serving up sandwiches, jacket potatoes and other snacks for four decades. **Rothbury Bakery** (High St) do great takeaway pies and sandwiches.

The **tourist office** (☎01669-620887; Church St; ⌚10am-5pm Apr-Oct) has a free exhibition on the Northumberland National Park.

Bus 144 runs hourly to and from Morpeth (30 minutes) Monday to Saturday.

Bellingham

The small, remote village of Bellingham (bellin-*jum*) is a pleasant-enough spot on the banks of the North Tyne, surrounded by beautiful, deserted countryside on all sides. It's an excellent launch pad for trips into the national park and a welcome refuelling halt on the Pennine Way.

The **Bellingham Heritage Centre** (☎01434-220050; Station Yard, Woodburn Rd; admission £3; ⌚9.30am-4.30pm Mon-Sat Apr-Sep;) houses a new **museum** with heaps of railway paraphernalia, an interesting section on the Border Reivers and mock-ups of old village shops. The heritage centre shares its premises with the tourist office.

The only other sights of note are the 12th-century **St Cuthbert's Church**, unique as it retains its original stone roof, and **St Cuthbert's Well**, outside the churchyard wall, which is alleged to have healing powers on account of its blessing by the saint.

The **Hareshaw Linn Walk** passes through a wooded valley and over six bridges, leading to a 9m-high waterfall 2.5 miles north of Bellingham (*linn* is an Old English name for waterfall).

Bellingham is popular with hikers so book ahead for accommodation in summer. Most of the B&Bs cluster around the village green.

Demesne Farm (☎01434-220107; www.demesnefarmcampsite.co.uk; Woodburn Rd; dm/pitch £16/12) is a working smallholding in the middle of the village but with a very comfortable 15-bed bunkhouse and lots of soft green grass for tents. There's also cycle storage, a drying room and kitchen. It's affiliated with the YHA.

The **Lyndale Guest House** (☎01434-220361; www.lyndaleguesthouse.co.uk; s/d from £35/65; 🅿📶) provides a cosy, homely experience and knowledgeable hosts Joy and Ken make you feel like a distant relative come to kip in the spare room.

Bellingham's pub grub is nothing to write home about so try the **Happy Valley** Chinese takeaway in Main St or the **Riverside Hall Hotel**, just outside the village heading towards Kielder, for superior fare.

The **tourist office** (01434-220616; Station Yard, Woodburn Rd; 9.30am-4.30pm Mon-Sat Apr-Sep) handles visitor inquiries (and is the same building as the heritage centre).

Kielder Water

Taken a shower or had a cup of tea while in the northeast? Chances are the water you used came from Kielder Water, Europe's largest artificial lake holding 200,000 million litres. Surrounding its 27-mile-long shoreline is England's largest forest, 150 million spruce and pine trees growing in nice, orderly fashion. Besides being busy supplying H2O and O2 for this part of the world, the lake and forest are the setting for one of England's largest outdoor-adventure playgrounds, with water parks, cycle trails, walking routes and plenty of birdwatching sites, but it's also a great place to escape humanity: you are often as much as 10 miles from the nearest village. In summer, however, your constant companion will be the insistent midge (mosquito-like insect): bring strong repellent.

Sights & Activities

Leaplish Waterside Park ACTIVITY CENTRE
(01434-251000) Most of the lake's activities are focused on this activity centre located a few miles northwest of Tower Knowe. It is a purpose-built complex with a heated outdoor pool, sauna, fishing and other water sports as well as restaurants, cafes and accommodation.

Birds of Prey Centre BIRD CENTRE
(www.discoverit.co.uk/falconry; Leaplish Waterside Park; admission £5; 10.30am-late afternoon) Come see flapping owls, falcons and hawks who are shown to the public three times daily.

FREE **Kielder Castle** CASTLE
(Kielder; 10am-5pm Apr-Oct) At the lake's northern end, a couple of miles from the Scottish border, is the drowsy village of Kielder and its castle, built in 1775 as a hunting lodge by the Duke of Northumberland. The building is now a Forestry Commission information centre with exhibitions on renewable energy, forestry, Kielder's birdlife and local architecture.

> **LAKESIDE GALLERY**
>
> The Kielder area claims to be the world's largest open-air gallery with 20 award-winning works of contemporary art and architecture dotting the surrounding landscape. Arguably the most striking and intriguing pieces are the **Minotaur Maze** in Kielder, James Turnell's **Skyspace** on the southern shore and the **Silvas Capitalis** (forest head), a giant decapitated larch wood bonce located in woodland on the northern shore, around 3 miles from Kielder. For more information and images of the pieces, log on to www.visitkielder.com.

Sleeping & Eating

Leaplish Waterside Park CARAVAN PARK £
(01434-251000; site per person £15, cabins £60, Reiver's Rest dm/d £17.50/38; Apr-Oct) The water park offers three distinct types of accommodation. The campsite is set among trees; the Reiver's Rest (formerly a fishing lodge) has en suite doubles and two dorms that all share a kitchen and a laundry, while the fully self-contained log cabins offer a bit of waterside luxury, complete with TVs and DVD players. The catch is that the cabins can only be rented for a minimum of three nights.

No 27 B&B ££
(01434-250366; www.staykielder.co.uk; 27 Castle Dr, Kielder; s/d £38/76) This cosy B&B near Kielder Castle has only the one room but the flexible owners are willing to house out-of-the-blue nomads in their self-catering property when there's space. Cycle storage, no-need-for-lunch breakfasts and a friendly send-off come as standard.

Kielder YHA YOUTH HOSTEL £
(0845 371 9126; www.yha.org.uk; Butteryhaugh, Kielder Village; dm £16) This well-equipped, activities-based hostel on the lake's northern shore has small dorms and a couple of four-bed rooms. Open year round.

Falstone Tea Rooms CAFE £
(Old School House, Falstone; mains £5) This characterful place serves tasty, home-cooked food in the old school house.

Duke's Pantry CAFE ££

(Kielder Castle; Kielder; mains £4.50-7.25) The cafe at the castle does a good line in no-nonsense, filling fare such as jacket potatoes, steak pie and lasagne.

Information

Tower Knowe Visitor Centre (01434-240436; www.visitkielder.com; parking £3; 10am-5pm Jun & Sep, to 6pm Jul-Aug, to 4pm Oct-Apr) Near the southeastern end of the lake, this visitor centre has plenty of information on the area, with lots of walking leaflets and maps, a cafe and a small exhibition on the history of the valley and lake. *Cycling at Kielder* and *Walking at Kielder* are useful leaflets (£2.70 each). They describe trails in and around the forest, their length and difficulty.

Getting There & Around

From Newcastle, bus 714 (two hours) goes directly to Kielder on Sundays and bank holidays, June to October. The bus leaves in the morning, turns into a shuttle between the various lake attractions and returns in the afternoon. Mondays and Thursdays a dial-a-ride service (01434-606156) operates between Bellingham and Kielder. A day's notice is required. Bus 880 (twice daily Tuesday, Friday and Saturday) runs from Hexham via Bellingham.

If driving, be aware that there is no petrol station in the Kielder – the nearest fuel is in Bellingham 18 miles away.

The **Osprey Ferry** (adult/child £6.40/4) navigates the lake (four per day Easter to October plus additional service June to August) between Tower Knowe, Leaplish and Belvedere on the northern shore, and is the best way to get a sense of its huge size.

Bike Place (01434-250457; www.thebikeplace.co.uk; Station Garage, Kielder; hire per day adult/child £20/15; 9.30am-5.30pm Easter-Sep) supplies detailed cycle trail maps for the entire Kielder area and they'll even pick you up in Newcastle.

Wooler

POP 1860

A harmonious, stone-terraced town, Wooler owes its sense of unified design to a devastating fire in 1863, which resulted in an almost complete rebuild. It is an excellent spot in which to catch your breath, especially as it is surrounded by some excellent forays into the nearby Cheviots (including a clamber to the top of the Cheviot, the highest peak in the range). It's also the midway point for the 65-mile St Cuthbert's Way, which runs from Melrose in Scotland to Holy Island on the coast.

Activities

A popular walk from Wooler takes in **Humbleton Hill**, the site of an Iron Age hill fort and the location of yet another battle (1402) between the Scots and the English. It's immortalised in 'The Ballad of Chevy Chase' and Shakespeare's *Henry IV*. There are great views of the wild Cheviot Hills to the south and plains to the north, merging into the horizon. The well-posted 4-mile trail starts and ends at the bus station (follow the signs to Wooler Common). It takes approximately two hours. Alternatively, the yearly **Chevy Chase** (www.woolerrunningclub.co.uk) is a classic 20-mile fell run with over 4000ft of accumulated climb, run at the beginning of July.

A more arduous hike leads to the top of the **Cheviot** (815m), 6 miles southeast. The top is barren and wild, but on a clear day you can see the castle at Bamburgh and as far out as Holy Island. It takes around four hours to reach the top from Wooler. Check with the tourist office for information before setting out.

Sleeping & Eating

Tilldale House B&B ££

(01668-281450; www.tilldalehouse.co.uk; 34-40 High St; s/d from £40/60) One of the houses to survive the fire of 1863 now contains comfortable, spacious rooms that radiate a welcoming golden hue. The five-star breakfast includes veggie and gluten free options.

Wooler YHA YOUTH HOSTEL £

(01668-281365; www.yha.org.uk; 30 Cheviot St; dm £14) In a low, red-brick building above the town, the northernmost YHA hostel (at least until the new Berwick hostel opens) contains 46 beds in a variety of rooms, a modern lounge and a small cafe.

Spice Village INDIAN RESTAURANT £

(3 Peth Head; mains from £5; dinner) There's bog-standard pub grub galore in Wooler, but for a bit more flavour, head for this small takeaway/restaurant that does spicy Indian and Bangladeshi dishes.

Information

Tourist office (01668-282123; www.wooler.org.uk; Cheviot Centre, 12 Padgepool Pl; 10am-4.30pm Easter-Oct) A mine of information on walks in the hills.

Getting There & Around

Wooler has good bus connections to the major towns in Northumberland. To reach Wooler from Newcastle change at Alnwick.

Alnwick Buses 470 and 473; nine daily Monday to Saturday.

Berwick Buses 464 and 267; 50 minutes, nine daily Monday to Saturday.

Cycle hire is available at **Haugh Head Garage** (01668-281316; per day from £15) in Haugh Head, 1 mile south of Wooler on the A697.

Around Wooler

Recently voted best castle in Europe by readers of the *Independent*, **Chillingham** (01668-215359; www.chillingham-castle.com; adult/child £7/3.50; noon-5pm Sun-Fri Easter-Sep) is steeped in history, warfare, torture and ghosts: it is said to be one of the country's most haunted places, with ghostly clientele ranging from a phantom funeral to Lady Mary Berkeley in search of her errant husband.

The current owner, Sir Humphrey Wakefield, has gone to great lengths to restore the castle to its eccentric, noble best. This followed a 50-year fallow period when the Grey family (into which Sir Humphrey married) abandoned it, despite having owned it since 1245, because they couldn't afford the upkeep.

Today's visitor is in for a real treat, from the extravagant medieval staterooms that have hosted a handful of kings in their day to the stone-flagged banquet halls, where many a turkey leg must surely have been hurled to the happy hounds. Below ground, Sir Humphrey has gleefully restored the grisly torture chambers, which have a polished rack and the none-too-happy face of an Iron Maiden. There's also a museum with a fantastically jumbled collection of objects – it's like stepping into the attic of a compulsive and well-travelled hoarder.

It's possible to stay at the medieval fortress in the seven apartments designed for guests, where the likes of Henry III and Edward I once snoozed. Prices vary depending on the luxury of the apartment; the **Grey Apartment** (£170) is the most expensive – it has a dining table to seat 12 – or there's the **Tower Apartment** (£130), in the Northwest Tower. All of the apartments are self-catering.

Chillingham is 6 miles southeast of Wooler. Bus 470 running between Alnwick and Wooler (three daily Monday to Saturday) stops at Chillingham.

NORTHUMBERLAND

The utterly wild and stunningly beautiful landscapes of Northumberland don't stop with the national park. Hard to imagine an undiscovered wilderness in a country so modern and populated, but as you cast your eye across the rugged interior you will see ne'er a trace of Man save the fortified houses and lonely villages that dot the horizon.

While the west is covered by the national park, the magnificent and pale sweeping coast to the east is the scene of long, stunning beaches, bookmarked by dramatic wind-worn castles and tiny islands offshore that really do have an air of magic about them. Hadrian's Wall emerges from the national park and slices through the south.

History

Northumberland takes its name from the Anglo-Saxon kingdom of Northumbria (north of the River Humber). For centuries it served as the battleground for the struggle between north and south. After the arrival of the Normans in the 11th century, large numbers of castles and *peles* were built and hundreds of these remain. All this turmoil made life a tad unsettled till the 18th century brought calm. Today the land's turbulent history has echoes all around the sparsely populated countryside.

Alnwick

POP 7770

Northumberland's historic ducal town, Alnwick (no tongue gymnastics: just say 'annick') is an elegant maze of narrow cobbled streets spread out beneath the watchful gaze of a colossal medieval castle. England's most perfect bookshop, the northeast's most visited attraction at Alnwick Garden and some olde-worlde emporiums attract secondhand book worms, antique fans, castle junkies and the green-fingered in equal measure, and there's even a little something for Harry Potter nerds.

Most of the action takes place around Bondgate Within, Bondgate Without and Clayport St with the castle to the north overlooking the River Aln.

Sights

Alnwick Castle CASTLE
(www.alnwickcastle.com; adult/child £12.50/5.50, with Alnwick Garden £20.80/5.50; ⏲10am-6pm Apr-Oct) The outwardly imposing ancestral home of the Duke of Northumberland and a favourite set for film-makers (it was Hogwarts for the first couple of Harry Potter films) has changed little since the 14th century. The interior is sumptuous and extravagant; the six rooms open to the public – staterooms, dining room, guard chamber and library – have an incredible display of Italian paintings, including Titian's *Ecce Homo* and many Canalettos.

A free Harry Potter tour runs every day at 14.30 and includes details of other productions – period drama *Elizabeth* and the British comedy series *Blackadder* to name but two – to have used the castle as a backdrop.

The castle is set in parklands designed by Lancelot 'Capability' Brown. The woodland walk offers some great aspects of the castle, or for a view looking up the River Aln, take the B1340 towards the coast.

Alnwick Garden GARDENS
(www.alnwickgarden.com; adult/child £9.50/free; ⏲10am-6pm Apr-Oct) As spectacular a bit of green-thumb artistry as you'll see in England, this is one of the northeast's great success stories. Since the project began in 2000, the 4.8-hectare walled garden has been transformed from a derelict site into a spectacle that easily exceeds the grandeur of the castle's 19th-century gardens, a series of magnificent green spaces surrounding the breathtaking Grand Cascade – 120 separate jets spurting over 30,000L of water down 21 weirs for everyone to marvel at and kids to splash around in.

There are a half-dozen other gardens, including the Franco-Italian-influenced **Ornamental Garden** (with more than 15,000 plants), the **Rose Garden** and the particularly fascinating **Poison Garden**, home to some of the deadliest – and most illegal – plants in the world, including cannabis, magic mushrooms, belladonna and even tobacco.

Bailiffgate Museum MUSEUM
(www.bailiffgatemuseum.co.uk; 14 Bailiffgate; adult/child £2.50/free; ⏲10am-5pm Easter-Oct) The three floors at this often overlooked museum near the castle are taken up with interesting exhibitions on coal mining, the history of Alnwick, Border Reivers and the railways as well as locally themed temporary shows.

Sleeping

Alnwick packs them in at weekends from Easter onwards so book ahead. B&Bs cluster near the castle.

TOP CHOICE **Alnwick Lodge** B&B ££
(☎01665-604363; www.alnwicklodge.com; West Cawledge Park, 2 miles S off the A1; s/d from £45/100; P 📶) Is it a B&B, is it a lonely Victorian farmstead, is it an antiques gallery? The answer is, it's all of these and more. The never-ending jumble of rooms, each one different and all containing restored antiques; the quirky touches such as free-standing baths with lids; the roaring fire in the Victorian guest lounge, the friendly, flexible owners and the cooked breakfasts around a huge circular banqueting table – all its features make this a truly unique place to stay. The catch – you'll need a car or taxi to get there.

White Swan Hotel HOTEL ££
(☎01665-602109; www.classiclodges.co.uk; Bondgate Within; s/d from £80/105; P 📶) Alnwick's top address is this 300-year-old coaching inn right in the heart of town. Its rooms are all of a pretty good standard (LCD screen TVs, DVD players and free wi-fi), but this spot stands out for its dining room, filched in its entirety from the *Olympic*, sister ship to the *Titanic*, elaborate panelling, ceiling and stained-glass windows included.

Blackmore's BOUTIQUE HOTEL ££
(☎01665-602395; www.blackmoresofalnwick.com; Bondgate Without; s/d £90/115; P 📶) Trendy Blackmore's motto of 'Eat well, sleep well and party hard' may be a touch incongruous in slow-paced Alnwick, but this takes nothing away from the 14 very comfortable rooms with boutique elements and up-to-the-minute bathrooms. The timber and leather bar-restaurant downstairs is where Alnwick's suited and booted come to booze and get hitched.

Eating & Drinking

Art House INTERNATIONAL ££
(www.arthouserestaurant.com; 14 Bondgate Within; mains £9-16 ⏲Thu-Mon) Located partially within the 15th-century Hotspur Tower (known locally as the Bondgate Tower), this bright, sharp-edged restaurant/art gallery offers simple but flavoursome combos such as salmon in white wine and pesto sauce, and chicken breast with wild mushrooms and tarragon. Ingredients are locally picked, caught and reared wherever possible. All the art on the walls is for sale.

Market Tavern PUB
(7 Fenkle St; stottie £6) Near Market Sq, this is the place to go for a traditional giant beef stottie (round loaf) sluiced down with a yard of real ale. B&B available (£30).

Ye Old Cross PUB
(Narrowgate) Known as 'Bottles', after the dusty bottles in the window, this is another atmospheric stottie-and-pint halt. Legend has it that 150 years ago the owner collapsed and died while trying to move the bottles and no one's dared attempt it since; the irony is that the old window is now behind plexiglass to stop revellers stealing them!

Shopping

Barter Books SECONDHAND BOOKSHOP
(☎01665-604888; www.barterbooks.co.uk; Alnwick Station; ⏲9am-7pm) One of the country's largest secondhand bookshops is the magnificent, sprawling Barter Books, housed in a Victorian railway station with coal fires, velvet ottomans and reading (once waiting) rooms. You could spend days in here.

Information

Tourist office (☎01665-511333; www.visitalnwick.org.uk; 2 The Shambles; ⏲9am-5pm Mon-Sat, 10am-4pm Sun) Located by the market place; staff can help find accommodation.

Getting There & Away

Alnwick's nearest train station is at Alnmouth, connected to Alnwick by bus every 15 minutes.

Berwick-upon-Tweed Buses 501 & 505; 50 minutes, 10 daily.

Newcastle Buses 501, 505, 518; one hour, two to three hourly.

Warkworth Buses 518 & 472, 25 minutes, twice hourly.

Warkworth

Biscuit-coloured Warkworth is little more than a cluster of houses around a loop in the River Coquet, but it makes for an impressive sight, especially if you arrive on the A1068 from Alnwick, when the village literally unfolds before you to reveal the craggy ruin of an enormous 14th-century castle.

A 'worm-eaten hold of ragged stone', **Warkworth Castle** (EH; adult/child £4.50/3.20; ⏲10am-5pm Apr-Sep) features in Shakespeare's *Henry IV* Parts I and II and will not disappoint modern visitors. Yes, it is still pretty worm-eaten and ragged, but it crowns an imposing site, high above the gentle, twisting river. *Elizabeth* (1998), starring Cate Blanchett, was filmed here.

Tiny, mystical, 14th-century **Warkworth Hermitage** (EH; adult/child £3.20/1.60; ⏲11am-5pm Wed & Sun Apr-Sep), carved into the rock, is a few hundred yards upriver. Follow the signs along the path, then take possibly the world's shortest ferry ride. It's a lovely stretch of water and you can hire a **rowing boat** (adult/child per 45min £5/3; ⏲Sat & Sun May-Sep).

Bus 518 links Newcastle (1½ hours, hourly), Warkworth, Alnmouth and Alnwick.

Craster

Sandy, salty Craster is a small sheltered fishing village about 6 miles north of Alnwick that is famous for its kippers. In the early 20th century, 2500 herring were smoked here *daily;* these days, it's mostly cigarettes that are smoked, but the kippers they do produce often grace the Queen's breakfast table no less.

The place to buy them is **Robson & Sons** (www.kipper.co.uk; 2 for around £8), which has been stoking oak-sawdust fires since 1865.

You can also sample the day's catch – crab and kipper pâté are particularly good – and contemplate the splendid views at the **Jolly Fisherman** (sandwiches £3-5).

For fishy facts and other local info, call into the **tourist office** (☎01665-576007; Quarry Car Park; ⏲10am-4.30pm Easter-Oct).

Bus 411 or 501 from Alnwick calls at Craster (30 minutes, around eight daily). A pay-and-display car park is the only place in Craster where it's possible to park your car.

Dunstanburgh Castle

The dramatic 1.5-mile walk along the coast from Craster (not accessible by car) is the most scenic path to the moody, weather beaten ruins of yet another atmospheric **castle** (EH & NT; adult/child £3.80/1.90; ⏲10am-5pm Apr-Sep). The haunting sight of the ruins, high on a basalt outcrop famous for its sea birds, can be seen for miles along this exhilarating stretch of tide-thrashed shoreline.

Dunstanburgh was once one of the largest border castles. Its construction began in 1314, it was strengthened during the Wars of the Roses, but then left to crumble. Only parts of the original wall and gatehouse keep are still standing; it was already a ruin by 1550, so it's a tribute to its builders that so much is left today.

You can also reach the castle on foot from Embleton (1.5 miles).

Embleton Bay

From Dunstanburgh, beautiful Embleton Bay, a pale wide arc of sand, stretches around to the endearing, sloping village of **Embleton**. The village is home to a cluster of houses and the stunning seaside **Dunstanburgh Castle Golf Club** (www.dunstanburgh.com; green fee weekday/weekend £26/30), first laid out in 1900 and improved upon by golf legend and 'inventor' of the dogleg, James Braid (1870–1950) in 1922. Buses 401 and 501 from Alnwick call here.

Past Embleton, the broad vanilla-coloured strand curves around to end at **Low-Newton-by-the-Sea**, a tiny whitewashed, National Trust–preserved village with a fine pub. Behind the bay is a path leading to the **Newton Pool Nature Reserve**, an important spot for breeding and migrating birds such as black-headed gulls and grasshopper warblers. There are a couple of hides where you can peer out at them. You can continue walking along the headland beyond Low Newton, where you'll find **Football Hole**, a delightful hidden beach between headlands.

Sleeping & Eating

Sportsman HOTEL ££
(01665-576588; www.sportsmanhotel.co.uk; 6 Sea lane, Embleton; s/d from £40/65) This large, relaxed place set up from the bay has a wide deck out the front and a spacious, plain wooden bar that serves award-winning local nosh (mains £12 to £17). Upstairs are 12 beautifully appointed rooms – nine of which look over the bay and golf course – and all have sturdy oak beds and handsome pine furniture.

Ship Inn PUB
(www.shipinnnewton.co.uk; Low-Newton-by-the-Sea) This wonderfully traditional ale house has a large open yard for fine weather, although it would take a real dose of sunshine to tear yourself away from the cosy interior. Local lobster (caught 50m away), Craster kippers and the superb ploughman's lunch made with cheddar from a local dairy are the highlights of the locally-themed menu.

Farne Islands

One of England's most incredible seabird conventions is found on a rocky archipelago of islands about 3 miles offshore from the undistinguished fishing village of **Seahouses**.

The best time to visit the **Farne Islands** (NT; admission £6, depending on island & time of year) is during breeding season (roughly May to July), when you can see feeding chicks of 20 species of seabird, including puffin, kittiwake, Arctic tern, eider duck, cormorant and gull. This is a quite extraordinary experience, for there are few places in the world where you can get so close to nesting seabirds. The islands are also home to a colony of grey seals.

To protect the islands from environmental damage, only two are accessible to the public: Inner Farne and Staple Island. Inner Farne is the more interesting of the two, as it is also the site of a tiny **chapel** (1370, restored 1848) to the memory of St Cuthbert, who lived here for a spell and died here in 687.

Information

The **tourist office** (01665-720884; Seafield car park; 10am-5pm Apr-Oct) near the harbour in Seahouses and a **National Trust Shop** (16 Main St; 10am-5pm Apr-Oct) are on hand to provide island-specific information.

Getting There & Away

There are various tours, from 1½-hour cruises to all-day specials, and they get going from 10am April to October. Crossings can be rough, and may be impossible in bad weather. Some of the boats have no proper cabin, so make sure you've got warm, waterproof clothing if there's a chance of rain. Also recommended is an old hat – those birds sure can ruin a head of hair!

Of the four operators that sail from the dock in Seahouses, **Billy Shiel** (01665-720308; www.farne-islands.com; 3hr tour adult/child £13/9, all-day tour with landing £25/15) is probably the best known – he even got an MBE for his troubles.

Bamburgh

POP 450

Cute little Bamburgh is dominated by its castle, a massive, imposing structure roosting high up on a basalt crag and a solid contender for England's best. The village itself – a tidy fist of houses around a pleasant green – will be forever associated with the valiant achievements of local lass, Grace Darling.

Bamburgh Castle CASTLE

(www.bamburghcastle.com; adult/child £8/4, audio guide £2.50; ⏲10am-5pm Mar-Oct) Northumberland's most dramatic castle was built around a powerful 11th-century Norman keep by Henry II, although its name is a derivative of Bebbanburgh, after the wife of Anglo-Saxon ruler Aedelfrip, whose fortified home occupied this basalt outcrop 500 years earlier. The castle played a key role in the border wars of the 13th and 14th centuries, and in 1464 was the first English castle to fall as the result of a sustained artillery attack, by Richard Neville, Earl of Warwick, during the Wars of the Roses. It was restored in the 19th century by the great industrialist Lord Armstrong, who died before work was completed. The castle is still home to the Armstrong family.

Once through the gates, head for the **museum** to view scraps of WWII German bombers washed up on Northumberland's beaches, plus exhibits illustrating just how the Armstrongs raked in their millions (ships, weapons, locomotives), before entering the castle proper. The 12 rooms and chambers inside are crammed with antique furniture, suits of armour, priceless ceramics and works of art, but top billing must go to the **King's Hall**, a stunning piece of 19th-century neo-Gothic fakery, all wood panelling, leaded windows and hefty beams supporting the roof.

RNLI Grace Darling Museum MUSEUM

(1 Radcliffe Rd; adult/child £2.75/1.75; ⏲10am-5pm) Born in Bamburgh, Grace Darling was the lighthouse keeper's daughter on Outer Farne who rowed out to the grounded, flailing SS *Forfarshire* in 1838 and saved its crew in the middle of a dreadful storm. This recently refurbished museum is dedicated to the plucky Victorian heroine and even has the actual coble (rowboat) in which she braved the churning North Sea, as well as a film on the events of that stormy night. Grace was born just three houses down from the museum and is buried in the churchyard opposite, her ornate wrought-iron and sandstone tomb built tall so as to be visible to passing ships.

Sleeping & Eating

Bamburgh has some fine places to snooze but for greater choice and lower rates, head for Seahouses (p772) 4 miles down the road.

Bamburgh Hall Farm B&B ££

(☎01668-214230; www.bamburghhallfarm.com; s/d £45/70; Ⓟ) This magnificent mini-mansion built in 1697 comes highly recommended for the sheer pleasure of the views, right down to the sea, and the huge breakfast, served in the very dining room where Jacobite officers met during the rebellion of 1715. Studies in understated elegance, the four rooms are a superb deal.

Greenhouse B&B ££

(☎01668-214513; www.bamburghholidays.co.uk; 5-6 Front St; r from £65; Ⓟ) With four smart and generously cut rooms sporting period features and a mix of views (rooms 1 and 2 overlooking the front are best), this is a comfortable place run by friendly owners. However, there's no discount for single occupancy.

Victoria Hotel HOTEL ££

(☎01668-214431; www.thevictoriahotelbamburgh.co.uk; Front St; s/d from £50/100; Ⓟ) Overlooking the village green is this handsome hotel with bedrooms decorated with quality antiques and – in the superior rooms – handcrafted four-posters. Here you'll also find the best restaurant in the village, with a surprisingly adventurous menu (mains £10 to £16) that blends local fare with exotic flavours.

You can stock up for a picnic at the **Pantry** (13 Front St; sandwiches £2.25-4.50); the **Copper Kettle** (22 Front St; afternoon tea £5-7) is a gift shop with a pleasant tearoom.

Getting There & Away

Alnwick Bus 401 or 501; one hour, four to six daily.

Newcastle Bus 501; 2½ hours, three daily Monday to Saturday, two Sunday. Stops at Alnwick and Seahouses.

Holy Island (Lindisfarne)

Holy Island is often referred to as an unearthly place, and while a lot of this talk is just that (and a little bit of bring-'em-in tourist bluster), there *is* something almost other-worldly about this small island (it's only 2 sq miles). It's slightly tricky to reach, as it's connected to the mainland by a narrow causeway that only appears at low tide. It's also fiercely desolate and isolated, barely any different from when St Aidan arrived to found a monastery in 635. As you cross the empty flats to get here, it's not difficult to imagine the marauding Vikings who repeatedly sacked the settlement between 793 and 875, when the monks finally took the hint and left. They carried with them the illuminated *Lindisfarne Gospels* (now in the British Library in London) and the miraculously preserved body of St Cuthbert, who lived here for a couple of years but preferred the hermit's life on Inner Farne. A priory was re-established in the 11th century but didn't survive the Dissolution in 1537.

Holy Island is this strange mix of magic and menace that attracts the pious and the curious; during summer weekends the tiny fishing village, built around the red-sandstone remains of the medieval priory, swarms with visitors. The island's peculiar isolation is best appreciated at high tide or out of season, when the wind-lashed, marram-covered dunes offer the same bleak existence as that taken on by St Aidan and his band of hardy monks.

Pay attention to the crossing-time information, posted at tourist offices and on notice boards throughout the area. Every year a handful of go-it-alone fools are caught midway by the incoming tide and have to abandon their cars.

Sights

Lindisfarne Priory PRIORY

(EH; adult/child £4.50/2.30; ⌚9.30am-5pm Apr-Sep) The skeletal, red and grey ruins of the priory are an eerie sight and give a fleeting impression of the isolated life lead by the Lindisfarne monks. The later 13th-century St Mary the Virgin Church is built on the site of the first church between the Tees and the Firth of Forth and the adjacent museum displays the remains of the first monastery and tells the story of the monastic community before and after the Dissolution.

Lindisfarne Heritage Centre HERITAGE CENTRE

(www.lindisfarne.org.uk; Marygate; adult/child £3/1; ⌚10am-5pm Apr-Oct, according to tides Nov-Mar) Twenty pages of the luminescent *Lindisfarne Gospels* can be flicked through on touch-screens here, though there's normally a queue for the two terminals. While you wait your turn there are fascinating exhibitions on the Vikings and the sacking of Lindisfarne in 793.

Lindisfarne Castle CASTLE

(NT; adult/child £6/3; ⌚10.30am-3pm or noon-4.30pm Tue-Sun Mar-Oct) Half a mile from the village stands this tiny, storybook castle, moulded onto a hunk of rock in 1550, and extended and converted by Sir Edwin Lutyens from 1902 to 1910 for Mr Hudson, the owner of *Country Life* magazine. You can imagine some decadent parties have graced its alluring rooms – Jay Gatsby would have been proud. Its opening times may be extended depending on the tide.

Sleeping & Eating

It's possible to stay on the island, but you'll need to book well in advance.

Open Gate HOTEL ££

(☎01289-389222; www.aidanandhilda.org; Marygate; s/d £40/65) This spacious Elizabethan stone farmhouse with comfortable rooms caters primarily to those looking for a contemplative experience – you're not as much charged a room rate as 'encouraged' to give the listed price as a donation. There's a small chapel in the basement and a room full of books on Celtic spirituality.

Manor House Hotel HOTEL ££

(☎01289-389207; www.manorhouselindisfarne.com; s/d £55/95) Check in at the bar before heading up the tartan-carpeted stairway to one of the 10 smart rooms, the six at the front enjoying spectacular castle views. The restaurant downstairs (mains £7 to £11) is a very popular tourist refuelling stop. Booking ahead essential.

Ship Inn PUB, B&B ££

(☎01289-389311; www.theshipinn-holyisland.co.uk; Marygate; s/d from £82/104) Four exceptionally comfortable rooms – one with a four-poster – sit above an 18th-century public house known here as the Tavern. There's good local seafood in the bar.

Shopping

St Aidan's Winery MEAD PRODUCERS

(www.lindisfarne-mead.co.uk) Sample and buy deliciously sweet Lindisfarne Mead, said to be a potent aphrodisiac, at the island's winery housed in a new modern complex.

Getting There & Away

Holy Island can be reached by bus 477 from Berwick (Wednesday and Saturday only, Monday to Saturday July and August). People taking cars across are requested to park in one of the signposted car parks (£4.40 per day). The sea covers the causeway and cuts the island off from the mainland for about five hours each day. Tide times are listed at tourist offices, in local newspapers and at each side of the crossing.

If arriving by car, a **shuttle bus** (£2; ⌚every 20min) runs from the car park to the castle.

Berwick-upon-Tweed

POP 11,665

The northernmost city in England is a salt-encrusted fortress town and the stubborn holder of two unique honours: it is the most fought-over settlement in European history (between 1174 and 1482 it changed hands 14 times between the Scots and the English); and its football team, Berwick Rangers, are the only English team to play in the Scottish League – albeit in lowly Division Three. Although firmly English since the 15th century, Berwick retains its own peculiar identity, an odd blend of Scottish and English with locals born south of the border very often speaking with a noticeable Scottish whirr.

Sights & Activities

FREE Berwick's Walls DEFENSIVE WALLS

(EH) Berwick's hefty Elizabethan walls were begun in 1558 to reinforce an earlier set built during the reign of Edward II. They represented state-of-the-art military technology of the day and were designed both to house artillery (in arrowhead-shaped bastions) and to withstand it (the walls are low and massively thick, but it's still a long way to fall).

You can walk almost the entire length of the walls, a circuit of about a mile. It's a must, with wonderful, wide-open views. Only a small fragment remains of the once mighty **border castle**, most of the building having been replaced by the train station.

Berwick Barracks MUSEUMS/GALLERIES

(EH; The Parade; adult/child £3.70/1.90; ⌚10am-5pm Apr-Sep) Designed by Nicholas Hawksmoor, the oldest purpose-built barracks (1717) in Britain now house an assortment of museums and art galleries.

The **By Beat of Drum** exhibition charges through the history of British soldiery from 1660 to 1900, while the **Regimental Museum** is only really for those with a burning interest in the King's Own Scottish Borderers. The **Berwick Museum and Art Gallery** romps through the town's history and holds 400 works of art from the Burrell collection (the other 9000 make up Glasgow's famous museum). The **Gymnasium Gallery** (⌚noon-4pm Wed-Sun) hosts big-name contemporary art exhibitions.

Cell Block Museum MUSEUM

(Marygate; adult/child £2/50p; ⌚tours 10.30am & 2pm Mon-Fri Apr-Sep) The original jail cells in the upper floor of the town hall (1750-61) have been preserved as a museum devoted to crime and punishment. Tours take in the public rooms, museum, jail and belfry.

FREE Lowry Trail TRAIL

Known primarily for populating the northwest's industrial landscapes with matchstick figures, some of LS Lowry's finest works are actually the result of his many visits over 40 years to Berwick. Most of the trail's information boards stand on the walls, but the route also crosses the 17th-century Old Bridge into the aptly grim suburbs of Tweedmouth and Spittal. Ask for a free map from the tourist office.

Sleeping

There's a cluster of fairly basic B&Bs in Church St. The new Granary development by the river will contain a brand-new YHA hostel expected to open in 2011.

TOP CHOICE No 1 Sallyport BOUTIQUE B&B £££

(☎01289-308827; www.sallyport.co.uk; 1 Sallyport, off Bridge St; r £110-150) Not just the best in town, but one of the best B&Bs in England, No 1 Sallyport has only six suites – each carefully appointed to fit a theme. The Manhattan Loft, crammed into the attic, makes the minimalist most of the confined space; the Lowry Room is a country-style Georgian classic; the Smuggler's Suite has a separate sitting room complete with widescreen TV, DVD players and plenty of space to lounge around in. The Tiffany Suite has a grand fireplace and the attic Mulberry Suite has a sexy freestanding bath. The downstairs **restaurant** (mains £8.95-14.95) is Berwick's finest serving Cheviot lamb, North Sea fish and homemade cakes and pastries. The ambitious owners are hoping to gain Northumberland's first Michelin star in 2011.

Berwick Backpackers HOSTEL ££

(☎01289-331481; www.berwickbackpackers.co.uk; 56-58 Bridge St; dm/s/d from £16.95/29.95/70; P@) This well-appointed hostel, basically a series of rooms in the outhouses of a Georgian home positioned around a central courtyard, has a variety of spick-and-span rooms including two mixed dorms. Highly recommended.

Eating & Drinking

Good dining is a little thin on the ground, but there are a few exceptions.

Berwick-Upon-Tweed

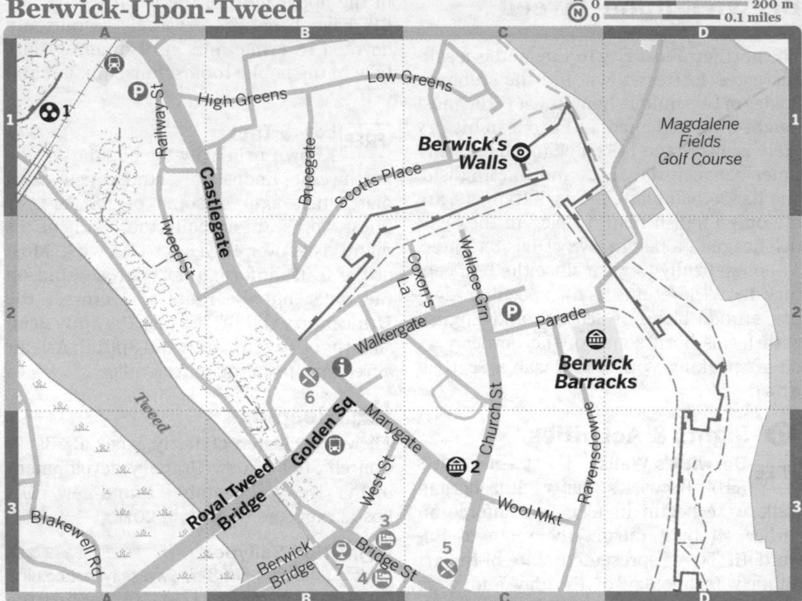

Berwick-Upon-Tweed

Top Sights
Berwick Barracks C2
Berwick's Walls C1

Sights
1 Border Castle Ruins A1
2 Cell Block Museum C3

Sleeping
3 Berwick Backpackers B3
4 No 1 Sallyport B3

Eating
5 Foxton's C3
6 Reivers Tryst B2

Drinking
7 Barrels Alehouse B3

Foxton's CONTINENTAL ££
(26 Hide Hill; mains £9-14.50; Mon-Sat) This decent brasserie-style restaurant has Continental dishes to complement the local fare, which means there's something for everyone.

Reivers Tryst BRITISH £
(119 Marygate; mains £4.70-9; Mon-Sat) From the hearty all-day breakfast through to homemade pies for lunch and the likes of gammon and pineapple in the evening, this place specialises in stodgy English cuisine – nothing fancy, but very good.

Barrels Alehouse PUB
(56 Bridge St) Berwick's best watering hole attracts a mixed, laid-back crowd who can be found supping real ales and micro-distilled gins and whiskies at all hours. There's regular live music in the atmospherically dingy basement bar.

Information

Berwick Library (Walkergate; closed Thu & Sun) Bring ID to access the internet.

Tourist office (01289-330733; www.visitnorthumberland.com; 106 Marygate; 10am-5pm Mon-Sat, 11am-3pm Sun Easter-Oct) Can help find accommodation and runs one-hour guided walks at 10am, 11.45am & 2pm on weekdays (£4).

Getting There & Away

Bus

Buses stop on Golden Sq (where Marygate becomes Castlegate).

Edinburgh National Express; £13.70, one hour 20 minutes, twice daily.

Holy Island Bus 477; 35 minutes, two services

on Wednesday and Saturday, Monday to Saturday in August.

London National Express; £35.30, eight hours, twice daily.

Newcastle Buses 505, 501 (via Alnwick); 2½ hours, nine daily.

Train

Berwick is almost exactly halfway between **Edinburgh** (£13.60, 50 minutes, half hourly) and **Newcastle** (£19.70, 50 minutes, half hourly) on the main east-coast London–Edinburgh line.

Getting Around

The best tool for getting around Berwick is at the end of your legs, but if you're feeling lazy try **Berwick Taxis** (01289-307771). **Wilson Cycles** (01289-331476; 17a Bridge St) hires out bikes for £15 a day.

Around Berwick-upon-Tweed

NORHAM CASTLE

Once considered the most dangerous place in the country, the pinkish ruins of **Norham Castle** (EH; admission free; 10am-5pm Apr-Sep) are quiet these days, but during the border wars it was besieged no less than 13 times, including a year-long siege by Robert the Bruce in 1318. The last attack came just three weeks before the Battle of Flodden and the castle was once again restored to the prince bishops of Durham, for whom it was originally built in 1160 to guard a swerving bend in the River Tweed.

The castle ruins are 6.5 miles southwest of Berwick on a minor road off the A698; bus 67 regularly passes Norham Castle from Berwick train station on its way to Galashiels in Scotland (six daily Monday to Saturday).

ETAL & FORD

The pretty villages of Etal and Ford are part of a 23.45-sq-mile working rural estate set between the coast and the Cheviots, a lush and ordered landscape that belies its ferocious, bloody history.

Etal (*eet*-le) perches at the estate's northern end, and its main attraction is the roofless 14th-century **castle** (EH; adult/child £3.70/1.90; 11am-4.30pm Apr-Oct). It was captured by the Scots just before the ferocious Battle of Flodden and has a striking border-warfare exhibition. It is 12 miles south of Berwick on the B6354.

About 1.5 miles southeast of here is Ford, home to the **Lady Waterford Hall** (adult/child £2/1.50; 11am-5pm Mar-Oct, other times by appointment), a fine Victorian schoolhouse decorated with biblical murals and pictures by Louisa Anna, Marchioness of Waterford. The imposing 14th-century **Ford Castle** is closed to the public.

If you're travelling with kids, take a spin on the toy-town **Heatherslaw Light Railway** (adult/child £6/4; hourly 10am-3pm Apr-Oct), which chugs from the Heatherslaw Corn Mill (about halfway between the two villages) to Etal Castle. The 3.5-mile return journey follows the river through pretty countryside.

Sleeping & Eating

Estate House B&B ££

(01890-820668; www.theestatehouse.info; Ford; s/d £55/75) This fine house near Lady Waterford Hall has three lovely bedrooms (all with handsome brass beds) overlooking a colourful, mature garden. An excellent choice – the owners have a plethora of local information.

Black Bull PUB

(Etal) This whitewashed, popular place is Northumberland's only thatched pub. It serves great pub food (mains £7 to £9, no food Tuesday) and pours a variety of well-kept ales.

Getting There & Away

Bus 267 between Berwick and Wooler stops at both Etal and Ford (four daily, Monday to Saturday).

CROOKHAM & AROUND

Unless you're a Scot or a historian, chances are you won't have heard of the Battle of Flodden, but this 1513 encounter between the Scots and the English – which left the English victorious and the Scots to count 10,000 dead, including James IV of Scotland and most of his nobles – was a watershed in the centuries-old scrap between the two. A large stone cross, a monument 'to the brave of both nations', surmounts an innocuous hill overlooking the battlefield and is the only memorial to the thousands used as arrow fodder.

Sleeping & Eating

TOP CHOICE **Coach House** B&B ££

(01890-820293; www.coachhousecrookham.com; Crookham; s/d from £54/78) This exquisite guesthouse spread about a 17th-century cottage, an old smithy and other outbuildings has a variety of rooms, from the traditional (with rare chestnut beams and country-style furniture) to contemporary layouts flavoured with Mediterranean and Indian touches. The food (dinner £22.95), beginning with an organic breakfast, is absolutely delicious and the equal of any restaurant around.

Getting There & Away

The battlefield is 1.5 miles west of Crookham, on a minor road off the A697; Crookham itself is 3 miles west of Ford. Bus 267, between Berwick-upon-Tweed and Wooler stops outside Crookham post office (six daily, 36 minutes).

Understand England

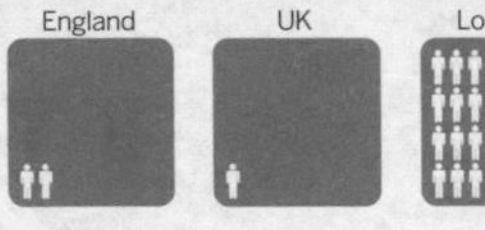

England Today

For England and the English, the first decade of the 21st century has been a time of significant change and national soul-searching. The year 2010 was especially pivotal, thanks to two key events: the World Cup and the General Election. And yes, they are listed in order of importance.

» Population: 51 million

» Size: 50,000 sq miles (130,000 sq km)

» Inflation: 2%

It's a Knock-out

First, the World Cup. In June 2010, the English players went to the world's greatest football tournament full of hope and glory, but they only just scraped through the first round and then got soundly whipped by old enemy Germany. Second, the general election. After 15 years of Labour government, the country saw an alignment between the Conservatives and Liberal Democrats, and a coalition government for the first time in modern history.

Honeymoon Days

To understand the significance of the 2010 election result, we need to rewind a little. The 1980s had been dominated by the Conservatives and the formidable Prime Minister Margaret Thatcher. Then, through the 1990s, the political pendulum swung the other way, culminating in a landslide victory in 1997 for the Labour party and its leader Tony Blair.

For the first four years, Mr Blair and Labour remained immensely popular and went on to win elections 2001 and 2005. A year later Mr Blair became the longest-serving Labour prime minister in British history.

Labour Pains

As the decade continued, the honeymoon period seemed a distant memory and the Labour government faced a seemingly unending string of crises. Most evident were the invasions of Iraq and Afghanistan, and

Manners

» **Queues** The English are notoriously polite, especially when it comes to queuing. Any attempt to 'jump the queue' will result in an outburst of tutting.

» **Bargaining** Haggling over the price of goods (but not food) is OK in markets, but rare in shops. Politeness is still key though.

Books

» *Notes from a Small Island* by Bill Bryson. It's dated, but this American's fond take on British behaviour is still spot on today.

» *Watching the English* by Kate Fox. A fascinating field guide to the nation's peculiar habits.

belief systems
(% of population)

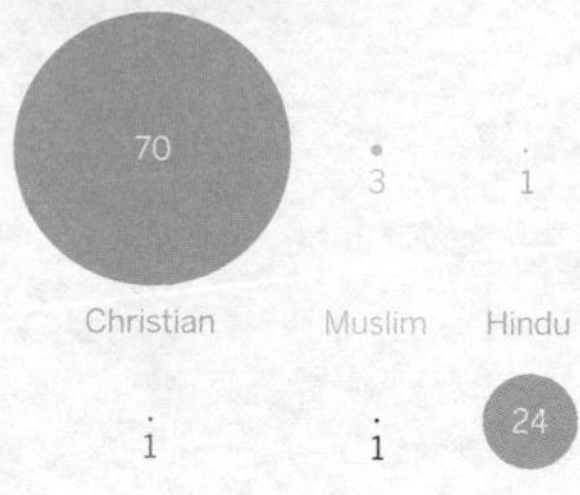

if England were 100 people

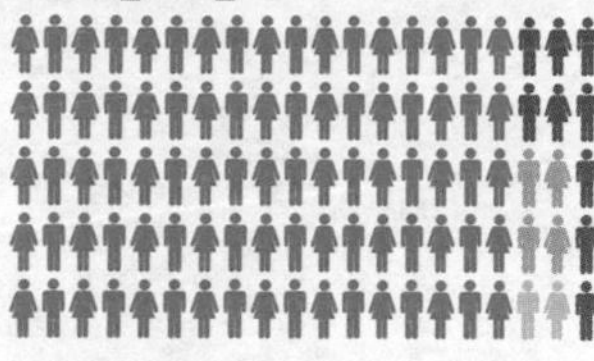

85 would be British
4 would be South Asian
2 would be African & Afro Caribbean
9 would be other

the threat of terrorism close at hand, epitomised by the London bombings on 7 July 2005, when more than 50 people were killed.

In June 2007 Tony Blair resigned as Labour leader, allowing Gordon Brown, for so long the prime-minister-in-waiting, to finally get the top job. His first three months in office were promising, but then policies seemed to go awry. The final nail in the Labour coffin was the Global Financial Crisis. Some commentators said the economic turbulence brought out the best in the fiscally-astute Mr Brown, and Britain weathered the storm better than other countries, but in the opinion polls it was too late.

Unexpected Bedfellows

And that brings us back to the start of this story: Labour lost the 2010 election, and the new government was a seminal coalition between the Conservatives and Liberal-Democrats – a result that very few political pundits would have ever predicted.

Unexpected or not, the new government got straight down to work, and despite coming from opposite sides of the centre ground, impressed most observers with laudable displays of collaboration. Foundation policies were based around the tenets of 'fairness' and 'choice' – most notably new laws allowing parents to set up their own schools, while in July 2010 a major reform of funding for the National Health Service was announced to give more flexibility to doctors and patients.

Home & Away

On the international front, the new government remained committed to keeping Britain's forces in Afghanistan, although public sympathy for UK involvement is waning here too. It's likely, however, that the biggest issue in British politics for the next few years will be the

» Total number of televisions: 30 million

» Total number of mobile phones: 90 million

» Average number of cups of tea per person per day: 3

» *I Never Knew That About England* by Christopher Winn. A treasure trove of bizarre Blighty-themed facts.

» *Eccentric Britain* by Benedict le Vay. A detailed and highly readable study of every folly, oddity and quirky custom the country has to offer.

» *The English* by Jeremy Paxman. A perceptive take on the national character by the BBC broadcaster known for his ferocious interviewing technique and razor-sharp wit.

aftereffects of the GFC. Speeches from newly-installed ministers promised 'straight-talking', but in reality refrained from too much detail. Most commentators – from all sides of the political spectrum – agree that the government will reduce spending and raise taxes more than it has so far admitted. For the people on the ground, it remains to be seen exactly what gets cut, and what gets spared.

Whither Albion?

Meanwhile, away from political battles, there are deeper schisms at work. For most English people, the difference between being British and being English is pretty hazy – and it has been for centuries – but in the wake of continuing devolution from the central UK government to regional assemblies in Scotland, Wales and Northern Ireland, the very identity of England has become a subject of fierce debate. What does English mean? What does it mean to be English? In an increasingly homogenised world, the people of England are being forced to reflect on the values, beliefs and institutions that bind the country together.

So while there may be choppy waters ahead, if there's one thing this plucky little nation has proven down the centuries, it's resilience (so long as there's a nice hot mug of tea to hand, of course). More than 2000 years of history are packed into this pocket-sized island, and no matter what the future may hold, the true jewels in England's crown – its country houses, castles and chocolate-box villages, its landmark monuments and buzzing music scene, its sweeping countryside, revitalised cities and extraordinary coastline – remain as bright and untarnished as ever. The wars are still raging, the economy's looking dicey and national identity is under the glass, but one thing's for certain – England's days are far from over yet.

» Average household weekly spend on fruit £3

» Average household weekly spend on alcohol £14

» Percentage of population overweight 60%

Top tunes

» *A New England* Billy Bragg

» *England My Home* The Levellers

» *I was Made in England* Elton John

» *Old England* The Waterboys

» *This is England* The Clash

» *Waterloo Sunset* The Kinks

» *England My Lionheart* Kate Bush

» *Village Green Preservation Society* Kate Rusby

» *London* The Smiths

Movies

» *Brief Encounter* (1945)

» *Passport to Pimlico* (1949)

» *This Sporting Life* (1961)

» *My Beautiful Laundrette* (1985)

» *Sense & Sensibility (1996)*

» *The Full Monty (1997)*

» *Elizabeth: The Golden Age (2007)*

History

England may be a small country on the edge of Europe, but it was never on the sidelines of history. For thousands of years, invaders and incomers have arrived, settled and made their mark. The result is England's fascinating mix of landscape, culture and language – a dynamic pattern that shaped the nation and continues to evolve today.

Among the earliest migrants were Neolithic peoples – thanks to lower sea levels they could cross the land bridge between England and the continent of Europe. Much later the Celts took more or less the same route, and after them came Roman invaders; they established the province of Britannia and left a legacy of spectacular ruins that can still be explored and admired by today's visitors.

After the Romans came a period once known as the Dark Ages (because it was seen as a time of cultural decline), but the Anglo-Saxon migration that followed was a key turning point in English history. Thanks to kings such as Alfred the Great, who battled against Viking invaders, and the later consolidation of separate Saxon kingdoms, the foundations were laid for the modern state we now call England.

Next came a pivotal date in English history – 1066 – when the country was invaded by the French Norman army of William the Conqueror. This led to the great constructions of the Medieval period – the sturdy castles and graceful cathedrals – that are such a feature on tourist itineraries today.

By the 18th century, the aristocrats no longer needed castles, so instead they built great country mansions as even more potent symbols of their power and wealth. Today, these 'stately homes' dot the English landscape, often containing vast hoards of art and priceless furniture, and set spectacularly at the heart of manicured parks.

For many visitors, this rich historic legacy – everything from Stonehenge and Hadrian's Wall to Canterbury Cathedral and the Tower of London – is England's main attraction, so this chapter concentrates

The Isles: A History by Norman Davies provides much-acclaimed and highly readable coverage of the past 10,000 years in England within the broader history of the British Isles.

TIMELINE

4000 BC

Neolithic peoples migrate from continental Europe. They differ significantly from previous arrivals: instead of hunting and moving on, they settle in one place and start farming.

c 500 BC

The Celts, a group originally from Central Europe, have by this time arrived in Britain. Indigenous peoples take on Celtic ways, and a Celtic-British culture is established.

c 55 BC

Relatively small groups of Roman invaders under the command of Emperor Julius Caesar make forays into southern England from the northern coast of Gaul (today's France).

on high-profile events. We also mention some historic locations you're likely to see on your travels, so you can get the most from your trip.

Stone Age & Iron Age

The history of England from 3000 BC to AD 2000 is well covered in *A History of Britain* by historian and TV star Simon Schama; it's an incisive and highly accessible three-volume set, analysing events in a modern context.

Stone tools discovered near Lowestoft in Suffolk show that human habitation in England stretches back at least 700,000 years, although exact dates depend somewhat on your definition of 'human'. These early peoples were nomadic hunter-gatherers, but by around 4000 BC, most had settled down, notably in open areas such as Salisbury Plain in southern England. Alongside their fields they built burial mounds (today called barrows), but their most enduring legacies are the great stone circles of Avebury (p298) and Stonehenge (p291), still clearly visible today.

Move on a millennium or two and it's the Iron Age. Better tools meant trees could be felled and more land turned over to farming. As landscapes altered, this was also a time of cultural change: a new wave of migrants – the Celts – arrived in Britain. Historians are unclear on their numbers, and it's not clear if the new arrivals absorbed the indigenous people, or vice versa. But the end result was the widespread adoption of Celtic language and culture, and the creation of a Celtic-British population – today often known as the Britons (or Ancient Britons to distinguish them from contemporary natives).

By around 100BC, the Britons had separated into about 20 different tribes, including the Cantiaci (in today's county of Kent), the Iceni (today's Norfolk) and the Brigantes (northwest England).

Notice the Latin-sounding names? That's because the tribal tags were handed out by the next arrivals on England's shores...

The Romans

Although there had been some earlier expeditionary campaigns, the main Roman invasion of England was in AD 43. They called their newly won province Britannia, and within a decade most of southern England was under Roman control. It wasn't a walkover, though: some locals fought back, most famously the warrior-queen Boudica, who led a rebel army against Londinium, the Roman port on the present site of London.

THREE IN ONE

The country of England (with Wales and Scotland) is *part of* the island of Great Britain. The words 'England' and 'Britain' are not synonymous, although visitors sometimes miss the distinction – as do a lot of English people (though never the Scottish or the Welsh). Getting a grip on this basic principle will ease your understanding of English history and culture, and make your travel here more enjoyable.

AD 43

Emperor Claudius leads the first proper Roman invasion of England. His army wages a ruthless campaign, and the Romans control most of southern England by AD 50.

60

The Iceni warrior queen Boudica (also known as Boadicea) leads a rebel army against the Romans, destroys the Roman town of Colchester and gets as far as their port at Londinium (now London).

122

Rather than conquer wild north British tribes, Emperor Hadrian settles for building a coast-to-coast barricade. For nearly 300 years, Hadrian's Wall marks the northernmost limit of the Roman Empire.

200

The Romans build a defensive wall around the city of London with four main entrance gates, still remembered today by the districts of Aldgate, Ludgate, Newgate and Bishopsgate.

Opposition was mostly sporadic, however, and no real threat to the Romans' military might. By around AD 80 Britannia comprised much of today's England and Wales. And although it's tempting to imagine noble natives battling courageously against occupying forces, Roman control and stability was probably welcomed by the general population, which was tired of feuding chiefs and insecure tribal territories.

Roman settlement in England would continue for almost four centuries, and intermarriage was common between locals and incomers (many from other parts of the empire – including modern-day Belgium, Spain and Syria – rather than Rome itself). A Romano-British population thus evolved, particularly in the towns, while indigenous Celtic-British culture remained in rural areas.

Along with stability and wealth, the Romans introduced another cultural facet – a new religion called Christianity – after it was recognised by Emperor Constantine in the 4th century. (Recent research, however, indicates that Celtic Christians may have brought the religion to Britain even earlier.) But by this time, although Romano-British culture was thriving in Britannia, back in its Mediterranean heartland the Empire was already in decline.

It was an untidy finale. The Romans were not driven out by the ancient Britons (after more than 300 years, Romano-British culture was so established there was nowhere for many to go 'home' to). In reality, Britannia was simply dumped by the rulers in Rome, and the colony slowly fizzled out. But historians are neat folk, and the end of Roman power in England is generally dated at AD 410.

Fledgling England

When Roman power faded, the province of Britannia went downhill. Romano-British towns were abandoned and rural areas became no-go zones as local warlords fought over fiefdoms. The vacuum didn't go unnoticed, and once again invaders crossed from the European mainland – this time Germanic tribes called Angles and Saxons.

Historians disagree on what happened next; either the Anglo-Saxons largely overcame or absorbed the Romano-British and Celts, or the indigenous tribes simply adopted Anglo-Saxon language and culture. Either way, by the late 6th century much of England was predominantly Anglo-Saxon, divided into separate kingdoms dominated by Wessex (in today's southern England), Mercia (today's Midlands) and Northumbria (today's northern England).

Some areas remained unaffected by the incomers, but the overall impact was immense. Today, the core of the English language is Anglo-Saxon, many place names have Anglo-Saxon roots, and the very term

STONEHENGE

Probably built around 3000 BC, Stonehenge has stood on Salisbury Plain for more than 5000 years, making it older than the Great Pyramids of Egypt.

c 410

As the classical world's greatest empire declines after more than three centuries of relative peace and prosperity, Roman rule ends in Britain with more of a whimper than a bang.

5th century

Teutonic tribes – known today as the Anglo-Saxons – from the area now called Germany migrate to England, and quickly spread across much of the country.

597

Pope Gregory sends missionary St Augustine to England to revive interest in Christianity among the southern Anglo-Saxons. His colleague St Aidan similarly converts many people in the north.

8th century

King Offa of Mercia orders the construction of a clear border between his kingdom and Wales – a defensive ditch called Offa's Dyke that is still visible today.

LEGACY OF THE LEGIONS

To control their new territory, the Romans built garrisons across England. Many developed into towns, later called 'chesters', today remembered by names like Winchester, Manchester and, of course, Chester. ('Cester' was a variation – hence Cirencester, Bicester, Leicester etc.) The Romans are also well known for their roads, initially built so soldiers could march quickly from place to place, and later so that trade could develop. Wherever possible the roads were straight lines (because it was efficient, not – as the old joke goes – to stop Ancient Britons hiding round corners) and included Ermine St between London and York, Watling St between Kent and Wales, and the Fosse Way between Exeter and Lincoln. As you travel around England, you'll notice many modern highways still follow Roman roads. In a country better known for old lanes and turnpike routes winding through the landscape, these ruler-straight highways clearly stand out on the map.

'Anglo-Saxon' has become a (much abused and factually incorrect) byword for 'pure English'.

The Vikings & Alfred the Great

In the 9th century England was yet again invaded by a bunch of pesky Continentals. This time it was the Vikings – a Nordic people from today's Scandinavia – and they quickly conquered the eastern and northeastern areas of England.

It's another classic historical image: blond men, big swords, horned helmets and rampant pillaging. School history books still give the impression that Vikings turned up, killed everyone, took everything, and left. There's some truth in that, but many Vikings settled and their legacy remains throughout much of northern England – in the form of local dialect (geographical terms such as 'fell' and 'dale' come from Norse *fjell* and *dalr*) and even in the traces of Nordic DNA in some of today's inhabitants.

By the middle of the century, the Vikings started to expand southwards into central England. Blocking their route were the Anglo-Saxon armies heading north, led by the king of Wessex, Alfred the Great – one of English history's best-known characters. Alfred's capital was Winchester; if you come to visit the famous cathedral (p247, look out for the nearby statue of Alfred overlooking the city centre.

The conflict that followed between the Saxons and the Vikings was seminal to the foundation of the nation-state of England, but it didn't all go King Alfred's way. For a few months he was on the run, disguised as a commoner, wading through swamps and hiding in forests. According to later chronicles, Alfred took shelter in a peasant woman's

850

Vikings come from what is today Denmark and conquer east and northeast England. They establish their capital at Yorvik, today's city of York.

927

Athelstan, grandson of Alfred the Great, son of Edward the Elder, is the first monarch to be crowned King of England, building on his ancestors' success in regaining Viking territory.

1066

Incumbent King Harold is defeated by an invading Norman army at the Battle of Hastings, and England finds itself with a new monarch: William the Conqueror.

1085–86

The Norman invaders compile the Domesday Book – a thorough census of England's stock and future potential; it's still a vital historical document today.

hovel and was given the task of watching cakes cook on the fire. But he started to think about ways to defeat the Vikings, got distracted, and the cakes were burnt. When the woman returned she was understandably angry. Only when the scolding got too much was Alfred forced to reveal himself as king. It was the stuff of legend, which is just what you need when the chips are down, and by 886 Alfred had turned the tables, garnered his forces and pushed the Vikings back to the north.

Thus England was divided in two: north and east were the Viking lands, known as 'Danelaw', while south and west was Anglo-Saxon territory. Alfred was hailed as king of the English – the first time the Anglo-Saxons regarded themselves as a truly united people.

Alfred's son and successor was Edward – known as Edward the Elder. After more battles, he gained control of the Danelaw, and thus became the first king to rule the whole country – a major milestone in English history. But it was hardly cause for celebration: the Vikings were still around, and later in the 10th century, more raids from Scandinavia threatened the fledgling English unity. Over the following decades, control swung from Saxon (King Edgar) to Dane (King Knut), and back to Saxon again (King Edward the Confessor). As England came to the end of the 1st millennium AD, the future was anything but certain.

Sarum by Edward Rutherford is a truly mammoth novel, covering the stories of five factional families through about 10,000 years of English history – from the building of Stonehenge and Salisbury Cathedral, right up to the 1980s.

1066 & All That

When King Edward the Confessor died, the crown passed to Harold, his brother-in-law. That should've settled things, but Edward had a cousin in Normandy (the northern part of today's France) called William, who thought *he* should have succeeded to the throne of England.

The end result was the 1066 Battle of Hastings, the most memorable of dates for anyone who has studied English history. William sailed from Normandy with an army and landed near the town of Hastings, on England's southern coast. The Saxons were defeated by the Norman army, and King Harold was killed – by an arrow in the eye, according to legend. William became king of England, earning himself the prestigious epithet Conqueror.

William's successor, William II, had a less auspicious reign; he was mysteriously assassinated during a hunting trip and succeeded by Henry I – the first of a long list of kings called Henry.

In the years after the invasion, the French-speaking Normans and the English-speaking Anglo-Saxons kept pretty much to themselves. At the top of the feudal system came the monarch, and below that came the nobles: barons and baronesses, dukes and duchesses, plus the bishops. Then came earls, knights and lords – and their ladies. At the bottom were peasants or 'serfs', and this strict hierarchy became the basis of a class system that to a certain extent still exists in England today.

London is another epic from Edward Rutherford – or rather around 50 separate mini-novels – each set in a key historical era; from the Roman invasion to the Blitz of WWII. Exhaustive and exhausting, but great for a sense of each period

1095

The start of the First Crusade – a campaign of Christian European armies against the Muslim occupation of Jerusalem and the 'Holy Land'. A series of crusades continues until 1272.

12th century

Oxford University founded. There's evidence of teaching in the area since 1096, but King Henry II's 1167 ban on students attending the University of Paris solidified Oxford's importance.

ROCCO FASANO

» The Gothic interior of Oxford's University Museum (p188)

MISSIONARY ENDEAVOURS

The invasion of the 'pagan' Anglo-Saxons forced the Christian religion (previously introduced by the Romans, and possibly by the Celts before them) out of England to the edges of the British Isles. The pope of the time, Gregory, decided this was a poor show and sent missionaries to revive interest in the faith in the late 6th century. One holy pioneer was St Augustine, who successfully converted Angles in Kent, and some good-looking specimens were sent to Rome as proof – giving rise to Pope Gregory's famous quip about Angles looking like angels. In northern England, another missionary, St Aidan, was even more successful. With admirable energy and fervour, he converted the entire populations of Mercia and Northumbria, and still had time to establish a monastery at Lindisfarne (see p773), a beautiful site on the coast.

Intermarriage was not unknown – Henry himself married a Saxon princess. Nonetheless, such unifying moves meant nothing after Henry's death: a struggle for succession followed, finally won by Henry II, who took the throne as the first king of the House of Plantagenet.

Royal & Holy Squabbling

The Celtic language was still being spoken in parts of southern England when the Normans invaded 500 years later.

The fight to follow Henry I established the long-standing English tradition of competition for the throne, and introduced an equally enduring tendency of bickering between royalty and the Church. Things came to a head in 1170 when Henry II had 'turbulent priest' Thomas Becket murdered in Canterbury Cathedral, still one of England's finest medieval cathedrals (p132).

Perhaps the next king, Richard I, wanted to make amends for his forebears' unholy sentiments by fighting against Muslim 'infidels' in the Holy Land (today known as Israel and the Palestinian territories, plus parts of Syria, Jordan and Lebanon). Unfortunately, he was too busy crusading to bother about governing England – although his bravery earned him the Richard the Lionheart sobriquet – and in his absence the country fell into disarray.

Richard was succeeded by his brother John, and things got even worse for the general population. According to legend, it was during this time that a noble named Robert of Loxley, better known as Robin Hood, hid in Sherwood Forest and engaged in a spot of wealth redistribution.

Plantagenet Progress

Although administratively competent, by the early 13th century King John's erratic rule was too much for the powerful barons, and they forced him to sign a document called the Magna Carta ('Great Charter') at Run-

1215

King John signs the Magna Carta, limiting the monarch's power for the first time in English history: an early step on the path towards constitutional rule.

1337–1453

England battles France in a long conflict known as the Hundred Years' War. It was actually a series of small conflicts. And it lasted for more than a century, too…

1348

The arrival of the Black Death. Commonly attributed to bubonic plague, the pandemic killed more than 1.5 million people, over a third of the country's population.

1381

Richard II confronted by the Peasants' Revolt. This attempt by commoners to overthrow the feudal system is brutally suppressed, further injuring an already deeply divided country.

nymede, near Windsor; you can still visit the site today (see the boxed text, p240). Intended as a set of handy ground rules, the Magna Carta became a fledgling bill of human rights and eventually led to the creation of Parliament – a body to rule the country, independent of the throne.

The next king was Henry III, followed in 1272 by Edward I – a skilled ruler and ambitious general. During a busy 35-year reign, he was a firm believer in English nationalism and unashamedly expansionist, leading campaigns into Wales and Scotland, where his ruthless activities earned him the title 'Hammer of the Scots'.

Edward I was succeeded by Edward II, who lacked his forebear's military success – his favouring of friends over barons didn't help. He failed in the marriage department, too, and came to a grisly end when his wife, Isabella, and her lover, Roger Mortimer, had him murdered. Fans of ghoulish ends can visit the very spot where it happened – Berkeley Castle (p213).

The Year 1000 by Robert Lacey and Danny Danziger looks hard and deep at English life a millennium ago. Apparently it was cold and damp then, too.

Houses of Lancaster & York

In 1399 the last of the Plantagenets, Richard II, was ousted by a powerful baron called Henry Bolingbroke, who became Henry IV – the first monarch of the House of Lancaster. He was followed, neatly, by Henry V, who decided it was time to finally end (or stir up) the Hundred Years' War, a long-standing conflict between England and France. Henry's defeat of France at the Battle of Agincourt and the patriotic speech he was given by Shakespeare in his namesake play ('Cry God for Harry, England and St George') ensured his position among the most famous English monarchs.

Still keeping things neat, Henry V was followed by Henry VI. His main claim to fame was overseeing the building of great places of worship – King's College Chapel (p403), in Cambridge, Eton Chapel (p239), near Windsor – and suffering from great bouts of insanity.

When the Hundred Years' War finally ground to a halt in 1453, you'd have thought things would be calm for a while. But no. Just a few years later, England was plunged into a civil conflict dubbed the Wars of the Roses.

Briefly it went like this: Henry VI of the House of Lancaster (emblem: a red rose) was challenged by Richard, Duke of York (emblem: a white

King Knut is better known as King Canute, famous for reputedly giving his regal power a test too far. He was carried to a beach and commanded the tide not to roll in. He got his feet wet.

LOOKING SOUTH

The arrival of William the Conqueror was a seminal event, as it marked the end of England's century-old ties to the countries of northern Europe. Perspective turned to France and the Mediterranean, with massive cultural implications that have lasted into our own time. In addition, the events capped an era of armed invasion. Since 1066, in the near-on thousand years to the present day, England has never again been successfully invaded by an overseas enemy.

1415

The invading English army under Henry V defeats the French army at the Battle of Agincourt – a crucial battle in the Hundred Years' War. (The war itself continues for almost another 40 years).

1459–71

The Wars of the Roses: a conflict between two competing dynasties – the Houses of Lancaster and York. The Yorkists are successful, and King Edward IV gains the throne.

1485

Henry Tudor defeats Richard III at the Battle of Bosworth to become King Henry VII, establishing the Tudor dynasty and ending York-Lancaster rivalry for the throne.

1509-47

The reign of King Henry VIII. The Pope's disapproval of Henry's serial marriage and divorce results in the English Reformation – the founding of the Church of England.

rose). Henry was weak and it was almost a walkover for Richard, but Henry's wife, Margaret of Anjou, was made of sterner mettle and her forces defeated the challenger. But it didn't rest there. Richard's son Edward entered with an army, turned the tables, drove out Henry, and became King Edward IV – the first monarch of the House of York.

Dark Deeds in the Tower

Life was never easy for the guy at the top. Edward IV hardly had time to catch his breath before facing a challenger to his own throne. Enter the scheming Earl of Warwick, who liked to be billed as 'the kingmaker'. In 1470 he teamed up with the energetic Margaret of Anjou to shuttle Edward into exile and bring Henry VI to the throne. But a year later Edward IV came bouncing back; he killed Warwick, captured Margaret and had Henry snuffed out in the Tower of London.

Although Edward IV's position seemed secure, he ruled for only a decade before being succeeded by his 12-year-old son, now Edward V. But the boy-king's reign was even shorter than his dad's. In 1483 he was mysteriously murdered, along with his brother, and once again the Tower of London was the scene of the crime.

With the 'little princes' dispatched, the throne was open for their dear old Uncle Richard. Whether he was the princes' killer remains the subject of debate, but his rule as Richard III was short-lived. Despite another famous Shakespearean sound bite ('A horse, a horse, my kingdom for a horse'), few tears were shed in 1485 when he was tumbled from the top job by a noble from Wales named Henry Tudor, who became King Henry VII.

Medieval Women by Henrietta Leyser looks through a female lens at the period of English history from AD 500 to 1500: a life of work, marriage, sex and children – not necessarily in that order.

Peace & Dissolution

There hadn't been a Henry on the throne for a while, and the new incumbent harked back to the days of his namesakes with a skilful reign. Following the Wars of the Roses, Henry VII's Tudor neutrality was important. He also mended fences with his northern neighbours by marrying off his daughter to James IV of Scotland, thereby linking the Tudor and Stewart lines.

Henry VII's successor, Henry VIII, is one of England's best-known monarchs, mainly thanks to his string of six wives – the result of a desperate quest for a male heir. He also had a profound impact on England's history; his excommunication from the Roman Catholic Church, and the split between the Church of England from Rome, was followed by the 'Dissolution' – the infamous closure or demolition of many monasteries – the ruins of which can still be seen in many parts of England today, at places such as Fountains Abbey (p610) and Rievaulx Abbey (p620) in Yorkshire.

1536 & 1543

English authority is exerted over Wales; the Laws in Wales Acts, also known as the Acts of Union (1535–42), formally tie the two countries as a single political entity.

1558–1603

The reign of Queen Elizabeth I, a period of boundless English optimism. Enter stage right playwright William Shakespeare. Exit due west navigators Walter Raleigh and Francis Drake.

1605

King James' attempts to smooth religious relations are set back by an anti-Catholic outcry following the infamous Gunpowder Plot, a terrorist attempt to blow up Parliament led by Guy Fawkes.

1644–49

English Civil War' Royalist forces supporting the king are pitted against Oliver Cromwell's army of 'parliamentarians'. Cromwell is victorious, and England becomes a republic.

The Elizabethan Age

Henry VIII was succeeded by his son Edward VI, then his daughter Mary I, but their reigns were short. And so Elizabeth, his third child, unexpectedly came to the throne.

As Elizabeth I, she inherited a nasty mess of religious strife and divided loyalties, but after an uncertain start she gained confidence and turned the country around. Refusing marriage, she borrowed biblical motifs and became known as the Virgin Queen – perhaps the first English monarch to create a cult image.

Highlights of her 45-year reign included the naval defeat of the Spanish Armada, the far-flung explorations of English seafarers Walter Raleigh and Francis Drake and the expansion of England's trading network (including the newly established colonies on the east coast of America) – not to mention a cultural flourishing, thanks to writers such as William Shakespeare and Christopher Marlowe.

Meanwhile, Elizabeth's cousin Mary (daughter of Scottish King James V, and a Catholic) had become Queen of Scotland. She'd spent her childhood in France and had married the French dauphin (crown prince), thereby becoming queen of France as well. Why stop at two? After her husband's death and so no longer France's queen, Mary returned to Scotland, and from there ambitiously claimed the English throne as well – on the grounds that Elizabeth was illegitimate.

Mary's plans failed, she was imprisoned and forced to abdicate, but escaped to England and appealed to Elizabeth for help. This could have been a rookie error, or she might have been advised by courtiers with their own agenda. Either way, it was a bad move. Mary was – not surprisingly – seen as a security risk and imprisoned once again. In an uncharacteristic display of indecision, before finally ordering her execution Elizabeth held Mary under arrest for 19 years – moving her frequently from house to house. As you travel around England today, you can visit many stately homes (and even a few pubs) that proudly claim, 'Mary Queen of Scots slept here'.

Shakespeare's *Henry V* was filmed most recently in 1989 – a superb epic, starring cinema darling Kenneth Branagh as the eponymous king. Also worth catching is the earlier movie of the same name starring Laurence Olivier, made in 1944 as a patriotic rallying cry.

United & Disunited Britain

When Elizabeth died in 1603, despite a bountiful reign, the Virgin Queen had failed to provide an heir. She was succeeded by her closest relative, the Scottish King James, the safely Protestant son of the murdered Mary. Thus, he became James I of England and VI of Scotland, the first English monarch of the House of Stuart (Mary's time in France had Gallicised the Stewart name). James did his best to soothe Catholic-Protestant tensions and united England, Wales and Scotland into one kingdom for the first time – another step towards British unity, at least on paper.

Today, 600 years after the Wars of the Roses, Yorkshire's symbol is still a white rose, while Lancashire's is still a red rose, and rivalry between the people of these two counties is still very strong – especially when it comes to cricket or football.

DAVID TOMLINSON

» The ornate stonework of the Houses of Parliament (p59)

1688

William of Orange and his wife, Mary, daughter of King James II, jointly ascend the throne after William defeats his father-in-law in the Glorious Revolution.

1721–42

Violent struggles for the throne are a thing of the past, and the Hanoverian kings increasingly rely on Parliament to govern the country. Robert Walpole becomes Britain's first prime minister.

The 1955 film version of Shakespeare's Richard III, staring Laurence Olivier and John Gielgud is well worth watching for the award-winning drama of its time, and a view on this turbulent period in English history.

But the divide between king and Parliament continued to smoulder, and the power struggle worsened during the reign of Charles I, eventually degenerating into the English Civil War. The antiroyalist (or 'parliamentarian') forces were led by Oliver Cromwell, a Puritan who preached against the excesses of the monarchy and established Church. His army (known as the Roundheads) was pitched against the king's forces (the Cavaliers) in a conflict that tore England apart – although it was the final civil war in English history. It ended with victory for the Roundheads, the king executed, and England declared a republic, with Cromwell hailed as 'Protector'.

The Return of the King

By 1653 Cromwell was finding Parliament too restricting and assumed dictatorial powers, much to his supporters' dismay. On his death in 1658, he was followed half-heartedly by his son, but in 1660 Parliament decided to re-establish the monarchy – as republican alternatives were proving far worse.

Charles II (the exiled son of Charles I) came to the throne, and his rule – known as 'the Restoration' – saw scientific and cultural activity bursting forth after the strait-laced ethics of Cromwell's time. Exploration and expansion were also on the agenda. Backed by the army and navy (which had been modernised by Cromwell), colonies stretched down the American coast, while the East India Company set up headquarters in Bombay, laying foundations for what was to become the British Empire.

The next king, James II, had a harder time. Attempts to ease restrictive laws on Catholics ended with his defeat at the Battle of the Boyne by William III, the Protestant king of Holland, aka William of Orange. William was married to James' daughter Mary, but it didn't stop him having a bash at his father-in-law.

RULING THE ROOST

A glance at the story of England's ruling dynasties clearly shows that life is never dull for the person at the top. Despite immense power and privilege, the position of monarch (or, perhaps worse, *potential* monarch) probably ranks as one of history's least safe occupations. English kings to meet an untimely end include Harold (killed in battle), William II (assassinated), Charles I (beheaded by Republicans), Edward V (murdered by an uncle), Richard II (probably starved to death), John (too much eating and drinking), James II (deposed), Edward II (dispatched by his queen and her lover) and William III (died after his horse tripped over a molehill). As you visit the castles and battlefields of England, you may feel a touch of sympathy – but only a touch – for those all-powerful figures continually looking over their shoulders.

1749
Author and magistrate Henry Fielding founds the Bow Street Runners, London's first professional police force. A 1792 Act of Parliament allowed the Bow Street model to spread across England.

1776–83
The American War of Independence is the British Empire's first major reverse, forcing England to withdraw from the world stage, a fact not missed by French ruler Napoleon.

1799–1815
The Napoleonic Wars see a weakened Britain threatened with invasion by Napoleon, whose ambitions are curtailed at the famous battles of Trafalgar (1805) and Waterloo (1815).

1837–1901
The reign of Queen Victoria. The British Empire – 'the Empire where the sun never sets' – expands from Canada through Africa and India to Australia and New Zealand.

William and Mary had equal rights to the throne, and their joint accession in 1688 was known as the Glorious Revolution. Lucky they were married or there might have been another civil war.

Empire Building

In 1694 Mary died, leaving just William as monarch. He died a few years later and was succeeded by his sister-in-law, Anne. During her reign, in 1707, the Act of Union was passed, linking the countries of England, Wales and Scotland under one Parliament – based in London – for the first time.

Queen Anne died without an heir in 1714, marking the end of the Stuart line. The throne passed to distant (but still safely Protestant) German relatives – the House of Hanover.

Meanwhile, the British Empire – which, despite its title, was predominantly an English entity – continued to grow in the Americas, as well as in Asia, while claims were made to Australia after James Cook's epic voyage in 1768.

The movie *Elizabeth,* directed by Shekhar Kapur (1998) and starring Cate Blanchett, covers the early years of the Virgin Queen's rule – as she graduates from princess to commanding monarch – a time of forbidden love, unwanted suitors, intrigue and death.

ELIZABETH

The Industrial Era

While the Empire expanded abroad, at home Britain had become the crucible of the Industrial Revolution. Steam power (patented by James Watt in 1781) and steam trains (launched by George Stephenson in 1830) transformed methods of production and transport, and the towns of the English Midlands became the first industrial cities.

The industrial growth led to Britain's first major period of internal migration, as vast numbers of people from the countryside came to the cities in search of work. At the same time, medical advances improved life expectancy, creating a sharp population increase, so for many ordinary people the effects of Britain's economic blossoming were dislocation and poverty.

But despite the social turmoil of the early 19th century, by the time Queen Victoria took the throne in 1837, Britain's factories and fleets dominated world trade. The rest of the 19th century was seen as Britain's Golden Age – a period of patriotic confidence not seen since the days of the last great queen, Elizabeth I.

In a final move of PR genius, the queen's chief spin doctor and most effective prime minister, Benjamin Disraeli, had Victoria crowned Empress of India. She'd never been to the subcontinent, but the British people simply loved the idea.

The times were optimistic, but it wasn't all tub-thumping jingoism. Disraeli and his successor, William Gladstone, also introduced social reforms to address the worst excesses of the Industrial Revolution. Education became universal, trade unions were legalised and the right to

1914
Archduke Franz Ferdinand of Austria is assassinated in the Balkan city of Sarajevo – the final spark in a decade-long crisis that starts the Great War, now called WWI.

1926
Increasing mistrust of the government, fuelled by soaring unemployment, leads to the General Strike. Millions of workers – train drivers, miners, shipbuilders – down tools and bring the country to a halt.

1939–45
WWII rages across Europe, and much of Africa and Asia. Britain and Allies, including America, Russia, Australia, India and New Zealand, eventually defeat the armies of Germany, Japan and Italy.

1945
WWII ends, and in the immediate postwar election the Labour Party under Clement Attlee defeats the Conservatives under Winston Churchill, despite the latter's pivotal rule in Britain's WWII victory.

vote was extended to commoners. Well, to male commoners – women didn't get the vote for another few decades. Disraeli and Gladstone may have been enlightened gentlemen, but they had their limits.

For details on the English monarchy *A Brief History of British Kings & Queens* by Mike Ashley provides a concise and comprehensive overview, plus timelines, biographies and family trees. Good for pub-quiz training too.

World War I

When Queen Victoria died in 1901, it seemed that all of Britain's energy fizzled out, too, and the country entered a period of decline. Meanwhile, in continental Europe, other states were more active: the military powers of Russia, Austro-Hungary, Turkey and Germany were sabre-rattling in the Balkan states, a dispute that eventually started WWI. When German forces entered Belgium, on their way to invade France, it meant Britain and the Allied countries were drawn in, and the 'Great War' became a vicious conflict of stalemate and horrendous slaughter.

By the war's weary end in 1918, more than a million Britons had died (not to mention millions more from many other countries), and there was hardly a street or village untouched by death, as the sobering lists of names on war memorials all over England still show. The conflict also added 'trench warfare' to the dictionary, and the divide that existed between aristocrat officers and their troops during the conflict, further deepened the huge gulf between the ruling and working classes when the war was over.

When the soldiers who did return from WWI found the social order back home little changed, their disillusion helped create a new political force – the Labour Party, representing the working class – which upset the balance long enjoyed by the Liberal and Conservative parties.

One of the finest novels about WWI is *Birdsong* by Sebastian Faulks. Understated, perfectly paced and intensely moving, it tells of passion, fear, waste, incompetent generals and the poor bloody infantry.

The Labour Party came to power for the first time, in coalition with the Liberals, in the 1923 election, with James Ramsay MacDonald as prime minister, but by the mid-1920s the Conservatives were back. The world economy was now in decline and industrial unrest had become widespread. When 500,000 workers marched in protest through the streets, the government's heavy-handed response included sending in the army, setting the stage for the style of industrial conflict that was to plague Britain for the next 50 years.

The situation worsened in the 1930s as the Great Depression meant another decade of misery and political upheaval, and even the royal family took a knock when Edward VIII abdicated in 1936 so he could marry Wallis Simpson, a woman who was twice divorced and – horror of horrors – American. The ensuing scandal was good for newspaper sales and hinted at the prolonged 'trial by media' that would be suffered by royals in the coming decades.

The throne was taken by Edward's less-than-charismatic brother, George VI, and Britain dithered through the rest of the decade, with mediocre government failing to confront the country's deep-set problems.

1946–48

The Labour Party nationalises key industries such as shipyards, coalmines and steel foundries. Britain's 'big four' train companies are combined into British Railways.

1948

Aneurin Bevan, the Health Minister in the Labour government, launches the National Health Service – free medical care for all – the core of Britain as a 'welfare state'.

1952

Princess Elizabeth becomes Queen Elizabeth II when her father, George VI, dies. Her coronation takes place in Westminster Abbey in June 1953.

1960–66

Overseas, the era of African and Caribbean independence brings the freedom of Nigeria, Tanzania, Jamaica, Trinidad & Tobago, Kenya, Malawi, Gambia and Barbados.

World War II

Meanwhile, on mainland Europe, Germany saw the rise of Adolf Hitler, leader of the Nazi party. Many feared another Great War, but Prime Minister Neville Chamberlain met the German leader in 1938 and promised Britain 'peace in our time'. He was wrong. The following year Hitler invaded Poland. Two days later Britain was once again at war with Germany.

The German army moved with astonishing speed, swept through Europe and pushed back British forces to the beaches of Dunkirk, in northern France, in June 1940. An extraordinary flotilla of rescue vessels turned total disaster into a brave defeat – and Dunkirk Day is still remembered with pride and sadness in Britain every year.

By mid-1940, most of Europe was controlled by Germany. In Russia, Stalin had negotiated a peace agreement. The USA was neutral, leaving Britain virtually isolated. Neville Chamberlain, reviled for his earlier 'appeasement' stance, stood aside to let a new prime minister, Winston Churchill, lead a coalition government.

The new leader was welcomed by the British people, but for many the war got worse before it got better. Between September 1940 and May 1941, the German air force launched a series of (mainly night-time) bombing raids on London and several other cities and ports, with the joint aim of destroying industrial targets and lowering public morale. During 'The Blitz', as it was known, more than a million houses were destroyed in the capital and more than 40,000 civilians were killed.

Despite the bombing, morale in Britain remained strong, thanks partly to Churchill's regular radio broadcasts, and in late 1941 the tide began to turn as the USA entered the war and Germany became bogged down on the eastern front fighting Russia. The following year, British forces were revitalised thanks to Churchill's focus on arms manufacturing, and the Germans were defeated in North Africa.

By 1944 Germany was in retreat. Britain and the USA controlled the skies, Russia pushed back from the east, and the Allies were again on the beaches of France. The Normandy landings (D-Day, as it's better remembered) marked the start of the liberation of Europe's western side, and in Churchill's words, 'the beginning of the end of the war'. By 1945 Hitler was dead and his forces were defeated. Two atomic bombs forced the surrender of Japan, and finally brought WWII to a dramatic and terrible close.

Responses during The Blitz included turning underground railway stations into bomb shelters and the evacuation of children from the cities to country areas, while retaliatory British bombing raids were carried out on German cities.

Handy Historic Websites

- » www.royal.gov.uk
- » www.bbc.co.uk/history
- » www.victorianweb.org
- » www.englishclub.com/english-language-history.htm

Swinging & Sliding

In Britain, despite the WWII victory, there was an unexpected swing on the political front. An electorate tired of war and hungry for change tumbled Churchill's Conservatives in favour of the Labour Party. But

1960s

At home, it's the era of Beatlemania. Successful songs such as 'I Want to Hold Your Hand' ensure the Beatles become household names in Britain, then America – then the world.

DENNIS JOHNSON

» The Abbey Rd zebra crossing made famous by The Beatles

1971

Britain adopts the 'decimal' currency (1 pound equals 100 pence) and drops the ancient system of 20 shillings or 240 pennies per pound, the centuries-old bane of school maths lessons.

change was gradual, and improvements slow in coming; food rationing, for example, continued well into the 1950s.

The impact of depleted reserves were felt overseas too, as parts of the British Empire became independent, including India and Pakistan in 1947 and Malaya in 1957, followed by much of Africa and the Caribbean. Through the next decade, people from these former colonies were drawn to England. In many cases they were specifically invited; postwar England was still rebuilding and needed the additional labour.

English explorers, missionaries and traders had 'been in India' since at least the 16th century, but the subcontinent became one of Britain's most important colonies from 1857 until independence in 1947, a period known as the British Raj.

But while the Empire's sun may have been setting, Britain's royal family was still going strong. In 1952 George VI was succeeded by his daughter, Elizabeth II, and following the trend set by earlier queens Elizabeth I and Victoria, she has remained on the throne for more than five decades, overseeing a period of massive social and economic change.

By the late 1950s, recovery was strong enough for Prime Minister Harold Macmillan to famously remind the British people they'd 'never had it so good'. Some saw this as a boast for a confident future, others as a warning about difficult times ahead. But many people didn't care either way when the 1960s arrived and grey old England was suddenly more fun and lively than it had been for generations – especially if you were over 10 and under 30. There was the music of the Beatles, The Rolling Stones, Cliff Richard, and The Shadows, while cinema audiences flocked to see Michael Caine, Peter Sellers and Glenda Jackson.

Alongside the glamour, 1960s business seemed swinging too, but by the 1970s decline had set in. A combination of inflation, an oil crisis and international competition revealed the weaknesses of Britain's economy, and a lot that was rotten in British society too. The ongoing struggle between the ruling classes and disgruntled working classes was brought to the boil once again; the rest of the decade was marked by strikes, disputes and general all-round gloom – especially when the electricity was cut, as power stations went short of fuel or workers walked out.

One of Us: A Biography of Mrs Thatcher by journalist and commentator Hugo Young covers the early life of the 'Iron Lady' and concentrates on her time in power – showing that her grip on events, and on her own party, wasn't quite as steely as it seemed.

Neither the Conservatives – also known as the Tories – under Prime Minister Edward Heath, nor Labour, under Prime Ministers Harold Wilson and Jim Callaghan, proved capable of controlling the strife. The British public had had enough, and the elections of May 1979 returned power to the Conservatives in a landslide result, led by a little-known politician named Margaret Thatcher.

The Thatcher Years

Soon everyone had heard of Margaret Thatcher, or Mrs Thatcher as she was known by her supporters. Love her or hate her, no one could argue that her methods weren't dramatic. The industries nationalised in the late 1940s were now seen as inefficient and a drain on resources, and

1970s
Much of the decade is characterised by inflation, inept governments (on the left and right), trade union disputes, strikes, shortages and blackouts, culminating in the 1978/79 'Winter of Discontent'.

1979
A Conservative government led by Margaret Thatcher wins the national election, a major milestone of Britain's 20th-century history, ushering in a decade of dramatic political and social change.

1982
Britain is victorious in war against Argentina over the invasion of the Falkland Islands, boosting patriotism and leading to a bout of flag-waving not seen since WWII.

1990
Mrs Thatcher ousted as leader, and the Conservative party enters a period of decline, thanks partly to the unpopular 'poll tax', but remains in power due to inept Labour opposition.

WINSTON CHURCHILL

Churchill was born in 1874. Although from an aristocratic family, Churchill's early years were not auspicious; he was famously a 'dunce' at school – an image he actively cultivated in later life.

As a young man Churchill joined the British Army and also acted as a war correspondent for various newspapers and wrote several books about his exploits. In 1901 he was elected to Parliament as a Conservative MP. In 1904 he defected to the Liberals, the main opposition party at the time. A year later, after a Liberal election victory, he became a government minister. Churchill rejoined the Conservatives in 1922, and held various ministerial positions through the rest of the 1920s. Notable statements during this period included calling Mussolini a 'genius' and Gandhi 'a half-naked fakir'.

Churchill criticised Prime Minister Neville Chamberlain's 1938 'appeasement' of Hitler and called for British rearmament to face a growing German threat, but his political life was generally quiet – so he concentrated on writing. His multivolume *History of the English-Speaking Peoples* was drafted during this period; although biased and flawed, it remains his best-known work.

In 1939 Britain entered WWII, and by 1940 Churchill was prime minister, taking additional responsibility as Minister of Defence. Hitler had expected an easy victory in the war, but Churchill's extraordinary dedication (not to mention his radio speeches – most famously offering 'nothing but blood, toil, sweat and tears' and promising to 'fight on the beaches...') inspired the British people to resist.

Between July and October 1940 the Royal Air Force withstood Germany's aerial raids to win what became known as the Battle of Britain – a major turning point in the war, and a chance for land forces to rebuild their strength. It was an audacious strategy, but it paid off and Churchill was lauded as a national hero – praise that continued to the end of the war, beyond his death in 1965, and up to today.

sold off with a sense of purpose that made Henry VIII's dissolution of the monasteries seem like a Sunday-school picnic.

Naturally, these moves were opposed by those working in the nationalised industries (and by many other sections of society) via strikes, marches and organised industrial disputes, but the Thatcher government also waged a relentless assault on the power of trade unions. At the time, unions were regarded as too powerful by many British people (presumably except those in the unions), so there was considerable public support for the new laws and restrictions introduced by the government to curb union activity.

The impact of the Thatcher government's twin-pronged industrial and trade-union policies were epitomised by the closure of coalmines throughout Britain – most notably in the English Midlands, Yorkshire,

1992
Labour remains divided between 'traditionalists' and 'modernists'. The Conservatives, under new leader John Major, confound the pundits and unexpectedly win the general election.

1997
The general election sees Tony Blair lead 'New' Labour to victory in the polls, with a record-breaking parliamentary majority, ending more than 20 years of Tory rule.

2003
Britain joins the USA in the invasion of Iraq, initially with some support from Parliament and the public – despite large anti-war demonstrations held in London and other cities.

2005
Public support for the Iraq war wanes, and the Labour government faces several internal crises, but still wins the general election for a historic third term.

London – The Biography by Peter Ackroyd is an absorbing and original 'warts-and-all' treatment of the capital as a living organism, approaching its history through intriguing themes such as drinking and crime. In fact, it's mainly warts.

South Wales and parts of Scotland – and the responding nationwide strike by miners in the early 1980s. It was one of the bitterest labour disputes in British history, but Mrs Thatcher was victorious, the unions never regained their power, and the pit closures went ahead. (Since 1984 around 140 coal pits have closed across Britain, with a quarter of a million jobs lost.)

Looking back from a 21st-century vantage point, most commentators agree that by economic measures Mrs Thatcher's policies were largely successful, but by social measures they were a failure. The newly competitive Britain created by the Thatcher government's monetarist policies was now also a greatly polarised Britain. On one side were the people who gained from the prosperous wave of jobs and opportunities in the 'new' industries – the financial, IT and services sectors – now the foundations of the country's growing economy; on the other side were those left drowning in its wake – the unemployed and dispossessed, as the 'old' industries such as mining and manufacturing became an increasingly small part of the country's economic picture.

Even Thatcher fans were occasionally unhappy about the brutal and uncompromising methods favoured by the 'Iron Lady', but any dissent had little impact and by 1988 she was the longest-serving British prime minister of the 20th century – although her repeated electoral victories were helped considerably by the Labour Party's ineffective campaigns and destructive internal struggles.

New Labour, New Millennium

The pendulum started to swing again in early 1990s. Margaret Thatcher was replaced as leader by John Major, but the voters still regarded Labour with suspicion, allowing the Conservatives to unexpectedly win the 1992 election. The result for Britain was another half decade of political stalemate, as the Tories imploded and Labour rebuilt on the sidelines.

Things Can Only Get Better by John O'Farrell is a witty, self-deprecating story of politics in 1980s and early '90s – the era Thatcher and Conservative domination – from a struggling Labour viewpoint.

It all came to a head in the 1997 election, when 'New' Labour swept to power under fresh-faced leader Tony Blair. After nearly 18 years of Tory rule, it really seemed to the majority of Brits that Labour's rallying call ('things can only get better') was true – and some people literally danced in the street when the results were announced.

Tony Blair and New Labour enjoyed an extended honeymoon period, and the next election (in 2001) was another walkover. The Conservative party continued to struggle, allowing Labour to win a historic third term in 2005, and a year later Mr Blair became the longest-serving Labour prime minister in British history. In 2010, a record 14 years of Labour rule came to an end, and a new coalition between the Conservative and Liberal-Democrat parties became the new government.

2007

Tony Blair, Britain's longest-serving Labour prime minister, resigns and Gordon Brown, Chancellor of the Exchequer, takes over as Labour leader and prime minister.

2010

Labour is narrowly defeated in the general election as the minority Liberal-Democrats align with the Conservatives to form the first coalition government in Britain's postwar history.

SEAN CAFFREY

» The grand Palace of Westminster (p59), London

The English Kitchen

Once upon a time, English food was highly regarded. In the later medieval period and 17th century, many people – especially the wealthy – ate a varied diet. Then along came the Industrial Revolution, with mass migration from the country to the city, and food quality took a nosedive; a legacy that means there's no English equivalent for the phrase bon appétit.

Today the tide has turned once again. A culinary landmark came in 2005, when food bible *Gourmet* magazine famously singled out London as having the best collection of restaurants in the world. In the years since then the choice for food lovers – whatever their budget – has continued to improve. London is now regarded as a global gastronomic capital, and it's increasingly easy to find decent food in other cities, towns and rural areas across England.

Having said that, a culinary heritage of ready-sliced white bread, fatty meats and vegetables boiled to death, all washed down by tea with four sugars, remains firmly in place in many parts of the country. But wherever you travel in England, for each greasy spoon or fast-food joint, there's a local pub or restaurant serving up enticing home-grown specialities. Epicures can splash out big bucks on fine dining, while the impecunious can also enjoy tasty eating that definitely won't break the bank.

According to leading organic-food campaign group the Soil Association (www.soilassociation.org), more than 85% of people in Britain want pesticide-free food. For more info, see www.whyorganic.org.

Eating in England

The infamous outbreaks of 'mad cow' disease in the 1990s are ancient history now, and British beef is once again exported to the world, but an upside of the bad press at the time was a massive surge in demand for good quality food. Wherever you go in England, you'll find a plethora of organic, natural, unadulterated, chemical-free, free-range, hand-reared, nonintensive products available in shops, markets, cafes and restaurants across the country.

Alongside this greater awareness of food quality and provenance, there have been other changes to English food thanks to outside influences. For decades most towns have boasted Chinese and Indian restaurants, so a vindaloo or a chow mein is no longer considered 'exotic'; in fact, curry is the most popular takeaway food, outstripping even fish and chips.

EATING PRICE BANDS

In restaurant reviews throughout this book, we've indicated the price band.

- » £ means a budget place where a main dish is less then £9
- » ££ means midrange; mains are £9 to £18
- » £££ means top end; mains are more than £18

As well as the food available in Indian restaurants (which in many cases are actually owned, run and staffed by Pakistanis or Bangladeshis), dishes from Japan, Korea or Thailand and other Asian countries have become available in more recent times too. From elsewhere in the world, there's been a growth in restaurants serving up South American, Middle Eastern, African and Caribbean cuisine. Closer to home, a wide range of Mediterranean dishes – from countries as diverse as Morocco and Greece – are commonplace, not only in smarter restaurants but also in everyday eateries.

The overall effect of these foreign influences has been the introduction to 'traditional' English cuisine of new techniques (eg steaming), new condiments (eg chilli or soy sauce), new implements (eg woks) and even revolutionary ingredients (eg crisp, fresh vegetables). So now we have 'modern British cuisine', in which even humble bangers and mash rise to new heights when handmade pork, apple and thyme-flavoured sausages are paired with lightly chopped fennel and new potatoes, as well as 'fusion' dishes whose native ingredients get new flavours from adding, for example, oriental spices.

CHICKEN TIKKA MASALA

Perhaps the best example of fusion cuisine is chicken tikka masala, the UK's favourite 'Indian' dish created specifically for the British palate and unheard of in India itself.

But beware the hype. While some restaurants in England experiment with new ideas and are undeniably excellent, others are not. Only a few months after *Gourmet* magazine called the capital 'the best place in the world to eat right now', one of the country's most respected food critics, the *Evening Standard*'s Fay Maschler, decried the domination of style over substance, and accused several top eateries of offering poor value for money. As any food fan will tell you, rather than forking out £30 in a restaurant for a 'modern European' concoction that tastes as though it came from a can, you're often better off spending £5 on a top-notch curry in Bradford or a homemade steak-and-ale pie in a country pub in Devon.

Of course, there's more to food than eating out. The lavishly illustrated food sections in weekend newspapers and the bookshop shelves groaning under the weight of countless new cookery books all indicate that food is now officially fashionable. Feeding on this is the current phenomenon of so-called 'celebrity chefs', including Hugh Fernley-Whittingstall, who famously scored a £2 million deal with his publishers in the heady pre-recession days of 2006, and Gordon Ramsay, who featured in a list of Britain's richest self-made entrepreneurs a few months later. They are not alone; every night on a TV channel near you a star of the kitchen demonstrates imaginative and simple techniques for producing stylish, tasty and healthy food.

In October 2009 Phaidon Press published *Coco; 10 World-Leading Masters Choose 100 Contemporary Chefs*. Of the up-and-coming culinary stars selected by the experts, 13 were based in London – presumably much to the chagrin of food-fans of New York (eight chefs selected) and Paris (five).

There's change afoot in the shops too. Supermarkets still dominate – four companies (Asda Wal-Mart, Morrisons, Sainsbury's, Tesco) account for around 80% of all grocery shopping – squeezing suppliers to sell at ever lower prices while forcing out old-fashioned butchers and bakers from high streets and neighbourhoods. But they're selling more organic food than ever before, and new labels show just how much fat, salt and sugar the foodstuffs contain.

Alongside these changes at the multiples there's an increase in the number of independent stores selling high-quality food, while the relatively new phenomenon of farmers markets create an opportunity for food producers to sell locally sourced meat, veg, fruit, eggs, honey and so on direct to the public. And they're not just in country towns where you might expect to see them, but in cities too: there are around 20 farmers markets in London alone.

But behind the scenes, and despite the growing availability of good food in shops, markets, pubs and restaurants, many English folk still have an odd attitude to eating at home. They love to sit on the sofa and *watch* TV food shows. Then, inspired, they rush out and buy all the TV-tie-in recipe books. Then on the way back, they pop into the supermarket and buy a stack of ready-made meals. Homemade food sounds great in theory, but in reality the recipe for dinner is more likely to be something like this: open freezer, take out package, bung in microwave, ping, eat.

In fact, more junk food and ready-made meals are consumed in the UK than in all the rest of the countries of Europe put together. So it's no surprise that the English are getting increasingly heavy, with over 60% of the adult population overweight and almost 25% obese. But despite the vast intakes, average nutrition rates are lower now than they were during 1950s postwar rationing.

So in summary, yes, as a local or a visitor you can definitely find great food in England. It's just that not all the English seem to like eating it.

Most farmers markets around England are certified as genuine by the Farmers' Retail & Markets Association (Farma). For a list of farmers markets around the country see www.farmersmarkets.net.

The Full English

Although grazing on a steady supply of snacks is increasingly commonplace in England, as it is in many other industrialised nations, the English culinary day is still punctuated by the three traditional main meals of breakfast, lunch and dinner. And just to keep you on your toes, those very same meals are also called – depending on social class and location – breakfast, dinner and tea.

Breakfast

Most working people make do with toast or a bowl of cereal before dashing to the office or factory, but visitors staying in B&Bs will undoubtedly encounter a phenomenon called the 'Full English Breakfast'. This usually consists of bacon, sausages, eggs, tomatoes, mushrooms, baked beans and fried bread. In northern England (if you're really lucky) you may get black pudding – see Regional Specialities, following. And just in case you thought this insufficient, it's still preceded by cereal, and followed by toast and marmalade.

If you don't feel like eating half a farmyard first thing in the morning it's OK to ask for just the egg and tomatoes, for example. Some B&Bs offer other alternatives such as kippers (smoked fish) or a 'continental breakfast' – which completely omits the cooked stuff and may even add something exotic such as croissants.

Like meat, but not battery pens? Go to the Royal Society for the Prevention of Cruelty to Animals (www.rspca.org.uk) and follow links to Freedom Food.

Lunch

For the midday meal, one of the many great inventions that England gave the world is the sandwich. Slapping a slice of cheese or ham between two bits of bread may seem a simple concept, but no one apparently thought of it until the 18th century: the Earl of Sandwich (his title comes from a town in southeast England that originally got its name from the Viking word for 'sandy beach'; see p144) ordered his servants to bring cold meat between bread so he could keep working at his desk or, as some

THE PIG, THE WHOLE SHEEP & NOTHING BUT THE COW

One of the many trends enjoyed by modern British cuisine is the revival of 'nose to tail' cooking – that is, using the whole animal, not just the more obvious cuts such as chops and fillet steaks. This does not mean boiling or grilling a pig or sheep all in one go – although spit-roasts are popular. It means utilising the parts that may at first seem unappetising or, frankly, inedible. So as well as dishes involving liver, heart, chitterlings (intestines) and other offal, traditional delights such as bone marrow on toast, or tripe (stomach) and onions once again grace the menus of fashionable restaurants. The movement is particularly spearheaded by chef Fergus Henderson at his St John restaurant in London (p109) and via his influential recipe book *Nose to Tail Eating: A Kind of British Cooking* and 2007's follow-up *Beyond Nose To Tail*.

historians claim, keep playing cards late at night. Of course, he didn't really invent the idea – various cultures around the world had been doing it for millennia – but the name stuck and the sandwich became a fashionable food for the aristocracy. Its popularity grew among the lower classes in the early days of the Industrial Revolution – labourers heading for mines and mills needed a handy way to carry their midday meal – and today it's the staple of office and factory workers everywhere.

A favourite sandwich ingredient is Marmite, a dark and pungent yeast extract that generations of English kids have loved or hated. Either way, it's a passion that continues through adulthood. In 2006, when the manufacturer of Marmite moved from selling the stuff in a near-spherical glass jar to a (much more practical) plastic tube, much was the consternation across the land. Similar to the Australian icon, Vegemite (but not the same – oh no, sir!), it's also popular on toast at breakfast and especially great for late-night munchies.

The Campaign for Real Ale promotes the understanding of traditional British beer. Look for endorsement stickers on pub windows, and for more info see www.camra.org.uk.

Another English classic that perhaps epitomises English food more than any other – especially in pubs – is the ploughman's lunch. Basically it's bread and cheese, and although hearty yokels probably did carry such food to the fields (no doubt wrapped in a red spotted handkerchief) over many centuries, the meal is actually a modern phenomenon. It was invented in the 1960s by the marketing chief of the national cheesemakers' organisation as a way to boost consumption, neatly cashing in on public nostalgia and fondness for tradition.

You can still find a basic ploughman's lunch offered in some pubs – and it undeniably goes well with a pint or two of local ale at lunchtime – but these days the meal has usually been smartened up to include butter, salad, pickle, pickled onion and dressings. At some pubs you get a selection of cheeses. You'll also find other variations, such as a farmer's lunch (bread and chicken), stockman's lunch (bread and ham), Frenchman's lunch (brie and baguette) and fisherman's lunch (you guessed it, with fish).

In the 16th century, Queen Elizabeth I decreed that mutton could only be served with bitter herbs – intended to stop people eating sheep in order to help the wool trade – but her subjects discovered mint sauce improved taste, and it's been roast lamb's favourite condiment ever since.

Dinner

For generations, a typical English dinner has been 'meat and two veg'. Dressed up as 'evening meal' or dressed down as 'cooked tea', there was little variation: the meat would be pork, beef or lamb, one of the veggies would be potatoes and the other would inevitably be carrots, cabbage or cauliflower – just as inevitably cooked long and hard. Although tastes and diets are changing, this classic combination still graces the tables of many English families several times a week.

Traditionally, the beef is roasted beef (that's why the French call the English 'les rosbif'), although meat consumption – and British farming – took a dive in 2000 and 2001 following the outbreak of mad-cow and foot-and-mouth disease. These events were still most notoriously recalled in 2005 by France's President Jacques Chirac; joking with fellow leaders at an international conference, he quipped about the British, 'The only thing they have done for European agriculture is mad

VEGETARIANS & VEGANS

It's official, vegetarians are no longer regarded as weird. Many restaurants and pubs in England have at least one token vegetarian dish (another meat-free lasagne, anyone?), but better places offer much more imaginative choices. Vegans will find the going trickier, except of course at dedicated veggie/vegan restaurants – and where possible we recommend good options throughout this book. For more ideas see www.happycow.com.

cow.' But despite Mr Chirac's derogatory comments, good-quality roasts from well-reared cattle grace menus once again.

And with the beef – especially at Sunday lunches – comes Yorkshire pudding. It's simply roast batter, but very tasty when properly cooked. Another classic English dish brings Yorkshire pudding and sausages together, with the delightful name of 'toad-in-the-hole'.

Yorkshire pudding also turns up at dinner in another guise, especially in pubs and cafes in northern England, where menus may offer a big bowl-shaped Yorkshire pudding filled with meat stew, beans or vegetables. You can even find Yorkshire puddings filled with curry – a favourite multicultural crossover that says something about English society today.

But perhaps the best-known classic English meal is fish and chips, often bought from the 'chippie' as a takeaway wrapped in paper to enjoy at home – especially popular with families on a Friday night. Later in the evening, epicures may order their fish and chips 'open' to eat immediately while walking back from the pub. For visitors, English fish and chips can be an acquired taste. Sometimes the chips can be limp and soggy, and fish can be greasy and tasteless, especially once you get away from the sea, but in towns with salt in the air this classic deep-fried delight is always worth trying.

Puddings

After the main course – usually at an evening meal, or if you're enjoying a hearty lunch – comes dessert or 'pudding'. A classic English pudding is rhubarb crumble, the juicy stem of a large-leafed garden plant, stewed and sweetened, then topped with a crunchy mix of flour, butter and more sugar – and served with custard or ice cream. For much of the 20th century, rhubarb was a very popular food, with overnight trains dubbed the 'rhubarb express' bringing huge cargos of the stuff to London and the cities of southern England from the farms of the north. The main growing area was between the Yorkshire towns of Leeds, Wakefield and Morely, known – inevitably – as the 'rhubarb triangle'. It fell out of fashion around the 1980s but is currently enjoying a renaissance in gourmet restaurants as well as humble kitchens.

Moving on to another sweet option, Bakewell pudding blundered into the recipe books around 1860 when a cook at the Rutland Arms Hotel in the Derbyshire town of Bakewell was making a strawberry tart, but mistakenly (some stories say drunkenly) spread the egg mixture on top of the jam instead of stirring it into the pastry. Especially in northern England, the Bakewell pudding (pudding, mark you, not 'Bakewell tart' as it's sometimes erroneously called) features regularly on local dessert menus and is certainly worth sampling.

Other favourite English puddings include treacle sponge, bread-and-butter pudding and plum pudding, a dome-shaped cake with fruit, nuts and brandy or rum, traditionally eaten at Christmas, when it's called – surprise, surprise – Christmas pudding. This pudding is steamed (rather than baked), cut into slices, and served with brandy butter. It's eaten after the traditional Christmas lunch of roast turkey, and shortly before the traditional sleep on the sofa when the annual Queen's speech airs on TV. Watch out for coins inserted in the pudding by superstitious cooks – if you bite one it means good luck for the next year, but it may play havoc with your fillings.

While key ingredients of most puddings are self-explanatory, they are perhaps not so obvious for another well-loved favourite: spotted dick. But fear not; while the origin of 'dick' in this context is unclear (it may be a corruption of 'dough' or derived from the German *dicht* – meaning thick – or even from 'spotted dog') but the ingredients are easy: it's just a white suet pudding dotted with black currants. Plus

YORKSHIRE PUDDING

In Yorkshire, the eponymous pudding is traditionally a *starter*, a reminder of days when food was scarce and the pudding was a pre-meal stomach-filler.

Sherry trifle was considered the height of sophistication at dinner parties of the 1970s, then fell out of fashion, but this combination of custard, fruit, sponge cake, whipped cream, and (of course) sherry is now considered a classic, and is enjoying a renaissance in many English restaurants.

sugar, of course. Most English puddings have loads of butter or loads of sugar, preferably both. Light, subtle and healthy? Not on your life.

And to polish off our tour de table, staying with the sweet stuff, a reminder that the international favourite banoffee pie (a delightfully sticky dessert made from bananas and toffee) is also an English invention, first developed in a pub in Sussex in southern England in the early 1970s. A plaque on the wall of the pub proudly commemorates this landmark culinary event.

Queen Elizabeth I reputedly had the kitchen at Hampton Court Palace moved because the smell of cooking food drifted into her bedroom and spoilt her clothes.

Regional Specialities

With England's large coastline, it's no surprise that seafood is a speciality in many parts of the country. If fish is your thing, head for Yorkshire's seaside resorts – particularly famous for huge servings of cod, despite it becoming an endangered species thanks to overfishing – while restaurants in Devon and Cornwall regularly conjure up prawns, lobster, oysters, mussels and scallops. Local seafood you may encounter elsewhere on your travels includes Norfolk crab, Northumberland kippers, and jellied eels in London.

Meat-based treats in northern and central England include Cumberland sausage – a tasty mix of minced pork and herbs, so large it has to be spiralled to fit on your plate – and Melton Mowbray pork pies (motto: 'gracious goodness for over 100 years') – cooked ham compressed in a casing of pastry and always eaten cold, ideally with pickle. A legal victory in 2005 ensured that only pies made in the eponymous Midlands town could carry the Melton Mowbray moniker – in the same way that fizzy wine from other regions can't be called Champagne.

Another English speciality that enjoys the same protection is Stilton – a strong white cheese, either plain or in a blue vein variety. Only five dairies in all of England – four in the Vale of Belvoir, and one in Derbyshire – are allowed to produce cheese with this name. Bizarrely, the cheese cannot be made in the village of Stilton in Cambridgeshire, although this is where it was first sold – hence the name.

Perhaps less appealing is black pudding, effectively a large sausage made from ground meat, offal, fat and blood, and traditionally served for breakfast. It's known in other countries as 'blood sausage', but the English version has a high content of oatmeal so that it doesn't fall apart in the pan when fried.

Rick Stein is a TV chef, energetic restaurateur and good-food evangelist. His books *Food Heroes* and *Food Heroes - Another Helping* extol small-scale producers and top-notch local food, from organic veg to wild boar sausages.

RICK STEIN

Eating Out

In England, 'eating out' means simply going to a restaurant or cafe – anywhere away from home. There's a huge choice across the country, and this section outlines just some of your options. For details on opening times, see p840. The tricky issue of tipping is covered on p844, while some pointers on restaurants' attitudes to kids are on p43.

Picnics & Self-Catering

When shopping for food, as well as the more obvious chain stores and corner shops, markets can be a great place for bargains – everything from dented tins of tomatoes to home-baked cakes and organic goat's cheese. Farmers markets are always worth a browse; they're a great way for producers to sell good food direct to consumers, with both sides avoiding the grip of the supermarkets.

Cafes & Teashops

The traditional English cafe is nothing like its continental European namesake. For a start, asking for a brandy with your coffee may cause confusion, as cafes in England rarely serve alcohol. Most are simple places serving simple meals such as meat pie, beans on toast, baked potato or omelette with chips (costing around £3 to £4) and stuff like sandwiches, cakes and other snacks (£1 to £2). Quality varies enormously: some cafes definitely earn their 'greasy spoon' handle, while others are neat and clean.

In London and some other cities, a rearguard of classic cafes – with formica tables, seats in booths, and decor unchanged from the their 1950s glory days – stand against the onslaught of the international chains. In rural areas, many market towns and villages have cafes catering for tourists, walkers, cyclists and other outdoor types, and in summer they're open every day. Whether you're in town or country, good English cafes are a wonderful institution and always worth a stop during your travels.

Smarter cafes are called teashops – also more often found in country areas – where you might pay a bit more for extras such as neat decor and table service.

As well as the traditional establishments, in most cities and towns you'll also find US-flavoured coffee shops – the inevitable Starbucks on every corner – and a growing number of Euro-style cafe-bars, serving decent lattes and espressos and offering bagels or ciabattas rather than beans on toast (you'll probably be able to get that brandy too). Some of these modern places even have outdoor chairs and tables – rather brave considering the narrow pavements and inclement weather much of England enjoys.

Eggs, Bacon, Chips & Beans by Russell Davies showcases 50 of the UK's finest traditional cafes, with tongue-in-cheek taster's notes on their various versions of the traditional fry-up.

Restaurants

London has scores of excellent restaurants that could hold their own in major cities worldwide, while places in Bath, Leeds and Manchester can give the capital a fair run for its money (actually, often for rather less money). We've taken great pleasure in seeking out some of the best and best-value restaurants in England, and have recommended a small selection throughout this book

Prices vary considerably across the country, with a main course in a straightforward restaurant costing around £9 or less, and anywhere between £10 and £18 at midrange places. Utterly excellent food, service and surroundings can be enjoyed for £20 to £50 – although in London you can, if you want, pay double this.

Teashops are your best bet for sampling a 'cream tea' – a plate of scones, clotted cream and jam, served with a pot of tea. This is known as a Devonshire tea in some other English-speaking countries, but not in England (except of course in the county of Devon, where it's a well-known – and much-hyped – local speciality).

Pubs & Gastropubs

Not so many years ago, a pub was the place to go for a drink. And that was it. If you felt peckish, your choice might be ham or cheese roll, with pickled onions if you were lucky. Today many pubs sell a wide range of food, and some pubs sell more food than drink. Pub food is often a good-value option, too, whether you want a toasted sandwich between museum visits in London, or a three-course meal in the evening after touring castles and stately homes in Yorkshire.

While the food in many pubs is good quality and good value, some places raised the bar to such a degree that a whole new genre of eatery – the gastropub – was born. While some gastropubs are almost

EARLY DOORS, LATE NIGHTS

Pubs in towns and country areas usually open daily, from 11am to 11pm Sunday to Thursday, sometimes to midnight or 1am Friday and Saturday. Most open all day, although some may shut from 3pm to 6pm. Throughout this book, we don't list pub opening and closing times unless they vary significantly from these hours.

In cities, some pubs open until midnight or later, but it's mostly bars and clubs that take advantage of new licensing laws ('the provision of late-night refreshment', as it's officially and charmingly called) to stay open to 1am, 2am or later. As every place is different, we list opening hours for all bars and clubs.

restaurants in style (with smart decor, neat menus and uniformed table service), others have gone for a more relaxed atmosphere, where you'll find mismatched cutlery, no tablecloths, waiters in T-shirts, and today's choices chalked up on a blackboard. And in true pub style, you order and pay at the bar, just as you do for your drinks. The key for all, though, is top-notch no-frills food. For visitors relaxing after a hard day doing the sights, nothing beats the luxury of a wholesome shepherd's pie washed down with a decent ale without the worry of guessing which fork to use.

Favourite Regional Beers – North & Central England

- » Black Sheep – Black Sheep Ale
- » Hook Norton – Hooky Bitter
- » Jennings – Cumberland Ale
- » Kelham Island – Pale Rider
- » Marston's – Pedigree
- » Timothy Taylor – Landlord

Drinking in England

Among alcoholic drinks, England is probably best known for its beer, and as you travel around the country, you should definitely try some local brew. English beer typically ranges from dark brown to bright orange in colour, and is often served at room temperature. Technically it's called ale and is more commonly called 'bitter'. This is to distinguish it from lager – the drink that most of the rest of the word calls 'beer' – which is generally yellow and served cold.

Bitter that's traditionally brewed and served is called 'real ale', to distinguish it from mass-produced brands, and there the many different varieties around England. But be ready! If you're used to the 'amber nectar' or 'king of beers', a local English brew may come as a shock – a warm, flat and expensive shock. This is partly to do with England's climate, and partly to do with the beer being served by hand pump rather than gas pressure. Most important, though, is the integral flavour: traditional English beer doesn't need to be chilled or fizzed to make it palatable.

Another key feature is that real ale must be looked after, usually meaning a willingness on the part of the pub manager or landlord to put in extra effort (often translating into extra effort on food, atmosphere, cleanliness and so on, too). But the extra effort is why many pubs don't serve real ale, so beware of places where bar staff give the barrels as much care as they give the condom machine in the toilets. There's honestly nothing worse than a bad pint of real ale.

Most English beers have an alcohol content of between 3.5% and 5% ABV (alcohol by volume) – though some get nearer 6%. The strongest beers include Duke of Brontë Ale, at a mammoth a 12.5% (yes, the same as wine), produced by the Old Bear Brewery in Keighley, Yorkshire.

If beer doesn't tickle your palate, try cider – available in sweet and dry varieties. In western parts of England, notably Herefordshire and the southwestern counties such as Devon and Somerset, you could try 'scrumpy', a very strong dry cider traditionally made from local apples. Many pubs serve it straight from the barrel.

On hot summer days, you could go for shandy – beer and lemonade mixed in equal quantities. You'll usually need to specify 'lager shandy' or 'bitter shandy'. It may seem an astonishing combination for outsiders,

NAME THAT PASTY

A favourite speciality in southwest England is the Cornish pasty. Originally a mix of cooked vegetables wrapped in pastry, it's often available in meat varieties (much to the scorn of the Cornish people) and now sold everywhere in England. Invented long before Tupperware, the pasty was an all-in-one-lunch pack that tin miners carried underground and left on a ledge ready for mealtime. So pasties weren't mixed up, they were marked with their owners' initials – always at one end, so the miner could eat half and safely leave the rest to snack on later without it mistakenly disappearing into the mouth of a workmate. Before going back to the surface, the miners traditionally left the last few crumbs of the pasty as a gift for the spirits of the mine, known as 'knockers', to ensure a safe shift the next day.

WHERE THERE'S SMOKE

All restaurants and cafes in England are nonsmoking throughout. Virtually all pubs have the same rule, which is why there's often a small crowd of smokers standing on the pavement outside. Some pubs provide specific outdoor smoking areas, ranging from a simple yard to elaborate gazebos with canvas walls and the full complement of lighting, heating, piped music and TV screens – where you'd never need to know you were 'outside' at all, apart from the pungent clouds of burning tobacco.

but it's very refreshing and of course not very strong. Another hybrid is 'snakebite', an equal mix of cider and lager, favoured by students as it's a cost-efficient way to get drunk – thanks to the lager's bubbles and the cider's strength – the very reason some pubs refuse to serve it.

Back to more sensible tipples, many visitors are surprised to learn that wine is produced in England, and has been since the time of the Romans. Today, more than 400 vineyards and wineries produce around two million bottles a year, many of which are highly regarded and frequently winning major awards. English white sparkling wines have been a particular success story in recent years; many are produced in the southeast of the country, where the chalky soil and climatic conditions are similar to those of the Champagne region in France.

Tipplers' tomes for your edification: *Good Beer Guide to Great Britain*, by the Campaign for Real Ale, *Good Pub Guide*, by Alisdair Aird and Fiona Stapley and *300 Beers to Try Before you Die*, by Roger Protz.

Tea for Two

In England, a drink means any ingestible liquid, so if you're from overseas and a local asks 'would you like a drink?', don't automatically expect a gin and tonic. They may well mean a 'cuppa' – a cup of tea – England's best-known beverage. Tea is sometimes billed as the national drink, although coffee is equally popular these days; the Brits consume 165 million cups a day and the British coffee market is worth almost £700 million a year – but with the prices some coffee shops charge, maybe that's not surprising. And a final word of warning: when you're ordering a coffee and the server says 'white or black', don't panic. It simply means 'do you want milk in it?'

Bars & Pubs

In England, the difference between a bar and a pub is sometimes vague, but generally bars are smarter, larger and louder than pubs, possibly with a younger crowd. Drinks are more expensive, too, unless there's a gallon-of-vodka-and-Red-Bull-for-a-fiver promotion – which there often is.

As well as beer, cider, wine and the other drinks mentioned in this chapter, pubs and bars offer the usual choice of spirits, often served with a 'mixer', producing English favourites such as gin and tonic, rum and coke or vodka and lime. These drinks are served in measures called 'singles' and 'doubles'. A single is 35ml – just over one US fluid ounce. A double is of course 70ml – still disappointingly small when compared to measures in other countries. To add further to your disappointment, the vast array of cocktail options, as found in America, is generally restricted to more upmarket city bars in England.

And while we're serving out warnings, here are two more: first, if you see a pub calling itself a 'free house', it's simply a place that doesn't belong to a brewery or pub company, and thus is 'free' to sell any brand of beer. Unfortunately, it doesn't mean the booze is free of charge. Second, remember that drinks in English pubs are ordered and paid for at the bar. You can always spot the freshly arrived tourists – they're the ones sitting forlornly at a empty table hoping to spot a server.

When it comes to gratuities, it's not usual to tip the waiter or waitress. However, if you're ordering a large round, or the service has been

Favourite Regional Beers – South, East & Western England

- Adnams – Southwold Bitter
- Arkell's – 3B
- Fuller's – London Pride
- St Austell – Tribute
- Shepherd Neame – Spitfire
- Wadworth – 6X

THE OLDEST PUB IN ENGLAND?

Many drinkers are often surprised to learn that the word 'pub', short for 'public house', although apparently steeped in history, dates only from the 19th century. But places selling beer have been around for much longer, and the 'oldest pub in England' is a hotly contested title.

One of the country's oldest pubs, with the paperwork to prove it, is Ye Olde Trip to Jerusalem in Nottingham (p454), which was serving ale to departing crusaders in the 12th century.

Other contenders sniff that Ye Olde Trip is a mere newcomer. A fine old inn called the Royalist Hotel in Stow-on-the-Wold, Gloucestershire (p194) claims to have been selling beer since AD 947, while another pub called Ye Olde Fighting Cocks in St Albans (Hertfordshire, p234) apparently dates back to the 8th century – although the 13th is more likely.

But then back comes Ye Olde Trip with a counterclaim: one of its bars is a cave hollowed out of living rock, and that's more than a million years old.

good all evening, you can say to the person behind the bar '... and one for yourself'. They may not have a drink, but they'll add the monetary equivalent to the total you pay and keep it as a tip.

Apart from good service, what makes a good pub? It's often surprisingly hard to pin down, but in our opinion the best pubs follow a remarkably simple formula: they offer a welcoming atmosphere, pleasant surroundings, a good range of hand-pulled beer and a good menu of snacks and meals – cooked on the premises, not shipped in by the truck full and defrosted in the microwave.

After months of painstaking research, this is the type of pub we recommend throughout this book. But, of course, there are many more pubs in England than even we could sample, and nothing beats the fun of doing your own research. So, armed with the advice in this chapter, we urge you to get out there and tipple your taste buds.

Food & Drink Glossary

aubergine	large purple-skinned vegetable; 'eggplant' in the USA and Australia
bangers	sausages (colloquial)
bap	a large, wide, flat, soft bread roll
bevvy	drink (originally from northern England)
bill	the total you need to pay after eating in a restaurant ('check' to Americans)
bitter	ale; a type of beer
black pudding	type of sausage made from dried blood and other ingredients
bun	bread roll, usually sweet, eg currant bun, cream bun
BYO	bring your own (usually in the context of bringing your own drink to a restaurant)
caff	abbreviated form of cafe
candy floss	light sugar-based confectionary; called 'cotton candy' in the USA, 'fairy floss' in Australia
chips	sliced, deep-fried potatoes, eaten hot (what Americans call 'fries')
cider	beer made from apples
clotted cream	cream so heavy or rich that it's become almost solid (but not sour)
corkage	a small charge levied by the restaurant when you BYO (bring your own)
courgette	green vegetable ('zucchini' to Americans)

cream cracker	white unsalted savoury biscuit
cream tea	cup of tea and a scone loaded with jam and cream
crisps	thin slices of fried potato bought in a packet, eaten cold; called 'chips' or 'potato chips' in the USA and Australia
crumpet	circular piece of doughy bread, toasted before eating, usually covered with butter
double cream	heavy or thick cream
dram	whisky measure
fish fingers	strips of fish pieces covered in breadcrumbs, usually bought frozen and cooked by frying or grilling
greasy spoon	cheap café (colloquial)
ice lolly	flavoured ice on a stick; called 'popsicle' in the USA, 'icy pole' in Australia
icing	thick, sweet and solid covering on a cake
jam	fruit conserve often spread on bread
jelly	sweet dessert of flavoured gelatine; called jello in the US
joint	cut of meat used for roasting
kippers	salted and smoked fish, traditionally herring
pickle	a thick, vinegary vegetable-based condiment
Pimms	popular English spirit mixed with lemonade, mint and fresh fruit
pint	beer (as in 'let me buy you a pint')
pop	fizzy drink (northern England)
salad cream	creamy vinegary salad dressing, much sharper than mayonnaise
scrumpy	a type of strong dry cider originally made in England's West Country; many pubs serve it straight from the barrel
shandy	beer and lemonade mixed together in equal quantities; when ordering, specify a bitter shandy or a lager shandy
shepherd's pie	two-layered dish with a ground beef and onion mixture on the bottom and mashed potato on the top, cooked in an oven
shout	to buy a group of people drinks, usually reciprocated (colloquial)
single cream	light cream (to distinguish from *double cream* and *clotted cream*)
snakebite	equal mix of cider and lager; favoured by students as it reputedly gets you drunk quickly
snug	usually a small separate room in a pub
squash	fruit drink concentrate mixed with water
stout	dark, full-bodied beer made from malt; Guinness is the most famous variety
swede	large root vegetable; sometimes called 'yellow turnip' or 'rutabaga' in the USA
sweets	what Americans call 'candy' and Australians call 'lollies' or 'cakes'
tipple	an old-fashioned word for drink, often used ironically, eg 'Do you fancy a tipple?'; a tippler is a drinker
treacle	molasses or dark syrup

Architecture in England

With an architectural heritage that stretches back three millennia or more, the many different buildings of England – from simple cottages to grand cathedrals – are an obvious highlight of any visit.

The construction of Stonehenge pushed the limits of technology in the Neolithic era. Some giant menhirs were brought from a great distance, while the standing stones were shaped slightly wider at the top to take account of perspective – a trick used by the Greeks many centuries later.

Early Foundations

The oldest buildings in the country are the grass-covered mounds of earth, called 'tumuli' or 'barrows', used as burial sites by England's prehistoric residents. These mounds – measuring anything from a rough semisphere just 2m high to much larger, elongated semi-ovoids 5m high and 10m long – are dotted across the countryside from Cornwall to Cumbria, and are espcecially common in chalk areas such as Salisbury Plain and the Wiltshire Downs in southern England.

Perhaps the most famous barrow– and certainly the largest and most mysterious – is Silbury Hill, near Marlborough. Historians are not sure exactly why this huge conical mound was built – there's no evidence of it actually being used for burial. Theories suggest it was used at cultural ceremonies or as part of the worship of deities in the style of South American pyramids, but whatever is original purpose, it's still very impressive today, many centuries after it was built.

Even more impressive than giant tumuli are another legacy of the Neolithic era: menhirs, or standing stones, especially well known when they're set out in rings. These include the iconic stone circle of Stonehenge and the even larger Avebury Stone Circle, both in Wiltshire.

Bronze Age & Iron Age

There are over a thousand Iron Age hill forts in England. Impressive examples include: Danebury Ring, Hampshire; Barbury Castle, Wiltshire; Uffington Castle, Oxfordshire; Carl Wark, Derbyshire and Cadbury Castle, Somerset.

After the large stone circles of the Neolithic era, the architecture of the Bronze Age that we can see today is on a more domestic scale. Hut circles from this period can still be seen in several parts of England, most notably on Dartmoor.

By the time we reach the Iron Age, the early peoples of England were organising themselves into clans or tribes. Their legacy includes the forts they built to defend territory and protect themselves from rival tribes or other invaders. Most forts consisted of a large circular or oval ditch, with a steep mound of earth behind. A famous example is Maiden Castle in Dorset.

The Roman Era

Roman remains are found in many English towns and cities, including Chester, Exeter and St Albans – as well as the lavish Roman spa and bathing complex in Bath. But England's largest and most impressive Roman relic is the 73-mile sweep of Hadrian's Wall, built in the 2nd century AD as a defensive line stretching coast to coast across the country.

Originally built to separate marauding Pictish warriors to the north of the wall (in modern Scotland) from the Empire's territories to the south, it later became as much a symbol of Roman power as a necessary defence mechanism. For more information on the wall, see p760).

Castles & Cathedrals

In the centuries following the Norman Invasion of 1066, England saw an explosion of architecture inspired by the two most pressing concerns of the day: worship and defence. Churches, abbeys, monasteries and minsters sprang up during the early Middle Ages, as did many landmark cathedrals, such as Salisbury and Canterbury, and York Minster.

As for castles, you're spoilt for choice: England's strongholds range from the atmospheric ruins of Tintagel and Dunstanburgh and the feudal keeps of Lancaster and Bamburgh to the large and sturdy fortresses of Warwick and Windsor. And then there's the most impressive of them all – the Tower of London, guardian of the capital for more than 1000 years. (p67).

England's Top Castles

- Alnwick Castle
- Bamburgh Castle
- Berkeley Castle
- Carlisle Castle
- Corfe Castle
- Ludlow Castle
- Richmond Castle
- Skipton Castle
- Tintagel Castle
- Tower of London
- Warwick Castle
- Windsor Castle

Stately Homes

The medieval period was tumultuous, but by around 1600 life became more settled, and the nobility started to have less need for their castles. While they were excellent for keeping out rivals or the common riff-raff, they were often too dark, cold and draughty to be comfortable. So many castles saw the home improvements of the day – the installation of larger windows, wider staircases and better drainage. Others were simply abandoned for a brand new dwelling next door; an example of this is Hardwick Hall in Derbyshire.

Following the Civil War, the trend away from castles gathered pace, as through the 17th century the landed gentry developed a taste for fine 'country houses' designed by the most famous architects of the day. Many became the 'stately homes' that are a major feature of the English landscape, and a major attraction for visitors. Among the most extravagant are Holkham Hall in Norfolk, Chatsworth House in Derbyshire, and Blenheim Palace in Oxfordshire.

The great stately homes all display the proportion, symmetry and architectural harmony so in vogue during the 17th and 18th centuries, styles later reflected in the fashionable town houses of the Georgian era – most notably in the city of Bath, where the stunning Royal Crescent is the epitome of the genre.

Victoriana

The Victorian era was a time of great building. A style called Victorian-Gothic developed, echoing the towers and spires that were such a feature of the original Gothic cathedrals. The most famous example of this style is the Palace of Westminster, better known as the Houses of Parliament, and the Tower of Big Ben, in London. Other highlights include London's Natural History Museum and St Pancras train station.

CHALK FIGURES

As you travel around England, look out for the chalk figures gracing many of the country's hilltops. They're made by cutting through the turf to reveal the white chalk soil below, so they're obviously found in chalk areas – most notably in southwestern England, especially the counties of Dorset and Wiltshire. Some figures, such as the Uffington White Horse, date from the Bronze Age, but most are more recent; the formidably endowed Cerne Abbas Giant is often thought to be an ancient pagan figure, although recent research suggests it was etched sometime in the 17th century.

Through the early 20th century, as England's cities grew in size and stature, the newly moneyed middle classes built streets and squares of smart town houses. Meanwhile, in other suburbs the first town planners oversaw the construction of endless terraces of red-brick two-up-two-down houses to accommodate the massive influx of workers required to fuel the country's factories – not especially scenic but perhaps the most enduring mark of all on the English architectural landscape today.

England's Finest Stately Homes

- Audley End House
- Blickling Hall
- Burghley House
- Blenheim Palace
- Castle Howard
- Chastleton House
- Chatsworth House
- Cotehele
- Harewood House
- Leeds Castle
- Snowshill Manor
- Waddesdon Manor

Postwar

During WWII many of England's cities were damaged by bombing, and the rebuilding that followed showed scant regard for the overall aesthetic of the cities, or for the lives of the people who lived in them. The rows of terraces were swept away in favour of high-rise tower blocks, while the 'brutalist' architects of the 1950s and '60s employed the modern and efficient materials of steel and concrete, leaving legacies such as London's South Bank Centre.

Perhaps this is why, on the whole, the English are conservative in their architectural tastes, and often resent ambitious or experimental designs, especially when they're applied to public buildings, or when form appears more important than function. But a familiar pattern often unfolds: after a few years of resentment, first comes a nickname, then grudging acceptance, and finally – once the locals have got used to it – comes pride and affection for the new building. The English just don't like to be rushed, that's all.

With this attitude in mind, over the last few decades, English architecture has started to redeem itself, and many big cities now have contemporary buildings their residents can enjoy and be proud of. Highlights in London's financial district include the bulging cone of the Swiss Re building (inevitably dubbed 'the Gherkin') and the former Millennium Dome (now rebranded as simply the O2), which has been transformed from a source of national embarrassment into one of the capital's leading live-music venues.

One simple English cottage thrust into the limelight was Gold Hill, Shaftsbury – thanks to a favourite TV ad for Hovis bread. Meanwhile, movie appearances of the main (and only) street in Wiltshire village Castle Combe range from 1967's *Dr Doolittle* to Steven Spielberg's latest blockbuster, *Warhorse*.

21st Century

Beyond London, many areas of England place a new importance on progressive, popular architecture as a part of wider regeneration. Top examples include Manchester's Imperial War Museum North, Birmingham's Bullring shopping centre, Cornwall's futuristic Eden Project, The Deep aquarium in Hull, and the Sage concert hall in Gateshead, Northeast England.

Skyscrapers are back in fashion again in many of England's cities: in the past few years Leeds, Manchester, Brighton and Birmingham all announced plans for new buildings over 200m high. Top of the heap, however, is the London Bridge Tower (because of its shape, it was quickly nicknamed 'the Shard'), which, at 306m, is set to become one of Europe's tallest buildings when it's completed around 2012.

But wait, there may be more. Although construction has yet to start, two more giant skyscrapers are planned, and yes, they already have

HOUSE & HOME

It's not all about big houses. Alongside the stately homes, ordinary domestic architecture from the 16th century onwards can also still be seen in rural areas: black-and-white 'half-timbered' houses still characterise counties such as Worcestershire, while brick-and-flint cottages pepper Suffolk and Sussex, and hardy centuries-old farms built with slate or local gritstone are a feature of areas such as Derbyshire and the Lake District.

nicknames. Ladies and gentlemen, I give you 'the Walkie-Talkie' and 'the Cheese-grater'. We look forward to seeing these new marvels for real some time in the next decade.

So London continues to grow upwards, and English architecture continues to push new boundaries of style and technology. The buildings may look a little different, but it's great to see the spirit of Stonehenge alive and well after all these years.

Glossary of English Architecture

aisle	passageway or open space along either side of a church's *nave*
apse	area for clergy, traditionally at the east end of the church
bailey	outermost wall of a castle
bar	gate (York, and some other northern cities)
barrel vault	semicircular arched roof
boss	covering for the meeting point of the ribs in a *vaulted* roof
brass	memorial consisting of a brass plate set into the floor or a tomb
buttress	vertical support for a wall; see also *flying buttress*
campanile	free-standing belfry or bell tower
chancel	eastern end of the church, usually reserved for choir and clergy
chantry	*chapel* established by a donor for use in their name after death
chapel	small church; shrine or area of worship off the main body of a cathedral
chapel of ease	*chapel* built for those who lived far away from the parish church
choir	area in the church where the choir is seated
cloister	covered walkway linking the church with adjacent monastic buildings
close	buildings grouped around a cathedral
cob	mixture of mud and straw for building
corbel	stone or wooden projection from a wall supporting a beam or arch
crossing	intersection of the *nave* and *transepts* in a church
EH	English Heritage
flying buttress	supporting *buttress* in the form of one side of an open arch
font	basin used for baptisms, often in a separate *baptistry*
frater	common or dining room in a medieval monastery
lady chapel	*chapel* dedicated to the Virgin Mary
lancet	pointed window in Early English style
lierne vault	*vault* containing many tertiary ribs
Martello tower	small, circular tower used for coastal defence
minster	church connected to a monastery
misericord	hinged choir seat with a bracket (often elaborately carved)
nave	main body of the church at the western end, where the congregation gather
NT	National Trust
oast house	building containing a kiln for drying hops
pargeting	decorative stucco plasterwork
pele	fortified house
presbytery	eastern area of *chancel* beyond the choir, where the clergy operate
precincts	see *close*
priory	religious house governed by a prior

pulpit	raised box where the priest gives sermons
quire	medieval term for *choir*
refectory	monastic dining room
reredos	literally 'behind the back'; backdrop to an altar
rood	archaic word for cross (in churches)
rood screen	screen carrying a *rood* or crucifix, separating *nave* from *chancel*
squint	angled opening in a wall or pillar to allow a view of a church's altar
transepts	north–south projections from a church's *nave*, giving church a cruciform (cross-shaped plan)
undercroft	vaulted underground room or cellar
vault	roof with arched ribs, usually in a decorative pattern
vestry	priest's robing room

The English Landscape

England maybe small, but even a relatively short journey can take you through a surprising mix of landscapes. Seeing the change – subtle in some areas, dramatic in others – as you travel through the landscape is one of this country's great drawcards.

Southern England's countryside is gently undulating, with a few hilly areas like the Cotswolds, and farmland between the towns and cities. East Anglia is mainly low and flat, while the Southwest Peninsula has wild moors and rich pastures – hence Devon's world-famous cream – with a rugged coast and sheltered beaches that make it a favourite holiday destination.

In England's north, farmland remains interspersed with towns and cities, but the landscape is bumpier. A line of large hills called the Pennines (fondly tagged 'the backbone of England') runs from Derbyshire to the Scottish border, and includes the peaty plateaus of the Peak District, the delightful valleys of the Yorkshire Dales and the frequently windswept but ruggedly beautiful moors of Northumberland.

Perhaps England's best-known landscape is the Lake District, a small but spectacular cluster of hills and mountains in the northwest, where Scafell Pike (a towering 978m) is England's highest peak.

National Parks

Back in 1810, English poet and outdoor fan William Wordsworth suggested that the wild landscape of the Lake District in Cumbria, northwest England, should be 'a sort of national property, in which every man has a right'. More than a century later, the Lake District did indeed become a national park, along with Dartmoor, Exmoor, the New Forest, Norfolk and Suffolk Broads, Northumberland, the North York Moors, the Peak District, the South Downs and the Yorkshire Dales.

But the term 'national park' can cause confusion. First, they are not state-owned: nearly all land is private, belonging to farmers, private

Comparing Coverage

These essential measurements may be handy for planning or perspective as you travel around:

» **England** 50,000 sq miles

» **Britain** 88,500 sq miles

» **UK** 95,000 sq miles

» **British Isles** 123,000 sq miles

By comparison, France is about 212,000 sq miles, Australia 2.7 million sq miles and the USA about 3.5 million sq miles.

BEACHES

England has a great many beaches – from tiny hidden coves in Cornwall to vast neon-lined strands such as Brighton or Blackpool. Other great beaches can be found in Devon, Somerset and along the south coast, in Suffolk, Norfolk, Lancashire, Yorkshire and Northumberland – each with its own distinct character. The best resort beaches earn the coveted international **Blue Flag** (www.blueflag.org) award, meaning sand and water are clean and unpolluted. Other parameters include the presence of lifeguards, litter bins and recycling facilities – meaning some wild beaches may not earn the award, but are stunning nonetheless.

estates and conservation organisations. Second, they are *not* areas of wilderness as in many other countries.

In England's national parks you'll see crop fields in lower areas and grazing sheep on the uplands, as well as roads, railways and villages, and even towns, quarries and factories in some parks. It's a reminder of the balance that needs to be struck in this crowded country between protecting the natural environment and catering for the people who live in it.

Despite these apparent anomalies, England's national parks still contain mountains, hills, downs, moors, woods, river valleys and other areas of quiet countryside, all ideal for long walks, easy rambles, cycle rides, sightseeing or just lounging around.

As well as national parks, other parts of the England are designated as Areas of Outstanding Natural Beauty (AONBs), the second tier of protected landscape after national parks. There are also Conservation Areas, Sites of Special Scientific Interest and many others that you'll undoubtedly come across as you travel around.

Top Areas of Outstanding Natural Beauty

- Chilterns
- Cornwall
- Cotswolds
- Isles of Scilly
- North Pennines
- Northumberland Coast
- Suffolk Coast
- Wye Valley

Wildlife

For a small country, England has a diverse range of plants and animals. Many native species are hidden away, but there are some undoubted gems – from lowland woods carpeted in shimmering bluebells to stately herds of deer on the high moors – and taking the time to have a closer look will enhance your trip enormously, especially if you have the time and inclination to enjoy some walking through the English landscape. For more ideas on this, see (p36).

Wildlife & Walking Books

- *Wildlife Walks*, published by the Wildlife Trusts
- *Walking In Britain*, Lonely Planet
- *Wildlife Walks in Britain*, published by the AA

Animals

In farmland areas, rabbits are everywhere, but if you're hiking through the countryside, be on the lookout for brown hares, an increasingly rare species. They're related to rabbits but much larger. Males who battle for territory by boxing on their hind legs in early spring are, of course, as 'mad as a March hare'.

Although hare numbers are on the decline, down on the riverbank the once-rare otter is making a comeback. Elsewhere, the black-and-white striped badger is under threat from farmers who believe they transmit bovine tuberculosis to cattle, although conservationists say the case is far from proven.

Common birds of farmland and similar landscapes (and urban gardens) include the robin, with its instantly recognisable red breast and cheerful whistle; the wren, whose loud trilling song belies its tiny size; and the yellowhammer, with a song that sounds like (if you use your

WILDLIFE IN YOUR POCKET

Is it a rabbit or a hare? A gull or a tern? Buttercup or cowslip? If you need to know a bit more about England's plant and animal kingdoms the following field guides are ideal for entry-level naturalists:

- *Complete Guide to British Wildlife* by Paul Sterry is portable and highly recommended, covering mammals, birds, fish, plants, snakes, insects and even fungi, with brief descriptions and excellent photos.
- If feathered friends are enough, the *Complete Guide to British Birds* by Paul Sterry has clear photos and descriptions, plus when and where each species may be seen.
- *Wildlife of the North Atlantic* by world-famous film-maker Tony Soper beautifully covers the animals seen from beach, boat and clifftop in the British Isles and beyond.
- The Collins GEM series includes handy little books on wildlife topics such as *Birds*, *Trees*, *Fish* and *Wild Flowers*.

'THE UNSPEAKABLE IN PURSUIT OF THE INEDIBLE'

Fox hunting has been a traditional English countryside activity (or a savage blood sport, depending on whom you talk to) for centuries, but it was banned in 2005 by a controversial law. As this activity killed only a small proportion of the total fox population, opinion is still divided on whether the ban has had any impact on numbers.

imagination) 'a-little-bit-of-bread-and-no-cheese'. In open fields, the warbling cry of a skylark is another classic, but now threatened, sound of the English outdoors. You're more likely to see a pheasant, a large bird originally introduced from Russia to the nobility's shooting estates, but now considered naturalised.

In woodland areas, mammals include the small white-spotted fallow deer and the even smaller roe deer. Woodland is full of birds too, but you'll hear them more than see them. Listen out for willow warblers (which have a warbling song with a descending cadence) and chiffchaffs (which, also not surprisingly, make a repetitive 'chiff chaff' noise).

If you hear rustling among the fallen leaves it might be a hedgehog – a cute-looking, spiny-backed insect eater – but it's an increasingly rare sound these days; conservationists say they'll be extinct in Britain by 2025, thanks to insecticides in farming, increased building in rural areas and hedgehogs' notoriously poor ability to safely cross roads.

In contrast, foxes are widespread and well adapted to a scavenging life in rural towns, and even city suburbs. Grey squirrels (introduced from North America) have also proved very adaptable, to the extent that native red squirrels are severely endangered because the greys eat all the food.

Perhaps unexpectedly, England is home to herds of 'wild' ponies, notably in the New Forest, Exmoor and Dartmoor, but although these animals roam free they are privately owned and regularly managed. There's even a pocket of wild goats near Lynmouth in Devon, where they've apparently gambolled merrily for almost 1000 years.

On mountains and high moors – including the Lake District and Northumberland – the most visible mammal is the red deer. Males of the species grow their famous large antlers between April and July, and shed them again in February. Also on the high ground, well known and easily recognised birds include the red grouse, which often hides in the heather until almost stepped on then flies away with a loud warning call, and the curlew, with its stately long legs and elegant curved bill. Look hard, and you may see beautifully camouflaged golden plovers, while the spectacular aerial displays of lapwings are impossible to miss.

Down by the sea, mammals include seals, and in areas such as Norfolk and Northumberland, boat trips to see their colonies are a popular attraction. Estuaries and mudflats are feeding grounds for numerous migrant wading birds, easily spotted are black-and-white oystercatchers with their long red bills, while flocks of ringed plovers skitter along the sand.

On the coastal cliffs in early summer, particularly in Cornwall and Yorkshire, countless thousands of guillemots, razorbills, kittiwakes and other breeding seabirds fight for space on crowded rock ledges, and the air is thick with their sound. Even if you're not into birdwatching, this is one of England's finest wildlife spectacles.

Plants

In the hill country of southern England and the limestone areas further north (such as the Peak District and Yorkshire Dales), the best place to see wildflowers are the fields that evade large-scale farming – many erupt with great profusions of cowslips and primroses in April and May.

Britain's Best Wildlife by Chris Pacham and Mike Dilger is a 'Top 40' countdown of favourites compiled by experts and the public, with details on when and where to see the country's wildlife at its finest.

Wildlife of Britain by George McGavin et al is subtitled 'the definitive visual guide'. Although too heavy to carry around, this beautiful photographic book is great for pre-trip inspiration or post-trip memories.

Perhaps surprisingly, England's most wooded county is Surrey, despite its proximity to London. The soil is too poor for agriculture, so while woodland areas elsewhere in England were cleared, Surrey's trees got a stay of execution.

SEA LIFE

Two seal species frequent English coasts: the larger grey seal, which is more often seen, and the misnamed common seal. Dolphins, porpoises, minke whales and basking sharks can also be seen off the western coasts, especially from about May to September when viewing conditions are better – although you may need to go with someone who knows where to look. Boat trips are available from many coastal holiday resorts.

Britain's new 'hedgerows' are the long strips of grass and bushes alongside motorways and major roads. Rarely trod by humans, they support rare flowers, thousands of insect species plus mice, shrews and other small mammals – so kestrels are often seen hovering nearby.

For woodland flowers, the best time is also April and May, before the leaf canopy is fully developed so sunlight can reach plants such as bluebells – a beautiful and internationally rare species. Another classic English plant is gorse: you can't miss the swaths of this spiky bush in heath areas like the New Forest. Its vivid yellow flowers show year-round.

In contrast, the blooming season for heather is quite short, but no less dramatic; through August and September areas such as the North York Moors and Dartmoor are covered in a riot of purple.

Environmental Issues

With England's long history of human occupation, it's not surprising that the country's appearance is almost totally the result of human interaction with the environment. Since the earliest times, people have been chopping down trees and creating fields for crops or animals, but the most dramatic changes in rural areas came after WWII in the late 1940s, continuing into the '50s and '60s, when a drive to be self-reliant in food meant new – intensive and large-scale – farming methods. The visible result: an ancient patchwork of small meadows became a landscape of vast prairies, as walls were demolished, woodlands felled, ponds filled, wetlands drained and, most notably, hedgerows ripped out.

In most cases the hedgerows were lines of dense bushes, shrubs and trees forming a network that stretched across the countryside, protecting fields from erosion, supporting a varied range of flowers, and providing shelter for numerous insects, birds and small mammals. But in the rush to improve farm yields, thousands of miles of hedgerows were destroyed in the postwar decades, and between the mid-1980s and the early 2000s another 25% disappeared.

Hedgerows have come to symbolise many other environmental issues in rural areas, and in recent years the destruction has abated, partly because farmers recognise their anti-erosion qualities, and partly because they're encouraged – with financial incentives from UK or European agencies – to 'set aside' such areas as wildlife havens.

Landscape & Environment Online

» www.wildaboutbritain.co.uk

» www.environment-agency.gov.uk

» www.nationalparks.gov.uk

» www.aonb.org.uk

In addition to hedgerow clearance, other farming techniques remain hot environmental issues. Studies have shown that the use of pesticides and intensive irrigation results in rivers running dry or being poisoned by run-off. Meanwhile, monocropping means vast fields have one type of grass and not another plant to be seen. These 'green deserts' support no insects, so in turn wild bird populations have plummeted. This is not a case of wizened old peasants recalling the idyllic days of their forbears; you only have to be over about 40 in England to remember a countryside where birds such as skylarks or lapwings were visibly much more numerous.

But all is not lost. In the face of apparently overwhelming odds, England still boasts great biodiversity, and some of the best wildlife habitats are protected (to a greater or lesser extent) by the creation of national parks and similar areas, or private reserves owned by conservation campaign groups such as the **Wildlife Trusts** (www.wildlifetrusts.org), **Woodland Trust** (www.woodland-trust.org), **National Trust**

ENGLAND'S TOP NATIONAL PARKS

NATIONAL PARK	FEATURES	ACTIVITIES	BEST TIME TO VISIT	PAGE
Dartmoor National Park	rolling hills, rocky outcrops and serene valleys; wild ponies, deer, peregrine falcons	walking, mountain biking, horse riding	May-Jun (wildflowers in bloom)	p356
Exmoor National Park	sweeping moors and craggy sea cliffs; red deer, wild ponies, horned sheep	horse riding, walking	Sep (heather in bloom)	p331
Lake District	majestic fells, rugged mountains and shimmering lakes; ospreys, red squirrels, golden eagles	water sports, walking, mountaineering, rock climbing	Sep-Oct (summer crowds have left and autumn colours abound)	p691
New Forest	woodlands and heath; wild ponies, otters, Dartford warbler, southern damselfly	walking, cycling, horse riding	Apr-Sep (lush vegetation, wild ponies grazing)	p258
Norfolk & Suffolk Broads	expansive shallow lakes, rivers and marshlands; water lilies, wildfowl, otters	walking, cycling, boating	Apr-May (birds most active)	p438
North York Moors National Park	heather-clad hills, deep-green valleys, lonely farms and isolated villages; merlins, curlews and golden plovers	walking, mountain biking	Aug-Sep (heather flowering)	p618
Northumberland National Park	wild rolling moors, heather and gorse; black grouse, red squirrels; Hadrian's Wall	walking, cycling, climbing	Apr-May (lambs) & Sep (heather flowering)	p765
Peak District National Park	high moors, tranquil dales, limestone caves; kestrels, badgers, grouse	walking, cycling, mountain biking, hang-gliding, rock climbing	Apr-May (even more lambs)	p484
South Downs National Park	rolling grassy chalky hills, chalky sea-cliffs, gorse, heather; Adonis blue butterfly	walking, mountain biking	Aug (when the heather blooms)	p158
Yorkshire Dales	rugged hills and lush valleys crossed by stone walls and dotted with monastic ruins	walking, cycling, climbing	Apr-May (you guessed it, when lambs outnumber visitors)	p582

(www.nationaltrust.org.uk) and the **Royal Society for the Protection of Birds** (www.rspb.org.uk). Many of these areas are open to the public – ideal spots for walking, birdwatching or simply enjoying the peace and beauty of the countryside – and well worth a visit as you travel around.

English Literature

The roots of England's literary heritage stretch back to Norse sagas and Early English epics such as *Beowulf*. As the English language spread around the world, especially in the colonial era, so too did English literature, so that the poetry and prose of this small country is surprisingly well known far from its original homeland.

As you travel around the country today you'll see numerous towns and cities with literary links, as well as humble villages and grand stately homes, not to mention forests, beaches and mountain ranges that feature in novels, poems and other works. Wherever possible in this chapter we've mentioned real places where you can experience something of the life of your favourite poets and novelists or even walk in the footsteps of their characters.

For extra insight while travelling, the *Oxford Literary Guide to Great Britain & Ireland* edited by Daniel Hahn and Nicholas Robins gives details of towns, villages and countryside immortalised by writers, from Chaucer's Canterbury and Austen's Bath to Philip Pullman's Oxford.

First Stars

Modern English literature starts around 1387 (yes, that is 'modern' in history-soaked England) when the nation's first literary giant, Geoffrey Chaucer, produced *The Canterbury Tales*. Still a classic today, this mammoth poem is a collection of fables, stories and morality tales using travelling pilgrims – the Knight, the Wife of Bath, the Nun's Priest and so on – as a narrative hook.

The next big name came two centuries later, when William Shakespeare entered the scene. Still England's best-known playwright, he also wrote about 150 poems. Perhaps his most famous poetic line is 'Shall I compare thee to a summer's day?' from Sonnet 18.

The 17th & 18th Centuries

The early 17th century saw the rise of the metaphysical poets, including John Donne, Andrew Marvell and George Herbert. Their vivid imagery and far-fetched 'conceits', or comparisons, daringly pushed the boundaries. In 'A Valediction: Forbidding Mourning', for instance, Donne compares the points of a compass with a pair of conjoined lovers. Racy stuff in its day.

Another key landmark came in 1667 with the publication of John Milton's *Paradise Lost,* an epic poem inspired by the biblical tale of Adam and Eve's expulsion from the Garden of Eden, swiftly followed in 1678 by the equally seminal *Pilgrim's Progress* by John Bunyan, an allegorical tale of the everyday Christian struggle. For mere mortals, reading these books in their entirety can be hard going, but they're worth dipping into for a taste of the rich language. On a rather more prosaic level, everyday London life of the time is richly captured in the wonderful *Diary of Samuel Pepys*.

During the early 18th century, English literature took on a new political edge, with works such as Alexander Pope's 'The Rape of the Lock' attacking the mores of contemporary society. Daniel Defoe wrote *Robinson Crusoe*, seen by many scholars as the first English novel. It's also a discussion on civilisation, colonialism and faith, and has been a travel-lit blockbuster since its publication in 1719. It was later parodied by the Anglo-Irish writer Jonathan Swift in his satirical study of human nature, *Gulliver's Travels*.

As the Pennine moors haunt Brontë novels, so the marshy Cambridgeshire Fens dominate *Waterland* by Graham Swift – a tale of personal and national history, betrayal and compassion, and rated a landmark work of the 1980s.

The Romantic & Gothic Era

As the Industrial Revolution began to take hold in the late 18th and early 19th century, the response from a new generation of writers was to draw inspiration from the natural world and the human imagination (in many cases helped along by a healthy dose of laudanum). Leading lights of the movement were William Blake, John Keats, Percy Bysshe Shelley, Lord Byron and Samuel Taylor Coleridge, and perhaps the best known of all, William Wordsworth, a resident of the English Lake District. His famous line from 'Daffodils', 'I wandered lonely as a cloud', was inspired by a hike in the hills.

Gothic literature took the power of the human imagination a step further – to create horror rather than joy. A classic Gothic text is Mary Shelley's *Frankenstein*, a cautionary tale about the dangers of human ambition and perverted technology, a meditation on a post-Enlightenment society facing up to a godless world, and often cited as the world's first work of science fiction.

Victoriana

Next came the reign of Queen Victoria and the era of industrial expansion, so key novels of the time explored social and political themes. Charles Dickens especially tackled many prevailing issues of his day: in *Oliver Twist*, he captures the lives of young thieves in the London slums; *Bleak House* is a critique of the English legal system; and *Hard Times* criticises the excesses of capitalism. At around the same time, but choosing a rural setting, George Eliot (the pen-name of Mary Anne Evans) wrote *The Mill on the Floss* – where the central character, Maggie Tulliver, looks for true love and struggles against society's expectations.

Meanwhile, Thomas Hardy's classic *Tess of the D'Urbervilles* deals with the peasantry's decline, and *The Trumpet Major* paints a picture of idyllic English country life interrupted by war and encroaching modernity. Many of Hardy's works are based in the fictionalised county

AUSTEN & THE BRONTËS

As the 19th century dawned, a new generation of writers used the trials and tribulations of English society as the basis for their novels. Best known and best loved are Jane Austen and the Brontë sisters.

Two centuries after her death, Jane Austen is still one of England's best-known novelists, thanks to her exquisite observations of class, society, love, friendship, intrigues and passions boiling under the stilted preserve of provincial middle-class social convention – and in no small part to an endless stream of movies and TV costume dramas based on her works, such as *Pride and Prejudice* and *Sense and Sensibility*. For visitors today, the location most associated with Jane Austen is the city of Bath – a beautiful place even without the literary link. As one of her heroines said, 'who can ever be tired of Bath?'.

Other major figures from this era are the Brontë sisters. Of the family's prodigious output, Emily Brontë's *Wuthering Heights* is the best known – an epic tale of obsession and revenge, where the dark and moody landscape plays a role as great as any human character. Charlotte Brontë's *Jane Eyre* and Anne Brontë's *The Tenant of Wildfell Hall* are classics of passion, mystery and love. Fans still flock to their former home in the Yorkshire town of Haworth, perched on the edge of the wild Pennine moors that inspired so many of their books.

of Wessex, largely based on today's Dorset and surrounding counties, where towns such as Dorchester are popular stops on tourist itineraries.

While Dickens and Hardy tackled issues at home, other writers explored Britain's rapidly expanding frontiers abroad, notably Rudyard Kipling, perhaps the classic chronicler of empire, in works such as *Gunga Din* and *The Jungle Book*.

Helen Fielding's book *Bridget Jones's Diary*, originally a series of newspaper articles, is a fond look at the heartache of a modern single woman's blundering search for love, and the epitome of the late-1990s 'chick-lit' genre. It's also very loosely based on *Pride and Prejudice* by Jane Austen. Very loosely.

The 20th Century

England – and its literature – changed forever following the devastating carnage of WWI. Patriotic poems such as Rupert Brooke's *The Soldier* ('If I should die, think only this of me...') gave way to excoriating dissections of the false glory of war in the work of Siegfried Sassoon and Wilfred Owen. Even Kipling recanted his unquestioning devotion to the English cause following the death of his only son in the war; his devastating refrain 'If any question why we died/Tell them, because our fathers lied' has since become a mantra for the anti-war movement.

The ideological chaos and social disruption of the postwar period fed into the fractured narratives of modernism. Perhaps the greatest English novelist of the interwar period is DH Lawrence, best known for *Sons and Lovers,* which follows the lives and loves of generations in the English Midlands as the country changes from rural idyll to an increasingly industrial landscape, and his controversial exploration of sexuality in *Lady Chatterley's Lover,* originally banned as 'obscene'.

Other highlights of the interwar years included EM Forster's *A Passage to India*, about the hopelessness of British colonial rule, Daphne du Maurier's romantic suspense novel *Rebecca,* set on the Cornish coast, and Evelyn Waugh's exploration of moral and social disintegration in *Vile Bodies* and *Brideshead Revisited*. Another major figure was Virginia Woolf; her best-known novel, *To the Lighthouse*, also set in Cornwall, examines the impact of war on English society, the emotional clash between men and women, and the need for artists to balance their creativity with the demands of real life. In a different world entirely, JRR Tolkien published *The Hobbit*, trumping it some 20 years later with his awesome trilogy *The Lord of the Rings*.

Graham Greene's novel *Brighton Rock* (1938) is a classic account of wayward English youth. For an even more shocking take, try Anthony Burgess' *A Clockwork Orange*, later infamously filmed by Stanley Kubrick in 1971 and withdrawn in the UK following a spate of violent copycat acts.

The chaos of WWII led to a new wave of self-examination and paranoia. George Orwell wrote his closely observed studies of totalitarian rule, *Animal Farm* and *1984* (the novel that gave Big Brother to the wider world), while the Cold War inspired Graham Greene's *Our Man in Havana*, in which a secret agent studies the workings of a vacuum cleaner to inspire fictitious spying reports.

Another spook of that period was Ian Fleming's full-blooded English hero James Bond – today better known as a movie franchise. He first appeared in 1953 in the book *Casino Royale*, then swashbuckled through numerous thrillers for another decade.

Alongside the novelists, the first half of the 20th century was a great time for poets. Big names include WH Auden's 'Funeral Blues' and TS Eliot's epic *The Wasteland*, although he is better know for *Old Possum's Book of Practical Cats* – turned into the musical *Cats* by Andrew Lloyd Webber. Different was the gritty verse of Ted Hughes, while fellow 1960s writer Roger McGough and friends determined to make art relevant to daily life and produced *The Mersey Sound* – landmark pop poetry for the streets.

The 1970s saw the arrival of two big names. Martin Amis, aged 24, published *The Rachel Papers* in 1974, and has been getting up the noses of the establishment ever since, while Ian McEwan debuted with *The Cement Garden* in 1978 and went on to find critical acclaim with finely observed studies of the English character such as *Atonement* and *On Chesil Beach*.

The New Millennium

As the 20th century came to a close, the nature of multicultural Britain proved a rich inspiration for contemporary novelists. Hanif Kurieshi sowed the seeds with his groundbreaking 1990 novel *The Buddha of Suburbia*, which examined the hopes and fears of a group of suburban Anglo-Asians in London. Other star novelists covering (loosely defined) 'multicultural England' themes include: Zadie Smith, who published her acclaimed debut *White Teeth* in 2000 followed by a string of literary best sellers, including *The Autograph Man*; Monica Ali, whose *Brick Lane* was shortlisted for the 2003 Man Booker Prize; Hari Kunzru, who received one of the largest advances in publishing history in 2002 for his debut *The Impressionist*; and Andrea Levy, winner of the 2004 Orange Prize for her novel *Small Island*, about a Jamaican couple settled in postwar London.

Other contemporary writers worth seeking out include: Will Self, known for his surreal, satirical novels, including his most recent book, *Liver*, a typically imaginative tale that explores the livers of four London characters in various stages of disease, decay and disintegration; David Mitchell, whose multilayered, time-bending *Cloud Atlas* marked him out as a writer to watch; and Sarah Waters, a gifted novelist who often places lesbian issues at the core of her work in books such as *Tipping the Velvet* and *Night Watch*.

At the more popular end is the best-selling author Nick Hornby, chronicling the fragilities and insecurities of the English middle-class male in novels like *Fever Pitch* and *High Fidelity*. Sebastian Faulks, meanwhile, established himself with his wartime novels *Birdsong* and *Charlotte Gray*. Faulks was recently chosen to write the first new James Bond novel in over 50 years to mark the centenary of Ian Fleming's birth; the resulting *Devil May Care* has since become one of the fastest selling hardbacks ever published, shifting over 44,000 copies in its first four days.

But even James Bond can't hold a candle to the literary phenomenon that is JK Rowling's *Harry Potter* series, the magical adventures that have entertained millions of children (and a fair few adults too) over the last decade. The books are the latest in a long line of English children's classics stretching back to the works of Lewis Carroll (*Alice's Adventures in Wonderland*), E Nesbit (*The Railway Children*), AA Milne (*Winnie-the-Pooh*), TH White (*The Once and Future King*) and CS Lewis (*The Chronicles of Narnia*). More recently, Philip Pullman's controversial *His Dark Materials* trilogy has also been a hit.

Alongside the work of English poets and novelists, it's impossible to overlook the recent trend for scurrilous celebrity autobiographies – penned by everyone from footballers to reality TV also-rans – a reminder of the increasing importance of hype over merit in the modern book market. But whatever you make of the literary qualities of these memoirs, it's hard to argue with the figures – the British public buys them by the bucket load.

For other worlds and other-worldly humour, try two of England's funniest – and most successful – writers: Douglas Adams (*The Hitchhiker's Guide to the Galaxy* and several sequels) and Terry Pratchett (the *Discworld* series).

Visual & Performing Arts

Cinema

Early Days

England had a number of successful directors in the early days of cinema. Many cut their teeth in the silent-film industry – including Alfred Hitchcock, who directed *Blackmail*, one of the first English 'talkies' in 1929 and went on to direct a string of films during the 1930s before migrating to Hollywood in the early 1940s.

During WWII, British films were dominated by patriotic stories designed to keep up morale on the Home Front: films like *Went the Day Well?* (1942), *In Which We Serve* (1942) and *We Dive at Dawn* (1943) are classics of the genre. During this period the precocious young director David Lean directed a series of striking Dickens adaptations and the classic tale of buttoned-up English passion, *Brief Encounter* (1945), before graduating to Hollywood epics, including *Lawrence of Arabia* and *Doctor Zhivago*. The war years also marked the start of one of the great partnerships of British cinema, between the English writer-director Michael Powell and the Hungarian-born scriptwriter Emeric Pressburger. During and after the war, they produced some of the most enduring British films, including *The Life and Death of Colonel Blimp* (1941), *A Matter of Life and Death* (1946) and *The Red Shoes* (1948).

The Ladykillers (1955) is a classic Ealing comedy about a band of hapless bank robbers holed up in a London guesthouse, and features Alec Guinness sporting quite possibly the most outrageous set of false teeth ever committed to celluloid.

After the War

Following the hardships of the war, English audiences were in the mood for escape and entertainment. During the late 1940s and early '50s, the domestic film industry specialised in eccentric English comedies epitomised by the work of Ealing Studios: notable titles include *Passport to Pimlico* (1949), *Kind Hearts and Coronets* (1949) and *The Titfield Thunderbolt* (1953). And in an England still struggling with rationing and food shortages, tales of heroic derring-do such as *The Dam Busters* (1955) and *Reach for the Sky* (1956) helped lighten the national mood.

Swinging Sixties

In the late 1950s 'British New Wave' and 'Free Cinema' explored the gritty realities of British life in an intimate, semi-documentary style, borrowing techniques from the 'kitchen-sink' theatre of the '50s and the vérité style of the French New Wave. Lindsay Anderson and Tony Richardson crystallised the movement in films such as *This Sporting Life* (1961) and *A Taste of Honey* (1961). At the other end of the spectrum were the *Carry On* films, the cinematic equivalent of the smutty seaside postcard, packed with bawdy gags and a revolving troupe of actors, including Barbara Windsor,

Sid James and Kenneth Williams. The 1960s also saw the birth of another classic English hero: James Bond, adapted from the Ian Fleming novels and ironically played by a Scotsman, Sean Connery.

Hard Times, Good Times

After the boom of the swinging '60s, English cinema entered troubled waters in the '70s. Dwindling production funds and increasing international competition meant that by the mid-1970s the only films being made in England were financed with foreign cash. Despite the hardships, new directors, including Ken Russell, Nic Roeg, Ken Loach and Mike Hodges, emerged, and the American director Stanley Kubrick produced some of his films in Britain, including *A Clockwork Orange* (1971).

The UK's biggest film magazine is *Empire* (www.empireonline.co.uk). For less mainstream opinion check out *Little White Lies* (www.littlewhitelies.co.uk).

In the 1980s the British film industry rediscovered its sense of self thanks partly to David Puttnam's Oscar success with *Chariots of Fire* in 1981. The newly established Channel Four invested in edgy films such as *My Beautiful Laundrette* (1985), and exciting new talents, including Neil Jordan, Mike Newell and American-born (member of the Monty Python team) Terry Gilliam. Meanwhile, the British producing duo of Ismail Merchant and James Ivory played Hollywood at its own game with epic tales including *Heat and Dust* (1983) and *A Room With A View* (1986), riding on the success of Richard Attenborough's big-budget *Gandhi* (1982), which bagged eight Academy Awards.

The 1990s saw another minor renaissance in English films, ushered in by the massively successful *Four Weddings and a Funeral* (1994), introducing Hugh Grant in his trademark role as a bumbling, self-deprecating Englishman, a character type he reprised in subsequent hits, including *Notting Hill*, *About a Boy* and *Love Actually*. All these films were co-financed by Working Title, a London-based production company which has become one of the big players of British cinema (and also unleashed Rowan Atkinson's hapless Mr Bean onto the global stage).

For movies about the English music scene, try: *Backbeat* (1994), The Beatles' early days; *Sid & Nancy* (1986), The Sex Pistols' bassist and his girlfriend; *Velvet Goldmine* (1998), the glam-rock era; *24 Hour Party People* (2002), the Manchester scene; and *Nowhere Boy* (2009), John Lennon pre-Beatles.

English cinema refocused its attention on domestic issues in the late 1990s. *Brassed Off* (1996) related the trials of a struggling colliery band; the smash-hit *The Full Monty* (1997) followed a troupe of laid-off steel workers turned male strippers; and *Billy Elliott* (2000) charted the story of an aspiring young ballet dancer striving to escape the slag-heaps and boarded-up factories of the industrial north. Films such as *East Is East* (1999) and *Bend It like Beckham* (2002) explored the tensions of modern multicultural Britain, while veteran British director Mike Leigh, known for his heavily improvised style, found success with *Life Is Sweet* (1991), *Naked* (1993) and the Palme d'Or winning *Secrets and Lies* (1996), in which an adopted black woman traces her white mother.

21st-Century Box

In the first decade of the 21st century, literary adaptations have continued to provide the richest seam of success in the English film industry. Hits of this genre include blockbuster adaptations of the Bridget Jones and Harry Potter books, as well as 2005's *The Constant Gardener* (based on a John Le Carré novel), 2007's *The Last King of Scotland* (featuring Forest Whittaker as Ugandan dictator Idi Amin), and *Atonement* (2008), a big-budget adaptation of Ian McEwan's novel.

Biopics are also a perennial favourite: recent big-screen subjects include Ian Curtis from Joy Division (*Control*, 2007), Elizabeth I (*Elizabeth: The Golden Age*, 2007), and even the Queen (in, er, *The Queen*, 2006).

But life remains tough for the British filmmaker, especially those at the low-budget end, and especially as the industry's support body, the UK Film Council, is one of many similar public sector organisations threatened with abolition in the harsh post-financial-crisis Britain of 2010. Nevertheless, names to look out for include Paul Greengrass,

THE PLASTICINE MAN

One of the great success stories of English TV and cinema has been Bristol-based animator Nick Park and the production company Aardman Animations, best known for the award-winning animations starring the man-and-dog duo Wallace and Gromit. This lovable pair first appeared in Park's graduation film, *A Grand Day Out* (1989), and went on to star in *The Wrong Trousers* (1993), *A Close Shave* (1995) and their feature debut, *Wallace & Gromit in The Curse of the Were-Rabbit* (2005). Known for their intricate plots, film homages and amazingly realistic animation, the Wallace and Gromit films scooped Nick Park four Oscars. Aardman Animations has also produced two successful animated features, *Chicken Run* (2000) and *Flushed Away* (2006), in partnership with Hollywood's DreamWorks studios.

Andrea Arnold, Stephen Daldry, Stephen Frears, Danny Boyle and Andrew Macdonald. Sam Taylor-Wood is another name to watch, thanks to her sensitive film *Nowhere Boy* (2009), about the early life of John Lennon.

Many talented names often take better-paid work abroad in order to finance home ventures, and genuinely British films about genuinely British subjects tend to struggle in an oversaturated marketplace: it's telling that two of Britain's best directors, Shane Meadows (*Dead Man's Shoes, This is England*) and Michael Winterbottom (*9 Songs, 24 Hour Party People*) have both yet to score a big splash at the box office.

The classic English youth movie is *Quadrophenia*, a visceral tale of Mods, Rockers, and pimped-up mopeds, with a top-notch soundtrack courtesy of The Who.

More success has come to the comedy trio of Simon Pegg, Edgar Wright and Nick Frost with their zombie homage *Shaun of The Dead* (2004) and its cop-flick follow-up *Hot Fuzz* (2007), while music video director Garth Jennings followed his adaptation of *The Hitchhiker's Guide to the Galaxy* (2005) with a low-budget tale of youthful friendship and shoestring moviemaking in *Son of Rambow* (2007).

Veteran directors like Mike Leigh and Ken Loach are still going strong: Leigh's *Vera Drake* (2004), about a housewife turned backstreet abortionist in 1950s Britain, won the Golden Lion at the Venice Film Festival, while Loach's *The Wind that Shakes the Barley* (2006), a hard-hitting account of the Irish struggle for independence, scooped the Palme d'Or at Cannes.

Meanwhile the oldest of English film franchises trundles on: a tough, toned 21st-century James Bond appeared in 2006 courtesy of Daniel Craig and the blockbuster *Casino Royale*. His next film, *Quantum of Solace* (2008), was due to be followed by another Bond movie (taking the total to more than 20) in 2010, but the project was delayed, keeping Bond fans on the edge of their seats for a little while longer than expected.

Television

If there's one thing the English excel at, it's the telly. Over the last 80-odd years of broadcasting, England has produced some of the world's finest programming, from classic comedy through to ground-breaking drama – and many of the world's most popular formats have their origins in English broadcasting (including the phenomenon known as reality TV).

The BBC is famous for its news and natural-history programming, symbolised by landmark series such as *Planet Earth* and *The Blue Planet* (helmed by the reassuring presence of David Attenborough, a national institution on British screens since the 1970s).

The big-budget costume drama is another Sunday-night staple: BBC viewers have been treated to adaptations of practically every Dickens, Austen and Thackeray novel in the canon over the last decade. More recently ITV has been making inroads into costume-drama territory, notably with Jane Austen's *Persuasion, Mansfield Park* and *Northanger Abbey*. Both channels are also known for their long-running 'soaps' – *Eastenders* (BBC), *Emmerdale* and *Coronation Street* (both ITV), which have collectively been running on British screens for well over a century.

Reality TV has dominated many channels in recent years, although the popularity of shows such as *Big Brother* and *I'm a Celebrity – Get Me Out of Here!* seems to be on the wane. On the flip side, talent and variety are making a big comeback, with programs like *Britain's Got Talent* and *Strictly Come Dancing* being syndicated all over the world (the latter under the brand of 'Dancing with the Stars'). Game shows are another big success story, with *Who Wants to be a Millionaire?* and *The Weakest Link* spawning countless foreign versions.

While the main channels of BBC1 and ITV concentrate on high-profile programming, BBC2 and Channel 4 tend to produce edgier and more experimental content. Both channels are known for their documentaries – Channel 4 has a particular penchant for shocking subject matter (one of the channel's most controversial recent programs was *Autopsy*, which did exactly what it said on the label). Comedy is another strong point – the satirical news quiz *Have I Got News For You* is still going strong after 15 years, while classic British comedies such as *Monty Python, Steptoe & Son* and *Only Fools & Horses* have more recently been joined in comedy's hall of fame by cult hits *The Mighty Boosh, The League of Gentlemen, I'm Alan Partridge, Ali G, Spaced* and Ricky Gervais' *The Office* and *Extras*.

Withnail and I is one of the great cult British comedies. Directed by Bruce Robinson, it stars Paul McGann and Richard E Grant as a pair of hapless out-of-work actors on a disastrous holiday to Wales.

Pop & Rock Music

England's been putting the world through its musical paces ever since a mop-haired four-piece from Liverpool tuned up their Rickenbackers and created The Beatles. And while some may claim that Elvis invented rock and roll, it was the Fab Four that transformed it into a global phenomenon, backed by the other bands of the 1960s 'British Invasion' – The Rolling Stones, The Who, Cream and The Kinks.

In the 1970s, glam rock swaggered onto the stage, led by Marc Bolan and David Bowie in their tight-fitting costumes and chameleonic guises, succeeded by art-rockers Roxy Music and anthemic popsters Queen and Elton John. Meanwhile Led Zeppelin laid down the blueprint for heavy metal and hard rock, and the psychedelia of the previous decade morphed into the spacey noodlings of prog rock, epitomised by Pink Floyd, Genesis and Yes. By the late 1970s the prog bands were looking out of touch in an England wracked by rampant unemployment,

HAMMER HORROR

The low-budget fright flicks produced by Hammer Film Productions are revered among horror fans across the globe. Founded in 1934, the company was best known for its string of horror flicks produced in the 1950s and '60s, starting with *The Quatermass Xperiment* (1955) and *The Curse of Frankenstein* (1957). The two stars of the latter – Peter Cushing as Dr Frankenstein and Christopher Lee as the Monster – would feature in many of Hammer's best films over the next 20 years.

Hammer produced some absolute classics of the horror genre, including a string of nine *Dracula* films (most of which star Lee as Dracula and Cushing as Van Helsing or his descendants) and six *Frankenstein* sequels.

The studio also launched the careers of several other notable actors (including Oliver Reed, who made his film debut in *The Curse of the Werewolf*, 1961) and inspired a legion of low-budget horror directors; Wes Craven, John Carpenter and Sam Raimi have all acknowledged Hammer films as an early influence. The studio even spawned its very own spoof, *Carry On Screaming* – the ultimate English seal of approval.

industrial unrest and the three-day week, and punk exploded onto the scene, summing up the general air of doom and gloom with nihilistic lyrics and short, sharp, three-chord tunes. The Sex Pistols produced one landmark album – *Never Mind the Bollocks, Here's the Sex Pistols* – and a clutch of (mostly banned) singles, plus a storm of controversy, ably assisted by other punk pioneers like The Clash, The Damned, The Buzzcocks and The Stranglers.

While punk burned itself out in a blaze of squealing guitars and ear-splitting feedback, New Wave acts including The Jam and Elvis Costello took up the torch, blending spiky tunes and sharp lyrics into a poppier, more radio-friendly sound. A little later, along came bands like The Specials, The Selecter and baggy-trousered rude boys Madness, mixing mixed punk, reggae and ska into Two Tone.

Britain's longest running soap is *Coronation Street*, which has charted everyday life in the fictional northern town of Weatherfield since 1960.

The big money and conspicuous consumption of Britain in the early 1980s bled over into the decade's pop scene. Big hair, shiny suits and shoulder pads became the uniform of the day, epitomised by Wham! (a boyish duo headed by an up-and-coming popster called George Michael), while frills and floppy fringes became hallmarks of the New Romantic bands such as Visage, Spandau Ballet, Duran Duran and Culture Club. At the same time, the advent of synthesisers and processed beats led to the development of a new electronic sound in the music of Depeche Mode and Human League.

But the glitz and glitter of '80s pop concealed a murky underbelly: bands like The Cure, Bauhaus, and Siouxsie and the Banshees employed doom-laden lyrics and apocalyptic riffs, while Britain's rock heritage inspired the birth of heavy-metal acts such as Iron Maiden, Judas Priest and Black Sabbath. The arch-priests of 'miserabilism', The Smiths – fronted by extravagantly quiffed wordsmith Morrissey – summed up the disaffection of mid-1980s England in classic albums such as *The Queen is Dead* and *Meat is Murder*.

The beats and bleeps of 1980s electronica fuelled the burgeoning dance-music scene of the early '90s. Pioneering artists such as New Order (risen from the ashes of Joy Division) and The Orb used synthesised sounds to inspire the soundtrack for the new, ecstasy-fuelled rave culture, centred on famous clubs like Manchester's Haçienda and London's Ministry of Sound. Subgenres such as trip-hop, drum and bass, jungle, house and big-beat cropped up in other UK cities, with key acts including Massive Attack, Portishead and the Chemical Brothers.

Manchester was also a focus for the burgeoning British 'indie' scene, driven by guitar-based bands such as The Charlatans, The Stone Roses, James, Happy Mondays and Manchester's most famous musical export, Oasis. In the late 1990s, indie segued into Britpop, a catch-all term covering several bands, with Oasis still at its head and now including the likes of Pulp, Supergrass and Blur, whose distinctively British music chimed with the country's new sense of optimism following the landslide election of New Labour in 1997. Noel Gallagher of Oasis famously had tea with Tony Blair, but the 'Cool Britannia' phenomenon was short-lived and well and truly over by the end of the '90s.

The first decade of the new millennium saw no let-up in the British music scene's continual shifting and reinventing, becoming ever more diverse thanks to the arrival of MySpace, iTunes and file sharing. Jazz, soul, R&B and hip-hop beats fused into a new 'urban' sound epitomised by artists like Jamelia, The Streets and Dizzee Rascal. On the pop side, singer-songwriters – such as Amy Winehouse, Damien Rice, Ed Harcourt, Katie Mellua, James Blunt and Duffy – made a comeback, while the spirit of shoe-gazing British indie stayed alive and well thanks to Keane, Foals, Editors and world-conquering Coldplay, while traces of punk and postpunk survived thanks to Franz Ferdinand, Razorlight, Babyshambles, Muse, Klaxons, Dirty Pretty Things and 2008's download phenomenon Arctic Monkeys.

As the wheel turns again, the swagger of the Manchester sound still echoes through the music of Primal Scream, Kaiser Chiefs, Kasabian, Doves and The (reformed) Verve, while other key bands include British Sea Power, The Ting Tings, Guillemots, Elbow and Radiohead. By the time you read this book half of the 'great new bands' of last year will have sunk without trace, and a fresh batch of unknowns will have risen to dominate the airwaves and download sites. One thing's for sure, the English music scene has never stood still, and it doesn't look like settling down any time soon.

Painting & Sculpture

Early Days

For many centuries, continental Europe – especially Holland, Spain, France and Italy – set the artistic agenda. The first artist with a truly English style and sensibility was arguably William Hogarth, whose riotous canvases exposed the vice and corruption of 18th-century London. His most celebrated work is *A Rake's Progress,* displayed today at Sir John Soane's Museum in London, kick-starting a long tradition of British caricatures that can be traced right through to the work of modern-day cartoonists such as Gerald Scarfe and Steve Bell.

While Hogarth was busy satirising society, other artists were hard at work showing it in its best light. The leading figures of 18th-century English portraiture were Sir Joshua Reynolds, Thomas Gainsborough, George Romney and George Stubbs, best known for his intricate studies of animals (particularly horses). Most of these artists are represented at Tate Britain or the National Gallery in London.

For movies about the English music scene, try: *Backbeat* (1994; the Beatles' early days), *Sid & Nancy* (1986; the Sex Pistols bassist and his girlfriend), *Velvet Goldmine* (1998; the glam-rock era), *24 Hour Party People* (2002; the Manchester scene) and *Nowhere Boy* (2009; John Lennon pre-Beatles).

The 19th Century

In the 19th century, leading painters favoured the English landscape. John Constable's idyllic depictions of the Suffolk countryside are summed up in *The Haywain* (National Gallery), while JMW Turner was fascinated by the effects of light and colour on English scenes, with his works becoming almost entirely abstract by the 1840s, vilified at the time but prefiguring the Impressionist movement that was to follow 50 years later.

While Turner was becoming more abstract, the Pre-Raphaelite movement of the late 19th century harked back to the figurative style of classical Italian and Flemish art, tying in with the prevailing Victorian taste for English fables, myths and fairy tales. Key members of the movement included Dante Gabriel Rosetti, John Everett Millais, and William Holman Hunt, all represented at London's Tate Britain or the Victoria & Albert Museum.

The 20th Century

In the tumultuous 20th century, English art became increasingly experimental. Francis Bacon placed Freudian psychoanalysis on the canvas in his portraits, while pioneering sculptors such as Henry Moore

BURNING BRIGHT

While some English artists fitted neatly into specific genres, the painter, writer, poet and visionary William Blake (1757–1827) occupied a world of his own, mixing fantastical landscapes and mythological scenes with motifs drawn from classical art, religious iconography and English legend. For more see www.blakearchive.org.

ANISH KAPOOR

The sculptor Anish Kapoor has been working in London since the 1970s, but his work appears around the world. He's best known for his large outdoor installations, which often feature curved shapes and reflective materials, such as highly polished steel. His recent works include a major new installation in London, called *Arcelor Mittal Orbit*, to celebrate the 2012 Olympic Games. Based on the five Olympic rings, at over 110m high it will be the largest piece of public art in Britain when completed.

and Barbara Hepworth experimented with natural forms and all kinds of new materials. Some of Moore's work can be seen at the Yorkshire Sculpture Park, and Hepworth is forever associated with St Ives. Other artists, including Patrick Heron and Terry Frost, developed their own version of abstract expressionism, while amateur artist LS Lowry was setting his strange 'matchstick men' among the smokestacks and terraces of northern England.

The mid-1950s and early '60s saw an explosion of English artists plundering TV, music, advertising and popular culture for inspiration. Leaders of this new 'pop art' movement included David Hockney, who used bold colours and simple lines to depict his dachshunds and swimming pools, and Peter Blake, who designed the cut-up collage cover for The Beatles' landmark album *Sgt Pepper's Lonely Hearts Club Band.* The '60s also saw the rise of sculptor Anthony Caro, who held his first, groundbreaking exhibition at the Whitechapel Art Gallery in 1963. Creating large abstract works in steel and bronze, he remains one of England's most influential sculptors.

The next big explosion in English art came in the 1990s, thanks partly to the interest (and money) of advertising tycoon and patron Charles Saatchi. Figureheads of the movement – dubbed, inevitably, 'Britart' – include Damien Hirst, famous for his pickled sharks, embalmed cows and more recently a diamond-encrusted skull; Tracey Emin, whose work has ranged from confessional videos to a tent entitled *All The People I Have Ever Slept With*; and the Chapman Brothers, known for their deformed child mannequins (often featuring genitalia in inappropriate places).

The British Film Institute (BFI; www.bfi.org.uk) is dedicated to promoting film and cinema in Britain, and publishes the monthly academic journal *Sight & Sound.*

Apart from Hirst, one of the few Britart figures to find mainstream success is Rachel Whiteread, known for her resin casts of everyday objects. In 2008 she was one of five artists short-listed for the 'Angel of the South', a £2 million project to create a huge outdoor sculpture in Kent to counterbalance the celebrated *Angel of the North* created by Antony Gormley. Whiteread's idea for the project was a plaster-cast of a house interior on an artificial hill, but the final selection went to Mark Wallinger, winner of the 2007 Turner Prize, for his *White Horse at Ebbsfleet.* As the name implies, this work is a white horse, true to life in everything except size. When finished it will be over 50m high – that's more than 30 times bigger than a real horse, so it should be clearly seen from the nearby A2 main road and the railway line between London and Paris. It's due for completion by 2012, although a petition raised by local residents in July 2010 called for the project to be stopped.

Theatre

However you budget your time and money, make sure that you see some English theatre as part of your travels. It easily lives up to its reputation as the finest in the world, and London is the international centre for theatrical arts – whatever New Yorkers say.

But first, let's set the stage with some history. Centuries after his death in 1616, English theatre's best-known name is, of course, William

Shakespeare. Originally from the Midlands, he made his name in London, where most of his plays were performed (at the Globe Theatre).

His brilliant plots and spectacular use of language, plus the sheer size of his canon of work (including classics such as *Hamlet, Romeo and Juliet, Henry V* and *A Midsummer Night's Dream*), have turned him into a national – and international – icon. Today, the Globe has now been rebuilt, so you can see Shakespeare's plays performed in Elizabethan style, and you can also catch his works at the theatre in his birthplace Stratford-upon-Avon, now forever linked with the Bard himself.

Later in the 17th century, following the English Civil War, the puritanical Oliver Cromwell closed the nation's theatres, but when the exiles king Charles II returned to the throne in 1660 – the period known as the Restoration – he reopened the doors and encouraged many radical innovations, including actresses (female roles had previously been played by boys). Bawdy comedies of the era satirised the upper classes and indulged in fabulously lewd jokes (William Wycherley's *The Country Wife* is a prime example). One of the leading actresses of the day, Nell Gwyn, became Charles II's mistress, and England's first female playwright, Aphra Behn, also emerged during this period.

In the 18th century, theatres were built in the larger English cities (the Bristol Old Vic and The Grand in Lancaster date from this time) but English drama went into something of a decline, mainly due to the rise in operas and burlesque entertainment. It wasn't until the Victorian era that serious drama came back into fashion; during the mid-19th century classical plays competed for space on London's stages with a broad mix of melodramas, comic operas, vaudeville and music hall.

Of the Victorian and Edwardian dramatists, the most famous names include George Bernard Shaw, Noel Coward and Oscar Wilde (everyone's heard of *The Importance of Being Earnest*, even if they haven't seen it).

During the early 20th century, the theatre soldiered on despite increasing competition from the cinema, but it wasn't until the 1950s that a new generation of English playwrights brought theatre back to life. The 'Angry Young Men', including John Osborne, Joe Orton and Terence Rattigan, railed against the injustices of mid-1950s Britain with a searing and confrontational new style of theatre. A contemporary was Harold Pinter, who developed a new dramatic style and perfectly captured the stuttering illogical diction of real-life conversation.

Other ground-breaking playwrights experimented with language and form during the 1960s and '70s – including Tom Stoppard *(Rosencrantz and Guildenstern are Dead)*, Peter Shaffer *(Amadeus)*, Michael Frayn *(Noises Off)* and Alan Ayckbourn *(The Norman Conquests)* – while emerging directors like Peter Hall and Peter Brook took new risks with

WHAT A PANTOMIME

If any English tradition is guaranteed to bemuse outsiders, it's the pantomime. This over-the-top Christmas spectacle graces stages throughout the land in December and January and traces its roots back to Celtic legends, medieval morality plays and the English music hall. The modern incarnation is usually based on a classic fairy tale and features a mix of saucy dialogue, comedy skits, song-and-dance routines and plenty of custard-pie humour, mixed in with topical gags for the grown-ups. Tradition dictates that the leading 'boy' is played by a woman, and the leading lady, or 'dame', played by a chap. B-list celebrities, struggling actors and soap stars famously make a small fortune hamming it up for the Christmas panto, and there are always a few staple routines that everyone knows and joins in ('Where's that dragon/wizard/pirate/lion?' – 'He's behind you!'). It's cheesy, daft and frequently rather surreal, but guaranteed to be great fun for the family. Oh, no, it isn't! Oh, yes, it is! Oh, no, it isn't!

dramatic staging. It was also a golden period for acting – the staid, declamatory style of the past steadily gave way to a new, edgy realism in the performances of Laurence Olivier and Richard Burton, succeeded by actors such as Antony Sher, Judi Dench, Glenda Jackson and Ian McKellen.

Many of these actors remain household names, although they're perhaps better-known for their appearances in big-budget films from America. Other notable English actors – including Ralph Fiennes, Brenda Blethyn, Toby Stephens and Simon Callow – also juggle high-paying Hollywood roles with theatrical appearances on the English stage.

It's not all one-way traffic though. Many major Hollywood stars have taken hefty pay cuts to tread the London boards – including Glenn Close, Nicole Kidman, Gwyneth Paltrow, Macaulay Culkin and Christian Slater. Kevin Spacey liked it so much he decided to take over a theatre; since 2004 he's been in charge at London's Old Vic.

Home-grown names to look out for in current English theatre include the sometimes controversial playwrights Mark Ravenhill, Katie Mitchell and Emma Rice. The best place to find their work, and other new or experimental productions, are London's smaller theatres like the Donmar Warehouse or the Royal Court Theatre.

Meanwhile, the West End, the heart of London's theatre-land, is mostly the preserve of classic plays and – especially – big musicals, from *Jesus Christ Superstar* in the 1970s to 2011's *Wizard of Oz* via crowd-pullers like *Cats*, *Les Mis*, *Chicago*, *Phantom of the Opera* and all the rest. Many of today's shows are based on the pop lexicon, from *We Will Rock You* to *Mamma Mia*, proving that all a lot of people want to do is have a fun night out and a jolly good singalong.

Sporting England

The English may have invented many of the world's favourite sports, or at least codified the modern rules – including cricket, tennis, rugby and football – but unfortunately the national teams aren't very good at playing them. Despite some standout success stories from the last decade, including victory at the Rugby World Cup in 2004, a long-awaited win against Australia in the 2005 Ashes cricket series, followed by another win against the Aussies in the Twenty20 cricket world cup in 2010, England has a poor track record in most major international sporting tournaments. And it says something about the nation's football prowess, and something about the nation itself, when the most revered date in the brain of every self-respecting fan is still England's victory in the World Cup, way back in 1966.

But even when England isn't winning, a poor result doesn't dull the enthusiasm of the fans. Every weekend, thousands of people turn out to cheer their favourite team, and sporting highlights such as the FA Cup, Wimbledon or the Derby keep the entire nation enthralled, while the phenomenal success of the swimmers, cyclists and rowers at the Beijing Olympics engendered an outbreak of patriotic sporting pride – helped of course by London's hosting of the next Games in 2012.

This section gives a brief overview of spectator sports you might encounter as part of your travels around England; the regional chapters have more details on specific football stadia, cricket grounds and so on. For information on participatory sports, see the Outdoor England chapter.

For the dates and details of major football and cricket matches, horse racing and other sporting fixtures across the country, a great place to start is the sports pages of www.britevents.com.

Football (Soccer)

Despite what the fans may say in Madrid or Sao Paulo, the English **Premier League** (www.premierleague.com) has some of the finest teams in the world, dominated in recent years by the four top teams – Arsenal, Liverpool, Chelsea and Manchester United – all (with the notable exception of Arsenal) owned by multimillionaire foreigners, whose limitless transfer budgets have allowed the clubs to attract many of the world's best – and now richest – players.

Down in quality from the Premiership, 72 other teams play in the English divisions called the Championship, League One and League Two.

The football season is the same for all divisions (August to May), so seeing a match can easily be tied into most visitors' itineraries, but tickets for the Premier League are like gold dust – your chances of bagging one are pretty much zilch unless you're a club member, or know someone who is. You're better off buying a ticket at one of the lower-division games – they're cheaper and more easily available. You can often buy tickets on the spot, or try the club websites or online agencies like www.ticketmaster.co.uk and www.myticketmarket.com.

For the latest lowdown on everything football, from the National 11's next game and major League competitions to grass-roots matches and where to buy a replica England shirt, consult the Football Association's website at www.thefa.com.

SOCK IT TO ME

The word 'soccer' (the favoured term in countries where 'football' means another game) is reputedly derived from 'Association'. The sport is still officially called Association Football, to distinguish it from Rugby Football, Gaelic football, American Football, Aussie Rules Football and so on. Another source is the word 'sock'; in medieval times this was a tough leather foot-cover worn by peasants – ideal for kicking around a pig's bladder in the park on a Saturday afternoon.

Cricket

Village greens, chaps in starched whites, and the *knick* of leather on willow – what could be more English than a cricket match? This quintessentially English sport has been played formally since the 18th century – although its roots are much older – and spread through the Commonwealth during Britain's colonial era. Australia, the Caribbean and the Indian subcontinent took to the game with gusto, and a century on, the former colonies still delight in giving the old country a good spanking on the cricket pitch.

While many English people follow cricket like a religion, to the uninitiated it's an impenetrable spectacle. Spread over one-day games or five-day 'test matches', progress seems so *slow* (surely, say the unbelievers, this is the game for which TV highlights were invented), and dominated by arcane terminology like innings, overs, googlies, outswingers, leg-byes and silly mid-offs. Nonetheless, at least one cricket match should feature in your travels around England. If you're patient and learn the intricacies, you could find cricket as enriching and enticing as all the Brits who remain glued to their radio or computer all summer, 'just to see how England's getting on'.

Causing ructions in the cricket world is the Twenty20 Cup, a new format which basically limits the time each team has to play, laying the emphasis on fast big-batting scores, rather than slow and careful run-building. While many traditionalists think this crowd-pleasing invention is changing the character of the game, there's no doubting its popularity – most Twenty20 matches sell out.

One-day games and international tests are played at grounds including Lords in London, Edgbaston in Birmingham and Headingley in Leeds. Tickets cost from £30 to well over £200. The County Championship pits together the best teams from around the country. Details are on the site of the **English Cricket Board** (www.ecb.co.uk). Tickets cost £15 to £25, and only the most crucial games tend to sell out.

Easiest option of all – and often the most enjoyable – is stumbling across a local game on a village green as you travel around the country. There's no charge for spectators, and no one will mind if you nip to the pub during a quiet period.

Queen Elizabeth II is a great horse-racing fan, and the royal stables have produced many winners, including around 20 victories at Ascot. The 2005 Grand National famously clashed with Prince Charles' marriage; rumours abound that the start was delayed so the Queen could attend the nuptials *and* see the race.

Horse Racing

The tradition of horse racing in England stretches back centuries, and there's a 'meeting' somewhere in England pretty much every day, and for all but the major events you should be able to get a ticket on the day – or buy in advance from the British Horse Racing Authority's site www.gototheraces.com, which also has lots of information about social events such as music festivals that coincide with the races.

The top event in the calendar is **Royal Ascot** (www.royalascot.co.uk) in mid-June, where the rich and famous come to see and be seen, and the fashion is almost as important as the nags – and even the Queen turns up to put a fiver each way on Lucky Boy in the 3.15.

Other highlights include the Grand National steeplechase at Aintree in early April, and the Derby, run at Epsom on the first Saturday in June. The latter is especially popular with the masses so, unlike Ascot, you won't see morning suits and outrageous hats anywhere.

Rugby

A wit once said that football was a gentlemen's game played by hooligans, while rugby was the other way around. That may be true, but rugby is very popular, especially since England became world champions in 2004, and nearly did it again in 2008, beaten in the final by South Africa. It's worth catching a game for the display of skill (OK, and brawn) and the fun atmosphere in the grounds.

There are two versions of the game: **Rugby Union** (www.rfu.com) is played more in southern England, Wales and Scotland, and traditionally the game of the middle and upper classes, while **Rugby League** (www.therfl.com) is played predominantly in northern England, traditionally by the working classes – although these days there's a lot of crossover. Both 'codes' trace their roots to a football match in 1823 at Rugby School, in Warwickshire. A player called William Webb Ellis, frustrated at the limitations of mere kicking, reputedly picked up the ball and ran with it towards the opponents' goal. True to the sense of English fair play, rather than Ellis being dismissed from the game, a whole new sport was developed around his tactic, and the Rugby Football Union was formally inaugurated in 1871. The Rugby World Cup is named the Webb Ellis trophy after this enterprising young tearaway.

Today, leading rugby union clubs include Leicester, Bath and Gloucester, while London has a host of good-quality teams (including Wasps and Saracens). In rugby league, teams to watch include the Wigan Warriors, Bradford Bulls and Leeds Rhinos. Tickets for games cost around £15 to £40 depending on the club's status and fortunes.

The international rugby union calendar is dominated by the annual Six Nations Championship between January and April, in which England does battle with neighbours Scotland, Wales, Ireland, France and Italy.

THE SWEET FA CUP

The Football Association held its first interclub knockout tournament in 1871. Fifteen clubs took part, playing for a nice piece of silverware called the FA Cup – then worth about £20.

Nowadays, around 600 clubs compete for this legendary and priceless trophy. It differs from many other competitions in that every team – from the lowest-ranking part-timers to the stars of the Premier League – is in with a chance. The preliminary rounds begin in August, and the world-famous Cup Final is held in May at the iconic Wembley Stadium in London.

The team with the most FA Cup victories is Manchester United, but public attention – and affection – is invariably focussed on the 'giant-killers' – minor clubs that claw their way up through the rounds, unexpectedly beating higher-ranking competitors. The best-known giant-killing event occurred in 1992, when Wrexham, then ranked 24th in Division 3, famously beat league champions Arsenal. Other shocks include nonleague Kidderminster Harriers' 1994 defeat of big boys Birmingham City, and Oldham Athletic beating premier leaguers Manchester City in 2005.

In recent years, the FA Cup has become one football competition among many. The Premier League and Champion's League (against European teams) have higher profiles, bigger kudos, and simply more money to play with. But – just as the country gets behind the English national side – nothing raises community spirit more than a town team doing better than expected. Gates are down, and perhaps the FA Cup will one day be consigned to history – but what a sweet and glorious history it's been!

THE ASHES

The historic test cricket series between England and Australia known as the Ashes has been played every other year since 1882 (bar a few interruptions during the World Wars). It is played alternately in England and Australia with each of the five matches in the series held at a different cricket ground, always in the summer in the host location.

The contest's name dates back to the landmark test match of 1882, won (for the very first time) by the Australians. Defeat of the mother country by the colonial upstarts was a source of profound national shock: a mock-obituary in the *Sporting Times* lamented the death of English cricket and referred to the sport's ashes being taken to Australia.

Later the name was given to a terracotta urn presented the following year to the English captain Ivo Bligh (later Lord Darnley), purportedly containing the cremated ashes of a stump or bail used in this landmark match. Since 1953 this hallowed relic has resided at the Marylebone Cricket Club (MCC) Museum at Lord's. Despite the vast importance given to winning the series, the urn itself is a diminutive six inches high (150cm).

The recent history of the Ashes is not without drama. After eight straight defeats, England won the series in 2005, then handed the prize straight back to the Aussies after a humiliating thrashing in 2007, before 'regaining the Ashes' once again in 2009. At the time of writing, it remains to be seen if it's Australia's turn for the urn in 2011.

Over 27 tonnes of strawberries and 7000L of cream are consumed every year during the two weeks of the Wimbledon Tennis Championships.

Tennis

Tennis is widely played at club and regional level, but the best-known tournament is the All England Championships – known to all as **Wimbledon** (www.wimbledon.org) – when tennis fever sweeps through the country in the last week of June and first week of July. There's something quintessentially English about the combination of grass courts, polite applause and umpires in boaters, with strawberries and cream devoured by the truckload.

Demand for seats at Wimbledon always outstrips supply, but to give everyone an equal chance the tickets are sold through a public ballot. You can also take your chance on the spot; about 6000 tickets are sold each day (but not the last four days), but you'll need to be an early riser – dedicated fans start queuing before dawn.

Survival Guide

Directory A-Z

Accommodation

B&Bs & Guesthouses

The B&B ('bed and breakfast') is a great British institution. At smaller places it's pretty much a room in somebody's house, and you'll really feel part of the family. Larger B&Bs may have around 10 rooms and more facilities (and sometimes a larger B&B will call itself a 'guesthouse').

Facilities usually reflect price: for around £20 per person you get a simple bedroom and share the bathroom; for around £25 to £30 you get a private bathroom – either down the hall or en suite.

B&B prices are usually quoted per person, based on two people sharing a room. Single rooms for solo travellers are harder to find, and attract a 20% to 50% premium. Some B&Bs simply won't take single people (unless you pay the full double-room price), especially in summer.

Here are some more B&B tips:

» In country areas, B&Bs might be in the heart of a village or an isolated farm; in cities it's usually a suburban house.

» Advance reservations are always preferred at B&Bs, and are essential during popular periods. Many require a minimum two nights at weekends.

» If a B&B is full, owners may recommend another place nearby (possibly a private house taking occasional guests, not in tourist listings).

ACCOMMODATION PRICE RANGES

The following price ranges have been used in our reviews of places to stay. Prices are all based on double room with private bathroom, in high season.

BUDGET	LONDON	ELSEWHERE
budget (£)	<£80	<£50
midrange (££)	£80-180	£50–130
top end (£££)	>£180	>£130

BOOK YOUR STAY ONLINE

For more accommodation reviews by Lonely Planet authors, check out hotels.lonelyplanet.com/England. You'll find independent reviews, as well recommendations on the best places to stay. Best of all, you can book online.

» In cities, some B&Bs are for long-term residents or people on welfare; they don't take passing tourists.

» In country areas, most B&Bs cater for walkers and cyclists, but some don't, so let them know if you'll be turning up with dirty boots or wheels.

» Some places reduce rates for longer stays (two or three nights).

» Most B&Bs serve enormous breakfasts; some offer packed lunches (around £5) and evening meals (around £12 to £15).

» If you're on a flexible itinerary and haven't booked in advance, most towns have a main drag of B&Bs; those with spare rooms hang up a 'Vacancies' sign.

» When booking, check where your B&B actually is. In country areas, postal addresses include the nearest town, which may be 20 miles away. Some B&B owners will pick you up by car for a small charge.

Bunkhouses & Camping Barns

A bunkhouse is a simple place to stay, handy for walkers, cyclists or anyone on a budget in the countryside. They usually have a communal sleeping area and bathroom, heating and cooking stoves. You provide the sleeping bag and possibly cooking gear.

Most charge around £10 per person per night.

Camping barns are even more basic: they're usually converted farm buildings, with sleeping platforms, a cooking area, and basic toilets outside. Take everything you'd need to camp except the tent. Charges are from around £5 per person.

Camping

The opportunities for camping in England are numerous – ideal if you're on a tight budget or simply enjoy the great outdoors. In rural areas, campsites range from farmers' fields with a tap and a basic toilet, costing as little as £3 per person per night, to smarter affairs with hot showers and many other facilities, charging up to £10.

Whatever your style, you'll usually need all your own kit. England doesn't really have huge sites of permanent tents, as found in France and some other European countries. That said, a few campsites in England also offer self-catering accommodation in chalets and caravans, or in more exotic options such as tepees and yurts. Some options are very smart and stylish – quickly dubbed 'glamping' by the UK travel press.

Hostels

There are two types of hostel in England: those run by the **Youth Hostel Association** (YHA; www.yha.org.uk) and independent hostels – most of which are listed in the **Independent Hostels** guidebook and website (www.independenthostelguide.co.uk). You'll find hostels in rural areas, towns and cities. They're aimed at all types of traveller and you don't have to be young.

Some hostels are purpose-built but many are converted cottages, country houses and even castles – often in wonderful locations. Facilities include showers, drying room, lounge and equipped self-catering kitchen. Sleeping is usually in dormitories. Many hostels also have twin or four-bed rooms, some with private bathroom.

INDEPENDENT HOSTELS

In rural areas some independent hostels are little more than simple bunkhouses (charging around £6), while others are almost up to B&B standard (£15 or more). In cities, independent backpacker hostels are usually aimed at young budget travellers. Most are open 24/7, with a lively atmosphere, good range of rooms (doubles or dorms), bar, cafe, internet computer, wi-fi and laundry. Prices are around £15 for a dorm bed, or £20 to £35 for a bed in a private room.

YHA HOSTELS

The simplest YHA hostels cost from £10. Larger hostels with more facilities are £15 to £20. London's YHA hostels cost from £25. All plus £3 if you're not a YHA member. Reservations and advance payments with credit card are usually possible.

You don't *have* to be a member of the YHA (or another Hostelling International organisation) to stay at YHA hostels, but it's usually worth joining. Annual YHA membership costs £16; under-26s and families get discounts. Throughout this book we have generally quoted the member rates for YHA hostels.

YHA prices (just like train fares) vary according to demand and season. Book early for a Tuesday night in May and you'll get the best rate. Book late for a weekend in August and you'll pay top price – if there's space at all. Throughout this book, we have generally quoted the cheaper rates (in line with those listed on the YHA's website); you may find yourself paying more.

YHA hostels tend to have complicated opening times and days, especially in remote locations or out of tourist season, so check before turning up.

Hotels

A hotel in England might be a small and simple place, perhaps a former farmhouse now stylishly converted, where peace and quiet – along with luxury – are guaranteed. Or it might be a huge country house with fancy facilities, grand staircases acres of grounds and stag heads on the wall.

Charges vary as much as quality and atmosphere. At the bargain end, you can find singles/doubles costing

NO SUCH THING AS A 'STANDARD' HOTEL RATE

It's worth noting that there's often no such thing as a 'standard' hotel rate. Many hotels, especially larger places or chains, vary prices according to demand – or have different rates for online, phone or walk-in bookings – just like airlines and train operators. So if you book early for a night when the hotel is likely to be quiet, rates are cheap. Try to book late, or aim for a public holiday weekend and you'll pay a lot. However, if you're prepared to be flexible and leave booking to the very last minute you can sometimes get a bargain as rates drop again. The end result, you can pay anything from £19 to £190 for the very same hotel room. With that in mind, the hotel rates we quote throughout this book are often guide prices only. (B&B prices tend to much more consistent.)

£30/40. Move up the scale and you'll pay £100/150 or beyond. More money doesn't always mean a better hotel though – whatever your budget, some are excellent value, while others overcharge.

If all you want is a place to put your head down, budget chain hotels can be a good option. Most are totally lacking in style or ambience, but who cares? You'll only be there for eight hours, and six of them you'll be asleep. Most offer rooms at variable prices based on demand; on a quiet night in November twin-bed rooms with private bathroom start at around £20, and at the height of the tourist season you'll pay £45 or more. Options include:

Etap Hotels (www.etaphotel.com)

Hotel Formule 1 (www.hotelformule1.com)

Premier Inn (www.premierinn.com)

Travelodge (www.travelodge.co.uk)

Pubs & Inns

As well as selling drinks, many pubs and inns offer lodging, particularly in country areas. Staying in a pub can be good fun – you're automatically at the centre of the community – although accommodation varies enormously.

Expect to pay around £20 per person at the cheap end, and around £30 to £35 for something better.

CONVENIENCE STORES

» London and other cities have 24/7 convenience stores.

» In smaller towns and in country areas, shops often shut for lunch (normally 1pm to 2pm) and on Wednesday or Thursday afternoon.

An advantage for solo tourists: pubs are more likely to have single rooms.

If a pub does B&B, it normally does evening meals, served in the bar or an adjoining restaurant.

Rental Accommodation

If you want to slow down and get to know a place, renting for a week or two can be ideal. Choose from neat apartments in towns and cities, or quaint old houses and farms (always called cottages, whatever the size) in country areas. Cottages for four people cost between £200 and £600 in high season. Rates fall at quieter times, and you may be able to rent for a long weekend. Handy websites:

Bed & Breakfast Nationwide (www.bedandbreakfastnationwide.com)

Cottages4U (www.cottages4u.co.uk)

Hoseasons (www.hoseasons.co.uk)

National Trust (www.nationaltrust.org.uk/accommodation)

Stilwell's (www.stilwell.co.uk)

University Accommodation

Many universities offer student accommodation to visitors during vacations. You usually get a functional single bedroom with private bathroom, and self-catering flats are also available.Prices range from £15 to £30 per person. A handy portal is www.universityrooms.co.uk.

Business Hours

Throughout this book, we don't list opening and closing times unless they vary significantly from the hours listed here.

Banks

» Monday to Friday, open at 9.30am until 4pm or 5pm.

» Saturday, main branches open 9.30am to 1pm.

» Sunday closed.

OPENING HOURS

Throughout this book we work on the basis that most restaurants and cafes are open for lunch or dinner or both, so precise opening times and days are given only if they differ markedly from the pattern outlined here.

Bars & Clubs

» In cities, bars (and some pubs) open until midnight or later, especially at weekends.

» Clubs stay open to 2am or beyond.

Cafes & Teashops

» In cities: from 7am to 6pm, sometimes later.

» In country areas: teashops open for lunch, and may stay open until 7pm or later in the summer.

» In winter months, country cafe hours are reduced; some close completely October to April (Easter).

Museums & Sights

» Large museums and sights usually open virtually every day of the year.

» Some smaller places open Saturday and Sunday but closed Monday and/or Tuesday.

» Smaller places open daily in high season; open weekends only or can be completely closed in low season.

Post Offices

» Monday to Friday, post offices keep same hours as shops.

» Saturday, 9am to 12.30. Main branches to 5pm.

» Sunday closed.

Climate

London

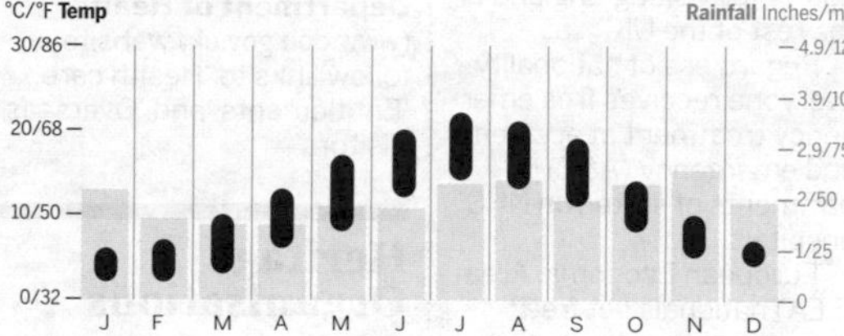

Newquay

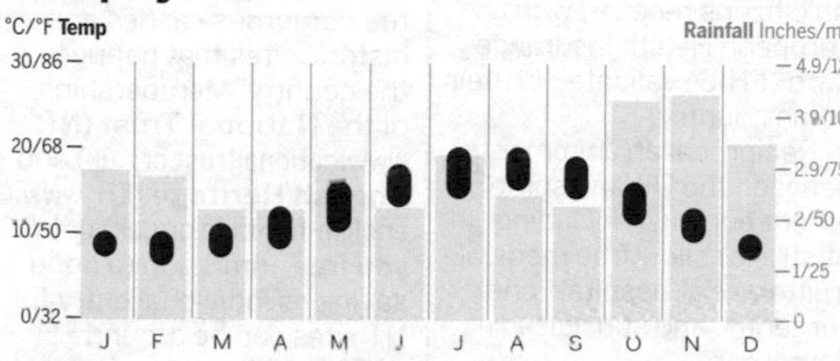

York

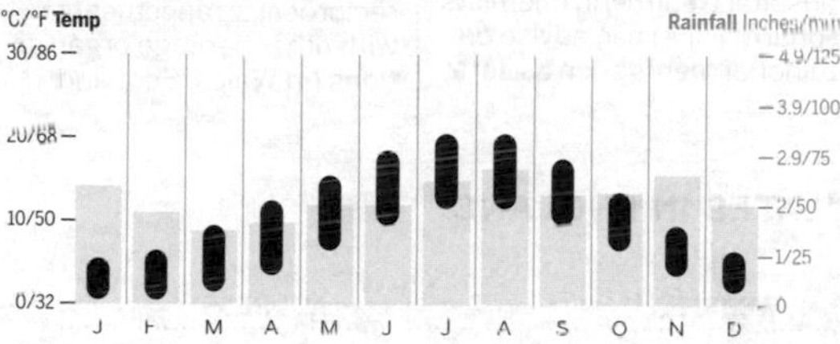

Pubs

» From 11am to 11pm Sunday to Thursday, sometimes to midnight or 1am Friday and Saturday.

» Some pubs shut from 3pm to 6pm.

Restaurants

» Monday to Sunday; some close Sunday evening, or all day Monday.

» Lunch (about noon to 3pm) and dinner (about 6pm to 11pm, to midnight or later in cities).

» Some restaurants open only for lunch or dinner.

» A few restaurants open at around 7am and serve breakfast, but mainly cafes do this.

Shops

» Monday to Friday, 9am to 5pm (5.30pm or 6pm in cities).

» Saturday, 9am to 5pm.

» Sunday, larger shops open 10am to 4pm.

Customs Regulations

The UK has a two-tier customs system: one for goods bought duty-free outside the EU; the other for goods bought in another European Union (EU) country where tax and duty is paid. Below is a summary of the rules; for more information go to www.hmce.gov.uk and search for 'Customs Allowances'.

Duty Free

For duty-free goods from *outside* the EU, the limits include 200 cigarettes, 2L of still wine, plus 1L of spirits or another 2L of wine, 60cc of perfume, and other duty-free goods (including beer) to the value of £300.

Tax & Duty Paid

There is no limit to the goods you can bring from *within* the EU (if taxes have been paid), but customs officials use the following guidelines to distinguish personal use from commercial imports: 3200 cigarettes, 200 cigars, 10L of spirits, 20L of fortified wine, 90L of wine and 110L of beer. Still enough to have one hell of a party

Electricity

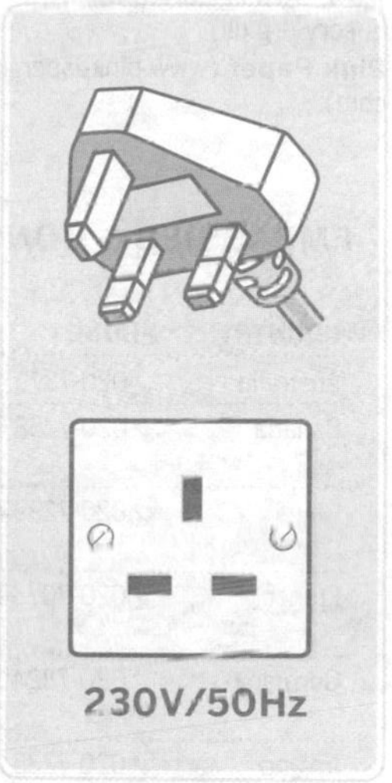

Embassies & Consulates

This is a selection of embassies, consulates and high commissions in London. For a complete list of embassies in the UK, see the website of the **Foreign & Commonwealth Office** (www.fco.gov.uk), which also lists Britain's diplomatic missions overseas.

Gay & Lesbian Travellers

England is a generally tolerant place for gays and lesbians. London, Manchester and Brighton have flourishing gay scenes, and in other sizeable cities (even some small towns) you'll find communities not entirely in the closet. That said, you'll still find pockets of homophobic hostility in some areas. Resources include the following:

Diva (www.divamag.co.uk)

Gay Times (www.gaytimes.co.uk)

London Lesbian & Gay Switchboard (020-7837 7324; www.llgs.org.uk or www.queery.org.uk)

Pink Paper (www.pinkpaper.com)

Health

No immunisations are mandatory for visiting England or the rest of the UK.

Regardless of nationality, everyone receives free emergency treatment at accident and emergency (A&E) departments of state-run NHS hospitals.

European Economic Area (EEA) nationals get free non-emergency treatment (ie the same service British citizens receive) with a European Health Insurance Card (EHIC) validated in their home country.

Reciprocal arrangements between the UK and some other countries (including Australia) allow free medical treatment at hospitals and surgeries, and subsidised dental care.

If you don't need full-on hospital treatment, chemists (pharmacies) can advise on minor ailments such as sore throats and earaches. In large cities, there's always at least one 24/7 chemist.

For more details see the **Department of Health** (www.doh.gov.uk) website – follow links to 'Health care', 'Entitlements' and 'Overseas Visitors'.

Heritage Organisations

A highlight of a journey through England is visiting the numerous castles and historic sites that pepper the country. Membership of the **National Trust** (NT; www.nationaltrust.org.uk) and **English Heritage** (EH; www.english-heritage.org.uk) gets you free admission (a good saving as individual entry to NT sites can be around £5, while EH sites range from free to about £6), as well as reciprocal arrangements with other heritage organisations (in Wales, Scotland

EMBASSIES & CONSULATES IN ENGLAND

COUNTRY	PHONE	WEBSITE	ADDRESS
Australia	020-7379 4334	www.australia.org.uk	The Strand, WC2B 4LA
Canada	020-7258 6600	www.canada.org.uk	1 Grosvenor Sq, W1X 0AB
China	020-7299 4049	www.chinese-embassy.org.uk	49-51 Portland Pl, London W1B 4JL
France	020-7073 1000	www.ambafrance-uk.org	58 Knightsbridge, SW1 7JT
Germany	020-7824 1300	www.london.diplo.de	23 Belgrave Sq, SW1X 8PX
Ireland	020-7235 2171	www.embassyofireland.co.uk	17 Grosvenor Pl, SW1X 7HR
Japan	020-7465 6500	www.uk.emb-japan.go.jp	101 Piccadilly, W1J 7JT
Netherlands	020-7590 3200	www.netherlands-embassy.org.uk	38 Hyde Park Gate, SW7 5DP
New Zealand	020-7930 8422	www.nzembassy.com/uk	80 Haymarket, SW1Y 4TQ
Poland	0870-774 2700	www.polishembassy.org.uk	47 Portland Pl, London W1B 1HQ
USA	020-7499 9000	www.usembassy.org.uk	24 Grosvenor Sq, W1A 1AE

TRAVEL HEALTH WEBSITES

Before visiting England from overseas, consult your government's travel health website:

Australia (www.dfat.gov.au/travel)

Canada (www.travelhealth.gc.ca)

USA (www.cdc.gov/travel/)

and beyond), information handbooks and so on. You can join at the first NT or EH site you visit.

The National Trust protects hundreds of historic buildings plus vast tracts of land with scenic importance. Annual membership costs £49 (with discounts for under-26s and families). A Touring Pass allows free entry to NT properties for one/two weeks (£21/26 per person); families and couples get cheaper rates.

English Heritage is a state-funded organisation responsible for numerous historic sites. Annual membership costs £44 (couples and seniors get discounts). An Overseas Visitors Pass allows free entry to most sites for seven/14 days for £20/25 (with cheaper rates for couples and families).

We have included the relevant acronym (NT or EH) in the information brackets after properties listed throughout this book.

Insurance

Although everyone receives free emergency treatment, regardless of nationality, travel insurance is still highly recommended. It will usually cover medical consultation and treatment at private clinics, which can be quicker than NHS places, and emergency dental care – as well as loss of baggage or valuable items and, most importantly, the cost of any emergency flights home. Worldwide travel insurance is available at www.lonelyplanet.com/travel_services. You can buy, extend and claim online any time – even if you're already on the road.

Internet Access

Internet cafes are surprisingly rare in England, especially away from big cities and tourist spots. Most charge from £1 per hour, and out in the sticks you can pay up to £5 per hour.

Public libraries often have computers with free internet access, but only for 30-minute slots, and demand is high. All the usual warnings apply about keystroke-capturing software and other security risks.

If you'll be using your laptop to get online, an increasing number of hotels, hostels, stations and coffee shops (even some trains) have wi-fi access, charging anything from nothing to £5 per hour.

Legal Matters

The age of consent is 16 (gay or straight). Travellers should note that they can be prosecuted under the law of their home country regarding age of consent, even when abroad.

You must be over 18 to buy alcohol and cigarettes. You usually have to be 18 to enter a pub or bar, although rules are different if you have a meal. Some bars and clubs are over-21 only.

Illegal drugs are widely available, especially in clubs. Cannabis possession is a criminal offence; punishment for carrying a small amount may be a warning, a fine or imprisonment. Dealers face stiffer penalties, as do people caught with other drugs.

Drink-driving is a serious offence. See p849 for more information about speed limits.

On buses and trains (including the London Underground), people without a valid ticket are fined on the spot – usually around £20.

CAN YOU DRINK THE WATER?

Tap water in England is safe unless there's a sign to the contrary (eg on trains). Don't drink from streams in the countryside – you never know if there's a dead sheep upstream.

Money

The currency of England (and Britain) is the pound sterling (£). Paper money comes in £5, £10, £20 and £50 denominations, although some shops don't accept £50s because fakes circulate.

Other currencies are rarely accepted, except some gift shops in London, which may take euros, US dollars, yen and other major currencies.

For a rundown of exchange rates and costs see Need to Know p19.

ATMs

ATMs (often called 'cash machines') are easy to find in cities and even small towns.

Watch out for ATMs that might have been tampered with; a common ruse is to attach a card-reader to the slot.

Credit & Debit Cards

Visa and MasterCard credit and debit cards are widely accepted in England. Smaller businesses, such as pubs or B&Bs, prefer debit cards (or charge a fee for credit cards), and some take cash or cheque only.

Nearly all credit and debit cards use a 'Chip and PIN' system (instead of signing). If your card isn't Chip and PIN enabled, you should be able to sign in the usual way, but some places may not accept your card.

Moneychangers

Cities and larger towns have banks and bureaus for changing your money (cash or travellers cheques) into pounds.

Check rates first; some bureaus offer poor rates or levy outrageous commissions.

You can also change money at some post offices – very handy in country areas, and exchange rates are fair.

Tipping

In England, you're not obliged to tip if the service or food was unsatisfactory (even if it's been automatically added to your bill as a 'service charge').

» Restaurants – around 10%. Also teashops and smarter cafes with full table service. At smarter restaurants waiters can get a bit sniffy if the tip isn't nearer 12% or even 15%.

» Taxis – 10%, or rounded up to the nearest pound, especially in London. It's less usual to tip minicab drivers.

» Toilet attendants – around 50p.

» Pubs – around 10% if you order food at the table and your meal is brought to you. If you order and pay at the bar (food or drinks), tips are not expected.

Travellers Cheques

Travellers cheques are safer than cash, but are rarely used in England, as credit/debit cards and ATMs have become the method of choice. They are rarely accepted for purchases (except at large hotels), so for cash you'll still need to go to a bank or change bureau.

Public Holidays

In England and Wales, most businesses and banks close on these official public holidays (hence the term 'bank holiday'):

New Year's Day 1 January

Easter March/April (Good Friday to Easter Monday inclusive)

May Day First Monday in May

Spring Bank Holiday Last Monday in May

Summer Bank Holiday Last Monday in August

Christmas Day 25 December

Boxing Day 26 December

» If a public holiday falls on a weekend, the nearest Monday is usually taken instead.

» On public holidays, some small museums and places of interest close, but larger attractions have their busiest times.

» If a place closes on Sunday, it'll probably be shut on bank holidays as well.

» Virtually everything – attractions, shops, banks, offices – closes on Christmas Day, although pubs are open at lunchtime.

» There's usually no public transport on Christmas Day, and a very minimal service on Boxing Day.

Roads get busy and hotel prices go up during school holidays. Exact dates vary from year to year and region to region, but are roughly:

Easter Holiday Week before and week after Easter.

Summer Holiday Third week of July to first week of September.

Christmas Holiday Mid-December to first week of January.

There are also three week-long 'half-term' school holidays – usually late February (or early March), late May and late October.

Safe Travel

England is a remarkably safe country, but crime is not unknown in London and other cities. When travelling by tube, tram or urban train service at night, choose a carriage containing other people.

Unlicensed minicabs – a bloke with a car earning money on the side – operate in large cities, but these are worth avoiding unless you know what you're doing. Annoyances include driving round in circles, then charging an enormous fare. Dangers include driving to a remote location then robbery or rape. To avoid this, use a metered taxi or phone a reputable minicab company and get an up-front quote for the ride.

Telephone Codes

In this book, area codes and individual numbers are listed together, separated by a hyphen.

Area codes in Britain do not have a standard format

GOVERNMENT TRAVEL ADVICE

The following government websites offer travel advisories and information on current hot spots.

Australian Department of Foreign Affairs (www.smarttraveller.gov.au)

British Foreign Office (www.fco.gov.uk/countryadvice)

Canadian Department of Foreign Affairs (www.dfait-maeci.gc.ca)

US State Department (http://travel.state.gov)

or length, eg ☎020 for London, ☎0161 for Manchester, ☎01225 for Bath, ☎015394 for Ambleside, followed as usual by the individual number.

Other codes:

» ☎0500 or ☎0800 – free calls

» ☎0845 – calls at local rate, wherever you're dialling from within the UK

» ☎087 – national rate

» ☎089 or ☎09 – premium rate

» ☎07 – mobile phones, more expensive than calling a landline

To call outside the UK dial ☎00, then the country code (☎1 for USA, ☎61 for Australia etc), the area code (you usually drop the initial zero) and the number.

» operator ☎100

» international operator ☎155 – also for reverse-charge (collect) calls

For directory inquiries, a host of agencies compete for your business and charge from 10p to 40p; numbers include ☎118 192, ☎118 118, ☎118 500 and ☎118 811.

Tourist Information

All English cities and towns, and some villages, have a tourist information centre (TIC). Some TICs are run by national parks and often have small exhibits about the area. You'll also see 'visitor welcome centres' or 'visitor information centres' – for ease we've called all these places 'tourist offices' in this book.

These places have helpful staff, books and maps for sale, leaflets to give away and loads of advice on things to see or do. They can also assist with booking accommodation. Most tourist offices keep regular business hours; in quiet areas they close from October to March, while in popular areas they open daily year-round.

TOURISM SITES

Before leaving home, check the informative, comprehensive and wide-ranging websites **VisitBritain** (www.visitbritain.com) and **EnjoyEngland** (www.enjoyengland.com), covering all the angles of national tourism, with links to numerous other sites.

For a list of all tourist offices around Britain see www.visitmap.info/tic.

Travellers with Disabilities

All new buildings have wheelchair access, and even hotels in grand old country houses often have lifts, ramps and other facilities. Smaller B&Bs are often harder to adapt, so you'll have less choice here.

Getting around in cities, new buses have low floors for easy access, but few have conductors who can lend a hand when you're getting on or off. Many taxis take wheelchairs, or just have more room in the back.

For long-distance travel, coaches may present problems if you can't walk, but the main operator, **National Express** (www.nationalexpress.com) has wheelchair-friendly coaches on many routes. For details, ring their dedicated Disabled Passenger Travel Helpline on ☎0121-423 8479 or try the website.

On most inter-city trains there's more room and better facilities, and usually station staff around; just have a word and they'll be happy to help.

Useful organisations:

Good Access Guide (www.goodaccessguide.co.uk)

Royal Association for Disability & Rehabilitation (RADAR; www.radar.org.uk) Published titles include *Holidays in Britain and Ireland*. Through RADAR you can get a key for 7000 public disabled toilets across the UK.

Tourism For All (www.tourismforall.org.uk)

Visas

If you're a European Economic Area (EEA) national, you don't need a visa to visit (or work in) England or any other part of the UK. Citizens of Australia, Canada, New Zealand, South Africa and the USA are given leave to enter the UK at their point of arrival for up to six months (three months for some nationalities), but are prohibited from working. For more info see www.ukvisas.gov.uk or www.ukba.homeoffice.gov.uk.

Work

Nationals of most European countries don't need a permit to work in England, but everyone else does.

Exceptions include most Commonwealth citizens with a UK-born parent; the 'Right of Abode' allows you to live and work in England and the rest of the UK.

Most Commonwealth citizens under 31 are eligible for a Working Holidaymaker Visa – valid for two years, you can work for a total of 12 months, and must be obtained in advance.

Useful websites are listed below. Also very handy is the 'Living & Working Abroad' thread on the Thorntree forum at lonelyplanet.com.

BUNAC (www.bunac.org)

Go Work Go Travel (www.goworkgotravel.com)

UK Border Agency (www.ukba.homeoffice.gov.uk)

UK Employment & Recruitment Agencies (www.employmentrecruitment.co.uk)

Working Holiday Guru (www.workingholidayguru.com)

Transport

GETTING THERE & AWAY

London is a global transport hub, so you can easily fly to England from just about anywhere. In recent years, the massive growth of budget ('no-frills') airlines has increased the number of routes – and reduced the fares – between England and other countries in Europe.

Your other main option for travel between England and mainland Europe is ferry, either port-to-port or combined with a long-distance bus trip, although journeys can be long and financial savings not huge compared with budget airfares. International trains are much more comfortable, and another 'green' option; the Channel Tunnel allows direct rail services between England, France and Belgium, with onward connections to many other European destinations.

Getting from England to Scotland and Wales is easy. The bus and train systems are fully integrated and in most cases you won't even know you've crossed the border. Passports are not required – although some Scots and Welsh may think they should be!

Flights, tours and rail tickets can be booked online at www.lonelyplanet.com/bookings.

Air

Airports

London's main airports:

Heathrow (LHR; www.heathrowairport.com) The world's busiest airport, and the UK's main airport for international flights; often chaotic and crowded. About 15 miles west of central London.

Gatwick (LGW; www.gatwickairport.com) The UK's number-two airport, also mainly for international flights, 30 miles south of central London.

Stansted (STN; www.stanstedairport.com) About 35 miles northeast of central London, mainly handling charter and budget European flights.

Luton (LTN; www.london-luton.co.uk) Some 35 miles north of central London, especially well-known as a holiday-flight airport.

CLIMATE CHANGE & TRAVEL

Every form of transport that relies on carbon-based fuel generates CO2, the main cause of human-induced climate change. Modern travel is dependent on aeroplanes and while they might use less fuel per kilometre per person than most cars, they travel much greater distances. It's not just CO2 emissions from aircraft that are the problem. The altitude at which aircraft emit gases (including CO2) and particles contributes significantly to their total impact on climate change. The Intergovernmental Panel on Climate Change believes aviation is responsible for 4.9% of climate change – double the effect of its CO2 emissions alone.

Lonely Planet regards travel as a global benefit. We encourage the use of more climate-friendly travel modes where possible and, together with other concerned partners across many industries, we support the carbon-offset scheme run by ClimateCare. Websites such as climatecare.org use 'carbon calculators' that allow people to offset the greenhouse gases they are responsible for with contributions to portfolios of climate-friendly initiatives throughout the developing world. Lonely Planet offsets the carbon footprint of all staff and author travel.

London City (LCY; www.londoncityairport.com) A few miles east of central London, specialising in flights to/from European and other UK airports.

For details on getting between these airports and central London, see p124.

Some planes on European and long-haul routes go direct to major regional airports including Manchester, while smaller regional airports such as Southampton and Birmingham are served by flights to and from continental Europe and Ireland.

Land

Bus & Coach

You can easily get between England and other European countries via long-distance bus or coach. The international network **Eurolines** (www.eurolines.com) connects a huge number of destinations; you can buy tickets online via one of the national operators.

Services to/from England are operated by **National Express** (www.nationalexpress.com). Some sample journey times to/from London:

Amsterdam 12 hours.
Barcelona 24 hours.
Dublin 12 hours.
Paris Eight hours

If you book early, and can be flexible with timings (ie travel when few other people want to) you can get some very good deals – some branded as 'fun fares' and 'promo fares'. For example, London to Paris or Amsterdam one way starts at just £18, although paying nearer £25 is more usual.

Train

CHANNEL TUNNEL SERVICES

The Channel Tunnel makes direct train travel between England and continental Europe a fast and enjoyable option. High-speed **Eurostar** (www.eurostar.com) passenger services hurtle at least 10 times daily between London and Paris (2½ hours) or Brussels (two hours). You can buy tickets from travel agencies, major train stations or direct from the Eurostar website. The normal single fare between London and Paris/Brussels is around £150, but if you buy in advance and travel at a less busy period, deals drop to around £90 return or even less. You can also buy 'through fare' tickets from many cities in England – for example York to Paris, or Manchester to Brussels. Very good train and hotel combination deals are available – bizarrely sometimes cheaper than train fare only.

Drivers use **Eurotunnel** (www.eurotunnel.com). At Folkestone in England or Calais in France, you drive onto a train, get carried through the tunnel and drive off at the other end. The trains run about four times an hour from 6am to 10pm, then hourly. Loading and unloading is an hour; the journey takes 35 minutes. You can book in advance online or pay on the spot. The one-way cost for a car and passengers is around £90 to £150 depending on the time of day (less busy times are cheaper); promotional fares often bring it nearer to £50.

TRAIN & FERRY CONNECTIONS

As well as Eurostar, many 'normal' trains run between England and mainland Europe. You buy one ticket, but get off the train at the port, walk onto a ferry, then get another train on the other side. The main route is Amsterdam–London (via Hook of Holland and Harwich).

Travelling between Ireland and England, the main train-ferry-train route is Dublin to London, via Dun Laoghaire and Holyhead. Ferries also run between Rosslare and Fishguard or Pembroke in Wales, with train connections on either side.

Sea

The main ferry routes between England and mainland Europe:

- » Dover–Calais or Boulogne (France)
- » Harwich–Hook of Holland (Netherlands)
- » Hull– Zeebrugge (Belgium)
- » Hull–Rotterdam (Netherlands)
- » Newcastle–Bergen (Norway)
- » Newcastle–Gothenberg (Sweden)
- » Portsmouth–Santander (Spain)
- » Portsmouth–Bilbao (Spain).

Routes to/from Ireland include Holyhead (Wales) to Dun Laoghaire.

Competition from Eurotunnel and budget airlines has forced ferry operators to discount heavily and offer flexible fares, meaning great bargains at quiet times of day or year. For example, the short cross-channel routes such as Dover to Calais or Boulogne can be as low as £20 for a car plus up to five passengers, although around £50 is more likely. If you're a foot passenger, or cycling, there's often less need to book ahead, and cheap fares on the short crossings start from about £10 each way.

Main operators:

Brittany Ferries (www.brittany-ferries.com)

DFDS Seaways (www.dfds.co.uk)

Irish Ferries (www.irishferries.com)

Norfolkline (www.norfolkline.com)

P&O Ferries (www.poferries.com)

Speedferries (www.speedferries.com)

Stena Line (www.stenaline.com)

Transmanche (www.transmancheferries.com)

A very handy option is www.ferrybooker.com, a single site covering all sea-ferry routes and operators, plus Eurotunnel.

GETTING AROUND

For getting around England your first decision is whether to go by car or public transport. While having your own car makes the best use of your time, and helps reach remote places, hire and fuel costs can be expensive for budget travellers – while the trials of traffic jams and parking in major cities hit everyone – so public transport is often the better way to go.

Your main public transport options are train and long-distance bus (called coach in England). Services between major towns and cities are generally good, although at 'peak' (busy) times you must book in advance to be sure of getting a ticket. Conversely, if you book ahead early and/or travel at 'off-peak' periods, tickets can be very cheap.

As long as you have time, by using a mix of train, coach, local bus, the odd taxi, walking and occasionally hiring a bike, you can get almost anywhere without having to drive. You'll certainly see more of the countryside than you might slogging along grey motorways.

Air

England's domestic air companies include British Airways, BMI, BMIbaby, easyJet and Ryanair, but flights around the country aren't really necessary for tourists; even if you're going from one end of the country to the other (eg London to Newcastle, or Manchester to Newquay) trains compare favourably with planes, once airport down-time is factored in. On costs, you might get a bargain airfare, but with advance planning trains can still be cheaper.

Bicycle

England is a compact country, and getting around by bicycle is perfectly feasible – and a great way to really see the country – if you've got time to spare. For more inspiration see p38.

Hiring a bike is easy in London; the capital is dotted with automatic docking stations where bikes can be hired on the spot – and they're free for the first 30 minutes. For info go to the Transport for London site (www.tfl.gov.uk) and follow the links to Cycling. Other hire options are listed at www.lcc.org.uk. Other tourist spots such as Oxford and Cambridge also have plentiful options. Rates start at about £10 per day, £20 for something half decent. Bike hire is also possible in country areas, especially at forestry sites and reservoirs now primarily used for leisure activities, for example Kielder Water in Northumberland and Grizedale Forest in the Lake District. In some areas, disused railway lines are now bike routes, notably the Peak District in Derbyshire.

Bus & Coach

If you're on a tight budget, long-distance buses (called coaches in England) are nearly always the cheapest way to get around, although they're also the slowest – sometimes by a considerable margin. Many towns have separate bus and coach stations; make sure you go to the right place!

National Express (www.nationalexpress.com/coach) is the main coach operator, with a wide network and frequent services between main centres. Fares vary: they're cheaper if you book in advance and travel at quieter times, and more expensive if you buy your ticket on the spot and it's Friday afternoon. As a guide, a 200-mile trip (eg London to York) will cost around £15 to £20 if you book a few days in advance.

Megabus (www.megabus.com) operates a budget-airline-style coach service between about 30 destinations around the country. Go at a quiet time, book early, and your ticket will be very cheap. Book later, for a busy time and...you get the picture.

For information about short-distance and local bus services see p850.

Bus Passes & Discounts

National Express offers discount passes to full-time students and under-26s, called Young Persons Coachcards. They cost £10 and get you 30% off standard adult fares. Also available are coachcards for people over 60, families and disabled travellers.

For touring the country, National Express offers BritXplorer passes, allowing unlimited travel for seven days (£79), 14 days (£139) and 28 days (£219). You don't need to book journeys in advance; if the coach has a spare seat, you can take it.

Car & Motorcycle

Travelling by car or motorbike means you can be independent and flexible, and reach remote places. Downsides for drivers include traffic jams and high parking costs in cities.

Hire

Compared with many countries (especially the USA), hire rates are expensive in England; you should expect to pay around £250 per week for a small car (unlimited mileage) but rates rise at

MOTORING ORGANISATIONS

Organisations include the **Automobile Association** (www.theaa.com) and the **Royal Automobile Club** (www.rac.co.uk); annual membership starts at around £35, including 24-hour roadside breakdown assistance. A greener alternative is the **Environmental Transport Association** (www.eta.co.uk); it provides all the usual services (breakdown assistance, roadside rescue, vehicle inspections etc) but doesn't campaign for more roads.

busy times and drop at quiet times. Some main players:

Avis (www.avis.co.uk)
Budget (www.budget.co.uk)
Europcar (www.europcar.co.uk)
Sixt (www.sixt.co.uk)
Thrifty (www.thrifty.co.uk)

Many international websites have separate web pages for customers in different countries, and the prices for a car in England on the UK webpages can differ from the same car's prices on the USA or Australia pages. You have to surf a lot of sites to find the best deals.

Another option is to look online for small local car-hire companies in England who can undercut the international franchises. Generally those in cities are cheaper than in rural areas. See Getting Around in the main city sections for more details, or see a rental-broker site such as **UK Car Hire** (www.ukcarhire.net).

Yet another option is to hire a motorhome or campervan. It's more expensive than hiring a car, but saves on accommodation costs, and gives almost unlimited freedom. Sites to check:

Cool Campervans (www.coolcampervans.com)
Just Go (www.justgo.uk.com)
Wild Horizon (www.wildhorizon.co.uk)

Parking

Many cities have short-stay and long-stay car parks; the latter are cheaper though may be less convenient. 'Park & Ride' systems allow you to park on the edge of the city then ride to the centre on regular buses provided for an all-in-one price.

Yellow lines (single or double) along the edge of the road indicate restrictions. Find the nearby sign that spells out when you can and can't park. In London and other big cities, traffic wardens operate with efficiency; if you park on the yellow lines at the wrong time, your car will be clamped or towed away, and it'll cost you £100 or more to get driving again. In some cities there are also red lines, which mean no stopping at all.

Roads & Rules

Motorways and main A-roads are dual carriageways and deliver you quickly from one end of the country to another. Lesser A-roads, B-roads and minor roads are much more scenic and fun, as you wind through the countryside from village to village – ideal for car or motorcycle touring. You can't travel fast, but you won't care.

A foreign driving licence is valid in England for up to 12 months. If you plan to bring a car from Europe, it's illegal to drive without (at least) third-party insurance. Some other important rules:

» drive on the left (!)
» wear fitted seat belts in cars
» wear crash helmets on motorcycles
» give way to your right at junctions and roundabouts
» always use the left-side lane on motorways and dual-carriageways, unless overtaking (although so many people ignore this rule, you'd think it didn't exist)
» don't use a mobile phone while driving unless it's fully hands-free (another rule frequently flouted).

Speed limits:

» 30mph (48km/h) in built-up areas
» 60mph (96km/h) on main roads
» 70mph (112km/h) on motorways and most (but not all) dual carriageways.

Drinking and driving is taken very seriously; you're allowed a minimum blood-alcohol level of 80mg/100mL (0.08%) – campaigners want it reduced to 50mg/100mL.

Hitching

Hitching is not as common as it used to be in England, maybe because more people have cars, maybe because few drivers give lifts any more. It's perfectly possible, however, if you don't mind long waits, although travellers should understand that they're taking a small but potentially serious risk, and we don't recommend it. If you decide to go by thumb, note that it's illegal to hitch on motorways; you must use approach roads or service stations.

Local Transport

English cities usually have good local public transport systems – a combination of bus, train and tram – often run by a confusing number of separate companies. Tourist offices can provide maps and information. More details are given in the city sections throughout this book.

Bus

There are good local bus networks year-round in cities and towns. Buses also run in some rural areas year-round, although timetables are designed to serve schools and businesses, so there can be few midday and weekend services (and they may stop running during school holidays), or buses may link local villages to a market town on only one day each week. In tourist spots (especially national parks) there are frequent services from Easter to September. It's always worth double-checking at a tourist office before planning your day's activities around a bus that may not actually be running.

In this book, along with the local bus route number, frequency and duration, we have provided indicative prices if the fare is over £5. If it's less than this, we have generally omitted the fare.

BUS PASSES

If you're taking a few local bus rides in a day of energetic sightseeing, day-passes (with names like Day Rover, Wayfarer or Explorer), are cheaper than buying several single tickets. If you plan to linger longer in one area, three-day passes are also available; often they can be bought on your first bus, and may include local rail services. It's always worth asking ticket clerks or bus drivers about your options.

Taxi

There are two sorts of taxi in England: the famous black cabs (some with advertising livery in other colours), which have meters and can be hailed in the street; and minicabs, which are cheaper but can only be called by phone. In London and other big cities, taxis cost £2 to £3 per mile. In rural areas it's about half that. The best place to find the local taxi's phone number is the local pub. Alternatively, call **National Cabline** (☎0800 123444) from a landline phone; the service pinpoints your location and transfers you to an approved local taxi company.

Also useful is www.traintaxi.co.uk – designed to help you 'bridge the final gap' between the train station and your hotel or other final destination.

STATION NAMES

London has several mainline train stations, such as Victoria, Paddington, King's Cross, Waterloo, Charing Cross and Liverpool St, positioned in a rough circle around the city's central area (and mostly linked by the Circle underground line). The stations' proper names are London Victoria, London Paddington, London King's Cross and so on, and this is how you'll see them on official timetables, information boards and booking websites – although the English never use the full names in everyday speech.

For clarity, in the destination chapters throughout this book we have used the full name for these London stations (except in the London chapter). This is also to help distinguish the London stations from stations in some other British cities that also share station names such as Victoria and Charing Cross.

BIKES ON TRAINS

Bicycles can be taken free of charge on most local urban trains (although they may not be allowed at peak times when the trains are too crowded with commuters) and on shorter trips in rural areas, on a first-come-first-served basis. Bike can be carried on long-distance train journeys free of charge as well, but advance booking is required for most conventional bikes. (Folding bikes can be carried on pretty much any train at any time.) In theory, this shouldn't be too much trouble as most long-distance rail trips are best bought in advance anyway, but you have to go a long way down the path of booking your seat, before you start booking your bike – only to find space isn't available. A better course of action is to buy in advance at a major rail station, where the booking clerk can help you through the options, or phone the relevant operator's Customer Service department. Have a large cup of coffee and a stress-reliever handy. And a final warning: when railways are being repaired, cancelled trains are replaced by buses – and they won't take bikes.

A very useful leaflet called 'Cycling by Train' is available at major stations or downloadable from www.nationalrail.co.uk/passenger_services/cyclists.html.

Train

For long-distance travel around England, trains are generally faster and more comfortable than coaches but can be more expensive, although with discount tickets they're competitive – and often take you through beautiful countryside. The English like to moan about their trains, but around 85% run on time. The other 15% that get delayed or cancelled mostly impact commuters rather than long-distance services.

About 20 different companies operate train services in Britain (for example: First Great Western runs from London to Bristol, Cornwall and South Wales; National Express East Coast runs London to Leeds, York and Scotland; Virgin Trains run the 'west coast' route from London to Birmingham, Carlisle and Scotland), while Network Rail operates track and stations. For some passengers this system can be confusing at first, but information and ticket-buying services are mostly centralised. If you have to change trains, or use two or more train operators, you still buy one ticket – valid for the whole of your journey. The main railcards are also accepted by all operators.

Your first stop should be **National Rail Enquiries** (☎08457 48 49 50; www.nationalrail.co.uk), the nationwide timetable and fare information service. This site also advertises special offers, and has real-time links to station departure boards. Once you've found the journey you need, links take you to the relevant train operator or to centralised ticketing services (eg, www.thetrainline.com, www.qjump.co.uk, www.raileasy.co.uk) to buy the ticket. To use these websites you always have to state a preferred time and day of travel, even if you don't mind when you go, but with a little delving around they can offer some real bargains.

You can also buy train tickets on the spot at stations, which is fine for short journeys, but discount tickets for longer trips are usually not available and must be bought in advance by phone or online.

For planning your trip, some very handy maps of the UK's rail network can be downloaded from the National Rail Enquiries website.

HOW MUCH TO...?

When travelling long-distance by train or bus/coach in England, it's important to realise that there's no such thing as a standard fare. Prices vary according to demand and when you buy your ticket. Book long in advance and travel on Tuesday mid-morning, and it's cheap. Buy your ticket on the spot late Friday afternoon, and it'll be a lot more expensive. Ferries use similar systems. Throughout this book, we have generally quoted *sample* fares somewhere in between the very cheapest and most expensive options. The price you pay will almost certainly be different.

Classes

There are two classes of rail travel: first and standard. First class costs around 50% more than standard and, except on very crowded trains, is not really worth it. At weekends some train operators offer 'upgrades' for an extra £10 to £15 on top of your standard class fare.

Costs & Reservations

For short journeys (under about 50 miles) it's usually best to buy tickets on the spot at train stations. For longer journeys, on-the-spot fares are always available, but tickets are much cheaper if bought in advance. Essentially, the earlier you book, the cheaper it gets. You can also save if you travel 'off-peak' (ie, the days and times that aren't busy). Advance purchase usually gets a reserved seat too. The cheapest fares are nonrefundable, so if you miss your train you'll have to buy a new ticket.

If you buy online, you can have the ticket posted (UK addresses only), or collect it at the station on the day of travel from automatic machines.

Whichever operator you travel with and wherever you buy tickets, these are the three main fare types:

Anytime Buy any time, travel any time.

Advance Buy ticket in advance, travel only on specific trains.

Off-peak Buy ticket any time, travel off-peak.

For an idea of the price difference, an Anytime single ticket from London to York will cost around £100 or more, an Off-peak around £80, while an Advance is around £20, and even less if you book early enough or don't mind arriving at midnight.

If train doesn't get you all the way to your destination, a **PlusBus** supplement (usually around £2) validates your train ticket for onward travel by bus – more convenient, and usually cheaper, than buying a separate bus ticket. For details see www.plusbus.info.

Train Passes

DISCOUNT PASSES

Local train passes usually cover rail networks around a city (many include bus travel too), and are mentioned in the individual city sections throughout this book. If you're staying in England for a while, passes known as 'railcards' are available:

16-25 Railcard For those aged 16 to 25, or a full-time UK student.

Family & Friends Railcard Covers up to four adults and four children travelling together.

Senior Railcard For anyone over 60.

These railcards cost around £26 (valid for one year, available from major stations or online) and get you a 33% discount on most train fares, except those already heavily discounted. With the Family card, adults get 33% and children get 60% discounts, so the fee is easily repaid in a couple of journeys. For full details on all discount passes see www.railcard.co.uk. Also available:

Disabled Person's Railcard (£18) You can get an application from stations or from the railcard website.

REGIONAL PASSES

Network Railcard For those concentrating their travels on southeast England (eg London to Dover, Weymouth, Cambridge or Oxford). Covers up to four adults and up to four children travelling together outside peak times.

NATIONAL PASSES

BritRail (www.britrail.com) For countrywide travel. Available to visitors from overseas (not in England). Must be bought in your country of origin from a specialist travel agency. Available in three different versions (England only; all Britain; UK and Ireland) for periods from four to 30 days.

almshouse – accommodation for the aged or needy

billion – the British billion is a million million (unlike the American billion – a thousand million)

bloke – man (colloquial)

bridleway – path or track that can be used by walkers, horse riders and cyclists

Brummie – native of Birmingham

bus – local bus; see also *coach*

chemist – pharmacist

circus – junction of several city streets, usually circular, and usually with a green or other feature at the centre

coach – long-distance bus

coasteering – adventurous activity that involves making your way around a rocky coastline by climbing, scrambling, jumping or swimming

DIY – do-it-yourself, ie home improvements

downs – rolling upland, characterised by lack of trees

duvet – quilt replacing sheets and blankets ('doona' to Australians)

evensong – daily evening service (Church of England)

fell race – tough running race through hills or moors

fen – drained or marshy low-lying flat land

fiver – five-pound note

flat – apartment (colloquial)

flip-flops – plastic sandals with a single strap over toes ('thongs' to Australians)

footpath – path through countryside or between houses in towns and cities, not beside a road (that's called a 'pavement')

guv, guvner – from governor, a colloquial but respectful term of address for owner or boss; can sometimes be used ironically

HI – Hostelling International (organisation)

hire – rent

inn – pub with accommodation

lift – machine for carrying people up and down in large buildings ('elevator' to Americans)

lock – part of a canal or river that can be closed off and the water levels changed to raise or lower boats

mad – insane (not angry, as in American English)

Marches – borderlands between England and Wales, after the Anglo-Saxon word *mearc*, meaning 'boundary'

motorway – major road linking cities (equivalent to 'interstate' or 'freeway')

motte – mound on which a castle was built

naff – inferior, in poor taste (colloquial)

NCN – National Cycle Network

OS – Ordnance Survey

p (pronounced 'pee') – pence (ie 2p is 'two p' not 'two pence' or 'tuppence')

pile – a large imposing building

postbus – minibus delivering the mail, also carrying passengers – found in remote areas

punter – customer (colloquial)

quid – pound (colloquial)

ramble – short easy walk

reiver – warrior or raider (historic term; northern England)

return ticket – round-trip ticket

RSPB – Royal Society for the Protection of Birds

sarsen – boulder, a geological remnant usually found in chalky areas (sometimes used in neolithic constructions eg Stonehenge and Avebury)

single ticket – one-way ticket

tenner – £10 note (colloquial)

tor – pointed hill

torch – flashlight

Tory – Conservative (political party)

towpath – path running beside a river or canal, where horses once towed barges

twitcher – obsessive birdwatcher

Tube, the – London's underground railway system (colloquial)

Underground, the – London's underground railway system

verderer – officer upholding law and order in the royal forests

wolds – open, rolling countryside

YHA – Youth Hostels Association

behind the scenes

SEND US YOUR FEEDBACK

We love to hear from travellers – your comments keep us on our toes and help make our books better. Our well-travelled team reads every word on what you loved or loathed about this book. Although we cannot reply individually to postal submissions, we always guarantee that your feedback goes straight to the appropriate authors, in time for the next edition. Each person who sends us information is thanked in the next edition – and the most useful submissions are rewarded with a free book.

Visit **lonelyplanet.com/contact** to submit your updates and suggestions or to ask for help. Our award-winning website also features inspirational travel stories, news and discussions.

Note: We may edit, reproduce and incorporate your comments in Lonely Planet products such as guidebooks, websites and digital products, so let us know if you don't want your comments reproduced or your name acknowledged. For a copy of our privacy policy visit lonelyplanet.com/privacy.

OUR READERS

Many thanks to the travellers who used the last edition and wrote to us with helpful hints, useful advice and interesting anecdotes:

A Helen Aesa, Victoria Atherstone, Peggie Atkins **B** Linzi Banks, Christoph Bauer, Jane Boulding, Hilary Bristow-Smith, JR Brown, Vicky Bull, Chris Byrom **C** Claudia Canevari, Fiona Casterton, Davide Cerruti, Seren Charrington-Greene, Camelia Chirtes, Katie Colburn, Lori Costantini, Steven Cottrell, Stephen Craddock, Anthony Cross, C Cunningham **D** Emma Dadds, Pam Daragan, John David, Ashley De Freitas, Alberto Della Santina, Monica Durksen **E** Lucy E, Jane Ellis, Jane Ellis, Sean Everett **F** Roy Fearnall, Anthony Fisher, Mark Fittall, Michael Fraser **G** Jo Gallagher, Sean Gardiner, Judi Goodchild, Carl Griffin, Neil Grosvenor **H** Jackie Hall, Lillian R Hall, Patti Harris, Craig Hayes, Tanja Herrmann, Christiane Hoffmann, John Hope, Michael Hornickel, Jay Howard, Shona Howes, Steve Hudson **J** Mollie Jameson, Tatiana Jardim, John & Valerie Johnson, Steve Johnson, Rick Jones **K** Robert Kettle **L** Vicki Lambert, Sarah Lang **M** Allison Mackay, Faisal Mahomed, Natalie Manifold, Will Marchant, Pascale Martineau, Meghan Maury, Trevor Mazzucchelli, Siobhan McDonald, Colleen McLaughlin, Sheila Melot, Rachael Metcalfe, Ina Meyerhof, Andrea Mikleova, Kevin Moreland, Pierre Morin, Mark Motileb **N** Dirk Nehls, Dave Newman, Daisy Nicholson, Henrik Norberg **O** Louise O'Reilly **P** Gary Padfield, Douglas Palardy, Trent Paton, Paul & Kumari Pease, Andrew Peters, Fiona Pouchard **Q** Moin Qazi **R** Minaz Ramzan, Stephen Reeve, Maricela Robles, Darren Ross **S** Barbara & Mark Sadler, Bekir Salgin, Frank Savery, Stephanie Schintler, Aaran Scott, Sally Searle, Caroline Sharp, Paula Smith, Margaret Snowball, Becky Spencer, Hayley Stead, Richard Stuttle, Anneli Sundqvist, Dave Swinfen, Ragnar Sydbrant **T** Roger Taylor, Naomi Timpany, Luke Tomkinson, Thu Trang **V** Angela Valente, Betsie Van Coillie, Anna Visciano, Nancy Voigts **W** Sue Wallis, Alasdair Warwood, Paul Watson, Tony Wheeler, Thomas Woodworth, Stephen Young.

AUTHOR THANKS

David Else

As always, massive appreciation goes to my wife Corinne, for joining me on many of my research trips around England, and for not minding when I locked myself away for 12 hours at a time to write this book – and for bringing coffee when it gets nearer 16 hours. Thanks also to the co-authors of this book; my name goes down as coordinating author, but I couldn't have done it without this team. And finally, thanks to Cliff Wilkinson my commissioning editor at Lonely Planet London, and to all the friendly faces in the production departments at Lonely Planet Melbourne who helped bring this book to final fruition.

Oliver Berry

Big thanks as always to everyone for keeping the home fires burning and the cups of tea coming, but biggest thanks as always to Susie Berry and Molly Berry. Big thanks also to lots of helpful people I met along the way or who helped me during the research of this book, including Sandrine Cofflard, Emmanuelle Bouvet, Claire Thomas-Chenard and Jean-François Carille. Lastly thanks to Cliff Wilkinson for the gig, David Else for steering the ship, and of course all my co-authors, along with the Hobo for keeping me company when all other lights went out.

Joe Bindloss

First up, thanks as always to my partner Linda and my little boy Tyler for going without bedtime stories while I was researching this book. In Shropshire, thanks to Tony and Petra Bindloss and my kid brothers Peter and Eddie, for providing a home away from home. Across the Midlands, thanks to all the travellers who provided top tips and recommendations. Thanks also to David Else, for fielding questions on the road, and to Clifton Wilkinson at Lonely Planet for calmly managing this new edition.

Fionn Davenport

A big thanks to Trevor Evers and the staff of Marketing Manchester, who were as helpful and as gracious as always. Thanks to Oliver Thomas for taking time out of his busy day to answer my questions. Thanks to the staff at the tourist offices in Liverpool, Blackpool, Douglas and elsewhere – you may not know why I asked so many questions, but your help in answering them is much appreciated. Thanks to Cliff, David and everyone else at Lonely Planet. And finally thanks to Caroline, who makes coming home the best bit of all.

Marc Di Duca

Big thanks must go to fellow Darlingtonian Clifton for entrusting me with the Northeast and Southeast chapters of this guide, and to David Else for his guidance throughout. A huge 'ta' to my parents Jacqueline and Paul in Whitley Bay for all their Tyneside insights and for letting me kip in their back bedroom between flits into the wilds of Northumberland. Undying gratitude goes to all the staff at tourist offices around the land, especially those in Brighton, Canterbury, Newcastle, Rye, Haltwhistle, Barnard Castle and Berwick. Also thanks to Madeleine in Berwick, Colin in Sandwich, my sister Selena in Darlington, Geoff in Killhope and inlaws Mykola and Vira in Kyiv for all their help. Last but certainly not least, heartfelt thanks must go to my wife Tanya and son Taras for all the long days we spend apart.

Belinda Dixon

It's always a true collaboration, so sincere thanks to all who've supported and advised along the way. As ever, tourist office staff have been unfailingly helpful, but particular thanks go to those at Portsmouth (Southsea), Poole, Salisbury, Lyme, Lulworth Cove and at the Dartmoor National Park – they even managed to explain the baffling complexities of the bus

This Book

This 6th edition of *England* was researched and written by David Else (coordinating author), Oliver Berry, Joe Bindloss, Fionn Davenport, Marc Di Duca, Belinda Dixon, Peter Dragicevich, Etain O'Carroll and Neil Wilson. The previous edition was also researched by Nana Luckham. The book was commissioned in Lonely Planet's London office, and produced by the following people:

Commissioning Editors Errol Hunt, Glenn van der Knijff, Clifton Wilkinson

Coordinating Editor Gina Tsarouhas

Coordinating Cartographer Alex Leung

Coordinating Layout Designer Jacqui Saunders

Managing Editors Imogen Bannister, Annelies Mertens

Managing Cartographers Adrian Persoglia, Amanda Sierp, Herman So

Managing Layout Designer Indra Kilfoyle

Assisting Editors Holly Alexander, Elisa Arduca, Kate Evans, Chris Girdler, Carly Hall, Trent Holden, Evan Jones, Amy Karafin, Ali Lemer, Shawn Low, Joanne Newell, Katie O'Connell, Susan Paterson, Charles Rawlings-Way, Erin Richards, Alison Ridgway, Louisa Syme, Angela Tinson, Branislava Vladisavljevic, Jeanette Wall

Assisting Cartographers Xavier Di Toro

Assisting Layout Designer Kerrianne Southway

Cover Research Naomi Parker

Internal Image Research Aude Vauconsant

Illustrator Javier Zarracina

Thanks to Mark Adams, Sasha Baskett, David Connolly, Stefanie Di Trocchio, Janine Eberle, Brigitte Ellemor, Joshua Geoghegan, Mark Germanchis, Michelle Glynn, Liz Heynes, Lauren Hunt, Laura Jane, David Kemp, Nic Lehman, John Mazzocchi, Wayne Murphy, Piers Pickard, Averil Robertson, Lachlan Ross, Michael Ruff, Julie Sheridan, Laura Stansfeld, John Taufa, Sam Trafford, Juan Winata, Emily K Wolman, Celia Wood, Nick Wood

82 timetable. Finally smiles to the AD, for serenity, sanity and sea swims.

Peter Dragicevich

Thanks to my London crew for assisting in 'researching' London's bars and restaurants, particularly Tim Benzie, Vanessa Irvine, Ed Lee and Sue Ostler. Special thanks are due to my inspiring Lonely Planet team-mates, especially Clifton Wilkinson, Laura Stansfeld, Herman So and David Else.

Etain O'Carroll

Sincere thanks to Peter Berry in Oxford and Mark Wilkinson in Norwich for giving me their time and inside tips for use in this book. Thanks to Pedro Honwana for all his help with the Cheltenham section and to all the staff in tourist offices across the country who answered my endless questions. Thanks to Cliff and David for making the whole process so smooth and to the inhouse staff who helped with legions of queries on the new styling. Lastly, thanks to Maria Leon Ferreiro for her endless patience and goodwill and to Mark, Osgur and Neven for company on the road and keeping me sane on return.

Neil Wilson

Thanks to the many Yorkshire folk who freely offered advice and recommendations; to the tourist office staff for answering dumb questions; and to eerie Andy Dextrous in York for his help – much appreciated. Thanks also to Lonely Planet's editors and cartographers, and to Carol for good company in many Yorkshire restaurants.

ACKNOWLEDGMENTS

Climate map data adapted from Peel MC, Finlayson BL & McMahon TA (2007) 'Updated World Map of the Köppen-Geiger Climate Classification', Hydrology and Earth System Sciences, 11, 163344.
Cover photograph: Views of cliffs and lighthouse along South Downs Way, Beachy head, Sussex/ Paul Bigland/LPI.
Illustrations pp666-7, pp668-9, pp670-1 by Javier Zarracina
Many of the images in this guide are available for licensing from Lonely Planet Images: www.lonelyplanetimages.com.

index

INDEX

Map Pages **p000**
Image Pages p000

H

Map Pages **p000**
Image Pages **p000**

Map Pages **p000**
Image Pages p000

N

Map Pages **p000**
Image Pages p000

Q

R

Y

Map Pages **p000**
Image Pages p000

how to use this book

These symbols will help you find the listings you want:

- Sights
- Activities
- Courses
- Tours
- Festivals & Events
- Sleeping
- Eating
- Drinking
- Entertainment
- Shopping
- Information/ Transport

These symbols give you the vital information for each listing:

- Telephone Numbers
- Opening Hours
- Parking
- Nonsmoking
- Air-Conditioning
- Internet Access
- Wi-Fi Access
- Swimming Pool
- Vegetarian Selection
- English-Language Menu
- Family-Friendly
- Pet-Friendly
- Bus
- Ferry
- Metro
- Subway
- London Tube
- Tram
- Train

Reviews are organised by author preference.

Look out for these icons:

TOP CHOICE Our author's recommendation

FREE No payment required

A green or sustainable option

Our authors have nominated these places as demonstrating a strong commitment to sustainability – for example by supporting local communities and producers, operating in an environmentally friendly way, or supporting conservation projects.

Map Legend

Sights
- Beach
- Buddhist
- Castle
- Christian
- Hindu
- Islamic
- Jewish
- Monument
- Museum/Gallery
- Ruin
- Winery/Vineyard
- Zoo
- Other Sight

Activities, Courses & Tours
- Diving/Snorkelling
- Canoeing/Kayaking
- Skiing
- Surfing
- Swimming/Pool
- Walking
- Windsurfing
- Other Activity/ Course/Tour

Sleeping
- Sleeping
- Camping

Eating
- Eating

Drinking
- Drinking
- Cafe

Entertainment
- Entertainment

Shopping
- Shopping

Information
- Bank
- Embassy/ Consulate
- Hospital/Medical
- Internet
- Police
- Post Office
- Telephone
- Toilet
- Tourist Information
- Other Information

Transport
- Airport
- Border Crossing
- Bus
- Cable Car/ Funicular
- Cycling
- Ferry
- Metro
- Monorail
- Parking
- Petrol Station
- Taxi
- Train/Railway
- Tram
- Other Transport

Routes
- Tollway
- Freeway
- Primary
- Secondary
- Tertiary
- Lane
- Unsealed Road
- Plaza/Mall
- Steps
- Tunnel
- Pedestrian Overpass
- Walking Tour
- Walking Tour Detour
- Path

Geographic
- Hut/Shelter
- Lighthouse
- Lookout
- Mountain/Volcano
- Oasis
- Park
- Pass
- Picnic Area
- Waterfall

Population
- Capital (National)
- Capital (State/Province)
- City/Large Town
- Town/Village

Boundaries
- International
- State/Province
- Disputed
- Regional/Suburb
- Marine Park
- Cliff
- Wall

Hydrography
- River, Creek
- Intermittent River
- Swamp/Mangrove
- Reef
- Canal
- Water
- Dry/Salt/ Intermittent Lake
- Glacier

Areas
- Beach/Desert
- Cemetery (Christian)
- Cemetery (Other)
- Park/Forest
- Sportsground
- Sight (Building)
- Top Sight (Building)

Marc Di Duca

Canterbury & the Southeast; Newcastle & the Northeast From Farnham to the Farne Islands, Marc topped and tailed his native land for this edition of *England*. Born a mile from the Stockton & Darlington railway, Marc spent a decade in central Europe before becoming a full-time travel-guide author based in the southeast. Chilling extremities in the nippy River Tees, sinking ale in Cinque Ports, scrambling along Hadrian's Wall and stalking Dickens across six counties all formed part of his research for this guide.

Read more about Marc at:
lonelyplanet.com/members/madidu

Belinda Dixon

Hampshire, New Forest, Isle of Wight, Dorset, Wiltshire (Wessex); Devon Belinda made a gleeful bolt for the southwest 17 years ago and has worked as a writer, journalist and local radio broadcaster there ever since. This is her sixth mission for Lonely Planet in the region, and it's seen her hugging sarsens in the stone circle at Avebury, rummaging for fossils at Lyme, and cresting tor tops on Dartmoor. All that and rigorously (very rigorously) testing all the food and drink she can manage.

Read more about Belinda at:
lonelyplanet.com/members/belindadixon

Peter Dragicevich

London After a dozen years reviewing music and restaurants for publications in New Zealand and Australia, London's bright lights and loud guitars could no longer be resisted. Like all good Kiwis, Peter got to know the city while surfing his way between friends' flats all over London, before finally putting down roots. He has contributed to 18 Lonely Planet titles, including *Walking in Britain* and the last edition of this book.

Read more about Peter at:
lonelyplanet.com/members/peterdragicevich

Etain O'Carroll

Oxford, Cotswolds & Around; Cambridge & East Anglia Travel writer and photographer Etain grew up in rural Ireland but now calls Oxford home. She has worked on more than 20 Lonely Planet books including numerous *England* and *Great Britain* guides as well as *Cycling Britain*. Her top tip? Oxford and the Cotswolds are expensive to live in but great places to visit on a budget. There are world-class museums, stunning architecture, gorgeous villages and ancient pubs – most of them free to visit.

Read more about Etain at:
lonelyplanet.com/members/EtainOCarroll

Neil Wilson

Yorkshire From rock-climbing trips to Yorkshire gritstone, to weekend getaways in York and Whitby, Neil has made many cross-border forays into 'God's own country' from his home in Scotland. Good weather on this research trip allowed a memorable ascent of Ingleborough with summit views to the Irish Sea, and a knee-trashing mountain-bike descent of the Pennine Way into Hawes. Neil is a full-time travel writer based in Edinburgh, and has written more than 40 guidebooks for various publishers.

Read more about Neil at:
lonelyplanet.com/members/neilwilson

OUR STORY

A beat-up old car, a few dollars in the pocket and a sense of adventure. In 1972 that's all Tony and Maureen Wheeler needed for the trip of a lifetime – across Europe and Asia overland to Australia. It took several months, and at the end – broke but inspired – they sat at their kitchen table writing and stapling together their first travel guide, *Across Asia on the Cheap*. Within a week they'd sold 1500 copies. Lonely Planet was born.

Today, Lonely Planet has offices in Melbourne, London and Oakland, with more than 600 staff and writers. We share Tony's belief that 'a great guidebook should do three things: inform, educate and amuse'.

OUR WRITERS

David Else

Coordinating Author As a professional writer, David has authored over 40 books, including several editions of Lonely Planet's *England*, *Great Britain* and *Walking in Britain*. His knowledge comes from a lifetime of travel around the country – often on foot – a passion dating from university years, when heading for the hills was always more attractive than visiting the library. Originally from London, David has lived in Yorkshire and Derbyshire, and is now a resident of the Cotswolds. For this current edition of *England*, David's research took him from Cornwall to Northumberland – via two favourite spots: Porthcurno Beach and the *Angel of the North*.

Read more about David at:
lonelyplanet.com/members/davidelse

Oliver Berry

Bristol, Bath & Somerset (Wessex); Cornwall; Cumbria & the Lake District Oliver is a writer and photographer based in Cornwall. Among many other projects for Lonely Planet, Oliver has written the 1st editions of *Devon, Cornwall & Southwest England* and *The Lake District*, and worked on several previous editions of the *England* and *Great Britain* guides. Research highlights for this edition were sampling some traditional 'scrumpy' on a Somerset cider farm and watching the sun rise over Glastonbury Tor. You can see some of his latest work at www.oliverberry.com.

Read more about Oliver at:
lonelyplanet.com/members/oliverberry

Joe Bindloss

Nottingham & the East Midlands; Birmingham, the West Midlands & the Marches Born of English stock, albeit in Cyprus, Joe spends a lot of time in the Marches, not least because his parents and brothers live in the sleepy village of Clun (hell, they even go Morris dancing). For this book, Joe juggled exploring rugged uplands and picturesque medieval villages with writing for newspapers and magazines and being a full-time dad in London. Joe has been writing guidebooks for Lonely Planet since 1999, covering everywhere from rural England to the high reaches of the Himalaya.

Read more about Joe at:
lonelyplanet.com/members/bindibhaji

Fionn Davenport

Manchester, Liverpool & the Northwest Fionn is an unashamed urban junky (urban philosophy: eat, stare, walk) – there are enough distractions in a good city to keep him entertained for years. Which is why he's been visiting and writing about northwest England for the guts of a decade – it's home to his favourite English city (Manchester) and his favourite football club (Liverpool). He also likes getting out of cities, and spots like the Wirral, northern Lancashire and the Isle of Man have enough countryside for anyone intent on getting away from Man's concrete footprint.

OVER PAGE MORE WRITERS

Published by Lonely Planet Publications Pty Ltd
ABN 36 005 607 983
6th edition – Mar 2011
ISBN 978 1 74179 567 7

10 9 8 7 6 5 4 3 2 1
Printed in China